ECONOMIC REPORT

OF THE

PRESIDENT

TRANSMITTED TO THE CONGRESS

FEBRUARY 2010

TOGETHER WITH

THE ANNUAL REPORT

OF THE

COUNCIL OF ECONOMIC ADVISERS

UNITED STATES GOVERNMENT PRINTING OFFICE

WASHINGTON : 2010

For sale by the Superintendent of Documents, U.S. Government Printing Office
Internet: bookstore.gpo.gov Phone: toll free (866) 512-1800; DC area (202) 512-1800
Fax: (202) 512-2104 Mail: Stop IDCC, Washington, DC 20402-0001

ISBN 978-0-16-084824-7

$$\smallint\!\!\!\!\!\smallint$$

C O N T E N T S

*For a detailed table of contents of the Council's Report, see page 15.

ECONOMIC REPORT
OF THE
PRESIDENT

ECONOMIC REPORT OF THE PRESIDENT

To the Congress of the United States:

As we begin a new year, the American people are still experiencing the effects of a recession as deep and painful as any we have known in generations. Traveling across this country, I have met countless men and women who have lost jobs these past two years. I have met small business owners struggling to pay for health care for their workers; seniors unable to afford prescriptions; parents worried about paying the bills and saving for their children's future and their own retirement. And the effects of this recession come in the aftermath of a decade of declining economic security for the middle class and those who aspire to it.

At the same time, over the past two years, we have also seen reason for hope: the resilience of the American people who have held fast—even in the face of hardship—to an unrelenting faith in the promise of our country.

It is that determination that has helped the American people overcome difficult periods in our Nation's history. And it is this persever-ance that remains our great strength today. After all, our workers are as productive as ever. American businesses are still leaders in innovation. Our potential is still unrivaled. Our task as a Nation—and our mission as an Administration—is to harness that innovative spirit, that productive energy, and that potential in order to create jobs, raise incomes, and foster economic growth that is sustained and broadly shared. It's not enough to move the economy from recession to recovery. We must rebuild the economy on a new and stronger foundation.

I can report that over the past year, this work has begun. In the coming year, this work continues. But to understand where we must go in the next year and beyond, it is important to remember where we began one year ago.

Last January, years of irresponsible risk-taking and debt-fueled speculation—unchecked by sound oversight—led to the near-collapse of our financial system. We were losing an average of 700,000 jobs each month. Over the course of one year, $13 trillion of Americans' household wealth had evaporated as stocks, pensions, and home values plummeted. Our gross domestic product was falling at the fastest rate in a quarter century. The flow of credit, vital to the functioning of businesses large and small, had ground to a halt. The fear among economists, from across the political spectrum, was that we could sink into a second Great Depression.

Immediately, we took a series of difficult steps to prevent that catastrophe for American families and businesses. We acted to get lending flowing again so ordinary Americans could get financing to buy homes and cars, to go to college, and to start businesses of their own; and so businesses, large and small, could access loans to make payroll, buy equipment, hire workers, and expand. We enacted measures to stem the tide of foreclosures in our housing market, helping responsible homeowners stay in their homes and helping to stop the broader decline in home values.

To achieve this, and to prevent an economic collapse, we were forced to use authority enacted under the previous Administration to extend assistance to some of the very banks and financial institutions whose actions had helped precipitate the turmoil. We also took steps to prevent the collapse of the American auto industry, which faced a crisis partly of its own making, to prevent another round of widespread job losses in an already fragile time. These decisions were not popular, but they were necessary. Indeed, the decision to stabilize the financial system helped to avert a larger catastrophe, and thanks to the efficient management of the rescue—with added transparency and accountability—we have recovered most of the money provided to banks.

In addition, even as we worked to address the crises in our banking sector, in our housing market, and in our auto industry, we also began attacking our economic crisis on a broader front. Less than one month after taking office, we enacted the most sweeping economic recovery package in history: the American Recovery and Reinvestment Act of 2009. The Recovery Act not only provided tax cuts to small businesses and 95 percent of working families and provided emergency relief to those out of work or without health insurance; it also began to lay a new foundation for long-term growth. With investments in health care, education, infrastructure, and clean energy, the Recovery Act has saved or created roughly two million jobs so far, and it has begun the hard work of transforming our economy to thrive in the modern, global era.

Because of these and other steps, we can safely say that we've avoided the depression many feared. Our economy is growing again, and the growth over the last three months was the strongest in six years. But while economic growth is important, it means nothing to somebody who has lost a job and can't find another. For Americans looking for work, a good job is the only good news that matters. And that's why our work is far from complete.

It is true that the steps we have taken have slowed the flood of job losses from 691,000 per month in the first quarter of 2009 to 69,000 in the last quarter. But stemming the tide of job loss isn't enough. More than 7 million jobs have been lost since the recession began two years ago. This represents not only a terrible human tragedy, but also a very deep hole from which we'll have to climb out. Until jobs are being created to replace those we've lost—until America is back at work—my Administration will not rest and this recovery will not be finished.

That's why I am continuing to call on the Congress to pass a jobs bill. I've proposed a package that includes tax relief for small businesses to spur hiring, that accelerates construction on roads, bridges, and waterways, and that creates incentives for homeowners to invest in energy efficiency, because this will create jobs, save families money, and reduce pollution that harms our environment.

It is also essential that as we promote private sector hiring, we continue to take steps to prevent layoffs of critical public servants like teachers, firefighters, and police officers, whose jobs are threatened by State and local budget shortfalls. To do otherwise would not only worsen unemployment and hamper our recovery; it would also undermine our communities. And we cannot forget the millions of people who have lost their jobs. The Recovery Act provided support for these families hardest-hit by this recession, and that support must continue.

At the same time, long before this crisis hit, middle-class families were under growing strain. For decades, Washington failed to address fundamental weaknesses in the economy: rising health care costs, growing dependence on foreign oil, an education system unable to prepare all of our children for the jobs of the future. In recent years, spending bills and tax cuts for the very wealthiest were approved without paying for any of it, leaving behind a mountain of debt. And while Wall Street gambled without regard for the consequences, Washington looked the other way.

As a result, the economy may have been working for some at the very top, but it was not working for all American families. Year after year, folks were forced to work longer hours, spend more time away from their loved ones, all while their incomes flat-lined and their sense of economic security evaporated. Growth in our country was neither sustained nor broadly shared. Instead of a prosperity powered by smart ideas and sound investments, growth was fueled in large part by a rapid rise in consumer borrowing and consumer spending.

Beneath the statistics are the stories of hardship I've heard all across America—hardships that began long before this recession hit two years ago. For too many, there has long been a sense that the American dream—a chance to make your own way, to work hard and support your family, save for college and retirement, own a home—was slipping away. And this sense of anxiety has been combined with a deep frustration that Washington either didn't notice, or didn't care enough to act.

These weaknesses have not only made our economy more susceptible to the kind of crisis we have been through. They have also meant that even in good times the economy did not produce nearly enough gains for middle-class families. Typical American families saw their standards of living stagnate, rather than rise as they had for generations. That is why, in the aftermath of this crisis, and after years of inaction, what is clear is that we cannot go back to business as usual.

That is why, as we strive to meet the crisis of the moment, we are continuing to lay a new foundation for prosperity: a foundation on which the middle class can prosper and grow, where if you are willing to work hard, you can find a good job, afford a home, send your children to world-class schools, afford high-quality health care, and enjoy retirement security in your later years. This is the heart of the American Dream, and it is at the core of our efforts to not only rebuild this economy—but to rebuild it stronger than before. And this work has already begun.

Already, we have made historic strides to reform and improve our education system. We have launched a Race to the Top in which schools are competing to create the most innovative programs, especially in math and science. We have already made college more affordable, even as we seek to increase student aid by ending a wasteful subsidy that serves only to line the pockets of lenders with tens of billions of taxpayer dollars. And I've proposed a new American Graduation Initiative and set this goal: by 2020, America will once again have the highest proportion of college graduates in the world. For we know that in this new century, growth will be powered not by what consumers can borrow and spend, but what talented, skilled workers can create and export.

Already, we have made historic strides to improve our health care system, essential to our economic prosperity. The burdens this system places on workers, businesses, and governments is simply unsustainable. And beyond the economic cost—which is vast—there is also a terrible human toll. That's why we've extended health insurance to millions more children; invested in health information technology through the Recovery Act to improve care and reduce costly errors; and provided the largest boost to medical research in our history. And I continue to fight to pass real, meaningful health insurance reforms that will get costs under control for families, businesses, and governments, protect people from the worst practices of insurance companies, and make coverage more affordable and secure for people with insurance, as well as those without it.

Already, we have begun to build a new clean energy economy. The Recovery Act included the largest investment in clean energy in history, investments that are today creating jobs across America in the industries that will power our future: developing wind energy, solar technology, and clean energy vehicles. But this work has only just begun. Other countries around the world understand that the nation that leads the clean energy economy will be the nation that leads the global economy. I want America to be that nation. That is why we are working toward legislation that will create new incentives to finally make renewable energy the profitable kind of energy in America. It's not only essential for our planet and our security, it's essential for our economy.

But this is not all we must do. For growth to be truly sustainable— for our prosperity to be truly shared and our living standards to actually rise—we need to move beyond an economy that is fueled by budget deficits and consumer demand. In other words, in order to create jobs and raise incomes for the middle class over the long run, we need to export more and borrow less from around the world, and we need to save more money and take on less debt here at home. As we rebuild, we must also rebalance. In order to achieve this, we'll need to grow this economy by growing our capacity to innovate in burgeoning industries, while putting a stop to irresponsible budget policies and financial dealings that have led us into such a deep fiscal and economic hole.

That begins with policies that will promote innovation throughout our economy. To spur the discoveries that will power new jobs, new businesses—and perhaps new industries—I have challenged both the public sector and the private sector to devote more resources to research and development. And to achieve this, my budget puts us on a path to double investment in key research agencies and makes the research and experimentation tax credit permanent. We are also pursuing policies that will help us export more of our goods around the world, especially by small businesses and farmers. And by harnessing the growth potential of international trade—while ensuring that other countries play by the rules and that all Americans share in the benefits—we will support millions of good, high-paying jobs.

But hand in hand with increasing our reliance on the Nation's ingenuity is decreasing our reliance on the Nation's credit card, as well as reining in the excess and abuse in our financial sector that led large firms to take on extraordinary risks and extraordinary liabilities.

When my Administration took office, the surpluses our Nation had enjoyed at the start of the last decade had disappeared as a result of the failure to pay for two large tax cuts, two wars, and a new entitlement program. And decades of neglect of rising health care costs had put our budget on an unsustainable path.

In the long term, we cannot have sustainable and durable economic growth without getting our fiscal house in order. That is why even as we increased our short-term deficit to rescue the economy, we have refused to go along with business as usual, taking responsibility for every dollar we spend. Last year, we combed the budget, cutting waste and excess wherever we could, a process that will continue in the coming years. We are pursuing health insurance reforms that are essential to reining in deficits. I've called for a fee to be paid by the largest financial firms so that the American people are fully repaid for bailing out the financial sector. And I've proposed a freeze on nonsecurity discretionary spending for three years, a bipartisan commission to address the long-term structural imbalance between expenditures and revenues, and the enactment of "pay-go" rules so that Congress has to account for every dollar it spends.

In addition, I've proposed a set of common sense reforms to prevent future financial crises. For while the financial system is far stronger today than it was one year ago, it is still operating under the same rules that led to its near-collapse. These are rules that allowed firms to act contrary to the interests of customers; to hide their exposure to debt through complex financial dealings that few understood; to benefit from taxpayer-insured deposits while making speculative investments to increase their own profits; and to take on risks so vast that they posed a threat to the entire economy and the jobs of tens of millions of Americans.

That is why we are seeking reforms to empower consumers with the benefit of a new consumer watchdog charged with making sure that financial information is clear and transparent; to close loopholes that allowed big financial firms to trade risky financial products like credit defaults swaps and other derivatives without any oversight; to identify system-wide risks that could cause a financial meltdown; to strengthen capital and liquidity requirements to make the system more stable; and to ensure that the failure of any large firm does not take the economy down with it. Never again will the American taxpayer be held hostage by a bank that is "too big to fail."

Through these reforms, we seek not to undermine our markets but to make them stronger: to promote a vibrant, fair, and transparent financial system that is far more resistant to the reckless, irresponsible activities that might lead to another meltdown. And these kinds of reforms are in the shared interest of firms on Wall Street and families on Main Street.

These have been a very tough two years. American families and businesses have paid a heavy price for failures of responsibility from Wall Street to Washington. Our task now is to move beyond these failures, to take responsibility for our future once more. That is how we will create new jobs in new industries, harnessing the incredible generative and creative capacity of our people. That is how we'll achieve greater economic security and opportunity for middle-class families in this country. That is how in this new century we will rebuild our economy stronger than ever before.

THE WHITE HOUSE
FEBRUARY 2010

THE ANNUAL REPORT
OF THE
COUNCIL OF ECONOMIC ADVISERS

LETTER OF TRANSMITTAL

COUNCIL OF ECONOMIC ADVISERS
Washington, D.C., February 11, 2010

MR. PRESIDENT:

The Council of Economic Advisers herewith submits its 2010 Annual Report in accordance of the Employment Act of 1946 as amended by the Full Employment and Balanced Growth Act of 1978.

Sincerely,

Christina D. Romer
Chair

Austan Goolsbee
Member

Cecilia Elena Rouse
Member

⚜

CONTENTS

LIST OF FIGURES

LIST OF TABLES

LIST OF BOXES

CHAPTER 1

TO RESCUE, REBALANCE, AND REBUILD

President Obama took office at a time of economic crisis. The recession that began in December 2007 had accelerated following the financial crisis in September 2008. By January 2009, 11.9 million people were unemployed and real gross domestic product (GDP) was falling at a breakneck pace. The possibility of a second Great Depression was frighteningly real.

In the first months of the Administration, the President and Congress took unprecedented actions to restore demand, stabilize financial markets, and put people back to work. Just 28 days after his inauguration, the President signed the American Recovery and Reinvestment Act of 2009, the boldest countercyclical fiscal stimulus in American history. The Financial Stability Plan, announced in February, included wide-ranging measures to strengthen the banking system, increase consumer and business lending, and stem foreclosures and support the housing market. These and a host of other actions stabilized the financial system, supported those most directly affected by the recession, and walked the economy back from the brink.

But the Administration always knew that stabilizing the economy would not be enough. The problems that led to the crisis were years in the making. Continued action will be necessary to return the economy to full employment. In the process, an important rebalancing will need to occur. For too many years, America's growth and prosperity were fed by a boom in consumer spending stemming from rising asset prices and easy credit. The Federal Government had likewise been living beyond its means, resulting in large and growing budget deficits. And our regulatory system had failed to keep up with financial innovation, allowing risky practices to endanger the system and the economy. For this reason, the Administration has sought to help restore the economy to health on a foundation of greater investment, fiscal responsibility, and a well-functioning and secure financial system.

Even this important rebalancing would not be sufficient. In addition to the problems that had set the stage for the crisis, long-term challenges had been ignored and the U.S. economy was failing at some of its central tasks. Our health care system was beset by steadily rising costs, and millions of Americans either had no health insurance at all or were unsure whether their coverage would be there when they needed it. Middle-class families had seen their real incomes stagnate during the previous eight years, while those at the top of the income distribution had seen their incomes soar. A failure to slow the consumption of fossil fuels had contributed to global warming and continued dependence on foreign oil. And a country built on its record of innovation was failing to invest enough in research and development.

The President has dedicated his Administration to dealing with these long-run problems as well. As the new decade opens, Congress has come closer than ever before to passing landmark legislation reforming the health insurance system. This legislation would make health insurance more secure for those who have it and affordable for those who do not, and it would slow the growth rate of health care costs. Over the past year, the Administration has also worked with Congress to make important new investments to sustain and improve K-12 education and community colleges, jump-start the transition to a clean energy economy, and spur innovation through increased research and development. These and numerous other initiatives will help to rebuild the American economy stronger than before and put us on the path to sustained growth and prosperity. Enacting these policies will help to ensure that our children and grandchildren inherit a country as full of promise and as economically secure as ever in our history.

RESCUING AN ECONOMY IN FREEFALL

In December 2007, the American economy entered what at first seemed likely to be a mild recession. As Figure 1-1 shows, real house prices (that is, house prices adjusted for inflation) had risen to unprecedented levels, almost doubling between 1997 and 2006. The rapid run-up in prices was accompanied by a residential construction boom and the proliferation of complex mortgages and mortgage-related financial assets. The fall of national house prices starting in early 2007, and the associated declines in the values of mortgage-backed and other related assets, led to a slowdown in the growth of consumer spending, increases in mortgage defaults and home foreclosures, significant strains on financial institutions, and reduced credit availability.

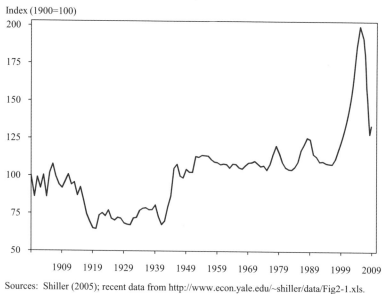

Figure 1-1
House Prices Adjusted for Inflation

Index (1900=100)

Sources: Shiller (2005); recent data from http://www.econ.yale.edu/~shiller/data/Fig2-1.xls.

By early 2008, the economy was contracting. Employment fell by an average of 137,000 jobs per month over the first eight months of 2008. Real GDP rose only anemically from the third quarter of 2007 to the second quarter of 2008.

Then in September 2008, the character of the downturn worsened dramatically. The collapse of Lehman Brothers and the near-collapse of American International Group (AIG) led to a seizing up of financial markets and plummeting consumer and business confidence. Parts of the financial system froze, and assets once assumed to be completely safe, such as money-market mutual funds, became unstable and subject to runs. Credit spreads, a common indicator of credit market stress, spiked to unprecedented levels in the fall of 2008. The value of the stock market plunged 24 percent in September and October, and another 15 percent by the end of January. As Figure 1-2 shows, over the final four months of 2008 and the first month of 2009, the economy lost, on average, a staggering 544,000 jobs per month, the highest level of job loss since the demobilization at the end of World War II. Real GDP fell at an increasingly rapid pace: an annual rate of 2.7 percent in the third quarter of 2008, 5.4 percent in the fourth quarter of 2008, and 6.4 percent in the first quarter of 2009.

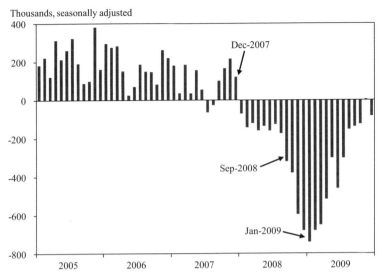

Figure 1-2
Monthly Change in Payroll Employment

Thousands, seasonally adjusted

Source: Department of Labor (Bureau of Labor Statistics), Current Employment Statistics survey Series CES0000000001.

Rescuing the Economy from the Great Recession

Thus, the first imperative of the new Administration upon taking office had to be to turn around an economy in freefall. Chapter 2 describes the unprecedented policy actions the Administration has taken, together with Congress and the Federal Reserve, to address the immediate crisis. The large fiscal stimulus in the American Recovery and Reinvestment Act, the programs to stabilize financial markets and restart lending, and the policies to assist small businesses and distressed homeowners have all played a role in generating one of the sharpest economic turnarounds in post–World War II history. Real GDP is growing again, job loss has moderated greatly, house prices appear to have stabilized, and credit spreads have almost returned to normal levels. A wide range of evidence indicates that in the absence of the aggressive policy actions, the recession and the attendant suffering of ordinary Americans would have been far more severe and could have led to catastrophe.

Yet, because the economy's downward momentum was so great and the barriers to robust growth from the weakened financial conditions of households and financial institutions are so strong, the economy remains distressed and many families continue to struggle. A change from freefall to growing GDP and moderating job losses is a dramatic improvement, but it is not nearly enough. Chapter 2 therefore also examines the challenges that remain in achieving a full recovery. It discusses some possible additional measures to spur private sector job creation.

Crisis and Recovery in the World Economy

In the early fall of 2008, there was hope that the impact of the crisis on the rest of the world would be limited. Those hopes were dashed during the months that followed. In the fourth quarter of 2008 and the first quarter of 2009, real GDP fell sharply—often at double-digit rates—in the United Kingdom, Germany, Japan, Taiwan, and elsewhere. The surprisingly rapid spread of the downturn to the rest of the world reduced the demand for U.S. exports sharply, and so magnified our economic contraction.

The worldwide crisis required a worldwide response. Chapter 3 describes both the actions taken by individual countries and those taken through international institutions and cooperation. As described in the leaders' statement from the September summit of the Group of Twenty (G-20) nations, the result was "the largest and most coordinated fiscal and monetary stimulus ever undertaken" (Group of Twenty 2009). Just as the actions in the United States have begun to turn the domestic economy around, these international actions appear to have put the worst of the global crisis behind us. But the firmness of the budding recovery varies considerably across countries, and significant challenges still remain.

REBALANCING THE ECONOMY ON THE PATH TO FULL EMPLOYMENT

The path from budding recovery to full employment will surely be a difficult one. The problems that sowed the seeds of the financial crisis need to be dealt with so that the economy emerges from the recession with a stronger, more durable prosperity. There needs to be a rebalancing of the economy away from low personal saving and large government budget deficits and toward investment. Our financial system must be strengthened both to provide the lending needed to support the recovery and to reduce the risk of future crises.

Saving and Investment

The expansion of the 2000s was fueled in part by high consumption. As Figure 1-3 shows, the share of GDP that takes the form of consumption has been on a generally upward trend for decades and reached unprecedented heights in the 2000s. The personal saving rate fell to exceptionally low levels, and trade deficits were large and persistent. A substantial amount of the remainder of GDP took the form of housing construction, which may have crowded out other kinds of investment. Such an expansion is not just unstable, as we have learned painfully over the past two years. It also contributes too little to increases in standards of living. Low investment in equipment and factories slows the growth of productivity and wages.

Figure 1-3
Personal Consumption Expenditures as a Share of GDP

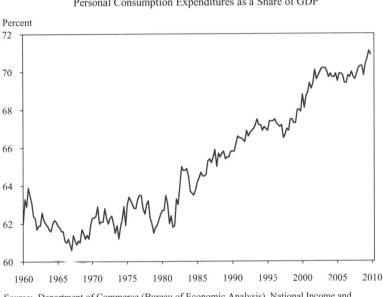

Source: Department of Commerce (Bureau of Economic Analysis), National Income and Product Accounts Table 1.1.10.

Chapter 4 examines the transition from consumption-driven growth to a greater emphasis on investment and exports. It discusses the likelihood that consumers will return to saving rates closer to the postwar average than to the very low rates of the early 2000s. It also describes the Administration's initiatives to encourage household saving. Greater personal saving will tend to encourage investment by helping to maintain low real interest rates. The increased investment will help to fill some of the gap in demand left by reduced consumption. Chapter 4 discusses additional Administration policies, such as investment tax incentives, designed to promote private investment. Higher saving relative to investment will reduce net international capital flows to the United States. Because net foreign borrowing must equal the current account deficit, lower net capital inflows imply a closer balance of exports and imports, which will help create further demand for American products. The Administration also supports aggressive export promotion measures to further increase demand for our exports. The end result of this rebalancing will be an economy that is more stable, more investment-oriented, and more export-oriented, and thus better for our future standards of living.

Addressing the Long-Run Fiscal Challenge

A key part of the rebalancing that must occur as the economy returns to full employment and beyond involves taming the Federal budget deficit. Figure 1-4 shows the actual and projected path of the budget surplus based on estimates released by the Congressional Budget Office (CBO) in January 2009, just before President Obama took office. As the figure makes clear, the budget surpluses of the late 1990s turned to substantial deficits in the 2000s, and the deficits were projected to grow even more sharply over the next three decades. As discussed in Chapter 5, the change to deficits in the 2000s largely reflects policy actions that were not paid for, such as the 2001 and 2003 tax cuts and the introduction of the Medicare prescription drug benefit. The projection of steadily increasing future deficits is largely due to the continuation of the decades-long trend of rising health care costs.

Figure 1-4
Actual and Projected Budget Surpluses in January 2009 under Previous Policy

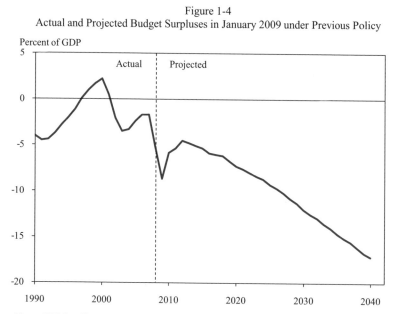

Note: CBO baseline surplus projection adjusted for CBO's estimates of costs of continued war spending, continuation of the 2001 and 2003 tax cuts, preventing scheduled cuts in Medicare's physician payment rates, and holding other discretionary outlays constant as a share of GDP.
Sources: Congressional Budget Office (2009a, 2009b).

Chapter 5 describes the likely consequences of these projected deficits over time and the importance of restoring fiscal discipline. It also discusses the President's plan for facing this challenge. A period of severe economic weakness is no time for a large fiscal contraction. Instead, the Nation must tackle the long-run deficit problem through actions that address the underlying sources of the problem over time. The single most important step that can be taken to reduce future deficits is to adopt health care reform that slows the growth rate of costs without compromising the quality of care. In addition, the President's fiscal 2011 budget includes other significant measures, such as allowing President Bush's tax cuts for the highest-income earners to expire, reforming international tax rules to discourage tax avoidance and encourage investment in the United States, and imposing a three-year freeze in nonsecurity discretionary spending; alongside a proposal for a bipartisan commission process to address the long-run gap between revenues and expenditures.

Building a Safer Financial System

Risky credit practices both encouraged some of the imprudent rise in consumption and homebuilding in the previous decade and set the stage for the financial crisis. Chapter 6 analyzes the role that financial intermediaries play in the economy and diagnoses what went wrong during the meltdown of financial markets. The crisis showed that the Nation's financial regulatory structure, much of which had not been fundamentally changed since the 1930s, failed to keep up with the evolution of financial markets. The current system provided too little protection for the economy from actions that could threaten financial stability and too little protection for ordinary Americans in their dealings with sophisticated and powerful financial institutions and other providers of credit. Strengthening our financial system is thus a key element of the rebalancing needed to assure stable, robust growth.

Chapter 6 discusses financial regulatory modernization. What is needed is a system where capital requirements and sensible rules are set in a way to control excessive risk-taking; where regulators can consider risks to the system as a whole and not just to individual institutions; where institutions cannot choose their regulators; where regulators no longer face the unacceptable choice between the disorganized, catastrophic failure of a financial institution and a taxpayer-funded bailout; and where a dedicated agency has consumer protection as its central mandate. For this reason, the President put forward a comprehensive plan for financial regulatory reform last June and is working with Congress to ensure passage of these critical reforms this year.

Rebuilding a Stronger Economy

Even before the crisis, the economy faced significant long-term challenges. As a result, it was doing poorly at providing rising standards of living for the vast majority of Americans. Figure 1-5 shows the evolution of before-tax real median family income since 1960. Beginning around 1970, slower productivity growth and rising income inequality caused incomes for most families to grow only slowly. After a half-decade of higher growth in the 1990s, the real income of the typical American family actually fell between 2000 and 2006.

Figure 1-5
Real Median Family Income

Notes: Income measure is total money income excluding capital gains and before taxes. Annual income deflated using CPI-U-RS.
Source: Department of Commerce (Census Bureau), Current Population Survey, Annual Social and Economic Supplement, Historical Income Table F-12.

A central focus of Administration policy both over the past year and for the years to come is to build a firmer foundation for the economy. The President is committed to policies that will raise living standards for all Americans.

Reforming Health Care

Health care is a key challenge that long predates the current economic crisis. The existing system has left many Americans who have health insurance inadequately covered, poorly protected against insurance industry abuses, and fearful of losing the insurance they have. And it has left tens of millions of Americans with no insurance coverage at all. The system also delivers too little benefit at too high a cost. Comparisons across countries and, especially, across regions of the United States reveal large differences in health care spending that are not associated with differences in health outcomes and that cannot be fully explained by factors such as differences in demographics, health status, income, or medical care prices. These large differences in spending suggest that up to nearly 30 percent of health care spending could be saved without adverse health consequences. The unnecessary growth of health care costs is eroding the growth of take-home pay and is central to our long-run fiscal challenges. These adverse effects will only become more severe if cost growth is not slowed.

To illustrate what could happen to workers' earnings in the absence of reform, Figure 1-6 shows the historical and projected paths of real total compensation per worker (which includes nonwage benefits such as health insurance) and total compensation net of health insurance premiums. As health insurance premiums absorb a growing fraction of workers' compensation, the remaining portion of compensation levels off and then starts to decline.

Figure 1-6
Total Compensation Including and Excluding Health Insurance

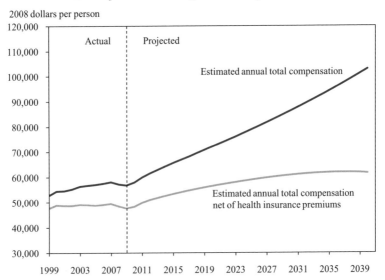

Note: Health insurance premiums include the employee- and employer-paid portions.
Sources: Actual data from Department of Labor (Bureau of Labor Statistics); Kaiser Family Foundation and Health Research and Educational Trust (2009); Department of Health and Human Services (Agency for Healthcare Research and Quality, Center for Financing, Access, and Cost Trends), 2008 Medical Expenditure Panel Survey-Insurance Component. Projections based on CEA calculations.

Chapter 7 describes the actions the Administration and Congress took in 2009 to begin the process of improvement, including an expansion of the Children's Health Insurance Program to provide access to health care for millions of children and important investments in the modernization of the health care system through the Recovery Act. It also describes the key elements of successful health insurance reform and discusses the progress that has been made on reform legislation. Successful reform involves making insurance more secure for those who have it and expanding coverage to those who lack it. It must include delivery system reforms, reductions in waste and improper payments in the Medicare system, and changes in consumer and firm incentives that will slow the growth rate of costs substantially, while maintaining and even improving quality. Slowing the growth rate of health care costs will have benefits throughout the economy: it will raise standards of living for families, help reduce the Federal budget deficit relative to what it otherwise would be, benefit state and local governments, and encourage job growth and improved macroeconomic performance.

Strengthening the American Labor Force

American workers have suffered greatly in the current recession. As described in Chapter 8, long-term unemployment is at record levels. The unemployment rate, which was 10 percent for the country as a whole in December, is far higher for blacks, Hispanics, and other demographic groups. The decline in house prices has eroded the nest eggs that many Americans had been counting on for their retirement. The Administration has initiated many actions to help support workers and their families through the recession and beyond. These actions range from extended and expanded unemployment insurance, to measures to make health insurance more affordable, to initiatives to promote retirement saving.

American workers also face the persistent problem of stagnating incomes. A key determinant of growth in standards of living is the rate of increase in the education and skills of our workforce. More and more jobs require education and training beyond the high school level, along with the ability to complete tasks that are open-ended and interactive. But, as Figure 1-7 shows, the years of education U.S. workers have brought to the labor market have risen little in the past four decades. And, as is well known, U.S. students lag behind those from many other countries in their performance on standardized tests.

Chapter 8 describes the Administration's initiatives to improve the skills of our workers. The Administration is pursuing reform to eliminate wasteful subsidies to student loan providers, the savings from which will fund new investments in education. The Administration has proposed a major initiative to support and improve community colleges, which are a neglected but critical link in our education system. It has also proposed increasing Pell Grants, and is taking steps to simplify the student aid application process so that eligible students are no longer discouraged by a complicated process from even applying for aid. All of these actions will help to achieve one of the President's key educational goals for the country—that the proportion of adults with a college degree be the largest in the world by 2020.

Figure 1-7
Mean Years of Schooling by Birth Cohort

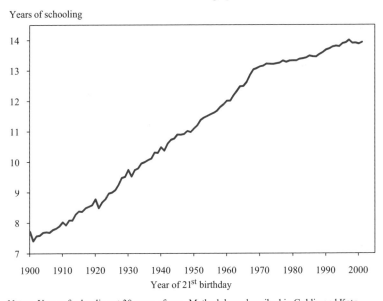

Notes: Years of schooling at 30 years of age. Methodology described in Goldin and Katz (2007).
Sources: Department of Commerce (Bureau of the Census), 1940-2000 Census IPUMS, 2005 CPS MORG; Goldin and Katz (2007).

Transforming the Energy Sector and Addressing Climate Change

Climate change and energy independence present a very different long-run challenge. Continued reliance on fossil fuels is leading to the buildup of greenhouse gases in the atmosphere and is changing our climate. Left unaddressed, these trends will have increasingly severe consequences over time. What is more, the United States imports the majority of the oil it uses, much of it from sources that are potentially subject to disruption.

Chapter 9 analyzes how economic policy can play a critical role in moving the United States toward a clean energy economy that is less dependent on fossil fuels and fossil fuel imports. Slowing climate change requires slowing the emission of greenhouse gases. A market-based approach, such as that supported by the Administration and currently working its way through Congress, can provide the signals needed to accomplish this slowing of emissions efficiently and with minimal disruptions.

The support for research and development (R&D) and incentives for investment in clean energy technologies and energy efficiency in the Recovery Act and the President's budget, as well as in the energy and climate legislation, can help foster the transition to a clean energy economy and spur growth in vital new industries. These new industries have the potential to reinvigorate the American manufacturing sector and generate secure, high-quality jobs.

Fostering Productivity Growth Through Innovation and Trade

The ultimate driver of growth in average standards of living is productivity growth. Increased investment in capital and in the skills of our workforce are two important sources of that growth. Chapter 10 examines two other sources of productivity gains: innovation and international trade.

Innovation comes from many sources. But a central one is investment in R&D. Figure 1-8 shows the share of GDP devoted to R&D over the past 50 years. In the mid-1960s, R&D constituted a larger share of total spending

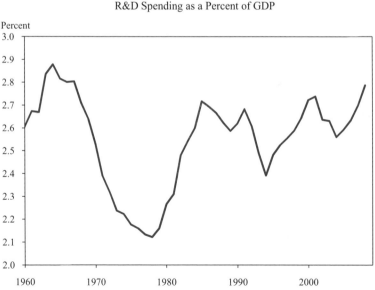

Figure 1-8
R&D Spending as a Percent of GDP

Note: Data for 2008 are preliminary.
Sources: National Science Foundation, Science and Engineering Indicators 2010 Tables 4-1 and 4-7.

than it has in the past decade. And in some other countries, such as Korea, Sweden, and Japan, R&D spending is a larger fraction of GDP than in the United States. The President is committed to raising the share of output devoted to R&D to 3 percent, so that America can continue to be a leader in new technologies and American workers and businesses can benefit from more rapid economic growth.

Through the Recovery Act and other measures, the Administration is investing both directly in basic scientific research and development and in the infrastructure to support that research. Most innovation, however, comes from the private sector. Here, the Administration is providing critical incentives for R&D both in general and in such vital areas as clean energy technologies. The Administration is also pursuing a wide range of policies to support the small businesses that contribute so much to technological progress—policies ranging from programs to maintain the flow of credit to small businesses to health insurance reform that will help level the playing field between small and large businesses.

Finally, international trade can be an important source of productivity growth and incentives for innovation. Trade has the potential to allow the U.S. economy to expand output in areas where it is more productive and to enable higher-productivity firms to expand. Access to a world market encourages American firms to invest in the research needed to become technological leaders. Through these routes, a free and fair trade regime can play an important part in lifting living standards in the long run. But for trade to play this role, it is essential to enforce existing trade rules and pursue policies that ensure that the benefits of trade are widely shared.

CONCLUSION

The past year has been one of great challenge for all Americans. Nearly every family has been touched in some way by the fallout from the crisis in financial markets, the drying up of credit, and the rise in unemployment. These challenges, moreover, have come after a decade in which ordinary Americans have seen their living standards stagnate, their health insurance become less secure, and their environment deteriorate.

The rest of this *Report* describes in more detail the actions the President has taken to end the recession, foster stable growth by rebalancing production and demand, and rebuild the foundation of the American economy. More fundamentally, it describes the work that remains to be done to create the prosperous, dynamic economy the American people need and deserve.

CHAPTER 2

RESCUING THE ECONOMY FROM THE GREAT RECESSION

The first and most fundamental task the Administration faced when President Obama took office was to rescue an economy in freefall. In November 2008, employment was declining at a rate of more than half a million jobs per month, and credit markets were stretched almost to the breaking point. As the economy entered 2009, the decline accelerated, with job loss in January reaching almost three-quarters of a million. The President responded by working with Congress to take unprecedented actions. These steps, together with measures taken by the Federal Reserve and other financial regulators, have succeeded in stabilizing the economy and beginning the process of healing a severely shaken economic and financial system. But much work remains. With high unemployment and continued job losses, it is clear that recovery must remain the key focus of 2010.

An Economy in Freefall

According to the National Bureau of Economic Research, the United States entered a recession in December 2007. Unlike most postwar recessions, this downturn was not caused by tight monetary policy aimed at curbing inflation. Although economists will surely analyze this downturn extensively in the years to come, there is widespread consensus that its central precipitating factor was a boom and bust in asset prices, especially house prices. The boom was fueled in part by irresponsible and in some cases predatory lending practices, risky investment strategies, faulty credit ratings, and lax regulation. When the boom ended, the result was widespread defaults and crippling blows to key financial institutions, magnifying the decline in house prices and causing enormous spillovers to the remainder of the economy.

The Run-Up to the Recession

The rise in house prices during the boom was remarkable. As Figure 2-1 shows, real house prices almost doubled between 1997 and 2006. By 2006, they were more than 50 percent above the highest level they had reached in the 20th century.

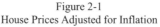

Figure 2-1
House Prices Adjusted for Inflation

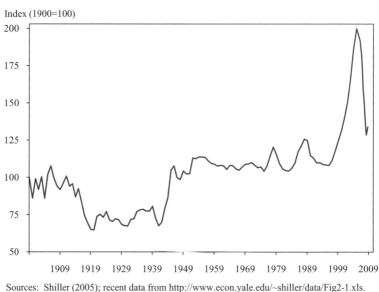

Sources: Shiller (2005); recent data from http://www.econ.yale.edu/~shiller/data/Fig2-1.xls.

Stock prices also rose rapidly. The Standard and Poor's (S&P) 500, for example, rose 101 percent between its low in 2002 and its high in 2007. That rise, though dramatic, was not unprecedented. Indeed, in the five years before its peak in March 2000, during the "tech bubble," the S&P 500 rose 205 percent, while the more technology-focused NASDAQ index rose 506 percent.

The run-up in asset prices was associated with a surge in construction and consumer spending. Residential construction rose sharply as developers responded to the increase in housing demand. From the fourth quarter of 2001 to the fourth quarter of 2005, the residential investment component of real GDP rose at an average annual rate of nearly 8 percent. Similarly, consumers responded to the increases in the value of their assets by continuing to spend freely. Saving rates, which had been declining since the early 1980s, fell to about 2 percent during the two years before the recession. This spending was facilitated by low interest rates and easy credit, with household borrowing rising faster than incomes.

The Downturn

House prices began to drop in some markets in 2006, and then nationally beginning in 2007. This process was gradual at first, with prices measured using the LoanPerformance house price index declining just 3½ percent nationally between January and June 2007. Lenders had lent aggressively during the boom, often providing mortgages whose soundness hinged on continued house price appreciation. As a result, the comparatively modest decline in house prices threatened large losses on subprime residential mortgages (the riskiest class of mortgages), as well as on the slightly higher-quality "Alt-A" mortgages. As the availability of mortgage credit tightened, the downward pressure on real estate prices intensified. National house prices declined 6 percent between June and December 2007.

The negative feedback between credit availability and the housing market weighed on household and business confidence, restraining consumer spending and business investment. Although residential construction led the slowdown in real activity through 2007, by early 2008 outlays for consumer goods and services and business equipment and software had decelerated sharply, and total employment was beginning to decline. Real gross domestic product (GDP) fell slightly in the first quarter of 2008.

In February 2008, Congress passed a temporary tax cut. Figure 2-2 shows real after-tax (or disposable) income and consumer spending before and after rebate checks were issued. Consumption was maintained despite a tremendous decline in household wealth over the same period. Total household and nonprofit net worth declined 9.1 percent between June 2007 and June 2008. Microeconomic studies of consumer behavior in this episode confirm the role of the tax rebate in maintaining spending (Broda and Parker 2008; Sahm, Shapiro, and Slemrod 2009). The fact that real GDP reversed course and grew in the second quarter of 2008 is further tribute to the helpfulness of the policy. But, in part because of the lack of robust, sustained stimulus, growth did not continue.

Financial institutions had invested heavily in assets whose values were tied to the value of mortgages. For many reasons—the opacity of the instruments, the complexity of financial institutions' balance sheets and their "off-balance-sheet" exposures, the failure of credit-rating agencies to accurately identify the riskiness of the assets, and poor regulatory oversight—the extent of the institutions' exposure to mortgage default risk was obscured. When mortgage defaults rose, the result was unexpectedly large losses to many financial institutions.

In the fall of 2008, the nature of the downturn changed dramatically. More rapid declines in asset prices generated further loss of confidence in the ability of some of the world's largest financial institutions to honor

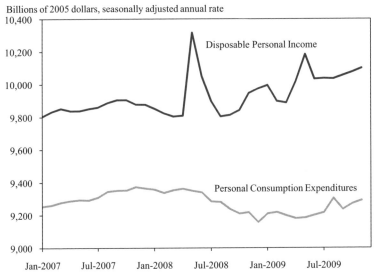

Figure 2-2
Income and Consumption Around the 2008 Tax Rebate

Billions of 2005 dollars, seasonally adjusted annual rate

Sources: Department of Commerce (Bureau of Economic Analysis), National Income and
Product Accounts Table 2.6, line 30, and Table 2.8.6, line 1.

their obligations. In September, the Lehman Brothers investment bank
declared bankruptcy, and other large financial firms (including American
International Group, Washington Mutual, and Merrill Lynch) were forced
to seek government aid or to merge with stronger institutions. What
followed was a rush to liquidity and a cascading of retrenchment that had
many of the features of a classic financial panic.

Risk spreads shot up to extraordinary levels. Figure 2-3 shows both
the TED spread and Moody's BAA-AAA spread. The TED spread is the
difference between the rate on short-term loans among banks and a safe
short-term Treasury interest rate. The BAA-AAA spread is the difference
between the interest rates on high-grade and medium-grade corporate
bonds. Both spreads rose dramatically during the heart of the panic. Indeed,
one way to put the spike in the BAA-AAA spread in perspective is to note
that the same spread barely moved during the Great Crash of the stock
market in 1929, and rose by only about half as much during the first wave of
banking panics in 1930 as it did in the fall of 2008.

The same loss of confidence shown by the rise in credit spreads
translated into declining asset prices of all sorts. The S&P 500 declined
29 percent in the second half of 2008. Real house prices tumbled another
11 percent over the same period (see Figure 2-1). All told, household and

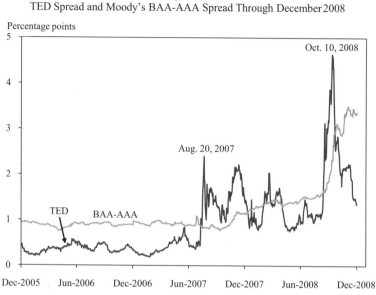

Figure 2-3
TED Spread and Moody's BAA-AAA Spread Through December 2008

Percentage points

Oct. 10, 2008

Aug. 20, 2007

TED   BAA-AAA

Dec-2005   Jun-2006   Dec-2006   Jun-2007   Dec-2007   Jun-2008   Dec-2008

Notes: The TED spread is defined as the three-month London Interbank Offered Rate
(Libor) less the yield on the three-month U.S. Treasury security. Moody's BAA-AAA
spread is the difference between Moody's indexes of yields on AAA and BAA rated
corporate bonds.
Source: Bloomberg.

nonprofit net worth declined 20 percent between December 2007 and December 2008, or by about $13 trillion. Again, a useful way to calibrate the size of this shock is to note that in 1929, household wealth declined only 3 percent—about one-seventh as much as in 2008. This is another indication that the shocks hitting the U.S. economy in 2008 were enormous.

The decline in wealth had a severe impact on consumer spending. This key component of aggregate demand, which accounts for roughly 70 percent of GDP and is traditionally quite stable, declined at an annual rate of 3.5 percent in the third quarter of 2008 and 3.1 percent in the fourth quarter. Some of this large decline may have also reflected the surge in uncertainty about future incomes. Not only did asset prices fall sharply, leading to the decline in wealth; they also became dramatically more volatile. The standard deviation of daily stock returns in the fourth quarter, for example, was 4.3 percentage points, even larger than in the first months of the Great Depression.

The financial panic led to a precipitous decline in lending. Bank credit continued to rise over the latter portion of 2008, as households and firms that had lost access to other forms of credit turned to banks. However, bank loans declined sharply in the first and second quarters of 2009 as banks tightened their terms and standards. Other sources of credit showed even more substantial declines. One particularly important market is that for commercial paper (short-term notes issued by firms to finance key operating costs such as payroll and inventory). The market for lower-tier nonfinancial (A2/P2) commercial paper collapsed in the fall of 2008, with the average daily value of new issues falling from $8.0 billion in the second quarter of 2008 to $4.3 billion in the fourth quarter. In addition, securitization of automobile loans, credit card receivables, student loans, and commercial mortgages ground to a halt.

This freezing of credit markets, together with the decline in wealth and confidence, caused consumer spending and residential investment to fall sharply. Real GDP declined at an annual rate of 2.7 percent in the third quarter of 2008, 5.4 percent in the fourth quarter, and 6.4 percent in the first quarter of 2009. Industrial production, which had been falling steadily over the first eight months of 2008, plummeted in the final four months—dropping at an annual rate of 18 percent.

Many industries were battered by the financial crisis and the resulting economic downturn. The American automobile industry was hit particularly hard. Sales of light motor vehicles, which had exceeded 16 million units every year from 1999 to 2007, fell to an annual rate of only 9.5 million in the first quarter of 2009. Employment in the motor vehicle and parts industry declined by 240,000 over the 12 months through January 2009. Two domestic manufacturers, General Motors (GM) and Chrysler, required emergency loans in late December 2008 and early January 2009 to avoid disorderly bankruptcy.

The most disturbing manifestation of the rapid slowdown in the economy was the dramatic increase in job loss. Over the first months of 2008, job losses were typically between 100,000 and 200,000 per month. In October, the economy lost 380,000 jobs; in November, 597,000 jobs. By January, the economy was losing jobs at a rate of 741,000 per month. Commensurate with this terrible rate of job loss, the unemployment rate rose rapidly—from 6.2 percent in September 2008 to 7.7 percent in January 2009. It then continued to rise by roughly one-half of a percentage point per month through the winter and spring; it reached 9.4 percent in May, and ended the year at 10.0 percent.

Wall Street and Main Street

As described in more detail later, policymakers have focused much of their response to the crisis on stabilizing the financial system. Many Americans are troubled by these policies. Because to a large extent it was the actions of credit market participants that led to the crisis, people ask why policymakers should take actions focused on restoring credit markets.

The basic reason for these policies is that the health of credit markets is critically important to the functioning of our economy. Large firms use commercial paper to finance their biweekly payrolls and pay suppliers for materials to keep production lines going. Small firms rely on bank loans to meet their payrolls and pay for supplies while they wait for payment of their accounts receivable. Home purchases depend on mortgages; automobile purchases depend on car loans; college educations depend on student loans; and purchases of everyday items depend on credit cards.

The events of the past two years provide a dramatic demonstration of the importance of credit in the modern economy. As the President said in his inaugural address, "Our workers are no less productive than when this crisis began. Our minds are no less inventive, our goods and services no less needed." Yet developments in financial markets—rises and falls in home and equity prices and in the availability of credit—have led to a collapse of spending, and hence to a precipitous decline in output and to unemployment for millions.

Numerous academic studies before the crisis had also shown that the availability of credit is critical to investment, hiring, and production. One study, for example, found that when a parent company earns high profits and so has less need to rely on credit, the additional funds lead to higher investment by subsidiaries in completely unrelated lines of business (Lamont 1997). Another found that when a small change in a firm's circumstances frees up a large amount of funds that would otherwise have to go to pension contributions, the result is a large change in spending on capital goods (Rauh 2006). Other studies have shown that when the Federal Reserve tightens monetary policy, small firms, which typically have more difficulty obtaining financing, are hit especially hard (Gertler and Gilchrist 1994), and firms without access to public debt markets cut their inventories much more sharply than firms that have such access (Kashyap, Lamont, and Stein 1994).

Research before the crisis had also found that financial market disruptions could affect the real economy. Ben Bernanke, who is now Chairman of the Federal Reserve, demonstrated a link between the disruption of lending caused by bank failures and the worsening of the Great Depression (Bernanke 1983). A smaller but more modern example is provided by the impact of Japan's financial crisis in the 1990s on the United States: construction lending, new construction, and construction employment were more adversely affected in U.S. states where subsidiaries of Japanese banks had a larger role, and thus where credit availability was more affected by the collapse of Japan's bubble (Peek and Rosengren 2000). That a financial disruption in a trading partner can have a detectable adverse impact on our economy through its impact on credit availability suggests that the effect of a full-fledged financial crisis at home would be enormous—an implication that, sadly, has proven to be correct.

Finally, microeconomic evidence from the recent crisis also shows the importance of the financial system to the real economy. For example, firms that happened to have long-term debt coming due after the crisis began, and thus faced high costs of refinancing, cut their investment much more than firms that did not (Almeida et al. 2009). Another study found that a majority of corporate chief financial officers surveyed reported that their firms faced financing constraints during the crisis, and that the constrained firms on average planned to reduce investment spending, research and development, and employment sharply compared with the unconstrained firms (Campello, Graham, and Harvey 2009).

In short, the goal of the policies to stabilize the financial system was not to help financial institutions. The goal was to help ordinary Americans. When the financial system is not working, individuals and businesses cannot get credit, demand and production plummet, and job losses skyrocket. Thus, an essential step in healing the real economy is to heal the financial system. The alternative of letting financial institutions suffer the consequences of their mistakes would have led to a collapse of credit markets and vastly greater suffering for millions and millions of Americans.

The policies to rescue the financial sector were, however, costly, and often had the side effect of benefiting the very institutions whose irresponsible actions contributed to the crisis. That is one reason that the President has endorsed a Financial Crisis Responsibility Fee on the largest financial firms to repay the Federal Government for its extraordinary actions. As discussed in Chapter 6, the Administration has also proposed a comprehensive plan for financial regulatory reform that will help ensure that Wall Street does not return to the risky practices that were a central cause of the recent crisis.

THE UNPRECEDENTED POLICY RESPONSE

Given the magnitude of the shocks that hit the economy in the fall of 2008 and the winter of 2009, the downturn could have turned into a second Great Depression. That it has not is a tribute to the aggressive and effective policy response. This response involved the Federal Reserve and other financial regulators, the Administration, and Congress. The policy tools were similarly multifaceted, including monetary policy, financial market interventions, fiscal policy, and policies targeted specifically at housing.

Monetary Policy

The first line of defense against a weak economy is the interest rate policy of the independent Federal Reserve. By increasing or decreasing the quantity of reserves it supplies to the banking system, the Federal Reserve can lower or raise the Federal funds rate, which is the interest rate at which banks lend to one another. The funds rate influences other interest rates in the economy and so has important effects on economic activity. Using changes in the target level of the funds rate as their main tool of counter-cyclical policy, monetary policymakers had kept inflation low and the real economy remarkably stable for more than two decades.

The Federal Reserve has used interest rate policy aggressively in the recent episode. The target level of the funds rate at the beginning of 2007 was 5¼ percent. The Federal Reserve cut the target by 1 percentage point over the last four months of 2007 and by an additional 2¼ percentage points over the first four months of 2008. After the events of September, it cut the target in three additional steps in October and December, bringing it to its current level of 0 to ¼ percent.

Conventional interest rate policy, however, could do little to deal with the enormous disruptions to credit markets. As a result, the Federal Reserve has used a range of unconventional tools to address those disruptions directly. For example, in March 2008, it created the Primary Dealer Credit Facility and the Term Securities Lending Facility to provide liquidity support for primary dealers (that is, financial institutions that trade directly with the Federal Reserve) and the key financial markets in which they operate. In October 2008, when the critical market for commercial paper threatened to stop functioning, the Federal Reserve responded by setting up the Commercial Paper Funding Facility to backstop the market.

Once the Federal Reserve's target for the funds rate was effectively lowered to zero in December 2008, there was another reason to use unconventional tools. Nominal interest rates generally cannot fall below zero: because holding currency guarantees a nominal return of zero, no one is willing to make loans at a negative nominal interest rate. As a result, when the Federal funds rate is zero, supplying more reserves does not drive it lower. Statistical estimates suggest that based on the Federal Reserve's usual response to inflation and unemployment, the subdued level of inflation and the weak state of the economy would have led the central bank to reduce its target for the funds rate by about an additional 5 percentage points if it could have (Rudebusch 2009).

This desire to provide further stimulus, coupled with the inability to use conventional interest rate policy, led the Federal Reserve to undertake large-scale asset purchases to reduce long-term interest rates. In March

2009, the Federal Reserve announced plans to purchase up to $300 billion of long-term Treasury debt; it also announced plans to increase its purchases of the debt of Fannie Mae, Freddie Mac, and the Federal Home Loan Banks (the government-sponsored enterprises, or GSEs, that support the mortgage market) to up to $200 billion, and its purchases of agency (that is, Fannie Mae, Freddie Mac, and Ginnie Mae) mortgage-backed securities to up to $1.25 trillion.

Finally, the Federal Reserve has attempted to manage expectations by providing information about its goals and the likely path of policy. Officials have consistently stressed their commitment to ensuring that inflation neither falls substantially below nor rises substantially above its usual level. In addition, the Federal Reserve has repeatedly stated that economic conditions "are likely to warrant exceptionally low levels of the Federal funds rate for an extended period." To the extent this statement provides market participants with information they did not already have, it is likely to keep longer-term interest rates lower than they otherwise would be.

One effect of the Federal Reserve's unconventional policies has been an enormous expansion of the quantity of assets on the Federal Reserve's balance sheet. Figure 2-4 shows the evolution of Federal Reserve asset holdings since the beginning of 2007. One can see both that asset holdings nearly tripled between January and December 2008 and that there was a dramatic move away from short-term Treasury securities.

Figure 2-4
Assets on the Federal Reserve's Balance Sheet

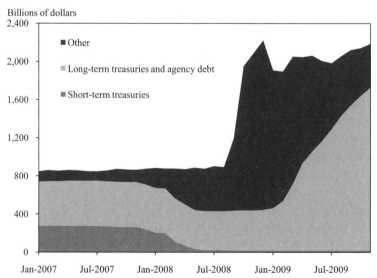

Billions of dollars

Notes: Agency debt refers to obligations of Fannie Mae, Freddie Mac, and the Federal Home Loan Banks. Agency mortgage-backed securities are also included in this category.
Source: Federal Reserve Board, H.4.1 Table 1.

The flip side of the large increase in the Federal Reserve's asset holdings is a large increase in the quantity of reserves it has supplied to the financial system. Some observers have expressed concern that the large expansion in reserves could lead to inflation. In this regard, two key points should be kept in mind. First, as already described, most statistical models suggest that the Federal Reserve's target interest rate would be substantially lower than it is today if it were not constrained by the fact that the Federal funds rate cannot fall below zero. As a result, monetary policy is in fact unusually tight given the state of the economy, not unusually loose. Second, the Federal Reserve has the tools it needs to prevent the reserves from leading to inflation. It can drain the reserves from the financial system through sales of the assets it has acquired or other actions. Indeed, despite the weak state of the economy, the return of credit market conditions toward normal is leading to the natural unwinding of some of the exceptional credit market programs. Another reliable way the Federal Reserve can keep the reserves from creating inflationary pressure is by using its relatively new ability to raise the interest rate it pays on reserves: banks will be unwilling to lend the reserves at low interest rates if they can obtain a higher return on their balances held at the Federal Reserve.

Financial Rescue

Efforts to stabilize the financial system have been a central part of the policy response. As just discussed, even before the financial crisis in September 2008, the Federal Reserve was taking steps to ease pressures on credit markets. The events of the fall led to even stronger actions. On September 7, Fannie Mae and Freddie Mac were placed in conservatorship under the Federal Housing Finance Agency to prevent a potentially severe disruption of mortgage lending. On September 16, concern about the potentially catastrophic effects of a disorderly failure of American International Group (AIG) caused the Federal Reserve to extend the firm an $85 billion line of credit. On September 19, concerns about the possibility of runs on money-market mutual funds led the Treasury to announce a temporary guarantee program for these funds.

On October 3, Congress passed and President Bush signed the Emergency Economic Stabilization Act of 2008. This Act provided up to $700 billion for the Troubled Asset Relief Program (TARP) for the purchase of distressed assets and for capital injections into financial institutions, although the second $350 billion required presidential notification to Congress and could be disallowed by a vote of both houses. The initial $350 billion was used mainly to purchase preferred equity shares in financial institutions, thereby providing the institutions with more capital to help them withstand the crisis.

At President-Elect Obama's request, President Bush notified Congress on January 12, 2009 of his plan to release the second $350 billion of TARP funds. With strong support from the incoming Administration, the Senate defeated a resolution disapproving the release. These funds provided policy-makers with critical resources needed to ensure financial stability.

On February 10, 2009, Secretary of the Treasury Timothy Geithner announced the Administration's Financial Stability Plan. The plan represented a new, comprehensive approach to the financial rescue that sought to tackle the interlocking sources of instability and increase credit flows. An overarching theme was a focus on transparency and accountability to rebuild confidence in financial markets and protect taxpayer resources.

A key element of the plan was the Supervisory Capital Assessment Program (or "stress test"). The purpose was to assess the capital needs of the country's 19 largest financial institutions should economic and financial conditions deteriorate further. Institutions that were found to need an additional capital buffer would be encouraged to raise private capital and would be provided with temporary government capital if those efforts did not succeed. This program was intended not just to examine the capital positions of the institutions and ensure that they obtained more capital if needed, but also to strengthen private investors' confidence in the soundness of the institutions' balance sheets, and so strengthen the institutions' ability to obtain private capital.

Another element of the plan was the Consumer and Business Lending Initiative, which was aimed at maintaining the flow of credit. In November 2008, the Federal Reserve had created the Term Asset-Backed Securities Loan Facility to help counteract the dramatic decline in securitized lending. In the February announcement of the Financial Stability Plan, the Treasury greatly expanded the resources of the not-yet-implemented facility. The Treasury increased its commitment to $100 billion to leverage up to $1 trillion of lending for businesses and households. By facilitating securitization, the program was designed to help unfreeze credit and lower interest rates for auto loans, credit card loans, student loans, and small business loans guaranteed by the Small Business Administration (SBA).

A third element of the plan was a Treasury partnership with the Federal Deposit Insurance Corporation and the Federal Reserve to create the Public-Private Investment Program. A central purpose was to remove troubled assets from the balance sheets of financial institutions, thereby reducing uncertainty about their financial strength and increasing their ability to raise capital and hence their willingness to lend. Partnership with the private sector served two important objectives: it leveraged scarce public funds, and it used private competition and incentives to ensure that the government did not overpay for assets.

There were two other key components of the Financial Stability Plan. One was a wide-ranging program to reduce mortgage interest rates and help responsible homeowners stay in their homes. These policies are described later in the section on housing policy. The other component was a range of measures to help small businesses. Many of these were included in the American Recovery and Reinvestment Act and are discussed in the section on fiscal stimulus.

Failure of the two troubled domestic automakers (GM and Chrysler) threatened economy-wide repercussions that would have been magnified by related problems at the automakers' associated financial institutions (GMAC and Chrysler Financial). To avoid these consequences, the Bush Administration set up the Auto Industry Financing Program within the TARP. This program extended $17.4 billion in funding to the two companies in late December 2008 and early January 2009. The program also extended $7.5 billion in funding to the two auto finance companies around the same time. Upon taking office, the Obama Administration required the automakers to submit plans for restructuring and a return to viability before additional funds were committed. To sustain the industry during this planning process, the Treasury established the Warranty Commitment Program to reassure consumers that warranties of the troubled firms would be honored. It also initiated the Auto Supplier Support Program to maintain stability in the auto supply base.

Over the spring of 2009, the Administration's Auto Task Force worked with GM and Chrysler to produce plans for viability. In the case of Chrysler, the task force determined that viability could be achieved by merging with the Italian automaker Fiat. For GM, the task force determined that substantial reductions in costs were necessary and charged the company with producing a more aggressive restructuring plan. For both companies, a quick, targeted bankruptcy was judged to be the most efficient and successful way to restructure. Chrysler filed for bankruptcy on April 30, 2009; GM, on June 1. In addition to concessions by all stakeholders, including workers, retirees, creditors, and suppliers, the U.S. Government invested substantial funds to bring about the orderly restructuring. In all, more than $80 billion of TARP funds had been authorized for the motor vehicle industry as of September 20, 2009.

Fiscal Stimulus

The signature element of the Administration's policy response to the crisis was the American Recovery and Reinvestment Act of 2009 (ARRA). The President signed the Recovery Act in Denver on February 17, just 28 days after taking office. At an estimated cost of $787 billion, the Act is the largest countercyclical fiscal action in American history. It provides tax cuts and increases in government spending equivalent to roughly 2 percent of GDP in 2009 and 2¼ percent of GDP in 2010. To put those figures in perspective, the largest expansionary swing in the budget during Franklin Roosevelt's New Deal was an increase in the deficit of about 1½ percent of GDP in fiscal 1936. That expansion, however, was counteracted the very next fiscal year by a contraction that was even larger.

The fiscal stimulus was designed to fill part of the shortfall in aggregate demand caused by the collapse of private demand and the Federal Reserve's inability to lower short-term interest rates further. It was part of a comprehensive package that included stabilizing the financial system, helping responsible homeowners avoid foreclosure, and aiding small businesses through tax relief and increased lending. The President set as a goal for the fiscal stimulus that it raise employment by 3½ million relative to what it otherwise would have been.

Several principles guided the design of the stimulus. One was that it be spread over two years, reflecting the Administration's view that the economy would need substantial support for more than one year. At the same time, the Administration also strongly supported keeping the stimulus explicitly temporary. It was not to be an excuse to permanently expand the size of government.

A second key principle was that the stimulus be well diversified. Different types of stimulus affect the economy in different ways. Individual tax cuts, for example, affect production and employment in a wide range of industries by encouraging households to spend more on consumer goods, while government investments in infrastructure directly increase construction activity and employment. In addition, underlying economic conditions affect the efficacy of fiscal policy in ways that can be quantitatively important and sometimes difficult to forecast. Likewise, different types of stimulus affect the economy with different speeds. For instance, aid to individuals directly affected by the recession tends to be spent relatively quickly, while new investment projects require more time. Because of the need to provide broad support to the economy over an extended period, the Administration supported a stimulus plan that included a broad range of fiscal actions.

A third principle was that emergency spending should aim to address long-term needs. Some spending, such as unemployment insurance, is aimed at helping those directly affected by the recession maintain a decent standard of living. But government investment spending should aim to create enduring capital investments that increase productivity and growth.

The Recovery Act reflected those guiding principles. The Congressional Budget Office (CBO) estimated that almost one-quarter of the stimulus would be spent by the end of the third quarter of 2009, and an additional half would be spent over the next four quarters (Congressional Budget Office 2009b). So far, the pace of the spending and tax cuts has largely matched CBO's estimates.

The final package was very well diversified. Roughly one-third took the form of tax cuts. The most significant of these was the Making Work Pay tax credit, which cut taxes for 95 percent of working families. Taxes for a typical family were reduced by $800 per couple for each of 2009 and 2010. Another provision of the bill provided roughly $14 billion for one-time payments of $250 to seniors, veterans, and people with disabilities. The macroeconomic effects of these payments are likely to be similar to those of tax cuts.

Businesses received important tax cuts as well. The most important of these was an extension of bonus depreciation, which reduced taxes on new investments by allowing firms to immediately deduct half the cost of property and equipment purchases. One advantage of such temporary investment incentives is that they can affect the timing of investment, moving some investment from future years when the economy does not have a deficiency of aggregate demand to the present, when it does.

In addition, because the financial market disruptions had a particularly paralyzing effect on the financial plans of small businesses, the Act included additional measures targeted specifically at those businesses. Tax cuts for small businesses included an expansion of provisions allowing for the carryback of net operating losses, a temporary 75 percent exclusion from capital gains taxes on small business stock, and the ability to immediately expense up to $250,000 of qualified investment purchases. In addition to reducing taxes, these provisions improve cash flow at firms facing credit constraints and provide extra incentives for individuals to invest in small businesses. The Act also included measures to help increase small business lending through the SBA. In particular, it raised to 90 percent the maximum guarantee on SBA general purpose and working capital loans (the 7(a) program) and eliminated fees on both 7(a) loans and loans for fixed-asset capital and real estate investment projects (the 504 program).

Another important part of the stimulus consisted of fiscal relief to state governments. Because almost every state has a balanced-budget requirement, the declines in revenues caused by the recession forced states to cut spending or raise taxes, thereby further contracting demand and magnifying the downturn. Federal fiscal relief can help prevent these contractionary responses, helping to maintain critical state services and state employment, prevent tax increases on families already suffering from the recession, and cushion the fall in demand. And because many states were already raising taxes and cutting spending when the ARRA was passed, the effects were likely to occur relatively quickly. The Act therefore included roughly $140 billion of state fiscal relief.

The Recovery Act also included approximately $90 billion of support for individuals directly affected by the recession. This support serves two critical purposes. First, it provides relief from the recession's devastating impact on families and individuals. Second, because the recipients typically spend this support quickly, it provides an immediate boost to the broader economy. Among the major components of this relief were an extension and expansion of unemployment insurance benefits, subsidies to help the unemployed continue to obtain health insurance, and additional funding for the Supplemental Nutritional Assistance Program. The Act also reduced taxes on unemployment insurance benefits, the effect of which is similar to an expansion of benefits.

Finally, the Recovery Act included direct government investment spending. Because government investment raises output in the short run both through its direct effects and by increasing the incomes and spending of the workers employed on the projects, its output effects are particularly large. In addition, because this type of stimulus is spent less quickly than other types, it will play a vital role in providing support to the economy after 2009. And by funding critical investments, this spending will raise the economy's output even in the long run.

The Act included funding both for traditional government investment projects, such as transportation infrastructure and basic scientific research, and for initial investments to jump-start private investment in emerging new areas, such as health information technology, a smart electrical grid, and clean energy technologies. The Act also included tax credits for specific types of private spending, such as home weatherization and advanced energy manufacturing, which are likely to have effects similar to direct government investment spending. Altogether, roughly one-third of the budget impact of the Recovery Act will take the form of these investments and tax credits.

Fiscal stimulus actions did not end with the passage and implementation of the Recovery Act. In June 2009, the Administration worked with Congress to set up the Car Allowance Rebate System (CARS). Commonly known as the "Cash for Clunkers" program, CARS gave rebates of up to $4,500 to consumers who replaced older cars and trucks with newer, more fuel-efficient models. The program was in effect for July and most of August. After the program's popularity led to quick exhaustion of the original funding of $1 billion, the funding was increased to $3 billion to allow more consumers to participate.

In November, the Worker, Homeownership, and Business Assistance Act of 2009 cut taxes for struggling businesses and strengthened the safety net for workers. In particular, the Act extended the net operating loss provisions of the Recovery Act that allowed small businesses to count their losses this year against taxes paid in previous years for an additional year, and expanded the benefit to medium and large businesses. The Act also provided up to 20 additional weeks of unemployment insurance benefits for workers who were reaching the end of their emergency unemployment benefits. In December, an amendment to the Department of Defense Appropriations Act of 2010 continued through the end of February 2010 the unemployment insurance provisions of the Recovery Act, the November extension of emergency benefits, and the COBRA subsidy program that helps unemployed workers maintain their health insurance. It also expanded the COBRA premium subsidy period from 9 to 15 months and extended the increased guarantees and fee waivers for SBA loans.

Housing Policy

The economic and financial crisis began in the housing market, and an important part of the policy response has been directed at that market. The Administration initiated the Making Home Affordable program (MHA) in March 2009. This program was designed to support low mortgage rates, keep millions of homeowners in their homes, and stabilize the housing market.

As described earlier, the Federal Reserve undertook large-scale purchases of GSE debt and mortgage-backed securities in an effort to reduce mortgage interest rates. At the same time, the Treasury Department made an increased funding commitment to the GSEs. This increased government support for the agencies also reduced their borrowing costs and so helped lower mortgage interest rates.

Importantly, MHA also included a program to help households take advantage of lower interest rates. The Home Affordable Refinance Program helps families whose homes have lost value and whose mortgage payments can be reduced by refinancing at historically low interest rates. This program expanded the opportunity to refinance to borrowers with loans owned or guaranteed by the GSEs who had a mortgage balance up to 125 percent of their home's current value.

Another key component of MHA is the Home Affordable Modification Program (HAMP), which is providing up to $75 billion to encourage loan modifications. It offers incentives to investors, lenders, servicers, and homeowners to encourage mortgage modifications in which all stakeholders share in the cost of ensuring that responsible homeowners can afford their monthly mortgage payments. To protect taxpayers, HAMP focuses on sound modifications. No payments are made by the government unless the modification lasts for at least three months, and all the payments are designed around the principle of "pay for success." All parties have aligned incentives under the program to achieve successful modifications at an affordable and sustainable level.

The Administration has supported additional programs to help the housing sector. The Recovery Act included an $8,000 first-time homebuyer's credit for home purchases made before December 1, 2009. As with temporary investment incentives, this credit can help the economy by changing the timing of decisions, bringing buyers into the housing market who were not planning on becoming homeowners until after 2009 or were postponing their purchases in light of the distress in the market. In November, this credit was expanded and extended by the Workers, Homeownership, and Business Assistance Act of 2009.

The Recovery Act also gave considerable resources to the Neighborhood Stabilization Program, a program administered by the Department of Housing and Urban Development to stabilize communities that have suffered from foreclosures and abandoned homes. The Administration also provided assistance to state and local housing finance agencies and their efforts to aid distressed homeowners, stimulate first-time home buying, and provide affordable rental homes. These agencies had faced a significant liquidity crisis resulting from disruptions in financial markets.

The Effects of the Policies

The condition of the American economy has changed dramatically in the past year. At the beginning of 2009, financial markets were functioning poorly, house prices were plummeting, and output and employment were in freefall. Today, financial markets have stabilized and credit is starting to flow again, house prices have leveled off, output is growing, and the employment situation is stabilizing. Because of the depth of the economy's fall, we are a long way from full recovery, and significant challenges remain. But the trajectory of the economy is vastly improved.

There is strong evidence that the policy response has been central to this turnaround. The actions to stabilize credit markets have prevented further destructive failures of major financial institutions and helped maintain lending in key areas. The housing and mortgage policies have kept hundreds of thousands of homeowners in their homes and brought mortgage rates to historic lows. The speed of the economy's change in direction has been remarkable and matches up well with the timing of the fiscal stimulus. And both direct estimates as well as the assessments of expert observers underscore the crucial role played by the stimulus.

The Financial Sector

Given the powerful impact of the financial sector on the real economy, a necessary first step to recovery of the real economy was recovery of the financial sector. And the financial sector has unquestionably begun to recover. Figure 2-5 extends the graph of the TED spread and the BAA-AAA spread shown in Figure 2-3 through December 2009. After spiking to unprecedented levels in October 2008, the TED spread fell rapidly over the next two months but remained substantially elevated at the beginning of 2009. It then declined gradually through August and is now at normal levels. This key indicator of the basic functioning of credit markets suggests substantial financial recovery. The BAA-AAA spread remained very high through April but then fell rapidly from April to September. This spread, which normally rises when the economy is weak because of higher corporate default risks, is now at levels comparable to those at the beginning of the recession and below its levels in much of 1990–91 and 2002–03. Thus, the current level of the spread appears to reflect mainly the weak state of the economy rather than any specific difficulties in credit markets.

Figure 2-5
TED Spread and Moody's BAA-AAA Spread Through December 2009

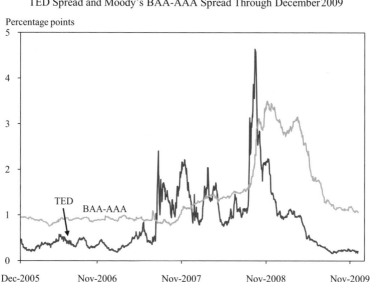

Notes: The TED spread is defined as the three-month London Interbank Offer Rate (LIBOR) less the yield on the three-month U.S. Treasury security. Moody's BAA-AAA spread is the difference between Moody's indexes of yields on AAA and BAA rated corporate bonds.
Source: Bloomberg.

Another broad indicator of the health of the financial system is the level of stock prices, which depend both on investors' expectations of future earnings and on their willingness to bear risk. Figure 2-6 shows the behavior of the S&P 500 stock price index since January 2006. This series declined by 18 percent from its peak in October 2007 through the end of August 2008, fell precipitously in September, and continued to fall through March 2009 as the economy deteriorated sharply and investors became extremely fearful. The stabilization of the economy and the restoration of more normal workings of financial markets have led to a sharp turnaround in stock prices. As of December 31, 2009, the S&P 500 was 65 percent above its low in March. As with the BAA-AAA spread, the current level of stock prices relative to their pre-recession level appears to reflect the weaker situation of the real economy rather than any specific problems with financial markets or investors' willingness to bear risk.

Figure 2-6
S&P 500 Stock Price Index

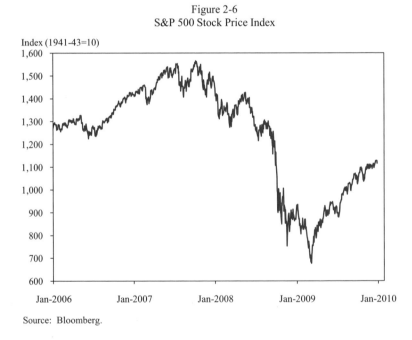

Index (1941-43=10)

Source: Bloomberg.

These indicators show that financial markets have evolved toward normalcy, which was a necessary step in stopping the economic freefall. But for the economy to recover fully, that is not enough: credit must be available to sound borrowers. On this front, the results are more mixed. Some sources of credit are coming back strongly, but others remain weak.

As described in more detail later, one critical market where policies have succeeded in lowering interest rates and maintaining credit flows is the mortgage market. Another market that has recovered substantially is the market for commercial paper. In late 2008 and early 2009, this market was functioning in large part because of the direct intervention of the Federal Reserve. By mid-January, the Federal Reserve's Commercial Paper Funding Facility (CPFF) was holding $350 billion of commercial paper. As credit conditions have stabilized, however, firms have been able to place their commercial paper privately on better terms than through the CPFF, and levels of commercial paper outstanding have remained stable even as the Federal Reserve has reduced its holdings to less than $15 billion. Nonetheless, quantities of commercial paper outstanding remain well below their pre-crisis levels.

Another crucial source of credit that has stabilized is the market for corporate bonds. As risk spreads have fallen, corporations have found it easier to obtain funding by issuing longer-term bonds than by issuing such instruments as commercial paper. As a result, corporate bond issuance, which fell sharply in the second half of 2008, is now running above pre-crisis levels.

An important financial market development occurred in response to the stress test conducted in the spring. This comprehensive review of the soundness of the Nation's 19 largest financial institutions, together with the public release of this information, strengthened private investors' confidence in the institutions. Partly as a result, the institutions were able to raise $55 billion in private common equity, improving their capital positions and their ability to lend.

The fact that financial institutions are increasingly able to raise private capital is reducing their need to rely on public capital. Only $7 billion of TARP funds have been extended to banks since January 20, 2009. Many financial institutions have repaid their TARP funds, and the expected cost of the program to the government has been revised down by approximately $200 billion since August 2009.

Policy initiatives have also had a clear impact on small business lending. Figure 2-7 shows the amount of SBA-guaranteed loans that have been made since October 2006. SBA loan volume experienced its first significant decrease in September and October 2007; following the failure of Lehman Brothers in September 2008, it fell by more than half. The recovery in small business lending coincided with the passage of the Recovery Act in February 2009. In the months between Lehman's fall and passage of the Recovery Act, average monthly loan volume was $830 million; immediately after passage, loan volume began to steadily recover and averaged $1.3 billion per month through September 2009. In September, loan volume reached $1.9 billion, which was the highest level since August 2007; this has since been exceeded by November 2009's monthly loan volume of

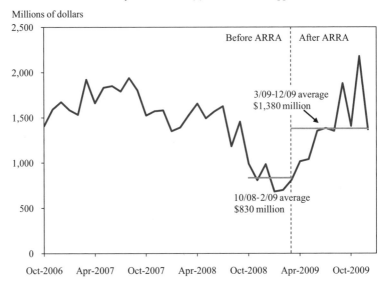

Figure 2-7
Monthly Gross SBA 7(a) and 504 Loan Approvals

Millions of dollars

Before ARRA | After ARRA

3/09-12/09 average
$1,380 million

10/08-2/09 average
$830 million

Source: Unpublished monthly data provided by the Small Business Administration.

$2.2 billion. In total, between February and December 2009 the SBA guaranteed nearly $15 billion in small business lending.

Nonetheless, overall credit conditions have not returned to normal. Many small business owners report continued difficulties in obtaining credit. In addition, the severity of the downturn is leading to elevated rates of failure of small banks, potentially disrupting their lending to small businesses and households. The market for asset-backed securities is also far from fully recovered. As a result, it is often hard for banks and other lenders to package and sell their loans, which forces them to hold a greater fraction of the loans they originate and thus limits their ability to lend.

One important source of data on credit availability is the Federal Reserve's Senior Loan Officer Opinion Survey on Bank Lending Practices. The survey, conducted every three months, examines whether banks are tightening lending standards, loosening them, or keeping them basically unchanged. The October 2008 survey found that the overwhelming majority of banks were tightening standards. This fraction has declined steadily, and by October 2009 less than 20 percent were reporting that they were tightening standards for commercial and industrial loans, though none reported loosening standards. Thus, credit conditions remain tight.

Housing

As described earlier, policymakers have taken unprecedented actions to maintain mortgage lending. One result has been a major shift in the composition of mortgage finance. In 2006, private institutions provided 60 percent of liquidity while the GSEs, the Federal Housing Agency (FHA), and the Veterans Administration (VA) provided the remaining 40 percent. As home prices began to decline nationally in 2007, private financing for mortgages began to dry up. As of November 2009, the mortgages guaranteed by the GSEs, FHA, and the VA accounted for nearly all mortgage originations. About 22 percent of mortgage originations are guaranteed by FHA or VA, up from less than 3 percent in 2006. About 75 percent of mortgage originations are guaranteed by the GSEs, up from less than 40 percent in 2006.

As Figure 2-8 shows, mortgage rates fell to historic lows in 2009—consistent with the government's increased funding commitment to Fannie Mae and Freddie Mac and the Federal Reserve's purchases of mortgage-backed securities. These low mortgage rates support home prices and thus benefit all homeowners. More directly, households that have refinanced their mortgages at the lower rates have obtained considerable savings. These savings have effects similar to tax cuts, improving households' financial positions and encouraging spending on other goods. With the help of the Home Affordable Refinance Program, approximately 3 million borrowers have refinanced, putting more than $6 billion of purchasing power at an annual rate into the hands of households.

Figure 2-8
30-Year Fixed Rate Mortgage Rate

Note: Contract interest rate for first mortgages.
Source: Freddie Mac, Primary Mortgage Market Survey.

In addition, the Home Affordable Modification Program has been successful in encouraging mortgage modifications. When the program was launched, the Administration estimated that it could offer help to as many as 3 million to 4 million borrowers through the end of 2012. On October 8, 2009, the Administration announced that servicers had begun more than 500,000 trial modifications, nearly a month ahead of the original goal. As of November, the monthly pace of trial modifications exceeded the monthly pace of completed foreclosures. Of course, not all trial modifications will become permanent, but the Administration is making every effort to ensure that as many sound modifications as possible do.

One important result of the policies aimed at the housing market and of the broader policies to support the economy is that the housing market appears to have stabilized. National home price indexes have been relatively steady for the past several months, as shown in Figure 2-9. The Federal Housing Finance Agency purchase-only house price index, which is constructed using only conforming mortgages (that is, mortgages eligible for purchase by the GSEs), has changed little since late 2008. The LoanPerformance house price index, another closely watched measure that uses conforming and nonconforming mortgages with coverage of repeat sales transactions for more than 85 percent of the population, rose 6 percent between March and August 2009 before declining slightly in recent months. In addition, the pace of sales of existing single-family homes has increased substantially. Sales in the fourth quarter of 2009 were 29 percent above their low in the first quarter of 2009 and comparable to levels in the first half of 2007.

Finally, there are signs of renewed building activity. After falling 81 percent from their peak in September 2005 to their low in January 2009, single-family housing permits (a leading indicator of housing construction) rose 49 percent through December 2009. Similarly, after falling for 14 consecutive quarters, the residential investment component of real GDP rose in the third and fourth quarters of 2009.

Inventories of vacant homes for sale remain at high levels, and many vacant homes are being held off the market and will likely be put up for sale as home prices increase. This overhang may lead to some additional price declines, although prices are unlikely to fall at the same rate as they did during the crisis. Thus, the recovery of the housing sector is likely to be slow. Of course, we should neither expect nor want the housing market to return to its pre-crisis condition. In the long run, as discussed in more detail in Chapter 4, neither the extraordinarily high levels of housing construction and price appreciation before the crisis nor the extraordinarily low levels of construction and the rapid price declines during the crisis are sustainable.

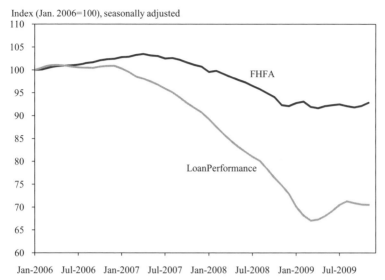

Figure 2-9
FHFA and LoanPerformance National House Price Indexes

Index (Jan. 2006=100), seasonally adjusted

FHFA

LoanPerformance

Jan-2006   Jul-2006   Jan-2007   Jul-2007   Jan-2008   Jul-2008   Jan-2009   Jul-2009

Sources: Federal Housing Finance Agency, purchase-only index; First American Core Logic
LoanPerformance.

Overall Economic Activity

The direction of overall economic activity changed dramatically over
the course of 2009. Figure 2-10 shows the quarterly growth rate of real GDP,
the broadest indicator of national production. After falling at an annual
rate of 6.4 percent in the first quarter, real GDP declined at a rate of just
0.7 percent in the second quarter. It then grew at a 2.2 percent rate in the
third quarter and a 5.7 percent rate in the fourth. Such a rapid turnaround
in growth is remarkable. The improvement in growth of 8.6 percentage
points from the first quarter to the third quarter (that is, the swing from
growth at a -6.4 percent rate to growth at a 2.2 percent rate) was the largest
since 1983. Similarly, the three-quarter improvement from the first quarter
to the fourth of 12.1 percentage points was the largest since 1981, and the
second largest since 1958.

One limitation of these simple statistics is that they do not account
for the usual dynamics of the economy. A more sophisticated way to gauge
the extent of the change in the economy's direction is to compare the path
the economy has followed with the predictions of a statistical model. There
are many ways to construct a baseline statistical forecast. The particular one
used here is a vector autoregression (or VAR) that includes the logarithms
of real GDP (in billions of chained 2005 dollars) and payroll employment (in
thousands, in the final month of the quarter), using four lags of each variable

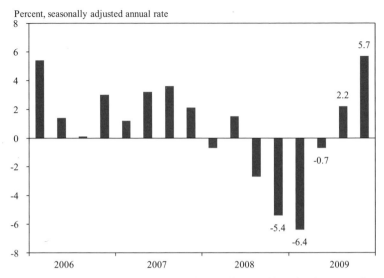

Figure 2-10
Real GDP Growth

Percent, seasonally adjusted annual rate

Source: Department of Commerce (Bureau of Economic Analysis), National Income and
Product Accounts Table 1.1.1, line 1.

and estimated over the period 1990:Q1–2007:Q4. Because the sample period
ends in the fourth quarter of 2007, the coefficient estimates used to construct
the forecast are not influenced by the current recession. Rather, they show
the normal joint short-run dynamics of real GDP and employment over an
extended period. GDP and employment are then forecast for the final three
quarters of 2009 using the estimated VAR and actual data through the first
quarter of the year. The resulting comparison of the actual and projected
paths of the economy shows the differences between the economy's actual
performance and what one would have expected given the situation as of
the first quarter and the economy's usual dynamics.[1] Although the results
presented here are based on one specific approach to constructing the
baseline projection, other reasonable approaches have similar implications.

This more sophisticated exercise also finds that the economy's
turnaround has been impressive. The statistical forecast based on the economy's normal dynamics projects growth at a -3.3 percent rate in the second
quarter of 2009, -0.5 percent in the third, and 1.3 percent in the fourth. In
all three quarters, actual growth was substantially higher than the projection.
Figure 2-11 shows that as a result, the *level* of GDP exceeded the projected
level by an increasing margin: 0.7 percent in the second quarter, 1.4 percent
in the third quarter, and 2.5 percent in the fourth.

---

[1] For more details on this approach and the model-based approach discussed later, see Council
of Economic Advisers (2010).

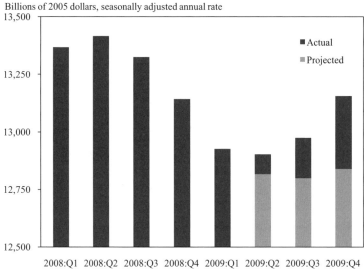

Figure 2-11
Real GDP: Actual and Statistical Baseline Projection

Billions of 2005 dollars, seasonally adjusted annual rate

Sources: Department of Commerce (Bureau of Economic Analysis), National Income and Product Accounts Table 1.1.6, line 1; CEA calculations. See Council of Economic Advisers (2010).

The gap between the actual and projected paths of GDP provides a rough way to estimate the effect of economic policy. The most obvious sources of the differences are the unprecedented policy actions. However, the gap reflects all unusual influences on GDP. For example, the rescue actions taken in other countries (described in Chapter 3) could have played a role in better American performance. At the same time, the continuing stringency in credit markets is likely lowering output relative to its usual cyclical patterns. Thus, while some factors work in the direction of causing the comparison of the economy's actual performance with its normal behavior to overstate the contribution of economic policy actions, others work in the opposite direction.

One way to estimate the specific impact of the Recovery Act is to use estimates from economic models. Mainstream estimates of economic multipliers for the effects of fiscal policy can be combined with figures on the stimulus to date to estimate how much the stimulus has contributed to growth. (For the financial and housing policies, this approach is not feasible, because the policies are so unprecedented that no estimates of their effects are readily available.) When this exercise is performed using the multipliers employed by the Council of Economic Advisers (CEA), which are based on mainstream economic models, the results suggest a critical role for the fiscal stimulus. They suggest that the Recovery Act contributed approximately 2.8

percentage points to *growth* in the second quarter, 3.9 percentage points in the third, and 1.8 percentage points in the fourth. As a result, this approach suggests that the *level* of GDP in the fourth quarter was slightly more than 2 percent higher than it would have been in the absence of the stimulus.

Knowledgeable outside observers agree that the Recovery Act has increased output substantially relative to what it otherwise would have been. For example, in November 2009, CBO estimated that the Act had raised the level of output in the third quarter by between 1.2 and 3.2 percent relative to the no-stimulus baseline (Congressional Budget Office 2009a). Private forecasters also generally estimate that the Act has raised output substantially.

A final way to look for the effects of the rescue policies on GDP is in the behavior of the components of GDP. Figure 2-12 shows the contribution of various components of GDP to overall GDP growth in each of the four quarters of 2009. One area where policy's role seems clear is in business investment in equipment and software. A key source of the turnaround in GDP is the change in this type of investment from a devastating 36 percent annual rate of decline in the first quarter to a 13 percent rate of increase by the fourth quarter. Two likely contributors to this change were the investment incentives in the Recovery Act and the many measures to stabilize the financial system and maintain lending. Similarly, the housing and financial

Figure 2-12
Contributions to Real GDP Growth

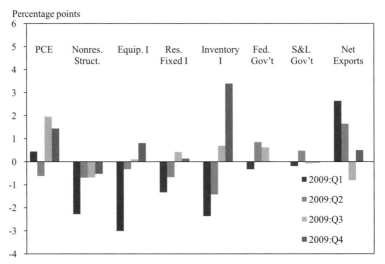

Notes: Bars sum to quarterly change in GDP growth (-6.4% in Q1; -0.7% in Q2; 2.2% in Q3; 5.7% in Q4). PCE is personal consumption expenditures; Nonres. Struct. is nonresidential fixed investment in structures; Equip I. is nonresidential fixed investment in equipment and software; Res. Fixed I is residential fixed investment; Inventory I is inventory investment; Federal Gov't is Federal Government purchases; S&L Gov't is state and local government purchases; Net Exports is net exports.
Source: Department of Commerce (Bureau of Economic Analysis), National Income and Product Accounts Table 1.1.2.

market policies were surely important to the swing in the growth of residential investment from a 38 percent annual rate of decline in the first quarter to increases in the third and fourth quarters.

Two other components showing evidence of the policies' effects are personal consumption expenditures and state and local government purchases. The Making Work Pay tax credit and the aid to individuals directly affected by the recession meant that households did not have to cut their consumption spending as much as they otherwise would have, and the Cash for Clunkers program provided important incentives for motor vehicle purchases in the third quarter. Consumption was little changed in the first two quarters of 2009 and then rose at a healthy 2.8 percent annual rate in the third quarter—driven in considerable part by a 44 percent rate of increase in purchases of motor vehicles and parts—and at a 2.0 percent rate in the fourth quarter. And, despite the dire budgetary situations of state and local governments, their purchases rose at the fastest pace in more than five years in the second quarter and were basically stable in the third and fourth quarters. This stability almost surely could not have occurred in the absence of the fiscal relief to the states.

The figure also shows the large role of inventory investment in magnifying macroeconomic fluctuations. When the economy goes into a recession, firms want to cut their inventories. As a result, inventory investment moves from its usual slightly positive level to sharply negative, contributing to the fall in output. Then, as firms moderate their inventory reductions, inventory investment rises—that is, becomes less negative—contributing to the recovery of output.

Finally, the turnaround in the automobile industry has been substantial. The Cash for Clunkers program appears to have generated a sharp increase in demand for automobiles in July and August 2009 (Council of Economic Advisers 2009). Sales of light motor vehicles averaged 12.6 million units at an annual rate during these two months, up from an annual rate of 9.6 million units in the second quarter. Although some observers had hypothesized that the July and August sales boost would be offset by a corresponding loss of sales in the months immediately following, sales in September (9.2 million at an annual rate) roughly matched the pace of sales in the first half of 2009, and sales subsequently rebounded to a 10.8 million unit annual pace in the fourth quarter. Employment in motor vehicles and parts hit a low of 633,300 in June 2009 and has increased modestly since then. In December 2009, employment was 655,200.

Both GM and Chrysler proceeded through bankruptcy in an efficient manner, and the new companies emerged far more quickly than outside experts thought would be possible. The companies are performing in line with their restructuring plans, and in November 2009, GM announced its intention to begin repaying the Federal Government earlier than originally expected. It made a first payment of $1 billion in December.

The Labor Market

The ultimate goal of the economic stabilization and recovery policies is to provide a job for every American who seeks one. The recession's impact on the labor market has been severe: employment in December 2009 was 7.2 million below its peak level two years earlier, and the unemployment rate was 10 percent. Moreover, although real GDP has begun to grow, employment losses are continuing.

Nonetheless, there is clear evidence that the labor market is stabilizing. Figure 2-13 shows the average monthly job loss by quarter since 2006. Average monthly job losses have moderated steadily, from a devastating 691,000 in the first quarter of 2009 to 428,000 in the second quarter, 199,000 in the third, and 69,000 in the fourth. The *change* in the average monthly change in employment from the first quarter to the third was the largest over any two-quarter period since 1980, and the change from the first to the fourth quarter was the largest three-quarter change since 1946. Given what we now know about the terrible rate of job loss over the winter, it would have been very difficult for the labor market to stabilize more rapidly than it has.

Figure 2-13
Average Monthly Change in Employment

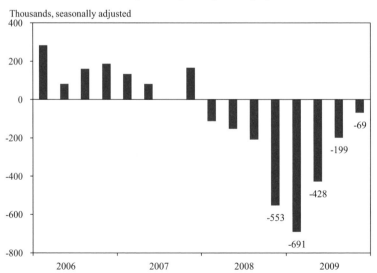

Source: Department of Labor (Bureau of Labor Statistics), Current Employment Statistics survey Series CES0000000001.

One can again use the VAR described earlier to obtain a more refined estimate of how the behavior of employment has differed from its usual pattern. This statistical procedure implies that given the economy's behavior through the first quarter of 2009 and its usual dynamics, one would have expected job losses of about 597,000 per month in the second quarter, 513,000 in the third quarter, and 379,000 in the fourth. Thus, actual employment as of the middle of the second quarter (May) was approximately 300,000 higher than one would have projected given the normal behavior of the economy; as of the middle of the third quarter (August), it was about 1.1 million higher; and as of the middle of the fourth quarter (November), it was about 2.1 million higher. As with the behavior of GDP, the portion of this difference that is attributable to the Recovery Act and other policies cannot be isolated from the portion resulting from other factors. But again, the difference could either understate or overstate the policies' contributions.

As with GDP, economic models can be used to focus specifically on the contributions of the Recovery Act. The results are shown in Figure 2-14. The CEA's multiplier estimates suggest that the Act raised employment relative to what it otherwise would have been by about 400,000 in the second quarter of 2009, 1.1 million in the third quarter, and 1.8 million in the fourth quarter. Again, these estimates are similar to other assessments. For example, CBO's November report estimated that the Act had raised

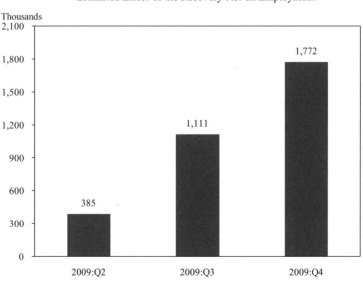

Figure 2-14
Estimated Effect of the Recovery Act on Employment

Note: The figure shows the estimated impact on employment relative to what otherwise would have happened.
Source: CEA calculations. See Council of Economic Advisers (2010).

employment in the third quarter by between 0.6 million and 1.6 million, relative to what otherwise would have happened.

A more complete picture of the process of labor market healing can be obtained by looking at labor market indicators beyond employment. Table 2-1 shows some of the main margins along which labor market recovery occurs. The margins are listed from left to right in the rough order in which they tend to adjust coming out of a recession. One of the first margins to respond is productivity—when demand begins to recover or moderates relative to the previous rate of decline, firms initially produce more with the same number of workers. Another early margin is initial claims for unemployment insurance—fewer workers are laid off. A somewhat later margin is the average workweek—firms start increasing production by increasing hours. The usual next step is temporary help employment—when firms decide to hire, they often begin with temporary help. Eventually total employment responds. The unemployment rate usually lags employment slightly because employment growth brings some discouraged workers back into the labor force and because the labor force naturally grows over time. The last item to adjust is usually the duration of unemployment spells, as workers who have been unemployed for extended periods finally find jobs.

The table shows that recovery from this recession is following the typical pattern, with labor market repair evident along the margins that typically respond early in a recovery. Productivity growth has surged as GDP has begun to increase and employment has continued to fall.

Table 2-1
Cyclically Sensitive Elements of Labor Market Adjustment

First to move ⟶ Last to move

	Produc-tivity growth, annual rate (percent)	Average monthly change					
		Initial UI claims (thou-sands/ week)	Work-week (hours)	Tempo-rary help employ-ment (thou-sands)	Total employ-ment (thou-sands)	Un-employ-ment rate (percent)	Average duration of unem-ployment (weeks)
2008:Q4	0.8	22	-0.10	-70	-553	0.39	0.3
2009:Q1	0.3	40	-0.07	-73	-691	0.42	0.4
2009:Q2	6.9	-15	-0.03	-28	-428	0.29	1.2
2009:Q3	8.1[p]	-22	0.03	5	-199	0.11	0.7
2009:Q4	7.5[e]	-30	0.03	49	-69	0.04	0.9

Notes: This table arranges the indicators according to the order in which they typically first move around business cycle turning points. Quarterly values for the average monthly change are measured from the last month in the previous quarter to the last month in the quarter. p is preliminary; e is estimate.
Sources: Department of Labor (Bureau of Labor Statistics), Series PRS85006092, and Employment Situation Tables A, A-9, and B-1; Department of Labor (Employment and Training Administration).

Initial unemployment insurance claims, which rose precipitously earlier in the recession, have begun to decline at an increasing rate. Likewise, the workweek has gone from shortening to lengthening, albeit slowly. Temporary help employment has changed from extreme declines to substantial increases. So far, total employment has shown a greatly moderating decline but has not yet risen. The pace of increase in the unemployment rate has slowed noticeably, but the unemployment rate has not yet fallen on a quarterly basis. Finally, increases in the duration of unemployment have not yet begun to moderate noticeably.

These data suggest that the labor market is beginning to move in the right direction, but much work remains to be done. The country is not yet seeing the substantial rises in total employment and declines in the unemployment rate that are the ultimate hallmark of robust labor market improvement. And, of course, even once all the indicators are moving solidly in the right direction, the labor market will still have a long way to go before it is fully recovered.

Signs of healing are also beginning to appear in the industrial composition of the stabilization of the labor market. Figure 2-15 shows the average monthly change in each of eight sectors in each of the four quarters of 2009. As one would expect of the beginnings of a recovery from a severe

Figure 2-15
Contributions to the Change in Employment

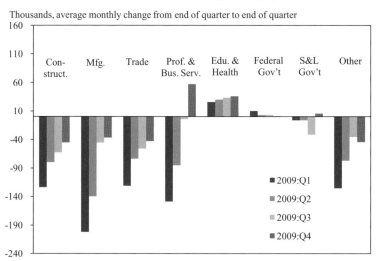

Notes: Bars sum to average monthly change in quarter (-691,000 in Q1; -428,000 in Q2; -199,000 in Q3; -69,000 in Q4). Construct. is construction; Mfg. is manufacturing; Trade is wholesale and retail trade, transportation, and utilities; Prof. & Bus. Serv. is professional and business services; Edu. & Health is education and health; Federal Gov't is Federal Government; S&L Gov't is state and local government.
Source: Department of Labor (Bureau of Labor Statistics), Employment Situation Table B-1.

recession, the moderation in job losses has been particularly pronounced in manufacturing and construction, two of the most cyclically sensitive sectors. There has also been a sharp turnaround in professional business services, driven largely by renewed employment growth in temporary help services.

One area where the Recovery Act appears to have had a direct impact on employment is in state and local government. Despite the enormous harm the recession has done to their budgets, employment in state and local governments has fallen relatively little. Indeed, employment in state and local government, particularly in public education, rose in the fourth quarter.

THE CHALLENGES AHEAD

The financial and economic rescue policies have helped avert an economic calamity and brought about a sharp change in the economy's direction. Output has begun growing again, and employment appears poised to do so as well. But even when the country has returned to a path of steadily growing output and employment, the economy will be far from fully recovered. Since the recession began in December 2007, 7.2 million jobs have been lost. It will take many months of robust job creation to erase that employment deficit. For this reason, it is important to explore policies to speed recovery and spur job creation.

Deteriorating Forecasts

This jobs deficit is much larger than the vast majority of observers anticipated at the end of 2008. This is not the result of a slow economic turn-around. On the contrary, as described above, the change in the economy's direction has been remarkably rapid given the economy's condition in the first quarter of 2009. Rather, the jobs deficit reflects two developments.

The first development is the unanticipated severity of the downturn in the real economy in 2008 and early 2009. Table 2-2 shows consensus fore-casts from November 2008 through February 2009, along with preliminary and actual estimates of real GDP growth. The table shows that the magni-tude of the fall in GDP in the fourth quarter of 2008 and the first quarter of 2009—driven in part by the unexpectedly strong spread of the crisis to the rest of the world—surprised most observers. The Blue Chip Consensus released in mid-December 2008 projected fourth quarter growth would be -4.1 percent and first quarter growth would be -2.4 percent. The actual values turned out to be -5.4 percent and -6.4 percent. The Blue Chip forecast released in mid-January also projected a substantially smaller decline in first quarter real GDP than actually occurred.

Table 2-2
Forecast and Actual Macroeconomic Outcomes

Real GDP Growth					
	2008:Q4	2009:Q1	2009:Q2	2009:Q3	2009:Q4
Blue Chip (11/10/08)	-2.8	-1.5	0.2	1.5	2.1
SPF (11/17/08)	-2.9	-1.1	0.8	0.9	2.3
Blue Chip (12/10/08)	-4.1	-2.4	-0.4	1.2	1.9
Blue Chip (1/10/09)	-5.2	-3.3	-0.8	1.2	2.2
SPF (2/13/09)	--	-5.2	-1.8	1.0	1.8
BEA Advance Estimate	-3.8	-6.1	-1.0	3.5	5.7
BEA Preliminary (2nd) Estimate	-6.2	-5.7	-1.0	2.8	--
Actual	**-5.4**	**-6.4**	**-0.7**	**2.2**	--

Unemployment Rate					
	2008:Q4	2009:Q1	2009:Q2	2009:Q3	2009:Q4
Blue Chip (11/10/08)	6.5	6.9	7.3	7.6	7.7
SPF (11/17/08)	6.6	7.0	7.4	7.6	7.7
Blue Chip (12/10/08)	6.7	7.3	7.7	8.0	8.1
Blue Chip (1/10/09)	6.9	7.4	7.9	8.3	8.4
SPF (2/13/09)	--	7.8	8.3	8.7	8.9
Actual	**6.9**	**8.2**	**9.3**	**9.7**	**10.0**

Notes: In the GDP panel, all numbers are in percent and are seasonally adjusted annual rates. In the unemployment panel, all numbers are in percent and are seasonally adjusted. SPF is the Survey of Professional Forecasters. Dashes indicate data are not available.

Sources: Blue Chip Economic Indicators; Survey of Professional Forecasters; Department of Commerce (Bureau of Economic Analysis), GDP news releases on 1/30/2009, 2/27/2009, 4/29/2009, 5/29/2009, 7/31/2009, 8/27/2009, 10/29/2009, 11/24/2009, 1/29/2010, and National Income and Product Accounts Table 1.1.1, line 1; Department of Labor (Bureau of Labor Statistics), Current Population Survey Series LNS14000000.

Part of the difficulty in forecasting resulted from large data revisions. The official GDP figures available at the end of January 2009 indicated that real GDP had fallen by just 0.2 percent over the four quarters of 2008; revised data now put the decline at 1.9 percent.

The Administration's economic forecast made in January 2009 and released with the fiscal 2010 budget, like the private forecasts, underestimated the speed of GDP decline in the first quarter. It also underestimated average growth over the remaining three quarters of 2009. For the four quarters of 2009, the Administration forecast overall growth of 0.3 percent; the actual value, according to the latest available data, is 0.1 percent.

The second development accounting for the unexpectedly large jobs deficit involves the behavior of the labor market given the behavior of GDP. Table 2-2 also shows consensus forecasts for the unemployment rate. These data indicate that as of December 2008, unemployment in the fourth quarter of 2009 was forecast to be 8.1 percent, dramatically less than the actual value of 10.0 percent. As of mid-January 2009, unemployment was forecast to be 8.4 percent in the fourth quarter. In its forecast made in

January 2009, the Administration unemployment forecast was similar to the consensus forecast.

Some of the unanticipated rise in unemployment was the result of the worse-than-expected GDP growth in 2008 and the beginning of 2009. CEA analysis, however, also suggests that the normal relationship between GDP and unemployment has fit poorly in the current recession. This relationship, termed Okun's law after former CEA Chair Arthur Okun who first identified it, suggests that a fall in GDP of 1 percent relative to its normal trend path is associated with a rise in the unemployment rate of about 0.5 percentage point after four quarters. Figure 2-16 shows the scatter plot of the four-quarter change in real GDP and the four-quarter change in the unemployment rate. The figure shows that although the fit of Okun's law is usually good, the relationship has broken down somewhat during this recession. The error was concentrated in 2009, when the unemployment rate increased considerably faster than might have been expected given the change in real GDP. CEA calculations suggest that as of the fourth quarter of 2009, the unemployment rate was approximately 1.7 percentage points higher than would have been expected given the behavior of real GDP since the business cycle peak in the fourth quarter of 2007.

This unusual rise in the unemployment rate does not appear to result from unusual behavior of the labor force. If anything, the labor force

Figure 2-16
Okun's Law, 2000-2009

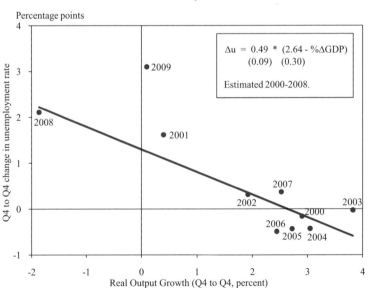

Sources: Department of Commerce (Bureau of Economic Analysis), National Income and Product Accounts Table 1.1.1, line 1; Department of Labor (Bureau of Labor Statistics), Current Population Survey Series LNS11000000 and LNS113000000; CEA calculations.

appears to have contracted somewhat more than usual given the path of the economy. Rather it reflects larger-than-typical falls in employment relative to the decline in GDP. This behavior is consistent with the tremendous increase in productivity during this episode, especially over the final three quarters of 2009. Indeed, labor productivity rose at a 6.9 percent annual rate in the second quarter and at an 8.1 percent rate in the third quarter; if productivity rose by a similar amount in the fourth quarter, as seems likely, the increase will have been one of the fastest over three quarters in postwar history.

The Administration Forecast

Looking forward, the Administration projects steady but moderate GDP growth over the near and medium term. Table 2-3 reports the Administration's forecast used in preparing the President's fiscal year 2011 budget. The table shows that GDP growth in 2010 is forecast to be 3 percent.

Table 2-3
Administration Economic Forecast

	Nominal GDP	Real GDP (chain-type)	GDP price index (chain-type)	Con-sumer price index (CPI-U)	Un-employ-ment rate (percent)	Interest rate, 91-day Treasury bills (percent)	Interest rate, 10-year Treasury notes (percent)	Nonfarm payroll employ-ment (average monthly change, Q4 to Q4, thou-sands)
	Percent change, Q4 to Q4				Level, calendar year			
2008 (actual)	0.1	-1.9	1.9	1.5	5.8	1.4	3.7	-189
2009	0.4	-0.5	0.9	1.4	9.3	0.2	3.3	-419
2010	4.0	3.0	1.0	1.3	10.0	0.4	3.9	95
2011	5.7	4.3	1.4	1.7	9.2	1.6	4.5	190
2012	6.1	4.3	1.7	2.0	8.2	3.0	5.0	251
2013	6.0	4.2	1.7	2.0	7.3	4.0	5.3	274
2014	5.7	3.9	1.7	2.0	6.5	4.1	5.3	267
2015	5.2	3.4	1.7	2.0	5.9	4.1	5.3	222
2016	5.0	3.1	1.8	2.1	5.5	4.1	5.3	181
2017	4.5	2.7	1.8	2.1	5.3	4.1	5.3	139
2018	4.5	2.6	1.8	2.1	5.2	4.1	5.3	113
2019	4.4	2.5	1.8	2.1	5.2	4.1	5.3	98
2020	4.3	2.5	1.8	2.1	5.2	4.1	5.3	93

Notes: Based on data available as of November 18, 2009. Interest rate on 91-day Treasury bills is measured on a secondary market discount basis. The figures do not reflect the upcoming BLS benchmark revision, which is expected to reduce 2008 and 2009 job growth by a cumulative 824,000 jobs.
Sources: CEA calculations; Department of Commerce (Bureau of Economic Analysis and Economics and Statistics Administration); Department of Labor (Bureau of Labor Statistics); Department of the Treasury; Office of Management and Budget.

The Administration estimates that normal or potential GDP growth will be roughly 2½ percent per year (see Box 2-1). Because projected GDP growth is only slightly stronger than potential growth, relatively little decline is projected in the unemployment rate during 2010. Indeed, it is possible that the rate will rise for a while as some discouraged workers return to the labor force, before starting to generally decline. Consistent with this, employment growth is projected to be roughly equal to normal trend growth of about 100,000 per month.

Box 2-1: Potential Real GDP Growth

The Administration forecast is based on the idea that real GDP fluctuates around a potential level that trends upward at a relatively steady rate. Over the budget window, potential real GDP is projected to grow at a 2.5 percent annual rate. Potential real GDP growth is a measure of the sustainable rate of growth of productive capacity.

The growth rate of the economy over the long run is determined by its supply side components, which include population, labor force participation, the ratio of nonfarm business employment to household employment, the length of the workweek, and labor productivity. The Administration's forecast for the contribution of the growth rates of these supply side factors to potential real GDP growth is shown in the accompanying table.

Components of Potential Real GDP Growth, 2009-2020

Component	Contribution (Percentage points)
Civilian noninstitutional population aged 16+	1.0
Labor force participation rate	-0.3
Employment rate	0.0
Ratio of nonfarm business employment to household employment	-0.0
Average weekly hours (nonfarm business)	-0.1
Output per hour (productivity, nonfarm business)	2.3
Ratio of real GDP to nonfarm business output	-0.4
SUM: Real GDP	2.5

Note: All contributions are in percentage points at an annual rate.
Sources: CEA calculations; Department of the Treasury; Office of Management and Budget.

Over the next 11 years, the working-age population is projected to grow 1.0 percent per year, the rate projected by the Census Bureau.

Continued on next page

Box 2-1, continued

The normal or potential labor force participation rate, which fell at a 0.3 percent annual rate during the past 8 years, is expected to continue declining at that pace. The continued projected decline results from the aging baby boom generation entering their retirement years. The potential employment rate (that is, 1 minus the normal or potential unemployment rate) is not expected to contribute to potential GDP growth because no change is anticipated in the unemployment rate consistent with stable inflation. The potential ratio of nonfarm business employment to household employment is also expected to be flat during the forecast horizon—consistent with its average behavior in the long run. This would be a change, however, from its puzzling 0.5 percent annual rate of decline during the past business cycle. The potential workweek is projected to edge down slightly (0.1 percent per year). This is a slightly shallower pace of decline than over the past 50 years, when it declined 0.3 percent per year. Over the 11-year projection interval, some firming of the workweek would be a natural labor market accommodation to the anticipated decline in labor force participation.

Potential growth of labor productivity is projected at 2.3 percent per year, a conservative forecast relative to its measured product-side growth rate (2.8 percent) between the past two business cycle peaks, but close to an alternative income-side measure of productivity growth (2.2 percent) during the same period. The ratio of real GDP to nonfarm business output is expected to continue to subtract from overall growth as it has over most long periods, because the nonfarm business sector generally grows faster than other sectors, such as government, households, and nonprofit institutions. Together, the sum of all of the components is the growth rate of potential real GDP, which is 2.5 percent per year.

As Table 2-3 shows, actual real GDP is projected to grow more rapidly than potential real GDP over most of the forecast horizon. The most important reason for the difference is that the actual employment rate is projected to rise as millions of workers who are currently unemployed return to employment and so contribute to GDP growth.

Traditionally, the large amount of slack would be expected to put substantial downward pressure on wage and price inflation. For this reason, inflation is projected to remain low in 2010. However, because inflationary expectations remain well anchored, inflation is not likely to slow dramatically or become negative (that is, turn into deflation).

In 2011, slightly higher GDP growth of approximately 4 percent is projected (again measured from fourth quarter to fourth quarter). Consistent with this, stronger employment growth and a more substantial decline in the unemployment rate are expected in 2011. However, because GDP growth is still not projected to be as robust as that following some other deep recessions, continued large output gaps are anticipated. This will limit the upward movement of the inflation rate toward a pace consistent with the Federal Reserve's long-term target inflation rate of about 2 percent. Moreover, employment growth is unlikely to be large enough to reduce the employment shortfall dramatically in 2011.

Responsible Policies to Spur Job Creation

This large employment gap and the prospects that it is likely to recede only slowly make a compelling case for additional measures to spur private sector job creation. The Administration is therefore exploring a range of possibilities and working with Congress to pass measures into law.

Several principles are guiding this process. First, at a time when the budget deficit is large and the country faces significant long-run fiscal challenges, measures must be cost-effective. Second, given that the employment consequences of the recession have been severe, measures must focus particularly on job creation. And third, measures must be tailored to the state of the economy: the policies that are appropriate when an economy is contracting rapidly may not be the same as those that are appropriate for an economy that is growing again but operating below capacity.

Guided by these principles, the Administration has identified three key priorities. One is a multifaceted program to jump-start job creation by small businesses, which are critical to growth and have been particularly harmed by the recession. Among the possible policies in this area are investment incentives, tax incentives for hiring, and additional steps to increase the availability of loans backed by the Small Business Administration. These policies may be particularly effective at a time when the economy is growing—so that the question for many firms is not whether to hire but when—and at a time when credit availability remains an important constraint.

Initiatives to encourage energy efficiency and clean energy are another priority. One proposal involves incentives for homeowners to retrofit their homes for energy efficiency. Because in many cases the effect of such incentives would be to lead homeowners to make cost-saving investments earlier than they otherwise would have, they might have an especially large impact. In addition, the employment effects would be concentrated in construction, an area that has been particularly hard-hit by the recession.

The Administration has also supported extending tax credits through the Department of Energy that promote the manufacture of advanced energy products and providing incentives to increase the energy efficiency of public and nonprofit buildings.

A third priority is infrastructure investment. The experience of the Recovery Act suggests that spending on infrastructure is an effective way to put people back to work while creating lasting investments that raise future productivity. For this reason, the Administration is supporting an additional investment of up to $50 billion in roads, bridges, airports, transit, rail, and water projects. Funneling some of these funds through programs such as the Transportation Investment Generating Economic Recovery (TIGER) program at the Department of Transportation, which is a competitive grant program, could offer a way to ensure that the projects with the highest returns receive top priority.

Finally, it is critical to maintain our support for the individuals and families most affected by the recession by extending the emergency funding for such programs as unemployment insurance and health insurance subsidies for the unemployed. This support not only cushions the worst effects of the downturn, but also boosts spending and so spurs job creation. Similarly, it is important to maintain support for state and local governments. The budgets of these governments remain under severe strain, and many are cutting back in anticipation of fiscal year 2011 deficits. Additional fiscal support could therefore have a rapid impact on spending, and would do so by maintaining crucial services and preventing harmful tax increases.

CONCLUSION

The recession that began at the end of 2007 became the "Great Recession" following the financial crisis in the fall of 2008. In the wake of the collapse of Lehman Brothers in September, American families faced devastating job losses, high unemployment, scarce credit, and lost wealth. Late 2008 and 2009 will be remembered as a time of great trial for American workers, businesses, and families.

But 2009 should also be remembered as a year when even more tragic losses and dislocation did not occur. As terrible as this recession has been, a second Great Depression would have been far worse. Had policymakers not responded as aggressively as they did to shore up the financial system, maintain demand, and provide relief to those directly harmed by the downturn, the outcome could have been much more dire.

As 2010 begins, there are strong signs that the American economy is starting to recover. Housing and financial markets appear to have stabilized and real GDP is growing again. The labor market also appears to be healing, showing the expected early pattern of response to output expansion.

With millions of Americans still unemployed, much work remains to restore the American economy to health. It will take a prolonged and robust GDP expansion to eliminate the large jobs deficit that has opened up over the course of the recession. Only when the unemployment rate has returned to normal levels and families are once again secure in their jobs, homes, and savings will this terrible recession truly be over.

CHAPTER 3

CRISIS AND RECOVERY IN THE WORLD ECONOMY

The financial crisis and recession have affected economies around the globe. The impact on the U.S. economy has been severe, but many areas of the world have fared even worse. The average growth rate of real gross domestic product (GDP) around the world was -6.2 percent at an annual rate in the fourth quarter of 2008 and -7.5 percent in the first quarter of 2009. All told, the world economy is expected to have contracted 1.1 percent in 2009 from the year before—the first annual decline in world output in more than half a century.[1] Although economic dislocations have been severe in one region or another at various times over the past 50 years, never in that time span has the annual output of the entire global economy contracted. But, as bad as the outcome has been, the decline would likely have been far larger if policymakers in the world's key economies had not acted forcefully to limit the impact of the crisis.

The global economic crisis started as a financial crisis, generally beginning in housing-related asset markets, and accelerated in the fall of 2008. After September 2008, interbank interest rates spiked, exchange rates shifted quickly, and the flows of capital across borders slowed dramatically. Trade flows also plummeted, falling even more dramatically than GDP. As a result, trade flows became a key transmission mechanism in the crisis, spreading macroeconomic distress to countries that were not primarily exposed to the financial shocks.

Policymakers around the world responded quickly, sometimes taking coordinated action, sometimes acting independently. Many central banks

---

[1] Quarterly figures are calculations of the Council of Economic Advisers based on a 64-country sample that represents 93 percent of world GDP. Annual average projections are from the International Monetary Fund (2009a). These projections indicate that from the fourth quarter of 2007 to the fourth quarter of 2008, world GDP contracted 0.1 percent, and from the fourth quarter of 2008 to the fourth quarter of 2009, world GDP expanded 0.8 percent. The contraction was strongest from the middle of 2008 to the middle of 2009; hence the annual average growth from 2008 to 2009 (-1.1 percent) is lower than the fourth-quarter-to-fourth-quarter numbers.

cut interest rates nearly to zero and expanded their balance sheets to try to stimulate lending and keep their economies going. They also lent large sums to one another to prevent dislocations caused by a lack of foreign currency in some markets. Beyond the central bank actions, governments intervened more broadly in banks and financial markets as well. Governments also spent large sums in fiscal stimulus to avoid massive drop-offs in aggregate demand. In a welcome development, they did not, however, restrict trade in an attempt to turn away imports.

The global economy is now seeing the beginnings of recovery. Financial markets have rebounded, trade is recovering, and GDP growth rates are again positive. Recovery is far from complete or certain, and some risks remain: lending is still constrained, and unemployment is painfully high. But, at the start of 2010, the world economy is no longer at the edge of collapse, and the elements of a sound recovery seem to be coming into place.

INTERNATIONAL DIMENSIONS OF THE CRISIS

The worldwide contraction had roots in many financial phenomena, and its rapid spread can be seen in a number of financial indicators. Borrowing costs increased, U.S. dollars were scarce in foreign markets, and exchange rates moved rapidly. Yet, despite problems in U.S. financial markets, there was no U.S. dollar crisis, and while currency markets moved rapidly, many of the emerging-market currency depreciations were temporary and not accompanied by cascading defaults. Thus, the world economy was better positioned for recovery than it might have been.

Spread of the Financial Shock

One of the early indicators of the crisis was the large spike in the interest rate banks charge one another that took place as the value of assets held on bank balance sheets came into question. After the investment bank Lehman Brothers declared bankruptcy in September 2008, banks grew even warier about lending to each other. This fear of lending to one another can be seen by comparing the interbank lending rate with the risk-free overnight interest rate. Similar to the TED spread, the Libor-OIS spread (the London interbank offered rate minus the overnight indexed swap) gives such a comparison for dollar loans, and comparable spreads are available for loans in other currencies. As Figure 3-1 shows, the spike in spreads for dollar loans was larger earlier, but the increase in interbank lending rates was sharp in dollars, pounds, and euros alike. Banks simply refused to lend to one another at low rates in these major financial systems. Furthermore, concerns about which firms might go bankrupt sent the cost of insuring

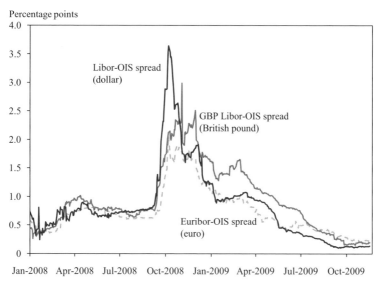

Figure 3-1
Interbank Market Rates

Percentage points

Libor-OIS spread
(dollar)

GBP Libor-OIS spread
(British pound)

Euribor-OIS spread
(euro)

Jan-2008   Apr-2008   Jul-2008   Oct-2008   Jan-2009   Apr-2009   Jul-2009   Oct-2009

Source: Bloomberg.

against a default on a bond soaring. Thus, costs of borrowing increased for even creditworthy borrowers, putting a strain on the ability of firms to finance themselves.

The Dollar Shortage. Beyond the difficulties of evaluating counter-party risk were the acute shortages of dollar liquidity outside the United States, which were reflected in a steep rise in the cost of exchanging foreign currency for dollars for a fixed period of time (a foreign currency swap). The reasons for the dollar shortage are complex but can be understood by looking at foreign banks' behavior before the crisis. During the boom years, non-U.S. banks acquired large amounts of dollar-denominated assets, often paying for these acquisitions with borrowed dollars rather than with their own currency, thus avoiding the currency mismatch risk of borrowing in one currency and having assets in another. Much of the dollar borrowing was short term and came from U.S. money-market funds. After investors began to pull their money out of these funds in the fall of 2008, that source of lending dried up, and banks were left trying to obtain dollars in other ways. This put pressure on the currency swap market.

Before the crisis, moreover, some banks funded purchases of U.S. assets directly through swaps. In a simplified version of the transaction, foreign banks borrow in their own currency (euros, for example), exchange that currency for dollars through a swap, and then use the dollars to buy U.S. assets. By using a swap market rather than simply purchasing currency, they even out the currency risk (McGuire and von Peter 2009),[2] but they are left with a funding risk. If no one will lend them dollars when their swap is due, they may have to sell their dollar assets (some of which may have fallen in value) to pay back the dollars they owe. When banks became very nervous about taking on risk, demand greatly increased the price of currency swaps.

Unwinding Carry Trades. As concerns about the stability of the financial markets heightened over the course of 2008, investors responded by trying to deleverage and reduce some of their exposed risky positions. The desire to undo risky positions coupled with the dollar shortage led to swift movements in currency markets, especially an unwinding of the "carry trade." In the carry trade, an investor borrows money in a low-interest-rate currency (for example, the Japanese yen), sells that currency for a higher-interest-rate currency (for example, the Australian dollar), and invests the money in that currency. If interest rates are 1 percent in Japan and 6 percent in Australia, the investor stands to collect a 5 percent profit if exchange rates do not move. Although economic theory suggests that currency movements should offset this expected profit, over short horizons, if the exchange rate does not move, investors can make a profit. This happened in the mid-2000s, and the carry trade became a favorite strategy for hedge funds and other investors.

The popularity of the trade became self-fulfilling as the continued flows of money into higher-interest-rate currencies helped them appreciate and made the trade even more profitable. But, as the crisis hit, investors tried to reduce their risk and leverage. This unwinding process meant rapid sales of high-interest-rate currencies and rapid purchases of low-interest-rate currencies. Currencies that had low interest rates and had been known as funding currencies (such as the Japanese yen) rose rapidly in value, and the currencies of a number of popular carry-trade destinations (such as Australia, Brazil, and Iceland) depreciated swiftly. Thus, as the crisis hit, borrowing became more expensive and currency markets were increasingly volatile.

The Dollar During the Crisis. Although in many ways the crisis was triggered within U.S. asset markets, the response was not a run on the U.S. dollar; instead the dollar strengthened notably. Some observers had argued that the high U.S. current account deficit and problems in the U.S. housing and other asset markets might lead to an unwillingness to hold U.S. assets more broadly, which could have triggered a depreciation of the dollar. But both the need for foreign banks to cover their dollar borrowing and the need for other investors to repay loans borrowed in dollars (including for carry trades) generated strong demand for dollars. Further, the desire to

---

[2] The swap means they have borrowed dollars and lent euros. In this way, they borrowed euros at home and lent them in the swap, and they owe dollars in the swap but also own dollar assets. Thus, their foreign currency position is balanced.

avoid risky investments at the height of the crisis led to a "flight to safety," with many investors buying dollars and U.S. Treasury bills. As seen in Figure 3-2, the trade-weighted value of the dollar increased 18 percent from July 2008 to its peak in March 2009. The movement of the dollar was broad-based, with sharp appreciations against most major trade partners; the main exceptions were Japan, where the yen appreciated even more against the world as the carry trade unwound, and China, which had reestablished its peg to the dollar in July of 2008 and therefore had a stable exchange rate against the dollar.

Figure 3-2
Nominal Trade-Weighted Dollar Index

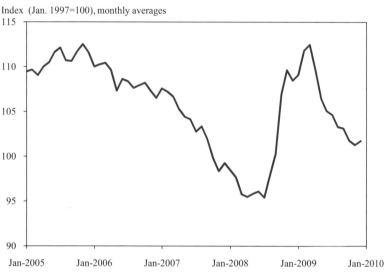

Note: The index is constructed such that an upward movement represents an appreciation of the dollar.
Source: Federal Reserve Board, G.5.

Currency Volatility in Emerging Markets. The deleveraging and fall in risk appetite contributed to large and in some cases sharp swings in the currencies of many emerging economies, but the impact of these large depreciations varied. Some of the sharpest depreciations, such as those in Brazil, Korea, and Mexico, were largely temporary. The currencies of all three countries depreciated more than 50 percent against the dollar between the end of July 2008 and February 2009, but by the end of November 2009 Korea's currency was down only 15 percent and Brazil's only 12 percent. Mexico was still 29 percent below its summer 2008 value.[3]

---

[3] The starting point for comparison is important. Korea had been depreciating in early 2008 as well, while Brazil and Mexico were appreciating. Thus, by the end of November 2009, Brazil had appreciated slightly from the start of 2008 while Korea had depreciated 24 percent and Mexico 18 percent.

Some countries with large current account deficits faced more pressure. The region with the sharpest declines in the value of its currencies against the dollar was Eastern Europe, where the currencies of Hungary, Poland, and Ukraine all depreciated more than 50 percent between July 2008 and February 2009, and others depreciated nearly as much. These large depreciations resulted in part from the strengthening of the dollar against the euro, as many of these countries are closely tied with Europe, but some of these currencies remained weak even when other countries started to strengthen against the dollar.

A large depreciation can especially lead to broad damage in an economy if there are negative balance-sheet effects. In this setting, a country may have few foreign assets but extensive liabilities denominated in foreign currency. As the exchange rate depreciates, the foreign currency loans become more expensive in local currency. This was particularly a concern in Eastern Europe, where many countries borrowed substantially in foreign currency leading up to the crisis. In Hungary, for example, many individuals took out mortgages in foreign currency. The depreciation of the Hungarian *forint* thus put pressure on both individuals and bank balance sheets. There was widespread concern that the Western European banks, such as those in Austria, that had made loans in Eastern Europe would face substantial losses. Both the Organisation for Economic Co-operation and Development (OECD) and the International Monetary Fund (IMF) warned of potentially serious bank problems in Austria because of these concerns. By the end of 2009, however, those concerns had not materialized. Austria has had to shore up its banks, but there has not been widespread contagion from Eastern Europe.

During the peak of the crisis, the spreads on emerging-market bonds spiked, but they returned toward more standard levels over time, and outright financial collapse was avoided. There are a number of reasons for the more contained impact of the exchange-rate movements during the crisis. In the past decade, many developing countries have reduced the currency mismatch on their balance sheets by borrowing less, increasing their stocks of foreign exchange reserves, and shifting away from debt finance (Lane and Shambaugh forthcoming). The improved fiscal positions of some countries likely also helped, as did the strong policy response and coordination described later. Some vulnerable countries also benefited from the strengthening of the IMF's lending capabilities (discussed later). The failure of this shock to turn into a series of deep sustained financial collapses across the emerging world was a welcome development that left the world economy better positioned for a quick turnaround.

The Collapse of World Trade

Despite this crisis's origins in the financial sector, trade rapidly became a crucial source of transmission of the crisis around the world. Exports collapsed in nearly every major trading country, and total world trade fell faster than it did during the Great Depression or any time since. From a peak in July 2008 to the low in February 2009, the nominal value of world goods exports fell 36 percent; the nominal value of U.S. goods exports fell 28 percent (imports fell 38 percent) over the same period. Even countries such as Germany, which did not experience their own housing bubble, experienced substantial trade contractions, which helped spread the crisis. The collapse in net exports in Germany and Japan contributed substantially to their declines in GDP, helping drive these countries into recession. In the fourth quarter of 2008, Germany's drop in net exports contributed 8.1 percentage points to a 9.4 percent decline in GDP (at an annual rate); Japan's net exports contributed 9.0 percentage points to a 10.2 percent GDP decline. Real exports fell even faster in the first quarter of 2009.

Figure 3-3 shows that the drop in the trade-to-GDP ratio during this crisis, from 28 percent to 23 percent in OECD countries, is unprecedented. Trade as a share of GDP had not dropped by more than 2 percentage points from the year before since at least 1970 (the earliest available data), suggesting trade's drop relative to GDP has been larger than in the past. Economists have noted that the responsiveness of trade to GDP has been

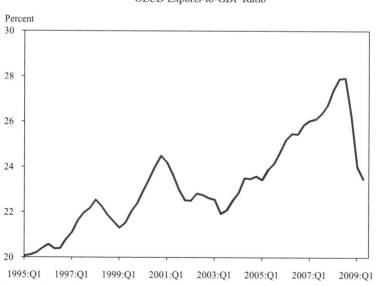

Figure 3-3
OECD Exports-to-GDP Ratio

Source: Organisation for Economic Co-operation and Development, Quarterly National Accounts.

rising over time. Three main reasons for the exceptionally large fall in trade, even given the decline in GDP, have been suggested (Freund 2009; Levchenko, Lewis, and Tesar 2009; and Baldwin 2009).

The first reason is the use of global supply chains (or vertical specialization), where parts of production are manufactured or assembled in different countries and intermediate inputs are shipped from country to country, often from one branch of a firm to another, and then sent to a final destination for finishing. In this case, a reduction in output of one car may involve a decrease in shipments far larger than the final value of that single car. For example, a country that imports $80 of inputs and adds $20 of value added before exporting a $100 good will see GDP fall by $20 if demand for that good disappears, but trade (measured as the average of imports and exports) will fall $90. If the decline in demand was concentrated in goods where global supply chains were particularly important, this could help account for the large fall in trade-to-GDP ratios. Estimates are that imported inputs account for, on average, 30 percent of the content of exports in OECD and major emerging market countries, although there is variation across countries within the OECD. Figure 3-4 shows that, with the exception of Ireland, the percentage by which trade declined for a country was

Figure 3-4
Vertical Specialization and the Collapse in Trade

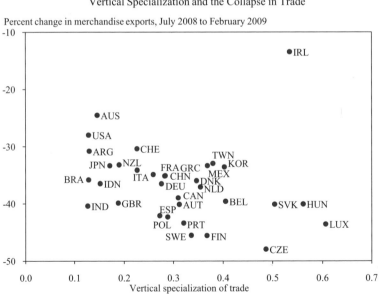

Notes: See text for definition of the vertical specialization of trade. Merchandise exports measured in dollars. Alternate data from Johnson and Noguera (2009), which include the degree to which exports themselves are intermediate inputs, show a similar picture.
Sources: Miroudot and Ragoussis (2009); country sources; CEA calculations.

strongly correlated with the extent of that country's vertical specialization (specifically defined as the degree of imported inputs used in exports).

Second, the disruption in global financial markets may have helped generate the trade collapse. Exporters typically require some form of financing to produce their export goods because importers will not pay for them before they arrive. Similarly, importers may need some sort of financing to bridge the gap between when they need to pay for goods and when they will be able to sell them on a domestic market. When liquidity tightened in world financial markets, the cost of trade finance increased. Little high-quality information is available for trade finance because it is typically arranged by banks or from one party to another, rather than through an organized exchange. The data that do exist show a drop in trade finance, but one that is not necessarily larger than the drop in overall trade. The drop in general financing available for producers and consumers, along with the impact of the recession on aggregate demand, may be factors as significant as the specifics of trade finance.[4]

Finally, the types of products that are traded may have been a critical factor in the trade collapse. Investment goods and consumer durables make up a substantial portion of merchandise trade, representing 57 percent of U.S. exports and 49 percent of U.S. imports in 2006. In a recession, investment spending by firms and purchases of durable goods by consumers often fall more sharply than other components of GDP. Because these investment and purchasing decisions are large and irreversible, they may be delayed until the economic situation is more clear. The drop in spending in these categories during this crisis has been far more severe than in previous recessions in the past 30 years in the United States. Paralleling the movements in overall demand, the collapse in the nominal value of trade was most severe in capital and durable goods and in chemicals and metals, and least severe in services and nondurable goods. The combination of the concentration of the spending reduction in these sectors and the sectors' importance in overall trade appears to be one source of the sharp fall in trade in the crisis.

The Collapse in Financial Flows

Trade in goods was not the only international flow to collapse. Financial trade evaporated in a way never before seen. U.S. outflows and inflows of finance rose steadily for decades as increasingly integrated capital markets grew in size and scope. By 2007, the average monthly gross purchases and sales of foreign long-term assets by American investors were

---

[4] See Mora and Powers (2009) for a discussion of trade finance in the recent crisis. Levchenko, Lewis, and Tesar (2009) find no support for the notion that trade credit played a role in the reduced trade flows for the United States during the crisis.

$1.4 trillion, and foreigners' purchases and sales of U.S. long-term assets were $4.9 trillion. Each group both bought and sold a considerable amount of their holdings, so that net purchases by Americans were $19 billion a month and net purchases by foreign investors were $84 billion a month.

When the crisis hit, there was a massive deglobalization of finance that was unprecedented and in many ways more extreme than the collapse in goods and services trade. Figure 3-5 shows that the scale of cross-border flows was cut in half after years of fairly steady climbing. Net purchases by both home and foreign investors actually became negative in the fall of 2008 (that is, there were more sales than purchases). Americans pulled funds home at such a fast pace that from July to November of 2008, Americans on net sold foreign assets worth $143 billion. Foreign investors also liquidated their positions, selling a net $92 billion in U.S. holdings. Hence, outflows from foreign investors returning to their home markets were offset in part by inflows from Americans bringing money back to the United States, likely reducing the impact of the outflows.

Figure 3-5
Cross-Border Gross Purchases and Sales of Long-Term Assets

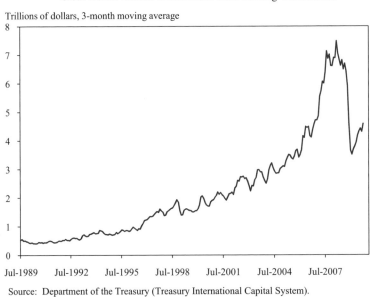

Trillions of dollars, 3-month moving average

Source: Department of the Treasury (Treasury International Capital System).

The Decline in Output Around the Globe

While the triggers of the crisis are generally considered financial in nature, these shocks were rapidly transmitted to the real economy. What had been a financial market shock or a trade collapse became a full-fledged recession in countries around the world. The financial disruption was so strong and swift in most countries that confidence fell as well. Confidence levels are measured in different ways across countries, but they were generally falling throughout 2008 and reached recent lows in the fall of 2008 and winter of 2009. In many countries, confidence had not been so low in more than a decade.

As noted, world GDP is estimated to have fallen roughly 1.1 percent in 2009 from the year before. The number for the annual average masks the shocking depth of the crisis in the winter of 2008–09, when GDP was contracting at an annual rate over 6 percent. In advanced economies, the crisis was even deeper; the IMF expects GDP to have contracted 3.4 percent in advanced economies for all of 2009. For OECD member countries, GDP fell at an annual rate of 7.2 percent in the fourth quarter of 2008 and 8.4 percent in the first quarter of 2009. Despite the historic nature of its collapse, the U.S. economy actually fared better than about half of OECD economies during those quarters. Figure 3-6 shows the decline in industrial production across major economies, with each of these economies in January 2009 more than 10 percent below its January 2008 level, and Japan faring far worse relative to the other major economies.

Figure 3-6
Industrial Production in Advanced Economies

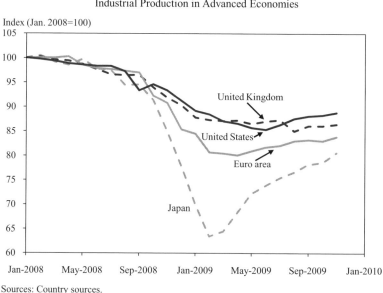

Sources: Country sources.

Some emerging market countries collapsed as well, with contractions at an annual rate of over 20 percent in Mexico, Russia, and Turkey, but the collapses were brief—lasting only a quarter or so. On average, the emerging and developing world was quite resilient to the crisis and is projected to have continued to expand in 2009 at a rate of 1.7 percent for the year (these countries contracted in the first quarter, but they began growing quickly in the second quarter). Some regions, such as developing Asia, continued to grow at a robust pace for the year as a whole (over 6 percent), but even that rate is considerably slower than their growth in the mid-2000s. Figure 3-7 shows that industrial production fell in Brazil and Mexico in a manner similar to that in industrial economies, but in China and India it merely stalled for a brief period and then accelerated again. This overall performance in the emerging world is a turnaround from previous crises, where recessions in the advanced countries were followed by sustained collapses in some emerging countries.

Figure 3-7
Industrial Production in Emerging Economies

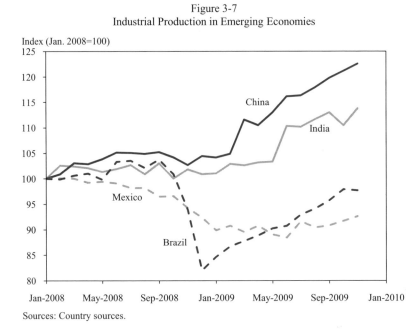

Index (Jan. 2008=100)

Sources: Country sources.

The combination of weak aggregate demand and falling energy prices has meant that price pressure has been starkly absent in this crisis. In fact, lower oil prices have meant that year-over-year inflation numbers were negative in most major countries until toward the end of 2009 (Figure 3-8). Core inflation rates—which exclude volatile energy and food prices—have also been quite low over the year and even negative in Japan. This lack of price pressure has left the world's central banks with more flexibility than they had in the 1970s recessions because they do not have pressing inflation problems to consider. Inflation has also been muted in emerging and developing countries relative to their history; it is estimated to be 5.5 percent over 2009 and is projected to fall slightly in 2010. As economies and commodity markets strengthened toward the end of 2009, inflation pressure grew in a limited number of countries but was not in any way widespread.

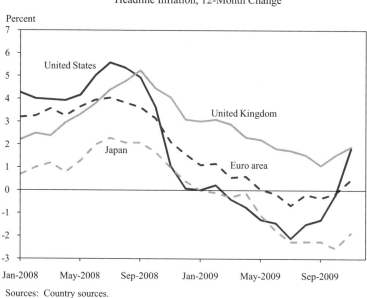

Figure 3-8
Headline Inflation, 12-Month Change

Sources: Country sources.

Policy Responses Around the Globe

Given the severity of the downturn, it is not surprising that policymakers responded with dramatic action. Central banks cut interest rates, governments spent considerable sums in the form of fiscal stimulus, and governments and central banks supported financial sectors with funds and guarantees. Many of these actions were coordinated as policymakers tried to prevent the financial market upheaval and recession from becoming a full-fledged depression.

Monetary Policy in the Crisis

The response of monetary authorities was both strong and swift across the globe. The major central banks coordinated a significant rate cut of 50 basis points on October 8, 2008, in an attempt to increase liquidity and to boost confidence by demonstrating that they were prepared to act decisively. During the crisis, every member of the Group of Twenty (G-20) major economies cut interest rates. By March 2009, the Federal Reserve, the Bank of Japan, and the Bank of England had all cut rates to 0.5 percent or less, with the Federal Reserve and the Bank of Japan approaching the zero nominal lower bound. The European Central Bank (ECB) responded slightly more slowly but still cut its policy rate more than 3 percentage points to 1 percent by May 2009 (Figure 3-9). Emerging market countries and major commodity exporters, whose economies were growing fast in the summer of 2008, moved as well, but not to the near-zero levels seen at the major central banks.

Figure 3-9
Policy Rates in Economies with Major Central Banks

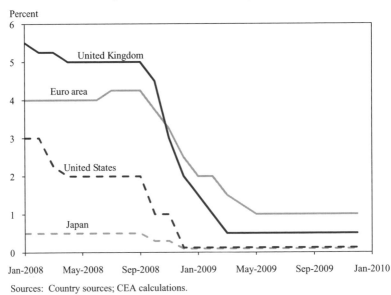

Sources: Country sources; CEA calculations.

Besides cutting interest rates, three of the largest central banks used nonstandard monetary policy as well. As Figure 3-10 shows, the Federal Reserve and the Bank of England more than doubled the size of their balance sheets in 2008 (see Chapter 2 for more details on the Federal Reserve's actions). The two banks bought large quantities of assets, substantially increasing the supply of reserves, and made loans against a variety of asset classes. The goal of these programs was to free up credit in markets that were being underserved through purchases of, or loans against, asset-backed securities and commercial paper. The ECB also expanded its balance sheet substantially (37 percent) in 2008 and made loans against a variety of assets, but it did not undertake the same level of quantitative easing as either the U.S. or U.K. central banks. The Bank of Japan did not expand its balance sheet on a similar scale.[5] While it did expand some of its lending programs in corporate bond markets, its policies were more oriented to financial markets than to quantitative monetary policy. As noted earlier, Japan's inflation rate has been negative.

Figure 3-10
Change in Central Bank Assets

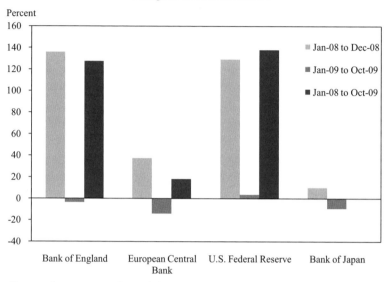

Sources: Country sources; CEA calculations.

As Figure 3-10 shows, the rapid growth of central bank balance sheets halted during 2009, but the central banks have not withdrawn the liquidity they injected into the system. Similarly, policy interest rates have remained constant since December 2008 in the United States and Japan and since the spring of 2009 in the euro area and the United Kingdom. Some commodity producers and smaller advanced nations with strong growth have begun to withdraw some monetary accommodation. Australia, Israel, and Norway have all raised policy interest rates. Also, authorities in countries such as China and India had not raised main policy rates as of the end of 2009, but they have made administrative changes that tightened lending to slow the expansion of credit as their economies began to grow more quickly.

In addition to lending support, authorities directly intervened to support the banking sectors in a number of countries. Countries took many actions on their own, ranging from the policies pursued in the United States such as the Troubled Asset Relief Program (discussed in Chapter 2), to direct takeovers of some banks in the United Kingdom, to the creation of other

---

[5] On December 1, 2009, the Bank of Japan announced a roughly $115 billion increase in lending, equivalent to a nearly 10 percent increase in its balance sheet. This increase was significant but still far below the actions taken by other major central banks.

entities to centralize some bad assets and clean the balance sheets of other banks in Switzerland and Ireland, to general support and guarantees in a wide range of countries.

Central Bank Liquidity Swaps

In addition to the coordination of rate cuts, one other important form of international coordination took place across central banks. As noted, a dollar funding shortage materialized abroad, as the normal channels for the transmission of dollar liquidity from U.S. markets to the global financial system broke down. This shortage presented a unique set of challenges to central banks. They could have simply provided domestic currency and left banks to sell it for dollars, but the foreign exchange swaps market in which such transactions are usually conducted was severely impaired. Alternatively, central banks could have used dollar reserves to provide foreign currency funds, but few advanced countries (outside of Japan) had sufficient foreign currency holdings to fully address the foreign currency funding needs of their banking systems.

Central banks whose currencies were in demand responded to the shortage by providing large amounts of liquidity to partner central banks through central bank liquidity swaps.[6] In many of these arrangements, the Federal Reserve purchased foreign currency in exchange for U.S. dollars and at the same time agreed to return the foreign currency for the same quantity of dollars at a specific date in the future. When foreign central banks drew dollars in this way to fund their auctions of dollar liquidity in local markets, the Federal Reserve received interest equal to what the foreign central banks were receiving on the lending operations. The Federal Reserve first used these swaps in late 2007 on a relatively small scale. But, as shown in Figure 3-11, from August 2008 through December 2008 these swaps increased from $67 billion to $553 billion. This massive supply of liquidity was larger than the available lending facilities of the IMF. The United States extended this program to major emerging market countries as well on October 29, 2008, providing lines of up to $30 billion each to Brazil, Mexico, Singapore, and Korea.

As the acute funding needs have subsided, nearly all of the central bank swaps have been unwound, and the Federal Reserve has announced that it anticipates that these swap arrangements will be closed by February 1, 2010. There was no long-term funding cost to the Federal Reserve from these swap lines; moreover, the Federal Reserve's counterparties in these transactions were the central banks of other countries, and the loans

---

[6] See Fender and Gyntelberg (2008) for a more comprehensive discussion.

were fully collateralized with foreign currency, so very little credit risk was involved in these transactions.

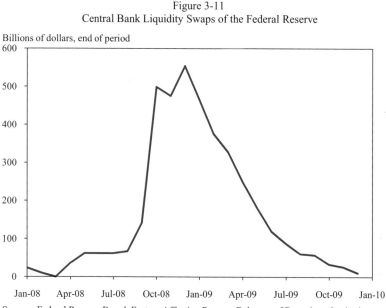

Figure 3-11
Central Bank Liquidity Swaps of the Federal Reserve

Billions of dollars, end of period

Source: Federal Reserve Board, Factors Affecting Reserve Balances of Depository Institutions and Condition Statements of Federal Reserve Banks, H.4.1 Table 1.

Although the dollar funding shortages were unique, the Federal Reserve was not the only central bank to provide swap lines. Some of the more notable examples include the European Central Bank, which made euros available to a number of central banks in Europe, among them the central banks of Denmark, Hungary, and Poland, that felt pressure for funding in euros; the Swedish central bank, which provided support to central banks in the Baltics; and the Swiss National Bank, which provided Swiss francs to the European Central Bank and Poland. Across Asia there was renewed interest in the Chiang Mai Initiative, under which various Asian central banks set up swap lines that could be used in an emergency. Despite the increases in these cross-Asian country swap lines, together they totaled $90 billion, far less than the available Federal Reserve swap lines, and they were not drawn on during the crisis. In sum, while existing institutional structures (IMF lending or reserves) appear to have been insufficient to meet this aspect of the crisis, the world's central banks innovated to take temporary actions that quelled market disruptions and avoided even sharper financial dislocation.

Fiscal Policy in the Crisis

In part because major central banks had pushed interest rates as low as they could go and in part because of the magnitude of the crisis, by the beginning of 2009, many countries decided to institute substantial fiscal stimulus. The hope was that government spending could step into the breach left by the collapse of private demand and provide the necessary lift to prevent a slide into a deep recession or worse.

Nearly every major country instituted stimulus, with the exception of some countries hampered by substantial public finance concerns, such as Hungary and Ireland. Every G-20 nation implemented substantial stimulus, with an unweighted average of 2.0 percent of GDP in 2009 (Table 3-1), and many other OECD nations also adopted stimulus plans. Among G-20 countries, China, Korea, Russia, and Saudi Arabia enacted the most extensive stimulus programs in 2009, all equivalent to more than 3 percent of GDP. The U.S. stimulus in 2009 (estimated at 2 percent of GDP) was greater than the OECD's estimate of its member country average (1.6 percent of GDP), but the same as the G-20 average and not quite as extensive as the four high-stimulus nations.

Table 3-1
2009 Fiscal Stimulus as Share of GDP, G-20 Members

Argentina	1.5%	Japan	2.9%
Australia	2.9%	Mexico	1.6%
Brazil	0.6%	Russia	4.1%
Canada	1.8%	Saudi Arabia	3.3%
China	3.1%	South Africa	3.0%
France	0.6%	South Korea	3.7%
Germany	1.6%	Turkey	2.0%
India	0.6%	United Kingdom	1.6%
Indonesia	1.4%	United States	2.0%
Italy	0.1%	**All G-20 Nations**	**2.0%**

Note: Values are average of International Monetary Fund and Organisation for Economic Co-operation and Development estimates for nations with expansionary fiscal policies.
Sources: Horton, Kumar, and Mauro (2009); Organisation for Economic Co-operation and Development (2009a).

Discretionary fiscal action was not the only form of fiscal stimulus; automatic stabilizers (unemployment insurance, welfare, reduction in taxes collected due to lower payrolls) are triggered when an economy slows down. The size of automatic stabilizers present in an economy appears to be negatively correlated with the size of discretionary stimulus. As Figure 3-12 shows, those countries that already had large automatic stabilizers in place appear to have adopted less discretionary fiscal stimulus, but they were obviously still providing substantial fiscal relief during the crisis.[7]

Figure 3-12
Tax Share and Discretionary Stimulus

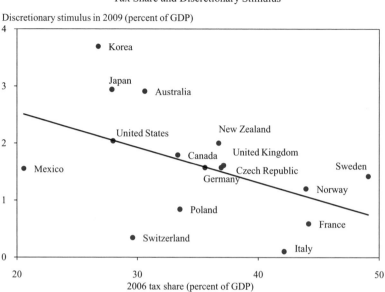

Discretionary stimulus in 2009 (percent of GDP)

2006 tax share (percent of GDP)

Notes: The regression line is stimulus = 3.8 - 0.06*(tax share). The coefficient on tax share is significant at the 90 percent confidence level. The R-squared is 0.23.
Sources: Organisation for Economic Co-operation and Development, Tax Database Table O.1; Organisation for Economic Co-operation and Development (2009a); Horton, Kumar, and Mauro (2009).

Stimulus is expected to fade slowly in 2010. Overall, the IMF estimates that advanced G-20 countries will spend 1.6 percent of GDP on discretionary stimulus in 2010, compared with 1.9 percent in 2009.[8] Emerging and developing G-20 countries will also spend 1.6 percent of GDP in 2010, compared with 2.2 percent in 2009. The IMF projects that among the G-20 countries that adopted large stimulus programs, only Germany, Korea, and Saudi Arabia will increase those programs in 2010. In addition, substantial stimulus will continue into 2010 in Australia, Canada, China, and the United

---

[7] The level of taxation in the economy is used as a proxy for automatic stabilizers. Countries with large levels of taxation see immediate automatic stabilizers because any lost income immediately reduces taxes. Those same countries often tend to have more generous social safety nets (funded by their higher taxes).

[8] The averages are calculated by the IMF using PPP GDP weights. That is, the IMF uses the size of an economy—evaluated at purchasing power parity exchange rates, which take into account different prices for different types of goods and services—to weight the different countries in the averages.

States.[9] Thus, substantial fiscal stimulus should continue to support the recovering world economy. The crucial question will be whether sufficient private demand has been rekindled by late 2010 to pick up the economic slack as stimulus unwinds.

Trade Policy in the Crisis

An extremely welcome development is the policy that was not called on during the crisis: trade protectionism. Frequently viewed as an accelerant of the Great Depression, protectionism has been largely absent during the current crisis. In the Great Depression, trade protectionism came into play after the crisis had started and was not a cause of the Depression itself (Eichengreen and Irwin 2009). But the extensive barriers that built up in the first few years of the Depression meant that as production rebounded, trade levels could not do so. In the current crisis, rather than respond to declining exports with increasing tariffs, countries left markets open, allowing for the possibility of a rebound in world trade. No major country has instituted dramatic trade restrictions. Furthermore, while antidumping and countervailing duty investigations have increased, the value of imports facing possible new import restrictions by G-20 countries stemming from new trade remedy investigations begun between 2008:Q1 and 2009:Q1 represents less than 0.5 percent of those countries' imports (Bown forthcoming).

THE ROLE OF INTERNATIONAL INSTITUTIONS

Rather than resort to beggar-thy-neighbor policies, this crisis has been characterized by international policy coordination. National policies did not take place in a vacuum; to the contrary, nations used a number of international institutions to coordinate and communicate their rescue efforts.

The G-20

The G-20, which includes 19 nations plus the European Union, was the locus of much of the coordination on trade policy, financial policy, and crisis response. Its membership is composed of most of the world's largest economies—both advanced and emerging—and makes up nearly 90 percent of world gross national product.

The first G-20 leaders' summit was held at the peak of the crisis in November 2008. At that point, G-20 countries committed to keep their markets open, adopt policies to support the global economy, and stabilize the financial sector. Leaders also began discussing financial reforms that would help prevent a repeat of the crisis.

---

[9] Japan has announced additional stimulus since these estimates and will also be providing extensive stimulus in 2010.

The second G-20 leaders' summit took place in April 2009 at the height of concern about rapid falls in GDP and trade. Leaders of the world's largest economies pledged to "do everything necessary to ensure recovery, to repair our financial systems and to maintain the global flow of capital." Furthermore, they committed to work together on tax and financial policies. Perhaps the most notable act of world coordination was the decision to provide substantial new funding to the IMF. U.S. leadership helped secure a commitment by the G-20 leaders to provide over $800 billion to fund multilateral banks broadly, with over $500 billion of those funds allocated to the IMF in particular.

In September 2009, the G-20 leaders met in Pittsburgh. They noted that international cooperation and national action had been critical in arresting the crisis and putting the world's economies on the path toward recovery. They also recognized that continued action was necessary, pledged to "sustain our strong policy response until a durable recovery is secured," and committed to avoid premature withdrawal of stimulus. The leaders also focused on the policies, regulations, and reforms that would be needed to ensure a strong recovery while avoiding the practices and vulnerabilities that gave rise to boom-bust cycles and the current crisis. They launched a new Framework for Strong, Sustainable, and Balanced Growth that committed the G-20 countries to work together to assess how their policies fit together and evaluate whether they were "collectively consistent with more sustainable and balanced growth." Further, the leaders committed to act together to improve the global financial system through financial regulatory reforms and actions to increase capital in the system.

Given the central role the G-20 had played in the response to the crisis, it is not surprising that the leaders agreed in Pittsburgh to make the G-20 the premier forum for their economic coordination. This shift reflects the growing importance of key emerging economies such as India and China—a shift that was reinforced by the agreement in Pittsburgh to realign quota shares and voting weights in the IMF and World Bank to better reflect shifts in the global economy.

The International Monetary Fund

The IMF's role has changed considerably over time, from being the shepherd of the world's Bretton Woods fixed exchange rate system to becoming a crisis manager. In a systemic bank run, a central bank sometimes steps in as the lender of last resort. The IMF is not a central bank and can neither print money nor regulate countries' behavior in advance of a crisis, but it has played a coordinating and funding role in many crises. As the scale of the current crisis became apparent, it was clear that the IMF's funds were insufficient to backstop a large systemic crisis, particularly in advanced nations. While it is still unlikely to be able to arrest a run on major advanced country financial systems, the increase in resources stemming from the G-20 summit has roughly tripled the resources available to the IMF and left it better suited to quell runs in individual countries.

As the IMF's resources were expanded, the institution took a number of concrete interventions. It set up emergency lines of credit (called Flexible Credit Lines) with Colombia, Mexico, and Poland, which in total are worth over $80 billion. These lines were intended to provide immediate liquidity in the event of a run by investors, but also to signal to the markets that funds were available, making a run less likely. Now, rather than have to go to the IMF for funds during a crisis, these countries are "pre-approved" for loans. In each of these countries, markets responded positively to the announcement of the credit lines, with the cost of insuring the countries' bonds narrowing (International Monetary Fund 2009b). The IMF also negotiated a set of standby agreements with 15 countries, committing a total of $75 billion to help them survive the economic crisis by smoothing current account adjustments and mitigating liquidity pressures. IMF analysis suggests that this program discouraged large exchange-rate swings in these countries (International Monetary Fund 2009b). These actions as well as the very existence of a better-funded global lender may have helped to keep the contraction short and to prevent sustained currency crises in many emerging nations.

THE BEGINNING OF RECOVERY AROUND THE GLOBE

In contrast to the Great Depression, where poor policy actions—monetary, fiscal, regulatory, and protectionist—helped turn a sharp global downturn into the worst worldwide collapse the modern economy has known, the recent massive policy response helped stop the spiraling of this Great Recession. Already financial markets have stabilized, GDP has begun to grow, and trade has begun to rebound. The crisis is far from over, however; most notably, employment in many countries is still distressingly weak. But the world economy appears to have avoided the outright collapse that was feared at one point and is now moving toward recovery.

The second quarter of 2009 saw the first hints of recovery in many countries. World average growth was 2.4 percent, and even OECD countries registered a positive 0.2 percent growth rate.[10] The rebound caught many by surprise. The IMF and the OECD had revised projections steadily

---

[10] World weighted average quarterly real GDP growth rates at a seasonally adjusted annual rate are from CEA calculations. The OECD growth rate is from the OECD quarterly national accounts database.

downward through the winter and spring, but by the middle of 2009 many economies had returned to growth. The one-quarter improvement in annualized growth of 5.7 percentage points (from -6.4 percent to -0.7 percent from the first to the second quarter of 2009) in the United States was one of the largest improvements in decades, but other countries that had deeper contractions rebounded even more. Annualized growth rates improved more than 14 percentage points in Germany and Japan, while growth rates rose more than 30 percentage points in Malaysia, Singapore, Taiwan, and Turkey. Other emerging markets, such as China, India, and Indonesia, which did not contract but faced lower growth during the crisis, rebounded to growth rates on par with their performance during the 2000s (if not the rapid booms of 2006–07).

Trade had collapsed quickly, and it has begun to rebound quickly as well. Beginning in March, when GDP was still falling rapidly, exports began to turn. From lows in February 2009, nominal world goods exports in dollar terms had grown 20 percent by October. U.S. nominal goods exports picked up later but had grown 17 percent from their April lows by October. As GDP began to rise, trade volume began to grow faster. Annualized growth for world real exports was 2.4 percent in the second quarter of 2009 and 16.8 percent in the third quarter. By comparison, world weighted average annualized real GDP growth in the second and third quarters of 2009 was 2.4 percent and 3.4 percent, respectively.

Financial markets are rebounding as well. Net cross-border financial flows are near their pre-crisis levels, and gross flows are increasing (although as of October 2009 they were still less than 80 percent of their average level in 2008). Libor-OIS spreads have fallen to more typical levels, and equivalent measures in other markets have subsided as well. Stock market indexes in the United States, Japan, the United Kingdom, and the European Union have all risen substantially. By October 2009, all were above their levels in October 2008, making up dramatic losses in early 2009. House prices have stabilized in most markets. Furthermore, the cost of insuring emerging-market bonds, which had spiked in the fall of 2008, is now back roughly to its pre-crisis level. The value of the dollar, which rose dramatically during the crisis, has retreated toward its value before the crisis (see Figure 3-2). From the end of March 2009 through December, the dollar depreciated 10 percent against a basket of currencies. The trade-weighted value is roughly at the same level as in the fall of 2007 and above its lows in 2008.

Potential financial problems still exist. Banks around the world may not have recognized all the losses on their balance sheets. The shock waves from the threatened default by Dubai World in November 2009 showed that there are still concerns in the market about potential bad debts on various entities' balance sheets. There also are concerns in some countries that asset prices may be rising ahead of fundamentals. But the crush of near-bankruptcy across the system has clearly eased.

The Impact of Fiscal Policy

The broad financial rescues and the monetary policy responses played crucial roles in stabilizing financial markets. Fiscal policy also played an essential role in the macroeconomic turnaround. A simple examination of G-20 advanced economies shows that while they all had broadly similar GDP contractions during the crisis, the high-stimulus countries—despite having much smaller automatic stabilizers—grew faster after the crisis than countries that adopted smaller stimulus packages. Table 3-2 shows the 2009 discretionary fiscal stimulus as a share of GDP, the tax share of GDP (which is a rough estimate of automatic stabilizers), as well as the GDP growth during the two quarters of crisis (2008:Q4 and 2009:Q1) and the second quarter of 2009 when growth resumed in many countries. Growth reappeared first in the high-stimulus G-20 countries.

Table 3-2
Stimulus and Growth in Advanced G-20 Countries

	Stimulus (% of GDP)	Stabilizers (% of GDP)	Growth during:	
			Crisis (%)	2009:Q2 (%)
High stimulus	3.2	28.4	-7.1	5.4
Mid stimulus	1.7	35.3	-8.3	-1.3
Low stimulus	0.3	43.2	-7.4	-0.3
United States	2.0	28.0	-5.9	-0.7

Notes: High countries are Australia, Japan, and Korea; middle countries are Canada, Germany, and the United Kingdom; low countries are France and Italy. Growth rates are annualized. Crisis refers to Q4:2008 and Q1:2009.
Sources: Organisation for Economic Co-operation and Development, Tax Database Table 0.1; Horton, Kumar, and Mauro (2009); Organisation for Economic Co-operation and Development (2009a); country sources.

Countries may have different typical growth patterns, however. Thus, to understand the impact of fiscal stimulus, one must estimate what would have happened had there been no stimulus—a counterfactual. Private sector expectations in November 2008—after the crisis had begun but before most stimulus packages were adopted—can serve as that counterfactual. Thus, one can compare actual growth minus predicted growth with the degree of stimulus to see whether those countries with large stimulus packages outperformed expectations once the stimulus policies were in place. The second quarter of 2009 is used as the test case. Figure 3-13 shows actual growth minus expected growth compared with 2009 discretionary fiscal

Figure 3-13
Outperforming Expectations and Stimulus

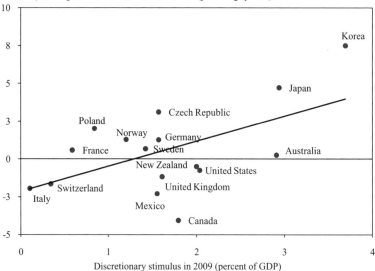

Actual Q2 GDP growth minus November forecast (percentage points)

Discretionary stimulus in 2009 (percent of GDP)

Notes: The regression line is (growth - forecast) = -2.1 + 1.65 * stimulus. The coefficient on stimulus is significant at the 95 percent confidence level. The R-squared is 0.31.
Sources: J.P. Morgan Global Data Watch, Global Economic Outlook Summary Table, November 7, 2008; Horton, Kumar, and Mauro (2009); Organisation for Economic Co-operation and Development (2009a); country sources; CEA calculations.

stimulus for the OECD countries for which private sector forecasts were available on a consistent date.[11] Countries with larger stimulus on average exceeded expectations to a greater degree than those with smaller stimulus packages. The two countries in this exercise with the largest stimulus packages, Korea and Japan, outperformed expectations by dramatic amounts. Countries such as Italy that had virtually no stimulus performed worse than most. Among non-OECD countries, China had one of the largest fiscal stimulus packages, and in the second quarter of 2009 its growth was both rapid and far in excess of what had been expected in November 2008. Fiscal

[11] Stimulus is measured as in Table 3-1, using IMF and OECD estimates of 2009 fiscal stimulus. Forecasts are from J.P.Morgan. See Council of Economic Advisers (2009) for more details. That report examines more countries and a set of time series forecasts in addition to the private sector (J.P.Morgan) forecasts. The results are quite similar with a simple time series forecast. Results are slightly weaker with a broader sample, but that is not surprising because the swings in the economies in emerging markets were quite severe and difficult to predict, and the stimulus policies may operate somewhat differently in those nations. Council of Economic Advisers (2009) used Brookings estimates as well as OECD and IMF, but those ceased being updated in March, and thus this analysis uses only IMF and OECD estimates. Using the June estimates alone slightly weakens the results because stimulus announced late in the second quarter likely had little impact on growth in that quarter.

stimulus seems to have been important in restarting world economic growth in the second quarter of 2009.

After the second quarter of 2009, the relationship between stimulus and growth weakens somewhat. High-stimulus countries still exceed expectations relative to low-stimulus countries, but the relationship is not statistically significant. It may be that quarterly growth projections made nearly a year in advance are not precise enough a measure of a third-quarter growth counterfactual.

The World Economy in the Near Term

While the return to GDP and export growth is encouraging, exports are still far below their level in the summer of 2008, and GDP is now far below its prior trend level. The IMF currently forecasts annual world growth of 3.1 percent in 2010; the OECD projects 3.4 percent.[12] For advanced countries, the forecasts are even more restrained: the IMF projects 1.3 percent, the OECD 1.9 percent for OECD countries. The IMF forecasts world trade to grow 2.5 percent in 2010; the OECD, 6.0 percent. These forecasts may be conservative. The IMF forecast would leave trade at a much lower share of GDP than before the crisis, and even if trade growth met the OECD's more aggressive forecast, trade would not reach its previous level as a share of GDP for some time. Given that trade declined faster than GDP in the crisis, it is possible it will continue to bounce back faster as well, surpassing these estimates.

How Fast Will Countries Grow? There is an open question about how fast countries will grow following the crisis. After typical recessions, the magnitude of a recovery often matches the depth of the drop. In this way, GDP returns not only to its previous growth rate, but to its previous trend path as well. If, however, the world's advanced economies emerge from the crisis only slowly and simply return to stable growth rates, output will be on a permanently lower path. A financial crisis could lower the future level of output by generating lower levels of labor, capital, or the productivity of those factors. If the economy returns to full employment, and productivity growth remains on trend, though, capital should eventually return to its pre-crisis path because the incentives to invest will be high. Thus, as long as the economy eventually returns to full employment, the long-run impact of the crisis chiefly rests on productivity growth in the years ahead. Chapter 10 discusses the prospects and importance of productivity in more detail.

Some research suggests financial crises may result in a slow growth pattern (International Monetary Fund 2009a), with substantial average

---

[12] IMF estimates are from International Monetary Fund (2009a). OECD estimates are from Organisation for Economic Co-operation and Development (2009b).

losses in the level of output in the years following a financial crisis. The same research, however, shows a wide variety of experiences following crises, with a substantial number of countries returning to or exceeding the pre-crisis trend level path of GDP. It is far too early to project the likely outcome of this recession and recovery, but there is hope that the aggressive policy responses and the potential for a sharp uptick in world trade—bouncing back with responsiveness similar in magnitude to its downturn—will return the path of GDP to previous trend levels in many economies.

Concerns about Unemployment. One reason for the great concern about the pace of growth after the recession is the current employment situation. What was a financial crisis and then a real economy and trade crisis has rapidly become a jobs crisis in many advanced economies. The OECD projects the average unemployment rate in OECD countries will have risen 2.3 percentage points from 2008 to 2009, with an average jobless rate of 8.2 percent in 2009. More worryingly, the OECD projects the group average will continue rising in 2010, and in some areas (such as the euro area) the jobless rate is expected to be even higher in 2011.

The United States has been an outlier in the extent to which the GDP contraction has turned into an employment contraction. Figure 3-14 shows the change in GDP and in the unemployment rate from the first quarter of 2008 to the second quarter of 2009. Typically, one would expect a line running from the upper left to the lower right because countries with small declines in GDP (or even increases) would have small increases in unemployment (lower right) and those with larger declines in GDP would have larger increases in unemployment (upper left). Countries broadly fit this pattern during the current crisis and recovery, but there are a number of aberrations. Germany saw a large contraction in GDP, and while growth has resumed, its one-year contraction was still sizable. Still, Germany's unemployment rate barely increased. In contrast, the United States suffered a relatively mild output contraction (for an OECD country), and yet it has had the largest jump in the unemployment rate outside of Iceland, Ireland, Spain, and Turkey, all of which had larger GDP declines.

There are several partial explanations for the large variation in the GDP-unemployment relationship across countries. The more flexible labor markets in the United States make the usual response of unemployment to output movements larger than in most other OECD countries; and, as discussed in Chapter 2, the rise in U.S. unemployment in the current episode has been unusually large given the output decline. Another factor is a policy response in some countries aimed at keeping current employees in current jobs. The extreme example of such a policy has been Germany's *Kurzarbeit* (short-time work) program, which subsidizes companies that put workers

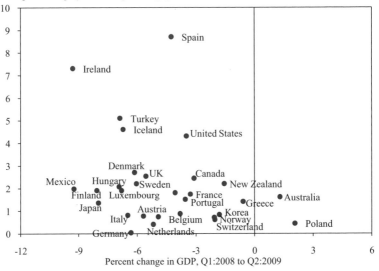

Figure 3-14
OECD Countries: GDP and Unemployment

Sources: Organisation for Economic Co-Operation and Development, Quarterly National Accounts and Key Short-Term Economic Indicators; country sources.

on shorter shifts rather than firing them. The OECD estimates the German unemployment rate would be roughly 1 percentage point higher without the program. Because such programs benefit only those who already have jobs, they could hold down unemployment at the cost of a more rigid labor market. Labor market flexibility is generally seen as allowing lower unemployment on average over the course of the business cycle and as permitting a more efficient distribution of labor resources, thus enhancing productivity.

Global Imbalances in the Crisis

In addition to the unambiguous signs of problems in the U.S. economy going into the crisis, there were clear signals that the global economy was not well balanced. Global growth was strong from 2002 to 2007, but the growth was not well distributed around the world economy, with fast growth in some emerging markets and sluggish growth in some advanced economies. Further, that growth came with mounting imbalances in saving and borrowing across the world. U.S. saving was very low, which led to substantial borrowing from the rest of the world. Home price bubbles and overborrowing were not exclusive to the United States; the United Kingdom, Spain, and many other economies also borrowed extensively, helping inflate asset prices in those economies. This borrowing was paired with very high saving in some countries, particularly in emerging Asia.

The extent to which the global imbalances were a cause of the crisis or represented a symptom of poor policy choices in different countries is a question of active debate (see Obstfeld and Rogoff 2009 for discussion). The current account (net borrowing from or lending to the rest of the world) can be defined as a country's saving minus its investment. Thus, some argue that forces in the rest of the world cannot be deterministic of a country's current account balance. A country saves or borrows based on its own choices. In this formulation, the imbalances were merely a symptom. In fact, some argued the imbalances were beneficial because savings were channeled away from inefficient financial markets in poor countries toward what were thought to be more efficient markets in rich countries. Conversely, some argue that the influx of global savings into the United States distorted incentives by keeping interest rates too low and led to overborrowing and asset bubbles. In this view, the imbalances played a leading role in the crisis.

The truth almost certainly lies somewhere in between. The influx of global savings into the United States did lower borrowing rates and encouraged more spending and less saving within the U.S. economy. This may have allowed the credit expansion and related asset price bubbles to continue longer than they could have otherwise. At the same time, even if the global savings in some sense led to U.S. borrowing, the failure of the financial system to use that borrowing productively and the failure of regulation to make sure risk was being treated appropriately were surely partly to blame for the crisis.

As the U.S. economy seeks to find a more sure footing and a growth path less dependent on borrowing and bubbles, world demand needs to be redistributed so that it is less dependent on the U.S. consumer and does not cause global imbalances to reappear and contribute to distortions in the economy. Fixing the imbalances can help provide more demand for the U.S. economy. But these imbalances also need to be treated as symptoms of deeper regulatory and policy failures. Fixing the imbalances alone will not prevent another crisis.

Since the onset of the crisis, the imbalances have partially unwound (the likely future path of the U.S. current account is discussed in more detail in Chapter 4). The U.S. current account deficit, which had built to over 6 percent of GDP in 2006, was on a downward path before the crisis struck in full force, falling to under 5 percent of GDP at the start of 2008. After the crisis hit, it fell below 3 percent of GDP in the first quarter of 2009. Major surplus countries—China, Germany, and Japan—have all seen a reduction in their current account surpluses from the highs of 2007. In all three cases, the surpluses have stabilized at substantial levels (in the range of 3–5 percent of GDP), but they are notably down from their highs. One essential part of the response to the crisis has been the substantial fiscal stimulus implemented by these three countries, which has helped demand in these countries stay stronger than it otherwise would have been.

Figure 3-15, which shows current account imbalances scaled to world GDP, demonstrates how much of total world excess saving or borrowing is attributable to individual countries. As the figure makes clear, by 2005 and 2006, the United States was borrowing nearly 2 percent of world GDP, and by the end of 2008, China was lending nearly 1 percent of world GDP. During the crisis, the surpluses of OPEC (Organization of Petroleum Exporting Countries) countries, Japan, and Germany contracted, and the United States is now borrowing less than 1 percent of world GDP. China's surplus is also smaller than before the crisis, but China is still lending nearly 0.5 percent of world GDP, and OPEC surpluses may rise as well. But by the third quarter of 2009, the degree of imbalance was substantially lower than just a year earlier. There is hope that the short-run moves in these current account balances are not simply cyclical factors that will return quickly to

Figure 3-15
Current Account Deficits or Surpluses

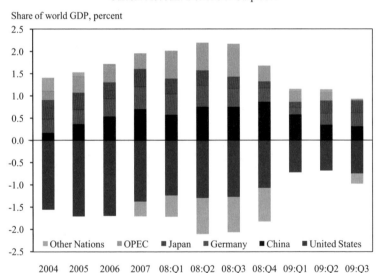

Notes: Sample limited by data availability. In the figure, OPEC includes Ecuador, Iran, Kuwait, Saudi Arabia, and Venezuela; and Other Nations includes all other countries with quarterly current account data. Third quarter 2009 data for both OPEC and Other Nations were incomplete at the time of writing.
Sources: Country sources; CEA estimates.

former levels but rather that they represent a more sustained rebalancing of world demand.

Net export growth is often a key source of growth propelling a country out of a financial crisis. But in a global crisis, not every country can increase exports and decrease imports simultaneously. Someone must buy the products that are being sold, and the world's current accounts must balance out. Thus far, the crisis has come with a reduction in imbalances, with strong growth and smaller surpluses in many surplus countries. Whether these shifts become a permanent part of the world economy or policies and growth models revert to the pattern of the 2000s will be an important area for policy coordination.

CONCLUSION

The period from September 2008 to the end of 2009 will be remembered as a historic period in the world economy. The drops in GDP and trade may stand for many decades as the largest worldwide economic crisis since the Great Depression. In contrast to the Depression, however, the history of the period may also show how aggressive policy action and international coordination can help turn the world economy from the edge of disaster. The recovery is unsteady and, especially with regard to unemployment, incomplete, but compared with a year ago, the positive shift in trends in the world economy has been dramatic.

CHAPTER 4

SAVING AND INVESTMENT

The United States appears poised to begin its recovery from the most severe recession since the Great Depression. But as discussed in Chapter 2, the recession has been unusually deep, and the crisis has caused declines in credit availability as well as weak consumer and business confidence. As a result, achieving the private spending necessary to support a robust and full recovery has been, and will continue to be, challenging.

Moreover, as the President has repeatedly emphasized, it is not enough simply to return to the path the economy was on before the slump. The growth that preceded the recession saw high consumption spending, low private saving, excessive housing construction, unsustainable run-ups in asset prices (especially for assets related directly or indirectly to housing), and high budget and trade deficits. That path was unstable—as we have learned at enormous cost—and undermined long-run prosperity. Thus, as the economy recovers, a rebalancing will be necessary. The composition of spending needs to be reoriented in a way that will put us on a path to sustained, stable prosperity.

In thinking about the twin challenges of recovery and reorientation, it is useful to consider the division of demand into its components. Overall or aggregate demand can be classified into personal consumption expenditures, residential investment, business investment, net exports, and government purchases of goods and services. Government purchases, which consist of such items as Federal expenditures on national defense and state and local spending on education, are relatively stable. This is especially true when one recalls that government transfers, such as spending on Medicare or Social Security, are not part of government purchases but rather are elements of personal income. Thus, it is the behavior of the remaining components that will be central to addressing the challenges of generating enough demand for recovery and a better composition of demand for long-run growth and stability.

This chapter lays out a picture of how the components of private demand behaved during the downturn and how they are likely to evolve as the economy recovers and once it returns to full employment. The chapter describes the transition that has already occurred away from low personal saving and high residential investment, as well as the transition that needs to occur toward greater business investment and net exports. It also describes the President's initiatives for encouraging the transitions necessary for long-run prosperity and stability.

THE PATH OF CONSUMPTION SPENDING

Figure 4-1 shows the share of gross domestic product (GDP) that takes the form of production of goods and services directly purchased by consumers. The figure has two key messages. First, consumption represents a substantial majority of output. As a result, movements in consumption play a central role in macroeconomic outcomes. Second, the fraction of output devoted to consumption has been rising over time, leaving less room for components that contribute to future standards of living. The behavior of consumption will therefore be central to addressing both the shorter-run challenge of generating a strong recovery and the longer-run challenge of rebalancing the economy.

Figure 4-1
Personal Consumption Expenditures as a Share of GDP

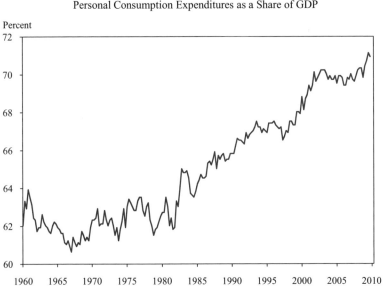

Source: Department of Commerce (Bureau of Economic Analysis), National Income and Product Accounts Table 1.1.10.

The Determinants of Saving

To understand the behavior of consumption, it is critical to consider how households divide their disposable income between consumption and saving. Figure 4-2 shows the personal saving rate (that is, the ratio of saving to disposable personal income) since 1960 (left axis), along with the ratio of household wealth to disposable personal income (right axis).

Figure 4-2
Personal Saving Rate Versus Wealth Ratio

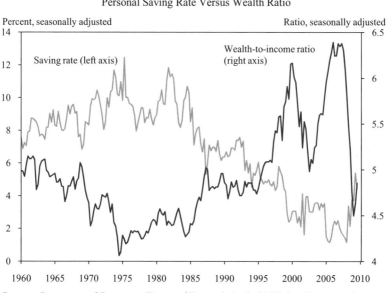

Sources: Department of Commerce (Bureau of Economic Analysis), National Income and Product Accounts Table 2.1; Federal Reserve Board, Flow of Funds Table B.100.

The big swings in wealth reflect asset market booms and busts. Much of the drop in wealth in the early 1970s reflects the stock market decline associated with the first oil price shock. The stock market booms of the mid-1980s and the late 1990s are obvious, as is the decline in stock prices in the early 2000s. The wealth decline in 2008–09 was the largest such experience in the sample, reflecting large contributions from falling house prices as well as stock prices.

Paralleling the behavior of the consumption-output ratio, the saving rate showed no strong trend before roughly 1980. But it has shown a marked downward trend since then. Economic theory suggests a variety of factors that should influence saving, most notably changes in the demographic structure of the population, the growth rate of income, and the real after-tax interest rate. None of these three factors, however, provides a compelling explanation for the fluctuations in the saving rate evident in the figure.

Indeed, some of the factors should probably have pushed saving up in recent decades, not down. A 1991 study, for example, predicted that the saving rate would rise as the baby boom generation entered its high-saving preretirement years (Auerbach, Cai, and Kotlikoff 1991). Instead, the saving rate fell steadily as the boomers approached retirement (the first boomers claimed early Social Security benefits in 2008).

Figure 4-2 suggests to the eye, and statistical analysis confirms, a strong negative association between the saving rate and the wealth-to-income ratio. This relationship has been interpreted as reflecting the effect of wealth on spending: a run-up in wealth leads to less need for saving. Such an interpretation is unsatisfying, however, because it leaves a key question unanswered: If wealth movements cause saving rate movements, what causes wealth movements? More broadly, it leaves open the possibility that both saving choices and asset price movements are a consequence of some deeper underlying force. For example, an increase in optimism about future economic conditions might lead both to a spending boom and to a general bidding up of asset prices. In that case, the true moving force would not be wealth changes per se; instead, both asset prices and saving would be responding to the increase in optimism.

Survey data measuring "consumer sentiment" or "consumer confidence" do, in fact, have substantial forecasting power for near-term spending growth, and are also associated with contemporaneous movements in asset prices (Carroll, Fuhrer, and Wilcox 1994). Such surveys are therefore a useful part of a macroeconomist's forecasting tool kit. But such surveys have not proven useful in explaining long-term trends like the secular decline in the saving rate.

Emerging economic research suggests another underlying explanation that may be more potent: movements in the availability of credit. A substantial academic literature has documented the expansion of credit since the era of financial liberalization that began in the early 1980s (Dynan 2009). Many factors have contributed to this expansion; perhaps the most prominent explanation (aside from the liberalization itself) is the telecommunications and computer revolutions, which together have permitted the construction of ever-more-detailed databases on consumer credit histories, giving creditors a far more precise ability to tailor credit offers to the personal characteristics of individual borrowers (Jappelli and Pagano 1993). A beneficial effect of this information revolution has been that many people who had previously been unable to obtain credit have for the first time been able to borrow to buy a home, to start a business, or to undertake many other useful activities (Edelberg 2006; Getter 2006).

A reduction in saving, however, is almost the inevitable consequence of a general increase in the ability to borrow. If there is less need to save for a down payment for a home, for a child's education, for unforeseen emergencies, or for spending of any other kind, then the likelihood is that less saving will be done. Of course, eventually the saving rate should mostly recover from any dip caused by a one-time increase in the availability of credit, because whatever extra debt was incurred must be paid back over time (and paying back debt is another form of saving). This recovery in saving, however, may take a long time. If, in the meantime, credit availability increases again, the gradual small increase in saving that reflects debt repayment could easily be obscured by the new drop in saving occasioned by the continuing expansion in credit availability.

How much of the decline in the saving rate was due to a gradual, but cumulatively large, increase in credit availability is not easy to determine, partly because an aggregate measure of credit availability is difficult to construct. Recent research on commercial lending has argued that a good measure of the change in credit supply is provided by the Federal Reserve's Senior Loan Officer Opinion Survey on Bank Lending Practices, in which managers at leading financial institutions are asked for their assessments of credit conditions for businesses (Lown and Morgan 2006). Building on that research, one study has proposed that a measure of the level of credit availability to consumers can be constructed simply by accumulating the sequence of readings from this survey's measure of credit availability to consumers (Muellbauer 2007).[1]

Economic theory suggests that one further element may be important in understanding spending and saving choices around times of recession: the intensity of consumers' precautionary motive for saving. Because the risk of becoming unemployed is perhaps the greatest threat to most people's future financial stability, the unemployment rate has sometimes been used as a proxy for the intensity of the precautionary saving motive.

Implications for Recent and Future Saving Behavior

Figure 4-3 shows the relationship between the measured saving rate and a simple statistical model that relates the saving rate to the wealth-to-income ratio, a slightly modified version of Muellbauer's credit availability index, and the unemployment rate. The statistical model is estimated over the sample period 1966:Q3 to 2009:Q3. All three variables have statistically important predictive power, with the two most important measures being the measure of credit conditions and the wealth-to-income ratio.

---

[1] Specifically, each quarter the survey asks about banks' willingness to make consumer install-ment loans now as opposed to three months ago.

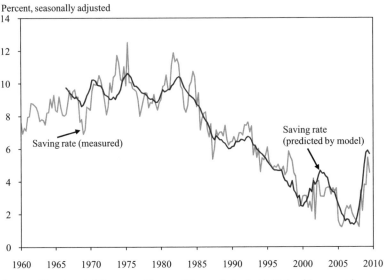

Figure 4-3
Personal Saving Rate: Actual Versus Model

Percent, seasonally adjusted

Saving rate (measured)

Saving rate
(predicted by model)

Sources: Department of Commerce (Bureau of Economic Analysis), National Income and
Product Accounts Table 2.1; CEA calculations.

Figure 4-4 uses this simple framework to ask what the path of the
saving rate might have looked like if the increase in credit availability and the
housing price boom had not occurred. (To be exact, the figure shows what
the model says the saving rate would have been if the wealth-to-income ratio
had remained constant from the first quarter of 2003 to the fourth quarter
of 2007, and if credit conditions had neither expanded nor contracted; the
first quarter of 2003 is chosen as the starting point because in that quarter
the wealth-to-income ratio was close to its average historical value.) In this
counterfactual history, the personal saving rate would have been, on average,
about 2 percentage points higher over the 2003–07 period.

Of course, a far more important consequence than the higher saving
rate might have been the avoidance of the financial and real disturbances
caused by the housing price boom and subsequent crash. But taking the
crash as given, Figure 4-3 shows that the model does a reasonably good job
in tracking the dynamics of the saving rate over the period since the business cycle peak. All three elements of the model contribute to the model's
predicted rise in the personal saving rate over the past couple of years: the
increase in the unemployment rate, the sharp drop in asset values evident
in Figure 4-2, and the steep drop in credit availability as measured by the
Senior Loan Officer Opinion Survey.

Figure 4-4
Actual Personal Saving Versus Counterfactual Personal Saving

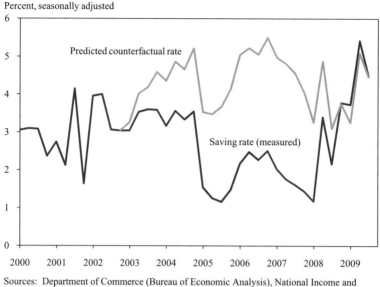

Percent, seasonally adjusted

Sources: Department of Commerce (Bureau of Economic Analysis), National Income and Product Accounts Table 2.1; CEA calculations.

The saving model also has implications for the future path of spending. Because of the important role it finds for credit availability, the model suggests that the speed of the recovery in spending is likely to be closely tied to the pace at which the financial sector returns to health. This point underscores a chief motivation for the Administration's efforts to repair the damage to the financial system: a full economic recovery is unlikely until and unless the financial system is repaired. The vital role that a healthy financial sector plays in the functioning of the economy explains the urgency with which the Administration has been pressing Congress to pass a comprehensive and effective reform of the financial regulatory system (see Chapter 6 for a detailed discussion of the Administration's proposals).

Over a longer time frame, a resumption seems unlikely of the past pattern in which credit growth persistently outpaces income growth. Instead, credit might reasonably be expected to expand, in the long run, at a pace that roughly matches the rate of income growth. Similarly, in keeping with the long-run stability of the wealth-to-income ratio evident in Figure 4-2, wealth plausibly might grow at roughly the same pace as income—or perhaps a bit faster if investment can sustain an increase in capital per worker. Finally, although unemployment is likely to remain above its normal rate for some time, it too can be expected to return to historically normal values in the medium run. Under these conditions, the model suggests that the personal saving rate will eventually stabilize somewhere in the range of 4 to 7 percent, somewhat below its level in the 1960s and 1970s, but well above its level over the past decade.

The saving rate has already risen sharply over the past two years (which reflects an even steeper drop in consumption than in income). As credit conditions and the unemployment rate return to normal, it is plausible to expect a temporary partial reversal of the recent increase, even if asset values do not return to their pre-crisis levels. It would not be surprising, therefore, if the saving rate dipped a bit over the next year or two before heading toward a higher long-run equilibrium value. The prospect of temporary fallback in the saving rate is also plausible as a consequence of the expected withdrawal of some of the temporary income support policies that were part of the stimulus package. On balance, however, the United States seems now to be on a trajectory that will eventually result in a more "normal," and more sustainable, pattern of household saving and spending than the one that has prevailed in recent years.

While the underlying economic forces sketched here seem likely to lead eventually to a higher saving rate even in the absence of policy changes, the Administration has proposed a variety of saving-promoting policy changes to enhance that trend over the longer term. These include increasing the availability of 401(k)-type saving plans and encouraging employers to gradually increase default contribution rates (and to ensure that new employees' default saving choices reflect sound financial planning). Economic research suggests that people assume that if their employer offers a retirement saving plan, the default saving rate in that plan probably reflects a reasonably good choice for them, unless their circumstances are unusual (Benartzi and Thaler 2004).

The Future of the Housing Market and Construction

The boom in construction spending that characterized the middle years of the past decade made a substantial contribution to growth while it lasted. When the residential investment engine began to sputter around the middle of 2006, and then to stall, the ensuing correction in the sector was correspondingly steep. With the benefit of hindsight, it is now clear that much of the mid-decade's frenetic activity was based on unsound financial decisions rather than sustainable economic developments. As a consequence, construction has declined to below-normal levels as the excesses work off. For the future, construction activity is expected to pick up and contribute to the economic recovery, although this activity is likely to be well below the very high levels it reached in the mid-2000s.

The Housing Market

The residential investment boom can be measured in several ways. As Figure 4-5 shows, new construction of single-family housing units soared in the first half of the 2000s. Builders were constructing 30 percent more single-family housing units a year in the expansion of the 2000s than in the 1990s boom. Housing investment as a share of GDP averaged more than 5.5 percent over the 2002–06 period, compared with an average of only 4.7 percent from 1950 to 2001. Figure 4-6 shows that from 1995 to 2005 the homeownership rate rose from 65 percent to 69 percent as mortgage underwriting standards loosened, especially in the later part of the period.

Figure 4-5
Single-Family Housing Starts

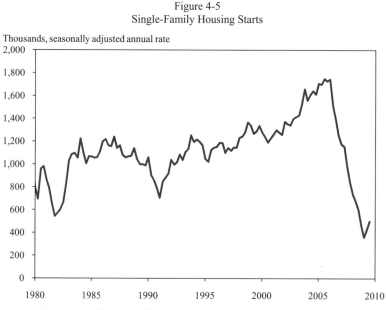

Source: Department of Commerce (Census Bureau), New Residential Construction Table 3.

It is now apparent that the mid-2000s level of new construction was unsustainable. Analysis by the Congressional Budget Office (2008) and Macroeconomic Advisers (2009) suggests the mid-2000s pace of starts was well in excess of the underlying pace of expansion in demand for new housing units based on household formation and other demographic drivers.

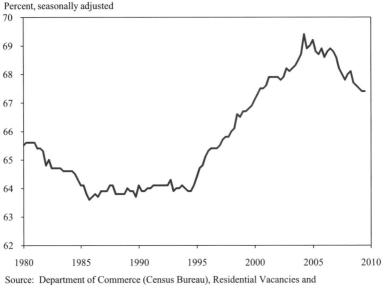

Figure 4-6
Homeownership Rate

Percent, seasonally adjusted

Source: Department of Commerce (Census Bureau), Residential Vacancies and
Homeownership Table 4.

The boom was followed by an equally dramatic bust. From their peak in the third quarter of 2005 to the first quarter of 2009, single-family housing starts fell by more than a factor of four. The homeownership rate reversed course, and by the second quarter of 2009 had returned to its 2000 level. The share of housing investment in GDP plummeted to 2.4 percent in the second quarter of 2009.

Just as the mid-decade's high levels of construction and housing market activity were not sustainable, the recent extremely low levels of construction will not persist indefinitely. In 2009, housing starts and the share of housing investment in GDP were well below their previous historical lows. In the long run, sounder underwriting standards will require more would-be homeowners to take time to save for a down payment before buying a home, suggesting that the homeownership rate will ultimately settle at a level lower than its recent peaks. Nonetheless, as the population grows and the housing stock depreciates, new residential construction will be required to meet demand. The analyses by the Congressional Budget Office (2008) and Macroeconomic Advisers (2009) suggest that the underlying demographic trend of household formation is consistent with growth in demand of between 1.1 million and 1.3 million new single-family housing units per year, more than double the pace of single-family housing starts in November 2009. Indeed, since the second quarter of 2009, housing construction has already rebounded a bit, making its first positive contribution to GDP growth in the third quarter of 2009 since the end of 2005. But, as described in Chapter 2, the stocks of new homes and existing homes for sale, vacant homes that are not currently on the market, and homes that are in the process of foreclosure and that are likely to be put on the market at some point remain high. As a result, construction demand is likely to rise to its long-run level only gradually while some demand is met by the stock of existing units.

In short, as the housing market stabilizes and returns to a more normal condition, its role as a major drag on economic growth seems to be ending, and it is likely to contribute to the recovery. But residential construction cannot be expected to be the engine for GDP growth that it was during the housing boom of the mid-2000s.

Commercial Real Estate

The market for commercial real estate has also suffered in the recession. Commercial real estate encompasses a wide range of properties, from small businesses that occupy a single stand-alone structure to large shopping malls owned by a consortium of investors.

Problems in the commercial real estate sector are less obviously a result of overbuilding than those in the residential sector; instead, they reflect the sharp decline in demand for commercial space and the overall decline in the economy. The value of commercial real estate increased notably between 2005 to 2007, spurred by easy credit conditions, as measured for example in the Senior Loan Officer Opinion Survey. By the end of 2004, the net number of banks reporting they had eased lending standards for commercial real estate loans was persistently larger than at any point in the history of the series. Most banks did not begin tightening standards again until the end of 2006. The relative quantity of financing also increased over this period; the ratio of the change in the value of commercial real estate mortgages to new construction, which should increase when debt financing becomes relatively attractive, reached a 45-year high in 2003 and then continued to climb, peaking at the end of 2005 at more than three times the historical average.[2]

In the nonresidential sector, high prices did not translate into a dramatic increase in new construction (Figure 4-7). Rather, existing owners of nonresidential properties used the cheap financing and price increases to refinance or sell. Several factors appear to have played a role in limiting

---

[2] The numerator of the ratio is the seasonally adjusted change in commercial and multifamily residential mortgages (Federal Reserve, Flow of Funds Tables F219 and F220). The denominator is seasonally adjusted construction of commercial and health care structures, multifamily structures, and miscellaneous other nonresidential structures (Department of Commerce, Bureau of Economic Analysis, National Income and Product Accounts Table 5.3.5). The median of the ratio from 1958 to 2000 is 0.46, while the 2005:Q4 value is 1.50.

new investment in this sector. First, a close look at Figure 4-7 shows that nonresidential construction has historically exhibited much less volatility than residential construction, a pattern that also held true during the recent boom. Second, developers seem to have been wary of overbuilding because of unhappy experiences in previous expansions. A final dampening factor has been that construction resources were tied up in the residential construction sector. Indeed, only when residential construction slowed in 2006 did nonresidential construction begin to show larger gains.

Figure 4-7
Fixed Investment in Structures by Type

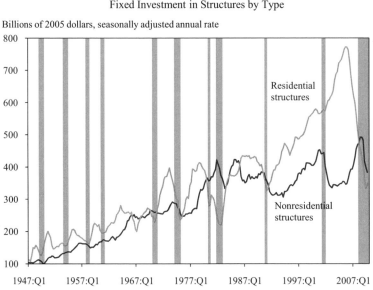

Note: Grey shading indicates recessions.
Source: Department of Commerce (Bureau of Economic Analysis), National Income and Product Accounts Table 5.3.6.

Commercial real estate values have declined dramatically since 2007. As Figure 4-8 shows, according to the Moody's/REAL Commercial Property Index, which tracks same-property price changes for commercial office, apartment, industrial, and retail buildings, commercial real estate prices fell 43 percent from their peak in October 2007 to September 2009. A steep increase in vacancy rates, stemming from weakness in the overall economy, has been one important reason for these declines in value: the commercial real estate services firm CB Richard Ellis reports that vacancy rates for offices increased from 12.6 percent in mid-2007 to 17.2 percent in the third quarter of 2009. Before the recession, vacancy rates were generally declining.

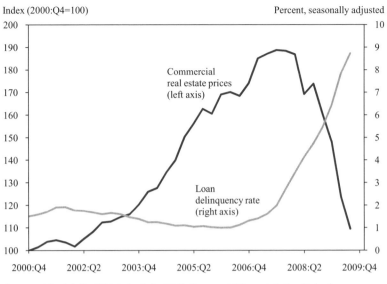

Figure 4-8
Commercial Real Estate Prices and Loan Delinquencies

Sources: Moody's/Real Estate Analytics LLC, Commercial Property Index; Federal
Reserve Board.

As commercial real estate values have declined, owners have found
it difficult to refinance their debt because loan balances now appear large
relative to the properties' value. Nearly half of the banks responding to the
Senior Loan Officer Opinion Survey in the third quarter of 2009 reported
that they continued to tighten standards on commercial real estate loans,
whereas none of the respondents reported having eased standards. Since
commercial real estate loans typically are relatively short term, an inability
to refinance debt has led to a sharp rise in delinquencies and foreclosures.
Figure 4-8 shows that the proportion of commercial real estate loans with
payments at least 30 days past due rose from about 1 percent during most
of the decade to almost 9 percent by the third quarter of 2009. Distress has
made lenders reluctant to provide financing for new projects. Overall, the
value of commercial and multifamily residential mortgages declined in each
of the first three quarters of 2009 (Federal Reserve Flow of Funds Tables
L.219 and L.220). Tight credit and the increase in sales of distressed properties have fed into further price declines, generating a negative feedback loop
between property values and conditions in the sector.

As private sources of funding have dried up, the Federal Reserve
has helped fill the gap through the Term Asset-Backed Securities Loan
Facility (TALF). In June 2009, the TALF made lending available to private
financial market participants against their holdings of existing commercial

mortgage-backed securities (CMBS), thereby increasing liquidity in the CMBS market. In November 2009, the TALF made its first loans against newly issued CMBS. The provision of TALF financing for these newly issued securities may prove particularly important in allowing borrowers to refinance.

The negative feedback loop between credit conditions, the sale of distressed commercial properties, and commercial property values may lead to further price declines. Eventually, however, a combination of economic recovery and an improvement in financing conditions should help prices stabilize. Still, as with the residential mortgage market, commercial real estate financing will likely not return any time soon to the easy terms that prevailed before the collapse. Experience in previous business cycles suggests that recovery of the sector will lag the economy as a whole.

BUSINESS INVESTMENT

If consumption and construction are not the drivers of growth going forward in the way they were in the early 2000s, two components of private demand are left to fill the gap: business investment excluding structures, and net exports.[3] Nonstructures investment could well become again (as it was in the 1990s) a driving force in the expansion of aggregate demand and economic production. And in the long run, its share in GDP could reach levels higher than those of the first part of the decade.

Investment in the Recovery

Investment spending (other than structures) plummeted in late 2008 and early 2009. This investment spending fell so low that, after accounting for depreciation, estimates of the absolute stock of capital showed stagnation in 2008 and even a decline in the first quarter of 2009. Falling spending in this category reflected falling business confidence, as indicated, for example, in the Federal Reserve Bank of Philadelphia's Business Outlook Diffusion Index; this index was negative every month from October 2008 to July 2009, signaling that more businesses thought conditions were deteriorating than thought they were improving. Similarly, the National Federation of Independent Business Index of Small Business Optimism hit its lowest point since 1980 in March 2009.

---

[3] In the National Income and Product Accounts, construction of commercial structures is classified as part of business investment. Given that the boom and bust were concentrated in residential and commercial construction, however, for discussing recent and prospective developments it is more useful to consider commercial construction investment together with residential investment, as was done in the previous section. Thus, the discussion that follows is largely concerned with nonstructures investment.

Investment of this kind firmed in the second half of 2009, coinciding with improvements in business confidence. Indeed, investment in equipment and software increased at a 13 percent annual rate in the fourth quarter. Nevertheless, the cumulative erosion has been so substantial that years of strong growth will be necessary to fully recover from the nadir. As a result, recovery of spending in this area is likely to make a substantial contribution to the recovery of the overall economy.

Investment in the Long Run

In the long run, the share of business investment is likely not just to return to its pre-recession levels, but to exceed them. During the boom of the 1990s, the share of business investment in equipment and software as a fraction of GDP rose from a post-Gulf-War recession low of 6.9 percent in 1991 to 9.6 percent in 2000. During that period, investment in information processing equipment and software made the largest contribution to the increase, as shown in Figure 4-9. Information technology (IT) investment grew an astounding 18 percent per year on average from 1991 to 2000. Other investment in equipment and software, which includes industrial, transportation, and construction equipment, accelerated as well, and grew as a share of GDP over this period. This high level of investment in the 1990s increased industrial capacity by an average of 4 percent per year.

As the figure shows, the boom came to an end at the beginning of the 2000s, when investment in every category of equipment and software fell sharply as a share of GDP. The recovery in business investment in equipment and software after the 2001 recession was weak. IT investment grew at a historically tepid pace of 6 percent per year from 2003 to 2007, far below pre-2000 growth rates. Non-IT investment growth was also muted, with spending on industrial equipment growing at an annual pace of only 3.7 percent from 2003 to 2007, down from an average of 5.4 percent in the 1990s. Investment in transportation equipment surpassed its 1999 peak only for one quarter in 2006. In the recovery following the 2001–02 recession, the peak value of non-IT equipment investment as a share of GDP was only 4.3 percent (in 2006), a level that does not even match the historical *average* value of that series in the period from 1980 to 2000. Production capacity in the sector grew an average of 0.6 percent per year from 2003 to 2007, substantially below the average pace of growth in the 1990s. Taken as a whole, these figures suggest that business investment may have been abnormally low over the course of the post-2001 expansion.

There are strong reasons to expect investment's role in the economy will be larger in the future. In the long run, the real interest rate will adjust to bring the demand for the economy's output in line with the economy's

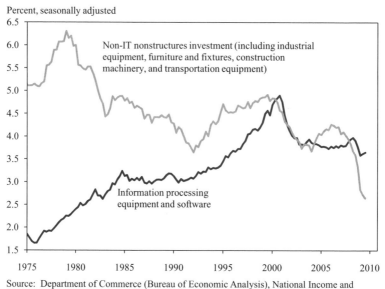

Figure 4-9
Nonstructures Investment as a Share of Nominal GDP

Percent, seasonally adjusted

Non-IT nonstructures investment (including industrial
equipment, furniture and fixtures, construction
machinery, and transportation equipment)

Information processing
equipment and software

Source: Department of Commerce (Bureau of Economic Analysis), National Income and
Product Accounts Table 5.3.5.

capacity. The increase in private saving described in the first part of the
chapter, together with the policies to tackle the long-run budget deficit that
are the subject of the next chapter, should help maintain low real interest
rates. By keeping the cost of investing low, these low real interest rates
should help to encourage investment.

At the same time, other forces should help increase investment at
a given cost of borrowing. A number of promising technological developments offer the prospect that businesses will be able to find many
productive purposes for new investments, ranging from new uses of wireless
electromagnetic spectrum, to new applications of medical and biological
discoveries opened up by DNA sequencing technologies, to environmentally
friendly technologies like new forms of production and distribution of clean
energy (see Chapter 10 for more on these subjects).

Another form of investment is business spending on research and
development (R&D). Such spending can be interpreted as investment in the
accumulation of "knowledge capital." Ideally, private investments in R&D
will dovetail with complementary public investments in knowledge capital
through basic research and scientific and technological infrastructure. The
Administration's commitment to fostering the connections between public
and private investments in knowledge production has been strongly signaled
in both the Recovery Act and the President's fiscal year 2010 budget (Office
of Management and Budget 2009). The Recovery Act included $18.3 billion

of direct spending on research, one of the largest direct increases in such spending in the Nation's history. In addition, more than $80 billion of Recovery Act funds were targeted toward technology and science infrastructure. The Administration's first budget proposed to double the research spending by three key science agencies: the National Science Foundation, the Department of Energy's Office of Science, and the Department of Commerce's National Institute of Standards and Technology. And to foster private sector innovation, the budget also included the full $74 billion cost of making the research and experimentation tax credit permanent in order to give businesses the certainty they need to invest, innovate, and grow.

With reduced demand from consumption and housing tending to make the real interest rate lower than it otherwise would be, and increased investment demand from the many newly developing technologies and incentives for R&D, a larger portion of the economy's output is likely to be devoted to investment. And, because business investment contributes not only to aggregate demand but also to aggregate supply and productivity, a larger role for investment will create a stronger economy going forward.

THE CURRENT ACCOUNT

The picture of future growth in the United States described in the previous sections depends less on borrowing and consumption than did growth in the past decade. This view has important implications for our interactions with other countries and the current account.

Determinants of the Current Account

The current account is the trade balance plus net income on overseas assets and unilateral transfers like foreign aid and remittances. The trade balance, or net exports, represents the bulk of the current account and is responsible for a large majority of short-run movements in it. To a first approximation, a current account deficit implies that the trade balance is negative or, equivalently, that our exports are less than our imports. At the same time, the current account deficit must also be matched by the net borrowing of the United States from the rest of the world. If we spend more than we earn, we must borrow the money to do so. In the national income accounting sense, the definition of the current account can be reduced to national saving minus investment (plus some measurement error).

This accounting definition provides a description but not an explanation of the drivers of the current account. One important driver is the business cycle. As Box 4-1 explains, over the last 30 years, the U.S. current account deficit tended to be larger when the economy was booming and unemployment was low. In a boom, investment tends to rise and saving tends to fall, generating a current account deficit. When the economy struggles, investment often falls and saving often rises, generating a surplus (or a smaller deficit). In countries that rely more on exports to drive their growth, an acceleration in growth can be associated with a rising current account surplus (or smaller deficit).

Current accounts do not need to be balanced in every country in every year. At any point in time, countries may offer more investment opportunities than their desired level of saving at a given interest rate can fund, making them net borrowers, resulting in a current account deficit. Other countries may have an excess of saving over desired investment, making them net lenders (a current account surplus). However, in the

---

Box 4-1: Unemployment and the Current Account

The relationship between the level of unemployment and the current account balance is complicated. People frequently argue that imports—and specifically the current account deficit—displace U.S. workers and generate higher unemployment. However, the main determinant of unemployment in the short and medium runs is the state of the business cycle. The scatter plot of the current account and the unemployment rate since 1980, shown in the accompanying figure, displays a positive relationship. Historically, a smaller current account deficit has coincided with a *higher* unemployment rate. Both were being driven by cyclical economic factors: in a recession, the current account balance improved, and unemployment was high. In a boom, the current account balance deteriorated, and unemployment was low. This usual pattern has been at work in the current recession. The U.S. current account deficit narrowed from 6.4 percent of GDP in the third quarter of 2006 to 2.8 percent of GDP in the second quarter of 2009. At the same time, unemployment *rose* from 4.6 percent to 9.3 percent.

The relationship between unemployment and the current account balance can be different in countries that have relied more heavily on exports for growth. For example, in Germany, the unemployment rate fell from 11.7 percent in 2005 to 9.0 percent in 2007 while the current account surplus rose from 5.1 percent of GDP to 7.9 percent. Likewise, in Japan, unemployment fell from 2005 to 2007 as the current account surplus rose. Given the slack in the U.S. economy, a shift toward a current account surplus could increase aggregate demand and help lower the unemployment rate.

Continued on next page

Box 4-1, continued

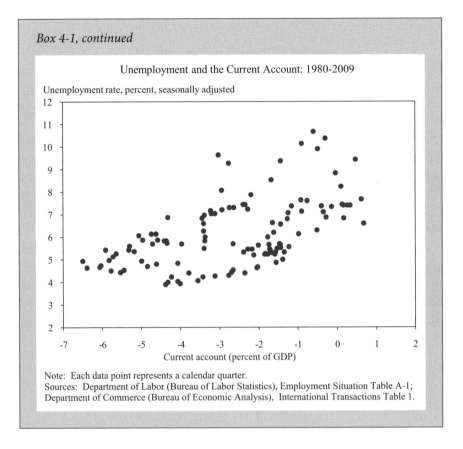

Unemployment and the Current Account: 1980-2009

Unemployment rate, percent, seasonally adjusted

Current account (percent of GDP)

Note: Each data point represents a calendar quarter.
Sources: Department of Labor (Bureau of Labor Statistics), Employment Situation Table A-1; Department of Commerce (Bureau of Economic Analysis), International Transactions Table 1.

long run, current accounts should tend toward balance, thereby allowing the net foreign investment position (total foreign assets minus total foreign liabilities) of borrowing nations to at least stabilize as a ratio to GDP and possibly to decline over time. Otherwise, creditor nations would be continually increasing the share of their wealth held as assets of debtor nations, and debtor nations would owe a larger and larger share of their production to foreign lenders and capital owners.

Thus, in the long run, one would expect the U.S. current account to move toward balance. As it does so, it will not cause the absolute level of our accumulated net foreign debt to decline unless the U.S. current account moves into surplus (which is of course possible). But, even if the long-run current account is merely in balance or a small deficit, the previous net foreign borrowing should still decline as a share of GDP as GDP rises. Further, so-called "valuation effects"—changes in asset values of foreign assets held by Americans or U.S. assets owned by foreign investors—also affect the ratio of foreign indebtedness to GDP.

The Current Account in the Recovery and in the Long Run

As the U.S. economy recovers from the current crisis, it is unlikely to return to current account deficits as large as those in the mid-2000s. Coming out of the 2001–02 recession, investment rose more quickly than saving, and the current account deficit widened to more than 6 percent of GDP (Figure 4-10). Investment had also declined slightly more than saving had before the current crisis hit, and the current account deficit moderated to less than 5 percent of GDP by the third quarter of 2007.[4] The gap narrowed rapidly as investment fell sharply during the crisis. The increase in the personal saving rate since the onset of the crisis has partly offset the large Federal budget deficit (which is negative government saving), so the current account deficit shrank to under 3 percent of GDP.

The specific path of the current account as the economy exits the crisis will depend on whether government and private saving rise ahead of, or along with, a rebound in private investment. But in the long run, the current account deficit is likely to be smaller than it was before the crisis. The likely rise in private and public saving relative to their pre-crisis levels

Figure 4-10
Saving, Investment, and the Current Account as a Percent of GDP

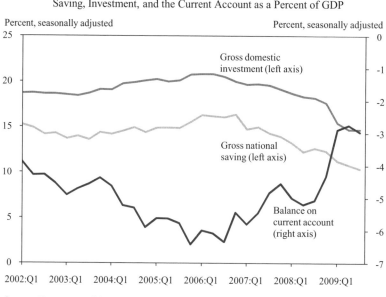

Source: Department of Commerce (Bureau of Economic Analysis), National Income and Product Accounts Table 5.1.

---

[4] There is also a statistical discrepancy between the saving-minus-investment gap and the current account. While this discrepancy is generally close to zero, it moved from slightly negative to slightly positive in this period, so that the measured current account moved more than the measured gap between saving and investment did.

implies an increase in national saving. Thus, saving is likely to more closely balance domestic investment, suggesting a transition to a smaller current account deficit than in the 2000s. Given that the current account deficit has already narrowed to roughly 3 percent of GDP—less than half its peak—the crucial challenge will be to avoid a reversion to a high-spending, low-saving economy. A successful shift toward a more balanced world growth model generated by increased consumption in nations with current account surpluses could improve net exports even more. This could bring the current account deficit toward its mid-1990s level of roughly 1 to 2 percent of U.S. GDP.

Exports can be expected to rise rapidly as the world economy recovers for a number of reasons. Just as trade typically falls faster than GDP in a recession (discussed in Chapter 3), it typically grows faster during a rebound. Trade-to-GDP ratios have fallen in the last year and can be expected to bounce back as the world economy recovers. This bounce-back alone will lead to rapid export growth. More generally, the crucial driver of exports is always the performance of the world economy. For U.S. goods and services to be bought abroad, demand in other countries must return robustly. This is one reason for the United States to strengthen its ties with fast-growing regions such as emerging East Asia. The faster our trade partners grow and the more we trade with fast-growing economies, the more demand for U.S. exports grows. Figure 4-11 shows the historical relationship between U.S. export growth and growth of non-U.S. world GDP.

The rebalancing of the U.S. economy is likely to be accompanied by a rebalancing of the world economy as well. It is reasonable to expect growth in East Asia to continue at a rapid rate but also to become more oriented toward domestic consumption and investment than it has been in the recent past. Some nations with large current account surpluses took steps to increase domestic demand during the crisis, and these efforts must be maintained and expanded if world growth is to rebalance. It is not a given that such a transition in world demand will take place. Concerted policy action will be needed, but if saving falls in countries with current account surpluses and spending rises, that should stimulate U.S. exports as well as take pressure off of the U.S. consumer as an engine of world growth.

Steps to Encourage Exports

The Administration is taking many concrete steps to encourage exports. The Trade Promotion Coordinating Committee brings government agencies together to help firms export. While the final decision of whether and how much to export is a market decision made by private businesses, the government can play a constructive role in many ways. The

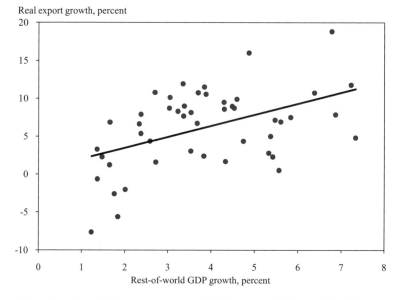

Figure 4-11
Growth of U.S. Exports and Rest-of-World Income: 1960-2008

Notes: Rest-of-world GDP constructed as world GDP in constant dollars less U.S. GDP.
Data are annual growth rates, 1960-2008. Best-fit linear regression equation is: export
growth = 0.5 + 1.5 (GDP growth).
Sources: World Bank, World Development Indicators; Department of Commerce (Bureau of
Economic Analysis), National Income and Product Accounts Table 1.1.6.

Export-Import Bank can help with financing; consular offices can provide
contacts, information, and advocacy; Commerce Department officials can
help firms negotiate hurdles; a combination of agencies can help small and
mid-sized businesses explore overseas markets. Much of the academic
literature in trade models a firm's decision to export as involving a substantial one-time fixed cost (Melitz 2003). The Administration is doing all that
it can to lower that initial fixed cost to help expand exports.

In addition, the Administration is pursuing possible trade agreements
and making the most of its current trade agreements to expand opportunities for American firms to export. Because U.S. trade barriers are relatively
low, new trade agreements often lower barriers abroad more than in the
United States, opening new paths for U.S. exports. As the Administration
works to expand U.S. market access through a world trade agreement in the
Doha round of multilateral trade talks, it continues to explore its options in
bilateral free trade agreements and regional frameworks, such as the Trans-
Pacific Partnership. The United States Trade Representative continues
to work through previously negotiated trade agreements to lower non-
tariff trade barriers and facilitate customs issues to make it easier for U.S.
businesses to export.

Not all of these developments will necessarily increase net exports (or the current account) of the United States. Since the current account equals net lending to or borrowing from the world, moving the current account balance requires adjustments in saving and investment as well as more opportunities to export. In the long run, increases in demand for U.S. exports resulting from export promotion or reduced trade barriers will generate higher standards of living, but through improved terms of trade, not an increase in net exports. Further, the simple recovery of world trade volumes will increase exports and imports alike. As discussed in Chapter 10, this increase in trade can increase productivity and living standards, but it will not change the current account. However, rapid world growth and declining current account surpluses abroad should lead to an increase in U.S. exports. This can help increase U.S. net exports and hence contribute to the recovery.

As with higher investment, lower current account deficits have important long-run benefits. Lower foreign indebtedness than the country otherwise would have had means reduced interest payments to foreigners. Equivalently, it means that foreigners have on net smaller claims on the output produced in the United States. Thus, lower current account deficits will raise standards of living in the long run.

CONCLUSION

Economic policy should not aim to return the economy to the path of unstable, unsustainable, unhealthy growth it was on before the wrenching events of the past two years. We should—and can—achieve something better. Growth that is not fueled by unsustainable borrowing, and growth that is based on productive investments, is more stable than the growth of recent decades. And growth that is associated with higher saving will lead to greater accumulation of wealth, and so greater growth in our standards of living.

CHAPTER 5

ADDRESSING THE LONG-RUN FISCAL CHALLENGE

After several years of budget surpluses, the Federal Government began running consistent, substantial deficits in the 2002 fiscal year. Because the deficits absorbed a significant portion of private saving, they were one reason that the economic expansion of the 2000s was led by consumption and foreign borrowing rather than investment and net exports. More troubling than the deficits of the recent past, however, is the long-term fiscal outlook the Administration inherited. Even before the increased spending necessary to rescue and stabilize the economy, the policy choices of the previous eight years and projected increases in spending on health care and Social Security had already put the government on a path of rising deficits and debt. Thus, a key step in rebalancing the economy and restoring its long-run health must be putting fiscal policy on a sound, sustainable footing.

This chapter discusses the fiscal challenges the Administration inherited, the dangers posed by large and growing deficits, and the Administration's measures and plans for addressing these challenges. The Administration and Congress are already taking important steps, most notably through their efforts toward comprehensive health care reform. The legislation currently under consideration addresses rapidly rising health care costs, which are one of the central drivers of the long-run fiscal problem. The fiscal problem is multifaceted, however, and was decades in the making. As a result, no single step can fully address it. Much work remains, and bipartisan cooperation will be essential.

The Long-Run Fiscal Challenge

When President Obama took office in January 2009, fiscal policy was on a deteriorating course. Figure 5-1 shows the grim outlook for the budget projected by the Congressional Budget Office (CBO) under the assumption that the policies then in effect would be continued.[1] As the figure makes clear, the budget was on an unsustainable trajectory.

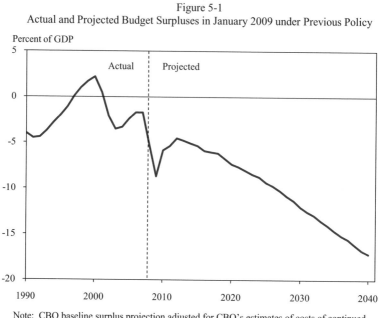

Figure 5-1
Actual and Projected Budget Surpluses in January 2009 under Previous Policy

Note: CBO baseline surplus projection adjusted for CBO's estimates of costs of continued war spending, continuation of the 2001 and 2003 tax cuts, avoiding scheduled cuts in Medicare's physician payment rates, and holding other discretionary outlays constant as a share of GDP.
Sources: Congressional Budget Office (2009a, 2009f).

The figure shows that CBO projected that the deficit would be severely affected in the short run by the economic crisis. The decline in output was projected to send tax revenues plummeting and spending for unemployment insurance, nutritional assistance, and other safety net programs soaring. As a result, the deficit was projected to spike to 9 percent of gross domestic product (GDP) in 2009 before falling as the economy recovered. It is natural for revenues to decline and government spending to rise during a recession. Indeed, these movements both mitigate the recession and cushion its impact on ordinary Americans.

---

[1] This figure presents the CBO January 2009 baseline budget outlook through 2019, adjusted to reflect CBO's estimates of the cost of extending expiring tax provisions including the 2001 and 2003 tax cuts and indexing the Alternative Minimum Tax (AMT) for inflation, reducing the number of troops in Iraq and Afghanistan to 75,000 by 2013, modifying Medicare's "sustainable growth rate" formula to avoid scheduled cuts in physician payment rates, holding other discretionary outlays constant as a share of gross domestic product, and the added interest costs resulting from these adjustments (Congressional Budget Office 2009a). After 2019, the figure presents CBO's June 2009 *Long-Term Budget Outlook* alternative fiscal scenario, which also reflects the costs of continuing these policies (Congressional Budget Office 2009f).

The key message of the figure, however, concerns the path of the deficit after the economy's projected recovery from the recession. The deficit was projected to fall to close to 4 percent of GDP in 2012 as the economy recovers, but then to reverse course, rising steadily by about 1 percent of GDP every two years. Figure 5-2 shows that if that path were followed, the ratio of the government's debt to GDP would surpass its level at the end of World War II within 20 years, and would continue growing rapidly thereafter. At some point along such a path, investors would no longer be willing to hold the government's debt at any reasonable interest rate. Thus, such a path is not feasible indefinitely.

Figure 5-2
Actual and Projected Government Debt Held by the Public under Previous Policy

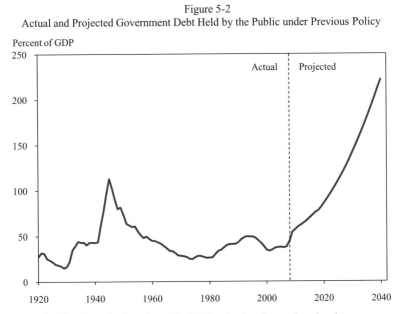

Note: CBO baseline projection adjusted for CBO's estimates of costs of continued war spending, continuation of the 2001 and 2003 tax cuts, avoiding scheduled cuts in Medicare's physician payment rates, and holding other discretionary outlays constant as a share of GDP.
Sources: Congressional Budget Office (2009a, 2009f).

Sources of the Long-Run Fiscal Challenge

The challenging long-run budget outlook the Administration inherited has two primary causes: the policy choices of the previous eight years and projected rising spending on Medicare, Medicaid, and Social Security. The policy choices under the previous administration contribute a substantial amount to the high projected deficits as a share of GDP, while rising spending for health care and Social Security is the main reason the deficits are projected to balloon over time. Both make large contributions to the difficult fiscal outlook.

The previous policy choices involved both spending and revenues. On the spending side, two decisions were particularly important. One was the failure to pay for the addition of a prescription drug benefit to Medicare, which is estimated to increase annual deficits over the next decade by an average of one-third of a percent of GDP, excluding interest, and more than that in the years thereafter (Congressional Budget Office 2009g; Council of Economic Advisers estimates). The other was the decision to fight two wars without taking any steps to pay for the costs—costs that so far have come close to $1 trillion. On the revenue side, the most important decisions were those that lowered taxes without making offsetting spending cuts. In particular, the 2001 and 2003 tax cuts have helped push revenues to their lowest level as a fraction of GDP at any point since 1950 (Office of Management and Budget 2010).

Figure 5-3 shows the impact on the budget deficit of these three major policies of the previous eight years that were not paid for: the 2001 and 2003 tax cuts (including the increased cost of Alternative Minimum Tax relief as a result of those tax cuts), the prescription drug benefit, and the spending for the wars in Iraq and Afghanistan (which for this analysis are assumed to wind down by 2013), both with and without the interest expense of financing these policies.[2] At their peak in 2007 and 2008, these policies worsened the government's fiscal position by almost 4 percent of GDP, and their effect, including interest, rises above 4 percent of GDP into the indefinite future. The fiscal outlook would be far better if these policies had been paid for. Indeed, Auerbach and Gale (2009) conclude that roughly half of the long-run fiscal shortfall in the outlook described earlier results from policy decisions made from 2001 to 2008.

The other main source of the long-run fiscal challenge is rising spending on Medicare, Medicaid, and Social Security. These burdens stem primarily from the rapid escalation of health care costs, combined with the aging of the population. Annual age-adjusted health care costs per Medicare enrollee grew 2.3 percentage points faster than the increase in per capita GDP from 1975 to 2007. If this rate of increase were to continue, Federal spending on Medicare and Medicaid alone would approach 40 percent of the Nation's income in 2085, which is clearly not sustainable

---

[2] The figure shows the annual cost (as a percent of GDP) of supplemental military expenditures for operations in Iraq and Afghanistan through 2009 and CBO's estimate of the cost of reducing the number of troops in Iraq and Afghanistan to 75,000 by 2013 thereafter; the cost of the Medicare Part D program net of offsetting receipts and Medicaid savings; the cost of the 2001 and 2003 tax cuts plus the additional cost of AMT relief associated with those tax cuts, as estimated by CBO; and the interest expense of financing these policies.

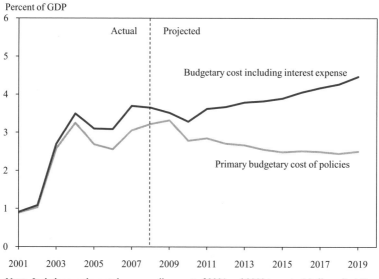

Figure 5-3
Budgetary Cost of Previous Administration Policy

Percent of GDP

Actual | Projected

Budgetary cost including interest expense

Primary budgetary cost of policies

Note: Includes supplemental war spending, cost of 2001 and 2003 tax cuts, Medicare Part D net of offsetting receipts and Medicaid savings, and related interest expense.
Sources: Belasco (2009); Congressional Budget Office (2009a, 2009g); CEA estimates.

(Congressional Budget Office 2009f). In addition, as a result of decreases in fertility and increases in longevity, the ratio of Social Security and Medicare beneficiaries to workers is rising, straining the financing of these programs.

Figure 5-4 projects the growth in spending in Medicare, Medicaid, and Social Security. Spending on the programs is projected to double as a share of GDP by 2050. Over the next 20 years, demographics—the retirement of the baby boom generation—is the larger cause of rising spending. But throughout, rising health care costs contribute to rising spending, and over the long term, they are by far the larger contributor to the deficit.

Other important factors have also contributed to the increase in entitlement spending. For example, the fraction of non-elderly adults receiving Social Security Disability Insurance (SSDI) benefits has approximately doubled since the mid-1980s, and the fraction of Social Security spending accounted for by SSDI benefits has increased from 10 to 17 percent. Beneficiaries of SSDI are also eligible for health insurance through Medicare. Total cash benefits paid to SSDI recipients were $106 billion in 2008 and an additional $63 billion was spent on their health care through Medicare. One contributor to the increase in disability enrollment was a 1984 change in the program's medical eligibility criteria, which allowed more applicants to qualify for benefits in subsequent years (Autor and Duggan 2006).

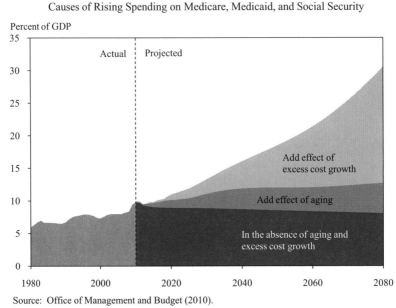

Figure 5-4
Causes of Rising Spending on Medicare, Medicaid, and Social Security

Source: Office of Management and Budget (2010).

The potential challenges to the budget from these three entitlement programs have been clear for decades. Yet, policymakers in previous administrations did little to address them. For example, in October 2000, CBO warned that spending on Medicare, Medicaid, and Social Security would more than double, rising from 7.5 percent of GDP in 1999 to over 16.7 percent in 2040; nine years later, their forecast for spending on these programs remains virtually unchanged (Congressional Budget Office 2000, 2009f).

All told, the Obama Administration inherited a very different budget outlook from the one left to the previous administration. Figure 5-5 compares the budget forecast in January 2001 (Congressional Budget Office 2001) with the budget outlook in January 2009 described above.[3] In 2001, CBO forecast a relatively bright fiscal future. After a decade of strong growth and responsible fiscal policy, the budget was substantially in surplus, and CBO analysts projected rising surpluses over the next decade, even under their more pessimistic policy alternatives. Rising health care costs would squeeze the budget only over the long term, and the retirement of the baby boom generation was still more than a decade away. The intervening time could have been used to pay off the national debt and accumulate

---

[3] The 2001 forecast includes the January 2001 baseline forecast adjusted to reflect CBO's estimated cost of holding nondiscretionary outlays constant as a share of nominal GDP. Starting in 2012, the deficit evolves according to the intermediate projection in the October 2000 *Long-Term Budget Outlook* (Congressional Budget Office 2000).

substantial assets in preparation. But policymakers chose a different path. They enacted policies that added trillions to the national debt and doubled the size of the long-run problem. Combined with a deteriorating economic forecast and technical reestimates, the result was a much worse budget outlook in January 2009 than in January 2001.

Figure 5-5
Budget Comparison: January 2001 and January 2009

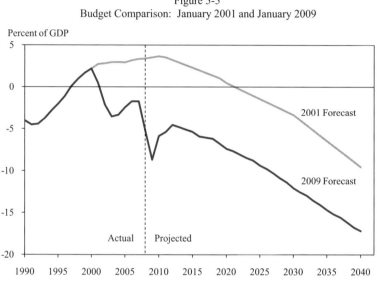

Note: CBO 2001 baseline projection adjusted for the cost of holding nondiscretionary outlays constant as a share of nominal GDP; CBO 2009 baseline projection adjusted for costs of continued war spending, continuation of 2001 and 2003 tax cuts, avoiding scheduled cuts in Medicare's physician payment rates, and holding nondiscretionary outlays constant as a share of nominal GDP.
Sources: Congressional Budget Office (2000, 2001, 2009a, 2009f).

The Role of the Recovery Act and Other Rescue Operations

One development that has had an important effect on the short-term budget outlook since January 2009 is the aggressive action the Administration and Congress have taken to combat the recession. By far the most important component of the response in terms of the budget is the American Recovery and Reinvestment Act of 2009. The Recovery Act cuts taxes and increases spending by about 2 percent of GDP in calendar year 2009 and by 2¼ percent of GDP in 2010.

Crucially, however, the budgetary impact of the Recovery Act will fade rapidly. As a result, it is at most a very small part of the long-run fiscal shortfall. By 2012, the tax cuts and spending under the Recovery Act will be less than one-third of 1 percent of GDP. Other rescue measures, such as extensions of programs providing additional support to those most directly affected by the recession, also contribute to the deficit in the short run. But these programs are much smaller than the Recovery Act. And like the Recovery Act, their budgetary impact will fade quickly.

Figure 5-6 shows the overall budgetary impact of the Recovery Act and other rescue measures, including interest on the additional debt from the higher short-run deficits resulting from the measures. The impact is substantial in 2009 and 2010 but then fades rapidly to about one-quarter of 1 percent of GDP. Moreover, because these estimates do not include the effects of the rescue measures in mitigating the downturn and speeding recovery—and thus raising incomes and tax revenues—they surely overstate the measures' impact on the budget outlook.

Figure 5-6
Effect of the Recovery Act on the Deficit

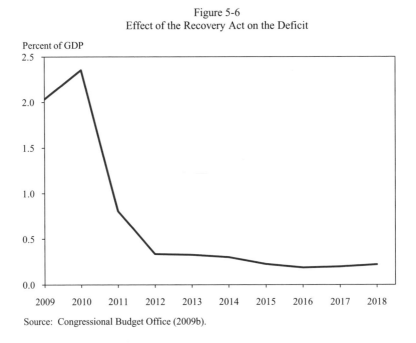

Source: Congressional Budget Office (2009b).

AN ANCHOR FOR FISCAL POLICY

The trajectory for fiscal policy that the Administration inherited, with budget deficits and government debt growing relative to the size of the economy, is clearly untenable. Change is essential. But there are many alternatives to the trajectory the Administration inherited. In thinking about what path fiscal policy should attempt to follow, it is therefore important to examine how deficits affect the economy and what policy paths are feasible.

The Effects of Budget Deficits

Two factors are critical in shaping the economic effects of budget deficits: the state of the economy, and the size and duration of the deficits. Consider first the state of the economy. A central lesson of macroeconomics is that in an economy operating below capacity, higher deficits raise output and employment. Transfer payments (such as unemployment benefits) and tax cuts encourage private consumption and investment spending. Government investments and other purchases contribute to higher output and employment directly and, by raising incomes, also encourage further private spending.

In the current situation, as discussed in Chapter 2, monetary policymakers are constrained because nominal interest rates cannot be lowered below zero, and so they are unlikely to raise interest rates quickly in response to fiscal expansion. As a result, the fiscal expansion attributable to the Recovery Act is likely to increase private investment as well as private consumption and government purchases. Finally, in a precarious environment like the one of the past year, expansionary fiscal policy may make the difference between an economy spiraling into depression and one embarking on a self-sustaining recovery, and so have a dramatic impact on outcomes. As described more fully in Chapter 2, these benefits of fiscal expansion were precisely the motivation for the Administration's pursuit of the Recovery Act and other stimulus policies over the past year.

When the economy is operating at normal capacity, the effects of higher budget deficits are very different. In such a setting, the stimulus from deficits leads not to higher output, but only (perhaps after a delay) to a change in the composition of output. To finance its deficits, the government must borrow money, competing against businesses and individuals seeking to finance new productive investments. As a result, deficits drive up interest rates, discouraging private investment. Hence, deficit spending diverts resources that would otherwise be invested in productive private capital—new business investments in plant, equipment, machinery, and software, or investments in human capital through education and training—into government purchases or private consumption. To the extent that the private investments nonetheless occur but are financed by borrowing from abroad, the country has the benefit of the capital, but at the cost of increased foreign indebtedness. The result is that Americans' claims on future output are lower.

In sum, in normal times, higher budget deficits impede the rebalancing of output toward investment and net exports described in Chapter 4; lower deficits contribute to that rebalancing. In addition, budget deficits were one source of the "global imbalances" discussed in Chapter 3 that have been implicated by some analysts as part of the cause of the financial and economic crisis. Finally, higher budget deficits and the higher levels of debt they imply may reduce policymakers' ability to turn to expansionary fiscal policy in the event of a crisis.

Although determining the impact of large budget deficits on capital formation and interest rates is a difficult and contentious issue, the bulk of the evidence points to important effects. For example, several studies find that increases in projected deficits raise interest rates (Wachtel and Young 1987; Engen and Hubbard 2005; Laubach 2009). A careful review concludes that the weight of the evidence indicates that budget deficits raise interest rates moderately (Gale and Orszag 2003). Examining the international evidence, another study reaches a similar conclusion (Ardagna, Caselli, and Lane 2007).

The economic impact of budget deficits depends not only on the condition of the economy but also on their magnitude and persistence. A moderate period of large deficits in a weak economy will speed recovery in the short run and leave the government with only modestly higher debt in the long run. Even in an economy operating at capacity, a temporary period of high deficits is manageable, as the experience of World War II shows compellingly. Once full employment was reached, the high wartime spending surely crowded out investment and thus caused standards of living after the war to be lower than they otherwise would have been. But that cost aside, the enormous temporary deficits that reached 30 percent of GDP at the peak of the war created no long-run problems.

In contrast, the effects of large deficits and debt that grow indefinitely and without bound relative to the size of the economy are very different— and potentially very dangerous. If a government tried to follow such a path, eventually its debt would exceed the amount investors were willing to hold at a reasonable interest rate. At that point, the situation would spiral out of control. Rising interest costs would worsen the fiscal situation; this would further reduce investors' willingness to hold the government's debt, raising interest costs further; and so on. Eventually, investors would be unwilling to hold the debt at any interest rate.

Feasible Long-Run Fiscal Policies

Investors have no qualms about holding some government debt. Indeed, many desire the safety of such an investment. And crucially, in an economy in which private incomes and wealth, as well as the government's tax base, are growing, the amount of debt investors are willing to hold also grows. Thus, the key to a sustainable deficit path is a fiscal policy that keeps the level of debt relative to the scale of the economy at levels where investors are willing to hold that debt at a reasonable interest rate. Most obviously, paths where the ratio of the deficit to GDP and the ratio of the debt to GDP grow without bound cannot be sustained. Equally, however, paths that would lead the debt-to-GDP ratio to stabilize, but at an extremely high level, are also not feasible.

Historical and international comparisons, as well as the very favorable terms on which investors are currently willing to lend to the United States, show that the Nation is not close to such problematic levels of indebtedness. In 2007, before the recession, the debt held by the public was 37 percent of nominal GDP. In 2015, because of the direct effects of the recession and, to a lesser extent, the fiscal stimulus, the President's budget projects the public debt (net of financial assets held by the government) will be 65 percent of GDP. By comparison, it was 113 percent of GDP at the end of World War II; in the United Kingdom, the ratio at the end of World War II was over 250 percent. Table 5-1 shows the projected 2010 government debt-to-GDP ratio (including state and local government debt) for a wide range of developed countries. Japan's debt-to-GDP ratio is 105 percent, Italy's is 101 percent, and Belgium's is 85 percent, and all of these are projected to rise. None of these countries enjoys the same depth and breadth of demand for its debt as the United States does, yet none has difficulty financing its debt. Thus, although it is hard to know the exact U.S. debt-to-GDP ratio that would begin to pose problems, it is clearly well above current levels.

Table 5-1
Government Debt-to-GDP Ratio in Selected OECD Countries (percent)

	2010
Belgium	85.4
Canada	32.6
France	60.7
Germany	54.7
Italy	100.8
Japan	104.6
Spain	41.6
Sweden	-13.1
United Kingdom	59.0
United States	65.2
Euro-area average	57.9
OECD average	57.6

Note: Numbers include state and local as well as Federal net government debt.
Source: Organisation for Economic Co-operation and Development (2009).

The Choice of a Fiscal Anchor

It is essential that the United States follow a fiscal policy that stabilizes the debt-to-GDP ratio at a feasible level. In thinking about the specific level of that ratio that policymakers should aim for, it is useful to think about the implications that different levels of the budget deficit have for the level of government debt in the long run. In particular, consider paths where the deficit as a percent of GDP stabilizes at some level. If the deficit-to-GDP ratio and the growth rate of nominal GDP are both steady, the debt-to-GDP ratio will settle down to the ratio of the deficit-to-GDP ratio to the growth rate of nominal GDP.[4] For example, if the deficit is 1 percent of GDP and nominal GDP is growing at 5 percent per year, the debt-to-GDP ratio will stabilize at 20 percent. Similarly, if the deficit-to-GDP ratio and the growth rate of nominal GDP are both 4 percent, the debt-to-GDP ratio will stabilize at 100 percent. Instead of thinking about various possible long-run targets for the debt-to-GDP ratio, policymakers can consider possible targets for the deficit-to-GDP ratio and their accompanying implications for the long-run debt-to-GDP ratio.

The choice among different deficit-to-GDP ratios involves tradeoffs. Lower deficits, and thus lower debt in the long run, have obvious advantages: a higher capital stock, lower foreign indebtedness, smaller global imbalances, and more fiscal room to maneuver. But lower deficits have disadvantages as well. They require smaller government programs, higher taxes, or both. Because Medicare, Medicaid, and Social Security will grow faster than GDP in coming decades even after the best efforts to make those programs as efficient as possible, significant cuts in government spending would impose substantial costs. And higher taxes can reduce incentives to work, save, and invest.

Based on these considerations, the Administration believes that an appropriate medium-run goal is to balance the primary budget—the budget excluding interest payments on the debt. Including interest payments, this target will result in total deficits of approximately 3 percent of GDP. With real GDP growth of about 2.5 percent per year and inflation of about

---

[4] To see this, consider the case where the deficit-to-GDP ratio equals the growth rate of GDP. Then the dollar amount of debt issued in a year (that is, the deficit) equals the dollar increase in GDP. If the debt-to-GDP ratio is 100 percent—the amount of debt outstanding equals GDP—then the percent increase in debt exactly equals the percent increase in GDP, and the debt-to-GDP ratio holds steady at 100 percent. If, however, the amount of debt outstanding is less than nominal GDP, then adding a dollar to the debt results in a larger percentage increase in the debt than does a dollar added to GDP. Hence, the debt-to-GDP ratio will rise. If the amount of debt outstanding is more than nominal GDP, then the percent increase in debt is smaller than the percent increase in GDP and the debt-to-GDP ratio falls. Thus, the debt-to-GDP ratio converges to the ratio of the deficit-to-GDP ratio to the growth rate of GDP, which in this case is 100 percent.

2 percent per year, nominal GDP growth will be about 4.5 percent per year in the long run. Thus a target for the total deficit-to-GDP ratio of 3 percent implies that the debt-to-GDP ratio will stabilize at less than 70 percent. Because the debt-to-GDP ratio is projected to rise to about 65 percent in a few years, such a target implies that the debt-to-GDP ratio will change little once the economy has recovered from the current recession. A debt-to-GDP ratio of around two-thirds is comfortably within the range of historical and international experience. It represents substantial fiscal discipline relative to the trajectory the Administration inherited. Stabilizing the ratio rather than continuing on a path where it is continually growing is imperative, and stabilizing it at around its post-crisis level has considerable benefits and is a natural focal point.

REACHING THE FISCAL TARGET

Bringing the primary budget into balance and keeping it there will not be easy. Noninterest spending outstrips tax revenues by a large margin in the budget inherited by the Administration. More importantly, the trajectory of policy implied that spending would continue to exceed revenues even after the economy had recovered and that the deficit would rise steadily for decades to come. The economic developments and policy decisions that put fiscal policy on that course took place over many years. Thus, moving policy back onto a sound path will not happen all at once.

General Principles

In broad terms, the right way to tackle the long-run fiscal problem is not through a sharp, immediate fiscal contraction, but through policies that steadily address the underlying drivers of deficits over time. Large spending cuts or tax increases are exactly the wrong medicine for an economy with high unemployment and considerable unused capacity: just as fiscal stimulus raises income and employment in such an environment, mistimed attempts at fiscal discipline have the opposite effects. Any short-run fiscal contraction can best be tolerated at a time when the Federal Reserve is no longer constrained by the zero bound on nominal interest rates, and so has the tools to counteract any contractionary macroeconomic impacts.

The dangers of a large immediate contraction are powerfully illustrated by America's experience in the Great Depression. In 1937, after four years of very rapid growth but with the economy still far from fully recovered, both fiscal and monetary policy turned sharply contractionary: the veterans' bonus program of the previous year was discontinued, Social Security taxes were collected for the first time, and the Federal Reserve doubled reserve requirements. The consequences of this premature policy tightening were devastating: real GDP fell by 3 percent in 1938, unemployment spiked from 14 percent to 19 percent, and the strong recovery was cut short.

The impact of actions taken today to gradually bring the long-run sources of the deficit problem under control would be very different. Such policies do not involve a sharp short-run contraction that could derail a nascent recovery. Because the effects cumulate over time, however, they can have a large effect on the long-term fiscal outlook.

Policies that provide gradual but permanent and growing deficit reduction have another potential advantage. By improving the outlook for the long-term performance of the economy, they can improve business and consumer confidence today. As a result, deficit-improving policies whose effects are felt mainly in the future can actually boost the economy in the short run. There is considerable evidence that such "expansionary fiscal contractions" are not just a theoretical possibility (see, for example, Giavazzi and Pagano 1990; Alesina and Perotti 1997; Romer and Romer forthcoming).

In keeping with these general considerations, the Administration is taking actions in three important areas that will have a material impact on the deficit in the medium and long terms.

Comprehensive Health Care Reform

The first and single most important step toward improving the country's long-run fiscal prospects is the enactment of comprehensive health care reform that will slow the growth rate of costs. Beyond the obvious importance for Americans' well-being and economic security, the health reform legislation being considered by Congress would save money. The rapid growth of health care costs is a central source of the country's fiscal difficulties. CBO has estimated that both the bill passed by the House in November 2009 and the bill passed by the Senate in December 2009 would significantly reduce the deficit over the next decade (Congressional Budget Office 2009e, 2009d). But the more important factor for the long-run fiscal situation is that, as discussed in more detail in Chapter 7, the bills contain crucial measures that experts believe will lead to lower growth in costs while expanding access to coverage, increasing affordability, and improving quality. Given the central role of rising health costs in the long-run deficit projections, these measures would therefore lead to substantial improvements in the budget situation over time.

In November 2009, CBO's analysis of the Senate health care bill found that "Medicare spending under the bill would increase at an average annual rate of roughly 6 percent during the next two decades—well below the roughly 8 percent annual growth rate of the past two decades" (Congressional Budget Office 2009c). In December, the Council of Economic Advisers estimated that the fundamental health care reform in the Senate bill would reduce the annual growth rate of Medicare and Medicaid costs by a full percentage point below what it would otherwise be in the coming decade, and by even more in the following decade (Council of Economic Advisers 2009b). These reductions reflect specific measures directed at identifiable sources of wasteful spending and fraud combined with institutional reforms that will help counter the forces leading to excessive cost growth.

Such a reduction in the growth rate of health care costs would have a more profound effect on the long-run fiscal situation of the country than virtually any other fiscal decision being contemplated today. Even if the slowdown in cost growth held steady at 1 percentage point annually rather than rising in the second decade, it would reduce the budget deficit in 2030 by about 2 percent of GDP relative to what it otherwise would be. In today's terms, this is equivalent to almost $300 billion per year. Most of these savings reflect the direct impact of lower health care costs on Federal spending. To the extent that health care reform also slows the growth of private sector health insurance costs, which are tax preferred, employees in the private sector will benefit from higher wages and the Treasury from increased revenues; this becomes a second source of budget savings. And these direct savings are magnified by lower interest costs resulting from the reduced debt accumulation in the years preceding 2030 (Council of Economic Advisers 2009a). The need to expand coverage would reduce the overall impact of health care reform on the budget deficit somewhat. However, these costs of expansion would be more than offset even within the coming decade. Thereafter, reform will lower the deficit by increasing amounts over time.

Restoring Balance to the Tax Code

The second major step the Administration is taking to address the long-run fiscal challenge is restoring balance to the tax code that has been lost since 2001. The 2001 and 2003 tax cuts disproportionately favored wealthy taxpayers. According to estimates from the Urban-Brookings Tax Policy Center (2010), in 2010 the 2001 and 2003 tax cuts will increase the after-tax income of the poorest 20 percent of the population by 0.5 percent (about $51), the middle 20 percent by 2.6 percent ($1,023), and the top 1 percent by 6.7 percent ($72,910). About 67 percent of the tax cuts went to the top 20 percent of taxpayers, and 26 percent to the top 1 percent.

These tax cuts for the wealthiest Americans took place when the incomes of ordinary Americans were stagnating and inequality was reaching almost unprecedented levels. In other words, the tax cuts exacerbated the broader trend rather than mitigated it.

The President has consistently maintained that the tax cuts went too far in cutting taxes for people making more than $250,000 per year and that the country could not afford the tax breaks given to that group over the past eight years. That is why one important plank of his fiscal responsibility framework is to rebalance the tax code, so that it is similar to what existed in the late 1990s for those making more than $250,000 per year. Specifically, the Administration has proposed letting the marginal tax rates on ordinary income and capital gains for people making more than $250,000 per year return to the levels they were in 2000. It has also proposed setting the tax rate on dividends for high-income taxpayers to the same 20 percent rate that would apply to capital gains—which is lower than the rate in the 1990s—and letting all other features of the 2001 and 2003 tax cuts expire for these taxpayers. In addition, it has proposed limiting the rate of deductions for high-income taxpayers to 28 percent, so that the wealthy do not obtain proportionately larger benefits from their deductions than other Americans do. None of these changes would take effect until 2011, so they would not affect disposable incomes as the economy recovers in 2010. Nonetheless, they would raise nearly $1 trillion over the next 10 years and even more over the longer run. Equivalently, they would reduce the budget deficit by more than 0.5 percent of GDP in the medium run and somewhat more over time.

As just discussed, most of these changes would merely bring the tax rates on high-income taxpayers back to their levels in the 1990s. To the extent that some go further, on balance they are more than offset by the fact that some common types of income—dividends, for example—will have rates significantly lower than in the 1990s. Looking at tax policy over U.S. postwar history more broadly shows even more clearly how moderate the proposed changes are. Figure 5-7 shows the top marginal tax rates on ordinary income and capital gains over time and their levels under the Administration's proposals. For ordinary income, a top rate of 39.6 percent, while higher than in the past eight years, is not high compared with the rates that prevailed during most of the past several decades and even during most of the Reagan administration. For capital gains, the 20 percent rate is lower than in many previous periods and is certainly not unusual. And for dividends, the 20 percent rate proposed by the Administration would be lower than under any other modern president save the last.

Figure 5-7
Top Statutory Tax Rates

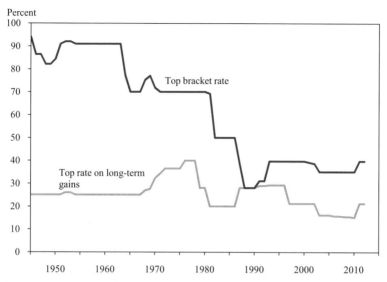

Note: The top rate on qualified dividends is equal to the top bracket rate until 2003; thereafter, it is equal to the top rate on long-term capital gains.
Source: Department of the Treasury, Internal Revenue Service (2009); Department of the Treasury, Office of Tax Analysis (2010).

Statutory marginal tax rates, however, provide only a partial picture of how the progressivity of the tax system has changed over time. The number of tax brackets has declined and the thresholds at which statutory bracket rates apply have changed; different sources of income, such as capital gains and dividends, are now treated differently in the tax code and taxed at lower rates; and exemption amounts and standard deductions have been adjusted. Moreover, the distribution of income across taxpayers and the composition of taxpayers' sources of income have changed significantly over time, making it difficult to disentangle the effects of statutory changes in the tax system from economic changes. To illustrate the impact of historical statutory tax changes in isolation, Figure 5-8 applies the tax rates for each year from 1960 to 2008 to a sample of taxpayers who filed returns in 2005, after adjusting for average wage growth.[5] The purpose is to show both how current taxpayers

---

[5] Average tax rates are calculated for nondependent, nonseparated filers with positive adjusted gross income in tax year 2005. Dollar figures are adjusted to the appropriate tax year using the Social Security Administration national average wage index (Social Security Administration 2009), and the tax due is estimated using the National Bureau of Economic Research's TAXSIM tax model. This tax model incorporates the major tax provisions affecting the vast majority of taxpayers and taxable income, and provides estimates of tax liabilities that closely match the historical distribution of taxes actually paid. However, the tax calculation ignores certain small tax provisions and certain accounting changes that broadened the definition of taxable income over time.

Figure 5-8
Evolution of Average Tax Rates

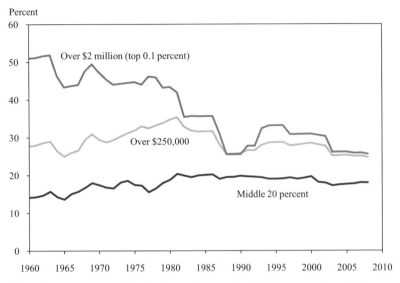

Notes: Average tax rates calculated each year for a sample of 2005 taxpayers after adjusting
for average wage growth. Dollar figures in 2009 dollars.
Sources: Department of the Treasury, Internal Revenue Service, Statistics of Income Public
Use File 2005; National Bureau of Economic Research TAXSIM (Feenburg and Coutts 1993);
CEA calculations.

would have fared under the tax rates that applied historically and how the
tax rates that applied to different income groups have changed over time.

This analysis suggests that the effective tax rates that applied to
high-income taxpayers reached their lowest levels in at least half a century in
2008. Under the tax laws that applied from 1960 to the mid-1980s, today's
taxpayers earning more than $250,000 would have paid an average of around
30 percent of their income in Federal income and payroll taxes, with modest
variations from year to year. Moreover, while the tax rates that applied to
these "ordinary" rich have fallen considerably, tax rates for the very rich have
declined much more. Figure 5-8 shows that taxpayers whose real incomes
put them in the top 0.1 percent of taxpayers today—the one-in-a-thousand
taxpayers with incomes above about $2 million in 2009 dollars—would have
paid more than 50 percent of their incomes in taxes in the early 1960s.

Average tax rates on high-income groups fell precipitously in the
mid-1980s, with the sharp decline in statutory marginal rates. At the
same time, the tax rates that would have applied to today's middle-income
taxpayers (the middle 20 percent of taxpayers in 2005, those making between
about $29,500 and $49,500 per year) increased, on balance, over the last half
century. The result is a compression in the tax burdens applied to taxpayers

with different incomes—the difference between the average tax rates on high-income groups and those on middle-class households is narrower than at any other time in modern history. All told, because of legislative changes in the tax code, the after-tax income of the very-high-income group—their disposable income and purchasing power—is more than 50 percent higher than it would have been under historical tax rates and brackets, while that of the middle class is slightly lower.

Under the Administration's proposals, tax rates on taxpayers earning more than $250,000 would be very close to the levels that prevailed in the 1990s, leaving statutory tax rates on higher-income taxpayers far below the levels that prevailed until the mid-1980s. The rebalancing of the tax code would not affect middle-class taxpayers—except, of course, to the extent that a better fiscal picture enhances medium- and long-term prospects for economic growth.

The need to restore balance is also evident in our corporate tax system, which encourages businesses to move jobs overseas and to transfer profits to tax havens abroad in order to avoid taxes at home. The Administration's plan to reform international tax laws would reduce these incentives.

Balance also requires that the largest and most highly levered financial firms reimburse taxpayers for the extraordinary assistance provided to them through the Troubled Asset Relief Program. The President has proposed a modest Financial Crisis Responsibility Fee to ensure that the cost of the financial rescue is not borne by taxpayers. Moreover, the fee would provide a deterrent against the excessive leverage that helped contribute to the crisis.

Eliminating Wasteful Spending

The third step the Administration is taking to confront the long-term deficit is cutting unnecessary spending. The President pledged to eliminate programs that are not working. Last year, the Administration either proposed or enacted cuts to 121 specific programs; these proposed cuts totaled $17 billion in the first year and hundreds of billions of dollars over the 10-year budget window. They include billions of dollars in terminations of defense programs such as the F-22 fighter aircraft and the new Presidential helicopter, cuts in subsidies for large, high-income agribusinesses, and more than $40 billion in savings over the next 10 years from eliminating unnecessary subsidies to financial institutions in the private student loan market.

In its fiscal 2011 budget, the Administration is proposing another important measure for spending restraint: a three-year freeze in all nonsecurity discretionary spending starting in 2011. The freeze would be a tough measure of shared sacrifice. By 2013, it would reduce overall nonsecurity funding by $30 billion per year relative to current inflation-adjusted funding levels.

The President also strongly supports restoring the pay-as-you-go requirement (PAYGO) that was in place in the 1990s. This law, which requires that lawmakers make the tough choices needed to offset the costs of new nonemergency spending or tax changes, helped move the government budget from deficit to surplus a decade ago. PAYGO is an important tool to force the government to live within its means and move the budget toward fiscal sustainability.

These measures mean that once the temporary rise in government spending necessitated by the economic crisis has ended, spending will be on a lower path than it otherwise would have been. Moreover, both the multiyear freeze and steps to identify additional unnecessary spending each year make the reduction gradual rather than sudden. As a result, the cumulative reduction is substantial, yet there is never a sudden, potentially disruptive drop in spending.

Conclusion: The Distance Still to Go

The actions the Administration has taken and is proposing would reduce deficits by more than $1 trillion over the next 10 years and by even more after that. These actions are significantly bolder steps toward deficit reduction than any taken in decades, and they will face serious opposition by those with vested interests. Even with these actions, however, the primary budget is forecast to remain in deficit in 2015. And the longer-run fiscal problem facing the country still centers on the growth of health care costs and the aging of the population. Thus, barring a substantial and sustained quickening of economic growth above its usual trend rate, further steps will be needed to get the deficit down to the target in the medium and long run.

Regardless of the form they take, these additional steps to reduce the deficit will involve sacrifices by a broad range of groups and significant compromise. Thus, a bipartisan effort will be essential. That is why the President is issuing an executive order creating a bipartisan fiscal commission to report back with a package of measures for additional deficit reduction. The charge to the commission is to propose both medium-term actions to close the gap between noninterest expenditures and tax revenues and additional steps to address the longer-term issues associated with rising health care costs, the aging of the population, and the persistent deficit. The commission's recommendations will form an important foundation on which to base policy decisions moving forward.

The Administration understands that addressing the long-run fiscal challenge will be a long and difficult task requiring commitment and shared sacrifice. But the President also believes that Americans deserve for and expect policymakers to deal with the ever-rising deficit. The changes eventually enacted will be central to the long-run preservation of both America's financial strength and the standards of living of ordinary Americans.

✥

C H A P T E R   6

BUILDING A SAFER
FINANCIAL SYSTEM

From the ashes of the Great Depression, our leaders built a national system of financial regulation. Before 1933, there was no national regulator for stock and bond markets, no required disclosure by public firms, no national oversight of mutual funds or investment advisors, no insurance for bank depositors, and few restrictions on the activities of banks or other financial institutions. By 1940, landmark legislation had created the Securities and Exchange Commission, the Federal Deposit Insurance Corporation, new and important powers for the Federal Reserve, and disclosure requirements for virtually every major player in financial markets. The pieces of this regulatory structure fit together in a relatively cohesive whole, and the United States enjoyed a long period of relative financial calm. In the 60 years before the Great Depression, our Nation experienced seven episodes of financial panic, in which many banks were forced to shut their windows and declined to redeem deposit accounts. In the nearly 80 years since the Depression, not a single financial crisis has risen to that level.

Although the system of regulation put together during the Depression served us well for many years, warning signs appeared periodically. The savings and loan crisis of the late 1980s and early 1990s showed how banking regulation itself can have unintended consequences. At that time, deregulation coupled with generous deposit insurance combined to create a dangerous pattern of risk-taking that eventually led to a large Federal bailout of the financial system. In 1998, the collapse of Long-Term Capital Management highlighted gaps in the regulatory structure and induced the Federal Reserve Bank of New York to organize an unprecedented private rescue of an unregulated hedge fund. In 2001, the collapse of Enron laid bare the complexity of the financial operations at seemingly nonfinancial corporations and posed new challenges for accountants, policymakers, and analysts. Regulatory changes in the past 30 years responded to the specific weaknesses demonstrated by these crises, but these changes were incremental and lacked a strategic plan. Throughout this period, the architecture created after the Great Depression was becoming increasingly inadequate to handle ongoing financial innovation. It was in this vacuum that financial innovation accelerated during the first decade of the 21st century.

The weaknesses in our outdated regulatory system nearly drove our economy into a second Great Depression. After the bankruptcy of Lehman Brothers in September 2008, credit markets froze and the Federal Government was forced to embark on increasingly aggressive intervention in financial markets. But as bad as the situation was, it could have been much worse. Courage and creativity during the depths of the crisis, and forceful stewardship by the Administration in the aftermath, have enabled our Nation to escape a second Great Depression. Chapter 2 of this report discusses the major elements of the Administration's recovery plan. This chapter focuses on the long-term changes necessary to prevent future crises.

What Is Financial Intermediation?

Suppose that the world woke up tomorrow to find all the banks gone, along with insurance companies, investment banks, mutual funds, and all the other institutions where ordinary people put their savings. What would happen? In the short run, people could keep their savings in mattresses and piggy banks, and the only apparent losses would be the forgone interest and dividends. But with no easy way to get the savings from piggy banks into productive investment, the economy would face bigger problems very quickly. Entrepreneurs with ideas would find it difficult to get capital. Large companies in need of money to restructure their operations would have no way to borrow against their future earnings. Young families would have no way to buy a house until they had personally saved enough to afford the whole thing. Our system of financial intermediation makes possible all those activities, and the infrastructure to perform that function is necessarily complex and costly.

The Economics of Financial Intermediation

Figure 6-1 is a simplified diagram of the main function of financial intermediation: transforming savings into investment. The ultimate source of funds is shown on the left: individuals and institutions that have the final claim on wealth and wish to save some of it for the future. The ultimate use of funds is shown on the right: the productive activities that need funds for investment. The middle of the diagram can be classified as "financial intermediation." Financial intermediation uses either markets (like the stock market) or institutions (like a bank) to channel savings into investment.

In each of these cases, financial intermediaries provide three important services: information production, liquidity transformation, and diversification. The paragraphs that follow use a concrete investment example to explain these services and define the terms used in the figure.

Figure 6-1
Financial Intermediation: Saving into Investment

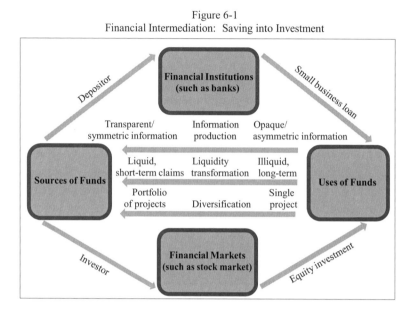

Suppose that an entrepreneur has an idea for a new company (right side of figure) to develop a new cancer treatment. The science behind this business is specialized and complicated. He could directly approach a wealthy individual with savings (left side of figure) and ask for an investment in his company. The potential investor would immediately face two difficult problems. The first is that she does not know the quality of the entrepreneur's idea. The entrepreneur is likely to know much more about the science than does the potential investor. Maybe the entrepreneur has already asked more than 100 potential investors and been turned down by all of them. Maybe he knows that the idea has little chance of commercial success but wants to try anyway for humanitarian reasons. The investor knows none of these things and cannot learn about them without putting in real effort. In this case, there would be asymmetric information between the investor and the entrepreneur at the time of the potential investment: economists call this a problem of adverse selection.

The second problem faced by the investor is that, after she makes the investment, she needs some way to monitor the entrepreneur and make sure he is using the money in the most efficient way. Perhaps the entrepreneur will decide to use the money for some other business or research purpose. How will the investor know? Even worse, what is to prevent the entrepreneur from using the funds for his personal benefit or taking the money without putting in any effort? In this case, there would be additional asymmetric information introduced after the investment was made: economists call this a problem of moral hazard.

To solve these adverse selection and moral hazard problems, the investor will need to expend some resources. She will need to study the technology, evaluate its chances for scientific and commercial success, and then carefully watch over the entrepreneur after the investment is made. These activities are difficult and costly, and there is no reason to believe that a typical source of funds (whose main qualification is that she has money to invest) would also be the best person to solve these problems. One important service of financial intermediation is to efficiently solve the adverse selection and moral hazard problems that come with the transformation of savings into investment. This chapter refers to this service as information production.

The second main service of financial intermediation is liquidity transformation. Consider how long it takes to develop a cancer treatment. In the United States, all new drug treatments must pass through a complex regulatory review stretched over many years. Even if a drug is eventually approved, the path to commercial success can take many more years. Most investors do not want to wait that long to see any return on their money. Individual investors have uncertain liquidity needs—jobs can be lost, family members can get sick—and even institutional investors are subject to performance evaluation over short periods. Overall, investment projects tend to have long production times, while investment sources prefer to have easy access to their money. Somebody, somewhere, must be willing to absorb the liquidity needs of the economy. In practice, these needs are provided by liquidity transformation: financial institutions and markets transform long-term (illiquid) investment projects into short-term (liquid) claims.

Liquidity transformation is also important for another, more worrisome, reason: it is the main source of the fragility that can lead to a financial crisis. Because most intermediaries have illiquid assets and liquid liabilities, any broad-based attempt by creditors to call liabilities at the same time creates an impossible situation for the intermediary. The classic example is a bank run, where holders of deposits (liquid liabilities) all "run" at the same time to withdraw their funds, leaving banks unable to sell the illiquid business loans and mortgages quickly enough to meet these demands. The same process can occur in a wide variety of nonbank institutions, as is discussed at length later in this chapter.

The third main service of financial intermediation is diversification. A single investment project can be very risky. In the case of the drug company, no investor would want her entire net worth riding on the success of just one technological project. Individual investors can minimize their risk by purchasing a diversified portfolio of investments. If, for example, an investor could pay 1 percent of the costs for 100 different drug-development projects, then her overall portfolio risk would be greatly reduced. Further diversification is achieved by dedicating only a small share of a portfolio to any given industry or country. Such diversification is a main service of most financial institutions, which take funds from many small sources and then invest across a wide variety of projects.

Types of Financial Intermediaries

Figure 6-2 plots nominal gross domestic product (GDP) in the United States against the total assets in the financial sector and a long list of institutional types, including banks, securities firms, mutual funds, money-market funds, mortgage pools, asset-backed-securities (ABS) issuers, insurance companies, and pension funds. Figure 6-3 plots the same set of intermediaries, this time as a percentage of the total assets held by the entire financial

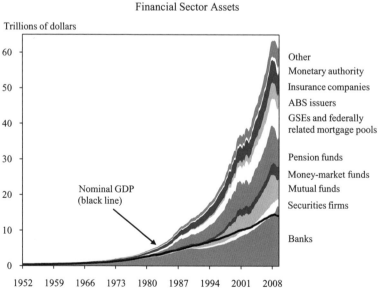

Figure 6-2
Financial Sector Assets

Sources: Federal Reserve Board, Flow of Funds; Department of Commerce (Bureau of Economic Analysis), National Income and Product Accounts Table 1.1.5.

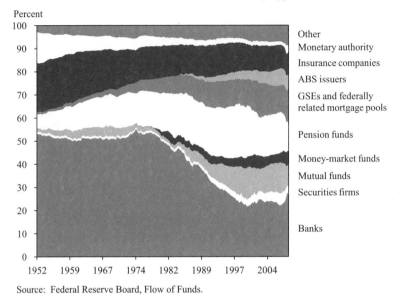

Figure 6-3
Share of Financial Sector Assets by Type

Percent

Other
Monetary authority
Insurance companies
ABS issuers
GSEs and federally
related mortgage pools

Pension funds

Money-market funds
Mutual funds
Securities firms

Banks

1952   1959   1967   1974   1982   1989   1997   2004

Source: Federal Reserve Board, Flow of Funds.

sector. All of these financial data are from the Federal Reserve's Flow of Funds.

These figures show several important trends. First, assets in the financial sector have grown much faster than GDP: from 1952 to 2009, nominal GDP grew by 4,000 percent and financial sector assets grew by 16,000 percent. This trend is important to remember in considering the regulation of finance. It would be helpful to know if the ratio of financial assets to GDP is "too big" or "too small," but no good evidence permits such a conclusion. Furthermore, modern developments in the financial system have allowed each dollar of underlying assets to multiply many times across an increasing chain of financial intermediation, so that any measurement of gross assets (as in Figure 6-2) is misleading as a measure of the "importance" of the financial sector. The concept of increasing intermediation chains is discussed later for specific institutional types.

A second important trend is that the assets held by banks grew at approximately the same rate as GDP. Nevertheless, because the overall size of the financial sector has increased, the percentage of financial sector assets held by banks has fallen over time. Third, Figure 6-3 shows the rising share of assets held by mutual funds, government sponsored enterprises (GSEs) and federally related mortgage pools, and issuers of asset-backed securities. Some of this growth can be attributed to the lengthening of the financial intermediation chain, as pension funds delegate asset management to mutual funds, banks sell mortgages to mortgage pools, and money-market funds purchase securities from these pools.

Three long-standing institutional types are banks, securities firms, and insurance companies. Banks, including commercial banks, bank holding companies, savings institutions (thrifts), and credit unions, are still the largest component of the financial sector, with $16.5 trillion in assets as of June 2009. Although bank assets represent 26.7 percent of the financial sector, their share has fallen precipitously since 1952, when it was 53.2 percent. Securities firms, also known as investment banks or broker-dealers, had $2.0 trillion in assets, comprising 3.2 percent of the sector in June 2009. This percentage was down considerably from an average of 5.1 percent in 2007, because most of the largest securities firms went bankrupt, were acquired by banks, or formally converted to banks during the crisis. Insurance companies have $5.9 trillion in assets, comprising 9.5 percent of the sector as of June 2009.

Mutual funds and pension funds are a second layer of intermediation, often standing in between investors and another institution or market. Mutual funds had $9.7 trillion in assets, comprising 15.7 percent of the sector, in June 2009, up from only 1.6 percent in 1952 and 3.1 percent in 1980. Mutual funds take money from retail investors and invest in public securities. An important subgroup of mutual funds are money-market funds (MMFs), which are broken out separately in these figures and in the underlying Federal Reserve data. In 1990, MMFs held less than $500 billion in assets; by June 2009, their total assets were $3.6 trillion, comprising 5.8 percent of total financial assets. MMFs invest only in relatively safe, short-term assets. Pension funds are a large and growing share of the sector, with assets of $8.3 trillion making up 13.5 percent of total financial assets in June 2009. Many pension assets are reinvested in mutual funds, so they show up twice in the overall totals. Thus, some of the growth in overall sector assets is driven by this extra step of intermediation.

The next category in Figure 6-2 is GSEs and federally related mortgage pools, with $8.4 trillion in assets in June 2009. Beginning in the 1930s, various nonbank sources emerged to buy mortgages on the secondary market. By the end of the 1970s, federally related mortgage pools—which include those established by GSEs known as Fannie Mae and Freddie Mac—had almost $100 billion in assets. The growth of GSEs added an extra layer to the financial intermediation of mortgages. Here, the bank provides a loan to a borrower but then resells this loan to a GSE. The bank may hold debt securities issued by the GSE, and the GSE creates a pool that holds the mortgage.

In addition to those created by GSEs, private mortgage pools, focusing on "subprime" borrowers, have grown substantially in the past 10 years.

These private mortgage pools issue securities backed by the mortgages; these securities, known as mortgage-backed securities (MBSs), are purchased and held by mutual funds or other financial intermediaries. They are one type of an asset-backed security managed by an ABS issuer. ABS issuers do not confine themselves to mortgages; they also pool and securitize auto loans, student loans, credit card debt, and many other types of debt. Twenty years ago, few ABS issuers existed, but by June 2009 they held $3.8 trillion in assets and comprised 6.2 percent of total financial sector assets.

The remaining categories in Figures 6-2 and 6-3 are the monetary authority (the Federal Reserve) and "other." As discussed in Chapter 2, the assets of the monetary authority increased rapidly during the crisis, but the increase is expected to be reversed as the Federal Reserve exits from its emergency programs and begins reducing the large stock of long-term securities it had purchased. The "other" category includes special purpose vehicles created to manage the emergency lending programs and various other minor groups of intermediaries.

Hedge funds are an increasingly important financial intermediary, but they are not included in Figures 6-2 and 6-3. Because of a lack of data on domestic hedge funds, the Federal Reserve classifies such funds as part of the household sector and computes the assets of this sector as a residual after everything else is added together and subtracted from total assets. The Federal Reserve is unable to get a clean number for hedge funds because they are largely unregulated private investment pools that are not required to report their holdings to any official source. Unofficial sources estimate the amount of assets held by hedge funds to have been $1.7 trillion in 2008, but in the absence of regulatory oversight, this estimate is less reliable than the other totals shown in Figure 6-2 (Hedge Fund Research 2009).

THE REGULATION OF FINANCIAL INTERMEDIATION IN THE UNITED STATES

Private institutions and markets should clearly play the central role in financial intermediation. But government also has a role. Economists generally favor government regulation of markets that exhibit a market failure of some kind. This chapter has already discussed two types of market failure: adverse selection and moral hazard. Both can be classified as special cases of asymmetric information, where different parties to a contract do not have the same information. The financial intermediation system alleviates asymmetric-information problems between savers and investors, but information can also be asymmetric between buyers and sellers of financial services. Just as physicians almost always know more than patients about medicine, and lawyers more than their clients about law, banks and financial advisors should be expected to know more than their investors about investment opportunities. For this reason, there will always be a consumer protection basis for some government regulation of financial services.

Consumer protection was an important motivation for several important pieces of Depression-era legislation. The first two, the Securities Act of 1933 and the Securities Exchange Act of 1934, set forth a long list of requirements for issuing and trading public securities. The list included many types of public disclosure that persist to this day, including information about executive compensation, stockholdings, balance sheets, and income statements. The 1934 Act also created the Securities and Exchange Commission (SEC), the agency responsible for enforcing the new rules. These securities laws were the first Federal laws to regulate organized financial exchanges.

With regulated markets came the growth of intermediaries to service them. These intermediaries gained Federal oversight with the Investment Advisers Act of 1940 (for publicly available investment advisory services) and the Investment Company Act of 1940 (for mutual funds). In total, these four pieces of legislation enacted between 1933 and 1940 represented a huge change in the regulatory structure of financial markets and in most cases can be considered attempts to lessen adverse selection and moral hazard problems between investors, intermediaries, and investments.

Depression-era laws also strengthened the national system of bank regulation, adding new elements to a long pre-Depression history of Federal regulation. Beginning with the National Bank Act of 1864, federally chartered banks have been examined regularly for capital adequacy. State-chartered banks received similar examinations from both state and Federal banking agencies. Such examinations are a form of microprudential regulation, with a focus on the safety and soundness of individual institutions in isolation and with the aim of reducing asymmetric-information problems. Few bank depositors have the time or incentive to conduct detailed reviews of their banks. When regulators conduct periodic reviews and publicize the results, they create a public good of information about the safety and soundness of individual banks. Furthermore, examinations and regulations can constrain excessive risk-taking by federally insured institutions, a moral hazard problem faced by the government, rather than by bank depositors, in part because of deposit insurance.

The microprudential approach, however, is not well suited to handle risks to the entire financial system. The next section of this chapter discusses in detail the spread of crises. For now, it is sufficient to think of a crisis as an occasion when there is a sudden increase in the asymmetric-information problem in the financial system, as can happen after a large economic shock or the failure of a major bank. The microprudential system of bank examination can alleviate asymmetric-information problems in normal times, but because the government relies on careful periodic examinations, staggered across banks, it does not have the capacity to examine all banks quickly after a shock or to evaluate the risk that a single bank failure will have on other institutions. Faced with a large economic shock, bank customers can rationally fear for the safety of their deposits. Since the upside of leaving one's money at a bank in such a situation is relatively small, but the downside—losing all one's money—is large, it is individually rational for depositors to withdraw their money when uncertainty increases. What is rational for individual depositors, however, puts an impossible strain on the whole banking system, since the liquidity transformation performed by banks cannot be quickly reversed; the illiquid loans and mortgages held by banks cannot immediately be returned to all depositors as cash.

One partial solution to the liquidity problem during banking crises is to create a "lender of last resort." This lender stands ready to make cash loans to banks that are backed by illiquid collateral: essentially, this lender serves as a new layer of liquidity transformation above the banks. This form of macroprudential policy was the traditional solution to banking crises in Europe in the 19th century but did not come to the United States until the Federal Reserve Act of 1913 created the first version of the Federal Reserve System as a lender of last resort.

But a lender of last resort, by itself, is unable to prevent bank runs across the entire system. Even illiquid collateral must be given a value by the lender—by law the Federal Reserve can only make secured loans—and if the entire system is failing at the same time, there may be no way for a central bank to estimate reasonable valuations quickly enough. A lender of last resort is designed to solve liquidity problems, not solvency problems, but in a severe crisis, these two problems can become inextricably tied together. (This problem arose during the current crisis, when Lehman Brothers was unable to provide enough collateral to qualify for sufficient Federal Reserve loans.) During the Great Depression, some 9,000 bank failures occurred between 1930 and 1933, well above the number of failures in earlier panics. Shortly after taking office in 1933, President Franklin Roosevelt gave his first "fireside chat" and implied a government guarantee for all bank deposits. The Banking Act of 1933 made the guarantee explicit by creating deposit insurance through a new agency, the Federal Deposit Insurance Corporation (FDIC). In the 75 years that followed, the United States averaged fewer than 30 commercial bank failures a year. The FDIC is a crucial piece of macroprudential regulation in that it provides a guarantee to all insured banks, regardless of the condition of any specific bank. Within the account limits of FDIC insurance, no depositor needs to worry about the soundness of her bank; thus, the FDIC guarantee eliminates most asymmetric-information problems that could lead to bank runs.

A constant tension in macroprudential regulation is that the attempt to prevent bank runs can itself lead to new forms of moral hazard. Because they have deposit insurance, small depositors no longer need to monitor the safety of their banks; therefore, unless regulators are watching carefully, the banks may take excessive risks with no fear of losing deposits. This latent problem was exacerbated during the 1980s by deregulation in the thrift industry. Following this deregulation, thrift institutions began aggressively seeking out deposits by paying ever-higher interest rates and then intermediating these deposits into speculative investments. This strategy allowed thrifts to use FDIC insurance to gamble for solvency, and when the investments failed, a wave of thrift failures swept through Texas, the Midwest, and New England in the 1980s and early 1990s. This wave, now known as the savings and loan crisis, represented the first significant increase in bank failures since the Great Depression. The failures, it should be noted, were not caused by bank runs—they were not driven by a liquidity mismatch between deposits and loans. Deposit insurance remained intact, and no insured deposit lost any money. Rather, the bank failures were caused by the insolvency of the banks, as they gambled and lost with (effectively) government money. Nevertheless, even in the absence of bank runs, many economists believe that the savings and loan crisis contributed to the "credit crunch" and recession of 1990–91.

There has been no fundamental restructuring of the Nation's financial regulatory system since the Great Depression. All changes since that time have been piecemeal responses to specific events, added individually onto the original superstructure. That regulatory stasis has led to four major gaps in the current system. First, many of the newer financial institutions— hedge funds, mortgage pools, asset-backed-securities issuers—have grown rapidly while being subject to only minimal Federal regulation. These new institutions suffer from many of the asymmetric-information problems that banks faced before the Depression-era reforms. Second, overlapping jurisdictions and mandates have led to regulatory competition between agencies and regulatory "shopping" by institutions. Such competition is yet another form of moral hazard—now centered on the regulators themselves. Third, regulators operate separately in functional silos of banking, insurance, and securities. Many of the largest institutions perform all these activities at once but are not subject to robust consolidated regulation and supervision. And finally, most of the regulatory system is microprudential and focused on the safety and soundness of specific institutions. No regulator is tasked with taking a macroprudential approach, which attempts to monitor, recognize, and alleviate risks to the financial system as a whole. Such macroprudential regulation would require explicit rules for the orderly resolution of all large financial institutions, not just the banks currently resolved by the FDIC. In short, because of these four gaps, the failure of one institution imposes negative externalities on others, and there is no coherent system for fixing these externalities.

Of the four gaps, the last requires the most urgent reform and the biggest change in regulatory thinking. The financial crisis made clear how rapidly failures can spread across institutions and affect the whole system. A primary challenge of macroprudential regulation is to recognize such "contagion" and categorize and counteract all the different ways it can manifest. The next section of the chapter turns to this task.

Financial Crises: The Collapse of Financial Intermediation

A financial crisis is a collapse of financial intermediation. In a crisis, the ability of the financial system to move savings into investment is severely impaired. In an extreme crisis, banks close their doors, financial markets shut down, businesses are unable to finance their operations, and households are challenged to find credit. A financial crisis can be triggered by events that are completely external to the financial system. If a large macroeconomic shock hits all banks at the same time, regulators can do little to control the damage. Some crises, however, are triggered or exacerbated by shocks to a small group of institutions that then spread to others. This spread, known as contagion, is a form of negative externality imposed by distressed institutions. The recent financial crisis involved three different types of contagion, referred to in this chapter as confidence contagion, counterparty contagion, and coordination contagion. A macroprudential regulator must have the tools to handle all three.

Confidence Contagion

The classic example of a "run on the bank" is shown in Figure 6-4. Banks are mostly financed by deposits, which are then lent out as loans to businesses and mortgages for homeowners. A bank's balance sheet has a maturity mismatch between assets (the loans) and liabilities (the deposits): the loans are long term, with payments coming over many years, while the deposits are short term and can be withdrawn at any time. The liquidity transformation service of the bank works in ordinary times but breaks down if all the depositors ask for their money back at the same time.

Figure 6-4
Confidence Contagion

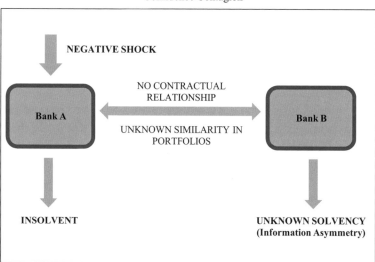

Suppose, for example, a depositor in Bank A hears a rumor that other depositors in Bank A are withdrawing their funds. He does not know the explanation. It might be that Bank A has a problem with solvency, that a fair accounting would show that its liabilities exceed its assets. Typically, a depositor does not have the necessary information to form an accurate judgment about solvency. So what does he do? The safe thing, in the absence of deposit insurance, is to go to the bank and take out his money. Perhaps these other depositors know something that he does not. If he waits too long, the bank will be out of cash and unable to redeem his account.

It is easy to see how the run at Bank A could lead to runs at other banks. The public spectacle of long lines of depositors waiting outside a bank is enough to make other banks' customers nervous—the negative externality on confidence. Perhaps Bank A had many real estate loans in some trouble area, and Bank B has an unknown number of similar loans. The issue here is that bank depositors do not want to take the risk of leaving their money in a failing bank. Unlike stock market investors, who expect to take risks and face complicated problems in forecasting the future path of company profits, bank depositors want their money to be safe and do not want to spend an enormous amount of time making sure that it is. The information production service of banks cannot quickly be replaced if the bank is in trouble. Banks, therefore, have historically been subject to runs, and the runs have spread quickly across banks, a phenomenon called confidence contagion.

Classic bank runs were commonplace in the United States before (and during) the Great Depression. In the post-FDIC world, bank failure has become a problem of insolvency, not illiquidity. FDIC insurance works almost perfectly up to a current limit of $250,000 for each account. What happens above this limit? What of the many corporations and investors who want a safe place to put their million-dollar and billion-dollar deposits? In the absence of insured accounts at this level, they choose such alternatives as money-market funds, collateralized short-term loans to financial institutions, and complex derivative transactions. In each of these cases, the effort to find safe, liquid investments can lead to situations that look identical to a classic bank run, but with different players. When a single investment bank (Bear Stearns in March 2008) or money-market fund (the Reserve Fund in September 2008) gets into solvency trouble, confidence can quickly erode at similar institutions. Macroprudential regulation must stop this confidence contagion or, at least, contain it to one segment of the financial system.

Counterparty Contagion

Counterparty contagion is illustrated in Figure 6-5. Here, Bank A owes $1 billion to Bank B, which owes $1 billion to Bank C, with this same debt going through the alphabet to Bank E. When Bank A goes out of business owing money to Bank B, then Bank B cannot pay Bank C. To the extent that Bank C lacks the information or the ability to insure against the failure of Bank A, that failure imposes an externality. One failure could lead to defaults all the way to Bank E. Such contagion seems particularly wasteful, because most of it could be averted by getting rid of all the steps in the middle: the only banks here with net exposure are Banks A and E; once the middle is eliminated, all that is left is a $1 billion debt of A to E.

Derivatives are an important modern vehicle for counterparty chains. A derivative is any security whose value is based completely on the value of one or more reference assets, rates, or indexes. For example, a simple derivative could be constructed as the promise by Party B to pay $1 to Party A if and only if the stock price of Company XYZ is above $200 a share on December 31, 2012. This contract is a derivative because its payoff is completely "derived" from the value of XYZ stock; the contract has no meaning that is independent of XYZ stock. Things begin to grow more complicated when Party A and Party B begin to make offsetting trades with other parties, creating counterparty exposures among the group of market participants. For example, Party B, having taken on the risk that XYZ will climb above $200 a share, may at some point decide to offset this risk by purchasing a similar option from Party C. Eventually, Party C makes the reverse trade with Party D, and soon the chain can extend across the alphabet.

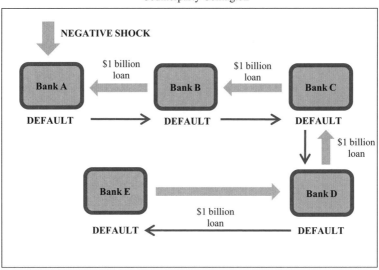

Figure 6-5
Counterparty Contagion

Coordination Contagion

Coordination contagion is illustrated in Figure 6-6. Here, Bank A owns many assets of Type I and Type II; Bank B owns many assets of Type II and Type III; and Bank C owns many assets of Type III and Type IV. Suppose that a negative shock to the value of Type I assets threatens the solvency of Bank A. In an effort to remain in business, Bank A begins to liquidate its portfolio by selling Type I and Type II assets. As is typical for banks, these underlying assets are relatively illiquid, so it is difficult for Bank A to sell substantial quantities without depressing the price of the assets. As the prices of Type II assets fall, Bank B is in a quandary. The market value of its assets is falling, and the regulators of Bank B may insist that it reduce its leverage or raise more capital. Bank B may then sell Type II and Type III assets to achieve this goal. Again, it is easy to see how this process could flow through the alphabet. Here the process is called coordination contagion because it is driven by the coordinated holdings of the banks, rather than by confidence of investors (in any particular bank) or the chains of contractual relationships (among banks) that lead to counterparty contagion. The externality occurs here only because the underlying assets are illiquid. With this illiquidity, the transactions of each player can significantly affect the price, and the forced sale by one bank harms all the others that own these assets.

Coordination contagion is exacerbated if failing institutions are forced to liquidate their positions quickly. In the fall of 2008, many large financial institutions had significant holdings of subprime housing and other

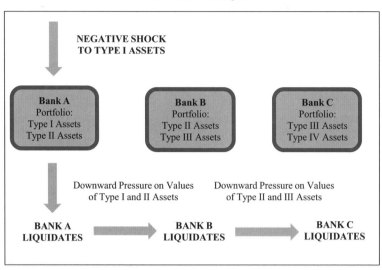

Figure 6-6
Coordination Contagion

structured instruments on their balance sheets. With capital scarce and uncertainty about the value of these assets high, distressed institutions faced pressure to sell these assets. If the most desperate institutions sold first, then the depressed prices of these sales would then place pressure on other institutions to mark down the values of these assets on their balance sheets, further exacerbating the problem. One partial solution to this coordination contagion would be to allow the most distressed institutions to exit their positions slowly, so as not to further destabilize the illiquid market for these assets. Such slow exits can be enabled by taking failing institutions into a form of receivership or conservatorship, an enhanced "resolution authority" for nonbank financial institutions that would be analogous to the FDIC process for failing depository institutions.

PREVENTING FUTURE CRISES: REGULATORY REFORM

The Financial Stability Plan and other policies to address the current crisis described in Chapter 2 have had a positive short-run effect on the financial system. To prevent future crises and achieve long-term stability, however, it will be necessary to fill the gaps in the current regulatory system. The Administration is working closely with Congress to build a regulatory system for the 21st century.[1] The plan for regulatory reform has five key parts, each covering a different aspect of the financial intermediation system illustrated by Figure 6-1. The parts of the plan are discussed below, with references back to the relevant sections of Figure 6-1.

Promote Robust Supervision and Regulation of Financial Firms

If the recent financial crisis has proven anything, it is that we have outgrown our Depression-era financial regulatory system. Although most of the largest, most interconnected, and most highly leveraged financial firms were subject to some form of supervision and regulation before the crisis, those forms of oversight proved inadequate and inconsistent. The financial institutions at the top of Figure 6-1 are a varied group that is no longer dominated by traditional commercial banks. A modern regulatory system must account for the entire group.

Three primary weaknesses inherent in the current system led to the crisis. First, capital and liquidity requirements for institutions were simply not high enough. Regulation failed because firms were not required to hold sufficient capital to cover trading assets, high-risk loans, and off-balance-sheet commitments, or to hold increased capital during good times in preparation for bad times. Nor were firms required to plan for liquidity shortages.

Second, various agencies shared responsibility for supervising the consolidated operations of large financial firms. This fragmentation of supervisory responsibility, in addition to loopholes in the legal definition of a "bank," made it possible for owners of banks and other insured depository institutions to shop for the most lenient regulator.

Finally, other types of financial institutions were subject to insufficient government oversight. Money-market funds were vulnerable to runs, but unlike their banking cousins, they lacked both regulators and insurers. Major investment banks were subject to a regulatory regime through the SEC that is now moot, since large independent investment banks no longer exist. Meanwhile, hedge funds and other private pools of capital operated completely outside the existing supervisory framework.

In combination, these three sets of weaknesses increased the likelihood that some firms would fail and made it less likely that problems at these firms would be detected early. This was a breakdown in the supervision under current authority over individual institutions. But glaring problems were also created by a lack of focus on large, interconnected, and highly leveraged institutions that could inflict harm both on the financial system and on the

---

[1] This section is based heavily on the Administration's white paper on financial reform (Department of the Treasury 2009).

economy if they failed. No regulators were tasked with responsibility for contagion, whether from confidence, counterparties, or coordination.

To solve these problems and ensure the long-term health of the financial system, the government must create a new foundation for the regulation of financial institutions. To do that, the Administration will promote more robust and consistent regulatory standards for all financial institutions. Not only should similar financial institutions face the same supervisory and regulatory standards, but the system can contain no gaps, loopholes, or opportunities for arbitrage.

The Administration has also proposed creating a Financial Services Oversight Council (FSOC). This body, chaired by the Secretary of the Treasury, would facilitate coordination of policy and resolution of disputes and identify emerging risks and gaps in supervision in firms and market activities. The heads of the principal Federal financial regulators would be members of the Council, which would benefit from a permanent staff at the Department of the Treasury.

Finally, the Federal Reserve's current supervisory authority for bank holding companies must evolve along with the financial system. Regardless of whether they own an insured depository institution, all large, interconnected firms whose failure may threaten the stability of the entire system should be subject to consolidated supervision by the Federal Reserve. To that end, the Administration proposes creating a single point of accountability for the consolidated supervision of all companies that own a bank. These firms should not be allowed or able to escape oversight of their risky activities by manipulating their legal structures.

Taken together, these proposals will help reduce the weaknesses in the financial regulatory system by more stringently regulating the largest, most interconnected, and most highly leveraged institutions. In effect, the Administration's proposals would operate on the simple principle that firms that could pose higher risks should be subject to higher standards. Furthermore, both the Federal Reserve and the FSOC would operate through a macroprudential prism and be wary of contagion in all its forms.

Establish Comprehensive Regulation of Financial Markets

The financial crisis followed a long and remarkable period of growth and innovation in the Nation's financial markets. These new financial markets, found in the bottom part of Figure 6-1, still rely on regulation put together in response to the Great Depression, when stocks and bonds were the main financial products for which there were significant markets. But over time, new financial instruments allowed credit risks to be spread widely, enabling investors to diversify their portfolios in new ways and allowing banks to shed exposures that once would have had to remain on their balance sheets. As discussed earlier, securitization allowed mortgages and other loans to be aggregated with similar loans, segmented, and sold in tranches to a large and diverse pool of new investors with varied risk preferences. Credit derivatives created a way for banks to transfer much of their credit exposure to third parties without the outright selling of the underlying assets. At the time, this innovation in the distribution of risk was perceived to increase financial stability, promote efficiency, and contribute to a better allocation of resources.

Far from transparently distributing risk, however, the innovations often resulted in opaque and complex risk concentrations. Furthermore, the innovations arose too rapidly for the market's infrastructure, which consists of payment, clearing, and settlement systems, to accommodate them, and for the Nation's financial supervisors to keep up with them. Furthermore, many individual financial institutions' risk management systems failed to keep up. The result was a disastrous buildup of risk in the over-the-counter (OTC) derivatives markets. In the run-up to the crisis, many believed these markets would distribute risk to those most able to bear it. Instead, these markets became a major source of counterparty contagion during the crisis.

In response to these problems, the Administration proposes creating a more coherent and coordinated regulatory framework for the markets for OTC derivatives and asset-backed securities. The Administration's proposal, which aims to improve both transparency and market discipline, would impose record-keeping and reporting requirements on all OTC derivatives. The Administration further proposes strengthening the prudential regulation of all dealers in the OTC derivative markets and requiring all standardized OTC derivative transactions to be executed in regulated and transparent venues and cleared through regulated central counterparties. The primary goal of these regulatory changes is to reduce the possibility of the sort of counterparty contagion seen in the recent crisis. Moving activity to a centralized clearinghouse can effectively break the chain of failures by netting out middleman parties. A successful clearinghouse can reduce the counterparty contagion illustrated in Figure 6-5 to a single debt owned by Bank A to Bank E, thus sparing Banks B, C, and D from the problems.

The Administration has also proposed enhancing the Federal Reserve's authority over market infrastructure to reduce the potential for contagion among financial firms and markets. After all, even a clearinghouse can fail, and regulators must be alert to this danger. Finally, the Administration proposes harmonizing the statutory and regulatory regimes between the futures and securities markets. Although important distinctions exist between the two, many differences in regulation between them are no longer justifiable. In particular, the growth and innovation in derivatives and derivatives markets have highlighted the need to address gaps and inconsistencies in the regulation of these products by the Commodity Futures Trading Commission (CFTC) and the SEC. In October 2009, the SEC and the CFTC issued a joint report identifying major areas necessary to reconcile their regulatory approaches and outlining a series of regulatory and statutory recommendations to narrow or where possible eliminate those differences.

Provide the Government with the Tools It Needs to Manage Financial Crises

During the recent crisis, the financial system was strained by the failure or near-failure of some of the largest and most interconnected financial firms. Thanks to lessons learned from past crises, the current system already has strong procedures for handling bank failure. However, when a bank holding company or other nonbank financial firm is in severe distress, it has only two options: obtain outside capital or file for bankruptcy. In a normal economic climate, these options would be suitable and would pose no consequences for broader financial stability. However, during a crisis, distressed institutions may be hard-pressed to raise sufficient private capital. Thus, if a large, interconnected bank holding company or other nonbank financial firm nears failure during a financial crisis, its only two options are untenable: to obtain emergency funding from the U.S. Government, as in the case of AIG; or to file for bankruptcy, as in the case of Lehman Brothers. Neither option manages the resolution of the firm in a manner that limits damage to the broader economy at minimal cost to the taxpayer.

This situation is unacceptable. A way must be found to address the potential failure of a bank holding company or other nonbank financial firm when the stability of the financial system is at risk. To solve this issue, the Administration proposes creating a new authority modeled on the existing authority of the FDIC. The Administration has also proposed that the Federal Reserve Board receive prior written approval from the Secretary of the Treasury for emergency lending under its "unusual and exigent circumstances" authority to improve accountability in the use of other crisis tools. The goal of these proposals is to allow for an orderly resolution of all large institutions—not just banks—so that the coordination contagion depicted in Figure 6-6 does not again threaten the entire financial system. Taking nonbank financial institutions into receivership or conservatorship would make it possible to sell assets slowly and with minimal disruption to the values of similar assets at otherwise healthy institutions.

Raise International Regulatory Standards and Improve International Cooperation

The system in Figure 6-1 cannot be managed by one country alone, because its interconnections are global. As the recent crisis has illustrated, financial stress can spread quickly and easily across borders. Yet regulation is still set largely in a national context and has failed to effectively adapt. Without consistent supervision and regulation, rational financial institutions will see opportunity in this situation and move their activities to jurisdictions with looser standards. This can create a "race to the bottom" situation.

The United States is addressing this issue by playing a strong leadership role in efforts to coordinate international financial policy through the Group of Twenty (G-20), the G-20's newly established Financial Stability Board, and the Basel Committee on Banking Supervision. The goal is to promote international initiatives compatible with the domestic regulatory reforms described in this report. These efforts have already borne fruit. In September, the G-20 met in Pittsburgh and agreed in principle to this goal. And while those processes are ongoing, significant progress has been made in agreements strengthening prudential requirements, including capital and liquidity standards; expanding the scope of regulation to nonbank financial institutions, hedge funds, and over-the-counter derivatives markets; and reinforcing international cooperation on the supervision of globally active firms.

Protect Consumers and Investors from Financial Abuse

Before the financial crisis, numerous Federal and state regulations protected consumers against fraud and promoted understanding of financial products like credit cards and mortgages. But as abusive practices spread, particularly in the subprime and nontraditional mortgage markets, the Nation's outdated regulatory framework proved inadequate in crucial ways. Although multiple agencies now have authority over consumer protection in financial products, the supervisory framework for enforcing those regulations has significant shortcomings rooted in history. State and Federal banking regulators have a primary mission to promote safe and sound banking practices—placing consumer protection in a subordinate position—while other agencies have a clear mission but limited tools and jurisdiction. In the run-up to the financial crisis, mortgage companies and other firms outside of the purview of bank regulation exploited the lack of clear accountability by selling subprime mortgages that were overly complicated and unsuited to borrowers' particular financial situations. Banks and thrifts eventually followed suit, with disastrous results for consumers and the financial system at large.

In 2009, Congress, the Administration, and numerous financial regulators took significant measures to address some of the most obvious inadequacies in the consumer protection framework. One notable achievement was the Credit Card Accountability, Responsibility, and Disclosure Act, signed into law by the President on May 22, 2009. This Act outlaws some of the most unfair and deceptive practices in the credit card industry. For example, it requires that payments be applied to the balances with the highest interest rate first; bans retroactive increases in interest rates for reasons having nothing to do with the cardholder's record with the credit card; prohibits a variety of gimmicks with due dates and "double-cycle fees"; and requires clearer disclosure and ensures consumer choice.

However, given the weaknesses that the recent financial crisis highlighted, it is clear that the consumer protection system needs comprehensive reform across all markets. For that reason the Administration has proposed creating a single regulatory agency, a Consumer Financial Protection Agency (CFPA), with the authority and accountability to make sure that consumer protection regulations are written fairly and enforced vigorously. The CFPA should reduce gaps in Federal supervision and enforcement, improve coordination with the states, set higher standards for financial intermediaries, and promote consistent regulation of similar products.

CONCLUSION

Our Nation's system of financial intermediation is a powerful engine for economic growth. Productive investment projects are risky, complex to evaluate and monitor, and require long periods of waiting with no returns and illiquid capital. Investors who provide the funds for these projects would be far less willing to do so if they had to absorb all these risks and costs. Bridging the gap between savings and investment requires the efforts of millions of talented professionals collectively performing the services of information production, liquidity transformation, and diversification. In the recent financial crisis this complex system broke down.

To prevent another such crisis from paralyzing our economy, the Administration has embarked on an ambitious plan to modernize the framework of financial regulation. The keystone of the new framework is an emphasis on macroprudential regulation. The regulatory system's past focus on individual institutions served the Nation well for many decades but is now outdated. A modern system that can meet the needs of the 21st century must have the tools to monitor and regulate the interconnections that cause financial crises.

CHAPTER 7

REFORMING HEALTH CARE

In recent years, rising health care costs in the United States have imposed tremendous economic burdens on families, employers, and governments at every level. The number of people without health insurance has also risen steadily, with recent estimates from the Census Bureau indicating that more than 46 million were uninsured in 2008.

With the severe recession exacerbating these problems, Congress and the President worked together during the past year to enact several health care policies to cushion the impact of the economic downturn on individuals and families. For example, just two weeks after taking office, the President signed into law an expansion of the Children's Health Insurance Program (CHIP), which will extend health insurance to nearly 4 million low- and middle-income uninsured children by 2013. Additionally, legislation that increased funding for COBRA (Consolidated Omnibus Budget Reconciliation Act) health insurance coverage allowed many working Americans who lost their jobs to receive subsidized health insurance for themselves and their families, helping to reduce the number of uninsured below what it otherwise would have been.

In late 2009, both the House and the Senate passed major health reform bills, bringing the United States closer to comprehensive health insurance reform than ever before. The legislation would expand insurance coverage to more than 30 million Americans, improve the quality of care and the security of insurance coverage for individuals with insurance, and reduce the growth rate of costs in both the private and public sectors. These reforms would improve the health and economic well-being of tens of millions of Americans, allow employers to pay higher wages to their employees and to hire more workers, and reduce the burden of rising health care costs on Federal, state, and local governments.

The Current State of the
U.S. Health Care Sector

Although health outcomes in the United States have improved steadily in recent decades, the U.S. health care sector is beset by rising spending, declining rates of health insurance coverage, and inefficiencies in the delivery of care. In the United States, as in most other developed countries, advances in medical care have contributed to increases in life expectancy and reductions in infant mortality. Yet the unrelenting rise in health care costs in both the private and public sectors has placed a steadily increasing burden on American families, businesses, and governments at all levels.

Rising Health Spending in the United States

For the past several decades, health care spending in the United States has consistently risen more rapidly than gross domestic product (GDP). Recent projections suggest that total spending in the U.S. health care sector exceeded $2.5 trillion in 2009, representing 17.6 percent of GDP (Sisko et al. 2009)—approximately twice its share in 1980 and a substantially greater portion of GDP than that of any other member of the Organisation for Economic Co-Operation and Development (OECD). As shown in Figure 7-1, estimates from the Congressional Budget Office (CBO) in June 2009 projected that this trend would continue in the absence of significant health insurance reform. More specifically, CBO estimated that health care spending would account for one-fourth of GDP by 2025 and one-third by 2040 (Congressional Budget Office 2009d).

The steady growth in health care spending has placed an increasingly heavy financial burden on individuals and families, with a steadily growing share of workers' total compensation going to health care costs. According to the most recent data from the U.S. Census Bureau, inflation-adjusted median household income in the United States declined 4.3 percent from 1999 to 2008 (from $52,587 to $50,303), and real weekly median earnings for full-time workers increased just 1.8 percent. During that same period, the real average total cost of employer-sponsored health insurance for a family policy rose by more than 69 percent (Kaiser Family Foundation and Health Research and Educational Trust 2009).

Because firms choose to compensate workers with either wages or benefits such as employer-sponsored health insurance, increasing health care costs tend to "crowd out" increases in wages. Therefore, these rapid

Figure 7-1
National Health Expenditures as a Share of GDP

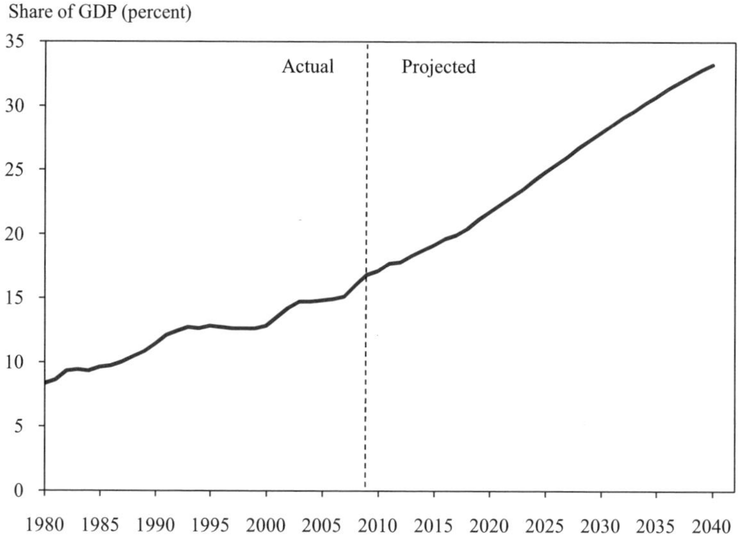

Share of GDP (percent)

Source: Congressional Budget Office (2009d).

increases in employer-sponsored health insurance premiums have resulted in much lower wage growth for workers.

When considering these divergent trends, it is also important to remember that workers typically pay a significant share of their health insurance premiums out of earnings. According to data from the Kaiser Family Foundation, the average employee share for an employer-sponsored family policy was 27 percent in both 1999 and 2008. In real dollars, the average total family premium increased by $5,200 during this nine-year period. Thus, the amount paid by the typical worker with employer-sponsored health insurance increased by more than $1,400 from 1999 to 2008. Subtracting these average employee contributions from median household income in each year gives a rough measure of "post-premium" median household income. By that measure, the decline in household income swells from 4.3 percent to 7.3 percent (that is, post-premium income fell from $50,566 to $46,879).

This point is further reinforced when one considers the implications of rapidly rising health care costs for the wage growth of workers in the years ahead. As Figure 7-2 shows, compensation net of health insurance premiums is projected to grow much less rapidly than total compensation, with the growth eventually turning negative by 2037.[1] Put simply, if health care costs continue to increase at the rate that they have in recent years, workers' take-home wages are likely to grow slowly and eventually decline.

Figure 7-2
Total Compensation Including and Excluding Health Insurance

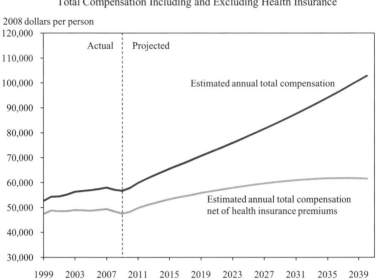

Note: Health insurance premiums include the employee- and employer-paid portions.
Sources: Actual data from Department of Labor (Bureau of Labor Statistics); Kaiser Family Foundation and Health Research and Educational Trust (2009); Department of Health and Human Services (Agency for Healthcare Research and Quality, Center for Financing, Access, and Cost Trends), 2008 Medical Expenditure Panel Survey-Insurance Component. Projections based on CEA calculations.

Rising health care spending has placed similar burdens on the 45 million aged and disabled beneficiaries of the Medicare program, whose inflation-adjusted premiums for Medicare Part B coverage—which covers outpatient costs including physician fees—rose 64 percent (from $1,411 to $2,314 per couple per year) between 1999 and 2008. During that same period, average inflation-adjusted Social Security benefits for retired workers grew less than 10 percent. Rising health insurance premiums are thus consuming larger shares of workers' total compensation and Medicare recipients' Social Security benefits alike.

---

[1] The upper curve of Figure 7-2 displays historical annual compensation per worker in the nonfarm business sector in constant 2008 dollars from 1999 through 2009, deflated with the CPI-U-RS. Real compensation per worker is projected using the Administration's forecast from 2009 through 2020 and at a 1.8 percent annual rate in the subsequent years. The lower curve plots historical real annual compensation per person net of average total premiums for employer-sponsored health insurance during the same period. The assumed growth rate of employer-sponsored premiums is 5 percent, which is slightly lower than the average annual rate as reported by the Kaiser Family Foundation during the 1999 to 2009 period.

The corrosive effects of rising health insurance premiums have not been limited to businesses and individuals. Increases in outlays for programs such as Medicare and Medicaid and rising expenditures for uncompensated care caused by increasing numbers of uninsured Americans have also strained the budgets of Federal, state, and local governments. The fraction of Federal spending devoted to health care rose from 11.1 percent in 1980 to 25.2 percent in 2008. In the absence of reform, this trend is projected to continue, resulting in lower spending on other programs, higher taxes, or increases in the Federal deficit.

The upward trend in health care spending has also posed problems for state governments, with spending on the means-tested Medicaid program now the second largest category of outlays in their budgets, just behind elementary and secondary education. Because virtually all state governments must balance their budgets each year, the rapid increases in Medicaid spending have forced lawmakers to decide whether to cut spending in areas such as public safety and education or to increase taxes.

If health care costs continue rising, the consequences for government budgets at the local, state, and Federal level could be dire. And as discussed in Chapter 5, projected increases in the costs of the Medicare and Medicaid programs are a key source of the Federal Government's long-term fiscal challenges.

Market Failures in the Current U.S. Health Care System: Theoretical Background

As described by Nobel Laureate Kenneth Arrow in a seminal 1963 paper, an individual's choice to purchase health insurance is rooted in the economics of risk and uncertainty. Over their lifetimes, people face substantial risks from events that are largely beyond their control. When possible, those who are risk-averse prefer to hedge against these risks by purchasing insurance (Arrow 1963).

Health care is no exception. When people become sick, they face potentially debilitating medical bills and often must stop working and forgo earnings. Moreover, medical expenses are not equally distributed: annual medical costs for most people are relatively small, but some people face ruinously large costs. Although total health care costs for the median respondent in the 2007 Medical Expenditure Panel Survey were less than $1,100, costs for those at the 90th percentile of the distribution were almost 14 times higher (Department of Health and Human Services 2009). As a result, risk-averse people prefer to trade an uncertain stream of expenses for medical care for the certainty of a regular insurance payment, which buys a policy that pays for the high cost of treatment during illness or injury. Economic theory and common sense suggest that purchasing health insurance to hedge the risk associated with the economic costs of poor health makes people better off.

Health insurance markets, however, do not function perfectly. The economics literature documents four primary impediments: adverse selection, moral hazard, the Samaritan's dilemma, and problems arising from incomplete insurance contracts. In a health insurance market characterized by these and other sources of inefficiency, well-designed government policy has the potential to reduce costs, improve efficiency, and benefit patients by stabilizing risk pools for insurance coverage and providing needed coverage to those who otherwise could not afford it.

Adverse Selection. In the case of adverse selection, buyers and sellers have asymmetric information about the characteristics of market participants. People with larger health risks want to buy more generous insurance, while those with smaller health risks want lower premiums for coverage. Insurers cannot perfectly determine whether a potential purchaser is a large or small health risk.

To understand how adverse selection can harm insurance markets, suppose that a group of individuals is given a choice to buy health insurance or pay for medical costs out-of-pocket. The insurance rates for the group will depend on the average cost of health care for those who elect to purchase insurance. The healthiest members of the group may decide that the insurance is too expensive, given their expected costs. If they choose not to get insurance, the average cost of care for those who purchase insurance will increase. As premiums increase, more and more healthy individuals may choose to leave the insurance market, further increasing average health care costs for those who purchase insurance. Over time, this winnowing process can lead to declining insurance rates and even an unraveling of health insurance markets. Without changes to the structure of insurance markets, the markets can break down, and fewer people can receive insurance than would be optimal. Subsidies to encourage individuals to purchase health insurance can help combat adverse selection, as can regulations requiring that individuals purchase insurance, because both ensure that healthier people enter the risk pool along with their less healthy counterparts.

Under current institutional arrangements, adverse selection is likely to be an especially large problem for small businesses and for people purchasing insurance in the individual market. In large firms, where employees are generally hired for reasons unrelated to their health, high- and low-risk employees are automatically pooled together, reducing the probability of low-risk employees opting out of coverage or high-risk workers facing extremely high premiums. In contrast, small employers cannot pool risk across a large group of workers, and thus the average risk of a given small firm's employee pool can be significantly above or below the population average. As such, similar to the market for individual insurance described above, firms with low-risk worker pools will tend to opt out of insurance coverage, leaving firms with high-risk pools to pay much higher premiums.

Moral Hazard. A second problem with health insurance is moral hazard: the tendency for some people to use more health care because they are insulated from its price. When individuals purchase insurance, they no longer pay the full cost of their medical care. As a result, insurance may induce some people to consume health care on which they place much less value than the actual cost of this care or discourage patients and their doctors from choosing the most efficient treatment. This extra consumption could increase average medical costs and, ultimately, insurance premiums. The presence of moral hazard suggests that research into which treatments deliver the greatest health benefits could encourage doctors and patients to adopt best practices.

Samaritan's Dilemma. A third source of inefficiency in the insurance market is that society's desire to treat all patients, even those who do not have insurance and cannot pay for their care, gives rise to the Samaritan's dilemma. Because governments and their citizens naturally wish to provide care for those who need it, people who lack insurance and cannot pay for medical care can still receive some care when they fall ill. Some people may even choose not to purchase insurance because they understand that emergency care may still be available to them. In the context of adverse selection, a low insurance rate is a *symptom* of underlying inefficiencies. Viewed through the lens of the Samaritan's dilemma, in contrast, the millions of uninsured Americans are one *source* of health care inefficiencies.

The burden of paying for some of this uncompensated care is passed on to people who do purchase insurance. The result is a "hidden tax" on health insurance premiums, which in turn exacerbates adverse selection by raising premiums for individuals who do not opt out of coverage. One estimate suggests that the total amount of uncompensated care for the uninsured was approximately $56 billion in 2008 (Hadley et al. 2008).

Incomplete Insurance Contracts. Many economic transactions involve a single, straightforward interaction between a buyer and a seller. In many purchases of goods, for example, the prospective buyer can look the good over carefully, decide whether or not to purchase it, and never interact with the seller again. Health insurance, in contrast, involves a complex relationship between an insurance company and a patient that can last years or even decades. It is not possible to foresee and spell out in detail every contingency that may arise and what is and is not covered.

When individuals are healthy, their medical costs are typically lower than their premiums, and these patients are profitable for insurance companies. When patients become ill, however, they may no longer be profitable. Insurance companies therefore have a financial incentive to find ways to deny care or drop coverage when individuals become sick, undermining the central purpose of insurance. For example, in most states, insurance companies can rescind coverage if individuals fail to list any medical conditions—even those they know nothing about—on their initial health status questionnaire. Entire families can lose vital health insurance coverage in this manner. A House committee investigation found that three large insurers rescinded nearly 20,000 policies over a five-year period, saving these companies $300 million that would otherwise have been paid out as claims (Waxman and Barton 2009).

A closely related problem is that insurance companies are reluctant to accept patients who may have high costs in the future. As a result, individuals with preexisting conditions find obtaining health insurance extremely expensive, regardless of whether the conditions are costly today. This is a major problem in the individual market for health insurance. Forty-four states now permit insurance companies to deny coverage, charge inflated premiums, or refuse to cover whole categories of illnesses because of preexisting medical conditions. A recent survey found that 36 percent of non-elderly adults attempting to purchase insurance in the individual market in the previous three years faced higher premiums or denial of coverage because of preexisting conditions (Doty et al. 2009). In another survey, 1 in 10 people with cancer said they could not obtain health coverage, and 6 percent said they lost their coverage because of being diagnosed with the disease (USA Today, Kaiser Family Foundation, and Harvard School of Public Health 2006). And the problem affects not only people with serious medical conditions, but also young and healthy people with relatively minor conditions such as allergies or asthma.

System-Wide Evidence of Inefficient Spending

While an extensive literature in economic theory makes the case for market failure in the provision of health insurance, a substantial body of evidence documents the pervasiveness of inefficient allocation of spending and resources throughout the health care system. Evidence that health care spending may be inefficient comes from analyses of the relationship between health care spending and health outcomes, both across states in our own Nation and across countries around the world.

Within the United States, research suggests that the substantially higher rates of health care utilization in some geographic areas are not associated with better health outcomes, even after accounting for differences in medical care prices, patient demographics, and regional rates of illness (Wennberg, Fisher, and Skinner 2002). Evidence from Medicare reveals that spending per enrollee varies widely across regions, without being clearly linked to differences in either medical needs or outcomes. One comparison of composite quality scores for medical centers and average spending per Medicare beneficiary found that facilities in states with low average costs are as likely or even more likely to provide recommended care for some common health problems than are similar facilities in states with high costs (Congressional Budget Office 2008). One study suggests that nearly 30 percent of Medicare's costs could be saved if Medicare per capita spending in all regions were equal to that in the lowest-cost areas (Wennberg, Fisher, and Skinner 2002).

Variations in spending tend to be more dramatic in cases where medical experts are uncertain about the best kind of treatment to administer. For instance, in the absence of medical consensus over the best use of imaging and diagnostic testing for heart attacks, use rates vary widely geographically, leading to corresponding variation in health spending. Research that helps medical providers understand and use the most effective treatment can help reduce this uncertainty, lower costs, and improve health outcomes.

Overuse of "supply-sensitive services," such as specialist care, diagnostic tests, and admissions to intensive care facilities among patients with chronic illnesses, as well as differences in social norms among local physicians, seems to drive up per capita spending in high-cost areas (Congressional Budget Office 2008). Moral hazard may help to explain some of the overuse of services that do not improve people's health status.

Health care spending also differs as a share of GDP across countries, without corresponding systematic differences in outcomes. For example, according to the United Nations, the estimated U.S. infant mortality rate of 6.3 per 1,000 infants for the 2005 to 2010 period is projected to be substantially higher than that in any other Group of Seven (G-7) country, as is the mortality rate among children under the age of five, as shown in Figure 7-3 (United Nations 2007). This variation is especially striking when one considers that the United States has the highest GDP per capita of any G-7 country. Although drawing direct conclusions from cross-country comparisons is difficult because of underlying health differences, this comparison further suggests that the United States could lower health care spending without sacrificing quality. Similarly, life expectancy is much lower in the United States than in other advanced economies. The OECD estimated life expectancy at birth in 2006 to be 78.1 years in the United States compared with an average of 80.7 in other G-7 countries (Organisation for Economic Co-operation and Development 2009).

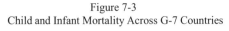

Figure 7-3
Child and Infant Mortality Across G-7 Countries

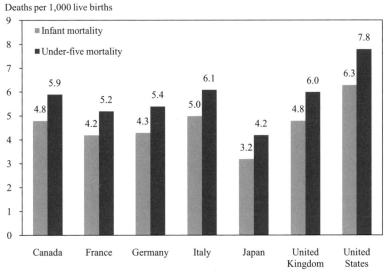

Source: United Nations (2007).

Recent research suggests that differences in health care systems account for at least part of these cross-country differences in life expectancy. For example, one study (Nolte and McKee 2008) analyzed mortality from causes that could be prevented by effective health care, which the authors term "amenable mortality." They found that the amenable mortality rate among men in the United States in 1997–98 was 8 percent higher than the average rate in 18 other industrialized countries. The corresponding rate among U.S. women was 17 percent higher than the average among these other 18 countries. Moreover, of all 19 countries considered, the United States had the smallest decline during the subsequent five years, with a decline of just 4 percent compared with an average decline of 16 percent across the remaining 18. The authors further estimated that if the U.S. improvement had been equal to the average improvement for the other countries, the number of preventable deaths in the United States would have been 75,000 lower in 2002. This finding suggests that the U.S. health care system has been improving much less rapidly than the systems in other industrialized countries in recent years.

A further indication that our health care system is in need of reform is that satisfaction with care has, if anything, been declining despite the substantial increases in spending. Not surprisingly, this decline in satisfaction has been concentrated among people without health insurance, whose ranks have swelled considerably during the past decade. For example, from 2000 to 2009, the fraction of uninsured U.S. residents reporting that they were satisfied with their health care fell from 36 to 26 percent. And not only has dissatisfaction with our health care system increased over time, it is also noticeably greater than dissatisfaction with systems in many other developed nations (Commonwealth Fund 2008).

Declining Coverage and Strains on Particular Groups and Sectors

The preceding analysis shows that at an aggregate level, there are major inefficiencies in the current health care system. But, because of the nature of the market failures in health care, the current system works particularly poorly in certain parts of the economy and places disproportionate burdens on certain groups. Moreover, because of rising costs, many of the strains are increasing over time.

Declining Coverage among Non-Elderly Adults. The rapid increase in health insurance premiums in recent years has caused many firms to stop offering health insurance to their workers, forcing employees either to pay higher prices for coverage in the individual market (which is often much less generous than coverage in the group market) or to go without health insurance entirely. According to the Kaiser Family Foundation, between 2000 and 2009, the share of firms offering health insurance to their workers fell from 69 to 60 percent. Furthermore, 8 percent of firms offering coverage in 2009 reported that they were somewhat or very likely to drop coverage in 2010.

Largely because of these falling offer rates, private health insurance coverage declined substantially during this same period. As shown in Figure 7-4, the fraction of non-elderly adults in the United States with private health insurance coverage fell from 75.5 percent in 2000 to 69.5 percent in 2008.

These numbers, however, provide just a snapshot of health insurance coverage in the United States because they measure the fraction of people who are uninsured at a point in time and thus obscure the fact that a large fraction of the population has been uninsured at some point in the past. According to recent research, at least 48 percent of non-elderly Americans were uninsured at some point between 1996 and 2006 (Department of the Treasury 2009).

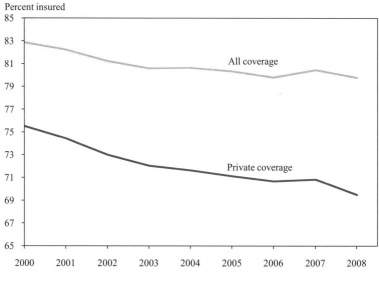

Figure 7-4
Insurance Rates of Non-Elderly Adults

Source: DeNavas-Walt, Proctor, and Smith (2009).

Although roughly half of the 2000–2008 decline in private coverage displayed in Figure 7-4 has been offset by an increase in public health insurance, the share of non-elderly adults without health insurance nevertheless rose from 17.2 to 20.3 percent. In other words, approximately 5.9 million more adults were uninsured in 2008 than would have been had the fraction uninsured remained constant since 2000. The decline in private health insurance coverage was similarly large among children, although it was more than offset by increases in public health insurance (most notably Medicaid and CHIP), so that less than 10 percent of children were uninsured by 2008 (DeNavas-Walt, Proctor, and Smith 2009).

The generosity of private health insurance coverage has also been declining in recent years. For example, from 2006 to 2009, the fraction of covered workers enrolled in an employer-sponsored plan with a deductible of $1,000 or greater for single coverage more than doubled, from 10 to 22 percent. The increase in deductibles was also striking among covered workers with family coverage. For example, during this same three-year period, the fraction of enrollees in preferred provider organizations with a deductible of $2,000 or more increased from 8 to 17 percent. Similar increases in cost-sharing were apparent for visits with primary care physicians. The fraction of covered workers with a copayment of $25 or more for an office visit with a primary care physician increased from 12 to 31 percent from 2004 to 2009. These rising costs in the private market fall disproportionately on the near-elderly, who have higher medical costs but are not eligible for Medicare. A recent study found that the average family premium in the individual market in 2009 for those aged 60–64 was 93 percent higher than the average family premium for individuals aged 35–39 (America's Health Insurance Plans 2009).

Low Insurance Coverage among Young Adults and Low-Income Individuals. Figure 7-5 shows the relationship between age and the fraction of people without health insurance in 2008. One striking pattern is the sharp and substantial rise in this fraction as individuals enter adulthood. For example, the share of 20-year-olds without health insurance is more than twice that of 17-year-olds (28 percent compared with 12 percent).

Figure 7-5
Percent of Americans Uninsured by Age

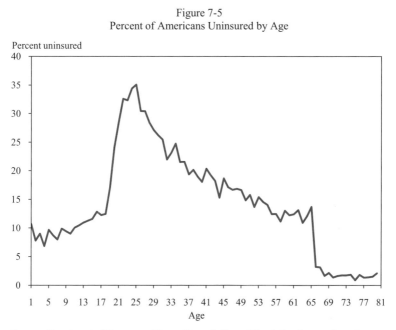

Source: Department of Commerce (Census Bureau), Current Population Survey, Annual Social and Economic Supplement.

Adverse selection is clearly a key source of this change. Many teenagers obtain insurance through their parents' employer-provided family policies, and so are in large pools. Many young adults, in contrast, do not have this coverage and are either jobless or work at jobs that do not offer health insurance; thus, they must either buy insurance on the individual market or go uninsured. As described above, health insurance coverage in the individual market can be very expensive because of adverse selection. Many young adults also have very low incomes, making the cost of coverage prohibitively high for them. Furthermore, because they are, on average, in very good health, young adults may be more tolerant than other groups of the risks associated with being uninsured.

The burden of rising costs also falls differentially on low-income individuals, who find it more difficult each year to afford coverage through employer plans or the individual market. Indeed, as shown in Figure 7-6, low-income individuals are substantially more likely to be uninsured than their higher-income counterparts. As the figure shows, non-elderly individuals below the Federal poverty line ($10,830 a year in income for an individual and $22,050 for a family of four in 2009) were five times as likely to be uninsured as their counterparts above 400 percent of the poverty line in 2008. These low rates of insurance coverage increase insurance premiums for other Americans because of the "hidden tax" that arises from the financing of uncompensated care.

Figure 7-6
Share of Non-Elderly Individuals Uninsured by Poverty Status

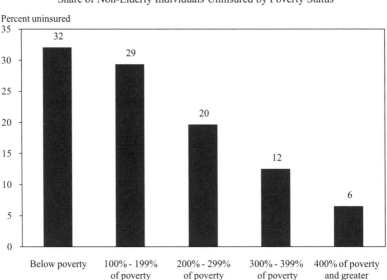

Source: Department of Commerce (Census Bureau), Current Population Survey, Annual Social and Economic Supplement.

The Elderly. Even those over the age of 65 are not protected from high costs, despite almost universal coverage through Medicare. Consider prescription drug expenses, for which the majority of Medicare recipients have coverage through Medicare Part D. As shown in Figure 7-7, after the initial deductible of $310, a standard Part D plan in 2010 covers 75 percent of the cost of drugs only up to $2,830 in annual prescription drug spending. After that, enrollees are responsible for all expenditures on prescriptions up to $6,440 in total drug spending (where out-of-pocket costs would be $4,550), at which point they qualify for catastrophic coverage with a modest copayment. Millions of beneficiaries fall into this coverage gap—termed the "donut hole"—every year, and as a result many may not be able to afford to fill needed prescriptions.

Figure 7-7
Medicare Part D Out-of-Pocket Costs by Total Prescription Drug Spending

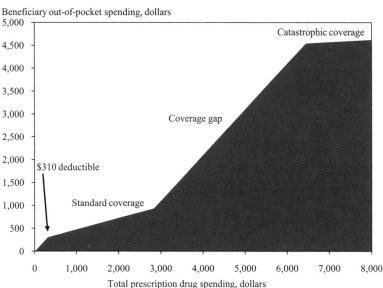

Note: Calculations based on a standard 2010 benefit design.
Source: Medicare Payment Advisory Commission, Part D Payment System, October 2009.

In 2007, one-quarter of Part D enrollees who filled one or more prescriptions but did not receive low-income subsidies had prescription drug expenses that were high enough to reach the coverage gap. For that reason, 3.8 million Medicare recipients reached the initial coverage limit and were required to pay the full cost of additional pharmaceutical treatments received while in the coverage gap, despite having insurance for prescription drug costs. One study found that in 2007, 15 percent of Part D enrollees in the coverage gap using pharmaceuticals in one or more of eight major drug classes stopped taking their medication (Hoadley et al. 2008).

Small Businesses. As described earlier, adverse selection is a serious problem for small businesses, which do not have large numbers of workers to pool risks. This problem manifests itself in two forms. The first is high costs. Because of high broker fees and administrative costs as well as adverse selection, small firms pay up to 18 percent more per worker for the same policy than do large firms (Gabel et al. 2006). The second is low coverage. Employees at small businesses are almost three times as likely as their counterparts at large firms to be uninsured (29 percent versus 11 percent, according to the March 2009 Current Population Survey). And among small businesses that do offer insurance, only 22 percent of covered workers are offered a choice of more than one type of plan (Kaiser Family Foundation and Health Research and Educational Trust 2009).

In recent years, small businesses and their employees have had an especially difficult time managing the rapidly rising cost of health care. Consistent with this, the share of firms with three to nine employees offering health insurance to their workers fell from 57 to 46 percent between 2000 and 2009.

As discussed in a Council of Economic Advisers report issued in July 2009, high insurance costs in the small-group market discourage entrepreneurs from launching their own companies, and the low availability of insurance discourages many people from working at small firms (Council of Economic Advisers 2009c). As a result, the current system discourages entrepreneurship and hurts the competitiveness of existing small businesses. Given the key role of small businesses in job creation and growth, this harms the entire economy.

Taken together, the trends summarized in this section demonstrate that in recent years the rapid rise in health insurance premiums has reduced the take-home pay of American workers and eaten into increases in Medicare recipients' Social Security benefits. Fewer firms are electing to offer health insurance to their workers, and those that do are reducing the generosity of that coverage through increased cost-sharing. Fewer individuals each year can afford to purchase health insurance coverage. The current system places small businesses at a competitive disadvantage. And finally, the steady increases in health care spending strain the budgets of families, businesses, and governments at every level, and demonstrate the need for health insurance reform that slows the growth rate of costs.

HEALTH POLICIES ENACTED IN 2009

Since taking office, the President has signed into law a series of provisions aimed at expanding health insurance coverage, improving the quality of care, and reducing the growth rate of health care spending. The

American Recovery and Reinvestment Act of 2009 provided vital support to those hit hardest by the economic downturn while helping to ensure access to doctors, nurses, and hospitals for Americans who lost jobs and income. At the same time, legislation extended health insurance coverage to millions of children, and improvements in health system quality and efficiency benefited the entire health care system. These necessary first steps have set the stage for a more fundamental reform of the U.S. health care system, one that will ensure access to affordable, high-quality coverage and that genuinely slows the growth rate of health care spending.

Expansion of the CHIP Program

Just two weeks after taking office, the President signed into law the Children's Health Insurance Program Reauthorization Act, which provides funding that expands access to nearly 4 million additional children by 2013. This guarantee of coverage also kept millions of children from losing insurance in the midst of the recession, when many workers lost employer-sponsored coverage for themselves and their dependents. An examination of data from recent surveys by the Centers for Disease Control and Prevention found that private coverage among children fell by 2.5 percentage points from the first six months of 2008 to the first six months of 2009. Despite the fall in private coverage, however, fewer children were uninsured during that six-month period in 2009, in large part because public coverage increased by 3 percentage points (Martinez and Cohen 2008, 2009).

Approximately 7 million children (1 in every 10) were uninsured in 2008 (DeNavas-Walt, Proctor, and Smith 2009). Once fully phased in, the CHIP reauthorization legislation signed by the President will lower that number by as much as half from the 2008 baseline. In the future, this new legislation will enhance the quality of medical care for children and improve their health. Research has convincingly shown that expanding health insurance to children is very cost-effective, because it not only increases access to care but also substantially lowers mortality (Currie and Gruber 1996a, 1996b).

Subsidized COBRA Coverage

In part because of the difficulty of purchasing health insurance on the individual market (owing to adverse selection), most Americans get health insurance through their own or a family member's job. And what is true for dependent children is true for their parents: when economic conditions deteriorate, the number of people with employer-sponsored health insurance tends to fall. However, unlike the case with children, during the current recession public coverage has only offset part of the reduction in private health insurance coverage among adults. Thus, the fraction of adults without health insurance has increased. Figure 7-8 uses survey data from Gallup to show that from the third quarter of 2008 to the first quarter of 2009, the share of U.S. adults without health insurance rose by 1.7 percentage points, from 14.4 to 16.1 percent, representing an estimated increase of 4.0 million uninsured individuals.

Figure 7-8
Share Uninsured among Adults Aged 18 and Over

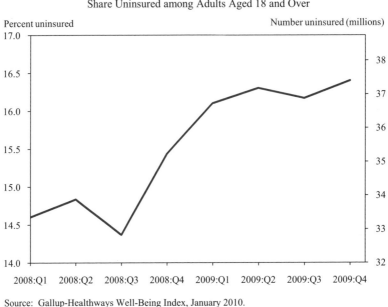

Source: Gallup-Healthways Well-Being Index, January 2010.

When workers at large firms lose their jobs, COBRA provisions give them the right to continue existing coverage for themselves and their families. However, they are often required to pay the full premium cost with no assistance from former employers and without favorable tax treatment of their insurance benefits. Thus, although a large fraction of workers who lose their jobs can still purchase health insurance through COBRA at group rates, many elect not to do so, likely because the coverage is not affordable to a family with a newly laid-off wage earner.

One provision of the American Recovery and Reinvestment Act addressed the recession-induced drop in employer-sponsored health insurance by subsidizing COBRA coverage so that individuals pay only 35 percent of their premium, with the Federal Government covering the remaining 65 percent. This large subsidy may partially explain why the growth in the share of American adults without health insurance slowed dramatically from the first to the fourth quarter of 2009, even while the unemployment rate continued to rise. While the average rate of uninsurance in 2009 was still 1.4 percentage points higher than the average in 2008, the rate was fairly constant throughout 2009. Thus, while the CHIP expansion was providing stable coverage to millions of children who would otherwise have lost it, the COBRA subsidy was further reinforcing access to coverage for working parents and families who faced unemployment.

Temporary Federal Medical Assistance Percentage (FMAP) Increase

Historically, declines in employer-sponsored health insurance have led to increases in the number of people who qualify for public health insurance through programs such as Medicaid, which insured 45.8 million U.S. residents in December 2007. Because almost half of all Medicaid spending is typically financed by state governments, state Medicaid spending tends to rise substantially when economic conditions deteriorate. Coupled with the recession-induced drop in state tax revenues, these increases in Medicaid enrollment place a considerable strain on state budgets. And because virtually every state is required to balance its budget each year, increases in Medicaid enrollment often leave states with little choice but to raise taxes, lay off employees, reduce spending on public safety, education, and other important priorities, or reduce Medicaid benefits, provider payments, or eligibility. These policies are especially problematic when the economy is in severe recession, because they can stifle economic recovery.

Figure 7-9 uses administrative data from all 50 states and the District of Columbia to contrast the growth in Medicaid enrollment in the months leading up to the start of the recession in December 2007 with the corresponding growth during the recession.[2] An examination of the data displayed in the figure reveals that, after growing from 45.2 million in September 2006 to 45.8 million in December 2007, the number of Medicaid recipients increased much more rapidly in the subsequent 21 months, and stood at 51.1 million in September 2009. This represents an increase of 253,000 Medicaid recipients per month during the recession, versus an average increase of just 36,000 per month in the preceding 15 months.

---

[2] Data on state Medicaid enrollment were derived from direct communication between the Council of Economic Advisers and state health departments in 50 states and the District of Columbia. Monthly enrollment from September 2006 through September 2009 was reported by all states with the exception of Vermont in the first 10 months considered. For each month from September 2006 through June 2007 in Vermont, the state's July 2007 Medicaid enrollment was used.

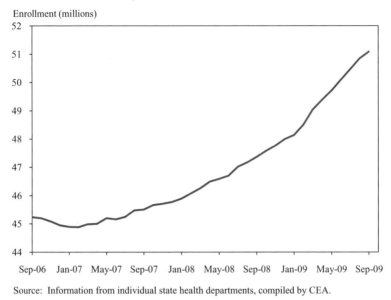

Figure 7-9
Monthly Medicaid Enrollment Across the States

Enrollment (millions)

Source: Information from individual state health departments, compiled by CEA.

To help states pay for an expanding Medicaid program without raising taxes or cutting key services, one important component of the Recovery Act was a temporary increase in each state's Federal Medical Assistance Percentage (FMAP), the share of Medicaid spending paid by the Federal Government. This fiscal relief allowed states to avoid cutbacks to their Medicaid programs or other adjustments that would have exacerbated the effects of the recession. The increased FMAPs were larger for states where unemployment increased the most, because their financial strains were greatest. To qualify for the increased FMAPs, states were required to maintain Medicaid eligibility at pre-recession levels.

A recent report by the Kaiser Family Foundation confirms that support from the Recovery Act—as well as the expansion of coverage for children enacted several weeks earlier in February 2009—was essential to preserving the ability of states to offer health insurance coverage to those most in need. In fact, more than half the states expanded access to health insurance coverage for low-income children, parents, and pregnant women in Medicaid and CHIP in 2009 (Ross and Jarlenski 2009).

Recovery Act Measures to Improve the Quality and Efficiency of Health Care

Beyond supporting jobless workers and their families in the midst of the recession, the Recovery Act addressed structural weaknesses in the health care system by investing in its infrastructure and its workforce. These investments will help to build a health care system with lower costs and better health outcomes for the long term.

For example, the Recovery Act invested $2 billion in health centers for new construction, renovation of existing facilities, and expansion of coverage. An additional $500 million was allocated to bolster the primary care workforce to improve access to primary care in underserved areas. The Act provided a further $1 billion in funding for public health activities to improve prevention and to incentivize wellness initiatives for those with chronic illness; both measures are aimed at improving the quality of care and ultimately bringing down costs. The Act also increased spending on comparative effectiveness research by $1.1 billion, to give doctors and patients access to the most credible and up-to-date information about which treatments are likely to work best.

One final component of the Recovery Act was the Health Information Technology for Economic and Clinical Health Act, which expanded the adoption and use of health information technology through infrastructure formation, information security improvements, and incentives for adoption and meaningful use of certified health information technology. This investment in developing computerized medical records will reduce health care spending and improve quality while securing patients' confidential information.

These investments build a foundation for comprehensive health insurance reform by adding to the ranks of doctors, nurses, and other health care providers, especially in critical fields like primary care, and in areas of the country with the greatest need for a more robust medical workforce. Moreover, the investments in comparative effectiveness research and health information technology will make it much easier for information and quality improvements to spread rapidly between doctors, medical practices, and hospitals across the public and private sectors. When combined with the wide range of delivery system changes included in health insurance reform legislation, these investments are expected to contain costs and improve quality over the long run.

In summary, legislation passed in 2009 helped extend or continue health insurance coverage for the workers, families, and children affected by the current recession. Rather than focusing solely on today's crisis, the legislation lays the groundwork for a reformed health care system that addresses the weaknesses, flaws, and inefficiencies of the status quo.

2009 HEALTH REFORM LEGISLATION

As this *Report* goes to press, Congress has come closer to passing comprehensive health insurance reform than ever before, with major bills having passed both the House and the Senate. As of this writing, whether those bills will lead to enactment of final legislation in the near future is uncertain. Nonetheless, the bills contain important features that would expand coverage, slow the growth rate of costs while improving the quality of care, and benefit individuals, businesses, and governments at every level. This section discusses the major features of the two bills—the House's Affordable Health Care for America Act and the Senate's Patient Protection and Affordable Care Act.

Insurance Market Reforms: Strengthening and Securing Coverage

Both the House and the Senate bills contain important features that would immediately expand coverage and increase access to preventive care. The legislation would also strengthen regulation of the health insurance market, improve consumer protections, and secure coverage for more than 30 million Americans. These regulations would correct insurance market failures by preventing health insurers from responding to adverse selection by raising rates and denying coverage, thus stabilizing risk pools to secure access to affordable coverage.

Both versions of the legislation provide immediate Federal support for a new program to provide coverage to uninsured Americans with preexisting conditions. Combined with strong new consumer protections, these measures would ensure that millions of Americans can immediately purchase coverage at more affordable prices despite their personal medical history or health risks. Health insurance reform also makes immediate investments in community health centers, which would improve access to coverage among the most vulnerable populations. Both the House and Senate versions of reform immediately create reinsurance programs for employer health plans, providing coverage for early retirees to prevent them from becoming uninsured before they are covered by Medicare. Additionally, reform legislation would immediately begin to reform delivery systems for health care and improve transparency and choice for consumers. For example, the Senate proposal would create a website that would help consumers compare coverage options by summarizing important aspects of each insurance contract in a consistent and easy-to-understand format.

New laws would help cover millions of young adults as they transition into the workforce by requiring insurers to allow extended family coverage for dependents through their mid-20s. The CBO and the Joint Committee on Taxation estimate that this requirement would lower average premiums per person in the large-group market by increasing the number of relatively healthy low-cost people in large-group pools (Congressional Budget Office 2009a).

In the years following reform, legislation would put into place strong new consumer protections to prevent denials of coverage or excessive costs for the less healthy. Insurers would be required to renew any policy for which the premium has been paid in full. Insurers could not refuse to renew because someone became sick, nor could they drop or water down insurance coverage for those who are or become ill. To prevent insurers from charging excessively high rates to the less healthy, reform legislation would also enact adjusted community rating rules for premiums.

Banning such treatment of individuals with preexisting conditions would not only allow insurance markets to better help individuals hedge against the risk of health care costs, but may also make the U.S. labor market more efficient. Without such protections, adults with preexisting conditions may be reluctant to change insurance providers and expose themselves to increased premiums. Workers who receive health insurance through their employers may therefore be less willing to change jobs, creating "job lock" that discourages desirable adjustments in the labor market.

In both versions of reform legislation, these provisions are linked with incentives for individuals to obtain coverage and for firms to insure their workers. While preventing insurance companies from discriminating based on preexisting conditions will help some of the neediest members of our society, in isolation these reforms could increase costs for individuals without preexisting conditions, potentially aggravating adverse selection. Without a responsibility to maintain health insurance coverage, individuals could forgo purchasing coverage until they fell ill, and thus not contribute to a shared insurance risk pool until their expected costs rose sharply. However, with restrictions on exclusions for preexisting conditions in place, high-cost individuals who sign up after falling ill could obtain coverage at low premiums. Thus, individuals who had contributed toward coverage would be faced with higher costs, potentially driving even more individuals out of coverage. To prevent a spiral of increasing costs and decreasing insurance rates resulting from adverse selection, both the House and the Senate bills establish a principle of joint individual and employer responsibility to obtain and provide insurance, and would provide subsidies and tax credits that would assist in this process.

The bills would address other features of many health plans that limit their ability to help individuals insure against financial risk. Currently, insurers can put yearly and lifetime limits on coverage. For people with diseases such as cancer, life-saving treatment is often very costly, and exceeding annual and lifetime benefit limits can lead to bankruptcy. This problem is especially severe in the individual and small-group markets, where insurers have more discretion in designing policies. Insurance plans that allow individuals to bankrupt themselves may be socially inefficient because of the Samaritan's dilemma: medical bills that are unpaid when a patient becomes bankrupt impose a hidden tax on other participants in the health care market.

In addition to these insurance market reforms, legislation passed by Congress would require coverage of preventive care and exempt preventive care benefits from deductibles and other cost-sharing requirements in Medicare and private insurance. Evidence suggests that not only are certain preventive care measures cost-effective, but they can also help to prevent diseases that are responsible for roughly half of yearly mortality in the United States (Mokdad et al. 2004). Some measures, such as smoking cessation programs, discussing aspirin use with high-risk adults, and childhood immunizations, may even lower total health care spending (Maciosek et al. 2006). Because many people change insurance companies several times over the course of their lives, insurance companies may underinvest in preventive care that is cost-effective but does not reduce medical costs until far in the future. By encouraging all insurance companies to invest in preventive care, health insurance reform would increase the efficiency of the health care sector.

Finally, reform legislation takes steps to make prescription drug coverage more affordable and secure for senior citizens. The legislation would increase the initial coverage limit under Medicare Part D by $500 in 2010 and also provide 50 percent price discounts for brand-name drugs in the "donut hole" discussed earlier. This discount would allow many Medicare Part D recipients to reduce their out-of-pocket spending on prescription drugs. Not only would fewer beneficiaries have to pay the full cost of their prescription drugs while in the donut hole, but those who do reach this coverage gap would also benefit from increased coverage before reaching that point.

In summary, within the first few years after passage, reform legislation in Congress would guarantee coverage for those with preexisting conditions, reform private insurance markets with strong consumer protections that would stabilize risk pools and mitigate adverse selection, and strengthen public coverage under Medicare.

Expansions in Health Insurance Coverage Through the Exchange

Central to both the House and the Senate bills is the health insurance exchange, which would allow individuals and employees of small businesses to choose among many different insurance plans. The exchange would provide a centralized marketplace to allow individuals, families, and small firms to pool together and purchase coverage much like larger firms do today, improving consumer choice and increasing pressure on insurers to offer lower prices and more generous benefits to attract customers. In its first year of operation, the exchange would be open to qualified individuals and small businesses.

Individuals and small businesses, which might otherwise purchase health insurance in the individual or small-group markets, would benefit from the economies of scale and greater buying leverage in the exchange, which could result in much lower premiums. The exchange would also provide transparent information on plan quality, out-of-pocket costs, covered benefits, and premiums for each offered plan, enabling individuals to select the plan that best fits their and their family's needs. The availability of easy-to-compare premium information would provide a powerful incentive for health insurers to price competitively, thus making coverage more affordable for participants in the exchange.

The new exchange would be especially beneficial for small business employees, who, as described earlier, face particularly severe challenges in the health insurance market. The bills would enable small businesses that meet certain criteria to purchase insurance through the exchange, allowing them and their workers to buy better coverage at lower costs. Moreover, many small businesses that provide health insurance for their employees would receive a tax credit to alleviate their disproportionately higher costs and to encourage coverage. The tax credit would lower the cost of coverage by as much as 50 percent. Reform would make it easier for small businesses to recruit talented workers and would also increase workers' incentives to start their own small businesses. A recent analysis of the Senate bill by the CBO found that premiums for a given amount of coverage for the same set of people or small businesses would fall in the individual and small-group markets as a result of reductions in administrative costs and increased competition in a centralized marketplace (Congressional Budget Office 2009a).

Most individuals who select a plan in the exchange would be eligible for subsidies that reduce the cost of their coverage. In both the House and

Senate bills, subsidies would be available to certain individuals and families with incomes below 400 percent of the Federal poverty line. The premium and out-of-pocket spending subsidies for plans purchased in the exchange would be larger for lower-income families, many of whom cannot afford the cost of a private plan. In addition, individuals with incomes below about 133 to 150 percent of the poverty line would be eligible for health insurance through the Medicaid program.

In the exchange, Federal subsidies would be tied to premiums for relatively lower-cost "reference" plans. Beneficiaries would, however, be able to buy more extensive coverage at an additional, unsubsidized cost.

Economic and Health Benefits of Expanding Health Insurance Coverage

CBO analyses of both the House and Senate bills indicate that, in part because of the creation of the exchanges and the expansion in Medicaid, more than 30 million Americans who would otherwise be uninsured would obtain coverage as a result of reform. These coverage expansions would improve not only the health and the economic well-being of affected individuals and families, but also the broader economy.

A comprehensive body of literature demonstrates that being uninsured leads to poorer medical treatment, worse health status, and higher mortality rates. Across a range of acute conditions and chronic diseases, uninsured Americans have worse outcomes, higher rates of preventable death, and lower-quality care. Additionally, being uninsured imposes on families a significant financial risk of bankruptcy caused by medical expenses.

Evidence from the state of Massachusetts—which expanded health insurance to all but 2.6 percent of its population in a 2006 reform effort—finds that expanding coverage increased regular medical care and lowered financial burdens for residents who gained coverage. Only 17.4 percent of adults with family incomes of less than 300 percent of the Federal poverty line reported forgoing care because of costs in 2008, compared with 27.3 percent in the pre-reform baseline in 2006 (Long and Masi 2009).

Taken together, this evidence strongly suggests that expanding coverage for Americans through health insurance reform would directly benefit millions of families by giving them access to the care they need to maintain their health without substantial financial burdens and risks. Moreover, because of the fixed costs of developing health care infrastructure such as trauma centers, increasing the share of people with health insurance can improve health outcomes for people with insurance as well.

Beyond the improvements for individuals and families, coverage expansions would produce benefits that extend throughout the entire economy. A CEA report in June 2009 estimated that economic gains from reduced financial risk for the uninsured totaled $40 billion per year (Council of Economic Advisers 2009a). Moreover, the CEA report found an economic value of more than $180 billion per year from averting preventable deaths caused by a lack of insurance. Taken together, these gains would far exceed the cost of extending coverage to the currently uninsured population.

The economic benefits of expanding coverage would extend to labor markets in the form of reduced absenteeism and greater productivity. According to the 2009 March Current Population Survey, 18.7 million non-elderly adults report having one or more disabilities that prevent or limit the work they can perform; of that total, 3.1 million lack health insurance. Approximately 50 percent of non-elderly adults who work report having at least one serious medical condition. Previous research has documented the indirect costs to employers of health-related productivity losses. Some of the costliest conditions—depression, migraines, and asthma—can often be effectively managed with prescription medications made more affordable by health insurance. This suggests that expanding access to coverage would improve productivity and labor supply by creating a healthier workforce that would lose fewer hours to preventable illnesses or disabilities.

Reducing the Growth Rate of Health Care Costs in the Public and Private Sectors

The House and Senate bills contain a number of provisions that would reduce the growth rate of health care spending in both the public and private sectors. Both bills create pilot programs in Medicare to bundle provider payments for an episode of care rather than for individual procedures. Under bundled payments, Medicare would provide a single reimbursement for an entire episode of care rather than multiple reimbursements for individual treatments. This payment strategy would give providers, organized around a hospital or group of physicians, a stronger incentive to coordinate and provide quality care efficiently rather than carry out low-value or unnecessary treatments and procedures. Recent research in the *New England Journal of Medicine* suggests that bundled payments could improve quality and substantially reduce health care spending (Hussey et al. 2009). The Department of Health and Human Services would be given authority to expand or extend successful pilot programs without additional legislative action.

Both bills also include measures that directly reduce waste in the current health care system. One example of such waste is the substantial overpayment to Medicare Advantage plans, which are currently paid an average of 14 percent more per recipient than traditional Medicare. The reform bills would reduce these overpayments, saving more than $100 billion between 2010 and 2019 (Congressional Budget Office 2009b). Reducing the overpayments would also lower Medicare recipients' Part B premiums below what they otherwise would be and would extend the solvency of the Medicare Trust Fund.

Another component of the legislation that has the potential to slow the growth rate of health care spending is the Independent Payment Advisory Board included in the Senate bill. This board would have the authority to propose changes to the Medicare program both to improve the quality of care and to reduce the growth rate of program spending. Absent Congressional action, these recommendations would be automatically implemented.

Using the the CEA analysis of the House and Senate bills along with projections from CBO about the level of Federal spending on Medicare, Medicaid, and CHIP, it is possible to estimate the effect of reform on the growth rate of Federal health care spending. Recent CEA analyses of the House and Senate bills find that reform would lower total Federal spending on Medicare, Medicaid, and CHIP by 2019 below what it otherwise would have been (Council of Economic Advisers 2009b). Moreover, between 2016 and 2019, both bills would lower the annual growth rate of Federal spending on these programs by approximately 1.0 percentage point. State and local governments would also benefit financially from health insurance reform, as described in Box 7-1.

Box 7-1: The Impact of Health Reform on State and Local Governments

Although slowing the growth in health care costs will help the long-run fiscal situation of the Federal Government, some observers worry about how reform will affect state and local governments. To help ensure that virtually all Americans receive health insurance, both the Senate and the House bills call for expanding Medicaid eligibility. Because Medicaid is partly funded by states, some state officials fear that the state fiscal situation will deteriorate as a consequence of reform.

As documented by a CEA report published in September (Council of Economic Advisers 2009d), however, health insurance reform would

Continued on next page

improve the fiscal health of state and local governments in at least three important ways. First, state and local governments are already spending billions of dollars each year providing coverage to the uninsured; these costs would fall significantly as a consequence of health reform. Second, encouraging all individuals to become insured would reduce the hidden tax paid by providers of health insurance. Because state and local governments employ more than 19 million people, the total savings from removing the hidden tax is likely to be substantial. Third, an excise tax on high-cost plans would boost workers' wages by billions of dollars each year and thus increase state income tax revenues.

To understand the net consequences of reform for the fiscal health of state and local governments, the CEA studied the impact of reform for 16 states that are diverse along many important dimensions: geographic, economic, and demographic. For every state studied, health reform would result in substantial savings for state and local governments.

In addition to these public savings, the reform proposals would reduce the growth of health care costs in the private sector. One important mechanism through which reform could reduce these costs is the excise tax on high-cost insurance plans included in the Senate bill. Under current tax law, employer compensation in the form of wages is subject to the income tax, while compensation in the form of employer-provided health care benefits is not. Individuals may therefore have an incentive to obtain more generous health insurance than they would if wages and health insurance faced more equal tax treatment. Absent other incentives for individuals to obtain insurance, the preferential tax treatment of health insurance may be beneficial, because it encourages firms to provide health insurance to their workers and facilitates pooling. Nonetheless, placing no limit on this subsidy likely leads to health insurance that is more generous than would be efficient in some cases.

To help contain the growth in the cost of these plans without jeopardizing the risk-pooling benefits, the Senate bill would impose a tax on only the most expensive employer-sponsored plans. Although only a small share of plans would be affected, CEA estimates based on data from the CBO suggest that the excise tax on high-cost insurance plans would reduce the growth rate of annual health care costs in the private sector by 0.5 percentage point per year from 2012 to 2018. The excise tax would encourage workers and their firms' human resources departments to be more watchful consumers and would give insurers a powerful incentive to price competitively. And to the extent that bundling, accountable care organizations, and other delivery system reforms in both the House and Senate bills would spill over to the private sector, it is likely that the rate of growth of health care spending in the private sector would fall by considerably more than 0.5 percentage point per year. Lower increases in private health insurance premiums would lead to substantially higher take-home earnings for workers.

Reform would also reduce private spending on health care in other important ways. As noted, encouraging all individuals to obtain health insurance would likely reduce average costs for people who are insured. Reducing the hidden tax on health insurance premiums imposed by uncompensated care for the uninsured, for example, would reduce the financial burden not only on state and local governments, but also on individuals. CBO estimates of the Senate legislation find that reform has the power to reduce small-group premiums by up to 2 percent and even large-group premiums by up to 3 percent. And according to research by the Business Roundtable, reforms similar to those included in both the House and Senate bills could reduce employer-sponsored health insurance costs for family coverage by as much as $3,000 per worker by 2019 relative to what those costs otherwise would have been.

The Economic Benefits of Slowing the Growth Rate of Health Care Costs

Reform as envisioned in both the House and Senate bills passed in late 2009 would substantially lower the growth rate of health care spending. Of course, spending would increase in the very short run as coverage was extended to more than 30 million Americans who would otherwise be uninsured. But, according to the CBO, these temporary increases would soon be more than offset by the slowdown in the growth rate of spending, with the net savings increasing over time (Congressional Budget Office 2009b, 2009c).

A report released by the CEA in June 2009 demonstrated that slowing the growth rate of health care costs would raise U.S. standards of living by freeing up resources that could be used to produce other goods and services. An examination of the cost reduction measures contained in the Senate bill suggests that the typical family would see its income increase by thousands of dollars per year by 2030. Total GDP would be substantially higher as well, driven upward by both increased efficiency and increased national saving.

Slowing the growth rate of health care costs would also lower the Federal budget deficit. Projections by the CBO of both the House and the Senate legislation suggest that the bills would lower the deficit substantially in the upcoming decade, and even more in the next decade. These savings would obviate large tax increases or cuts in other important priority areas. As discussed in Chapter 5, it would be the single most important step toward addressing the Nation's long-run fiscal challenges.

Finally, reform that genuinely slows the growth of health care costs could increase employment for a period of time by lowering the unemployment rate that is consistent with steady inflation. These effects could be important, with CEA estimates suggesting an increase of more than 300,000 jobs for a period of time if health care costs grew by 1 percentage point less each year.

CONCLUSION

In recent years, health care costs in the Nation's private and public sectors have been rising at an unsustainable rate, and the fraction of Americans who are uninsured has steadily increased. These trends have imposed tremendous burdens on individuals, employers, and governments at every level, and the problems have grown yet more severe during the past two years with the onset of the worst recession since the Great Depression.

Last year, the President signed into law several policies that have cushioned the worst of the economic downturn, including an expansion in the Children's Health Insurance Program and an extension of COBRA coverage for displaced workers and their families. Other policies, such as increased funding for health information technology, will improve the long-run efficiency and quality of the health care sector.

Legislation passed by both the House and the Senate in late 2009 would expand health insurance coverage to tens of millions of Americans while slowing the growth rate of health care costs. These reforms would improve the health and the economic well-being of individuals and families, help small businesses, stimulate job creation, and ease strains on Federal, state, and local governments imposed by rapidly rising health care costs.

$$\curlyvee$$

C H A P T E R   8

STRENGTHENING THE AMERICAN LABOR FORCE

The recession has been extremely difficult for American workers and families. One in ten workers is now unemployed, wages and hours worked have fallen, and many families are struggling to make ends meet. Making matters worse, the recession followed a sustained period of rising inequality and stagnation in the living standards of typical American workers. A central challenge in coming years will be to smooth the transition to a sustainable growth path with more widely shared prosperity.

As we begin to recover from the recession, we will see a new and much-changed labor market. Some industries that grew unsustainably large in recent years, such as construction and finance, will recover but will not immediately return to past employment levels. The same may be true for traditional manufacturing, which has been shrinking as a share of the economy for decades. The pace of employment decline will surely moderate after the recession, but many former workers in traditional manufacturing will need to transition into new, growing sectors.

In the place of the declining industries will come new opportunities for American workers. Health care will remain an important source of growth in the labor market, as will high-technology sectors including clean energy industries and advanced manufacturing. Well-trained and highly skilled workers will be best positioned to secure good jobs in these new and growing sectors. The best way to prepare our workforce for the challenges and opportunities that lie ahead is by strengthening our education system, creating a seamless, efficient path for every American from childhood to entry into the labor market as a skilled worker ready to meet the needs of the new labor market.

Both individuals and the economy as a whole benefit from increased educational attainment and improved school quality. A focus on access, equity, and quality for all American students, from early childhood through high school and into postsecondary education and training throughout workers' careers, will help ensure that the benefits of economic growth are widely shared.

CHALLENGES FACING AMERICAN WORKERS

The last few years have been a challenging time for American workers, with the high unemployment of the current recession compounding longer-run trends toward increased insecurity and inequality.

Unemployment

As of December 2009, the unemployment rate was 10.0 percent, a rate that has been exceeded only once since the Great Depression. As high as it is, however, this rate understates just how weak the labor market is. Many Americans who would like to work have given up hope of finding a job and have dropped out of the labor force; others who would like full-time jobs have settled for part-time work. Figure 8-1 shows both the conventional unemployment rate and a broader measure of labor underutilization that includes not just unemployed workers but also those who would like jobs

Figure 8-1
Unemployment and Underemployment Rates

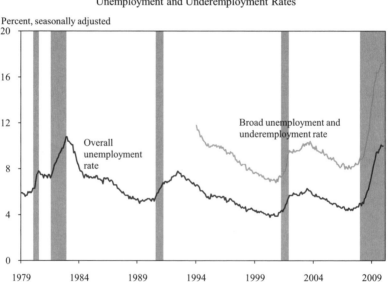

Notes: Grey shading indicates recessions. The overall unemployment rate represents the share of the labor force that is unemployed (those actively looking for work). The broad unemployment rate is a variant of the overall unemployment rate that adds marginally attached workers (those not actively looking for a job, but want one and have looked for one recently) as well as workers employed part-time for economic reasons to the numerator (the "unemployed"), and adds marginally attached workers to the denominator (the "labor force").
Source: Department of Labor (Bureau of Labor Statistics), Employment Situation Table A-12, Series U-3 and U-6.

but have given up looking for work and those who are employed part-time for economic reasons. This measure indicates that more than one in six potential workers are unemployed or underemployed. Another measure of labor market conditions that accounts for those who have given up looking for work is the employment-to-population ratio. In December, fewer than six in ten adults were employed, the lowest ratio since 1983. A final useful labor market indicator is the number of long-term unemployed—those without jobs for 27 weeks or more. More than one-third of unemployed Americans have been seeking work for more than 26 weeks, the highest share since the series began in 1948.

The employment situation is even worse for members of racial and ethnic minorities. Figure 8-2 shows the unemployment rate for whites, blacks, Hispanics, and Asians. While the unemployment rate for whites topped out at 9.4 percent in October 2009 and has declined slightly since then, the rate for blacks exceeds 16 percent and has continued to rise, while that for Hispanics is nearly 13 percent. The disproportionate impact of the current recession on blacks and Hispanics mirrors that seen in past business cycles. It is critical that all Americans be able to participate fully and equally in our economic recovery.

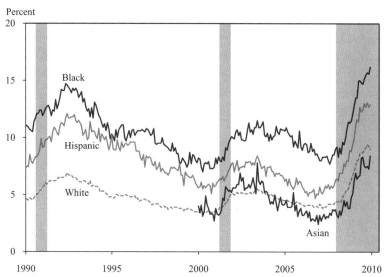

Figure 8-2
Unemployment Rates by Race

Notes: Grey shading indicates recessions. Hispanics may be of any race. Respondents with multiple races are excluded from the white, black, and Asian categories. Series for whites, blacks, and Hispanics are seasonally adjusted. Asian series is not seasonally adjusted and is not available before 2000.
Source: Department of Labor (Bureau of Labor Statistics), Employment Situation Table A-2.

Even a quick return to job growth will not immediately eliminate employment problems, as it will take time to create the millions of new jobs needed to return to normal employment levels. Many workers will have difficulty finding work for some time to come. Extended periods of high unemployment and low job creation rates mean that many displaced workers will exhaust their unemployment insurance benefits before jobs become available in large numbers. After months or even years of unemployment, most who exhaust their benefits will likely have used up whatever savings they had when they lost their jobs. Many will be forced to turn to public assistance—Temporary Assistance for Needy Families, Supplemental Nutritional Assistance (formerly known as food stamps), or other similar programs—to make ends meet.

Sustained periods of low labor demand also have negative repercussions for the long-run health of the economy. Mounting evidence indicates that displacement during bad economic times leads to long-run reductions in workers' productivity (Jacobson, LaLonde, and Sullivan 1993), likely because the displaced workers lose job skills, fall out of habits needed for successful employment, and have trouble convincing employers that they will be good employees. The resulting loss of "human capital" reduces workers' earning power, even after the economy recovers.

Deep downturns have particularly large effects on young Americans. The unemployment rate for teenagers in December was 27.1 percent. Research shows that teens who first enter the labor market during a recession can have trouble getting their feet onto the first rung of the career ladder, leaving them a step or more behind throughout their lives (Kahn forthcoming; Oreopoulos, von Wachter, and Heisz 2006; Oyer 2006). There is also evidence that when parents lose their jobs, their children's long-run economic opportunities suffer (Oreopoulos, Page, and Stevens 2008).

Sectoral Change

The Great Recession has aggravated an already challenging trend: sectoral shifts that are changing the nature of work. While most American workers were once engaged in producing food and manufactured goods, often through physical labor that did not require a great deal of training, the United States is increasingly a knowledge-based society where workers produce services using analytical skills. The changing economy offers tremendous opportunities for American workers in high technology, in the new clean energy economy, in health care, and in other high-skill fields.

Accompanying these shifts in the composition of employment have been changes in the institutions that govern the labor market. The prototypical American career once involved working for a single employer for many years, backed by a union that bargained for steady wage increases and for a pension that promised a stable, guaranteed income in retirement. The labor market has changed. Fewer than one in seven workers belongs to a union, and most people can count on changing employers several times over their careers. Moreover, the vast majority of retirement plans are now "defined contribution," meaning that workers' retirement incomes depend on the success of their individual investment decisions and on the performance of asset markets as a whole. This shift has meant added risk for workers, particularly those whose planned retirements coincide with downturns in asset prices.

Stagnating Incomes for Middle-Class Families

A final major challenge facing American workers is the decades-long stagnation in living standards for typical families and the related increase in inequality. Figure 8-3 offers two looks at income trends over the past half century. First, it shows real median family income—the level at which half of families have higher income and half have lower income—over time. The median rose steadily until 1970, but then the rate of growth slowed substantially, and since 2000, the median has actually fallen.

One determinant of family income is the number of individuals working outside of the home. Female labor force participation has risen dramatically: in 1960, just over 40 percent of adult women (aged 18–54) participated in the labor force; by 2000, approximately three-quarters did. This increase in female labor force participation contributed to the rise in family incomes. However, the female labor force participation rate has been roughly stable since 2000, and there are not likely to be future increases in participation as dramatic as those seen in the past. Further increases in family incomes will likely rely on growth in individual earnings.

The other two series in Figure 8-3 show the median earnings for men and women working full-time, year-round jobs. Real median female year-round earnings have grown steadily by about 1.1 percent per year on average since 1960, reflecting in part the gradual leveling of labor market barriers to women's career advancement. But real male earnings have been essentially flat since the early 1970s. One source of the stagnation of median male earnings and the reduced growth rate of median female earnings is that productivity growth slowed betwen 1973 and 1995 (Chapter 10). But this is not a complete explanation. Even at a reduced growth rate, American workers' productivity has more than doubled in the last 40 years.

A partial explanation for the divergence between productivity and earnings is the rapid rise in health care costs in recent years: an ever-greater share of the compensation paid by employers has gone toward health

Figure 8-3
Real Median Family Income and Median Individual Earnings

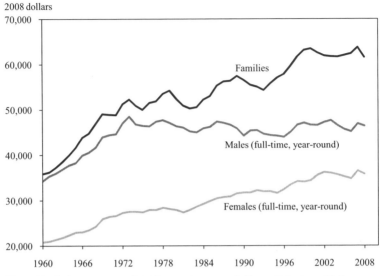

Notes: Family income measure is total money income excluding capital gains and before
taxes. Median earnings series are for full-time, year-round workers; prior to 1989, only
civilian workers are included. All series are deflated using CPI-U-RS.
Sources: Department of Commerce (Census Bureau), Income, Poverty, and Health Insurance
Coverage in the United States Table A-2; Current Population Survey, Annual Social and
Economic Supplement, Historical Income Table F-12.

insurance premiums, which have risen much faster than inflation. This
makes health reform an urgent priority. As discussed in Chapter 7, the
proposals under consideration in Congress will slow the growth in health
care costs, allowing American workers to realize more of the benefits of their
hard work through increased take-home pay.

A second explanation is that per capita earnings are distributed in
an increasingly unequal way, with ever-smaller shares going to workers in
the middle and bottom of the distribution (Kopczuk, Saez, and Song forthcoming). Earnings inequality is compounded by inequality in nonlabor
income, including dividends, interest, and capital gains. Figure 8-4 shows
that in recent years nearly half of all income—including both wages and
salaries and nonlabor income—has gone to 10 percent of families. The top
1 percent of families now receive nearly 25 percent of income, up from
less than 10 percent in the 1970s (Piketty and Saez 2003). Today's income
concentration is of a form not seen since the 1920s. Although there is
nothing inherently wrong with high incomes at the top of the distribution,
they are problematic if they come at the expense of the rest of workers.
A major challenge for American public policy is to ensure that prosperity is
again broadly shared.

Figure 8-4
Share of Pre-Tax Income Going to the Top 10 Percent of Families

Percent of total pre-tax income

Note: Includes capital gains.
Sources: Piketty and Saez (2003); recent data from http://elsa.berkeley.edu/~saez/TabFig2007.xls.

POLICIES TO SUPPORT WORKERS

The Administration's first priority upon taking office was to strengthen the economy and the labor market, helping to provide jobs for those who need them. According to Council of Economic Advisers estimates, the American Recovery and Reinvestment Act of 2009 had created or saved between 1.5 million and 2 million jobs as of the fourth quarter of 2009 (Council of Economic Advisers 2010).

At the same time, the Administration has worked to strengthen the safety net for those who remain unemployed. The Recovery Act provided unprecedented support for the jobless, with increased benefits for every unemployment insurance recipient, the longest extension of unemployment benefits in history, an expansion of the Supplemental Nutrition Assistance Program, and assistance with health insurance premiums for those who have lost their jobs. These provisions have directly helped millions of out-of-work Americans pay for housing, put food on the table, and maintain access to medical care. Moreover, because the unemployed are likely to spend any benefits they receive, these provisions have supported increased economic activity, strengthening the labor market and helping to create the job openings that will be needed to move people back into work. The safety net provisions in the Recovery Act are scheduled to expire at the end of

February 2010, but because of the ongoing weakness in the labor market, the Administration is working with Congress to extend them further.

The Recovery Act also included provisions to reform the unemployment insurance system, making it work more effectively in today's economy. These provisions extend unemployment insurance eligibility to many low-wage and part-time workers who were not previously eligible. These and other recent initiatives will also make it possible for many unemployed workers to draw out-of-work benefits while participating in training that prepares them to enter new fields.

Even after the labor market recovers, the dynamic American economy will continue to pose challenges—while also creating opportunities—for workers. Rapid technological change will cause shifts in the labor market, forcing some workers into unanticipated mid-life career changes. Policy can help to ease these transitions. Most important, it can ensure that workers who may switch careers several times during their lifetimes are able to maintain health insurance and to support themselves in retirement. As discussed in Chapter 7, comprehensive health care reform will eliminate preexisting conditions restrictions in health insurance and improve access to insurance in the individual market. These changes will make it much easier for people to maintain insurance when they change jobs or pursue entrepreneurial opportunities.

Declines in stock prices and home values have put serious pressure on many Americans' retirement plans and have highlighted the importance of improved retirement security. The Administration has proposed several measures to increase saving by low- and middle-income workers. Efforts include expanded access to retirement plans along with rule changes to streamline enrollment in 401(k) and IRA programs, facilitate simple saving strategies, and reorient program default options to emphasize saving. And, most important, the Administration is committed to protecting Social Security, thus ensuring that it can provide a reliable source of income for future retirees, as it has for their parents and grandparents.

Health and retirement security need to be accompanied by labor market institutions that support and protect workers. Labor unions have long been a force helping to raise standards of living for middle-class families. They remain important, and we need to reinforce the principle that workers who wish to join a union should have the right to do so.

Another set of institutions in need of attention is our immigration system. The current framework absorbs considerable resources but does not serve anyone—native workers, employers, taxpayers, or potential immigrants—well. Particular problems are posed by the presence of large numbers of unauthorized immigrants and the lengthy queues—some over 20 years—for legal residency.

Reform of the immigration system can strengthen our economy and labor market. Reform should provide a path for those who are currently here illegally to come out of the shadows. It should include strengthened border controls and better enforcement of laws against employing undocumented workers, along with programs to help immigrants and their children quickly integrate into their communities and American society. Future immigration policy should be more responsive to our economy's changing needs. Reform of the employment-based visa and permanent residency programs will also help reduce the incentives to immigrate illegally by giving potential immigrants a more viable legal path into the United States.

EDUCATION AND TRAINING: THE GROUNDWORK FOR LONG-TERM PROSPERITY

Rebuilding our economy on a more sustainable basis, investing in future productivity, fostering technological and other forms of innovation, and reforming our health care system to deliver better outcomes at lower costs are all crucial to long-run increases in living standards, and all are discussed elsewhere in this report. But one fundamental component of a strategy to ensure balanced, sustained, and widely shared growth is a robust system of education and training. The positive link between education and worker productivity—the cornerstone of economic prosperity—is well established. In fact, research has credited education with up to one-third of the productivity growth in the United States from the 1950s to the 1990s (Jones 2002).

Benefits of Education

At the individual level, there is a strong relationship between educational attainment and earnings (Card 1999). The earnings premium shows up at all levels of education. Those who complete one year of post-secondary education earn more than those who stop after high school, while those who complete two years or finish degrees earn more still. And job training for the unemployed has been shown by rigorous studies to raise participants' future earnings (Manpower Demonstration Research Corporation 1983; Jacobson, LaLonde, and Sullivan 2005).

The earnings premium associated with education is far larger than the cost—in tuition and forgone earnings—of remaining in school (Barrow and Rouse 2005), and it has grown in recent decades. Figure 8-5 shows the trends in the average annual earnings of individuals with high school diplomas but no college and of those with bachelor's degrees. In the mid-1960s, college graduates earned roughly 50 percent more than high school graduates, on average; by 2008, the premium had more than doubled.

Figure 8-5
Total Wage and Salary Income by Educational Group

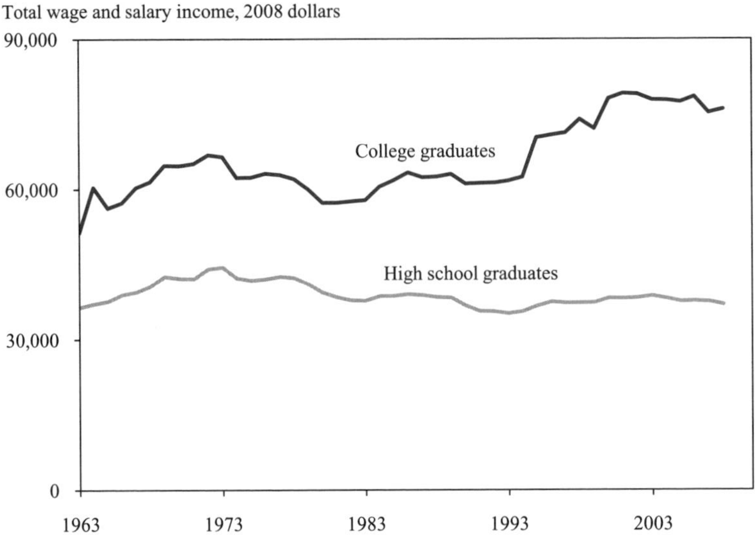

Total wage and salary income, 2008 dollars

Notes: Figures for full-time workers aged 25-65 who worked 50-52 weeks in the calendar
year. Before 1991, education groups are defined based on the highest grade of school or year
of college completed. Beginning in 1991, groups are defined based on the highest degree or
diploma earned. Incomes are deflated using the CPI-U.
Source: Department of Labor (Bureau of Labor Statistics), March Current Population Survey,
1964-2009.

Education has other important benefits besides increased earnings.
For example, recent studies have found that education improves people's
health (Cutler and Lleras-Muney 2006; Grossman 2005). The explanation
may be that better educated people make better health-related decisions,
such as exercising or not smoking, or that education allows for easier navi-
gation of a complex health care system. Education's benefits also extend
beyond the individual. More educated people commit fewer crimes, vote
more, and are more likely to support free speech (Dee 2004; Lochner
and Moretti 2004). They also make their neighbors and coworkers more
productive (Moretti 2004).

Trends in U.S. Educational Attainment

The United States has historically had the world's best education
system. Although most European countries once limited advanced education to the economic elite, the United States has historically made it broadly
available. U.S secondary schools have been free and generally accessible since early in the 20th century. By the 1950s, nearly 80 percent of
older teens (aged 15–19) in the United States were enrolled in secondary
school, compared with fewer than 40 percent in Western Europe. The

widespread expansion of state colleges and universities, begun under the Morrill Land Grant Act of 1862, led to even further advances in American education. Average educational attainment of people born in 1975 was over five years higher than that of those born in 1895. About 50 percent of the gain was attributable to increases in high school education, about 30 percent to increases in college and postcollege education, and the remainder to continued increases in elementary education (Goldin and Katz 2008). During the second half of the 20th century, as educational attainment rose worldwide, the United States became a clear leader in graduate education, attracting the brightest students from around the world. Some remained in the United States, adding importantly to the Nation's human capital stock and its diversity, while others returned to their home countries and used the education they got here to help increase prosperity there.

Harvard economists Claudia Goldin and Lawrence Katz contend that America's strong educational system helped make the United States the richest nation in the world (Goldin and Katz 2008). Over the past several decades, however, U.S. leadership in education has slipped. Although the Nation remains preeminent in postgraduate education, we can no longer claim to be home to the most educated people in the world.

For decades, the number of educated American workers grew faster than did the demand for them. But beginning with the cohort that completed its schooling in the early 1970s, the growth rate in the supply of educated Americans slowed significantly. This can be seen in Figure 8-6, which shows the mean years of schooling of Americans by year of birth. High school and college graduation rates, which grew steadily for many decades, began to stagnate, and younger generations no longer graduate at significantly higher rates than did previous generations. This slowdown in the growth of educational attainment has contributed to rising income inequality, as the shortage of college-educated workers has meant rising wages for high-skill work and falling wages for work requiring less education. The current recession may provide an opportunity to reverse this slowdown but only if our education system can keep up with increased demand (Box 8-1).

Meanwhile, other developed countries have continued to improve their educational outcomes, and the United States has slipped behind several other advanced countries at both the high school and postsecondary levels. Among the cohort born between 1943 and 1952—a group that largely completed its education by the late 1970s—the United States leads the world in the share with at least a bachelor's degree or the equivalent. In more recent cohorts, the percentage completing college has been roughly stable in the United States while increasing substantially in several peer countries. Figure 8-7 shows that only 40 percent of Americans born between 1973 and

Figure 8-6
Mean Years of Schooling by Birth Cohort

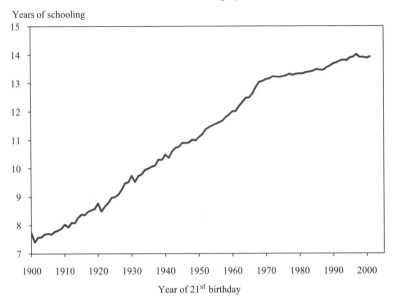

Notes: Years of schooling at 30 years of age. Methodology described in Goldin and Katz (2007). Graph shows estimates of the average years of schooling at 30 years of age for each birth cohort, obtained from regressions of the log of mean years of schooling by birth cohort-year cell on a full set of birth cohort dummies and a quartic in age. Sample includes all native-born residents aged 25 to 64 in the 1940-2000 decennial census IPUMS samples and the 2005 CPS MORG. For further details on the method and data processing, see Goldin and Katz (2008, Figure 1.4) and DeLong, Goldin, and Katz (2003, Figure 2.1).
Sources: Department of Commerce (Bureau of the Census), 1940-2000 Census IPUMS, 2005 CPS MORG; Goldin and Katz (2007).

Box 8-1: The Recession's Impact on the Education System

Today's weak labor market is likely to lead to short- and medium-run increases in school enrollments, as high unemployment pushes many young people to increase their job skills through further education. Indeed, college enrollments rose substantially in 2008 relative to 2007, and preliminary reports suggest further increases in 2009. The resulting increase in educational attainment will offer long-run benefits for the economy, because today's students will be more productive workers when labor demand returns to full strength.

In the short run, however, elevated enrollments are placing strains on colleges, particularly the two-year colleges that are seeing most of the enrollment increase, as colleges' costs are rising at the same time state

Continued on next page

x

Continued on next page

funding is being cut. Elementary and secondary schools are under similar strains. In part because of reduced state funding, schools employed roughly 70,000 fewer teachers and teachers' assistants in October 2009 than a year earlier, even though student enrollments were up. The reduction in per-pupil resources at both levels is an unfortunate budgetary response. At this time of high unemployment, it is desirable to encourage human capital formation, not make it more difficult. The State Fiscal Stabilization Fund, part of the Recovery Act, is helping in this regard, and recipients credit the Act with creating or saving at least 325,000 education jobs through the third quarter of 2009.

Figure 8-7
Educational Attainment by Birth Cohort, 2007

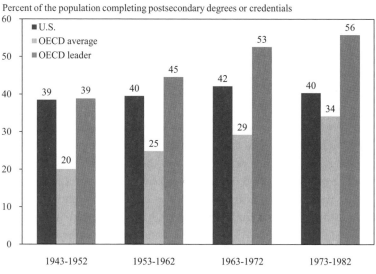

Percent of the population completing postsecondary degrees or credentials

Notes: Postsecondary degrees or credentials include only those of normal duration of two years or more and correspond to the Organisation for Economic Co-operation and Development (OECD) tertiary (types A and B) and advanced research qualifications. U.S. data reflect associate's, bachelor's, and more advanced degrees.
Sources: Organisation for Economic Co-operation and Development (2009); OECD Indicators Table A1.3a.

1982 have completed associate's degrees or better. Equivalent attainment rates are higher in nine other countries, led by Canada and Korea, where 56 percent completed some postsecondary degree or extended certificate program. High school graduation rates show a similar pattern, with the United States slipping from the top rank to the middle in recent decades.

U.S. Student Achievement

U.S. student achievement, as measured by assessments that capture how much students know at particular ages or grades, has improved notably in recent years, even as attainment has stagnated. The most reliable barometer is the National Assessment of Education Progress (NAEP), which has been administered consistently for more than three decades. Figure 8-8 shows average NAEP math scores for students at three different ages from 1978 through 2008. The performance of 9-year-olds (who are typically enrolled in 4th grade) and 13-year-olds (typically 8th grade) has improved over the past 35 years. The size of the achievement gains is impressive. Nearly three-quarters of 13-year-olds in 2008 scored above the 1978 median, with similar gains throughout the distribution. The performance of 17-year-olds (typically 12th graders) has also improved, although the gain was smaller.

Despite recent progress, American students are not doing as well as they should. In addition to average performance, the NAEP program measures the fraction of students who attain target achievement levels defined based on the skills that children at each age and grade should have mastered. A student is judged "proficient" if he or she demonstrates age- or grade-appropriate competency over challenging subject matter and shows an ability to apply knowledge to real-world situations. In the most recent tests, only 31 percent of 8th graders were proficient in reading and only 34 percent in math. Proficiency rates are similar in 4th grade.

For some subgroups, proficiency rates were much lower. Only 12 percent of black students and 17 percent of Hispanics were proficient in math in 8th grade. The low achievement in these subgroups is also reflected in low attainment. In 2000, only 81 percent of black young adults (aged 30–34) had graduated from high school, and only 15 percent had bachelor's degrees. Although racial and ethnic gaps have narrowed importantly in recent decades—the black-white and Hispanic-white mathematics gaps at age 13 in the NAEP long-term trend data are each only two-thirds as large as in 1978—the low attainment and achievement of black and Hispanic students remain disturbing evidence of educational inequality in our society. Our future prosperity depends on ensuring that American children from all backgrounds have the opportunity to become productive workers.

Nowhere does low performance more acutely affect the health of the U.S. economy than in the areas of science, technology, engineering, and mathematics (known commonly by the acronym STEM). Employers frequently report that they have difficulty finding Americans with the qualifications needed for technical jobs and are forced to look abroad for suitably skilled workers. Indeed, international comparisons show that other countries achieve higher outcomes in STEM skills than we do. In

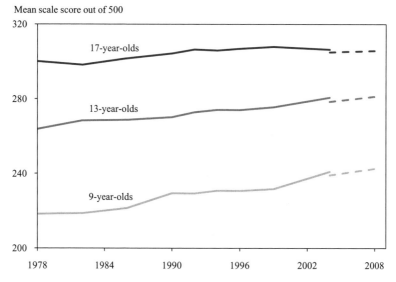

Figure 8-8
Long-Term Trend Math Performance

Mean scale score out of 500

Notes: In 2004 and thereafter, accommodations were made available for students with disabilities and for English language learners, and other changes in test administration conditions were introduced. Dashed lines represent data from tests given under the new conditions.
Source: Department of Education (Institute of Education Sciences, National Center for Education Statistics), National Assessment of Educational Progress (NAEP), Long-Term Trend Mathematics Assessments.

2006, U.S. 15-year-olds scored well below the Organisation for Economic Co-operation and Development (OECD) average for science literacy on the Programme for International Student Assessment, and behind most other OECD nations on critical skills and competencies, such as explaining scientific phenomena and using scientific evidence.

A Path Toward Improved Educational Performance

Concerned about the impact of stagnating educational outcomes on U.S. economic growth, the President has pledged to return our Nation to the path of increasing educational attainment. He has challenged every young American to commit to at least one year of higher education or career training. He also has set ambitious goals: by 2020, America should "once again have the highest proportion of college graduates in the world" (Obama 2009a), and U.S. students should move "from the middle to the top of the pack in science and math" (Obama 2009b). Meeting these challenges will require substantial commitment and reform, not just at the postsecondary level but also in elementary and high schools and even in early childhood programs.

Postsecondary Education

The Nation's postsecondary education system encompasses a diverse group of institutions, including public, nonprofit, and for-profit organizations offering education ranging from short-term skill refresher programs up to doctoral degrees.

In many of our peer countries, postsecondary education is entirely or largely state funded, with little direct cost to the student. U.S. postsecondary students, however, are generally charged tuition and fees, which have risen substantially in real terms over the past three decades. It is important to keep in mind that most of our students do not pay full tuition, as more than 60 percent of full-time students receive grant aid, and millions more also benefit from Federal tax credits and deductions for tuition. But increases in financial aid and Federal assistance have not kept up with rising costs, and the net price of attendance at four-year public colleges has risen nearly 20 percent over the past decade (College Board 2009).

Young people may have trouble financing expensive investments in college education even when these investments will pay off through increased long-term earnings. Thus, rising college costs represent an important barrier to enrollment. One study indicates that a $1,000 reduction in net college costs increases the probability of attending college by 5 percentage points and leads students to complete about one-fifth of a year more college (Dynarski 2003). Thus the dramatic increase in the price of college has likely had an adverse impact on college attendance and completion. Moreover, the impact of cost increases is not evenly distributed: while students from high-income families can relatively easily absorb the increases, students from lower-income families are disproportionately deterred.

The rising cost of college is affecting educational attainment and will continue to do so unless we find ways to make college more affordable. To this end, the Administration has secured historic investments in student aid, including more than $100 billion over the next 10 years for more generous Pell Grants, much of it financed through the elimination of wasteful subsidies to private lenders in the student loan program. This will ensure that virtually all students eligible for Pell Grants will receive larger awards. In addition, the Administration is taking steps to dramatically simplify the student aid application process, the complexity of which deters many aid-eligible students from even applying. This simplification will help millions more students benefit from the Federal investments in college accessibility and affordability.

Tuition is not the only barrier to college completion. A great many students, including nearly half of those at two-year institutions, begin college but fail to graduate. Completion rates are particularly low for low-income students. One way to raise completion rates is through better design of the institutional environment. Recent rigorous studies have shown that improvements such as enhanced student services, changes in how classes are organized, innovations in how remedial education is structured, and basing some portion of financial aid on student performance can all contribute to improved persistence (Scrivener et al. 2008; Scrivener, Sommo, and Collado 2009; Richburg-Hayes et al. 2009).

Training and Adult Education

An often-overlooked component of the Nation's education system, one in which the government makes a major investment, is job training and adult education. In 2009, the Federal Government devoted more than $17 billion to job training and employment services and spent substantial additional funds on Pell Grants for vocational and adult education students. Training is provided by a diverse set of institutions, including proprietary (for-profit) schools, four-year colleges, community-based organizations, and public vocational and technical schools. Box 8-2 discusses a particularly important type of training provider, community colleges.

Studies have documented that training and adult education programs improve participants' labor market outcomes. For example, a recent study found that Workforce Investment Act training programs for adults boosted employment and earnings, on average, although results varied substantially across states (Heinrich, Mueser, and Troske 2008). Evidence is also growing that state training programs for adults can have large positive impacts on long-term earnings (Hotz, Imbens, and Klerman 2006; Dyke et al. 2006).

Education and training for adults play critical roles in helping displaced workers regain employment in the short term and in helping them obtain and refresh their skills in the face of an ever-changing work-place. For example, one study of displaced workers in Washington State suggests that attending a community college after displacement during the 1990s increased long-term earnings about 9 percent for men and about 13 percent for women (Jacobson, LaLonde, and Sullivan 2005). The benefits were greatest for academic courses in math and science, as well as for courses related to the health professions, technical trades (such as air conditioner repair), and technical professions (such as software development).

Although research demonstrates the value of training programs, there is no doubt that the current system could be more effective. Five strategies that could improve effectiveness are: aligning goals across different elements of the education and training system and constructing a cumulative curriculum; collaborating with employers to ensure that curricula are aligned with workforce needs and regional economies; making sure that scheduling is flexible and that curricula meet the needs of older and nontraditional students; providing incentives and flexibility for institutions and programs to continually improve and innovate; and establishing a stronger accountability system that measures the right things, makes performance data available in an easily understood format, and does not create perverse incentives to avoid serving populations that most need assistance. Reauthorization of the Workforce Investment Act will provide an opportunity to implement these strategies.

Box 8-2: Community Colleges: A Crucial Component of Our Higher Education System

Community colleges are an important but often overlooked component of the Nation's postsecondary education system. These colleges may offer academic programs preparing students to transfer to four-year colleges to complete bachelor's degrees, academic and vocational programs leading to terminal associate's degrees or certificates, remedial education for those who want to attend college but who left high school insufficiently prepared, and short-term job training or other educational experiences. Most also offer contract training in which they work directly with the public sector, employers, and other clients (such as prisons) to develop and provide training for specific occupations or purposes.

Community colleges are public institutions that typically charge very low tuition and primarily serve commuters, which makes them accessible to people who do not have the resources for a four-year college. They generally have "open door" admissions policies, requiring only a high school diploma or an ability to benefit from the educational experience. This makes them a good choice for older and nontraditional students, as well as for potential students who want to pursue additional education and build their human capital but want or need to do so at relatively low cost.

More than 35 percent of first-time college freshmen enroll at community colleges. These colleges also serve about 35 percent of individuals receiving job training through the Workforce Investment Act, along with a notable proportion of adults attending adult basic education, English as a second language, and General Educational Development

Continued on next page

Box 8-2, continued

(GED) preparation classes. Researchers have estimated that attending a community college significantly raises earnings, even for individuals who do not complete degrees (Kane and Rouse 1999; Marcotte et al. 2005).

Community colleges will form the linchpin of efforts to increase college attendance and graduation rates. The Administration has proposed a new program of competitive grants for implementing college completion initiatives, with a focus on community colleges. Along with the sorts of strategies mentioned above for training programs more generally, community college initiatives could include building better partnerships between colleges, businesses, the workforce investment system, and other workforce partners to create career pathways for workers; expanding course offerings including those built on partnerships between colleges and high schools; and stronger accountability for results. These strategies will help both to strengthen colleges and to raise completion rates. The proposed program also recognizes the need to learn from such investment and therefore supports record levels of funding for research to evaluate the initiatives' effectiveness.

Elementary and Secondary Education

Students who leave high school with inadequate academic preparation face greater challenges to success in postsecondary training. In 2001, nearly one-third of first-year college students in the United States needed to take remedial classes in reading, writing, or mathematics, at an estimated cost of more than $1 billion (Bettinger and Long 2007). The need for remediation is a clear warning sign that a student may later drop out. In one study, students who needed the most remediation were only about half as likely to complete college as their peers who were better prepared (Adelman 1998). Of course, students who leave high school well prepared are more successful in the labor market as well as in college.

The task of improving college and labor market preparedness begins in elementary and secondary school, if not earlier. Among the most important contributors to enhanced student outcomes is effective teaching. Common sense and research both recognize the importance of high-quality teachers, and yet too few teachers reach that standard. Improvements are needed in teacher training, recruitment, evaluation, and in-service professional development.

Not only is the supply of high-quality teachers insufficient but their distribution across schools is inequitable. Frequently, schools with high concentrations of minority and low-income students, the very schools that need quality teachers the most, cannot recruit and retain skilled educators. In New York State, 21 percent of black students had teachers who failed their general knowledge certification exam on the first attempt, compared with 7 percent of white students (Lankford, Loeb, and Wyckoff 2002). A particular problem is high teacher turnover: high-poverty and high-minority schools have much higher turnover than do schools with more advantaged students. Some districts have begun experimenting with financial incentives for teaching in high-need schools; these efforts need to be rigorously evaluated and, if they are found to be successful, disseminated widely.

Improving teacher quality, however, is not the only promising strategy for change. Others include extending both the school day and the school year. Many successful strategies have emerged from schools that were given freedom to explore new and creative approaches to long-standing problems. Although traditional public schools can be agents for change, the public charter school model is tailor-made for such innovation. The Nation's experience with charter schools has been fairly brief, but evidence to date suggests that some of these schools have found successful strategies for raising student achievement. An important future challenge will be to take these strategies and other innovative school models to scale, even as schools continue to search for ever-better approaches.

Although most reforms in recent years have focused on elementary schools, high school reform is now rising to the top of the education policy agenda. Promising approaches to improving secondary education include programs that offer opportunities for accelerated instruction and individualized learning, programs to expand access to early college coursework before finishing high school, residential schools for disadvantaged students, and specialty career-focused academies.

An environment that supports innovation must be coupled with strong accountability. Some innovations are bound to be unsuccessful, and indeed there is substantial variation in the quality of both public and charter schools. Strong accountability systems that promote effective instructional approaches can provide incentives for all school stakeholders to perform at their best and help to identify struggling schools in need of intervention. Systems are needed to identify failing schools, based on high-quality student assessments as well as other metrics. At the same time, accountability strategies must be carefully crafted to discourage "teaching to the test" and other approaches that aim at the measures used for evaluating schools rather than at true student learning. Accountability strategies must also recognize that student achievement reflects family, community, and peer influences as well as that of the school.

Providing incentives for schools identified as failing to improve can significantly improve student outcomes. Several states have done just that. Sixteen years ago, Massachusetts began setting curriculum frameworks and holding schools accountable for student performance. Massachusetts students have historically scored above the national average on various academic achievement measures, but since passing school accountability reform, Massachusetts has moved even farther ahead. In Florida, too, a strong school accountability plan, implemented in 1999, has shown positive results (Figlio and Rouse 2006; Rouse et al. 2007).

The Recovery Act included an unprecedented Federal investment in elementary and secondary education. The Race to the Top Fund provides competitive grants to reward and encourage states that have taken strong measures to improve teacher quality, develop meaningful incentives, incorporate data into decisionmaking, and raise student achievement in low-achieving schools. The upcoming reauthorization of the Elementary and Secondary Education Act provides an opportunity to make further progress.

Early Childhood Education

High-quality elementary and secondary schools are necessary, but they are not enough. In recent years, researchers and educators have learned a great deal about how important the school readiness of entering kindergarteners is to later academic and labor market success. School readiness involves both academic skills, as measured by vocabulary size, complexity of spoken language, and basic counting, and social and emotional skills such as the ability to follow directions and self-regulate. Children who arrive at school without these skills lack the foundation on which later learning will build.

Recent research indicates that as many as 45 percent of entering kindergarteners are ill-prepared to succeed in school (Hair et al. 2006). Reducing the share of at-risk preschoolers is critical to strengthening America's educational system and its labor market in the long run. High-quality early childhood interventions can significantly improve school readiness, especially for low-income children. Intensive programs that combine high-quality preschool with home visits and parenting support have been shown to raise children's later test scores and educational attainment and also to reduce teen pregnancy rates and criminality (Karoly et al. 1998; Schweinhart et al. 1985).

The programs on which the most compelling research is based include small classes, highly educated teachers with training in early childhood education, and stimulating curricula. They feature parent training components that help parents reinforce what the teachers do in the classroom. The programs also assist teachers in identifying health and behavior problems that can inhibit children's intellectual and emotional development. Importantly, even intensive, expensive programs are cost-effective. For example, one particularly intensive program was found to produce $2.50 in long-run savings for taxpayers for every dollar spent, because in adulthood the participating children earned higher incomes, used fewer educational and government resources, and had lower health care costs (Barnett and Masse 2007).

Less intensive programs can be effective as well. The Head Start program provides an academically enriching preschool environment for 3- and 4-year-olds, at a cost in 2008 of only about $7,000 per child per year. Although the quality of Head Start centers varies widely, studies have found that attendance at a well-run center improves children's later-life outcomes (Currie and Thomas 1995).

Ensuring that all families have access to the services and support they need to help prepare their children for kindergarten will require a strong system of high-quality preschools and other early-learning centers. Providers must be held to high standards and given the resources—including qualified staff and teachers—needed for success. And when children leave their preschool and prekindergarten programs, they must have access to quality kindergartens that ease the transition to elementary school.

Conclusion

The recession has taken a severe toll on American workers and many will continue to suffer from its effects for some time to come. A strong safety net will be essential to helping working families through this trying time. As the economy strengthens, we must rebuild our labor market institutions in ways that ensure that prosperity and economic security are more widely shared.

Going forward, workers who have strong analytic and interactive skills will be best able to secure good jobs and to contribute to continued U.S. prosperity. Education must begin in preschool, because children's long-run success depends on arriving in kindergarten ready to learn, and be available throughout adulthood, because our increasingly dynamic economy requires lifelong learning. The Administration's education agenda will strengthen our education and training institutions at all levels.

C H A P T E R   9

TRANSFORMING THE ENERGY SECTOR AND ADDRESSING CLIMATE CHANGE

The President has called climate change "one of the defining challenges of our time." If steps are not taken to reduce atmospheric concentrations of carbon dioxide (CO_2) and other greenhouse gases, scientists project that the world could face a significant increase in the global average surface temperature. Projections indicate that CO_2 concentrations may double from pre-industrial levels as early as 2050, and that the higher concentrations are associated with a likely long-run temperature increase of 2 to 4.5 °C (3.6 to 8.1 °F). With temperatures at that level, climate change will lead to a range of negative impacts, including increased mortality rates, reduced agricultural yields in many parts of the world, and rising sea levels that could inundate low-lying coastal areas.

The planet has not experienced such rapid warming on a global scale in many thousands of years, and never as a result of emissions from human activity. By far the largest contribution to this warming comes from carbon-intensive fossil fuels, which the world depends on for cooking, heating and cooling homes and offices, transportation, generating electricity, and manufacturing products such as cement and steel.

The potential for significant damages if emissions from these activities are not curbed makes it crucial for the world to transform the energy sector. This transformation will entail developing entirely new industries and making major changes in the way energy is produced, distributed, and used. New technologies will be developed and new jobs created. The United States can play a leadership role in these efforts and become a world leader in clean energy technologies. The transformation to a clean energy economy will also reduce our Nation's dependence on oil and improve national security, and could reduce other pollutants in addition to greenhouse gases.

As this transformation unfolds, two market failures provide a motivation for government policy. First, greenhouse gas emissions are a classic example of a negative externality. As emitters of greenhouse gases contribute to climate change, they impose costs on others that are not taken into account when making decisions about how to produce and consume energy-intensive goods. Second, the development of new technologies has positive externalities. As discussed in Chapter 10, the developers of new technologies generally capture much less than the full benefit of their ideas to consumers, firms, and future innovators, and thus underinvest in research and development.

This diagnosis of the market failures underlying climate change provides clear guidance about the role of policy in the area. First, policy should take steps to ensure that the market provides the correct signals to greenhouse gas emitters about the full cost of their emissions. Second, policy should actively promote the development of new technologies. One way to accomplish these goals is through a market-based approach to reducing greenhouse gases combined with government incentives to promote research and development of new clean energy technologies. Once policy has ensured that markets are providing the correct signals and incentives, the operation of market forces can find the most effective and efficient paths to the clean energy economy. The Administration's policies in this area are guided by these principles.

GREENHOUSE GAS EMISSIONS, CLIMATE, AND ECONOMIC WELL-BEING

The world's dependence on carbon-intensive fuels is projected to continue to increase global average temperature as greenhouse gas emissions build in the atmosphere. These emissions are particularly problematic because many are long-lived: for instance, it will take a century for slightly more than half of the carbon dioxide now in the atmosphere to be naturally removed. The atmospheric buildup of greenhouse gases since the start of the industrial revolution has already raised average global temperature by roughly 0.8 °C (1.4 °F). If the concentrations of all greenhouse gases and aerosols resulting from human activity could somehow be kept constant at current levels, the temperature would still go up about another 0.4 °C (0.7 °F) by the end of the century. It is important to note that the overall impact of today's emissions would be even higher were it not for the offsetting net cooling effect of increases in atmospheric aerosols such as particulate matter caused by the incomplete combustion of fossil fuels in coal-fired power plants.

But keeping atmospheric concentrations constant at today's level is virtually impossible. Any additional greenhouse gas emissions contribute to atmospheric concentrations. And because of projected economic growth, particularly in developing countries, greenhouse gas emissions will continue to grow. Moreover, the sources of atmospheric aerosols that have partly offset the greenhouse warming experienced so far are not likely to grow apace because governments around the world are taking actions to curb these emissions to improve public health and control acid rain.

Greenhouse Gases

The principal long-lived greenhouse gases whose concentrations have been affected by human activity are carbon dioxide, methane, nitrous oxide, and halocarbons. Sulfur hexafluoride, though emitted in smaller quantities, is also a very potent greenhouse gas. All have increased significantly from pre-industrial levels. Carbon dioxide is emitted when fossil fuel is burned to heat and cool homes, fuel vehicles, and manufacture products such as cement and steel. Deforestation also releases carbon dioxide stored in trees and soil. The primary sources of methane and nitrous oxide are agricultural practices, natural gas use, and landfills. Halocarbons originate from refrigeration and industrial processes, while sulfur hexafluoride emissions mainly stem from electrical and industrial applications.

The pre-industrial atmospheric concentration of carbon dioxide was about 280 parts per million (ppm), meaning that 280 out of every million molecules of gas in the atmosphere were carbon dioxide. As of December 2009, its concentration had increased to about 387 ppm. Taking into account other long-lived greenhouse gases would result in a higher warming potential, but the net cooling effect of aerosols that have been added by humans to the atmosphere nearly cancels the effect of those other gases. Thus, the overall effect of human activity on the atmosphere to date is (coincidentally) about the same as that of the carbon dioxide increase alone.

A variety of models project that, absent climate policy, atmospheric concentrations of carbon dioxide will continue to grow, reaching levels ranging from 610 to 1030 ppm by 2100 (Figure 9-1). When the warming effects of other long-lived greenhouse gases are included, this range is equivalent to 830 to 1530 ppm. The breadth of the range reflects uncertainty about future energy supply, energy demand, and the future behavior of the carbon cycle.[1]

---

[1] Underlying uncertainty about future energy supply is uncertainty regarding the costs and penetration rates of technology, and resource availability. Uncertainty about future energy demand is driven by uncertainty regarding growth in population, gross domestic product, and energy efficiency.

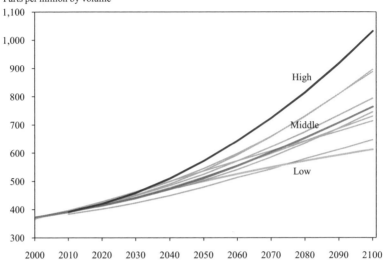

Figure 9-1
Projected Global Carbon Dioxide Concentrations with No Additional Action

Parts per million by volume

Note: The figure shows baseline projections from 10 different models, with the models that produce the highest, middle, and lowest atmospheric concentration of carbon dioxide in 2100 noted.
Source: Stanford Energy Modeling Forum, EMF 22 International Scenarios, 2009.

Temperature Change

The implications of large increases in greenhouse gas concentrations for temperature change are quite serious. There is a consensus among scientists that a doubling of CO_2 concentrations (or any equivalent combination of greenhouse gases) above the pre-industrial level of 280 ppm is likely to increase global average surface temperature by 2 to 4.5 °C (3.6 to 8.1 °F), with a best estimate of about 3 °C (5.4 °F).[2] Given much higher projections of greenhouse gas concentrations by the end of the century, a recent study projects that the global average temperature in 2100 is likely to be 4.2 to 8.1 °C (7.6 to 14.6 °F) above pre-industrial levels, absent effective policies to reduce emissions (Webster et al. 2009).

Increases in global average temperature mask variability by region. For instance, absent effective policy to reduce greenhouse gas emissions, mid-continent temperature increases are likely to be about 30 to 60 percent higher than the global average, while increases in parts of the far North (for instance, parts of Alaska, northern Canada, and Russia) are expected to be double the global average. The power of the strongest hurricanes and

---

[2] These values express what is likely to happen in equilibrium. Average surface temperature does not reach a new equilibrium for some decades after any given increase in the concentration of heat-trapping gases because of the large thermal inertia of the oceans.

typhoons is likely to grow, as are the frequency and intensity of extreme weather events such as heat waves, heavy precipitation, floods, and droughts. One study, for example, estimates that the number of days that mean temperature (calculated as the average of the daily minimum and daily maximum) in the United States will exceed 90 °F will increase from about one day a year between 1968 and 2002 to over 20 days a year by the end of the century (Deschênes and Greenstone 2008).

As the increase in global average temperature warms seawater and expands its volume, sea levels are projected to rise. Melting glaciers also contribute to sea-level rise. Sea level has already risen about 0.6 feet since 1900; it is projected to rise another 0.6 to 1.9 feet because of volume expansion and glacial melt by the end of the century. These estimates exclude possible rapid ice loss from the Greenland and Antarctic ice sheets, events that are highly uncertain but that could cause another 2 feet or more of sea level rise by 2100. Without expensive adaptation, low-lying land in coastal areas around the world could become permanently flooded as a result.

Impact on Economic Well-Being

Although predicting future economic impacts associated with increases in global average temperature involves a large degree of uncertainty, these economic effects are likely to be significant and largely negative, and to vary substantially by region. Even for countries that may be less vulnerable, large negative economic impacts in other regions will inevitably jeopardize their security and well-being. For instance, the temperature extremes and other changes in climate patterns associated with global average temperature increases of 2 °C (3.6 °F) or more are projected to increase mortality rates and reduce agricultural productivity in many regions, threaten the health and sustainability of many ecosystems, and necessitate expensive measures to adapt to these changes. Box 9-1 discusses recent research on projected physical and economic impacts in the United States.

Some regions of the world are expected to be particularly hard-hit. For example, low-lying and island countries are especially vulnerable to sea-level rise. Further, developing countries, especially those outside moderate temperature zones, may be especially poorly equipped to confront temperature changes. Recent research, for example, suggests that India may experience substantial declines in agricultural yields and increases in mortality rates (Guiteras 2009; Burgess et al. 2009).

These projected changes are predicated on likely increases in global mean temperature. Particularly worrisome is the possibility of much greater temperature change, should more extreme projections prove accurate. Although more drastic increases are less likely, their consequences could be devastating. For example, the costs of climate change are expected to grow nonlinearly (that is, more rapidly) as temperatures rise (Box 9-2).

In the United States, continued reliance on petroleum-based fuels poses challenges that go beyond climate change. It makes the economy susceptible to potentially costly spikes in crude oil prices and imposes significant national security costs. A panel of retired senior military officers and national security experts concluded that unabated climate change may act as a "threat multiplier" to foment further instability in some of the world's most unstable regions (CNA Corporation 2007). Fossil fuel consumption is also associated with other forms of pollution that harm human health, such as particulate, sulfur dioxide, and mercury emissions from coal-powered electricity generation.

Box 9-1: Climate Change in the United States and Potential Impacts

The average temperature in the United States has risen more than 1 °C (2 °F) over the past 50 years. However, this increase masks considerable regional variation. For instance, the temperature increase in Alaska has been more than twice the U.S. average. By the end of the century, the United Nations Intergovernmental Panel on Climate Change projects that average continental U.S. temperatures will increase by another 1.5 to 4.5 °C (about 2.7 to 8.1 °F) absent climate policy (Intergovernmental Panel on Climate Change 2007). Greater increases are possible, depending in part on how fast emissions rise over time. Climate change will likely bring substantial changes to water resources, energy supply, transportation, agriculture, ecosystems, and public health. Potential effects on U.S. water availability and agriculture are described below (Karl, Melillo, and Peterson 2009).

Precipitation already has increased an average of 5 percent over the past 50 years, with increases of up to 25 percent in parts of the Northeast and Midwest and decreases of up to 20 percent in parts of the Southeast. In the future, these trends will likely be amplified. The amount of rain falling in the heaviest downpours has increased an average of 20 percent over the past century, a trend that is expected to continue. In addition, Atlantic hurricanes and the strongest cold-season storms in the North are likely to become more powerful. In recent decades, the West has seen more droughts, greater wildfire frequency, and a longer fire season. Increases in temperature and reductions in rainfall frequency will likely exacerbate future droughts and wildfires.

Continued on next page

Box 9-1, continued

Although warmer temperatures may extend the growing season in the United States for many crops, large increases in temperature also may harm growth and yields. One study finds that yields are relatively unaffected by changes in mean temperature, but that they are vulnerable to an increase in the number of very hot days (Schlenker and Roberts 2009). That said, another study finds that expected changes in temperature in the United States will have a relatively small impact on overall agricultural profits (Deschênes and Greenstone 2007). Neither study accounts for the possible increase in yields from elevated carbon dioxide levels or the possible decrease in yields from increased pests, weeds, and disease.

Climate change is also likely to bring increased weather uncertainty. Extreme weather events—droughts and downpours—may have catastrophic effects on crops in some years. Growing crops in warmer climates requires more water, which will be particularly challenging in regions such as the Southeast that will likely face decreased water availability.

American farmers have substantial capacity for innovation and are already taking steps to adapt to climate change. For instance, they are changing planting dates and adopting crop varieties with greater resistance to heat or drought. They can also undertake more elaborate change. In areas projected to become hotter and drier, some farmers have returned to dryland farming (instead of irrigation) to help the soil absorb more moisture from the rain. How well the private sector can adapt to the effects of climate change and at what cost is still an open question.

Box 9-2: Expected Consumption Loss Associated with Temperature Increase

One major uncertainty regarding climate change is the relationship between temperature change and living standards, usually measured as total consumption. The highly respected PAGE model produces an estimate of this relationship (see Box 9-2 figure). Specifically, it reports the expected decline in consumption as a fraction of GDP in the year 2100. The range of these estimates is represented by the dotted lines that represent the 5th and 95th percentile of the damage estimates. The range reflects uncertainty about the sensitivity of the climate system to increased greenhouse gas concentrations, the probability of catastrophic events, and several other factors.

Continued on next page

Box 9-2, continued

The figure reveals that the projected losses for the most likely range of temperature changes are relatively modest. For example, at the Intergovernmental Panel on Climate Change's most likely temperature increase of 3 °C for a doubling of CO_2 concentration (concentrations in 2100 are likely to be higher), the projected decline is 1.5 percent of GDP.

The projected relationship between temperature changes and consumption losses is nonlinear—that is, the projected losses grow more rapidly as temperature increases. For example, while the projected loss for the first 3 °C is 1.5 percent, the loss at 6 °C is five times higher. And the estimated loss associated with an increase of 9 °C is about 20 percent with a 90 percent confidence interval of 8 to 38 percent. These large losses at higher temperatures reflect the increased probability of especially harmful events, such as large-scale changes in ice sheets or vegetation, or releases of methane from thawing permafrost and warming oceans. Overall, it is evident that policy based on the most likely outcomes may not adequately protect society because such estimates fail to reflect the harms at higher temperatures.

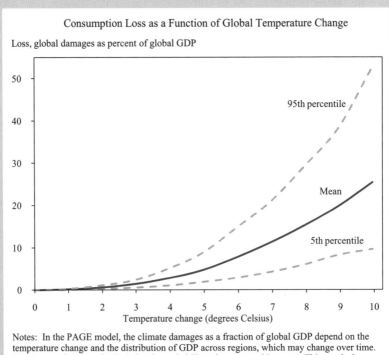

Consumption Loss as a Function of Global Temperature Change

Loss, global damages as percent of global GDP

Notes: In the PAGE model, the climate damages as a fraction of global GDP depend on the temperature change and the distribution of GDP across regions, which may change over time. The damage function also includes the probability of a catastrophic event. This graph shows the distribution of damages as a fraction of GDP in year 2100 using the default scenario from PAGE 2002.
Source: Hope (2006).

Jump-Starting the Transition to Clean Energy

To make the transition to a clean energy economy, the United States and the rest of the world need to reduce their reliance on carbon-intensive fossil fuels. The American Reinvestment and Recovery Act of 2009 provides a jump-start to this transition by providing about $60 billion in direct spending and $30 billion in tax credits (Council of Economic Advisers 2010). These Recovery Act investments were carefully chosen and provide a soup-to-nuts approach across a spectrum of energy-related activities, ranging from taking advantage of existing opportunities to improve energy efficiency to investing in innovative high-technology solutions that are currently little more than ideas. These investments will help create a new generation of jobs, reduce dependence on oil, enhance national security, and protect the world from the dangers of climate change. Ultimately, the investments will put the United States on a path to becoming a global leader in clean energy.

Recovery Act Investments in Clean Energy

A market-based approach to reducing greenhouse gases (discussed in detail later) will provide incentives for research and development (R&D) into new clean energy technologies as firms search for ever cheaper ways to address the negative externality associated with their emissions. However, as already described, there is a separate externality in the area of R&D. Because it is difficult for the person or firm doing research to capture all of the returns, the private market supplies too little R&D—particularly for more basic forms of R&D, less so as ideas move toward demonstration and deployment. In this case, government R&D policies can complement the use of a market-based approach to reducing greenhouse gas emissions and yield large benefits to society. A policy that broadly incentivizes energy R&D is more likely to maximize social returns than a narrow one targeted at a specific technology because it allows the market, rather than the government, to pick winners. Likewise, funding efforts in support of basic R&D are less likely to crowd out private investment because differences between private and social returns to innovation are largest for basic R&D.

In its 2011 proposed budget, the Administration has stated a commitment to fund R&D as part of its comprehensive approach to transform the way we use and produce energy while addressing climate change. The Recovery Act investments begun in 2009 are a first step in this clean energy transformation. They fall into eight categories that are briefly described here.

Energy Efficiency. The Recovery Act promotes energy efficiency through investments that reduce energy consumption in many sectors of the economy. For instance, the Act appropriates $5 billion to the Weatherization Assistance Program to pay up to $6,500 per dwelling unit for energy efficiency retrofits in low-income homes. The Recovery Act also appropriates $3.2 billion to the Energy Efficiency and Conservation Block Grant program, most of which will go to U.S. states, territories, local governments, and Indian tribes to fund projects that improve energy efficiency, reduce energy use, and lower fossil fuel emissions.

Renewable Generation. The Recovery Act investments in renewable energy generation also are leading to the installation of wind turbines, solar panels, and other renewable energy sources. The Energy Information Administration projects that the fraction of the Nation's electricity generated from renewable energy, excluding conventional hydroelectric power, will grow from 3 percent in 2008 to almost 7 percent in 2012 in large part because of the renewal of Federal tax credits and the funding of new loan guarantees for renewable energy through the Recovery Act (Department of Energy 2009a).

Grid Modernization. As the United States transitions to greater use of intermittent renewable energy sources such as wind and solar, the Recovery Act is financing the construction of new transmission lines that can support electricity generated by renewable energy. The Act is also investing in new technologies that will improve electricity storage capabilities and the monitoring of electricity use through "smart grid" devices, such as sophisticated electric meters. These investments will improve the reliability, flexibility, and efficiency of the Nation's electricity grid.

Advanced Vehicles and Fuels Technologies. The Recovery Act is funding research on and deployment of the next generation of automobile batteries, advanced biofuels, plug-in hybrids, and all-electric vehicles, as well as the necessary support infrastructure. These efforts are expected to reduce the Nation's dependence on oil in the transportation sector.

Traditional Transit and High-Speed Rail. Grants from the Recovery Act also will help upgrade the reliability and service of public transit and conventional intercity railroad systems. For example, $8 billion is going to improve existing, or build new, high-speed rail in 100- to 600-mile intercity corridors. Investments in high-speed rail and public transit will increase energy efficiency by improving both access and reliability, thus making it possible for more people to switch to rail or public transit from autos or other less energy-efficient forms of transportation.

Carbon Capture and Storage. One approach to limiting greenhouse gas emissions is to capture and store carbon from fossil-fuel combustion to keep it from entering the atmosphere. The abundance of coal reserves in the United States makes developing such technologies and overcoming barriers to their use a particular priority. For instance, technology to capture carbon dioxide emissions has been used in industrial applications but has not been used on a commercial scale to capture emissions from power generation. Likewise, although some carbon has been stored deep in the ocean or underground in depleted oil reservoirs, questions remain about the permanence of these and other types of storage. The Recovery Act is funding crucial research, development, and demonstration of these technologies.

Innovation and Job Training. The Recovery Act is also investing in the science and technology needed to build the foundation for the clean energy economy. For instance, a total of $400 million has been allocated to the Advanced Research Projects Agency-Energy (ARPA-E) program, which funds creative new research ideas aimed at accelerating the pace of innovation in advanced energy technologies that would not be funded by industry because of technical or financial uncertainty. The Recovery Act also helps fund the training of workers for jobs in the energy efficiency and clean energy industries of the future.

Clean Energy Equipment Manufacturing. The Recovery Act investments are increasing the Nation's capacity to manufacture wind turbines, solar panels, electric vehicles, batteries, and other clean energy components domestically. As the United States transitions away from fossil fuels, demand for advanced energy products will grow, and these investments in clean energy will help American manufacturers participate in supplying the needed goods.

Total Recovery Act Energy Investments. The Recovery Act is investing in 56 projects and activities that are related to transitioning the economy to clean energy. Forty-five are spending provisions with a total appropriation of $60.7 billion, and another 11 are tax incentives that the Office of Tax Analysis estimates will cost $29.5 billion through fiscal year 2019, for a total investment of over $90 billion. In some cases, a relatively small amount of Federal investment leverages a larger amount of non-Federal support. Throughout this section, only the expected subsidy cost of the Federal investment is counted toward the appropriation.[3]

The largest clean energy investments from the Recovery Act go to renewable energy generation and transmission, energy efficiency, and transit. Figure 9-2 illustrates how this $90 billion investment is distributed across the eight categories of projects described above, along with a ninth "other" category containing programs that do not fit elsewhere.

---

[3] Because of the public nature of the Bonneville and Western Area Power Administrations, the accounting of clean energy investments described here measures the projected drawdown of the borrowing authority to these agencies as the Recovery Act appropriation.

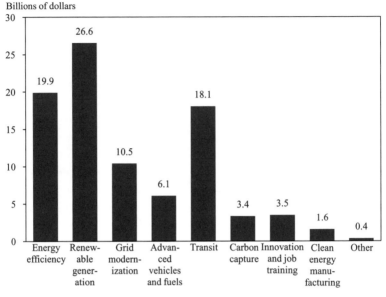

Figure 9-2
Recovery Act Clean Energy Appropriations by Category

Source: Council of Economic Advisers (2010).

Because most of the clean energy investments involve grants and contracts that require that proposals be reviewed before funds are expended, not all of the money appropriated for these investments could be spent immediately. Thus, as with the Recovery Act more generally, only a portion of the appropriation has been spent. Over $31 billion has been obligated and over $5 billion has been outlayed through the end of 2009.[4]

Short-Run Macroeconomic Effects of the Clean Energy Investments

Using a macroeconomic model, the Council of Economic Advisers (CEA) estimates that the approximately $90 billion of Recovery Act investments will save or create about 720,000 job-years by the end of 2012 (a job-year is one job for one year). Projects in the renewable energy generation and transmission, energy efficiency, and transit categories create the most job-years. Approximately two-thirds of the job-years represent work on clean energy projects, either by workers employed directly on the projects or by workers at suppliers to the projects. These macroeconomic benefits make it clear that the Administration has made a tremendous down payment on the clean energy transformation.

---

[4] *Obligated* means that the money is available to recipients once they make expenditures, and *outlayed* means the government has reimbursed recipients for their expenditures. Energy-related tax reductions to date are included in the totals obligated and outlayed by the end of 2009.

OTHER DOMESTIC ACTIONS TO
MITIGATE CLIMATE CHANGE

In his first year in office, the President took several other significant and concrete steps to transform the energy sector and address climate change. Significantly, the Environmental Protection Agency (EPA) issued two findings in December 2009. The first finding was that six greenhouse gases endanger public health and welfare. The second finding was that the emissions of these greenhouse gases from motor vehicles cause or contribute to pollution that threatens public health and welfare. These findings do not in and of themselves trigger any requirements for emitters, but they lay the foundation for regulating greenhouse gas emissions.

Following up on these findings, the Administration has proposed the first mandatory greenhouse gas emission standards for new passenger vehicles. The standards are expected to be finalized in the spring of 2010. By model year 2016, new cars and light trucks sold in the United States will be required to meet a fleet-wide tailpipe emissions limit equivalent to a standard of about 35.5 miles per gallon if met entirely through fuel economy improvements. The EPA estimates that these standards will save about 36 billion gallons of fuel and reduce vehicle greenhouse gas emissions by about 760 million metric tons in CO_2-equivalent terms over the lifetime of the vehicles.

The Administration also proposed renewable fuel standards consistent with the Energy Independence and Security Act (EISA), which requires that a minimum volume of renewable fuel be added to gasoline sold in the United States. Renewable fuels are derived from bio-based feedstocks such as corn, soy, sugar cane, or cellulose that have fewer life-cycle greenhouse gas emissions than the gasoline or diesel they replace. When fully implemented, the standards will increase the volume of renewable fuel blended into gasoline from 9 billion gallons in 2008 to 36 billion gallons by 2022.

The Administration also has been proactive in establishing minimum energy efficiency standards for a wide variety of consumer products and commercial equipment. For instance, standards were proposed or finalized in 2009 for microwave ovens, dishwashers, small electric motors, lighting, vending machines, residential water heaters, and commercial clothes washers, among others. Overall, these actions will reduce energy consumption and, in turn, greenhouse gas emissions. The Energy Information Administration's 2009 Annual Energy Outlook projected that by 2030, higher fuel economy and lighting efficiency standards will contribute to lowering energy use per capita by 10 percent, compared with fairly stable energy use per capita between 1980 and 2008 (Department of Energy

2009b). The 2010 Annual Energy Outlook highlights appliance and building efficiency standards as one reason for lower projected carbon dioxide emissions growth, underscoring the benefits of these regulations (Department of Energy 2009a).

Beginning in 2010, the United States will begin collecting comprehensive high-quality data on greenhouse gases from large emitters in many sectors of the economy (for instance, electricity generators and cement producers). When fully implemented, this program will cover about 85 percent of U.S. emissions. The information supplied will provide a basis for formulating policy on how best to reduce emissions in the future. It will also be a valuable tool to allow industry to track emissions over time. Specifically, these data will make it possible for industry and government to identify the cheapest ways to reduce greenhouse gas emissions.

Finally, the President issued an Executive Order requiring Federal agencies to set and meet aggressive goals for greenhouse gas emission reductions. Importantly, agencies are instructed to pursue reductions that lower energy expenses and save taxpayers money.

MARKET-BASED APPROACHES TO ADVANCE THE CLEAN ENERGY TRANSFORMATION AND ADDRESS CLIMATE CHANGE

Greenhouse gas emissions, as noted, are a classic example of a negative externality. Emitters of greenhouse gases contribute to climate change, thus imposing a cost on others that is not accounted for when making decisions about how to produce and consume energy-intensive goods. For this reason, policymakers should ensure that the market provides the correct signals to greenhouse-gas emitters about the full cost of their emissions. Once policy has ensured that markets are providing the correct signals and incentives, the operation of market forces can find the most effective and efficient paths to the clean energy economy. The President has included a market-based cap-and-trade approach in his 2010 and 2011 budgets as a way to accomplish this goal. This section describes the basics of this approach, including several potential ways to minimize compliance costs. It then discusses a specific proposal consistent with the President's goals for reducing greenhouse gas emissions.

Cap-and-Trade Program Basics

A cap-and-trade approach sets a limit on, or caps, total annual aggregate greenhouse gas emissions and then divides the cap into emission allowances. These allowances are allocated to firms through some combination of an auction and free allocation.[5] Firms may trade the allowances among themselves but are required to hold an allowance for each ton of greenhouse gas they emit. The aggregate cap limits the number of allowances available, ensuring their scarcity and thus establishing a price in the market for allowances. In this way, a cap-and-trade approach provides certainty in the quantity of emission reductions but allows the price of allowances to fluctuate with changes in the demand and supply.

Creating a market for greenhouse gas emissions gives firms flexibility in how they reduce emissions. Absent other regulatory requirements, a firm subject to the cap can choose to comply by changing its input mix (for instance, switching from coal to natural gas), modifying the underlying technology used in production (using more energy-efficient equipment, for example), or purchasing allowances from other entities with lower abatement costs. Such flexibility reaps rewards. A cap-and-trade program induces firms to seek out and exploit the lowest-cost ways of cutting emissions. It takes advantage of the profit motive and leverages private sector imagination and ingenuity to find ways to lower emissions.

Cap-and-trade programs already have proven successful. The United States has been using a cap-and-trade approach to reduce sulfur dioxide (SO_2) emissions since 1995. One study found that using a cap-and-trade approach instead of a performance standard to reduce sulfur dioxide emissions caused some firms to move away from putting scrubbers on their smokestacks to cheaper ways of meeting the cap, such as by blending different fuels (Burtraw and Palmer 2004). As a result, compliance costs of the SO_2 cap-and-trade program have been dramatically lower than predicted.

Finally, a cap-and-trade approach promotes innovation. A carbon price will give firms the certainty they need to make riskier long-term investments that could identify novel and substantially cheaper ways to reduce emissions. Evidence shows that pricing sulfur dioxide emissions through a cap-and-trade approach has produced patentable innovations as firms search for ever cheaper ways to abate (Burtraw and Szambelan 2009).

In the case of greenhouse gases, possible innovations range from new techniques to capture and store carbon generated by coal-burning electricity plants, to carbon-eating trees and algae, to the development of new types of renewable fuels. Indeed, such innovation—and the opportunity it provides

---

[5] In his fiscal year 2011 proposed budget, the President supports using allowance revenue to compensate vulnerable families, communities, and businesses during the transition to the clean energy economy, as well as in support of clean energy technologies and adapting to the impacts of climate change.

to make the United States a world leader in clean energy technologies—is a key motivation for the Administration's energy and climate policies.

Ways to Contain Costs in an Effective Cap-and-Trade System

There are a wide variety of ways to contain costs within a cap-and-trade framework. For instance, cap-and-trade programs may incorporate banking and borrowing of emission allowances over time, set ceilings or floors on allowance prices, or permit the use of offsets as ways to smooth the costs of compliance over time. A brief review of these mechanisms follows.

Banking and Borrowing. A cap-and-trade approach can be designed to give polluters flexibility in the timing of emission reductions through banking and borrowing. To limit allowance price volatility, sources can make greater reductions early if it is cheaper to do so and bank their allowances for future use. Likewise, firms can manage costs by borrowing against future reductions, allowing them to emit more today in return for more drastic reductions later.

Evidence shows that banking has played a particularly powerful role in helping firms to hedge uncertainty in the costs of the SO_2 cap-and-trade program over time. Anticipating that the cap originally set in 1995 would become more stringent in 2000, firms began to bank allowances for future use soon after the system was put in place. By 1999, almost 70 percent of available allowances in the market had been banked. Once the more stringent cap was in place, the banked allowances were drawn down to meet the cap, with about a 40 percent decrease in the size of the allowance bank between 2000 and 2005 (Environmental Protection Agency 2006).

In contrast, the inability of firms to bank or borrow in Southern California's nitrous oxide market played a significant role in increased price volatility during the State's electricity crisis in 2000 when firms met soaring demand for electricity by running old, dirty generators. One study found that the absence of banking and borrowing was an important contributing factor to the roughly tenfold increase in the price of nitrous oxide allowances, resulting in power plants subject to the cap eventually seeking exemption from the program (Ellerman, Joskow, and Harrison 2003).

Price Ceilings or Floors. While banking and borrowing allow firms to smooth costs over time, they may not guard against unexpected and potentially longer-lasting changes in allowance prices caused by such factors as a recession or economic boom, fuel price fluctuations, or unexpected variation in the pace of technological development. Consequently, cap-and-trade systems often include protections against prices that are deemed too high. For example, in the Northeast's greenhouse gas trading system, allowance prices above certain thresholds trigger additional flexibilities that reduce compliance costs.[6]

Another way for a cap-and-trade program to mitigate the effects of unexpected changes would be to specify an upper or lower limit, or both, on allowance prices. An upper limit protects firms and consumers from unexpectedly high prices. When the price reaches the upper limit, additional allowances are sold to prevent further escalation. A lower limit on allowance prices ensures that cheap abatement opportunities continue to be pursued. For example, cap-and-trade legislation recently passed by the U.S. House of Representatives reserves a small share of allowances to be auctioned if the price rises above a predetermined threshold and also sets a minimum price for allowances that are auctioned. One study finds that, for a given cumulative emissions reduction, a combined price ceiling and floor can reduce costs by almost 20 percent compared with a cap-and-trade program without any cost-containment mechanisms (Fell and Morgenstern 2009). On the other hand, it is possible that a floor or ceiling can cause total emissions to differ from the legislated cap.

Offsets. Offsets also can be an important cost-containment feature of a cap-and-trade program. Offsets are credits generated by reducing emissions in a sector outside the program; they can be purchased by a firm subject to the cap to meet its compliance obligations. Because greenhouse gases are global pollutants—they cause the same damage no matter where they are emitted—offsets offer the appealing prospect of achieving specified emissions reductions at a lower cost.

The purchase of offsets from the forestry and agricultural sectors could play a potentially important role in reducing the compliance costs of firms subject to the cap (Kinderman et al. 2008; Environmental Protection Agency 2009). And under some cap-and-trade programs, domestic firms may purchase international offsets to meet their compliance obligations. This possibility may encourage a foreign country to build a solar power plant rather than a coal plant so that it can sell the offsets in the U.S. market.

Despite these important advantages, however, it is crucial that the claimed reductions from offsets be real—otherwise the system will effectively provide payments without actually reducing emissions. Indeed, Europe's experience with a project-based approach to international offsets suggests that concerns about the environmental integrity of claimed

---

[6] Above $7 per ton (in 2005 dollars), a firm can cover up to 5 percent of its emissions with domestic offsets, up from 3.3 percent. At $10 per ton (in 2005 dollars plus a 2 percent increase per year), this amount increases to 10 percent of emissions and may include international offsets.

emissions reductions are well founded (Box 9-3).[7] If offsets are going to be included as part of a cap-and-trade program, substantial investments in rigorous monitoring methods, such as combining remote sensing with on-the-ground monitoring, to verify greenhouse gas reductions are crucial.

Box 9-3: The European Union's Experience with Emissions Trading

One of the pillars of the President's proposed response to climate change is a cap-and-trade system to reduce U.S. emissions of greenhouse gases. The European Union's Emission Trading Scheme (ETS), the world's first mandatory cap-and-trade program for carbon dioxide emissions, was launched in 2005 to meet emission reduction targets agreed to under the Kyoto Protocol. The first phase of the ETS—from 2005 to 2007—applied to several high-emitting industrial sectors, including power generation, in 25 countries and covered just over 40 percent of all European Union (EU) emissions. Although data limitations and uncertainty over baseline emissions preclude researchers from assessing the precise magnitude of the reductions, one estimate suggests that the ETS reduced EU emissions by about 4 percent in 2005 and 2006 relative to what the level would have been in its absence. Because of the flexibility offered under the cap-and-trade program, these reductions occurred where it was cheapest to achieve them. That said, the ETS offers three important cautionary lessons as the United States explores how best to implement its own cap-and-trade system.

One lesson is the importance of carefully establishing a baseline for current and future emissions, so that the price sends an accurate signal to firms regarding how much to abate and innovate based on the expected future value of reductions. During the first phase of the ETS, EU countries allocated allowances based on firms' estimates of their historic emissions. In April 2006, when monitoring data became available, the data showed that actual emissions were already below the cap. Allowance prices immediately fell from about €30 ($38) per metric ton to less than €10 ($13) before settling at €15–€20 ($19–$25) for the next few months.

The EU experience also demonstrates that distributing nearly all allowances to industry at no cost can lead to large windfall profits. The European Union distributed nearly 100 percent of allowances free to

Continued on next page

---

[7] Cap-and-trade programs that allow project-level offsets are particularly susceptible to crediting activity that would have occurred anyway or that is replaced by high-carbon activities elsewhere (leakage). One way to reduce the potential for leakage is a sector- or country-based framework, in which sectors or governments receive credit in exchange for implementing policies to reduce emissions. The legislation passed by the U.S. House of Representatives includes a sector-based approach to international offsets.

firms subject to the cap in Phase 1 and only auctioned a small portion of allowances for Phase 2 (2008–12). One estimate (Point Carbon Advisory Services 2008) suggests that during Phase 2, electricity generators in Germany will reap the highest windfall profits of all participating EU countries, on the order of €14 billion to €34 billion ($20 billion to $49 billion). In countries with low-greenhouse-gas emitters, electricity generators are expected to benefit less. For instance, in Spain, windfall profits are estimated to be about €1 billion to €4 billion ($1 billion to $6 billion). In Phase 3 (2013–20), the European Union plans to auction the majority of allowances.

Finally, it is important to ensure that any offsets from domestic and international sources reflect real reductions. Otherwise, they may endanger the environmental integrity of the cap. The ETS allows limited use of project-based international offsets from the United Nations' Clean Development Mechanism (CDM) in place of domestic emission reductions. A review of a random sample of offset project proposals in the CDM program from 2004 to 2007 estimated that "additionality" was unlikely or questionable for roughly 40 percent of registered projects, representing 20 percent of emissions reductions, meaning they would have occurred anyway (Schneider 2007). Although the CDM has worked to improve its accounting procedures over time, the EU's experience demonstrates the importance of designing an offsets program carefully.

Coverage of Gases and Industries

Although carbon dioxide made up about 83 percent of U.S. greenhouse emissions in 2008, a cap-and-trade approach that gives firms flexibility in where they reduce emissions, both in terms of the greenhouse gas and the economic sector, can lower firms' compliance costs. One study found that achieving an emission goal by cutting both methane and carbon dioxide emissions rather than carbon dioxide alone could reduce firms' abatement costs in the United States by over 25 percent in the medium run (Hayhoe et al. 1999).

Costs are also affected by the number of industries covered by the cap, with the general principle being that greater coverage lowers the marginal cost of emissions reductions. A recent study comparing alternative ways to achieve a 5 percent reduction in emissions found that the cap-and-trade program's costs to the economy were twice as large when manufacturing was excluded as they were under an economy-wide approach (Pizer et al. 2006).

The American Clean Energy and Security Act

In June 2009, the U.S. House of Representatives passed legislation—the American Clean Energy and Security Act (ACES)—that includes a cap-and-trade program consistent with the President's goal of reducing greenhouse gas emissions by more than 80 percent by 2050, and the Senate is currently engaged in a bipartisan effort to develop a bill.

Projected Climate Benefits. Based on two analyses of the ACES legislation, U.S. actions would reduce cumulative greenhouse gas emissions by approximately 110 billion to 150 billion metric tons in CO_2-equivalents by 2050 (Paltsev et al. 2009; Environmental Protection Agency 2009). The EPA estimates that emission reductions of this magnitude, when combined with comparable action by other countries consistent with reducing world emissions by 50 percent in 2050, is expected to limit warming in 2100 to less than 2 °C (3.6 °F) relative to the pre-industrial global average temperature, with a likely range of about 1.0 to 2.5 °C (1.8 to 4.5 °F).

To derive the possible benefits associated with the U.S. contribution to these emission reductions, the CEA calculates that the ACES will result in approximately $1.6 trillion to $2.0 trillion of avoided global damages in present value terms between 2012 and 2050 (in 2005 dollars).[8] The value of avoided damages includes such benefits as lower mortality rates, higher agricultural yields, money saved on adaptation measures, and the reduced likelihood of small-probability but high-impact catastrophic events. Further, the benefits will be significantly larger if U.S. policy induces other countries to undertake reductions in greenhouse gas emissions.

Projected Economic Costs. The estimated cost of meeting the caps outlined in the ACES legislation is relatively small. Recent research suggests that the ACES will result in a loss of consumption on the order of 1 to 2 percent in 2050 (Environmental Protection Agency 2009; Paltsev et al. 2009). On a per household basis, the average annual consumption loss would be between $80 and $400 a year between 2012 and 2050 (in 2005 dollars).

---

[8] The CEA uses estimates of the projected decline in emissions between 2012 and 2050 based on the President's proposed reductions in emissions and uses the central estimate of $20 a ton for a unit of carbon dioxide emitted in 2007 (in 2007 dollars) that was recently developed as an interim value for regulatory analyses (Department of Energy 2009c). Additionally, it assumes that the benefit of reducing one additional ton of carbon dioxide grows at 3 percent over time and that future damages from current emissions are discounted using an average of 5 percent. Several Federal agencies have used these values in recent proposed rulemakings but have requested comment prior to the final rulemaking, so these estimates may be revised.

International Action on Climate Change
Is Needed

Greenhouse gas emissions impose global risks. As a result, just as U.S. efforts to reduce emissions benefit other countries, actions that other countries take to mitigate emissions benefit the United States. Given the global nature of the problem and the declining U.S. share of greenhouse gas emissions, U.S. actions alone to reduce those emissions are insufficient to mitigate the most serious risks from climate change.

Developing countries such as China and India are responsible for a growing proportion of emissions because of their heavy reliance on carbon-intensive fuels, such as coal (Figure 9-3). In 1992, China's carbon dioxide emissions from fossil fuel combustion were half those of the United States and represented 12 percent of global emissions. By 2008, China's carbon dioxide emissions represented 22 percent of global emissions from fossil fuels, exceeding the U.S. share of 19 percent and the European share of 15 percent. China's share of global emissions is projected to grow to about 29 percent by 2030 absent new emission mitigation policies. By contrast, the U.S. share of global emissions is projected to fall to about 15 percent by 2030 even absent new emission mitigation policy. Thus, cooperation by both

Figure 9-3
United States, China, and World Carbon Dioxide Emissions

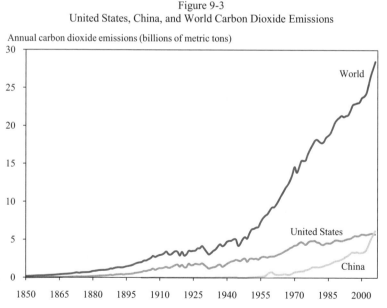

Annual carbon dioxide emissions (billions of metric tons)

Notes: The figure includes carbon dioxide emissions from fossil fuel consumption, cement manufacturing, and natural gas flaring. Notably, this figure does not include changes in carbon dioxide emissions from land-use change.
Source: World Resources Institute, Climate Analysis Indicators Tool.

past and future contributors to emissions will be required to stabilize the atmospheric concentrations of greenhouse gases.

In keeping with this goal, the Administration has actively pursued partnerships with major developed and emerging economies to advance efforts to reduce greenhouse gas emissions and promote economic development that lowers emission intensity.

Partnerships with Major Developed and Emerging Economies

The President has worked to further a series of international agreements to address climate change. For example, he launched the Major Economies Forum on Energy and Climate to engage 17 developed and emerging economies in a dialogue on climate change. In July, the leaders of these countries agreed that greenhouse gas emissions should peak in developed and developing countries alike, and recognized the scientific view that the increase in global average temperature above pre-industrial levels ought not to exceed 2 °C (3.6 °F). They also agreed to coordinate and dramatically increase investment in research, development, and deployment of low-carbon energy technologies with a goal of doubling such investment by 2015. Finally, the leaders agreed to mobilize financial resources in support of mitigation and adaptation activities, recognizing that the group should be responsive to developing-country needs in this area.

Also in July, leaders from the Group of Eight (G-8) countries agreed to undertake robust aggregate and individual medium-term emission reductions consistent with the objective of cutting global emissions by at least 50 percent by 2050. Additionally, under the Montreal Protocol, the United States jointly proposed with Canada and Mexico to phase down emissions of hydrofluorocarbons, a potent greenhouse gas used in refrigeration, fire suppression, and other industrial activities. This action alone would achieve about 10 percent of the greenhouse gas emission reductions needed to meet the agreed G-8 goal of a 50 percent reduction by 2050.

In December, the Administration worked with major emerging economies, including Brazil, China, India, and South Africa, developed countries, and other regions around the world to secure agreement on the Copenhagen Accord. For the first time, the international community established a long-term goal to limit warming of global average temperature to no more than 2 °C (3.6 °F). Also for the first time, all major economies agreed to take action to address climate change. Under the Accord, both developed and major emerging economies are in the process of submitting their emission mitigation commitments and actions to reduce greenhouse gas emissions. Every two years, developing countries will report on emission mitigation efforts, which will be subject to international consultation and analysis under clearly defined guidelines. Establishing transparent review of developed and developing country mitigation activities will help ensure that countries stand behind their commitments.

Furthermore, under the Accord, in the context of meaningful mitigation actions and transparency, developed countries committed to a goal of jointly mobilizing $100 billion a year in funding from a variety of private and public sources for developing countries by 2020. This funding will build on an immediate effort by developed countries to support forestry, adaptation, and emissions mitigation with funding approaching $30 billion sometime in the 2010 to 2012 timeframe. There will be a special focus on directing this funding to the poorest and most vulnerable developing countries.

Phasing Out Fossil Fuel Subsidies

The United States also spearheaded an agreement in September to phase out fossil fuel subsidies among G-20 countries, a goal seconded by countries in the Asian-Pacific Economic Cooperation (APEC) in November. The G-20 also called on all nations to phase out such subsidies worldwide. Fossil fuel subsidies are particularly large in non-OECD countries, such as India and Russia. Twenty of the largest non-OECD governments spent about $300 billion on fossil fuel subsidies in 2007. Together, this coordinated action to reduce subsidies can free up resources, especially in developing countries, to target other social needs such as public health and education. One model estimates that eliminating fossil fuel subsidies in the major non-OECD countries alone would reduce greenhouse gas emissions by more than 7 billion metric tons of CO_2-equivalent, enough to fulfill almost 15 percent of the agreed-upon G-8 goal of reducing global emissions by 50 percent by 2050 (Organisation for Economic Co-operation and Development 2009).

In the United States, these subsidies—including tax credits, deductions, expensing practices, and exemptions—are worth about $44 billion in tax revenues between 2010 and 2019. Their elimination will help put cleaner fuels, such as those derived from renewable sources, on a more equal footing and reduce wasteful consumption of fossil-fuel based energy caused by underpricing. Proper pricing of fossil fuels will also help reduce reliance on petroleum, thus enhancing energy security and aiding in the achievement of climate mitigation goals.

CONCLUSION

Today's economy is dependent on carbon-intensive fuels that are directly linked to an increase in global average temperature. Continued reliance on these fuels will have a range of negative impacts, including increased mortality rates, reduced agricultural productivity in many locations, higher sea levels, and the need for costly adaptation efforts. For these reasons, a clean energy transformation is essential.

Through his comprehensive plan, the President has set the country on course to achieve this goal. He has taken several significant and concrete steps to transform the energy sector and address climate change through the American Reinvestment and Recovery Act and through targeted regulation. To address externalities associated with greenhouse gas emissions, the President has proposed a market-based cap-and-trade approach. These combined efforts will stimulate the research and development necessary to advance new clean energy technologies. Because of the global nature of the climate change problem, the Administration is also actively pursuing partnerships with other countries to advance efforts to transition the world to clean energy and reduce greenhouse gas emissions.

C H A P T E R   1 0

FOSTERING PRODUCTIVITY GROWTH THROUGH INNOVATION AND TRADE

Americans have always believed in building a better future. Each generation has strived to pass on higher standards of living to their children than they themselves experienced. And for most of American history, this goal has been realized. Per capita income has risen strongly for most of the past two centuries.

Such economic growth stems from a number of factors. Investment in skills and education, or human capital, is a key determinant. The United States has a long history of investing in people, and this has enabled American workers to be among the most productive in the world. Investment in physical capital is also important. The tremendous accumulation of machines, buildings, and infrastructure has been a source of America's prosperity, and times of particularly great investment, such as the 1950s and 1960s, have been times of particularly rapid advances in standards of living.

Because investing in people and capital is important to the maintenance and growth of standards of living, the President has fashioned an ambitious agenda of improvements in education, incentives for investment, and financial regulatory reform to ensure that we have the financial system needed to support such investment. These initiatives have been described in detail in earlier chapters.

But as important as investments in labor and capital have been and will continue to be, they are not the only sources of growth. A third, more amorphous factor has also played a central role in American economic growth: advances in the overall productivity of that labor and capital. One need only think of a few of the technological changes of the past century—the airplane, antibiotics, computers, fiber-optic cables, and the Internet—to see that technological discovery and innovation are central to improved standards of living. Such innovations not only make us richer as a country, they have the potential to fundamentally alter the very way we live our lives and interact with one another.

As discussed throughout this *Report,* in the past decade American economic growth has slowed in important ways. American families saw their median income actually fall from 2000 to 2006. An important part of restoring growth and increases in standards of living is spurring innovation and increases in productivity. American firms and universities will naturally play the leading role in this endeavor. But that does not mean government has no role to play. Indeed, overwhelming evidence shows that innovation creates positive "externalities"—benefits for others beyond the individuals or firms who originally produce new ideas. Since inventors do not reap the full rewards, on its own the market will produce less innovation than is optimal. Public policy therefore has a powerful role to play in fostering pursuit of the myriad possibilities for scientific, technical, and analytical advances.

At its best, trade between regions of the country and across borders can also be an engine of growth. Trade has the potential to allow the U.S. economy to expand output in areas where it is more productive and to enable higher-productivity firms to expand. Access to a world market encourages American firms to invest in the research needed to become technological leaders. Through these routes, a free and fair trade regime can play an important part in lifting living standards in the long run.

Based on an understanding that progress springs from achieving the proper balance between generous rewards for the creation of new ideas and encouraging the best of those ideas to spread widely, the Administration has formulated a comprehensive "innovation agenda" that reaches far beyond the traditional scope of science and technology policy. This agenda touches everything from improvements in the Patent and Trademark Office, to increased government investments in research and development (R&D), to engaging the world economy in ways that ensure that the United States achieves the maximum benefits from trade's productivity-enhancing potential. This chapter discusses the key components of the agenda in detail.

All advances in productivity, whether from scientific breakthroughs, changes in the organization of firms, or increased international trade, involve losers as well as winners. Because productivity growth is the critical source of improved standards of living, the most effective way to address the painful impacts for those harmed by progress is not to stifle new ideas or trade. Rather, it is to build a robust system of support that can help ease the transition from employment in declining firms and industries to jobs in new, higher-paying, higher-productivity areas. Even more important are broad-based policies that ensure that the gains from rising productivity are widely shared: progressive taxation, a health care system that provides security and stability, a strong educational system, and a secure social safety net.

For too many years, our Nation has ignored necessary reforms in these broad-based policies and underinvested in areas such as health care and education, which are essential to ensuring that middle-class families will benefit from productivity advances. That is why the Obama Administration has set as a central economic priority rebuilding our economy on a firmer foundation. The Administration's innovation agenda must go hand in hand with progress in those areas as well.

THE ROLE OF PRODUCTIVITY GROWTH IN DRIVING LIVING STANDARDS

In the long run, the critical determinant of living standards is labor productivity—the amount of goods and services produced by an average worker in a fixed period of time, such as an hour or a 40-hour week. Figure 10-1 provides striking visual confirmation of this hypothesis. It shows that over U.S. history since the early 20th century, sustained increases in labor productivity have translated nearly one-for-one into increases in income per person.

Figure 10-1
Non-Farm Labor Productivity and Per Capita Income

Note: Productivity represents total output per unit of labor, 1901-1946, and non-farm business sector only, 1947-2008.
Sources: Department of Commerce (1973); Department of Commerce (Bureau of Economic Analysis), National Income and Product Accounts Table 7.1; Department of Labor (Bureau of Labor Statistics), Productivity and Costs Table A.

The importance of labor productivity to living standards may seem obvious, or even tautological, but it is not. In principle, increases in income per person could come not from more output per unit of labor input, but from more labor input per person—that is, from increases in the fraction of the population that is working or increases in each worker's hours. But both the historical evidence from the United States and the evidence from across a wide range of countries show that differences in labor input per person account for at most a small fraction of income differences.

Recent Trends in Productivity in the United States

Since labor productivity is the key driver of standards of living in the long run, it is important to discern the underlying trends in productivity. This task is complicated by the fact that in the short run, productivity depends on more than those underlying trends. It is powerfully influenced by the state of the business cycle, as well as by other factors (including simple measurement error) that leave no lasting mark on productivity.

Figure 10-2 shows the growth rate of labor productivity from four quarters earlier over the last 62 years. One immediate message is that although the overall pattern of productivity is strongly upward (as shown clearly by Figure 10-1), there is enormous short-run variation in productivity growth.

Figure 10-2
Labor Productivity Growth since 1947

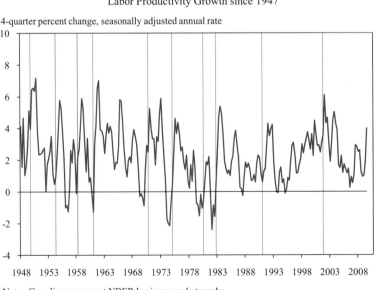

4-quarter percent change, seasonally adjusted annual rate

Note: Grey lines represent NBER business cycle troughs.
Source: Department of Labor (Bureau of Labor Statistics), Productivity and Costs Table A.

A more subtle message is that the average or trend rate of productivity growth is not constant but changes substantially over extended periods. It is conventional to divide the era from the beginning of the sample until about 1995 into two periods: the "immediate postwar" period from 1947 through 1972, and the "productivity growth slowdown" period from 1973 through 1995. In the immediate postwar period, the average rate of productivity growth was 2.8 percent per year. During the productivity growth slowdown, it was only 1.4 percent.

This division into different periods lets one see the cumulative importance of even seemingly modest changes in productivity growth. For example, if the high productivity growth of the immediate postwar period had continued through 1995 instead of slowing, the level of productivity in 1995—and hence standards of living—would have been more than one-third higher than they actually were.

The pattern of productivity growth since 1995 is somewhat complicated. From 1996:Q1 to the last available observation (2009:Q3), it averaged 2.7 percent per year, almost equal to its rate over the immediate postwar period. But that rapid growth was concentrated in the first part of the period. In the first eight years (1996:Q1 to 2003:Q4), productivity growth averaged 3.3 percent; in the four years before the business cycle peak (2004:Q1 to 2007:Q4), it averaged only 1.7 percent. A four-year period is too short to confidently determine underlying trends. But productivity growth in the years leading up to the recession was not strong enough to generate robust increases in standards of living.

A final pattern revealed by Figure 10-2 is a relationship between productivity growth and the business cycle. Productivity growth tends to fall during recessions and surge near their ends (marked by the vertical lines in Figure 10-2). This pattern has been operating strongly in the current recession. Productivity growth averaged less than 1 percent at an annual rate over the first five quarters of the recession, but then surged in 2009:Q2 and 2009:Q3, and appears to have remained high in 2009:Q4.

This recent experience highlights the importance of distinguishing between cyclical movements in productivity and longer-term movements: the pattern in productivity growth in 2009 largely reflects the fact that employment moves more slowly than production over the business cycle. The sluggishness of employment growth has meant that even as output reached its low point and began to recover, employment continued to decline. This cyclical improvement in productivity is obviously of a different character than the secular improvements that are the source of long-run increases in standards of living. Over the course of 2009, standards of living clearly did not follow productivity closely. But once the cyclical dynamics play themselves out, the usual long-term role of productivity growth in driving income growth is bound to reassert itself. An important goal of policy is to make the long-term path of productivity as favorable as possible.

Sources of Productivity Growth

Productivity growth is the overwhelming determinant of the progress of economic well-being over extended periods. It is therefore imperative to understand what determines productivity growth. Three sources have been identified as key.

The first source is the accumulation of physical capital—the machines, tools, computers, factories, infrastructure, and so on that workers use to produce output. Each year, some of our Nation's economic output takes the form of these capital goods. When workers have more or better capital to work with, they are more productive.

The second source is the accumulation of human capital—workers' education, skills, and training. The accumulation of human capital is just as much an investment as the accumulation of physical capital is. When some of the economy's output takes the form of physical capital goods rather than consumption, we are forgoing some consumption today in exchange for the ability to produce more in the future. Likewise, when students and teachers are in a classroom, or when an experienced worker is taking time to train a new hire, resources that could be used to produce goods for current consumption are being used instead for activities that increase future productive capacity. And just as a worker with better equipment is more productive, so too is a worker with more skills.

The third source of productivity growth is increases in the amount that can be produced from given amounts of physical and human capital. This factor goes by various names, such as "total factor productivity growth" or "the Solow residual." It encompasses all the forces that cause changes in how much an economy produces from its stocks of physical and human capital. Most obviously, it encompasses advances in knowledge and tech-nology. These advances in knowledge and technology allow factory workers to build better automobiles and electronics from the same raw materials; they allow doctors to provide more accurate diagnoses and prescribe better treatments in the same office visit; and much more.

But total factor productivity growth includes more than advances in knowledge and technology. For example, if an economy faces an increase in crime, individuals may devote more of their skills and physical capital to protecting the goods they have rather than producing more goods, and so total factor productivity growth may be low or even negative. If a country switches from central planning to a market-based economy, then workers and capital are likely to be allocated more effectively, and so output given the economy's stocks of physical and human capital may increase greatly. Changes in these types of "organizational capital" (or "institutional" or "social" capital) are potentially critical determinants of total factor productivity growth.

Research has not just identified changes in these three factors (physical capital, human capital, and total factor productivity) as critical determinants of productivity growth; it has also come to a fairly clear view about their relative importance. Perhaps surprisingly, the ranking of the three factors appears to be the same whether one is trying to understand the enormous growth in productivity over extended periods in the United States (for example, Jones 2002), or the vast differences in the level of productivity across countries (for example, Hall and Jones 1999).[1]

The factor that is most obvious and easiest to quantify—physical capital accumulation—turns out to be only moderately important. Differences in the fraction of output devoted to physical capital investment account for some portion of both long-run productivity growth and cross-country productivity differences, and increases in investment can have a significant impact on productivity growth, and hence on standards of living. At the same time, the evidence suggests that the other factors are even more important.[2]

One of those more important factors is human capital accumulation. Increases in the education and skills of the workforce play a substantial role in the long-term growth of labor productivity, and cross-country differences in human capital per worker are important to cross-country differences in labor productivity. Thus, increases in human capital investment through a stronger educational system and greater educational attainment at all levels, together with lifetime learning, provide another powerful route to raising productivity growth and standards of living.

The most important determinant is not physical or human capital accumulation, but changes in how much can be produced with them—that is, total factor productivity growth. Again, this finding applies to both long-term growth and cross-country differences. At an intuitive level, this result is not surprising. It seems very plausible that the most important reason we are so much more productive than our forebears is that, for reasons ranging

---

[1] See also Klenow and Rodríguez-Clare 1997; Hendricks 2002; Caselli 2005; and Hsieh and Klenow 2007.

[2] There is a subtlety here. When total factor productivity or human capital improves, the result is higher output, which then leads to more physical capital investment if the fraction of the economy's output that is invested does not change. The decompositions that find a moderate role for physical capital assign these indirect effects of total factor productivity and human capital investment to those factors, and not to physical capital. If those effects are instead assigned to physical capital, its importance increases greatly.

from advances in basic scientific knowledge to improved ways of organizing the workplace, we have found vastly better ways of producing output from a given set of inputs. Likewise, it is likely that a key reason the United States outperformed the Soviet Union economically in the postwar period was not that the United States was better at channeling its productive capacity into producing capital goods and its children into education (both of which the Soviet Union did on a very large scale), but that the United States' free-market institutions led it to produce more from its inputs, and led to myriad innovations that widened the productivity gap over time.

This discussion implies that in order to foster improvements in standards of living, policy should foster investment in physical capital, investment in human capital, and crucially, improvements in total factor productivity. Physical and human capital investment are discussed in earlier chapters—most notably Chapter 4 (as well as Chapters 5 and 6) in the case of physical capital investment, and Chapter 8 in the case of human capital. The remainder of this chapter turns to measures to improve total factor productivity. Such improvements in total factor productivity can be described broadly as "innovations."

Fostering Productivity Growth Through Innovation

Because total factor productivity reflects all determinants of labor productivity other than physical and human capital, it has a wide range of elements. As a result, there are many avenues along which well-designed policies can work to improve total factor productivity. It is for this reason that the Administration has proposed a comprehensive innovation agenda (Box 10-1).

Box 10-1: Overview of the Administration's Innovation Agenda

On a September 21 visit to New York's Hudson Valley Community College, President Obama presented the first comprehensive description of the Administration's Innovation Agenda, the conceptual framework underpinning the wide range of initiatives that the Administration has undertaken that share a common aim of fostering innovation.

The Agenda has three elements. The first is a commitment to invest in the building blocks of innovation, including basic scientific research and infrastructure, as articulated in detail in the body of this chapter.

Continued on next page

The second is a recognition of the vital role that competitive markets and a healthy environment for entrepreneurial risk-taking play in spurring innovation; reform of the Patent Office, improving the accessibility and usefulness of government statistics, and increasing the predictability and transparency of government policy are all parts of this effort. The final part of the agenda is a particular focus on innovation targeted toward specific national priorities, including the development of alternative energy sources, reducing costs and improving medical care through the use of health information technology, the creation of a "smart grid" that will allow more efficient use of existing energy generation capacity, and initiatives aimed at inventing cleaner and more fuel-efficient transportation technologies.

The Agenda builds on over $100 billion of funds appropriated in the American Recovery and Reinvestment Act of 2009 for the support of innovation, education, and technological and scientific infrastructure. It also encompasses directives to regulatory and executive branch agencies designed to help them refocus their missions to support the Agenda in whatever ways are most appropriate to their usual activities. A final key tool is the commitment to science-based, data-driven policymaking that brings to bear all the intellectual, statistical, informational, and analytical resources necessary to make sure that government policies achieve their stated aims as efficiently and effectively as possible.

The Importance of Basic Research

One uncontroversial conclusion of work on the determinants of productivity growth is that the payoff to investment in basic scientific and technological research has been vast, at least in some fields and over the long run. Breakthroughs on fundamental questions of physics, chemistry, biology, and other sciences have powered the transformations of economic production that underlie much of the productivity growth measured (however imperfectly) in economic statistics (Nordhaus 1997; Nelson and Romer 1996).

The Administration has taken that lesson to heart in its support for basic research in science and technology, especially in two areas where the need for progress is pressing: energy and biomedical research. The Department of Energy has created a new Advanced Research Projects Agency-Energy (ARPA-E), with the objective of pursuing breakthroughs that could fundamentally change the way we use and produce energy. In the medical and biological sciences, the Administration has ended restrictions on Federal funding for embryonic stem cell research, and in September 2009 it announced $5 billion in grants under the American Recovery and Reinvestment Act to fund cutting-edge medical research.

Across all areas, the Recovery Act included $18.3 billion for research funding. Because the Administration's commitment to evidence-based policymaking will require substantial improvements in the ability to reliably measure economic outcomes, the Act committed $1 billion to the 2010 Census as a first step in a longer-term effort to revamp the Nation's statistical infrastructure—a process that will not only improve policymaking but will also help private businesses make better decisions (for example, about where to locate new production or sales facilities).

In addition, the fiscal year 2011 budget enhances research funding in numerous ways. First, it continues to work to fulfill the President's pledge to double the budgets of three key science agencies (the National Science Foundation, the Department of Energy's Office of Science, and the Department of Commerce's National Institute of Standards and Technology). Second, it boosts funding for biomedical research at the National Institutes of Health by $1 billion to $32.1 billion. Third, it reinvigorates climate change research through increased investments in earth observations and climate science in agencies such as the U.S. Geological Survey and the National Oceanic and Atmospheric Administration. Fourth, it funds potentially groundbreaking discoveries with a boost to Department of Defense basic research and $300 million for the Department of Energy's ARPA-E program. Finally, it supports world-class agricultural research for national needs such as food safety and bioenergy with $429 million for the competitive research grants program in the Department of Agriculture's new National Institute of Food and Agriculture.

As part of the innovation agenda, and to ensure that the increased research funds are spent well, the Administration has also instructed agencies to work on constructing a set of systematic tools to track the long-term results of federally sponsored research, such as journal articles published and cited, patents obtained, medical advances achieved, or other measurable consequences (particularly in areas of national importance such as health or energy). Although the fruits of this effort will not be available for a number of years, the project is one of the most promising in the Administration's efforts at turning the evaluation of scientific research into a "science of science."

Private Research and Experimentation

Scientific breakthroughs are only the first step in producing improvements in total factor productivity and hence living standards. Benjamin Franklin's discovery that lightning was a form of electricity did not produce an immediate reduction in damage from electrical storms; much further research and development was necessary to turn that discovery into the lightning rod (though by late in his life Franklin was able to observe a flourishing industry that had been built upon his insight).

Measuring the returns to the economy as a whole from private research and experimentation is almost as formidable a challenge as measuring the returns to basic research. But most studies find that aggregate returns to such spending are much higher than the returns to ordinary investments in physical capital. Some work estimates the aggregate returns at 50 percent or higher (Hall, Mairesse, and Mohnen 2009).

These returns are mostly not received by the firms or individuals who pay for the work, because the ideas ultimately benefit others in many ways whose value is not captured through markets. Economic theory provides a clear prescription for policy toward activities that have measurable positive externalities: the activities should be subsidized.

This is the logic behind the research and experimentation (R&E) tax credit that has been an off-and-on part of the tax code for many years. But the credit's effectiveness has been hampered by chronic uncertainty about how long it will remain in force. Partly for budgetary accounting reasons, the R&E tax credit has been treated for many years as a temporary provision that was scheduled to expire at some point in the near future. Yet each year (except for 1995), Congress and the President have agreed (sometimes at the last minute) to extend the credit. The effect has been to substantially increase the uncertainty that firms face about the costs that they will end up paying for their research and experimentation projects; this uncertainty can have a serious negative effect on research, which is already a highly uncertain investment. The problem is particularly acute for the kinds of projects that might be expected to have the highest returns: long-term projects that require continuing expenditures over many years. For such projects, uncertainty about whether the R&E tax credit will be in place through the duration of the project can make the difference between pursuing or abandoning the research. The Administration therefore supports efforts in Congress to make the R&E tax credit permanent, so that the highest-return long-run projects can be confidently started without uncertainty about whether the credit will be there for the duration.

The importance of both public and private R&D spending for innovation and improvements in standards of living forms the basis for a key Administration goal. In a speech in May 2009 to the National Academy of Sciences, the President articulated the ambition of boosting total national investment in research and development to 3 percent of gross domestic product. As can be seen from Figure 10-3, this is a rate that would exceed even the peak rates reached in the 1960s. As described earlier, the American Recovery and Reinvestment Act began the Federal contribution with a historic increase in direct funding for scientific and technological research, as well as major investments in technological and scientific infrastructure detailed below. But reaching the President's goal will require not just an increase in the Federal Government's role; equally important is the need for a resurgence of entrepreneurial and corporate investment in research. The Administration's consequent focus on creating the best possible environment for private sector innovation is one of the many novel aspects of its innovation agenda.

Figure 10-3
R&D Spending as a Percent of GDP

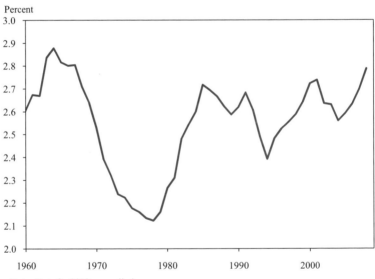

Note: Data for 2008 are preliminary.
Sources: National Science Foundation, Science and Engineering Indicators 2010 Tables 4-1 and 4-7.

Protection of Intellectual Property Rights

A subsidy like the R&E credit is one way to address underinvestment caused by the fact that the inventor of a new technology does not reap all the benefits of that invention. An older approach is embodied in the American system of patents and copyrights that had its origins in the Constitution (and before that, in the English legal system).

One leading scholar (Jones 2001) has argued that the invention of ways to protect intellectual property may have been a trigger for the industrial revolution that led to the modern era of economic growth. In this interpretation of history, the creation of a legal system that could protect intellectual property may have been one of the most important "technological" developments in human history. Though this interpretation can be debated, the practical implication is surely correct: achieving the proper balance between the private and the societal rewards from innovation is a critical element in creating and sustaining long-run economic growth.

The existing U.S. patent system developed over many years in response to the needs of an industrial economy. That system has been under considerable strain in the past couple of decades as the United States and the world have moved increasingly toward a "knowledge-based" economy. The Patent and Trademark Office (PTO) has been required to answer many questions that could not have been imagined in 1952 when the current patent statute was written, such as how and whether to grant patents for human genes or for Internet advertising tools. Further, the sheer volume of information necessary to evaluate a patent application, which might now arrive from any country in the world and might rely on ideas that even an expert might be unfamiliar with, has made the PTO's job increasingly daunting. As a result of these challenges, the agency currently faces a backlog of over 700,000 unexamined applications. Waiting times on a patent application can extend to four years or more. The costs that such waiting times impose on firms are substantial; and delays impose a particularly large burden on startup firms that rely on patents to attract venture capital funding—precisely the kind of firms that the Administration's innovation agenda is particularly designed to help.

While the PTO has made progress in responding to these problems, most notably by developing a "peer review" system modeled on academic publishing, observers agree that the patent system is in need of an overhaul. The Administration has endorsed the aims of bills pending in Congress that would address many of these problems, particularly by giving the PTO authority to set fees that cover the cost of application processing, and also by barring diversion of fees to projects unrelated to PTO activities. The PTO is also in the process of creating an Office of the Chief Economist, which will provide a mechanism for better integration into patent policy of economic research on how to properly reward innovation without stifling the widespread use of good ideas.

In recognition of the role of innovation and intellectual property in advancing continued U.S. leadership in the global economy, in 2008

Congress created the Office of the United States Intellectual Property Enforcement Coordinator. This office is charged with creating and implementing a strategy to coordinate and enhance enforcement of intellectual property rights in the United States and overseas. By ensuring that the Administration has a coordinated strategy, this office will work to ensure that the effort of American workers and businesses to produce creative and innovative products and services is valued fairly around the world.

Spurring Progress in National Priority Areas

Much of the Administration's innovation agenda is aimed at creating a general economic environment that encourages innovation across the board. But the Administration has also focused special attention on certain areas where particular national needs are urgent. These include investments in building a "smart grid" to enhance the reliability, flexibility, and efficiency of the electricity transmission grid; research on renewable energy technologies like wind, solar, and biofuels; and support for research into advanced vehicle technologies. These investments are motivated not only by the perception that technological breakthroughs are possible and would be highly valuable, but also by the enormous potential benefits that such breakthroughs could have in terms of enhancing national security, mitigating pollution, and stemming climate change. These are also investments that have a direct impact on creating high-paying, durable jobs—something that is particularly valuable at a time of high unemployment. Thus, as noted in Chapter 9, investments in the clean energy transformation involve two layers of externalities: innovators fail to receive the full economic benefits of their breakthroughs as measured by market valuation, and the market valuation itself understates the true social benefits of the breakthroughs.

Another priority, given the looming threat that health care spending poses to the Federal budget, is developing technologies for measuring and monitoring health more efficiently. Through the Recovery Act, the Administration has allocated substantial funds to development of a 21st-century system of medical recordkeeping that should jump-start work in this area.

Increasing Openness and Transparency

To noneconomists, the idea that the legal system or the Patent Office is a form of technology seems a bit of a stretch. Even more challenging is the idea that a society's overall degree of openness and transparency may be a key determinant of economic progress. Yet a substantial body of economic research has found that measures of openness and transparency in governmental policymaking processes have a strong association with growth outcomes.

There are several reasons why this may be so. One fairly simple one is that openness and transparency make it more difficult for special interests to achieve their aims at the expense of the public. Another view, which is not in conflict with the first, is that the process of requiring policies to be explained and encouraging wide discussion about them yields new ideas and improvements of existing ideas that might not otherwise have occurred even to the cleverest and most well-motivated public servant.

A more speculative proposition is that a commitment to openness and transparency on the part of the government is a form of investment in the kind of "organizational capital" described earlier. Economic research has found a strong correlation between measures of governmental transparency or openness and private sector productivity. Interpretations of this relationship are a matter of debate; some scholars argue that higher levels of productivity and income cause citizens to demand better government; others argue that both governmental openness and private productivity are a reflection of deeper unmeasured forces; and some advocate the straightforward view that open and transparent government has a direct effect in producing greater private sector efficiency.

The Administration's commitment in this area has been on full display in the unprecedented openness and transparency surrounding implementation of the Recovery Act. The most obvious manifestation of this transparency is the creation of the independent Recovery Accountability and Transparency Board charged with monitoring and reporting on the government spending under the Act. Likewise, the requirement that recipients report on job creation and retention each quarter provides a new source of information on the employment impact of the Act. The knowledge generated by the data collection and measurement under the Recovery Act will be valuable in assessing economic policymaking for years to come.

The principles of openness, accountability, and public input are far broader than just the Recovery Act, however. The Administration's "open government" initiative aims to harness the power of the Internet to bring the same commitment to transparency and accountability to every part of the Federal Government. New tools for this purpose are being developed not only by government agencies but by the private sector, by open source software programmers, and by citizens around the country. It seems plausible that eventually the new kinds of openness and transparency made possible by new forms of technology will have the same kinds of positive effects on growth that openness and transparency seem to have had across countries in the past.

TRADE AS AN ENGINE OF PRODUCTIVITY GROWTH
AND HIGHER LIVING STANDARDS

Specialization has long been understood to be an important source of productivity growth. In his *Wealth of Nations,* Adam Smith (1776) extolled the virtues of specialization in the pin factory where many different specialized laborers were involved in producing a simple pin. Perhaps the most important form of specialization is a transition from a subsistence society, where people produce all their consumption goods themselves, to a market economy, where people focus on particular skills and occupations and depend on purchases for their daily needs. Another significant transition, though, is one from a country that must produce everything its inhabitants want to consume toward one that specializes in particular goods and services and sells them on global markets for other goods and services.

Increases in trade and increases in GDP tend to go hand in hand, but untangling whether economic growth is generating more trade or whether trade is lifting growth is a difficult task. Creative research, however, has been able to demonstrate the causal role trade plays in increasing the amount a society can produce. One study demonstrated that countries that were geographically better suited for trade (because of their proximity to trading partners, access to ports, and the like) have higher levels of GDP (Frankel and Romer 1999). Another demonstrated that the same relationship can be seen across time (Feyrer 2009).[3]

Initially, trade was about introducing products (such as spices) from one market to another, providing consumers with choices they previously did not have. Still today, trade can offer consumers different goods and different varieties of products already available to them and bring new technology from other countries. By allowing countries to specialize based on skills or endowments, trade can also allow countries to improve their standards of living. Trade can also help a country increase its overall output by allowing firms or industries to take advantage of economies of scale or by encouraging the growth of more productive firms. Thus, trade has the potential to increase the overall quantity of goods and services that a given economy can produce with its resources—and hence increase the overall standard of living—making global commerce a cooperative, not a competitive venture. A clear rules-based system with enforcement of those rules can help ensure that trade is mutually beneficial.

---

[3] The transition from sea to air traffic for much of the world's trade has meant more of a collapsing of distance for some nations than others. Because some sea-based trading routes are inconvenient, a shift to air transport has increased trade more for some nations than others. Controlling for other features, countries whose trade has increased due to this transition have grown faster than other countries.

While the act of specializing should lift living standards over time, it requires shifting resources from one sector to another, and so can generate short-run dislocations. As a result, it is essential to strengthen both targeted and more general policies that seek to ensure all can benefit from increases in trade. For this reason, after this section describes the productivity-enhancing benefits trade can generate for the U.S. economy, the following section discusses how progressive taxation and a strong social safety net are crucial counterparts to productivity change of all types.

The United States and International Trade

Because of its massive size, the United States can engage in a considerable amount of specialization and trade within its own economy. Historically, foreign trade as a share of GDP has been smaller in the United States than in most other countries. In 1970, exports as a share of GDP for the average member of the Organisation for Economic Co-operation and Development (OECD) was 25 percent, while in the United States, the share was just 6 percent. By 2008, exports had increased to 13 percent of the U.S. economy (see Figure 10-4). Although that share is still relatively small, the increase in trade over the past four decades has meant that even in a large country like the United States, global commerce is an important part of the economy and—as discussed below—can be an important source of productivity growth.

Figure 10-4
Exports as a Share of GDP

Source: Department of Commerce (Bureau of Economic Analysis), National Income and Product Accounts Table 1.1.10.

Millions of American workers contribute to the production of goods and services that are exported to foreign markets, and their jobs, on average, pay higher wages than a typical job. The Commerce Department estimates that in 2008 U.S. exports represented the work of roughly 10 million American workers. The majority of these export-supported jobs were related to the export of goods; millions more were related to services exports and nearly a million were related to agricultural exports. The manufacturing sector is particularly connected to exports; 20 to 30 percent of manufacturing employment in the United States in 2008 was supported by exports. These estimates represent the number of job-equivalents based on total hours needed to produce the volume of exports. Because few workers produce exclusively exports or inputs for exports, the number of workers who are involved with exports is likely much larger than 10 million.

Currently, the U.S. economy is far from full employment, and any increased production could generate an increase in jobs. Chapter 4 discusses how an increase in exports may be an important part of GDP growth in the medium term. In the long run, though, the principal contribution of an increase in the trade share will be the increase in productivity and living standards it can generate. Thus, the rise in the export share of the economy from 6 percent in 1970 to 13 percent today represents specialization, as some workers who produced goods for domestic use have moved into export sectors. The following sections describe the ways in which trade can increase productivity.

Sources of Productivity Growth from International Trade

Productivity growth can come from a number of channels. Trade can allow increased specialization; it can allow increased scale of production; and it can allow more productive firms to grow rapidly, increasing their share of the economy.

Specialization. In the United States, a primary source of trade-related productivity growth is specialization. The concept of Ricardian comparative advantage—that nations specialize in producing the goods that they can produce cheaply relative to other goods—can be seen in a number of aspects of U.S. trade. America makes far more aircraft, grain, plastics, and equipment (optical, photographic, and medical) than it consumes. In these product areas, the United States has a substantial trade surplus, totaling over $100 billion in 2008. Conversely, the United States produces less electrical equipment, clothing, furniture, and toys than it consumes, and therefore imports more of these goods than it exports. If America cut its production of aircraft, where it has a comparative advantage, by the $50 billion it currently exports on net and instead tried to produce more of the goods we currently import, productivity would likely be lower.

Specialization also takes place within industries. For example, within the broad category of "electrical machinery and equipment," America imports telephones (including cell phones) and computer monitors, but exports electronic integrated circuits. Specialization can even take place within more narrow product classifications (for example, computer memory). Advanced countries with higher wages tend to produce and export more high-quality products even as they import lower-cost, lower-quality products from abroad in the same product type. Economists refer to this within-product differentiation as the "quality ladder," and extensive research in recent years has noted this pattern of specialization within products (Schott 2004). Over time, high-skill countries climb the quality ladder, making higher-quality products and increasingly importing low-skill products.

For example, consider the category "electrically erasable programmable read-only memory." The United States both imports and exports billions of dollars worth of products in this category every year, but the average unit price of the exports is roughly three times the average unit price of the imports. The U.S. products may have bigger memories with more complex production processes or be of higher quality than the cheaper imports. In any event, the imports and exports do not appear to be overlapping. Again, such a division of labor allows for higher standards of living across the world.

Intra-Industry Trade. Beyond specialization, trade can generate productivity advances in a number of ways. One important channel is that trade can allow companies to achieve a scale of production that they could not attain by selling just to the local market, thus increasing their productivity. Within any given economy, there is a limit to the quantity of a specific good that the domestic market will want to consume. The ability to manufacture more of a product than domestic consumption supports and exchange it for other products—even ones that are extremely similar to the exported good—can be quite beneficial. It results in economies of scale that can be internal to a firm, where one company grows quite large and productive at making one good, or to a region, where a particular good tends to be made in a given physical location as a substantial amount of expertise builds up there.

Trade in which different quality or simply different brand products are traded in both directions, known as intra-industry trade, represents between 40 and 50 percent of trade in the world economy. For the manufacturing industry of the United States, that figure is even higher. As Figure 10-5 shows, intra-industry foreign trade moved from roughly 65 percent of U.S.

manufacturing trade in the 1980s to roughly 75 percent in 2001. Frequently, this means two very similar countries engaging in trade with each other. Five of the seven largest U.S. trading partners are advanced economies; in fact, despite some observers' focus on low-wage country imports, roughly 50 percent of U.S. imports come from other advanced economies. These countries often have similar endowments of labor and are generally able to use the same technology, but narrow specialization within product classes, different brands, or differences in resource allocations allows for productive exchange.

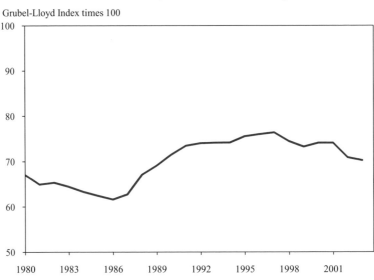

Figure 10-5
Intra-Industry Trade, U.S. Manufacturing

Source: Organisation for Economic Co-operation and Development, Structural Analysis (STAN) database.

Firm Productivity. Trade can also allow productive firms to grow relative to less productive firms as they increase their scale. A new literature on "heterogeneous firms" has focused less on differences in endowments or comparative advantage across countries and more on how firms within an economy respond to trade. A crucial insight in this literature is that most firms do not engage in trade, but those that do are on average more productive and pay higher wages. This literature shows that when a country opens to trade, more productive firms grow relative to less productive firms, thus shifting labor and other resources to the better organized firms and increasing overall productivity. Even if workers do not switch industries, they move from firms that are either poorly managed or that use less advanced technology and production processes toward the more productive firms. Thus, firm-level evidence demonstrates that trade allows not only economy-wide advances through resource allocation, but also allows within-industry productivity advances through reallocation of resources across firms. This shift has clear welfare-enhancing impacts; see Bernard et al. (2007) for a general overview of this literature.

Vertical Specialization. Thus far, the discussion regarding sources of productivity growth in international trade has assumed that finished goods are being bought and sold across borders. The world of trade, though, has changed substantially. Today, multinational corporations (U.S. or foreign-based) are involved in 64 percent of U.S. goods trade (imports and exports), and fully 19 percent of U.S. goods exports are sales from a U.S. multinational firm to its affiliates abroad. An increase in international vertical specialization, where firms have production in multiple countries and break up the production of a particular good into stages across different countries, has contributed significantly to growth in world trade. The process can be within a large firm or intermediate inputs can be bought and sold on the market. Decreased trade costs have made it easier to break up the value chain of production as various parts of production can be done in different places and an in-process good can be shipped many times before final assembly. One study estimates that roughly one-third of the growth in world trade from 1970 to 1990 was attributable to the growth in vertical-specialization exports (Hummels, Ishii, and Yi 2001). Calculations about the extent of vertical specialization vary from estimates that 30 percent of OECD exports contain imported inputs to estimates that intermediate inputs account for up to 60 percent of world trade.[4]

A trade system in which the same firms are both importers and exporters complicates considerations of the impacts of trade on different groups, as comparative advantage may not matter as much for a particular good as for a particular task or piece of the production process. Specialization by process should allow the United States to focus on jobs oriented toward the processes that match the human capital, physical capital, and technology in the United States, again increasing productivity. But it has also raised fears that the process of adjustment could be disruptive, as a broader range of jobs could be exposed to international competition. The crucial policy goal is to harness the benefits of trade and ensure that its benefits are shared broadly by all Americans.

---

[4] The 30 percent figure refers specifically to the share of exports that is made from imported inputs—sometimes called the vertical specialization of exports. The larger figure includes the volume of trade that is imports of intermediate goods used in the production of goods for either exports or the home market.

Encouraging Trade and Enforcing Trade Agreements

All of these aspects of trade highlight its potential to contribute to the long-run expansion of productivity in the United States. Many of the advantages of increased trade come from opening foreign markets to the products of U.S. workers. The best way to guarantee reliable access is through negotiated trade agreements and consistent enforcement of existing trade rules. As noted in Chapter 3, one positive development in the recent crisis is that, for the most part, countries did not resort to protectionism; that is, they did not close their markets to imports. Had they done so, the dislocation in U.S. employment would likely have been much worse. As it was, U.S. imports of goods and services fell 34 percent and exports dropped 26 percent from July 2008 to April 2009. From their peak in the third quarter of 2008 until the trough in the second quarter of 2009, the nominal value of exports of goods and services fell more than $400 billion at an annual rate, a drop of almost 3 percent of GDP. Imports also dropped substantially. In the long run, such a decline in world trade would be harmful for the U.S. economy. If trade had stayed at that depressed level, with lower trade surpluses in the United States' main export goods and smaller trade deficits in our import goods, the long-run dislocations from the crisis would have been worse than now expected. But U.S. exports are rebounding, opening the possibility that many workers who lost jobs in the crisis may find employment in the same productive industries where they were before the crisis.

Several explanations have been offered for this avoidance of protectionism during the crisis. One is the availability of macroeconomic policy tools such as fiscal and monetary policy (Eichengreen and Irwin 2009); another is the public commitments made by leaders at the Group of Twenty summits to avoid protectionist strategies. But the clear and concrete rules-based trade system was helpful as well. That rules-based system, embodied by the World Trade Organization (WTO) and by other trade commitments, allows the United States to take steps to ensure that other countries will abide by their obligations. It is also designed to give U.S. workers and firms confidence about the economic environment they will be facing and confidence that commitments made when trade agreements are negotiated will be kept. In addition, creating predictable and enforceable markets for innovative and creative works grounded in intellectual property rights is essential to spurring and protecting U.S. investments in technology and innovation.

The Administration recognizes that simply negotiating trade frameworks is not enough; robust enforcement of trade rules is an important part of our engagement in the world economy. The Administration has taken many trade enforcement actions recently. For example, the

Administration has continued pressing a WTO case that challenged China's treatment of U.S. auto parts exports. The ruling in this case resulted in China having to change its policies and increase its openness to U.S. exports. The United States (joined by Mexico and the European Union) has also initiated an action challenging China's use of subsidies and taxes to keep input costs low for firms in China, which lowers the cost of final goods from China relative to the world. Further, the Administration takes very seriously the "Special 301" process under which it monitors the protection and enforcement of intellectual property rights. In 2009, it added Canada to the priority watch list because Canada has not implemented key proposals to improve enforcement and protection of intellectual property rights. Actions like these represent the Administration's intent (made explicit, for example, in United States Trade Representative Ronald Kirk's speeches[5]) to enforce trade rules and aggressively pursue actions to open markets to U.S. exports.

As noted in Chapter 4, the Administration is currently pursuing these and other options to expand American exports, recognizing that increasing exports will be a key part of the U.S. growth model. Increases in our exports in the short run can help to return the economy to full employment. Over the longer run, increases in trade provide avenues for the United States to increase productivity through specialization, scale, and firm effects, and in turn, increase standards of living for American families.

Currently, a number of other trade expansion opportunities exist for the United States. The Administration supports a strong market-opening agreement for both goods and services in the WTO Doha Round negotiations and is continuing to work with U.S. trade partners on potential free trade agreements. Because the United States is a relatively open economy, negotiated trade deals often involve substantial improvements in access for U.S. exports to other countries relative to the market opening made by the United States.

It is also important that these trade frameworks protect productivity-enhancing innovation through adequate provisions for intellectual property rights and that they reflect our values regarding workers and the environment. An example of the Administration's actions to improve the world's trading regime is seen in the way the Administration is working to engage our trading partners across the Pacific region in a new regional agreement (the Trans-Pacific Partnership). It will be a high-standards agreement that expands trade in a way that is beneficial to the economy, workers, small businesses, and farmers, and is consistent with the values of the United States.

In addition to benefits to the United States, trade benefits our trade partners. This is of direct benefit to Americans in the sense that as these

---

[5] See for example his speech at Mon Valley Works—Edgar Thomson Plant on July 16, 2009.

economies grow, they can grow as a destination for U.S. exports. Trade can also have large benefits for the poorest countries. In particular, multilateral agreements that open trade flows between developing countries can have substantial impacts on poorer countries, and trade relations with the United States can be a crucial part of the path to development for the poorest countries. For example, the African Growth and Opportunity Act seeks to increase two-way trade with poor nations in sub-Saharan Africa, help integrate these countries into the global economy, and do so in a way that improves their institutions and reduces poverty. As development in the poorest nations of the world is in our national interest strategically, economically, and morally, trade presents win-win opportunities to advance development.

Ensuring the Gains from Productivity Growth Are Widely Shared

Any productivity advance—be it from technological change, trade, or other factors—will have different impacts across the economy. As discussed earlier, productivity advances are crucial to an increase in living standards. Still, those firms that do not make a specific advance will likely contract or fail, and some workers in the affected industry may face losses. Likewise, international trade can have disparate effects across industries, firms, and workers. In both cases, society on average will be better off because the economy is able to generate a higher standard of living. But the recent stagnation in median real wages despite positive productivity growth (discussed in Chapter 8) highlights the challenge of ensuring that the gains from productivity growth are widely spread.

The potential for productivity advances to generate disparities in outcomes suggests the need for strong social policy to support those who do not immediately benefit and to ensure that gains from trade and productivity advances are shared by all. Because identifying directly impacted individuals is difficult, the logical response to productivity advances is a strong social safety net that ensures that all benefit from the rise in living standards. Trade theory suggests that trade liberalization can generate gains that are large enough that they can be shared in a way that every member of society is made better off. In the past, however, the gains from our trade policies have not been shared sufficiently, and technological change and globalization have left many behind.

Trade adjustment assistance, worker retraining, and temporary relief programs are ways the Federal Government can and does support those who do not benefit from these advances. The Administration has supported trade adjustment assistance, which provides additional unemployment funds, retraining, and health coverage assistance, and has made trade adjustment assistance available to a wider set of employees through the Trade and Globalization Adjustment Assistance Act of 2009.

These specific institutions, though, are not enough. More broad-based policy must ensure that as the economy grows in the long run, it enhances living standards for all citizens. Progressive taxation—which can be justified in many ways—is supported by the uneven outcomes from productivity advances and globalization. Those whose incomes rise can pay a larger share of total taxes and still be better off than before the gains. By doing so, they support lower taxes for others whose incomes may have declined. This process makes everyone better off and thus supports innovation and open borders by minimizing the number of people who feel threatened by productivity advances and therefore oppose them.

For example, the ability to sell books across borders certainly enhanced the income J.K. Rowling was able to collect from writing the famous Harry Potter books. Had she been able to sell her books only in the United Kingdom, her audience and income would have been much smaller. In addition, millions of American readers benefited from the increased consumer choice and the ability to purchase her books. Similarly, more Americans can work as well-paid aircraft engineers or manufacturing employees for Boeing or as technology specialists for Apple because those firms are able to sell on a world market. At the same time, it is distinctly possible that some American authors who would have captured a larger share of the "magic-oriented book" market had there been no trade in literature were crowded out by Rowling's success, or that some handheld music device engineer in the United Kingdom has had to find another career because of Apple's success.

A progressive tax rate combined with trade allows those who realize substantial income gains from globalization to still prosper a great deal relative to the state where there is no trade and incomes are taxed at a flat rate. And it does so while making sure that those who face lower incomes from globalization also obtain benefits—not just through the lower prices and expanded choices associated with trade, but also through lower taxation.

Beyond a progressive tax rate, a strong social safety net can cushion the disruption generated by a dynamic economy. Unemployment insurance can provide temporary income. A robust health care system can ensure that temporary dislocations do not generate drastic consequences. And a vibrant education system can prepare workers for changing economic needs.

Conclusion

Advances in productivity are crucial to increasing the living standards of all Americans—to building a better future. Innovation initiatives, such as increased research and development, targeted investments, stronger intellectual property rights, and harnessing trade's productivity-enhancing potential, are all essential parts of lifting living standards in the long run. But to ensure living standards are rising for all, a dynamic open economy depends on a robust social infrastructure. Education improvements described in Chapter 8 are crucial to creating a well-trained labor force able to thrive in a flexible economy where innovation and trade may reshape industries over time. A sound health care system is needed to provide the certainty that changing jobs will not mean a loss of health services. And a productive, well-regulated financial system is essential to allocate capital to growing sectors. Thus, the initiatives being taken today as part of the Administration's rescue-and-rebuild programs are not meant only to correct the problems of today, but to set the stage for strong growth over decades to come.

REFERENCES

Chapter 1
To Rescue, Rebalance, and Rebuild

Congressional Budget Office. 2009a. *The Budget and Economic Outlook: Fiscal Years 2009 to 2019.*

————. 2009b. *The Long-Term Budget Outlook.*

Goldin, Claudia, and Lawrence F. Katz. 2007. "Long-Run Changes in the Wage Structure: Narrowing, Widening, Polarizing." *Brookings Papers on Economic Activity*, no. 2: 135–67.

Group of Twenty. 2009. "Leaders' Statement: The Pittsburgh Summit." September 24–25 (www.g20.org/Documents/pittsburgh_summit_leaders_statement_250909.pdf).

Kaiser Family Foundation and Health Research and Educational Trust. 2009. *Employer Health Benefits: 2009 Annual Survey.* Menlo Park, CA, and Chicago, IL: Henry J. Kaiser Family Foundation and Health Research and Educational Trust.

Shiller, Robert J. 2005. *Irrational Exuberance.* 2nd ed. Princeton University Press.

Chapter 2
Rescuing the Economy from the Great Recession

Almeida, Heitor, et al. 2009. "Corporate Debt Maturity and the Real Effects of the 2007 Credit Crisis." Working Paper 14990. Cambridge, MA: National Bureau of Economic Research (May).

Bernanke, Ben S. 1983. "Nonmonetary Effects of the Financial Crisis in the Propagation of the Great Depression." *American Economic Review* 73, no. 3: 257–76.

Broda, Christian, and Jonathan Parker. 2008. "The Impact of the 2008 Tax Rebates on Consumer Spending: Preliminary Evidence." Working Paper. University of Chicago, Graduate School of Business (July).

Campello, Murillo, John Graham, and Campbell R. Harvey. 2009. "The Real Effects of Financial Constraints: Evidence from a Financial Crisis." Working Paper 15552. Cambridge, MA: National Bureau of Economic Research (December).

Congressional Budget Office. 2009a. "Estimated Impact of the American Recovery and Reinvestment Act on Employment and Economic Output as of September 2009." November.

———. 2009b. Letter to the Honorable Charles E. Grassley. "Estimated Macroeconomic Impacts of the American Recovery and Reinvestment Act of 2009." March 2.

Council of Economic Advisers. 2009. "Economic Analysis of the Car Allowance Rebate System ('Cash for Clunkers')." September.

———. 2010. "The Economic Impact of the American Recovery and Reinvestment Act of 2009." Second Quarterly Report to Congress. January.

Gertler, Mark, and Simon Gilchrist. 1994. "Monetary Policy, Business Cycles, and the Behavior of Small Manufacturing Firms." *Quarterly Journal of Economics* 109, no. 2: 309–40.

Kashyap, Anil K, Owen A. Lamont, and Jeremy C. Stein. 1994. "Credit Conditions and the Cyclical Behavior of Inventories." *Quarterly Journal of Economics* 109, no. 3: 565–92.

Lamont, Owen A. 1997. "Cash Flow and Investment: Evidence from Internal Capital Markets." *Journal of Finance* 52, no. 1: 83–109.

Peek, Joe, and Eric S. Rosengren. 2000. "Collateral Damage: Effects of the Japanese Bank Crisis on Real Activity in the United States." *American Economic Review* 90, no. 1: 30–45.

Rauh, Joshua D. 2006. "Investment and Financing Constraints: Evidence from the Funding of Corporate Pension Plans." *Journal of Finance* 61, no. 1: 33–71.

Rudebusch, Glenn D. 2009. "The Fed's Monetary Policy Response to the Current Crisis." FRBSF Economic Letter 2009-17. Federal Reserve Bank of San Francisco (May).

Sahm, Claudia R., Matthew D. Shapiro, and Joel B. Slemrod. 2009. "Household Response to the 2008 Tax Rebate: Survey Evidence and Aggregate Implications." Working Paper 15421. Cambridge, MA: National Bureau of Economic Research (October).

Shiller, Robert J. 2005. *Irrational Exuberance.* 2nd ed. Princeton University Press.

⸻ ◆ ◆ ◆ ⸻

Chapter 3
Crisis and Recovery in the World Economy

Baldwin, Richard, ed. 2009. *The Great Trade Collapse: Causes, Consequences and Prospects.* VoxEU.org Ebook.

Bown, Chad P. Forthcoming. "The Global Resort to Antidumping, Safeguards, and Other Trade Remedies Amidst the Economic Crisis." In *Trade Implications of Policy Responses to the Crisis,* edited by Simon J. Evenett and Bernard Hoekman.

Council of Economic Advisers. 2009. "The Effects of Fiscal Stimulus: A Cross-Country Perspective." September.

Eichengreen, Barry, and Douglas A. Irwin. 2009. "The Slide to Protectionism in the Great Depression: Who Succumbed and Why?" Working Paper 15142. Cambridge, MA: National Bureau of Economic Research (July).

Fender, Ingo, and Jacob Gyntelberg. 2008. "Overview: Global Financial Crisis Spurs Unprecedented Policy Actions." *BIS Quarterly Review* (December): 1–24.

Freund, Caroline. 2009. "Demystifying the Collapse in Trade." VoxEU.org.

Horton, Mark, Manmohan Kumar, and Paolo Mauro. 2009. "The State of Public Finances: A Cross-Country Fiscal Monitor." IMF Staff Position Note SPN/09/21. Washington, DC: International Monetary Fund (July).

International Monetary Fund. 2009a. *World Economic Outlook: October 2009.* Washington, DC.

⸻ (Strategy, Policy and Review Department). 2009b. "Review of Recent Crisis Programs." Washington, DC. September.

Johnson, Robert C., and Guillermo Noguera. 2009. "Accounting for Intermediates: Production Sharing and Trade in Value Added." Working Paper. Princeton University and University of California, Berkeley (May).

Lane, Philip R., and Jay C. Shambaugh. Forthcoming. "Financial Exchange Rates and International Currency Exposures." *American Economic Review.*

Levchenko, Andrei A., Logan Lewis, and Linda L. Tesar. 2009. "The Collapse of International Trade During the 2008–2009 Crisis: In Search of the Smoking Gun." Research Seminar in International Economics Discussion Paper 592. University of Michigan (October).

McGuire, Patrick, and Goetz von Peter. 2009. "The U.S. Dollar Shortage in Global Banking." *BIS Quarterly Review* (March): 47–63.

Miroudot, Sébastien, and Alexandros Ragoussis. 2009. "Vertical Trade, Trade Costs and FDI." Trade Policy Working Paper 89. Paris: Organisation for Economic Co-operation and Development (July).

Mora, Jesse, and William Powers. 2009. "Did Trade Credit Problems Deepen the Great Trade Collapse?" In *The Great Trade Collapse: Causes, Consequences and Prospects,* edited by Richard Baldwin. VoxEU.org Ebook.

Obstfeld, Maurice, and Kenneth Rogoff. 2009. "Global Imbalances and the Financial Crisis: Products of Common Causes." Discussion Paper 7606. Washington, DC: Center for Economic Policy Research (December).

Organisation for Economic Co-operation and Development. 2009a. *Economic Outlook No. 85.* Paris.

———. 2009b. *Economic Outlook No. 86.* Paris.

CHAPTER 4
SAVING AND INVESTMENT

Auerbach, Alan J., Jinyong Cai, and Laurence J. Kotlikoff. 1991. "U.S. Demographics and Saving: Predictions of Three Saving Models." *Carnegie-Rochester Conference Series on Public Policy* 34, no. 1: 135–56.

Benartzi, Shlomo, and Richard Thaler. 2004. "Save More Tomorrow: Using Behavioral Economics to Increase Employee Savings." *Journal of Political Economy* 112, no. S1: S164–87.

Carroll, Christopher D., Jeffrey C. Fuhrer, and David W. Wilcox. 1994. "Does Consumer Sentiment Forecast Household Spending? If So, Why?" *American Economic Review* 84, no. 5: 1397–408.

Congressional Budget Office. 2008. "The Outlook for Housing Starts, 2009 to 2012." Background Paper. November.

Dynan, Karen E. 2009. "Changing Household Financial Opportunities and Economic Security." *Journal of Economic Perspectives* 23, no. 4: 49–68.

Edelberg, Wendy. 2006. "'Risk-Based Pricing of Interest Rates for Consumer Loans." *Journal of Monetary Economics* 53, no. 8: 2283–98.

Getter, Darryl. 2006. "Consumer Credit Risk and Pricing." *Journal of Consumer Affairs* 40, no. 1: 41–63.

Jappelli, Tullio, and Marco Pagano. 1993. "Information Sharing in Credit Markets." *Journal of Finance* 48, no. 5: 1693–718.

Lown, Cara S., and Donald P. Morgan. 2006. "The Credit Cycle and the Business Cycle: New Findings Using the Loan Officer Opinion Survey." *Journal of Money, Credit, and Banking* 38, no. 6: 1575–97.

Macroeconomic Advisers. 2009. "The Trough in Housing Starts: Are We There Yet?" *Macro Focus* 4, no. 5: 1–9.

Melitz, Marc J. 2003. "The Impact of Trade on Intra-Industry Reallocations and Aggregate Industry Productivity." *Econometrica* 71, no. 6: 1695–725.

Muellbauer, John N. 2007. "Housing, Credit and Consumer Expenditure." In *Housing, Housing Finance, and Monetary Policy*, pp. 267–334. Kansas City: Federal Reserve Bank of Kansas City.

Office of Management and Budget. 2009. *The Budget of the United States, Fiscal Year 2010.*

CHAPTER 5
ADDRESSING THE LONG-RUN FISCAL CHALLENGE

Alesina, Alberto, and Roberto Perotti. 1997. "Fiscal Adjustments in OECD Countries: Composition and Macroeconomic Effects." *IMF Staff Papers* 44, no. 2: 210–48.

Ardagna, Silvia, Francesco Caselli, and Timothy Lane. 2007. "Fiscal Discipline and the Cost of Public Debt Service: Some Estimates for OECD Countries." *B.E. Journal of Macroeconomics* 7, no. 1 (Topics), Article 28.

Auerbach, Alan J., and William G. Gale. 2009. "The Economic Crisis and the Fiscal Crisis: 2009 and Beyond, An Update." Working Paper. Brookings Institution, Washington, DC, and University of California, Berkeley (September).

Autor, David H., and Mark G. Duggan. 2006. "The Growth in the Social Security Disability Rolls: A Fiscal Crisis Unfolding." *Journal of Economic Perspectives* 20, no. 3: 71–96.

Belasco, Amy. 2009. "The Cost of Iraq, Afghanistan, and Other Global War on Terror Operations since 9/11." Washington, DC: Congressional Research Service. September.

Congressional Budget Office. 2000. *The Long-Term Budget Outlook.*

———. 2001. *The Budget and Economic Outlook: Fiscal Years 2002–2011.*

———. 2009a. *The Budget and Economic Outlook: Fiscal Years 2009 to 2019.*

———. 2009b. Letter to the Honorable Charles E. Grassley. "Estimated Macroeconomic Impacts of the American Recovery and Reinvestment Act of 2009." March 2.

———. 2009c. Letter to the Honorable Harry Reid. "Patient Protection and Affordable Care Act." November 18.

———. 2009d. Letter to the Honorable Harry Reid. "Patient Protection and Affordable Care Act, Incorporating the Manager's Amendment." December 19.

———. 2009e. Letter to the Honorable John D. Dingell. "H.R. 3962, Affordable Health Care for America Act." November 20.

———. 2009f. *The Long-Term Budget Outlook.*

————. 2009g. *A Preliminary Analysis of the President's Budget and an Update of CBO's Budget and Economic Outlook.* Supplemental Data on Spending Projections, Medicare Baseline. (www.cbo.gov/budget/factsheets/2009b/medicare.pdf).

Council of Economic Advisers. 2009a. "The Economic Case for Health Care Reform." June.

————. 2009b. "The Economic Case for Health Care Reform: Update." December.

Department of the Treasury (Internal Revenue Service). 2009. *Statistics of Income Bulletin* 28, no. 4.

———— (Office of Tax Analysis). 2010. "Capital Gains and Taxes Paid on Capital Gains for Returns with Positive Net Capital Gains, 1954-2007." January. (www.treasury.gov/offices/tax-policy/library/capgain1-2010.pdf).

Engen, Eric M., and R. Glenn Hubbard. 2005. "Federal Government Debt and Interest Rates." *NBER Macroeconomics Annual* 19: 83–138.

Feenberg, Daniel, and Elizabeth Coutts. 1993. "An Introduction to the TAXSIM Model." *Journal of Policy Analysis and Management* 12, no. 1: 189–94.

Gale, William G., and Peter R. Orszag. 2003. "Economic Effects of Sustained Budget Deficits." *National Tax Journal* 56, no. 3: 463–85.

Giavazzi, Francesco, and Marco Pagano. 1990. "Can Severe Fiscal Contractions Be Expansionary? Tales of Two Small European Countries." *NBER Macroeconomics Annual* 5: 75–111.

Laubach, Thomas. 2009. "New Evidence on the Interest Rate Effects of Budget Deficits and Debt." *Journal of the European Economic Association* 7, no. 4: 858–85.

Office of Management and Budget. 2010. *Budget of the U.S. Government, Fiscal Year 2011.*

Organisation for Economic Co-operation and Development. 2009. *Economic Outlook No. 86.* Paris.

Romer, Christina D., and David H. Romer. Forthcoming. "The Macroeconomic Effects of Tax Changes: Estimates Based on a New Measure of Fiscal Shocks." *American Economic Review.*

Social Security Administration. 2009. *National Average Wage Index.* (www.socialsecurity.gov/OACT/COLA/AWI.html).

Urban-Brookings Tax Policy Center. 2010. "2001–2008 Individual Income and Estate Tax Cuts with AMT Patch Distribution of Federal Tax Change by Cash Income Percentile, 2010." Microsimulation Model. Washington, DC.

Wachtel, Paul, and John Young. 1987. "Deficit Announcements and Interest Rates." *American Economic Review* 77, no. 5: 1007–12.

Chapter 6
Building a Safer Financial System

Department of the Treasury. 2009. *Financial Regulatory Reform: A New Foundation, Rebuilding Financial Supervision and Regulation.*

Hedge Fund Research. 2009. *HFR Market Microstructure Hedge Fund Industry Report—Year End 2008.* Chicago.

Chapter 7
Reforming Health Care

America's Health Insurance Plans (Center for Policy and Research). 2009. "Individual Health Insurance 2009: A Comprehensive Survey of Premiums, Availability, and Benefits." Washington, DC.

Arrow, Kenneth. 1963. "Uncertainty and the Welfare Economics of Medical Care." *American Economic Review* 53, no. 5: 941–73.

Commonwealth Fund. 2008. "2008 International Health Policy Survey of Sicker Adults." New York.

Congressional Budget Office. 2008. "Opportunities to Increase Efficiency in Health Care." Statement of Peter R. Orszag at the Health Reform Summit of the Senate Committee on Finance. June 16 (www.cbo. gov/ftpdocs/93xx/doc9384/06-16-HealthSummit.pdf).

———. 2009a. Letter to the Honorable Evan Bayh. "An Analysis of Health Insurance Premiums under the Patient Protection and Affordable Care Act." November 30.

———. 2009b. Letter to the Honorable Harry Reid. "Patient Protection and Affordable Care Act, Incorporating the Manager's Amendment." December 19.

———. 2009c. Letter to the Honorable John D. Dingell. "H.R. 3962, Affordable Health Care for America Act." November 20.

———. 2009d. *The Long-Term Budget Outlook.*

Council of Economic Advisers. 2009a. "The Economic Case for Health Care Reform." June.

———. 2009b. "The Economic Case for Health Care Reform: Update." December.

———. 2009c. "The Economic Effects of Health Care Reform on Small Businesses and Their Employees." July.

———. 2009d. "The Impact of Health Insurance Reform on State and Local Governments." September.

Currie, Janet, and Jonathan Gruber. 1996a. "Health Insurance Eligibility, Utilization of Medical Care, and Child Health." *Quarterly Journal of Economics* 111, no. 2: 431–66.

———. 1996b. "Saving Babies: The Efficacy and Cost of Recent Changes in the Medicaid Eligibility of Pregnant Women." *Journal of Political Economy* 104, no. 6: 1263–96.

DeNavas-Walt, Carmen, Bernadette D. Proctor, and Jessica C. Smith. 2009. *Income, Poverty, and Health Insurance Coverage in the United States: 2008.* Department of Commerce, Census Bureau.

Department of Health and Human Services (Agency for Healthcare Research and Quality, Center for Financing, Access and Cost Trends). 2009. 2007 Medical Expenditure Panel Survey—Household Component.

Department of the Treasury. 2009. "The Risk of Losing Health Insurance over a Decade: New Findings from Longitudinal Data." September.

Doty, Michelle, et al. 2009. "Failure to Protect: Why the Individual Insurance Market Is Not a Viable Option for Most U.S. Families." New York: Commonwealth Fund. July.

Gabel, Jon, et al. 2006. "Generosity and Adjusted Premiums in Job-Based Insurance: Hawaii Is Up, Wyoming Is Down." *Health Affairs* 25, no. 3: 832–43.

Hadley, Jack, et al. 2008. "Covering the Uninsured in 2008: Current Costs, Sources of Payment, and Incremental Costs." *Health Affairs* Web Exclusive 27, no. 5: w399–415.

Hoadley, Jack, et al. 2008. "The Medicare Part D Coverage Gap: Costs and Consequences in 2007." Menlo Park, CA: Kaiser Family Foundation and Health Research and Educational Trust.

Hussey, Peter S., et al. 2009. "Controlling U.S. Health Care Spending— Separating Promising from Unpromising Approaches." *New England Journal of Medicine* 361, no. 22: 2109–11.

Kaiser Family Foundation and Health Research and Educational Trust. 2009. *Employer Health Benefits: 2009 Annual Survey.* Menlo Park, CA, and Chicago, IL: Henry J. Kaiser Family Foundation and Health Research and Educational Trust.

Long, Sharon K., and Paul B. Masi. 2009. "Access and Affordability: An Update on Health Reform in Massachusetts, Fall 2008." *Health Affairs* Web Exclusive 28, no. 4: w578–87.

Maciosek, Michael V., et al. 2006. "Priorities among Effective Clinical Preventive Services: Results of a Systematic Review and Analysis." *American Journal of Preventive Medicine* 31, no. 1: 52–61.

Martinez, Michael E., and Robin A. Cohen. 2008. "Health Insurance Coverage: Early Release of Estimates from the National Health Interview Survey, January–June 2008." Centers for Disease Control and Prevention, National Center for Health Statistics. December.

———. 2009. "Health Insurance Coverage: Early Release of Estimates from the National Health Interview Survey, January–June 2009." Centers for Disease Control and Prevention, National Center for Health Statistics. December.

Mokdad, Ali H., et al. 2004. "Actual Causes of Death in the United States, 2000." *Journal of the American Medical Association* 291, no. 10: 1238–45.

Nolte, Ellen, and C. Martin McKee. 2008. "Measuring the Health of Nations: Updating an Earlier Analysis." *Health Affairs* 27, no. 1: 58–71.

Organisation for Economic Co-operation and Development (Directorate for Employment, Labour and Social Affairs). 2009. *OECD Health Data 2009.* Paris.

Ross, Donna Cohen, and Marian Jarlenski. 2009. *A Foundation for Health Reform: Findings of a 50 State Survey of Eligibility Rules, Enrollment and Renewal Procedures, and Cost-Sharing Practices in Medicaid and CHIP for Children and Parents During 2009.* Washington, DC: Kaiser Family Foundation and Health Research and Educational Trust, Commission on Medicaid and the Uninsured.

Sisko, Andrea, et al. 2009. "Health Spending Projections Through 2018: Recession Effects Add Uncertainty to the Outlook." *Health Affairs* Web Exclusive 28, no. 2: w346–57.

United Nations (Economic and Social Affairs, Population Division). 2007. "World Population Prospects: The 2006 Revision." New York.

USA Today, Kaiser Family Foundation and Health Research and Educational Trust, and Harvard School of Public Health. 2006. *National Survey of Households Affected by Cancer.* (www.kff.org/kaiserpolls/pomr112006pkg.cfm).

Waxman, Henry J., and Joe Barton. 2009. "Memorandum to Members and Staff of the Subcommittee on Oversight and Investigations: Supplemental Information Regarding the Individual Health Insurance Market," U.S. House of Representatives, Committee on Energy and Commerce. June 16.

Wennberg, John, E., Elliot S. Fisher, and Jonathan S. Skinner. 2002. "Geography and the Debate over Medicare Reform." *Health Affairs* Web Exclusive (February): w96–114.

<hr />

CHAPTER 8
STRENGTHENING THE AMERICAN LABOR FORCE

Adelman, Clifford. 1998. "The Kiss of Death? An Alternative View of College Remediation." *National Crosstalk* 6, no. 3: 11.

Barnett, W. Steven, and Leonard N. Masse. 2007. "Comparative Benefit-Cost Analysis of the Abecedarian Program and Its Policy Implications." *Economics of Education Review* 26, no. 1: 113–25.

Barrow, Lisa, and Cecilia Rouse. 2005. "Does College Still Pay?" *Economists' Voice* 2, no. 4, Article 3.

Bettinger, Eric P., and Bridget Terry Long. 2007. "Institutional Responses to Reduce Inequalities in College Outcomes: Remedial and Developmental Courses in Higher Education." In *Economic Inequality and Higher Education: Access, Persistence, and Success,* edited by Stacy Dickert-Conlin and Ross Rubenstein, pp. 69–100. New York: Russell Sage Foundation Press.

Card, David. 1999. "The Causal Effect of Education on Earnings." In *Handbook of Labor Economics,* Vol. 3, edited by Orley Ashenfelter and David Card, pp. 1801–63. Amsterdam: Elsevier Science.

College Board. 2009. *Trends in College Pricing 2009.* Washington, DC.

Council of Economic Advisers. 2010. "The Economic Impact of the American Recovery and Reinvestment Act of 2009." Second Quarterly Report to Congress. January.

Currie, Janet, and Duncan Thomas. 1995. "Does Head Start Make a Difference?" *American Economic Review* 85, no. 3: 341–64.

Cutler, David, and Adriana Lleras-Muney. 2006. "Education and Health: Evaluating Theories and Evidence." Working Paper 12352. Cambridge, MA: National Bureau of Economic Research (July).

Dee, Thomas S. 2004. "Are There Civic Returns to Education?" *Journal of Public Economics* 88, no. 9–10: 1697–720.

DeLong, J. Bradford, Claudia Goldin, and Lawrence F. Katz. 2003. "Sustaining U.S. Economic Growth." In *Agenda for the Nation,* edited by Henry J. Aaron, James M. Lindsay, and Pietro S. Nivola, pp. 17–60. Washington, DC: Brookings Institution.

Dyke, Andrew, et al. 2006. "The Effects of Welfare-to-Work Program Activities on Labor Market Outcomes." *Journal of Labor Economics* 24, no. 3: 567–608.

Dynarski, Susan. 2003. "Does Aid Matter? Measuring the Effect of Student Aid on College Attendance and Completion." *American Economic Review* 93, no. 1: 279–88.

Figlio, David, and Cecilia Rouse. 2006. "Do Accountability and Voucher Threats Improve Low-Performing Schools?" *Journal of Public Economics* 90, no. 1–2: 239–55.

Goldin, Claudia, and Lawrence F. Katz. 2007. "Long-Run Changes in the Wage Structure: Narrowing, Widening, Polarizing." *Brookings Papers on Economic Activity,* no. 2: 135–67.

———. 2008. *The Race Between Education and Technology.* Cambridge, MA: Belknap Press of Harvard University Press.

Grossman, Michael. 2005. "Education and Nonmarket Outcomes." Working Paper 11582. Cambridge, MA: National Bureau of Economic Research (August).

Hair, Elizabeth, et al. 2006. "Children's School Readiness in the ECLS-K: Predictions to Academic, Health, and Social Outcomes in First Grade." *Early Childhood Research Quarterly* 21, no. 4: 431–54.

Heinrich, Carolyn, Peter Mueser, and Kenneth Troske. 2008. "Workforce Investment Act Non-Experimental Net Impact Evaluation: Final Report." Columbia, MD: IMPAQ International.

Hotz, V. Joseph, Guido Imbens, and Jacob Klerman. 2006. "Evaluating the Differential Effects of Alternative Welfare-to-Work Training Components: A Reanalysis of the California GAIN Program." *Journal of Labor Economics* 24, no. 3: 521–66.

Jacobson, Louis, Robert J. LaLonde, and Daniel G. Sullivan. 1993. "Earnings Losses of Displaced Workers." *American Economic Review* 83, no. 4: 685–709.

———. 2005. "Estimating the Returns to Community College Schooling for Displaced Workers." *Journal of Econometrics* 125, no. 1–2: 271–304.

Jones, Charles I. 2002. "Sources of U.S. Economic Growth in a World of Ideas." *American Economic Review* 92, no. 1: 220–39.

Kahn, Lisa. Forthcoming. "The Long-Term Labor Market Consequences of Graduating from College in a Bad Economy." *Labour Economics.*

Kane, Thomas J., and Cecilia E. Rouse. 1999. "The Community College: Educating Students at the Margin Between College and Work." *Journal of Economic Perspectives* 13, no. 1: 63–84.

Karoly, Lynn A., et al. 1998. *Investing in Our Children: What We Know and Don't Know about the Costs and Benefits of Early Childhood Interventions.* Santa Monica, CA: RAND.

Kopczuk, Wojciech, Emmanuel Saez, and Jae Song. Forthcoming. "Earnings Inequality and Mobility in the United States: Evidence from Social Security Data since 1937." *Quarterly Journal of Economics.*

Lankford, Hamilton, Susanna Loeb, and James Wyckoff. 2002. "Teacher Sorting and the Plight of Urban Schools: A Descriptive Analysis." *Educational Evaluation and Policy Analysis* 22, no. 1: 37–62.

Lochner, Lance, and Enrico Moretti. 2004. "The Effect of Education on Crime: Evidence from Prison Inmates, Arrests, and Self-Reports." *American Economic Review* 94, no. 1: 155–89.

Manpower Demonstration Research Corporation. 1983. *Summary and Findings of the National Supported Work Demonstration.* Cambridge, MA: Ballinger.

Marcotte, Dave E., et al. 2005. "The Returns of a Community College Education: Evidence from the National Education Longitudinal Survey." *Educational Evaluation and Policy Analysis* 27, no. 2: 157–76.

Moretti, Enrico. 2004. "Estimating the Social Return to Higher Education: Evidence from Longitudinal and Repeated Cross-Sectional Data." *Journal of Econometrics* 121, no. 1–2: 175–212.

Obama, President Barack. 2009a. "Address to Joint Session of Congress." Washington, DC, February 24 (www.whitehouse.gov/the_press_office/remarks-of-president-barack-obama-address-to-joint-session-of-congress).

———. 2009b. "Remarks at the Annual Meeting of the National Academy of Sciences." Washington, DC, April 27 (www.whitehouse.gov/the_press_office/Remarks-by-the-President-at-the-National-Academy-of-Sciences-Annual-Meeting).

Oreopoulos, Philip, Marianne Page, and Ann Huff Stevens. 2008. "The Intergenerational Effects of Worker Displacement." *Journal of Labor Economics* 26, no. 3: 455–500.

Oreopoulos, Philip, Till von Wachter, and Andrew Heisz. 2006. "The Short- and Long-Term Career Effects of Graduating in a Recession: Hysteresis and Heterogeneity in the Market for College Graduates." Working Paper 12159. Cambridge, MA: National Bureau of Economic Research (April).

Organisation for Economic Co-operation and Development. 2009. *Education at a Glance 2009: OECD Indicators.* Paris.

Oyer, Paul. 2006. "Initial Labour Market Conditions and Long-Term Outcomes for Economists." *Journal of Economic Perspectives* 20, no. 3: 143–60.

Piketty, Thomas, and Emmanuel Saez. 2003. "Income Inequality in the United States: 1913–1998." *Quarterly Journal of Economics* 118, no. 1: 1–39.

Richburg-Hayes, LaShawn, et al. 2009. "Rewarding Persistence: Effects of a Performance-Based Scholarship Program for Low-Income Parents." New York: MDRC.

Rouse, Cecilia, et al. 2007. "Feeling the Florida Heat? How Low-Performing Schools Respond to Voucher and Accountability Pressure." Working Paper 13681. Cambridge, MA: National Bureau of Economic Research (December).

Schweinhart, Lawrence, et al. 1985. "Effects of the Perry Preschool Program on Youths Through Age 19." *Topics in Early Childhood Special Education* 5, no. 2: 26–35.

Scrivener, Susan, Colleen Sommo, and Herbert Collado. 2009. "Getting Back on Track: Effects of a Community College Program for Probationary Students." New York: MDRC. April.

Scrivener, Susan, et al. 2008. "A Good Start: Two-Year Effects of a Freshman Learning Community Program at Kingsborough Community College." New York: MDRC. March.

Chapter 9
Transforming the Energy Sector and Addressing Climate Change

Burgess, Robin, et al. 2009. "Weather and Death in India: Mechanisms and Implications for Climate Change." Working Paper. Massachusetts Institute of Technology (April).

Burtraw, Dallas, and Karen Palmer. 2004. "SO_2 Cap-and-Trade Program in the United States: A 'Living Legend' of Market Effectiveness." In *Choosing Environmental Policy: Comparing Instruments and Outcomes in the United States and Europe*, edited by Winston Harrington, Richard Morgenstern, and Thomas Sterner, pp. 41–66. Washington, DC: Resources for the Future Press.

Burtraw, Dallas, and Sarah Jo Szambelan. 2009. "U.S. Emissions Trading Markets for SO_2 and NO_X." Discussion Paper 09-40. Washington, DC: Resources for the Future (October).

CNA Corporation. 2007. *National Security and the Threat of Climate Change*. Alexandria, VA.

Council of Economic Advisers. 2010. "The Economic Impact of the American Recovery and Reinvestment Act of 2009." Second Quarterly Report to Congress. January.

Department of Energy (Energy Information Administration). 2009a. *Annual Energy Outlook 2010: Early Release Overview.* DOE/EIA-0383.

———— (Energy Information Administration). 2009b. *Annual Energy Outlook 2009 with Projections to 2030.* DOE/EIA-0383.

————. 2009c. "Energy Conservation Standards for Refrigerated Bottled or Canned Beverage Vending Machines, Final Rule." *Federal Register* 74, no. 167: 44914–68.

Deschênes, Olivier, and Michael Greenstone. 2007. "The Economic Impacts of Climate Change: Evidence from Agricultural Output and Random Fluctuations in Weather." *American Economic Review* 97, no. 1: 354–85.

————. 2008. "Climate Change, Mortality and Adaptation: Evidence from Annual Fluctuations in Weather in the U.S." Working Paper 07-19. Massachusetts Institute of Technology, Department of Economics (December).

Ellerman, A. Denny, Paul Joskow, and David Harrison. 2003. *Emissions Trading in the U.S.: Experience, Lessons, and Consideration for Greenhouse Gases.* Washington, DC: Pew Center on Global Climate Change.

Environmental Protection Agency. 2006. "Acid Rain Program: 2005 Progress Report." EPA-430-R-06-015.

————. 2009. "EPA Analysis of the American Clean Energy and Security Act of 2009 H.R. 2454 in the 111th Congress." June.

Fell, Harrison, and Richard Morgenstern. 2009. "Alternative Approaches to Cost Containment in a Cap-and-Trade System." Discussion Paper 09-14. Washington, DC: Resources for the Future (April).

Guiteras, Raymond. 2009. "The Impact of Climate Change on Indian Agriculture." Working Paper. University of Maryland (September).

Hayhoe, Katherine, et al. 1999. "Costs of Multi-Greenhouse Gas Reduction Targets for the USA." *Science* 286, no. 5441: 905–06.

Hope, Chris. 2006. "The Marginal Impact of CO_2 from PAGE2002: An Integrated Assessment Model Incorporating the IPCC's Five Reasons for Concern." *Integrated Assessment Journal* 6, no. 1: 19–56.

Intergovernmental Panel on Climate Change. 2007. "Summary for Policymakers." In *Climate Change 2007: The Physical Science Basis, Contribution of Working Group I to the Fourth Assessment Report of the Intergovernmental Panel on Climate Change.* Cambridge University Press.

Karl, Thomas R., Jerry M. Melillo, and Thomas C. Peterson, eds. 2009. *Global Climate Change Impacts in the United States.* U.S. Global Change Research Program. Cambridge University Press.

Kinderman, Georg, et al. 2008. "Global Cost Estimates of Reducing Carbon Emissions Through Avoided Deforestation." *Proceedings of the National Academy of Sciences* 105, no. 30: 10302–07.

Organisation for Economic Co-operation and Development. 2009. *The Economics of Climate Change Mitigation: Policies and Options for Global Action Beyond 2012.* Paris.

Paltsev, Sergey, et al. 2009. "The Cost of Climate Policy in the United States." Report 173. Massachusetts Institute of Technology, Joint Program on the Science and Policy of Global Change (April).

Pizer, William, et al. 2006. "Modeling Economy-Wide Versus Sectoral Climate Policies Using Combined Aggregate-Sectoral Models." *Energy Journal* 27, no. 3: 135–68.

Point Carbon Advisory Services. 2008. "EU ETS Phase II—The Potential and Scale of Windfall Profits in the Power Sector." Report for the World Wildlife Foundation. Oslo. March.

Schlenker, Wolfram, and Michael J. Roberts. 2009. "Nonlinear Temperature Effects Indicate Severe Damages to U.S. Crop Yields under Climate Change." *Proceedings of the National Academy of Sciences* 106, no. 37: 15594–608.

Schneider, Lambert. 2007. "Is the CDM Fulfilling Its Environmental and Sustainable Development Objectives? An Evaluation of the CDM and Options for Improvement." Report prepared for the World Wildlife Foundation. Berlin: Öko-Institut. November.

Webster, Mort, et al. 2009. "Analysis of Climate Policy Targets under Uncertainty." Report 180. Massachusetts Institute of Technology, Joint Program on the Science and Policy of Global Change (September).

CHAPTER 10
FOSTERING PRODUCTIVITY GROWTH THROUGH INNOVATION AND TRADE

Bernard, Andrew, et al. 2007. "Firms in International Trade." *Journal of Economic Perspectives* 21, no. 3: 105–30.

Caselli, Francesco. 2005. "Accounting for Cross-Country Income Differences." In *Handbook of Economic Growth*, edited by Philippe Aghion and Steven N. Durlauf, pp. 679–741. Amsterdam: Elsevier.

Department of Commerce (Bureau of Economic Analysis). 1973. *Long Term Economic Growth: 1860-1970.*

Eichengreen, Barry, and Douglas A. Irwin. 2009. "The Slide to Protectionism in the Great Depression: Who Succumbed and Why?" Working Paper 15142. Cambridge, MA: National Bureau of Economic Research (July).

Feyrer, James. 2009. "Trade and Income: Exploiting Time Series in Geography." Working Paper 14910. Cambridge, MA: National Bureau of Economic Research (October).

Frankel, Jeffrey A., and David Romer. 1999. "Does Trade Cause Growth?" *American Economic Review* 89, no. 3: 379–99.

Hall, Bronwyn H., Jacques Mairesse, and Pierre Mohnen. 2009. "Measuring the Returns to R&D." Working Paper 15622. Cambridge, MA: National Bureau of Economic Research (December).

Hall, Robert E., and Charles I. Jones. 1999. "Why Do Some Countries Produce So Much More Output per Worker than Others?" *Quarterly Journal of Economics* 114, no. 1: 83–116.

Hendricks, Lutz. 2002. "How Important Is Human Capital for Development? Evidence from Immigrant Earnings." *American Economic Review* 92, no. 1: 198–219.

Hsieh, Chang-Tai, and Peter J. Klenow. 2007. "Relative Prices and Relative Prosperity." *American Economic Review* 97, no. 3: 562–85.

Hummels, David, Jun Ishii, and Kei-Mu Yi. 2001. "The Nature and Growth of Vertical Specialization in World Trade." *Journal of International Economics* 54, no. 1: 75–96.

Jones, Charles I. 2001. "Was an Industrial Revolution Inevitable? Economic Growth over the Very Long Run." *B.E. Journal of Macroeconomics* 1, no. 2 (Advances), Article 1.

————. 2002. "Sources of U.S. Economic Growth in a World of Ideas." *American Economic Review* 92, no. 1: 220–39.

Klenow, Peter J., and Andrés Rodríguez-Clare. 1997. "The Neoclassical Revival in Growth Economics: Has It Gone Too Far?" *NBER Macroeconomics Annual* 12: 73–103.

Nelson, Richard R., and Paul M. Romer. 1996. "Science, Economic Growth, and Public Policy." In *Technology, R&D, and the Economy*, edited by Bruce L. R. Smith and Claude E. Barfield, pp. 49–74. Washington, DC: Brookings Institution and American Enterprise Institute.

Nordhaus, William D. 1997. "Do Real-Output and Real-Wage Measures Capture Reality? The History of Lighting Suggests Not." In *The Economics of New Goods*, edited by Robert J. Gordon and Timothy F. Bresnahan, pp. 29–66. University of Chicago Press for the National Bureau of Economic Research.

Schott, Peter. 2004. "Across-Product Versus Within-Product Specialization in International Trade." *Quarterly Journal of Economics* 119, no. 2: 647–78.

Smith, Adam. 1776. *An Inquiry into the Nature and Causes of the Wealth of Nations*. Reprint, edited by Edwin Cannan. University of Chicago Press, 1976.

APPENDIX A

REPORT TO THE PRESIDENT ON THE ACTIVITIES OF THE COUNCIL OF ECONOMIC ADVISERS DURING 2009

LETTER OF TRANSMITTAL

COUNCIL OF ECONOMIC ADVISERS
Washington, D.C., December 31, 2009

MR. PRESIDENT:

The Council of Economic Advisers submits this report on its activities during calendar year 2009 in accordance with the requirements of the Congress, as set forth in section 10(d) of the Employment Act of 1946 as amended by the Full Employment and Balanced Growth Act of 1978.

Sincerely,

Christina D. Romer, *Chair*
Austan Goolsbee, *Member*
Cecilia Elena Rouse, *Member*

Council Members and Their Dates of Service

Name	Position	Oath of office date	Separation date
Edwin G. Nourse	Chairman	August 9, 1946	November 1, 1949
Leon H. Keyserling	Vice Chairman	August 9, 1946	
	Acting Chairman	November 2, 1949	
	Chairman	May 10, 1950	January 20, 1953
John D. Clark	Member	August 9, 1946	
	Vice Chairman	May 10, 1950	February 11, 1953
Roy Blough	Member	June 29, 1950	August 20, 1952
Robert C. Turner	Member	September 8, 1952	January 20, 1953
Arthur F. Burns	Chairman	March 19, 1953	December 1, 1956
Neil H. Jacoby	Member	September 15, 1953	February 9, 1955
Walter W. Stewart	Member	December 2, 1953	April 29, 1955
Raymond J. Saulnier	Member	April 4, 1955	
	Chairman	December 3, 1956	January 20, 1961
Joseph S. Davis	Member	May 2, 1955	October 31, 1958
Paul W. McCracken	Member	December 3, 1956	January 31, 1959
Karl Brandt	Member	November 1, 1958	January 20, 1961
Henry C. Wallich	Member	May 7, 1959	January 20, 1961
Walter W. Heller	Chairman	January 29, 1961	November 15, 1964
James Tobin	Member	January 29, 1961	July 31, 1962
Kermit Gordon	Member	January 29, 1961	December 27, 1962
Gardner Ackley	Member	August 3, 1962	
	Chairman	November 16, 1964	February 15, 1968
John P. Lewis	Member	May 17, 1963	August 31, 1964
Otto Eckstein	Member	September 2, 1964	February 1, 1966
Arthur M. Okun	Member	November 16, 1964	
	Chairman	February 15, 1968	January 20, 1969
James S. Duesenberry	Member	February 2, 1966	June 30, 1968
Merton J. Peck	Member	February 15, 1968	January 20, 1969
Warren L. Smith	Member	July 1, 1968	January 20, 1969
Paul W. McCracken	Chairman	February 4, 1969	December 31, 1971
Hendrik S. Houthakker	Member	February 4, 1969	July 15, 1971
Herbert Stein	Member	February 4, 1969	
	Chairman	January 1, 1972	August 31, 1974
Ezra Solomon	Member	September 9, 1971	March 26, 1973
Marina v.N. Whitman	Member	March 13, 1972	August 15, 1973
Gary L. Seevers	Member	July 23, 1973	April 15, 1975
William J. Fellner	Member	October 31, 1973	February 25, 1975
Alan Greenspan	Chairman	September 4, 1974	January 20, 1977
Paul W. MacAvoy	Member	June 13, 1975	November 15, 1976
Burton G. Malkiel	Member	July 22, 1975	January 20, 1977
Charles L. Schultze	Chairman	January 22, 1977	January 20, 1981
William D. Nordhaus	Member	March 18, 1977	February 4, 1979
Lyle E. Gramley	Member	March 18, 1977	May 27, 1980

Council Members and Their Dates of Service

Name	Position	Oath of office date	Separation date
George C. Eads	Member	June 6, 1979	January 20, 1981
Stephen M. Goldfeld	Member	August 20, 1980	January 20, 1981
Murray L. Weidenbaum	Chairman	February 27, 1981	August 25, 1982
William A. Niskanen	Member	June 12, 1981	March 30, 1985
Jerry L. Jordan	Member	July 14, 1981	July 31, 1982
Martin Feldstein	Chairman	October 14, 1982	July 10, 1984
William Poole	Member	December 10, 1982	January 20, 1985
Beryl W. Sprinkel	Chairman	April 18, 1985	January 20, 1989
Thomas Gale Moore	Member	July 1, 1985	May 1, 1989
Michael L. Mussa	Member	August 18, 1986	September 19, 1988
Michael J. Boskin	Chairman	February 2, 1989	January 12, 1993
John B. Taylor	Member	June 9, 1989	August 2, 1991
Richard L. Schmalensee	Member	October 3, 1989	June 21, 1991
David F. Bradford	Member	November 13, 1991	January 20, 1993
Paul Wonnacott	Member	November 13, 1991	January 20, 1993
Laura D'Andrea Tyson	Chair	February 5, 1993	April 22, 1995
Alan S. Blinder	Member	July 27, 1993	June 26, 1994
Joseph E. Stiglitz	Member	July 27, 1993	
	Chairman	June 28, 1995	February 10, 1997
Martin N. Baily	Member	June 30, 1995	August 30, 1996
Alicia H. Munnell	Member	January 29, 1996	August 1, 1997
Janet L. Yellen	Chair	February 18, 1997	August 3, 1999
Jeffrey A. Frankel	Member	April 23, 1997	March 2, 1999
Rebecca M. Blank	Member	October 22, 1998	July 9, 1999
Martin N. Baily	Chairman	August 12, 1999	January 19, 2001
Robert Z. Lawrence	Member	August 12, 1999	January 12, 2001
Kathryn L. Shaw	Member	May 31, 2000	January 19, 2001
R. Glenn Hubbard	Chairman	May 11, 2001	February 28, 2003
Mark B. McClellan	Member	July 25, 2001	November 13, 2002
Randall S. Kroszner	Member	November 30, 2001	July 1, 2003
N. Gregory Mankiw	Chairman	May 29, 2003	February 18, 2005
Kristin J. Forbes	Member	November 21, 2003	June 3, 2005
Harvey S. Rosen	Member	November 21, 2003	
	Chairman	February 23, 2005	June 10, 2005
Ben S. Bernanke	Chairman	June 21, 2005	January 31, 2006
Katherine Baicker	Member	November 18, 2005	July 11, 2007
Matthew J. Slaughter	Member	November 18, 2005	March 1, 2007
Edward P. Lazear	Chairman	February 27, 2006	January 20, 2009
Donald B. Marron	Member	July 17, 2008	January 20, 2009
Christina D. Romer	Chair	January 29, 2009	
Austan Goolsbee	Member	March 11, 2009	
Cecilia E. Rouse	Member	March 11, 2009	

Report to the President
on the Activities of the
Council of Economic Advisers
During 2009

The Council of Economic Advisers was established by the Employment Act of 1946 to provide the President with objective economic analysis and advice on the development and implementation of a wide range of domestic and international economic policy issues.

The Chair of the Council

Christina D. Romer was nominated as Chair of the Council by the President on January 20, 2009. She was confirmed by the Senate on January 28, and took the oath of office on January 29. Dr. Romer is on a leave of absence from the University of California, Berkeley, where she is the Class of 1957-Garff B. Wilson Professor of Economics.

The Chair is a member of the President's Cabinet and is responsible for communicating the Council's views on economic matters directly to the President through personal discussions and written reports. Dr. Romer represents the Council at the daily Presidential economics briefing, daily White House senior staff meetings, budget meetings, Cabinet meetings, a variety of inter-agency meetings, and other formal and informal meetings with the President, the Vice President, and other senior government officials. She also meets frequently with members of Congress in both formal hearings and informal meetings to discuss economic issues and Administration priorities. She travels within the United States and overseas to present the Administration's views on the economy. Dr. Romer is the Council's chief public spokesperson. She directs the work of the Council and exercises ultimate responsibility for the work of the professional staff.

Dr. Romer succeeded Edward P. Lazear, whose tenure ended with the inauguration of the new President. Dr. Lazear returned to Stanford University, where he is the Jack Steele Parker Professor of Human Resources Management and Economics in the Graduate School of Business and the Morris Arnold Cox Senior Fellow at the Hoover Institution.

The Members of the Council

The other Members of the Council are Austan Goolsbee and Cecilia Rouse. They were nominated by the President on January 20, 2009, confirmed by the Senate on March 10, and took their oaths of office on March 11. Dr. Goolsbee also serves as the Staff Director and Chief Economist of the President's Economic Recovery Advisory Board. Dr. Goolsbee is on a leave of absence from the University of Chicago, where he is the Robert P. Gwinn Professor of Economics in the Booth School of Business. Dr. Rouse is on a leave of absence from Princeton University, where she is the Theodore A. Wells '29 Professor of Economics and Public Affairs. The Members represent the Council at a wide variety of meetings and frequently attend meetings with the President and the Vice President.

The Chair and the Members work as a team on most economic policy issues. The Chair works on the whole range of issues under the Council's purview, with a particular focus on macroeconomics and health care. Dr. Goolsbee focuses especially on issues related to housing, financial markets, and tax policy. Dr. Rouse focuses especially on issues related to labor markets, education, and international trade.

The term of Donald B. Marron as a Member of the Council ended with the inauguration of the new President. He is currently president of Marron Economics, LLC.

Areas of Activity

Macroeconomic Policies

A central function of the Council is to advise the President on all major macroeconomic issues and developments. The Council is actively involved in all aspects of macroeconomic policy. In 2009, the central macroeconomic issues included monitoring the financial and economic crisis; formulating the policy response, including the American Recovery and Reinvestment Act of 2009, the Financial Stability Plan, and additional measures targeted to spur job creation and deal with problems in specific sectors; evaluating the effects of the policies and the economy's response; health insurance reform; and setting priorities for the budget. In this process, the Council works closely with the Department of the Treasury, the Office of Management and Budget, the National Economic Council, White House senior staff, and other agencies and officials.

The Council prepares for the President, the Vice President, and the White House senior staff a daily economic briefing memo analyzing current economic developments, and almost-daily memos on key economic data releases. The Chair also makes more in-depth presentations on the state of the economy to these officials and to the Cabinet.

The Council, the Department of Treasury, and the Office of Management and Budget—the Administration's economic "troika"— are responsible for producing the economic forecasts that underlie the Administration's budget proposals. The Council initiates the forecasting process twice each year, consulting with a wide variety of outside sources, including leading private sector forecasters and other government agencies.

The Council issued a series of reports in 2009. Among those most directly related to macroeconomic policy were a report issued in May on estimation methodology for the jobs impact of specific programs of the Recovery Act; a report in June on the economic effects of comprehensive health insurance reform; a report in September on the macroeconomic effects of the Recovery Act; and three shorter reports accompanying that report focusing on the effects of state fiscal relief, the effects of the "Cash for Clunkers" program, and the cross-country experience with fiscal policy in the crisis.

The Council continued its efforts to improve the public's understanding of economic developments and of the Administration's economic policies through briefings with the economic and financial press, discussions with outside economists, and presentations to outside organizations. The Chair and Members also regularly met to exchange views on the macroeconomy with the Chairman and Members of the Board of Governors of the Federal Reserve System.

Microeconomic Policies

Throughout the year, the Council was an active participant in the analysis and consideration of a broad range of microeconomic policy issues. The Council was actively engaged in policy discussions on health insurance reform, financial regulatory reform, clean energy, the environment, education, and numerous labor market issues. As with macroeconomic policy, the Council works closely with other economic agencies, White House senior staff, and other agencies on these issues. Among the specific microeconomic issues that received particular attention in 2009 were small business lending; foreclosure mitigation and prevention; unemployment insurance; the condition and prospects of the American automobile industry; the role of cost-benefit analysis in regulatory policy; estimating the social benefits of reduced carbon emissions; reform of K-12 education; student financial aid; community colleges; potential developments in the U.S. labor market over the next five to ten years; and key indicators of family well-being in the recession and accompanying policy responses.

Many of the reports issued by the Council in 2009 were primarily concerned with microeconomic issues. In addition to its major health care report in June, the Council issued three other reports on health insurance reform over the course of the year—one on its impact on small businesses and their employees in July, one on its impact on state and local governments in September, and an update of the June report in December. The Council also issued an extensive report on the "jobs of tomorrow" in July and a report on simplifying student aid in September.

International Economic Policies

The Council was involved in a range of international trade and finance issues, with a particular emphasis on the consequences of the international financial crisis and the related global economic slowdown. The Council was an active participant in discussions at global and bilateral levels. Council Members and staff regularly met with economists, policy officials, and government officials of other countries to discuss issues relating to the global economy and participated in the first Strategic and Economic Dialogue with China in July 2009.

The Council was particularly active in examining policies that could help speed the global economy out of the current crisis. It carefully tracked developments in the global economy and considered the potential medium-run impacts of the current crisis. It was also an active participant in the Presidential Study Directive examining the development policies of the United States Government, providing analysis and support to the effort to review the interactions between the United States and countries in the developing world.

On the international trade front, the Council was an active participant in the trade policy process, occupying a position on the Trade Policy Staff Committee and the Trade Policy Review Group. The Council provided analysis and recommendations on a range of trade-related issues involving the enforcement of existing trade agreements, reviews of current U.S. trade policies, and consideration of future policies. The Council was also an active participant on the Trade Promotion Coordinating Committee, helping to examine the ways in which exports may support economic growth in the years to come. In the area of investment and security, the Council participated on the Committee on Foreign Investment in the United States (CFIUS), discussing individual cases before CFIUS.

The Council is a leading participant in the Organisation for Economic Co-operation and Development (OECD), an important forum for economic cooperation among high-income industrial economies. Dr. Romer is chair of the OECD's Economic Policy Committee, and Council staff participate actively in working-party meetings on macroeconomic policy and coordination.

Public Information

The Council's annual *Economic Report of the President* is an important vehicle for presenting the Administration's domestic and international economic policies. It is available for purchase through the Government Printing Office, and is viewable on-line at www.gpoaccess.gov/eop.

The Council prepared numerous reports in 2009, and the Chair and Members gave numerous public speeches and testified to Congress. The reports, texts of speeches, and written statements accompanying testimony are available at the Council's website, www.whitehouse.gov/cea.

Finally, the Council publishes the monthly *Economic Indicators*, which is available on-line at www.gpoaccess.gov/indicators.

The Staff of the Council of Economic Advisers

The staff of the Council consists of the senior staff, senior economists, staff economists, research assistants, analysts, and the administrative and support staff. The staff at the end of 2009 were:

Senior Staff

Senior staff play key managerial and analytical roles at the Council. They direct operations, perform central Council functions, and represent the Council in meetings with other agencies and White House offices.

Nan M. Gibson .... Chief of Staff
Michael B. Greenstone .... Chief Economist
Steven N. Braun .... Director of Macroeconomic Forecasting
Adrienne Pilot .... Director of Statistical Office

Senior Economists

Senior economists are Ph.D. economists on leave from academic institutions, government agencies, or private research institutions. They participate actively in the policy process, represent the Council in interagency meetings, and have primary responsibility for the economic analysis and reports prepared by the Council. Each senior economist is typically a primary author of one of the chapters in this *Report*.

Christopher D. Carroll .... Macroeconomics
Mark G. Duggan .... Health
W. Adam Looney .... Public Finance, Tax Policy
Andrew Metrick .... Finance
Jesse M. Rothstein .... Labor, Education, Welfare
Jay C. Shambaugh .... International Macroeconomics and Trade
Ann Wolverton .... Energy, Environment, Natural Resources

Staff Economists

Staff economists are typically graduate students on leave from their Ph.D. training in economics. They conduct advanced statistical analysis, contribute to reports, and generally support the research and analysis mission of the Council.

Sharon E. Boyd .... Health
Gabriel Chodorow-Reich .... International Macroeconomics and Trade
Laura J. Feiveson .... Macroeconomics, Finance
Joshua K. Goldman .... Energy, Environment, Infrastructure
Sarena F. Goodman .... Education, Labor, Public Finance
Joshua K. Hausman .... Macroeconomics
Zachary D. Liscow .... Public Finance, Labor, Environment
William G. Woolston .... Health, Education

Research Assistants

Research assistants are typically college graduates with significant coursework in economics. They conduct statistical analysis and data collection, and generally support the research and analysis mission of the Council. Both staff economists and research assistants contribute to this *Report* and play a crucial role in ensuring the accuracy of all Council documents.

Peter N. Ganong .... Labor, Public Finance, Environment
Clare M. Hove .... Macroeconomics
Michael P. Shapiro .... Health, International Economics

Statistical Office

The Statistical Office gathers, administers, and produces statistical information for the Council. Duties include preparing the statistical appendix to the *Economic Report of the President* and the monthly publication *Economic Indicators*. The staff also creates background materials for economic analysis and verifies statistical content in Presidential memoranda. The Office serves as the Council's liaison to the statistical community.

Brian A. Amorosi .... Program Analyst
Dagmara A. Mocala .... Program Analyst

Administrative Office

The Administrative Office provides general support for the Council's activities. This includes financial management, ethics, human resource management, travel, operations of facilities, security, information technology, and telecommunications management support.

Rosemary M. Rogers .... Administrative Officer
Archana A. Snyder .... Financial Officer
Doris T. Searles .... Information Management Specialist

Office of the Chair

Julie B. Siegel .... Special Assistant to the Chair
Lisa D. Branch .... Executive Assistant to the Members and Assistant to the Chief Economist

Staff Support

Sharon K. Thomas .... Administrative Support Assistant

Other Staff

Brenda Szittya and Martha Gottron provided editorial assistance in the preparation of the 2010 *Economic Report of the President.*

C. Bennett Blau and Gabrielle A. Elul served as staff assistants. Mr. Blau also served as editor of the Morning Economic Bulletin.

Student interns provide invaluable help with research projects, day-to-day operations, and fact-checking. Interns during the year were: Michael D. Arena; Jana Curry; Samantha G. Ellner; Brett B. Flagg; Karen R. Li; Devin K. Mattson; Allison L. Moore; Seth H. Werfel; Carl C. Wheeler; Kie C. Riedel; Rebecca A. Wilson; Yuelan L. Wu; and Allen Yang.

DEPARTURES

Jane E. Ihrig left her position as Chief Economist of the Council in January to return to the Federal Reserve Board. Pierce E. Scranton left his position as Chief of Staff in January. He was succeeded by Karen Anderson, who left the Council in November for maternity leave.

The senior economists who resigned during the year (with their institutions after leaving the Council in parentheses) were: Jean M. Abraham (University of Minnesota); Scott J. Adams (University of Wisconsin);

Benjamin N. Dennis (Department of the Treasury); Erik W. Durbin (Sullivan and Cromwell, LLP); Wendy M. Edelberg (Financial Crisis Inquiry Commission); Elizabeth A. Kopits (Environmental Protection Agency); Michael S. Piwowar (Senate Banking Committee); William M. Powers (International Trade Commission); and Robert P. Rebelein (Vassar College).

The staff economists who resigned during 2009 were Kristopher J. Dawsey, Elizabeth Schultz, and Brian Waters. Those who served as research assistants at the Council and resigned during 2009 were Michael Love and Aditi P. Sen.

There were three retirements at the Council in 2009: Alice Williams, Sandy Daigle and Mary Jones. Ms. Williams devoted 39 years and Ms. Daigle 23 years to the Council. Their untiring commitment, dedication, and loyalty in serving the Council, the Chairs, and the people of the United States over the years was extraordinary and will be greatly missed. Ms. Jones's 23 years of dedication to the senior economists and Council Members was a testament to her commitment to the Council and was greatly appreciated.

STATISTICAL TABLES RELATING TO INCOME, EMPLOYMENT, AND PRODUCTION

⚜

C O N T E N T S

NATIONAL INCOME OR EXPENDITURE

NATIONAL INCOME OR EXPENDITURE—*Continued*

POPULATION, EMPLOYMENT, WAGES, AND PRODUCTIVITY

PRODUCTION AND BUSINESS ACTIVITY

PRICES

MONEY STOCK, CREDIT, AND FINANCE

GOVERNMENT FINANCE

CORPORATE PROFITS AND FINANCE

AGRICULTURE

AGRICULTURE—*Continued*

INTERNATIONAL STATISTICS

General Notes
Detail in these tables may not add to totals because of rounding.

Because of the formula used for calculating real gross domestic product (GDP), the chained (2005) dollar estimates for the detailed components do not add to the chained-dollar value of GDP or to any intermediate aggregate. The Department of Commerce (Bureau of Economic Analysis) no longer publishes chained-dollar estimates prior to 1995, except for selected series.

Unless otherwise noted, all dollar figures are in current dollars.

Symbols used:
    P Preliminary.
    ... Not available (also, not applicable).

Data in these tables reflect revisions made by the source agencies through January 29, 2010. In particular, tables containing national income and product accounts (NIPA) estimates reflect revisions released by the Department of Commerce in July 2009.

National Income or Expenditure
Table B–1. Gross domestic product, 1960–2009

[Billions of dollars, except as noted; quarterly data at seasonally adjusted annual rates]

Year or quarter	Gross domestic product	Personal consumption expenditures Total	Goods	Services	Gross private domestic investment Total	Fixed investment Total	Nonresidential Total	Structures	Equipment and software	Residential	Change in private inventories
1960	526.4	331.8	177.0	154.8	78.9	75.7	49.4	19.6	29.8	26.3	3.2
1961	544.8	342.2	178.8	163.4	78.2	75.2	48.8	19.7	29.1	26.4	3.0
1962	585.7	363.3	189.0	174.4	88.1	82.0	53.1	20.8	32.3	29.0	6.1
1963	617.8	382.7	198.2	184.6	93.8	88.1	56.0	21.2	34.8	32.1	5.6
1964	663.6	411.5	212.3	199.2	102.1	97.2	63.0	23.7	39.2	34.3	4.8
1965	719.1	443.8	229.7	214.1	118.2	109.0	74.8	28.3	46.5	34.2	9.2
1966	787.7	480.9	249.6	231.3	131.3	117.7	85.4	31.3	54.0	32.3	13.6
1967	832.4	507.8	259.0	248.8	128.6	118.7	86.4	31.5	54.9	32.4	9.9
1968	909.8	558.0	284.6	273.4	141.2	132.1	93.4	33.6	59.9	38.7	9.1
1969	984.4	605.1	304.7	300.4	156.4	147.3	104.7	37.7	67.0	42.6	9.2
1970	1,038.3	648.3	318.8	329.5	152.4	150.4	109.0	40.3	68.7	41.4	2.0
1971	1,126.8	701.6	342.1	359.5	178.2	169.9	114.1	42.7	71.5	55.8	8.3
1972	1,237.9	770.2	373.8	396.4	207.6	198.5	128.8	47.2	81.7	69.7	9.1
1973	1,382.3	852.0	416.6	435.4	244.5	228.6	153.3	55.0	98.3	75.3	15.9
1974	1,499.5	932.9	451.5	481.4	249.4	235.4	169.5	61.2	108.2	66.0	14.0
1975	1,637.7	1,033.8	491.3	542.5	230.2	236.5	173.7	61.4	112.4	62.7	–6.3
1976	1,824.6	1,151.3	546.3	604.9	292.0	274.8	192.4	65.9	126.4	82.5	17.1
1977	2,030.1	1,277.8	600.4	677.4	361.3	339.0	228.7	74.6	154.1	110.3	22.3
1978	2,293.8	1,427.6	663.6	764.1	438.0	412.2	280.6	93.6	187.0	131.6	25.8
1979	2,562.2	1,591.2	737.9	853.2	492.9	474.9	333.9	117.7	216.2	141.0	18.0
1980	2,788.1	1,755.8	799.8	956.0	479.3	485.6	362.4	136.2	226.2	123.2	–6.3
1981	3,126.8	1,939.5	869.4	1,070.1	572.4	542.6	420.0	167.3	252.7	122.6	29.8
1982	3,253.2	2,075.5	899.3	1,176.2	517.2	532.1	426.5	177.6	248.9	105.7	–14.9
1983	3,534.6	2,288.6	973.8	1,314.8	564.3	570.1	417.2	154.3	262.9	152.9	–5.8
1984	3,930.9	2,501.1	1,063.7	1,437.4	735.6	670.2	489.6	177.4	312.2	180.6	65.4
1985	4,217.5	2,717.6	1,137.6	1,580.0	736.2	714.4	526.2	194.5	331.7	188.2	21.8
1986	4,460.1	2,896.7	1,195.6	1,701.1	746.5	739.9	519.8	176.5	343.3	220.1	6.6
1987	4,736.4	3,097.0	1,256.3	1,840.7	785.0	757.8	524.1	174.2	349.9	233.7	27.1
1988	5,100.4	3,350.1	1,337.3	2,012.7	821.6	803.1	563.8	182.8	381.0	239.3	18.5
1989	5,482.1	3,594.5	1,423.8	2,170.7	874.9	847.3	607.7	193.7	414.0	239.5	27.7
1990	5,800.5	3,835.5	1,491.3	2,344.2	861.0	846.4	622.4	202.9	419.5	224.0	14.5
1991	5,992.1	3,980.1	1,497.4	2,482.6	802.9	803.3	598.2	183.6	414.6	205.1	–.4
1992	6,342.3	4,236.9	1,563.3	2,673.6	864.8	848.5	612.1	172.6	439.6	236.3	16.3
1993	6,667.4	4,483.6	1,642.3	2,841.2	953.3	932.5	666.6	177.2	489.4	266.0	20.8
1994	7,085.2	4,750.8	1,746.6	3,004.3	1,097.3	1,033.5	731.4	186.8	544.6	302.1	63.8
1995	7,414.7	4,987.3	1,815.5	3,171.7	1,144.0	1,112.9	810.0	207.3	602.8	302.9	31.2
1996	7,838.5	5,273.6	1,917.7	3,355.9	1,240.2	1,209.4	875.4	224.6	650.8	334.1	30.8
1997	8,332.4	5,570.6	2,006.8	3,563.9	1,388.7	1,317.7	968.6	250.3	718.3	349.1	71.0
1998	8,793.5	5,918.5	2,110.0	3,808.5	1,510.8	1,447.1	1,061.1	275.1	786.0	385.9	63.7
1999	9,353.5	6,342.8	2,290.0	4,052.8	1,641.5	1,580.7	1,154.9	283.9	871.0	425.8	60.8
2000	9,951.5	6,830.4	2,459.1	4,371.2	1,772.2	1,717.7	1,268.7	318.1	950.5	449.0	54.5
2001	10,286.2	7,148.8	2,534.0	4,614.8	1,661.9	1,700.2	1,227.8	329.7	898.1	472.4	–38.3
2002	10,642.3	7,439.2	2,610.0	4,829.2	1,647.0	1,634.9	1,125.4	282.8	842.7	509.5	12.0
2003	11,142.1	7,804.0	2,727.4	5,076.6	1,729.7	1,713.3	1,135.7	281.9	853.8	577.6	16.4
2004	11,867.8	8,285.1	2,892.3	5,392.8	1,968.6	1,903.6	1,223.0	306.7	916.4	680.6	64.9
2005	12,638.4	8,819.0	3,073.9	5,745.1	2,172.2	2,122.3	1,347.3	351.8	995.6	775.0	50.0
2006	13,398.9	9,322.7	3,221.7	6,100.9	2,327.2	2,267.2	1,505.3	433.7	1,071.7	761.9	60.0
2007	14,077.6	9,826.4	3,365.0	6,461.4	2,288.5	2,269.1	1,640.2	535.4	1,104.8	629.0	19.4
2008	14,441.4	10,129.9	3,403.2	6,726.8	2,136.1	2,170.8	1,693.6	609.5	1,084.1	477.2	–34.8
2009 ᵖ	14,258.7	10,092.6	3,257.6	6,835.0	1,622.9	1,747.9	1,386.6	480.7	906.0	361.3	–125.0
2006: I	13,183.5	9,148.2	3,180.8	5,967.4	2,336.5	2,270.6	1,457.2	396.8	1,060.5	813.3	66.0
II	13,347.8	9,266.6	3,205.5	6,060.1	2,352.1	2,279.7	1,495.3	428.6	1,066.7	784.4	72.4
III	13,452.9	9,391.8	3,250.5	6,141.3	2,333.5	2,264.4	1,522.7	447.6	1,075.1	741.7	69.1
IV	13,611.5	9,484.1	3,249.1	6,235.0	2,286.5	2,254.2	1,546.1	461.7	1,084.4	708.1	32.3
2007: I	13,795.6	9,658.5	3,306.3	6,352.2	2,267.2	2,254.1	1,574.1	489.5	1,084.6	680.0	13.1
II	13,997.2	9,762.5	3,338.2	6,424.3	2,302.0	2,278.6	1,623.5	519.9	1,103.5	655.1	23.5
III	14,179.9	9,865.6	3,366.6	6,499.0	2,311.9	2,280.8	1,665.2	556.1	1,109.1	615.6	31.0
IV	14,337.9	10,019.2	3,448.9	6,570.3	2,272.9	2,263.0	1,697.9	575.9	1,122.0	565.2	9.8
2008: I	14,373.9	10,095.1	3,447.2	6,647.9	2,214.8	2,223.0	1,705.0	586.3	1,118.7	518.1	–8.2
II	14,497.8	10,194.7	3,474.9	6,719.8	2,164.6	2,214.0	1,719.7	610.6	1,109.2	494.2	–49.3
III	14,546.7	10,220.1	3,463.0	6,757.1	2,142.7	2,179.7	1,711.0	620.4	1,090.6	468.6	–37.0
IV	14,347.3	10,009.8	3,227.5	6,782.3	2,022.1	2,066.6	1,638.7	620.7	1,018.0	427.8	–44.5
2009: I	14,178.0	9,987.7	3,197.7	6,790.0	1,689.9	1,817.2	1,442.6	533.1	909.5	374.6	–127.4
II	14,151.2	9,999.3	3,193.8	6,805.6	1,561.5	1,737.7	1,391.8	494.8	897.0	345.9	–176.2
III	14,242.1	10,132.9	3,292.3	6,840.6	1,556.1	1,712.6	1,353.9	457.9	895.9	358.8	–156.5
IV ᵖ	14,463.4	10,250.5	3,346.8	6,903.7	1,684.0	1,724.0	1,358.2	436.8	921.5	365.7	–40.0

See next page for continuation of table.

[Billions of dollars, except as noted; quarterly data at seasonally adjusted annual rates]

Year or quarter	Net exports of goods and services			Government consumption expenditures and gross investment					Final sales of domestic product	Gross domestic purchases [1]	Addendum: Gross national product [2]	Percent change from preceding period	
	Net exports	Exports	Imports	Total	Federal			State and local				Gross domestic product	Gross domestic purchases [1]
					Total	National defense	Non-defense						
1960	4.2	27.0	22.8	111.5	64.1	53.3	10.7	47.5	523.2	522.2	529.6	3.9	3.2
1961	4.9	27.6	22.7	119.5	67.9	56.5	11.4	51.6	541.8	539.8	548.3	3.5	3.4
1962	4.1	29.1	25.0	130.1	75.2	61.1	14.1	54.9	579.6	581.6	589.7	7.5	7.7
1963	4.9	31.1	26.1	136.4	76.9	61.0	15.9	59.5	612.1	612.8	622.2	5.5	5.4
1964	6.9	35.0	28.1	143.2	78.4	60.2	18.2	64.8	658.8	656.7	668.6	7.4	7.2
1965	5.6	37.1	31.5	151.4	80.4	60.6	19.8	71.0	709.9	713.5	724.4	8.4	8.6
1966	3.9	40.9	37.1	171.6	92.4	71.7	20.8	79.2	774.1	783.8	792.8	9.5	9.9
1967	3.6	43.5	39.9	192.5	104.6	83.4	21.2	87.9	822.6	828.9	837.8	5.7	5.8
1968	1.4	47.9	46.6	209.3	111.3	89.2	22.0	98.0	900.8	908.5	915.9	9.3	9.6
1969	1.4	51.9	50.5	221.4	113.3	89.5	23.8	108.2	975.3	983.0	990.5	8.2	8.2
1970	4.0	59.7	55.8	233.7	113.4	87.6	25.8	120.3	1,036.3	1,034.4	1,044.7	5.5	5.2
1971	.6	63.0	62.3	246.4	113.6	84.6	29.1	132.8	1,118.6	1,126.2	1,134.4	8.5	8.9
1972	–3.4	70.8	74.2	263.4	119.6	86.9	32.7	143.8	1,228.8	1,241.3	1,246.4	9.9	10.2
1973	4.1	95.3	91.2	281.7	122.5	88.1	34.3	159.2	1,366.4	1,378.2	1,394.9	11.7	11.0
1974	–.8	126.7	127.5	317.9	134.5	95.6	39.0	183.4	1,485.5	1,500.3	1,515.0	8.5	8.9
1975	16.0	138.7	122.7	357.7	149.0	103.9	45.1	208.7	1,644.0	1,621.7	1,650.7	9.2	8.1
1976	–1.6	149.5	151.1	383.0	159.7	111.1	48.6	223.3	1,807.5	1,826.2	1,841.4	11.4	12.6
1977	–23.1	159.4	182.4	414.1	175.4	120.9	54.5	238.7	2,007.8	2,053.2	2,050.4	11.3	12.4
1978	–25.4	186.9	212.3	453.6	190.9	130.5	60.4	262.7	2,268.0	2,319.1	2,315.3	13.0	13.0
1979	–22.5	230.1	252.7	500.7	210.6	145.2	65.4	290.2	2,544.2	2,584.8	2,594.2	11.7	11.5
1980	–13.1	280.8	293.8	566.1	243.7	168.0	75.8	322.4	2,794.5	2,801.2	2,822.3	8.8	8.4
1981	–12.5	305.2	317.8	627.5	280.2	196.2	83.9	347.3	3,097.0	3,139.4	3,159.8	12.1	12.1
1982	–20.0	283.2	303.2	680.4	310.8	225.9	84.9	369.7	3,268.1	3,273.2	3,289.7	4.0	4.3
1983	–51.7	277.0	328.6	733.4	342.9	250.6	92.3	390.5	3,540.4	3,586.3	3,571.7	8.7	9.6
1984	–102.7	302.4	405.1	796.9	374.3	281.5	92.7	422.6	3,865.5	4,033.6	3,967.2	11.2	12.5
1985	–115.2	302.0	417.2	878.9	412.8	311.2	101.6	466.1	4,195.6	4,332.7	4,244.0	7.3	7.4
1986	–132.5	320.3	452.9	949.3	438.4	330.8	107.6	510.9	4,453.5	4,592.6	4,477.7	5.8	6.0
1987	–145.0	363.8	508.7	999.4	459.5	350.0	109.6	539.9	4,709.2	4,881.3	4,754.0	6.2	6.3
1988	–110.1	443.9	554.0	1,038.9	461.6	354.7	106.8	577.3	5,081.9	5,210.5	5,123.8	7.7	6.7
1989	–87.9	503.1	591.0	1,100.6	481.4	362.1	119.3	619.2	5,454.5	5,570.0	5,508.1	7.5	6.9
1990	–77.6	552.1	629.7	1,181.7	507.5	373.9	133.6	674.2	5,786.0	5,878.1	5,835.0	5.8	5.5
1991	–27.0	596.6	623.5	1,236.1	526.6	383.1	143.4	709.5	5,992.5	6,019.5	6,022.0	3.3	2.4
1992	–32.8	635.0	667.8	1,273.5	532.9	376.8	156.1	740.6	6,326.0	6,375.1	6,374.4	5.8	5.9
1993	–64.4	655.6	720.0	1,294.8	525.0	363.0	162.0	769.8	6,646.5	6,731.7	6,698.5	5.1	5.6
1994	–92.7	720.7	813.4	1,329.8	518.6	353.8	164.8	811.2	7,021.4	7,177.9	7,109.2	6.3	6.6
1995	–90.7	811.9	902.6	1,374.0	518.8	348.8	170.0	855.3	7,383.5	7,505.3	7,444.3	4.7	4.6
1996	–96.3	867.7	964.0	1,421.0	527.0	354.8	172.2	894.0	7,807.7	7,934.8	7,870.1	5.7	5.7
1997	–101.4	954.4	1,055.8	1,474.4	531.0	349.8	181.1	943.5	8,261.4	8,433.7	8,355.8	6.3	6.3
1998	–161.8	953.9	1,115.7	1,526.1	531.0	346.1	184.9	995.0	8,729.8	8,955.3	8,810.8	5.5	6.2
1999	–262.1	989.3	1,251.4	1,631.3	554.9	361.1	193.8	1,076.3	9,292.7	9,615.6	9,381.3	6.4	7.4
2000	–382.1	1,093.2	1,475.3	1,731.0	576.1	371.0	205.0	1,154.9	9,896.9	10,333.5	9,989.2	6.4	7.5
2001	–371.0	1,027.7	1,398.7	1,846.4	611.7	393.0	218.7	1,234.7	10,324.5	10,657.2	10,338.1	3.4	3.1
2002	–427.2	1,003.0	1,430.2	1,983.3	680.6	437.7	242.9	1,302.7	10,630.3	11,069.5	10,691.4	3.5	3.9
2003	–504.1	1,041.0	1,545.1	2,112.6	756.5	497.9	258.5	1,356.1	11,125.8	11,646.3	11,210.8	4.7	5.2
2004	–618.7	1,180.2	1,798.9	2,232.8	824.6	550.8	273.9	1,408.2	11,802.8	12,486.4	11,959.0	6.5	7.2
2005	–722.7	1,305.1	2,027.8	2,369.9	876.3	589.0	287.3	1,493.6	12,588.4	13,361.1	12,735.5	6.5	7.0
2006	–769.3	1,471.0	2,240.3	2,518.4	931.7	624.9	306.8	1,586.7	13,339.0	14,168.2	13,471.3	6.0	6.0
2007	–713.8	1,655.9	2,369.7	2,676.5	976.7	662.1	314.5	1,699.8	14,058.3	14,791.4	14,193.3	5.1	4.4
2008	–707.8	1,831.1	2,538.9	2,883.2	1,082.6	737.9	344.7	1,800.6	14,476.2	15,149.2	14,583.3	2.6	2.4
2009 *p*	–390.1	1,560.0	1,950.1	2,933.3	1,144.9	779.1	365.8	1,788.4	14,383.7	14,648.8	....	–1.3	–3.3
2006: I	–775.8	1,414.0	2,189.8	2,474.5	928.5	615.5	313.0	1,546.1	13,117.5	13,959.3	13,264.0	8.6	7.6
II	–781.4	1,456.0	2,237.4	2,510.5	930.3	624.1	306.2	1,580.2	13,275.4	14,129.2	13,423.3	5.1	5.0
III	–805.7	1,476.0	2,281.7	2,533.3	932.2	623.3	308.9	1,601.2	13,383.8	14,258.6	13,514.8	3.2	3.7
IV	–714.3	1,538.2	2,252.5	2,555.2	935.9	636.6	299.3	1,619.4	13,579.2	14,325.8	13,683.2	4.8	1.9
2007: I	–729.4	1,564.9	2,294.3	2,599.3	942.8	636.7	306.1	1,656.5	13,782.5	14,525.0	13,859.5	5.5	5.7
II	–724.8	1,602.1	2,326.9	2,657.4	968.1	656.6	311.6	1,689.3	13,973.7	14,722.0	14,073.3	6.0	5.5
III	–698.4	1,685.2	2,383.6	2,700.9	991.4	674.4	317.0	1,709.5	14,148.8	14,878.3	14,318.3	5.3	4.3
IV	–702.5	1,771.6	2,474.0	2,748.3	1,004.3	680.8	323.6	1,743.9	14,328.0	15,040.3	14,522.2	4.5	4.4
2008: I	–744.4	1,803.6	2,548.1	2,808.4	1,038.3	703.6	334.8	1,770.1	14,382.1	15,118.3	14,544.9	1.0	2.1
II	–738.7	1,901.5	2,640.2	2,877.1	1,069.5	725.6	343.9	1,807.6	14,547.1	15,236.4	14,626.6	3.5	3.2
III	–757.5	1,913.1	2,670.5	2,941.4	1,108.3	763.6	344.7	1,833.1	14,583.7	15,304.2	14,707.5	1.4	1.8
IV	–590.5	1,706.2	2,296.7	2,905.9	1,114.3	758.9	355.3	1,791.7	14,391.8	14,937.8	14,454.3	–5.4	–9.2
2009: I	–378.5	1,509.3	1,887.9	2,879.0	1,106.7	750.7	356.0	1,772.3	14,305.3	14,556.5	14,277.9	–4.6	–9.8
II	–339.1	1,493.7	1,832.8	2,929.4	1,138.3	776.2	362.1	1,791.2	14,327.4	14,490.3	14,243.8	–.8	–1.8
III	–402.2	1,573.8	1,976.0	2,955.4	1,164.3	795.8	368.5	1,791.1	14,398.7	14,644.3	14,363.7	2.6	4.3
IV *p*	–440.5	1,663.4	2,103.9	2,969.5	1,170.4	793.8	376.5	1,799.1	14,503.4	14,903.9	....	6.4	7.3

[1] Gross domestic product (GDP) less exports of goods and services plus imports of goods and services.
[2] GDP plus net income receipts from rest of the world.

Source: Department of Commerce (Bureau of Economic Analysis).

TABLE B–2. Real gross domestic product, 1960–2009

[Billions of chained (2005) dollars, except as noted; quarterly data at seasonally adjusted annual rates]

Year or quarter	Gross domestic product	Personal consumption expenditures			Gross private domestic investment						Change in private inventories
		Total	Goods	Services	Total	Fixed investment					
						Total	Nonresidential			Residential	
							Total	Structures	Equipment and software		
1960	2,830.9	1,784.4			296.5						
1961	2,896.9	1,821.2			294.6						
1962	3,072.4	1,911.2			332.0						
1963	3,206.7	1,989.9			354.3						
1964	3,392.3	2,108.4			383.5						
1965	3,610.1	2,241.8			437.3						
1966	3,845.3	2,369.0			475.8						
1967	3,942.5	2,440.0			454.1						
1968	4,133.4	2,580.7			480.5						
1969	4,261.8	2,677.4			508.5						
1970	4,269.9	2,740.2			475.1						
1971	4,413.3	2,844.6			529.3						
1972	4,647.7	3,019.5			591.9						
1973	4,917.0	3,169.1			661.3						
1974	4,889.9	3,142.8			612.6						
1975	4,879.5	3,214.1			504.1						
1976	5,141.3	3,393.1			605.9						
1977	5,377.7	3,535.9			697.4						
1978	5,677.6	3,691.8			781.5						
1979	5,855.0	3,779.5			806.4						
1980	5,839.0	3,766.2			717.9						
1981	5,987.2	3,823.3			782.4						
1982	5,870.9	3,876.7			672.8						
1983	6,136.2	4,098.3			735.5						
1984	6,577.1	4,315.6			952.1						
1985	6,849.3	4,540.4			943.3						
1986	7,086.5	4,724.5			936.9						
1987	7,313.3	4,870.3			965.7						
1988	7,613.9	5,066.6			988.5						
1989	7,885.9	5,209.9			1,028.1						
1990	8,033.9	5,316.2			993.5						
1991	8,015.1	5,324.2			912.7						
1992	8,287.1	5,505.7			986.7						
1993	8,523.4	5,701.2			1,074.8						
1994	8,870.7	5,918.9			1,220.9						
1995	9,093.7	6,079.0	1,898.6	4,208.2	1,258.9	1,235.7	792.2	342.0	493.0	456.1	32.1
1996	9,433.9	6,291.2	1,983.6	4,331.4	1,370.3	1,346.5	866.2	361.4	545.4	492.5	31.2
1997	9,854.3	6,523.4	2,078.2	4,465.0	1,540.8	1,470.8	970.8	387.9	620.4	501.8	77.4
1998	10,283.5	6,865.5	2,218.6	4,661.8	1,695.1	1,630.4	1,087.4	407.7	710.4	540.4	71.6
1999	10,779.8	7,240.9	2,395.3	4,852.8	1,844.3	1,782.1	1,200.9	408.2	810.9	574.2	68.5
2000	11,226.0	7,608.1	2,521.7	5,093.3	1,970.3	1,913.8	1,318.5	440.0	895.8	580.0	60.2
2001	11,347.2	7,813.9	2,600.9	5,218.7	1,831.9	1,877.6	1,281.8	433.3	866.9	583.3	−41.8
2002	11,553.0	8,021.9	2,706.6	5,318.1	1,807.0	1,798.1	1,180.2	356.6	830.3	613.8	12.8
2003	11,840.7	8,247.6	2,829.9	5,418.4	1,871.6	1,856.2	1,191.0	343.0	851.4	664.3	17.3
2004	12,263.8	8,532.7	2,955.3	5,577.6	2,058.2	1,992.5	1,263.0	346.7	917.3	729.5	66.3
2005	12,638.4	8,819.0	3,073.9	5,745.1	2,172.2	2,122.3	1,347.3	351.8	995.6	775.0	50.0
2006	12,976.2	9,073.5	3,173.9	5,899.7	2,230.4	2,171.3	1,453.9	384.0	1,069.6	718.2	59.4
2007	13,254.1	9,313.9	3,273.7	6,040.8	2,146.2	2,126.3	1,544.3	441.4	1,097.0	585.0	19.5
2008	13,312.2	9,290.9	3,206.0	6,083.1	1,989.4	2,018.4	1,569.7	486.8	1,068.6	451.1	−25.9
2009 ᵖ	12,988.7	9,237.3	3,143.7	6,090.5	1,522.8	1,646.7	1,289.1	391.0	887.9	359.1	−111.7
2006: I	12,915.9	8,986.6	3,145.7	5,841.0	2,264.7	2,200.2	1,424.9	364.8	1,060.7	775.2	65.8
II	12,962.5	9,035.0	3,150.8	5,884.2	2,261.2	2,189.9	1,450.3	383.7	1,066.3	740.1	72.5
III	12,965.9	9,090.7	3,176.4	5,914.3	2,229.6	2,162.2	1,466.0	393.2	1,072.0	697.4	67.5
IV	13,060.7	9,181.6	3,222.5	5,959.4	2,166.0	2,132.9	1,474.5	394.6	1,079.3	660.2	31.8
2007: I	13,099.9	9,265.1	3,253.9	6,011.7	2,132.6	2,118.8	1,489.6	409.2	1,078.1	631.7	14.5
II	13,204.0	9,291.5	3,255.4	6,036.2	2,162.2	2,137.7	1,530.3	430.7	1,095.2	610.4	23.3
III	13,321.1	9,335.6	3,280.6	6,055.5	2,166.5	2,135.6	1,565.8	456.8	1,101.3	572.9	29.8
IV	13,391.2	9,363.6	3,304.8	6,059.7	2,123.4	2,113.0	1,591.3	469.1	1,113.3	525.0	10.3
2008: I	13,366.9	9,349.6	3,262.1	6,087.1	2,082.9	2,079.2	1,598.9	476.8	1,111.9	483.2	.6
II	13,415.3	9,351.0	3,257.8	6,092.5	2,026.5	2,064.8	1,604.4	493.2	1,097.7	462.9	−37.1
III	13,324.6	9,267.7	3,193.6	6,072.4	1,990.7	2,020.4	1,579.2	493.1	1,071.0	443.3	−29.7
IV	13,141.9	9,195.3	3,110.4	6,080.4	1,857.7	1,909.3	1,496.1	484.0	993.7	415.0	−37.4
2009: I	12,925.4	9,209.2	3,129.8	6,076.0	1,558.5	1,687.5	1,321.2	419.4	887.5	367.9	−113.9
II	12,901.5	9,189.0	3,105.4	6,078.8	1,456.7	1,631.9	1,288.4	400.0	876.5	344.4	−160.2
III	12,973.0	9,252.6	3,159.6	6,090.6	1,474.4	1,626.7	1,269.0	380.2	879.8	359.6	−139.2
IV ᵖ	13,155.0	9,298.5	3,180.0	6,116.4	1,601.8	1,640.6	1,278.1	364.6	907.7	364.6	−33.5

See next page for continuation of table.

[Billions of chained (2005) dollars, except as noted; quarterly data at seasonally adjusted annual rates]

Year or quarter	Net exports of goods and services			Government consumption expenditures and gross investment					Final sales of domestic product	Gross domestic purchases [1]	Addendum: Gross national product [2]	Percent change from preceding period	
	Net exports	Exports	Imports	Total	Federal			State and local				Gross domestic product	Gross domestic purchases [1]
					Total	National defense	Non-defense						
1960	....	98.5	114.5	871.0	....	....	....	....	2,836.6	2,867.6	2,850.6	2.5	1.8
1961	....	99.0	113.8	914.8	....	....	....	....	2,904.6	2,933.3	2,918.6	2.3	2.3
1962	....	104.0	126.7	971.1	....	....	....	....	3,064.9	3,119.0	3,096.8	6.1	6.3
1963	....	111.5	130.1	996.1	....	....	....	....	3,202.6	3,248.8	3,232.8	4.4	4.2
1964	....	124.6	137.0	1,018.0	....	....	....	....	3,393.7	3,426.3	3,420.4	5.8	5.5
1965	....	128.1	151.6	1,048.7	....	....	....	....	3,590.7	3,659.2	3,639.5	6.4	6.8
1966	....	137.0	174.1	1,141.1	....	....	....	....	3,806.6	3,910.2	3,873.1	6.5	6.9
1967	....	140.1	186.8	1,228.7	....	....	....	....	3,923.3	4,018.2	3,971.1	2.5	2.8
1968	....	151.1	214.7	1,267.2	....	....	....	....	4,119.4	4,225.6	4,164.1	4.8	5.2
1969	....	158.4	226.9	1,264.3	....	....	....	....	4,248.6	4,358.6	4,291.6	3.1	3.1
1970	....	175.5	236.6	1,233.7	....	....	....	....	4,287.9	4,352.0	4,299.4	.2	−.2
1971	....	178.4	249.2	1,206.9	....	....	....	....	4,407.4	4,506.9	4,446.0	3.4	3.6
1972	....	191.8	277.2	1,198.1	....	....	....	....	4,640.6	4,755.8	4,682.9	5.3	5.5
1973	....	228.0	290.1	1,193.9	....	....	....	....	4,888.2	4,991.2	4,964.5	5.8	5.0
1974	....	246.0	283.5	1,224.0	....	....	....	....	4,874.1	4,926.2	4,944.0	−.6	−1.3
1975	....	244.5	252.0	1,251.6	....	....	....	....	4,926.3	4,872.0	4,921.4	−.2	−1.1
1976	....	255.1	301.3	1,257.2	....	....	....	....	5,120.2	5,189.2	5,191.2	5.4	6.5
1977	....	261.3	334.2	1,271.0	....	....	....	....	5,344.9	5,464.4	5,433.7	4.6	5.3
1978	....	288.8	363.2	1,308.4	....	....	....	....	5,639.7	5,763.2	5,733.2	5.6	5.5
1979	....	317.5	369.2	1,332.8	....	....	....	....	5,841.2	5,903.3	5,930.2	3.1	2.4
1980	....	351.7	344.7	1,358.8	....	....	....	....	5,878.7	5,789.6	5,913.4	−.3	−1.9
1981	....	356.0	353.8	1,371.2	....	....	....	....	5,959.5	5,944.7	6,052.5	2.5	2.7
1982	....	328.8	349.3	1,395.3	....	....	....	....	5,923.8	5,865.4	5,939.1	−1.9	−1.3
1983	....	320.3	393.4	1,446.3	....	....	....	....	6,172.9	6,208.3	6,202.3	4.5	5.8
1984	....	346.4	489.1	1,494.9	....	....	....	....	6,495.6	6,745.4	6,639.8	7.2	8.7
1985	....	357.0	520.9	1,599.0	....	....	....	....	6,838.9	7,045.3	6,893.9	4.1	4.4
1986	....	384.4	565.4	1,696.2	....	....	....	....	7,098.7	7,303.3	7,116.5	3.5	3.7
1987	....	425.7	598.9	1,737.1	....	....	....	....	7,296.2	7,518.4	7,342.2	3.2	2.9
1988	....	493.9	622.4	1,758.9	....	....	....	....	7,607.8	7,758.8	7,650.4	4.1	3.2
1989	....	550.6	649.8	1,806.8	....	....	....	....	7,867.5	7,990.9	7,924.0	3.6	3.0
1990	....	600.2	673.0	1,864.0	....	....	....	....	8,032.7	8,104.6	8,081.8	1.9	1.4
1991	....	640.0	672.0	1,884.4	....	....	....	....	8,034.8	8,034.6	8,055.6	−.2	−.9
1992	....	684.0	719.2	1,893.2	....	....	....	....	8,284.3	8,309.6	8,326.4	3.4	3.4
1993	....	706.4	781.4	1,878.2	....	....	....	....	8,515.3	8,592.9	8,563.2	2.9	3.4
1994	....	768.0	874.6	1,878.0	....	....	....	....	8,809.2	8,976.0	8,900.5	4.1	4.5
1995	−98.8	845.7	944.5	1,888.9	704.1	476.8	227.5	1,183.6	9,073.2	9,189.0	9,129.4	2.5	2.4
1996	−110.7	916.0	1,026.7	1,907.9	696.0	470.4	225.7	1,211.1	9,412.5	9,542.0	9,471.1	3.7	3.8
1997	−139.8	1,025.1	1,165.0	1,943.8	689.1	457.2	231.9	1,254.3	9,782.6	9,992.8	9,881.8	4.5	4.7
1998	−252.6	1,048.5	1,301.1	1,985.0	681.4	447.5	233.7	1,303.8	10,217.1	10,539.9	10,304.0	4.4	5.5
1999	−356.6	1,094.3	1,450.9	2,056.1	694.6	455.8	238.7	1,361.8	10,715.7	11,141.1	10,812.1	4.8	5.7
2000	−451.6	1,188.3	1,639.9	2,097.8	698.1	453.5	244.4	1,400.1	11,167.5	11,681.4	11,268.8	4.1	4.8
2001	−472.1	1,121.6	1,593.8	2,178.3	726.5	470.7	255.5	1,452.3	11,391.7	11,825.7	11,404.6	1.1	1.2
2002	−548.8	1,099.2	1,648.0	2,279.6	779.5	505.3	273.9	1,500.6	11,543.5	12,107.7	11,606.9	1.8	2.4
2003	−603.9	1,116.8	1,720.7	2,330.5	831.1	549.2	281.7	1,499.7	11,824.8	12,449.2	11,914.2	2.5	2.8
2004	−688.0	1,222.8	1,910.8	2,362.0	865.0	580.4	284.6	1,497.1	12,198.2	12,952.5	12,358.5	3.6	4.0
2005	−722.7	1,305.1	2,027.8	2,369.9	876.3	589.0	287.3	1,493.6	12,588.4	13,361.1	12,735.5	3.1	3.2
2006	−729.2	1,422.0	2,151.2	2,402.1	894.9	598.4	296.6	1,507.2	12,917.1	13,705.7	13,046.1	2.7	2.6
2007	−647.7	1,546.1	2,193.8	2,443.1	906.4	611.5	294.9	1,536.7	13,234.3	13,901.6	13,362.8	2.1	1.4
2008	−494.3	1,629.3	2,123.5	2,518.1	975.9	659.4	316.4	1,543.7	13,341.2	13,801.2	13,442.6	.4	−.7
2009 *p*	−353.8	1,468.6	1,822.5	2,566.4	1,026.7	695.1	331.4	1,542.8	13,115.2	13,335.8	....	−2.4	−3.4
2006: I	−732.6	1,388.8	2,121.3	2,397.1	900.5	595.6	305.0	1,496.6	12,851.3	13,648.7	12,994.2	5.4	4.7
II	−732.8	1,412.1	2,144.9	2,399.1	892.8	597.2	295.7	1,506.3	12,891.0	13,695.5	13,035.4	1.4	1.4
III	−756.5	1,414.1	2,170.5	2,402.7	892.0	594.3	297.7	1,510.8	12,898.3	13,722.8	13,025.1	.1	.8
IV	−694.9	1,473.2	2,168.1	2,409.4	894.4	606.5	287.8	1,515.0	13,027.8	13,755.7	13,129.5	3.0	1.0
2007: I	−705.0	1,485.9	2,190.8	2,409.5	882.8	594.7	288.1	1,526.5	13,086.4	13,805.0	13,160.5	1.2	1.4
II	−683.4	1,504.8	2,188.1	2,435.4	898.7	607.1	291.6	1,536.5	13,179.6	13,887.6	13,275.9	3.2	2.4
III	−638.4	1,569.9	2,208.3	2,458.9	919.0	621.7	297.2	1,540.0	13,290.3	13,959.7	13,451.5	3.6	2.1
IV	−564.0	1,624.0	2,188.0	2,468.7	925.1	622.4	302.7	1,543.7	13,381.1	13,954.2	13,563.3	2.1	−.2
2008: I	−550.9	1,623.4	2,174.3	2,484.7	943.4	634.8	308.6	1,541.9	13,363.5	13,916.4	13,525.4	−.7	−1.1
II	−476.0	1,670.4	2,146.5	2,506.9	961.3	645.6	315.8	1,546.6	13,453.5	13,885.5	13,533.7	1.5	−.9
III	−479.2	1,655.2	2,134.4	2,536.6	991.6	675.4	315.9	1,547.0	13,354.3	13,798.8	13,470.7	−2.7	−2.5
IV	−470.9	1,568.0	2,038.9	2,544.0	1,007.3	681.7	325.4	1,539.3	13,193.5	13,604.0	13,240.5	−5.4	−5.5
2009: I	−386.5	1,434.5	1,821.0	2,527.2	996.3	672.8	323.4	1,533.3	13,055.8	13,303.1	13,018.1	−6.4	−8.6
II	−330.4	1,419.5	1,749.8	2,568.6	1,023.5	695.2	328.2	1,548.0	13,077.8	13,225.9	12,986.8	−.7	−2.3
III	−357.4	1,478.8	1,836.2	2,585.5	1,043.3	709.3	333.8	1,545.5	13,127.2	13,323.8	13,084.0	2.2	3.0
IV *p*	−341.1	1,541.6	1,882.7	2,584.4	1,043.5	703.1	340.4	1,544.3	13,200.2	13,490.3	....	5.7	5.1

[1] Gross domestic product (GDP) less exports of goods and services plus imports of goods and services.

[2] GDP plus net income receipts from rest of the world.

Source: Department of Commerce (Bureau of Economic Analysis).

TABLE B–3. Quantity and price indexes for gross domestic product, and percent changes, 1960–2009

[Quarterly data are seasonally adjusted]

Year or quarter	Index numbers, 2005=100					Percent change from preceding period [1]				
	Gross domestic product (GDP)			Personal consumption expenditures (PCE)		Gross domestic product (GDP)			Personal consumption expenditures (PCE)	
	Real GDP (chain-type quantity index)	GDP chain-type price index	GDP implicit price deflator	PCE chain-type price index	PCE less food and energy price index	Real GDP (chain-type quantity index)	GDP chain-type price index	GDP implicit price deflator	PCE chain-type price index	PCE less food and energy price index
1960	22.399	18.604	18.596	18.606	19.024	2.5	1.4	1.4	1.6	1.8
1961	22.921	18.814	18.805	18.801	19.262	2.3	1.1	1.1	1.0	1.3
1962	24.310	19.071	19.062	19.023	19.525	6.1	1.4	1.4	1.2	1.4
1963	25.373	19.273	19.265	19.245	19.778	4.4	1.1	1.1	1.2	1.3
1964	26.841	19.572	19.563	19.527	20.081	5.8	1.6	1.5	1.5	1.5
1965	28.565	19.928	19.919	19.810	20.335	6.4	1.8	1.8	1.4	1.3
1966	30.426	20.493	20.484	20.313	20.795	6.5	2.8	2.8	2.5	2.3
1967	31.195	21.124	21.115	20.824	21.432	2.5	3.1	3.1	2.5	3.1
1968	32.705	22.022	22.012	21.636	22.351	4.8	4.3	4.2	3.9	4.3
1969	33.721	23.110	23.099	22.616	23.400	3.1	4.9	4.9	4.5	4.7
1970	33.786	24.328	24.317	23.674	24.498	.2	5.3	5.3	4.7	4.7
1971	34.920	25.545	25.533	24.680	25.651	3.4	5.0	5.0	4.2	4.7
1972	36.775	26.647	26.634	25.525	26.480	5.3	4.3	4.3	3.4	3.2
1973	38.905	28.124	28.112	26.901	27.492	5.8	5.5	5.5	5.4	3.8
1974	38.691	30.664	30.664	29.703	29.673	–.6	9.0	9.1	10.4	7.9
1975	38.609	33.577	33.563	32.184	32.159	–.2	9.5	9.5	8.4	8.4
1976	40.680	35.505	35.489	33.950	34.114	5.4	5.7	5.7	5.5	6.1
1977	42.550	37.764	37.751	36.155	36.303	4.6	6.4	6.4	6.5	6.4
1978	44.924	40.413	40.400	38.687	38.731	5.6	7.0	7.0	7.0	6.7
1979	46.328	43.773	43.761	42.118	41.550	3.1	8.3	8.3	8.9	7.3
1980	46.200	47.776	47.751	46.641	45.356	–.3	9.1	9.1	10.7	9.2
1981	47.373	52.281	52.225	50.810	49.318	2.5	9.4	9.4	8.9	8.7
1982	46.453	55.467	55.412	53.615	52.501	–1.9	6.1	6.1	5.5	6.5
1983	48.552	57.655	57.603	55.923	55.220	4.5	3.9	4.0	4.3	5.2
1984	52.041	59.823	59.766	58.038	57.513	7.2	3.8	3.8	3.8	4.2
1985	54.194	61.633	61.576	59.938	59.695	4.1	3.0	3.0	3.3	3.8
1986	56.071	63.003	62.937	61.399	61.945	3.5	2.2	2.2	2.4	3.8
1987	57.866	64.763	64.764	63.589	64.300	3.2	2.8	2.9	3.6	3.8
1988	60.244	66.990	66.988	66.121	67.088	4.1	3.4	3.4	4.0	4.3
1989	62.397	69.520	69.518	68.994	69.856	3.6	3.8	3.8	4.3	4.1
1990	63.568	72.213	72.201	72.147	72.838	1.9	3.9	3.9	4.6	4.3
1991	63.419	74.762	74.760	74.755	75.673	–.2	3.5	3.5	3.6	3.9
1992	65.571	76.537	76.533	76.954	78.218	3.4	2.4	2.4	2.9	3.4
1993	67.441	78.222	78.224	78.643	80.068	2.9	2.2	2.2	2.2	2.4
1994	70.188	79.867	79.872	80.265	81.836	4.1	2.1	2.1	2.1	2.2
1995	71.953	81.533	81.536	82.041	83.721	2.5	2.1	2.1	2.2	2.3
1996	74.645	83.083	83.088	83.826	85.346	3.7	1.9	1.9	2.2	1.9
1997	77.972	84.554	84.555	85.395	86.981	4.5	1.8	1.8	1.9	1.9
1998	81.367	85.507	85.511	86.207	88.242	4.4	1.1	1.1	1.0	1.4
1999	85.295	86.766	86.768	87.596	89.555	4.8	1.5	1.5	1.6	1.5
2000	88.825	88.648	88.647	89.777	91.111	4.1	2.2	2.2	2.5	1.7
2001	89.783	90.654	90.650	91.488	92.739	1.1	2.3	2.3	1.9	1.8
2002	91.412	92.113	92.118	92.736	94.345	1.8	1.6	1.6	1.4	1.7
2003	93.688	94.099	94.100	94.622	95.784	2.5	2.2	2.2	2.0	1.5
2004	97.036	96.769	96.770	97.098	97.788	3.6	2.8	2.8	2.6	2.1
2005	100.000	100.000	100.000	100.000	100.000	3.1	3.3	3.3	3.0	2.3
2006	102.673	103.263	103.257	102.746	102.292	2.7	3.3	3.3	2.7	2.3
2007	104.872	106.221	106.214	105.502	104.699	2.1	2.9	2.9	2.7	2.4
2008	105.331	108.481	108.483	109.031	107.207	.4	2.1	2.1	3.3	2.4
2009 ᵖ	102.772	109.754	109.777	109.252	108.828	–2.4	1.2	1.2	.2	1.5
2006: I	102.196	102.071	102.071	101.803	101.325	5.4	3.0	3.0	1.7	2.0
II	102.564	102.980	102.973	102.567	102.057	1.4	3.6	3.6	3.0	2.9
III	102.592	103.763	103.756	103.316	102.630	.1	3.1	3.1	3.0	2.3
IV	103.341	104.237	104.218	103.298	103.154	3.0	1.8	1.8	–.1	2.1
2007: I	103.652	105.327	105.310	104.250	103.862	1.2	4.2	4.3	3.7	2.8
II	104.475	106.026	106.008	105.074	104.318	3.2	2.7	2.7	3.2	1.8
III	105.402	106.460	106.447	105.681	104.904	3.6	1.6	1.7	2.3	2.3
IV	105.957	107.072	107.069	107.005	105.714	2.1	2.3	2.4	5.1	3.1
2008: I	105.764	107.577	107.534	107.974	106.333	–.7	1.9	1.7	3.7	2.4
II	106.147	108.061	108.069	109.021	106.976	1.5	1.8	2.0	3.9	2.4
III	105.430	109.130	109.172	110.273	107.652	–2.7	4.0	4.1	4.7	2.6
IV	103.984	109.155	109.172	108.855	107.866	–5.4	.1	.0	–5.0	.8
2009: I	102.271	109.661	109.691	108.449	108.173	–6.4	1.9	1.9	–1.5	1.1
II	102.082	109.656	109.686	108.814	108.712	–.7	.0	.0	1.4	2.0
III	102.648	109.763	109.783	109.510	109.027	2.2	.4	.4	2.6	1.2
IV ᵖ	104.088	109.934	109.946	110.235	109.400	5.7	.6	.6	2.7	1.4

[1] Quarterly percent changes are at annual rates.

Source: Department of Commerce (Bureau of Economic Analysis).

TABLE B–4. Percent changes in real gross domestic product, 1960–2009

[Percent change from preceding period; quarterly data at seasonally adjusted annual rates]

Year or quarter	Gross domestic product	Personal consumption expenditures			Gross private domestic investment					Exports and imports of goods and services		Government consumption expenditures and gross investment		
					Nonresidential fixed									
		Total	Goods	Services	Total	Structures	Equipment and software	Residential fixed		Exports	Imports	Total	Federal	State and local
1960	2.5	2.7	1.8	3.9	5.7	8.0	4.2	-7.1		17.4	1.3	0.2	-2.7	4.4
1961	2.3	2.1	.6	3.7	-.6	1.4	-1.9	.3		.5	-.7	5.0	4.2	6.2
1962	6.1	4.9	5.1	4.7	8.7	4.6	11.6	9.6		5.0	11.4	6.2	8.5	3.1
1963	4.4	4.1	4.0	4.2	5.6	1.2	8.4	11.8		7.2	2.7	2.6	.1	6.0
1964	5.8	6.0	6.0	6.0	11.9	10.4	12.8	5.8		11.8	5.3	2.2	-1.3	6.8
1965	6.4	6.3	7.1	5.5	17.4	15.9	18.3	-2.9		2.8	10.6	3.0	.0	6.7
1966	6.5	5.7	6.3	5.0	12.5	6.8	16.0	-8.9		6.9	14.9	8.8	11.1	6.3
1967	2.5	3.0	2.0	4.1	-1.3	-2.5	-.7	-3.1		2.3	7.3	7.7	10.0	5.1
1968	4.8	5.8	6.2	5.3	4.5	1.4	6.2	13.6		7.9	14.9	3.1	.8	5.9
1969	3.1	3.7	3.1	4.5	7.6	5.4	8.8	3.0		4.8	5.7	-.2	-3.4	3.4
1970	.2	2.3	.8	3.9	-.5	.3	-1.0	-6.0		10.7	4.3	-2.4	-7.4	2.8
1971	3.4	3.8	4.2	3.5	.0	-1.6	1.0	27.4		1.7	5.3	-2.2	-7.7	3.1
1972	5.3	6.2	6.5	5.8	9.2	3.1	12.9	17.8		7.5	11.3	-.7	-4.1	2.2
1973	5.8	5.0	5.2	4.7	14.6	8.2	18.3	-.6		18.9	4.6	-.4	-4.2	2.9
1974	-.6	-.8	-3.6	1.9	.8	-2.2	2.6	-20.6		7.9	-2.3	2.5	.9	3.8
1975	-.2	2.3	.7	3.8	-9.9	-10.5	-9.5	-13.0		-.6	-11.1	2.3	.3	3.7
1976	5.4	5.6	7.0	4.3	4.9	2.4	6.3	23.5		4.4	19.6	.4	.0	.7
1977	4.6	4.2	4.3	4.1	11.3	4.1	15.1	21.5		2.4	10.9	1.1	2.1	.4
1978	5.6	4.4	4.1	4.7	15.0	14.4	15.2	6.3		10.5	8.7	2.9	2.5	3.3
1979	3.1	2.4	1.6	3.1	10.1	12.7	8.7	-3.7		9.9	1.7	1.9	2.4	1.5
1980	-.3	-.4	-2.5	1.5	-.3	5.9	-3.6	-21.2		10.8	-6.6	1.9	4.7	-.1
1981	2.5	1.5	1.2	1.8	5.7	8.0	4.3	-8.0		1.2	2.6	.9	4.8	-2.0
1982	-1.9	1.4	.7	1.9	-3.8	-1.6	-5.2	-18.2		-7.6	-1.3	1.8	3.9	.0
1983	4.5	5.7	6.4	5.2	-1.3	-10.8	5.4	41.4		-2.6	12.6	3.7	6.6	1.2
1984	7.2	5.3	7.2	3.9	17.6	13.9	19.8	14.8		8.2	24.3	3.4	3.1	3.6
1985	4.1	5.2	5.3	5.2	6.6	7.1	6.4	1.6		3.0	6.5	7.0	7.8	6.2
1986	3.5	4.1	5.6	3.0	-2.9	-11.0	1.9	12.3		7.7	8.5	6.1	5.7	6.4
1987	3.2	3.1	1.8	4.0	-.1	-2.9	1.4	2.0		10.8	5.9	2.4	3.6	1.4
1988	4.1	4.0	3.7	4.2	5.2	.7	7.5	-1.0		16.0	3.9	1.3	-1.6	3.7
1989	3.6	2.8	2.5	3.0	5.6	2.0	7.3	-3.0		11.5	4.4	2.7	1.6	3.7
1990	1.9	2.0	.6	3.0	.5	1.5	.0	-8.6		9.0	3.6	3.2	2.0	4.1
1991	-.2	.1	-2.0	1.5	-5.4	-11.1	-2.6	-9.6		6.6	-.1	1.1	-.2	2.1
1992	3.4	3.4	3.2	3.6	3.2	-6.0	7.3	13.8		6.9	7.0	.5	-1.8	2.2
1993	2.9	3.6	4.2	3.2	8.7	-.6	12.5	8.2		3.3	8.6	-.8	-3.9	1.5
1994	4.1	3.8	5.3	3.0	9.2	1.8	11.9	9.7		8.7	11.9	.0	-3.8	2.6
1995	2.5	2.7	3.0	2.5	10.5	6.4	12.0	-3.3		10.1	8.0	.6	-2.7	2.7
1996	3.7	3.5	4.5	2.9	9.3	5.7	10.6	8.0		8.3	8.7	1.0	-1.2	2.3
1997	4.5	3.7	4.8	3.1	12.1	7.3	13.8	1.9		11.9	13.5	1.9	-1.0	3.6
1998	4.4	5.2	6.8	4.4	12.0	5.1	14.5	7.7		2.3	11.7	2.1	-1.1	3.9
1999	4.8	5.5	8.0	4.1	10.4	.1	14.1	6.3		4.4	11.5	3.6	1.9	4.5
2000	4.1	5.1	5.3	5.0	9.8	7.8	10.5	1.0		8.6	13.0	2.0	.5	2.8
2001	1.1	2.7	3.1	2.5	-2.8	-1.5	-3.2	.6		-5.6	-2.8	3.8	4.1	3.7
2002	1.8	2.7	4.1	1.9	-7.9	-17.7	-4.2	5.2		-2.0	3.4	4.7	7.3	3.3
2003	2.5	2.8	4.6	1.9	.9	-3.8	2.5	8.2		1.6	4.4	2.2	6.6	-.1
2004	3.6	3.5	4.4	2.9	6.0	1.1	7.7	9.8		9.5	11.0	1.4	4.1	-.2
2005	3.1	3.4	4.0	3.0	6.7	1.4	8.5	6.2		6.7	6.1	.3	1.3	-.2
2006	2.7	2.9	3.3	2.7	7.9	9.2	7.4	-7.3		9.0	6.1	1.4	2.1	.9
2007	2.1	2.6	3.1	2.4	6.2	14.9	2.6	-18.5		8.7	2.0	1.7	1.3	2.0
2008	.4	-.2	-2.1	.7	1.6	10.3	-2.6	-22.9		5.4	-3.2	3.1	7.7	.5
2009 ᵖ	-2.4	-.6	-1.9	.1	-17.9	-19.7	-16.9	-20.4		-9.9	-14.2	1.9	5.2	-.1
2006: I	5.4	4.5	7.5	2.9	18.0	18.9	17.8	-4.2		16.5	7.8	4.1	11.9	-.3
II	1.4	2.2	.7	3.0	7.3	22.4	2.1	-16.9		6.9	4.5	.3	-3.4	2.6
III	.1	2.5	3.3	2.1	4.4	10.3	2.2	-21.2		.6	4.9	.6	-.4	1.2
IV	3.0	4.1	5.9	3.1	2.3	1.5	2.8	-19.7		17.8	-.5	1.1	1.1	1.1
2007: I	1.2	3.7	3.9	3.6	4.2	15.6	-.5	-16.2		3.5	4.3	.0	-5.1	3.1
II	3.2	1.1	.2	1.6	11.4	22.7	6.5	-12.9		5.2	-.5	4.4	7.4	2.7
III	3.6	1.9	3.1	1.3	9.6	26.6	2.2	-22.4		18.5	3.7	3.9	9.3	.9
IV	2.1	1.2	3.0	.3	6.7	11.2	4.5	-29.5		14.5	-3.6	1.6	2.7	1.0
2008: I	-.7	-.6	-5.1	1.8	1.9	6.8	-.5	-28.2		-.1	-2.5	2.6	8.1	-.5
II	1.5	.1	-.5	.4	1.4	14.5	-5.0	-15.8		12.1	-5.0	3.6	7.8	1.2
III	-2.7	-3.5	-7.7	-1.3	-6.1	-.1	-9.4	-15.9		-3.6	-2.2	4.8	13.2	.1
IV	-5.4	-3.1	-10.0	.5	-19.5	-7.2	-25.9	-23.2		-19.5	-16.7	1.2	6.5	-2.0
2009: I	-6.4	.6	2.5	-.3	-39.2	-43.6	-36.4	-38.2		-29.9	-36.4	-2.6	-4.3	-1.5
II	-.7	-.9	-3.1	.2	-9.6	-17.3	-4.9	-23.3		-4.1	-14.7	6.7	11.4	3.9
III	2.2	2.8	7.2	.8	-5.9	-18.4	1.5	18.9		17.8	21.3	2.6	8.0	-.6
IV ᵖ	5.7	2.0	2.6	1.7	2.9	-15.4	13.3	5.7		18.1	10.5	-.2	.1	-.3

Note: Percent changes based on unrounded data.

Source: Department of Commerce (Bureau of Economic Analysis).

National Income or Expenditure | 333

TABLE B–5. Contributions to percent change in real gross domestic product, 1960–2009

[Percentage points, except as noted; quarterly data at seasonally adjusted annual rates]

Year or quarter	Gross domestic product (percent change)	Personal consumption expenditures			Gross private domestic investment							Change in private inventories
		Total	Goods	Services	Total	Fixed investment					Residential	
							Total	Nonresidential				
								Total	Structures	Equipment and software		
1960	2.5	1.72	0.60	1.13	0.00	0.13	0.52	0.28	0.24	−0.39	−0.13	
1961	2.3	1.30	.21	1.09	−.10	−.04	−.06	.05	−.11	.01	−.05	
1962	6.1	3.10	1.68	1.42	1.81	1.24	.78	.16	.61	.46	.57	
1963	4.4	2.56	1.29	1.27	1.00	1.08	.50	.04	.46	.58	−.08	
1964	5.8	3.69	1.91	1.78	1.25	1.37	1.07	.36	.71	.30	−.13	
1965	6.4	3.91	2.26	1.66	2.16	1.50	1.65	.57	1.07	−.15	.66	
1966	6.5	3.50	2.02	1.48	1.44	.87	1.29	.27	1.02	−.43	.58	
1967	2.5	1.82	.62	1.21	−.76	−.28	−.15	−.10	−.05	−.13	−.49	
1968	4.8	3.51	1.92	1.59	.90	.99	.46	.05	.41	.53	−.10	
1969	3.1	2.29	.95	1.34	.90	.90	.78	.20	.58	.13	.00	
1970	.2	1.44	.24	1.19	−1.04	−.31	−.06	.01	−.07	−.26	−.73	
1971	3.4	2.37	1.27	1.10	1.67	1.10	.00	−.06	.07	1.10	.58	
1972	5.3	3.81	1.97	1.84	1.87	1.81	.93	.12	.81	.89	.06	
1973	5.8	3.08	1.57	1.51	1.96	1.47	1.50	.31	1.19	−.04	.50	
1974	−.6	−.52	−1.12	.60	−1.31	−1.04	.09	−.09	.18	−1.13	−.27	
1975	−.2	1.40	.20	1.20	−2.98	−1.71	−1.14	−.43	−.70	−.57	−1.27	
1976	5.4	3.51	2.08	1.43	2.84	1.42	.52	.09	.43	.90	1.41	
1977	4.6	2.66	1.28	1.38	2.43	2.18	1.19	.15	1.04	.99	.25	
1978	5.6	2.77	1.22	1.56	2.16	2.04	1.69	.54	1.15	.35	.12	
1979	3.1	1.48	.47	1.02	.61	1.02	1.23	.53	.71	−.21	−.41	
1980	−.3	−.22	−.74	.52	−2.12	−1.21	−.03	.27	−.30	−1.17	−.91	
1981	2.5	.95	.34	.62	1.55	.39	.74	.40	.34	−.35	1.16	
1982	−1.9	.86	.19	.67	−2.55	−1.21	−.50	−.09	−.42	−.71	−1.34	
1983	4.5	3.65	1.74	1.91	1.45	1.17	−.17	−.57	.41	1.33	.29	
1984	7.2	3.43	1.97	1.47	4.63	2.68	2.05	.60	1.45	.64	1.95	
1985	4.1	3.32	1.41	1.90	−.17	.89	.82	.32	.50	.07	−1.06	
1986	3.5	2.62	1.49	1.13	−.12	.20	−.36	−.50	.15	.55	−.32	
1987	3.2	2.01	.48	1.53	.51	.09	−.01	−.11	.10	.10	.42	
1988	4.1	2.64	.98	1.66	.39	.53	.58	.02	.55	−.05	−.14	
1989	3.6	1.86	.66	1.20	.64	.47	.61	.07	.54	−.14	.17	
1990	1.9	1.34	.16	1.18	−.53	−.32	.05	.05	.00	−.37	−.21	
1991	−.2	.10	−.51	.61	−1.20	−.94	−.57	−.39	−.18	−.37	−.26	
1992	3.4	2.27	.78	1.49	1.07	.79	.31	−.18	.50	.47	.29	
1993	2.9	2.37	1.02	1.35	1.21	1.14	.83	−.02	.85	.31	.07	
1994	4.1	2.57	1.29	1.27	1.94	1.30	.91	.05	.86	.39	.63	
1995	2.5	1.81	.73	1.08	.48	.94	1.08	.17	.91	−.14	−.46	
1996	3.7	2.35	1.09	1.26	1.35	1.33	1.01	.16	.85	.33	.02	
1997	4.5	2.48	1.16	1.33	1.95	1.41	1.33	.21	1.12	.08	.54	
1998	4.4	3.50	1.61	1.90	1.65	1.70	1.38	.16	1.22	.32	−.05	
1999	4.8	3.68	1.90	1.78	1.50	1.52	1.24	.00	1.24	.28	−.02	
2000	4.1	3.44	1.29	2.15	1.19	1.24	1.20	.24	.96	.05	−.05	
2001	1.1	1.85	.77	1.09	−1.24	−.32	−.35	−.05	−.30	.03	−.92	
2002	1.8	1.85	.99	.86	−.22	−.70	−.94	−.58	−.36	.24	.48	
2003	2.5	1.97	1.11	.86	.55	.49	.10	−.10	.20	.40	.06	
2004	3.6	2.42	1.08	1.34	1.55	1.13	.61	.03	.58	.52	.42	
2005	3.1	2.34	.97	1.37	.92	1.05	.69	.04	.65	.36	−.13	
2006	2.7	2.01	.78	1.22	.46	.39	.84	.27	.58	−.45	.07	
2007	2.1	1.84	.75	1.09	−.65	−.35	.70	.49	.20	−1.05	−.30	
2008	.4	−.17	−.50	.32	−1.18	−.81	.19	.39	−.20	−1.00	−.37	
2009 p	−2.4	−.40	−.46	.06	−3.49	−2.75	−2.09	−.83	−1.27	−.65	−.74	
2006: I	5.4	3.08	1.76	1.32	1.08	1.57	1.84	.52	1.32	−.27	−.49	
II	1.4	1.48	.15	1.33	−.11	−.32	.80	.63	.17	−1.12	.22	
III	.1	1.70	.78	.92	−.99	−.86	.49	.32	.17	−1.36	−.13	
IV	3.0	2.79	1.39	1.40	−1.99	−.91	.27	.05	.22	−1.18	−1.08	
2007: I	1.2	2.54	.93	1.61	−1.05	−.43	.46	.50	−.04	−.89	−.61	
II	3.2	.81	.05	.76	.92	.59	1.25	.75	.51	−.66	.32	
III	3.6	1.35	.75	.60	.14	−.04	1.10	.91	.19	−1.14	.19	
IV	2.1	.86	.71	.15	−1.29	−.66	.78	.42	.36	−1.44	−.63	
2008: I	−.7	−.39	−1.24	.85	−1.20	−.99	.25	.27	−.02	−1.24	−.21	
II	1.5	.06	−.12	.17	−1.66	−.41	.19	.56	−.38	−.60	−1.25	
III	−2.7	−2.49	−1.89	−.60	−1.04	−1.30	−.73	.00	−.73	−.57	.26	
IV	−5.4	−2.15	−2.41	.26	−3.91	−3.28	−2.47	−.31	−2.15	−.81	−.64	
2009: I	−6.4	.44	.56	−.13	−8.98	−6.62	−5.29	−2.28	−3.01	−1.33	−2.36	
II	−.7	−.62	−.71	.09	−3.10	−1.68	−1.01	−.69	−.32	−.67	−1.42	
III	2.2	1.96	1.59	.37	.54	−.15	−.59	−.68	.10	.43	.69	
IV p	5.7	1.44	.61	.83	3.82	.43	.29	−.52	.81	.14	3.39	

See next page for continuation of table.

[Percentage points, except as noted; quarterly data at seasonally adjusted annual rates]

Year or quarter	Net exports	Exports			Imports			Total	Federal			State and local
		Total	Goods	Services	Total	Goods	Services		Total	National defense	Non-defense	
1960	0.72	0.78	0.76	0.02	−0.06	0.05	−0.11	0.04	−0.35	−0.17	−0.18	0.39
1961	.06	.03	.02	.01	.03	.00	.02	1.07	.51	.45	.06	.56
1962	−.21	.25	.17	.08	−.47	−.40	−.07	1.36	1.07	.63	.44	.29
1963	.24	.35	.29	.06	−.12	−.12	.00	.58	.01	−.25	.26	.57
1964	.36	.59	.52	.07	−.23	−.19	−.04	.49	−.17	−.39	.23	.65
1965	−.30	.15	.02	.13	−.45	−.41	−.04	.65	−.01	−.19	.19	.66
1966	−.29	.36	.27	.09	−.65	−.49	−.16	1.87	1.24	1.21	.03	.63
1967	−.22	.12	.02	.10	−.34	−.17	−.16	1.68	1.17	1.19	−.02	.51
1968	−.30	.41	.30	.10	−.71	−.68	−.03	.73	.10	.16	−.06	.63
1969	−.04	.25	.20	.05	−.29	−.20	−.09	−.05	−.42	−.49	.06	.37
1970	.34	.56	.44	.12	−.22	−.15	−.07	−.55	−.86	−.83	−.03	.31
1971	−.19	.10	−.02	.11	−.29	−.33	.04	−.50	−.85	−.97	.12	.36
1972	−.21	.42	.43	−.01	−.63	−.57	−.06	−.16	−.42	−.60	.18	.26
1973	.82	1.12	1.01	.11	−.29	−.34	.05	−.08	−.41	−.39	−.02	.33
1974	.75	.58	.46	.12	.18	.17	.00	.52	.08	−.05	.13	.44
1975	.89	−.05	−.16	.10	.94	.87	.07	.48	.03	−.06	.09	.45
1976	−1.08	.37	.31	.05	−1.45	−1.35	−.10	.10	.00	−.02	.03	.09
1977	−.72	.20	.08	.11	−.92	−.84	−.07	.23	.19	.07	.12	.04
1978	.05	.82	.68	.15	−.78	−.67	−.11	.60	.22	.05	.16	.38
1979	.66	.82	.77	.06	−.16	−.14	−.02	.37	.20	.17	.03	.17
1980	1.68	.97	.86	.11	.71	.67	.04	.38	.39	.25	.14	−.01
1981	−.15	.12	−.09	.21	−.27	−.18	−.09	.19	.42	.38	.04	−.23
1982	−.60	−.73	−.67	−.06	.12	.20	−.08	.35	.35	.48	−.13	.01
1983	−1.35	−.22	−.19	−.03	−1.13	−1.01	−.13	.76	.63	.50	.13	.13
1984	−1.58	.63	.46	.17	−2.21	−1.83	−.39	.70	.30	.35	−.05	.40
1985	−.42	.23	.20	.02	−.65	−.52	−.13	1.41	.74	.60	.14	.67
1986	−.30	.54	.26	.28	−.84	−.82	−.02	1.27	.55	.47	.08	.71
1987	.16	.77	.56	.21	−.61	−.39	−.22	.51	.35	.35	.00	.17
1988	.82	1.24	1.04	.20	−.43	−.36	−.07	.26	−.16	−.03	−.12	.42
1989	.52	.99	.75	.24	−.48	−.38	−.09	.55	.14	−.03	.17	.41
1990	.43	.81	.56	.26	−.38	−.26	−.13	.64	.18	.00	.18	.46
1991	.64	.63	.46	.16	.02	−.04	.05	.22	−.02	−.07	.05	.24
1992	−.05	.68	.52	.16	−.72	−.78	.06	.10	−.16	−.32	.16	.26
1993	−.57	.32	.23	.10	−.90	−.85	−.05	−.16	−.33	−.31	−.02	.17
1994	−.43	.85	.67	.19	−1.28	−1.18	−.10	.00	−.30	−.27	−.04	.30
1995	.11	1.03	.85	.19	−.92	−.86	−.06	.11	−.20	−.19	−.01	.30
1996	−.15	.90	.68	.22	−1.04	−.94	−.10	.19	−.08	−.06	−.02	.27
1997	−.32	1.30	1.11	.19	−1.62	−1.44	−.17	.34	−.07	−.13	.06	.41
1998	−1.18	.26	.18	.08	−1.43	−1.21	−.22	.38	−.07	−.09	.02	.45
1999	−.99	.47	.29	.18	−1.45	−1.31	−.14	.63	.12	.07	.04	.51
2000	−.85	.91	.82	.08	−1.76	−1.52	−.24	.36	.03	−.02	.05	.33
2001	−.20	−.61	−.48	−.13	.41	.39	.02	.67	.24	.14	.09	.43
2002	−.65	−.20	−.25	.05	−.46	−.42	−.04	.84	.44	.28	.15	.40
2003	−.45	.15	.12	.03	−.60	−.55	−.04	.42	.43	.36	.07	−.01
2004	−.66	.89	.55	.34	−1.55	−1.29	−.26	.26	.28	.26	.02	−.02
2005	−.27	.67	.52	.15	−.94	−.87	−.07	.06	.09	.07	.02	−.03
2006	−.05	.93	.68	.25	−.98	−.80	−.18	.26	.15	.07	.07	.11
2007	.63	.96	.57	.39	−.33	−.24	−.09	.32	.09	.10	−.01	.23
2008 *p*	1.20	.64	.48	.16	.56	.58	−.02	.59	.53	.37	.16	.06
2009 *p*	1.08	−1.21	−1.04	−.16	2.28	2.18	.10	.38	.39	.28	.11	−.01
2006: I	.44	1.64	1.23	.41	−1.20	−.81	−.39	.75	.79	.46	.32	−.03
II	.02	.72	.54	.18	−.70	−.66	−.05	.06	−.24	.05	−.29	.30
III	−.71	.06	.01	.05	−.78	−.74	−.04	.11	−.03	−.09	.06	.14
IV	1.94	1.84	.96	.87	.10	.35	−.25	.21	.08	.38	−.30	.14
2007: I	−.29	.39	.23	.16	−.68	−.67	−.01	.00	−.36	−.37	.01	.36
II	.66	.58	.48	.10	.08	.13	−.05	.82	.50	.39	.11	.32
III	1.36	1.99	1.11	.88	−.63	−.41	−.22	.75	.63	.46	.17	.11
IV	2.24	1.65	.97	.68	.60	.51	.08	.31	.19	.03	.16	.12
2008: I	.36	−.02	.34	−.36	.38	.46	−.08	.51	.56	.39	.17	−.05
II	2.35	1.47	1.17	.30	.88	.67	.21	.71	.55	.34	.21	.15
III	−.10	−.48	−.17	−.31	.38	.55	−.17	.95	.93	.93	.00	.01
IV	.45	−2.67	−2.50	−.17	3.12	3.09	.03	.24	.49	.20	.29	−.25
2009: I	2.64	−3.95	−3.41	−.54	6.58	6.25	.34	−.52	−.33	−.27	−.06	−.19
II	1.65	−.45	−.45	.00	2.09	1.89	.21	1.33	.85	.70	.15	.48
III	−.81	1.78	1.58	.20	−2.59	−2.41	−.18	.55	.62	.45	.17	−.08
IV *p*	.50	1.90	1.90	.00	−1.41	−1.55	.14	−.02	.02	−.19	.21	−.04

Source: Department of Commerce (Bureau of Economic Analysis).

TABLE B–6. Chain-type quantity indexes for gross domestic product, 1960–2009

[Index numbers, 2005=100; quarterly data seasonally adjusted]

Year or quarter	Gross domestic product	Personal consumption expenditures			Gross private domestic investment					
		Total	Goods	Services	Total	Fixed investment				Resi-dential
						Total	Nonresidential			
							Total	Structures	Equipment and software	
1960	22.399	20.233	19.767	19.850	13.650	13.974	10.796	48.488	5.499	26.167
1961	22.921	20.650	19.892	20.581	13.561	13.931	10.729	49.151	5.393	26.240
1962	24.310	21.671	20.915	21.554	15.283	15.190	11.666	51.393	6.017	28.756
1963	25.373	22.564	21.750	22.470	16.309	16.367	12.315	51.986	6.524	32.145
1964	26.841	23.908	23.047	23.807	17.654	17.948	13.777	57.399	7.356	34.013
1965	28.565	25.420	24.679	25.122	20.131	19.781	16.177	66.553	8.705	33.020
1966	30.426	26.862	26.245	26.367	21.905	20.915	18.200	71.109	10.098	30.065
1967	31.195	27.667	26.758	27.451	20.903	20.530	17.955	69.313	10.031	29.119
1968	32.705	29.263	28.415	28.915	22.120	21.962	18.756	70.299	10.656	33.089
1969	33.721	30.359	29.283	30.204	23.409	23.329	20.181	74.096	11.598	34.066
1970	33.786	31.071	29.514	31.385	21.871	22.838	20.073	74.300	11.482	32.028
1971	34.920	32.255	30.749	32.469	24.365	24.568	20.074	73.082	11.596	40.811
1972	36.775	34.239	32.760	34.346	27.250	27.522	21.917	75.359	13.092	48.064
1973	38.905	35.935	34.457	35.974	30.443	30.037	25.106	81.520	15.494	47.756
1974	38.691	35.637	33.200	36.664	28.200	28.159	25.316	79.755	15.890	37.897
1975	38.609	36.445	33.425	38.040	23.205	25.135	22.814	71.355	14.377	32.977
1976	40.680	38.475	35.766	39.672	27.893	27.613	23.931	73.073	15.276	40.743
1977	42.550	40.094	37.301	41.312	32.107	31.582	26.632	76.079	17.577	49.490
1978	44.924	41.862	38.842	43.234	35.978	35.406	30.618	87.058	20.253	52.606
1979	46.328	42.857	39.464	44.555	37.125	37.404	33.702	98.098	22.022	50.676
1980	46.200	42.705	38.464	45.241	33.047	34.974	33.613	103.837	21.230	39.952
1981	47.373	43.353	38.919	46.053	36.019	35.756	35.528	112.161	22.133	36.749
1982	46.453	43.958	39.190	46.950	30.972	33.249	34.190	110.325	20.982	30.077
1983	48.552	46.471	41.684	49.407	33.857	35.673	33.748	98.404	22.111	42.527
1984	52.041	48.935	44.608	51.341	43.833	41.698	39.704	112.125	26.497	48.839
1985	54.194	51.484	47.039	53.996	43.425	43.891	42.336	120.095	28.180	49.612
1986	56.071	53.572	49.670	55.602	43.129	44.402	41.126	106.935	28.714	55.699
1987	57.866	55.225	50.564	57.818	44.458	44.646	41.096	103.859	29.107	56.811
1988	60.244	57.451	52.442	60.272	45.504	46.118	43.245	104.539	31.302	56.235
1989	62.397	59.075	53.766	62.098	47.330	47.504	45.660	106.616	33.596	54.528
1990	63.568	60.281	54.099	63.942	45.736	46.512	45.885	108.187	33.607	49.823
1991	63.419	60.371	53.025	64.899	42.016	43.496	43.425	96.150	32.743	45.035
1992	65.571	62.430	54.696	67.212	45.421	46.075	44.811	90.354	35.129	51.267
1993	67.441	64.647	56.969	69.363	49.481	50.024	48.723	89.768	39.515	55.454
1994	70.188	67.115	59.973	71.433	56.204	54.703	53.207	91.405	44.227	60.845
1995	71.953	68.931	61.765	73.249	57.955	58.226	58.801	97.235	49.519	58.854
1996	74.645	71.336	64.530	75.394	63.082	63.448	64.293	102.744	54.782	63.554
1997	77.972	73.970	67.607	77.719	70.932	69.302	72.053	110.280	62.315	64.756
1998	81.367	77.849	72.175	81.145	78.034	76.822	80.707	115.911	71.358	69.737
1999	85.295	82.106	77.924	84.469	84.903	83.969	89.129	116.049	81.451	74.098
2000	88.825	86.270	82.034	88.654	90.704	90.178	97.864	125.101	89.976	74.839
2001	89.783	88.603	84.611	90.837	84.333	88.470	95.137	123.191	87.073	75.263
2002	91.412	90.962	88.050	92.568	83.185	84.726	87.593	101.377	83.397	79.210
2003	93.688	93.520	92.060	94.314	86.162	87.464	88.398	97.514	85.516	85.724
2004	97.036	96.754	96.141	97.084	94.753	93.884	93.743	98.571	92.141	94.136
2005	100.000	100.000	100.000	100.000	100.000	100.000	100.000	100.000	100.000	100.000
2006	102.673	102.886	103.251	102.692	102.678	102.309	107.913	109.180	107.434	92.679
2007	104.872	105.612	106.499	105.147	98.801	100.189	114.617	125.495	110.184	75.490
2008	105.331	105.351	104.296	105.883	91.585	95.106	116.502	138.392	107.332	58.213
2009 ᵖ	102.772	104.744	102.270	106.012	70.104	77.590	95.681	111.171	89.181	46.341
2006: I	102.196	101.901	102.335	101.670	104.258	103.670	105.759	103.696	106.542	100.031
II	102.564	102.450	102.501	102.421	104.098	103.186	107.643	109.068	107.101	95.502
III	102.592	103.081	103.334	102.945	102.643	101.880	108.811	111.771	107.681	89.988
IV	103.341	104.112	104.835	103.731	99.712	100.499	109.440	112.185	108.414	85.194
2007: I	103.652	105.059	105.854	104.641	98.176	99.838	110.561	116.327	108.285	81.521
II	104.475	105.358	105.904	105.068	99.539	100.726	113.579	122.437	110.007	78.764
III	105.402	105.858	106.724	105.403	99.736	100.626	116.219	129.869	110.615	73.932
IV	105.957	106.175	107.513	105.477	97.753	99.564	118.109	133.348	111.829	67.745
2008: I	105.764	106.016	106.121	105.953	95.887	97.969	118.674	135.559	111.685	62.355
II	106.147	106.032	105.983	106.047	93.292	97.291	119.083	140.215	110.258	59.738
III	105.430	105.088	103.895	105.697	91.643	95.199	117.210	140.191	107.577	57.208
IV	103.984	104.267	101.186	105.837	85.519	89.964	111.040	137.603	99.808	53.549
2009: I	102.271	104.425	101.817	105.761	71.746	79.514	98.061	119.243	89.143	47.478
II	102.082	104.196	101.023	105.809	67.059	76.895	95.623	113.716	88.036	44.436
III	102.648	104.917	102.789	106.014	67.874	76.647	94.183	108.074	88.370	46.403
IVᵖ	104.088	105.437	103.451	106.464	73.738	77.304	94.858	103.650	91.174	47.046

See next page for continuation of table.

TABLE B–6. Chain-type quantity indexes for gross domestic product, 1960–2009—*Continued*

[Index numbers, 2005=100; quarterly data seasonally adjusted]

Year or quarter	Exports of goods and services			Imports of goods and services			Government consumption expenditures and gross investment				
							Total	Federal			State and local
	Total	Goods	Services	Total	Goods	Services		Total	National defense	Non-defense	
1960	7.548	7.139	8.500	5.649	4.224	14.535	36.751	53.496	67.385	26.830	26.338
1961	7.588	7.175	8.552	5.611	4.218	14.287	38.600	55.739	70.368	27.642	27.961
1962	7.971	7.494	9.141	6.248	4.843	14.954	40.977	60.488	74.623	33.377	28.818
1963	8.541	8.083	9.605	6.416	5.039	14.943	42.032	60.526	72.838	36.946	30.552
1964	9.547	9.190	10.180	6.757	5.372	15.328	42.958	59.725	69.951	40.157	32.626
1965	9.815	9.239	11.215	7.476	6.132	15.779	44.250	59.697	68.481	42.878	34.813
1966	10.495	9.880	11.986	8.587	7.099	17.783	48.149	66.303	78.306	43.320	36.998
1967	10.737	9.927	12.932	9.213	7.473	19.957	51.844	72.903	88.567	42.913	38.868
1968	11.580	10.713	13.925	10.586	9.016	20.315	53.472	73.491	90.001	41.897	41.168
1969	12.140	11.274	14.442	11.189	9.510	21.596	53.347	70.969	85.556	43.019	42.557
1970	13.445	12.560	15.729	11.666	9.882	22.722	52.059	65.738	77.800	42.567	43.738
1971	13.674	12.511	16.942	12.289	10.711	22.075	50.926	60.677	68.981	44.575	45.077
1972	14.700	13.856	16.835	13.672	12.168	23.011	50.556	58.197	63.588	47.722	46.068
1973	17.471	17.038	18.025	14.306	13.027	22.235	50.379	55.748	60.061	47.429	47.381
1974	18.852	18.391	19.432	13.982	12.665	22.210	51.648	56.243	59.595	49.891	49.164
1975	18.732	17.964	20.626	12.428	11.069	21.247	52.812	56.426	59.030	51.594	50.970
1976	19.550	18.817	21.236	14.858	13.572	22.714	53.049	56.453	58.828	52.085	51.346
1977	20.021	19.063	22.606	16.483	15.226	23.846	53.630	57.647	59.511	54.324	51.532
1978	22.132	21.193	24.496	17.911	16.591	25.546	55.210	59.092	60.019	57.700	53.216
1979	24.326	23.697	25.250	18.208	16.876	25.897	56.241	60.519	61.845	58.309	53.998
1980	26.946	26.521	26.826	16.999	15.623	25.319	57.337	63.390	64.541	61.573	53.958
1981	27.277	26.234	29.683	17.446	15.945	26.778	57.860	66.420	68.628	62.396	52.873
1982	25.193	23.863	28.860	17.226	15.544	28.205	58.876	68.989	73.814	59.402	52.898
1983	24.543	23.177	28.380	19.400	17.656	30.483	61.027	73.561	79.110	62.471	53.514
1984	26.546	25.009	30.911	24.122	21.927	38.126	63.078	75.829	82.971	61.279	55.444
1985	27.352	25.931	31.279	25.687	23.299	41.026	67.471	81.771	90.002	64.900	58.879
1986	29.451	27.263	35.820	27.883	25.687	41.488	71.573	86.407	95.766	67.130	62.669
1987	32.619	30.286	39.390	29.532	26.878	46.378	73.300	89.477	100.301	67.081	63.575
1988	37.844	35.992	42.939	30.693	27.966	47.954	74.220	88.010	99.826	63.499	65.933
1989	42.193	40.281	47.375	32.045	29.171	50.278	76.240	89.379	99.335	68.795	68.340
1990	45.989	43.671	52.372	33.191	30.020	53.564	78.655	91.185	99.305	74.465	71.112
1991	49.042	46.685	55.505	33.142	30.156	52.173	79.514	91.000	98.214	76.170	72.585
1992	52.410	50.177	58.496	35.466	32.999	50.768	79.885	89.351	93.351	81.218	74.156
1993	54.127	51.812	60.437	38.532	36.301	52.124	79.253	85.842	88.401	80.687	75.244
1994	58.847	56.853	64.275	43.129	41.149	54.901	79.245	82.555	84.072	79.525	77.197
1995	64.805	63.505	68.316	46.580	44.855	56.556	79.705	80.353	80.936	79.207	79.247
1996	70.186	69.106	73.101	50.631	49.060	59.514	80.507	79.423	79.856	78.577	81.090
1997	78.550	79.042	77.436	57.450	56.130	64.687	82.020	78.641	77.618	80.737	83.980
1998	80.343	80.805	79.303	64.165	62.780	71.721	83.759	77.758	75.978	81.374	87.291
1999	83.849	83.880	83.857	71.550	70.609	76.569	86.761	79.270	77.386	83.095	91.179
2000	91.054	93.182	86.102	80.871	80.086	84.955	88.519	79.661	76.986	85.066	93.744
2001	85.946	87.414	82.534	78.596	77.530	84.292	91.917	82.901	79.908	88.945	97.236
2002	84.224	84.268	84.115	81.270	80.409	85.837	96.192	88.953	85.782	95.357	100.473
2003	85.574	85.773	85.107	84.857	84.363	87.474	98.336	94.839	93.243	98.071	100.408
2004	93.698	93.025	95.237	94.231	93.660	97.252	99.668	98.710	98.535	99.067	100.234
2005	100.000	100.000	100.000	100.000	100.000	100.000	100.000	100.000	100.000	100.000	100.000
2006	108.962	109.416	107.935	106.086	105.904	107.059	101.359	102.127	101.588	103.237	100.910
2007	118.472	117.512	120.644	108.188	107.709	110.754	103.090	103.434	103.806	102.653	102.886
2008	124.842	124.436	125.759	104.721	103.472	111.478	106.252	111.362	111.939	110.153	103.355
2009 *p*	112.532	108.933	120.467	89.874	86.599	107.225	108.293	117.158	118.003	115.381	103.293
2006: I	106.415	107.085	104.897	104.613	104.376	105.888	101.147	102.763	101.115	106.163	100.205
II	108.200	109.021	106.339	105.774	105.665	106.358	101.232	101.887	101.384	102.927	100.851
III	108.353	109.069	106.729	107.040	107.100	106.715	101.386	101.792	100.892	103.653	101.149
IV	112.882	112.488	113.773	106.917	106.476	109.276	101.670	102.066	102.963	100.203	101.437
2007: I	113.856	113.311	115.087	108.041	107.792	109.381	101.671	100.738	100.952	100.282	102.203
II	115.302	115.048	115.871	107.907	107.527	109.950	102.764	102.558	103.059	101.505	102.875
III	120.293	119.075	123.050	108.904	108.277	112.250	103.757	104.871	105.546	103.457	103.110
IV	124.436	122.613	128.568	107.901	107.239	111.435	104.169	105.570	105.668	105.367	103.356
2008: I	124.395	123.873	125.587	107.225	106.290	112.249	104.845	107.654	107.760	107.442	103.234
II	127.997	128.016	127.965	105.853	105.035	110.211	105.782	109.698	109.597	109.925	103.549
III	126.828	127.446	125.429	105.259	104.045	111.849	107.036	113.152	114.668	109.956	103.576
IV	120.149	118.407	124.054	100.547	98.517	111.605	107.346	114.946	115.732	113.288	103.061
2009: I	109.922	105.520	119.619	89.804	86.326	108.238	106.639	113.693	114.219	112.576	102.660
II	108.766	103.817	119.649	86.292	82.520	106.160	108.386	116.801	118.014	114.259	103.640
III	113.315	109.695	121.293	90.554	87.270	107.962	109.097	119.057	120.419	116.203	103.479
IV *p*	118.127	116.699	121.308	92.846	90.279	106.542	109.051	119.080	119.360	118.487	103.394

Source: Department of Commerce (Bureau of Economic Analysis).

TABLE B–7. Chain-type price indexes for gross domestic product, 1960–2009

[Index numbers, 2005=100, except as noted; quarterly data seasonally adjusted]

Year or quarter	Gross domestic product	Personal consumption expenditures			Gross private domestic investment					
						Fixed investment				
		Total	Goods	Services	Total	Total	Nonresidential			Residential
							Total	Structures	Equipment and software	
1960	18.604	18.606	29.144	13.581	26.607	25.530	33.978	11.516	54.445	12.962
1961	18.814	18.801	29.253	13.827	26.533	25.449	33.783	11.446	54.146	12.983
1962	19.071	19.023	29.404	14.090	26.548	25.465	33.788	11.537	53.878	13.003
1963	19.273	19.245	29.648	14.306	26.463	25.391	33.784	11.636	53.581	12.901
1964	19.572	19.527	29.971	14.573	26.613	25.545	33.955	11.801	53.558	13.003
1965	19.928	19.810	30.286	14.846	27.037	25.981	34.342	12.143	53.607	13.372
1966	20.493	20.313	30.953	15.277	27.592	26.528	34.854	12.580	53.749	13.857
1967	21.124	20.824	31.499	15.786	28.320	27.271	35.741	12.973	54.940	14.339
1968	22.022	21.636	32.597	16.468	29.378	28.367	36.999	13.621	56.416	15.100
1969	23.110	22.616	33.860	17.326	30.770	29.767	38.527	14.518	57.985	16.144
1970	24.328	23.674	35.152	18.287	32.072	31.047	40.348	15.473	60.119	16.666
1971	25.545	24.680	36.208	19.285	33.671	32.611	42.246	16.664	61.905	17.632
1972	26.647	25.525	37.135	20.103	35.077	34.009	43.673	17.863	62.651	18.703
1973	28.124	26.901	39.350	21.078	36.972	35.888	45.355	19.247	63.716	20.359
1974	30.669	29.703	44.261	22.868	40.648	39.422	49.733	21.910	68.414	22.460
1975	33.577	32.184	47.837	24.836	45.666	44.361	56.581	24.534	78.523	24.547
1976	35.505	33.950	49.709	26.558	48.190	46.932	59.718	25.741	83.143	26.124
1977	37.764	36.155	52.363	28.560	51.805	50.616	63.805	27.973	88.083	28.759
1978	40.413	38.687	55.576	30.779	56.030	54.891	68.078	30.675	92.731	32.281
1979	43.773	42.118	60.832	33.353	61.099	59.866	73.606	34.238	98.610	35.902
1980	47.776	46.641	67.644	36.805	66.836	65.468	80.098	37.421	107.032	39.789
1981	52.281	50.810	72.669	40.558	73.154	71.551	87.832	42.567	114.681	43.036
1982	55.467	53.615	74.650	43.712	76.899	75.468	92.670	45.927	119.155	45.340
1983	57.655	55.923	75.997	46.433	76.706	75.349	91.843	44.757	119.406	46.380
1984	59.823	58.038	77.435	48.850	77.256	75.790	91.621	45.147	118.364	47.714
1985	61.633	59.938	78.677	51.053	78.047	76.744	92.340	46.219	118.221	48.944
1986	63.003	61.399	78.309	53.378	79.737	78.579	93.908	47.106	120.094	50.994
1987	64.763	63.589	80.827	55.413	81.263	80.036	94.753	47.863	120.750	53.079
1988	66.990	66.121	82.958	58.127	83.120	82.111	96.857	49.895	122.256	54.913
1989	69.520	68.994	86.150	60.844	85.107	84.099	98.890	51.848	123.786	56.680
1990	72.213	72.147	89.678	63.812	86.747	85.808	100.783	53.522	125.389	58.011
1991	74.762	74.755	91.870	66.586	87.981	87.082	102.341	54.491	127.178	58.771
1992	76.537	76.954	92.978	69.240	87.672	86.831	101.488	54.502	125.681	59.486
1993	78.222	78.643	93.786	71.299	88.673	87.838	101.540	56.103	124.408	61.890
1994	79.867	80.265	94.740	73.205	89.828	89.023	102.029	58.089	123.695	64.069
1995	81.533	82.041	95.625	75.370	90.840	90.060	102.247	60.601	122.265	66.403
1996	83.083	83.826	96.676	77.479	90.455	89.817	101.054	62.141	119.323	67.828
1997	84.554	85.395	96.563	79.817	90.120	89.589	99.775	64.516	115.788	69.557
1998	85.507	86.207	95.106	81.695	89.109	88.756	97.587	67.480	110.641	71.412
1999	86.766	87.596	95.603	83.515	88.989	88.700	96.173	69.559	107.406	74.151
2000	88.648	89.777	97.520	85.824	89.954	89.751	96.219	72.298	106.114	77.415
2001	90.654	91.488	97.429	88.428	90.748	90.553	95.788	76.087	103.603	80.994
2002	92.113	92.736	96.430	90.807	91.118	90.924	95.363	79.292	101.494	83.002
2003	94.099	94.622	96.380	93.692	92.411	92.301	95.355	82.174	100.287	86.953
2004	96.769	97.098	97.867	96.687	95.632	95.541	96.834	88.441	99.897	93.296
2005	100.000	100.000	100.000	100.000	100.000	100.000	100.000	100.000	100.000	100.000
2006	103.263	102.746	101.508	103.411	104.371	104.419	103.534	112.922	100.194	106.081
2007	106.221	105.502	102.789	106.964	106.677	106.718	106.209	121.275	100.715	107.513
2008	108.481	109.031	106.150	110.582	107.355	107.551	107.897	125.207	101.455	105.779
2009 ᵖ	109.754	109.252	103.632	112.221	106.458	106.114	107.510	122.759	102.010	100.687
2006: I	102.071	101.803	101.116	102.171	103.139	103.195	102.279	108.823	99.977	104.890
II	102.980	102.567	101.765	102.998	104.026	104.089	103.112	111.791	100.042	105.940
III	103.763	103.316	102.329	103.844	104.666	104.713	103.878	113.962	100.285	106.295
IV	104.237	103.298	100.822	104.630	105.653	105.677	104.868	117.111	100.472	107.199
2007: I	105.327	104.250	101.612	105.668	106.375	106.380	105.686	119.716	100.611	107.604
II	106.026	105.074	102.548	106.433	106.547	106.591	106.104	120.794	100.766	107.307
III	106.460	105.681	102.627	107.327	106.761	106.803	106.354	121.786	100.712	107.455
IV	107.072	107.005	104.370	108.427	107.024	107.096	106.693	122.804	100.769	107.686
2008: I	107.577	107.974	105.689	109.213	106.586	106.909	106.617	122.976	100.590	107.271
II	108.061	109.021	106.678	110.296	106.745	107.210	107.161	123.800	101.019	106.838
III	109.130	110.273	108.451	111.275	107.350	107.866	108.314	125.814	101.797	105.807
IV	109.155	108.855	103.784	111.542	108.738	108.217	109.498	128.238	102.415	103.198
2009: I	109.661	108.449	102.186	111.749	108.245	107.668	109.154	127.092	102.450	101.915
II	109.656	108.814	102.864	111.954	107.019	106.463	107.993	123.706	102.304	100.554
III	109.763	109.510	104.216	112.312	105.465	105.265	106.656	120.451	101.802	99.863
IV ᵖ	109.934	110.235	105.264	112.869	105.102	105.062	106.238	119.786	101.485	100.417

See next page for continuation of table.

TABLE B–7. Chain-type price indexes for gross domestic product, 1960–2009—*Continued*

[Index numbers, 2005=100, except as noted; quarterly data seasonally adjusted]

Year or quarter	Exports and imports of goods and services		Government consumption expenditures and gross investment					Final sales of domestic product	Gross domestic purchases [1]		Percent change [2]		
	Exports	Imports	Total	Federal			State and local		Total	Less food and energy	Gross domestic product	Gross domestic purchases [1]	
				Total	National defense	Non-defense						Total	Less food and energy
1960	27.453	19.941	12.809	13.677	13.440	13.946	12.066	18.455	18.220		1.4	1.4	
1961	27.871	19.941	13.065	13.908	13.633	14.359	12.357	18.663	18.412		1.1	1.1	
1962	27.940	19.706	13.398	14.202	13.897	14.783	12.743	18.920	18.654		1.4	1.3	
1963	27.877	20.088	13.690	14.506	14.209	15.037	13.028	19.125	18.871		1.1	1.2	
1964	28.107	20.512	14.070	14.995	14.620	15.798	13.293	19.424	19.175		1.6	1.6	
1965	29.001	20.797	14.444	15.379	15.024	16.104	13.662	19.781	19.507		1.8	1.7	
1966	29.877	21.281	15.044	15.914	15.535	16.708	14.334	20.346	20.054		2.8	2.8	
1967	31.022	21.364	15.671	16.386	15.994	17.215	15.137	20.978	20.637		3.1	2.9	
1968	31.698	21.689	16.520	17.287	16.834	18.327	15.945	21.880	21.508		4.3	4.2	
1969	32.771	22.254	17.517	18.226	17.757	19.284	17.013	22.968	22.563		4.9	4.9	
1970	34.027	23.570	18.945	19.699	19.116	21.143	18.411	24.182	23.778		5.3	5.4	
1971	35.283	25.017	20.421	21.383	20.810	22.746	19.720	25.394	25.000		5.0	5.1	
1972	36.928	26.770	21.989	23.471	23.209	23.892	20.896	26.494	26.112		4.3	4.4	
1973	41.784	31.423	23.594	25.080	24.911	25.231	22.495	27.968	27.623		5.5	5.8	
1974	51.478	44.957	25.977	27.315	27.223	27.245	24.970	30.493	30.459		9.0	10.3	
1975	56.738	48.699	28.586	30.158	29.880	30.505	27.410	33.389	33.300		9.5	9.3	
1976	58.600	50.165	30.469	32.302	32.057	32.549	29.114	35.320	35.208		5.7	5.7	
1977	60.987	54.586	32.583	34.742	34.486	34.993	31.005	37.582	37.586		6.4	6.8	
1978	64.703	58.440	34.670	36.888	36.908	36.514	33.042	40.232	40.252		7.0	7.1	
1979	72.490	68.434	37.575	39.727	39.853	39.100	35.976	43.576	43.797		8.3	8.8	
1980	79.843	85.240	41.669	43.900	44.179	42.906	40.002	47.557	48.408		9.1	10.5	
1981	85.744	89.822	45.768	48.165	48.542	46.917	43.975	52.029	52.864		9.4	9.2	
1982	86.138	86.794	48.775	51.434	51.953	49.825	46.786	55.233	55.859	55.358	6.1	5.7	
1983	86.478	83.541	50.717	53.218	53.775	51.501	48.857	57.414	57.817	57.517	3.9	3.5	3.9
1984	87.280	82.820	53.319	56.358	57.603	52.779	51.034	59.573	59.854	59.650	3.8	3.5	3.7
1985	84.609	80.100	54.974	57.635	58.696	54.574	53.002	61.414	61.553	61.521	3.0	2.8	3.1
1986	83.342	80.097	55.977	57.938	58.642	55.915	54.577	62.802	62.948	63.407	2.2	2.3	3.1
1987	85.451	84.948	57.541	58.642	59.236	56.953	56.849	64.552	64.923	65.447	2.8	3.1	3.2
1988	89.876	89.011	59.924	59.884	60.326	58.679	58.621	66.807	67.159	67.839	3.4	3.4	3.7
1989	91.373	90.956	60.924	61.504	61.882	60.497	60.654	69.338	69.706	70.282	3.8	3.8	3.6
1990	91.993	93.563	63.405	63.548	63.917	62.568	63.474	72.040	72.540	72.977	3.9	4.1	3.8
1991	93.212	92.783	65.606	66.070	66.222	65.672	65.443	74.592	74.977	75.470	3.5	3.3	3.4
1992	92.833	92.856	67.276	68.101	68.522	67.034	66.856	76.371	76.724	77.450	2.4	2.4	2.6
1993	92.808	92.144	68.949	69.830	69.712	70.002	68.494	78.057	78.339	79.156	2.2	2.1	2.2
1994	93.842	93.009	70.819	71.725	71.438	72.267	70.351	79.707	79.962	80.873	2.1	2.1	2.2
1995	95.997	95.557	72.753	73.717	73.161	74.830	72.252	81.379	81.674	82.647	2.1	2.1	2.2
1996	94.727	93.891	74.488	75.763	75.431	76.406	73.806	82.953	83.150	84.001	1.9	1.8	1.6
1997	93.103	90.627	75.854	77.047	76.517	78.095	75.219	84.449	84.397	85.266	1.8	1.5	1.5
1998	90.972	85.748	76.879	77.931	77.328	79.120	76.320	85.443	84.962	86.093	1.1	.7	1.0
1999	90.408	86.250	79.337	79.886	79.225	81.188	79.036	86.720	86.304	87.384	1.5	1.6	1.5
2000	91.999	89.963	82.513	82.524	81.821	83.907	82.482	88.623	88.463	89.163	2.2	2.5	2.0
2001	91.627	87.762	84.764	84.201	83.484	85.612	85.019	90.631	90.123	90.769	2.3	1.9	1.8
2002	91.253	86.784	87.003	87.318	86.624	88.689	86.810	92.089	91.422	92.300	1.6	1.4	1.7
2003	93.216	89.796	90.650	91.024	90.659	91.774	90.425	94.089	93.550	94.177	2.2	2.3	2.0
2004	96.517	94.144	94.531	95.335	94.895	96.234	94.062	96.759	96.400	96.762	2.8	3.0	2.7
2005	100.000	100.000	100.000	100.000	100.000	100.000	100.000	100.000	100.000	100.000	3.3	3.7	3.3
2006	103.447	104.144	104.842	104.107	104.421	103.468	105.276	103.266	103.380	103.157	3.3	3.4	3.2
2007	107.103	108.017	109.552	107.754	108.286	106.672	110.615	106.226	106.408	105.984	2.9	2.9	2.7
2008 *p*	112.389	119.559	114.502	110.938	111.913	108.935	116.642	108.507	109.765	108.689	2.1	3.2	2.6
2009 *p*	106.243	107.022	114.298	111.516	112.089	110.360	115.923	109.666	109.823	109.508	1.2	.1	.8
2006: I	101.828	103.243	103.232	103.101	103.336	102.622	103.307	102.075	102.275	102.022	3.0	2.8	3.1
II	103.125	104.322	104.644	104.187	104.499	103.551	104.916	102.985	103.173	102.913	3.6	3.6	3.5
III	104.395	105.121	105.437	104.502	104.883	103.728	105.990	103.767	103.910	103.538	3.1	2.9	2.5
IV	104.438	103.889	106.055	104.637	104.965	103.972	106.892	104.237	104.162	104.153	1.8	1.0	2.4
2007: I	105.355	104.711	106.808	106.808	107.089	106.243	108.527	105.325	105.229	105.073	4.2	4.2	3.6
II	106.516	106.332	109.129	107.737	108.172	106.858	109.944	106.032	106.024	105.635	2.7	3.1	2.2
III	107.396	107.937	109.854	107.896	108.493	106.678	111.009	106.465	106.592	106.187	1.6	2.2	2.1
IV	109.144	113.088	111.336	108.577	109.389	106.908	112.975	107.080	107.786	107.040	2.3	4.6	3.3
2008: I	111.156	117.234	113.038	110.077	110.857	108.469	114.803	107.623	108.678	107.743	1.9	3.4	2.7
II	113.890	123.069	114.772	111.265	112.402	108.922	116.877	108.127	109.722	108.544	1.8	3.9	3.0
III	115.638	125.203	115.963	111.587	113.059	109.149	118.493	109.202	110.871	109.317	4.0	4.3	2.9
IV	108.871	112.730	114.233	110.628	111.334	109.198	116.396	109.078	109.790	109.151	.1	-3.8	-.6
2009: I	105.265	103.746	113.924	111.084	111.584	110.085	115.587	109.566	109.395	109.215	1.9	-1.4	.2
II	105.284	104.821	114.051	111.238	111.664	110.320	115.713	109.550	109.533	109.439	.0	.5	.8
III	106.473	107.688	114.312	111.601	112.195	110.401	115.889	109.681	109.895	109.521	.4	1.3	.3
IV *p*	107.952	111.830	114.905	112.164	112.914	110.635	116.501	109.868	110.470	109.856	.6	2.1	1.2

[1] Gross domestic product (GDP) less exports of goods and services plus imports of goods and services.
[2] Quarterly percent changes are at annual rates.

Source: Department of Commerce (Bureau of Economic Analysis).

TABLE B–8. Gross domestic product by major type of product, 1960–2009

[Billions of dollars; quarterly data at seasonally adjusted annual rates]

Year or quarter	Gross domestic product	Final sales of domestic product	Change in private inventories	Goods Total: Total	Goods Total: Final sales	Goods Total: Change in private inventories	Durable goods: Final sales	Durable goods: Change in private inventories[1]	Nondurable goods: Final sales	Nondurable goods: Change in private inventories[1]	Services[2]	Structures
1960	526.4	523.2	3.2	227.5	224.3	3.2	92.5	1.7	131.7	1.6	237.0	61.9
1961	544.8	541.8	3.0	230.6	227.6	3.0	92.6	−.1	135.0	3.0	250.6	63.6
1962	585.7	579.6	6.1	247.4	241.3	6.1	102.0	3.4	139.3	2.7	270.4	67.8
1963	617.8	612.1	5.6	258.5	252.9	5.6	108.6	2.6	144.3	3.0	286.6	72.7
1964	663.6	658.8	4.8	277.8	273.0	4.8	119.3	3.8	153.7	1.0	307.4	78.4
1965	719.1	709.9	9.2	304.3	295.1	9.2	131.6	6.2	163.5	3.0	330.1	84.7
1966	787.7	774.1	13.6	337.1	323.5	13.6	145.4	10.0	178.0	3.6	362.6	88.0
1967	832.4	822.6	9.9	345.4	335.5	9.9	150.0	4.8	185.5	5.0	397.5	89.6
1968	909.8	900.8	9.1	370.8	361.7	9.1	162.8	4.5	198.9	4.5	439.1	100.0
1969	984.4	975.3	9.2	397.6	388.4	9.2	175.7	6.0	212.7	3.2	478.6	108.3
1970	1,038.3	1,036.3	2.0	408.7	406.7	2.0	178.6	−.2	228.2	2.2	519.9	109.7
1971	1,126.8	1,118.6	8.3	432.6	424.4	8.3	186.7	2.9	237.7	5.3	565.8	128.4
1972	1,237.9	1,228.8	9.1	472.0	462.9	9.1	208.4	6.4	254.5	2.7	619.0	146.9
1973	1,382.3	1,366.4	15.9	547.1	531.2	15.9	243.6	13.0	287.6	2.9	672.2	162.9
1974	1,499.5	1,485.5	14.0	588.0	574.0	14.0	262.4	10.9	311.7	3.1	745.8	165.6
1975	1,637.7	1,644.0	−6.3	628.6	634.8	−6.3	293.2	−7.5	341.6	1.2	842.4	166.7
1976	1,824.6	1,807.5	17.1	706.6	689.5	17.1	330.9	10.8	358.6	6.3	926.8	191.2
1977	2,030.1	2,007.8	22.3	773.5	751.2	22.3	374.6	9.5	376.6	12.8	1,029.9	226.8
1978	2,293.8	2,268.0	25.8	872.6	846.8	25.8	424.9	18.2	422.0	7.6	1,147.2	273.9
1979	2,562.2	2,544.2	18.0	977.2	959.2	18.0	483.9	12.8	475.3	5.2	1,271.7	313.3
1980	2,788.1	2,794.5	−6.3	1,035.2	1,041.5	−6.3	512.3	−2.3	529.2	−4.0	1,431.6	321.3
1981	3,126.8	3,097.0	29.8	1,167.3	1,137.5	29.8	554.8	7.3	582.6	22.5	1,606.9	352.6
1982	3,253.2	3,268.1	−14.9	1,148.8	1,163.7	−14.9	552.5	−16.0	611.2	1.1	1,759.9	344.5
1983	3,534.6	3,540.4	−5.8	1,226.9	1,232.6	−5.8	592.3	2.5	640.3	−8.2	1,939.1	368.7
1984	3,930.9	3,865.5	65.4	1,402.2	1,336.8	65.4	665.9	41.4	670.9	24.0	2,102.9	425.8
1985	4,217.5	4,195.6	21.8	1,452.8	1,431.0	21.8	727.9	4.4	703.1	17.4	2,305.9	458.7
1986	4,460.1	4,453.5	6.6	1,491.2	1,484.7	6.6	758.3	−1.9	726.4	8.4	2,488.7	480.1
1987	4,736.4	4,709.2	27.1	1,570.7	1,543.6	27.1	785.3	22.9	758.3	4.2	2,668.0	497.6
1988	5,100.4	5,081.9	18.5	1,703.7	1,685.2	18.5	863.3	22.7	821.9	−4.3	2,881.7	515.0
1989	5,482.1	5,454.5	27.7	1,851.9	1,824.2	27.7	939.7	20.0	884.5	7.7	3,101.2	529.0
1990	5,800.5	5,786.0	14.5	1,923.1	1,908.5	14.5	973.2	7.7	935.3	6.8	3,343.9	533.5
1991	5,992.1	5,992.5	−.4	1,943.5	1,943.9	−.4	967.6	−13.6	976.3	13.2	3,548.6	499.9
1992	6,342.3	6,326.0	16.3	2,031.5	2,015.1	16.3	1,010.7	−3.0	1,004.4	19.3	3,788.1	522.7
1993	6,667.4	6,646.5	20.8	2,124.2	2,103.4	20.8	1,072.9	17.1	1,030.4	3.7	3,985.1	558.1
1994	7,085.2	7,021.4	63.8	2,290.7	2,226.9	63.8	1,149.8	35.7	1,077.1	28.1	4,187.2	607.3
1995	7,414.7	7,383.5	31.2	2,379.5	2,348.3	31.2	1,225.9	33.6	1,122.4	−2.4	4,396.7	638.5
1996	7,838.5	7,807.7	30.8	2,516.3	2,485.5	30.8	1,321.0	19.1	1,164.5	11.7	4,625.5	696.7
1997	8,332.4	8,261.4	71.0	2,701.2	2,630.2	71.0	1,430.7	40.0	1,199.5	31.0	4,882.5	748.6
1998	8,793.5	8,729.8	63.7	2,819.2	2,755.5	63.7	1,524.2	39.3	1,231.3	24.4	5,159.7	814.5
1999	9,353.5	9,292.7	60.8	2,990.1	2,929.3	60.8	1,633.8	37.4	1,295.5	23.4	5,485.1	878.2
2000	9,951.5	9,896.9	54.5	3,124.5	3,070.0	54.5	1,734.4	35.6	1,335.6	19.0	5,878.0	949.0
2001	10,286.2	10,324.5	−38.3	3,077.6	3,115.9	−38.3	1,731.5	−44.4	1,384.4	6.2	6,208.7	999.9
2002	10,642.3	10,630.3	12.0	3,101.2	3,089.1	12.0	1,678.9	17.7	1,410.3	−5.6	6,535.5	1,005.7
2003	11,142.1	11,125.8	16.4	3,170.1	3,153.7	16.4	1,694.2	13.0	1,459.5	3.3	6,891.7	1,080.4
2004	11,867.8	11,802.8	64.9	3,333.9	3,269.0	64.9	1,748.0	37.3	1,521.1	27.6	7,319.3	1,214.5
2005	12,638.4	12,588.4	50.0	3,472.9	3,422.9	50.0	1,855.9	35.2	1,567.0	14.7	7,802.1	1,363.4
2006	13,398.9	13,339.0	60.0	3,660.7	3,600.7	60.0	1,951.5	25.9	1,649.3	34.0	8,285.5	1,452.7
2007	14,077.6	14,058.3	19.4	3,814.1	3,794.7	19.4	2,040.1	7.6	1,754.6	11.8	8,810.8	1,452.8
2008	14,441.4	14,476.2	−34.8	3,783.8	3,818.6	−34.8	2,032.0	10.3	1,786.6	−45.1	9,265.4	1,392.2
2009 ᴾ	14,258.7	14,383.7	−125.0	3,696.8	3,821.8	−125.0	1,906.0	−94.9	1,915.9	−30.1	9,397.3	1,164.6
2006: I	13,183.5	13,117.5	66.0	3,615.0	3,549.0	66.0	1,938.9	20.9	1,610.1	45.1	8,114.2	1,454.3
II	13,347.8	13,275.4	72.4	3,646.9	3,574.5	72.4	1,943.2	33.7	1,631.3	38.7	8,229.7	1,471.3
III	13,452.9	13,383.8	69.1	3,667.4	3,598.3	69.1	1,945.8	44.1	1,652.5	25.0	8,335.7	1,449.7
IV	13,611.5	13,579.2	32.3	3,713.5	3,681.2	32.3	1,977.9	5.1	1,703.3	27.3	8,462.4	1,435.6
2007: I	13,795.6	13,782.5	13.1	3,726.7	3,713.6	13.1	1,986.4	11.2	1,727.3	1.9	8,620.5	1,448.4
II	13,997.2	13,973.7	23.5	3,796.5	3,773.1	23.5	2,032.5	−9.2	1,740.5	32.6	8,738.5	1,462.2
III	14,179.9	14,148.8	31.0	3,844.8	3,813.7	31.0	2,047.4	11.0	1,766.3	20.1	8,872.1	1,463.0
IV	14,337.9	14,328.0	9.8	3,888.3	3,878.4	9.8	2,094.2	17.3	1,784.2	−7.5	9,012.2	1,437.4
2008: I	14,373.9	14,382.1	−8.2	3,842.5	3,850.7	−8.2	2,076.7	16.5	1,774.0	−24.7	9,131.8	1,399.5
II	14,497.8	14,547.1	−49.3	3,825.2	3,874.6	−49.3	2,073.1	−22.0	1,801.4	−27.3	9,263.3	1,409.3
III	14,546.7	14,583.7	−37.0	3,806.1	3,843.0	−37.0	2,042.3	35.9	1,800.7	−72.9	9,340.8	1,399.8
IV	14,347.3	14,391.8	−44.5	3,661.4	3,705.9	−44.5	1,935.7	10.8	1,770.2	−55.3	9,325.7	1,360.2
2009: I	14,178.0	14,305.3	−127.4	3,649.3	3,776.7	−127.4	1,905.2	−122.7	1,871.5	−4.6	9,308.8	1,219.9
II	14,151.2	14,327.4	−176.2	3,625.7	3,801.9	−176.2	1,898.8	−129.0	1,903.1	−47.2	9,358.4	1,167.0
III	14,242.1	14,398.7	−156.5	3,679.9	3,836.4	−156.5	1,911.9	−100.2	1,924.6	−56.3	9,417.0	1,145.3
IV ᴾ	14,463.4	14,503.4	−40.0	3,832.4	3,872.4	−40.0	1,908.0	−27.7	1,964.4	−12.3	9,504.9	1,126.1

[1] Estimates for durable and nondurable goods for 1996 and earlier periods are based on the Standard Industrial Classification (SIC); later estimates are based on the North American Industry Classification System (NAICS).

[2] Includes government consumption expenditures, which are for services (such as education and national defense) produced by government. In current dollars, these services are valued at their cost of production.

Source: Department of Commerce (Bureau of Economic Analysis).

TABLE B–9. Real gross domestic product by major type of product, 1960–2009

[Billions of chained (2005) dollars; quarterly data at seasonally adjusted annual rates]

Year or quarter	Gross domestic product	Final sales of domestic product	Change in private inventories	Goods Total			Durable goods		Nondurable goods		Services[2]	Structures
				Total	Final sales	Change in private inventories	Final sales	Change in private inventories[1]	Final sales	Change in private inventories[1]		
1960	2,830.9	2,836.6	11.8	603.2							1,835.7	509.9
1961	2,896.9	2,904.6	10.6	608.2							1,902.6	524.1
1962	3,072.4	3,064.9	21.9	649.3							2,007.2	554.2
1963	3,206.7	3,202.6	20.3	675.1							2,090.3	591.7
1964	3,392.3	3,393.7	17.3	720.3							2,189.4	631.5
1965	3,610.1	3,590.7	32.9	780.7							2,299.1	663.1
1966	3,845.3	3,806.6	47.1	848.6							2,441.0	663.9
1967	3,942.5	3,923.3	33.9	850.9							2,576.9	654.2
1968	4,133.4	4,119.4	30.8	884.9							2,712.7	694.5
1969	4,261.8	4,248.6	30.3	915.4							2,800.8	703.3
1970	4,269.9	4,287.9	5.6	907.7							2,858.2	673.0
1971	4,413.3	4,407.4	25.0	934.7							2,926.8	735.5
1972	4,647.7	4,640.6	25.7	998.5							3,034.7	790.2
1973	4,917.0	4,888.2	39.0	1,104.7							3,125.5	807.1
1974	4,889.9	4,874.1	29.1	1,094.1							3,194.6	723.4
1975	4,879.5	4,926.3	–12.8	1,066.8							3,309.1	657.6
1976	5,141.3	5,120.2	34.3	1,150.5							3,400.2	719.2
1977	5,377.7	5,344.9	43.1	1,205.8							3,517.0	787.2
1978	5,677.6	5,639.7	45.6	1,286.8							3,651.5	862.8
1979	5,855.0	5,841.2	28.0	1,322.5							3,740.1	887.4
1980	5,839.0	5,878.7	–9.3	1,328.3							3,811.2	823.0
1981	5,987.2	5,959.5	39.0	1,388.2							3,887.4	811.9
1982	5,870.9	5,923.3	–19.7	1,316.8							3,956.9	742.6
1983	6,136.2	6,172.9	–7.7	1,373.7							4,120.1	796.3
1984	6,577.1	6,495.6	78.3	1,544.0							4,234.1	903.9
1985	6,849.3	6,838.9	25.4	1,581.0							4,448.8	951.0
1986	7,086.5	7,098.7	8.5	1,627.1							4,635.2	965.1
1987	7,313.3	7,296.2	33.2	1,692.7							4,785.3	969.3
1988	7,613.9	7,607.8	21.9	1,798.0							4,961.3	967.6
1989	7,885.9	7,867.5	30.6	1,900.2							5,114.8	961.0
1990	8,033.9	8,032.7	16.6	1,920.1							5,269.3	941.9
1991	8,015.1	8,034.8	–1.4	1,887.6							5,363.0	869.1
1992	8,287.1	8,284.3	17.9	1,962.7							5,521.7	902.4
1993	8,523.4	8,515.3	22.3	2,040.3							5,647.9	930.5
1994	8,870.7	8,809.2	69.3	2,183.8							5,781.2	978.4
1995	9,093.7	9,073.2	32.1	2,264.0	2,241.1	32.1	1,023.0	31.4	1,260.0	–3.3	5,902.5	988.9
1996	9,433.9	9,412.5	31.2	2,387.7	2,363.9	31.2	1,110.9	17.9	1,286.7	12.5	6,045.3	1,053.1
1997	9,854.3	9,782.6	77.4	2,573.9	2,509.8	77.4	1,222.7	40.2	1,309.9	36.1	6,208.3	1,097.8
1998	10,283.5	10,217.1	71.6	2,723.0	2,663.0	71.6	1,341.5	40.6	1,334.3	29.5	6,421.7	1,155.1
1999	10,779.8	10,715.7	68.5	2,914.0	2,855.8	68.5	1,476.4	39.5	1,385.0	27.7	6,663.6	1,202.2
2000	11,226.0	11,167.5	60.2	3,056.3	3,002.8	60.2	1,590.5	37.7	1,411.8	21.4	6,918.7	1,245.3
2001	11,347.2	11,391.7	–41.8	3,006.9	3,043.6	–41.8	1,614.7	–46.4	1,428.2	7.3	7,095.4	1,254.1
2002	11,553.0	11,543.5	12.8	3,059.2	3,047.4	12.8	1,656.0	18.1	1,451.9	–6.4	7,275.6	1,223.2
2003	11,840.7	11,824.8	17.3	3,164.0	3,146.1	17.3	1,656.3	13.5	1,490.5	3.6	7,416.0	1,263.6
2004	12,263.8	12,198.2	66.3	3,326.2	3,260.9	66.3	1,740.4	38.1	1,520.6	28.1	7,613.1	1,325.6
2005	12,638.4	12,588.4	50.0	3,472.9	3,422.9	50.0	1,855.9	35.2	1,567.0	14.7	7,802.1	1,363.4
2006	12,976.2	12,917.1	59.4	3,652.7	3,593.5	59.4	1,964.4	25.2	1,629.2	34.1	7,985.0	1,341.1
2007	13,254.1	13,234.3	19.5	3,789.7	3,771.6	19.5	2,080.7	7.6	1,691.7	11.8	8,192.7	1,281.4
2008	13,312.2	13,341.2	–25.9	3,805.1	3,839.5	–25.9	2,106.7	9.4	1,732.9	–33.7	8,314.8	1,205.4
2009 ᵖ	12,988.7	13,115.2	–111.7	3,615.6	3,755.3	–111.7	1,981.3	–88.9	1,767.2	–24.7	8,354.0	1,026.7
2006: I	12,915.9	12,851.3	65.8	3,624.5	3,559.5	65.8	1,943.8	20.6	1,615.9	45.1	7,918.5	1,374.0
II	12,962.5	12,891.0	72.5	3,640.6	3,568.5	72.5	1,953.8	32.9	1,614.9	39.7	7,957.8	1,365.4
III	12,965.9	12,898.3	67.5	3,640.9	3,573.0	67.5	1,962.4	42.4	1,611.0	25.1	7,996.6	1,330.7
IV	13,060.7	13,027.8	31.8	3,704.9	3,672.9	31.8	1,997.6	5.2	1,675.0	26.6	8,067.2	1,294.4
2007: I	13,099.9	13,086.4	14.5	3,697.4	3,685.8	14.5	2,009.7	11.1	1,675.8	3.2	8,120.4	1,287.3
II	13,204.0	13,179.6	23.3	3,753.3	3,730.3	23.3	2,063.3	–8.2	1,668.1	30.8	8,163.1	1,294.5
III	13,321.1	13,290.3	29.8	3,818.9	3,789.2	29.8	2,097.1	10.7	1,693.1	18.8	8,224.8	1,287.6
IV	13,391.2	13,381.1	10.3	3,889.1	3,881.3	10.3	2,152.9	16.7	1,729.8	–5.6	8,262.3	1,256.3
2008: I	13,366.9	13,363.5	.6	3,871.4	3,870.6	.6	2,141.2	15.2	1,730.5	–13.7	8,292.1	1,221.2
II	13,415.3	13,453.5	–37.1	3,885.6	3,930.0	–37.1	2,156.8	–19.6	1,773.4	–18.4	8,322.9	1,225.3
III	13,324.6	13,354.3	–29.7	3,815.5	3,850.5	–29.7	2,121.2	32.8	1,730.1	–57.8	8,315.1	1,208.0
IV	13,141.9	13,193.5	–37.4	3,648.1	3,706.7	–37.4	2,007.5	9.2	1,697.5	–45.1	8,329.3	1,167.0
2009: I	12,925.4	13,055.8	–113.9	3,566.4	3,710.2	–113.9	1,973.9	–115.3	1,731.3	–1.7	8,311.4	1,051.8
II	12,901.5	13,077.8	–160.2	3,537.3	3,730.3	–160.2	1,965.9	–121.8	1,757.5	–40.8	8,341.8	1,025.2
III	12,973.0	13,127.2	–139.2	3,592.1	3,761.5	–139.2	1,993.5	–93.1	1,762.2	–47.6	8,363.7	1,023.1
IV ᵖ	13,155.0	13,200.2	–33.5	3,766.7	3,819.2	–33.5	1,991.8	–25.4	1,817.8	–8.6	8,399.0	1,006.8

[1] Estimates for durable and nondurable goods for 1996 and earlier periods are based on the Standard Industrial Classification (SIC); later estimates are based on the North American Industry Classification System (NAICS).
[2] Includes government consumption expenditures, which are for services (such as education and national defense) produced by government. In current dollars, these services are valued at their cost of production.

Source: Department of Commerce (Bureau of Economic Analysis).

TABLE B–10. Gross value added by sector, 1960–2009

[Billions of dollars; quarterly data at seasonally adjusted annual rates]

Year or quarter	Gross domestic product	Business [1]			Households and institutions			General government [3]			Addendum: Gross housing value added
		Total	Nonfarm [1]	Farm	Total	House-holds	Nonprofit institutions serving households [2]	Total	Federal	State and local	
1960	526.4	419.9	401.7	18.2	44.5	32.6	12.0	62.0	33.0	28.9	39.9
1961	544.8	431.4	413.1	18.3	47.3	34.6	12.8	66.0	34.4	31.6	42.8
1962	585.7	463.9	445.5	18.4	51.0	37.0	14.0	70.7	36.5	34.2	46.0
1963	617.8	488.0	469.5	18.5	54.3	39.1	15.2	75.5	38.4	37.1	48.9
1964	663.6	524.9	507.5	17.3	57.7	41.2	16.5	81.1	40.7	40.4	51.6
1965	719.1	570.7	550.7	19.9	61.8	43.6	18.2	86.6	42.4	44.2	54.9
1966	787.7	624.3	603.5	20.8	66.6	46.2	20.4	96.8	47.2	49.6	58.2
1967	832.4	653.6	633.5	20.1	71.8	49.1	22.7	107.0	51.5	55.5	62.1
1968	909.8	713.5	693.0	20.5	77.5	51.9	25.6	118.8	56.3	62.5	65.9
1969	984.4	769.1	746.3	22.8	85.4	56.0	29.4	130.0	59.9	70.0	71.3
1970	1,038.3	802.2	778.5	23.7	92.6	59.8	32.8	143.5	64.0	79.5	76.7
1971	1,126.8	868.3	842.9	25.4	102.2	65.5	36.7	156.4	67.7	88.6	83.9
1972	1,237.9	957.1	927.5	29.7	111.4	70.8	40.5	169.4	71.5	97.9	91.1
1973	1,382.3	1,077.4	1,030.6	46.8	121.7	76.5	45.2	183.2	73.9	109.3	98.3
1974	1,499.5	1,164.5	1,120.3	44.2	133.6	83.0	50.6	201.3	79.6	121.8	106.8
1975	1,637.7	1,265.8	1,220.1	45.6	147.5	90.8	56.7	224.5	87.3	137.2	117.2
1976	1,824.6	1,420.7	1,377.7	43.0	160.5	98.7	61.8	243.5	93.8	149.7	126.6
1977	2,030.1	1,590.0	1,546.5	43.5	175.5	107.9	67.6	264.6	102.0	162.6	140.5
1978	2,293.8	1,809.4	1,758.7	50.7	196.9	121.3	75.6	287.5	109.7	177.8	155.5
1979	2,562.2	2,028.5	1,968.4	60.1	220.8	136.0	84.8	313.0	117.6	195.4	172.9
1980	2,788.1	2,186.1	2,134.7	51.4	253.5	156.5	97.0	348.5	131.2	217.3	199.8
1981	3,126.8	2,454.0	2,389.0	65.0	287.5	177.8	109.7	385.3	147.4	237.9	228.8
1982	3,253.2	2,514.9	2,454.5	60.4	319.3	196.7	122.7	419.0	161.2	257.7	255.7
1983	3,534.6	2,741.1	2,696.2	44.9	348.2	212.5	135.6	445.4	171.2	274.1	277.7
1984	3,930.9	3,065.5	3,001.3	64.2	380.3	231.0	149.3	485.1	192.1	293.1	301.3
1985	4,217.5	3,283.9	3,220.5	63.4	410.1	250.3	159.8	523.4	205.0	318.4	333.1
1986	4,460.1	3,461.5	3,402.1	59.5	442.3	268.0	174.3	556.3	212.6	343.7	359.7
1987	4,736.4	3,662.0	3,600.5	61.5	482.8	288.0	194.8	591.5	223.3	368.2	385.5
1988	5,100.4	3,940.2	3,879.4	60.7	529.7	313.1	216.6	630.6	234.8	395.8	415.3
1989	5,482.1	4,235.7	4,162.0	73.8	574.2	337.2	237.0	672.2	246.4	425.8	443.4
1990	5,800.5	4,453.9	4,376.6	77.3	624.0	363.3	260.6	722.7	258.8	463.9	477.8
1991	5,992.1	4,558.6	4,488.0	70.6	665.9	383.7	282.2	767.6	274.8	492.8	508.1
1992	6,342.3	4,829.2	4,748.9	80.4	711.1	405.3	305.9	801.9	282.0	519.9	538.6
1993	6,667.4	5,084.1	5,012.7	71.4	752.1	428.3	323.8	831.2	285.2	546.0	562.9
1994	7,085.2	5,425.2	5,341.3	83.9	800.0	461.3	338.7	859.9	285.2	574.7	602.6
1995	7,414.7	5,677.8	5,608.7	69.1	852.1	492.2	359.9	884.8	283.6	601.2	640.7
1996	7,838.5	6,030.2	5,936.9	93.3	897.0	519.8	377.2	911.3	287.6	623.7	671.3
1997	8,332.4	6,442.8	6,354.9	87.9	949.2	550.9	398.3	940.3	290.0	650.3	708.6
1998	8,793.5	6,810.8	6,731.6	79.2	1,010.1	583.9	426.3	972.5	292.2	680.3	745.3
1999	9,353.5	7,249.0	7,177.8	71.2	1,082.9	628.4	454.5	1,021.6	300.4	721.2	798.3
2000	9,951.5	7,715.5	7,641.9	73.6	1,157.2	673.5	483.7	1,078.8	315.1	763.7	849.9
2001	10,286.2	7,913.6	7,837.4	76.2	1,232.9	719.5	513.4	1,139.6	324.9	814.7	904.4
2002	10,642.3	8,132.8	8,060.5	72.3	1,298.0	746.0	552.1	1,211.4	351.8	859.6	932.5
2003	11,142.1	8,502.8	8,410.3	92.4	1,347.2	762.7	584.5	1,292.2	382.9	909.3	938.2
2004	11,867.8	9,084.6	8,966.4	118.3	1,423.8	806.0	617.7	1,359.3	412.0	947.3	988.7
2005	12,638.4	9,695.5	9,593.5	102.0	1,506.4	864.4	642.0	1,436.5	438.7	997.7	1,054.0
2006	13,398.9	10,284.1	10,191.1	93.1	1,602.9	924.8	678.1	1,512.0	460.6	1,051.3	1,130.8
2007	14,077.6	10,789.0	10,672.8	116.2	1,686.9	973.7	713.1	1,601.8	485.7	1,116.0	1,205.4
2008	14,441.4	10,953.1	10,821.0	132.1	1,799.9	1,048.7	751.2	1,688.4	515.2	1,173.2	1,306.5
2009 [p]	14,258.7	10,668.7	10,562.2	106.5	1,830.0	1,062.2	767.7	1,760.0	558.7	1,201.3	1,331.3
2006: I	13,183.5	10,129.8	10,043.0	86.7	1,570.4	906.0	664.4	1,483.2	455.8	1,027.5	1,104.9
II	13,347.8	10,246.9	10,156.4	90.6	1,599.3	924.3	675.0	1,501.6	459.7	1,041.9	1,127.8
III	13,452.9	10,311.9	10,218.2	93.6	1,619.6	938.4	681.2	1,521.4	462.4	1,059.0	1,146.7
IV	13,611.5	10,447.9	10,346.6	101.3	1,622.0	930.4	691.6	1,541.6	464.7	1,076.9	1,143.7
2007: I	13,795.6	10,572.3	10,462.3	110.0	1,648.7	947.4	701.3	1,574.5	480.7	1,093.8	1,166.8
II	13,997.2	10,737.4	10,626.8	110.6	1,666.4	958.3	708.1	1,593.4	484.0	1,109.3	1,185.6
III	14,179.9	10,872.9	10,758.4	114.5	1,697.6	981.7	716.0	1,609.3	487.3	1,122.0	1,217.5
IV	14,337.9	10,973.3	10,843.9	129.5	1,734.6	1,007.6	727.0	1,629.9	490.9	1,139.0	1,251.8
2008: I	14,373.9	10,952.7	10,809.7	143.1	1,761.5	1,025.0	736.5	1,659.7	505.3	1,154.4	1,274.6
II	14,497.8	11,022.1	10,889.6	132.6	1,796.2	1,050.6	745.5	1,679.5	511.8	1,167.7	1,306.2
III	14,546.7	11,034.7	10,901.6	133.0	1,812.4	1,057.1	755.3	1,699.6	518.5	1,181.1	1,318.3
IV	14,347.3	10,802.9	10,683.3	119.6	1,829.5	1,062.0	767.5	1,715.0	525.2	1,189.7	1,326.9
2009: I	14,178.0	10,614.2	10,510.4	103.8	1,823.9	1,063.4	760.5	1,739.8	543.8	1,196.0	1,330.0
II	14,151.2	10,578.5	10,473.0	105.5	1,814.7	1,054.5	760.1	1,758.0	554.3	1,203.8	1,322.9
III	14,242.1	10,641.0	10,540.6	100.4	1,836.5	1,065.6	770.9	1,764.7	563.6	1,201.1	1,335.6
IV [p]	14,463.4	10,840.9	10,724.7	116.2	1,844.8	1,065.4	779.4	1,777.7	573.3	1,204.4	1,336.8

[1] Gross domestic business value added equals gross domestic product excluding gross value added of households and institutions and of general government. Nonfarm value added equals gross domestic business value added excluding gross farm value added.
[2] Equals compensation of employees of nonprofit institutions, the rental value of nonresidential fixed assets owned and used by nonprofit institutions serving households, and rental income of persons for tenant-occupied housing owned by nonprofit institutions.
[3] Equals compensation of general government employees plus general government consumption of fixed capital.

Source: Department of Commerce (Bureau of Economic Analysis).

TABLE B–11. Real gross value added by sector, 1960–2009

[Billions of chained (2005) dollars; quarterly data at seasonally adjusted annual rates]

Year or quarter	Gross domestic product	Business [1] Total	Business [1] Nonfarm [1]	Business [1] Farm	Households and institutions Total	Households and institutions House-holds	Households and institutions Nonprofit institutions serving house-holds [2]	General government [3] Total	General government [3] Federal	General government [3] State and local	Adden-dum: Gross housing value added
1960	2,830.9	1,928.1	1,889.6	25.1	335.6	197.3	135.2	670.5	369.8	310.5	237.2
1961	2,896.9	1,965.8	1,927.3	25.4	349.6	206.5	139.2	694.2	377.6	326.5	250.5
1962	3,072.4	2,092.6	2,058.9	24.9	368.9	217.9	146.6	721.3	393.2	338.5	265.9
1963	3,206.7	2,189.2	2,155.2	25.7	384.0	226.9	152.6	742.8	396.7	356.1	278.9
1964	3,392.3	2,328.0	2,299.7	24.9	399.9	236.0	159.4	768.4	400.7	377.5	291.6
1965	3,610.1	2,492.3	2,462.6	26.5	419.7	246.9	168.6	794.2	403.4	400.5	307.1
1966	3,845.3	2,661.0	2,638.6	25.5	438.9	256.8	178.5	843.9	429.9	424.2	320.9
1967	3,942.5	2,712.0	2,684.1	27.6	457.1	267.1	186.6	888.7	457.9	442.1	335.6
1968	4,133.4	2,846.8	2,824.8	26.6	480.1	274.6	204.9	923.6	465.7	468.6	348.3
1969	4,261.8	2,934.0	2,910.9	27.5	501.2	285.9	214.9	947.2	467.1	490.0	364.6
1970	4,269.9	2,933.3	2,907.7	28.3	510.2	292.6	216.7	950.8	447.1	511.7	376.6
1971	4,413.3	3,046.0	3,018.2	29.8	531.7	305.9	224.5	952.4	426.5	532.5	393.6
1972	4,647.7	3,242.1	3,218.8	29.8	554.8	319.1	234.4	950.6	405.8	550.9	412.5
1973	4,917.0	3,469.4	3,454.8	29.5	574.6	330.6	242.7	954.9	390.7	570.2	427.8
1974	4,889.9	3,417.5	3,404.1	28.8	597.7	345.0	251.0	974.4	389.4	590.9	448.5
1975	4,879.5	3,385.6	3,348.6	34.3	617.9	354.2	262.5	990.1	387.3	608.9	462.2
1976	5,141.3	3,609.2	3,583.4	32.7	628.2	360.9	265.8	998.7	387.9	616.9	469.3
1977	5,377.7	3,810.1	3,783.0	34.5	637.5	365.0	271.3	1,009.2	389.0	626.4	481.2
1978	5,677.6	4,050.1	4,032.5	33.3	666.4	387.4	276.7	1,028.5	393.9	641.0	503.2
1979	5,855.0	4,184.6	4,159.7	36.3	695.3	405.0	287.8	1,039.5	393.5	652.4	523.0
1980	5,839.0	4,137.4	4,114.9	35.2	730.9	430.6	297.1	1,054.4	399.7	661.2	555.0
1981	5,987.2	4,252.5	4,202.5	46.5	754.1	444.1	306.8	1,060.2	405.9	660.9	576.7
1982	5,870.9	4,123.7	4,066.9	48.8	778.9	452.1	324.3	1,071.0	412.5	665.2	592.3
1983	6,136.2	4,345.8	4,328.5	31.9	801.0	460.5	338.5	1,077.9	422.0	662.5	605.4
1984	6,577.1	4,723.2	4,684.5	43.3	826.8	476.4	348.3	1,091.3	431.6	666.4	624.6
1985	6,849.3	4,942.5	4,886.4	52.9	841.2	487.4	351.2	1,122.5	443.9	685.6	649.1
1986	7,086.5	5,126.9	5,076.1	50.8	863.4	493.7	368.0	1,150.1	451.8	705.4	661.1
1987	7,313.3	5,295.7	5,245.2	51.3	895.8	506.8	388.0	1,175.3	463.6	719.0	676.8
1988	7,613.9	5,522.7	5,484.5	45.6	937.2	525.7	411.1	1,205.8	469.3	743.6	696.4
1989	7,885.9	5,727.3	5,678.1	52.3	974.8	542.0	432.9	1,234.6	475.1	766.4	712.2
1990	8,033.9	5,815.3	5,759.9	56.0	1,009.6	555.7	454.9	1,266.2	483.8	789.2	730.2
1991	8,015.1	5,764.3	5,707.0	56.9	1,038.5	572.0	467.4	1,279.4	486.7	799.4	754.6
1992	8,287.1	5,991.8	5,921.3	66.2	1,071.4	589.0	483.5	1,283.7	476.5	813.0	776.7
1993	8,523.4	6,185.0	6,128.2	57.8	1,106.9	603.5	504.9	1,286.5	467.4	824.2	789.1
1994	8,870.7	6,488.2	6,414.2	70.5	1,140.0	631.9	508.7	1,286.8	452.2	838.5	821.7
1995	9,093.7	6,670.8	6,617.8	56.4	1,175.5	651.3	524.8	1,287.7	435.1	855.1	846.9
1996	9,433.9	6,974.6	6,909.4	65.3	1,199.8	665.4	535.0	1,289.8	423.2	868.4	860.4
1997	9,854.3	7,335.7	7,261.4	72.5	1,240.5	687.6	553.5	1,299.6	415.2	885.6	885.6
1998	10,283.5	7,702.4	7,633.5	69.4	1,280.2	703.7	577.8	1,314.3	410.4	904.6	900.9
1999	10,779.8	8,132.8	8,060.6	72.8	1,325.5	740.3	585.3	1,326.3	407.1	919.5	942.3
2000	11,226.0	8,500.9	8,417.8	83.5	1,376.2	774.1	601.8	1,349.4	410.5	939.0	977.8
2001	11,347.2	8,569.1	8,491.9	77.7	1,407.0	793.1	613.4	1,373.7	412.1	961.3	997.8
2002	11,553.0	8,736.6	8,655.9	81.2	1,417.3	789.9	627.7	1,401.4	420.2	980.9	988.5
2003	11,840.7	9,005.9	8,914.8	91.6	1,417.8	787.1	631.1	1,418.2	431.5	986.7	969.3
2004	12,263.8	9,379.9	9,282.0	97.9	1,457.4	821.7	635.9	1,426.8	435.8	991.0	1,008.4
2005	12,638.4	9,695.5	9,593.5	102.0	1,506.4	864.4	642.0	1,436.5	438.7	997.7	1,054.0
2006	12,976.2	9,991.7	9,892.3	99.1	1,539.8	898.0	642.0	1,445.0	438.4	1,006.5	1,098.6
2007	13,254.1	10,215.9	10,123.7	91.6	1,573.9	919.5	654.5	1,465.5	441.8	1,023.7	1,136.8
2008	13,312.2	10,214.8	10,109.2	103.4	1,598.6	931.3	667.4	1,497.5	459.2	1,038.3	1,154.0
2009 ᵖ	12,988.7	9,855.8	9,741.7	111.4	1,600.7	924.3	676.6	1,525.3	487.3	1,038.2	1,150.1
2006: I	12,915.9	9,944.7	9,850.1	93.8	1,533.8	890.6	643.3	1,437.6	436.4	1,001.2	1,086.4
II	12,962.5	9,980.3	9,873.8	107.3	1,542.3	900.8	641.8	1,440.1	436.6	1,003.5	1,099.8
III	12,965.9	9,971.3	9,871.4	99.5	1,546.1	905.7	640.7	1,448.7	440.4	1,008.3	1,107.7
IV	13,060.7	10,070.6	9,974.0	96.0	1,537.0	894.8	642.4	1,453.5	440.5	1,013.1	1,100.3
2007: I	13,099.9	10,090.8	9,995.8	94.4	1,552.4	905.2	647.4	1,456.9	439.4	1,017.5	1,115.1
II	13,204.0	10,176.9	10,086.1	90.8	1,565.7	912.5	653.5	1,461.8	438.9	1,022.9	1,128.0
III	13,321.1	10,270.2	10,183.9	87.2	1,583.1	925.7	657.7	1,468.5	443.3	1,025.2	1,146.0
IV	13,391.2	10,323.5	10,229.1	93.9	1,593.9	934.8	659.4	1,474.6	445.4	1,029.3	1,158.1
2008: I	13,366.9	10,289.9	10,185.0	102.3	1,592.4	930.2	662.5	1,484.8	450.2	1,034.6	1,152.3
II	13,415.3	10,318.1	10,219.2	98.0	1,604.4	938.0	666.5	1,492.7	455.1	1,037.6	1,160.6
III	13,324.6	10,220.8	10,115.1	103.4	1,599.7	930.0	669.9	1,502.7	462.3	1,040.4	1,153.0
IV	13,141.9	10,030.6	9,917.5	110.0	1,597.8	927.2	670.8	1,509.7	469.1	1,040.6	1,150.1
2009: I	12,925.4	9,804.7	9,692.7	109.1	1,599.4	928.2	671.3	1,514.2	474.6	1,039.7	1,152.1
II	12,901.5	9,779.3	9,666.4	110.1	1,590.4	916.9	673.7	1,524.2	484.1	1,040.3	1,141.6
III	12,973.0	9,833.6	9,718.5	112.6	1,603.7	925.6	678.3	1,528.1	492.2	1,036.2	1,152.0
IV ᵖ	13,155.0	10,005.6	9,889.1	113.8	1,609.2	926.5	682.9	1,534.5	498.2	1,036.7	1,154.7

[1] Gross domestic business value added equals gross domestic product excluding gross value added of households and institutions and of general government. Nonfarm value added equals gross domestic business value added excluding gross farm value added.
[2] Equals compensation of employees of nonprofit institutions, the rental value of nonresidential fixed assets owned and used by nonprofit institutions serving households, and rental income of persons for tenant-occupied housing owned by nonprofit institutions.
[3] Equals compensation of general government employees plus general government consumption of fixed capital.

Source: Department of Commerce (Bureau of Economic Analysis).

[Billions of dollars; except as noted]

Year	Gross domestic product	Total private industries	Agriculture, forestry, fishing, and hunting	Mining	Construction	Manufacturing Total manufacturing	Durable goods	Non-durable goods	Utilities	Wholesale trade	Retail trade
						Value added					
1979	2,563.3	2,217.7	70.6	58.4	127.0	543.8	331.1	212.7	51.9	175.8	193.2
1980	2,789.5	2,405.8	62.0	91.3	130.3	556.6	333.9	222.7	60.0	188.7	200.9
1981	3,128.4	2,702.5	75.4	122.9	131.8	616.5	370.4	246.1	70.7	208.3	221.0
1982	3,255.0	2,792.6	71.3	120.0	128.8	603.2	353.4	249.8	81.7	207.9	229.9
1983	3,536.7	3,043.5	57.1	103.1	139.8	653.1	379.3	273.8	91.6	222.9	261.6
1984	3,933.2	3,395.1	77.1	107.2	164.4	724.0	443.5	280.5	102.3	249.4	293.6
1985	4,220.3	3,637.0	77.1	105.4	184.6	740.3	449.2	291.1	109.2	268.3	318.7
1986	4,462.8	3,842.9	74.2	68.9	207.7	766.0	459.3	306.7	114.4	278.5	336.6
1987	4,739.5	4,080.4	79.8	71.5	218.2	811.3	483.8	327.5	123.0	285.3	349.9
1988	5,103.8	4,399.1	80.2	71.4	232.7	876.9	519.0	357.9	122.8	318.1	366.0
1989	5,484.4	4,732.3	92.8	76.0	244.8	927.3	543.2	384.1	135.9	337.4	389.0
1990	5,803.1	4,997.8	96.7	84.9	248.5	947.4	542.7	404.7	142.9	347.7	398.8
1991	5,995.9	5,138.7	89.2	76.0	230.2	957.5	540.9	416.6	152.5	360.5	405.5
1992	6,337.7	5,440.4	99.6	71.3	232.5	996.7	562.8	433.8	157.4	378.9	430.0
1993	6,657.4	5,729.3	93.1	72.1	248.3	1,039.9	593.1	446.8	165.3	401.2	458.0
1994	7,072.2	6,110.5	105.6	73.6	274.4	1,118.8	647.7	471.1	174.6	442.7	493.3
1995	7,397.6	6,407.2	93.1	74.1	287.0	1,177.3	677.2	500.0	181.5	457.0	514.9
1996	7,816.9	6,795.2	113.8	87.5	311.7	1,209.4	706.5	502.9	183.3	489.1	543.8
1997	8,304.3	7,247.5	110.7	92.6	337.6	1,279.8	755.5	524.3	179.6	521.2	574.2
1998	8,747.0	7,652.5	102.4	74.8	374.4	1,343.9	806.9	537.0	180.8	542.9	598.6
1999	9,268.4	8,127.2	93.8	85.4	406.6	1,373.1	820.4	552.7	185.4	577.7	635.5
2000	9,817.0	8,614.3	98.0	121.3	435.9	1,426.2	865.3	560.9	189.3	591.7	662.4
2001	10,128.0	8,869.7	97.9	118.7	469.5	1,341.3	778.9	562.5	202.3	607.1	691.6
2002	10,469.6	9,131.2	95.4	106.5	482.3	1,352.6	774.8	577.9	207.3	615.4	719.6
2003	10,960.8	9,542.3	114.4	143.3	496.2	1,359.3	771.8	587.5	220.0	637.0	751.5
2004	11,685.9	10,194.3	142.2	171.3	539.2	1,427.9	807.5	620.4	240.3	686.7	776.9
2005	12,421.9	10,853.1	133.3	223.8	605.4	1,480.6	845.1	635.5	239.5	722.4	824.7
2006	13,178.4	11,529.3	121.6	262.4	646.0	1,577.4	899.4	678.0	272.7	773.2	866.5
2007	13,807.5	12,064.6	167.9	275.0	610.8	1,616.8	922.0	694.9	281.4	805.3	892.5
2008	14,264.6	12,424.6	157.7	325.3	581.5	1,637.7	914.7	723.0	306.0	818.8	885.5
	Percent					Industry value added as a percentage of GDP (percent)					
1979	100.0	86.5	2.8	2.3	5.0	21.2	12.9	8.3	2.0	6.9	7.5
1980	100.0	86.2	2.2	3.3	4.7	20.0	12.0	8.0	2.2	6.8	7.2
1981	100.0	86.4	2.4	3.9	4.2	19.7	11.8	7.9	2.3	6.7	7.1
1982	100.0	85.8	2.2	3.7	4.0	18.5	10.9	7.7	2.5	6.4	7.1
1983	100.0	86.1	1.6	2.9	4.0	18.5	10.7	7.7	2.6	6.3	7.4
1984	100.0	86.3	2.0	2.7	4.2	18.4	11.3	7.1	2.6	6.3	7.5
1985	100.0	86.2	1.8	2.5	4.4	17.5	10.6	6.9	2.6	6.4	7.6
1986	100.0	86.1	1.7	1.5	4.7	17.2	10.3	6.9	2.6	6.2	7.5
1987	100.0	86.1	1.7	1.5	4.6	17.1	10.2	6.9	2.6	6.0	7.4
1988	100.0	86.2	1.6	1.4	4.6	17.2	10.2	7.0	2.4	6.2	7.2
1989	100.0	86.3	1.7	1.4	4.5	16.9	9.9	7.0	2.5	6.2	7.1
1990	100.0	86.1	1.7	1.5	4.3	16.3	9.4	7.0	2.5	6.0	6.9
1991	100.0	85.7	1.5	1.3	3.8	16.0	9.0	6.9	2.5	6.0	6.8
1992	100.0	85.8	1.6	1.1	3.7	15.7	8.9	6.8	2.5	6.0	6.8
1993	100.0	86.1	1.4	1.1	3.7	15.6	8.9	6.7	2.5	6.0	6.9
1994	100.0	86.4	1.5	1.0	3.9	15.8	9.2	6.7	2.5	6.3	7.0
1995	100.0	86.6	1.3	1.0	3.9	15.9	9.2	6.8	2.5	6.2	7.0
1996	100.0	86.9	1.5	1.1	4.0	15.5	9.0	6.4	2.3	6.3	7.0
1997	100.0	87.3	1.3	1.1	4.1	15.4	9.1	6.3	2.2	6.3	6.9
1998	100.0	87.5	1.2	.9	4.3	15.4	9.2	6.1	2.1	6.2	6.8
1999	100.0	87.7	1.0	.9	4.4	14.8	8.9	6.0	2.0	6.2	6.9
2000	100.0	87.7	1.0	1.2	4.4	14.5	8.8	5.7	1.9	6.0	6.7
2001	100.0	87.6	1.0	1.2	4.6	13.2	7.7	5.6	2.0	6.0	6.8
2002	100.0	87.2	.9	1.0	4.6	12.9	7.4	5.5	2.0	5.9	6.9
2003	100.0	87.1	1.0	1.3	4.5	12.4	7.0	5.4	2.0	5.8	6.9
2004	100.0	87.2	1.2	1.5	4.6	12.2	6.9	5.3	2.1	5.9	6.6
2005	100.0	87.4	1.1	1.8	4.9	11.9	6.8	5.1	1.9	5.8	6.6
2006	100.0	87.5	.9	2.0	4.9	12.0	6.8	5.1	2.1	5.9	6.6
2007	100.0	87.4	1.2	2.0	4.4	11.7	6.7	5.0	2.0	5.8	6.5
2008	100.0	87.1	1.1	2.3	4.1	11.5	6.4	5.1	2.1	5.7	6.2

[1] Consists of agriculture, forestry, fishing, and hunting; mining; construction; and manufacturing.
[2] Consists of utilities; wholesale trade; retail trade; transportation and warehousing; information; finance, insurance, real estate, rental, and leasing; professional and business services; educational services, health care, and social assistance; arts, entertainment, recreation, accommodation, and food services; and other services, except government.

Note: Data shown in Tables B–12 and B–13 do not reflect the benchmark revision of the National Income and Product Accounts released in July 2009. For details see *Survey of Current Business*, May 2009.

See next page for continuation of table.

TABLE B–12. Gross domestic product (GDP) by industry, value added, in current dollars and as a percentage of GDP, 1979–2008—*Continued*

[Billions of dollars; except as noted]

Year	Transportation and warehousing	Information	Finance, insurance, real estate, rental, and leasing	Professional and business services	Educational services, health care, and social assistance	Arts, entertainment, recreation, accommodation, and food services	Other services, except government	Government	Private goods-producing industries [1]	Private services-producing industries [2]
			Private industries—Continued							
					Value added					
1979	96.6	90.3	390.3	164.0	120.5	77.1	58.2	345.7	799.7	1,417.9
1980	102.3	99.0	442.4	186.3	139.7	83.5	62.6	383.7	840.2	1,565.6
1981	109.9	112.7	498.4	213.2	159.9	93.5	68.5	425.9	946.6	1,755.9
1982	105.9	123.6	539.9	230.9	177.9	100.9	70.7	462.4	923.3	1,869.3
1983	117.8	140.0	604.6	262.5	198.3	112.0	79.2	493.1	953.1	2,090.5
1984	131.4	147.1	670.2	303.8	214.1	121.2	89.3	538.1	1,072.7	2,322.3
1985	136.3	162.9	729.7	340.8	231.3	134.3	98.0	583.3	1,107.4	2,529.5
1986	145.6	173.1	795.1	378.8	252.0	144.9	107.2	620.0	1,116.7	2,726.1
1987	151.1	185.0	840.3	414.1	286.5	152.1	112.3	659.1	1,180.8	2,899.5
1988	161.1	194.0	910.1	466.3	309.1	165.9	124.4	704.7	1,261.3	3,137.8
1989	164.1	210.4	975.4	518.0	347.0	180.2	133.9	752.0	1,341.0	3,391.4
1990	169.4	225.1	1,042.1	569.8	386.7	195.2	142.6	805.3	1,377.4	3,620.4
1991	178.2	235.2	1,103.6	579.3	424.8	202.2	144.2	857.2	1,352.8	3,785.9
1992	186.6	250.9	1,177.4	626.7	463.5	216.2	153.0	897.3	1,400.4	4,040.5
1993	201.0	272.6	1,241.5	659.1	488.0	225.5	163.7	928.1	1,453.4	4,275.9
1994	218.0	294.0	1,297.8	698.4	511.1	235.0	173.2	961.8	1,572.4	4,538.0
1995	226.3	307.6	1,383.0	743.1	533.3	248.3	180.9	990.4	1,631.4	4,775.8
1996	235.2	335.7	1,470.7	810.1	552.5	264.4	188.1	1,021.6	1,722.4	5,072.8
1997	253.7	347.8	1,593.3	896.5	573.1	289.8	197.4	1,056.8	1,820.8	5,426.8
1998	273.7	381.6	1,684.6	976.2	601.5	306.0	211.1	1,094.5	1,895.4	5,757.1
1999	287.4	439.3	1,798.4	1,064.5	634.5	327.8	217.8	1,141.2	1,958.9	6,168.3
2000	301.6	458.3	1,931.0	1,140.8	678.4	350.1	229.1	1,202.7	2,081.5	6,532.8
2001	296.9	476.9	2,059.2	1,165.9	739.3	361.5	241.5	1,258.3	2,027.5	6,842.2
2002	304.6	483.0	2,141.9	1,189.0	799.6	381.5	252.5	1,338.4	2,036.9	7,094.3
2003	316.6	489.1	2,244.6	1,248.9	857.3	398.9	265.3	1,418.4	2,113.3	7,429.1
2004	344.6	530.6	2,378.8	1,338.2	916.3	427.5	273.9	1,491.6	2,280.6	7,913.7
2005	364.7	557.8	2,527.9	1,463.9	969.7	451.8	287.5	1,568.8	2,443.2	8,409.9
2006	387.4	559.6	2,685.8	1,566.4	1,025.8	484.9	299.5	1,649.1	2,607.4	8,921.8
2007	407.2	586.3	2,811.2	1,694.1	1,087.0	513.3	315.6	1,742.9	2,670.6	9,394.0
2008	414.9	622.0	2,848.4	1,805.8	1,157.9	536.3	326.8	1,840.0	2,702.2	9,722.4
					Industry value added as a percentage of GDP (percent)					
1979	3.8	3.5	15.2	6.4	4.7	3.0	2.3	13.5	31.2	55.3
1980	3.7	3.5	15.9	6.7	5.0	3.0	2.2	13.8	30.1	56.1
1981	3.5	3.6	15.9	6.8	5.1	3.0	2.2	13.6	30.3	56.1
1982	3.3	3.8	16.6	7.1	5.5	3.1	2.2	14.2	28.4	57.4
1983	3.3	4.0	17.1	7.4	5.6	3.2	2.2	13.9	26.9	59.1
1984	3.3	3.7	17.0	7.7	5.4	3.1	2.3	13.7	27.3	59.0
1985	3.2	3.9	17.3	8.1	5.5	3.2	2.3	13.8	26.2	59.9
1986	3.3	3.9	17.8	8.5	5.6	3.2	2.4	13.9	25.0	61.1
1987	3.2	3.9	17.7	8.7	6.0	3.2	2.4	13.9	24.9	61.2
1988	3.2	3.8	17.8	9.1	6.1	3.3	2.4	13.8	24.7	61.5
1989	3.0	3.8	17.8	9.4	6.3	3.3	2.4	13.7	24.5	61.8
1990	2.9	3.9	18.0	9.8	6.7	3.4	2.5	13.9	23.7	62.4
1991	3.0	3.9	18.4	9.7	7.1	3.4	2.4	14.3	22.6	63.1
1992	2.9	4.0	18.6	9.9	7.3	3.4	2.4	14.2	22.1	63.8
1993	3.0	4.1	18.6	9.9	7.3	3.4	2.5	13.9	21.8	64.2
1994	3.1	4.2	18.4	9.9	7.2	3.3	2.4	13.6	22.2	64.2
1995	3.1	4.2	18.7	10.0	7.2	3.4	2.4	13.4	22.1	64.6
1996	3.0	4.3	18.8	10.4	7.1	3.4	2.4	13.1	22.0	64.9
1997	3.1	4.2	19.2	10.8	6.9	3.5	2.4	12.7	21.9	65.3
1998	3.1	4.4	19.3	11.2	6.9	3.5	2.4	12.5	21.7	65.8
1999	3.1	4.7	19.4	11.5	6.8	3.5	2.3	12.3	21.1	66.6
2000	3.1	4.7	19.7	11.6	6.9	3.6	2.3	12.3	21.2	66.5
2001	2.9	4.7	20.3	11.5	7.3	3.6	2.4	12.4	20.0	67.6
2002	2.9	4.6	20.5	11.4	7.6	3.6	2.4	12.8	19.5	67.8
2003	2.9	4.5	20.5	11.4	7.8	3.6	2.4	12.9	19.3	67.8
2004	2.9	4.5	20.4	11.5	7.8	3.7	2.3	12.8	19.5	67.7
2005	2.9	4.5	20.4	11.8	7.8	3.6	2.3	12.6	19.7	67.7
2006	2.9	4.2	20.4	11.9	7.8	3.7	2.3	12.5	19.8	67.7
2007	2.9	4.2	20.4	12.3	7.9	3.7	2.3	12.6	19.3	68.0
2008	2.9	4.4	20.0	12.7	8.1	3.8	2.3	12.9	18.9	68.2

Note (cont'd): Value added is the contribution of each private industry and of government to GDP. Value added is equal to an industry's gross output minus its intermediate inputs. Current-dollar value added is calculated as the sum of distributions by an industry to its labor and capital, which are derived from the components of gross domestic income.

Value added industry data shown in Tables B–12 and B–13 are based on the 1997 North American Industry Classification System (NAICS). GDP by industry data based on the Standard Industrial Classification (SIC) are available from the Department of Commerce, Bureau of Economic Analysis.

Source: Department of Commerce (Bureau of Economic Analysis).

Year	Gross domestic product	Total private industries	Agriculture, forestry, fishing, and hunting	Mining	Construction	Total manufacturing	Durable goods	Non-durable goods	Utilities	Wholesale trade	Retail trade
						Private industries					
						Manufacturing					
			Chain-type quantity indexes for value added (2000=100)								
1979	52.699	50.606	48.573	79.749	81.174	50.843	40.808	70.282	54.661	39.888	40.701
1980	52.579	50.321	47.543	89.978	74.626	48.190	38.476	67.152	51.968	39.782	38.907
1981	53.904	51.720	59.731	90.260	67.939	50.480	39.563	72.303	51.733	42.074	40.035
1982	52.860	50.422	62.961	86.329	59.460	46.795	35.645	69.864	50.698	42.096	39.951
1983	55.249	52.785	43.338	81.175	62.805	50.455	37.953	76.660	52.706	43.770	44.123
1984	59.220	56.789	57.105	88.849	72.200	55.084	44.042	76.466	57.341	47.143	48.265
1985	61.666	59.383	69.555	93.077	79.043	56.582	45.187	78.688	60.940	49.523	51.232
1986	63.804	61.137	68.605	87.529	81.818	56.516	45.550	77.515	64.406	54.486	54.187
1987	65.958	63.367	71.483	91.661	82.448	60.746	48.859	83.572	72.315	53.070	52.138
1988	68.684	66.299	64.678	99.992	85.435	64.212	52.843	85.425	70.613	56.444	56.545
1989	71.116	68.710	71.099	97.072	87.646	65.033	53.696	86.109	79.002	58.603	58.838
1990	72.451	69.905	74.689	96.157	86.543	64.299	52.963	85.419	84.447	57.318	59.794
1991	72.329	69.779	75.398	97.638	79.137	63.412	51.496	85.835	85.285	59.387	59.483
1992	74.734	72.363	83.114	95.694	80.026	65.508	52.742	89.669	85.362	65.037	62.960
1993	76.731	74.291	72.838	97.020	82.010	68.255	55.173	92.943	85.814	67.135	65.351
1994	79.816	77.765	84.616	105.327	86.586	73.496	60.173	98.369	89.518	71.346	69.806
1995	81.814	79.722	73.099	105.681	86.312	76.819	65.218	97.783	93.835	70.800	72.974
1996	84.842	83.179	80.041	98.850	90.694	79.682	69.120	98.443	95.405	77.261	79.407
1997	88.658	87.362	88.315	102.463	93.267	84.518	75.335	100.438	91.161	85.648	86.039
1998	92.359	91.662	86.287	101.682	97.087	90.181	84.355	99.762	90.481	95.431	90.399
1999	96.469	96.183	89.163	104.300	99.411	94.104	89.627	101.298	94.672	100.412	95.686
2000	100.000	100.000	100.000	100.000	100.000	100.000	100.000	100.000	100.000	100.000	100.000
2001	100.751	100.908	93.661	94.715	100.163	94.436	94.031	95.034	95.081	107.003	106.970
2002	102.362	102.354	98.767	88.719	98.201	97.066	95.663	99.056	99.144	108.059	109.294
2003	104.931	105.068	106.173	87.922	96.189	98.168	98.169	98.265	105.990	110.380	113.559
2004	108.748	109.198	113.287	88.770	96.430	103.653	103.873	103.468	112.076	112.614	116.533
2005	111.944	113.068	122.911	85.440	95.996	104.543	109.622	98.292	105.443	116.279	126.923
2006	115.054	116.591	116.434	91.760	92.039	110.312	118.547	100.388	106.638	116.980	133.983
2007	117.388	118.990	124.524	91.835	81.769	113.488	124.191	100.819	107.881	117.968	140.077
2008	118.692	119.678	123.854	91.056	77.183	110.382	122.621	96.166	109.945	116.240	139.396
			Percent change from year earlier								
1979	3.2	3.7	7.8	−10.3	3.5	3.4	1.6	6.4	−8.3	7.6	0.1
1980	−.2	−.6	−2.1	12.8	−8.1	−5.2	−5.7	−4.5	−4.9	−.3	−4.4
1981	2.5	2.8	25.6	.3	−9.0	4.8	2.8	7.7	−.5	5.8	2.9
1982	−1.9	−2.5	5.4	−4.4	−12.5	−7.3	−9.9	−3.4	−2.0	.1	−.2
1983	4.5	4.7	−31.2	−6.0	5.6	7.8	6.5	9.7	4.0	4.0	10.4
1984	7.2	7.6	31.8	9.5	15.0	9.2	16.0	−.3	8.8	7.7	9.4
1985	4.1	4.6	21.8	4.8	9.5	2.7	2.6	2.9	6.3	5.0	6.1
1986	3.5	3.0	−1.4	−6.0	3.5	−.1	.8	−1.5	5.7	10.0	5.8
1987	3.4	3.6	4.2	4.7	.8	7.5	7.3	7.8	12.3	−2.6	−3.8
1988	4.1	4.6	−9.5	9.1	3.6	5.7	8.2	2.2	−2.4	6.4	8.5
1989	3.5	3.6	9.9	−2.9	2.6	1.3	1.6	.8	11.9	3.8	4.1
1990	1.9	1.7	5.0	−.9	−1.3	−1.1	−1.4	−.8	6.9	−2.2	1.6
1991	−.2	−.2	.9	1.5	−8.6	−1.4	−2.8	.5	1.0	3.6	−.5
1992	3.3	3.7	10.2	−2.0	1.1	3.3	2.4	4.5	.1	9.5	5.8
1993	2.7	2.7	−12.4	1.4	2.5	4.2	4.6	3.7	.5	3.2	3.8
1994	4.0	4.7	16.2	8.6	5.6	7.7	9.1	5.8	4.3	6.3	6.8
1995	2.5	2.5	−13.6	.3	−.3	4.5	8.4	−.6	4.8	−.8	4.5
1996	3.7	4.3	9.5	−6.5	5.1	3.7	6.0	.7	1.7	9.1	8.8
1997	4.5	5.0	10.3	3.7	2.8	6.1	9.0	2.0	−4.4	10.9	8.4
1998	4.2	4.9	−2.3	−.8	4.1	6.7	12.0	−.7	−.7	11.4	5.1
1999	4.5	4.9	3.3	2.6	2.4	4.4	6.2	1.5	4.6	5.2	5.8
2000	3.7	4.0	12.2	−4.1	.6	6.3	11.6	−1.3	5.6	−.4	4.5
2001	.8	.9	−6.3	−5.3	.2	−5.6	−6.0	−5.0	−4.9	7.0	7.0
2002	1.6	1.4	5.5	−6.3	−2.0	2.8	1.7	4.2	4.3	1.0	2.2
2003	2.5	2.7	7.5	−.9	−2.0	1.1	2.6	−.8	6.9	2.1	3.9
2004	3.6	3.9	6.7	1.0	.3	5.6	5.8	5.3	5.7	2.0	2.6
2005	2.9	3.5	8.5	−3.8	−.5	.9	5.5	−5.0	−5.9	3.3	8.9
2006	2.8	3.1	−5.3	7.4	−4.1	5.5	8.1	2.1	1.1	.6	5.6
2007	2.0	2.1	6.9	.1	−11.2	2.9	4.8	.4	1.2	.8	4.5
2008	1.1	.6	−.5	−.8	−5.6	−2.7	−1.3	−4.6	1.9	−1.5	−.5

[1] Consists of agriculture, forestry, fishing, and hunting; mining; construction; and manufacturing.
[2] Consists of utilities; wholesale trade; retail trade; transportation and warehousing; information; finance, insurance, real estate, rental, and leasing; professional and business services; educational services, health care, and social assistance; arts, entertainment, recreation, accommodation, and food services; and other services, except government.

See next page for continuation of table.

Year	Transportation and warehousing	Information	Finance, insurance, real estate, rental, and leasing	Professional and business services	Educational services, health care, and social assistance	Arts, entertainment, recreation, accommodation, and food services	Other services, except government	Government	Private goods-producing industries[1]	Private services-producing industries[2]
					Private industries—Continued					
	Chain-type quantity indexes for value added (2000=100)									
1979	48.252	34.231	52.965	39.387	63.234	53.512	75.703	77.721	56.085	48.120
1980	47.232	36.394	55.414	40.529	66.887	52.407	74.411	79.023	53.880	48.764
1981	46.178	38.257	56.573	41.554	68.455	54.193	72.329	79.328	55.783	49.923
1982	43.855	38.155	56.986	41.345	68.856	55.695	69.103	79.456	52.029	49.794
1983	49.486	41.017	58.734	44.142	71.153	59.784	72.470	80.178	53.361	52.637
1984	52.121	40.717	61.282	48.913	72.366	62.194	77.498	81.038	59.454	55.727
1985	52.715	42.039	62.812	52.748	73.629	66.167	80.936	83.172	62.569	58.104
1986	53.021	42.672	63.965	56.860	75.166	69.642	82.885	85.105	62.534	60.576
1987	55.690	45.764	65.941	60.050	80.273	68.742	84.221	86.753	66.173	62.256
1988	57.990	47.649	68.652	64.420	80.570	71.515	89.044	88.812	69.104	65.186
1989	59.507	51.150	70.359	68.787	84.002	73.872	92.188	90.984	70.366	68.033
1990	62.281	53.420	71.877	72.073	87.047	76.063	94.369	93.215	69.858	69.877
1991	65.060	54.441	73.051	69.786	89.285	74.232	91.258	93.658	68.214	70.319
1992	68.758	57.568	74.863	72.008	91.728	77.250	92.502	94.134	70.330	73.074
1993	71.988	61.445	76.931	73.224	92.199	78.787	95.195	94.055	72.128	75.047
1994	77.827	65.223	78.506	75.430	92.413	80.604	98.624	94.407	77.818	77.745
1995	80.473	67.996	80.732	77.382	93.503	83.542	99.714	94.250	79.572	79.773
1996	84.585	72.714	82.893	82.053	94.144	86.796	99.072	94.768	82.596	83.377
1997	88.373	74.559	86.786	87.432	94.809	90.310	99.291	95.864	87.229	87.407
1998	91.454	82.252	90.201	91.976	95.603	93.446	101.871	96.923	91.878	91.591
1999	95.301	95.467	94.994	96.898	97.304	96.836	100.236	98.009	95.402	96.434
2000	100.000	100.000	100.000	100.000	100.000	100.000	100.000	100.000	100.000	100.000
2001	97.354	104.034	103.858	99.346	103.186	99.292	98.337	100.794	95.654	102.584
2002	99.531	106.263	104.800	99.192	107.527	101.022	98.667	102.467	96.853	104.107
2003	101.534	109.430	107.288	103.554	112.257	104.138	100.615	103.776	97.402	107.496
2004	110.780	122.221	110.433	107.750	115.949	108.114	100.770	104.252	101.328	111.692
2005	115.253	132.881	115.054	113.709	119.231	110.366	102.776	104.962	101.915	116.624
2006	117.627	136.503	119.756	117.579	123.043	114.158	102.381	105.509	104.628	120.414
2007	120.592	147.542	122.183	122.646	125.627	116.126	102.756	106.914	103.880	123.870
2008	116.091	155.211	122.100	129.361	131.207	118.049	103.026	109.033	100.718	125.879
	Percent change from year earlier									
1979	5.6	8.6	5.2	6.8	4.2	2.8	0.8	1.3	2.7	4.2
1980	−2.1	6.3	4.6	2.9	5.8	−2.1	−1.7	1.7	−3.9	1.3
1981	−2.2	5.1	2.1	2.5	2.3	3.4	−2.8	.4	3.5	2.4
1982	−5.0	−.3	.7	−.5	.6	2.8	−4.5	.2	−6.7	−.3
1983	12.8	7.5	3.1	6.8	3.3	7.3	4.9	.9	2.6	5.7
1984	5.3	−.7	4.3	10.8	1.7	4.0	6.9	1.1	11.4	5.9
1985	1.1	3.2	2.5	7.8	1.7	6.4	4.4	2.6	5.2	4.3
1986	.6	1.5	1.8	7.8	2.1	5.3	2.4	2.3	−.1	4.3
1987	5.0	7.2	3.1	5.6	6.8	−1.3	1.6	1.9	5.8	2.8
1988	4.1	4.1	4.1	7.3	.4	4.0	5.7	2.4	4.4	4.7
1989	2.6	7.3	2.5	6.8	4.3	3.3	3.5	2.4	1.8	4.4
1990	4.7	4.4	2.2	4.8	3.6	3.0	2.4	2.5	−.7	2.7
1991	4.5	1.9	1.6	−3.2	2.6	−2.4	−3.3	.5	−2.4	.6
1992	5.7	5.7	2.5	3.2	2.7	4.1	1.4	.5	3.1	3.9
1993	4.7	6.7	2.8	1.7	.5	2.0	2.9	−.1	2.6	2.7
1994	8.1	6.1	2.0	3.0	.2	2.3	3.6	.4	7.9	3.6
1995	3.4	4.3	2.8	2.6	1.2	3.6	1.1	−.2	2.3	2.6
1996	5.1	6.9	2.7	6.0	.7	3.9	−.6	.5	3.8	4.5
1997	4.5	2.5	4.7	6.6	.7	4.0	.2	1.2	5.6	4.8
1998	3.5	10.3	3.9	5.2	.8	3.5	2.6	1.1	5.3	4.8
1999	4.2	16.1	5.3	5.4	1.8	3.6	−1.6	1.1	3.8	5.3
2000	4.9	4.7	5.3	3.2	2.8	3.3	−.2	2.0	4.8	3.7
2001	−2.6	4.0	3.9	−.7	3.2	−.7	−1.7	.8	−4.3	2.6
2002	2.2	2.1	.9	−.2	4.2	1.7	.3	1.7	1.3	1.5
2003	2.0	3.0	2.4	4.4	4.4	3.1	2.0	1.3	.6	3.3
2004	9.1	11.7	2.9	4.1	3.3	3.8	.2	.5	4.0	3.9
2005	4.0	8.7	4.2	5.5	2.8	2.1	2.0	.7	.6	4.4
2006	2.1	2.7	4.1	3.4	3.2	3.4	−.4	.5	2.7	3.2
2007	2.5	8.1	2.0	4.3	2.1	1.7	.4	1.3	−.7	2.9
2008	−3.7	5.2	−.1	5.5	4.4	1.7	.3	2.0	−3.0	1.6

Note: Data are based on the 1997 North American Industry Classification System (NAICS).
See Note, Table B–12.

Source: Department of Commerce (Bureau of Economic Analysis).

TABLE B–14. Gross value added of nonfinancial corporate business, 1960–2009

[Billions of dollars; quarterly data at seasonally adjusted annual rates]

Year or quarter	Gross value added of non-financial corpo-rate busi-ness [1]	Con-sump-tion of fixed capital	Net value added						Corporate profits with inven-tory valuation and capital consumption adjustments			Addenda		
			Total	Com-pensa-tion of employ-ees	Taxes on produc-tion and imports less sub-sidies	Net operating surplus						Profits before tax	Inven-tory valua-tion adjust-ment	Capital con-sumption adjust-ment
						Total	Net interest and miscel-laneous pay-ments	Busi-ness current transfer pay-ments	Total	Taxes on corpo-rate rate income	Profits after tax [2]			
1960	276.4	23.1	253.3	180.4	26.6	46.3	3.2	1.4	41.7	19.1	22.6	40.1	−0.2	1.9
1961	283.7	23.7	260.1	184.5	27.6	47.9	3.7	1.5	42.7	19.4	23.3	39.9	.3	2.5
1962	309.8	24.5	285.2	199.3	29.9	56.1	4.3	1.7	50.1	20.6	29.5	44.6	.0	5.4
1963	329.9	25.6	304.3	210.1	31.7	62.5	4.7	1.7	56.1	22.8	33.4	49.7	.1	6.4
1964	356.1	27.0	329.0	225.7	33.9	69.5	5.2	2.0	62.4	23.9	38.5	55.9	−.5	7.0
1965	391.2	29.1	362.1	245.4	36.0	80.7	5.8	2.2	72.7	27.1	45.5	66.1	−1.2	7.8
1966	429.0	31.9	397.1	272.9	37.0	87.2	7.0	2.7	77.5	29.5	48.0	71.4	−2.1	8.1
1967	451.2	35.2	416.0	291.1	39.3	85.6	8.4	2.8	74.4	27.8	46.5	67.6	−1.6	8.3
1968	497.8	38.7	459.1	321.9	45.5	91.7	9.7	3.1	78.9	33.5	45.4	74.0	−3.7	8.6
1969	540.5	42.9	497.5	357.1	50.2	90.3	12.7	3.2	74.4	33.3	41.0	71.2	−5.9	9.1
1970	558.3	47.5	510.8	376.5	54.2	80.1	16.6	3.3	60.2	27.3	32.9	58.5	−6.6	8.3
1971	603.0	52.0	551.1	399.4	59.5	92.1	17.6	3.7	70.8	30.0	40.8	67.4	−4.6	8.0
1972	669.4	56.5	613.0	443.9	63.7	105.4	18.6	4.0	82.8	33.8	49.0	79.5	−6.6	9.9
1973	750.8	63.1	687.6	502.2	70.1	115.4	21.8	4.7	88.9	40.4	48.5	99.5	−19.6	9.0
1974	809.8	74.2	735.7	552.2	74.4	109.1	27.5	4.1	77.5	42.8	34.6	110.2	−38.2	5.5
1975	876.7	88.6	788.0	575.5	80.2	132.4	28.4	5.0	98.9	41.9	57.0	110.7	−10.5	−1.2
1976	989.7	97.8	892.0	651.4	86.7	153.9	26.0	7.0	121.0	53.5	67.5	138.2	−14.1	−3.2
1977	1,119.4	110.1	1,009.2	735.3	94.6	179.3	28.5	9.0	141.9	60.6	81.3	159.5	−15.7	−1.9
1978	1,272.7	125.1	1,147.5	845.1	102.7	199.7	33.4	9.5	156.8	67.6	89.2	183.7	−23.7	−3.2
1979	1,414.4	144.3	1,270.2	958.4	108.8	203.0	41.8	9.5	151.8	70.6	81.2	197.2	−40.1	−5.3
1980	1,534.5	166.7	1,367.8	1,047.2	121.5	199.1	54.2	10.2	134.7	68.2	66.5	184.1	−42.1	−7.2
1981	1,742.2	192.4	1,549.8	1,157.6	146.7	245.5	67.2	11.4	166.8	66.0	100.8	185.0	−24.6	6.5
1982	1,802.6	212.8	1,589.8	1,200.4	152.9	236.5	77.4	8.8	150.2	48.8	101.5	140.0	−7.5	17.8
1983	1,929.1	219.3	1,709.8	1,263.1	168.0	278.7	77.0	10.5	191.2	61.7	129.5	163.4	−7.4	35.2
1984	2,161.4	228.8	1,932.6	1,400.0	185.0	347.5	86.0	11.7	249.8	75.9	173.9	197.6	−4.0	56.2
1985	2,293.9	244.0	2,049.9	1,496.1	196.6	357.2	91.5	16.1	249.6	71.1	178.6	173.5	.0	76.2
1986	2,383.2	258.0	2,125.2	1,575.4	204.6	345.2	98.5	27.3	219.5	76.2	143.2	149.7	7.1	62.7
1987	2,551.0	270.0	2,280.9	1,678.4	216.8	385.6	95.9	29.9	259.9	94.2	165.7	213.5	−16.2	62.6
1988	2,765.4	287.3	2,478.1	1,804.7	233.8	439.6	107.9	27.4	304.3	104.0	200.3	264.1	−22.2	62.3
1989	2,899.2	303.9	2,595.3	1,905.7	248.2	441.5	133.9	24.0	283.5	101.2	182.3	243.1	−16.3	56.7
1990	3,035.2	321.0	2,714.2	2,005.5	263.5	445.2	143.1	25.4	276.7	98.5	178.3	243.3	−12.9	46.3
1991	3,104.1	336.1	2,768.0	2,044.8	285.7	437.5	139.6	26.6	271.3	88.6	182.7	226.8	4.9	39.6
1992	3,241.1	344.1	2,897.0	2,152.9	302.5	441.6	114.2	31.3	296.1	94.4	201.7	258.6	−2.8	40.3
1993	3,398.4	359.0	3,039.3	2,244.0	318.0	477.3	99.8	30.1	347.5	108.0	239.5	308.7	−4.0	42.9
1994	3,677.6	380.1	3,297.5	2,382.1	347.8	567.5	98.8	35.3	433.5	132.4	301.1	391.9	−12.4	54.0
1995	3,888.0	408.3	3,479.7	2,511.5	354.2	614.0	112.7	30.7	470.6	140.3	330.3	431.2	−18.3	57.6
1996	4,119.4	435.1	3,684.4	2,631.3	365.6	687.5	112.1	38.0	537.4	152.9	384.5	471.3	3.1	63.0
1997	4,412.5	466.9	3,945.6	2,814.6	381.0	750.0	124.7	39.2	586.2	161.4	424.8	506.8	14.1	65.3
1998	4,668.3	499.9	4,168.5	3,049.7	393.1	725.7	146.8	35.2	543.7	158.7	385.1	460.5	15.7	67.5
1999	4,955.5	539.3	4,416.3	3,256.5	414.6	745.1	164.5	47.1	533.5	171.4	362.1	468.6	−4.0	68.9
2000	5,279.4	590.1	4,689.4	3,541.8	439.4	708.2	192.8	47.9	467.5	170.2	297.3	432.5	−16.8	51.8
2001	5,252.5	632.0	4,620.5	3,559.4	434.5	626.7	197.7	58.9	370.1	111.2	258.8	315.1	8.0	47.0
2002	5,307.7	654.5	4,653.1	3,544.2	461.9	647.1	163.7	56.3	427.2	97.1	330.1	342.3	−2.6	87.5
2003	5,503.7	669.0	4,834.7	3,651.3	484.2	699.2	147.9	65.2	486.1	132.9	353.2	425.9	−11.3	71.5
2004	5,877.5	695.6	5,181.9	3,786.7	517.7	877.5	134.4	65.5	677.5	187.0	490.6	662.1	−34.3	49.7
2005	6,302.8	743.0	5,559.8	3,976.3	558.4	1,025.1	148.2	79.3	797.6	271.9	525.8	957.1	−30.7	−128.8
2006	6,740.3	800.9	5,939.4	4,182.3	593.3	1,163.7	164.0	75.8	923.9	307.6	616.2	1,117.9	−38.0	−156.0
2007	6,970.1	849.4	6,120.6	4,364.2	612.8	1,143.7	228.1	68.6	846.9	299.3	547.6	1,058.9	−44.0	−167.9
2008	6,971.5	898.4	6,073.0	4,427.9	621.0	1,024.1	242.1	70.4	711.6	237.8	473.8	806.7	−38.2	−56.8
2009 p		901.7		4,212.3	601.9			77.7						−113.3
2006: I	6,629.5	781.1	5,848.5	4,131.8	583.7	1,132.9	152.6	78.4	902.0	294.1	607.8	1,101.8	−33.4	−166.5
II	6,668.1	794.8	5,873.3	4,153.0	591.1	1,129.2	157.8	76.4	894.9	308.8	586.2	1,096.7	−48.4	−153.3
III	6,811.8	807.8	6,004.0	4,180.3	596.3	1,227.3	164.8	74.9	987.6	329.3	658.3	1,179.3	−42.3	−149.4
IV	6,851.8	820.1	6,031.7	4,264.2	602.0	1,165.5	180.9	73.5	911.1	298.3	612.7	1,093.8	−28.0	−154.8
2007: I	6,909.3	831.6	6,077.7	4,314.0	604.8	1,159.0	201.2	70.3	887.5	313.3	574.1	1,081.2	−42.2	−151.5
II	6,988.8	843.4	6,145.4	4,345.1	610.5	1,189.7	223.6	68.4	897.7	305.3	592.4	1,091.2	−29.5	−163.9
III	6,949.7	855.3	6,094.4	4,365.4	614.8	1,114.1	236.6	67.5	810.1	284.4	525.7	1,009.6	−25.3	−174.1
IV	7,032.6	867.5	6,165.1	4,432.2	620.9	1,112.0	251.2	68.4	792.4	294.2	498.1	1,053.5	−79.0	−182.1
2008: I	6,934.9	879.8	6,055.1	4,429.6	618.5	1,006.9	242.1	68.1	696.7	255.9	440.8	851.6	−107.9	−47.0
II	6,974.4	892.2	6,082.2	4,431.6	623.5	1,027.1	246.0	68.3	712.8	263.1	449.7	895.6	−129.6	−53.2
III	7,042.4	904.6	6,137.8	4,440.4	627.8	1,069.6	233.3	68.7	767.6	254.5	513.1	882.0	−54.5	−60.0
IV	6,934.1	917.1	6,017.0	4,410.1	614.2	992.7	246.8	76.5	669.4	177.7	491.6	597.4	139.2	−67.2
2009: I	6,703.8	916.7	5,787.1	4,238.5	602.7	945.8	237.4	79.2	629.2	197.9	431.3	676.9	81.1	−128.7
II	6,671.9	903.0	5,768.9	4,194.4	603.1	971.4	229.2	83.2	659.0	217.0	442.1	755.2	18.1	−114.2
III	6,665.2	894.0	5,771.2	4,198.3	593.9	979.0	219.2	73.1	686.6	227.0	459.6	809.4	−17.1	−105.7
IV p		893.2		4,218.0	607.8			75.3						−104.5

[1] Estimates for nonfinancial corporate business for 2000 and earlier periods are based on the Standard Industrial Classification (SIC); later estimates are based on the North American Industry Classification System (NAICS).
[2] With inventory valuation and capital consumption adjustments.

Source: Department of Commerce (Bureau of Economic Analysis).

TABLE B–15. Gross value added and price, costs, and profits of nonfinancial corporate business, 1960–2009

[Quarterly data at seasonally adjusted annual rates]

Year or quarter	Gross value added of nonfinancial corporate business (billions of dollars) [1]		Price per unit of real gross value added of nonfinancial corporate business (dollars) [1, 2]								
				Compensation of employees (unit labor cost)	Unit nonlabor cost				Corporate profits with inventory valuation and capital consumption adjustments [4]		
	Current dollars	Chained (2005) dollars	Total		Total	Consumption of fixed capital	Taxes on production and imports [3]	Net interest and miscellaneous payments	Total	Taxes on corporate income	Profits after tax [5]
1960	276.4	1,075.0	0.257	0.168	0.050	0.021	0.026	0.003	0.039	0.018	0.021
1961	283.7	1,099.2	.258	.168	.052	.022	.027	.003	.039	.018	.021
1962	309.8	1,193.2	.260	.167	.051	.021	.026	.004	.042	.017	.025
1963	329.9	1,264.9	.261	.166	.050	.020	.026	.004	.044	.018	.026
1964	356.1	1,354.2	.263	.167	.050	.020	.026	.004	.046	.018	.028
1965	391.2	1,466.7	.267	.167	.050	.020	.026	.004	.050	.019	.031
1966	429.0	1,571.9	.273	.174	.049	.020	.025	.004	.049	.019	.031
1967	451.2	1,614.3	.279	.180	.053	.022	.026	.005	.046	.017	.029
1968	497.8	1,719.0	.290	.187	.057	.023	.028	.006	.046	.020	.026
1969	540.5	1,788.5	.302	.200	.061	.024	.030	.007	.042	.019	.023
1970	558.3	1,774.1	.315	.212	.068	.027	.032	.009	.034	.015	.019
1971	603.0	1,847.3	.326	.216	.072	.028	.034	.010	.038	.016	.022
1972	669.4	1,988.5	.337	.223	.071	.028	.034	.009	.042	.017	.025
1973	750.8	2,111.0	.356	.238	.075	.030	.035	.010	.042	.019	.023
1974	809.8	2,077.6	.390	.266	.087	.036	.038	.013	.037	.021	.017
1975	876.7	2,047.1	.428	.281	.099	.043	.042	.014	.048	.020	.028
1976	989.7	2,214.4	.447	.294	.098	.044	.042	.012	.055	.024	.030
1977	1,119.4	2,378.5	.471	.309	.102	.046	.044	.012	.060	.025	.034
1978	1,272.7	2,534.0	.502	.334	.106	.049	.044	.013	.062	.027	.035
1979	1,414.4	2,612.4	.541	.367	.116	.055	.045	.016	.058	.027	.031
1980	1,534.5	2,584.7	.594	.405	.136	.064	.051	.021	.052	.026	.026
1981	1,742.2	2,687.9	.648	.431	.156	.072	.059	.025	.062	.025	.038
1982	1,802.6	2,622.6	.687	.458	.173	.081	.062	.030	.057	.019	.039
1983	1,929.1	2,746.2	.702	.460	.173	.080	.065	.028	.070	.022	.047
1984	2,161.4	2,989.4	.723	.468	.172	.077	.066	.029	.084	.025	.058
1985	2,293.9	3,120.3	.735	.479	.175	.078	.068	.029	.080	.023	.057
1986	2,383.2	3,197.9	.745	.493	.185	.081	.073	.031	.069	.024	.045
1987	2,551.0	3,364.7	.758	.499	.181	.080	.073	.028	.077	.028	.049
1988	2,765.4	3,560.4	.777	.507	.184	.081	.073	.030	.085	.029	.056
1989	2,899.2	3,618.2	.801	.527	.196	.084	.075	.037	.078	.028	.050
1990	3,035.2	3,672.6	.826	.546	.205	.087	.079	.039	.075	.027	.049
1991	3,104.1	3,655.5	.849	.559	.215	.092	.085	.038	.074	.024	.050
1992	3,241.1	3,768.0	.860	.571	.210	.091	.089	.030	.079	.025	.054
1993	3,398.4	3,866.5	.879	.580	.209	.093	.090	.026	.090	.028	.062
1994	3,677.6	4,115.3	.894	.579	.209	.092	.093	.024	.105	.032	.073
1995	3,888.0	4,309.4	.902	.583	.210	.095	.089	.026	.109	.033	.077
1996	4,119.4	4,548.0	.906	.579	.210	.096	.089	.025	.118	.034	.085
1997	4,412.5	4,843.8	.911	.581	.209	.096	.087	.026	.121	.033	.088
1998	4,668.3	5,123.5	.911	.595	.211	.098	.084	.029	.106	.031	.075
1999	4,955.5	5,422.5	.914	.601	.214	.099	.085	.030	.098	.032	.067
2000	5,279.4	5,707.9	.925	.621	.222	.103	.085	.034	.082	.030	.052
2001	5,252.5	5,604.6	.937	.635	.236	.113	.088	.035	.066	.020	.046
2002	5,307.7	5,629.3	.943	.630	.237	.116	.092	.029	.076	.017	.059
2003	5,503.7	5,767.4	.954	.633	.237	.116	.095	.026	.084	.023	.061
2004	5,877.5	6,040.4	.973	.627	.234	.115	.097	.022	.112	.031	.081
2005	6,302.8	6,302.8	1.000	.631	.243	.118	.101	.024	.127	.043	.083
2006	6,740.3	6,536.5	1.031	.640	.250	.123	.102	.025	.141	.047	.094
2007	6,970.1	6,649.4	1.048	.656	.264	.128	.102	.034	.127	.045	.082
2008	6,971.5	6,675.5	1.044	.663	.275	.135	.104	.036	.107	.036	.071
2006: I	6,629.5	6,505.1	1.019	.635	.245	.120	.102	.023	.139	.045	.093
II	6,668.1	6,480.0	1.029	.641	.250	.123	.103	.024	.138	.048	.090
III	6,811.8	6,567.2	1.037	.637	.250	.123	.102	.025	.150	.050	.100
IV	6,851.8	6,593.8	1.039	.647	.253	.124	.102	.027	.138	.045	.093
2007: I	6,909.3	6,597.4	1.047	.654	.258	.126	.102	.030	.135	.047	.087
II	6,988.8	6,649.8	1.051	.653	.263	.127	.102	.034	.135	.046	.089
III	6,949.7	6,624.9	1.049	.659	.268	.129	.103	.036	.122	.043	.079
IV	7,032.6	6,725.5	1.046	.659	.268	.129	.102	.037	.118	.044	.074
2008: I	6,934.9	6,664.3	1.041	.665	.271	.132	.103	.036	.105	.038	.066
II	6,974.4	6,735.8	1.035	.658	.272	.132	.103	.037	.106	.039	.067
III	7,042.4	6,722.6	1.048	.661	.274	.135	.104	.035	.114	.038	.076
IV	6,934.1	6,579.3	1.054	.670	.282	.139	.105	.038	.102	.027	.075
2009: I	6,703.8	6,278.8	1.068	.675	.293	.146	.109	.038	.100	.032	.069
II	6,671.9	6,269.8	1.064	.669	.290	.144	.109	.037	.105	.035	.071
III	6,665.2	6,291.5	1.059	.667	.283	.142	.106	.035	.109	.036	.073

[1] Estimates for nonfinancial corporate business for 2000 and earlier periods are based on the Standard Industrial Classification (SIC); later estimates are based on the North American Industry Classification System (NAICS).
[2] The implicit price deflator for gross value added of nonfinancial corporate business divided by 100.
[3] Less subsidies plus business current transfer payments.
[4] Unit profits from current production.
[5] With inventory valuation and capital consumption adjustments.

Source: Department of Commerce (Bureau of Economic Analysis).

TABLE B–16. Personal consumption expenditures, 1960–2009

[Billions of dollars; quarterly data at seasonally adjusted annual rates]

Year or quarter	Personal consumption expenditures	Goods						Services					Addendum: Personal consumption expenditures excluding food and energy [2]
		Total	Durable		Nondurable			Total	Household consumption expenditures				
			Total [1]	Motor vehicles and parts	Total [1]	Food and beverages purchased for off-premises consumption	Gasoline and other energy goods		Total [1]	Housing and utilities	Health care	Financial services and insurance	
1960	331.8	177.0	45.6	19.6	131.4	62.6	15.8	154.8	149.5	56.7	16.0	13.6	245.1
1961	342.2	178.8	44.2	17.7	134.6	63.7	15.7	163.4	157.9	60.3	17.1	14.8	253.8
1962	363.3	189.0	49.5	21.4	139.5	64.7	16.3	174.4	168.7	64.5	19.1	15.4	272.9
1963	382.7	198.2	54.2	24.2	143.9	65.9	16.9	184.6	178.6	68.2	21.0	15.9	290.0
1964	411.5	212.3	59.6	25.8	152.7	69.5	17.7	199.2	192.5	72.1	24.2	17.7	313.8
1965	443.8	229.7	66.4	29.6	163.3	74.4	19.1	214.1	206.9	76.6	26.0	19.4	339.3
1966	480.9	249.6	71.7	29.9	177.9	80.6	20.7	231.3	223.5	81.2	28.7	21.3	368.1
1967	507.8	259.0	74.0	29.6	185.0	82.6	21.9	248.8	240.4	86.3	31.9	22.8	391.1
1968	558.0	284.6	84.8	35.4	199.8	88.8	23.2	273.4	264.0	92.7	36.6	25.8	432.9
1969	605.1	304.7	90.5	37.4	214.2	95.4	25.0	300.4	290.4	101.0	42.1	28.5	470.8
1970	648.3	318.8	90.0	34.5	228.8	103.5	26.3	329.5	318.4	109.4	47.7	31.1	503.3
1971	701.6	342.1	102.4	43.2	239.7	107.1	27.6	359.5	347.2	120.0	53.7	34.1	550.1
1972	770.2	373.8	116.4	49.4	257.4	114.5	29.4	396.4	382.8	131.2	59.8	38.3	607.9
1973	852.0	416.6	130.5	54.4	286.1	126.7	34.3	435.4	420.7	143.5	67.2	41.5	670.9
1974	932.9	451.5	130.2	48.2	321.4	143.0	43.8	481.4	465.0	158.6	76.1	45.9	722.4
1975	1,033.8	491.3	142.2	52.6	349.2	156.6	48.0	542.5	524.4	176.5	89.0	54.0	800.6
1976	1,151.3	546.3	168.6	68.2	377.7	167.3	53.0	604.9	584.9	194.7	101.8	59.3	898.3
1977	1,277.8	600.4	192.0	79.8	408.4	179.8	57.8	677.4	655.6	217.8	115.7	67.8	1,002.5
1978	1,427.6	663.6	213.3	89.2	450.2	196.1	61.5	764.1	739.6	244.3	131.2	80.6	1,127.8
1979	1,591.2	737.9	226.3	90.2	511.6	218.4	80.4	853.2	825.4	273.4	148.8	87.6	1,245.4
1980	1,755.8	799.8	226.4	84.4	573.4	239.2	101.9	956.0	924.1	311.8	171.7	95.6	1,358.3
1981	1,939.5	869.4	243.9	93.0	625.4	255.3	113.4	1,070.1	1,033.9	352.0	201.9	102.0	1,507.1
1982	2,075.5	899.3	253.0	100.0	646.3	267.1	108.4	1,176.2	1,136.1	387.0	225.2	116.3	1,627.2
1983	2,288.6	973.8	295.0	122.9	678.8	277.0	106.5	1,314.8	1,271.9	421.2	253.1	145.9	1,824.2
1984	2,501.1	1,063.7	342.2	147.2	721.5	291.1	108.2	1,437.4	1,389.8	458.3	276.5	156.6	2,016.9
1985	2,717.6	1,137.6	380.4	170.1	757.2	303.0	110.5	1,580.0	1,529.7	500.7	302.2	180.5	2,215.1
1986	2,896.7	1,195.6	421.4	187.5	774.2	316.4	91.2	1,701.1	1,645.8	535.7	330.2	196.7	2,401.8
1987	3,097.0	1,256.3	442.0	188.2	814.3	324.3	96.4	1,840.7	1,782.1	571.8	366.0	207.1	2,587.3
1988	3,350.1	1,337.3	475.1	202.2	862.3	342.8	99.9	2,012.7	1,946.0	614.5	410.1	219.4	2,813.2
1989	3,594.5	1,423.8	494.3	207.8	929.5	365.4	110.4	2,170.7	2,099.0	655.6	451.2	235.7	3,019.8
1990	3,835.5	1,491.3	497.1	205.1	994.2	391.2	124.2	2,344.2	2,264.5	696.4	506.2	253.2	3,221.3
1991	3,980.1	1,497.4	477.2	185.7	1,020.3	403.0	121.1	2,482.6	2,398.4	735.5	555.8	282.0	3,351.1
1992	4,236.9	1,563.3	508.1	204.8	1,055.2	404.5	125.0	2,673.6	2,581.3	771.2	612.8	311.8	3,601.1
1993	4,483.6	1,642.3	551.5	224.7	1,090.8	413.5	126.9	2,841.2	2,746.6	814.5	648.8	341.0	3,828.2
1994	4,750.8	1,746.6	607.2	249.8	1,139.4	432.1	129.2	3,004.3	2,901.9	866.5	680.5	349.0	4,072.3
1995	4,987.3	1,815.5	635.7	255.7	1,179.8	443.7	133.4	3,171.7	3,064.6	913.8	719.9	364.7	4,291.9
1996	5,273.6	1,917.7	676.3	273.5	1,241.4	461.9	144.7	3,355.9	3,240.2	961.2	752.1	393.6	4,542.0
1997	5,570.6	2,006.8	715.5	293.1	1,291.2	474.8	147.7	3,563.9	3,451.6	1,009.9	790.9	431.3	4,821.6
1998	5,918.5	2,110.0	780.0	320.2	1,330.0	486.5	133.4	3,808.5	3,677.5	1,065.2	832.0	469.6	5,173.5
1999	6,342.8	2,290.0	857.4	350.7	1,432.6	513.6	148.8	4,052.8	3,907.4	1,125.0	863.6	514.2	5,554.6
2000	6,830.4	2,459.1	915.8	363.2	1,543.4	537.5	188.8	4,371.2	4,205.9	1,198.6	918.4	570.0	5,966.4
2001	7,148.8	2,534.0	946.3	383.3	1,587.7	559.7	183.6	4,614.8	4,428.6	1,287.7	996.6	562.8	6,255.9
2002	7,439.2	2,610.0	992.1	401.3	1,617.9	569.6	174.6	4,829.2	4,624.2	1,334.8	1,082.9	576.2	6,549.4
2003	7,804.0	2,727.4	1,014.8	401.5	1,712.6	593.1	209.6	5,076.6	4,864.8	1,393.8	1,149.3	601.8	6,840.9
2004	8,285.1	2,892.3	1,061.6	404.7	1,830.7	628.2	249.9	5,392.8	5,182.8	1,462.2	1,229.7	667.5	7,238.8
2005	8,819.0	3,073.9	1,105.5	409.6	1,968.4	665.0	304.8	5,745.1	5,531.0	1,582.8	1,316.0	712.6	7,658.8
2006	9,322.7	3,221.7	1,133.0	397.1	2,088.7	698.0	336.9	6,100.9	5,860.6	1,686.0	1,380.7	752.4	8,086.9
2007	9,826.4	3,365.0	1,160.5	400.3	2,204.5	740.1	368.0	6,461.4	6,207.9	1,763.1	1,469.6	824.2	8,508.2
2008	10,129.9	3,403.2	1,095.2	342.3	2,308.0	784.3	413.0	6,726.8	6,448.0	1,843.7	1,554.2	835.6	8,709.1
2009 [p]	10,092.6	3,257.6	1,034.4	312.6	2,223.3	790.1	307.4	6,835.0	6,569.7	1,878.3	1,626.0	828.5	8,782.2
2006: I	9,148.2	3,180.8	1,132.5	395.5	2,048.3	684.9	324.5	5,967.4	5,740.2	1,645.8	1,360.6	733.4	7,941.2
II	9,266.6	3,206.5	1,125.1	394.5	2,081.4	692.3	343.3	6,060.1	5,822.9	1,677.0	1,374.4	745.0	8,029.5
III	9,391.8	3,250.5	1,132.4	400.4	2,118.1	699.8	363.3	6,141.3	5,893.1	1,705.7	1,383.6	753.0	8,122.1
IV	9,484.1	3,249.1	1,142.2	398.1	2,106.9	714.8	316.7	6,235.0	5,986.2	1,715.3	1,404.4	778.1	8,254.8
2007: I	9,658.5	3,306.3	1,153.0	399.6	2,153.3	727.1	335.2	6,352.2	6,103.7	1,741.4	1,442.9	799.3	8,386.4
II	9,762.5	3,338.2	1,154.9	401.3	2,183.3	732.1	362.4	6,424.3	6,179.5	1,755.8	1,458.4	819.5	8,456.4
III	9,865.6	3,366.6	1,161.4	398.3	2,205.2	742.7	365.4	6,499.0	6,242.8	1,770.4	1,475.2	835.3	8,545.7
IV	10,019.2	3,448.9	1,172.7	401.9	2,276.2	758.4	408.8	6,570.3	6,305.8	1,784.8	1,501.7	842.8	8,644.3
2008: I	10,095.1	3,447.2	1,145.8	382.7	2,301.4	770.1	427.8	6,647.9	6,377.5	1,811.9	1,531.6	839.6	8,681.9
II	10,194.7	3,474.9	1,126.5	357.5	2,348.4	786.3	441.9	6,719.8	6,446.1	1,838.6	1,551.0	842.1	8,741.1
III	10,220.1	3,463.0	1,088.5	332.7	2,374.5	793.4	461.4	6,757.1	6,474.5	1,852.2	1,559.3	837.3	8,741.8
IV	10,009.8	3,227.5	1,019.9	296.4	2,207.6	787.5	321.2	6,782.3	6,494.1	1,872.1	1,574.9	823.5	8,671.4
2009: I	9,987.7	3,197.7	1,025.2	300.6	2,172.4	786.5	271.0	6,790.0	6,522.0	1,878.8	1,598.0	816.7	8,705.8
II	9,999.3	3,193.8	1,011.5	299.5	2,182.2	786.3	279.4	6,805.6	6,545.9	1,871.1	1,622.6	824.9	8,727.9
III	10,132.9	3,292.3	1,051.3	331.7	2,241.0	789.4	324.4	6,840.6	6,575.7	1,872.5	1,633.0	832.4	8,816.6
IV [p]	10,250.5	3,346.8	1,049.3	318.5	2,297.5	798.0	354.9	6,903.7	6,635.3	1,890.6	1,650.3	839.8	8,878.3

[1] Includes other items not shown separately.
[2] Food consists of food and beverages purchased for off-premises consumption; food services, which include purchased meals and beverages, are not classified as food.

Source: Department of Commerce (Bureau of Economic Analysis).

Table B–17. Real personal consumption expenditures, 1995–2009

[Billions of chained (2005) dollars; quarterly data at seasonally adjusted annual rates]

Year or quarter	Personal consumption expenditures	Goods — Total	Goods — Durable — Total¹	Goods — Durable — Motor vehicles and parts	Goods — Nondurable — Total¹	Goods — Nondurable — Food and beverages purchased for off-premises consumption	Goods — Nondurable — Gasoline and other energy goods	Services — Total	Services — Household consumption expenditures — Total¹	Services — Household consumption expenditures — Housing and utilities	Services — Health care	Services — Financial services and insurance	Addendum: Personal consumption expenditures excluding food and energy²
1995	6,079.0	1,898.6	511.6	255.6	1,437.8	548.5	264.3	4,208.2	4,068.6	1,234.9	947.5	489.4	5,126.4
1996	6,291.2	1,983.6	549.8	268.0	1,479.4	554.0	268.5	4,331.4	4,183.3	1,261.7	967.1	507.8	5,321.9
1997	6,523.4	2,078.2	594.7	286.1	1,522.9	558.9	273.9	4,465.0	4,327.2	1,290.4	997.1	525.2	5,543.3
1998	6,865.5	2,218.6	667.2	316.1	1,580.3	565.5	283.8	4,661.8	4,510.6	1,329.8	1,029.5	558.6	5,862.9
1999	7,240.9	2,395.3	753.8	345.1	1,660.9	587.4	292.5	4,852.8	4,690.4	1,371.8	1,045.6	605.6	6,202.5
2000	7,608.1	2,521.7	819.9	356.1	1,714.7	600.6	287.1	5,093.3	4,917.8	1,413.7	1,081.5	665.4	6,548.6
2001	7,813.9	2,600.9	864.4	374.3	1,745.6	607.6	289.2	5,218.7	5,028.8	1,451.5	1,135.4	660.7	6,745.7
2002	8,021.9	2,706.6	930.0	394.0	1,780.2	609.0	294.0	5,318.1	5,109.3	1,462.0	1,202.3	658.3	6,941.9
2003	8,247.6	2,829.9	986.1	405.3	1,845.6	622.4	302.2	5,418.4	5,199.0	1,480.2	1,229.4	657.8	7,142.0
2004	8,532.7	2,955.3	1,051.0	411.3	1,904.6	639.2	306.5	5,577.6	5,359.3	1,512.8	1,268.6	691.8	7,402.6
2005	8,819.0	3,073.9	1,105.5	409.6	1,968.4	665.0	304.8	5,745.1	5,531.0	1,582.8	1,316.0	712.6	7,658.8
2006	9,073.5	3,173.9	1,150.4	396.6	2,023.6	686.2	298.4	5,899.7	5,664.4	1,616.7	1,340.0	735.4	7,905.7
2007	9,313.9	3,273.7	1,199.9	402.4	2,074.8	700.7	300.7	6,040.8	5,796.1	1,631.8	1,375.5	772.3	8,126.3
2008	9,290.9	3,206.0	1,146.3	347.5	2,057.3	700.7	287.4	6,083.1	5,817.6	1,647.2	1,416.4	759.8	8,123.6
2009 ᵖ	9,237.3	3,143.7	1,100.5	316.8	2,037.3	697.1	292.7	6,090.5	5,833.9	1,657.6	1,446.2	758.7	8,069.3
2006: I	8,986.6	3,145.7	1,142.3	393.3	2,003.7	676.7	296.4	5,841.0	5,618.2	1,598.9	1,337.3	726.0	7,837.8
II	9,035.0	3,150.8	1,139.4	393.2	2,011.6	684.2	297.2	5,884.2	5,652.1	1,617.8	1,339.2	731.3	7,868.0
III	9,090.7	3,176.4	1,152.1	400.3	2,024.5	686.6	300.0	5,914.3	5,671.4	1,627.6	1,335.8	735.6	7,914.3
IV	9,181.6	3,222.5	1,167.9	399.7	2,054.7	697.5	299.9	5,959.4	5,716.0	1,622.5	1,347.7	748.8	8,002.8
2007: I	9,265.1	3,253.9	1,183.7	402.4	2,070.3	700.8	301.5	6,011.7	5,770.8	1,629.3	1,365.1	762.8	8,074.9
II	9,291.5	3,255.4	1,189.9	404.1	2,066.1	696.2	301.3	6,036.2	5,799.2	1,630.1	1,371.7	776.7	8,106.7
III	9,335.6	3,280.6	1,205.0	400.5	2,076.8	699.2	301.5	6,055.5	5,809.8	1,634.6	1,377.6	779.1	8,146.4
IV	9,363.6	3,304.8	1,221.2	402.6	2,086.0	706.6	298.5	6,059.7	5,804.8	1,633.1	1,387.6	770.5	8,177.1
2008: I	9,349.6	3,262.1	1,193.2	384.4	2,070.1	708.0	292.6	6,087.1	5,827.3	1,643.8	1,409.0	766.1	8,164.7
II	9,351.0	3,257.8	1,175.7	361.4	2,081.4	708.9	289.9	6,092.5	5,831.2	1,647.3	1,418.2	763.8	8,170.8
III	9,267.7	3,193.6	1,139.6	337.8	2,051.5	699.6	280.1	6,072.4	5,805.2	1,641.6	1,416.1	758.5	8,120.1
IV	9,195.3	3,110.4	1,076.8	306.2	2,026.1	686.4	287.2	6,080.4	5,806.6	1,656.3	1,422.4	750.6	8,038.7
2009: I	9,209.2	3,129.8	1,087.2	311.2	2,035.5	687.4	293.2	6,076.0	5,817.2	1,656.9	1,434.3	751.4	8,047.7
II	9,189.0	3,105.4	1,071.7	306.2	2,025.7	693.5	294.0	6,078.8	5,826.7	1,651.8	1,448.2	756.1	8,028.2
III	9,252.6	3,159.6	1,122.7	335.2	2,033.3	700.1	292.7	6,090.6	5,834.3	1,654.0	1,448.6	761.8	8,086.3
IV ᵖ	9,298.5	3,180.0	1,120.3	314.7	2,054.6	707.3	290.7	6,116.4	5,857.2	1,667.8	1,453.7	765.5	8,115.1

¹ Includes other items not shown separately.

² Food consists of food and beverages purchased for off-premises consumption; food services, which include purchased meals and beverages, are not classified as food.

Note: See Table B–2 for data for total personal consumption expenditures for 1960–94.

Source: Department of Commerce (Bureau of Economic Analysis).

Year or quarter	Private fixed investment	Nonresidential										Residential		
		Total nonresidential	Structures	Equipment and software									Structures	
				Total	Information processing equipment and software				Industrial equipment	Transportation equipment	Other equipment	Total residential [1]	Total [1]	Single family
					Total	Computers and peripheral equipment	Software	Other						
1960	75.7	49.4	19.6	29.8	4.9	0.2	0.1	4.6	9.4	8.5	7.1	26.3	25.8	14.9
1961	75.2	48.8	19.7	29.1	5.3	.3	.2	4.8	8.8	8.0	7.0	26.4	25.9	14.1
1962	82.0	53.1	20.8	32.3	5.7	.3	.2	5.1	9.3	9.8	7.5	29.0	28.4	15.1
1963	88.1	56.0	21.2	34.8	6.5	.7	.4	5.4	10.0	9.4	8.8	32.1	31.5	16.0
1964	97.2	63.0	23.7	39.2	7.4	.9	.5	5.9	11.4	10.6	9.9	34.3	33.6	17.6
1965	109.0	74.8	28.3	46.5	8.5	1.2	.7	6.7	13.7	13.2	11.0	34.2	33.5	17.8
1966	117.7	85.4	31.3	54.0	10.7	1.7	1.0	8.0	16.2	14.5	12.7	32.3	31.6	16.6
1967	118.7	86.4	31.5	54.9	11.3	1.9	1.2	8.2	16.9	14.3	12.4	32.4	31.6	16.8
1968	132.1	93.4	33.6	59.9	11.9	1.9	1.3	8.7	17.3	17.6	13.0	38.7	37.9	19.5
1969	147.3	104.7	37.7	67.0	14.6	2.4	1.8	10.4	19.1	18.9	14.4	42.6	41.6	19.7
1970	150.4	109.0	40.3	68.7	16.6	2.7	2.3	11.6	20.3	16.2	15.6	41.4	40.2	17.5
1971	169.9	114.1	42.7	71.5	17.3	2.8	2.4	12.2	19.5	18.4	16.3	55.8	54.5	25.8
1972	198.5	128.8	47.2	81.7	19.5	3.5	2.8	13.2	21.4	21.8	19.0	69.7	68.1	32.8
1973	228.6	153.3	55.0	98.3	23.1	3.5	3.2	16.3	26.0	26.6	22.6	75.3	73.6	35.2
1974	235.4	169.5	61.2	108.2	27.0	3.9	3.9	19.2	30.7	26.3	24.3	66.0	64.1	29.7
1975	236.5	173.7	61.4	112.4	28.5	3.6	4.8	20.2	31.3	25.2	27.4	62.7	60.8	29.6
1976	274.8	192.4	65.9	126.4	32.7	4.4	5.2	23.1	34.1	30.0	29.6	82.5	80.4	43.9
1977	339.0	228.7	74.6	154.1	39.2	5.7	5.5	28.0	39.4	39.3	36.3	110.3	107.9	62.2
1978	412.2	280.6	93.6	187.0	48.7	7.6	6.3	34.8	47.7	47.3	43.2	131.6	128.9	72.8
1979	474.9	333.9	117.7	216.2	58.5	10.2	8.1	40.2	56.2	53.6	47.9	141.0	137.8	72.3
1980	485.6	362.4	136.2	226.2	68.8	12.5	9.8	46.4	60.7	48.4	48.3	123.2	119.8	52.9
1981	542.6	420.0	167.3	252.7	81.5	17.1	11.8	52.5	65.5	50.6	55.2	122.6	118.9	52.0
1982	532.1	426.5	177.6	248.9	88.3	18.9	14.0	55.3	62.7	46.8	51.2	105.7	102.0	41.5
1983	570.1	417.2	154.3	262.9	100.1	23.9	16.4	59.8	58.9	53.5	50.4	152.9	148.6	72.5
1984	670.2	489.6	177.4	312.2	121.5	31.6	20.4	69.6	68.1	64.4	58.1	180.6	175.9	86.4
1985	714.4	526.2	194.5	331.7	130.3	33.7	23.8	72.9	72.5	69.0	59.9	188.2	183.1	87.4
1986	739.9	519.8	176.5	343.3	136.8	33.4	25.6	77.7	75.4	70.5	60.7	220.1	214.6	104.1
1987	757.8	524.1	174.2	349.9	141.2	35.8	29.0	76.4	76.7	68.1	63.9	233.7	227.9	117.2
1988	803.1	563.8	182.8	381.0	154.9	38.0	34.2	82.8	84.2	72.9	69.0	239.3	233.2	120.1
1989	847.3	607.7	193.7	414.0	172.6	43.1	41.9	87.6	93.3	67.9	80.2	239.5	233.4	120.9
1990	846.4	622.4	202.9	419.5	177.2	38.6	47.6	90.9	92.1	70.0	80.2	224.0	218.0	112.9
1991	803.3	598.2	183.6	414.6	182.9	37.7	53.7	91.5	89.3	71.5	70.8	205.1	199.4	99.4
1992	848.5	612.1	172.6	439.6	199.9	44.0	57.9	98.1	93.0	74.7	72.0	236.3	230.4	122.0
1993	932.5	666.6	177.2	489.4	217.6	47.9	64.3	105.4	102.2	89.4	80.2	266.0	259.9	140.1
1994	1,033.5	731.4	186.8	544.6	235.2	52.4	68.3	114.6	113.6	107.7	88.1	302.1	295.9	162.3
1995	1,112.9	810.0	207.3	602.8	263.0	66.1	74.6	122.3	129.0	116.1	94.7	302.9	296.5	153.5
1996	1,209.4	875.4	224.6	650.8	290.1	72.8	85.5	131.9	136.5	123.2	101.0	334.1	327.7	170.8
1997	1,317.7	968.6	250.3	718.3	330.3	81.4	107.5	141.4	140.4	135.5	112.1	349.1	342.8	175.2
1998	1,447.1	1,061.1	275.1	786.0	366.1	87.9	126.0	152.2	147.4	147.1	125.4	385.9	379.2	199.4
1999	1,580.7	1,154.9	283.9	871.0	417.1	97.2	157.3	162.5	149.1	174.4	130.4	425.8	418.5	223.8
2000	1,717.7	1,268.7	318.1	950.5	478.2	103.2	184.5	190.6	162.9	170.8	138.6	449.0	441.2	236.8
2001	1,700.2	1,227.8	329.7	898.1	452.5	87.6	186.6	178.4	151.9	154.2	139.5	472.4	464.4	249.1
2002	1,634.9	1,125.4	282.8	842.7	419.8	79.7	183.0	157.0	141.7	141.6	139.6	509.5	501.3	265.9
2003	1,713.3	1,135.7	281.9	853.8	430.9	77.6	191.3	162.0	142.6	132.9	147.5	577.6	569.1	310.6
2004	1,903.6	1,223.0	306.7	916.4	455.3	80.2	205.7	169.4	142.0	161.1	157.9	680.6	671.4	377.6
2005	2,122.3	1,347.3	351.8	995.6	475.3	78.9	218.0	178.4	159.6	181.7	178.9	775.0	765.2	433.5
2006	2,267.2	1,505.3	433.7	1,071.7	505.2	84.9	229.8	190.6	178.4	198.2	189.8	761.9	751.6	416.0
2007	2,269.1	1,640.2	535.4	1,104.8	537.4	89.2	245.6	202.5	193.2	181.7	192.6	629.0	618.6	305.2
2008	2,170.8	1,693.6	609.5	1,084.1	562.9	86.7	264.1	212.1	193.8	132.3	195.1	477.2	467.2	185.8
2009 ᵖ	1,747.9	1,386.6	480.7	906.0	519.9	74.7	241.8	203.4	150.4	72.4	163.2	361.3	352.0	105.2
2006: I	2,270.6	1,457.2	396.8	1,060.5	498.7	84.0	223.3	191.4	168.0	203.8	190.0	813.3	803.0	465.6
II	2,279.7	1,495.3	428.6	1,066.7	500.5	84.1	227.5	188.9	180.7	195.5	190.0	784.4	774.2	435.2
III	2,264.4	1,522.7	447.6	1,075.1	510.1	86.7	232.1	191.4	181.4	195.3	188.2	741.7	731.4	398.7
IV	2,254.2	1,546.1	461.7	1,084.4	511.6	84.8	236.2	190.5	183.7	198.2	191.0	708.1	697.8	364.5
2007: I	2,254.1	1,574.1	489.5	1,084.6	525.1	88.8	238.3	197.9	182.1	192.3	185.2	680.0	669.6	339.8
II	2,278.6	1,623.5	519.9	1,103.5	530.1	86.9	242.6	200.6	198.8	183.0	191.6	655.1	644.8	324.0
III	2,280.8	1,665.2	556.1	1,109.1	538.4	88.2	246.7	203.6	199.0	176.5	195.2	615.6	605.3	298.0
IV	2,263.0	1,697.9	575.9	1,122.0	555.8	93.1	254.8	208.0	192.9	175.1	198.2	565.2	554.8	259.1
2008: I	2,223.0	1,705.0	586.3	1,118.7	566.3	93.7	263.2	209.5	195.3	164.3	192.7	518.1	507.9	220.5
II	2,214.0	1,719.7	610.6	1,109.2	576.2	92.9	268.0	215.3	197.3	143.8	192.0	494.2	484.0	197.4
III	2,179.7	1,711.0	620.4	1,090.6	568.8	84.3	266.4	218.1	194.8	125.9	201.1	468.6	458.7	176.0
IV	2,066.6	1,638.7	620.7	1,018.0	540.2	75.8	258.7	205.6	187.9	95.3	194.7	427.8	418.3	149.1
2009: I	1,817.2	1,442.6	533.1	909.5	508.3	71.1	240.5	196.7	157.8	65.4	178.0	374.6	365.2	111.8
II	1,737.7	1,391.8	494.8	897.0	512.2	72.0	240.2	200.1	151.4	70.6	162.7	345.9	336.8	93.1
III	1,712.6	1,353.9	457.9	895.9	519.0	72.5	241.4	205.1	146.5	73.2	157.2	358.8	349.6	105.2
IV ᵖ	1,724.0	1,358.2	436.8	921.5	540.3	83.3	245.1	211.9	145.9	80.5	154.8	365.7	356.5	110.9

[1] Includes other items not shown separately.

Source: Department of Commerce (Bureau of Economic Analysis).

TABLE B–19. Real private fixed investment by type, 1995–2009

[Billions of chained (2005) dollars; quarterly data at seasonally adjusted annual rates]

Year or quarter	Private fixed investment	Total nonresidential	Structures	Equipment and software					Industrial equipment	Transportation equipment	Other equipment	Residential		
				Total	Information processing equipment and software							Total residential[2]	Structures	
					Total	Computers and peripheral equipment[1]	Software	Other					Total[2]	Single family
1995	1,235.7	792.2	342.0	493.0	149.5	....	66.9	93.7	145.5	131.5	110.6	456.1	450.1	240.2
1996	1,346.5	866.2	361.4	545.4	179.1	....	78.5	102.7	150.9	136.8	114.8	492.5	486.8	262.4
1997	1,470.8	970.8	387.9	620.4	220.8	....	101.7	111.5	154.1	148.2	125.9	501.8	496.3	261.6
1998	1,630.4	1,087.4	407.7	710.4	271.1	....	122.8	125.5	160.8	162.0	138.8	540.4	534.5	290.1
1999	1,782.1	1,200.9	408.2	810.9	332.0	....	151.5	139.9	161.8	190.3	142.4	574.2	567.5	311.5
2000	1,913.8	1,318.5	440.0	895.8	391.9	....	172.4	168.4	175.8	186.2	150.4	580.0	572.6	315.0
2001	1,877.6	1,281.8	433.3	866.9	390.2	....	173.7	163.2	162.8	169.6	149.3	583.3	575.6	315.4
2002	1,798.1	1,180.2	356.6	830.3	379.3	....	173.4	148.4	151.9	154.2	148.2	613.8	605.9	327.7
2003	1,856.2	1,191.0	343.0	851.4	405.0	....	185.6	156.4	151.6	140.4	155.0	664.3	655.9	362.6
2004	1,992.5	1,263.0	346.7	917.3	443.1	....	204.6	168.1	147.4	162.3	164.4	729.5	720.1	406.1
2005	2,122.3	1,347.3	351.8	995.6	475.3	....	218.0	178.4	159.6	181.7	178.9	775.0	765.2	433.5
2006	2,171.3	1,453.9	384.0	1,069.6	514.8	....	227.1	191.2	172.9	196.5	185.5	718.2	708.1	391.1
2007	2,126.3	1,544.3	441.4	1,097.0	555.7	....	241.5	202.3	180.9	177.4	184.1	585.0	575.0	283.9
2008	2,018.4	1,569.7	486.8	1,068.6	588.8	....	257.0	211.1	174.7	128.9	180.3	451.1	441.5	179.7
2009 ᵖ	1,646.7	1,289.1	391.0	887.9	553.7	....	238.3	202.3	133.9	66.1	148.8	359.1	350.0	108.8
2006: I	2,200.2	1,424.9	364.8	1,060.7	505.7	....	222.4	192.2	165.1	202.6	187.3	775.2	764.9	442.4
II	2,189.9	1,450.3	383.7	1,066.3	508.9	....	224.8	189.8	176.2	194.1	187.0	740.1	730.0	409.4
III	2,162.2	1,466.0	393.2	1,072.0	520.4	....	228.5	191.9	174.7	193.7	183.4	697.4	687.3	374.6
IV	2,132.9	1,474.5	394.6	1,079.3	524.1	....	232.8	191.0	175.6	195.5	184.3	660.2	650.2	338.0
2007: I	2,118.8	1,489.6	409.2	1,078.1	540.2	....	235.0	198.4	172.4	188.2	178.3	631.7	621.6	314.0
II	2,137.7	1,530.3	430.7	1,095.2	546.9	....	238.9	200.3	186.9	178.1	183.7	610.4	600.4	301.6
III	2,135.6	1,565.8	456.8	1,101.3	558.2	....	242.6	203.1	185.9	171.8	186.4	572.9	562.9	277.9
IV	2,113.0	1,591.3	469.1	1,113.3	577.5	....	249.6	207.4	178.6	171.5	188.0	525.0	515.0	242.1
2008: I	2,079.2	1,598.9	476.8	1,111.9	591.7	....	257.3	209.2	179.3	161.9	182.3	483.2	473.3	208.6
II	2,064.8	1,604.4	493.2	1,097.7	601.3	....	260.3	214.2	178.6	141.0	180.9	462.9	453.0	189.1
III	2,020.4	1,579.2	493.1	1,071.0	594.5	....	258.3	216.7	173.7	121.7	185.4	443.3	433.7	171.8
IV	1,909.3	1,496.1	484.0	993.7	567.6	....	252.2	204.3	167.2	90.9	172.6	415.0	405.8	149.4
2009: I	1,687.5	1,321.2	419.4	887.5	537.5	....	235.5	195.8	140.8	59.8	157.3	367.9	358.9	112.9
II	1,631.9	1,288.4	400.0	876.5	544.8	....	236.2	199.1	135.2	62.7	144.0	344.4	335.5	96.3
III	1,626.7	1,269.0	380.2	879.8	554.9	....	239.2	203.9	130.4	66.0	140.1	359.6	350.5	110.4
IV ᵖ	1,640.6	1,278.1	364.6	907.7	577.6	....	242.2	210.5	129.2	76.0	137.9	364.6	355.2	115.5

[1] For information on this component, see *Survey of Current Business* Table 5.3.6, Table 5.3.1 (for growth rates), Table 5.3.2 (for contributions), and Table 5.3.3 (for quantity indexes).

[2] Includes other items not shown separately.

Source: Department of Commerce (Bureau of Economic Analysis).

TABLE B–20. Government consumption expenditures and gross investment by type,
1960–2009

[Billions of dollars; quarterly data at seasonally adjusted annual rates]

Year or quarter	Total	Federal Total	National defense Total	National defense Consumption expenditures	National defense Gross investment Structures	National defense Gross investment Equipment and software	Nondefense Total	Nondefense Consumption expenditures	Nondefense Gross investment Structures	Nondefense Gross investment Equipment and software	State and local Total	State and local Consumption expenditures	State and local Structures	State and local Gross investment Equipment and software
1960	111.5	64.1	53.3	41.0	2.2	10.1	10.7	8.7	1.7	0.3	47.5	33.5	12.7	1.2
1961	119.5	67.9	56.5	42.7	2.4	11.5	11.4	9.0	1.9	.6	51.6	36.6	13.8	1.3
1962	130.1	75.2	61.1	46.6	2.0	12.5	14.1	11.3	2.1	.8	54.9	39.0	14.5	1.3
1963	136.4	76.9	61.0	48.3	1.6	11.0	15.9	12.4	2.3	1.2	59.5	41.9	16.0	1.5
1964	143.2	78.4	60.2	48.8	1.3	10.2	18.2	14.0	2.5	1.6	64.8	45.8	17.2	1.8
1965	151.4	80.4	60.6	50.6	1.1	8.9	19.8	15.1	2.8	1.9	71.0	50.2	19.0	1.9
1966	171.6	92.4	71.7	59.9	1.3	10.5	20.8	15.9	2.8	2.1	79.2	56.1	21.0	2.1
1967	192.5	104.6	83.4	69.9	1.2	12.3	21.2	17.0	2.2	1.9	87.9	62.6	23.0	2.3
1968	209.3	111.3	89.2	77.1	1.2	10.9	22.0	18.2	2.1	1.7	98.0	70.4	25.2	2.4
1969	221.4	113.3	89.5	78.1	1.5	9.9	23.8	20.2	1.9	1.7	108.2	79.8	25.6	2.7
1970	233.7	113.4	87.6	76.5	1.3	9.8	25.8	22.1	2.1	1.7	120.3	91.5	25.8	3.0
1971	246.4	113.6	84.6	77.1	1.8	5.7	29.1	24.9	2.5	1.7	132.8	102.7	27.0	3.1
1972	263.4	119.6	86.9	79.5	1.8	5.7	32.7	28.2	2.7	1.8	143.8	113.2	27.1	3.5
1973	281.7	122.5	88.1	79.4	2.1	6.6	34.3	29.4	3.1	1.8	159.2	126.0	29.1	4.1
1974	317.9	134.5	95.6	84.5	2.2	8.9	39.0	33.4	3.4	2.2	183.4	143.7	34.7	4.9
1975	357.7	149.0	103.9	90.9	2.3	10.7	45.1	38.7	4.1	2.4	208.7	165.1	38.1	5.5
1976	383.0	159.7	111.1	95.8	2.1	13.2	48.6	41.4	4.6	2.7	223.3	179.5	38.1	5.7
1977	414.1	175.4	120.9	104.2	2.4	14.4	54.5	46.5	5.0	3.0	238.7	195.9	36.9	5.9
1978	453.6	190.9	130.5	112.7	2.5	15.3	60.4	50.6	6.1	3.7	262.7	213.2	42.8	6.6
1979	500.7	210.6	145.2	123.8	2.5	18.9	65.4	55.1	6.3	4.0	290.2	233.3	49.0	7.8
1980	566.1	243.7	168.0	143.7	3.2	21.1	75.8	63.8	7.1	4.9	322.4	258.4	55.1	8.9
1981	627.5	280.2	196.2	167.3	3.2	25.7	83.9	71.0	7.7	5.3	347.3	282.3	55.4	9.5
1982	680.4	310.8	225.9	191.1	4.0	30.8	84.9	72.1	6.8	6.0	369.7	304.9	54.2	10.6
1983	733.4	342.9	250.6	208.7	4.8	37.1	92.3	77.7	6.7	7.8	390.5	324.1	54.2	12.2
1984	796.9	374.3	281.5	232.8	4.9	43.8	92.7	77.1	7.0	8.7	422.6	347.7	60.5	14.4
1985	878.9	412.8	311.2	253.7	6.2	51.3	101.6	84.7	7.3	9.6	466.1	381.8	67.6	16.8
1986	949.3	438.4	330.8	267.9	6.8	56.1	107.6	90.1	8.0	9.5	510.9	418.1	74.2	18.6
1987	999.4	459.5	350.0	283.6	7.7	58.8	109.6	90.1	9.0	10.4	539.9	441.4	78.8	19.6
1988	1,038.9	461.6	354.7	293.5	7.4	53.9	106.8	88.3	6.8	11.7	577.3	471.0	84.8	21.5
1989	1,100.6	481.4	362.1	299.4	6.4	56.3	119.3	99.1	6.9	13.4	619.2	504.5	88.7	26.0
1990	1,181.7	507.5	373.9	308.0	6.1	59.8	133.6	111.0	8.0	14.6	674.2	547.0	98.5	28.7
1991	1,236.1	526.6	383.1	319.7	4.6	58.8	143.4	118.6	9.2	15.7	709.5	577.5	103.2	28.9
1992	1,273.5	532.9	376.8	315.2	5.2	56.3	156.1	128.9	10.3	16.9	740.6	606.2	104.2	30.1
1993	1,294.8	525.0	363.0	307.5	5.3	50.1	162.0	133.7	11.2	17.0	769.8	634.2	104.5	31.2
1994	1,329.8	518.6	353.8	300.8	5.8	47.2	164.8	139.9	10.2	14.7	811.2	668.2	108.7	34.3
1995	1,374.0	518.8	348.8	297.0	6.7	45.1	170.0	143.2	10.8	16.0	855.3	701.3	117.3	36.7
1996	1,421.0	527.0	354.8	303.2	6.3	45.4	172.2	143.4	11.3	17.5	894.0	730.2	126.8	36.9
1997	1,474.4	531.0	349.8	304.5	6.1	39.2	181.1	153.0	9.9	18.2	943.5	764.5	139.5	39.4
1998	1,526.1	531.0	346.1	300.3	5.8	39.9	184.9	154.3	10.8	19.9	995.0	808.6	143.6	42.9
1999	1,631.3	554.9	361.1	313.0	5.4	42.8	193.8	160.3	10.7	22.7	1,076.3	870.6	159.7	46.1
2000	1,731.0	576.1	371.0	321.8	5.4	43.8	205.0	174.2	8.3	22.6	1,154.9	930.6	176.0	48.3
2001	1,846.4	611.7	393.0	342.0	5.3	45.6	218.7	188.1	8.1	22.5	1,234.7	994.2	192.3	48.2
2002	1,983.5	680.6	437.7	380.7	5.8	51.2	242.9	209.8	9.9	23.2	1,302.7	1,049.4	205.8	47.5
2003	2,112.6	756.5	497.9	435.2	7.3	55.4	258.5	225.1	10.3	23.1	1,356.1	1,096.5	211.8	47.8
2004	2,232.8	824.6	550.8	481.2	7.1	62.4	273.9	240.2	9.1	24.6	1,408.2	1,139.1	220.2	48.9
2005	2,369.9	876.3	589.0	514.8	7.5	66.8	287.3	251.0	8.3	28.0	1,493.6	1,212.0	230.8	50.8
2006	2,518.4	931.7	624.9	543.9	8.1	72.9	306.8	267.1	9.5	30.2	1,586.7	1,282.3	249.9	54.5
2007	2,676.5	976.7	662.1	574.9	10.5	76.8	314.5	273.9	11.1	29.5	1,699.8	1,366.1	277.2	56.4
2008	2,883.2	1,082.6	737.9	634.0	12.9	91.0	344.7	300.4	11.7	32.5	1,800.6	1,452.4	290.9	57.3
2009 ᵖ	2,933.3	1,144.9	779.1	666.8	16.7	95.5	365.8	320.0	13.2	32.6	1,788.4	1,430.9	301.9	55.5
2006: I	2,474.5	928.5	615.5	538.3	7.5	69.7	313.0	272.1	8.6	32.3	1,546.1	1,254.5	238.4	53.2
II	2,510.5	930.3	624.1	541.2	8.0	74.8	306.2	267.2	9.2	29.7	1,580.2	1,274.6	251.3	54.3
III	2,533.3	932.2	623.3	543.7	7.8	71.8	308.9	269.4	9.3	30.2	1,601.2	1,292.7	253.6	54.9
IV	2,555.2	935.9	636.6	552.3	8.9	75.4	299.3	259.8	10.8	28.7	1,619.4	1,307.6	256.3	55.5
2007: I	2,599.3	942.8	637.7	554.3	9.5	73.0	306.1	266.8	10.4	28.8	1,656.5	1,331.2	269.4	56.0
II	2,657.4	968.1	656.6	568.8	10.9	76.9	311.6	271.2	10.9	29.5	1,689.3	1,357.3	275.7	56.3
III	2,700.9	991.4	674.4	585.1	10.5	78.8	317.0	275.6	11.7	29.7	1,709.5	1,373.6	279.4	56.5
IV	2,748.3	1,004.3	680.8	591.4	10.9	78.5	323.6	282.1	11.3	30.2	1,743.9	1,402.5	284.5	56.9
2008: I	2,808.4	1,038.3	703.6	609.7	11.5	82.4	334.8	293.5	10.4	30.9	1,770.1	1,429.3	283.5	57.3
II	2,877.1	1,069.5	725.6	622.4	12.1	91.1	343.9	300.8	11.1	32.0	1,807.6	1,458.3	291.5	57.7
III	2,941.4	1,108.3	763.6	655.2	13.0	95.3	344.7	300.7	12.3	31.7	1,833.1	1,480.4	295.4	57.3
IV	2,905.9	1,114.3	758.9	648.8	14.8	95.3	355.3	306.6	13.2	35.6	1,791.7	1,441.7	293.2	56.8
2009: I	2,879.0	1,106.7	750.7	642.9	15.8	91.9	356.0	311.3	13.2	31.5	1,772.3	1,424.4	292.5	55.4
II	2,929.4	1,138.3	776.2	662.7	16.4	97.2	362.1	316.4	13.2	32.4	1,791.2	1,429.9	305.8	55.4
III	2,955.4	1,164.3	795.8	679.3	18.5	98.0	368.5	321.9	13.3	33.2	1,791.1	1,429.8	305.9	55.4
IV ᵖ	2,969.5	1,170.4	793.8	682.4	16.3	95.1	376.5	330.3	13.0	33.2	1,799.1	1,439.7	303.5	55.9

Source: Department of Commerce (Bureau of Economic Analysis).

TABLE B–21. Real government consumption expenditures and gross investment by type, 1995–2009

[Billions of chained (2005) dollars; quarterly data at seasonally adjusted annual rates]

Year or quarter	Total	Government consumption expenditures and gross investment												
		Federal									State and local			
		Total	National defense				Nondefense				Total	Con-sumption expen-ditures	Gross investment	
			Total	Con-sumption expen-ditures	Gross investment		Total	Con-sumption expen-ditures	Gross investment				Struc-tures	Equip-ment and soft-ware
					Struc-tures	Equip-ment and soft-ware			Struc-tures	Equip-ment and soft-ware				
1995	1,888.9	704.1	476.8	424.5	10.1	43.7	227.5	201.2	15.7	13.7	1,183.6	983.0	175.4	29.1
1996	1,907.9	696.0	470.4	418.5	9.2	43.8	225.7	196.2	15.9	15.5	1,211.1	1,001.0	184.3	29.9
1997	1,943.8	689.1	457.2	412.2	8.7	38.9	231.9	203.2	13.8	16.6	1,254.3	1,027.7	196.7	33.1
1998	1,985.0	681.4	447.5	401.2	8.1	40.1	233.7	201.2	14.5	18.7	1,303.8	1,070.8	196.5	37.7
1999	2,056.1	694.6	455.8	407.6	7.2	42.4	238.7	202.9	14.0	21.7	1,361.8	1,109.5	210.9	41.8
2000	2,097.8	698.1	453.5	403.9	6.9	43.6	244.4	212.4	10.4	21.5	1,400.1	1,133.7	222.2	44.3
2001	2,178.3	726.5	470.7	418.5	6.5	46.3	255.5	224.2	9.8	21.6	1,452.3	1,172.6	234.8	45.3
2002	2,279.6	779.5	505.3	445.8	7.0	52.7	273.9	239.7	11.8	22.7	1,500.6	1,211.3	244.2	45.8
2003	2,330.5	831.1	549.2	484.1	8.5	57.0	281.7	247.1	11.9	23.0	1,499.7	1,207.5	245.5	47.2
2004	2,362.0	865.0	580.4	509.4	7.8	63.3	284.6	250.2	9.9	24.6	1,497.1	1,207.4	241.3	48.6
2005	2,369.9	876.3	589.0	514.8	7.5	66.8	287.3	251.0	8.3	28.0	1,493.6	1,212.0	230.8	50.8
2006	2,402.1	894.9	598.4	519.1	7.5	71.9	296.6	257.5	8.8	30.3	1,507.2	1,220.7	231.4	55.2
2007	2,443.1	906.4	611.5	527.4	9.1	75.0	294.9	255.2	9.8	29.9	1,536.7	1,242.6	236.9	57.4
2008	2,518.1	975.9	659.4	561.6	11.0	87.2	316.4	273.5	9.9	33.2	1,543.7	1,251.5	234.6	58.0
2009 p	2,566.4	1,026.7	695.1	589.4	14.3	91.8	331.4	286.9	11.0	33.4	1,542.8	1,249.4	237.0	56.0
2006: I	2,397.1	900.5	595.6	519.2	7.1	69.3	305.0	264.4	8.3	32.4	1,496.6	1,214.1	228.9	53.7
II	2,399.1	892.8	597.2	515.9	7.5	73.9	295.7	257.3	8.7	29.7	1,506.3	1,216.5	234.9	54.8
III	2,402.7	892.0	594.3	516.7	7.2	70.4	297.7	259.0	8.6	30.1	1,510.8	1,222.3	232.8	55.8
IV	2,409.4	894.4	606.5	524.5	8.0	74.1	287.8	249.2	9.8	28.8	1,515.0	1,230.0	229.1	56.3
2007: I	2,409.5	882.8	594.7	514.6	8.4	71.6	288.1	249.7	9.3	29.0	1,526.5	1,235.6	234.3	56.8
II	2,435.4	898.7	607.1	522.2	9.6	75.4	291.6	252.1	9.7	29.8	1,536.5	1,242.3	237.2	57.2
III	2,458.9	919.0	621.7	535.9	9.2	76.8	297.2	256.8	10.3	30.1	1,540.0	1,245.1	237.6	57.6
IV	2,468.7	925.1	622.4	536.7	9.4	76.4	302.7	262.2	9.8	30.6	1,543.7	1,247.4	238.4	58.1
2008: I	2,484.7	943.4	634.8	545.4	9.8	79.7	308.6	268.4	8.9	31.4	1,541.9	1,249.6	234.3	58.5
II	2,506.9	961.3	645.6	548.4	10.4	87.4	315.8	273.8	9.4	32.6	1,546.6	1,250.1	238.1	58.7
III	2,536.6	991.6	675.4	574.0	11.1	90.9	315.9	273.3	10.3	32.2	1,547.0	1,252.5	236.8	58.0
IV	2,544.0	1,007.3	681.7	578.7	12.7	90.8	325.4	278.4	10.8	36.5	1,539.3	1,253.6	229.4	57.0
2009: I	2,527.2	996.3	672.8	571.5	13.2	88.4	323.4	280.1	10.8	32.3	1,533.3	1,252.3	226.2	55.7
II	2,568.6	1,023.5	695.2	588.2	13.9	93.5	328.2	284.0	11.0	33.2	1,548.0	1,252.7	239.0	55.7
III	2,585.5	1,043.3	709.3	599.6	15.9	94.1	333.8	288.3	11.3	34.1	1,545.5	1,246.6	242.2	55.8
IV p	2,584.4	1,043.5	703.1	598.2	14.0	91.1	340.4	295.2	11.1	33.9	1,544.3	1,246.1	240.8	56.7

Note: See Table B–2 for data for total government consumption expenditures and gross investment for 1960–94.

Source: Department of Commerce (Bureau of Economic Analysis).

TABLE B–22. Private inventories and domestic final sales by industry, 1960–2009

[Billions of dollars, except as noted; seasonally adjusted]

Quarter	Private inventories [1]								Final sales of domestic business [3]	Ratio of private inventories to final sales of domestic business	
	Total [2]	Farm	Mining, utilities, and construction [2]	Manufac-turing	Wholesale trade	Retail trade	Other indus-tries [2]	Non-farm [2]		Total	Non-farm
Fourth quarter:											
1960	136.4	42.9		48.7	16.9	21.9	6.1	93.5	32.3	4.22	2.89
1961	139.8	44.6		50.1	17.3	21.3	6.6	95.2	33.9	4.12	2.81
1962	147.4	47.0		53.2	18.0	22.7	6.6	100.5	35.6	4.14	2.82
1963	149.9	44.4		55.1	19.5	23.9	7.1	105.5	37.9	3.95	2.78
1964	154.5	42.2		58.6	20.8	25.2	7.7	112.2	40.8	3.79	2.75
1965	169.4	47.2		63.4	22.5	28.0	8.3	122.2	44.9	3.77	2.72
1966	185.6	47.3		73.0	25.8	30.6	8.9	138.3	47.4	3.92	2.92
1967	194.8	45.7		79.9	28.1	30.9	10.1	149.1	49.9	3.90	2.99
1968	208.1	48.8		85.1	29.3	34.2	10.6	159.3	55.0	3.79	2.90
1969	227.4	52.8		92.6	32.5	37.5	12.0	174.6	58.7	3.88	2.98
1970	235.7	52.4		95.5	36.4	38.5	12.9	183.3	61.9	3.81	2.96
1971	253.7	59.3		96.6	39.4	44.7	13.7	194.4	67.5	3.76	2.88
1972	283.6	73.7		102.1	43.1	49.8	14.8	209.9	75.7	3.74	2.77
1973	351.5	102.2		121.5	51.7	58.4	17.7	249.4	83.7	4.20	2.98
1974	405.6	87.6		162.6	66.9	63.9	24.7	318.1	89.8	4.52	3.54
1975	408.5	89.5		162.2	66.5	64.4	25.9	319.0	101.1	4.04	3.16
1976	439.6	85.3		178.7	74.1	73.0	28.5	354.2	111.2	3.95	3.19
1977	482.0	90.6		193.2	84.0	80.9	33.3	391.4	124.0	3.89	3.16
1978	570.9	119.3		219.8	99.0	94.1	38.8	451.7	143.6	3.98	3.15
1979	667.6	134.9		261.8	119.5	104.7	46.6	532.6	159.4	4.19	3.34
1980	739.0	140.3		293.4	139.4	111.7	54.1	598.7	174.1	4.24	3.44
1981	779.1	127.4		313.1	148.8	123.2	66.6	651.7	186.7	4.17	3.49
1982	773.9	131.3		304.6	147.9	123.2	66.8	642.6	194.8	3.97	3.30
1983	796.9	131.7		308.9	153.4	137.6	65.2	665.1	215.7	3.69	3.08
1984	869.0	131.4		344.5	169.1	157.0	66.9	737.6	233.6	3.72	3.16
1985	875.9	125.8		333.3	175.9	171.4	69.5	750.2	249.5	3.51	3.01
1986	858.0	113.0		320.6	182.0	176.2	66.3	745.1	264.2	3.25	2.82
1987	924.2	119.9		339.6	195.8	199.1	69.9	804.4	277.7	3.33	2.90
1988	999.7	130.7		372.4	213.9	213.2	69.5	869.1	304.1	3.29	2.86
1989	1,044.3	129.6		390.5	222.8	231.4	70.1	914.7	322.8	3.23	2.83
1990	1,082.0	133.1		404.5	236.8	236.6	71.0	948.9	335.9	3.22	2.82
1991	1,057.2	123.2		384.1	239.2	240.2	70.5	934.0	345.7	3.06	2.70
1992	1,082.6	133.1		377.6	248.3	249.4	74.3	949.5	370.9	2.92	2.56
1993	1,116.0	132.3		380.1	258.6	268.6	76.5	983.7	391.4	2.85	2.51
1994	1,194.5	134.5		404.3	281.5	293.6	80.6	1,060.0	413.9	2.89	2.56
1995	1,257.2	131.1		424.5	303.7	312.2	85.6	1,126.1	436.0	2.88	2.58
NAICS:											
1996	1,284.7	136.6	31.1	421.0	285.1	328.7	82.1	1,148.1	465.6	2.76	2.47
1997	1,327.3	136.9	33.0	432.0	302.5	335.9	87.1	1,190.4	492.2	2.70	2.42
1998	1,341.6	120.5	36.6	432.3	312.0	349.2	91.1	1,221.1	525.8	2.55	2.32
1999	1,432.7	124.3	38.5	457.6	334.8	377.7	99.8	1,308.4	557.2	2.57	2.35
2000	1,524.0	132.1	42.3	476.5	357.7	400.8	114.6	1,391.8	588.3	2.59	2.37
2001	1,447.3	126.2	45.3	440.9	335.8	386.0	113.0	1,321.1	603.0	2.40	2.19
2002	1,489.1	135.9	46.5	443.7	343.2	408.0	111.8	1,353.2	608.5	2.45	2.22
2003	1,545.7	151.0	54.7	447.6	352.6	425.5	114.3	1,394.7	646.3	2.39	2.16
2004	1,681.5	157.2	64.1	487.2	388.9	460.9	123.2	1,524.3	685.2	2.45	2.22
2005	1,804.6	165.2	81.7	531.5	422.8	473.7	129.8	1,639.4	728.7	2.48	2.25
2006: I	1,820.2	158.4	79.2	543.4	430.3	478.0	130.8	1,661.8	745.2	2.44	2.23
II	1,861.7	157.6	81.5	561.5	444.3	483.0	133.9	1,704.2	753.7	2.47	2.26
III	1,896.9	165.3	86.3	571.4	450.0	487.8	136.2	1,731.6	758.7	2.50	2.28
IV	1,917.1	165.1	90.7	575.7	456.4	491.6	137.7	1,752.0	771.9	2.48	2.27
2007: I	1,951.8	177.4	94.5	581.9	463.7	494.1	140.2	1,774.5	784.3	2.49	2.26
II	1,972.6	175.1	98.1	590.7	468.2	498.0	142.5	1,797.5	795.0	2.48	2.26
III	2,003.9	183.3	94.4	599.0	477.3	506.1	143.8	1,820.6	804.7	2.49	2.26
IV	2,070.6	188.4	95.3	625.3	499.9	513.6	148.2	1,882.2	813.7	2.54	2.31
2008: I	2,124.9	195.8	102.9	646.1	514.2	514.3	151.6	1,929.1	810.9	2.62	2.38
II	2,199.7	210.0	114.5	673.3	531.0	516.4	154.6	1,989.8	818.3	2.69	2.43
III	2,177.8	200.9	114.6	655.3	528.2	520.7	158.2	1,976.9	814.4	2.67	2.43
IV	2,015.9	178.4	100.1	592.8	482.7	506.4	155.5	1,837.5	800.0	2.52	2.30
2009: I	1,948.1	171.9	96.4	575.8	464.3	489.7	150.0	1,776.1	794.1	2.45	2.24
II	1,912.2	171.6	96.8	567.4	449.6	478.5	148.3	1,740.6	792.5	2.41	2.20
III	1,892.3	168.6	97.7	564.3	436.6	477.1	147.9	1,723.7	795.3	2.38	2.17
IV [p]	1,914.2	167.0	98.1	570.0	445.6	484.5	148.9	1,747.2	801.3	2.39	2.18

[1] Inventories at end of quarter. Quarter-to-quarter change calculated from this table is not the current-dollar change in private inventories component of gross domestic product (GDP). The former is the difference between two inventory stocks, each valued at its respective end-of-quarter prices. The latter is the change in the physical volume of inventories valued at average prices of the quarter. In addition, changes calculated from this table are at quarterly rates, whereas change in private inventories is stated at annual rates.

[2] Inventories of construction, mining, and utilities establishments are included in other industries through 1995.

[3] Quarterly totals at monthly rates. Final sales of domestic business equals final sales of domestic product less gross output of general government, gross value added of nonprofit institutions, compensation paid to domestic workers, and space rent for owner-occupied housing. Includes a small amount of final sales by farm and by government enterprises.

Note: The industry classification of inventories is on an establishment basis. Estimates through 1995 are based on the Standard Industrial Classification (SIC). Beginning with 1996, estimates are based on the North American Industry Classification System (NAICS).

Source: Department of Commerce (Bureau of Economic Analysis).

TABLE B–23. Real private inventories and domestic final sales by industry, 1960–2009

[Billions of chained (2005) dollars, except as noted; seasonally adjusted]

Quarter	Private inventories [1]								Final sales of domestic business [3]	Ratio of private inventories to final sales of domestic business	
	Total [2]	Farm	Mining, utilities, and construc- tion [2]	Manufac- turing	Wholesale trade	Retail trade	Other indus- tries [2]	Non- farm [2]		Total	Non- farm
Fourth quarter:											
1960	487.9	133.3		164.7	66.5	69.5	35.8	338.3	144.8	3.37	2.34
1961	498.5	135.8		169.6	68.4	68.2	39.5	346.1	151.2	3.30	2.29
1962	520.4	137.6		180.9	71.6	73.0	39.4	366.5	157.0	3.31	2.33
1963	540.6	139.0		187.8	77.5	77.0	42.1	385.5	166.3	3.25	2.32
1964	557.9	135.1		198.2	82.2	81.1	44.7	407.3	176.4	3.16	2.31
1965	590.8	137.7		212.2	87.8	89.3	46.6	437.8	191.6	3.08	2.29
1966	637.9	136.3		240.6	99.5	96.6	47.9	487.9	195.7	3.26	2.49
1967	671.8	138.8		259.6	107.7	96.6	53.5	519.5	200.6	3.35	2.59
1968	702.6	142.9		271.5	111.5	104.8	55.1	545.9	211.5	3.32	2.58
1969	732.9	142.9		284.1	119.7	112.1	57.9	576.8	215.8	3.40	2.67
1970	738.5	140.5		284.0	128.7	112.2	58.6	585.5	218.4	3.38	2.68
1971	763.5	144.6		280.6	135.5	127.4	60.7	606.1	229.6	3.33	2.64
1972	789.1	145.0		288.3	141.6	137.3	63.7	632.8	248.7	3.17	2.54
1973	828.1	146.8		309.6	145.4	148.4	67.0	673.3	257.4	3.22	2.62
1974	857.2	142.4		333.0	158.9	146.2	71.4	712.3	247.8	3.46	2.87
1975	844.4	148.2		324.6	152.1	138.8	73.3	690.9	259.6	3.25	2.66
1976	878.7	146.6		340.1	162.2	149.5	74.0	728.5	272.4	3.23	2.67
1977	921.8	153.9		349.6	175.3	158.1	79.6	764.2	286.7	3.21	2.67
1978	967.4	155.9		365.6	189.3	168.7	84.4	809.1	308.2	3.14	2.63
1979	995.4	160.2		379.7	198.7	168.6	84.3	832.8	315.4	3.16	2.64
1980	986.0	153.0		380.1	204.0	163.8	82.9	832.4	315.1	3.13	2.64
1981	1,025.0	163.1		385.2	209.8	172.8	92.3	860.6	312.8	3.28	2.75
1982	1,005.3	170.6		367.9	207.2	168.9	89.4	833.3	311.6	3.23	2.67
1983	997.7	153.1		367.5	206.3	182.7	88.3	844.0	335.2	2.98	2.52
1984	1,075.9	159.4		399.4	222.8	205.0	89.7	916.3	353.5	3.04	2.59
1985	1,101.3	166.5		392.4	229.2	220.8	94.8	934.7	369.9	2.98	2.53
1986	1,109.8	164.2		388.3	237.7	224.3	98.3	945.1	383.8	2.89	2.46
1987	1,143.0	155.1		397.6	245.4	246.1	100.8	986.2	394.3	2.90	2.50
1988	1,164.9	142.0		416.2	254.9	253.9	99.3	1,021.6	414.7	2.81	2.46
1989	1,195.6	142.0		431.8	258.5	268.8	94.8	1,052.4	426.9	2.80	2.47
1990	1,212.1	148.6		441.6	267.2	267.2	91.2	1,066.4	428.2	2.83	2.49
1991	1,210.7	146.7		434.2	271.5	267.7	94.8	1,066.8	428.0	2.83	2.49
1992	1,228.6	153.8		429.0	280.3	272.5	97.7	1,077.7	451.1	2.72	2.39
1993	1,250.8	146.3		432.9	286.5	288.3	101.2	1,107.6	466.9	2.68	2.37
1994	1,320.1	160.0		446.3	302.7	309.4	106.1	1,163.4	485.5	2.72	2.40
1995	1,352.2	147.0		461.7	316.2	321.9	108.6	1,207.7	503.4	2.69	2.40
NAICS:											
1996	1,383.4	155.3	47.6	465.7	298.0	335.3	87.6	1,230.9	529.2	2.61	2.33
1997	1,460.8	159.0	50.1	490.0	324.9	349.5	93.2	1,304.4	551.4	2.65	2.37
1998	1,532.4	160.6	59.1	507.6	348.6	364.7	99.0	1,373.9	586.2	2.61	2.34
1999	1,600.9	156.9	57.1	523.8	369.7	390.5	106.6	1,444.7	616.4	2.60	2.34
2000	1,661.1	155.2	54.3	531.9	390.4	411.1	119.3	1,505.9	638.7	2.60	2.36
2001	1,619.4	155.3	65.1	505.7	376.8	400.5	119.1	1,464.4	645.1	2.51	2.27
2002	1,632.1	152.2	61.0	500.5	376.7	424.2	118.0	1,480.0	645.5	2.53	2.29
2003	1,649.5	152.4	68.2	492.0	376.3	441.5	119.6	1,497.2	676.7	2.44	2.21
2004	1,715.8	160.3	69.6	498.0	396.8	465.2	126.0	1,555.6	698.6	2.46	2.23
2005	1,765.8	160.4	73.4	519.0	415.0	469.8	128.3	1,605.4	719.8	2.45	2.23
2006: I	1,782.2	161.3	75.8	523.7	419.5	472.7	129.0	1,621.0	732.7	2.43	2.21
II	1,800.4	159.3	81.0	529.5	424.5	474.8	130.7	1,641.1	736.1	2.45	2.23
III	1,817.2	157.7	85.9	534.3	428.7	473.8	131.9	1,659.5	735.9	2.47	2.26
IV	1,825.2	156.7	90.3	536.0	428.3	480.6	132.9	1,668.6	746.3	2.45	2.24
2007: I	1,828.8	158.2	92.0	535.2	429.0	479.7	134.2	1,670.7	751.2	2.43	2.22
II	1,834.6	157.1	93.4	537.2	429.5	481.9	135.2	1,677.7	757.1	2.42	2.22
III	1,842.1	156.4	91.7	539.1	432.3	486.9	135.5	1,685.8	764.0	2.41	2.21
IV	1,844.7	155.9	89.9	541.0	434.7	486.4	136.4	1,689.0	770.4	2.39	2.19
2008: I	1,844.8	152.8	90.5	548.6	433.2	482.1	137.1	1,692.6	766.5	2.41	2.21
II	1,835.5	152.4	91.1	542.8	432.8	478.6	137.2	1,683.6	772.4	2.38	2.18
III	1,828.1	151.1	90.3	535.1	433.8	480.0	137.6	1,677.5	760.7	2.40	2.21
IV	1,818.8	150.7	87.5	537.1	429.6	474.6	138.9	1,668.6	746.0	2.44	2.24
2009: I	1,790.3	150.7	89.2	529.9	419.0	462.8	138.1	1,639.8	734.7	2.44	2.23
II	1,750.2	151.3	91.1	520.0	400.8	450.0	136.6	1,599.1	734.3	2.38	2.18
III	1,715.4	151.8	92.1	506.2	384.1	445.7	135.6	1,563.7	737.2	2.33	2.12
IV ᵖ	1,707.1	150.2	89.0	503.3	383.5	446.1	134.8	1,556.9	742.4	2.30	2.10

[1] Inventories at end of quarter. Quarter-to-quarter changes calculated from this table are at quarterly rates, whereas the change in private inventories component of gross domestic product (GDP) is stated at annual rates.

[2] Inventories of construction, mining, and utilities establishments are included in other industries through 1995.

[3] Quarterly totals at monthly rates. Final sales of domestic business equals final sales of domestic product less gross output of general government, gross value added of nonprofit institutions, compensation paid to domestic workers, and space rent for owner-occupied housing. Includes a small amount of final sales by farm and by government enterprises.

Note: The industry classification of inventories is on an establishment basis. Estimates through 1995 are based on the Standard Industrial Classification (SIC). Beginning with 1996, estimates are based on the North American Industry Classification System (NAICS).
See *Survey of Current Business*, Tables 5.7.6A and 5.7.6B, for detailed information on calculation of the chained (2005) dollar inventory series.

Source: Department of Commerce (Bureau of Economic Analysis).

TABLE B–24. Foreign transactions in the national income and product accounts, 1960–2009

[Billions of dollars; quarterly data at seasonally adjusted annual rates]

Year or quarter	Current receipts from rest of the world					Current payments to rest of the world									Balance on current account, NIPA[2]
	Total	Exports of goods and services			Income receipts	Total	Imports of goods and services			Income payments	Current taxes and transfer payments to rest of the world (net)				
		Total	Goods[1]	Services[1]			Total	Goods[1]	Services[1]		Total	From persons (net)	From government (net)	From business (net)	
1960	31.9	27.0	20.5	6.6	4.9	28.8	22.8	15.2	7.6	1.8	4.1	0.5	3.6	0.1	3.2
1961	32.9	27.6	20.9	6.7	5.3	28.7	22.7	15.1	7.6	1.8	4.2	.5	3.6	.1	4.2
1962	35.0	29.1	21.7	7.4	5.9	31.2	25.0	16.9	8.1	1.8	4.4	.6	3.7	.1	3.8
1963	37.6	31.1	23.3	7.7	6.5	32.7	26.1	17.7	8.4	2.1	4.5	.7	3.7	.1	4.9
1964	42.3	35.0	26.7	8.3	7.2	34.8	28.1	19.4	8.7	2.3	4.4	.7	3.5	.2	7.5
1965	45.0	37.1	27.8	9.4	7.9	38.9	31.5	22.2	9.3	2.6	4.7	.8	3.8	.2	6.2
1966	49.0	40.9	30.7	10.2	8.1	45.2	37.1	26.3	10.7	3.0	5.1	.8	4.1	.2	3.8
1967	52.1	43.5	32.2	11.3	8.7	48.7	39.9	27.8	12.2	3.3	5.5	1.0	4.2	.2	3.5
1968	58.0	47.9	35.3	12.6	10.1	56.5	46.6	33.9	12.6	4.0	5.9	1.0	4.6	.3	1.5
1969	63.7	51.9	38.3	13.7	11.8	62.1	50.5	36.8	13.7	5.7	5.9	1.1	4.5	.3	1.6
1970	72.5	59.7	44.5	15.2	12.8	68.8	55.8	40.9	14.9	6.4	6.6	1.3	4.9	.4	3.7
1971	77.0	63.0	45.6	17.4	14.0	76.7	62.3	46.6	15.8	6.4	7.9	1.4	6.1	.4	.3
1972	87.1	70.8	51.8	19.0	16.3	91.2	74.2	56.9	17.3	7.7	9.2	1.4	7.4	.5	−4.0
1973	118.8	95.3	73.9	21.3	23.5	109.9	91.2	71.8	19.3	10.9	7.9	1.6	5.6	.7	8.9
1974	156.5	126.7	101.0	25.7	29.8	150.5	127.5	104.5	22.9	14.3	8.7	1.4	6.4	1.0	6.0
1975	166.7	138.7	109.6	29.1	28.0	146.9	122.7	99.0	23.7	15.0	9.1	1.3	7.1	.7	19.8
1976	181.9	149.5	117.8	31.7	32.4	174.8	151.1	124.6	26.5	15.5	8.1	1.4	5.7	1.1	7.1
1977	196.6	159.4	123.7	35.7	37.2	207.5	182.4	152.6	29.8	16.9	8.1	1.4	5.3	1.4	−10.9
1978	233.1	186.9	145.4	41.5	46.3	245.8	212.3	177.4	34.8	24.7	8.8	1.6	5.9	1.4	−12.6
1979	298.5	230.1	184.0	46.1	68.3	299.6	252.7	212.8	39.9	36.4	10.6	1.7	6.8	2.0	−1.2
1980	359.9	280.8	225.8	55.0	79.1	351.4	293.8	248.6	45.3	44.9	12.6	2.0	8.3	2.4	8.5
1981	397.3	305.2	239.1	66.1	92.0	393.9	317.8	267.8	49.9	59.1	17.0	5.6	8.3	3.2	3.4
1982	384.2	283.2	215.0	68.2	101.0	387.5	303.2	250.5	52.6	64.5	19.8	6.7	9.7	3.4	−3.3
1983	378.9	277.0	207.3	69.7	101.9	413.9	328.6	272.7	56.0	64.8	20.5	7.0	10.1	3.4	−35.1
1984	424.2	302.4	225.6	76.7	121.9	514.3	405.1	336.3	68.8	85.6	23.6	7.9	12.2	3.5	−90.1
1985	414.5	302.0	222.2	79.8	112.4	528.8	417.2	343.3	73.9	85.9	25.7	8.3	14.4	2.9	−114.3
1986	431.3	320.3	226.0	94.3	111.0	574.0	452.9	370.0	82.9	93.4	27.8	9.1	15.4	3.2	−142.7
1987	486.6	363.8	257.5	106.2	122.8	640.7	508.7	414.8	93.9	105.2	26.8	10.0	13.4	3.4	−154.1
1988	595.5	443.9	325.8	118.1	151.6	711.2	554.0	452.1	101.9	128.3	29.0	10.8	13.7	4.5	−115.7
1989	680.3	503.1	369.4	133.8	177.2	772.7	591.0	484.8	106.2	151.2	30.4	11.6	14.2	4.6	−92.4
1990	740.6	552.1	396.6	155.5	188.5	815.6	629.7	508.1	121.7	154.1	31.7	12.2	14.7	4.8	−74.9
1991	764.7	596.6	423.6	173.0	168.1	756.9	623.5	500.7	122.8	138.2	−4.9	14.1	−24.0	5.0	7.9
1992	786.8	635.0	448.0	187.0	151.8	832.4	667.8	544.9	122.9	122.7	41.9	14.5	22.0	5.4	−45.6
1993	810.8	655.6	459.9	195.7	155.2	889.4	720.0	592.8	127.2	124.0	45.4	17.1	22.9	5.4	−78.6
1994	904.8	720.7	510.1	210.6	184.1	1,019.5	813.4	676.8	136.6	160.0	46.1	18.9	21.1	6.0	−114.7
1995	1,041.1	811.9	583.3	228.6	229.3	1,146.2	902.6	757.4	145.1	199.6	44.1	20.3	15.6	8.2	−105.1
1996	1,113.5	867.7	618.3	249.3	245.8	1,227.6	964.0	807.4	156.5	214.2	49.5	22.6	20.0	6.9	−114.1
1997	1,233.9	954.4	687.7	266.7	279.5	1,363.3	1,055.8	885.7	170.1	256.1	51.4	25.7	16.7	9.1	−129.3
1998	1,240.1	953.9	680.9	273.0	286.2	1,444.6	1,115.7	930.8	184.9	268.9	60.0	29.7	17.4	13.0	−204.5
1999	1,308.8	989.3	697.2	292.1	319.5	1,600.7	1,251.4	1,047.7	203.7	291.7	57.6	32.2	18.0	7.4	−291.9
2000	1,473.7	1,093.2	784.3	308.9	380.5	1,884.1	1,475.3	1,246.5	228.8	342.8	66.1	34.6	20.0	11.4	−410.4
2001	1,350.8	1,027.7	731.2	296.5	323.0	1,742.4	1,398.7	1,171.7	227.0	271.1	72.6	38.1	16.2	18.3	−391.6
2002	1,316.5	1,003.0	700.3	302.7	313.5	1,768.1	1,430.2	1,193.9	236.3	264.4	73.5	40.6	21.6	11.3	−451.6
2003	1,394.4	1,041.0	726.8	314.2	353.3	1,910.5	1,545.1	1,289.3	255.9	284.6	80.7	41.2	25.8	13.7	−516.1
2004	1,628.8	1,180.2	817.0	363.2	448.6	2,253.4	1,798.9	1,501.7	297.3	357.4	97.1	43.6	27.2	26.3	−624.6
2005	1,878.1	1,305.1	906.1	399.0	573.0	2,618.6	2,027.8	1,708.0	319.8	475.9	115.0	48.4	35.3	31.3	−740.5
2006	2,192.1	1,471.0	1,024.4	446.6	721.1	2,990.5	2,240.3	1,884.9	355.4	648.6	101.5	51.6	28.8	21.1	−798.4
2007	2,517.7	1,655.9	1,139.4	516.5	861.8	3,242.4	2,369.7	1,987.7	382.1	746.0	126.6	58.7	36.5	31.4	−724.7
2008 ᵖ	2,640.3	1,831.1	1,266.9	564.2	809.2	3,347.6	2,538.9	2,126.4	412.4	667.3	141.4	64.5	40.8	36.2	−707.2
2009 ᵖ		1,560.0	1,035.1	524.9			1,950.1	1,569.8	380.4		142.6	62.7	50.5	29.5	
2006: I	2,073.0	1,414.0	985.1	428.9	659.0	2,862.6	2,189.8	1,842.9	346.9	578.5	94.3	46.8	26.9	20.6	−789.6
II	2,172.4	1,456.0	1,016.5	439.6	716.4	2,983.5	2,237.4	1,884.3	353.1	640.9	105.1	52.2	33.6	19.4	−811.0
III	2,217.6	1,476.0	1,030.6	445.3	741.6	3,070.9	2,281.7	1,925.0	356.6	679.7	109.5	52.7	34.6	22.3	−853.3
IV	2,305.3	1,538.2	1,065.4	472.8	767.2	3,045.0	2,252.5	1,887.5	365.0	695.5	97.1	54.8	20.1	22.2	−739.7
2007: I	2,352.8	1,564.9	1,081.4	483.4	787.9	3,152.2	2,294.3	1,926.9	367.4	724.0	133.9	57.8	46.2	29.9	−799.3
II	2,454.2	1,602.1	1,109.4	492.7	852.1	3,216.8	2,326.9	1,951.1	375.8	776.0	113.9	57.9	26.1	29.9	−762.6
III	2,582.8	1,685.2	1,156.6	528.6	897.6	3,267.6	2,383.6	1,993.8	389.8	759.1	124.8	58.7	32.4	33.7	−684.8
IV	2,681.0	1,771.6	1,210.4	561.2	909.4	3,332.9	2,474.0	2,078.9	395.2	725.1	133.8	60.4	41.2	32.1	−651.9
2008: I	2,660.0	1,803.6	1,247.3	556.3	856.3	3,377.4	2,548.1	2,143.1	404.9	685.3	144.0	63.1	43.8	37.1	−717.4
II	2,742.0	1,901.5	1,326.2	575.3	840.5	3,495.3	2,640.2	2,226.8	413.4	711.6	143.6	66.2	43.0	34.4	−753.3
III	2,738.6	1,913.1	1,338.5	574.6	825.6	3,475.8	2,670.5	2,243.3	427.2	664.8	140.4	66.7	37.2	36.5	−737.1
IV	2,420.7	1,706.2	1,155.7	550.5	714.4	3,041.7	2,296.7	1,892.5	404.2	607.4	137.5	61.8	39.1	36.6	−621.0
2009: I	2,089.0	1,509.3	989.5	519.8	579.6	2,498.5	1,887.9	1,508.2	379.6	479.7	130.9	63.8	35.9	31.2	−409.5
II	2,065.0	1,493.7	978.1	515.6	571.3	2,454.5	1,832.8	1,461.1	371.7	478.6	143.0	63.1	50.4	29.6	−389.5
III	2,164.4	1,573.8	1,045.2	528.5	590.6	2,589.8	1,976.0	1,592.8	383.1	469.1	144.8	61.9	54.0	28.9	−425.5
IV ᵖ		1,663.4	1,127.6	535.8			2,103.9	1,716.9	387.0		131.5	61.9	41.5	28.1	

[1] Certain goods, primarily military equipment purchased and sold by the Federal Government, are included in services. Beginning with 1986, repairs and alterations of equipment were reclassified from goods to services.
[2] National income and product accounts (NIPA).

Source: Department of Commerce (Bureau of Economic Analysis).

TABLE B–25. Real exports and imports of goods and services, 1995–2009

[Billions of chained (2005) dollars; quarterly data at seasonally adjusted annual rates]

Year or quarter	Exports of goods and services					Imports of goods and services				
	Total	Goods [1]			Services [1]	Total	Goods [1]			Services [1]
		Total	Durable goods	Non-durable goods			Total	Durable goods	Non-durable goods	
1995	845.7	575.4	363.6	216.2	272.6	944.5	766.1	422.9	360.0	180.9
1996	916.0	626.2	405.4	223.4	291.7	1,026.7	837.9	468.1	384.1	190.3
1997	1,025.1	716.2	478.7	237.9	308.9	1,165.0	958.7	545.4	424.1	206.9
1998	1,048.5	732.2	494.2	237.6	316.4	1,301.1	1,072.3	617.2	462.9	229.4
1999	1,094.3	760.0	517.8	240.8	334.6	1,450.9	1,206.0	707.1	500.2	244.9
2000	1,188.3	844.3	584.6	256.5	343.5	1,639.9	1,367.9	814.8	549.2	271.7
2001	1,121.6	792.0	535.9	255.2	329.3	1,593.8	1,324.2	764.5	564.2	269.6
2002	1,099.2	763.5	505.6	259.1	335.6	1,648.0	1,373.4	796.5	580.2	274.5
2003	1,116.8	777.2	514.5	263.8	339.6	1,720.7	1,440.9	830.6	615.2	279.8
2004	1,222.8	842.9	571.0	272.2	380.0	1,910.8	1,599.7	945.0	655.8	311.0
2005	1,305.1	906.1	624.9	281.2	399.0	2,027.8	1,708.0	1,025.4	682.6	319.8
2006	1,422.0	991.4	691.9	299.6	430.6	2,151.2	1,808.8	1,115.3	694.5	342.4
2007	1,546.1	1,064.8	749.1	316.1	481.3	2,193.8	1,839.6	1,139.8	701.4	354.2
2008	1,629.3	1,127.5	784.0	342.7	501.7	2,123.5	1,767.3	1,089.2	678.5	356.5
2009 ᵖ	1,468.6	987.0	650.9	331.6	480.6	1,822.5	1,479.1	858.8	612.5	342.9
2006: I	1,388.8	970.3	678.3	292.1	418.5	2,121.3	1,782.7	1,103.2	681.2	338.6
II	1,412.1	987.8	688.2	299.7	424.3	2,144.9	1,804.7	1,109.0	696.7	340.1
III	1,414.1	988.3	688.4	299.9	425.8	2,170.5	1,829.3	1,116.8	712.6	341.3
IV	1,473.2	1,019.2	712.7	306.7	453.9	2,168.1	1,818.6	1,132.3	687.6	349.5
2007: I	1,485.9	1,026.7	721.5	305.6	459.2	2,190.8	1,841.1	1,141.5	700.6	349.8
II	1,504.8	1,042.4	732.0	310.7	462.3	2,188.1	1,836.5	1,127.8	709.0	351.6
III	1,569.9	1,078.9	758.4	320.9	490.9	2,208.3	1,849.4	1,144.3	706.4	359.0
IV	1,624.0	1,111.0	784.6	327.2	512.9	2,188.0	1,831.6	1,145.5	689.6	356.4
2008: I	1,623.4	1,122.4	783.3	338.6	501.1	2,174.3	1,815.4	1,132.0	686.7	359.0
II	1,670.4	1,159.9	808.3	351.0	510.5	2,146.5	1,794.0	1,122.3	676.4	352.5
III	1,655.2	1,154.8	807.0	347.8	500.4	2,134.4	1,777.1	1,097.6	680.2	357.7
IV	1,568.0	1,072.9	737.4	333.3	494.9	2,038.9	1,682.6	1,004.7	670.7	356.9
2009: I	1,434.5	956.1	637.3	314.9	477.2	1,821.0	1,474.4	835.3	629.4	346.2
II	1,419.5	940.7	611.4	324.0	477.4	1,749.8	1,409.4	798.1	602.1	339.5
III	1,478.8	993.9	651.8	337.2	483.9	1,836.2	1,490.6	863.5	618.4	345.3
IV ᵖ	1,541.6	1,057.4	702.9	350.2	484.0	1,882.7	1,541.9	938.3	600.0	340.7

[1] Certain goods, primarily military equipment purchased and sold by the Federal Government, are included in services. Beginning with 1986, repairs and alterations of equipment were reclassified from goods to services.

Note: See Table B–2 for data for total exports of goods and services and total imports of goods and services for 1960–94.

Source: Department of Commerce (Bureau of Economic Analysis).

TABLE B-26. Relation of gross domestic product, gross national product, net national product, and national income, 1960–2009

[Billions of dollars; quarterly data at seasonally adjusted annual rates]

Year or quarter	Gross domestic product	Plus: Income receipts from rest of the world	Less: Income payments to rest of the world	Equals: Gross national product	Less: Consumption of fixed capital			Equals: Net national product	Less: Statistical discrepancy	Equals: National income
					Total	Private	Government			
1960	526.4	4.9	1.8	529.6	56.6	41.6	15.0	473.0	−1.0	473.9
1961	544.8	5.3	1.8	548.3	58.2	42.6	15.6	490.1	−.6	490.7
1962	585.7	5.9	1.8	589.7	60.6	44.1	16.5	529.2	.3	528.9
1963	617.8	6.5	2.1	622.2	63.3	45.9	17.5	558.9	−.8	559.7
1964	663.6	7.2	2.3	668.6	66.4	48.3	18.1	602.2	.8	601.4
1965	719.1	7.9	2.6	724.4	70.7	51.9	18.9	653.7	1.5	652.2
1966	787.7	8.1	3.0	792.8	76.5	56.5	20.0	716.3	6.2	710.1
1967	832.4	8.7	3.3	837.8	82.9	61.6	21.4	754.9	4.5	750.4
1968	909.8	10.1	4.0	915.9	90.4	67.4	23.0	825.5	4.3	821.2
1969	984.4	11.8	5.7	990.5	99.2	74.5	24.7	891.4	2.9	888.5
1970	1,038.3	12.8	6.4	1,044.7	108.3	81.7	26.6	936.4	6.9	929.5
1971	1,126.8	14.0	6.4	1,134.4	117.8	89.5	28.2	1,016.6	11.0	1,005.6
1972	1,237.9	16.3	7.7	1,246.4	127.2	97.7	29.4	1,119.3	8.9	1,110.3
1973	1,382.3	23.5	10.9	1,394.9	140.8	109.5	31.3	1,254.1	8.0	1,246.1
1974	1,499.5	29.8	14.3	1,515.0	163.7	127.8	35.9	1,351.3	9.8	1,341.5
1975	1,637.7	28.0	15.0	1,650.7	190.4	150.4	39.9	1,460.3	16.3	1,444.0
1976	1,824.6	32.4	15.5	1,841.4	208.2	165.5	42.6	1,633.3	23.5	1,609.8
1977	2,030.1	37.2	16.9	2,050.4	231.8	186.1	45.6	1,818.6	21.2	1,797.4
1978	2,293.8	46.3	24.7	2,315.3	261.4	212.0	49.5	2,053.9	26.1	2,027.9
1979	2,562.2	68.3	36.4	2,594.2	298.9	244.5	54.4	2,295.3	47.0	2,248.3
1980	2,788.1	79.1	44.9	2,822.3	344.1	282.3	61.8	2,478.2	45.3	2,433.0
1981	3,126.8	92.0	59.1	3,159.8	393.3	323.2	70.1	2,766.4	36.6	2,729.8
1982	3,253.2	101.0	64.5	3,289.7	433.5	356.4	77.1	2,856.2	4.8	2,851.4
1983	3,534.6	101.9	64.8	3,571.7	451.1	369.5	81.6	3,120.6	49.7	3,070.9
1984	3,930.9	121.9	85.6	3,967.2	474.3	387.5	86.9	3,492.8	31.5	3,461.3
1985	4,217.5	112.4	85.9	4,244.0	505.4	412.8	92.7	3,738.6	42.3	3,696.3
1986	4,460.1	111.0	93.4	4,477.7	538.5	439.1	99.4	3,939.2	67.7	3,871.5
1987	4,736.4	122.8	105.2	4,754.0	571.1	464.5	106.6	4,182.9	32.9	4,150.0
1988	5,100.4	151.6	128.3	5,123.8	611.0	497.1	113.9	4,512.8	−9.5	4,522.3
1989	5,482.1	177.2	151.2	5,508.1	651.5	529.6	121.8	4,856.6	56.1	4,800.5
1990	5,800.5	188.5	154.1	5,835.0	691.2	560.4	130.8	5,143.7	84.2	5,059.5
1991	5,992.1	168.1	138.2	6,022.0	724.4	585.4	138.9	5,297.6	79.7	5,217.9
1992	6,342.3	151.8	122.7	6,371.4	744.4	599.9	144.5	5,627.1	110.0	5,517.1
1993	6,667.4	155.2	124.0	6,698.5	778.0	626.4	151.6	5,920.5	135.8	5,784.7
1994	7,085.2	184.1	160.0	7,109.2	819.2	661.0	158.2	6,290.1	108.8	6,181.3
1995	7,414.7	229.3	199.6	7,444.3	869.5	704.6	164.8	6,574.9	52.5	6,522.3
1996	7,838.5	245.8	214.2	7,870.1	912.5	743.4	169.2	6,957.6	25.9	6,931.7
1997	8,332.4	279.5	256.1	8,355.8	963.8	789.7	174.1	7,392.0	−14.0	7,406.0
1998	8,793.5	286.2	268.9	8,810.8	1,020.5	841.6	179.0	7,790.3	−85.3	7,875.6
1999	9,353.5	319.5	291.7	9,381.3	1,094.4	907.2	187.2	8,286.9	−71.1	8,358.0
2000	9,951.5	380.5	342.8	9,989.2	1,184.3	986.8	197.5	8,804.9	−134.0	8,938.9
2001	10,286.2	323.0	271.1	10,338.1	1,256.2	1,051.6	204.6	9,081.9	−103.4	9,185.2
2002	10,642.3	313.5	264.4	10,691.4	1,305.0	1,094.0	210.9	9,386.4	−22.1	9,408.5
2003	11,142.1	353.3	284.6	11,210.8	1,354.1	1,135.9	218.1	9,856.8	16.6	9,840.2
2004	11,867.8	448.6	357.4	11,959.0	1,432.8	1,200.9	231.9	10,526.2	−7.8	10,534.0
2005	12,638.4	573.0	475.9	12,735.5	1,541.4	1,290.8	250.6	11,194.2	−79.7	11,273.8
2006	13,398.9	721.1	648.6	13,471.3	1,660.7	1,391.4	269.3	11,810.7	−220.6	12,031.2
2007	14,077.6	861.8	746.0	14,193.3	1,760.0	1,469.6	290.4	12,433.3	−14.8	12,448.2
2008	14,441.4	809.2	667.3	14,583.3	1,847.1	1,536.2	310.9	12,736.2	101.0	12,635.2
2009 ᵖ	14,258.7	....	....	....	1,863.7	1,538.4	325.3	....	....	....
2006: I	13,183.5	659.0	578.5	13,264.0	1,618.0	1,357.4	260.6	11,646.0	−192.2	11,838.2
II	13,347.8	716.4	640.9	13,423.3	1,648.2	1,381.1	267.1	11,775.2	−190.7	11,965.9
III	13,452.9	741.6	679.7	13,514.8	1,675.2	1,403.2	272.0	11,839.6	−253.4	12,093.0
IV	13,611.5	767.2	695.5	13,683.2	1,701.3	1,423.9	277.4	11,981.9	−246.0	12,227.9
2007: I	13,795.6	787.9	724.0	13,859.5	1,726.7	1,443.1	283.7	12,132.8	−121.1	12,253.9
II	13,997.2	852.1	776.0	14,073.3	1,749.4	1,461.4	288.0	12,324.0	−97.1	12,421.1
III	14,179.9	897.6	759.1	14,318.3	1,771.2	1,478.7	292.5	12,547.2	64.9	12,482.2
IV	14,337.9	909.4	725.1	14,522.2	1,792.8	1,495.1	297.6	12,729.4	94.0	12,635.4
2008: I	14,373.9	856.3	685.3	14,544.9	1,813.6	1,510.6	303.0	12,731.2	69.8	12,661.5
II	14,497.8	840.5	711.6	14,626.6	1,835.6	1,527.0	308.5	12,791.1	126.7	12,664.4
III	14,546.7	825.6	664.8	14,707.5	1,858.2	1,544.4	313.8	12,849.3	68.3	12,781.0
IV	14,347.3	714.4	607.4	14,454.3	1,881.0	1,562.6	318.4	12,573.3	139.4	12,433.9
2009: I	14,178.0	579.6	479.7	14,277.9	1,883.6	1,561.3	322.3	12,394.3	185.4	12,208.9
II	14,151.2	571.3	478.6	14,243.8	1,864.0	1,540.5	323.5	12,379.8	161.7	12,218.1
III	14,242.1	590.6	469.1	14,363.7	1,850.7	1,525.5	325.2	12,512.9	163.2	12,349.7
IV ᵖ	14,463.4	....	....	....	1,856.4	1,526.3	330.1	....	....	....

Source: Department of Commerce (Bureau of Economic Analysis).

TABLE B–27. Relation of national income and personal income, 1960–2009

[Billions of dollars; quarterly data at seasonally adjusted annual rates]

Year or quarter	National income	Less: Corporate profits with inventory valuation and capital consumption adjustments	Less: Taxes on production and imports less subsidies	Less: Contributions for government social insurance, domestic	Less: Net interest and miscellaneous payments on assets	Less: Business current transfer payments (net)	Less: Current surplus of government enterprises	Wage accruals less disbursements	Plus: Personal income receipts on assets	Plus: Personal current transfer receipts	Equals: Personal income
1960	473.9	53.1	43.4	16.4	10.6	1.9	0.9	0.0	37.9	25.7	411.3
1961	490.7	54.2	45.0	17.0	12.5	2.0	.8	.0	40.1	29.5	428.8
1962	528.9	62.3	48.1	19.1	14.2	2.2	.9	.0	44.1	30.4	456.4
1963	559.7	68.3	51.2	21.7	15.2	2.7	1.4	.0	47.9	32.2	479.5
1964	601.4	75.5	54.5	22.4	17.4	3.1	1.3	.0	53.8	33.5	514.3
1965	652.2	86.5	57.7	23.4	19.6	3.6	1.3	.0	59.4	36.2	555.5
1966	710.1	92.5	59.3	31.3	22.4	3.5	1.0	.0	64.1	39.6	603.8
1967	750.4	90.2	64.1	34.9	25.5	3.8	.9	.0	69.0	48.0	648.1
1968	821.2	97.3	72.2	38.7	27.1	4.3	1.2	.0	75.2	56.1	711.7
1969	888.5	94.5	79.3	44.1	32.7	4.9	1.0	.0	84.1	62.3	778.3
1970	929.5	82.5	86.6	46.4	39.1	4.5	.0	.0	93.5	74.7	838.6
1971	1,005.6	96.1	95.8	51.2	43.9	4.3	–.2	.6	101.0	88.1	903.1
1972	1,110.3	111.4	101.3	59.2	47.9	4.9	.5	.0	109.6	97.9	992.6
1973	1,246.1	124.5	112.0	75.5	55.2	6.0	–.4	–.1	124.7	112.6	1,110.5
1974	1,341.5	115.1	121.6	85.2	70.8	7.1	–.9	–.5	146.4	133.3	1,222.7
1975	1,444.0	133.3	130.8	89.3	81.6	9.4	–3.2	.1	162.2	170.0	1,334.9
1976	1,609.8	161.6	141.3	101.3	85.5	9.5	–1.8	.1	178.4	184.0	1,474.7
1977	1,797.4	191.8	152.6	113.1	101.1	8.5	–2.7	.1	205.3	194.2	1,632.5
1978	2,027.9	218.4	162.0	131.3	115.0	10.8	–2.2	.3	234.8	209.6	1,836.7
1979	2,248.3	225.4	171.6	152.7	138.9	13.3	–2.9	–.2	274.7	235.3	2,059.5
1980	2,433.0	201.4	190.5	166.2	181.8	14.7	–5.1	.0	338.7	279.5	2,301.5
1981	2,729.8	223.3	224.2	195.7	232.3	17.9	–5.6	.1	421.9	318.4	2,582.3
1982	2,851.4	205.7	225.9	208.9	271.1	20.6	–4.5	.0	488.4	354.8	2,766.8
1983	3,070.9	259.8	242.0	226.0	285.3	22.6	–3.2	–.4	529.6	383.7	2,952.2
1984	3,461.3	318.6	268.7	257.5	327.1	30.3	–1.9	.2	607.9	400.1	3,268.9
1985	3,696.3	332.5	286.8	281.4	341.5	35.2	.6	–.2	653.2	424.9	3,496.7
1986	3,871.5	314.1	298.5	303.4	367.1	36.9	.9	.0	694.5	451.0	3,696.0
1987	4,150.0	367.8	317.3	323.1	366.7	34.1	.2	.0	715.8	467.6	3,924.4
1988	4,522.3	426.6	345.0	361.5	385.3	33.6	2.6	.0	767.0	496.5	4,231.2
1989	4,800.5	425.6	371.4	385.2	434.1	39.2	4.9	.0	874.8	542.6	4,557.5
1990	5,059.5	434.4	398.0	410.1	444.2	40.1	1.6	.1	920.8	594.9	4,846.7
1991	5,217.9	457.3	429.6	430.2	418.2	39.9	5.7	–.1	928.6	665.9	5,031.5
1992	5,517.1	496.2	453.3	455.0	387.7	40.7	8.2	–15.8	909.7	745.8	5,347.3
1993	5,784.7	543.7	466.4	477.4	364.6	40.5	8.7	6.4	900.5	790.8	5,568.1
1994	6,181.3	628.2	512.7	508.2	362.2	41.9	9.6	17.6	947.7	826.4	5,874.8
1995	6,522.3	716.2	523.1	532.8	358.3	45.8	13.1	16.4	1,005.4	878.9	6,200.9
1996	6,931.7	801.5	545.5	555.1	371.1	53.8	14.4	3.6	1,080.7	924.1	6,591.6
1997	7,406.0	884.8	577.8	587.2	407.6	51.3	14.1	–2.9	1,165.5	949.2	7,000.7
1998	7,875.6	812.4	603.1	624.7	479.3	65.2	13.3	–.7	1,269.2	977.9	7,525.4
1999	8,358.0	856.3	628.4	661.3	481.4	69.0	14.1	5.2	1,246.8	1,021.6	7,910.8
2000	8,938.9	819.2	662.7	705.8	539.3	87.0	9.1	.0	1,360.7	1,083.0	8,559.4
2001	9,185.2	784.2	669.0	733.2	544.4	101.3	4.0	.0	1,346.0	1,188.1	8,883.3
2002	9,408.5	872.2	721.4	751.5	506.4	82.4	6.3	.0	1,309.6	1,282.1	9,060.1
2003	9,840.2	977.8	757.7	778.9	504.1	76.1	7.0	15.0	1,312.9	1,341.7	9,378.1
2004	10,534.0	1,246.9	817.0	827.3	461.6	81.7	1.2	–15.0	1,408.5	1,415.5	9,937.2
2005	11,273.8	1,456.1	869.3	872.7	543.0	95.9	–3.5	5.0	1,542.0	1,508.6	10,485.9
2006	12,031.2	1,608.3	935.5	921.8	652.2	83.0	–4.2	1.3	1,829.7	1,605.0	11,268.1
2007	12,448.2	1,541.7	974.0	959.3	739.2	102.2	–6.6	–6.3	2,031.5	1,718.0	11,894.1
2008	12,635.2	1,360.4	993.8	990.6	815.1	118.8	–6.9	–5.0	1,994.4	1,875.9	12,238.8
2009 ᵖ	....	....	964.3	973.2	786.2	134.0	–8.1	5.0	1,791.5	2,106.9	12,072.1
2006: I	11,838.2	1,590.9	916.0	915.4	608.9	82.8	–2.4	–20.0	1,711.1	1,569.0	11,026.7
II	11,965.9	1,597.7	931.9	917.4	654.4	79.3	–3.8	.0	1,812.2	1,597.9	11,204.0
III	12,093.0	1,655.1	941.9	920.8	661.6	83.6	–4.7	.0	1,881.3	1,620.7	11,336.9
IV	12,227.9	1,589.6	952.1	933.8	684.0	86.1	–6.0	25.0	1,909.0	1,632.4	11,504.8
2007: I	12,253.9	1,535.4	966.0	952.5	690.6	97.8	–8.4	–25.0	1,968.2	1,693.8	11,706.9
II	12,421.1	1,594.9	966.9	953.7	711.3	99.0	–6.9	.0	2,022.0	1,699.1	11,823.4
III	12,482.2	1,537.1	976.1	958.6	756.0	105.0	–4.9	.0	2,065.8	1,725.5	11,945.6
IV	12,635.4	1,499.4	986.8	972.6	798.9	107.0	–6.0	.0	2,069.8	1,753.7	12,100.3
2008: I	12,661.5	1,459.7	989.3	985.3	790.7	114.8	–5.6	.0	2,020.8	1,794.1	12,142.2
II	12,664.4	1,403.7	997.9	988.9	809.0	112.6	–6.3	.0	1,997.3	1,937.0	12,292.9
III	12,781.0	1,454.6	1,005.7	994.9	806.1	116.0	–6.9	.0	2,001.4	1,874.3	12,286.6
IV	12,433.9	1,123.6	982.1	993.3	854.7	131.8	–8.9	–20.0	1,958.1	1,898.0	12,233.5
2009: I	12,208.9	1,182.7	963.2	969.7	826.2	137.9	–10.7	20.0	1,845.5	1,987.3	11,952.7
II	12,218.1	1,226.5	964.6	970.9	784.4	145.4	–8.8	.0	1,773.4	2,140.3	12,048.8
III	12,349.7	1,358.9	955.4	974.0	759.7	124.8	–6.3	.0	1,763.1	2,137.5	12,083.9
IV ᵖ	....	....	973.8	978.4	774.7	128.1	–6.6	.0	1,784.0	2,162.5	12,203.1

Source: Department of Commerce (Bureau of Economic Analysis).

TABLE B–28. National income by type of income, 1960–2009

[Billions of dollars; quarterly data at seasonally adjusted annual rates]

Year or quarter	National income	Compensation of employees								Proprietors' income with inventory valuation and capital consumption adjustments			Rental income of persons with capital consumption adjustment
		Total	Wage and salary accruals			Supplements to wages and salaries				Total	Farm	Non-farm	
			Total	Government	Other	Total	Employer contributions for employee pension and insurance funds	Employer contributions for government social insurance					
1960	473.9	296.4	272.9	49.2	223.7	23.6	14.3	9.3	50.7	10.6	40.1	17.0
1961	490.7	305.3	280.5	52.5	228.0	24.8	15.2	9.6	53.2	11.2	42.0	17.7
1962	528.9	327.1	299.4	56.3	243.0	27.8	16.6	11.2	55.3	11.2	44.1	18.6
1963	559.7	345.2	314.9	60.0	254.8	30.4	18.0	12.4	56.5	11.0	45.5	19.3
1964	601.4	370.7	337.8	64.9	272.9	32.9	20.3	12.6	59.4	9.8	49.6	19.4
1965	652.2	399.5	363.8	69.9	293.8	35.7	22.7	13.1	63.9	12.0	51.9	19.9
1966	710.1	442.7	400.3	78.4	321.9	42.3	25.5	16.8	68.2	13.0	55.2	20.5
1967	750.4	475.1	429.0	86.5	342.5	46.1	28.1	18.0	69.8	11.6	58.2	20.9
1968	821.2	524.3	472.0	96.7	375.3	52.3	32.4	20.0	74.2	11.7	62.5	20.6
1969	888.5	577.6	518.3	105.6	412.7	59.3	36.5	22.8	77.5	12.8	64.7	20.9
1970	929.5	617.2	551.6	117.2	434.3	65.7	41.8	23.8	78.5	12.9	65.6	21.1
1971	1,005.6	658.9	584.5	126.8	457.8	74.4	47.9	26.4	84.7	13.4	71.3	22.2
1972	1,110.3	725.1	638.8	137.9	500.9	86.4	55.2	31.2	96.0	17.0	79.0	23.1
1973	1,246.1	811.2	708.8	148.8	560.0	102.5	62.7	39.8	113.6	29.1	84.6	23.9
1974	1,341.5	890.2	772.3	160.5	611.8	118.0	73.3	44.7	113.5	23.5	90.0	24.0
1975	1,444.0	949.1	814.8	176.2	638.6	134.3	87.6	46.7	119.6	22.0	97.6	23.4
1976	1,609.8	1,059.3	899.7	188.9	710.8	159.6	105.2	54.4	132.2	17.2	115.0	22.1
1977	1,797.4	1,180.5	994.2	202.6	791.6	186.4	125.3	61.1	146.0	16.0	130.1	19.6
1978	2,027.9	1,335.5	1,120.6	220.0	900.6	214.9	143.4	71.5	167.5	19.9	147.6	20.9
1979	2,248.3	1,498.3	1,253.3	237.1	1,016.2	245.0	162.4	82.6	181.1	22.2	159.0	22.6
1980	2,433.0	1,647.6	1,373.4	261.5	1,112.0	274.2	185.2	88.9	173.5	11.7	161.8	28.5
1981	2,729.8	1,819.7	1,511.4	285.8	1,225.5	308.3	204.7	103.6	181.6	19.0	162.6	36.5
1982	2,851.4	1,919.6	1,587.5	307.5	1,280.0	332.1	222.4	109.8	174.8	13.3	161.5	38.1
1983	3,070.9	2,035.5	1,677.5	324.8	1,352.7	358.0	238.1	119.9	190.7	6.2	184.5	38.2
1984	3,461.3	2,245.4	1,844.9	348.1	1,496.8	400.5	261.5	139.0	233.1	20.9	212.1	40.0
1985	3,696.3	2,411.7	1,982.6	373.9	1,608.7	429.2	281.5	147.7	246.1	21.0	225.1	41.9
1986	3,871.5	2,557.7	2,102.3	397.2	1,705.1	455.3	297.5	157.9	262.6	22.8	239.7	33.8
1987	4,150.0	2,735.6	2,256.3	423.1	1,833.1	479.4	313.1	166.3	294.2	28.9	265.3	34.2
1988	4,522.3	2,954.2	2,439.8	452.0	1,987.7	514.4	329.7	184.6	334.8	26.8	308.0	40.2
1989	4,800.5	3,131.3	2,583.1	481.1	2,101.9	548.3	354.6	193.7	351.6	33.0	318.6	42.4
1990	5,059.5	3,326.3	2,741.2	519.0	2,222.2	585.1	378.6	206.5	365.1	32.2	333.0	49.8
1991	5,217.9	3,438.3	2,814.5	548.8	2,265.7	623.9	408.7	215.1	367.3	27.5	339.8	61.6
1992	5,517.1	3,631.4	2,957.8	572.0	2,385.8	673.6	445.2	228.4	414.9	35.8	379.1	84.6
1993	5,784.7	3,797.1	3,083.0	589.0	2,494.0	714.1	474.4	239.7	449.6	32.0	417.6	114.1
1994	6,181.3	3,998.5	3,248.5	609.5	2,639.0	750.1	495.9	254.1	485.1	35.6	449.5	142.9
1995	6,522.3	4,195.2	3,434.4	629.0	2,805.4	760.8	496.7	264.1	516.0	23.4	492.6	154.6
1996	6,931.7	4,391.4	3,620.0	648.1	2,971.9	771.4	496.6	274.8	583.7	38.4	545.2	170.4
1997	7,406.0	4,665.6	3,873.6	671.8	3,201.8	792.0	502.4	289.6	628.2	32.6	595.6	176.5
1998	7,875.6	5,023.2	4,180.9	701.2	3,479.7	842.3	535.1	307.2	687.5	28.9	658.7	191.5
1999	8,358.0	5,353.9	4,465.2	733.7	3,731.5	888.8	565.4	323.3	746.8	28.5	718.3	208.2
2000	8,938.9	5,788.8	4,827.7	779.7	4,048.0	961.2	615.9	345.2	817.5	29.6	787.8	215.3
2001	9,185.2	5,979.3	4,952.2	821.9	4,130.3	1,027.1	669.1	358.0	870.7	30.5	840.2	232.4
2002	9,408.5	6,110.8	4,997.3	873.1	4,124.2	1,113.5	747.4	366.1	890.3	18.5	871.8	218.7
2003	9,840.2	6,382.6	5,154.6	913.3	4,241.3	1,228.0	845.6	382.4	930.6	36.5	894.1	204.2
2004	10,534.0	6,693.4	5,410.7	952.8	4,457.9	1,282.7	874.6	408.1	1,033.8	49.7	984.1	198.4
2005	11,273.8	7,065.0	5,706.0	991.5	4,714.5	1,359.1	931.6	427.5	1,069.8	43.9	1,025.9	178.2
2006	12,031.2	7,477.0	6,070.1	1,035.2	5,035.0	1,406.9	960.1	446.7	1,133.0	29.3	1,103.6	146.5
2007	12,448.2	7,856.5	6,402.6	1,089.1	5,313.5	1,453.8	993.0	460.8	1,096.4	39.4	1,056.9	144.9
2008	12,635.2	8,037.4	6,540.8	1,141.3	5,399.6	1,496.6	1,023.9	472.7	1,106.3	48.7	1,057.5	210.4
2009 ᵖ		7,841.3	6,335.6	1,182.5	5,153.1	1,505.7	1,043.9	461.8	1,042.3	29.9	1,012.4	268.3
2006: I	11,838.2	7,353.7	5,958.9	1,019.0	4,939.9	1,394.8	950.7	444.1	1,126.9	28.4	1,098.5	161.3
II	11,965.9	7,419.9	6,018.6	1,028.3	4,990.3	1,401.3	956.8	444.5	1,133.2	28.4	1,104.8	153.2
III	12,093.0	7,484.1	6,075.4	1,041.0	5,034.5	1,408.7	962.7	445.9	1,131.2	28.4	1,102.8	140.3
IV	12,227.2	7,650.3	6,227.6	1,052.3	5,175.4	1,422.6	970.4	452.2	1,140.6	32.2	1,108.4	131.2
2007: I	12,253.9	7,757.2	6,318.6	1,073.2	5,245.3	1,438.6	980.5	458.1	1,094.2	36.7	1,057.5	121.1
II	12,421.1	7,819.7	6,372.2	1,084.2	5,288.0	1,447.5	989.4	458.2	1,096.0	35.7	1,060.3	140.3
III	12,482.2	7,869.6	6,412.5	1,093.2	5,319.4	1,457.1	996.9	460.2	1,093.2	37.5	1,055.7	150.2
IV	12,635.4	7,979.3	6,507.3	1,105.8	5,401.4	1,472.1	1,005.2	466.9	1,102.1	47.9	1,054.2	168.0
2008: I	12,661.5	8,017.5	6,533.0	1,125.3	5,407.7	1,484.5	1,014.0	470.5	1,115.2	57.2	1,057.9	179.9
II	12,664.4	8,032.8	6,539.2	1,136.4	5,402.8	1,493.5	1,021.7	471.8	1,111.9	49.4	1,062.5	202.8
III	12,781.0	8,069.1	6,567.7	1,148.5	5,419.2	1,501.4	1,026.7	474.7	1,114.4	49.3	1,065.1	222.2
IV	12,433.9	8,030.3	6,523.5	1,154.9	5,368.6	1,506.8	1,033.2	473.6	1,083.6	39.0	1,044.5	236.7
2009: I	12,208.9	7,825.8	6,327.8	1,171.8	5,156.0	1,498.0	1,037.8	460.2	1,037.8	27.3	1,010.5	245.9
II	12,218.1	7,815.9	6,313.1	1,184.4	5,128.8	1,502.8	1,042.0	460.8	1,028.0	28.9	999.1	262.0
III	12,349.7	7,841.5	6,333.2	1,184.8	5,148.4	1,508.3	1,046.1	462.2	1,037.9	25.8	1,012.0	277.9
IVᵖ		7,882.1	6,368.2	1,189.0	5,179.2	1,513.8	1,049.8	464.1	1,065.5	37.4	1,028.1	287.4

See next page for continuation of table.

TABLE B–28. National income by type of income, 1960–2009—*Continued*

[Billions of dollars; quarterly data at seasonally adjusted annual rates]

Year or quarter	Corporate profits with inventory valuation and capital consumption adjustments								Capital con-sump-tion adjust-ment	Net interest and miscel-laneous pay-ments	Taxes on produc-tion and imports	Less: Sub-sidies	Busi-ness current transfer pay-ments (net)	Current surplus of govern-ment enter-prises
	Total	Profits with inventory valuation adjustment and without capital consumption adjustment												
		Total	Profits					Inven-tory valua-tion adjust-ment						
			Profits before tax	Taxes on corpo-rate income	Profits after tax									
					Total	Net divi-dends	Undis-tributed profits							
1960	53.1	51.5	51.6	22.8	28.8	13.4	15.5	−0.2	1.6	10.6	44.5	1.1	1.9	0.9
1961	54.2	51.8	51.6	22.9	28.7	13.9	14.8	.3	2.3	12.5	47.0	2.0	2.0	.8
1962	62.3	57.0	57.0	24.1	32.9	15.0	17.9	.0	5.3	14.2	50.4	2.3	2.2	.9
1963	68.3	62.1	62.1	26.4	35.7	16.2	19.5	.1	6.2	15.2	53.4	2.2	2.7	1.4
1964	75.5	68.6	69.1	28.2	40.9	18.2	22.7	−.5	6.9	17.4	57.3	2.7	3.1	1.3
1965	86.5	78.9	80.2	31.1	49.1	20.2	28.9	−1.2	7.6	19.6	60.7	3.0	3.6	1.3
1966	92.5	84.6	86.7	33.9	52.8	20.7	32.1	−2.1	8.0	22.4	63.2	3.9	3.5	1.0
1967	90.2	82.0	83.5	32.9	50.6	21.5	29.1	−1.6	8.2	25.5	67.9	3.8	3.8	.9
1968	97.3	88.8	92.4	39.6	52.8	23.5	29.3	−3.7	8.5	27.1	76.4	4.2	4.3	1.2
1969	94.5	85.5	91.4	40.0	51.4	24.2	27.2	−5.9	9.0	32.7	83.9	4.5	4.9	1.0
1970	82.5	74.4	81.0	34.8	46.2	24.3	21.9	−6.6	8.1	39.1	91.4	4.8	4.5	.0
1971	96.1	88.3	92.9	38.2	54.7	25.0	29.7	−4.6	7.8	43.9	100.5	4.7	4.3	−.2
1972	111.4	101.6	108.2	42.3	65.9	26.8	39.0	−6.6	9.8	47.9	107.9	6.6	4.9	.5
1973	124.5	115.4	135.0	50.0	85.0	29.9	55.1	−19.6	9.1	55.2	117.2	5.2	6.0	−.4
1974	115.1	109.6	147.8	52.8	95.0	33.2	61.8	−38.2	5.6	70.8	124.9	3.3	7.1	−.9
1975	133.3	135.0	145.5	51.6	93.9	33.0	60.9	−10.5	−1.7	81.6	135.3	4.5	9.4	−3.2
1976	161.6	165.6	179.7	65.3	114.5	39.0	75.4	−14.1	−4.0	85.5	146.4	5.1	9.5	−1.8
1977	191.8	194.8	210.5	74.4	136.1	44.8	91.3	−15.7	−3.0	101.1	159.7	7.1	8.5	−2.7
1978	218.4	222.4	246.1	84.9	161.3	50.8	110.5	−23.7	−4.0	115.0	170.9	8.9	10.8	−2.2
1979	225.4	232.0	272.1	90.0	182.1	57.5	124.6	−40.1	−6.6	138.9	180.1	8.5	13.3	−2.9
1980	201.4	211.4	253.5	87.2	166.4	64.1	102.3	−42.1	−10.0	181.8	200.3	9.8	14.7	−5.1
1981	223.3	219.1	243.7	84.3	159.4	73.8	85.6	−24.6	4.2	232.3	235.6	11.5	17.9	−5.6
1982	205.7	191.1	198.6	66.5	132.1	77.7	54.4	−7.5	14.6	271.1	240.9	15.0	20.6	−4.5
1983	259.8	226.6	234.0	80.6	153.4	83.5	69.9	−7.4	33.3	285.3	263.3	21.3	22.6	−3.2
1984	318.6	264.6	268.6	97.5	171.1	90.8	80.3	−4.0	54.0	327.1	289.8	21.1	30.3	−1.9
1985	332.5	257.5	257.5	99.4	158.1	97.6	60.5	.0	75.1	341.5	308.1	21.4	35.2	.6
1986	314.1	253.0	246.0	109.7	136.3	106.2	30.1	7.1	61.1	367.1	323.4	24.9	36.9	.9
1987	367.8	306.9	323.1	130.4	192.7	112.3	80.3	−16.2	61.0	366.7	347.5	30.3	34.1	.2
1988	426.6	367.7	389.9	141.6	248.3	129.9	118.4	−22.2	58.9	385.3	374.5	29.5	33.6	2.6
1989	425.6	374.1	390.5	146.1	244.4	158.0	86.4	−16.3	51.5	434.1	398.9	27.4	39.2	4.9
1990	434.4	398.8	411.7	145.4	266.3	169.1	97.2	−12.9	35.7	444.2	425.0	27.0	40.1	1.6
1991	457.3	430.3	425.4	138.6	286.8	180.7	106.1	4.9	27.0	418.2	457.1	27.5	39.9	5.7
1992	496.2	471.6	474.4	148.7	325.7	188.0	137.7	−2.8	24.6	387.7	483.4	30.1	40.7	8.2
1993	543.7	515.0	519.0	171.0	348.0	202.9	145.1	−4.0	28.7	364.6	503.1	36.7	40.5	8.7
1994	628.2	586.6	599.0	193.1	405.9	235.7	170.2	−12.4	41.6	362.2	545.2	32.5	41.9	9.6
1995	716.2	666.0	684.3	217.8	466.5	254.4	212.1	−18.3	50.2	358.3	557.9	34.8	45.8	13.1
1996	801.5	743.8	740.7	231.5	509.3	297.7	211.5	3.1	57.7	371.1	580.8	35.2	53.8	14.4
1997	884.8	815.9	801.8	245.4	556.3	331.2	225.1	14.1	69.0	407.6	611.6	33.8	51.3	14.1
1998	812.4	738.6	722.9	248.4	474.5	351.5	123.1	15.7	73.8	479.3	639.5	36.4	65.2	13.3
1999	856.3	776.6	780.5	258.8	521.7	337.4	184.3	−4.0	79.7	481.4	673.6	45.2	69.0	14.1
2000	819.2	755.7	772.5	265.1	507.4	377.9	129.5	−16.8	63.6	539.3	708.6	45.8	87.0	9.1
2001	784.2	720.8	712.7	203.3	509.4	370.9	138.5	8.0	63.4	544.4	727.7	58.7	101.3	4.0
2002	872.2	762.8	765.3	192.3	573.0	399.3	173.8	−2.6	109.4	506.4	762.8	41.4	82.4	6.3
2003	977.8	892.2	903.5	243.8	659.7	424.9	234.8	−11.3	85.6	504.1	806.8	49.1	76.1	7.0
2004	1,246.9	1,195.1	1,229.4	306.1	923.3	550.3	373.0	−34.3	51.8	461.6	863.4	46.4	81.7	1.2
2005	1,456.1	1,609.5	1,640.2	412.4	1,227.8	557.3	670.5	−30.7	−153.4	543.0	930.2	60.9	95.9	−3.5
2006	1,608.3	1,784.7	1,822.7	473.3	1,349.5	704.8	644.7	−38.0	−176.4	652.2	986.8	51.4	83.0	−4.2
2007	1,541.7	1,730.4	1,774.4	451.5	1,322.8	767.8	555.1	−44.0	−188.7	739.2	1,028.7	54.8	102.2	−6.6
2008	1,360.4	1,424.5	1,462.7	292.2	1,170.6	689.9	480.7	−38.2	−64.1	815.1	1,047.3	53.5	118.8	−6.9
2009 *p*	....	....	....	....	....	576.1	....	....	−127.7	786.2	1,023.9	59.7	134.0	−8.1
2006: I	1,590.9	1,781.9	1,815.3	460.7	1,354.6	646.4	708.2	−33.4	−191.0	608.9	971.5	55.6	82.8	−2.4
II	1,597.7	1,771.4	1,819.8	475.1	1,344.7	691.1	653.6	−48.4	−173.7	654.4	983.3	51.4	79.3	−3.8
III	1,655.1	1,822.8	1,865.1	496.6	1,368.5	727.1	641.4	−42.3	−167.7	661.6	991.6	49.8	83.6	−4.7
IV	1,589.6	1,762.7	1,790.7	460.7	1,330.0	754.5	575.5	−28.0	−173.2	684.0	1,000.7	48.7	86.1	−6.0
2007: I	1,535.4	1,705.4	1,747.6	469.5	1,278.1	772.6	505.5	−42.2	−170.0	690.6	1,015.3	49.2	97.8	−8.4
II	1,594.9	1,779.1	1,808.6	466.5	1,342.1	778.1	564.0	−29.5	−184.2	711.3	1,025.2	58.3	99.0	−6.9
III	1,537.1	1,732.9	1,758.2	440.0	1,318.2	770.6	547.6	−25.3	−195.8	756.0	1,032.2	56.0	105.0	−4.9
IV	1,499.4	1,704.1	1,783.1	430.1	1,353.0	749.9	603.2	−79.0	−204.7	798.9	1,042.3	55.4	107.0	−6.0
2008: I	1,459.7	1,512.9	1,620.8	323.2	1,297.6	719.4	578.2	−107.9	−53.2	790.7	1,042.5	53.1	114.8	−5.6
II	1,403.7	1,463.8	1,593.5	317.5	1,276.0	693.7	582.3	−129.6	−60.1	809.0	1,050.8	52.9	112.6	−6.3
III	1,454.6	1,522.2	1,576.6	304.8	1,271.9	676.6	595.3	−54.5	−67.6	806.1	1,058.5	52.9	116.0	−6.9
IV	1,123.6	1,199.3	1,060.1	223.3	836.8	669.9	166.9	139.2	−75.6	854.7	1,037.3	55.2	131.8	−8.9
2009: I	1,182.7	1,327.6	1,246.5	270.3	976.1	618.1	358.0	81.1	−144.9	826.2	1,018.6	55.5	137.9	−10.7
II	1,226.5	1,355.1	1,337.1	305.9	1,031.1	556.0	475.1	18.1	−128.6	784.4	1,019.6	54.9	145.4	−8.8
III	1,358.9	1,477.8	1,495.0	321.0	1,173.9	549.9	624.1	−17.1	−118.9	759.7	1,023.1	67.7	124.8	−6.3
IV *p*	....	....	....	....	....	580.5	....	....	−118.3	774.7	1,034.3	60.5	128.1	−6.6

Source: Department of Commerce (Bureau of Economic Analysis).

Table B–29. Sources of personal income, 1960–2009

[Billions of dollars; quarterly data at seasonally adjusted annual rates]

Year or quarter	Personal income	Compensation of employees, received							Proprietors' income with inventory valuation and capital consumption adjustments			Rental income of persons with capital consumption adjustment
		Total	Wage and salary disbursements			Supplements to wages and salaries			Total	Farm	Non-farm	
			Total	Private industries	Government	Total	Employer contributions for employee pension and insurance funds	Employer contributions for government social insurance				
1960	411.3	296.4	272.9	223.7	49.2	23.6	14.3	9.3	50.7	10.6	40.1	17.0
1961	428.8	305.3	280.5	228.0	52.5	24.8	15.2	9.6	53.2	11.2	42.0	17.7
1962	456.4	327.1	299.4	243.0	56.3	27.8	16.6	11.2	55.3	11.2	44.1	18.6
1963	479.5	345.2	314.9	254.8	60.0	30.4	18.0	12.4	56.5	11.0	45.5	19.3
1964	514.3	370.7	337.8	272.9	64.9	32.9	20.3	12.6	59.4	9.8	49.6	19.4
1965	555.5	399.5	363.8	293.8	69.9	35.7	22.7	13.1	63.9	12.0	51.9	19.9
1966	603.8	442.7	400.3	321.9	78.4	42.3	25.5	16.8	68.2	13.0	55.2	20.5
1967	648.1	475.1	429.0	342.5	86.5	46.1	28.1	18.0	69.8	11.6	58.2	20.9
1968	711.7	524.3	472.0	375.3	96.7	52.3	32.4	20.0	74.2	11.7	62.5	20.6
1969	778.3	577.6	518.3	412.7	105.6	59.3	36.5	22.8	77.5	12.8	64.7	20.9
1970	838.6	617.2	551.6	434.3	117.2	65.7	41.8	23.8	78.5	12.9	65.6	21.1
1971	903.1	658.3	584.0	457.4	126.6	74.4	47.9	26.4	84.7	13.4	71.3	22.2
1972	992.6	725.1	638.8	501.2	137.6	86.4	55.2	31.2	96.0	17.0	79.0	23.1
1973	1,110.5	811.3	708.8	560.0	148.8	102.5	62.7	39.8	113.6	29.1	84.6	23.9
1974	1,222.7	890.7	772.8	611.8	161.0	118.0	73.3	44.7	113.5	23.5	90.0	24.0
1975	1,334.9	949.0	814.7	638.6	176.1	134.3	87.6	46.7	119.6	22.0	97.6	23.4
1976	1,474.7	1,059.2	899.6	710.8	188.8	159.6	105.2	54.4	132.2	17.2	115.0	22.1
1977	1,632.5	1,180.4	994.1	791.6	202.5	186.4	125.3	61.1	146.0	16.0	130.1	19.6
1978	1,836.7	1,335.2	1,120.3	900.6	219.7	214.9	143.4	71.5	167.5	19.9	147.6	20.9
1979	2,059.5	1,498.5	1,253.5	1,016.2	237.3	245.0	162.4	82.6	181.1	22.2	159.0	22.6
1980	2,301.5	1,647.6	1,373.5	1,112.0	261.5	274.2	185.2	88.9	173.5	11.7	161.8	28.5
1981	2,582.3	1,819.6	1,511.3	1,225.5	285.8	308.3	204.7	103.6	181.6	19.0	162.6	36.5
1982	2,766.8	1,919.6	1,587.5	1,280.0	307.5	332.1	222.4	109.8	174.8	13.3	161.5	38.1
1983	2,952.2	2,036.0	1,678.0	1,352.7	325.2	358.0	238.1	119.9	190.7	6.2	184.5	38.2
1984	3,268.9	2,245.2	1,844.7	1,496.8	347.9	400.5	261.5	139.0	233.1	20.9	212.1	40.0
1985	3,496.7	2,412.0	1,982.8	1,608.7	374.1	429.2	281.5	147.7	246.1	21.0	225.1	41.9
1986	3,696.0	2,557.7	2,102.3	1,705.1	397.2	455.3	297.5	157.9	262.6	22.8	239.7	33.8
1987	3,924.4	2,735.6	2,256.3	1,833.1	423.1	479.4	313.1	166.3	294.2	28.9	265.3	34.2
1988	4,231.2	2,954.2	2,439.8	1,987.7	452.0	514.4	329.7	184.6	334.8	26.8	308.0	40.2
1989	4,557.5	3,131.3	2,583.1	2,101.9	481.1	548.3	354.6	193.7	351.6	33.0	318.6	42.4
1990	4,846.7	3,326.2	2,741.1	2,222.2	519.0	585.1	378.6	206.5	365.1	32.2	333.0	49.8
1991	5,031.5	3,438.4	2,814.5	2,265.7	548.8	623.9	408.7	215.1	367.3	27.5	339.8	61.6
1992	5,347.3	3,647.2	2,973.5	2,401.5	572.0	673.6	445.2	228.4	414.9	35.8	379.1	84.6
1993	5,568.1	3,790.6	3,076.6	2,487.6	589.0	714.1	474.4	239.7	449.6	32.0	417.6	114.1
1994	5,874.8	3,980.9	3,230.8	2,621.3	609.5	750.1	495.9	254.1	485.1	35.6	449.5	142.9
1995	6,200.9	4,178.8	3,418.0	2,789.0	629.0	760.8	496.7	264.1	516.0	23.4	492.6	154.6
1996	6,591.6	4,387.7	3,616.3	2,968.3	648.1	771.4	496.6	274.8	583.7	38.4	545.2	170.4
1997	7,000.7	4,668.6	3,876.6	3,204.8	671.8	792.0	502.4	289.6	628.2	32.6	595.6	176.5
1998	7,525.4	5,023.9	4,181.6	3,480.4	701.2	842.3	535.1	307.2	687.5	28.9	658.7	191.5
1999	7,910.8	5,348.8	4,460.0	3,726.3	733.7	888.8	565.4	323.3	746.8	28.5	718.3	208.2
2000	8,559.4	5,788.8	4,827.7	4,048.0	779.7	961.2	615.9	345.2	817.5	29.6	787.8	215.3
2001	8,883.3	5,979.3	4,952.2	4,130.3	821.9	1,027.1	669.1	358.0	870.7	30.5	840.2	232.4
2002	9,060.1	6,110.8	4,997.3	4,124.2	873.1	1,113.5	747.4	366.1	890.3	18.5	871.8	218.7
2003	9,378.1	6,367.6	5,139.6	4,226.3	913.3	1,228.0	845.6	382.4	930.6	36.5	894.1	204.2
2004	9,937.2	6,708.4	5,425.7	4,472.9	952.8	1,282.7	874.6	408.1	1,033.8	49.7	984.1	198.4
2005	10,485.9	7,060.0	5,701.0	4,709.5	991.5	1,359.1	931.6	427.5	1,069.8	43.9	1,025.9	178.2
2006	11,268.1	7,475.7	6,068.9	5,033.7	1,035.2	1,406.9	960.1	446.7	1,133.0	29.3	1,103.6	146.5
2007	11,894.1	7,862.7	6,408.9	5,319.8	1,089.1	1,453.8	993.0	460.8	1,096.4	39.4	1,056.9	144.9
2008	12,238.8	8,042.4	6,545.9	5,404.6	1,141.3	1,496.6	1,023.9	472.7	1,106.3	48.7	1,057.5	210.4
2009 ᵖ	12,072.1	7,836.3	6,330.6	5,148.1	1,182.5	1,505.7	1,043.9	461.8	1,042.3	29.9	1,012.4	268.3
2006: I	11,026.7	7,373.7	5,978.9	4,959.9	1,019.0	1,394.8	950.7	444.1	1,126.9	28.4	1,098.5	161.3
II	11,204.0	7,419.9	6,018.6	4,990.3	1,028.3	1,401.3	956.8	444.5	1,133.2	28.4	1,104.8	153.2
III	11,336.9	7,484.1	6,075.4	5,034.5	1,041.0	1,408.7	962.7	445.9	1,131.2	28.4	1,102.8	140.3
IV	11,504.8	7,625.3	6,202.6	5,150.4	1,052.3	1,422.6	970.4	452.2	1,140.6	32.2	1,108.4	131.2
2007: I	11,706.9	7,782.2	6,343.6	5,270.3	1,073.2	1,438.6	980.5	458.1	1,094.2	36.7	1,057.5	121.1
II	11,823.4	7,819.7	6,372.2	5,288.0	1,084.2	1,447.5	989.4	458.2	1,096.0	35.7	1,060.3	140.3
III	11,945.6	7,869.6	6,412.5	5,319.4	1,093.2	1,457.1	996.9	460.2	1,093.2	37.5	1,055.7	150.2
IV	12,100.3	7,979.3	6,507.3	5,401.4	1,105.8	1,472.1	1,005.2	466.9	1,102.1	47.9	1,054.2	168.0
2008: I	12,142.2	8,017.5	6,533.0	5,407.7	1,125.3	1,484.5	1,014.0	470.5	1,115.2	57.2	1,057.9	179.9
II	12,292.9	8,032.8	6,539.2	5,402.8	1,136.4	1,493.5	1,021.7	471.8	1,111.9	49.4	1,062.5	202.8
III	12,286.6	8,069.1	6,567.7	5,419.2	1,148.5	1,501.4	1,026.7	474.7	1,114.4	49.3	1,065.1	222.2
IV	12,233.5	8,050.3	6,543.5	5,388.6	1,154.9	1,506.8	1,033.2	473.6	1,083.6	39.0	1,044.5	236.7
2009: I	11,952.7	7,805.8	6,307.8	5,136.0	1,171.8	1,498.0	1,037.8	460.2	1,037.8	27.3	1,010.5	245.9
II	12,048.8	7,815.9	6,313.1	5,128.8	1,184.4	1,502.8	1,042.0	460.8	1,028.0	28.9	999.1	262.0
III	12,083.9	7,841.5	6,333.2	5,148.4	1,184.8	1,508.3	1,046.1	462.2	1,037.9	25.8	1,012.0	277.9
IV ᵖ	12,203.1	7,882.1	6,368.2	5,179.2	1,189.0	1,513.8	1,049.8	464.1	1,065.5	37.4	1,028.1	287.4

See next page for continuation of table.

TABLE B–29. Sources of personal income, 1960–2009—*Continued*

[Billions of dollars; quarterly data at seasonally adjusted annual rates]

Year or quarter	Personal income receipts on assets — Total	Personal interest income	Personal dividend income	Personal current transfer receipts — Total	Gov. social benefits — Total	Old-age, survivors, disability, and health insurance benefits	Government unemployment insurance benefits	Veterans benefits	Family assistance [1]	Other	Other current transfer receipts, from business (net)	Less: Contributions for government social insurance, domestic
1960	37.9	24.5	13.4	25.7	24.4	11.1	3.0	4.6	1.0	4.7	1.3	16.4
1961	40.1	26.2	13.9	29.5	28.1	12.6	4.3	5.0	1.1	5.1	1.4	17.0
1962	44.1	29.1	15.0	30.4	28.8	14.3	3.1	4.7	1.3	5.5	1.5	19.1
1963	47.9	31.7	16.2	32.2	30.3	15.2	3.0	4.8	1.4	5.9	1.9	21.7
1964	53.8	35.6	18.2	33.5	31.3	16.0	2.7	4.7	1.5	6.4	2.2	22.4
1965	59.4	39.2	20.2	36.2	33.9	18.1	2.3	4.9	1.7	7.0	2.3	23.4
1966	64.1	43.4	20.7	39.6	37.5	20.8	1.9	4.9	1.9	8.1	2.1	31.3
1967	69.0	47.5	21.5	48.0	45.8	25.8	2.2	5.6	2.3	9.9	2.3	34.9
1968	75.2	51.6	23.5	56.1	53.3	30.5	2.1	5.9	2.8	11.9	2.8	38.7
1969	84.1	59.9	24.2	62.3	59.0	33.1	2.2	6.7	3.5	13.4	3.3	44.1
1970	93.5	69.2	24.3	74.7	71.7	38.6	4.0	7.7	4.8	16.6	2.9	46.4
1971	101.0	75.9	25.0	88.1	85.4	44.7	5.8	8.8	6.2	20.0	2.7	51.2
1972	109.6	82.8	26.8	97.9	94.8	49.8	5.7	9.7	6.9	22.7	3.1	59.2
1973	124.7	94.8	29.9	112.6	108.6	60.9	4.4	10.4	7.2	25.7	3.9	75.5
1974	146.4	113.2	33.2	133.3	128.6	70.3	6.8	11.8	8.0	31.7	4.7	85.2
1975	162.2	129.3	32.9	170.0	163.1	81.5	17.6	14.5	9.3	40.2	6.8	89.3
1976	178.4	139.5	39.0	184.0	177.3	93.3	15.8	14.4	10.1	43.7	6.7	101.3
1977	205.3	160.6	44.7	194.2	189.1	105.3	12.7	13.8	10.6	46.7	5.1	113.1
1978	234.8	184.0	50.7	209.6	203.2	116.9	9.1	13.9	10.8	52.5	6.5	131.3
1979	274.7	217.3	57.4	235.3	227.1	132.5	9.4	14.4	11.1	59.6	8.2	152.7
1980	338.7	274.7	64.0	279.5	270.8	154.8	15.7	15.0	12.5	72.8	8.6	166.2
1981	421.9	348.3	73.6	318.4	307.2	182.1	15.6	16.1	13.1	80.2	11.2	195.7
1982	488.4	410.8	77.6	354.8	342.4	204.6	25.1	16.4	12.9	83.4	12.4	208.9
1983	529.6	446.3	83.3	383.7	369.9	222.2	26.2	16.6	13.8	91.0	13.8	226.0
1984	607.9	517.2	90.6	400.1	380.4	237.8	15.9	16.4	14.5	95.9	19.7	257.5
1985	653.2	555.8	97.4	424.9	402.6	253.0	15.7	16.7	15.2	102.0	22.3	281.4
1986	694.5	588.4	106.0	451.0	428.0	268.9	16.3	16.7	16.1	109.9	22.9	303.4
1987	715.8	603.6	112.2	467.6	447.4	282.6	14.5	16.6	16.4	117.3	20.2	323.1
1988	767.0	637.3	129.7	496.5	475.9	300.2	13.2	16.9	16.9	128.7	20.6	361.5
1989	874.8	717.0	157.8	542.6	519.4	325.6	14.3	17.3	17.5	144.8	23.2	385.2
1990	920.8	751.9	168.8	594.9	572.7	351.8	18.0	17.8	19.2	165.9	22.2	410.1
1991	928.6	748.2	180.3	665.9	648.2	381.7	26.6	18.3	21.1	200.5	17.6	430.2
1992	909.7	722.2	187.6	745.8	729.5	414.4	38.9	19.3	22.2	234.6	16.3	455.0
1993	900.5	698.1	202.3	790.8	776.7	444.7	34.1	20.0	22.8	255.0	14.1	477.4
1994	947.7	712.7	235.0	826.4	813.1	476.6	23.5	20.1	23.2	269.7	13.3	508.2
1995	1,005.4	751.9	253.4	878.9	860.2	508.9	21.4	20.9	22.6	286.4	18.7	532.8
1996	1,080.7	784.4	296.4	924.1	901.2	536.9	22.0	21.7	20.3	300.3	22.9	555.1
1997	1,165.5	835.8	329.7	949.2	929.8	563.5	19.9	22.6	17.9	306.0	19.4	587.2
1998	1,269.2	919.3	349.8	977.9	951.9	574.7	19.5	23.5	17.4	316.8	26.0	624.7
1999	1,246.8	910.9	335.9	1,021.6	987.6	586.6	20.3	24.3	17.9	336.4	34.0	661.3
2000	1,360.7	984.2	376.5	1,083.0	1,040.6	620.5	20.6	25.2	18.4	355.9	42.4	705.8
2001	1,346.0	976.5	369.5	1,188.1	1,141.3	667.7	31.7	26.8	18.1	397.1	46.8	733.2
2002	1,309.6	911.9	397.7	1,282.1	1,247.9	706.1	53.2	29.8	17.7	441.1	34.2	751.5
2003	1,312.9	889.8	423.1	1,341.7	1,316.0	740.4	52.8	32.2	18.4	472.3	25.7	778.9
2004	1,408.5	860.2	548.3	1,415.5	1,398.6	790.2	36.0	34.5	18.4	519.6	16.9	827.3
2005	1,542.0	987.0	555.0	1,508.6	1,482.7	844.7	31.3	36.8	18.2	551.7	25.8	872.7
2006	1,829.7	1,127.5	702.2	1,605.0	1,583.6	943.3	29.9	39.3	18.2	552.9	21.4	921.8
2007	2,031.5	1,266.4	765.1	1,718.0	1,687.8	1,003.7	32.3	42.1	18.5	591.2	30.2	959.3
2008 *p*	1,994.4	1,308.0	686.4	1,875.9	1,843.2	1,070.3	50.6	45.6	18.9	657.9	32.6	990.6
2009 *p*	1,791.5	1,236.9	554.6	2,106.9	2,074.2	1,156.7	120.3	51.5	19.8	725.9	32.7	973.2
2006: I	1,711.1	1,067.2	643.9	1,569.0	1,547.3	917.5	29.6	38.9	18.2	543.1	21.7	915.4
II	1,817.2	1,128.7	688.5	1,597.9	1,578.0	941.6	29.4	39.2	18.2	549.6	19.8	917.4
III	1,881.3	1,156.8	724.5	1,620.7	1,600.1	950.7	30.4	39.5	18.2	561.3	20.6	920.8
IV	1,909.0	1,157.2	751.9	1,632.4	1,609.1	963.4	30.3	39.7	18.3	557.4	23.3	933.8
2007: I	1,968.2	1,198.3	769.9	1,693.8	1,666.7	981.0	31.4	41.0	18.4	595.0	27.1	952.5
II	2,022.0	1,246.5	775.5	1,699.1	1,669.3	998.2	31.2	42.0	18.4	579.5	29.8	953.7
III	2,065.8	1,297.9	767.9	1,725.5	1,693.9	1,012.7	32.8	42.2	18.5	587.7	31.6	958.6
IV	2,069.8	1,322.8	747.0	1,753.7	1,721.2	1,023.1	33.9	43.0	18.6	602.7	32.4	972.6
2008: I	2,020.8	1,304.6	716.2	1,794.1	1,761.5	1,049.1	35.7	44.8	18.6	613.3	32.6	985.3
II	1,997.3	1,306.6	690.7	1,937.0	1,904.4	1,064.5	38.7	45.0	18.8	737.5	32.6	988.9
III	2,001.4	1,327.8	673.7	1,874.3	1,841.7	1,080.5	57.7	46.1	18.9	638.5	32.6	994.9
IV	1,958.1	1,292.9	665.2	1,898.0	1,865.3	1,087.0	70.3	46.5	19.2	642.3	32.7	993.3
2009: I	1,845.5	1,243.4	602.1	1,987.3	1,954.7	1,128.5	96.2	50.3	19.5	660.4	32.5	969.7
II	1,773.4	1,241.1	532.3	2,140.3	2,107.7	1,151.1	122.5	50.5	19.7	763.9	32.7	970.9
III	1,763.1	1,234.9	528.2	2,137.5	2,104.7	1,165.8	135.7	52.0	19.9	731.2	32.8	974.0
IV *p*	1,784.0	1,228.2	555.8	2,162.5	2,129.6	1,181.5	126.7	53.3	20.1	748.1	32.9	978.4

[1] Consists of aid to families with dependent children and, beginning in 1996, assistance programs operating under the Personal Responsibility and Work Opportunity Reconciliation Act of 1996.

Source: Department of Commerce (Bureau of Economic Analysis).

Table B–30. Disposition of personal income, 1960–2009

[Billions of dollars, except as noted; quarterly data at seasonally adjusted annual rates]

Year or quarter	Personal income	Less: Personal current taxes	Equals: Disposable personal income	Less: Personal outlays — Total	Personal consumption expenditures	Personal interest payments [1]	Personal current transfer payments	Equals: Personal saving	Percent of disposable personal income [2] — Personal outlays Total	Personal consumption expenditures	Personal saving
1960	411.3	46.1	365.2	338.9	331.8	6.2	0.8	26.3	92.8	90.9	7.2
1961	428.8	47.3	381.6	349.7	342.2	6.5	1.0	31.9	91.6	89.7	8.4
1962	456.4	51.6	404.9	371.4	363.3	7.0	1.1	33.5	91.7	89.7	8.3
1963	479.5	54.6	425.0	391.8	382.7	7.9	1.2	33.1	92.2	90.0	7.8
1964	514.3	52.1	462.3	421.7	411.5	8.9	1.3	40.5	91.2	89.0	8.8
1965	555.5	57.7	497.8	455.1	443.8	9.9	1.4	42.7	91.4	89.2	8.6
1966	603.8	66.4	537.4	493.1	480.9	10.7	1.6	44.3	91.8	89.5	8.2
1967	648.1	73.0	575.1	520.9	507.8	11.1	2.0	54.2	90.6	88.3	9.4
1968	711.7	87.0	624.7	572.2	558.0	12.2	2.0	52.5	91.6	89.3	8.4
1969	778.3	104.5	673.8	621.4	605.1	14.0	2.2	52.5	92.2	89.8	7.8
1970	838.6	103.1	735.5	666.1	648.3	15.2	2.6	69.4	90.6	88.1	9.4
1971	903.1	101.7	801.4	721.0	701.6	16.6	2.8	80.4	90.0	87.5	10.0
1972	992.6	123.6	869.0	791.5	770.2	18.1	3.2	77.5	91.1	88.6	8.9
1973	1,110.5	132.4	978.1	875.2	852.0	19.8	3.4	102.9	89.5	87.1	10.5
1974	1,222.7	151.0	1,071.7	957.5	932.9	21.2	3.4	114.2	89.3	87.0	10.7
1975	1,334.9	147.6	1,187.3	1,061.3	1,033.8	23.7	3.8	125.9	89.4	87.1	10.6
1976	1,474.7	172.3	1,302.3	1,179.6	1,151.3	23.9	4.4	122.8	90.6	88.4	9.4
1977	1,632.5	197.5	1,435.0	1,309.7	1,277.8	27.0	4.8	125.3	91.3	89.0	8.7
1978	1,836.7	229.4	1,607.3	1,465.0	1,427.6	31.9	5.4	142.4	91.1	88.8	8.9
1979	2,059.5	268.7	1,790.9	1,633.4	1,591.2	36.2	6.0	157.5	91.2	88.8	8.8
1980	2,301.5	298.9	2,002.7	1,806.4	1,755.8	43.6	6.9	196.3	90.2	87.7	9.8
1981	2,582.3	345.2	2,237.1	2,000.4	1,939.5	49.3	11.5	236.7	89.4	86.7	10.6
1982	2,766.8	354.1	2,412.7	2,148.8	2,075.5	59.5	13.8	263.9	89.1	86.0	10.9
1983	2,952.2	352.3	2,599.8	2,372.9	2,288.6	69.2	15.1	226.9	91.3	88.0	8.7
1984	3,268.9	377.4	2,891.5	2,595.2	2,501.1	77.0	17.1	296.3	89.8	86.5	10.2
1985	3,496.7	417.3	3,079.3	2,825.7	2,717.6	89.4	18.8	253.6	91.8	88.3	8.2
1986	3,696.0	437.2	3,258.8	3,012.4	2,896.7	94.5	21.1	246.5	92.4	88.9	7.6
1987	3,924.4	489.1	3,435.3	3,211.9	3,097.0	91.7	23.2	223.4	93.5	90.2	6.5
1988	4,231.2	504.9	3,726.3	3,469.7	3,350.1	94.0	25.6	256.6	93.1	89.9	6.9
1989	4,557.5	566.1	3,991.4	3,726.4	3,594.5	103.9	28.0	265.0	93.4	90.1	6.6
1990	4,846.7	592.7	4,254.0	3,977.3	3,835.5	111.3	30.6	276.7	93.5	90.2	6.5
1991	5,031.5	586.6	4,444.9	4,131.7	3,980.1	115.0	36.7	313.2	93.0	89.5	7.0
1992	5,347.3	610.5	4,736.7	4,388.7	4,236.9	111.3	40.5	348.1	92.7	89.4	7.3
1993	5,568.1	646.5	4,921.6	4,636.2	4,483.6	107.0	45.6	285.4	94.2	91.1	5.8
1994	5,874.8	690.5	5,184.3	4,913.6	4,750.8	113.0	49.8	270.7	94.8	91.6	5.2
1995	6,200.9	743.9	5,457.0	5,170.8	4,987.3	130.6	52.9	286.3	94.8	91.4	5.2
1996	6,591.6	832.0	5,759.6	5,478.5	5,273.6	147.3	57.6	281.1	95.1	91.6	4.9
1997	7,000.7	926.2	6,074.6	5,794.2	5,570.6	159.7	63.9	280.4	95.4	91.7	4.6
1998	7,525.4	1,026.4	6,498.9	6,157.5	5,918.5	169.5	69.5	341.5	94.7	91.1	5.3
1999	7,910.8	1,107.5	6,803.3	6,595.5	6,342.8	176.5	76.2	207.8	96.9	93.2	3.1
2000	8,559.4	1,232.3	7,327.2	7,114.1	6,830.4	200.3	83.4	213.1	97.1	93.2	2.9
2001	8,883.3	1,234.8	7,648.5	7,443.5	7,148.8	200.7	91.0	204.9	97.3	93.5	2.7
2002	9,060.1	1,050.4	8,009.7	7,727.5	7,439.2	191.3	97.0	282.2	96.5	92.9	3.5
2003	9,378.1	1,000.3	8,377.8	8,088.0	7,804.0	182.7	101.3	289.8	96.5	93.2	3.5
2004	9,937.2	1,047.8	8,889.4	8,585.7	8,285.1	190.3	110.3	303.7	96.6	93.2	3.4
2005	10,485.9	1,208.6	9,277.3	9,149.6	8,819.0	210.8	119.8	127.7	98.6	95.1	1.4
2006	11,268.1	1,352.4	9,915.7	9,680.7	9,322.7	230.1	128.0	235.0	97.6	94.0	2.4
2007	11,894.1	1,490.9	10,403.1	10,224.3	9,826.4	256.8	141.0	178.9	98.3	94.5	1.7
2008	12,238.8	1,432.4	10,806.4	10,520.0	10,129.9	237.7	152.3	286.4	97.3	93.7	2.7
2009 ᴾ	12,072.1	1,107.6	10,964.5	10,461.8	10,092.6	214.3	154.9	502.7	95.4	92.0	4.6
2006: I	11,026.7	1,321.5	9,705.2	9,493.5	9,148.2	223.9	121.4	211.7	97.8	94.3	2.2
II	11,204.0	1,340.2	9,863.8	9,618.2	9,266.6	223.7	127.8	245.6	97.5	93.9	2.5
III	11,336.9	1,354.3	9,982.5	9,754.9	9,391.8	233.5	129.6	227.7	97.7	94.1	2.3
IV	11,504.8	1,393.5	10,111.2	9,856.4	9,484.1	239.2	133.2	254.8	97.5	93.8	2.5
2007: I	11,706.9	1,459.5	10,247.4	10,038.3	9,658.5	242.1	137.8	209.1	98.0	94.3	2.0
II	11,823.4	1,481.8	10,341.7	10,158.2	9,762.5	256.2	139.4	183.5	98.2	94.4	1.8
III	11,945.6	1,500.7	10,445.0	10,275.6	9,865.6	268.2	141.8	169.4	98.4	94.5	1.6
IV	12,100.3	1,521.9	10,578.4	10,425.0	10,019.2	260.7	145.0	153.5	98.5	94.7	1.5
2008: I	12,142.2	1,531.8	10,610.4	10,484.1	10,095.1	239.8	149.2	126.3	98.8	95.1	1.2
II	12,292.9	1,326.2	10,966.7	10,592.2	10,194.7	243.9	153.6	374.4	96.6	93.0	3.4
III	12,286.6	1,437.3	10,849.3	10,613.6	10,220.1	238.3	155.2	235.7	97.8	94.2	2.2
IV	12,233.5	1,434.3	10,799.1	10,389.9	10,009.8	228.8	151.3	409.2	96.2	92.7	3.8
2009: I	11,952.7	1,187.3	10,765.4	10,362.3	9,987.7	220.4	154.2	403.1	96.3	92.8	3.7
II	12,048.8	1,082.6	10,966.2	10,370.5	9,999.3	216.7	154.5	595.7	94.6	91.2	5.4
III	12,083.9	1,086.1	10,997.8	10,502.8	10,132.9	215.5	154.4	495.0	95.5	92.1	4.5
IV ᴾ	12,203.1	1,074.4	11,128.6	10,611.8	10,250.5	204.7	156.6	516.9	95.4	92.1	4.6

[1] Consists of nonmortgage interest paid by households.
[2] Percents based on data in millions of dollars.

Source: Department of Commerce (Bureau of Economic Analysis).

TABLE B–31. Total and per capita disposable personal income and personal consumption expenditures, and per capita gross domestic product, in current and real dollars, 1960–2009

[Quarterly data at seasonally adjusted annual rates, except as noted]

Year or quarter	Disposable personal income Total (billions of dollars) Current dollars	Disposable personal income Total (billions of dollars) Chained (2005) dollars	Disposable personal income Per capita (dollars) Current dollars	Disposable personal income Per capita (dollars) Chained (2005) dollars	Personal consumption expenditures Total (billions of dollars) Current dollars	Personal consumption expenditures Total (billions of dollars) Chained (2005) dollars	Personal consumption expenditures Per capita (dollars) Current dollars	Personal consumption expenditures Per capita (dollars) Chained (2005) dollars	Gross domestic product per capita (dollars) Current dollars	Gross domestic product per capita (dollars) Chained (2005) dollars	Population (thousands)[1]
1960	365.2	1,963.9	2,020	10,865	331.8	1,784.4	1,836	9,871	2,912	15,661	180,760
1961	381.6	2,030.8	2,077	11,052	342.2	1,821.2	1,862	9,911	2,965	15,766	183,742
1962	404.9	2,129.6	2,170	11,413	363.3	1,911.2	1,947	10,243	3,139	16,466	186,590
1963	425.0	2,209.5	2,245	11,672	382.7	1,989.9	2,022	10,512	3,263	16,940	189,300
1964	462.3	2,368.7	2,408	12,342	411.5	2,108.4	2,144	10,985	3,458	17,675	191,927
1965	497.8	2,514.7	2,562	12,939	443.8	2,241.8	2,284	11,535	3,700	18,576	194,347
1966	537.4	2,647.3	2,733	13,465	480.9	2,369.0	2,446	12,050	4,007	19,559	196,599
1967	575.1	2,763.5	2,894	13,904	507.8	2,440.0	2,555	12,276	4,188	19,836	198,752
1968	624.7	2,889.2	3,112	14,392	558.0	2,580.7	2,780	12,856	4,532	20,590	200,745
1969	673.8	2,981.4	3,324	14,706	605.1	2,677.4	2,985	13,206	4,856	21,021	202,736
1970	735.5	3,108.8	3,586	15,158	648.3	2,740.2	3,161	13,361	5,063	20,820	205,089
1971	801.4	3,249.1	3,859	15,644	701.6	2,844.6	3,378	13,696	5,425	21,249	207,692
1972	869.0	3,406.6	4,140	16,228	770.2	3,019.5	3,669	14,384	5,897	22,140	209,924
1973	978.1	3,638.2	4,615	17,166	852.0	3,169.1	4,020	14,953	6,522	23,200	211,939
1974	1,071.7	3,610.2	5,010	16,878	932.9	3,142.8	4,362	14,693	7,010	22,861	213,898
1975	1,187.3	3,691.3	5,497	17,091	1,033.8	3,214.1	4,786	14,881	7,583	22,592	215,981
1976	1,302.3	3,838.3	5,972	17,600	1,151.3	3,393.1	5,279	15,558	8,366	23,575	218,086
1977	1,435.0	3,970.7	6,514	18,025	1,277.8	3,535.9	5,801	16,051	9,216	24,412	220,289
1978	1,607.3	4,156.5	7,220	18,670	1,427.6	3,691.8	6,413	16,583	10,303	25,503	222,629
1979	1,790.9	4,253.8	7,956	18,897	1,591.2	3,779.5	7,069	16,790	11,382	26,010	225,106
1980	2,002.7	4,295.6	8,794	18,863	1,755.8	3,766.2	7,710	16,538	12,243	25,640	227,726
1981	2,237.1	4,410.0	9,726	19,173	1,939.5	3,823.3	8,432	16,623	13,594	26,030	230,008
1982	2,412.7	4,506.5	10,390	19,406	2,075.5	3,876.7	8,938	16,694	14,009	25,282	232,218
1983	2,599.8	4,655.7	11,095	19,868	2,288.6	4,098.3	9,766	17,489	15,084	26,186	234,333
1984	2,891.5	4,989.1	12,232	21,105	2,501.1	4,315.6	10,580	18,256	16,629	27,823	236,394
1985	3,079.3	5,144.8	12,911	21,571	2,717.6	4,540.4	11,394	19,031	17,683	28,717	238,506
1986	3,258.8	5,315.0	13,540	22,083	2,896.7	4,724.5	12,036	19,630	18,531	29,443	240,683
1987	3,435.3	5,402.4	14,146	22,246	3,097.0	4,870.3	12,753	20,055	19,504	30,115	242,843
1988	3,726.3	5,635.6	15,206	22,997	3,350.1	5,066.6	13,670	20,675	20,813	31,069	245,061
1989	3,991.4	5,785.1	16,134	23,385	3,594.5	5,209.9	14,530	21,060	22,160	31,877	247,387
1990	4,254.0	5,896.3	17,004	23,568	3,835.5	5,316.2	15,331	21,249	23,185	32,112	250,181
1991	4,444.9	5,945.9	17,532	23,453	3,980.1	5,324.2	15,699	21,000	23,635	31,614	253,530
1992	4,736.7	6,155.3	18,436	23,958	4,236.9	5,505.7	16,491	21,432	24,686	32,255	256,922
1993	4,921.6	6,258.2	18,909	24,044	4,483.6	5,701.2	17,226	21,904	25,616	32,747	260,282
1994	5,184.3	6,459.0	19,678	24,517	4,750.8	5,918.9	18,033	22,466	26,893	33,671	263,455
1995	5,457.0	6,651.6	20,470	24,951	4,987.3	6,079.0	18,708	22,803	27,813	34,112	266,588
1996	5,759.6	6,870.9	21,355	25,475	5,273.6	6,291.2	19,553	23,325	29,062	34,977	269,714
1997	6,074.6	7,113.5	22,255	26,061	5,570.6	6,523.4	20,408	23,899	30,526	36,102	272,958
1998	6,498.9	7,538.8	23,534	27,299	5,918.5	6,865.5	21,432	24,861	31,843	37,238	276,154
1999	6,803.3	7,766.7	24,356	27,805	6,342.8	7,240.9	22,707	25,923	33,486	38,592	279,328
2000	7,327.2	8,161.5	25,944	28,899	6,830.4	7,608.1	24,185	26,939	35,237	39,750	282,418
2001	7,648.5	8,360.1	26,805	29,299	7,148.8	7,813.9	25,054	27,385	36,049	39,768	285,335
2002	8,009.7	8,637.1	27,799	29,976	7,439.2	8,021.9	25,819	27,841	36,935	40,096	288,133
2003	8,377.8	8,853.9	28,805	30,442	7,804.0	8,247.6	26,832	28,357	38,310	40,711	290,845
2004	8,889.4	9,155.1	30,287	31,193	8,285.1	8,532.7	28,228	29,072	40,435	41,784	293,502
2005	9,277.3	9,277.3	31,318	31,318	8,819.0	8,819.0	29,771	29,771	42,664	42,664	296,229
2006	9,915.7	9,650.7	33,157	32,271	9,322.7	9,073.5	31,174	30,341	44,805	43,391	299,052
2007	10,403.1	9,860.6	34,445	32,648	9,826.4	9,313.9	32,535	30,838	46,611	43,884	302,025
2008	10,806.4	9,911.3	35,450	32,514	10,129.9	9,290.9	33,231	30,479	47,375	43,671	304,831
2009 ᵖ	10,964.5	10,035.3	35,659	32,637	10,092.6	9,237.3	32,823	30,042	46,372	42,242	307,484
2006: I	9,705.2	9,533.8	32,572	31,997	9,148.2	8,986.6	30,703	30,161	44,246	43,348	297,959
II	9,863.8	9,617.3	33,031	32,205	9,266.6	9,035.0	31,031	30,255	44,698	43,407	298,625
III	9,982.5	9,662.5	33,341	32,272	9,391.8	9,090.7	31,367	30,362	44,931	43,305	299,411
IV	10,111.2	9,788.8	33,680	32,606	9,484.1	9,181.6	31,591	30,584	45,340	43,505	300,213
2007: I	10,247.4	9,830.2	34,055	32,668	9,658.5	9,265.1	32,097	30,790	45,846	43,534	300,913
II	10,341.7	9,842.7	34,287	32,633	9,762.5	9,291.5	32,367	30,806	46,407	43,777	301,617
III	10,445.0	9,883.9	34,540	32,684	9,865.6	9,335.6	32,624	30,871	46,890	44,050	302,406
IV	10,578.4	9,886.2	34,893	32,610	10,019.2	9,363.6	33,049	30,886	47,294	44,171	303,166
2008: I	10,610.4	9,826.8	34,925	32,345	10,095.1	9,349.6	33,228	30,774	47,312	43,997	303,810
II	10,966.7	10,059.0	36,022	33,041	10,194.7	9,351.0	33,486	30,715	47,620	44,065	304,445
III	10,849.3	9,838.3	35,551	32,238	10,220.1	9,267.7	33,489	30,368	47,666	43,662	305,177
IV	10,799.1	9,920.4	35,304	32,431	10,009.8	9,195.3	32,724	30,061	46,904	42,963	305,890
2009: I	10,765.4	9,926.4	35,124	32,387	9,987.7	9,209.2	32,587	30,047	46,258	42,172	306,496
II	10,966.2	10,077.5	35,709	32,815	9,999.3	9,189.0	32,560	29,922	46,080	42,011	307,101
III	10,997.8	10,042.3	35,728	32,625	10,132.9	9,252.6	32,919	30,059	46,268	42,146	307,815
IV ᵖ	11,128.6	10,095.1	36,071	32,721	10,250.5	9,298.5	33,225	30,139	46,880	42,639	308,522

[1] Population of the United States including Armed Forces overseas; includes Alaska and Hawaii beginning in 1960. Annual data are averages of quarterly data. Quarterly data are averages for the period.

Source: Department of Commerce (Bureau of Economic Analysis and Bureau of the Census).

National Income or Expenditure | 367

TABLE B–32. Gross saving and investment, 1960–2009

[Billions of dollars, except as noted; quarterly data at seasonally adjusted annual rates]

Year or quarter	Total gross saving	Gross saving — Net saving — Total net saving	Net private saving — Total	Net private saving — Personal saving	Net private saving — Undistributed corporate profits[1]	Net private saving — Wage accruals less disbursements	Net government saving — Total	Net government saving — Federal	Net government saving — State and local	Consumption of fixed capital — Total	Consumption of fixed capital — Private	Consumption of fixed capital — Government
1960	111.3	54.7	43.3	26.3	16.9	0.0	11.4	7.1	4.3	56.6	41.6	15.0
1961	114.3	56.1	49.3	31.9	17.4	.0	6.8	2.6	4.3	58.2	42.6	15.6
1962	124.9	64.3	56.7	33.5	23.2	.0	7.7	2.4	5.2	60.6	44.1	16.5
1963	133.2	69.8	58.8	33.1	25.7	.0	11.0	5.3	5.7	63.3	45.9	17.5
1964	143.4	77.0	69.7	40.5	29.2	.0	7.3	.9	6.4	66.4	48.3	18.1
1965	158.5	87.7	78.0	42.7	35.3	.0	9.8	3.2	6.5	70.7	51.9	18.9
1966	168.7	92.3	82.3	44.3	38.0	.0	10.0	2.3	7.8	76.5	56.5	20.0
1967	170.6	87.6	89.9	54.2	35.8	.0	-2.3	-9.3	7.0	82.9	61.6	21.4
1968	182.0	91.6	86.6	52.5	34.1	.0	5.1	-2.4	7.5	90.4	67.4	23.0
1969	198.4	99.3	82.7	52.5	30.3	.0	16.5	8.6	8.0	99.2	74.5	24.7
1970	192.8	84.5	92.9	69.4	23.4	.0	-8.4	-15.5	7.1	108.3	81.7	26.6
1971	209.2	91.5	113.7	80.4	32.9	.4	-22.2	-28.7	6.5	117.8	89.5	28.2
1972	237.3	110.1	119.4	77.5	42.2	-.3	-9.3	-24.9	15.6	127.2	97.7	29.4
1973	292.2	151.4	147.5	102.9	44.6	.0	3.9	-11.8	15.7	140.8	109.5	31.3
1974	301.8	138.1	143.3	114.2	29.1	.0	-5.2	-14.5	9.3	163.7	127.8	35.9
1975	296.9	106.5	174.6	125.9	48.7	.0	-68.2	-70.6	2.5	190.4	150.4	39.9
1976	342.0	133.8	180.1	122.8	57.3	.0	-46.3	-53.7	7.4	208.2	165.5	42.6
1977	396.7	164.9	197.9	125.3	72.6	.0	-33.0	-46.1	13.1	231.8	186.1	45.6
1978	476.3	214.9	225.2	142.4	82.8	.0	-10.2	-28.9	18.7	261.4	212.0	49.5
1979	533.2	234.3	235.3	157.5	77.8	.0	-1.0	-14.0	13.0	298.9	244.5	54.4
1980	542.7	198.6	246.5	196.3	50.2	.0	-47.8	-56.6	8.8	344.1	282.3	61.8
1981	646.1	252.7	301.9	236.7	65.2	.0	-49.2	-56.8	7.6	393.3	323.2	70.1
1982	621.5	187.9	325.4	263.9	61.5	.0	-137.5	-135.3	-2.2	433.5	356.4	77.1
1983	602.4	151.3	322.6	226.9	95.7	.0	-171.4	-176.2	4.9	451.1	369.5	81.6
1984	753.4	279.0	426.5	296.3	130.3	.0	-147.5	-171.5	23.9	474.3	387.5	86.9
1985	738.4	232.9	389.2	253.6	135.6	.0	-156.3	-178.6	22.4	505.4	412.8	92.7
1986	709.3	170.8	344.7	246.5	98.3	.0	-173.9	-194.6	20.7	538.5	439.1	99.4
1987	782.3	211.2	348.5	223.4	125.1	.0	-137.4	-149.3	12.0	571.1	464.5	106.6
1988	901.5	290.5	411.7	256.6	155.1	.0	-121.2	-138.4	17.2	611.0	497.1	113.9
1989	924.1	272.7	386.5	265.0	121.5	.0	-113.8	-133.9	20.1	651.5	529.6	121.8
1990	917.6	226.4	396.7	276.7	120.0	.0	-170.3	-176.4	6.2	691.2	560.4	130.8
1991	951.3	227.0	451.2	313.2	138.0	.0	-224.2	-218.4	-5.8	724.4	585.4	138.9
1992	932.3	187.9	491.8	348.1	159.5	-15.8	-303.9	-302.5	-1.4	744.4	599.9	144.5
1993	958.4	180.4	461.6	285.4	169.7	6.4	-281.2	-280.2	-.9	778.0	626.4	151.6
1994	1,094.7	275.5	487.7	270.7	199.4	17.6	-212.2	-220.4	8.2	819.2	661.0	158.2
1995	1,219.0	349.6	546.6	286.3	243.9	16.4	-197.0	-206.2	9.2	869.5	704.6	164.8
1996	1,344.4	431.8	557.1	281.1	272.3	3.6	-125.3	-148.2	23.0	912.5	743.4	169.2
1997	1,525.7	561.9	585.7	280.4	308.2	-2.9	-23.8	-60.1	36.3	963.8	789.7	174.1
1998	1,654.4	633.9	553.4	341.5	212.6	-.7	80.5	33.6	46.9	1,020.5	841.6	179.0
1999	1,708.0	613.6	473.0	207.8	260.1	5.2	140.6	98.8	41.8	1,094.4	907.2	187.2
2000	1,800.1	615.8	389.4	213.1	176.3	.0	226.5	185.2	41.3	1,184.3	986.8	197.5
2001	1,695.7	439.4	414.9	204.9	210.0	.0	24.6	40.5	-15.9	1,256.2	1,051.6	204.6
2002	1,560.9	255.9	562.8	282.2	280.6	.0	-306.9	-252.8	-54.1	1,305.0	1,094.0	210.9
2003	1,552.8	198.7	613.9	289.8	309.2	15.0	-415.2	-376.4	-38.8	1,354.1	1,135.9	218.1
2004	1,724.2	291.4	679.2	303.7	390.5	-15.0	-387.8	-379.5	-8.4	1,432.8	1,200.9	231.9
2005	1,903.4	362.0	619.1	127.7	486.4	5.0	-257.1	-283.0	25.9	1,541.4	1,290.8	250.6
2006	2,174.4	513.7	666.5	235.0	430.3	1.3	-152.7	-203.8	51.0	1,660.7	1,391.4	269.3
2007	2,040.2	280.2	495.0	178.9	322.4	-6.3	-214.8	-236.5	21.7	1,760.0	1,469.6	290.4
2008	1,824.1	-23.0	659.8	286.4	378.3	-5.0	-682.7	-642.6	-40.2	1,847.1	1,536.2	310.9
2009 p	....	....	....	....	502.7	5.0	....	....	....	1,863.7	1,538.4	325.3
2006: I	2,148.9	530.9	675.6	211.7	483.9	-20.0	-144.7	-207.3	62.6	1,618.0	1,357.4	260.6
II	2,159.2	511.0	677.2	245.6	431.5	.0	-166.2	-229.4	63.2	1,648.2	1,381.1	267.1
III	2,161.2	485.9	659.0	227.7	431.4	.0	-173.1	-215.5	42.4	1,675.2	1,403.2	272.0
IV	2,228.4	527.1	654.1	254.8	374.3	25.0	-127.0	-163.0	35.9	1,701.3	1,423.9	277.4
2007: I	2,036.1	309.3	477.4	209.1	293.3	-25.0	-168.1	-200.9	32.8	1,726.7	1,443.1	283.7
II	2,096.8	347.4	533.8	183.5	350.3	.0	-186.3	-221.3	34.9	1,749.4	1,461.4	288.0
III	2,028.7	257.5	495.9	169.4	326.5	.0	-238.4	-258.8	20.3	1,771.2	1,478.7	292.5
IV	1,999.3	206.5	472.9	153.5	319.4	.0	-266.3	-265.0	-1.3	1,792.8	1,495.1	297.6
2008: I	1,903.5	89.9	543.4	126.3	417.1	.0	-453.5	-433.5	-20.1	1,813.6	1,510.6	303.0
II	1,780.1	-55.5	767.0	374.4	392.6	.0	-822.5	-796.9	-25.5	1,835.6	1,527.0	308.5
III	1,842.4	-15.8	709.0	235.7	473.2	.0	-724.8	-665.7	-59.0	1,858.2	1,544.4	313.8
IV	1,770.5	-110.5	619.7	409.2	230.5	-20.0	-730.2	-674.1	-56.1	1,881.0	1,562.6	318.4
2009: I	1,595.3	-288.3	717.4	403.1	294.2	20.0	-1,005.7	-969.1	-36.6	1,883.6	1,561.3	322.3
II	1,530.7	-333.3	960.2	595.7	364.5	.0	-1,293.5	-1,268.9	-24.6	1,864.0	1,540.5	323.5
III	1,491.7	-359.0	983.0	495.0	488.0	.0	-1,342.0	-1,327.0	-14.9	1,850.7	1,525.5	325.2
IV p	....	....	....	....	516.9	.0	....	....	....	1,856.4	1,526.3	330.1

[1] With inventory valuation and capital consumption adjustments.

See next page for continuation of table.

TABLE B–32. Gross saving and investment, 1960–2009—*Continued*

[Billions of dollars, except as noted; quarterly data at seasonally adjusted annual rates]

Year or quarter	Gross domestic investment, capital account transactions, and net lending, NIPA [2]							Addenda:						
	Gross domestic investment			Capital account transactions (net) [4]	Net lending or net borrowing (–), NIPA [2,5]	Statistical discrepancy	Gross private saving	Gross government saving			Net domestic investment	Gross saving as a percent of gross national income	Net saving as a percent of gross national income
	Total	Total	Gross private domestic investment	Gross government investment [3]					Total	Federal	State and local			
1960	110.3	107.2	78.9	28.3	....	3.2	–1.0	84.9	26.4	17.7	8.7	50.6	21.0	10.3
1961	113.7	109.5	78.2	31.3	....	4.2	–.6	91.9	22.4	13.4	9.0	51.3	20.8	10.2
1962	125.2	121.4	88.1	33.3	....	3.8	.3	100.8	24.1	13.9	10.3	60.9	21.2	10.9
1963	132.3	127.4	93.8	33.6	....	4.9	–.8	104.7	28.4	17.4	11.1	64.1	21.4	11.2
1964	144.2	136.7	102.1	34.6	....	7.5	.8	118.0	25.4	13.2	12.1	70.3	21.5	11.5
1965	160.0	153.8	118.2	35.6	....	6.2	1.5	129.8	28.6	15.9	12.8	83.1	21.9	12.1
1966	174.9	171.1	131.3	39.8	....	3.8	6.2	138.7	30.0	15.3	14.6	94.6	21.5	11.7
1967	175.1	171.6	128.6	43.0	....	3.5	4.5	151.5	19.1	4.5	14.5	88.6	20.5	10.5
1968	186.4	184.8	141.2	43.6	....	1.5	4.3	154.0	28.0	12.2	15.8	94.4	20.0	10.1
1969	201.3	199.7	156.4	43.3	....	1.6	2.9	157.2	41.2	23.9	17.3	100.5	20.1	10.0
1970	199.7	196.0	152.4	43.6	....	3.7	6.9	174.6	18.2	.6	17.7	87.6	18.6	8.1
1971	220.2	219.9	178.2	41.8	....	.3	11.0	203.2	6.0	–12.2	18.3	102.2	18.6	8.1
1972	246.2	250.2	207.6	42.6	....	–4.0	8.9	217.1	20.2	–8.3	28.5	123.1	19.2	8.9
1973	300.2	291.3	244.5	46.8	....	8.9	8.0	257.0	35.2	5.2	30.0	150.6	21.1	10.9
1974	311.6	305.7	249.4	56.3	....	6.0	9.8	271.1	30.7	3.7	27.0	142.0	20.1	9.2
1975	313.2	293.3	230.2	63.1	....	19.8	16.3	325.1	–28.2	–50.9	22.7	102.9	18.2	6.5
1976	365.4	358.4	292.0	66.4	....	7.1	23.5	345.6	–3.7	–32.3	28.6	150.2	18.8	7.4
1977	417.9	428.8	361.3	67.5	....	–10.9	21.2	384.1	12.6	–23.1	35.7	197.1	19.6	8.1
1978	502.4	515.0	438.0	77.1	....	–12.6	26.1	437.1	39.2	–3.9	43.2	253.6	20.8	9.4
1979	580.2	581.4	492.9	88.5	....	–1.2	47.0	479.7	53.5	13.0	40.5	282.4	20.9	9.2
1980	588.0	579.5	479.3	100.3	....	8.5	45.3	528.8	14.0	–26.6	40.6	235.4	19.5	7.2
1981	682.6	679.3	572.4	106.9	....	3.4	36.6	625.2	20.9	–23.0	43.8	285.9	20.7	8.1
1982	626.2	629.5	517.2	112.3	–0.1	–3.2	4.8	681.9	–60.4	–97.7	37.3	196.0	18.9	5.7
1983	652.1	687.2	564.3	122.9	–.1	–35.0	49.7	692.2	–89.8	–135.6	45.8	236.0	17.1	4.3
1984	784.9	875.0	735.6	139.4	–.1	–89.9	31.5	814.0	–60.6	–126.9	66.3	400.6	19.1	7.1
1985	780.7	895.0	736.2	158.8	–.2	–114.1	42.3	802.0	–63.6	–130.6	67.0	389.5	17.6	5.5
1986	777.1	919.7	746.5	173.2	–.2	–142.5	67.7	783.8	–74.5	–143.0	68.6	381.3	16.1	3.9
1987	815.1	969.2	785.0	184.3	–.2	–153.9	32.9	813.0	–30.8	–94.2	63.4	398.1	16.6	4.5
1988	892.0	1,007.7	821.6	186.1	–.4	–115.4	–9.5	908.8	–7.3	–79.3	72.0	396.7	17.6	5.7
1989	980.3	1,072.6	874.9	197.7	–.2	–92.2	56.1	916.1	8.0	–70.6	78.7	421.2	17.0	5.0
1990	1,001.8	1,076.7	861.0	215.7	6.7	–81.6	84.2	957.1	–39.5	–108.7	69.2	385.5	16.0	3.9
1991	1,031.0	1,023.2	802.9	220.3	4.6	3.2	79.7	1,036.6	–85.3	–146.4	61.1	298.8	16.0	3.8
1992	1,042.3	1,087.9	864.8	223.1	–.8	–44.8	110.0	1,091.7	–159.4	–227.9	68.5	343.5	14.9	3.0
1993	1,094.2	1,172.8	953.3	219.4	1.5	–80.0	135.8	1,088.0	–129.5	–202.4	72.9	394.8	14.6	2.7
1994	1,203.5	1,318.2	1,097.3	220.9	1.9	–116.6	108.8	1,148.6	–53.9	–140.3	86.4	499.0	15.6	3.9
1995	1,271.6	1,376.6	1,144.0	232.6	1.1	–106.2	52.5	1,251.2	–32.2	–124.5	92.3	507.2	16.5	4.7
1996	1,370.3	1,484.4	1,240.2	244.2	.9	–115.1	25.9	1,300.5	43.9	–66.3	110.2	571.9	17.1	5.5
1997	1,511.7	1,641.0	1,388.7	252.4	1.2	–130.6	–14.0	1,375.4	150.3	22.4	127.9	677.2	18.2	6.7
1998	1,569.1	1,773.6	1,510.8	262.9	1.0	–205.5	–85.3	1,394.9	259.5	116.4	143.1	753.1	18.6	7.1
1999	1,637.0	1,928.9	1,641.5	287.4	5.2	–297.1	–71.1	1,380.3	327.8	183.9	143.9	834.5	18.1	6.5
2000	1,666.2	2,076.5	1,772.2	304.3	1.4	–411.7	–134.0	1,376.2	424.0	273.0	151.0	892.2	17.8	6.1
2001	1,592.3	1,984.0	1,661.9	322.0	–11.7	–380.0	–103.4	1,466.5	229.2	129.1	100.1	727.7	16.2	4.2
2002	1,538.9	1,990.4	1,647.0	343.5	1.8	–453.4	–22.1	1,656.8	–95.9	–163.6	67.7	685.4	14.6	2.4
2003	1,569.4	2,085.5	1,729.7	355.8	3.8	–519.9	16.6	1,749.8	–197.1	–285.5	88.4	731.4	13.9	1.8
2004	1,716.3	2,340.9	1,968.6	372.4	–1.1	–623.5	–7.8	1,880.1	–155.9	–284.6	128.7	908.2	14.4	2.4
2005	1,823.7	2,564.2	2,172.2	392.0	–11.1	–729.5	–79.7	1,909.9	–6.5	–182.6	176.1	1,022.9	14.9	2.8
2006	1,953.8	2,752.2	2,327.2	425.1	4.2	–802.6	–220.6	2,057.9	116.5	–97.2	213.8	1,091.6	15.9	3.8
2007	2,025.4	2,750.0	2,288.5	461.6	2.2	–726.8	–14.8	1,964.6	75.6	–123.9	199.5	990.0	14.4	2.0
2008	1,925.2	2,632.4	2,136.1	496.3	–.4	–706.8	101.0	2,195.9	–371.8	–522.8	151.0	785.3	12.6	–.2
2009 *p*	....	2,138.4	1,622.9	515.5	....	....	....	....	....	....	....	274.7	....	....
2006: I	1,956.7	2,746.2	2,336.5	409.7	7.2	–796.7	–192.2	2,033.0	115.9	–103.5	219.4	1,128.2	16.0	3.9
II	1,968.5	2,779.5	2,352.1	427.4	4.3	–815.4	–190.7	2,058.2	101.0	–123.4	224.4	1,131.3	15.9	3.8
III	1,907.7	2,761.1	2,333.5	427.6	2.4	–855.8	–253.4	2,062.2	98.9	–107.7	206.6	1,085.8	15.7	3.5
IV	1,982.4	2,722.1	2,286.5	435.6	2.8	–742.5	–246.0	2,078.0	150.4	–54.2	204.7	1,020.8	16.0	3.8
2007: I	1,914.9	2,714.3	2,267.2	447.1	2.5	–801.8	–121.1	1,920.5	115.6	–90.6	206.2	987.5	14.6	2.2
II	1,999.7	2,762.3	2,302.0	460.2	.8	–763.3	–97.1	1,995.1	101.7	–109.6	211.2	1,012.9	14.8	2.5
III	2,093.6	2,778.4	2,311.9	466.6	2.8	–687.6	64.9	1,974.6	54.0	–145.5	199.6	1,007.2	14.2	1.8
IV	2,093.3	2,745.2	2,272.9	472.3	2.7	–654.6	94.0	1,968.0	31.3	–149.8	181.1	952.4	13.9	1.4
2008: I	1,973.2	2,690.7	2,214.8	475.9	2.8	–720.3	69.8	2,054.0	–150.5	–316.2	165.7	877.1	13.2	.6
II	1,906.8	2,660.2	2,164.6	495.5	3.0	–756.4	126.7	2,294.1	–514.0	–677.3	163.3	824.6	12.3	–.4
III	1,910.6	2,647.8	2,142.7	505.0	–11.6	–725.5	68.3	2,253.3	–411.0	–544.7	133.7	789.6	12.6	–.1
IV	1,909.9	2,530.9	2,022.1	508.9	4.0	–625.1	139.4	2,182.3	–411.8	–553.0	141.2	650.0	12.4	–.8
2009: I	1,780.8	2,190.3	1,689.9	500.4	3.1	–412.6	185.4	2,278.7	–683.4	–846.6	163.2	306.7	11.3	–2.0
II	1,692.4	2,082.0	1,561.5	520.4	3.0	–392.5	161.7	2,500.7	–970.0	–1,144.9	174.9	218.0	10.9	–2.4
III	1,654.9	2,080.4	1,556.1	524.3	2.9	–428.4	163.2	2,508.5	–1,016.8	–1,201.0	184.2	229.7	10.5	–2.5
IV *p*	....	2,201.0	1,684.0	517.0	....	....	....	....	....	....	....	344.6	....	....

[2] National income and product accounts (NIPA).
[3] For details on government investment, see Table B–20.
[4] Consists of capital transfers and the acquisition and disposal of nonproduced nonfinancial assets.
[5] Prior to 1982, equals the balance on current account, NIPA (see Table B–24).

Source: Department of Commerce (Bureau of Economic Analysis).

TABLE B–33. Median money income (in 2008 dollars) and poverty status of families and people, by race, selected years, 1996–2008

Year	Families[1] Number (millions)	Families Median money income (in 2008 dollars)[2]	Below poverty level Total Number (millions)	Below poverty level Total Percent	Below poverty level Female householder Number (millions)	Below poverty level Female householder Percent	People below poverty level Number (millions)	People below poverty level Percent	Males All people	Males Year-round full-time workers	Females All people	Females Year-round full-time workers
ALL RACES												
1996	70.2	$57,801	7.7	11.0	4.2	32.6	36.5	13.7	$32,568	$45,829	$17,511	$34,073
1997	70.9	59,613	7.3	10.3	4.0	31.6	35.6	13.3	33,723	47,146	18,329	34,815
1998	71.6	61,653	7.2	10.0	3.8	29.9	34.5	12.7	34,947	47,822	19,035	35,426
1999[3]	73.2	63,099	6.8	9.3	3.6	27.8	32.8	11.9	35,268	48,393	19,776	35,362
2000[4]	73.8	63,430	6.4	8.7	3.3	25.4	31.6	11.3	35,437	48,625	20,084	36,412
2001	74.3	62,519	6.8	9.2	3.5	26.4	32.9	11.7	35,391	48,812	20,205	36,995
2002	75.6	61,852	7.2	9.6	3.6	26.5	34.6	12.1	34,993	48,480	20,121	37,066
2003	76.2	61,671	7.6	10.0	3.9	28.0	35.9	12.5	35,040	48,587	20,205	37,055
2004[5]	76.9	61,623	7.8	10.2	4.0	28.3	37.0	12.7	34,784	47,495	20,138	36,608
2005	77.4	61,976	7.7	9.9	4.0	28.7	37.0	12.6	34,493	46,529	20,487	36,678
2006	78.5	62,372	7.7	9.8	4.1	28.3	36.5	12.3	34,455	48,010	21,373	37,364
2007	77.9	63,712	7.6	9.8	4.1	28.3	37.3	12.5	34,472	48,000	21,726	37,557
2008	78.9	61,521	8.1	10.3	4.2	28.7	39.8	13.2	33,161	47,779	20,867	36,688
WHITE												
1996	58.9	61,158	5.1	8.6	2.3	27.3	24.7	11.2	34,092	47,472	17,711	34,651
1997	59.5	62,536	5.0	8.4	2.3	27.7	24.4	11.0	34,930	48,310	18,448	35,405
1998	60.1	64,669	4.8	8.0	2.1	24.9	23.5	10.5	36,469	49,067	19,282	36,018
1999[3]	61.1	66,004	4.4	7.3	1.9	22.5	22.2	9.8	37,039	50,670	19,838	36,181
2000[4]	61.3	66,302	4.3	7.1	1.8	21.2	21.6	9.5	37,255	50,328	20,104	37,448
2001	61.6	65,754	4.6	7.4	1.9	22.4	22.7	9.9	36,776	49,607	20,251	37,517
Alone[6]												
2002	62.3	65,386	4.9	7.8	2.0	22.6	23.5	10.2	36,363	49,518	20,152	37,580
2003	62.6	65,286	5.1	8.1	2.2	24.0	24.3	10.5	35,977	49,335	20,396	37,686
2004[5]	63.1	64,657	5.3	8.4	2.3	24.7	25.3	10.8	35,729	48,554	20,175	37,309
2005	63.4	65,420	5.1	8.0	2.3	25.3	24.9	10.6	35,490	48,192	20,590	37,609
2006	64.1	65,440	5.1	8.0	2.4	25.1	24.4	10.3	36,140	49,051	21,445	37,937
2007	63.6	66,903	5.0	7.9	2.3	24.7	25.1	10.5	36,491	49,050	21,879	38,139
2008	64.2	65,000	5.4	8.4	2.4	25.2	27.0	11.2	35,120	49,924	20,950	37,210
Alone or in combination[6]												
2002	63.0	65,166	5.0	7.9	2.1	22.6	24.1	10.3	36,283	49,448	20,113	37,566
2003	63.5	65,094	5.2	8.1	2.2	24.2	25.0	10.6	35,891	49,261	20,359	37,672
2004[5]	64.0	64,500	5.4	8.5	2.3	24.8	26.1	10.9	35,651	48,429	20,140	37,266
2005	64.3	65,208	5.2	8.1	2.4	25.5	25.6	10.7	35,406	48,021	20,535	37,530
2006	65.0	65,352	5.2	8.0	2.4	25.0	25.2	10.4	35,959	48,982	21,399	37,899
2007	64.4	66,702	5.2	8.0	2.4	24.8	25.9	10.6	36,377	48,980	21,818	38,104
2008	65.0	64,804	5.5	8.5	2.4	25.4	27.9	11.3	35,013	49,755	20,921	37,177
BLACK												
1996	8.5	36,241	2.2	26.1	1.7	43.7	9.7	28.4	22,534	37,080	16,086	30,049
1997	8.4	38,257	2.0	23.6	1.6	39.8	9.1	26.5	24,205	35,976	17,453	30,448
1998	8.5	38,788	2.0	23.4	1.6	40.8	9.1	26.1	25,487	36,240	17,330	31,480
1999[3]	8.7	41,156	1.9	21.8	1.5	39.2	8.4	23.6	26,414	38,965	19,093	32,487
2000[4]	8.7	42,105	1.7	19.3	1.3	34.3	8.0	22.5	26,685	38,120	19,856	32,195
2001	8.8	40,860	1.8	20.7	1.4	35.2	8.1	22.7	26,106	38,821	19,801	33,197
Alone[6]												
2002	8.9	40,123	1.9	21.5	1.4	35.8	8.6	24.1	25,805	38,217	20,022	33,062
2003	8.9	40,235	2.0	22.3	1.5	36.9	8.8	24.4	25,739	39,135	19,411	32,336
2004[5]	8.9	40,064	2.0	22.8	1.5	37.6	9.0	24.7	25,864	36,157	19,787	33,222
2005	9.1	39,113	2.0	22.1	1.5	36.1	9.2	24.9	24,984	37,755	19,445	33,487
2006	9.3	40,867	2.0	21.6	1.5	36.6	9.0	24.3	26,765	37,885	20,400	33,036
2007	9.3	41,685	2.0	22.1	1.5	37.3	9.2	24.5	26,814	38,148	20,511	32,805
2008	9.4	39,879	2.1	22.0	1.5	37.2	9.4	24.7	25,254	38,612	20,197	32,186
Alone or in combination[6]												
2002	9.1	40,254	2.0	21.4	1.5	35.7	8.9	23.9	25,742	38,258	19,952	33,156
2003	9.1	40,514	2.0	22.1	1.5	36.8	9.1	24.3	25,679	39,176	19,363	32,399
2004[5]	9.1	40,261	2.1	22.8	1.5	37.6	9.4	24.7	25,890	36,146	19,773	33,276
2005	9.3	39,256	2.1	22.0	1.5	36.2	9.5	24.7	24,935	37,657	19,405	33,491
2006	9.5	41,135	2.0	21.5	1.5	36.4	9.4	24.2	26,777	37,921	20,359	33,087
2007	9.5	41,767	2.1	22.0	1.6	37.2	9.7	24.4	26,783	38,193	20,469	32,889
2008	9.6	39,936	2.1	21.9	1.6	37.1	9.9	24.6	25,118	38,365	20,203	32,204

[1] The term "family" refers to a group of two or more persons related by birth, marriage, or adoption and residing together. Every family must include a reference person.
[2] Current dollar median money income adjusted by consumer price index research series (CPI-U-RS).
[3] Reflects implementation of Census 2000–based population controls comparable with succeeding years.
[4] Reflects household sample expansion.
[5] For 2004, figures are revised to reflect a correction to the weights in the 2005 Annual Social and Economic Supplement.
[6] Data are for "white alone," for "white alone or in combination," for "black alone," and for "black alone or in combination." ("Black" is also "black or African American.") Beginning with data for 2002 the Current Population Survey allowed respondents to choose more than one race; for earlier years respondents could report only one race group.

Note: Poverty thresholds are updated each year to reflect changes in the consumer price index (CPI-U).
For details see publication Series P–60 on the Current Population Survey and Annual Social and Economic Supplements.

Source: Department of Commerce (Bureau of the Census).

TABLE B–34. Population by age group, 1933–2009

[Thousands of persons]

July 1	Total	Age (years)						
		Under 5	5–15	16–19	20–24	25–44	45–64	65 and over
1933	125,579	10,612	26,897	9,302	11,152	37,319	22,933	7,363
1939	130,880	10,418	25,179	9,822	11,519	39,354	25,823	8,764
1940	132,122	10,579	24,811	9,895	11,690	39,868	26,249	9,031
1941	133,402	10,850	24,516	9,840	11,807	40,383	26,718	9,288
1942	134,860	11,301	24,231	9,730	11,955	40,861	27,196	9,584
1943	136,739	12,016	24,093	9,607	12,064	41,420	27,671	9,867
1944	138,397	12,524	23,949	9,561	12,062	42,016	28,138	10,147
1945	139,928	12,979	23,907	9,361	12,036	42,521	28,630	10,494
1946	141,389	13,244	24,103	9,119	12,004	43,027	29,064	10,828
1947	144,126	14,406	24,468	9,097	11,814	43,657	29,498	11,185
1948	146,631	14,919	25,209	8,952	11,794	44,288	29,931	11,538
1949	149,188	15,607	25,852	8,788	11,700	44,916	30,405	11,921
1950	152,271	16,410	26,721	8,542	11,680	45,672	30,849	12,397
1951	154,878	17,333	27,279	8,446	11,552	46,103	31,362	12,803
1952	157,553	17,312	28,894	8,414	11,350	46,495	31,884	13,203
1953	160,184	17,638	30,227	8,460	11,062	46,786	32,394	13,617
1954	163,026	18,057	31,480	8,637	10,832	47,001	32,942	14,076
1955	165,931	18,566	32,682	8,744	10,714	47,194	33,506	14,525
1956	168,903	19,003	33,994	8,916	10,616	47,379	34,057	14,938
1957	171,984	19,494	35,272	9,195	10,603	47,440	34,591	15,388
1958	174,882	19,887	36,445	9,543	10,756	47,337	35,109	15,806
1959	177,830	20,175	37,368	10,215	10,969	47,192	35,663	16,248
1960	180,671	20,341	38,494	10,683	11,134	47,140	36,203	16,675
1961	183,691	20,522	39,765	11,025	11,483	47,084	36,722	17,089
1962	186,538	20,469	41,205	11,180	11,959	47,013	37,255	17,457
1963	189,242	20,342	41,626	12,007	12,714	46,994	37,782	17,778
1964	191,889	20,165	42,297	12,736	13,269	46,958	38,338	18,127
1965	194,303	19,824	42,938	13,516	13,746	46,912	38,916	18,451
1966	196,560	19,208	43,702	14,311	14,050	47,001	39,534	18,755
1967	198,712	18,563	44,244	14,200	15,248	47,194	40,193	19,071
1968	200,706	17,913	44,622	14,452	15,786	47,721	40,846	19,365
1969	202,677	17,376	44,840	14,800	16,480	48,064	41,437	19,680
1970	205,052	17,166	44,816	15,289	17,202	48,473	41,999	20,107
1971	207,661	17,244	44,591	15,688	18,159	48,936	42,482	20,561
1972	209,896	17,101	44,203	16,039	18,153	50,482	42,898	21,020
1973	211,909	16,851	43,582	16,446	18,521	51,749	43,235	21,525
1974	213,854	16,487	42,989	16,769	18,975	53,051	43,522	22,061
1975	215,973	16,121	42,508	17,017	19,527	54,302	43,801	22,696
1976	218,035	15,617	42,099	17,194	19,986	55,852	44,008	23,278
1977	220,239	15,564	41,298	17,276	20,499	57,561	44,150	23,892
1978	222,585	15,735	40,428	17,288	20,946	59,400	44,286	24,502
1979	225,055	16,063	39,552	17,242	21,297	61,379	44,390	25,134
1980	227,726	16,451	38,838	17,167	21,590	63,470	44,504	25,707
1981	229,966	16,893	38,144	16,812	21,869	65,528	44,500	26,221
1982	232,188	17,228	37,784	16,332	21,902	67,692	44,462	26,787
1983	234,307	17,547	37,526	15,823	21,844	69,733	44,474	27,361
1984	236,348	17,695	37,461	15,295	21,737	71,735	44,547	27,878
1985	238,466	17,842	37,450	15,005	21,478	73,673	44,602	28,416
1986	240,651	17,963	37,404	15,024	20,942	75,651	44,660	29,008
1987	242,804	18,052	37,333	15,215	20,385	77,338	44,854	29,626
1988	245,021	18,195	37,593	15,198	19,846	78,595	45,471	30,124
1989	247,342	18,508	37,972	14,913	19,442	79,943	45,882	30,682
1990	250,132	18,856	38,632	14,466	19,323	81,291	46,316	31,247
1991	253,493	19,208	39,349	13,992	19,414	82,844	46,874	31,812
1992	256,894	19,528	40,161	13,781	19,314	83,201	48,553	32,356
1993	260,255	19,729	40,904	13,953	19,101	83,766	49,899	32,902
1994	263,436	19,777	41,689	14,228	18,758	84,334	51,318	33,331
1995	266,557	19,627	42,510	14,522	18,391	84,933	52,806	33,769
1996	269,667	19,408	43,172	15,057	17,965	85,527	54,396	34,143
1997	272,912	19,233	43,833	15,433	17,992	85,737	56,283	34,402
1998	276,115	19,145	44,332	15,856	18,250	85,663	58,249	34,619
1999	279,295	19,136	44,755	16,164	18,672	85,408	60,362	34,798
2000 [1]	282,385	19,186	45,152	16,213	19,186	85,153	62,417	35,077
2001 [1]	285,267	19,348	45,178	16,252	19,855	84,889	64,414	35,332
2002 [1]	288,028	19,534	45,125	16,302	20,367	84,557	66,553	35,591
2003 [1]	290,704	19,770	45,040	16,349	20,769	84,202	68,623	35,952
2004 [1]	293,310	20,059	44,881	16,497	20,964	83,953	70,654	36,301
2005 [1]	295,994	20,301	44,709	16,632	21,038	83,776	72,786	36,752
2006 [1]	298,766	20,436	44,533	16,945	21,072	83,730	74,787	37,264
2007 [1]	301,714	20,730	44,390	17,200	21,111	83,724	76,616	37,942
2008 [1]	304,483	21,006	44,320	17,330	21,204	83,676	78,077	38,870
2009 [1]	307,226	21,268	44,371	17,319	21,424	83,565	79,651	39,628

[1] Revised total population data are available as follows: 2000, 282,385; 2001, 285,309; 2002, 288,105; 2003, 290,820; 2004, 293,463; 2005, 296,186; 2006, 298,996; 2007, 302,004; 2008, 304,798; and 2009, 307,439.

Note: Includes Armed Forces overseas beginning with 1940. Includes Alaska and Hawaii beginning with 1950.
All estimates are consistent with decennial census enumerations.

Source: Department of Commerce (Bureau of the Census).

TABLE B–35. Civilian population and labor force, 1929–2009

[Monthly data seasonally adjusted, except as noted]

Year or month	Civilian noninsti-tutional population [1]	Civilian labor force					Not in labor force	Civilian labor force participa-tion rate [2]	Civilian employ-ment/ population ratio [3]	Unemploy-ment rate, civilian workers [4]
		Total	Employment			Un-employ-ment				
			Total	Agricultural	Non-agricultural					
		Thousands of persons 14 years of age and over							Percent	
1929	....	49,180	47,630	10,450	37,180	1,550	....	....	....	3.2
1933	....	51,590	38,760	10,090	28,670	12,830	....	....	....	24.9
1939	....	55,230	45,750	9,610	36,140	9,480	....	....	....	17.2
1940	99,840	55,640	47,520	9,540	37,980	8,120	44,200	55.7	47.6	14.6
1941	99,900	55,910	50,350	9,100	41,250	5,560	43,990	56.0	50.4	9.9
1942	98,640	56,410	53,750	9,250	44,500	2,660	42,230	57.2	54.5	4.7
1943	94,640	55,540	54,470	9,080	45,390	1,070	39,100	58.7	57.6	1.9
1944	93,220	54,630	53,960	8,950	45,010	670	38,590	58.6	57.9	1.2
1945	94,090	53,860	52,820	8,580	44,240	1,040	40,230	57.2	56.1	1.9
1946	103,070	57,520	55,250	8,320	46,930	2,270	45,550	55.8	53.6	3.9
1947	106,018	60,168	57,812	8,256	49,557	2,356	45,850	56.8	54.5	3.9
		Thousands of persons 16 years of age and over								
1947	101,827	59,350	57,038	7,890	49,148	2,311	42,477	58.3	56.0	3.9
1948	103,068	60,621	58,343	7,629	50,714	2,276	42,447	58.8	56.6	3.8
1949	103,994	61,286	57,651	7,658	49,993	3,637	42,708	58.9	55.4	5.9
1950	104,995	62,208	58,918	7,160	51,758	3,288	42,787	59.2	56.1	5.3
1951	104,621	62,017	59,961	6,726	53,235	2,055	42,604	59.2	57.3	3.3
1952	105,231	62,138	60,250	6,500	53,749	1,883	43,093	59.0	57.3	3.0
1953 [5]	107,056	63,015	61,179	6,260	54,919	1,834	44,041	58.9	57.1	2.9
1954	108,321	63,643	60,109	6,205	53,904	3,532	44,678	58.8	55.5	5.5
1955	109,683	65,023	62,170	6,450	55,722	2,852	44,660	59.3	56.7	4.4
1956	110,954	66,552	63,799	6,283	57,514	2,750	44,402	60.0	57.5	4.1
1957	112,265	66,929	64,071	5,947	58,123	2,859	45,336	59.6	57.1	4.3
1958	113,727	67,639	63,036	5,586	57,450	4,602	46,088	59.5	55.4	6.8
1959	115,329	68,369	64,630	5,565	59,065	3,740	46,960	59.3	56.0	5.5
1960 [5]	117,245	69,628	65,778	5,458	60,318	3,852	47,617	59.4	56.1	5.5
1961	118,771	70,459	65,746	5,200	60,546	4,714	48,312	59.3	55.4	6.7
1962 [5]	120,153	70,614	66,702	4,944	61,759	3,911	49,539	58.8	55.5	5.5
1963	122,416	71,833	67,762	4,687	63,076	4,070	50,583	58.7	55.4	5.7
1964	124,485	73,091	69,305	4,523	64,782	3,786	51,394	58.7	55.7	5.2
1965	126,513	74,455	71,088	4,361	66,726	3,366	52,058	58.9	56.2	4.5
1966	128,058	75,770	72,895	3,979	68,915	2,875	52,288	59.2	56.9	3.8
1967	129,874	77,347	74,372	3,844	70,527	2,975	52,527	59.6	57.3	3.8
1968	132,028	78,737	75,920	3,817	72,103	2,817	53,291	59.6	57.5	3.6
1969	134,335	80,734	77,902	3,606	74,296	2,832	53,602	60.1	58.0	3.5
1970	137,085	82,771	78,678	3,463	75,215	4,093	54,315	60.4	57.4	4.9
1971	140,216	84,382	79,367	3,394	75,972	5,016	55,834	60.2	56.6	5.9
1972 [5]	144,126	87,034	82,153	3,484	78,669	4,882	57,091	60.4	57.0	5.6
1973 [5]	147,096	89,429	85,064	3,470	81,594	4,365	57,667	60.8	57.8	4.9
1974	150,120	91,949	86,794	3,515	83,279	5,156	58,171	61.3	57.8	5.6
1975	153,153	93,775	85,846	3,408	82,438	7,929	59,377	61.2	56.1	8.5
1976	156,150	96,158	88,752	3,331	85,421	7,406	59,991	61.6	56.8	7.7
1977	159,033	99,009	92,017	3,283	88,734	6,991	60,025	62.3	57.9	7.1
1978 [5]	161,910	102,251	96,048	3,387	92,661	6,202	59,659	63.2	59.3	6.1
1979	164,863	104,962	98,824	3,347	95,477	6,137	59,900	63.7	59.9	5.8
1980	167,745	106,940	99,303	3,364	95,938	7,637	60,806	63.8	59.2	7.1
1981	170,130	108,670	100,397	3,368	97,030	8,273	61,460	63.9	59.0	7.6
1982	172,271	110,204	99,526	3,401	96,125	10,678	62,067	64.0	57.8	9.7
1983	174,215	111,550	100,834	3,383	97,450	10,717	62,665	64.0	57.9	9.6
1984	176,383	113,544	105,005	3,321	101,685	8,539	62,839	64.4	59.5	7.5
1985	178,206	115,461	107,150	3,179	103,971	8,312	62,744	64.8	60.1	7.2
1986 [5]	180,587	117,834	109,597	3,163	106,434	8,237	62,752	65.3	60.7	7.0
1987	182,753	119,865	112,440	3,208	109,232	7,425	62,888	65.6	61.5	6.2
1988	184,613	121,669	114,968	3,169	111,800	6,701	62,944	65.9	62.3	5.5
1989	186,393	123,869	117,342	3,199	114,142	6,528	62,523	66.5	63.0	5.3
1990 [5]	189,164	125,840	118,793	3,223	115,570	7,047	63,324	66.5	62.8	5.6
1991	190,925	126,346	117,718	3,269	114,449	8,628	64,578	66.2	61.7	6.8
1992	192,805	128,105	118,492	3,247	115,245	9,613	64,700	66.4	61.5	7.5
1993	194,838	129,200	120,259	3,115	117,144	8,940	65,638	66.3	61.7	6.9
1994 [5]	196,814	131,056	123,060	3,409	119,651	7,996	65,758	66.6	62.5	6.1
1995	198,584	132,304	124,900	3,440	121,460	7,404	66,280	66.6	62.9	5.6
1996	200,591	133,943	126,708	3,443	123,264	7,236	66,647	66.8	63.2	5.4
1997 [5]	203,133	136,297	129,558	3,399	126,159	6,739	66,837	67.1	63.8	4.9
1998 [5]	205,220	137,673	131,463	3,378	128,085	6,210	67,547	67.1	64.1	4.5
1999 [5]	207,753	139,368	133,488	3,281	130,207	5,880	68,385	67.1	64.3	4.2

[1] Not seasonally adjusted.
[2] Civilian labor force as percent of civilian noninstitutional population.
[3] Civilian employment as percent of civilian noninstitutional population.
[4] Unemployed as percent of civilian labor force.

See next page for continuation of table.

Year or month	Civilian noninstitutional population [1]	Civilian labor force Total	Employment Total	Employment Agricultural	Employment Non-agricultural	Unemployment	Not in labor force	Civilian labor force participation rate [2]	Civilian employment/ population ratio [3]	Unemployment rate, civilian workers [4]
	Thousands of persons 16 years of age and over							Percent		
2000 [5,6]	212,577	142,583	136,891	2,464	134,427	5,692	69,994	67.1	64.4	4.0
2001	215,092	143,734	136,933	2,299	134,635	6,801	71,359	66.8	63.7	4.7
2002	217,570	144,863	136,485	2,311	134,174	8,378	72,707	66.6	62.7	5.8
2003 [5]	221,168	146,510	137,736	2,275	135,461	8,774	74,658	66.2	62.3	6.0
2004 [5]	223,357	147,401	139,252	2,232	137,020	8,149	75,956	66.0	62.3	5.5
2005 [5]	226,082	149,320	141,730	2,197	139,532	7,591	76,762	66.0	62.7	5.1
2006 [5]	228,815	151,428	144,427	2,206	142,221	7,001	77,387	66.2	63.1	4.6
2007 [5]	231,867	153,124	146,047	2,095	143,952	7,078	78,743	66.0	63.0	4.6
2008 [5]	233,788	154,287	145,362	2,168	143,194	8,924	79,501	66.0	62.2	5.8
2009 [5]	235,801	154,142	139,877	2,103	137,775	14,265	81,659	65.4	59.3	9.3
2006: Jan [5]	227,553	150,201	143,142	2,163	140,932	7,059	77,352	66.0	62.9	4.7
Feb	227,763	150,629	143,444	2,180	141,251	7,185	77,135	66.1	63.0	4.8
Mar	227,975	150,839	143,765	2,157	141,573	7,075	77,136	66.2	63.1	4.7
Apr	228,199	150,915	143,794	2,253	141,461	7,122	77,284	66.1	63.0	4.7
May	228,428	151,085	144,108	2,198	141,889	6,977	77,343	66.1	63.1	4.6
June	228,671	151,368	144,370	2,258	142,065	6,998	77,303	66.2	63.1	4.6
July	228,912	151,383	144,229	2,280	142,083	7,154	77,529	66.1	63.0	4.7
Aug	229,167	151,729	144,631	2,237	142,442	7,097	77,439	66.2	63.1	4.7
Sept	229,420	151,650	144,797	2,176	142,640	6,853	77,770	66.1	63.1	4.5
Oct	229,675	152,020	145,292	2,179	143,188	6,728	77,655	66.2	63.3	4.4
Nov	229,905	152,360	145,477	2,159	143,280	6,883	77,545	66.3	63.3	4.5
Dec	230,108	152,698	145,914	2,226	143,661	6,784	77,410	66.4	63.4	4.4
2007: Jan [5]	230,650	153,117	146,032	2,214	143,757	7,085	77,533	66.4	63.3	4.6
Feb	230,834	152,941	146,043	2,302	143,738	6,898	77,893	66.3	63.3	4.5
Mar	231,034	153,093	146,368	2,188	144,155	6,725	77,940	66.3	63.4	4.4
Apr	231,253	152,531	145,686	2,077	143,545	6,845	78,721	66.0	63.0	4.5
May	231,480	152,717	145,952	2,088	143,843	6,765	78,763	66.0	63.1	4.4
June	231,713	153,045	146,079	1,951	144,137	6,966	78,668	66.0	63.0	4.6
July	231,958	153,039	145,926	2,017	144,033	7,113	78,919	66.0	62.9	4.6
Aug	232,211	152,781	145,685	1,861	143,856	7,096	79,429	65.8	62.7	4.6
Sept	232,461	153,393	146,193	2,077	144,117	7,200	79,067	66.0	62.9	4.7
Oct	232,715	153,158	145,885	2,113	143,846	7,273	79,557	65.8	62.7	4.7
Nov	232,939	153,767	146,483	2,138	144,347	7,284	79,172	66.0	62.9	4.7
Dec	233,156	153,869	146,173	2,207	143,926	7,696	79,286	66.0	62.7	5.0
2008: Jan [5]	232,616	154,048	146,421	2,205	144,146	7,628	78,568	66.2	62.9	5.0
Feb	232,809	153,600	146,165	2,202	143,965	7,435	79,209	66.0	62.8	4.8
Mar	232,995	153,966	146,173	2,190	143,976	7,793	79,029	66.1	62.7	5.1
Apr	233,198	153,936	146,306	2,122	144,129	7,631	79,262	66.0	62.7	5.0
May	233,405	154,420	146,023	2,125	143,888	8,397	78,985	66.2	62.6	5.4
June	233,627	154,327	145,768	2,126	143,639	8,560	79,300	66.1	62.4	5.5
July	233,864	154,410	145,515	2,141	143,422	8,895	79,454	66.0	62.2	5.8
Aug	234,107	154,696	145,187	2,148	143,045	9,509	79,411	66.1	62.0	6.1
Sept	234,360	154,590	145,021	2,207	142,793	9,569	79,770	66.0	61.9	6.2
Oct	234,612	154,849	144,677	2,192	142,576	10,172	79,764	66.0	61.7	6.6
Nov	234,828	154,524	143,907	2,195	141,742	10,617	80,304	65.8	61.3	6.9
Dec	235,035	154,587	143,188	2,185	140,975	11,400	80,448	65.8	60.9	7.4
2009: Jan [5]	234,739	154,140	142,221	2,147	140,014	11,919	80,599	65.7	60.6	7.7
Feb	234,913	154,401	141,687	2,148	139,559	12,714	80,512	65.7	60.3	8.2
Mar	235,086	154,164	140,854	2,051	138,830	13,310	80,922	65.6	59.9	8.6
Apr	235,271	154,718	140,902	2,143	138,762	13,816	80,554	65.8	59.9	8.9
May	235,452	154,956	140,438	2,166	138,287	14,518	80,496	65.8	59.6	9.4
June	235,655	154,759	140,038	2,154	137,825	14,721	80,895	65.7	59.4	9.5
July	235,870	154,351	139,817	2,138	137,629	14,534	81,519	65.4	59.3	9.4
Aug	236,087	154,426	139,433	2,095	137,285	14,993	81,661	65.4	59.1	9.7
Sept	236,322	153,927	138,768	2,009	136,752	15,159	82,396	65.1	58.7	9.8
Oct	236,550	153,854	138,242	2,041	136,311	15,612	82,696	65.0	58.4	10.1
Nov	236,743	153,720	138,381	2,086	136,357	15,340	83,022	64.9	58.5	10.0
Dec	236,924	153,059	137,792	2,056	135,717	15,267	83,865	64.6	58.2	10.0

[5] Not strictly comparable with earlier data due to population adjustments or other changes. See *Employment and Earnings* or population control adjustments to the Current Population Survey (CPS) at http://www.bls.gov/cps/documentation.htm#concepts for details on breaks in series.

[6] Beginning in 2000, data for agricultural employment are for agricultural and related industries; data for this series and for nonagricultural employment are not strictly comparable with data for earlier years. Because of independent seasonal adjustment for these two series, monthly data will not add to total civilian employment.

Note: Labor force data in Tables B–35 through B–44 are based on household interviews and relate to the calendar week including the 12th of the month. For definitions of terms, area samples used, historical comparability of the data, comparability with other series, etc., see *Employment and Earnings* or population control adjustments to the CPS at http://www.bls.gov/cps/documentation.htm#concepts.

Source: Department of Labor (Bureau of Labor Statistics).

TABLE B–36. Civilian employment and unemployment by sex and age, 1962–2009

[Thousands of persons 16 years of age and over; monthly data seasonally adjusted]

Year or month	Civilian employment							Unemployment						
	Total	Males			Females			Total	Males			Females		
		Total	16–19 years	20 years and over	Total	16–19 years	20 years and over		Total	16–19 years	20 years and over	Total	16–19 years	20 years and over
1962	66,702	44,177	2,362	41,815	22,525	1,833	20,693	3,911	2,423	408	2,016	1,488	313	1,175
1963	67,762	44,657	2,406	42,251	23,105	1,849	21,257	4,070	2,472	501	1,971	1,598	383	1,216
1964	69,305	45,474	2,587	42,886	23,831	1,929	21,903	3,786	2,205	487	1,718	1,581	385	1,195
1965	71,088	46,340	2,918	43,422	24,748	2,118	22,630	3,366	1,914	479	1,435	1,452	395	1,056
1966	72,895	46,919	3,253	43,668	25,976	2,468	23,510	2,875	1,551	432	1,120	1,324	405	921
1967	74,372	47,479	3,186	44,294	26,893	2,496	24,397	2,975	1,508	448	1,060	1,468	391	1,078
1968	75,920	48,114	3,255	44,859	27,807	2,526	25,281	2,817	1,419	426	993	1,397	412	985
1969	77,902	48,818	3,430	45,388	29,084	2,687	26,397	2,832	1,403	440	963	1,429	413	1,015
1970	78,678	48,990	3,409	45,581	29,688	2,735	26,952	4,093	2,238	599	1,638	1,855	506	1,349
1971	79,367	49,390	3,478	45,912	29,976	2,730	27,246	5,016	2,789	693	2,097	2,227	568	1,658
1972	82,153	50,896	3,765	47,130	31,257	2,980	28,276	4,882	2,659	711	1,948	2,222	598	1,625
1973	85,064	52,349	4,039	48,310	32,715	3,231	29,484	4,365	2,275	653	1,624	2,089	583	1,507
1974	86,794	53,024	4,103	48,922	33,769	3,345	30,424	5,156	2,714	757	1,957	2,441	665	1,777
1975	85,846	51,857	3,839	48,018	33,989	3,263	30,726	7,929	4,442	966	3,476	3,486	802	2,684
1976	88,752	53,138	3,947	49,190	35,615	3,389	32,226	7,406	4,036	939	3,098	3,369	780	2,588
1977	92,017	54,728	4,174	50,555	37,289	3,514	33,775	6,991	3,667	874	2,794	3,324	789	2,535
1978	96,048	56,479	4,336	52,143	39,569	3,734	35,836	6,202	3,142	813	2,328	3,061	769	2,292
1979	98,824	57,607	4,300	53,308	41,217	3,783	37,434	6,137	3,120	811	2,308	3,018	743	2,276
1980	99,303	57,186	4,085	53,101	42,117	3,625	38,492	7,637	4,267	913	3,353	3,370	755	2,615
1981	100,397	57,397	3,815	53,582	43,000	3,411	39,590	8,273	4,577	962	3,615	3,696	800	2,895
1982	99,526	56,271	3,379	52,891	43,256	3,170	40,086	10,678	6,179	1,090	5,089	4,499	886	3,613
1983	100,834	56,787	3,300	53,487	44,047	3,043	41,004	10,717	6,260	1,003	5,257	4,457	825	3,632
1984	105,005	59,091	3,322	55,769	45,915	3,122	42,793	8,539	4,744	812	3,932	3,794	687	3,107
1985	107,150	59,891	3,328	56,562	47,259	3,105	44,154	8,312	4,521	806	3,715	3,791	661	3,129
1986	109,597	60,892	3,323	57,569	48,706	3,149	45,556	8,237	4,530	779	3,751	3,707	675	3,032
1987	112,440	62,107	3,381	58,726	50,334	3,260	47,074	7,425	4,101	732	3,369	3,324	616	2,709
1988	114,968	63,273	3,492	59,781	51,696	3,313	48,383	6,701	3,655	667	2,987	3,046	558	2,487
1989	117,342	64,315	3,477	60,837	53,027	3,282	49,745	6,528	3,525	658	2,867	3,003	536	2,467
1990	118,793	65,104	3,427	61,678	53,689	3,154	50,535	7,047	3,906	667	3,239	3,140	544	2,596
1991	117,718	64,223	3,044	61,178	53,496	2,862	50,634	8,628	4,946	751	4,195	3,683	608	3,074
1992	118,492	64,440	2,944	61,496	54,052	2,724	51,328	9,613	5,523	806	4,717	4,090	621	3,469
1993	120,259	65,349	2,994	62,355	54,910	2,811	52,099	8,940	5,055	768	4,287	3,885	597	3,288
1994	123,060	66,450	3,156	63,294	56,610	3,005	53,606	7,996	4,367	740	3,627	3,629	580	3,049
1995	124,900	67,377	3,292	64,085	57,523	3,127	54,396	7,404	3,983	744	3,239	3,421	602	2,819
1996	126,708	68,207	3,310	64,897	58,501	3,190	55,311	7,236	3,880	733	3,146	3,356	573	2,783
1997	129,558	69,685	3,401	66,284	59,873	3,260	56,613	6,739	3,577	694	2,882	3,162	577	2,585
1998	131,463	70,693	3,558	67,135	60,771	3,493	57,278	6,210	3,266	686	2,580	2,944	519	2,424
1999	133,488	71,446	3,685	67,761	62,042	3,487	58,555	5,880	3,066	633	2,433	2,814	529	2,285
2000	136,891	73,305	3,671	69,634	63,586	3,519	60,067	5,692	2,975	599	2,376	2,717	483	2,235
2001	136,933	73,196	3,420	69,776	63,737	3,320	60,417	6,801	3,690	650	3,040	3,111	512	2,599
2002	136,485	72,903	3,169	69,734	63,582	3,162	60,420	8,378	4,597	700	3,896	3,781	553	3,228
2003	137,736	73,332	2,917	70,415	64,404	3,002	61,402	8,774	4,906	697	4,209	3,868	554	3,314
2004	139,252	74,524	2,952	71,572	64,728	2,955	61,773	8,149	4,456	664	3,791	3,694	543	3,150
2005	141,730	75,973	2,923	73,050	65,757	3,055	62,702	7,591	4,059	667	3,392	3,531	519	3,013
2006	144,427	77,502	3,071	74,431	66,925	3,091	63,834	7,001	3,753	622	3,131	3,247	496	2,751
2007	146,047	78,254	2,917	75,337	67,792	2,994	64,799	7,078	3,882	623	3,259	3,196	478	2,718
2008	145,362	77,486	2,736	74,750	67,876	2,837	65,039	8,924	5,033	736	4,297	3,891	549	3,342
2009	139,877	73,670	2,328	71,341	66,208	2,509	63,699	14,265	8,453	898	7,555	5,811	654	5,157
2008: Jan	146,421	78,259	2,782	75,477	68,162	2,981	65,181	7,628	4,238	749	3,489	3,390	501	2,889
Feb	146,165	78,224	2,785	75,439	67,941	2,900	65,041	7,435	4,070	629	3,441	3,365	494	2,871
Mar	146,173	78,101	2,794	75,306	68,072	2,945	65,127	7,793	4,253	604	3,649	3,540	487	3,054
Apr	146,306	78,104	2,872	75,232	68,202	3,024	65,178	7,631	4,232	593	3,639	3,398	495	2,903
May	146,023	77,959	2,915	75,044	68,064	2,912	65,152	8,397	4,619	766	3,853	3,779	591	3,187
June	145,768	77,769	2,769	75,000	67,998	2,820	65,178	8,560	4,777	740	4,037	3,783	568	3,215
July	145,515	77,646	2,681	74,964	67,869	2,802	65,067	8,895	5,128	850	4,278	3,767	587	3,180
Aug	145,187	77,436	2,737	74,698	67,752	2,796	64,956	9,509	5,253	714	4,540	4,256	579	3,677
Sept	145,021	77,205	2,725	74,480	67,816	2,801	65,015	9,569	5,603	739	4,864	3,967	579	3,388
Oct	144,677	76,902	2,661	74,241	67,775	2,772	65,003	10,172	5,918	851	5,067	4,254	531	3,723
Nov	143,907	76,407	2,557	73,850	67,500	2,694	64,806	10,617	6,153	800	5,353	4,464	538	3,926
Dec	143,188	75,812	2,575	73,237	67,376	2,632	64,744	11,400	6,650	778	5,871	4,750	590	4,160
2009: Jan	142,221	75,118	2,492	72,625	67,103	2,713	64,391	11,919	6,948	805	6,144	4,971	569	4,402
Feb	141,687	74,756	2,490	72,266	66,931	2,693	64,238	12,714	7,425	831	6,593	5,290	614	4,676
Mar	140,854	74,072	2,405	71,667	66,782	2,673	64,110	13,310	7,852	840	7,013	5,458	595	4,863
Apr	140,902	74,107	2,442	71,665	66,794	2,647	64,147	13,816	8,295	854	7,441	5,521	563	4,957
May	140,438	73,974	2,423	71,552	66,463	2,617	63,847	14,518	8,689	902	7,787	5,829	616	5,213
June	140,038	73,727	2,373	71,354	66,311	2,570	63,741	14,721	8,749	857	7,892	5,972	729	5,243
July	139,817	73,613	2,357	71,255	66,205	2,519	63,685	14,534	8,642	914	7,728	5,892	667	5,225
Aug	139,433	73,436	2,294	71,142	65,997	2,446	63,552	14,993	9,031	976	8,055	5,962	667	5,295
Sept	138,768	73,120	2,259	70,861	65,648	2,368	63,280	15,159	9,077	961	8,116	6,081	675	5,406
Oct	138,242	72,844	2,182	70,662	65,398	2,266	63,133	15,612	9,340	978	8,362	6,271	717	5,554
Nov	138,381	72,794	2,131	70,662	65,587	2,318	63,269	15,340	9,171	932	8,239	6,169	695	5,473
Dec	137,792	72,499	2,108	70,391	65,293	2,294	62,998	15,267	8,955	944	8,011	6,312	690	5,622

Note: See footnote 5 and Note, Table B–35.

Source: Department of Labor (Bureau of Labor Statistics).

[Thousands of persons 16 years of age and over; monthly data seasonally adjusted]

Year or month	All civilian workers	White [1] Total	White [1] Males	White [1] Females	White [1] Both sexes 16–19	Black and other [1] Total	Black and other [1] Males	Black and other [1] Females	Black and other [1] Both sexes 16–19	Black or African American [1] Total	Black or African American [1] Males	Black or African American [1] Females	Black or African American [1] Both sexes 16–19
1962	66,702	59,698	40,016	19,682	3,774	7,003	4,160	2,843	420				
1963	67,762	60,622	40,428	20,194	3,851	7,140	4,229	2,911	404				
1964	69,305	61,922	41,115	20,807	4,076	7,383	4,359	3,024	440				
1965	71,088	63,446	41,844	21,602	4,562	7,643	4,496	3,147	474				
1966	72,895	65,021	42,331	22,690	5,176	7,877	4,588	3,289	545				
1967	74,372	66,361	42,833	23,528	5,114	8,011	4,646	3,365	568				
1968	75,920	67,750	43,411	24,339	5,195	8,169	4,702	3,467	584				
1969	77,902	69,518	44,048	25,470	5,508	8,384	4,770	3,614	609				
1970	78,678	70,217	44,178	26,039	5,571	8,464	4,813	3,650	574				
1971	79,367	70,878	44,595	26,283	5,670	8,488	4,796	3,692	538				
1972	82,153	73,370	45,944	27,426	6,173	8,783	4,952	3,832	573	7,802	4,368	3,433	509
1973	85,064	75,708	47,085	28,623	6,623	9,356	5,265	4,092	647	8,128	4,527	3,601	570
1974	86,794	77,184	47,674	29,511	6,796	9,610	5,352	4,258	652	8,203	4,527	3,677	554
1975	85,846	76,411	46,697	29,714	6,487	9,435	5,161	4,275	615	7,894	4,275	3,618	507
1976	88,752	78,853	47,775	31,078	6,724	9,899	5,363	4,536	611	8,227	4,404	3,823	508
1977	92,017	81,700	49,150	32,550	7,068	10,317	5,579	4,739	619	8,540	4,565	3,975	508
1978	96,048	84,936	50,544	34,392	7,367	11,112	5,936	5,177	703	9,102	4,796	4,307	571
1979	98,824	87,259	51,452	35,807	7,356	11,565	6,156	5,409	727	9,359	4,923	4,436	579
1980	99,303	87,715	51,127	36,587	7,021	11,588	6,059	5,529	689	9,313	4,798	4,515	547
1981	100,397	88,709	51,315	37,394	6,588	11,688	6,083	5,606	637	9,355	4,794	4,561	505
1982	99,526	87,903	50,287	37,615	5,984	11,624	5,983	5,641	565	9,189	4,637	4,552	428
1983	100,834	88,893	50,621	38,272	5,799	11,941	6,166	5,775	543	9,375	4,753	4,622	416
1984	105,005	92,120	52,462	39,659	5,836	12,885	6,629	6,256	607	10,119	5,124	4,995	474
1985	107,150	93,736	53,046	40,690	5,768	13,414	6,845	6,569	666	10,501	5,270	5,231	532
1986	109,597	95,660	53,785	41,876	5,792	13,937	7,107	6,830	681	10,814	5,428	5,386	536
1987	112,440	97,789	54,647	43,142	5,898	14,652	7,459	7,192	742	11,309	5,661	5,648	587
1988	114,968	99,812	55,550	44,262	6,030	15,156	7,722	7,434	774	11,658	5,824	5,834	601
1989	117,342	101,584	56,352	45,232	5,946	15,757	7,963	7,795	813	11,953	5,928	6,025	625
1990	118,793	102,261	56,703	45,558	5,779	16,533	8,401	8,131	801	12,175	5,995	6,180	598
1991	117,718	101,182	55,797	45,385	5,216	16,536	8,426	8,110	690	12,074	5,961	6,113	494
1992	118,492	101,669	55,959	45,710	4,985	16,823	8,482	8,342	684	12,151	5,930	6,221	492
1993	120,259	103,045	56,656	46,390	5,113	17,214	8,693	8,521	691	12,382	6,047	6,334	494
1994	123,060	105,190	57,452	47,738	5,398	17,870	8,998	8,872	763	12,835	6,241	6,595	552
1995	124,900	106,490	58,146	48,344	5,593	18,409	9,231	9,179	826	13,279	6,422	6,857	586
1996	126,708	107,808	58,888	48,920	5,667	18,900	9,319	9,580	832	13,542	6,456	7,086	613
1997	129,558	109,856	59,998	49,859	5,807	19,701	9,687	10,014	853	13,969	6,607	7,362	631
1998	131,463	110,931	60,604	50,327	6,089	20,532	10,089	10,443	962	14,556	6,871	7,685	736
1999	133,488	112,235	61,139	51,096	6,204	21,253	10,307	10,945	968	15,056	7,027	8,029	691
2000	136,891	114,424	62,289	52,136	6,160					15,156	7,082	8,073	711
2001	136,933	114,430	62,212	52,218	5,817					15,006	6,938	8,068	637
2002	136,485	114,013	61,849	52,164	5,441					14,872	6,959	7,914	611
2003	137,736	114,235	61,866	52,369	5,064					14,739	6,820	7,919	516
2004	139,252	115,239	62,712	52,527	5,039					14,909	6,912	7,997	520
2005	141,730	116,949	63,763	53,186	5,105					15,313	7,155	8,158	536
2006	144,427	118,833	64,883	53,950	5,215					15,765	7,354	8,410	618
2007	146,047	119,792	65,289	54,503	4,990					16,051	7,500	8,551	566
2008	145,362	119,126	64,624	54,501	4,697					15,953	7,398	8,554	541
2009	139,877	114,996	61,630	53,366	4,138					15,025	6,817	8,208	442
2008: Jan	146,421	119,926	65,220	54,706	4,797					16,079	7,554	8,524	573
Feb	146,165	119,665	65,161	54,504	4,788					16,165	7,560	8,604	572
Mar	146,173	119,695	65,135	54,559	4,839					16,127	7,477	8,650	527
Apr	146,306	119,676	65,040	54,636	4,961					16,218	7,533	8,685	573
May	146,023	119,624	65,029	54,595	4,910					16,030	7,448	8,582	558
June	145,768	119,441	64,837	54,604	4,729					16,026	7,462	8,563	527
July	145,515	119,382	64,885	54,497	4,623					15,950	7,377	8,573	533
Aug	145,187	119,016	64,580	54,436	4,642					16,024	7,495	8,529	594
Sept	145,021	119,031	64,368	54,663	4,607					15,742	7,329	8,413	564
Oct	144,677	118,697	64,153	54,543	4,609					15,787	7,286	8,501	535
Nov	143,907	118,018	63,789	54,229	4,487					15,676	7,150	8,526	473
Dec	143,188	117,335	63,284	54,050	4,421					15,646	7,126	8,520	483
2009: Jan	142,221	116,709	62,836	53,873	4,409					15,463	7,014	8,449	496
Feb	141,687	116,427	62,487	53,939	4,494					15,296	6,940	8,356	455
Mar	140,854	115,663	61,908	53,755	4,346					15,176	6,865	8,311	461
Apr	140,902	115,896	62,019	53,877	4,300					15,119	6,839	8,281	496
May	140,438	115,451	61,895	53,557	4,315					15,066	6,822	8,244	442
June	140,038	115,102	61,665	53,437	4,205					15,048	6,792	8,255	448
July	139,817	114,984	61,648	53,336	4,140					15,050	6,832	8,219	476
Aug	139,433	114,784	61,510	53,274	4,060					14,914	6,745	8,169	460
Sept	138,768	114,215	61,237	52,979	3,980					14,754	6,694	8,060	401
Oct	138,242	113,754	60,953	52,801	3,816					14,763	6,748	8,015	409
Nov	138,381	113,669	60,833	52,836	3,820					14,904	6,757	8,148	373
Dec	137,792	113,339	60,598	52,741	3,804					14,758	6,765	7,992	379

[1] Beginning in 2003, persons who selected this race group only. Prior to 2003, persons who selected more than one race were included in the group they identified as the main race. Data for "black or African American" were for "black" prior to 2003. Data discontinued for "black and other" series. See *Employment and Earnings* or concepts and methodology of the Current Population Survey (CPS) at http://www.bls.gov/cps/documentation.htm#concepts for details.

Note: Beginning with data for 2000, detail will not sum to total because data for all race groups are not shown here.
See footnote 5 and Note, Table B–35.

Source: Department of Labor (Bureau of Labor Statistics).

Table B–38. Unemployment by demographic characteristic, 1962–2009

[Thousands of persons 16 years of age and over; monthly data seasonally adjusted]

Year or month	All civilian workers	White [1] Total	Males	Females	Both sexes 16–19	Black and other [1] Total	Males	Females	Both sexes 16–19	Black or African American [1] Total	Males	Females	Both sexes 16–19
1962	3,911	3,052	1,915	1,137	580	861	509	352	142	....	....	....	....
1963	4,070	3,208	1,976	1,232	708	863	496	367	176	....	....	....	....
1964	3,786	2,999	1,779	1,220	708	787	426	361	165	....	....	....	....
1965	3,366	2,691	1,556	1,135	705	678	360	318	171	....	....	....	....
1966	2,875	2,255	1,241	1,014	651	622	310	312	186	....	....	....	....
1967	2,975	2,338	1,208	1,130	635	638	300	338	203	....	....	....	....
1968	2,817	2,226	1,142	1,084	644	590	277	313	194	....	....	....	....
1969	2,832	2,260	1,137	1,123	660	571	267	304	193	....	....	....	....
1970	4,093	3,339	1,857	1,482	871	754	380	374	235	....	....	....	....
1971	5,016	4,085	2,309	1,777	1,011	930	481	450	249	....	....	....	....
1972	4,882	3,906	2,173	1,733	1,021	977	486	491	288	906	448	458	279
1973	4,365	3,442	1,836	1,606	955	924	440	484	280	846	395	451	262
1974	5,156	4,097	2,169	1,927	1,104	1,058	544	514	318	965	494	470	297
1975	7,929	6,421	3,627	2,794	1,413	1,507	815	692	355	1,369	741	629	330
1976	7,406	5,914	3,258	2,656	1,364	1,492	779	713	355	1,334	698	637	330
1977	6,991	5,441	2,883	2,558	1,284	1,550	784	766	379	1,393	698	695	354
1978	6,202	4,698	2,411	2,287	1,189	1,505	731	774	394	1,330	641	690	360
1979	6,137	4,664	2,405	2,260	1,193	1,473	714	759	362	1,319	636	683	333
1980	7,637	5,884	3,345	2,540	1,291	1,752	922	830	377	1,553	815	738	343
1981	8,273	6,343	3,580	2,762	1,374	1,930	997	933	388	1,731	891	840	357
1982	10,678	8,241	4,846	3,395	1,534	2,437	1,334	1,104	443	2,142	1,167	975	396
1983	10,717	8,128	4,859	3,270	1,387	2,588	1,401	1,187	441	2,272	1,213	1,059	392
1984	8,539	6,372	3,600	2,772	1,116	2,167	1,144	1,022	384	1,914	1,003	911	353
1985	8,312	6,191	3,426	2,765	1,074	2,121	1,095	1,026	394	1,864	951	913	357
1986	8,237	6,140	3,433	2,708	1,070	2,097	1,097	999	383	1,840	946	894	347
1987	7,425	5,501	3,132	2,369	995	1,924	969	955	353	1,684	826	858	312
1988	6,701	4,944	2,766	2,177	910	1,757	888	869	316	1,547	771	776	288
1989	6,528	4,770	2,636	2,135	863	1,757	889	868	331	1,544	773	772	300
1990	7,047	5,186	2,935	2,251	903	1,860	971	889	308	1,565	806	758	268
1991	8,628	6,560	3,859	2,701	1,029	2,068	1,087	981	330	1,723	890	833	280
1992	9,613	7,169	4,209	2,959	1,037	2,444	1,314	1,130	390	2,011	1,067	944	324
1993	8,940	6,655	3,828	2,827	992	2,285	1,227	1,058	373	1,844	971	872	313
1994	7,996	5,892	3,275	2,617	960	2,104	1,092	1,011	360	1,666	848	818	300
1995	7,404	5,459	2,999	2,460	952	1,945	984	961	394	1,538	762	777	325
1996	7,236	5,300	2,896	2,404	939	1,936	984	952	367	1,592	808	784	310
1997	6,739	4,836	2,641	2,195	912	1,903	935	967	359	1,560	747	813	302
1998	6,210	4,484	2,431	2,053	876	1,726	835	891	329	1,426	671	756	281
1999	5,880	4,273	2,274	1,999	844	1,606	792	814	318	1,309	626	684	268
2000	5,692	4,121	2,177	1,944	795	....	....	....	....	1,241	620	621	230
2001	6,801	4,969	2,754	2,215	845	....	....	....	....	1,416	709	706	260
2002	8,378	6,137	3,459	2,678	925	....	....	....	....	1,693	835	858	260
2003	8,774	6,311	3,643	2,668	909	....	....	....	....	1,787	891	895	255
2004	8,149	5,847	3,282	2,565	890	....	....	....	....	1,729	860	868	241
2005	7,591	5,350	2,931	2,419	845	....	....	....	....	1,700	844	856	267
2006	7,001	5,002	2,730	2,271	794	....	....	....	....	1,549	774	775	253
2007	7,078	5,143	2,869	2,274	805	....	....	....	....	1,445	752	693	235
2008	8,924	6,509	3,727	2,782	947	....	....	....	....	1,788	949	839	246
2009	14,265	10,648	6,421	4,227	1,157	....	....	....	....	2,606	1,448	1,159	288
2008: Jan	7,628	5,536	3,124	2,412	907	....	....	....	....	1,620	845	775	296
Feb	7,435	5,461	3,058	2,403	803	....	....	....	....	1,462	749	713	253
Mar	7,793	5,585	3,097	2,488	733	....	....	....	....	1,619	810	809	249
Apr	7,631	5,543	3,143	2,400	827	....	....	....	....	1,534	762	772	190
May	8,397	6,071	3,418	2,652	992	....	....	....	....	1,698	867	831	262
June	8,560	6,222	3,514	2,708	969	....	....	....	....	1,660	897	763	223
July	8,895	6,525	3,801	2,724	1,085	....	....	....	....	1,758	979	779	261
Aug	9,509	6,882	3,878	3,004	955	....	....	....	....	1,934	974	960	254
Sept	9,569	6,868	4,119	2,749	974	....	....	....	....	2,027	1,094	933	242
Oct	10,172	7,523	4,420	3,103	1,017	....	....	....	....	2,017	1,115	902	267
Nov	10,617	7,875	4,637	3,238	1,018	....	....	....	....	2,031	1,122	910	220
Dec	11,400	8,458	4,901	3,557	1,033	....	....	....	....	2,150	1,226	924	241
2009: Jan	11,919	8,815	5,177	3,638	1,006	....	....	....	....	2,278	1,307	971	288
Feb	12,714	9,408	5,575	3,834	1,077	....	....	....	....	2,396	1,365	1,031	289
Mar	13,310	9,996	5,932	4,064	1,107	....	....	....	....	2,367	1,362	1,005	228
Apr	13,816	10,213	6,196	4,017	1,075	....	....	....	....	2,676	1,538	1,138	268
May	14,518	10,874	6,625	4,250	1,127	....	....	....	....	2,650	1,490	1,161	294
June	14,721	10,986	6,712	4,274	1,163	....	....	....	....	2,617	1,444	1,173	280
July	14,534	10,927	6,677	4,251	1,202	....	....	....	....	2,600	1,397	1,203	270
Aug	14,993	11,254	6,907	4,347	1,303	....	....	....	....	2,682	1,499	1,184	247
Sept	15,159	11,366	6,985	4,381	1,212	....	....	....	....	2,701	1,468	1,233	287
Oct	15,612	11,813	7,213	4,600	1,279	....	....	....	....	2,754	1,496	1,257	298
Nov	15,340	11,589	7,037	4,552	1,142	....	....	....	....	2,757	1,559	1,198	370
Dec	15,267	11,266	6,707	4,559	1,174	....	....	....	....	2,843	1,505	1,337	356

[1] See footnote 1 and Note, Table B–37.

Note: See footnote 5 and Note, Table B–35.

Source: Department of Labor (Bureau of Labor Statistics).

[Percent [1]; monthly data seasonally adjusted]

Year or month	Labor force participation rate							Employment/population ratio						
	All civilian workers	Males	Females	Both sexes 16–19 years	White[2]	Black and other[2]	Black or African American[2]	All civilian workers	Males	Females	Both sexes 16–19 years	White[2]	Black and other[2]	Black or African American[2]
1962	58.8	82.0	37.9	46.1	58.3	63.2	....	55.5	77.7	35.6	39.4	55.4	56.3	....
1963	58.7	81.4	38.3	45.2	58.2	63.0	....	55.4	77.1	35.8	37.4	55.3	56.2	....
1964	58.7	81.0	38.7	44.5	58.2	63.1	....	55.7	77.3	36.3	37.3	55.5	57.0	....
1965	58.9	80.7	39.3	45.7	58.4	62.9	....	56.2	77.5	37.1	38.9	56.0	57.8	....
1966	59.2	80.4	40.3	48.2	58.7	63.0	....	56.9	77.9	38.3	42.1	56.8	58.4	....
1967	59.6	80.4	41.1	48.4	59.2	62.8	....	57.3	78.0	39.0	42.2	57.2	58.2	....
1968	59.6	80.1	41.6	48.3	59.3	62.2	....	57.5	77.8	39.6	42.2	57.4	58.0	....
1969	60.1	79.8	42.7	49.4	59.9	62.1	....	58.0	77.6	40.7	43.4	58.0	58.1	....
1970	60.4	79.7	43.3	49.9	60.2	61.8	....	57.4	76.2	40.8	42.3	57.5	56.8	....
1971	60.2	79.1	43.4	49.7	60.1	60.9	....	56.6	74.9	40.4	41.3	56.8	54.9	....
1972	60.4	78.9	43.9	51.9	60.4	60.2	59.9	57.0	75.0	41.0	43.5	57.4	54.1	53.7
1973	60.8	78.8	44.7	53.7	60.8	60.5	60.2	57.8	75.5	42.0	45.9	58.2	55.0	54.5
1974	61.3	78.7	45.7	54.8	61.4	60.3	59.8	57.8	74.9	42.6	46.0	58.3	54.3	53.5
1975	61.2	77.9	46.3	54.0	61.5	59.6	58.8	56.1	71.7	42.0	43.3	56.7	51.4	50.1
1976	61.6	77.5	47.3	54.5	61.8	59.8	59.0	56.8	72.0	43.2	44.2	57.5	52.0	50.8
1977	62.3	77.7	48.4	56.0	62.5	60.4	59.8	57.9	72.8	44.5	46.1	58.6	52.5	51.4
1978	63.2	77.9	50.0	57.8	63.3	62.2	61.5	59.3	73.8	46.4	48.3	60.0	54.7	53.6
1979	63.7	77.8	50.9	57.9	63.9	62.2	61.4	59.9	73.8	47.5	48.5	60.6	55.2	53.8
1980	63.8	77.4	51.5	56.7	64.1	61.7	61.0	59.2	72.0	47.7	46.6	60.0	53.6	52.3
1981	63.9	77.0	52.1	55.4	64.3	61.3	60.8	59.0	71.3	48.0	44.6	60.0	52.6	51.3
1982	64.0	76.6	52.6	54.1	64.3	61.6	61.0	57.8	69.0	47.7	41.5	58.8	50.9	49.4
1983	64.0	76.4	52.9	53.5	64.3	62.1	61.5	57.9	68.8	48.0	41.5	58.9	51.0	49.5
1984	64.4	76.4	53.6	53.9	64.6	62.6	62.2	59.5	70.7	49.5	43.7	60.5	53.6	52.3
1985	64.8	76.3	54.5	54.5	65.0	63.3	62.9	60.1	70.9	50.4	44.4	61.0	54.7	53.4
1986	65.3	76.3	55.3	54.7	65.5	63.7	63.3	60.7	71.0	51.4	44.6	61.5	55.4	54.1
1987	65.6	76.2	56.0	54.7	65.8	64.3	63.8	61.5	71.5	52.5	45.5	62.3	56.8	55.6
1988	65.9	76.2	56.6	55.3	66.2	64.0	63.8	62.3	72.0	53.4	46.8	63.1	57.4	56.3
1989	66.5	76.4	57.4	55.9	66.7	64.7	64.2	63.0	72.5	54.3	47.5	63.8	58.2	56.9
1990	66.5	76.4	57.5	53.7	66.9	64.4	64.0	62.8	72.0	54.3	45.3	63.7	57.9	56.7
1991	66.2	75.8	57.4	51.6	66.6	63.8	63.3	61.7	70.4	53.7	42.0	62.6	56.7	55.4
1992	66.4	75.8	57.8	51.3	66.8	64.6	63.9	61.5	69.8	53.8	41.0	62.4	56.4	54.9
1993	66.3	75.4	57.9	51.5	66.8	63.8	63.2	61.7	70.0	54.1	41.7	62.7	56.3	55.0
1994	66.6	75.1	58.8	52.7	67.1	63.9	63.4	62.5	70.4	55.3	43.4	63.5	57.2	56.1
1995	66.6	75.0	58.9	53.5	67.1	64.3	63.7	62.9	70.8	55.6	44.2	63.8	58.1	57.1
1996	66.8	74.9	59.3	52.3	67.2	64.6	64.1	63.2	70.9	56.0	43.5	64.1	58.6	57.4
1997	67.1	75.0	59.8	51.6	67.5	65.2	64.7	63.8	71.3	56.8	43.4	64.6	59.4	58.2
1998	67.1	74.9	59.8	52.8	67.3	66.0	65.6	64.1	71.6	57.1	45.1	64.7	60.9	59.7
1999	67.1	74.7	60.0	52.0	67.3	65.9	65.8	64.3	71.6	57.4	44.7	64.8	61.3	60.6
2000	67.1	74.8	59.9	52.0	67.3	....	65.8	64.4	71.9	57.5	45.2	64.9	....	60.9
2001	66.8	74.4	59.8	49.6	67.0	....	65.3	63.7	70.9	57.0	42.3	64.2	....	59.7
2002	66.6	74.1	59.6	47.4	66.8	....	64.8	62.7	69.7	56.3	39.6	63.4	....	58.1
2003	66.2	73.5	59.5	44.5	66.5	....	64.3	62.3	68.9	56.1	36.8	63.0	....	57.4
2004	66.0	73.3	59.2	43.9	66.3	....	63.8	62.3	69.2	56.0	36.4	63.1	....	57.2
2005	66.0	73.3	59.3	43.7	66.3	....	64.2	62.7	69.6	56.2	36.5	63.4	....	57.7
2006	66.2	73.5	59.4	43.7	66.5	....	64.1	63.1	70.1	56.6	36.9	63.8	....	58.4
2007	66.0	73.2	59.3	41.3	66.4	....	63.7	63.0	69.8	56.6	34.8	63.6	....	58.4
2008	66.0	73.0	59.5	40.2	66.3	....	63.7	62.2	68.5	56.2	32.6	62.8	....	57.3
2009	65.4	72.0	59.2	37.5	65.8	....	62.4	59.3	64.5	54.4	28.4	60.2	....	53.2
2008: Jan	66.2	73.3	59.6	41.2	66.5	....	64.0	62.9	69.6	56.7	33.9	63.5	....	58.2
Feb	66.0	73.1	59.3	40.0	66.2	....	63.7	62.8	69.5	56.5	33.4	63.3	....	58.4
Mar	66.1	73.1	59.5	40.1	66.3	....	64.0	62.7	69.3	56.6	33.7	63.3	....	58.2
Apr	66.0	73.0	59.5	41.0	66.2	....	64.0	62.7	69.2	56.6	34.6	63.3	....	58.5
May	66.2	73.1	59.6	42.1	66.4	....	63.8	62.6	69.0	56.5	34.1	63.2	....	57.7
June	66.1	73.0	59.5	40.4	66.3	....	63.6	62.4	68.8	56.4	32.7	63.1	....	57.6
July	66.0	73.2	59.3	40.5	66.4	....	63.6	62.2	68.6	56.2	32.1	63.0	....	57.3
Aug	66.1	73.0	59.6	39.9	66.4	....	64.4	62.0	68.4	56.1	32.4	62.7	....	57.4
Sept	66.0	73.0	59.4	40.0	66.3	....	63.6	61.9	68.1	56.1	32.3	62.7	....	56.3
Oct	66.0	72.9	59.5	39.8	66.4	....	63.6	61.7	67.7	56.0	31.8	62.4	....	56.4
Nov	65.8	72.6	59.4	38.5	66.2	....	63.2	61.3	67.2	55.7	30.7	62.0	....	55.9
Dec	65.8	72.5	59.5	38.4	66.1	....	63.4	60.9	66.6	55.6	30.4	61.6	....	55.8
2009: Jan	65.7	72.3	59.5	38.5	66.0	....	63.2	60.6	66.1	55.4	30.4	61.4	....	55.1
Feb	65.7	72.3	59.6	38.8	66.1	....	63.0	60.3	65.8	55.2	30.3	61.2	....	54.5
Mar	65.6	72.0	59.5	38.1	66.0	....	62.4	59.9	65.1	55.0	29.7	60.7	....	54.0
Apr	65.8	72.4	59.6	38.1	66.2	....	63.2	59.9	65.1	55.0	29.8	60.8	....	53.7
May	65.8	72.5	59.5	38.4	66.3	....	62.9	59.4	64.9	54.7	29.5	60.6	....	53.5
June	65.7	72.3	59.4	38.3	66.1	....	62.6	59.4	64.6	54.5	29.0	60.3	....	53.3
July	65.4	72.0	59.2	37.9	65.9	....	62.5	59.3	64.5	54.4	28.6	60.2	....	53.3
Aug	65.4	72.2	59.1	37.5	66.0	....	62.2	59.1	64.3	54.2	27.8	60.1	....	52.7
Sept	65.1	71.8	58.8	36.8	65.7	....	61.6	58.7	63.9	53.8	27.2	59.7	....	52.1
Oct	65.0	71.8	58.7	36.1	65.6	....	61.7	58.4	63.6	53.6	26.1	59.4	....	52.0
Nov	64.9	71.5	58.8	35.8	65.4	....	62.2	58.5	63.5	53.7	26.2	59.4	....	52.5
Dec	64.6	71.0	58.6	35.6	65.0	....	61.9	58.2	63.2	53.4	25.9	59.1	....	51.9

[1] Civilian labor force or civilian employment as percent of civilian noninstitutional population in group specified.
[2] See footnote 1, Table B–37.

Note: Data relate to persons 16 years of age and over.
See footnote 5 and Note, Table B–35.

Source: Department of Labor (Bureau of Labor Statistics).

Table B–40. Civilian labor force participation rate by demographic characteristic, 1968–2009

[Percent [1]; monthly data seasonally adjusted]

Year or month	All civilian workers	White [2] Total	White Males Total	White Males 16–19 years	White Males 20 years and over	White Females Total	White Females 16–19 years	White Females 20 years and over	Black and other or black or African American [2] Total	Males Total	Males 16–19 years	Males 20 years and over	Females Total	Females 16–19 years	Females 20 years and over
									Black and other [2]						
1968	59.6	59.3	80.4	55.9	83.2	40.7	43.0	40.4	62.2	77.7	49.7	82.2	49.3	34.8	51.4
1969	60.1	59.9	80.2	56.8	83.0	41.8	44.6	41.5	62.1	76.9	49.6	81.4	49.8	34.6	52.0
1970	60.4	60.2	80.0	57.5	82.8	42.6	45.6	42.2	61.8	76.5	47.4	81.4	49.5	34.1	51.8
1971	60.2	60.1	79.6	57.9	82.3	42.6	45.4	42.3	60.9	74.9	44.7	80.0	49.2	31.2	51.8
1972	60.4	60.4	79.6	60.1	82.0	43.2	48.1	42.7	60.2	73.9	46.0	78.6	48.8	32.3	51.2
									Black or African American [2]						
1972	60.4	60.4	79.6	60.1	82.0	43.2	48.1	42.7	59.9	73.6	46.3	78.5	48.7	32.2	51.2
1973	60.8	60.8	79.4	62.0	81.6	44.1	50.1	43.5	60.2	73.4	45.7	78.4	49.3	34.2	51.6
1974	61.3	61.4	79.4	62.9	81.4	45.2	51.7	44.4	59.8	72.9	46.7	77.6	49.0	33.4	51.4
1975	61.2	61.5	78.7	61.9	80.7	45.9	51.5	45.3	58.8	70.9	42.6	76.0	48.8	34.2	51.1
1976	61.6	61.8	78.4	62.3	80.3	46.9	52.8	46.2	59.0	70.0	41.3	75.4	49.8	32.9	52.5
1977	62.3	62.5	78.5	64.0	80.2	48.0	54.5	47.3	59.8	70.6	43.2	75.6	50.8	32.9	53.6
1978	63.2	63.3	78.6	65.0	80.1	49.4	56.7	48.7	61.5	71.5	44.9	76.2	53.1	37.3	55.5
1979	63.7	63.9	78.6	64.8	80.1	50.5	57.4	49.8	61.4	71.3	43.6	76.3	53.1	36.8	55.4
1980	63.8	64.1	78.2	63.7	79.8	51.2	56.2	50.6	61.0	70.3	43.2	75.1	53.1	34.9	55.6
1981	63.9	64.3	77.9	62.4	79.5	51.9	55.4	51.5	60.8	70.0	41.6	74.5	53.5	34.0	56.0
1982	64.0	64.3	77.4	60.0	79.2	52.4	55.0	52.2	61.0	70.1	39.8	74.7	53.7	33.5	56.2
1983	64.0	64.3	77.1	59.4	78.9	52.7	54.5	52.5	61.5	70.6	39.9	75.2	54.2	33.0	56.8
1984	64.4	64.6	77.1	59.0	78.7	53.3	55.4	53.1	62.2	70.8	41.7	74.8	55.2	35.0	57.6
1985	64.8	65.0	77.0	59.7	78.5	54.1	55.2	54.0	62.9	70.8	44.6	74.4	56.5	37.9	58.6
1986	65.3	65.5	76.9	59.3	78.5	55.0	56.3	54.9	63.3	71.2	43.7	74.8	56.9	39.1	58.9
1987	65.6	65.8	76.8	59.0	78.4	55.7	56.5	55.6	63.8	71.1	43.6	74.7	58.0	39.6	60.0
1988	65.9	66.2	76.9	60.0	78.3	56.4	57.2	56.3	63.8	71.0	43.8	74.6	58.0	37.9	60.1
1989	66.5	66.7	77.1	61.0	78.5	57.2	57.1	57.2	64.2	71.0	44.6	74.4	58.7	40.4	60.6
1990	66.5	66.9	77.1	59.6	78.5	57.4	55.3	57.6	64.0	71.0	40.7	75.0	58.3	36.8	60.6
1991	66.2	66.6	76.5	57.3	78.0	57.4	54.1	57.6	63.3	70.4	37.3	74.6	57.5	33.5	60.0
1992	66.4	66.8	76.5	56.9	78.0	57.7	52.5	58.1	63.9	70.7	40.6	74.3	58.5	35.2	60.8
1993	66.3	66.8	76.2	56.6	77.7	58.0	53.5	58.3	63.2	69.6	39.5	73.2	57.9	34.6	60.2
1994	66.6	67.1	75.9	57.7	77.3	58.9	55.1	59.2	63.4	69.1	40.8	72.5	58.7	36.3	60.9
1995	66.6	67.1	75.7	58.5	77.1	59.0	55.5	59.2	63.7	69.0	40.1	72.5	59.5	39.8	61.4
1996	66.8	67.2	75.8	57.1	77.3	59.1	54.7	59.4	64.1	68.7	39.5	72.3	60.4	38.9	62.6
1997	67.1	67.5	75.9	56.1	77.5	59.5	54.1	59.9	64.7	68.3	37.4	72.2	61.7	39.9	64.0
1998	67.1	67.3	75.6	56.6	77.2	59.4	55.4	59.7	65.6	69.0	40.7	72.5	62.8	42.5	64.8
1999	67.1	67.3	75.6	56.4	77.2	59.6	54.5	59.9	65.8	68.7	38.6	72.4	63.5	38.8	66.1
2000	67.1	67.3	75.5	56.7	77.1	59.5	54.5	59.9	65.8	69.2	39.2	72.8	63.1	39.6	65.4
2001	66.8	67.0	75.1	53.7	76.9	59.4	52.4	59.9	65.3	68.4	37.9	72.1	62.8	37.3	65.2
2002	66.6	66.8	74.8	50.3	76.7	59.3	50.8	60.0	64.8	68.4	37.3	72.1	61.8	34.7	64.4
2003	66.2	66.5	74.2	47.5	76.3	59.2	47.9	59.9	64.3	67.3	31.1	71.5	61.9	33.7	64.6
2004	66.0	66.3	74.1	47.4	76.2	58.9	46.7	59.7	63.8	66.7	30.0	70.9	61.5	32.8	64.2
2005	66.0	66.3	74.1	46.2	76.2	58.9	47.6	59.7	64.2	67.3	32.6	71.3	61.6	32.2	64.4
2006	66.2	66.5	74.3	46.9	76.4	59.0	46.6	59.9	64.1	67.0	32.3	71.1	61.7	35.6	64.2
2007	66.0	66.4	74.0	44.3	76.3	59.0	44.6	60.1	63.7	66.8	29.4	71.2	61.1	31.2	64.0
2008	66.0	66.3	73.7	43.0	76.1	59.2	43.3	60.3	63.7	66.7	29.1	71.1	61.3	29.7	64.3
2009	65.4	65.8	72.8	40.3	75.3	59.1	40.9	60.4	62.4	65.0	26.4	69.6	60.3	27.9	63.4
2008: Jan	66.2	66.5	74.0	42.3	76.5	59.2	45.2	60.2	64.0	67.7	37.8	71.2	61.1	27.7	64.3
Feb	66.0	66.2	73.8	42.2	76.3	59.0	43.5	60.1	63.7	66.8	28.0	71.4	61.1	33.9	63.8
Mar	66.1	66.3	73.8	42.1	76.3	59.1	43.2	60.2	64.0	66.6	26.2	71.3	62.0	31.9	64.9
Apr	66.0	66.2	73.7	43.8	76.0	59.0	44.8	60.0	64.0	66.5	25.5	71.4	61.9	31.5	64.8
May	66.2	66.4	73.9	45.8	76.1	59.2	44.4	60.3	63.8	66.6	30.4	70.9	61.5	31.0	64.5
June	66.1	66.3	73.8	43.9	76.1	59.2	43.2	60.4	63.6	66.9	28.2	71.4	60.9	27.8	64.1
July	66.0	66.4	74.1	44.0	76.4	59.1	43.2	60.2	63.6	66.7	29.5	71.1	61.0	29.9	64.0
Aug	66.1	66.4	73.7	42.6	76.1	59.3	42.9	60.4	64.4	67.5	31.1	71.8	61.8	32.1	64.7
Sept	66.0	66.3	73.7	42.5	76.1	59.2	42.8	60.4	63.6	67.0	30.0	71.4	60.8	30.0	63.8
Oct	66.0	66.4	73.7	42.8	76.1	59.4	43.1	60.5	63.6	66.7	31.9	70.9	61.1	27.9	64.3
Nov	65.8	66.2	73.5	42.4	75.9	59.2	41.6	60.4	63.2	65.6	24.9	70.4	61.2	26.7	64.5
Dec	65.8	66.1	73.2	41.7	75.6	59.3	41.5	60.5	63.4	66.2	26.7	70.8	61.2	27.1	64.5
2009: Jan	65.7	66.0	73.1	41.3	75.5	59.2	41.5	60.4	63.2	66.0	27.5	70.5	61.0	30.7	63.9
Feb	65.7	66.1	73.1	41.7	75.5	59.4	43.6	60.6	63.0	65.8	27.0	70.3	60.7	28.3	63.9
Mar	65.6	66.0	72.8	40.8	75.3	59.4	42.6	60.6	62.4	65.1	23.5	70.0	60.2	27.6	63.3
Apr	65.8	66.2	73.2	40.3	75.7	59.5	42.0	60.7	63.2	66.2	29.2	70.5	60.8	27.7	64.0
May	65.8	66.3	73.4	41.8	75.9	59.4	41.6	60.6	62.9	65.6	25.0	70.3	60.6	29.7	63.6
June	65.7	66.1	73.2	40.3	75.7	59.2	42.1	60.4	62.6	64.9	25.2	69.5	60.7	29.0	63.8
July	65.4	65.9	73.1	40.9	75.6	59.1	41.1	60.3	62.5	64.7	26.7	69.2	60.6	28.9	63.7
Aug	65.4	66.0	73.1	41.8	75.5	59.1	40.5	60.4	62.2	64.8	25.0	69.4	60.1	27.8	63.2
Sept	65.1	65.7	72.9	40.3	75.4	58.8	39.5	60.1	61.6	64.0	25.8	68.4	59.6	25.6	62.9
Oct	65.0	65.6	72.7	39.6	75.3	58.8	38.7	60.2	61.7	64.6	26.1	69.0	59.4	26.7	62.5
Nov	64.9	65.4	72.4	37.5	75.0	58.7	38.9	60.1	62.2	65.0	30.2	69.0	59.8	25.5	63.1
Dec	64.6	65.0	71.7	37.8	74.3	58.6	39.0	60.0	61.9	64.6	27.6	68.8	59.7	27.5	62.7

[1] Civilian labor force as percent of civilian noninstitutional population in group specified.
[2] See footnote 1, Table B–37.

Note: Data relate to persons 16 years of age and over.
See footnote 5 and Note, Table B–35.

Source: Department of Labor (Bureau of Labor Statistics).

TABLE B–41. Civilian employment/population ratio by demographic characteristic, 1968–2009

[Percent [1]; monthly data seasonally adjusted]

Year or month	All civilian workers	White [2]						Black and other or black or African American [2]						
		Total	Males			Females			Total	Males			Females		
			Total	16–19 years	20 years and over	Total	16–19 years	20 years and over	Total	Total	16–19 years	20 years and over	Total	16–19 years	20 years and over
									Black and other [2]						
1968	57.5	57.4	78.3	50.3	81.6	38.9	37.8	39.1	58.0	73.3	38.7	78.9	45.2	24.7	48.2
1969	58.0	58.0	78.2	51.1	81.4	40.1	39.5	40.1	58.1	72.8	39.0	78.4	45.9	25.1	48.9
1970	57.4	57.5	76.8	49.6	80.1	40.3	39.5	40.4	56.8	70.9	35.5	76.8	44.9	22.4	48.2
1971	56.6	56.8	75.7	49.2	79.0	39.9	38.6	40.1	54.9	68.1	31.8	74.2	43.9	20.2	47.3
1972	57.0	57.4	76.0	51.5	79.0	40.7	41.3	40.6	54.1	67.3	32.4	73.2	43.3	19.9	46.7
									Black or African American [2]						
1972	57.0	57.4	76.0	51.5	79.0	40.7	41.3	40.6	53.7	66.8	31.6	73.0	43.0	19.2	46.5
1973	57.8	58.2	76.5	54.3	79.2	41.8	43.6	41.6	54.5	67.5	32.8	73.7	43.8	22.0	47.2
1974	57.8	58.3	75.9	54.4	78.6	42.4	44.3	42.2	53.5	65.8	31.4	71.9	43.5	20.9	46.9
1975	56.1	56.7	73.0	50.6	75.7	42.0	42.5	41.9	50.1	60.6	26.3	66.5	41.6	20.2	44.9
1976	56.8	57.5	73.4	51.5	76.0	43.2	44.2	43.1	50.8	60.6	25.8	66.8	42.8	19.2	46.4
1977	57.9	58.6	74.1	54.4	76.5	44.5	45.9	44.4	51.4	61.4	26.4	67.5	43.3	18.5	47.0
1978	59.3	60.0	75.0	56.3	77.2	46.3	48.5	46.1	53.6	63.3	28.5	69.1	45.8	22.1	49.3
1979	59.9	60.6	75.1	55.7	77.3	47.5	49.4	47.3	53.8	63.4	28.7	69.1	46.0	22.4	49.3
1980	59.2	60.0	73.4	53.4	75.6	47.8	47.9	47.8	52.3	60.4	27.0	65.8	45.7	21.0	49.1
1981	59.0	60.0	72.8	51.3	75.1	48.3	46.2	48.5	51.3	59.1	24.6	64.5	45.1	19.7	48.5
1982	57.8	58.8	70.6	47.0	73.0	48.1	44.6	48.4	49.4	56.0	20.3	61.4	44.2	17.7	47.5
1983	57.9	58.9	70.4	47.4	72.6	48.5	44.5	48.9	49.5	56.3	20.4	61.6	44.1	17.0	47.4
1984	59.5	60.5	72.1	49.1	74.3	49.8	47.0	50.0	52.3	59.2	23.9	64.1	46.7	20.1	49.8
1985	60.1	61.0	72.3	49.9	74.3	50.7	47.1	51.0	53.4	60.0	26.3	64.6	48.1	23.1	50.9
1986	60.7	61.5	72.3	49.6	74.3	51.7	47.9	52.0	54.1	60.6	26.5	65.1	48.8	23.8	51.6
1987	61.5	62.3	72.7	49.9	74.7	52.8	49.0	53.1	55.6	62.0	28.5	66.4	50.3	25.8	53.0
1988	62.3	63.1	73.2	51.7	75.1	53.8	50.2	54.0	56.3	62.7	29.4	67.1	51.2	25.8	53.9
1989	63.0	63.8	73.7	52.6	75.4	54.6	50.5	54.9	56.9	62.8	30.4	67.0	52.0	27.1	54.6
1990	62.8	63.7	73.3	51.0	75.1	54.7	48.3	55.2	56.7	62.6	27.7	67.1	51.9	25.8	54.7
1991	61.7	62.6	71.6	47.2	73.5	54.2	45.9	54.8	55.4	61.3	23.8	65.9	50.6	21.5	53.6
1992	61.5	62.4	71.1	46.4	73.1	54.2	44.2	54.9	54.9	59.9	23.6	64.3	50.8	22.1	53.6
1993	61.7	62.7	71.4	46.6	73.3	54.6	45.7	55.2	55.0	60.0	23.6	64.3	50.9	21.6	53.8
1994	62.5	63.5	71.8	48.3	73.6	55.8	47.5	56.4	56.1	60.8	25.4	65.0	52.3	24.5	55.0
1995	62.9	63.8	72.0	49.4	73.8	56.1	48.1	56.7	57.1	61.7	25.2	66.1	53.4	26.1	56.1
1996	63.2	64.1	72.3	48.2	74.2	56.3	47.6	57.0	57.4	61.1	24.9	65.5	54.4	27.1	57.1
1997	63.8	64.6	72.7	48.1	74.7	57.0	47.2	57.8	58.2	61.4	23.7	66.1	55.6	28.5	58.4
1998	64.1	64.7	72.7	48.6	74.7	57.1	49.3	57.7	59.7	62.9	28.4	67.1	57.2	31.8	59.7
1999	64.3	64.8	72.8	49.3	74.8	57.3	48.3	58.0	60.6	63.1	26.7	67.5	58.6	29.0	61.5
2000	64.4	64.9	73.0	49.5	74.9	57.4	48.8	58.0	60.9	63.6	28.9	67.7	58.6	30.6	61.3
2001	63.7	64.2	72.0	46.2	74.0	57.0	46.5	57.7	59.7	62.1	26.4	66.3	57.8	27.0	60.7
2002	62.7	63.4	70.8	42.3	73.1	56.4	44.1	57.3	58.1	61.1	25.6	65.2	55.8	24.9	58.7
2003	62.3	63.0	70.1	39.4	72.5	56.3	41.5	57.3	57.4	59.5	19.9	64.1	55.6	23.4	58.6
2004	62.3	63.1	70.4	39.7	72.8	56.1	40.3	57.2	57.2	59.3	19.3	63.9	55.5	23.6	58.5
2005	62.7	63.4	70.8	38.8	73.3	56.3	41.4	57.7	57.7	60.2	20.8	64.7	55.7	22.4	58.9
2006	63.1	63.8	71.3	40.0	73.7	56.6	41.1	57.7	58.4	60.6	21.7	65.2	56.5	26.4	59.4
2007	63.0	63.6	70.9	37.3	73.5	56.7	39.2	57.9	58.4	60.7	19.5	65.5	56.5	23.3	59.8
2008	62.2	62.8	69.7	34.8	72.4	56.3	37.1	57.7	57.3	59.1	18.7	63.9	55.8	21.7	59.1
2009	59.3	60.2	66.0	30.2	68.7	54.8	33.4	56.3	53.2	53.7	14.3	58.2	52.8	18.6	56.1
2008: Jan	62.9	63.5	70.7	34.2	73.5	56.7	39.4	57.9	58.2	60.9	23.4	65.3	56.0	19.8	59.5
Feb	62.8	63.3	70.5	35.1	73.3	56.5	38.3	57.8	58.4	60.8	19.3	65.7	56.4	23.6	59.6
Mar	62.7	63.3	70.5	36.0	73.1	56.5	38.1	57.8	58.2	60.1	16.0	65.3	56.7	23.5	59.9
Apr	62.7	63.3	70.3	37.0	72.9	56.5	38.9	57.8	58.5	60.4	18.5	65.4	56.8	24.3	60.0
May	62.6	63.2	70.2	37.6	72.8	56.5	37.5	57.8	57.7	59.7	18.4	64.5	56.1	23.3	59.3
June	62.4	63.1	70.0	35.6	72.6	56.4	36.7	57.8	57.6	59.7	18.2	64.6	55.9	21.2	59.3
July	62.2	63.0	70.0	34.2	72.7	56.3	36.5	57.7	57.3	58.9	18.1	63.7	55.9	21.7	59.2
Aug	62.0	62.7	69.6	34.3	72.3	56.2	36.6	57.6	57.4	59.8	21.8	64.2	55.5	22.5	58.8
Sept	61.9	62.7	69.3	34.1	72.0	56.4	36.3	57.8	56.3	58.3	20.2	62.8	54.7	21.8	57.9
Oct	61.7	62.4	69.0	33.4	71.7	56.2	37.0	57.6	56.4	57.9	19.3	62.4	55.2	20.5	58.6
Nov	61.3	62.0	68.5	33.3	71.2	55.8	35.2	57.3	55.9	56.7	14.3	61.7	55.3	20.8	58.6
Dec	60.9	61.6	67.9	32.8	70.6	55.6	34.7	57.1	55.8	56.4	17.3	61.1	55.2	18.6	58.7
2009: Jan	60.6	61.4	67.5	32.2	70.2	55.4	35.2	56.9	55.1	55.6	15.3	60.4	54.7	21.5	57.9
Feb	60.3	61.2	67.1	32.3	69.8	55.5	36.5	56.8	54.5	55.0	14.7	59.7	54.1	19.1	57.4
Mar	59.9	60.7	66.4	31.2	69.2	55.3	35.4	56.7	54.0	54.3	13.7	59.1	53.7	20.4	56.9
Apr	59.9	60.8	66.5	31.1	69.2	55.4	34.8	56.8	53.7	54.0	17.0	58.4	53.5	19.9	56.7
May	59.6	60.6	66.3	31.5	69.0	55.0	34.7	56.4	53.5	53.8	13.5	58.5	53.2	19.3	56.4
June	59.4	60.3	66.0	30.5	68.8	54.9	34.1	56.3	53.3	53.5	13.9	58.1	53.2	19.4	56.4
July	59.3	60.2	66.0	30.2	68.7	54.7	33.4	56.2	53.3	53.7	16.2	58.1	52.9	19.2	56.1
Aug	59.1	60.1	65.8	30.1	68.5	54.6	32.3	56.2	52.7	53.0	13.3	57.6	52.5	21.0	55.5
Sept	58.7	59.7	65.4	29.5	68.1	54.3	31.7	55.8	52.1	52.5	12.7	57.1	51.7	17.2	55.0
Oct	58.4	59.4	65.1	28.3	67.8	54.0	30.4	55.7	52.0	52.8	14.7	57.2	51.4	15.8	54.8
Nov	58.5	59.4	64.9	27.7	67.7	54.1	31.2	55.6	52.5	52.8	12.9	57.4	52.2	15.0	55.7
Dec	58.2	59.1	64.6	27.5	67.4	53.9	31.3	55.5	51.9	52.8	13.2	57.4	51.1	15.2	54.5

[1] Civilian employment as percent of civilian noninstitutional population in group specified.
[2] See footnote 1, Table B–37.

Note: Data relate to persons 16 years of age and over.
See footnote 5 and Note, Table B–35.

Source: Department of Labor (Bureau of Labor Statistics).

TABLE B–42. Civilian unemployment rate, 1962–2009

[Percent [1]; monthly data seasonally adjusted, except as noted]

Year or month	All civilian workers	Males Total	Males 16–19 years	Males 20 years and over	Females Total	Females 16–19 years	Females 20 years and over	Both sexes 16–19 years	White [2]	Black and other [2]	Black or African American [2]	Asian (NSA) [2,3]	Hispanic or Latino ethnicity [4]	Married men, spouse present	Women who maintain families (NSA) [3]
1962	5.5	5.2	14.7	4.6	6.2	14.6	5.4	14.7	4.9	10.9				3.6	
1963	5.7	5.2	17.2	4.5	6.5	17.2	5.4	17.2	5.0	10.8				3.4	
1964	5.2	4.6	15.8	3.9	6.2	16.6	5.2	16.2	4.6	9.6				2.8	
1965	4.5	4.0	14.1	3.2	5.5	15.7	4.5	14.8	4.1	8.1				2.4	
1966	3.8	3.2	11.7	2.5	4.8	14.1	3.8	12.8	3.4	7.3				1.9	
1967	3.8	3.1	12.3	2.3	5.2	13.5	4.2	12.9	3.4	7.4				1.8	4.9
1968	3.6	2.9	11.6	2.2	4.8	14.0	3.8	12.7	3.2	6.7				1.6	4.4
1969	3.5	2.8	11.4	2.1	4.7	13.3	3.7	12.2	3.1	6.4				1.5	4.4
1970	4.9	4.4	15.0	3.5	5.9	15.6	4.8	15.3	4.5	8.2				2.6	5.4
1971	5.9	5.3	16.6	4.4	6.9	17.2	5.7	16.9	5.4	9.9				3.2	7.3
1972	5.6	5.0	15.9	4.0	6.6	16.7	5.4	16.2	5.1	10.0	10.4			2.8	7.2
1973	4.9	4.2	13.9	3.3	6.0	15.3	4.9	14.5	4.3	9.0	9.4		7.5	2.3	7.1
1974	5.6	4.9	15.6	3.8	6.7	16.6	5.5	16.0	5.0	9.9	10.5		8.1	2.7	7.0
1975	8.5	7.9	20.1	6.8	9.3	19.7	8.0	19.9	7.8	13.8	14.8		12.2	5.1	10.0
1976	7.7	7.1	19.2	5.9	8.6	18.7	7.4	19.0	7.0	13.1	14.0		11.5	4.2	10.1
1977	7.1	6.3	17.3	5.2	8.2	18.3	7.0	17.8	6.2	13.1	14.0		10.1	3.6	9.4
1978	6.1	5.3	15.8	4.3	7.2	17.1	6.0	16.4	5.2	11.9	12.8		9.1	2.8	8.5
1979	5.8	5.1	15.9	4.2	6.8	16.4	5.7	16.1	5.1	11.3	12.3		8.3	2.8	8.3
1980	7.1	6.9	18.3	5.9	7.4	17.2	6.4	17.8	6.3	13.1	14.3		10.1	4.2	9.2
1981	7.6	7.4	20.1	6.3	7.9	19.0	6.8	19.6	6.7	14.2	15.6		10.4	4.3	10.4
1982	9.7	9.9	24.4	8.8	9.4	21.9	8.3	23.2	8.6	17.3	18.9		13.8	6.5	11.7
1983	9.6	9.9	23.3	8.9	9.2	21.3	8.1	22.4	8.4	17.8	19.5		13.7	6.5	12.2
1984	7.5	7.4	19.6	6.6	7.6	18.0	6.8	18.9	6.5	14.4	15.9		10.7	4.6	10.3
1985	7.2	7.0	19.5	6.2	7.4	17.6	6.6	18.6	6.2	13.7	15.1		10.5	4.3	10.4
1986	7.0	6.9	19.0	6.1	7.1	17.6	6.2	18.3	6.0	13.1	14.5		10.6	4.4	9.8
1987	6.2	6.2	17.8	5.4	6.2	15.9	5.4	16.9	5.3	11.6	13.0		8.8	3.9	9.2
1988	5.5	5.5	16.0	4.8	5.6	14.4	4.9	15.3	4.7	10.4	11.7		8.2	3.3	8.1
1989	5.3	5.2	15.9	4.5	5.4	14.0	4.7	15.0	4.5	10.0	11.4		8.0	3.0	8.1
1990	5.6	5.7	16.3	5.0	5.5	14.7	4.9	15.5	4.8	10.1	11.4		8.2	3.4	8.3
1991	6.8	7.2	19.8	6.4	6.4	17.5	5.7	18.7	6.1	11.1	12.5		10.0	4.4	9.3
1992	7.5	7.9	21.5	7.1	7.0	18.6	6.3	20.1	6.6	12.7	14.2		11.6	5.1	10.0
1993	6.9	7.2	20.4	6.4	6.6	17.5	5.9	19.0	6.1	11.7	13.0		10.8	4.4	9.7
1994	6.1	6.2	19.0	5.4	6.0	16.2	5.4	17.6	5.3	10.5	11.5		9.9	3.7	8.9
1995	5.6	5.6	18.4	4.8	5.6	16.1	4.9	17.3	4.9	9.6	10.4		9.3	3.3	8.0
1996	5.4	5.4	18.1	4.6	5.4	15.2	4.8	16.7	4.7	9.3	10.5		8.9	3.0	8.2
1997	4.9	4.9	16.9	4.2	5.0	15.0	4.4	16.0	4.2	8.8	10.0		7.7	2.7	8.1
1998	4.5	4.4	16.2	3.7	4.6	12.9	4.1	14.6	3.9	7.8	8.9		7.2	2.4	7.2
1999	4.2	4.1	14.7	3.5	4.3	13.2	3.8	13.9	3.7	7.0	8.0		6.4	2.2	6.4
2000	4.0	3.9	14.0	3.3	4.1	12.1	3.6	13.1	3.5		7.6	3.6	5.7	2.0	5.9
2001	4.7	4.8	16.0	4.2	4.7	13.4	4.1	14.7	4.2		8.6	4.5	6.6	2.7	6.6
2002	5.8	5.9	18.1	5.3	5.6	14.9	5.1	16.5	5.1		10.2	5.9	7.5	3.6	8.0
2003	6.0	6.3	19.3	5.6	5.7	15.6	5.1	17.5	5.2		10.8	6.0	7.7	3.8	8.5
2004	5.5	5.6	18.4	5.0	5.4	15.5	4.9	17.0	4.8		10.4	4.4	7.0	3.1	8.0
2005	5.1	5.1	18.6	4.4	5.1	14.5	4.6	16.6	4.4		10.0	4.0	6.0	2.8	7.8
2006	4.6	4.6	16.9	4.0	4.6	13.8	4.1	15.4	4.0		8.9	3.0	5.2	2.4	7.1
2007	4.6	4.7	17.6	4.1	4.5	13.8	4.0	15.7	4.1		8.3	3.2	5.6	2.5	6.5
2008	5.8	6.1	21.2	5.4	5.4	16.2	4.9	18.7	5.2		10.1	4.0	7.6	3.4	8.0
2009	9.3	10.3	27.8	9.6	8.1	20.7	7.5	24.3	8.5		14.8	7.3	12.1	6.6	11.5
2008: Jan	5.0	5.1	21.2	4.4	4.7	14.4	4.2	17.8	4.4		9.2	3.2	6.4	2.7	7.0
Feb	4.8	4.9	18.4	4.4	4.7	14.6	4.2	16.5	4.4		8.3	3.0	6.2	2.7	6.7
Mar	5.1	5.2	17.8	4.6	4.9	14.2	4.5	16.0	4.5		9.1	3.6	6.9	2.9	7.1
Apr	5.0	5.1	17.1	4.6	4.7	14.1	4.3	15.6	4.4		8.6	3.2	6.9	2.8	6.8
May	5.4	5.6	20.8	4.9	5.3	16.9	4.7	18.9	4.8		9.6	3.8	6.9	2.9	6.9
June	5.5	5.8	21.1	5.1	5.3	16.8	4.7	19.0	5.0		9.4	4.5	7.7	3.0	7.9
July	5.8	6.2	24.1	5.4	5.3	17.3	4.7	20.8	5.2		9.9	4.0	7.5	3.3	8.5
Aug	6.1	6.4	20.7	5.7	5.9	17.2	5.4	18.9	5.5		10.8	4.4	8.0	3.6	9.6
Sept	6.2	6.8	21.3	6.1	5.5	17.1	5.0	19.3	5.5		11.4	3.8	8.0	3.9	8.2
Oct	6.6	7.1	24.2	6.4	5.9	16.1	5.4	20.3	6.0		11.3	3.8	8.9	4.1	8.8
Nov	6.9	7.5	23.8	6.8	6.2	16.6	5.7	20.3	6.3		11.5	4.8	8.8	4.3	9.3
Dec	7.4	8.1	23.2	7.4	6.6	18.3	6.0	20.8	6.7		12.1	5.1	9.4	4.6	9.5
2009: Jan	7.7	8.5	24.4	7.8	6.9	17.3	6.4	20.9	7.0		12.8	6.2	9.9	5.1	10.3
Feb	8.2	9.0	25.0	8.4	7.3	18.6	6.8	21.8	7.5		13.5	6.9	11.0	5.6	10.3
Mar	8.6	9.6	25.9	8.9	7.6	18.2	7.1	22.0	8.0		13.5	6.4	11.6	6.0	10.8
Apr	8.9	10.1	25.9	9.4	7.6	17.6	7.2	21.8	8.1		15.0	6.6	11.4	6.3	10.0
May	9.4	10.5	27.1	9.8	8.1	19.1	7.5	23.2	8.6		15.0	6.7	12.7	6.7	11.0
June	9.5	10.6	26.5	10.0	8.3	22.1	7.6	24.3	8.7		14.8	8.2	12.3	6.9	11.7
July	9.4	10.5	27.9	9.8	8.2	20.9	7.6	24.5	8.7		14.7	8.3	12.4	6.9	12.6
Aug	9.7	11.0	29.9	10.2	8.3	21.4	7.7	25.7	8.9		15.2	7.5	13.0	7.1	12.2
Sept	9.8	11.0	29.9	10.3	8.5	22.2	7.9	26.1	9.1		15.5	7.4	12.7	7.3	11.6
Oct	10.1	11.4	31.0	10.6	8.8	24.0	8.1	27.6	9.4		15.7	7.5	13.1	7.5	12.9
Nov	10.0	11.2	30.4	10.4	8.6	23.1	8.0	26.8	9.3		15.6	7.3	12.7	7.5	11.4
Dec	10.0	11.0	30.9	10.2	8.8	23.1	8.2	27.1	9.0		16.2	8.4	12.9	7.3	13.0

[1] Unemployed as percent of civilian labor force in group specified.
[2] See footnote 1, Table B–37.
[3] Not seasonally adjusted (NSA).
[4] Persons whose ethnicity is identified as Hispanic or Latino may be of any race.

Note: Data relate to persons 16 years of age and over.
See footnote 5 and Note, Table B–35.

Source: Department of Labor (Bureau of Labor Statistics).

TABLE B–43. Civilian unemployment rate by demographic characteristic, 1968–2009

[Percent [1]; monthly data seasonally adjusted]

Year or month	All civilian workers	White [2] Total	Males Total	Males 16–19 years	Males 20 years and over	Females Total	Females 16–19 years	Females 20 years and over	Black and other or black or African American [2] Total	Males Total	Males 16–19 years	Males 20 years and over	Females Total	Females 16–19 years	Females 20 years and over
									Black and other [2]						
1968	3.6	3.2	2.6	10.1	2.0	4.3	12.1	3.4	6.7	5.6	22.1	3.9	8.3	28.7	6.3
1969	3.5	3.1	2.5	10.0	1.9	4.2	11.5	3.4	6.4	5.3	21.4	3.7	7.8	27.6	5.8
1970	4.9	4.5	4.0	13.7	3.2	5.4	13.4	4.4	8.2	7.3	25.0	5.6	9.3	34.5	6.9
1971	5.9	5.4	4.9	15.1	4.0	6.3	15.1	5.3	9.9	9.1	28.8	7.3	10.9	35.4	8.7
1972	5.6	5.1	4.5	14.2	3.6	5.9	14.2	4.9	10.0	8.9	29.7	6.3	11.4	38.4	8.8
									Black or African American [2]						
1972	5.6	5.1	4.5	14.2	3.6	5.9	14.2	4.9	10.4	9.3	31.7	7.0	11.8	40.5	9.0
1973	4.9	4.3	3.8	12.3	3.0	5.3	13.0	4.3	9.4	8.0	27.8	6.0	11.1	36.1	8.6
1974	5.6	5.0	4.4	13.5	3.5	6.1	14.5	5.1	10.5	9.8	33.1	7.4	11.3	37.4	8.8
1975	8.5	7.8	7.2	18.3	6.2	8.6	17.4	7.5	14.8	14.8	38.1	12.5	14.8	41.0	12.2
1976	7.7	7.0	6.4	17.3	5.4	7.9	16.4	6.8	14.0	13.7	37.5	11.4	14.3	41.6	11.7
1977	7.1	6.2	5.5	15.0	4.7	7.3	15.9	6.2	14.0	13.3	39.2	10.7	14.9	43.4	12.3
1978	6.1	5.2	4.6	13.5	3.7	6.2	14.4	5.2	12.8	11.8	36.7	9.3	13.8	40.8	11.2
1979	5.8	5.1	4.5	13.9	3.6	5.9	14.0	5.0	12.3	11.4	34.2	9.3	13.3	39.1	10.9
1980	7.1	6.3	6.1	16.2	5.3	6.5	14.8	5.6	14.3	14.5	37.5	12.4	14.0	39.8	11.9
1981	7.6	6.7	6.5	17.9	5.6	6.9	16.6	5.9	15.6	15.7	40.7	13.5	15.6	42.2	13.4
1982	9.7	8.6	8.8	21.7	7.8	8.3	19.0	7.3	18.9	20.1	48.9	17.8	17.6	47.1	15.4
1983	9.6	8.4	8.8	20.2	7.9	7.9	18.3	6.9	19.5	20.3	48.8	18.1	18.6	48.2	16.5
1984	7.5	6.5	6.4	16.8	5.7	6.5	15.2	5.8	15.9	16.4	42.7	14.3	15.4	42.6	13.5
1985	7.2	6.2	6.1	16.5	5.4	6.4	14.8	5.7	15.1	15.3	41.0	13.2	14.9	39.2	13.1
1986	7.0	6.0	6.0	16.3	5.3	6.1	14.9	5.4	14.5	14.8	39.3	12.9	14.2	39.2	12.4
1987	6.2	5.3	5.4	15.5	4.8	5.2	13.4	4.6	13.0	12.7	34.4	11.1	13.2	34.9	11.6
1988	5.5	4.7	4.7	13.9	4.1	4.7	12.3	4.1	11.7	11.7	32.7	10.1	11.7	32.0	10.4
1989	5.3	4.5	4.5	13.7	3.9	4.5	11.5	4.0	11.4	11.5	31.9	10.0	11.4	33.0	9.8
1990	5.6	4.8	4.9	14.3	4.3	4.7	12.6	4.1	11.4	11.9	31.9	10.4	10.9	29.9	9.7
1991	6.8	6.1	6.5	17.6	5.8	5.6	15.2	5.0	12.5	13.0	36.3	11.5	12.0	36.0	10.6
1992	7.5	6.6	7.0	18.5	6.4	6.1	15.8	5.5	14.2	15.2	42.0	13.5	13.2	37.2	11.8
1993	6.9	6.1	6.3	17.7	5.7	5.7	14.7	5.2	13.0	13.8	40.1	12.1	12.1	37.4	10.7
1994	6.1	5.3	5.4	16.3	4.8	5.2	13.8	4.6	11.5	12.0	37.6	10.3	11.0	32.6	9.8
1995	5.6	4.9	4.9	15.6	4.3	4.8	13.4	4.3	10.4	10.6	37.1	8.8	10.2	34.3	8.6
1996	5.4	4.7	4.7	15.5	4.1	4.7	12.9	4.1	10.5	11.1	36.9	9.4	10.0	30.3	8.7
1997	4.9	4.2	4.2	14.3	3.6	4.2	12.8	3.7	10.0	10.2	36.5	8.5	9.9	28.7	8.8
1998	4.5	3.9	3.9	14.1	3.2	3.9	10.9	3.4	8.9	8.9	30.1	7.4	9.0	25.3	7.9
1999	4.2	3.7	3.6	12.6	3.0	3.8	11.3	3.3	8.0	8.2	30.9	6.7	7.8	25.1	6.8
2000	4.0	3.5	3.4	12.3	2.8	3.6	10.4	3.1	7.6	8.0	26.2	6.9	7.1	22.8	6.2
2001	4.7	4.2	4.2	13.9	3.7	4.1	11.4	3.6	8.6	9.3	30.4	8.0	8.1	27.5	7.0
2002	5.8	5.1	5.3	15.9	4.7	4.9	13.1	4.4	10.2	10.7	31.3	9.5	9.8	28.3	8.8
2003	6.0	5.2	5.6	17.1	5.0	4.8	13.3	4.4	10.8	11.6	36.0	10.3	10.2	30.3	9.2
2004	5.5	4.8	5.0	16.3	4.4	4.7	13.6	4.2	10.4	11.1	35.6	9.9	9.8	28.2	8.9
2005	5.1	4.4	4.4	16.1	3.8	4.4	12.3	3.9	10.0	10.5	36.3	9.2	9.5	30.3	8.5
2006	4.6	4.0	4.0	14.6	3.5	4.0	11.7	3.6	8.9	9.5	32.7	8.3	8.4	25.9	7.5
2007	4.6	4.1	4.2	15.7	3.7	4.0	12.1	3.6	8.3	9.1	33.8	7.9	7.5	25.3	6.7
2008	5.8	5.2	5.5	19.1	4.9	4.9	14.4	4.4	10.1	11.4	35.9	10.2	8.9	26.8	8.1
2009	9.3	8.5	9.4	25.2	8.8	7.3	18.4	6.8	14.8	17.5	46.0	16.3	12.4	33.4	11.5
2008: Jan	5.0	4.4	4.6	19.1	3.9	4.2	12.8	3.8	9.2	10.1	38.0	8.3	8.3	28.7	7.5
Feb	4.8	4.4	4.5	16.8	4.0	4.2	11.9	3.8	8.3	9.0	31.1	8.0	7.7	30.3	6.5
Mar	5.1	4.5	4.5	14.5	4.1	4.4	11.8	4.0	9.1	9.8	39.1	8.5	8.6	26.5	7.7
Apr	5.0	4.4	4.6	15.4	4.1	4.2	13.2	3.7	8.6	9.2	27.4	8.4	8.2	22.9	7.5
May	5.4	4.8	5.0	18.1	4.4	4.6	15.4	4.1	9.6	10.4	39.4	9.0	8.8	24.7	8.1
June	5.5	5.0	5.1	18.9	4.5	4.7	15.0	4.2	9.4	10.7	35.5	9.6	8.2	24.0	7.5
July	5.8	5.2	5.5	22.3	4.8	4.8	15.5	4.2	9.9	11.7	38.7	10.4	8.3	27.3	7.5
Aug	6.1	5.5	5.7	19.5	5.1	5.2	14.5	4.8	10.8	11.5	29.8	10.6	10.1	30.1	9.2
Sept	6.2	5.5	6.0	19.7	5.4	4.8	15.2	4.3	11.4	13.0	32.8	12.0	10.0	27.3	9.2
Oct	6.6	6.0	6.4	21.8	5.8	5.4	14.2	4.9	11.3	13.3	39.5	11.9	9.6	26.3	8.9
Nov	6.9	6.3	6.8	21.4	6.1	5.6	15.4	5.2	11.5	13.6	42.5	12.4	9.6	21.9	9.2
Dec	7.4	6.7	7.2	21.5	6.6	6.2	16.3	5.7	12.1	14.7	35.3	13.8	9.8	31.3	8.9
2009: Jan	7.7	7.0	7.6	22.0	7.0	6.3	15.0	5.9	12.8	15.7	44.4	14.4	10.3	30.1	9.4
Feb	8.2	7.5	8.2	22.4	7.6	6.6	16.3	6.1	13.5	16.4	45.6	15.1	11.0	32.5	10.1
Mar	8.6	8.0	8.7	23.5	8.1	7.0	17.1	6.5	13.5	16.6	41.7	15.6	10.8	26.0	10.1
Apr	8.9	8.1	9.1	22.9	8.5	6.9	17.1	6.4	15.0	18.4	41.7	17.2	12.1	28.2	11.4
May	9.4	8.6	9.7	24.6	9.0	7.4	16.6	6.9	15.0	17.9	46.2	16.7	12.3	34.8	11.3
June	9.5	8.7	9.8	24.4	9.2	7.4	19.0	6.8	14.8	17.5	44.8	16.4	12.4	33.1	11.5
July	9.4	8.7	9.8	26.1	9.1	7.4	18.7	6.8	14.7	17.0	39.2	16.0	12.8	33.5	11.9
Aug	9.7	8.9	10.1	28.1	9.3	7.5	20.2	7.0	15.2	18.2	46.8	17.0	12.7	24.5	12.2
Sept	9.8	9.1	10.2	26.8	9.6	7.6	19.7	7.1	15.5	18.0	50.8	16.5	13.3	32.7	12.5
Oct	10.1	9.4	10.6	28.6	9.9	8.0	21.4	7.4	15.7	18.1	43.6	17.0	13.6	40.7	12.5
Nov	10.0	9.3	10.4	26.0	9.8	7.9	20.0	7.4	15.6	18.7	57.1	16.8	12.8	41.4	11.7
Dec	10.0	9.0	10.0	27.4	9.3	8.0	19.8	7.4	16.2	18.2	52.2	16.6	14.3	44.8	13.1

[1] Unemployed as percent of civilian labor force in group specified.
[2] See footnote 1, Table B–37.

Note: Data relate to persons 16 years of age and over.
See footnote 5 and Note, Table B–35.

Source: Department of Labor (Bureau of Labor Statistics).

TABLE B–44. Unemployment by duration and reason, 1962–2009

[Thousands of persons, except as noted; monthly data seasonally adjusted [1]]

Year or month	Un-employ-ment	Duration of unemployment						Reason for unemployment					
		Less than 5 weeks	5–14 weeks	15–26 weeks	27 weeks and over	Average (mean) duration (weeks)	Median duration (weeks)	Job losers [3]			Job leavers	Re-entrants	New entrants
								Total	On layoff	Other			
1962	3,911	1,663	1,134	534	585	14.7	....	....	....	....	....	....	....
1963	4,070	1,751	1,231	535	553	14.0	....	....	....	....	....	....	....
1964	3,786	1,697	1,117	491	482	13.3	....	....	....	....	....	....	....
1965	3,366	1,628	983	404	351	11.8	....	....	....	....	....	....	....
1966	2,875	1,573	779	287	239	10.4	....	....	....	....	....	....	....
1967 [2]	2,975	1,634	893	271	177	8.7	2.3	1,229	394	836	438	945	396
1968	2,817	1,594	810	256	156	8.4	4.5	1,070	334	736	431	909	407
1969	2,832	1,629	827	242	133	7.8	4.4	1,017	339	678	436	965	413
1970	4,093	2,139	1,290	428	235	8.6	4.9	1,811	675	1,137	550	1,228	504
1971	5,016	2,245	1,585	668	519	11.3	6.3	2,323	735	1,588	590	1,472	630
1972	4,882	2,242	1,472	601	566	12.0	6.2	2,108	582	1,526	641	1,456	677
1973	4,365	2,224	1,314	483	343	10.0	5.2	1,694	472	1,221	683	1,340	649
1974	5,156	2,604	1,597	574	381	9.8	5.2	2,242	746	1,495	768	1,463	681
1975	7,929	2,940	2,484	1,303	1,203	14.2	8.4	4,386	1,671	2,714	827	1,892	823
1976	7,406	2,844	2,196	1,018	1,348	15.8	8.2	3,679	1,050	2,628	903	1,928	895
1977	6,991	2,919	2,132	913	1,028	14.3	7.0	3,166	865	2,300	909	1,963	953
1978	6,202	2,865	1,923	766	648	11.9	5.9	2,585	712	1,873	874	1,857	885
1979	6,137	2,950	1,946	706	535	10.8	5.4	2,635	851	1,784	880	1,806	817
1980	7,637	3,295	2,470	1,052	820	11.9	6.5	3,947	1,488	2,459	891	1,927	872
1981	8,273	3,449	2,539	1,122	1,162	13.7	6.9	4,267	1,430	2,837	923	2,102	981
1982	10,678	3,883	3,311	1,708	1,776	15.6	8.7	6,268	2,127	4,141	840	2,384	1,185
1983	10,717	3,570	2,937	1,652	2,559	20.0	10.1	6,258	1,780	4,478	830	2,412	1,216
1984	8,539	3,350	2,451	1,104	1,634	18.2	7.9	4,421	1,171	3,250	823	2,184	1,110
1985	8,312	3,498	2,509	1,025	1,280	15.6	6.8	4,139	1,157	2,982	877	2,256	1,039
1986	8,237	3,448	2,557	1,045	1,187	15.0	6.9	4,033	1,090	2,943	1,015	2,160	1,029
1987	7,425	3,246	2,196	943	1,040	14.5	6.5	3,566	943	2,623	965	1,974	920
1988	6,701	3,084	2,007	801	809	13.5	5.9	3,092	851	2,241	983	1,809	816
1989	6,528	3,174	1,978	730	646	11.9	4.8	2,983	850	2,133	1,024	1,843	677
1990	7,047	3,265	2,257	822	703	12.0	5.3	3,387	1,028	2,359	1,041	1,930	688
1991	8,628	3,480	2,791	1,246	1,111	13.7	6.8	4,694	1,292	3,402	1,004	2,139	792
1992	9,613	3,376	2,830	1,453	1,954	17.7	8.7	5,389	1,260	4,129	1,002	2,285	937
1993	8,940	3,262	2,584	1,297	1,798	18.0	8.3	4,848	1,115	3,733	976	2,198	919
1994	7,996	2,728	2,408	1,237	1,623	18.8	9.2	3,815	977	2,838	791	2,786	604
1995	7,404	2,700	2,342	1,085	1,278	16.6	8.3	3,476	1,030	2,446	824	2,525	579
1996	7,236	2,633	2,287	1,053	1,262	16.7	8.3	3,370	1,021	2,349	774	2,512	580
1997	6,739	2,538	2,138	995	1,067	15.8	8.0	3,037	931	2,106	795	2,338	569
1998	6,210	2,622	1,950	763	875	14.5	6.7	2,822	866	1,957	734	2,132	520
1999	5,880	2,568	1,832	755	725	13.4	6.4	2,622	848	1,774	783	2,005	469
2000	5,692	2,558	1,815	669	649	12.6	5.9	2,517	852	1,664	780	1,961	434
2001	6,801	2,853	2,196	951	801	13.1	6.8	3,476	1,067	2,409	835	2,031	459
2002	8,378	2,893	2,580	1,369	1,535	16.6	9.1	4,607	1,124	3,483	866	2,368	536
2003	8,774	2,785	2,612	1,442	1,936	19.2	10.1	4,838	1,121	3,717	818	2,477	641
2004	8,149	2,696	2,382	1,293	1,779	19.6	9.8	4,197	998	3,199	858	2,408	686
2005	7,591	2,667	2,304	1,130	1,490	18.4	8.9	3,667	933	2,734	872	2,386	666
2006	7,001	2,614	2,121	1,031	1,235	16.8	8.3	3,321	921	2,400	827	2,237	616
2007	7,078	2,542	2,232	1,061	1,243	16.8	8.5	3,515	976	2,539	793	2,142	627
2008	8,924	2,932	2,804	1,427	1,761	17.9	9.4	4,789	1,176	3,614	896	2,472	766
2009	14,265	3,165	3,828	2,775	4,496	24.4	15.1	9,160	1,630	7,530	882	3,187	1,035
2008: Jan	7,628	2,619	2,399	1,157	1,382	17.5	9.0	3,874	1,055	2,819	831	2,202	685
Feb	7,435	2,623	2,378	1,106	1,313	16.9	8.6	3,870	996	2,875	781	2,113	660
Mar	7,793	2,759	2,494	1,156	1,316	16.4	8.4	4,144	1,065	3,078	794	2,123	705
Apr	7,631	2,468	2,504	1,294	1,374	17.0	9.3	4,016	1,094	2,922	860	2,128	631
May	8,397	3,259	2,416	1,193	1,579	16.8	8.1	4,209	1,093	3,117	877	2,485	807
June	8,560	2,751	2,980	1,309	1,603	17.4	9.4	4,386	1,095	3,291	858	2,506	771
July	8,895	2,872	2,834	1,427	1,679	17.1	9.7	4,589	1,041	3,549	871	2,703	829
Aug	9,509	3,291	2,848	1,570	1,860	17.7	9.4	4,958	1,262	3,695	1,014	2,657	826
Sept	9,569	2,916	3,073	1,613	2,014	18.6	10.2	5,275	1,366	3,909	982	2,594	811
Oct	10,172	3,098	3,115	1,770	2,270	19.8	10.5	5,763	1,330	4,433	936	2,651	826
Nov	10,617	3,312	3,307	1,776	2,214	18.7	9.9	6,266	1,442	4,824	924	2,697	735
Dec	11,400	3,294	3,535	1,987	2,612	19.6	10.7	6,729	1,550	5,179	1,007	2,802	820
2009: Jan	11,919	3,633	3,622	2,073	2,689	19.9	10.6	7,251	1,468	5,784	912	2,792	792
Feb	12,714	3,364	3,961	2,405	2,964	20.0	11.4	7,878	1,519	6,359	820	2,912	1,016
Mar	13,310	3,314	4,032	2,574	3,241	20.8	11.9	8,434	1,581	6,853	884	3,017	881
Apr	13,816	3,284	3,962	2,571	3,725	21.8	13.1	8,867	1,638	7,229	887	3,127	919
May	14,518	3,219	4,300	2,983	4,030	22.9	14.9	9,428	1,842	7,586	909	3,200	977
June	14,721	3,152	3,994	3,404	4,440	24.4	18.2	9,562	1,741	7,821	822	3,322	969
July	14,534	3,181	3,539	2,847	4,972	25.3	15.9	9,549	1,670	7,880	882	3,306	994
Aug	14,993	2,992	4,093	2,825	5,024	25.2	15.5	9,814	1,704	8,110	835	3,294	1,096
Sept	15,159	2,938	3,838	2,958	5,447	26.5	17.8	10,236	1,918	8,318	869	3,255	1,134
Oct	15,612	3,131	3,671	3,184	5,620	27.2	19.0	10,261	1,671	8,590	909	3,461	1,114
Nov	15,340	2,774	3,517	3,075	5,901	28.6	20.2	9,965	1,548	8,418	929	3,221	1,270
Dec	15,267	2,929	3,486	2,840	6,130	29.1	20.5	9,701	1,558	8,143	932	3,334	1,270

[1] Because of independent seasonal adjustment of the various series, detail will not sum to totals.
[2] For 1967, the sum of the unemployed categorized by reason for unemployment does not equal total unemployment.
[3] Beginning with January 1994, job losers and persons who completed temporary jobs.

Note: Data relate to persons 16 years of age and over.
See footnote 5 and Note, Table B–35.

Source: Department of Labor (Bureau of Labor Statistics).

TABLE B–45. Unemployment insurance programs, selected data, 1980–2009

[Thousands of persons, except as noted]

Year or month	All programs [1]		Regular State programs						
	Insured unemployment (weekly average) [2]	Total benefits paid (millions of dollars)	Covered employment [3]	Insured unemployment (weekly average) [2]	Initial claims (weekly average)	Exhaustions (weekly average) [4]	Insured unemployment as percent of covered employment	Benefits paid	
								Total (millions of dollars)	Average weekly check (dollars) [5]
1980	3,521	16,668	86,918	3,356	488	59	3.9	14,887	99.06
1981	3,248	15,910	87,783	3,045	460	57	3.5	14,568	106.61
1982	4,836	26,649	86,148	4,059	583	80	4.7	21,769	119.34
1983	5,216	31,615	86,867	3,395	438	80	3.9	19,025	123.59
1984	3,160	18,201	91,378	2,475	377	50	2.7	13,642	123.47
1985	2,751	16,441	94,027	2,617	397	49	2.8	14,941	128.09
1986	2,667	16,325	95,946	2,621	378	52	2.7	16,188	135.65
1987	2,349	14,632	98,760	2,300	328	46	2.3	14,561	140.39
1988	2,122	13,500	101,987	2,081	310	38	2.0	13,483	144.74
1989	2,158	14,618	104,750	2,156	330	37	2.1	14,603	151.43
1990	2,527	18,452	106,325	2,522	388	45	2.4	18,413	161.20
1991	3,514	27,004	104,642	3,342	447	67	3.2	25,924	169.56
1992	4,906	39,669	105,187	3,245	408	74	3.1	26,048	173.38
1993	4,188	34,649	107,263	2,751	341	62	2.6	22,599	179.41
1994	2,941	24,261	110,526	2,670	340	57	2.4	22,338	181.91
1995	2,648	22,026	113,504	2,572	357	51	2.3	21,925	187.04
1996	2,656	22,397	116,078	2,595	356	53	2.2	22,349	189.27
1997	2,372	20,333	119,159	2,323	323	48	1.9	20,287	192.84
1998	2,264	20,091	122,427	2,222	321	44	1.8	20,017	200.58
1999	2,223	21,037	125,280	2,188	298	44	1.7	21,001	212.10
2000	2,143	21,005	128,054	2,110	301	41	1.6	20,983	221.01
2001	3,012	32,227	127,923	2,974	404	54	2.3	32,135	238.07
2002	4,453	53,350	126,545	3,585	407	85	2.8	42,266	256.79
2003	4,400	53,352	126,084	3,531	404	85	2.8	41,896	261.67
2004	3,103	36,495	127,618	2,950	345	68	2.3	35,034	262.50
2005	2,709	32,154	129,929	2,661	328	55	2.0	32,098	266.63
2006	2,521	30,917	132,177	2,476	313	51	1.9	30,852	277.20
2007	2,612	33,212	133,688	2,572	324	51	1.9	33,156	287.73
2008 ᵖ	3,898	51,798	133,076	3,306	424	66	2.5	43,764	297.10
2009 ᵖ	8,943	139,826	127,507	5,724	565	141	4.5	80,681	309.85
2008: Jan	3,764	3,873.8	131,879	3,712	516	65	2.8	3,867.8	297.86
Feb	3,422	3,558.2	132,366	3,378	359	56	2.6	3,551.3	300.02
Mar	3,735	3,781.6	132,979	3,689	356	63	2.8	3,774.8	299.60
Apr	3,346	3,568.6	133,635	3,304	381	71	2.5	3,560.6	298.80
May	2,938	2,996.2	134,678	2,901	349	64	2.2	2,989.6	297.40
June	3,269	3,149.2	134,871	3,228	392	65	2.4	3,143.0	293.66
July	3,839	3,844.8	132,182	3,421	459	76	2.6	3,467.2	290.97
Aug	4,789	4,737.2	132,707	3,301	375	69	2.5	3,199.2	290.65
Sept	5,075	5,289.3	133,449	3,441	424	76	2.6	3,494.5	294.80
Oct	4,562	4,719.4	133,279	3,387	506	78	2.5	3,432.1	297.24
Nov	4,693	4,515.6	132,740	3,778	558	75	2.8	3,623.0	297.88
Dec	7,245	7,763.9	132,142	5,441	838	99	4.1	5,660.6	302.32
2009: Jan	7,857	8,445.8	127,642	5,870	804	98	4.6	6,211.3	306.17
Feb	7,986	8,807.0	127,235	6,050	644	98	4.8	6,524.8	308.16
Mar	10,177	11,947.7	127,156	7,557	680	128	5.9	8,243.2	305.93
Apr	9,150	11,288.2	127,227	6,634	641	134	5.2	7,426.2	313.24
May	9,336	11,305.2	127,949	6,497	567	150	5.1	7,065.9	315.16
June	10,240	12,827.4	127,834	6,833	636	174	5.3	7,688.3	312.75
July	10,021	12,543.3		6,443	627	187		7,110.6	311.54
Aug	10,794	12,788.3		6,449	500	193		6,765.3	308.69
Sept	9,852	12,540.7		5,556	479	182		6,222.1	310.93
Oct	9,146	11,181.6		5,072	531	163		5,382.8	309.53
Nov	10,467	12,257.5		5,632	548	162		5,701.8	306.69
Dec ᵖ	11,238	13,893.4		5,814	694	163		6,338.6	308.41

[1] Includes State Unemployment Insurance (State), Unemployment Compensation for Federal Employees (UCFE), Unemployment Compensation for Ex-service members (UCX), and Federal and State extended benefit programs. Also includes temporary Federal emergency programs: Federal Supplemental Compensation (1982-1985), Emergency Unemployment Compensation (EUC, 1992-1993), Temporary Extended Unemployment Compensation (2002-2004), EUC 2008 (2008-2009), and Federal Additional Compensation (2009).
[2] The number of people continuing to receive benefits.
[3] Workers covered by regular State Unemployment Insurance programs.
[4] Individuals receiving final payments in benefit year.
[5] For total unemployment only. Excludes partial payments.

Note: Includes data for the District of Columbia, Puerto Rico, and the Virgin Islands.

Source: Department of Labor (Employment and Training Administration).

TABLE B–46. Employees on nonagricultural payrolls, by major industry, 1962–2009

[Thousands of persons; monthly data seasonally adjusted]

Year or month	Total	Goods-producing industries						Service-providing industries		
		Total	Mining and logging	Con-struc-tion	Manufacturing			Total	Trade, transportation, and utilities [1]	
					Total	Durable goods	Nondurable goods		Total	Retail trade
1962	55,659	19,203	709	2,997	15,498	9,099	6,399	36,455	11,215	5,672
1963	56,764	19,385	694	3,060	15,631	9,226	6,405	37,379	11,367	5,781
1964	58,391	19,733	697	3,148	15,888	9,414	6,474	38,658	11,677	5,977
1965	60,874	20,595	694	3,284	16,617	9,973	6,644	40,279	12,139	6,262
1966	64,020	21,740	690	3,371	17,680	10,803	6,878	42,280	12,611	6,530
1967	65,931	21,882	679	3,305	17,897	10,952	6,945	44,049	12,950	6,711
1968	68,023	22,292	671	3,410	18,211	11,137	7,074	45,731	13,334	6,977
1969	70,512	22,893	683	3,637	18,573	11,396	7,177	47,619	13,853	7,295
1970	71,006	22,179	677	3,654	17,848	10,762	7,086	48,827	14,144	7,463
1971	71,335	21,602	658	3,770	17,174	10,229	6,944	49,734	14,318	7,657
1972	73,798	22,299	672	3,957	17,669	10,630	7,039	51,499	14,788	8,038
1973	76,912	23,450	693	4,167	18,589	11,414	7,176	53,462	15,349	8,371
1974	78,389	23,364	755	4,095	18,514	11,432	7,082	55,025	15,693	8,536
1975	77,069	21,318	802	3,608	16,909	10,266	6,643	55,751	15,606	8,600
1976	79,502	22,025	832	3,662	17,531	10,640	6,891	57,477	16,128	8,966
1977	82,593	22,972	865	3,940	18,167	11,132	7,035	59,620	16,765	9,359
1978	86,826	24,156	902	4,322	18,932	11,770	7,162	62,670	17,658	9,879
1979	89,932	24,997	1,008	4,562	19,426	12,220	7,206	64,935	18,303	10,180
1980	90,528	24,263	1,077	4,454	18,733	11,679	7,054	66,265	18,413	10,244
1981	91,289	24,118	1,180	4,304	18,634	11,611	7,023	67,172	18,604	10,364
1982	89,677	22,550	1,163	4,024	17,363	10,610	6,753	67,127	18,457	10,372
1983	90,280	22,110	997	4,065	17,048	10,326	6,722	68,171	18,668	10,635
1984	94,530	23,435	1,014	4,501	17,920	11,050	6,870	71,095	19,653	11,223
1985	97,511	23,585	974	4,793	17,819	11,034	6,784	73,926	20,379	11,733
1986	99,474	23,318	829	4,937	17,552	10,795	6,757	76,156	20,795	12,078
1987	102,088	23,470	771	5,090	17,609	10,767	6,842	78,618	21,302	12,419
1988	105,345	23,909	770	5,233	17,906	10,969	6,938	81,436	21,974	12,808
1989	108,014	24,045	750	5,309	17,985	11,004	6,981	83,969	22,510	13,108
1990	109,487	23,723	765	5,263	17,695	10,737	6,958	85,764	22,666	13,182
1991	108,375	22,588	739	4,780	17,068	10,220	6,848	85,787	22,281	12,896
1992	108,726	22,095	689	4,608	16,799	9,946	6,853	86,631	22,125	12,828
1993	110,844	22,219	666	4,779	16,774	9,901	6,872	88,625	22,378	13,021
1994	114,291	22,774	659	5,095	17,020	10,132	6,889	91,517	23,128	13,491
1995	117,298	23,156	641	5,274	17,241	10,373	6,868	94,142	23,834	13,897
1996	119,708	23,409	637	5,536	17,237	10,486	6,751	96,299	24,239	14,143
1997	122,776	23,886	654	5,813	17,419	10,705	6,714	98,890	24,700	14,389
1998	125,930	24,354	645	6,149	17,560	10,911	6,649	101,576	25,186	14,609
1999	128,993	24,465	598	6,545	17,322	10,831	6,491	104,528	25,771	14,970
2000	131,785	24,649	599	6,787	17,263	10,877	6,386	107,136	26,225	15,280
2001	131,826	23,873	606	6,826	16,441	10,336	6,105	107,952	25,983	15,239
2002	130,341	22,557	583	6,716	15,259	9,485	5,774	107,784	25,497	15,025
2003	129,999	21,816	572	6,735	14,510	8,964	5,546	108,183	25,287	14,917
2004	131,435	21,882	591	6,976	14,315	8,925	5,390	109,553	25,533	15,058
2005	133,703	22,190	628	7,336	14,226	8,956	5,271	111,513	25,959	15,280
2006	136,086	22,531	684	7,691	14,155	8,981	5,174	113,556	26,276	15,353
2007	137,598	22,233	724	7,630	13,879	8,808	5,071	115,366	26,630	15,520
2008	137,066	21,419	774	7,215	13,431	8,476	4,955	115,646	26,385	15,356
2009 ᴾ	131,997	18,938	727	6,234	11,978	7,360	4,618	113,059	25,263	14,774
2008: Jan	138,080	21,981	748	7,489	13,744	8,710	5,034	116,099	26,711	15,572
Feb	137,936	21,887	750	7,445	13,692	8,673	5,019	116,049	26,655	15,526
Mar	137,814	21,800	756	7,401	13,643	8,637	5,006	116,014	26,629	15,506
Apr	137,654	21,679	756	7,337	13,586	8,587	4,999	115,975	26,562	15,458
May	137,517	21,612	763	7,293	13,556	8,567	4,989	115,905	26,503	15,420
June	137,356	21,507	770	7,232	13,505	8,533	4,972	115,849	26,467	15,404
July	137,228	21,432	777	7,201	13,454	8,502	4,952	115,796	26,425	15,380
Aug	137,053	21,351	787	7,177	13,387	8,439	4,948	115,702	26,354	15,335
Sept	136,732	21,247	794	7,131	13,322	8,392	4,930	115,485	26,257	15,278
Oct	136,352	21,063	794	7,066	13,203	8,300	4,903	115,289	26,157	15,217
Nov	135,755	20,814	793	6,939	13,082	8,216	4,866	114,941	26,005	15,126
Dec	135,074	20,532	789	6,841	12,902	8,085	4,817	114,542	25,843	15,038
2009: Jan	134,333	20,127	781	6,706	12,640	7,881	4,759	114,206	25,735	14,992
Feb	133,652	19,832	771	6,593	12,468	7,753	4,715	113,820	25,605	14,934
Mar	133,000	19,520	754	6,470	12,296	7,620	4,676	113,480	25,479	14,872
Apr	132,481	19,253	740	6,367	12,146	7,490	4,656	113,228	25,371	14,840
May	132,178	19,041	731	6,310	12,000	7,372	4,628	113,137	25,308	14,812
June	131,715	18,829	721	6,231	11,877	7,271	4,606	112,886	25,258	14,792
July	131,411	18,713	715	6,162	11,836	7,248	4,588	112,698	25,174	14,747
Aug	131,257	18,583	706	6,096	11,781	7,204	4,577	112,674	25,146	14,726
Sept	131,118	18,488	705	6,043	11,740	7,169	4,571	112,630	25,090	14,686
Oct	130,991	18,379	700	5,987	11,692	7,134	4,558	112,612	25,031	14,647
Nov ᴾ	130,995	18,321	704	5,960	11,657	7,105	4,552	112,674	24,999	14,633
Dec ᴾ	130,910	18,240	703	5,907	11,630	7,089	4,541	112,670	24,962	14,623

[1] Includes wholesale trade, transportation and warehousing, and utilities, not shown separately.

Note: Data in Tables B–46 and B–47 are based on reports from employing establishments and relate to full- and part-time wage and salary workers in nonagricultural establishments who received pay for any part of the pay period that includes the 12th of the month. Not comparable with labor force data (Tables B–35 through B–44), which include proprietors, self-employed persons, unpaid family workers, and private household workers; which count persons as employed when they are not at work because of industrial disputes, bad weather, etc., even if they are not paid for the time off; which are based on a

See next page for continuation of table.

[Thousands of persons; monthly data seasonally adjusted]

Year or month	Information	Financial activities	Profes-sional and business services	Education and health services	Leisure and hospitality	Other services	Government Total	Federal	State	Local
							Service-providing industries—Continued			
1962	1,723	2,656	3,885	3,172	3,557	1,243	9,004	2,455	1,669	4,881
1963	1,735	2,731	3,990	3,288	3,639	1,288	9,341	2,473	1,747	5,121
1964	1,766	2,811	4,137	3,438	3,772	1,346	9,711	2,463	1,856	5,392
1965	1,824	2,878	4,306	3,587	3,951	1,404	10,191	2,495	1,996	5,700
1966	1,908	2,961	4,517	3,770	4,127	1,475	10,910	2,690	2,141	6,080
1967	1,955	3,087	4,720	3,986	4,269	1,558	11,525	2,852	2,302	6,371
1968	1,991	3,234	4,918	4,191	4,453	1,638	11,972	2,871	2,442	6,660
1969	2,048	3,404	5,156	4,428	4,670	1,731	12,330	2,893	2,533	6,904
1970	2,041	3,532	5,267	4,577	4,789	1,789	12,687	2,865	2,664	7,158
1971	2,009	3,651	5,328	4,675	4,914	1,827	13,012	2,828	2,747	7,437
1972	2,056	3,784	5,523	4,863	5,121	1,900	13,465	2,815	2,859	7,790
1973	2,135	3,920	5,774	5,092	5,341	1,990	13,862	2,794	2,923	8,146
1974	2,160	4,023	5,974	5,322	5,471	2,078	14,303	2,858	3,039	8,407
1975	2,061	4,047	6,034	5,497	5,544	2,144	14,820	2,882	3,179	8,758
1976	2,111	4,155	6,287	5,756	5,794	2,244	15,001	2,863	3,273	8,865
1977	2,185	4,348	6,587	6,052	6,065	2,359	15,258	2,859	3,377	9,023
1978	2,287	4,599	6,972	6,427	6,411	2,505	15,812	2,893	3,474	9,446
1979	2,375	4,843	7,312	6,767	6,631	2,637	16,068	2,894	3,541	9,633
1980	2,361	5,025	7,544	7,072	6,721	2,755	16,375	3,000	3,610	9,765
1981	2,382	5,163	7,782	7,357	6,840	2,865	16,180	2,922	3,640	9,619
1982	2,317	5,209	7,848	7,515	6,874	2,924	15,982	2,884	3,640	9,458
1983	2,253	5,334	8,039	7,766	7,078	3,021	16,011	2,915	3,662	9,434
1984	2,398	5,553	8,464	8,193	7,489	3,186	16,159	2,943	3,734	9,482
1985	2,437	5,815	8,871	8,657	7,869	3,366	16,533	3,014	3,832	9,687
1986	2,445	6,128	9,211	9,061	8,156	3,523	16,838	3,044	3,893	9,901
1987	2,507	6,385	9,608	9,515	8,446	3,699	17,156	3,089	3,967	10,100
1988	2,585	6,500	10,090	10,063	8,778	3,907	17,540	3,124	4,076	10,339
1989	2,622	6,562	10,555	10,616	9,062	4,116	17,927	3,136	4,182	10,609
1990	2,688	6,614	10,848	10,984	9,288	4,261	18,415	3,196	4,305	10,914
1991	2,677	6,558	10,714	11,506	9,256	4,249	18,545	3,110	4,355	11,081
1992	2,641	6,540	10,970	11,891	9,437	4,240	18,787	3,111	4,408	11,267
1993	2,668	6,709	11,495	12,303	9,732	4,350	18,989	3,063	4,488	11,438
1994	2,738	6,867	12,174	12,807	10,100	4,428	19,275	3,018	4,576	11,682
1995	2,843	6,827	12,844	13,289	10,501	4,572	19,432	2,949	4,635	11,849
1996	2,940	6,969	13,462	13,683	10,777	4,690	19,539	2,877	4,606	12,056
1997	3,084	7,178	14,335	14,087	11,018	4,825	19,664	2,806	4,582	12,276
1998	3,218	7,462	15,147	14,446	11,232	4,976	19,909	2,772	4,612	12,525
1999	3,419	7,648	15,957	14,798	11,543	5,087	20,307	2,769	4,709	12,829
2000	3,630	7,687	16,666	15,109	11,862	5,168	20,790	2,865	4,786	13,139
2001	3,629	7,808	16,476	15,645	12,036	5,258	21,118	2,764	4,905	13,449
2002	3,395	7,847	15,976	16,199	11,986	5,372	21,513	2,766	5,029	13,718
2003	3,188	7,977	15,987	16,588	12,173	5,401	21,583	2,761	5,002	13,820
2004	3,118	8,031	16,394	16,953	12,493	5,409	21,621	2,730	4,982	13,909
2005	3,061	8,153	16,954	17,372	12,816	5,395	21,804	2,732	5,032	14,041
2006	3,038	8,328	17,566	17,826	13,110	5,438	21,974	2,732	5,075	14,167
2007	3,032	8,301	17,942	18,322	13,427	5,494	22,218	2,734	5,122	14,362
2008 ᵖ	2,997	8,146	17,778	18,855	13,459	5,528	22,500	2,764	5,178	14,557
2009 ᵖ	2,856	7,773	16,779	19,272	13,180	5,412	22,516	2,830	5,182	14,504
2008: Jan	3,022	8,229	18,069	18,613	13,534	5,524	22,391	2,737	5,157	14,497
Feb	3,025	8,211	18,018	18,657	13,529	5,533	22,421	2,746	5,153	14,522
Mar	3,023	8,204	17,954	18,698	13,528	5,537	22,441	2,751	5,152	14,538
Apr	3,017	8,190	17,950	18,752	13,512	5,541	22,451	2,758	5,159	14,534
May	3,013	8,179	17,887	18,798	13,495	5,542	22,488	2,763	5,167	14,558
June	3,006	8,162	17,824	18,843	13,490	5,535	22,522	2,765	5,175	14,582
July	2,995	8,154	17,788	18,888	13,473	5,536	22,537	2,776	5,184	14,577
Aug	2,990	8,141	17,727	18,950	13,454	5,530	22,556	2,768	5,204	14,584
Sept	2,986	8,115	17,675	18,957	13,428	5,532	22,535	2,771	5,192	14,572
Oct	2,982	8,088	17,612	18,981	13,395	5,535	22,539	2,775	5,194	14,570
Nov	2,965	8,043	17,488	19,044	13,344	5,509	22,543	2,783	5,197	14,563
Dec	2,940	8,010	17,356	19,080	13,304	5,477	22,532	2,778	5,196	14,558
2009: Jan	2,924	7,954	17,205	19,119	13,268	5,461	22,540	2,793	5,192	14,555
Feb	2,918	7,898	17,029	19,138	13,236	5,449	22,547	2,796	5,192	14,559
Mar	2,905	7,857	16,910	19,158	13,202	5,426	22,543	2,808	5,186	14,549
Apr	2,884	7,811	16,783	19,175	13,168	5,420	22,616	2,876	5,189	14,551
May	2,858	7,784	16,756	19,215	13,195	5,416	22,605	2,860	5,189	14,556
June	2,845	7,751	16,655	19,248	13,176	5,420	22,533	2,817	5,174	14,542
July	2,834	7,737	16,624	19,262	13,177	5,415	22,475	2,826	5,149	14,500
Aug	2,829	7,714	16,618	19,312	13,163	5,405	22,487	2,825	5,172	14,490
Sept	2,828	7,703	16,642	19,348	13,176	5,395	22,448	2,827	5,173	14,448
Oct	2,826	7,697	16,675	19,384	13,134	5,381	22,484	2,844	5,179	14,461
Nov ᵖ	2,812	7,691	16,764	19,421	13,121	5,378	22,488	2,839	5,180	14,469
Dec ᵖ	2,806	7,695	16,814	19,456	13,096	5,374	22,467	2,830	5,177	14,460

Note (cont'd): sample of the working-age population; and which count persons only once—as employed, unemployed, or not in the labor force. In the data shown here, persons who work at more than one job are counted each time they appear on a payroll.

Establishment data for employment, hours, and earnings are classified based on the 2007 North American Industry Classification System (NAICS). For further description and details see *Employment and Earnings*.

Source: Department of Labor (Bureau of Labor Statistics).

TABLE B–47. Hours and earnings in private nonagricultural industries, 1962–2009 [1]

[Monthly data seasonally adjusted]

Year or month	Average weekly hours			Average hourly earnings			Average weekly earnings, total private			
	Total private	Manufacturing		Total private		Manu-facturing (current dollars)	Level		Percent change from year earlier	
		Total	Overtime	Current dollars	1982 dollars [2]		Current dollars	1982 dollars [2]	Current dollars	1982 dollars [2]
1962		40.5	2.8			$2.27				
1963		40.6	2.8			2.34				
1964	38.5	40.8	3.1	$2.53	$7.86	2.41	$97.41	$302.52		
1965	38.6	41.2	3.6	2.63	8.04	2.49	101.52	310.46	4.2	2.6
1966	38.5	41.4	3.9	2.73	8.13	2.60	105.11	312.83	3.5	.8
1967	37.9	40.6	3.3	2.85	8.21	2.71	108.02	311.30	2.8	−.5
1968	37.7	40.7	3.5	3.02	8.37	2.89	113.85	315.37	5.4	1.3
1969	37.5	40.6	3.6	3.22	8.45	3.07	120.75	316.93	6.1	.5
1970	37.0	39.8	2.9	3.40	8.46	3.23	125.80	312.94	4.2	−1.3
1971	36.8	39.9	2.9	3.63	8.64	3.45	133.58	318.05	6.2	1.6
1972	36.9	40.6	3.4	3.90	8.99	3.70	143.91	331.59	7.7	4.3
1973	36.9	40.7	3.8	4.14	8.98	3.97	152.77	331.39	6.2	−.1
1974	36.4	40.0	3.2	4.43	8.65	4.31	161.25	314.94	5.6	−5.0
1975	36.0	39.5	2.6	4.73	8.48	4.71	170.28	305.16	5.6	−3.1
1976	36.1	40.1	3.1	5.06	8.58	5.09	182.67	309.61	7.3	1.5
1977	35.9	40.3	3.4	5.44	8.66	5.55	195.30	310.99	6.9	.4
1978	35.8	40.4	3.6	5.88	8.69	6.05	210.50	310.93	7.8	.0
1979	35.6	40.2	3.3	6.34	8.41	6.57	225.70	299.34	7.2	−3.7
1980	35.2	39.7	2.8	6.85	8.00	7.15	241.12	281.68	6.8	−5.9
1981	35.2	39.8	2.8	7.44	7.89	7.86	261.89	277.72	8.6	−1.4
1982	34.7	38.9	2.3	7.87	7.87	8.36	273.09	273.09	4.3	−1.7
1983	34.9	40.1	2.9	8.20	7.96	8.70	286.18	277.84	4.8	1.7
1984	35.1	40.7	3.4	8.49	7.96	9.05	298.00	279.55	4.1	.6
1985	34.9	40.5	3.3	8.74	7.92	9.40	305.03	276.55	2.4	−1.1
1986	34.7	40.7	3.4	8.93	7.97	9.59	309.87	276.42	1.6	.0
1987	34.7	40.9	3.7	9.14	7.87	9.77	317.16	273.18	2.4	−1.2
1988	34.6	41.0	3.8	9.44	7.82	10.05	326.62	270.60	3.0	−.9
1989	34.5	40.9	3.8	9.80	7.75	10.35	338.10	267.27	3.5	−1.2
1990	34.3	40.5	3.9	10.20	7.66	10.78	349.75	262.77	3.4	−1.7
1991	34.1	40.4	3.8	10.52	7.59	11.13	358.51	258.67	2.5	−1.6
1992	34.2	40.7	4.0	10.77	7.55	11.40	368.25	258.24	2.7	−.2
1993	34.3	41.1	4.4	11.05	7.54	11.70	378.91	258.47	2.9	.1
1994	34.5	41.7	5.0	11.34	7.54	12.04	391.22	260.29	3.2	.7
1995	34.3	41.3	4.7	11.65	7.54	12.34	400.07	258.78	2.3	−.6
1996	34.3	41.3	4.8	12.04	7.57	12.75	413.28	259.92	3.3	.4
1997	34.5	41.7	5.1	12.51	7.69	13.14	431.86	265.60	4.5	2.2
1998	34.5	41.4	4.9	13.01	7.89	13.45	448.56	272.18	3.9	2.5
1999	34.3	41.4	4.9	13.49	8.01	13.85	463.15	275.03	3.3	1.0
2000	34.3	41.3	4.7	14.02	8.04	14.32	481.01	275.97	3.9	.3
2001	34.0	40.3	4.0	14.54	8.12	14.76	493.79	275.71	2.7	−.1
2002	33.9	40.5	4.2	14.97	8.25	15.29	506.75	279.20	2.6	1.3
2003	33.7	40.4	4.2	15.37	8.28	15.74	518.06	279.13	2.2	.0
2004	33.7	40.8	4.6	15.69	8.24	16.14	529.09	277.88	2.1	−.4
2005	33.8	40.7	4.6	16.13	8.18	16.56	544.33	276.17	2.9	−.6
2006	33.9	41.1	4.4	16.76	8.24	16.81	567.87	279.19	4.3	1.1
2007	33.9	41.2	4.2	17.43	8.33	17.26	590.04	281.97	3.9	1.0
2008	33.6	40.8	3.7	18.08	8.30	17.74	607.99	279.14	3.0	−1.0
2009 [p]	33.1	39.8	2.9	18.60	8.60	18.21	616.37	284.91	1.4	2.1
2008: Jan	33.7	41.1	4.1	17.77	8.27	17.52	598.85	278.60	3.5	−1.2
Feb	33.8	41.2	4.1	17.83	8.28	17.58	602.65	279.85	3.8	−.7
Mar	33.8	41.2	4.0	17.90	8.28	17.64	605.02	279.82	3.6	−.7
Apr	33.8	41.0	4.0	17.94	8.29	17.64	606.37	280.03	3.8	−.4
May	33.7	40.9	3.9	17.99	8.27	17.68	606.26	278.56	3.1	−1.1
June	33.6	40.9	3.8	18.04	8.20	17.73	606.14	275.59	2.6	−2.5
July	33.6	41.0	3.7	18.10	8.16	17.80	608.16	274.31	2.9	−2.9
Aug	33.7	40.8	3.7	18.18	8.20	17.78	612.67	276.47	3.5	−2.2
Sept	33.6	40.5	3.5	18.21	8.21	17.81	611.86	275.99	3.0	−2.3
Oct	33.5	40.4	3.5	18.28	8.33	17.89	612.38	279.11	2.9	−.9
Nov	33.4	40.2	3.2	18.34	8.54	17.94	612.56	285.23	2.6	2.0
Dec	33.3	39.9	2.9	18.40	8.65	17.96	612.72	288.12	2.4	3.1
2009: Jan	33.3	39.8	2.9	18.43	8.64	17.99	613.72	287.60	2.5	3.2
Feb	33.3	39.5	2.7	18.46	8.61	18.07	614.72	286.80	2.0	2.5
Mar	33.1	39.4	2.6	18.50	8.64	18.10	612.35	286.10	1.2	2.2
Apr	33.1	39.6	2.7	18.50	8.65	18.11	612.35	286.16	1.0	2.2
May	33.1	39.4	2.8	18.53	8.65	18.11	613.34	286.25	1.2	2.8
June	33.0	39.5	2.8	18.54	8.57	18.13	611.82	282.94	.9	2.7
July	33.1	39.9	2.9	18.59	8.59	18.27	615.33	284.48	1.2	3.7
Aug	33.1	39.9	3.0	18.66	8.58	18.27	617.65	283.98	.8	2.7
Sept	33.1	40.0	3.0	18.68	8.57	18.36	618.31	283.77	1.1	2.8
Oct	33.0	40.1	3.2	18.74	8.57	18.35	618.42	282.88	1.0	1.4
Nov [p]	33.2	40.4	3.4	18.77	8.54	18.41	623.16	283.59	1.7	−.6
Dec [p]	33.2	40.4	3.4	18.80	8.54	18.40	624.16	283.58	1.9	−1.6

[1] For production or nonsupervisory workers; total includes private industry groups shown in Table B–46.
[2] Current dollars divided by the consumer price index for urban wage earners and clerical workers on a 1982=100 base.
Note: See Note, Table B–46.
Source: Department of Labor (Bureau of Labor Statistics).

TABLE B–48. Employment cost index, private industry, 1995–2009

Year and month	Total private			Goods-producing			Service-providing [1]			Manufacturing		
	Total compensation	Wages and salaries	Benefits [2]	Total compensation	Wages and salaries	Benefits [2]	Total compensation	Wages and salaries	Benefits [2]	Total compensation	Wages and salaries	Benefits [2]
Indexes on SIC basis, December 2005=100; not seasonally adjusted												
December:												
1995	70.2	72.2	65.7	70.7	73.7	65.2	70.0	71.7	66.0	70.8	73.9	65.0
1996	72.4	74.7	67.0	72.7	76.0	66.4	72.3	74.2	67.3	72.9	76.3	66.5
1997	74.9	77.6	68.5	74.5	78.3	67.3	75.1	77.4	69.2	74.6	78.6	67.4
1998	77.5	80.6	70.2	76.5	81.1	68.1	78.0	80.5	71.4	76.6	81.3	67.9
1999	80.2	83.5	72.6	79.1	83.8	70.5	80.6	83.4	73.8	79.2	84.1	70.3
2000	83.6	86.7	76.7	82.6	87.1	74.3	84.2	86.6	78.1	82.3	87.1	73.6
2001	87.1	90.0	80.6	85.7	90.2	77.3	87.8	89.9	82.5	85.3	90.2	76.3
Indexes on NAICS basis, December 2005=100; not seasonally adjusted												
2001 [3]	87.3	89.9	81.3	86.0	90.0	78.5	87.8	89.8	82.4	85.5	90.2	77.2
2002	90.0	92.2	84.7	89.0	92.6	82.3	90.4	92.1	85.8	88.7	92.8	81.3
2003	93.6	95.1	90.2	92.6	94.9	88.2	94.0	95.2	91.0	92.4	95.1	87.3
2004	97.2	97.6	96.2	96.9	97.2	96.3	97.3	97.7	96.1	96.9	97.4	96.0
2005	100.0	100.0	100.0	100.0	100.0	100.0	100.0	100.0	100.0	100.0	100.0	100.0
2006	103.2	103.2	103.1	102.5	102.9	101.7	103.4	103.3	103.7	101.8	102.3	100.8
2007	106.3	106.6	105.6	105.0	106.0	103.2	106.7	106.8	106.6	103.8	104.9	101.7
2008	108.9	109.4	107.7	107.5	109.0	104.7	109.4	109.6	108.9	105.9	107.7	102.5
2009	110.2	110.9	108.8	108.6	110.0	105.8	110.8	111.1	109.9	107.0	108.9	103.6
2009: Mar	109.3	109.8	108.2	107.9	109.2	105.4	109.8	110.0	109.3	106.5	108.1	103.5
June	109.6	110.1	108.4	108.2	109.5	105.7	110.1	110.3	109.5	106.7	108.4	103.6
Sept	110.0	110.6	108.7	108.4	109.8	105.7	110.5	110.8	109.9	106.8	108.6	103.4
Dec	110.2	110.9	108.8	108.6	110.0	105.8	110.8	111.1	109.9	107.0	108.9	103.6
Indexes on NAICS basis, December 2005=100; seasonally adjusted												
2008: Mar	107.2	107.6	106.5	106.1	107.1	104.0	107.6	107.7	107.4	104.6	105.9	102.3
June	107.9	108.4	106.9	106.6	107.8	104.3	108.4	108.5	108.0	105.1	106.6	102.2
Sept	108.6	109.1	107.5	107.2	108.5	104.5	109.1	109.2	108.7	105.6	107.3	102.4
Dec	109.1	109.6	107.9	107.7	109.2	104.9	109.6	109.7	109.1	106.0	107.9	102.6
2009: Mar	109.3	109.8	108.1	108.0	109.3	105.4	109.8	110.0	109.2	106.4	108.1	103.4
June	109.5	110.0	108.3	108.1	109.4	105.6	110.0	110.2	109.3	106.6	108.3	103.6
Sept	110.0	110.5	108.6	108.3	109.8	105.6	110.5	110.7	109.8	106.8	108.6	103.4
Dec	110.4	111.0	109.0	108.8	110.3	106.0	111.0	111.3	110.2	107.2	109.1	103.7
Percent change from 12 months earlier, not seasonally adjusted												
December:												
SIC:												
1995	2.5	2.8	2.2	2.5	2.8	1.7	2.8	3.0	2.5	2.6	2.9	1.7
1996	3.1	3.5	2.0	2.8	3.1	1.8	3.3	3.5	2.0	3.0	3.2	2.3
1997	3.5	3.9	2.2	2.5	3.0	1.4	3.9	4.3	2.8	2.3	3.0	1.4
1998	3.5	3.9	2.5	2.7	3.6	1.2	3.9	4.0	3.2	2.7	3.4	.7
1999	3.5	3.6	3.4	3.4	3.3	3.5	3.3	3.6	3.4	3.4	3.4	3.5
2000	4.2	3.8	5.6	4.4	3.9	5.4	4.5	3.8	5.8	3.9	3.6	4.7
2001	4.2	3.8	5.1	3.8	3.6	4.0	4.3	3.8	5.6	3.6	3.6	3.7
NAICS:												
2001 [3]	4.1	3.8	5.2	3.6	3.6	3.7	4.4	3.8	5.6	3.4	3.6	3.5
2002	3.1	2.6	4.2	3.5	2.9	4.8	3.0	2.6	4.1	3.7	2.9	5.3
2003	4.0	3.1	6.5	4.0	2.5	7.2	4.0	3.4	6.1	4.2	2.5	7.4
2004	3.8	2.6	6.7	4.6	2.4	9.2	3.5	2.6	5.6	4.9	2.4	10.0
2005	2.9	2.5	4.0	3.2	2.9	3.8	2.8	2.4	4.1	3.2	2.7	4.2
2006	3.2	3.2	3.1	2.5	2.9	1.7	3.4	3.3	3.7	1.8	2.3	.8
2007	3.0	3.3	2.4	2.4	3.0	1.5	3.2	3.4	2.8	2.0	2.5	.9
2008	2.4	2.6	2.0	2.4	2.8	1.5	2.5	2.6	2.2	2.0	2.7	.8
2009	1.2	1.4	1.0	1.0	.9	1.1	1.3	1.4	.9	1.0	1.1	1.1
2009: Mar	1.9	2.0	1.6	1.7	2.0	1.3	1.9	2.1	1.6	1.7	2.1	1.2
June	1.5	1.6	1.3	1.3	1.4	1.2	1.5	1.6	1.3	1.5	1.6	1.4
Sept	1.2	1.4	1.1	1.1	1.1	1.1	1.3	1.4	1.1	1.1	1.1	1.1
Dec	1.2	1.4	1.0	1.0	.9	1.1	1.3	1.4	.9	1.0	1.1	1.1
Percent change from 3 months earlier, seasonally adjusted												
2008: Mar	0.7	0.8	0.6	0.9	0.8	0.6	0.7	0.7	0.5	0.7	0.8	0.6
June	.7	.7	.4	.5	.7	.3	.7	.7	.6	.5	.7	−.1
Sept	.6	.6	.6	.6	.6	.2	.6	.6	.6	.5	.7	.2
Dec	.5	.5	.4	.5	.6	.4	.5	.5	.4	.4	.6	.2
2009: Mar	.2	.2	.2	.3	.1	.5	.2	.3	.1	.4	.2	.8
June	.2	.2	.2	.1	.1	.2	.2	.2	.1	.2	.2	.2
Sept	.5	.5	.3	.2	.4	.0	.5	.5	.5	.2	.3	−.2
Dec	.4	.5	.4	.5	.5	.4	.5	.5	.4	.4	.5	.3

[1] On Standard Industrial Classification (SIC) basis, data are for service-producing industries.
[2] Employer costs for employee benefits.
[3] Data on North American Industry Classification System (NAICS) basis available beginning with 2001; not strictly comparable with earlier data shown on SIC basis.

Note: Changes effective with the release of March 2006 data (in April 2006) include changing industry classification to NAICS from SIC and rebasing data to December 2005=100. Historical SIC data are available through December 2005.
Data exclude farm and household workers.

Source: Department of Labor (Bureau of Labor Statistics).

Table B–49. Productivity and related data, business and nonfarm business sectors, 1960–2009

[Index numbers, 1992=100; quarterly data seasonally adjusted]

Year or quarter	Output per hour of all persons — Business sector	Output per hour of all persons — Nonfarm business sector	Output [1] — Business sector	Output [1] — Nonfarm business sector	Hours of all persons [2] — Business sector	Hours of all persons [2] — Nonfarm business sector	Compensation per hour [3] — Business sector	Compensation per hour [3] — Nonfarm business sector	Real compensation per hour [4] — Business sector	Real compensation per hour [4] — Nonfarm business sector	Unit labor costs — Business sector	Unit labor costs — Nonfarm business sector	Implicit price deflator [5] — Business sector	Implicit price deflator [5] — Nonfarm business sector
1960	49.1	52.1	32.2	31.9	65.6	61.2	13.9	14.5	61.4	64.0	28.4	27.8	27.0	26.5
1961	50.8	53.7	32.8	32.5	64.6	60.6	14.5	15.0	63.2	65.5	28.5	27.9	27.2	26.7
1962	53.1	56.2	34.9	34.8	65.8	61.9	15.1	15.6	65.3	67.4	28.4	27.7	27.5	27.0
1963	55.2	58.1	36.5	36.4	66.2	62.6	15.6	16.1	66.8	68.8	28.3	27.7	27.7	27.2
1964	57.0	59.8	38.9	38.8	68.1	64.9	16.2	16.6	68.4	70.0	28.5	27.8	28.0	27.5
1965	59.1	61.7	41.6	41.6	70.4	67.4	16.8	17.2	69.8	71.2	28.5	27.8	28.4	27.9
1966	61.5	63.9	44.4	44.6	72.3	69.8	18.0	18.2	72.4	73.3	29.2	28.5	29.1	28.5
1967	62.8	65.0	45.3	45.3	72.1	69.7	19.0	19.3	74.3	75.3	30.2	29.6	29.9	29.4
1968	65.0	67.2	47.5	47.7	73.2	71.0	20.5	20.8	77.0	77.9	31.6	30.9	31.1	30.6
1969	65.3	67.3	49.0	49.2	75.0	73.0	22.0	22.2	78.1	78.9	33.6	32.9	32.5	32.0
1970	66.6	68.3	49.0	49.1	73.5	71.9	23.6	23.8	79.6	80.0	35.5	34.8	33.9	33.4
1971	69.3	71.1	50.8	51.0	73.3	71.7	25.1	25.3	81.0	81.5	36.2	35.6	35.4	34.8
1972	71.6	73.4	54.1	54.4	75.6	74.0	26.7	26.9	83.5	84.1	37.3	36.7	36.6	35.9
1973	73.7	75.7	57.9	58.3	78.5	77.0	29.0	29.1	85.2	85.6	39.3	38.4	38.5	37.2
1974	72.5	74.5	57.0	57.5	78.7	77.2	31.8	31.9	84.1	84.6	43.8	42.9	42.3	41.0
1975	75.1	76.6	56.5	56.6	75.3	73.9	35.0	35.2	85.0	85.4	46.6	45.9	46.4	45.4
1976	77.5	79.1	60.2	60.5	77.8	76.5	38.0	38.1	87.3	87.5	49.1	48.2	48.8	47.9
1977	78.8	80.4	63.6	63.9	80.7	79.5	41.1	41.2	88.5	88.9	52.1	51.3	51.8	51.0
1978	79.6	81.4	67.6	68.1	84.9	83.7	44.6	44.9	89.9	90.4	56.0	55.1	55.4	54.4
1979	79.6	81.1	69.8	70.2	87.7	86.6	48.9	49.1	89.9	90.2	61.4	60.5	60.1	59.0
1980	79.4	80.9	69.1	69.5	87.0	85.9	54.1	54.3	89.5	89.9	68.1	67.2	65.6	64.7
1981	81.1	82.0	71.0	71.0	87.6	86.6	59.2	59.6	89.5	90.0	73.1	72.7	71.6	70.9
1982	80.4	81.1	68.8	68.7	85.6	84.7	63.5	63.8	90.5	90.9	79.0	78.7	75.7	75.3
1983	83.3	84.7	72.5	73.1	87.1	86.3	66.1	66.5	90.3	90.9	79.4	78.5	78.3	77.7
1984	85.5	86.4	78.8	79.1	92.2	91.6	68.9	69.2	90.5	90.9	80.6	80.1	80.5	79.9
1985	87.5	87.8	82.5	82.5	94.3	94.0	72.1	72.3	91.6	91.8	82.5	82.3	82.4	82.2
1986	90.0	90.5	85.6	85.7	95.1	94.7	75.8	76.1	94.5	94.9	84.3	84.1	83.8	83.6
1987	90.3	90.8	88.4	88.6	97.9	97.6	78.6	78.8	94.8	95.1	87.1	86.8	85.8	85.6
1988	91.6	92.3	92.2	92.6	100.6	100.4	82.7	82.8	96.2	96.3	90.3	89.7	88.5	88.2
1989	92.6	93.0	95.6	95.9	103.3	103.1	84.9	84.9	94.7	94.7	91.7	91.3	91.8	91.4
1990	94.5	94.7	97.1	97.3	102.7	102.7	90.3	90.2	96.0	95.8	95.6	95.2	95.0	94.7
1991	96.0	96.2	96.2	96.4	100.2	100.2	95.0	94.9	97.4	97.3	98.9	98.7	98.1	98.1
1992	100.0	100.0	100.0	100.0	100.0	100.0	100.0	100.0	100.0	100.0	100.0	100.0	100.0	100.0
1993	100.5	100.6	103.2	103.5	102.7	102.9	102.2	102.0	99.8	99.6	101.7	101.4	102.0	102.0
1994	101.4	101.6	108.3	108.3	106.8	106.6	103.8	103.8	99.2	99.2	102.3	102.2	103.7	103.8
1995	101.5	102.0	111.3	111.8	109.7	109.6	105.9	106.0	98.8	98.9	104.4	103.9	105.6	105.7
1996	104.4	104.6	116.4	116.7	111.5	111.5	109.5	109.5	99.5	99.5	104.9	104.6	107.3	107.1
1997	106.3	106.2	122.4	122.6	115.2	115.4	113.1	112.9	100.6	100.4	106.4	106.3	109.0	109.1
1998	109.4	109.4	128.6	128.9	117.5	117.9	120.0	119.7	105.3	105.0	109.6	109.4	109.7	110.0
1999	113.3	113.0	135.7	136.1	119.8	120.5	125.4	124.8	107.8	107.3	110.7	110.5	110.6	111.0
2000	117.2	116.8	141.9	142.2	121.0	121.7	134.6	134.1	111.9	111.5	114.8	114.8	112.6	113.2
2001	120.7	120.2	143.0	143.4	118.4	119.3	140.9	140.1	114.0	113.3	116.7	116.5	114.6	115.1
2002	126.2	125.7	145.8	146.2	115.6	116.3	145.3	144.5	115.6	115.0	115.1	115.0	115.5	116.1
2003	131.0	130.3	150.3	150.6	114.7	115.5	152.3	151.4	118.6	117.9	116.2	116.2	117.1	117.6
2004	134.9	134.0	156.5	156.8	116.1	117.0	157.6	156.6	119.5	118.7	116.9	116.8	120.2	120.4
2005	137.1	136.2	161.8	162.0	118.0	118.9	163.8	162.8	120.2	119.4	119.5	119.5	124.1	124.7
2006	138.5	137.5	166.8	167.1	120.4	121.5	170.1	169.0	120.8	120.0	122.8	122.9	127.7	128.5
2007	141.0	140.1	170.5	171.0	120.9	122.1	177.3	176.0	122.4	121.6	125.7	125.7	131.0	131.5
2008	143.6	142.6	170.5	170.7	118.7	119.7	182.1	181.0	121.1	120.4	126.8	126.9	133.0	133.5
2006: I	138.5	137.5	166.0	166.4	119.8	121.0	168.4	167.1	120.8	119.9	121.6	121.5	126.4	127.1
II	138.7	137.7	166.6	166.8	120.1	121.1	169.1	168.0	120.3	119.6	121.9	122.0	127.4	128.3
III	138.0	137.0	166.4	166.7	120.6	121.7	169.7	168.6	119.7	118.9	123.0	123.0	128.3	129.1
IV	138.7	137.8	168.1	168.4	121.2	122.2	173.3	172.3	122.5	121.8	124.9	125.0	128.7	129.3
2007: I	139.0	138.2	168.4	168.8	121.2	122.1	175.2	174.2	122.7	122.1	126.0	126.0	130.0	130.5
II	140.2	139.2	169.8	170.3	121.2	122.4	176.5	175.1	122.4	121.4	125.9	125.8	130.9	131.4
III	142.1	141.1	171.4	172.0	120.6	121.9	177.8	176.3	122.6	121.5	125.1	125.0	131.4	131.7
IV	142.6	141.8	172.3	172.8	120.8	121.9	179.6	178.5	122.1	121.3	125.9	125.9	131.9	132.2
2008: I	142.7	141.7	171.7	172.0	120.3	121.4	180.3	179.2	121.2	120.5	126.3	126.4	132.1	132.3
II	143.8	142.8	172.2	172.6	119.8	120.8	181.0	179.8	120.4	119.6	125.9	125.9	132.5	132.9
III	143.9	142.8	170.6	170.8	118.6	119.6	183.0	181.8	119.9	119.1	127.2	127.3	134.0	134.4
IV	144.2	143.1	167.4	167.5	116.1	117.0	184.2	183.1	123.3	122.6	127.7	128.0	133.6	134.3
2009: I	144.3	143.2	163.6	163.7	113.4	114.3	182.0	180.9	122.6	121.9	126.1	126.3	134.3	135.2
II	146.7	145.6	163.2	163.2	111.3	112.1	184.9	183.9	124.1	123.5	126.1	126.3	134.2	135.1
III	149.7	148.5	164.5	164.4	109.9	110.7	187.6	186.4	124.8	124.0	125.3	125.5	134.3	135.3

[1] Output refers to real gross domestic product in the sector.

[2] Hours at work of all persons engaged in sector, including hours of proprietors and unpaid family workers. Estimates based primarily on establishment data.

[3] Wages and salaries of employees plus employers' contributions for social insurance and private benefit plans. Also includes an estimate of wages, salaries, and supplemental payments for the self-employed.

[4] Hourly compensation divided by the consumer price index for all urban consumers for recent quarters. The trend from 1978–2008 is based on the consumer price index research series (CPI-U-RS).

[5] Current dollar output divided by the output index.

Source: Department of Labor (Bureau of Labor Statistics).

Changes in productivity and related data, business and nonfarm business sectors, 1960–2009

[Percent change from preceding period; quarterly data at seasonally adjusted annual rates]

Year or quarter	Output per hour of all persons		Output[1]		Hours of all persons[2]		Compensation per hour[3]		Real compensation per hour[4]		Unit labor costs		Implicit price deflator[5]	
	Business sector	Nonfarm business sector	Business sector	Nonfarm business sector	Business sector	Nonfarm business sector	Business sector	Nonfarm business sector	Business sector	Nonfarm business sector	Business sector	Nonfarm business sector	Business sector	Nonfarm business sector
1960	1.7	1.2	1.9	1.8	0.2	0.6	4.2	4.3	2.4	2.5	2.4	3.1	1.1	1.1
1961	3.5	3.1	1.9	2.0	-1.5	-1.1	3.9	3.3	2.8	2.3	.4	.2	.8	.8
1962	4.6	4.5	6.5	6.8	1.8	2.2	4.4	4.0	3.4	3.0	-.1	-.5	1.0	1.0
1963	3.9	3.5	4.6	4.7	.7	1.1	3.6	3.4	2.2	2.1	-.3	-.1	.5	.7
1964	3.4	2.9	6.3	6.7	2.9	3.7	3.8	3.1	2.4	1.8	.4	.2	1.1	1.3
1965	3.5	3.1	7.1	7.1	3.4	3.9	3.7	3.3	2.1	1.7	.2	.2	1.6	1.3
1966	4.1	3.6	6.8	7.1	2.6	3.5	6.7	5.9	3.8	3.0	2.6	2.3	2.5	2.3
1967	2.2	1.7	1.9	1.7	-.3	.0	5.7	5.8	2.5	2.7	3.4	4.0	2.7	3.2
1968	3.4	3.4	5.0	5.2	1.5	1.8	8.1	7.8	3.7	3.5	4.5	4.3	4.0	3.9
1969	.5	.2	3.1	3.0	2.5	2.9	7.0	6.8	1.4	1.3	6.5	6.6	4.6	4.5
1970	2.0	1.5	.0	-.1	-2.0	-1.6	7.7	7.2	1.9	1.4	5.6	5.6	4.3	4.4
1971	4.1	4.0	3.8	3.8	-.3	-.2	6.3	6.4	1.8	1.9	2.1	2.3	4.2	4.3
1972	3.2	3.3	6.4	6.6	3.1	3.2	6.3	6.5	3.0	3.2	3.0	3.1	3.6	3.2
1973	3.1	3.1	7.0	7.3	3.8	4.1	8.4	8.1	2.1	1.8	5.2	4.9	5.2	3.5
1974	-1.7	-1.6	-1.5	-1.5	.2	.1	9.6	9.8	-1.3	-1.2	11.5	11.6	9.7	10.3
1975	3.5	2.8	-.9	-1.6	-4.3	-4.3	10.2	10.1	1.0	.9	6.5	7.1	9.7	10.7
1976	3.2	3.3	6.6	7.0	3.3	3.6	8.6	8.4	2.7	2.5	5.3	4.9	5.3	5.5
1977	1.7	1.6	5.6	5.6	3.8	3.9	8.0	8.1	1.4	1.5	6.2	6.5	6.0	6.3
1978	1.1	1.3	6.3	6.6	5.1	5.2	8.7	8.8	1.5	1.7	7.5	7.4	7.1	6.7
1979	-.1	-.4	3.3	3.2	3.4	3.6	9.6	9.4	.0	-.1	9.6	9.9	8.5	8.5
1980	-.3	-.3	-1.1	-1.1	-.9	-.8	10.7	10.7	-.4	-.4	10.9	11.0	9.0	9.6
1981	2.1	1.4	2.8	2.1	.7	.7	9.5	9.7	.0	.1	7.3	8.1	9.2	9.6
1982	-.8	-1.1	-3.0	-3.2	-2.3	-2.2	7.2	7.1	1.1	1.0	8.1	8.3	5.7	6.2
1983	3.6	4.4	5.4	6.4	1.8	1.9	4.1	4.2	-.1	-.1	.5	-.2	3.4	3.2
1984	2.7	2.0	8.7	8.2	5.8	6.1	4.2	4.1	.1	.0	1.5	2.0	2.9	2.9
1985	2.3	1.6	4.6	4.3	2.3	2.6	4.7	4.4	1.2	1.0	2.4	2.8	2.4	2.9
1986	2.9	3.1	3.7	3.9	.8	.8	5.1	5.2	3.3	3.4	2.2	2.1	1.6	1.7
1987	.3	.3	3.3	3.3	3.0	3.0	3.6	3.6	.2	.2	3.3	3.3	2.4	2.4
1988	1.5	1.6	4.3	4.6	2.7	2.9	5.2	5.0	1.5	1.3	3.7	3.3	3.2	3.0
1989	1.0	.8	3.7	3.5	2.6	2.7	2.7	2.6	-1.6	-1.7	1.6	1.8	3.7	3.6
1990	2.1	1.8	1.5	1.4	-.6	-.4	6.4	6.2	1.4	1.1	4.2	4.3	3.6	3.7
1991	1.5	1.5	-.9	-.9	-2.4	-2.4	5.1	5.3	1.5	1.6	3.5	3.7	3.3	3.5
1992	4.2	4.0	3.9	3.8	-.2	-.2	5.3	5.4	2.7	2.8	1.1	1.3	1.9	2.0
1993	.5	.6	3.2	3.5	2.7	2.9	2.2	2.0	-.2	-.5	1.7	1.4	2.0	2.0
1994	.9	1.0	4.9	4.7	4.0	3.6	1.5	1.8	-.6	-.3	.6	.8	1.7	1.8
1995	.0	.4	2.8	3.2	2.8	2.8	2.1	2.1	-.3	-.3	2.0	1.7	1.8	1.8
1996	2.9	2.6	4.6	4.4	1.6	1.8	3.4	3.3	.7	.6	.5	.7	1.6	1.4
1997	1.8	1.5	5.2	5.1	3.4	3.5	3.2	3.1	1.1	.9	1.5	1.6	1.6	1.9
1998	3.0	2.9	5.0	5.1	2.0	2.1	6.1	6.0	4.6	4.5	3.0	3.0	.7	.8
1999	3.5	3.3	5.6	5.6	2.0	2.2	4.5	4.3	2.4	2.2	.9	.9	.8	1.0
2000	3.5	3.4	4.5	4.4	1.0	1.0	7.4	7.4	3.9	4.0	3.7	3.9	1.8	1.9
2001	3.0	2.9	.8	.9	-2.1	-2.0	4.7	4.5	1.8	1.6	1.7	1.5	1.8	1.7
2002	4.5	4.6	2.0	1.9	-2.4	-2.5	3.1	3.2	1.5	1.5	-1.3	-1.3	.8	.9
2003	3.8	3.7	3.1	3.0	-.7	-.6	4.8	4.8	2.5	2.5	.9	1.1	1.4	1.3
2004	2.9	2.8	4.2	4.1	1.2	1.3	3.5	3.4	.8	.7	.6	.5	2.6	2.4
2005	1.7	1.7	3.4	3.4	1.6	1.7	4.0	4.0	.6	.6	2.2	2.3	3.2	3.5
2006	1.0	.9	3.1	3.1	2.1	2.2	3.8	3.8	.5	.5	2.8	2.8	2.9	3.0
2007	1.8	1.8	2.2	2.3	.4	.5	4.2	4.2	1.3	1.3	2.4	2.3	2.6	2.3
2008	1.9	1.8	.0	-.1	-1.9	-1.9	2.7	2.8	-1.1	-1.0	.8	1.0	1.5	1.5
2006: I	2.8	2.8	6.5	6.8	3.6	3.9	5.8	5.5	3.7	3.5	2.9	2.6	2.0	2.2
II	.6	.6	1.4	1.0	.8	.4	1.6	2.1	-1.6	-1.1	1.0	1.5	3.2	3.6
III	-2.2	-1.9	-.4	-.1	1.9	1.9	1.4	1.4	-2.3	-2.3	3.8	3.4	2.9	2.6
IV	2.1	2.4	4.0	4.2	1.9	1.8	8.8	9.1	9.9	10.2	6.5	6.5	1.3	.9
2007: I	.9	1.2	.8	.9	-.1	-.3	4.4	4.7	.6	.8	3.5	3.5	4.0	3.6
II	3.5	2.8	3.5	3.7	.0	.9	3.1	2.0	-1.1	-2.1	-.4	-.7	2.8	2.7
III	5.5	5.5	3.7	3.9	-1.7	-1.5	3.0	2.7	.6	.3	-2.4	-2.7	1.4	1.1
IV	1.6	2.0	2.1	1.8	.5	-.2	4.3	5.0	-1.4	-.7	2.6	3.0	1.6	1.4
2008: I	.2	-.1	-1.3	-1.7	-1.5	-1.6	1.5	1.7	-3.0	-2.8	1.3	1.7	.6	.5
II	3.1	3.1	1.1	1.3	-1.9	-1.7	1.6	1.3	-2.8	-3.0	-1.5	-1.8	1.4	1.6
III	.3	-.1	-3.7	-4.0	-4.0	-3.9	4.5	4.5	-1.6	-1.6	4.2	4.6	4.3	4.6
IV	.8	.8	-7.2	-7.6	-8.0	-8.3	2.6	2.9	12.0	12.3	1.8	2.0	-1.0	-.2
2009: I	.2	.3	-8.7	-8.8	-8.9	-9.0	-4.7	-4.7	-2.4	-2.4	-4.9	-5.0	2.1	2.7
II	6.8	6.9	-1.0	-1.1	-7.4	-7.5	6.7	6.9	5.3	5.5	-.2	.0	-.3	-.3
III	8.5	8.1	3.1	2.9	-5.0	-4.8	5.8	5.4	2.1	1.8	-2.4	-2.5	.2	.5

[1] Output refers to real gross domestic product in the sector.
[2] Hours at work of all persons engaged in the sector. See footnote 2, Table B–49.
[3] Wages and salaries of employees plus employers' contributions for social insurance and private benefit plans. Also includes an estimate of wages, salaries, and supplemental payments for the self-employed.
[4] Hourly compensation divided by a consumer price index. See footnote 4, Table B–49.
[5] Current dollar output divided by the output index.

Note: Percent changes are based on original data and may differ slightly from percent changes based on indexes in Table B–49.

Source: Department of Labor (Bureau of Labor Statistics).

PRODUCTION AND BUSINESS ACTIVITY
TABLE B–51. Industrial production indexes, major industry divisions, 1962–2009

[2002=100; monthly data seasonally adjusted]

Year or month	Total industrial production [1]	Manufacturing				Mining	Utilities
		Total [1]	Durable	Nondurable	Other (non-NAICS) [1]		
1962	28.4	25.8					
1963	30.1	27.4					
1964	32.1	29.3					
1965	35.3	32.4					
1966	38.4	35.4					
1967	39.2	36.1					
1968	41.4	38.1					
1969	43.3	39.8					
1970	41.9	38.0					
1971	42.5	38.6					
1972	46.6	42.6	31.4	60.9	68.3	107.8	50.3
1973	50.4	46.4	35.3	63.8	70.5	108.3	53.2
1974	50.2	46.3	35.1	64.1	71.0	106.8	53.0
1975	45.8	41.5	30.5	59.4	67.5	104.2	54.0
1976	49.4	45.2	33.4	64.9	69.6	105.0	56.4
1977	53.1	49.1	36.6	69.3	76.3	107.4	58.7
1978	56.0	52.1	39.5	71.8	78.9	110.8	60.2
1979	57.7	53.7	41.5	72.2	80.6	114.1	61.6
1980	56.3	51.8	39.7	70.0	83.4	116.2	62.0
1981	57.0	52.4	40.1	70.6	85.4	119.2	62.9
1982	54.1	49.5	36.7	69.6	86.4	113.3	60.9
1983	55.6	51.9	38.5	72.8	88.8	107.3	61.4
1984	60.5	57.0	44.0	76.2	92.8	114.3	65.0
1985	61.3	57.9	44.9	76.6	96.5	112.0	66.4
1986	61.9	59.2	45.7	78.8	98.4	103.9	67.0
1987	65.1	62.5	48.4	83.0	104.1	104.8	70.1
1988	68.4	65.9	52.0	85.8	103.6	107.5	74.1
1989	69.1	66.4	52.6	86.3	102.1	106.2	76.4
1990	69.7	67.0	52.8	87.7	100.9	107.8	77.9
1991	68.7	65.6	51.2	87.4	96.8	105.4	79.8
1992	70.6	68.0	53.8	89.6	94.8	103.1	79.7
1993	72.9	70.4	56.8	90.9	95.5	103.0	82.6
1994	76.8	74.5	61.6	94.0	94.7	105.4	84.2
1995	80.4	78.5	66.9	95.7	94.7	105.3	87.2
1996	84.0	82.2	72.8	96.0	93.8	107.1	89.7
1997	90.1	89.2	81.6	99.5	101.7	108.9	89.7
1998	95.4	95.1	90.2	101.0	107.8	107.2	92.0
1999	99.5	99.9	97.8	101.7	110.9	101.6	94.7
2000	103.7	104.4	105.2	102.2	112.6	104.2	97.4
2001	100.1	100.1	100.4	98.9	105.7	104.8	97.0
2002	100.0	100.0	100.0	100.0	100.0	100.0	100.0
2003	101.3	101.3	102.7	100.1	97.1	100.2	101.9
2004	103.8	104.3	107.0	102.0	97.9	99.6	103.3
2005	107.2	108.5	112.8	104.8	97.6	98.3	105.4
2006	109.7	111.2	117.8	105.7	96.6	101.5	104.8
2007	111.3	112.7	120.2	106.7	95.3	102.1	108.3
2008	108.8	109.1	116.3	103.6	89.9	104.2	108.6
2009 ᵖ	98.2	96.7	96.7	98.0	75.5	97.9	106.6
2008: Jan	112.3	113.4	121.9	106.6	93.9	104.2	110.9
Feb	112.0	112.8	121.2	106.2	93.5	105.0	111.4
Mar	111.6	112.7	121.0	106.1	93.6	104.7	108.8
Apr	111.0	111.7	119.3	105.8	91.8	104.9	109.7
May	110.7	111.5	118.9	105.9	90.8	104.9	108.2
June	110.4	111.0	119.0	104.9	90.8	104.8	109.4
July	110.4	110.8	119.0	104.5	89.3	106.9	107.9
Aug	109.2	109.7	117.2	104.1	88.9	106.4	104.3
Sept	104.8	105.7	113.7	99.3	88.1	96.4	105.7
Oct	106.2	106.0	110.8	102.7	86.9	103.5	107.1
Nov	104.8	103.6	108.2	100.3	86.4	105.4	109.1
Dec	102.4	100.6	105.3	97.0	84.6	103.4	111.3
2009: Jan	100.1	97.8	99.9	96.7	81.4	102.8	111.5
Feb	99.3	97.7	98.7	97.7	80.4	101.3	106.4
Mar	97.7	96.1	96.4	96.9	76.1	98.7	106.1
Apr	97.2	95.7	95.7	97.0	75.1	96.1	106.4
May	96.2	94.8	93.7	97.1	74.4	95.1	104.3
June	95.8	94.4	92.9	97.2	74.4	93.7	103.8
July	96.9	95.9	96.3	97.1	73.6	95.1	102.8
Aug ᵖ	98.3	97.3	97.5	98.6	74.5	97.0	103.4
Sept ᵖ	98.9	98.0	98.5	99.0	75.0	96.8	104.1
Oct ᵖ	99.1	97.8	98.1	99.2	73.5	96.8	106.8
Nov ᵖ	99.7	98.7	98.8	100.3	74.7	98.6	104.2
Dec ᵖ	100.3	98.7	98.8	100.2	73.4	98.8	110.4

[1] Total industry and total manufacturing series include manufacturing as defined in the North American Industry Classification System (NAICS) plus those industries—logging and newspaper, periodical, book, and directory publishing—that have traditionally been considered to be manufacturing and included in the industrial sector.

Note: Data based on NAICS; see footnote 1.

Source: Board of Governors of the Federal Reserve System.

Table B–52. Industrial production indexes, market groupings, 1962–2009

[2002=100; monthly data seasonally adjusted]

Year or month	Total industrial production	Final products Total	Consumer goods Total	Automotive products	Other durable goods	Nondurable goods	Equipment Total [1]	Business	Defense and space	Nonindustrial supplies Total	Construction	Business	Materials Total	Nonenergy	Energy
1962	28.4	27.5	34.8	24.2	22.1	41.3	18.6	12.8	57.1	28.9	39.3	24.5	28.3	....	54.3
1963	30.1	29.1	36.7	26.5	23.8	43.2	19.7	13.5	61.5	30.5	41.1	26.1	30.1	....	57.5
1964	32.1	30.7	38.8	27.8	26.0	45.3	20.8	15.1	59.6	32.5	43.6	28.0	32.5	....	59.8
1965	35.3	33.7	41.8	34.2	29.5	47.2	23.5	17.3	65.9	34.6	46.3	29.8	36.2	....	62.6
1966	38.4	36.9	44.0	34.1	32.5	49.5	27.4	20.0	77.5	36.7	48.2	32.1	39.5	....	66.5
1967	39.2	38.4	45.0	29.9	32.9	52.0	29.1	20.4	88.4	38.2	49.5	33.8	39.1	32.3	68.8
1968	41.4	40.3	47.7	35.7	35.2	54.1	30.0	21.3	88.6	40.4	52.1	35.9	41.7	34.6	72.0
1969	43.3	41.6	49.5	35.8	37.5	55.9	30.8	22.7	84.3	42.6	54.3	38.2	44.1	36.8	75.6
1970	41.9	40.1	49.0	30.2	36.4	56.9	28.6	21.8	71.4	41.9	52.4	38.3	42.6	34.6	79.4
1971	42.5	40.4	51.8	38.4	38.5	58.5	26.8	20.8	64.2	43.2	54.1	39.5	43.2	35.3	80.1
1972	46.6	43.9	56.0	41.4	44.1	62.2	29.3	23.6	62.4	48.2	61.4	43.5	47.6	39.5	83.1
1973	50.4	47.3	58.5	45.0	47.1	64.1	33.4	27.4	68.4	51.6	66.6	46.2	51.9	43.8	85.2
1974	50.2	47.2	56.8	38.9	44.3	64.2	35.1	29.0	70.6	51.1	65.0	46.1	51.8	43.7	84.8
1975	45.8	44.6	54.5	37.5	38.8	63.1	32.1	25.9	71.2	45.9	55.1	42.5	46.1	37.5	84.0
1976	49.4	47.7	59.0	42.7	43.6	67.0	33.7	27.6	69.1	49.0	59.3	45.3	50.1	41.8	85.9
1977	53.1	51.6	62.7	48.3	48.7	69.4	37.7	31.9	61.9	53.2	64.6	49.1	53.6	45.2	88.6
1978	56.0	54.7	64.6	48.0	50.9	71.9	41.9	36.0	63.0	56.2	68.3	51.7	56.3	48.2	89.7
1979	57.7	56.6	63.7	43.2	51.2	71.5	46.8	40.5	67.5	57.9	70.0	53.5	57.8	49.5	92.1
1980	56.3	56.3	61.3	33.3	47.5	71.6	49.1	41.5	80.2	55.6	64.8	52.3	55.7	46.6	92.8
1981	57.0	57.7	61.7	34.3	47.9	71.9	51.4	42.8	86.9	56.2	63.7	53.5	56.0	46.7	93.7
1982	54.1	56.4	61.5	33.3	44.4	73.1	48.9	39.1	103.9	54.2	57.8	52.9	51.7	42.1	89.7
1983	55.6	57.5	63.8	38.7	48.1	73.9	48.6	39.3	104.6	57.1	61.9	55.4	53.0	45.0	86.9
1984	60.5	62.3	66.7	43.2	53.7	75.4	55.5	45.2	119.8	62.1	67.3	60.2	58.1	50.1	92.4
1985	61.3	63.8	67.3	43.2	53.7	76.4	58.3	46.9	134.0	63.7	69.0	61.8	58.0	50.2	91.9
1986	61.9	64.8	69.7	46.4	56.9	78.2	57.4	46.1	142.4	65.8	71.3	63.8	57.9	51.1	88.2
1987	65.1	67.8	72.6	49.5	59.9	81.0	60.6	49.3	145.4	69.8	75.9	67.6	61.0	54.5	90.3
1988	68.4	71.5	75.4	52.1	63.1	83.6	65.5	54.4	146.9	72.1	77.7	70.1	64.4	58.0	93.4
1989	69.1	72.3	75.7	54.2	63.8	83.4	67.1	56.3	147.1	72.8	77.4	71.1	64.9	58.4	94.3
1990	69.7	73.1	76.0	50.8	63.7	84.8	68.6	58.4	142.0	73.9	76.8	72.8	65.3	58.5	96.2
1991	68.7	72.2	75.9	47.4	61.9	86.0	66.3	57.4	131.5	72.1	72.6	71.8	64.3	57.2	96.3
1992	70.6	73.9	78.2	55.5	64.7	86.6	67.0	59.6	122.0	74.1	75.7	73.5	66.4	60.0	95.4
1993	72.9	76.2	80.7	61.3	69.2	87.8	69.1	62.3	115.3	76.7	79.0	75.8	68.6	62.7	95.7
1994	76.8	79.4	84.3	68.7	74.9	90.0	71.7	66.0	108.3	80.3	84.7	78.8	73.1	67.7	97.2
1995	80.4	82.8	86.9	70.8	79.4	92.2	76.4	71.7	105.2	83.3	86.7	82.1	77.2	72.4	98.7
1996	84.0	85.9	88.6	73.0	83.1	93.4	82.2	78.5	102.0	86.7	90.5	85.2	81.2	76.9	100.2
1997	90.1	91.6	91.8	78.5	88.5	95.6	92.5	90.3	100.7	92.3	95.0	91.3	87.8	85.0	100.0
1998	95.4	96.9	95.2	83.7	95.5	97.6	101.8	100.5	100.1	97.5	100.1	96.5	93.1	91.4	100.4
1999	99.5	99.6	97.1	91.7	100.5	97.6	106.0	106.4	102.2	101.2	102.7	100.6	98.7	98.5	99.9
2000	103.7	102.8	99.1	93.7	104.5	99.2	111.9	114.7	91.3	105.2	105.0	105.2	104.0	104.8	101.5
2001	100.1	100.8	98.1	90.8	98.8	99.4	107.7	108.0	100.0	100.7	100.1	101.0	99.1	98.7	100.3
2002	100.0	100.0	100.0	100.0	100.0	100.0	100.0	100.0	100.0	100.0	100.0	100.0	100.0	100.0	100.0
2003	101.3	101.3	101.4	105.6	101.0	100.6	101.0	100.0	100.7	101.1	99.7	101.7	101.3	101.8	100.0
2004	103.8	103.4	102.7	105.2	104.4	101.8	100.5	105.3	104.7	103.3	102.0	103.8	104.5	106.4	99.6
2005	107.2	106.5	105.4	103.0	107.7	105.3	113.5	112.6	115.8	107.1	106.6	107.3	107.0	110.7	98.4
2006	109.7	110.3	105.8	99.5	109.0	106.2	122.5	123.2	113.4	108.7	109.0	108.5	109.5	113.7	100.0
2007	111.3	111.9	106.8	101.5	107.9	107.4	125.8	126.4	117.6	108.9	106.9	109.9	111.7	116.0	101.8
2008	108.8	109.7	104.0	87.7	100.9	106.9	125.4	125.0	120.6	104.6	100.1	106.7	109.6	111.8	103.6
2009 ᵖ	98.2	101.6	98.8	71.1	85.1	104.9	109.1	108.9	120.9	91.5	82.2	95.9	97.6	94.5	100.9
2008: Jan	112.3	112.9	106.9	99.4	105.9	108.2	129.4	130.2	122.3	108.5	105.0	110.2	113.2	117.1	104.2
Feb	112.0	112.5	106.7	98.6	104.5	108.2	128.7	129.8	120.5	108.0	104.0	109.9	113.1	116.5	104.9
Mar	111.6	111.9	105.6	92.8	104.5	107.6	129.7	130.8	120.7	107.5	103.3	109.4	112.9	116.3	104.6
Apr	111.0	111.1	105.0	87.6	104.2	107.7	128.0	128.4	120.8	106.9	102.1	109.1	112.4	115.6	104.6
May	110.7	110.8	104.7	87.9	103.8	107.3	128.0	128.4	120.2	106.3	102.2	108.3	112.1	115.1	104.6
June	110.4	110.9	104.8	90.9	103.2	107.1	128.1	128.2	121.9	105.7	101.7	107.6	111.7	114.8	104.0
July	110.4	110.6	104.5	92.4	103.0	106.6	127.4	127.4	120.2	105.7	102.4	107.3	111.9	114.4	105.2
Aug	109.2	109.0	102.7	83.1	101.0	105.9	126.6	126.2	120.8	104.9	101.2	106.6	110.9	113.5	104.0
Sept	104.8	106.3	101.4	84.2	98.7	104.3	119.9	117.7	118.9	102.6	99.1	104.3	104.8	107.8	96.2
Oct	106.2	107.0	103.0	81.5	97.2	107.0	117.6	114.8	120.4	102.2	97.8	104.3	106.9	108.2	102.3
Nov	104.8	106.7	102.0	79.0	93.7	106.7	119.5	117.6	120.0	99.8	93.6	102.8	104.7	103.7	104.3
Dec	102.4	106.1	100.6	74.5	90.5	106.0	121.6	120.8	119.9	96.5	89.1	100.1	101.0	98.0	104.2
2009: Jan	100.1	103.4	98.6	58.7	90.0	105.9	116.7	115.7	120.5	94.7	85.8	98.9	99.0	95.4	103.6
Feb	99.3	102.7	98.7	64.2	87.7	105.5	113.6	113.6	118.4	93.2	84.6	97.3	98.5	95.3	102.2
Mar	97.7	101.6	98.3	66.2	85.6	105.0	110.3	110.6	119.2	91.4	82.7	95.6	96.5	92.7	101.3
Apr	97.2	100.7	97.9	66.4	85.7	104.4	108.2	108.5	119.0	91.1	82.0	95.5	96.2	92.9	100.1
May	96.2	99.5	96.9	63.5	84.3	103.8	106.2	106.2	119.7	90.5	82.1	94.5	95.2	92.0	99.0
June	95.8	98.9	96.3	61.3	83.7	103.5	105.7	105.8	119.8	90.5	82.1	94.6	94.7	91.7	98.0
July	96.9	100.1	97.3	72.6	84.8	102.8	107.3	107.3	122.0	90.7	82.5	94.7	96.4	93.9	98.2
Aug ᵖ	98.3	101.5	98.7	76.8	83.8	104.2	108.7	108.8	123.4	91.1	82.8	95.0	97.9	95.4	99.8
Sept ᵖ	98.9	102.3	99.7	81.7	84.3	104.7	108.9	108.4	125.4	90.9	81.8	95.3	98.7	96.2	100.6
Oct ᵖ	99.1	102.8	100.3	80.0	84.4	105.7	109.3	109.0	124.5	90.7	80.5	95.6	98.8	96.1	101.0
Nov ᵖ	99.7	102.7	100.3	81.9	85.5	105.2	108.8	108.2	123.0	91.5	81.7	96.2	100.0	97.8	101.0
Dec ᵖ	100.3	103.4	100.9	81.5	84.4	106.2	109.8	109.2	122.6	91.6	80.1	97.2	100.8	98.2	102.8

[1] Includes other items not shown separately.

Note: See footnote 1 and Note, Table B–51.

Source: Board of Governors of the Federal Reserve System.

TABLE B–53. Industrial production indexes, selected manufacturing industries, 1967–2009

[2002=100; monthly data seasonally adjusted]

Year or month	Durable manufacturing								Nondurable manufacturing					
	Primary metal		Fabricated metal products	Machinery	Computer and electronic products		Transportation equipment		Apparel	Paper	Printing and support	Chemical	Plastics and rubber products	Food
	Total	Iron and steel products			Total	Selected high-technology[1]	Total	Motor vehicles and parts						
1967	....	....	....	....	0.3	....	....	....	....	....	....	....	....	....
1968	....	....	....	....	.3	....	....	....	....	....	....	....	....	....
1969	....	....	....	....	.3	....	....	....	....	....	....	....	....	....
1970	....	....	....	....	.3	....	....	....	....	....	....	....	....	....
1971	....	....	....	....	.3	....	....	....	....	....	....	....	....	....
1972	122.0	129.1	69.1	68.0	1.4	.3	53.1	44.3	169.9	66.3	51.6	47.8	34.9	58.7
1973	142.0	154.8	76.3	78.5	1.7	.4	60.7	50.7	175.1	71.6	54.2	52.3	39.2	58.8
1974	145.6	165.4	75.0	82.4	1.9	.5	55.9	43.5	163.0	74.7	52.6	54.4	38.2	59.4
1975	113.0	122.7	64.8	71.8	1.7	.5	50.7	38.0	159.5	64.6	49.1	47.8	32.7	58.3
1976	120.0	127.3	69.4	74.9	2.0	.6	56.8	48.5	168.5	71.4	52.7	53.5	36.2	63.0
1977	121.2	124.4	75.3	81.8	2.6	.8	61.7	55.1	179.1	74.5	57.1	58.2	42.6	64.1
1978	129.0	133.6	79.0	88.1	3.1	1.0	65.7	57.4	184.3	77.9	60.4	61.1	44.1	66.1
1979	132.1	138.3	82.5	93.0	3.9	1.3	66.3	52.6	174.6	79.0	62.2	62.5	43.4	65.4
1980	116.1	117.3	77.8	88.5	4.7	1.6	58.8	38.8	177.2	78.8	62.7	59.1	38.6	66.6
1981	116.2	121.6	77.3	87.6	5.4	1.9	56.6	37.8	176.2	79.9	64.3	60.1	40.9	67.5
1982	82.2	74.7	69.2	73.3	6.1	2.2	52.1	34.1	178.5	78.6	69.1	56.2	40.2	70.1
1983	84.2	75.4	69.8	66.1	7.1	2.6	57.5	43.5	183.7	83.7	74.3	60.1	43.7	70.9
1984	92.3	83.0	75.9	77.2	8.7	3.4	65.3	52.2	186.3	87.9	80.9	63.6	50.5	72.3
1985	85.2	77.1	77.0	77.4	9.3	3.6	68.7	54.2	179.0	86.2	84.2	63.1	52.5	74.9
1986	83.2	75.2	76.5	76.2	9.6	3.7	70.3	54.1	181.1	89.8	88.4	65.9	54.7	76.1
1987	89.7	85.7	77.9	77.8	11.0	4.5	72.9	56.1	182.3	92.7	94.9	71.0	60.6	77.7
1988	100.2	99.7	81.9	85.7	12.3	5.4	77.4	59.9	179.1	96.4	98.0	75.1	63.2	79.7
1989	97.9	96.2	81.3	88.8	12.7	5.7	78.9	59.3	170.2	97.4	98.4	76.5	65.4	79.9
1990	96.7	95.1	80.3	86.7	13.8	6.4	76.5	55.8	166.8	97.4	102.1	78.3	67.2	82.3
1991	90.8	86.9	76.6	81.4	14.3	6.9	73.4	53.3	167.7	97.6	98.9	78.0	66.5	83.8
1992	93.0	90.9	79.0	81.1	16.1	8.2	76.1	60.7	170.9	100.0	104.3	79.2	71.6	85.4
1993	97.5	96.4	82.0	87.2	17.7	9.6	78.3	67.0	174.9	101.1	104.6	80.1	76.7	87.6
1994	104.9	103.9	89.1	95.5	20.7	12.1	82.0	77.0	178.4	105.5	105.7	82.2	83.0	88.2
1995	106.0	105.6	94.6	102.2	26.7	16.9	82.1	79.3	178.6	107.0	107.3	83.5	85.1	90.4
1996	108.6	108.1	98.0	105.8	34.5	24.1	83.6	79.9	173.6	103.7	108.0	85.3	87.9	88.6
1997	113.3	111.4	102.5	111.6	46.1	35.3	91.1	86.1	171.6	105.9	110.2	90.3	93.4	91.0
1998	115.3	111.2	105.8	114.5	59.2	49.1	99.2	90.6	162.5	106.7	111.5	91.8	96.7	95.0
1999	115.1	111.9	106.4	112.0	77.2	70.0	104.6	100.5	155.6	107.6	112.4	93.6	101.9	96.0
2000	111.4	110.8	110.7	117.7	101.4	98.3	99.7	99.9	148.0	105.3	113.1	95.0	102.9	97.7
2001	99.5	96.8	102.6	104.2	103.3	101.3	96.2	91.4	126.9	99.3	106.3	93.4	96.9	97.7
2002	100.0	100.0	100.0	100.0	100.0	100.0	100.0	100.0	100.0	100.0	100.0	100.0	100.0	100.0
2003	99.1	101.2	98.7	99.7	114.3	120.5	101.0	103.5	92.8	96.8	96.2	101.3	100.3	101.0
2004	110.0	118.2	98.9	103.7	129.9	137.9	100.7	103.7	79.8	97.6	96.9	105.6	101.5	101.1
2005	108.0	110.1	103.4	110.2	144.5	158.8	104.5	103.9	76.9	97.5	99.2	109.3	102.3	104.2
2006	112.6	119.3	109.0	115.5	163.8	189.1	104.2	100.2	75.3	97.6	99.8	112.7	102.9	105.4
2007	110.0	115.8	112.1	116.4	176.7	213.7	106.1	97.4	76.5	95.9	100.6	114.1	104.7	109.5
2008	102.4	105.2	110.1	109.4	192.9	238.0	96.1	83.3	72.6	92.1	93.9	108.8	99.1	111.1
2009 p	67.3	59.9	89.4	85.7	172.9	204.1	79.6	59.9	62.3	82.1	80.2	104.2	84.2	110.7
2008: Jan	113.2	121.8	113.6	114.9	191.0	237.5	106.4	94.6	75.9	95.5	98.6	114.0	103.5	111.3
Feb	111.9	123.4	113.5	113.6	194.0	242.2	105.2	94.2	75.3	94.0	97.1	113.2	102.9	111.4
Mar	110.6	119.6	113.6	114.8	197.5	248.1	101.6	88.7	74.0	94.8	98.0	112.6	101.9	112.4
Apr	109.7	118.0	112.6	111.2	199.2	251.2	98.2	83.9	73.1	94.1	96.9	112.2	100.9	112.2
May	107.8	114.5	112.1	110.9	199.4	250.3	97.9	83.9	71.5	96.2	96.4	112.1	100.8	111.5
June	107.9	114.3	110.5	110.6	199.0	248.4	100.1	86.4	72.5	94.3	93.4	111.0	101.2	111.2
July	110.1	118.9	109.8	109.2	198.0	246.6	100.9	88.7	73.7	94.0	91.9	110.6	101.5	110.5
Aug	108.6	116.9	110.2	110.2	196.6	243.6	94.6	79.2	74.2	94.2	93.0	109.7	99.4	110.7
Sept	102.0	104.9	109.2	107.3	194.2	240.0	88.2	79.9	72.8	91.3	92.3	101.0	97.7	110.4
Oct	93.2	88.5	107.3	106.1	188.4	228.4	85.1	76.9	71.4	89.7	91.9	106.7	96.0	111.8
Nov	81.4	68.3	106.0	104.0	180.7	214.3	86.5	74.2	69.6	85.9	90.6	103.2	93.7	111.7
Dec	71.9	53.3	102.4	99.7	176.2	204.9	88.3	69.2	67.7	81.3	87.4	98.7	89.4	108.6
2009: Jan	67.3	48.4	98.2	96.2	174.9	204.2	75.3	51.2	65.5	80.1	85.3	99.8	88.2	108.3
Feb	64.5	49.0	95.6	94.0	171.6	199.5	77.7	55.8	64.5	82.9	82.7	101.6	86.0	109.5
Mar	60.7	44.8	91.3	88.7	171.4	200.4	78.0	56.7	64.7	78.9	81.6	101.3	83.4	109.0
Apr	60.3	43.5	89.4	86.6	172.5	203.6	77.3	56.6	63.1	78.2	80.1	102.7	82.9	109.8
May	59.2	45.9	87.5	83.9	170.3	199.0	74.0	52.4	63.6	80.9	79.6	102.4	82.2	110.9
June	61.1	53.0	87.2	82.0	169.6	199.7	72.3	49.5	59.5	82.5	80.2	103.1	82.2	110.3
July	68.0	64.3	87.2	82.6	173.3	205.5	80.4	61.1	60.9	82.6	79.9	103.8	83.2	109.2
Aug p	71.7	69.9	87.6	84.2	174.2	205.8	82.3	63.6	61.3	84.4	80.2	105.1	83.6	111.8
Sept p	73.4	73.7	88.2	83.1	173.8	204.4	86.2	69.0	61.4	83.7	79.4	106.5	84.2	111.7
Oct p	74.3	78.6	88.0	85.0	174.1	206.2	84.6	67.3	60.9	81.7	79.2	106.5	85.3	113.0
Nov p	77.8	80.0	87.9	83.5	173.9	206.4	85.0	68.3	61.6	85.8	79.0	108.3	86.2	112.9
Dec p	78.1	80.8	88.7	85.4	176.7	211.4	85.1	68.3	61.9	84.0	78.5	109.7	86.6	112.0

[1] Computers and peripheral equipment, communications equipment, and semiconductors and related electronic components.

Note: See footnote 1 and Note, Table B–51.

Source: Board of Governors of the Federal Reserve System.

TABLE B–54. Capacity utilization rates, 1962–2009

[Percent [1]; monthly data seasonally adjusted]

Year or month	Total industry [2]	Manufacturing Total [2]	Durable goods	Nondurable goods	Other (non-NAICS) [2]	Mining	Utilities	Crude	Primary and semi-finished	Finished
1962	....	81.4	....	....	....	....	....	....	81.5	81.6
1963	....	83.5	....	....	....	....	....	....	83.8	83.4
1964	....	85.6	....	....	....	....	....	....	87.8	84.6
1965	....	89.5	....	....	....	....	....	....	91.0	88.8
1966	....	91.1	....	....	....	....	....	....	91.4	91.1
1967	87.0	87.2	87.5	86.3	....	81.2	94.5	81.1	85.0	88.2
1968	87.4	87.1	87.3	86.5	....	83.6	95.1	83.4	86.8	87.1
1969	87.4	86.7	87.1	86.2	....	86.7	96.8	85.6	88.1	85.6
1970	81.3	79.5	77.7	82.2	....	89.1	96.3	85.1	81.5	78.2
1971	79.7	78.0	75.5	81.9	....	87.8	94.7	84.3	81.7	75.7
1972	84.7	83.4	82.1	85.3	85.8	90.7	95.3	88.5	88.2	79.7
1973	88.3	87.6	88.5	86.6	84.7	91.6	93.3	90.4	92.1	83.1
1974	85.1	84.4	84.6	84.2	82.8	90.9	86.9	91.1	87.4	80.1
1975	75.7	73.5	71.6	76.0	77.2	89.0	85.1	83.9	75.1	73.5
1976	79.7	78.2	76.3	81.0	77.5	89.4	85.5	86.9	80.0	76.7
1977	83.4	82.4	81.2	84.2	83.3	89.5	86.6	88.9	84.5	79.9
1978	85.0	84.3	83.8	84.9	85.0	89.6	86.9	88.4	86.2	82.1
1979	85.0	84.0	84.1	83.6	85.7	91.1	87.0	89.3	86.0	81.8
1980	80.7	78.7	77.6	79.5	87.1	91.1	85.5	88.9	78.8	79.5
1981	79.6	77.0	75.2	78.8	87.5	90.8	84.4	89.1	77.3	77.6
1982	73.7	70.9	66.6	76.3	87.4	84.2	80.2	82.2	70.5	73.3
1983	74.9	73.5	68.7	79.5	88.1	79.8	79.6	79.8	74.5	73.3
1984	80.5	79.4	76.8	82.4	89.5	85.7	82.1	85.6	81.1	77.4
1985	79.3	78.2	75.7	80.8	90.3	84.3	81.8	83.9	79.7	76.8
1986	78.6	78.4	75.3	81.9	88.9	77.6	81.0	79.3	79.7	77.1
1987	81.2	81.0	77.6	84.8	90.7	80.3	83.6	83.1	82.8	78.7
1988	84.3	84.0	82.0	86.1	88.6	84.3	86.6	86.8	85.8	81.6
1989	83.7	83.2	81.6	85.0	85.3	85.3	86.8	87.3	84.7	81.4
1990	82.5	81.7	79.4	84.4	83.8	86.9	86.5	88.2	82.7	80.6
1991	79.8	78.4	75.1	82.4	81.0	85.1	87.8	85.6	79.8	78.0
1992	80.4	79.5	76.9	82.7	80.0	84.6	86.3	85.6	81.5	77.9
1993	81.5	80.4	78.6	82.6	81.2	85.9	88.3	85.9	83.5	78.0
1994	83.5	82.7	81.7	84.3	81.1	87.7	88.4	88.2	86.5	79.0
1995	84.0	83.2	82.5	84.3	82.0	88.1	89.3	89.0	86.6	79.7
1996	83.4	82.2	81.8	82.9	80.7	90.4	90.8	88.8	85.8	79.2
1997	84.2	83.2	82.7	83.6	84.9	91.4	90.3	90.7	86.2	80.2
1998	83.0	81.8	81.2	82.2	85.6	89.2	92.7	87.7	84.3	80.4
1999	81.9	80.7	80.4	80.3	86.1	86.1	94.1	86.6	84.2	78.3
2000	81.7	80.1	80.0	79.1	87.9	90.7	93.8	88.5	84.4	77.1
2001	76.1	73.8	71.4	75.8	83.4	90.4	89.6	85.3	77.4	72.5
2002	74.6	72.7	69.3	76.3	80.8	86.1	87.7	82.7	76.6	70.7
2003	75.8	73.7	70.6	76.9	82.0	88.0	86.0	84.4	77.7	71.6
2004	77.9	76.2	73.5	78.6	84.5	88.3	84.8	86.1	79.8	73.3
2005	80.1	78.6	76.3	80.6	84.4	88.6	85.2	86.5	81.7	76.0
2006	80.9	79.4	77.9	80.7	83.0	90.4	83.4	88.3	81.7	77.1
2007	80.6	79.0	77.2	80.8	81.3	89.2	85.4	87.8	81.0	77.5
2008	77.6	75.1	72.6	77.7	76.0	90.1	83.8	86.5	77.3	74.1
2009 [p]	70.2	66.9	60.4	74.1	64.0	84.2	80.2	82.0	67.5	68.5
2008: Jan	80.5	78.5	76.8	80.2	79.8	90.6	86.5	88.8	80.6	77.1
Feb	80.2	78.0	76.1	79.8	79.3	91.2	86.7	88.9	80.3	76.6
Mar	79.8	77.8	75.8	79.7	79.4	90.8	84.5	88.8	79.6	76.3
Apr	79.2	77.0	74.6	79.4	77.8	90.9	85.1	88.5	79.4	75.2
May	78.9	76.7	74.3	79.4	76.8	90.8	83.7	88.6	78.8	75.0
June	78.7	76.3	74.2	78.6	76.7	90.7	84.4	87.6	78.7	74.9
July	78.6	76.1	74.1	78.3	75.4	92.3	83.1	88.7	78.3	74.6
Aug	77.6	75.3	73.0	77.9	75.0	91.8	80.2	88.3	77.1	73.7
Sept	74.5	72.5	70.7	74.3	74.3	83.1	81.2	78.7	74.9	72.2
Oct	75.4	72.7	68.8	76.8	73.3	89.2	82.1	84.7	75.4	71.5
Nov	74.4	71.1	67.2	75.1	72.9	90.7	83.5	84.7	73.5	71.2
Dec	72.7	69.0	65.4	72.6	71.3	89.0	85.1	82.1	71.4	70.3
2009: Jan	71.1	67.1	62.0	72.4	68.7	88.4	85.1	81.5	69.7	68.5
Feb	70.6	67.1	61.2	73.2	67.8	87.1	81.1	81.7	68.5	68.6
Mar	69.5	66.0	59.9	72.8	64.2	84.9	80.8	79.5	67.1	68.2
Apr	69.2	65.8	59.4	72.9	63.4	82.7	80.9	79.5	67.0	67.6
May	68.5	65.3	58.2	73.2	62.9	81.9	79.2	79.8	65.9	67.0
June	68.3	65.1	57.8	73.3	63.0	80.7	78.7	79.5	65.8	66.6
July	69.2	66.2	59.9	73.4	62.4	82.0	77.8	81.0	66.5	67.6
Aug [p]	70.2	67.2	60.7	74.6	63.2	83.8	78.2	82.7	67.1	68.9
Sept [p]	70.8	67.8	61.4	75.1	63.7	83.7	78.5	83.9	67.6	69.3
Oct [p]	71.0	67.8	61.2	75.4	62.5	83.8	80.5	83.8	67.9	69.5
Nov [p]	71.5	68.5	61.7	76.4	63.6	85.5	78.4	85.6	68.2	69.9
Dec [p]	72.0	68.6	61.8	76.5	62.6	85.7	82.9	86.1	68.9	70.2

[1] Output as percent of capacity.
[2] See footnote 1 and Note, Table B–51.

Source: Board of Governors of the Federal Reserve System.

[Value put in place, billions of dollars; monthly data at seasonally adjusted annual rates]

Year or month	Total new construction	Private construction									Public construction		
		Total	Residential buildings [1]		Nonresidential buildings and other construction						Total	Federal	State and local
			Total [2]	New housing units [3]	Total	Lodging	Office	Commercial [4]	Manufacturing	Other [5]			
1964	75.1	54.9	30.5	24.1	24.4						20.2	3.7	16.5
1965	81.9	60.0	30.2	23.8	29.7						21.9	3.9	18.0
1966	85.8	61.9	28.6	21.8	33.3						23.8	3.8	20.0
1967	87.2	61.8	28.7	21.5	33.1						25.4	3.3	22.1
1968	96.8	69.4	34.2	26.7	35.2						27.4	3.2	24.2
1969	104.9	77.2	37.2	29.2	39.9						27.8	3.2	24.6
1970	105.9	78.0	35.9	27.1	42.1						27.9	3.1	24.8
1971	122.4	92.7	48.5	38.7	44.2						29.7	3.8	25.9
1972	139.1	109.1	60.7	50.1	48.4						30.0	4.2	25.8
1973	153.8	121.4	65.1	54.6	56.3						32.3	4.7	27.6
1974	155.2	117.0	56.0	43.4	61.1						38.1	5.1	33.0
1975	152.6	109.3	51.6	36.3	57.8						43.3	6.1	37.2
1976	172.1	128.2	68.3	50.8	59.9						44.0	6.8	37.2
1977	200.5	157.4	92.0	72.2	65.4						43.1	7.1	36.0
1978	239.9	189.7	109.8	85.6	79.9						50.1	8.1	42.0
1979	272.9	216.2	116.4	89.3	99.8						56.6	8.6	48.1
1980	273.9	210.3	100.4	69.6	109.9						63.6	9.6	54.0
1981	289.1	224.4	99.2	69.4	125.1						64.7	10.4	54.3
1982	279.3	216.3	84.7	57.0	131.6						63.1	10.0	53.1
1983	311.9	248.4	125.8	95.0	122.6						63.5	10.6	52.9
1984	370.2	300.0	155.0	114.6	144.9						70.2	11.2	59.0
1985	403.4	325.6	160.5	115.9	165.1						77.8	12.0	65.8
1986	433.5	348.9	190.7	135.2	158.2						84.6	12.4	72.2
1987	446.6	356.0	199.7	142.7	156.3						90.6	14.1	76.6
1988	462.0	367.3	204.5	142.4	162.8						94.7	12.3	82.5
1989	477.5	379.3	204.3	143.2	175.1						98.2	12.2	86.0
1990	476.8	369.3	191.1	132.1	178.2						107.5	12.1	95.4
1991	432.6	322.5	166.3	114.6	156.2						110.1	12.8	97.3
1992	463.7	347.8	199.4	135.1	148.4						115.8	14.4	101.5
1993	485.5	358.2	208.2	150.9	150.0	4.6	20.0	34.4	23.4	67.7	127.4	14.4	112.9
1994	531.9	401.5	241.0	176.4	160.4	4.7	20.4	39.6	28.8	66.9	130.4	14.4	116.0
1995	548.7	408.7	228.1	171.4	180.5	7.1	23.0	44.1	35.4	70.9	140.0	15.8	124.3
1996	599.7	453.0	257.5	191.1	195.5	10.9	26.5	49.4	38.1	70.6	146.7	15.3	131.4
1997	631.9	478.4	264.7	198.1	213.7	12.9	32.8	53.1	37.6	77.3	153.4	14.1	139.4
1998	688.5	533.7	296.3	224.0	237.4	14.8	40.4	55.7	40.5	86.0	154.8	14.3	140.5
1999	744.6	575.5	326.3	251.3	249.2	16.0	45.1	59.4	35.1	93.7	169.1	14.0	155.1
2000	802.8	621.4	346.1	265.0	275.3	16.3	52.4	64.1	37.6	104.9	181.3	14.2	167.2
2001	840.2	638.3	364.4	279.4	273.9	14.5	49.7	63.6	37.8	108.2	201.9	15.1	186.8
2002	847.9	634.4	396.7	298.8	237.7	10.5	35.3	59.0	22.7	110.2	213.4	16.6	196.9
2003	891.5	675.4	446.0	345.7	229.3	9.9	30.6	57.5	21.4	109.9	216.1	17.9	198.2
2004	991.6	771.4	532.9	417.5	238.5	12.0	32.9	63.2	23.7	106.8	220.2	18.3	201.8
2005	1,102.7	868.5	611.9	480.8	256.6	12.7	37.3	66.6	29.9	110.2	234.2	17.3	216.9
2006	1,167.6	912.2	613.7	468.8	298.4	17.6	45.7	73.4	35.1	126.7	255.4	17.6	237.8
2007	1,150.7	861.6	493.2	354.1	368.4	27.5	53.8	85.9	45.3	155.9	289.1	20.6	268.5
2008	1,072.1	766.2	350.1	229.9	416.1	35.4	57.1	81.5	60.8	181.4	306.0	23.8	282.1
2008: Jan	1,095.5	802.8	396.6	279.0	406.2	31.5	57.9	88.1	52.9	175.9	292.7	21.4	271.3
Feb	1,092.1	797.6	385.8	261.0	411.8	32.5	58.0	88.2	54.3	178.8	294.5	21.7	272.8
Mar	1,095.2	791.0	383.1	259.4	407.8	34.0	56.6	85.1	53.6	178.5	304.2	21.1	283.1
Apr	1,091.1	787.7	373.4	251.0	414.3	36.1	57.3	87.5	55.3	178.1	303.4	22.7	280.7
May	1,090.7	786.2	363.5	244.6	422.7	37.4	57.0	85.2	57.1	186.0	304.5	22.8	281.6
June	1,075.6	769.5	351.7	237.1	417.8	37.7	57.5	84.0	58.4	180.2	306.1	22.7	283.4
July	1,070.2	759.8	339.9	231.1	419.9	37.0	57.9	82.8	57.3	185.0	310.4	24.9	285.5
Aug	1,066.1	756.4	340.2	220.7	416.2	37.4	58.0	79.9	61.1	179.8	309.7	24.8	284.9
Sept	1,081.2	773.6	350.4	212.9	423.2	36.8	58.4	77.9	65.8	184.3	307.6	23.6	283.9
Oct	1,064.1	754.1	327.7	204.7	426.3	36.6	56.5	76.5	71.0	185.8	310.0	25.0	285.1
Nov	1,037.3	726.8	310.5	192.1	416.4	35.7	55.8	73.5	70.6	180.7	310.5	26.2	284.3
Dec	1,002.1	696.6	292.3	176.2	404.3	31.8	51.6	71.0	70.2	179.7	305.6	28.3	277.3
2009: Jan	974.3	673.8	278.8	162.6	395.1	29.2	49.0	66.7	77.3	172.9	300.4	27.0	273.4
Feb	970.4	660.9	260.8	147.9	400.1	29.1	48.4	66.5	81.3	174.7	309.5	27.5	282.1
Mar	966.7	650.4	248.9	139.2	401.5	31.2	48.1	65.0	82.0	175.3	316.3	27.2	289.1
Apr	971.4	654.1	252.7	130.7	401.5	30.2	43.7	62.1	84.1	181.3	317.2	25.5	291.7
May	958.3	639.8	241.4	123.4	398.4	28.4	44.1	58.8	85.4	181.8	318.5	27.0	291.5
June	945.1	619.5	237.0	125.4	382.6	27.4	42.1	53.5	78.6	180.9	325.6	29.1	296.5
July	934.2	608.4	237.3	131.0	371.2	24.3	40.0	51.8	77.6	177.4	325.8	29.9	295.9
Aug	925.5	605.2	244.7	133.4	360.5	23.2	39.3	48.8	72.6	176.6	320.4	27.7	292.7
Sept	910.5	590.5	243.2	134.0	347.2	21.6	35.3	48.0	67.9	174.3	320.0	27.7	292.3
Oct [p]	905.6	585.5	254.9	135.2	330.6	19.6	34.8	44.2	65.6	166.4	320.1	27.0	293.1
Nov [p]	900.1	581.2	250.7	135.7	330.5	19.3	34.0	43.7	65.7	167.8	318.8	27.3	291.6

[1] Includes farm residential buildings.
[2] Includes residential improvements, not shown separately.
[3] New single- and multi-family units.
[4] Including farm.
[5] Health care, educational, religious, public safety, amusement and recreation, transportation, communication, power, highway and street, sewage and waste disposal, water supply, and conservation and development.

Note: Data beginning with 1993 reflect reclassification.

Source: Department of Commerce (Bureau of the Census).

TABLE B–56. New private housing units started, authorized, and completed and houses sold, 1962–2009

[Thousands; monthly data at seasonally adjusted annual rates]

Year or month	New housing units started — Total	New housing units started — Type of structure — 1 unit	New housing units started — Type of structure — 2 to 4 units[2]	New housing units started — Type of structure — 5 units or more	New housing units authorized[1] — Total	New housing units authorized[1] — Type of structure — 1 unit	New housing units authorized[1] — Type of structure — 2 to 4 units	New housing units authorized[1] — Type of structure — 5 units or more	New housing units completed	New houses sold
1962	1,462.9	991.4	471.5		1,186.6	716.2	87.1	383.3		
1963	1,603.2	1,012.4	590.8		1,334.7	750.2	118.9	465.6		560
1964	1,528.8	970.5	108.3	450.0	1,285.8	720.1	100.8	464.9		565
1965	1,472.8	963.7	86.7	422.5	1,240.6	709.9	84.8	445.9		575
1966	1,164.9	778.6	61.2	325.1	971.9	563.2	61.0	347.7		461
1967	1,291.6	843.9	71.7	376.1	1,141.0	650.6	73.0	417.5		487
1968	1,507.6	899.4	80.7	527.3	1,353.4	694.7	84.3	574.4	1,319.8	490
1969	1,466.8	810.6	85.1	571.2	1,322.3	624.8	85.2	612.4	1,399.0	448
1970	1,433.6	812.9	84.9	535.9	1,351.5	646.8	88.1	616.7	1,418.4	485
1971	2,052.2	1,151.0	120.5	780.9	1,924.6	906.1	132.9	885.7	1,706.1	656
1972	2,356.6	1,309.2	141.2	906.2	2,218.9	1,033.1	148.6	1,037.2	2,003.9	718
1973	2,045.3	1,132.0	118.2	795.0	1,819.5	882.1	117.0	820.5	2,100.5	634
1974	1,337.7	888.1	68.0	381.6	1,074.4	643.8	64.3	366.2	1,728.5	519
1975	1,160.4	892.2	64.0	204.3	939.2	675.5	63.9	199.8	1,317.2	549
1976	1,537.5	1,162.4	85.8	289.2	1,296.2	893.6	93.1	309.5	1,377.2	646
1977	1,987.1	1,450.9	121.7	414.4	1,690.0	1,126.1	121.3	442.7	1,657.1	819
1978	2,020.3	1,433.3	125.1	462.0	1,800.5	1,182.6	130.6	487.3	1,867.5	817
1979	1,745.1	1,194.1	122.0	429.0	1,551.8	981.5	125.4	444.8	1,870.8	709
1980	1,292.2	852.2	109.5	330.5	1,190.6	710.4	114.5	365.7	1,501.6	545
1981	1,084.2	705.4	91.2	287.7	985.5	564.3	101.8	319.4	1,265.7	436
1982	1,062.2	662.6	80.1	319.6	1,000.5	546.4	88.3	365.8	1,005.5	412
1983	1,703.0	1,067.6	113.5	522.0	1,605.2	901.5	133.6	570.1	1,390.3	623
1984	1,749.5	1,084.2	121.4	543.9	1,681.8	922.4	142.6	616.8	1,652.2	639
1985	1,741.8	1,072.4	93.5	576.0	1,733.3	956.6	120.1	656.6	1,703.3	688
1986	1,805.4	1,179.4	84.0	542.0	1,769.4	1,077.6	108.4	583.5	1,756.4	750
1987	1,620.5	1,146.4	65.1	408.7	1,534.8	1,024.4	89.3	421.1	1,668.8	671
1988	1,488.1	1,081.3	58.7	348.0	1,455.6	993.8	75.7	386.1	1,529.8	676
1989	1,376.1	1,003.3	55.3	317.6	1,338.4	931.7	67.0	339.8	1,422.8	650
1990	1,192.7	894.8	37.6	260.4	1,110.8	793.9	54.3	262.6	1,308.0	534
1991	1,013.9	840.4	35.6	137.9	948.8	753.5	43.1	152.1	1,090.8	509
1992	1,199.7	1,029.9	30.9	139.0	1,094.9	910.7	45.8	138.4	1,157.5	610
1993	1,287.6	1,125.7	29.4	132.6	1,199.1	986.5	52.3	160.2	1,192.7	666
1994	1,457.0	1,198.4	35.2	223.5	1,371.6	1,068.5	62.2	241.0	1,346.9	670
1995	1,354.1	1,076.2	33.8	244.1	1,332.5	997.3	63.7	271.5	1,312.6	667
1996	1,476.8	1,160.9	45.3	270.8	1,425.6	1,069.5	65.8	290.3	1,412.9	757
1997	1,474.0	1,133.7	44.5	295.8	1,441.1	1,062.4	68.5	310.3	1,400.5	804
1998	1,616.9	1,271.4	42.6	302.9	1,612.3	1,187.6	69.2	355.5	1,474.2	886
1999	1,640.9	1,302.4	31.9	306.6	1,663.5	1,246.7	65.8	351.1	1,604.9	880
2000	1,568.7	1,230.9	38.7	299.1	1,592.3	1,198.1	64.9	329.3	1,573.7	877
2001	1,602.7	1,273.3	36.6	292.8	1,636.7	1,235.6	66.0	335.2	1,570.8	908
2002	1,704.9	1,358.6	38.5	307.9	1,747.7	1,332.6	73.7	341.4	1,648.4	973
2003	1,847.7	1,499.0	33.5	315.2	1,889.2	1,460.9	82.5	345.8	1,678.7	1,086
2004	1,955.8	1,610.5	42.3	303.0	2,070.1	1,613.4	90.4	366.2	1,841.9	1,203
2005	2,068.3	1,715.8	41.1	311.4	2,155.3	1,682.0	84.0	389.3	1,931.4	1,283
2006	1,800.9	1,465.4	42.7	292.8	1,838.9	1,378.2	76.6	384.1	1,979.4	1,051
2007	1,355.0	1,046.0	31.7	277.3	1,398.4	979.9	59.6	359.0	1,502.8	776
2008	905.5	622.0	17.5	266.0	905.4	575.6	34.4	295.4	1,119.7	485
2009 ᵖ	553.8	443.5	11.4	98.8	572.2	435.1	19.9	117.2	796.0	374
2008: Jan	1,083	764	27	292	1,102	711	41	350	1,338	608
Feb	1,100	722	29	349	1,015	665	39	311	1,266	576
Mar	993	717	16	260	968	634	36	298	1,195	509
Apr	1,001	676	15	310	991	647	39	305	1,028	533
May	971	679	19	273	978	629	35	314	1,139	509
June	1,078	655	22	401	1,174	605	36	533	1,131	488
July	933	632	14	287	924	575	35	314	1,089	500
Aug	849	612	15	222	857	548	34	275	1,018	444
Sept	822	549	19	254	806	529	38	239	1,148	436
Oct	763	534	10	219	729	470	33	226	1,055	409
Nov	655	457	18	180	630	422	21	187	1,084	390
Dec	556	393	9	154	564	370	20	174	1,028	374
2009: Jan	488	357	13	118	531	342	20	169	778	329
Feb	574	357	13	204	550	381	17	152	828	354
Mar	521	361	31	129	511	360	20	131	833	332
Apr	479	388	11	80	498	378	18	102	846	345
May	551	409	9	133	518	406	18	94	812	371
June	590	478	11	101	570	433	23	114	794	399
July	593	506	15	72	564	463	18	83	785	419
Aug	581	481	6	94	580	464	19	97	785	408
Sept	586	508	9	69	575	452	19	104	723	391
Oct	524	471	4	49	551	449	16	86	750	408
Nov ᵖ	580	490	10	80	589	469	25	95	865	370
Dec ᵖ	557	456	9	92	653	505	18	130	768	342

[1] Authorized by issuance of local building permits in permit-issuing places: 20,000 places beginning with 2004; 19,000 for 1994–2003; 17,000 for 1984–93; 16,000 for 1978–83; 14,000 for 1972–77; 13,000 for 1967–71; 12,000 for 1963–66; and 10,000 prior to 1963.
[2] Monthly data derived.

Note: Data beginning with 1999 for new housing units started and completed and for new houses sold are based on new estimation methods and are not directly comparable with earlier data.

Source: Department of Commerce (Bureau of the Census).

TABLE B–57. Manufacturing and trade sales and inventories, 1968–2009

[Amounts in millions of dollars; monthly data seasonally adjusted]

Year or month	Total manufacturing and trade			Manufacturing			Merchant wholesalers [1]			Retail trade			Retail and food services sales
	Sales [2]	Inventories [3]	Ratio [4]	Sales [2]	Inventories [3]	Ratio [4]	Sales [2]	Inventories [3]	Ratio [4]	Sales [2,5]	Inventories [3]	Ratio [4]	
SIC: [6]													
1968	98,685	156,611	1.59	50,229	90,560	1.80	21,012	27,166	1.29	27,445	38,885	1.42	
1969	105,690	170,400	1.61	53,501	98,145	1.83	22,818	29,800	1.31	29,371	42,455	1.45	
1970	108,221	178,594	1.65	52,805	101,599	1.92	24,167	33,354	1.38	31,249	43,641	1.40	
1971	116,895	188,991	1.62	55,906	102,567	1.83	26,492	36,568	1.38	34,497	49,856	1.45	
1972	131,081	203,227	1.55	63,027	108,121	1.72	29,866	40,297	1.35	38,189	54,809	1.44	
1973	153,677	234,406	1.53	72,931	124,499	1.71	38,115	46,918	1.23	42,631	62,989	1.48	
1974	177,912	287,144	1.61	84,790	157,625	1.86	47,982	58,667	1.22	45,141	70,852	1.57	
1975	182,198	288,992	1.59	86,589	159,708	1.84	46,634	57,774	1.24	48,975	71,510	1.46	
1976	204,150	318,345	1.56	98,797	174,636	1.77	50,698	64,622	1.27	54,655	79,087	1.45	
1977	229,513	350,706	1.53	113,201	188,378	1.66	56,136	73,179	1.30	60,176	89,149	1.48	
1978	260,320	400,931	1.54	126,905	211,691	1.67	66,413	86,934	1.31	67,002	102,306	1.53	
1979	297,701	452,640	1.52	143,936	242,157	1.68	79,051	99,679	1.26	74,713	110,804	1.48	
1980	327,233	508,924	1.56	154,391	265,215	1.72	93,099	122,631	1.32	79,743	121,078	1.52	
1981	355,822	545,786	1.53	168,129	283,413	1.69	101,180	129,654	1.28	86,514	132,719	1.53	
1982	347,625	573,908	1.67	163,351	311,852	1.95	95,211	127,428	1.36	89,062	134,628	1.49	
1983	369,286	590,287	1.56	172,547	312,379	1.78	99,225	130,075	1.28	97,514	147,833	1.44	
1984	410,124	649,780	1.53	190,682	339,516	1.73	112,199	142,452	1.23	107,243	167,812	1.49	
1985	422,583	664,039	1.56	194,538	334,749	1.73	113,459	147,409	1.28	114,586	181,881	1.52	
1986	430,419	662,738	1.55	194,657	322,654	1.68	114,960	153,574	1.32	120,803	186,510	1.56	
1987	457,735	709,848	1.50	206,326	338,109	1.59	122,968	163,903	1.29	128,442	207,836	1.55	
1988	497,157	767,222	1.49	224,619	369,374	1.57	134,521	178,801	1.30	138,017	219,047	1.54	
1989	527,039	815,455	1.52	236,698	391,212	1.63	143,760	187,009	1.28	146,581	237,234	1.58	
1990	545,909	840,594	1.52	242,686	405,073	1.65	149,506	195,833	1.29	153,718	239,688	1.56	
1991	542,815	834,609	1.53	239,847	390,950	1.65	148,306	200,448	1.33	154,661	243,211	1.54	
1992	567,176	842,809	1.48	250,394	382,510	1.54	154,150	208,302	1.32	162,632	251,997	1.52	
NAICS: [6]													
1992	540,573	836,992	1.53	242,002	378,709	1.57	147,261	196,914	1.31	151,310	261,369	1.67	168,261
1993	567,580	864,028	1.50	251,708	379,660	1.50	154,018	204,842	1.30	161,854	279,526	1.68	179,858
1994	610,253	927,330	1.46	269,843	399,910	1.44	164,575	221,978	1.29	175,835	305,442	1.66	194,638
1995	655,097	986,089	1.48	289,973	424,772	1.44	179,915	238,392	1.29	185,209	322,925	1.72	204,677
1996	687,350	1,005,506	1.46	299,766	430,446	1.43	190,362	241,050	1.27	197,222	334,010	1.67	217,463
1997	723,879	1,046,750	1.42	319,558	443,566	1.37	198,154	258,575	1.26	206,167	344,609	1.64	227,670
1998	742,837	1,078,738	1.43	324,984	449,065	1.39	202,260	272,404	1.31	215,592	357,269	1.62	238,278
1999	786,634	1,138,982	1.40	335,991	463,625	1.35	216,597	290,318	1.30	234,046	385,039	1.59	257,797
2000	834,325	1,198,022	1.41	350,715	481,673	1.35	234,546	309,462	1.29	249,063	406,887	1.59	274,518
2001	818,615	1,120,422	1.43	330,875	427,720	1.38	232,996	297,927	1.32	255,644	394,775	1.58	282,131
2002	823,714	1,140,904	1.36	326,227	422,724	1.28	236,294	301,891	1.26	261,194	416,289	1.55	288,845
2003	853,596	1,147,981	1.34	334,616	407,967	1.24	246,857	307,642	1.23	272,123	432,372	1.56	301,264
2004	923,319	1,239,685	1.30	359,081	440,330	1.19	274,710	337,983	1.18	289,528	461,372	1.56	320,526
2005	1,000,368	1,306,598	1.27	395,173	472,398	1.16	297,915	362,451	1.18	307,280	471,749	1.51	340,057
2006	1,064,187	1,390,670	1.28	418,330	510,865	1.19	323,396	392,291	1.17	322,461	487,514	1.50	357,284
2007	1,102,196	1,446,313	1.28	423,423	529,957	1.23	345,871	416,632	1.16	332,902	499,724	1.49	369,385
2008	1,136,984	1,455,753	1.32	431,929	541,767	1.28	375,059	429,572	1.17	329,996	484,414	1.52	367,741
2008: Jan	1,156,058	1,463,157	1.27	439,923	537,072	1.22	377,061	426,408	1.12	339,035	503,669	1.49	376,262
Feb	1,143,322	1,472,661	1.29	434,265	541,454	1.25	372,986	426,580	1.14	336,071	504,627	1.50	373,140
Mar	1,156,608	1,474,830	1.28	439,275	546,023	1.24	379,712	426,601	1.12	337,621	502,206	1.49	374,845
Apr	1,171,292	1,484,308	1.27	448,658	547,716	1.22	384,205	432,149	1.12	338,429	504,443	1.49	376,009
May	1,177,041	1,488,099	1.26	449,729	550,178	1.22	388,406	435,311	1.12	338,906	502,610	1.48	376,662
June	1,187,363	1,495,812	1.26	452,979	554,737	1.22	396,296	439,195	1.11	338,088	501,880	1.48	376,055
July	1,185,470	1,510,101	1.27	457,116	558,252	1.22	392,275	443,913	1.13	336,079	507,936	1.51	374,103
Aug	1,160,334	1,511,162	1.30	440,921	561,150	1.27	386,097	446,873	1.16	333,356	503,144	1.51	371,311
Sept	1,134,171	1,506,344	1.33	429,156	559,091	1.30	377,364	444,618	1.18	327,651	502,635	1.53	365,855
Oct	1,090,431	1,495,342	1.37	412,885	556,012	1.35	360,753	438,760	1.22	316,793	500,570	1.58	354,744
Nov	1,026,879	1,475,847	1.44	384,413	551,297	1.43	325,256	433,890	1.29	307,210	490,660	1.60	345,175
Dec	996,571	1,455,753	1.46	373,446	541,767	1.45	325,672	429,572	1.32	297,453	484,414	1.63	335,016
2009: Jan	985,402	1,437,899	1.46	363,750	535,486	1.47	317,731	425,915	1.34	303,921	476,498	1.57	342,017
Feb	986,065	1,417,350	1.44	362,685	527,872	1.46	318,491	418,539	1.31	304,889	470,939	1.54	343,438
Mar	969,020	1,399,094	1.44	357,240	521,501	1.46	310,723	411,092	1.32	301,057	466,501	1.55	339,228
Apr	968,183	1,381,276	1.43	357,324	515,642	1.44	310,742	405,559	1.31	300,117	460,035	1.53	338,344
May	967,835	1,364,131	1.41	354,190	511,305	1.44	312,050	400,795	1.28	301,595	452,031	1.50	339,873
June	977,786	1,344,127	1.37	360,117	505,009	1.40	312,941	399,366	1.25	304,728	446,625	1.47	342,912
July	981,770	1,329,165	1.35	362,611	500,593	1.38	314,709	386,330	1.23	304,450	442,242	1.45	342,489
Aug	993,217	1,308,296	1.32	362,269	496,549	1.37	318,069	381,146	1.20	312,879	430,601	1.38	350,800
Sept	994,916	1,303,701	1.31	366,882	492,559	1.34	322,169	378,281	1.17	305,865	432,861	1.42	343,687
Oct	1,006,760	1,307,801	1.30	370,294	494,397	1.34	326,645	380,574	1.17	309,821	432,830	1.40	347,641
Nov [p]	1,027,359	1,313,168	1.28	374,174	495,143	1.32	337,396	386,263	1.14	315,789	431,762	1.37	353,951

[1] Excludes manufacturers' sales branches and offices.

[2] Annual data are averages of monthly not seasonally adjusted figures.

[3] Seasonally adjusted, end of period. Inventories beginning with January 1982 for manufacturing and December 1980 for wholesale and retail trade are not comparable with earlier periods.

[4] Inventory/sales ratio. Monthly inventories are inventories at the end of the month to sales for the month. Annual data beginning with 1982 are the average of monthly ratios for the year. Annual data for 1967–81 are the ratio of December inventories to monthly average sales for the year.

[5] Food services included on Standard Industrial Classification (SIC) basis and excluded on North American Industry Classification System (NAICS) basis. See last column for retail and food services sales.

[6] Effective in 2001, data classified based on NAICS. Data on NAICS basis available beginning with 1992. Earlier data based on SIC. Data on both NAICS and SIC basis include semiconductors.

Source: Department of Commerce (Bureau of the Census).

TABLE B–58. Manufacturers' shipments and inventories, 1968–2009

[Millions of dollars; monthly data seasonally adjusted]

Year or month	Shipments[1]			Inventories[2]								
					Durable goods industries				Nondurable goods industries			
	Total	Durable goods industries	Non-durable goods industries	Total	Total	Materials and supplies	Work in process	Finished goods	Total	Materials and supplies	Work in process	Finished goods
SIC:[3]												
1968	50,229	27,624	22,605	90,560	58,732	17,344	27,213	14,175	31,828	12,328	4,852	14,648
1969	53,501	29,403	24,098	98,145	64,598	18,636	30,282	15,680	33,547	12,753	5,120	15,674
1970	52,805	28,156	24,649	101,599	66,651	19,149	29,745	17,757	34,948	13,168	5,271	16,509
1971	55,906	29,924	25,982	102,567	66,136	19,679	28,550	17,907	36,431	13,686	5,678	17,067
1972	63,027	33,987	29,040	108,121	70,067	20,807	30,713	18,547	38,054	14,677	5,998	17,379
1973	72,931	39,635	33,296	124,499	81,192	25,944	35,490	19,758	43,307	18,147	6,729	18,431
1974	84,790	44,173	40,617	157,625	101,493	35,070	42,530	23,893	56,132	23,744	8,189	24,199
1975	86,589	43,598	42,991	159,708	102,590	33,903	43,227	25,460	57,118	23,565	8,834	24,719
1976	98,797	50,623	48,174	174,636	111,988	37,457	46,074	28,457	62,648	25,847	9,929	26,872
1977	113,201	59,168	54,033	188,378	120,877	40,186	50,226	30,465	67,501	27,387	10,961	29,153
1978	126,905	67,731	59,174	211,691	138,181	45,198	58,848	34,135	73,510	29,619	12,085	31,806
1979	143,936	75,927	68,009	242,157	160,734	52,670	69,325	38,739	81,423	32,814	13,910	34,699
1980	154,391	77,419	76,972	265,215	174,788	55,173	76,945	42,670	90,427	36,606	15,884	37,937
1981	168,129	83,727	84,402	283,413	186,443	57,998	80,998	47,447	96,970	38,165	16,194	42,611
1982	163,351	79,212	84,139	311,852	200,444	59,136	86,707	54,601	111,408	44,039	18,612	48,757
1983	172,547	85,481	87,066	312,379	199,854	60,325	86,899	52,630	112,525	44,816	18,691	49,018
1984	190,682	97,940	92,742	339,516	221,330	66,031	98,251	57,048	118,186	45,692	19,328	53,166
1985	194,538	101,279	93,259	334,749	218,193	63,904	98,162	56,127	116,556	44,106	19,442	53,008
1986	194,657	103,238	91,419	322,654	211,997	61,331	97,000	53,666	110,657	42,335	18,124	50,198
1987	206,326	108,128	98,198	338,109	220,799	63,562	102,393	54,844	117,310	45,319	19,270	52,721
1988	224,619	118,458	106,161	369,374	242,468	69,611	112,958	59,899	126,906	49,396	20,559	56,951
1989	236,698	123,158	113,540	391,212	257,513	72,435	122,251	62,827	133,699	50,674	21,653	61,372
1990	242,686	123,776	118,910	405,073	263,209	73,559	124,130	65,520	141,864	52,645	22,817	66,402
1991	239,847	121,000	118,847	390,950	250,019	70,834	114,960	64,225	140,931	53,011	22,815	65,105
1992	250,394	128,489	121,905	382,510	238,105	69,459	104,424	64,222	144,405	54,007	23,532	66,866
NAICS:[3]												
1992	242,002	126,572	115,430	378,709	238,102	69,737	104,211	64,154	140,607	53,179	23,304	64,124
1993	251,708	133,712	117,996	379,660	238,737	72,657	101,999	64,081	140,923	54,289	23,305	63,329
1994	269,843	147,005	122,838	399,910	253,141	78,573	106,556	68,012	146,769	57,161	24,383	65,225
1995	289,973	158,568	131,405	424,772	267,358	85,473	106,658	75,227	157,414	60,725	25,755	70,934
1996	299,766	164,883	134,883	430,446	272,495	86,226	110,563	75,706	157,951	59,101	26,438	72,412
1997	319,558	178,949	140,610	443,566	281,074	92,292	109,960	78,822	162,492	60,160	28,478	73,854
1998	324,984	185,966	139,019	449,065	290,700	93,629	115,235	81,836	158,365	58,223	27,044	73,098
1999	335,991	193,895	142,096	463,625	296,553	97,959	114,111	84,483	167,072	61,098	28,741	77,233
2000	350,715	197,807	152,908	481,673	306,727	106,214	111,196	89,317	174,946	61,509	30,015	83,422
2001	330,875	181,201	149,674	427,720	267,533	91,194	93,776	82,563	160,187	55,798	27,056	77,333
2002	326,227	176,968	149,259	422,724	260,265	88,512	92,231	79,522	162,459	56,593	27,793	78,073
2003	334,616	178,549	156,067	407,967	246,712	82,301	88,499	75,912	161,255	56,899	26,965	77,391
2004	359,081	188,722	170,359	440,330	264,794	92,129	90,932	81,733	175,536	61,760	29,821	83,955
2005	395,173	202,070	193,103	472,398	283,220	98,134	98,590	86,496	189,178	66,502	32,668	90,008
2006	418,330	213,408	204,923	510,865	309,320	108,592	104,910	95,818	201,545	69,816	35,968	95,761
2007	423,423	213,572	209,851	529,957	319,923	109,057	113,569	97,297	210,034	73,222	38,106	98,706
2008	431,929	207,801	224,128	541,767	342,699	115,800	130,373	96,526	199,068	68,138	36,423	94,507
2008: Jan	439,923	215,887	224,036	537,072	321,132	109,728	114,690	96,714	215,940	75,588	40,448	99,904
Feb	434,265	212,974	221,291	541,454	323,203	110,129	116,281	96,793	218,251	75,794	41,745	100,712
Mar	439,275	212,170	227,105	546,023	326,847	111,359	118,462	97,026	219,176	75,691	41,634	101,851
Apr	448,658	214,371	234,287	547,716	329,380	112,303	120,140	96,937	218,336	75,688	40,883	101,765
May	449,729	213,192	236,537	550,178	331,525	112,846	121,409	97,270	218,653	76,358	42,147	100,148
June	452,979	212,691	240,288	554,737	333,786	113,958	122,319	97,509	220,951	76,274	41,114	103,563
July	457,116	214,430	242,686	558,252	336,804	115,823	123,246	97,735	221,448	76,073	42,417	102,958
Aug	440,921	206,941	233,980	561,150	339,813	116,182	124,636	98,995	221,337	75,837	42,223	103,277
Sept	429,156	206,450	222,706	559,091	340,723	116,712	125,223	98,788	218,368	76,113	41,480	100,775
Oct	412,885	198,521	214,364	556,012	341,408	116,664	126,525	98,219	214,604	74,097	39,533	100,974
Nov	384,413	190,015	194,398	551,297	341,207	116,702	127,358	97,147	210,090	71,562	38,404	100,124
Dec	373,446	189,253	184,193	541,767	342,699	115,800	130,373	96,526	199,068	68,138	36,423	94,507
2009: Jan	363,750	177,696	186,054	535,486	338,475	115,240	129,265	93,970	197,011	66,897	37,221	92,893
Feb	362,685	176,094	186,591	527,872	334,112	114,345	127,694	92,073	193,760	65,599	36,648	91,513
Mar	357,240	173,884	183,356	521,501	328,422	112,272	125,769	90,381	193,079	64,949	37,122	91,008
Apr	357,324	173,480	183,844	515,642	324,569	110,135	125,256	89,178	191,073	64,050	37,212	89,811
May	354,190	169,440	184,750	511,305	320,714	108,234	124,856	87,624	190,591	64,106	37,160	89,325
June	360,117	169,672	190,445	505,009	315,984	106,139	124,091	85,754	189,025	63,838	36,685	88,502
July	362,611	174,982	187,629	500,593	312,367	103,840	123,880	84,647	188,226	64,118	36,454	87,654
Aug	362,269	172,366	189,903	496,549	308,133	102,920	121,442	83,771	188,416	63,832	36,872	87,712
Sept	366,882	174,914	191,968	492,559	305,056	102,367	120,306	82,383	187,503	63,632	37,166	86,705
Oct	370,294	175,345	194,949	494,397	304,023	101,161	120,971	81,891	190,374	64,548	38,065	87,761
Nov[p]	374,174	175,747	198,427	495,143	303,120	100,262	121,261	81,597	192,023	65,850	38,465	87,708

[1] Annual data are averages of monthly not seasonally adjusted figures.

[2] Seasonally adjusted, end of period. Data beginning with 1982 are not comparable with earlier data.

[3] Effective in 2001, data classified based on North American Industry Classification System (NAICS). Data on NAICS basis available beginning with 1992. Earlier data based on Standard Industrial Classification (SIC). Data on both NAICS and SIC basis include semiconductors.

Source: Department of Commerce (Bureau of the Census).

TABLE B-59. Manufacturers' new and unfilled orders, 1968–2009

[Amounts in millions of dollars; monthly data seasonally adjusted]

Year or month	New orders [1] Total	Durable goods industries Total	Durable goods industries Capital goods, nondefense	Nondurable goods industries	Unfilled orders [2] Total	Durable goods industries	Nondurable goods industries	Unfilled orders to shipments ratio [2] Total	Durable goods industries	Nondurable goods industries
SIC: [3]										
1968	50,657	28,051	6,314	22,606	108,377	104,393	3,984	3.79	4.58	0.69
1969	53,990	29,876	7,046	24,114	114,341	110,161	4,180	3.71	4.45	.69
1970	52,022	27,340	6,072	24,682	105,008	100,412	4,596	3.61	4.36	.76
1971	55,921	29,905	6,682	26,016	105,247	100,225	5,022	3.32	4.00	.76
1972	64,182	35,038	7,745	29,144	119,349	113,034	6,315	3.26	3.85	.86
1973	76,003	42,627	9,926	33,376	156,561	149,204	7,357	3.80	4.51	.91
1974	87,327	46,862	11,594	40,465	187,043	181,519	5,524	4.09	4.93	.62
1975	85,139	41,957	9,886	43,181	169,546	161,664	7,882	3.69	4.45	.82
1976	99,513	51,307	11,490	48,206	178,128	169,857	8,271	3.24	3.88	.74
1977	115,109	61,035	13,681	54,073	202,024	193,323	8,701	3.24	3.85	.71
1978	131,629	72,278	17,588	59,351	259,169	248,281	10,888	3.57	4.20	.81
1979	147,604	79,483	21,154	68,121	303,593	291,321	12,272	3.89	4.62	.82
1980	156,359	79,392	21,135	76,967	327,416	315,202	12,214	3.85	4.58	.75
1981	168,025	83,654	21,806	84,371	326,547	314,707	11,840	3.87	4.68	.69
1982	162,140	78,064	19,213	84,077	311,887	300,798	11,089	3.84	4.74	.62
1983	175,451	88,140	19,624	87,311	347,273	333,114	14,159	3.53	4.29	.69
1984	192,879	100,164	23,669	92,715	373,529	359,651	13,878	3.60	4.37	.64
1985	195,706	102,356	24,545	93,351	387,196	372,097	15,099	3.67	4.47	.68
1986	195,204	103,647	23,982	91,557	393,515	376,699	16,816	3.59	4.41	.70
1987	209,389	110,809	26,094	98,579	430,426	408,688	21,738	3.63	4.43	.83
1988	228,270	122,076	31,108	106,194	474,154	452,150	22,004	3.64	4.46	.76
1989	239,572	126,055	32,988	113,516	508,849	487,098	21,751	3.96	4.85	.77
1990	244,507	125,583	33,331	118,924	531,131	509,124	22,007	4.15	5.15	.76
1991	238,805	119,849	30,471	118,957	519,199	495,802	23,397	4.08	5.07	.79
1992	248,212	126,308	31,524	121,905	492,893	469,381	23,512	3.51	4.30	.75
NAICS: [3]										
1992	....	128,672	40,681	....	451,273	....	....	5.14	....	....
1993	246,668	128,672	40,681	....	425,979	....	....	4.66	....	....
1994	266,641	143,803	45,175	....	434,979	....	....	4.21	....	....
1995	285,542	154,137	51,011	....	447,411	....	....	3.97	....	....
1996	297,282	162,399	54,066	....	488,726	....	....	4.14	....	....
1997	314,986	174,377	60,697	....	512,916	....	....	4.04	....	....
1998	317,345	178,327	62,133	....	496,083	....	....	3.97	....	....
1999	329,770	187,674	64,392	....	505,498	....	....	3.76	....	....
2000	346,789	193,881	69,278	....	549,445	....	....	3.87	....	....
2001	322,746	173,072	58,246	....	514,262	....	....	4.21	....	....
2002	316,809	167,550	51,817	....	462,056	....	....	4.05	....	....
2003	330,369	174,302	52,894	....	477,557	....	....	3.92	....	....
2004	354,619	184,261	56,094	....	496,395	....	....	3.88	....	....
2005	395,401	202,298	65,770	....	572,827	....	....	3.84	....	....
2006	419,793	214,871	71,725	....	660,243	....	....	4.17	....	....
2007	427,597	217,746	74,288	....	772,982	....	....	4.80	....	....
2008	429,343	205,216	69,132	....	798,967	....	....	5.45	....	....
2008: Jan	442,055	218,019	75,327	....	780,822	....	....	5.14	....	....
Feb	438,780	217,489	74,657	....	790,370	....	....	5.24	....	....
Mar	445,319	218,214	75,574	....	801,204	....	....	5.27	....	....
Apr	449,119	214,832	73,624	....	807,250	....	....	5.27	....	....
May	450,956	214,419	73,707	....	813,304	....	....	5.30	....	....
June	454,835	214,547	70,983	....	819,087	....	....	5.31	....	....
July	455,354	212,668	72,441	....	822,963	....	....	5.32	....	....
Aug	436,596	202,616	67,788	....	823,183	....	....	5.50	....	....
Sept	425,853	203,147	66,885	....	823,768	....	....	5.53	....	....
Oct	400,753	186,389	62,576	....	816,392	....	....	5.73	....	....
Nov	374,334	179,936	60,071	....	810,059	....	....	5.93	....	....
Dec	357,472	173,279	54,895	....	798,967	....	....	5.87	....	....
2009: Jan	345,563	159,509	49,783	....	784,714	....	....	6.14	....	....
Feb	347,187	160,596	49,733	....	772,059	....	....	6.04	....	....
Mar	341,319	157,963	49,773	....	759,101	....	....	6.01	....	....
Apr	343,818	159,974	48,324	....	749,752	....	....	6.04	....	....
May	348,109	163,359	52,945	....	747,473	....	....	6.13	....	....
June	350,431	159,986	52,369	....	740,349	....	....	5.99	....	....
July	356,836	169,207	57,030	....	739,445	....	....	5.90	....	....
Aug	353,923	164,020	52,185	....	735,313	....	....	5.93	....	....
Sept	360,153	168,185	54,383	....	732,138	....	....	5.75	....	....
Oct	363,047	168,098	55,458	....	729,336	....	....	5.75	....	....
Nov [p]	365,295	166,868	53,819	....	724,534	....	....	5.69	....	....

[1] Annual data are averages of monthly not seasonally adjusted figures.

[2] Unfilled orders are seasonally adjusted, end of period. Ratios are unfilled orders at end of period to shipments for period (excludes industries with no unfilled orders). Annual ratios relate to seasonally adjusted data for December.

[3] Effective in 2001, data classified based on North American Industry Classification System (NAICS). Data on NAICS basis available beginning with 1992. Earlier data based on the Standard Industrial Classification (SIC). Data on SIC basis include semiconductors. Data on NAICS basis do not include semiconductors.

Note: For NAICS basis data beginning with 1992, because there are no unfilled orders for manufacturers' nondurable goods, manufacturers' nondurable new orders and nondurable shipments are the same (see Table B–58).

Source: Department of Commerce (Bureau of the Census).

TABLE B–60. Consumer price indexes for major expenditure classes, 1965–2009

[For all urban consumers; 1982–84=100, except as noted]

Year or month	All items	Food and beverages Total[1]	Food	Apparel	Housing	Transportation	Medical care	Recreation[2]	Education and communication[2]	Other goods and services	Energy[3]
1965	31.5	....	32.2	47.8	....	31.9	25.2	....	....	....	22.9
1966	32.4	....	33.8	49.0	....	32.3	26.3	....	....	....	23.3
1967	33.4	35.0	34.1	51.0	30.8	33.3	28.2	....	....	35.1	23.8
1968	34.8	36.2	35.3	53.7	32.0	34.3	29.9	....	....	36.9	24.2
1969	36.7	38.1	37.1	56.8	34.0	35.7	31.9	....	....	38.7	24.8
1970	38.8	40.1	39.2	59.2	36.4	37.5	34.0	....	....	40.9	25.5
1971	40.5	41.4	40.4	61.1	38.0	39.5	36.1	....	....	42.9	26.5
1972	41.8	43.1	42.1	62.3	39.4	39.9	37.3	....	....	44.7	27.2
1973	44.4	48.8	48.2	64.6	41.2	41.2	38.8	....	....	46.4	29.4
1974	49.3	55.5	55.1	69.4	45.8	45.8	42.4	....	....	49.8	38.1
1975	53.8	60.2	59.8	72.5	50.7	50.1	47.5	....	....	53.9	42.1
1976	56.9	62.1	61.6	75.2	53.8	55.1	52.0	....	....	57.0	45.1
1977	60.6	65.8	65.5	78.6	57.4	59.0	57.0	....	....	60.4	49.4
1978	65.2	72.2	72.0	81.4	62.4	61.7	61.8	....	....	64.3	52.5
1979	72.6	79.9	79.9	84.9	70.1	70.5	67.5	....	....	68.9	65.7
1980	82.4	86.7	86.8	90.9	81.1	83.1	74.9	....	....	75.2	86.0
1981	90.9	93.5	93.6	95.3	90.4	93.2	82.9	....	....	82.6	97.7
1982	96.5	97.3	97.4	97.8	96.9	97.0	92.5	....	....	91.1	99.2
1983	99.6	99.5	99.4	100.2	99.5	99.3	100.6	....	....	101.1	99.9
1984	103.9	103.2	103.2	102.1	103.6	103.7	106.8	....	....	107.9	100.9
1985	107.6	105.6	105.6	105.0	107.7	106.4	113.5	....	....	114.5	101.6
1986	109.6	109.1	109.0	105.9	110.9	102.3	122.0	....	....	121.4	88.2
1987	113.6	113.5	113.5	110.6	114.2	105.4	130.1	....	....	128.5	88.6
1988	118.3	118.2	118.2	115.4	118.5	108.7	138.6	....	....	137.0	89.3
1989	124.0	124.9	125.1	118.6	123.0	114.1	149.3	....	....	147.7	94.3
1990	130.7	132.1	132.4	124.1	128.5	120.5	162.8	....	....	159.0	102.1
1991	136.2	136.8	136.3	128.7	133.6	123.8	177.0	....	....	171.6	102.5
1992	140.3	138.7	137.9	131.9	137.5	126.5	190.1	....	....	183.3	103.0
1993	144.5	141.6	140.9	133.7	141.2	130.4	201.4	90.7	85.5	192.9	104.2
1994	148.2	144.9	144.3	133.4	144.8	134.3	211.0	92.7	88.8	198.5	104.6
1995	152.4	148.9	148.4	132.0	148.5	139.1	220.5	94.5	92.2	206.9	105.2
1996	156.9	153.7	153.3	131.7	152.8	143.0	228.2	97.4	95.3	215.4	110.1
1997	160.5	157.7	157.3	132.9	156.8	144.3	234.6	99.6	98.4	224.8	111.5
1998	163.0	161.1	160.7	133.0	160.4	141.6	242.1	101.1	100.3	237.7	102.9
1999	166.6	164.6	164.1	131.3	163.9	144.4	250.6	102.0	101.2	258.3	106.6
2000	172.2	168.4	167.8	129.6	169.6	153.3	260.8	103.3	102.5	271.1	124.6
2001	177.1	173.6	173.1	127.3	176.4	154.3	272.8	104.9	105.2	282.6	129.3
2002	179.9	176.8	176.2	124.0	180.3	152.9	285.6	106.2	107.9	293.2	121.7
2003	184.0	180.5	180.0	120.9	184.8	157.6	297.1	107.5	109.8	298.7	136.5
2004	188.9	186.6	186.2	120.4	189.5	163.1	310.1	108.6	111.6	304.7	151.4
2005	195.3	191.2	190.7	119.5	195.7	173.9	323.2	109.4	113.7	313.4	177.1
2006	201.6	195.7	195.2	119.5	203.2	180.9	336.2	110.9	116.8	321.7	196.9
2007	207.342	203.300	202.916	118.998	209.586	184.682	351.054	111.443	119.577	333.328	207.723
2008	215.303	214.225	214.106	118.907	216.264	195.549	364.065	113.254	123.631	345.381	236.666
2009	214.537	218.249	217.955	120.078	217.057	179.252	375.613	114.272	127.393	368.586	193.126
2008: Jan	211.080	208.837	208.618	115.795	212.244	190.839	360.459	112.083	121.762	339.052	219.465
Feb	211.693	209.462	209.166	117.839	213.026	190.520	362.155	112.365	121.766	340.191	219.311
Mar	213.528	209.692	209.385	120.881	214.389	195.189	363.000	112.731	121.832	341.827	230.505
Apr	214.823	211.365	211.102	122.113	214.890	198.608	363.184	112.874	122.073	343.410	240.194
May	216.632	212.251	212.054	120.752	215.809	205.262	363.396	112.987	122.348	344.709	257.106
June	218.815	213.383	213.243	117.019	217.941	211.787	363.616	112.991	122.828	345.885	275.621
July	219.964	215.326	215.299	114.357	219.610	212.806	363.963	113.277	123.445	346.810	280.833
Aug	219.086	216.419	216.422	116.376	219.148	206.739	364.477	113.786	124.653	346.990	266.283
Sept	218.783	217.672	217.696	121.168	218.184	203.861	365.036	114.032	125.505	348.166	258.020
Oct	216.573	218.039	218.738	122.243	217.383	192.709	365.746	114.169	125.686	349.276	231.561
Nov	212.425	218.752	218.749	121.262	216.467	173.644	366.613	114.078	125.758	349.040	189.938
Dec	210.228	218.839	218.805	117.078	216.073	164.628	367.133	113.674	125.921	349.220	171.158
2009: Jan	211.143	219.729	219.675	114.764	216.928	166.738	369.830	113.822	126.151	350.259	174.622
Feb	212.193	219.333	219.205	118.825	217.180	169.542	372.405	114.461	126.190	351.223	178.741
Mar	212.709	218.794	218.600	122.545	217.374	169.647	373.189	114.625	126.187	361.156	177.454
Apr	213.240	218.364	218.162	123.208	217.126	171.987	374.170	114.261	126.273	370.606	179.704
May	213.856	218.076	217.826	121.751	216.971	175.997	375.026	114.264	126.467	369.901	186.909
June	215.693	218.030	217.740	118.799	218.071	183.735	375.093	114.643	126.519	370.595	205.408
July	215.351	217.608	217.257	115.620	218.085	182.798	375.739	114.619	126.914	372.894	201.938
Aug	215.834	217.701	217.350	117.130	217.827	184.386	376.537	114.755	128.128	372.699	204.971
Sept	215.969	217.617	217.218	122.476	217.178	183.932	377.727	114.629	129.035	374.219	202.243
Oct	216.177	217.957	217.526	123.998	216.612	185.362	378.552	114.157	129.128	375.444	199.198
Nov	216.330	217.733	217.265	122.465	215.808	188.587	379.575	113.820	128.845	376.702	204.026
Dec	215.949	218.049	217.637	119.357	215.523	188.318	379.516	113.212	128.883	377.330	202.301

[1] Includes alcoholic beverages, not shown separately.
[2] December 1997=100.
[3] Household energy—gas (piped), electricity, fuel oil, etc.—and motor fuel. Motor oil, coolant, etc. also included through 1982.

Note: Data beginning with 1983 incorporate a rental equivalence measure for homeowners' costs.
Series reflect changes in composition and renaming beginning in 1998, and formula and methodology changes beginning in 1999.

Source: Department of Labor (Bureau of Labor Statistics).

TABLE B–61. Consumer price indexes for selected expenditure classes, 1965–2009

[For all urban consumers; 1982–84=100, except as noted]

Year or month	Food and beverages — Total[1]	Food — Total	Food — At home	Food — Away from home	Housing — Total[2]	Shelter — Total[2]	Shelter — Rent of primary residence	Shelter — Owners' equivalent rent of primary residence[3]	Fuels and utilities — Total[2]	Household energy — Total[2]	Household energy — Gas (piped) and electricity
1965	....	32.2	33.5	28.4	....	27.0	40.9	....	26.6	....	23.5
1966	....	33.8	35.2	29.7	....	27.8	41.5	....	26.7	....	23.6
1967	35.0	34.1	35.1	31.3	30.8	28.8	42.2	....	27.1	21.4	23.7
1968	36.2	35.3	36.3	32.9	32.0	30.1	43.3	....	27.4	21.7	23.9
1969	38.1	37.1	38.0	34.9	34.0	32.6	44.7	....	28.0	22.1	24.3
1970	40.1	39.2	39.9	37.5	36.4	35.5	46.5	....	29.1	23.1	25.4
1971	41.4	40.4	40.9	39.4	38.0	37.0	48.7	....	31.1	24.7	27.1
1972	43.1	42.1	42.7	41.0	39.4	38.7	50.4	....	32.5	25.7	28.5
1973	48.8	48.2	49.7	44.2	41.2	40.5	52.5	....	34.3	27.5	29.9
1974	55.5	55.1	57.1	49.8	45.8	44.4	55.2	....	40.7	34.4	34.5
1975	60.2	59.8	61.8	54.5	50.7	48.8	58.0	....	45.4	39.4	40.1
1976	62.1	61.6	63.1	58.2	53.8	51.5	61.1	....	49.4	43.3	44.7
1977	65.8	65.5	66.8	62.6	57.4	54.9	64.8	....	54.7	49.0	50.5
1978	72.2	72.0	73.8	68.3	62.4	60.5	69.3	....	58.5	53.0	55.0
1979	79.9	79.9	81.8	75.9	70.1	68.9	74.3	....	64.8	61.3	61.0
1980	86.7	86.8	88.4	83.4	81.1	81.0	80.9	....	75.4	74.8	71.4
1981	93.5	93.6	94.8	90.9	90.4	90.5	87.9	....	86.4	87.2	81.9
1982	97.3	97.4	98.1	95.8	96.9	96.9	94.6	....	94.9	95.6	93.2
1983	99.5	99.4	99.1	100.0	99.5	99.1	100.1	102.5	100.2	100.5	101.5
1984	103.2	103.2	102.8	104.2	103.6	104.0	105.3	107.3	104.8	104.0	105.4
1985	105.6	105.6	104.3	108.3	107.7	109.8	111.8	113.2	106.5	104.5	107.1
1986	109.1	109.0	107.3	112.5	110.9	115.8	118.3	119.4	104.1	99.2	105.7
1987	113.5	113.5	111.9	117.0	114.2	121.3	123.1	124.8	103.0	97.3	103.8
1988	118.2	118.2	116.6	121.8	118.5	127.1	127.8	131.1	104.4	98.0	104.6
1989	124.9	125.1	124.2	127.4	123.0	132.8	132.8	137.4	107.8	100.9	107.5
1990	132.1	132.4	132.3	133.4	128.5	140.0	138.4	144.8	111.6	104.5	109.3
1991	136.8	136.3	135.8	137.9	133.6	146.3	143.3	150.4	115.3	106.7	112.6
1992	138.7	137.9	136.8	140.7	137.5	151.2	146.9	155.5	117.8	108.1	114.8
1993	141.6	140.9	140.1	143.2	141.2	155.7	150.3	160.5	121.3	111.2	118.5
1994	144.9	144.3	144.1	145.7	144.8	160.5	154.0	165.8	122.8	111.7	119.2
1995	148.9	148.4	148.8	149.0	148.5	165.7	157.8	171.3	123.7	111.5	119.2
1996	153.7	153.3	154.3	152.7	152.8	171.0	162.0	176.8	127.5	115.2	122.1
1997	157.7	157.3	158.1	157.0	156.8	176.3	166.7	181.9	130.8	117.9	125.1
1998	161.1	160.7	161.1	161.1	160.4	182.1	172.1	187.8	128.5	113.7	121.2
1999	164.6	164.1	164.2	165.1	163.9	187.3	177.5	192.9	128.8	113.5	120.9
2000	168.4	167.8	167.9	169.0	169.6	193.4	183.9	198.7	137.9	122.8	128.0
2001	173.6	173.1	173.4	173.9	176.4	200.6	192.1	206.3	150.2	135.4	142.4
2002	176.8	176.2	175.6	178.3	180.3	208.1	199.7	214.7	143.6	127.2	134.4
2003	180.5	180.0	179.4	182.1	184.8	213.1	205.5	219.9	154.5	138.2	145.0
2004	186.6	186.2	186.2	187.5	189.5	218.8	211.0	224.9	161.9	144.4	150.6
2005	191.2	190.7	189.8	193.4	195.7	224.4	217.3	230.2	179.0	161.6	166.5
2006	195.7	195.2	193.1	199.4	203.2	232.1	225.1	238.2	194.7	177.1	182.1
2007	203.300	202.916	201.245	206.659	209.586	240.611	234.679	246.235	200.632	181.744	186.262
2008	214.225	214.106	214.125	215.769	216.264	246.666	243.271	252.426	220.018	200.808	202.212
2009	218.249	217.955	215.124	223.272	217.057	249.354	248.812	256.610	210.696	188.113	193.563
2008: Jan	208.837	208.618	207.983	211.070	212.244	243.871	239.850	250.106	204.796	185.107	186.475
Feb	209.462	209.166	208.329	211.878	213.026	244.786	240.325	250.481	205.795	185.994	187.376
Mar	209.692	209.385	208.203	212.537	214.389	245.995	240.874	250.966	209.221	189.693	190.105
Apr	211.365	211.102	210.851	213.083	214.890	246.004	241.474	251.418	213.302	194.121	194.379
May	212.251	212.054	211.863	213.967	215.809	246.069	241.803	251.576	219.881	201.212	200.999
June	213.383	213.243	213.171	215.015	217.941	247.083	242.640	252.170	231.412	213.762	213.375
July	215.326	215.299	215.785	216.376	219.610	248.075	243.367	252.504	239.039	221.742	221.805
Aug	216.419	216.422	217.259	217.063	219.148	247.985	244.181	252.957	235.650	217.455	218.656
Sept	217.672	217.696	218.629	218.225	218.184	247.737	244.926	253.493	228.450	209.501	210.950
Oct	218.705	218.738	219.660	219.290	217.383	247.844	245.855	253.902	221.199	201.176	203.503
Nov	218.752	218.749	219.086	220.043	216.467	247.463	246.681	254.669	216.285	195.599	199.435
Dec	218.839	218.805	218.683	220.684	216.073	247.085	247.278	254.875	215.184	194.335	199.487
2009: Jan	219.729	219.675	219.744	221.319	216.928	248.292	247.974	255.500	215.232	194.149	199.791
Feb	219.333	219.205	218.389	221.968	217.180	248.878	248.305	255.779	213.520	192.168	197.886
Mar	218.794	218.600	217.110	222.216	217.374	249.597	248.639	256.321	210.501	188.736	194.752
Apr	218.364	218.162	215.783	222.905	217.126	249.855	248.899	256.622	207.175	184.903	190.686
May	218.076	217.826	215.088	223.023	216.971	249.779	249.069	256.875	206.358	183.783	189.619
June	218.030	217.740	214.824	223.163	218.071	250.243	249.092	256.981	212.677	190.647	196.754
July	217.608	217.257	213.815	223.345	218.085	250.310	248.994	256.872	212.961	190.534	196.767
Aug	217.701	217.350	213.722	223.675	217.827	250.248	249.029	257.155	212.661	189.735	195.475
Sept	217.617	217.218	213.227	224.003	217.178	249.501	248.965	256.865	211.618	188.509	194.176
Oct	217.957	217.526	213.605	224.224	216.612	249.474	248.888	256.890	207.937	184.146	188.963
Nov	217.733	217.265	212.816	224.633	215.808	248.211	248.886	256.731	208.955	185.165	189.166
Dec	218.049	217.637	213.359	224.789	215.523	247.863	248.999	256.727	208.760	184.886	188.724

[1] Includes alcoholic beverages, not shown separately.
[2] Includes other items not shown separately.
[3] December 1982=100.

See next page for continuation of table.

TABLE B–61. Consumer price indexes for selected expenditure classes, 1965–2009—*Continued*

[For all urban consumers; 1982-84=100, except as noted]

Year or month	Transportation Total	Private transportation Total²	New vehicles Total²	New cars	Used cars and trucks	Motor fuel	Public transportation	Medical care Total	Medical care commodities	Medical care services
1965	31.9	32.5	49.8	49.7	29.8	25.1	25.2	25.2	45.0	22.7
1966	32.3	32.9	48.9	48.8	29.0	25.6	26.1	26.3	45.1	23.9
1967	33.3	33.8	49.3	49.3	29.9	26.4	27.4	28.2	44.9	26.0
1968	34.3	34.8	50.7	50.7	....	26.8	28.7	29.9	45.0	27.9
1969	35.7	36.0	51.5	51.5	30.9	27.6	30.9	31.9	45.4	30.2
1970	37.5	37.5	53.1	53.0	31.2	27.9	35.2	34.0	46.5	32.3
1971	39.5	39.4	55.3	55.2	33.0	28.1	37.8	36.1	47.3	34.7
1972	39.9	39.7	54.8	54.7	33.1	28.4	39.3	37.3	47.4	35.9
1973	41.2	41.0	54.8	54.8	35.2	31.2	39.7	38.8	47.5	37.5
1974	45.8	46.2	58.0	57.9	36.7	42.2	40.6	42.4	49.2	41.4
1975	50.1	50.6	63.0	62.9	43.8	45.1	43.5	47.5	53.3	46.6
1976	55.1	55.6	67.0	66.9	50.3	47.0	47.8	52.0	56.5	51.3
1977	59.0	59.7	70.5	70.4	54.7	49.7	50.0	57.0	60.2	56.4
1978	61.7	62.5	75.9	75.8	55.8	51.8	51.5	61.8	64.4	61.2
1979	70.5	71.7	81.9	81.8	60.2	70.1	54.9	67.5	69.0	67.2
1980	83.1	84.2	88.5	88.4	62.3	97.4	69.0	74.9	75.4	74.8
1981	93.2	93.8	93.9	93.7	76.9	108.5	85.6	82.9	83.7	82.8
1982	97.0	97.1	97.5	97.4	88.8	102.8	94.9	92.5	92.3	92.6
1983	99.3	99.3	99.9	99.9	98.7	99.4	99.5	100.6	100.2	100.7
1984	103.7	103.6	102.6	102.8	112.5	97.9	105.7	106.8	107.5	106.7
1985	106.4	106.2	106.1	106.1	113.7	98.7	110.5	113.5	115.2	113.2
1986	102.3	101.2	110.6	110.6	108.8	77.1	117.0	122.0	122.8	121.9
1987	105.4	104.2	114.4	114.6	113.1	80.2	121.1	130.1	131.0	130.0
1988	108.7	107.6	116.5	116.9	118.0	80.9	123.3	138.6	139.9	138.3
1989	114.1	112.9	119.2	119.2	120.4	88.5	129.5	149.3	150.8	148.9
1990	120.5	118.8	121.4	121.0	117.6	101.2	142.6	162.8	163.4	162.7
1991	123.8	121.9	126.0	125.3	118.1	99.4	148.9	177.0	176.8	177.1
1992	126.5	124.6	129.2	128.4	123.2	99.0	151.4	190.1	188.1	190.5
1993	130.4	127.5	132.7	131.5	133.9	98.0	167.0	201.4	195.0	202.9
1994	134.3	131.4	137.6	136.0	141.7	98.5	172.0	211.0	200.7	213.4
1995	139.1	136.3	141.0	139.0	156.5	100.0	175.9	220.5	204.5	224.2
1996	143.0	140.0	143.7	141.4	157.0	106.3	181.9	228.2	210.4	232.4
1997	144.3	141.0	144.3	141.7	151.1	106.2	186.7	234.6	215.3	239.1
1998	141.6	137.9	143.4	140.7	150.6	92.2	190.3	242.1	221.8	246.8
1999	144.4	140.5	142.9	139.6	152.0	100.7	197.7	250.6	230.7	255.1
2000	153.3	149.1	142.8	139.6	155.8	129.3	209.6	260.8	238.1	266.0
2001	154.3	150.0	142.1	138.9	158.7	124.7	210.6	272.8	247.6	278.8
2002	152.9	148.8	140.0	137.3	152.0	116.6	207.4	285.6	256.4	292.9
2003	157.6	153.6	137.9	134.7	142.9	135.8	209.3	297.1	262.8	306.0
2004	163.1	159.4	137.1	133.9	133.3	160.4	209.1	310.1	269.3	321.3
2005	173.9	170.2	137.9	135.2	139.4	195.7	217.3	323.2	276.0	336.7
2006	180.9	177.0	137.6	136.4	140.0	221.0	226.6	336.2	285.9	350.6
2007	184.682	180.778	136.254	135.865	135.747	239.070	230.002	351.054	289.999	369.302
2008	195.549	191.039	134.194	135.401	133.951	279.652	250.549	364.065	296.045	384.943
2009	179.252	174.762	135.623	136.685	126.973	201.978	236.348	375.613	305.108	397.299
2008: Jan	190.839	186.978	136.827	136.363	137.203	260.523	234.334	360.459	295.355	380.135
Feb	190.520	186.571	136.279	136.009	137.248	259.242	235.724	362.155	296.130	382.196
Mar	195.189	191.067	135.727	135.645	137.225	278.739	242.929	363.000	297.308	382.872
Apr	198.608	194.574	135.175	135.329	136.787	294.291	244.164	363.184	296.951	383.292
May	205.262	201.133	134.669	135.144	136.325	322.124	251.600	363.396	294.896	384.505
June	211.787	207.257	134.516	135.235	135.980	347.418	264.681	363.616	295.194	384.685
July	212.806	208.038	134.397	135.800	135.840	349.731	270.002	363.963	294.777	385.361
Aug	206.739	201.779	133.404	135.481	135.405	323.822	268.487	364.477	295.003	385.990
Sept	203.861	199.153	132.399	134.994	132.916	315.078	261.318	365.036	295.461	386.579
Oct	192.709	187.976	132.264	134.837	129.733	268.537	252.323	365.746	295.791	387.440
Nov	173.644	168.527	132.359	135.041	126.869	187.189	243.385	366.613	297.317	387.992
Dec	164.628	159.411	132.308	134.930	125.883	149.132	237.638	367.133	298.361	388.267
2009: Jan	166.738	161.788	133.273	135.637	124.863	156.604	234.394	369.830	299.998	391.365
Feb	169.542	164.871	134.186	135.984	122.837	167.395	231.529	372.405	302.184	394.047
Mar	169.647	165.023	134.611	135.947	121.061	168.404	230.735	373.189	302.908	394.837
Apr	171.987	167.516	134.863	136.037	121.213	177.272	229.827	374.170	303.979	395.753
May	175.997	171.757	135.162	136.172	122.650	193.609	228.878	375.026	304.697	396.648
June	183.735	179.649	135.719	136.486	124.323	225.021	232.540	375.093	304.683	396.750
July	182.798	178.330	136.055	136.844	125.061	217.860	238.932	375.739	304.229	397.868
Aug	184.386	179.987	134.080	134.666	128.028	225.089	238.997	376.537	305.797	398.303
Sept	183.932	179.466	134.576	135.041	129.369	220.690	239.855	377.727	307.671	399.160
Oct	185.362	180.896	137.268	137.851	132.689	219.015	241.060	378.552	308.379	400.015
Nov	188.587	184.099	138.831	139.821	134.173	228.050	244.226	379.575	308.546	401.392
Dec	188.318	183.766	138.857	139.728	137.406	224.730	245.203	379.516	308.221	401.452

Source: Department of Labor (Bureau of Labor Statistics).

Table B–62. Consumer price indexes for commodities, services, and special groups, 1965–2009

[For all urban consumers; 1982–84=100, except as noted]

Year or month	All items (CPI-U)[1]	Commodities		Services	Special indexes				All items		
		All commodities	Commodities less food		All items less food	All items less energy	All items less food and energy	All items less medical care	CPI-U-X1 (Dec. 1982 =97.6)[2]	CPI-U-RS (Dec. 1977 =100)[3]	C-CPI-U (Dec. 1999 =100)[4]
1965	31.5	35.2	37.2	26.6	31.6	32.5	32.7	32.0	34.2		
1966	32.4	36.1	37.7	27.6	32.3	33.5	33.5	33.0	35.2		
1967	33.4	36.8	38.6	28.8	33.4	34.4	34.7	33.7	36.3		
1968	34.8	38.1	40.0	30.3	34.9	35.9	36.3	35.1	37.7		
1969	36.7	39.9	41.7	32.4	36.8	38.0	38.4	37.0	39.4		
1970	38.8	41.7	43.4	35.0	39.0	40.3	40.8	39.2	41.3		
1971	40.5	43.2	45.1	37.0	40.8	42.0	42.7	40.8	43.1		
1972	41.8	44.5	46.1	38.4	42.0	43.4	44.0	42.1	44.4		
1973	44.4	47.8	47.7	40.1	43.7	46.1	45.6	44.8	47.2		
1974	49.3	53.5	52.8	43.8	48.0	50.6	49.4	49.8	51.9		
1975	53.8	58.2	57.6	48.0	52.5	55.1	53.9	54.3	56.2		
1976	56.9	60.7	60.5	52.0	56.0	58.2	57.4	57.2	59.4		
1977	60.6	64.2	63.8	56.0	59.6	61.9	61.0	60.8	63.2		
1978	65.2	68.8	67.5	60.8	63.9	66.7	65.5	65.4	67.5	104.4	
1979	72.6	76.6	75.3	67.5	71.2	73.4	71.9	72.9	74.0	114.4	
1980	82.4	86.0	85.7	77.9	81.5	81.9	80.8	82.8	82.3	127.1	
1981	90.9	93.2	93.1	88.1	90.4	90.1	89.2	91.4	90.1	139.2	
1982	96.5	97.0	96.9	96.0	96.3	96.1	95.8	96.8	95.6	147.6	
1983	99.6	99.8	100.0	99.4	99.7	99.6	99.6	99.6	99.6	153.9	
1984	103.9	103.2	103.1	104.6	104.0	104.3	104.6	103.7	103.9	160.2	
1985	107.6	105.4	105.2	109.9	108.0	108.4	109.1	107.2	107.6	165.7	
1986	109.6	104.4	101.7	115.4	109.8	112.6	113.5	108.8	109.6	168.7	
1987	113.6	107.7	104.3	120.2	113.6	117.2	118.2	112.6	113.6	174.4	
1988	118.3	111.5	107.7	125.7	118.3	122.3	123.4	117.0	118.3	180.8	
1989	124.0	116.7	112.0	131.9	123.7	128.1	129.0	122.4	124.0	188.6	
1990	130.7	122.8	117.4	139.2	130.3	134.7	135.5	128.8	130.7	198.0	
1991	136.2	126.6	121.3	146.3	136.1	140.9	142.1	133.8	136.2	205.1	
1992	140.3	129.1	124.2	152.0	140.8	145.4	147.3	137.5	140.3	210.3	
1993	144.5	131.5	126.3	157.9	145.1	150.0	152.2	141.2	144.5	215.5	
1994	148.2	133.8	127.9	163.1	149.0	154.1	156.5	144.7	148.2	220.1	
1995	152.4	136.4	129.8	168.7	153.1	158.7	161.2	148.6	152.4	225.4	
1996	156.9	139.9	132.6	174.1	157.5	163.1	165.6	152.8	156.9	231.4	
1997	160.5	141.8	133.4	179.4	161.1	167.1	169.5	156.3	160.5	236.4	
1998	163.0	141.9	132.0	184.2	163.4	170.9	173.4	158.6	163.0	239.7	
1999	166.6	144.4	134.0	188.8	167.0	174.4	177.0	162.0	166.6	244.7	
2000	172.2	149.2	139.2	195.3	173.0	178.6	181.3	167.3	172.2	252.9	102.0
2001	177.1	150.7	138.9	203.4	177.8	183.5	186.1	171.9	177.1	260.0	104.3
2002	179.9	149.7	136.0	209.8	180.5	187.7	190.5	174.3	179.9	264.2	105.6
2003	184.0	151.2	136.5	216.5	184.7	190.6	193.2	178.1	184.0	270.1	107.8
2004	188.9	154.7	138.8	222.8	189.4	194.4	196.6	182.7	188.9	277.4	110.5
2005	195.3	160.2	144.5	230.1	196.0	198.7	200.9	188.7	195.3	286.7	113.7
2006	201.6	164.0	148.0	238.9	202.7	203.7	205.9	194.7	201.6	296.1	117.0
2007	207.342	167.509	149.720	246.848	208.098	208.925	210.729	200.080	207.342	304.5	119.957
2008	215.303	174.764	155.310	255.498	215.528	214.751	215.572	207.777	215.303	316.2	123.880
2009	214.537	169.698	147.071	259.154	214.008	218.433	219.235	206.555	214.537	315.0	
2008: Jan	211.080	171.179	152.531	250.648	211.512	211.846	213.138	203.569	211.080	310.0	121.868
Feb	211.693	171.530	152.799	251.527	212.136	212.545	213.866	204.136	211.693	310.9	122.224
Mar	213.528	173.884	155.881	252.817	214.236	213.420	214.866	205.992	213.528	313.6	123.177
Apr	214.823	175.838	157.870	253.426	215.462	213.851	215.059	207.317	214.823	315.5	123.817
May	216.632	178.341	160.880	254.509	217.411	214.101	215.180	209.170	216.632	318.1	124.617
June	218.815	180.534	163.385	256.668	219.757	214.600	215.553	211.408	218.815	321.3	125.554
July	219.964	181.087	163.364	258.422	220.758	215.335	216.045	212.576	219.964	323.0	126.088
Aug	219.086	179.148	160.341	258.638	219.552	215.873	216.476	211.653	219.086	321.7	125.815
Sept	218.783	179.117	159.825	258.059	218.991	216.397	216.862	211.321	218.783	321.3	125.746
Oct	216.573	175.257	154.250	257.559	216.250	216.695	217.023	209.021	216.573	318.0	124.757
Nov	212.425	167.673	144.055	256.967	211.421	216.417	216.690	204.721	212.425	311.9	122.257
Dec	210.228	163.582	138.536	256.731	208.855	215.930	216.100	202.442	210.228	308.7	120.634
2009: Jan	211.143	164.360	139.258	257.780	209.777	216.586	216.719	203.281	211.143	310.1	121.208
Feb	212.193	165.891	141.491	258.328	211.076	217.325	217.685	204.265	212.193	311.6	121.901
Mar	212.709	166.645	142.728	258.597	211.775	218.033	218.639	204.766	212.709	312.4	122.182
Apr	213.240	167.816	144.059	258.466	212.464	218.388	219.143	205.275	213.240	313.1	122.506
May	213.856	169.060	146.261	258.433	213.236	218.323	219.128	205.876	213.856	314.0	122.898
June	215.693	171.593	149.697	259.544	215.389	218.440	219.283	207.764	215.693	316.7	123.967
July	215.351	170.483	148.386	259.992	215.069	218.421	219.350	207.388	215.351	316.2	123.711
Aug	215.834	171.081	149.155	260.355	215.617	218.642	219.596	207.855	215.834	316.9	123.955
Sept	215.969	171.559	149.846	260.136	215.795	219.076	220.137	207.949	215.969	317.1	124.021
Oct	216.177	172.252	150.663	259.844	215.986	219.624	220.731	208.131	216.177	317.5	124.179
Nov	216.330	173.061	151.847	259.323	216.207	219.291	220.384	208.250	216.330	317.7	124.231
Dec	215.949	172.572	151.052	259.055	215.703	219.048	220.025	207.860	215.949	317.1	123.965

[1] Consumer price index, all urban consumers.

[2] CPI-U-X1 reflects a rental equivalence approach to homeowners' costs for the CPI-U for years prior to 1983, the first year for which the official index incorporates such a measure. CPI-U-X1 is rebased to the December 1982 value of the CPI-U (1982–84=100) and is identical with CPI-U data from December 1982 forward. Data prior to 1967 estimated by moving the series at the same rate as the CPI-U for each year.

[3] Consumer price index research series (CPI-U-RS) using current methods introduced in June 1999. Data for 2009 are preliminary. All data are subject to revision annually.

[4] Chained consumer price index (C-CPI-U) introduced in August 2002. Data for 2008 and 2009 are subject to revision.

Source: Department of Labor (Bureau of Labor Statistics).

TABLE B–63. Changes in special consumer price indexes, 1965–2009

[For all urban consumers; percent change]

Year or month	All items Dec. to Dec.[1]	All items Year to year	All items less food Dec. to Dec.[1]	All items less food Year to year	All items less energy Dec. to Dec.[1]	All items less energy Year to year	All items less food and energy Dec. to Dec.[1]	All items less food and energy Year to year	All items less medical care Dec. to Dec.[1]	All items less medical care Year to year
1965	1.9	1.6	1.6	1.6	1.9	1.6	1.5	1.2	1.9	1.6
1966	3.5	2.9	3.5	2.2	3.4	3.1	3.3	2.4	3.4	3.1
1967	3.0	3.1	3.3	3.4	3.2	2.7	3.8	3.6	2.7	2.1
1968	4.7	4.2	5.0	4.5	4.9	4.4	5.1	4.6	4.7	4.2
1969	6.2	5.5	5.6	5.4	6.5	5.8	6.2	5.8	6.1	5.4
1970	5.6	5.7	6.6	6.0	5.4	6.1	6.6	6.3	5.2	5.9
1971	3.3	4.4	3.0	4.6	3.4	4.2	3.1	4.7	3.2	4.1
1972	3.4	3.2	2.9	2.9	3.5	3.3	3.0	3.0	3.4	3.2
1973	8.7	6.2	5.6	4.0	8.2	6.2	4.7	3.6	9.1	6.4
1974	12.3	11.0	12.2	9.8	11.7	9.8	11.1	8.3	12.2	11.2
1975	6.9	9.1	7.3	9.4	6.6	8.9	6.7	9.1	6.7	9.0
1976	4.9	5.8	6.1	6.7	4.8	5.6	6.1	6.5	4.5	5.3
1977	6.7	6.5	6.4	6.4	6.7	6.4	6.5	6.3	6.7	6.3
1978	9.0	7.6	8.3	7.2	9.1	7.8	8.5	7.4	9.1	7.6
1979	13.3	11.3	14.0	11.4	11.1	10.0	11.3	9.8	13.4	11.5
1980	12.5	13.5	13.0	14.5	11.7	11.6	12.2	12.4	12.5	13.6
1981	8.9	10.3	9.8	10.9	8.5	10.0	9.5	10.4	8.8	10.4
1982	3.8	6.2	4.1	6.5	4.2	6.7	4.5	7.4	3.6	5.9
1983	3.8	3.2	4.1	3.5	4.5	3.6	4.8	4.0	3.6	2.9
1984	3.9	4.3	3.9	4.3	4.4	4.7	4.7	5.0	3.9	4.1
1985	3.8	3.6	4.1	3.8	4.0	3.9	4.3	4.3	3.5	3.4
1986	1.1	1.9	.5	1.7	3.8	3.9	3.8	4.0	.7	1.5
1987	4.4	3.6	4.6	3.5	4.1	4.1	4.2	4.1	4.3	3.5
1988	4.4	4.1	4.2	4.1	4.7	4.4	4.7	4.4	4.2	3.9
1989	4.6	4.8	4.5	4.6	4.6	4.7	4.4	4.5	4.5	4.6
1990	6.1	5.4	6.3	5.3	5.2	5.2	5.2	5.0	5.9	5.2
1991	3.1	4.2	3.3	4.5	3.9	4.6	4.4	4.9	2.7	3.9
1992	2.9	3.0	3.2	3.5	3.0	3.2	3.3	3.7	2.7	2.8
1993	2.7	3.0	2.7	3.1	3.1	3.2	3.2	3.3	2.6	2.7
1994	2.7	2.6	2.6	2.7	2.6	2.7	2.6	2.8	2.5	2.5
1995	2.5	2.8	2.7	2.8	2.9	3.0	3.0	3.0	2.5	2.7
1996	3.3	3.0	3.1	2.9	2.9	2.8	2.6	2.7	3.3	2.8
1997	1.7	2.3	1.8	2.3	2.1	2.5	2.2	2.4	1.6	2.3
1998	1.6	1.6	1.5	1.4	2.4	2.3	2.4	2.3	1.5	1.5
1999	2.7	2.2	2.8	2.2	2.0	2.0	1.9	2.1	2.6	2.1
2000	3.4	3.4	3.5	3.6	2.6	2.4	2.6	2.4	3.3	3.3
2001	1.6	2.8	1.3	2.8	2.8	2.7	2.7	2.6	1.4	2.7
2002	2.4	1.6	2.6	1.5	1.8	2.3	1.9	2.4	2.2	1.4
2003	1.9	2.3	1.5	2.3	1.5	1.5	1.1	1.4	1.8	2.2
2004	3.3	2.7	3.4	2.5	2.2	2.0	2.2	1.8	3.2	2.6
2005	3.4	3.4	3.6	3.5	2.2	2.2	2.2	2.2	3.3	3.3
2006	2.5	3.2	2.6	3.4	2.5	2.5	2.6	2.5	2.5	3.2
2007	4.1	2.8	4.0	2.7	2.8	2.6	2.4	2.3	4.0	2.8
2008	.1	3.8	-.8	3.6	2.4	2.8	1.8	2.3	-.1	3.8
2009	2.7	-.4	3.3	-.7	1.4	1.7	1.8	1.7	2.7	-.6

Percent change from preceding month

Year or month	Unadjusted	Seasonally adjusted	Unadjusted	Seasonally adjusted	Unadjusted	Seasonally adjusted	Unadjusted	Seasonally adjusted	Unadjusted	Seasonally adjusted
2008: Jan	0.5	0.4	0.4	0.3	0.5	0.3	0.4	0.3	0.5	0.3
Feb	.3	.2	.3	.1	.3	.1	.3	.1	.3	.2
Mar	.9	.4	1.0	.4	.4	.2	.5	.2	.9	.4
Apr	.6	.2	.6	.0	.2	.2	.1	.1	.6	.2
May	.8	.5	.9	.5	.1	.2	.1	.2	.8	.5
June	1.0	.9	1.1	1.0	.2	.3	.2	.3	1.1	1.0
July	.5	.7	.5	.7	.3	.4	.2	.3	.6	.8
Aug	-.4	.0	-.5	-.1	.2	.2	.2	.2	-.4	.0
Sept	-.1	.0	-.3	.0	.2	.2	.2	.1	-.2	.0
Oct	-1.0	-.8	-1.3	-1.0	.1	.1	.1	.0	-1.1	-.9
Nov	-1.9	-1.7	-2.2	-2.0	-.1	.1	-.2	.1	-2.1	-1.8
Dec	-1.0	-.8	-1.2	-.9	-.2	.0	-.3	.0	-1.1	-.9
2009: Jan	.4	.3	.4	.3	.3	.2	.3	.2	.4	.3
Feb	.5	.4	.6	.5	.3	.1	.4	.2	.5	.4
Mar	.2	-.1	.3	-.1	.3	.1	.4	.2	.2	-.2
Apr	.2	.0	.3	.0	.2	.2	.2	.3	.2	.0
May	.3	.1	.4	.2	.0	.1	.0	.1	.3	.1
June	.9	.7	1.0	.9	.1	.2	.1	.2	.9	.8
July	-.2	.0	-.1	.0	.0	.0	.0	.1	-.2	.0
Aug	.2	.4	.3	.5	.1	.1	.1	.1	.2	.5
Sept	.1	.2	.1	.2	.2	.1	.2	.2	.0	.2
Oct	.1	.3	.1	.3	.2	.1	.3	.2	.1	.3
Nov	.1	.4	.1	.5	-.2	.0	-.2	.0	.1	.4
Dec	-.2	.1	-.2	.1	-.1	.1	-.2	.1	-.2	.1

[1] Changes from December to December are based on unadjusted indexes.

Source: Department of Labor (Bureau of Labor Statistics).

TABLE B-64. Changes in consumer price indexes for commodities and services, 1933–2009

[For all urban consumers: percent change]

Year	All items		Commodities				Services				Medical care [2]		Energy [3]	
			Total		Food		Total		Medical care					
	Dec. to Dec. [1]	Year to year	Dec. to Dec. [1]	Year to year	Dec. to Dec. [1]	Year to year	Dec. to Dec. [1]	Year to year	Dec. to Dec. [1]	Year to year	Dec. to Dec. [1]	Year to year	Dec. to Dec. [1]	Year to year
1933	0.8	−5.1	....	....	6.9	−2.8	....	....	....	....	....	....	....	....
1939	.0	−1.4	−0.7	−2.0	−2.5	−2.5	0.0	0.0	1.2	1.2	1.0	0.0	....	....
1940	.7	.7	1.4	.7	2.5	1.7	.8	.8	.0	.0	.0	1.0	....	....
1941	9.9	5.0	13.3	6.7	15.7	9.2	2.4	.8	1.2	.0	1.0	.0	....	....
1942	9.0	10.9	12.9	14.5	17.9	17.6	2.3	3.1	3.5	3.5	3.8	2.9	....	....
1943	3.0	6.1	4.2	9.3	3.0	11.0	2.3	2.3	5.6	4.5	4.6	4.7	....	....
1944	2.3	1.7	2.0	1.0	.0	−1.2	2.2	2.2	3.2	4.3	2.6	3.6	....	....
1945	2.2	2.3	2.9	3.0	3.5	2.4	.7	1.5	3.1	3.1	2.6	2.6	....	....
1946	18.1	8.3	24.8	10.6	31.3	14.5	3.6	1.4	9.0	5.1	8.3	5.0	....	....
1947	8.8	14.4	10.3	20.5	11.3	21.7	5.6	4.3	6.4	8.7	6.9	8.0	....	....
1948	3.0	8.1	1.7	7.2	−.8	8.3	5.9	6.1	6.9	7.1	5.8	6.7	....	....
1949	−2.1	−1.2	−4.1	−2.7	−3.9	−4.2	3.7	5.1	1.6	3.3	1.4	2.8	....	....
1950	5.9	1.3	7.8	.7	9.8	1.6	3.6	3.0	4.0	2.4	3.4	2.0	....	....
1951	6.0	7.9	5.9	9.0	7.1	11.0	5.2	5.3	5.3	4.7	5.8	5.3	....	....
1952	.8	1.9	−.9	1.3	−1.0	1.8	4.4	4.5	5.8	6.7	4.3	5.0	....	....
1953	.7	.8	−.3	−.3	−1.1	−1.4	4.2	4.3	3.4	3.5	3.5	3.6	....	....
1954	−.7	.7	−1.6	−.9	−1.8	−.4	2.0	3.1	2.6	3.4	2.3	2.9	....	....
1955	.4	−.4	−.3	−.9	−.7	−1.4	2.0	2.0	3.2	2.6	3.3	2.2	....	....
1956	3.0	1.5	2.6	1.0	2.9	.7	3.4	2.5	3.8	3.8	3.2	3.8	....	....
1957	2.9	3.3	2.8	3.2	2.8	3.2	4.2	4.3	4.8	4.3	4.7	4.2	....	....
1958	1.8	2.8	1.2	2.1	2.4	4.5	2.7	3.7	4.6	5.3	4.5	4.6	....	....
1959	1.7	.7	.6	.0	−1.0	−1.7	3.9	3.1	4.9	4.5	3.8	4.4	4.7	1.9
1960	1.4	1.7	1.2	.9	3.1	1.0	2.5	3.4	3.7	4.3	3.2	3.7	1.3	2.3
1961	.7	1.0	.0	.6	−.7	1.3	2.1	1.7	3.5	3.6	3.1	2.7	−1.3	.4
1962	1.3	1.0	.9	.9	1.3	.7	1.6	2.0	2.9	3.5	2.2	2.6	2.2	.4
1963	1.6	1.3	1.5	.9	2.0	1.6	2.4	2.0	2.8	2.9	2.5	2.6	−.9	.0
1964	1.0	1.3	.9	1.2	1.3	1.3	1.6	2.0	2.3	2.3	2.1	2.1	.0	−.4
1965	1.9	1.6	1.4	1.1	3.5	2.2	2.7	2.3	3.6	3.2	2.8	2.4	1.8	1.8
1966	3.5	2.9	2.5	2.6	4.0	5.0	4.8	3.8	8.3	5.3	6.7	4.4	1.7	1.7
1967	3.0	3.1	2.5	1.9	1.2	.9	4.3	4.3	8.0	8.8	6.3	7.2	1.7	2.1
1968	4.7	4.2	4.0	3.5	4.4	3.5	5.8	5.2	7.1	7.3	6.2	6.0	1.7	1.7
1969	6.2	5.5	5.4	4.7	7.0	5.1	7.7	6.9	7.3	8.2	6.2	6.7	2.9	2.5
1970	5.6	5.7	3.9	4.5	2.3	5.7	8.1	8.0	8.1	7.0	7.4	6.6	4.8	2.8
1971	3.3	4.4	2.8	3.6	4.3	3.1	4.1	5.7	5.4	7.4	4.6	6.2	3.1	3.9
1972	3.4	3.2	3.4	3.0	4.6	4.2	3.4	3.8	3.7	3.5	3.3	3.3	2.6	2.6
1973	8.7	6.2	10.4	7.4	20.3	14.5	6.2	4.4	6.0	4.5	5.3	4.0	17.0	8.1
1974	12.3	11.0	12.8	11.9	12.0	14.3	11.4	9.2	13.2	10.4	12.6	9.3	21.6	29.6
1975	6.9	9.1	6.2	8.8	6.6	8.5	8.2	9.6	10.3	12.6	9.8	12.0	11.4	10.5
1976	4.9	5.8	3.3	4.3	.5	3.0	7.2	8.3	10.8	10.1	10.0	9.5	7.1	7.1
1977	6.7	6.5	6.1	5.8	8.1	6.3	8.0	7.7	9.0	9.9	8.9	9.6	7.2	9.5
1978	9.0	7.6	8.8	7.2	11.8	9.9	9.3	8.6	9.3	8.5	8.8	8.4	7.9	6.3
1979	13.3	11.3	13.0	11.3	10.2	11.0	13.6	11.0	10.5	9.8	10.1	9.2	37.5	25.1
1980	12.5	13.5	11.0	12.3	10.2	8.6	14.2	15.4	10.1	11.3	9.9	11.0	18.0	30.9
1981	8.9	10.3	6.0	8.4	4.3	7.8	13.0	13.1	12.6	10.7	12.5	10.7	11.9	13.6
1982	3.8	6.2	3.6	4.1	3.1	4.1	4.3	9.0	11.2	11.8	11.0	11.6	1.3	1.5
1983	3.8	3.2	2.9	2.9	2.7	2.1	4.8	3.5	6.2	8.7	6.4	8.8	−.5	.7
1984	3.9	4.3	2.7	3.4	3.8	3.8	5.4	5.2	5.8	6.0	6.1	6.2	.2	1.0
1985	3.8	3.6	2.5	2.1	2.6	2.3	5.1	5.1	6.8	6.1	6.8	6.3	1.8	.7
1986	1.1	1.9	−2.0	−.9	3.8	3.2	4.5	5.0	7.9	7.7	7.7	7.5	−19.7	−13.2
1987	4.4	3.6	4.6	3.2	3.5	4.1	4.3	4.2	5.6	6.6	5.8	6.6	8.2	.5
1988	4.4	4.1	3.8	3.5	5.2	4.1	4.8	4.6	6.9	6.4	6.9	6.5	.5	.8
1989	4.6	4.8	4.1	4.7	5.6	5.8	5.1	4.9	8.6	7.7	8.5	7.7	5.1	5.6
1990	6.1	5.4	6.6	5.2	5.3	5.8	5.7	5.5	9.9	9.3	9.6	9.0	18.1	8.3
1991	3.1	4.2	1.2	3.1	1.9	2.9	4.6	5.1	8.0	8.9	7.9	8.7	−7.4	.4
1992	2.9	3.0	2.0	2.0	1.5	1.2	3.6	3.9	7.0	7.6	6.6	7.4	2.0	.5
1993	2.7	3.0	1.5	1.9	2.9	2.2	3.8	3.9	5.9	6.5	5.4	5.9	−1.4	1.2
1994	2.7	2.6	2.3	1.7	2.9	2.4	2.9	3.3	5.4	5.2	4.9	4.8	2.2	.4
1995	2.5	2.8	1.4	1.9	2.1	2.8	3.5	3.4	4.4	5.1	3.9	4.5	−1.3	.6
1996	3.3	3.0	3.2	2.6	4.3	3.3	3.3	3.2	3.2	3.7	3.0	3.5	8.6	4.7
1997	1.7	2.3	.2	1.4	1.5	2.6	2.8	3.0	2.9	2.9	2.8	2.8	−3.4	1.3
1998	1.6	1.6	.4	.1	2.3	2.2	2.6	2.7	3.2	3.2	3.4	3.2	−8.8	−7.7
1999	2.7	2.2	2.7	1.8	1.9	2.1	2.6	2.5	3.6	3.4	3.7	3.5	13.4	3.6
2000	3.4	3.4	2.7	3.3	2.8	2.3	3.9	3.4	4.6	4.3	4.2	4.1	14.2	16.9
2001	1.6	2.8	−1.4	1.0	2.8	3.2	3.7	4.1	4.8	4.8	4.7	4.6	−13.0	3.8
2002	2.4	1.6	1.2	−.7	1.5	1.8	3.2	3.1	5.6	5.1	5.0	4.7	10.7	−5.9
2003	1.9	2.3	.5	1.0	3.6	2.2	2.8	3.2	4.2	4.5	3.7	4.0	6.9	12.2
2004	3.3	2.7	3.6	2.3	2.7	3.4	3.1	2.9	4.9	5.0	4.2	4.4	16.6	10.9
2005	3.4	3.4	2.7	3.6	2.3	2.4	3.8	3.3	4.5	4.8	4.3	4.2	17.1	17.0
2006	2.5	3.2	1.3	2.4	2.1	2.4	3.4	3.8	4.1	4.1	3.6	4.0	2.9	11.2
2007	4.1	2.8	5.2	2.1	4.9	4.0	3.3	3.3	5.9	5.3	5.2	4.4	17.4	5.5
2008	.1	3.8	−4.1	4.3	5.9	5.5	3.0	3.5	3.0	4.2	2.6	3.7	−21.3	13.9
2009	2.7	−.4	5.5	−2.9	−.5	1.8	.9	1.4	3.4	3.2	3.4	3.2	18.2	−18.4

[1] Changes from December to December are based on unadjusted indexes.
[2] Commodities and services.
[3] Household energy—gas (piped), electricity, fuel oil, etc.—and motor fuel. Motor oil, coolant, etc. also included through 1982.

Source: Department of Labor (Bureau of Labor Statistics).

TABLE B–65. Producer price indexes by stage of processing, 1965–2009

[1982=100]

Year or month	Total finished goods	Finished goods									Total finished consumer goods
		Consumer foods			Finished goods excluding consumer foods						
		Total	Crude	Processed	Total	Consumer goods				Capital equipment	
						Total	Durable	Nondurable		
1965	34.1	36.8	39.0	36.8	....	33.6	43.2	28.8	33.8		34.2
1966	35.2	39.2	41.5	39.2	....	34.1	43.4	29.3	34.6		35.4
1967	35.6	38.5	39.6	38.8	35.0	34.7	44.1	30.0	35.8		35.6
1968	36.6	40.0	42.5	40.0	35.9	35.5	45.1	30.6	37.0		36.5
1969	38.0	42.4	45.9	42.3	36.9	36.3	45.9	31.5	38.3		37.9
1970	39.3	43.8	46.0	43.9	38.2	37.4	47.2	32.5	40.1		39.1
1971	40.5	44.5	45.8	44.7	39.6	38.7	48.9	33.5	41.7		40.2
1972	41.8	46.9	48.0	47.2	40.4	39.4	50.0	34.1	42.8		41.5
1973	45.6	56.5	63.6	55.8	42.0	41.2	50.9	36.1	44.2		46.0
1974	52.6	64.4	71.6	63.9	48.8	48.2	55.5	44.0	50.5		53.1
1975	58.2	69.8	71.7	70.3	54.7	53.2	61.0	48.9	58.2		58.2
1976	60.8	69.6	76.7	69.0	58.1	56.5	63.7	52.4	62.1		60.4
1977	64.7	73.3	79.5	72.7	62.2	60.6	67.4	56.8	66.1		64.3
1978	69.8	79.9	85.8	79.4	66.7	64.9	73.6	60.0	71.3		69.4
1979	77.6	87.3	92.3	86.8	74.6	73.5	80.8	69.3	77.5		77.5
1980	88.0	92.4	93.9	92.3	86.7	87.1	91.0	85.1	85.8		88.6
1981	96.1	97.8	104.4	97.2	95.6	96.1	96.4	95.8	94.6		96.6
1982	100.0	100.0	100.0	100.0	100.0	100.0	100.0	100.0	100.0		100.0
1983	101.6	101.0	102.4	100.9	101.8	101.2	102.8	100.5	102.8		101.3
1984	103.7	105.4	111.4	104.9	103.2	102.2	104.5	101.1	105.2		103.3
1985	104.7	104.6	102.9	104.8	104.6	103.3	106.5	101.7	107.5		103.8
1986	103.2	107.3	105.6	107.4	101.9	98.5	108.9	93.3	109.7		101.4
1987	105.4	109.5	107.1	109.6	104.0	100.7	111.5	94.9	111.7		103.6
1988	108.0	112.6	109.8	112.7	106.5	103.1	113.8	97.3	114.3		106.2
1989	113.6	118.7	119.6	118.6	111.8	108.9	117.6	103.8	118.8		112.1
1990	119.2	124.4	123.0	124.4	117.4	115.3	120.4	111.5	122.9		118.2
1991	121.7	124.1	119.3	124.4	120.9	118.7	123.9	115.0	126.7		120.5
1992	123.2	123.3	107.6	124.4	123.1	120.8	125.7	117.3	129.1		121.7
1993	124.7	125.7	114.4	126.5	124.4	121.7	128.0	117.6	131.4		123.0
1994	125.5	126.8	111.3	127.9	125.1	121.6	130.9	116.2	134.1		123.3
1995	127.9	129.0	118.8	129.8	127.5	124.0	132.7	118.8	136.7		125.6
1996	131.3	133.6	129.2	133.8	130.5	127.6	134.2	123.3	138.3		129.5
1997	131.8	134.5	126.6	135.1	130.9	128.2	133.7	124.3	138.2		130.2
1998	130.7	134.3	127.2	134.8	129.5	126.4	132.9	122.2	137.6		128.9
1999	133.0	135.1	125.5	135.9	132.3	130.5	133.0	127.9	137.6		132.0
2000	138.0	137.2	123.5	138.3	138.1	138.4	133.9	138.7	138.8		138.2
2001	140.7	141.3	127.7	142.4	140.4	141.4	134.0	142.8	139.7		141.5
2002	138.9	140.1	128.5	141.0	138.3	138.8	133.0	139.8	139.1		139.4
2003	143.3	145.9	130.0	147.2	142.4	144.7	133.1	148.4	139.5		145.3
2004	148.5	152.7	138.2	153.9	147.2	150.9	135.0	156.6	141.4		151.7
2005	155.7	155.7	140.2	156.9	155.5	161.9	136.6	172.0	144.6		160.4
2006	160.4	156.7	151.3	157.1	161.0	169.2	136.9	182.6	146.9		166.0
2007	166.6	167.0	170.2	166.7	166.2	175.6	138.3	191.7	149.5		173.5
2008	177.1	178.3	175.5	178.6	176.6	189.1	141.2	210.5	153.8		186.3
2009 ᵖ	172.6	175.5	157.8	177.3	171.2	179.6	144.3	194.3	156.8		179.2
2008: Jan	172.0	174.5	199.3	172.1	171.0	181.9	140.1	200.3	151.4		180.1
Feb	172.3	173.6	180.6	173.0	171.7	182.7	140.2	201.4	151.8		180.4
Mar	175.1	176.0	194.3	174.2	174.6	187.1	139.9	208.2	151.8		184.2
Apr	176.5	175.5	177.6	175.3	176.4	189.6	140.5	211.7	152.4		185.8
May	179.8	177.6	172.1	178.2	180.1	195.0	140.3	220.0	152.7		190.3
June	182.4	180.0	183.0	179.7	182.8	199.0	139.7	226.4	152.7		193.8
July	185.1	181.0	164.1	182.7	185.9	203.4	139.6	233.1	153.3		197.2
Aug	182.2	181.3	159.8	183.5	182.2	197.5	140.2	223.9	153.9		193.2
Sept	182.2	181.5	168.9	182.8	182.1	197.2	140.3	223.4	154.3		193.0
Oct	177.4	180.7	170.0	181.8	176.3	187.0	144.8	205.4	157.0		185.5
Nov	172.0	179.8	175.2	180.3	169.6	177.0	144.2	190.6	156.9		178.2
Dec	168.8	177.7	161.7	179.4	166.1	171.5	144.4	182.1	157.2		173.7
2009: Jan	170.4	177.7	169.7	178.4	168.0	174.4	144.3	186.5	157.4		175.8
Feb	169.9	175.0	155.6	177.0	168.0	174.5	144.3	186.6	157.2		175.2
Mar	169.1	173.8	155.0	175.8	167.2	173.5	144.1	185.2	156.9		174.2
Apr	170.3	175.9	165.4	176.9	168.3	175.2	144.4	187.7	156.8		176.0
May	171.1	174.0	134.6	178.3	169.7	177.5	144.2	191.2	156.3		177.3
June	174.3	176.1	156.2	178.2	173.1	182.7	144.7	198.7	156.6		181.7
July	172.4	173.5	141.8	177.0	171.3	180.2	143.3	195.7	155.9		179.2
Aug	174.2	173.9	145.5	177.0	173.4	183.3	143.8	200.1	156.4		181.6
Sept ¹	173.4	173.9	145.0	177.0	172.5	181.9	143.1	198.4	156.1		180.6
Oct ¹	174.1	175.9	165.4	176.9	172.9	182.0	145.0	197.6	157.2		181.2
Nov ¹	176.2	176.8	173.4	177.0	175.2	185.3	145.6	202.2	157.6		183.9
Dec ¹	176.2	179.7	186.6	178.7	174.6	184.6	144.9	201.4	157.2		184.1

¹ Data have been revised through August 2009; data are subject to revision four months after date of original publication.

See next page for continuation of table.

Year or month	Intermediate materials, supplies, and components								Crude materials for further processing				
	Total	Foods and feeds[2]	Other	Materials and components		Processed fuels and lubricants	Containers	Supplies	Total	Foodstuffs and feedstuffs	Other		
				For manufacturing	For construction						Total	Fuel	Other
1965	31.2	....	30.7	33.6	32.8	16.5	33.5	35.0	31.1	39.2	....	10.6	27.7
1966	32.0	....	31.3	34.3	33.6	16.8	34.5	36.5	33.1	42.7	....	10.9	28.3
1967	32.2	41.8	31.7	34.5	34.0	16.9	35.0	36.8	31.3	40.3	21.1	11.3	26.5
1968	33.0	41.5	32.5	35.3	35.7	16.5	35.9	37.1	31.8	40.9	21.6	11.5	27.1
1969	34.1	42.9	33.6	36.5	37.7	16.6	37.2	37.8	33.9	44.1	22.5	12.0	28.4
1970	35.4	45.6	34.8	38.0	38.3	17.7	39.0	39.7	35.2	45.2	23.8	13.8	29.1
1971	36.8	46.7	36.2	38.9	40.8	19.5	40.8	40.8	36.0	46.1	24.7	15.7	29.4
1972	38.2	49.5	37.7	40.4	43.0	20.1	42.7	42.5	39.9	51.5	27.0	16.8	32.3
1973	42.4	70.3	40.6	44.1	46.5	22.2	45.2	51.7	54.5	72.6	34.3	18.6	42.9
1974	52.5	83.6	50.5	56.0	55.0	33.6	53.3	56.8	61.4	76.4	44.1	24.8	54.5
1975	58.0	81.6	56.6	61.7	60.1	39.4	60.0	61.8	61.6	77.4	43.7	30.6	50.0
1976	60.9	77.4	60.0	64.0	64.1	42.3	63.1	65.8	63.4	76.8	48.2	34.5	54.9
1977	64.9	79.6	64.1	67.4	69.3	47.7	65.9	69.3	65.5	77.5	51.7	42.0	56.3
1978	69.5	84.8	68.6	72.0	76.5	49.9	71.0	72.9	73.4	87.3	57.5	48.2	61.9
1979	78.4	94.5	77.4	80.9	84.2	61.6	79.4	80.2	85.9	100.0	69.6	57.3	75.5
1980	90.3	105.5	89.4	91.7	91.3	85.0	89.1	89.9	95.3	104.6	84.6	69.4	91.8
1981	98.6	104.6	98.2	98.7	97.9	100.6	96.7	96.9	103.0	103.9	101.8	84.8	109.8
1982	100.0	100.0	100.0	100.0	100.0	100.0	100.0	100.0	100.0	100.0	100.0	100.0	100.0
1983	100.6	103.6	100.5	101.2	102.8	95.4	100.4	101.8	101.3	101.8	100.7	105.1	98.8
1984	103.1	105.7	103.0	104.1	105.6	95.7	105.9	104.1	103.5	104.7	102.2	105.1	101.0
1985	102.7	97.3	103.0	103.3	107.3	92.8	109.0	104.4	95.8	94.8	96.9	102.7	94.3
1986	99.1	96.2	99.3	102.2	108.1	72.7	110.3	105.6	87.7	93.2	81.6	92.2	76.0
1987	101.5	99.2	101.7	105.3	109.8	73.3	114.5	107.7	93.7	96.2	87.9	84.1	88.5
1988	107.1	109.5	106.9	113.2	116.1	71.2	120.1	113.7	96.0	106.1	85.5	82.1	85.9
1989	112.0	113.8	111.9	118.1	121.3	76.4	125.4	118.1	103.1	111.2	93.4	85.3	95.8
1990	114.5	113.3	114.5	118.7	122.9	85.9	127.7	119.4	108.9	113.1	101.5	84.8	107.3
1991	114.4	111.1	114.6	118.1	124.5	85.3	128.1	121.4	101.2	105.5	94.6	82.9	97.5
1992	114.7	110.7	114.9	117.9	126.5	84.5	127.7	122.7	100.4	105.1	93.5	84.0	94.2
1993	116.2	112.7	116.4	118.9	132.0	84.7	126.4	125.0	102.4	108.4	94.7	87.1	94.1
1994	118.5	114.8	118.7	122.1	136.6	83.1	129.7	127.0	101.8	106.5	94.8	82.4	97.0
1995	124.9	114.8	125.5	130.4	142.1	84.2	148.8	132.1	102.7	105.8	96.8	72.1	105.8
1996	125.7	128.1	125.6	128.6	143.6	90.0	141.1	135.9	113.8	121.5	104.5	92.6	105.7
1997	125.6	125.4	125.7	128.3	146.5	89.3	136.0	135.9	111.1	112.2	106.4	101.3	103.5
1998	123.0	116.2	123.4	126.1	146.8	81.1	140.8	134.8	96.8	103.9	88.4	86.7	84.5
1999	123.2	111.1	123.9	124.6	148.9	84.6	142.5	134.2	98.2	98.7	94.3	91.2	91.1
2000	129.2	111.7	130.1	128.1	150.7	102.0	151.6	136.9	120.6	100.2	130.4	136.9	118.0
2001	129.7	115.9	130.5	127.4	150.6	104.5	153.1	138.7	121.0	106.1	126.8	151.4	101.5
2002	127.8	115.5	128.5	126.1	151.3	96.3	152.1	138.9	108.1	99.5	111.4	117.3	101.0
2003	133.7	125.9	134.2	129.7	153.6	112.6	153.7	141.5	135.3	113.5	148.2	185.7	116.9
2004	142.6	137.1	143.0	137.9	166.4	124.3	159.3	146.7	159.0	127.0	179.2	211.4	149.2
2005	154.0	133.8	155.1	146.0	176.6	150.0	167.1	151.9	182.2	122.7	223.4	279.7	176.7
2006	164.0	135.2	165.4	155.9	188.4	162.8	175.0	157.0	184.8	119.3	230.6	241.5	210.0
2007	170.7	154.4	171.5	162.4	192.5	173.9	180.3	161.7	207.1	146.7	246.3	236.8	238.7
2008	188.3	181.6	188.7	177.2	205.4	206.2	191.8	173.8	251.8	163.4	313.9	298.3	308.5
2009 ᵖ	172.6	165.9	173.1	162.8	202.9	162.3	195.8	172.2	175.0	134.4	197.1	165.6	211.0
2008: Jan	177.8	170.6	178.2	168.4	194.4	188.6	185.1	166.8	235.5	162.6	283.8	253.9	288.0
Feb	179.1	175.0	179.4	170.1	195.7	189.0	185.7	168.1	245.5	165.4	299.9	283.5	295.6
Mar	184.5	180.3	184.7	173.1	197.3	206.1	185.9	170.0	262.1	169.2	327.7	306.9	324.6
Apr	187.3	180.5	187.7	175.5	200.2	211.8	187.0	171.3	274.6	168.1	352.4	329.1	349.6
May	192.8	184.5	193.3	179.1	203.3	227.3	187.6	173.1	293.1	173.2	382.4	369.2	372.4
June	197.2	186.6	197.8	182.4	206.5	238.4	189.2	174.6	301.2	178.1	393.0	378.5	383.3
July	203.1	195.5	203.6	187.4	209.8	250.1	191.9	178.3	313.3	178.9	414.9	410.3	398.5
Aug	199.4	194.3	199.7	188.7	212.9	225.2	195.0	178.9	274.6	170.6	350.0	309.5	357.2
Sept	198.6	190.0	199.1	186.7	214.0	224.5	198.4	179.0	254.2	167.6	314.2	273.1	323.5
Oct	189.0	179.9	189.5	180.3	212.2	193.9	199.1	177.0	212.0	147.9	253.9	235.7	252.8
Nov	179.2	174.7	179.4	171.1	210.2	168.7	199.0	175.3	183.3	144.2	203.2	205.7	192.4
Dec	171.6	167.9	171.8	163.7	207.9	151.2	198.1	173.4	172.6	135.5	191.6	223.8	164.2
2009: Jan	171.4	165.8	171.8	162.7	207.0	153.4	200.8	172.9	170.2	136.1	186.5	217.1	160.3
Feb	169.7	164.6	170.1	161.0	204.8	150.7	199.5	172.3	160.7	133.3	171.5	178.9	160.9
Mar	168.0	163.5	168.4	159.5	204.2	146.5	198.4	171.9	160.1	131.0	172.6	158.3	176.2
Apr	168.6	164.5	168.9	158.9	203.2	151.4	197.6	172.0	163.9	136.5	174.6	152.8	182.9
May	170.2	167.3	170.4	160.1	202.8	156.5	196.1	172.3	171.5	140.5	184.7	147.7	202.6
June	172.7	169.3	172.9	160.9	202.0	167.0	195.4	172.8	179.8	141.0	199.8	150.6	225.1
July	172.3	166.5	172.7	161.6	201.9	164.1	194.3	172.2	172.9	133.2	194.5	159.8	210.2
Aug	174.8	166.1	175.5	163.8	201.5	172.2	193.5	171.9	178.4	130.2	207.5	156.0	234.1
Sept ¹	175.3	165.7	176.1	165.6	201.8	170.0	193.5	172.1	174.1	127.3	202.3	138.7	237.6
Oct ¹	174.8	164.8	175.6	165.1	201.9	169.3	193.8	171.7	182.2	131.6	213.2	154.6	244.6
Nov ¹	176.3	163.5	177.2	166.4	201.4	173.8	193.1	171.8	192.0	133.7	229.6	182.8	252.2
Dec ¹	176.7	167.8	177.3	167.4	202.2	172.1	193.0	172.5	193.8	138.6	228.3	190.5	244.7

[2] Intermediate materials for food manufacturing and feeds.

Source: Department of Labor (Bureau of Labor Statistics).

TABLE B–66. Producer price indexes by stage of processing, special groups, 1974–2009

[1982=100]

Year or month	Finished goods						Intermediate materials, supplies, and components				Crude materials for further processing			
	Total	Foods	Energy	Excluding foods and energy			Total	Foods and feeds[1]	Energy	Other	Total	Food-stuffs and feed-stuffs	Energy	Other
				Total	Capital equip-ment	Con-sumer goods exclud-ing foods and energy								
1974	52.6	64.4	26.2	53.6	50.5	55.5	52.5	83.6	33.1	54.0	61.4	76.4	27.8	83.3
1975	58.2	69.8	30.7	59.7	58.2	60.6	58.0	81.6	38.7	60.2	61.6	77.4	33.3	69.3
1976	60.8	69.6	34.3	63.1	62.1	63.7	60.9	77.4	41.5	63.8	63.4	76.8	35.3	80.2
1977	64.7	73.3	39.7	66.9	66.1	67.3	64.9	79.6	46.8	67.6	65.5	77.5	40.4	79.8
1978	69.8	79.9	42.3	71.9	71.3	72.2	69.5	84.8	49.1	72.5	73.4	87.3	45.2	87.8
1979	77.6	87.3	57.1	78.3	77.5	78.8	78.4	94.5	61.1	80.7	85.9	100.0	54.9	106.2
1980	88.0	92.4	85.2	87.1	85.8	87.8	90.3	105.5	84.9	90.3	95.3	104.6	73.1	113.1
1981	96.1	97.8	101.5	94.6	94.6	94.6	98.6	104.6	100.5	97.7	103.0	103.9	97.7	111.7
1982	100.0	100.0	100.0	100.0	100.0	100.0	100.0	100.0	100.0	100.0	100.0	100.0	100.0	100.0
1983	101.6	101.0	95.2	103.0	102.8	103.1	100.6	103.6	95.3	101.6	101.3	101.8	98.7	105.3
1984	103.7	105.4	91.2	105.5	105.2	105.7	103.1	105.7	95.5	104.7	103.5	104.7	98.0	111.7
1985	104.7	104.6	87.6	108.1	107.5	108.4	102.7	97.3	92.6	105.2	95.8	94.8	93.3	104.9
1986	103.2	107.3	63.0	110.6	109.7	111.1	99.1	96.2	72.6	104.9	87.7	93.2	71.8	103.1
1987	105.4	109.5	61.8	113.3	111.7	114.2	101.5	99.2	73.0	107.8	93.7	96.2	75.0	115.7
1988	108.0	112.6	59.8	117.0	114.3	118.5	107.1	109.5	70.9	115.2	96.0	106.1	67.7	133.0
1989	113.6	118.7	65.7	122.1	118.8	124.0	112.0	113.8	76.1	120.2	103.1	111.2	75.9	137.9
1990	119.2	124.4	75.0	126.6	122.9	128.8	114.5	113.3	85.5	120.9	108.9	113.1	85.9	136.3
1991	121.7	124.1	78.1	131.1	126.7	133.7	114.4	111.1	85.1	121.4	101.2	105.5	80.4	128.2
1992	123.2	123.3	77.8	134.2	129.1	137.3	114.7	110.7	84.3	122.0	100.4	105.1	78.8	128.4
1993	124.7	125.7	78.0	135.8	131.4	138.5	116.2	112.7	84.6	123.8	102.4	108.4	76.7	140.2
1994	125.5	126.8	77.0	137.1	134.1	139.0	118.5	114.8	83.0	127.1	101.8	106.5	72.1	156.2
1995	127.9	129.0	78.1	140.0	136.7	141.9	124.9	114.8	84.1	135.2	102.7	105.8	69.4	173.6
1996	131.3	133.6	83.2	142.0	138.3	144.3	125.7	128.1	89.8	134.0	113.8	121.5	85.0	155.8
1997	131.8	134.5	83.4	142.4	138.2	145.1	125.6	125.4	89.0	134.2	111.1	112.2	87.3	156.5
1998	130.7	134.3	75.1	143.7	137.6	147.7	123.0	116.2	80.8	133.5	96.8	103.9	68.6	142.1
1999	133.0	135.1	78.8	146.1	137.6	151.7	123.2	111.1	84.3	133.1	98.2	98.7	78.5	135.2
2000	138.0	137.2	94.1	148.0	138.8	154.0	129.2	111.7	101.7	136.6	120.6	100.2	122.1	145.2
2001	140.7	141.3	96.7	150.0	139.7	156.9	129.7	115.9	104.1	136.4	121.0	106.1	122.3	130.7
2002	138.9	140.1	88.8	150.2	139.1	157.6	127.8	115.5	95.9	135.8	108.1	99.5	102.0	135.7
2003	143.3	145.9	102.0	150.5	139.5	157.9	133.7	125.9	111.9	138.5	135.3	113.5	147.2	152.5
2004	148.5	152.7	113.0	152.7	141.4	160.3	142.6	137.1	123.2	146.5	159.0	127.0	174.6	193.0
2005	155.7	155.7	132.6	154.4	144.6	164.3	154.0	133.8	149.2	154.6	182.2	122.7	234.0	202.4
2006	160.4	156.7	145.9	158.7	146.9	166.7	164.0	135.2	162.8	163.8	184.8	119.3	226.9	244.5
2007	166.6	167.0	156.3	161.7	149.5	170.0	170.7	154.4	174.6	168.4	207.1	146.7	232.8	282.6
2008	177.1	178.3	178.7	167.2	153.8	176.4	188.3	181.6	208.1	180.9	251.8	163.4	309.4	324.4
2009 ᵖ	172.6	175.5	147.2	171.5	156.8	181.6	172.6	165.9	162.8	173.4	175.0	134.4	176.3	248.6
2008: Jan	172.0	174.5	166.6	164.4	151.4	173.2	177.8	170.6	190.5	172.5	235.5	162.6	273.6	307.3
Feb	172.3	173.6	167.2	165.0	151.8	174.0	179.1	175.0	191.5	173.7	245.5	165.4	291.7	319.7
Mar	175.1	176.0	177.5	165.1	151.8	174.1	184.5	180.3	208.6	175.8	262.1	169.2	325.4	332.1
Apr	176.5	175.5	182.4	165.7	152.4	174.8	187.3	180.5	213.4	178.3	274.6	168.1	346.1	366.7
May	179.8	177.6	194.8	166.1	152.7	175.2	192.8	184.5	228.7	181.2	293.1	173.2	386.1	372.4
June	182.4	180.0	204.6	166.0	152.7	175.2	197.2	186.6	240.3	183.8	301.2	178.1	400.4	373.8
July	185.1	181.0	214.0	166.7	153.3	175.9	203.1	195.5	253.5	187.5	313.3	178.9	426.5	386.1
Aug	182.2	181.3	198.6	167.4	153.9	176.6	199.4	194.3	231.3	188.7	274.6	170.6	339.1	374.2
Sept	182.2	181.5	197.0	167.9	154.3	177.2	198.6	190.0	227.5	188.8	254.2	167.6	303.7	337.5
Oct	177.4	180.7	167.8	170.8	157.0	180.2	189.0	179.9	197.4	184.8	212.0	147.9	244.4	276.7
Nov	172.0	179.8	144.1	170.6	156.9	180.0	179.2	174.7	167.3	180.2	183.3	144.2	194.9	224.8
Dec	168.8	177.7	130.6	170.8	157.2	180.1	171.6	167.9	147.7	175.9	172.6	135.5	181.1	221.3
2009: Jan	170.4	177.7	136.4	171.3	157.4	180.7	171.4	165.8	152.2	174.6	170.2	136.1	173.0	225.2
Feb	169.9	175.0	136.3	171.3	157.2	181.0	169.7	164.6	149.3	173.4	160.7	133.3	152.1	224.9
Mar	169.1	173.8	133.2	171.4	156.9	181.4	168.0	163.5	144.1	172.6	160.1	131.0	153.3	222.9
Apr	170.3	175.9	137.2	171.4	156.8	181.5	168.6	164.5	149.5	171.8	163.9	136.5	155.0	224.4
May	171.1	174.0	142.9	171.1	156.3	181.3	170.2	167.3	157.2	171.6	171.5	140.5	164.2	234.9
June	174.3	176.1	154.4	171.4	156.6	181.7	172.7	169.3	167.8	171.9	179.8	141.0	181.2	242.6
July	172.4	173.5	149.6	170.8	155.9	181.1	172.3	166.5	165.3	172.3	172.9	133.2	173.0	247.1
Aug	174.2	173.9	156.1	171.2	156.1	181.5	174.8	166.1	174.5	173.3	178.4	130.2	184.1	263.6
Sept²	173.4	173.9	153.5	170.9	156.1	181.1	175.3	165.7	172.0	174.7	174.1	127.3	174.3	271.1
Oct²	174.1	175.9	152.0	172.0	157.2	182.3	174.8	164.8	171.1	174.5	182.2	131.6	188.5	272.3
Nov²	176.2	176.8	158.4	172.6	157.6	183.1	176.3	165.5	176.4	174.9	192.0	133.7	211.4	270.4
Dec²	176.2	179.7	156.8	172.4	157.2	183.0	176.7	167.8	174.5	175.7	193.8	138.6	205.2	284.2

[1] Intermediate materials for food manufacturing and feeds.
[2] Data have been revised through August 2009; data are subject to revision four months after date of original publication.

Source: Department of Labor (Bureau of Labor Statistics).

TABLE B–67. Producer price indexes for major commodity groups, 1965–2009

[1982=100]

Year or month	Farm products and processed foods and feeds			Industrial commodities				
	Total	Farm products	Processed foods and feeds	Total	Textile products and apparel	Hides, skins, leather, and related products	Fuels and related products and power	Chemicals and allied products [1]
1965	39.0	40.7	38.0	30.9	48.8	35.9	13.8	33.9
1966	41.6	43.7	40.2	31.5	48.9	39.4	14.1	34.0
1967	40.2	41.3	39.8	32.0	48.9	38.1	14.4	34.2
1968	41.1	42.3	40.6	32.8	50.7	39.3	14.3	34.1
1969	43.4	45.0	42.7	33.9	51.8	41.5	14.6	34.2
1970	44.9	45.8	44.6	35.2	52.4	42.0	15.3	35.0
1971	45.8	46.6	45.5	36.5	53.3	43.4	16.6	35.6
1972	49.2	51.6	48.0	37.8	55.5	50.0	17.1	35.6
1973	63.9	72.7	58.9	40.3	60.5	54.5	19.4	37.6
1974	71.3	77.4	68.0	49.2	68.0	55.2	30.1	50.2
1975	74.0	77.0	72.6	54.9	67.4	56.5	35.4	62.0
1976	73.6	78.8	70.8	58.4	72.4	63.9	38.3	64.0
1977	75.9	79.4	74.0	62.5	75.3	68.3	43.6	65.9
1978	83.0	87.7	80.6	67.0	78.1	76.1	46.5	68.0
1979	92.3	99.6	88.5	75.7	82.5	96.1	58.9	76.0
1980	98.3	102.9	95.9	88.0	89.7	94.7	82.8	89.0
1981	101.1	105.2	98.9	97.4	97.6	99.3	100.2	98.4
1982	100.0	100.0	100.0	100.0	100.0	100.0	100.0	100.0
1983	102.0	102.4	101.8	101.1	100.3	103.2	95.9	100.3
1984	105.5	105.5	105.4	103.3	102.7	109.0	94.8	102.9
1985	100.7	95.1	103.5	103.7	102.9	108.9	91.4	103.7
1986	101.2	92.9	105.4	100.0	103.2	113.0	69.8	102.6
1987	103.7	95.5	107.9	102.6	105.1	120.4	70.2	106.4
1988	110.0	104.9	112.7	106.3	109.2	131.4	66.7	116.3
1989	115.4	110.9	117.8	111.6	112.3	136.3	72.9	123.0
1990	118.6	112.2	121.9	115.8	115.0	141.7	82.3	123.6
1991	116.4	105.7	121.9	116.5	116.3	138.9	81.2	125.6
1992	115.9	103.6	122.1	117.4	117.8	140.4	80.4	125.9
1993	118.4	107.1	124.0	119.0	118.0	143.7	80.0	128.2
1994	119.1	106.3	125.5	120.7	118.3	148.5	77.8	132.1
1995	120.5	107.4	127.0	125.5	120.8	153.7	78.0	142.5
1996	129.7	122.4	133.3	127.3	122.4	150.5	85.8	142.1
1997	127.0	112.9	134.0	127.7	122.6	154.2	86.1	143.6
1998	122.7	104.6	131.6	124.8	122.9	148.0	75.3	143.9
1999	120.3	98.4	131.1	126.5	121.1	146.0	80.5	144.2
2000	122.0	99.5	133.1	134.8	121.4	151.5	103.5	151.0
2001	126.2	103.8	137.3	135.7	121.3	158.4	105.3	151.8
2002	123.9	99.0	136.2	132.4	119.9	157.6	93.2	151.9
2003	132.8	111.5	143.4	139.1	119.8	162.3	112.9	161.8
2004	142.0	123.3	151.2	147.6	121.0	164.5	126.9	174.4
2005	141.3	118.5	153.1	160.2	122.8	165.4	156.4	192.0
2006	141.2	117.0	153.8	168.8	124.5	168.4	166.7	205.8
2007	157.8	143.4	165.1	175.1	125.8	173.6	177.6	214.8
2008	173.8	161.3	180.5	192.3	128.9	173.1	214.6	245.5
2009 ᴾ	161.4	134.5	176.2	174.9	129.5	156.7	158.9	229.7
2008: Jan	169.8	164.2	172.7	182.8	126.9	172.2	195.9	229.2
Feb	171.1	164.4	174.6	184.6	127.1	172.5	199.5	231.3
Mar	174.5	169.6	176.9	190.2	127.2	172.5	217.1	235.6
Apr	174.0	166.7	177.8	193.8	127.6	172.9	224.7	240.4
May	177.1	169.7	180.8	200.0	128.2	172.9	243.2	246.5
June	180.4	176.2	182.4	204.0	128.2	174.8	254.8	252.7
July	182.6	174.3	187.0	209.5	129.1	175.0	268.7	262.8
Aug	179.4	164.7	187.3	202.4	130.1	174.9	237.9	263.3
Sept	178.0	163.5	185.9	200.1	131.0	175.2	230.2	264.2
Oct	169.3	145.3	182.5	189.3	130.7	175.1	194.5	252.5
Nov	166.9	143.1	180.0	178.4	130.7	169.6	162.6	239.3
Dec	162.2	133.9	177.7	172.3	130.2	168.9	145.7	227.6
2009: Jan	162.4	136.4	176.8	172.6	130.2	157.0	148.5	226.8
Feb	160.4	132.8	175.5	170.8	129.9	157.0	143.6	226.5
Mar	158.9	130.6	174.4	169.5	129.4	157.9	140.2	225.8
Apr	161.8	136.8	175.5	170.3	129.7	153.6	144.8	225.2
May	163.4	137.8	177.4	172.0	129.1	153.8	152.2	225.8
June	165.2	142.1	177.9	175.5	129.6	151.9	165.0	227.8
July	160.3	131.6	176.2	174.6	129.1	153.1	160.7	230.0
Aug	159.6	130.1	175.9	177.7	129.4	155.2	169.6	231.1
Sept [2]	158.1	126.3	175.7	177.5	129.5	159.0	165.8	234.1
Oct [2]	160.5	133.0	175.6	177.9	129.4	160.1	166.9	231.9
Nov [2]	161.6	135.6	175.9	180.5	129.5	159.2	175.8	234.5
Dec [2]	164.8	141.1	177.7	180.4	129.6	162.2	173.3	237.1

[1] Prices for some items in this grouping are lagged and refer to one month earlier than the index month.
[2] Data have been revised through August 2009; data are subject to revision four months after date of original publication.

See next page for continuation of table.

TABLE B–67. Producer price indexes for major commodity groups, 1965–2009—*Continued*

[1982=100]

Year or month	Rubber and plastic products	Lumber and wood products	Pulp, paper, and allied products	Metals and metal products	Machinery and equipment	Furniture and household durables	Non-metallic mineral products	Transportation equipment Total	Motor vehicles and equipment	Miscellaneous products
1965	39.7	33.7	33.3	32.0	33.7	46.8	30.4	....	39.2	34.7
1966	40.5	35.2	34.2	32.8	34.7	47.4	30.7	....	39.2	35.3
1967	41.4	35.1	34.6	33.2	35.9	48.3	31.2	....	39.8	36.2
1968	42.8	39.8	35.0	34.0	37.0	49.7	32.4	....	40.9	37.0
1969	43.6	44.0	36.0	36.0	38.2	50.7	33.6	40.4	41.7	38.1
1970	44.9	39.9	37.5	38.7	40.0	51.9	35.3	41.9	43.3	39.8
1971	45.2	44.7	38.1	39.4	41.4	53.1	38.2	44.2	45.7	40.8
1972	45.3	50.7	39.3	40.9	42.3	53.8	39.4	45.5	47.0	41.5
1973	46.6	62.2	42.3	44.0	43.7	55.7	40.7	46.1	47.4	43.3
1974	56.4	64.5	52.5	57.0	50.0	61.8	47.8	50.3	51.4	48.1
1975	62.2	62.1	59.0	61.5	57.9	67.5	54.4	56.7	57.6	53.4
1976	66.0	72.2	62.1	65.0	61.3	70.3	58.2	60.5	61.2	55.6
1977	69.4	83.0	64.6	69.3	65.2	73.2	62.6	64.6	65.2	59.4
1978	72.4	96.9	67.7	75.3	70.3	77.5	69.6	69.5	70.0	66.7
1979	80.5	105.5	75.9	86.0	76.7	82.8	77.6	75.3	75.8	75.5
1980	90.1	101.5	86.3	95.0	86.0	90.7	88.4	82.9	83.1	93.6
1981	96.4	102.8	94.8	99.6	94.4	95.9	96.7	94.3	94.6	96.1
1982	100.0	100.0	100.0	100.0	100.0	100.0	100.0	100.0	100.0	100.0
1983	100.8	107.9	103.3	101.8	102.7	103.4	101.6	102.8	102.2	104.8
1984	102.3	108.0	110.3	104.8	105.1	105.7	105.4	105.2	104.1	107.0
1985	101.9	106.6	113.3	104.4	107.2	107.1	108.6	107.9	106.4	109.4
1986	101.9	107.2	116.1	103.2	108.8	108.2	110.0	110.5	109.1	111.6
1987	103.0	112.8	121.8	107.1	110.4	109.9	110.0	112.5	111.7	114.9
1988	109.3	118.9	130.4	118.7	113.2	113.1	111.2	114.3	113.1	120.2
1989	112.6	126.7	137.8	124.1	117.4	116.9	112.6	117.7	116.2	126.5
1990	113.6	129.7	141.2	122.9	120.7	119.2	114.7	121.5	118.2	134.2
1991	115.1	132.1	142.9	120.2	123.0	121.2	117.2	126.4	122.1	140.8
1992	115.1	146.6	145.2	119.2	123.4	122.2	117.3	130.4	124.9	145.3
1993	116.0	174.0	147.3	119.2	124.0	123.7	120.0	133.7	128.0	145.4
1994	117.6	180.0	152.5	124.8	125.1	126.1	124.2	137.2	131.4	141.9
1995	124.3	178.1	172.2	134.5	126.6	128.2	129.0	139.7	133.0	145.4
1996	123.8	176.1	168.7	131.0	126.5	130.4	131.0	141.7	134.1	147.7
1997	123.2	183.8	167.9	131.8	125.9	130.8	133.2	141.6	132.7	150.9
1998	122.6	179.1	171.7	127.8	124.9	131.3	135.4	141.2	131.4	156.0
1999	122.5	183.6	174.1	124.6	124.3	131.7	138.9	141.8	131.7	166.6
2000	125.5	178.2	183.7	128.1	124.0	132.6	142.5	143.8	132.3	170.8
2001	127.2	174.4	184.8	125.4	123.7	133.2	144.3	145.2	131.5	181.3
2002	126.8	173.3	185.9	125.9	122.9	133.5	146.2	144.6	129.9	182.4
2003	130.1	177.4	190.0	129.2	121.9	133.9	148.2	145.7	129.6	179.6
2004	133.8	195.6	195.7	149.6	122.1	135.1	153.2	148.6	131.0	183.2
2005	143.8	196.5	202.6	160.8	123.7	139.4	164.2	151.0	131.5	195.1
2006	153.8	194.4	209.8	181.6	126.2	142.6	179.9	152.6	131.0	205.6
2007	155.0	192.4	216.9	193.5	127.3	144.7	186.2	155.0	132.2	210.3
2008	165.9	191.3	226.8	213.0	129.7	148.9	197.1	158.6	134.1	216.6
2009 *p*	165.1	183.0	225.5	186.9	131.3	153.1	202.4	162.2	137.0	217.4
2008: Jan	159.2	189.3	222.3	197.5	127.8	145.7	188.5	157.5	133.7	212.7
Feb	159.9	189.1	223.4	201.8	128.3	146.1	188.8	157.5	133.7	213.3
Mar	160.6	189.9	224.0	208.0	128.5	146.4	189.5	156.8	132.9	214.8
Apr	161.3	190.5	224.9	217.6	128.7	147.2	191.0	157.6	133.6	214.9
May	162.8	193.8	225.2	223.4	129.2	147.3	192.1	157.5	133.3	216.4
June	164.0	194.6	225.7	226.9	129.6	148.0	194.4	156.7	132.1	217.1
July	167.4	193.5	227.0	231.8	130.4	149.3	198.8	156.7	131.8	218.3
Aug	169.7	193.5	229.6	230.9	130.5	150.3	202.7	157.6	132.4	218.4
Sept	171.6	193.7	231.1	223.7	130.7	151.0	204.4	157.8	132.4	218.3
Oct	172.5	191.1	230.9	209.1	130.9	151.8	205.0	162.8	138.4	218.8
Nov	172.1	188.9	228.8	195.9	131.1	152.1	205.3	162.4	137.5	218.1
Dec	169.8	188.0	228.0	189.7	131.0	152.1	204.6	162.8	137.6	218.0
2009: Jan	167.5	185.3	228.0	187.0	131.4	152.9	205.8	162.8	137.2	218.0
Feb	165.3	183.5	227.0	183.9	131.3	153.3	203.8	162.7	137.0	219.0
Mar	164.9	181.7	226.7	181.7	131.5	153.3	203.9	162.2	136.6	220.0
Apr	164.5	181.2	225.8	179.9	131.3	153.4	203.7	162.3	136.9	217.9
May	163.9	180.9	224.8	180.5	131.3	153.3	203.4	161.8	136.8	216.6
June	163.7	180.8	224.5	181.7	131.1	153.1	202.5	162.3	137.5	216.4
July	163.9	182.8	224.0	183.5	131.2	153.1	202.1	160.9	135.7	216.2
Aug	164.5	183.0	224.4	189.1	131.2	152.6	201.2	161.6	136.4	215.9
Sept [2]	165.7	184.1	225.5	192.8	131.4	152.9	200.8	161.0	135.7	216.7
Oct [2]	165.9	183.6	224.7	193.6	131.2	153.3	200.6	163.0	138.1	216.9
Nov [2]	165.6	184.4	225.0	193.3	131.3	153.2	200.0	163.4	138.5	217.5
Dec [2]	166.1	184.9	225.1	196.0	131.4	153.2	200.6	162.8	137.6	217.9

Source: Department of Labor (Bureau of Labor Statistics).

Prices | 409

TABLE B–68. Changes in producer price indexes for finished goods, 1969–2009

[Percent change]

Year or month	Total finished goods		Finished consumer foods		Finished goods excluding consumer foods						Finished energy goods		Finished goods excluding foods and energy	
					Total		Consumer goods		Capital equipment					
	Dec. to Dec.[1]	Year to year	Dec. to Dec.[1]	Year to year	Dec. to Dec.[1]	Year to year	Dec. to Dec.[1]	Year to year	Dec. to Dec.[1]	Year to year	Dec. to Dec.[1]	Year to year	Dec. to Dec.[1]	Year to year
1969	4.9	3.8	8.1	6.0	3.3	2.8	2.8	2.3	4.8	3.5	....	....	....	....
1970	2.1	3.4	−2.3	3.3	4.3	3.5	3.8	3.0	4.8	4.7	....	....	....	....
1971	3.3	3.1	5.8	1.6	2.0	3.7	2.1	3.5	2.4	4.0	....	....	....	....
1972	3.9	3.2	7.9	5.4	2.3	2.0	2.1	1.8	2.1	2.6	....	....	....	....
1973	11.7	9.1	22.7	20.5	6.6	4.0	7.5	4.6	5.1	3.3	....	....	....	....
1974	18.3	15.4	12.8	14.0	21.1	16.2	20.3	17.0	22.7	14.3	....	....	17.7	11.4
1975	6.6	10.6	5.6	8.4	7.2	12.1	6.8	10.4	8.1	15.2	16.3	17.2	6.0	11.4
1976	3.8	4.5	−2.5	−.3	6.2	6.2	6.0	6.2	6.5	6.7	11.6	11.7	5.7	5.7
1977	6.7	6.4	6.9	5.3	6.8	7.1	6.7	7.3	7.2	6.4	12.0	15.7	6.2	6.0
1978	9.3	7.9	11.7	9.0	8.3	7.2	8.5	7.1	8.0	7.9	8.5	6.5	8.4	7.5
1979	12.8	11.2	7.4	9.3	14.8	11.8	17.6	13.3	8.8	8.7	58.1	35.0	9.4	8.9
1980	11.8	13.4	7.5	5.8	13.4	16.2	14.1	18.5	11.4	10.7	27.9	49.2	10.8	11.2
1981	7.1	9.2	1.5	5.8	8.7	10.3	8.6	10.3	9.2	10.3	14.1	14.1	7.7	8.6
1982	3.6	4.1	2.0	2.2	4.2	4.6	4.2	4.1	3.9	5.7	−.1	−1.5	4.9	5.7
1983	.6	1.6	2.3	1.0	.0	1.8	−.9	1.2	2.0	2.8	−9.2	−4.8	1.9	3.0
1984	1.7	2.1	3.5	4.4	1.1	1.4	.8	1.0	1.8	2.3	−4.2	−4.2	2.0	2.4
1985	1.8	1.0	.6	−.8	2.2	1.4	2.1	1.1	2.7	2.2	−.2	−3.9	2.7	2.5
1986	−2.3	−1.4	2.8	2.6	−4.0	−2.6	−6.6	−4.6	2.1	2.0	−38.1	−28.1	2.7	2.3
1987	2.2	2.1	−.2	2.1	3.2	2.1	4.1	2.2	1.3	1.8	11.2	−1.9	2.1	2.4
1988	4.0	2.5	5.7	2.8	3.2	2.4	3.1	2.4	3.6	2.3	−3.6	−3.2	4.3	3.3
1989	4.9	5.2	5.2	5.4	4.8	5.0	5.3	5.6	3.8	3.9	9.5	9.9	4.2	4.4
1990	5.7	4.9	2.6	4.8	6.9	5.0	8.7	5.9	3.4	3.5	30.7	14.2	3.5	3.7
1991	−.1	2.1	−1.5	−.2	.3	3.0	−.7	2.9	2.5	3.1	−9.6	4.1	3.1	3.6
1992	1.6	1.2	1.6	−.6	1.6	1.8	1.6	1.8	1.7	1.9	−.3	−.4	2.0	2.4
1993	.2	1.2	2.4	1.9	−.4	1.1	−1.4	.7	1.8	1.8	−4.1	.3	.4	1.2
1994	1.7	.6	1.1	.9	1.9	.6	2.0	−.1	2.0	2.1	3.5	−1.3	1.6	1.0
1995	2.3	1.9	1.9	1.7	2.3	1.9	2.3	2.0	2.2	1.9	1.1	1.4	2.6	2.1
1996	2.8	2.7	3.4	3.6	2.6	2.4	3.7	2.9	.4	1.2	11.7	6.5	.6	1.4
1997	−1.2	.4	−.8	.7	−1.2	.3	−1.5	.5	−.6	−.1	−6.4	.2	.0	.3
1998	.0	−.8	.1	−.1	−.1	−1.1	−.1	−1.4	.0	−.4	−11.7	−10.0	2.5	.9
1999	2.9	1.8	.8	.6	3.5	2.2	5.1	3.2	.3	.0	18.1	4.9	.9	1.7
2000	3.6	3.8	1.7	1.6	4.1	4.4	5.5	6.1	1.2	.9	16.6	19.4	1.3	1.3
2001	−1.6	2.0	1.8	3.0	−2.6	1.7	−3.9	2.2	.0	.6	−17.1	2.8	.9	1.4
2002	1.2	−1.3	−.6	−.8	1.7	−1.5	2.9	−1.8	−.6	−.4	12.3	−8.2	−.5	.1
2003	4.0	3.2	7.7	4.1	3.0	3.0	4.1	4.3	.8	.3	11.4	14.9	1.0	.2
2004	4.2	3.6	3.1	4.7	4.5	3.4	5.5	4.3	2.4	1.4	13.4	10.8	2.3	1.5
2005	5.4	4.8	1.7	2.0	6.4	5.6	8.8	7.3	1.2	2.3	23.9	17.3	1.4	2.4
2006	1.1	3.0	1.7	.6	1.0	3.5	.4	4.5	2.3	1.6	−2.0	10.0	2.0	1.5
2007	6.2	3.9	7.6	6.6	5.8	3.2	7.7	3.8	1.4	1.8	17.8	7.1	2.0	1.9
2008	−.9	6.3	3.2	6.8	−2.1	6.3	−4.8	7.7	4.3	2.9	−20.3	14.3	4.5	3.4
2009 p	4.4	−2.5	1.1	−1.6	5.1	−3.1	7.6	−5.0	.0	2.0	20.1	−17.6	.9	2.6

	Percent change from preceding month													
	Unadjusted	Seasonally adjusted	Unadjusted	Seasonally adjusted	Unadjusted	Seasonally adjusted	Unadjusted	Seasonally adjusted	Unadjusted	Seasonally adjusted	Unadjusted	Seasonally adjusted	Unadjusted	Seasonally adjusted
2008: Jan	0.9	0.9	1.3	1.5	0.8	0.7	1.0	0.8	0.5	0.5	1.7	1.3	0.6	0.5
Feb	.2	.4	−.5	−.5	.4	.8	.4	.9	.3	.4	.4	1.4	.4	.5
Mar	1.6	.9	1.4	1.2	1.7	.7	2.4	1.0	.0	.1	6.2	2.4	.1	.1
Apr	.8	.2	−.3	.2	1.0	.2	1.3	.1	.4	.5	2.8	−.4	.4	.5
May	1.9	1.5	1.2	.7	2.1	1.7	2.8	2.3	.2	.3	6.8	5.2	.2	.3
June	1.4	1.3	1.4	1.2	1.5	1.3	2.1	1.8	.0	.3	5.0	4.3	−.1	.2
July	1.5	1.3	.6	.6	1.7	1.5	2.2	1.9	.4	.5	4.6	3.8	.4	.6
Aug	−1.6	−.5	.2	.2	−2.0	−.7	−2.9	−1.2	.4	.4	−7.2	−3.4	.4	.5
Sept	.0	−.1	−.1	.0	−.1	−.1	−.2	−.3	.3	.4	−.8	−1.3	.3	.4
Oct	−2.6	−2.6	−.4	.1	−3.2	−3.3	−5.2	−4.9	1.7	.6	−14.8	−12.8	1.7	.5
Nov	−3.0	−2.7	−.5	−.5	−3.8	−3.3	−5.3	−4.7	−.1	.0	−14.1	−12.4	−.1	.0
Dec	−1.9	−1.8	−1.2	−1.2	−2.1	−1.9	−3.1	−3.0	.2	.4	−9.4	−9.1	.1	.3
2009: Jan	.9	.9	.0	.1	1.1	1.1	1.7	1.6	.1	.1	4.4	4.1	.3	.2
Feb	−.3	−.1	−1.5	−1.6	.0	.3	.1	.4	−.1	.0	−.1	.9	.0	.1
Mar	−.5	−.9	−.7	−.8	−.5	−1.0	−.6	−1.4	−.2	−.1	−2.3	−4.7	.1	.1
Apr	.7	.4	1.2	1.5	.7	.2	1.0	.2	−.1	.1	3.0	.4	.0	.1
May	.5	.2	−1.1	−1.5	.8	.5	1.3	.9	−.3	−.2	4.2	2.7	−.2	−.1
June	1.9	1.7	1.2	1.1	2.0	1.8	2.9	2.5	.2	.4	8.0	6.6	.2	.4
July	−1.1	−1.2	−1.5	−1.5	−1.0	−1.0	−1.4	−1.4	−.4	−.3	−3.1	−3.8	−.4	−.2
Aug	1.0	1.9	.2	.3	1.2	2.2	1.7	3.0	.3	.4	4.3	8.1	.2	.3
Sept[2] ...	−.5	−.5	.0	−.1	−.5	−.6	−.8	−.8	−.2	−.1	−1.7	−2.0	−.2	−.1
Oct[2] ...	.4	.3	1.2	1.6	.2	.0	.1	.3	.7	−.7	−1.0	1.6	.6	−.6
Nov[2] ...	1.2	1.8	.5	.5	1.3	2.1	1.8	3.0	.3	.4	4.2	6.9	.3	.5
Dec[2] ...	.0	.2	1.6	1.4	−.3	−.1	−.4	−.2	−.3	−.1	−1.0	−.4	−.1	.0

[1] Changes from December to December are based on unadjusted indexes.
[2] Data have been revised through August 2009; data are subject to revision four months after date of original publication.

Source: Department of Labor (Bureau of Labor Statistics).

Money Stock, Credit, and Finance

Table B–69. Money stock and debt measures, 1970–2009

[Averages of daily figures, except debt end-of-period basis; billions of dollars, seasonally adjusted]

Year and month	M1 — Sum of currency, demand deposits, travelers checks, and other checkable deposits (OCDs)	M2 — M1 plus retail MMMF balances, savings deposits (including MMDAs), and small time deposits [2]	Debt [1] — Debt of domestic nonfinancial sectors	Percent change — From year or 6 months earlier [3] — M1	Percent change — From year or 6 months earlier [3] — M2	Percent change — From previous period [4] — Debt
December:						
1970	214.4	626.5	1,420.2			
1971	228.3	710.3	1,555.2	6.5	13.4	9.5
1972	249.2	802.3	1,711.2	9.2	13.0	10.0
1973	262.9	855.5	1,895.5	5.5	6.6	10.7
1974	274.2	902.1	2,069.9	4.3	5.4	9.2
1975	287.1	1,016.2	2,261.8	4.7	12.6	9.3
1976	306.2	1,152.0	2,505.3	6.7	13.4	10.8
1977	330.9	1,270.3	2,826.6	8.1	10.3	12.8
1978	357.3	1,366.0	3,211.2	8.0	7.5	13.8
1979	381.8	1,473.7	3,603.0	6.9	7.9	12.2
1980	408.5	1,599.8	3,953.5	7.0	8.6	9.5
1981	436.7	1,755.5	4,361.7	6.9	9.7	10.4
1982	474.8	1,909.3	4,783.4	8.7	8.8	10.4
1983	521.4	2,125.7	5,359.2	9.8	11.3	12.0
1984	551.6	2,308.8	6,146.2	5.8	8.6	14.8
1985	619.8	2,494.6	7,123.1	12.4	8.0	15.6
1986	724.7	2,731.4	7,966.3	16.9	9.5	11.9
1987	750.2	2,830.8	8,670.1	3.5	3.6	9.0
1988	786.7	2,993.9	9,450.7	4.9	5.8	9.0
1989	792.9	3,158.4	10,152.1	.8	5.5	7.2
1990	824.7	3,276.8	10,834.9	4.0	3.7	6.5
1991	897.0	3,377.0	11,301.4	8.8	3.1	4.3
1992	1,024.9	3,430.2	11,816.5	14.3	1.6	4.5
1993	1,129.6	3,480.7	12,391.4	10.2	1.5	4.7
1994	1,150.6	3,496.5	12,973.6	1.9	.5	4.6
1995	1,127.5	3,640.3	13,667.5	−2.0	4.1	5.2
1996	1,081.6	3,819.6	14,399.8	−4.1	4.9	5.4
1997	1,072.8	4,033.0	15,210.8	−.8	5.6	5.6
1998	1,095.8	4,376.3	16,216.4	2.1	8.5	6.6
1999	1,122.7	4,634.6	17,291.6	2.5	5.9	6.4
2000	1,087.7	4,917.9	18,167.3	−3.1	6.1	5.0
2001	1,182.2	5,434.1	19,302.3	8.7	10.5	6.3
2002	1,220.4	5,785.9	20,710.2	3.2	6.5	7.3
2003	1,306.9	6,073.7	22,420.4	7.1	5.0	8.1
2004	1,377.1	6,415.2	24,426.9	5.4	5.6	8.9
2005	1,375.3	6,679.2	26,756.1	−.1	4.1	9.5
2006	1,367.9	7,079.5	29,151.3	−.5	6.0	9.0
2007	1,375.8	7,509.4	31,694.5	.6	6.1	8.7
2008	1,594.7	8,241.6	33,564.9	15.9	9.8	5.9
2009	1,693.3	8,524.3		6.2	3.4	
2008: Jan	1,381.1	7,542.3		1.8	6.3	
Feb	1,387.0	7,631.7		2.2	7.1	
Mar	1,389.7	7,691.6	32,131.5	2.5	7.6	5.5
Apr	1,392.1	7,716.3		1.9	7.3	
May	1,391.5	7,739.0		2.3	7.1	
June	1,398.1	7,751.1	32,395.8	3.2	6.4	3.3
July	1,415.1	7,802.7		4.9	6.9	
Aug	1,400.0	7,790.6		1.9	4.2	
Sept	1,459.5	7,898.2	33,062.1	10.0	5.4	8.2
Oct	1,472.7	8,014.7		11.6	7.7	
Nov	1,518.1	8,065.3		18.2	8.4	
Dec	1,594.7	8,241.6	33,564.9	28.1	12.7	6.1
2009: Jan	1,573.8	8,302.6		22.4	12.8	
Feb	1,562.1	8,340.7		23.2	14.1	
Mar	1,564.3	8,392.7	33,932.0	14.4	12.5	4.3
Apr	1,592.7	8,343.7		16.3	8.2	
May	1,593.0	8,416.1		9.9	8.7	
June	1,641.0	8,442.2	34,310.5	5.8	4.9	4.5
July	1,649.9	8,436.5		9.7	3.2	
Aug	1,648.3	8,413.2		11.0	1.7	
Sept	1,660.8	8,452.3	34,551.9	12.3	1.4	2.8
Oct	1,673.8	8,481.3		10.2	3.3	
Nov	1,685.6	8,508.9		11.6	2.2	
Dec	1,693.3	8,524.3		6.4	1.9	

[1] Consists of outstanding credit market debt of the U.S. Government, State and local governments, and private nonfinancial sectors.
[2] Money market mutual fund (MMMF). Money market deposit account (MMDA).
[3] Annual changes are from December to December; monthly changes are from six months earlier at a simple annual rate.
[4] Annual changes are from fourth quarter to fourth quarter. Quarterly changes are from previous quarter at annual rate.

Note: The Federal Reserve no longer publishes the M3 monetary aggregate and most of its components. Institutional money market mutual funds is published as a memorandum item in the H.6 release, and the component on large-denomination time deposits is published in other Federal Reserve Board releases. For details, see H.6 release of March 23, 2006.

Source: Board of Governors of the Federal Reserve System.

Table B–70. Components of money stock measures, 1970–2009

[Averages of daily figures; billions of dollars, seasonally adjusted]

Year and month	Currency	Nonbank travelers checks	Demand deposits	Other checkable deposits (OCDs)		
				Total	At commercial banks	At thrift institutions
December:						
1970	48.6	0.9	164.7	0.1	0.0	0.1
1971	52.0	1.0	175.1	.2	.0	.2
1972	56.2	1.2	191.6	.2	.0	.2
1973	60.8	1.4	200.3	.3	.0	.3
1974	67.0	1.7	205.1	.4	.2	.4
1975	72.8	2.1	211.3	.9	.4	.5
1976	79.5	2.6	221.5	2.7	1.3	1.4
1977	87.4	2.9	236.4	4.2	1.8	2.3
1978	96.0	3.3	249.5	8.5	5.3	3.1
1979	104.8	3.5	256.6	16.8	12.7	4.2
1980	115.3	3.9	261.2	28.1	20.8	7.3
1981	122.5	4.1	231.4	78.7	63.0	15.6
1982	132.5	4.1	234.1	104.1	80.5	23.6
1983	146.2	4.7	238.5	132.1	97.3	34.8
1984	156.1	5.0	243.4	147.1	104.7	42.4
1985	167.7	5.6	266.9	179.5	124.7	54.9
1986	180.4	6.1	302.9	235.2	161.0	74.2
1987	196.7	6.6	287.7	259.2	178.2	81.0
1988	212.0	7.0	287.1	280.6	192.5	88.1
1989	222.3	6.9	278.6	285.1	197.4	87.7
1990	246.5	7.7	276.8	293.7	208.7	85.0
1991	267.1	7.7	289.6	332.5	241.6	90.9
1992	292.1	8.2	340.0	384.6	280.8	103.8
1993	321.6	8.0	385.4	414.6	302.6	112.0
1994	354.5	8.6	383.6	404.0	297.4	106.6
1995	372.8	9.0	389.0	356.6	249.0	107.6
1996	394.7	8.8	402.3	275.9	172.1	103.8
1997	425.4	8.4	393.8	245.2	148.3	96.9
1998	460.5	8.5	376.7	250.0	143.9	106.1
1999	517.9	8.6	352.9	243.3	139.7	103.7
2000	531.2	8.3	309.9	238.4	133.2	105.2
2001	581.1	8.0	335.7	257.4	142.0	115.4
2002	626.3	7.8	306.8	279.6	154.3	125.3
2003	662.5	7.7	326.4	310.3	175.2	135.0
2004	697.7	7.5	343.5	328.3	187.0	141.3
2005	724.1	7.2	325.0	319.1	180.9	138.2
2006	749.6	6.7	305.3	306.3	177.7	128.6
2007	759.8	6.3	301.9	307.8	174.4	133.5
2008	815.3	5.5	459.7	314.3	180.2	134.1
2009	862.1	5.1	441.7	384.5	233.9	150.6
2008: Jan	757.2	6.2	306.7	311.0	175.6	135.4
Feb	757.0	6.2	310.8	313.0	177.2	135.9
Mar	759.1	6.2	311.8	312.6	177.5	135.1
Apr	758.8	6.1	314.4	312.8	177.3	135.5
May	762.7	6.2	309.1	313.4	175.2	138.2
June	768.4	6.1	311.7	312.0	176.3	135.7
July	774.9	5.9	320.8	313.5	175.8	137.7
Aug	776.7	5.9	311.5	306.0	170.1	135.9
Sept	781.1	5.8	359.6	313.0	175.7	137.3
Oct	796.6	5.7	360.2	310.2	175.2	135.0
Nov	806.3	5.6	399.6	306.6	171.5	135.1
Dec	815.3	5.5	459.7	314.3	180.2	134.1
2009: Jan	827.2	5.5	428.4	312.7	177.0	135.7
Feb	836.8	5.5	397.3	322.4	182.2	140.3
Mar	842.9	5.4	390.5	325.5	184.5	141.0
Apr	847.8	5.3	406.2	333.3	191.6	141.6
May	849.2	5.3	401.9	336.7	195.1	141.5
June	852.3	5.2	434.0	349.5	210.4	139.1
July	854.2	5.1	435.7	354.9	215.2	139.8
Aug	857.7	5.1	426.9	358.6	219.1	139.5
Sept	861.4	5.1	430.4	363.9	222.2	141.7
Oct	862.6	5.1	432.2	373.9	226.2	147.6
Nov	861.7	5.1	434.5	384.3	236.3	148.0
Dec	862.1	5.1	441.7	384.5	233.9	150.6

See next page for continuation of table.

TABLE B–70. Components of money stock measures, 1970–2009—*Continued*

[Averages of daily figures; billions of dollars, seasonally adjusted]

Year and month	Savings deposits [1]			Small-denomination time deposits [2]			Retail money funds	Institutional money funds [3]
	Total	At commercial banks	At thrift institutions	Total	At commercial banks	At thrift institutions		
December:								
1970	261.0	98.6	162.3	151.2	79.3	71.9	0.0	0.0
1971	292.2	112.8	179.4	189.7	94.7	95.1	.0	.0
1972	321.4	124.8	196.6	231.6	108.2	123.5	.0	.0
1973	326.8	128.0	198.7	265.8	116.8	149.0	.1	.0
1974	338.6	136.8	201.8	287.9	123.1	164.8	1.4	.2
1975	388.9	161.2	227.6	337.9	142.3	195.5	2.4	.5
1976	453.2	201.8	251.4	390.7	155.5	235.2	1.8	.6
1977	492.2	218.8	273.4	445.5	167.5	278.0	1.8	1.0
1978	481.9	216.5	265.4	521.0	185.1	335.8	5.8	3.5
1979	423.8	195.0	228.8	634.3	235.5	398.7	33.9	10.4
1980	400.3	185.7	214.5	728.5	286.2	442.3	62.5	16.0
1981	343.9	159.0	184.9	823.1	347.7	475.4	151.7	38.2
1982	400.1	190.1	210.0	850.9	379.9	471.0	183.4	48.8
1983	684.9	363.2	321.7	784.1	350.9	433.1	135.3	40.9
1984	704.7	389.3	315.4	888.8	387.9	500.9	163.8	63.7
1985	815.3	456.6	358.6	885.7	386.4	499.3	173.8	66.7
1986	940.9	533.5	407.4	858.4	369.4	489.0	207.5	87.5
1987	937.4	534.8	402.6	921.0	391.7	529.3	222.1	94.6
1988	926.4	542.4	383.9	1,037.1	451.2	585.9	243.7	94.7
1989	893.7	541.1	352.6	1,151.3	533.8	617.6	320.4	112.4
1990	922.9	581.3	341.6	1,173.3	610.7	562.6	356.0	141.6
1991	1,044.5	664.8	379.6	1,065.3	602.2	463.1	370.2	190.9
1992	1,187.2	754.2	433.1	867.7	508.1	359.7	350.4	215.4
1993	1,219.3	785.3	434.0	781.5	467.9	313.6	350.3	219.9
1994	1,151.3	752.8	398.5	817.5	503.6	313.9	377.0	214.8
1995	1,135.9	774.8	361.0	932.4	575.8	356.5	444.7	268.0
1996	1,275.2	906.4	368.9	947.9	594.2	353.7	514.8	328.6
1997	1,402.1	1,023.2	378.9	967.6	625.5	342.2	590.4	403.1
1998	1,605.3	1,188.7	416.6	951.3	626.4	324.9	723.9	555.2
1999	1,739.2	1,288.2	451.0	955.2	636.9	318.3	817.5	660.7
2000	1,878.4	1,424.4	454.0	1,046.0	700.8	345.3	905.8	814.8
2001	2,309.2	1,738.5	570.7	974.6	636.1	338.5	968.1	1,216.4
2002	2,773.6	2,060.0	713.6	894.7	591.3	303.5	897.1	1,266.7
2003	3,162.9	2,338.1	824.8	817.9	541.8	276.1	786.0	1,127.5
2004	3,507.2	2,631.7	875.5	827.7	551.4	276.3	703.2	1,079.8
2005	3,604.9	2,775.9	829.0	992.0	645.2	346.8	706.9	1,151.3
2006	3,697.8	2,913.7	784.0	1,203.7	778.8	425.0	810.2	1,357.7
2007	3,876.2	3,047.4	828.8	1,272.7	856.2	416.5	984.7	1,913.9
2008	4,112.0	3,339.2	772.7	1,452.7	1,074.2	378.5	1,082.2	2,409.7
2009	4,849.0	4,006.9	842.2	1,168.4	851.5	316.9	813.5	2,219.7
2008: Jan	3,876.7	3,043.2	833.5	1,279.6	858.9	420.7	1,004.8	1,933.5
Feb	3,914.9	3,076.5	838.3	1,285.6	863.4	422.2	1,042.2	2,059.8
Mar	3,965.8	3,113.0	852.9	1,278.0	859.2	418.8	1,058.1	2,130.5
Apr	3,969.2	3,112.6	856.6	1,277.3	858.0	419.3	1,077.7	2,173.1
May	4,003.7	3,121.5	882.2	1,276.6	859.6	417.0	1,067.2	2,201.3
June	4,018.0	3,121.4	896.6	1,274.1	862.9	411.3	1,060.7	2,232.7
July	4,037.3	3,134.2	903.1	1,285.2	878.4	406.8	1,065.0	2,248.3
Aug	4,018.5	3,126.5	892.0	1,312.6	903.9	408.7	1,059.4	2,272.3
Sept	4,045.2	3,180.8	864.3	1,336.3	932.0	404.3	1,057.3	2,233.9
Oct	4,050.0	3,263.3	786.7	1,397.1	1,024.6	372.5	1,094.8	2,225.4
Nov	4,031.8	3,260.5	771.2	1,430.4	1,052.6	377.8	1,085.0	2,334.4
Dec	4,112.0	3,339.2	772.7	1,452.7	1,074.2	378.5	1,082.2	2,409.7
2009: Jan	4,207.3	3,428.8	778.5	1,445.6	1,065.9	379.7	1,075.9	2,472.3
Feb	4,284.8	3,495.1	789.8	1,437.6	1,056.0	381.6	1,056.2	2,494.7
Mar	4,356.1	3,552.1	804.0	1,424.9	1,042.6	382.4	1,047.4	2,501.6
Apr	4,326.4	3,520.9	805.4	1,404.9	1,027.9	377.0	1,019.8	2,514.2
May	4,438.4	3,621.3	817.2	1,384.3	1,021.4	362.9	1,000.4	2,528.5
June	4,466.8	3,640.9	825.9	1,361.5	1,003.2	358.4	972.8	2,511.3
July	4,506.5	3,671.9	834.6	1,333.9	980.5	353.4	946.3	2,492.2
Aug	4,546.0	3,715.5	830.5	1,303.9	961.9	342.0	915.0	2,447.0
Sept	4,632.3	3,789.6	842.7	1,268.0	935.6	332.4	891.1	2,407.3
Oct	4,716.5	3,861.1	855.4	1,229.2	901.8	327.4	861.8	2,339.2
Nov	4,787.9	3,952.1	835.8	1,197.6	876.8	320.7	837.9	2,281.0
Dec	4,849.0	4,006.9	842.2	1,168.4	851.5	316.9	813.5	2,219.7

[1] Savings deposits including money market deposit accounts (MMDAs); data prior to 1982 are savings deposits only.
[2] Small-denomination deposits are those issued in amounts of less than $100,000.
[3] Institutional money funds are not part of non-M1 M2.

Note: See also Table B–69.

Source: Board of Governors of the Federal Reserve System.

TABLE B–71. Aggregate reserves of depository institutions and the monetary base, 1979–2009

[Averages of daily figures [1]; millions of dollars; seasonally adjusted, except as noted]

| Year and month | Adjusted for changes in reserve requirements [2] | | | | | Borrowings from the Federal Reserve (NSA) [3] | | | | | | | |
| | Reserves of depository institutions | | | | Monetary base | Total [4] | Term auction credit | Primary | Other borrowings from the Federal Reserve [5] | | | | |
	Total	Non-borrowed	Required	Excess (NSA) [3]					Primary dealer and other broker-dealer credit [6]	Asset-backed commercial paper money market mutual fund liquidity facility	Credit extended to American International Group, Inc., net [7]	Term asset-backed securities loan facility, net [8]
December:												
1979	20,720	19,248	20,279	442	131,143	1,473						
1980	22,015	20,325	21,501	514	142,004	1,690						
1981	22,443	21,807	22,124	319	149,021	636						
1982	23,600	22,966	23,100	500	160,127	634						
1983	25,367	24,593	24,806	561	175,467	774						
1984	26,913	23,727	26,078	835	187,252	3,186						
1985	31,569	30,250	30,505	1,063	203,555	1,318						
1986	38,840	38,014	37,667	1,173	223,416	827						
1987	38,913	38,135	37,893	1,019	239,829	777						
1988	40,453	38,738	39,392	1,061	256,897	1,716						
1989	40,486	40,221	39,545	941	267,774	265						
1990	41,766	41,440	40,101	1,665	293,278	326						
1991	45,516	45,324	44,526	990	317,543	192						
1992	54,421	54,298	53,267	1,154	350,882	124						
1993	60,566	60,484	59,497	1,069	386,586	82						
1994	59,466	59,257	58,295	1,171	418,313	209						
1995	56,483	56,226	55,193	1,290	434,610	257						
1996	50,185	50,030	48,766	1,418	452,088	155						
1997	46,875	46,551	45,189	1,687	479,996	324						
1998	45,172	45,055	43,659	1,512	513,954	117						
1999	42,173	41,852	40,879	1,294	593,740	9 320						
2000	38,724	38,515	37,399	1,325	584,984	210						
2001	41,428	41,361	39,785	1,643	635,567	67						
2002	40,339	40,259	38,331	2,008	681,648	80						
2003	42,630	42,585	41,583	1,047	720,391	46		17				
2004	46,540	46,478	44,631	1,909	759,378	63		11				
2005	45,089	44,920	43,188	1,901	787,579	169		97				
2006	43,220	43,029	41,357	1,863	812,411	191		111				
2007	43,214	27,783	41,429	1,784	824,373	15,431	11,613	3,787				
2008	820,306	166,740	52,972	767,333	1,654,068	653,565	438,327	88,245	47,631	32,102	47,206	
2009	1,138,633	968,706	63,187	1,075,446	2,017,698	169,927	82,014	19,025	0	0	22,023	46,310
2008: Jan	42,289	−3,371	40,641	1,648	820,299	45,659	44,516	1,137				
Feb	43,397	−16,760	41,782	1,615	820,953	60,157	60,000	155				
Mar	45,119	−49,405	42,474	2,644	824,824	94,524	75,484	1,617	16,168			
Apr	44,789	−90,620	43,052	1,737	823,692	135,410	100,000	9,624	25,764			
May	45,708	−110,073	43,869	1,838	827,435	155,780	127,419	14,076	14,238			
June	45,674	−125,604	43,449	2,225	833,059	171,278	150,000	14,225	6,908			
July	45,274	−120,390	43,361	1,913	839,687	165,664	150,000	15,204	255			
Aug	46,258	−121,821	43,382	1,876	843,236	168,078	150,000	17,980	0			
Sept	103,583	−186,522	44,101	59,483	905,225	290,105	149,814	32,632	53,473	31,877	22,187	
Oct	315,458	−332,861	48,299	267,159	1,130,444	648,319	244,778	94,017	114,953	117,457	77,047	
Nov	609,305	−89,480	50,484	558,821	1,435,013	698,786	393,088	95,839	60,655	71,009	78,070	
Dec	820,306	166,740	52,972	767,333	1,654,068	653,565	438,327	88,245	47,631	32,102	47,206	
2009: Jan	856,993	293,496	58,813	798,180	1,702,465	563,496	403,523	70,436	33,061	17,745	38,690	
Feb	699,935	117,438	56,486	643,449	1,555,039	582,497	438,822	65,463	26,250	13,533	38,414	
Mar	779,497	167,385	54,891	724,605	1,640,732	612,111	477,049	62,513	20,292	7,857	43,328	1,061
Apr	881,019	322,825	56,658	824,362	1,747,298	558,194	444,933	47,324	10,918	4,267	45,057	5,649
May	900,866	375,418	56,797	844,068	1,768,832	525,448	403,970	40,124	701	23,347	44,915	12,367
June	809,196	370,473	57,840	751,355	1,679,687	438,722	316,868	37,302	0	18,891	43,057	22,552
July	794,995	428,023	62,015	732,980	1,666,475	366,961	255,119	34,366	0	6,230	43,108	27,993
Aug	828,466	497,017	62,639	765,827	1,703,377	331,450	224,490	32,147	0	184	40,021	33,898
Sept	922,473	615,646	62,408	860,065	1,800,961	306,827	196,731	29,243	0	79	39,074	41,036
Oct	1,056,405	791,347	61,673	994,732	1,936,564	265,058	155,396	25,163	0	28	41,222	42,765
Nov	1,140,488	923,181	63,200	1,077,288	2,018,813	217,307	110,049	20,434	0	0	43,222	43,497
Dec	1,138,633	968,706	63,187	1,075,446	2,017,698	169,927	82,014	19,025	0	0	22,023	46,310

[1] Data are prorated averages of biweekly (maintenance period) averages of daily figures.

[2] Aggregate reserves incorporate adjustments for discontinuities associated with regulatory changes to reserve requirements. For details on aggregate reserves series see *Federal Reserve Bulletin*.

[3] Not seasonally adjusted (NSA).

[4] Includes secondary, seasonal, other credit extensions, and adjustment not shown separately.

[5] Does not include credit extensions made by the Federal Reserve Bank of New York to Maiden Lane LLC, Maiden Lane II LLC, Maiden Lane III LLC, and Commercial Paper Funding Facility LLC.

[6] Includes credit extended through the Primary Dealer Credit Facility and credit extended to certain other broker-dealers.

[7] Includes outstanding principal and capitalized interest net of unamortized deferred commitment fees and allowance for loan restructuring. Excludes credit extended to consolidated LLCs as described in footnote 5.

[8] Includes credit extended by Federal Reserve Bank of New York to eligible borrowers through the Term Asset-Backed Securities Loan Facility, net of unamortized deferred administrative fees.

[9] Total includes borrowing under the terms and conditions established for the Century Date Change Special Liquidity Facility in effect from October 1, 1999 through April 7, 2000.

Source: Board of Governors of the Federal Reserve System.

TABLE B–72. Bank credit at all commercial banks, 1972–2009

[Monthly average; billions of dollars, seasonally adjusted [1]]

Year and month	Total bank credit	Securities in bank credit [2]			Loans and leases in bank credit						
		Total securities	U.S. Treasury and agency securities	Other securities	Total loans and leases [3]	Commercial and industrial loans	Real estate loans			Consumer loans [6]	Other loans and leases [7]
							Total [4]	Revolving home equity loans	Commercial loans [5]		
December:											
1972	561.8	159.7	86.9	72.8	402.0	133.1	96.9	....	....	85.3	86.8
1973	643.1	166.9	90.1	76.8	476.2	161.2	117.0			98.4	99.7
1974	707.5	172.1	88.2	83.9	535.4	191.3	129.8			102.1	112.2
1975	737.8	204.9	118.1	86.8	532.9	183.4	134.1			104.3	111.1
1976	798.6	226.7	137.5	89.1	571.9	185.2	148.5			115.8	122.3
1977	885.6	234.3	137.5	96.8	651.3	204.7	175.1			138.0	133.5
1978	1,003.8	240.2	138.3	101.9	763.6	237.2	210.5			164.4	151.5
1979	1,119.0	258.5	146.8	111.7	860.5	279.6	241.7			183.7	155.5
1980	1,217.8	294.2	172.2	121.9	923.7	312.0	262.3			178.6	170.8
1981	1,298.6	307.6	180.5	127.0	991.1	350.2	283.6			182.0	175.2
1982	1,398.5	334.5	203.2	131.3	1,063.9	392.0	299.7			187.6	184.6
1983	1,550.2	398.7	261.2	137.5	1,151.5	413.8	330.4			212.7	194.7
1984	1,715.4	401.3	260.5	140.7	1,314.1	472.8	376.1			253.5	211.6
1985	1,902.2	450.0	271.5	178.5	1,452.1	499.8	425.4			294.4	232.5
1986	2,084.7	503.0	309.7	193.3	1,581.7	536.5	493.3			315.2	236.6
1987	2,229.3	527.7	335.6	192.0	1,701.6	566.6	585.9	30.8		327.8	221.4
1988	2,405.7	547.7	359.5	188.2	1,858.0	604.4	665.0	40.0		355.3	233.3
1989	2,569.7	569.4	400.6	168.8	2,000.3	635.5	760.0	50.4		373.5	231.3
1990	2,704.9	615.8	458.5	157.3	2,089.1	638.2	841.7	62.2		375.6	233.6
1991	2,815.8	724.5	560.0	164.5	2,091.3	617.6	869.1	70.5		363.6	241.1
1992	2,916.1	821.0	661.3	159.7	2,095.1	598.0	887.9	73.8		354.7	254.4
1993	3,070.5	891.3	725.0	166.3	2,179.2	585.4	929.9	73.3		386.4	277.5
1994	3,238.2	889.1	713.6	175.5	2,349.1	643.6	986.6	75.2		443.7	275.1
1995	3,470.8	891.3	693.4	197.9	2,579.5	715.2	1,062.0	79.1		484.4	317.9
1996	3,635.7	887.6	692.3	195.3	2,748.1	778.4	1,121.9	85.4		505.4	342.4
1997	3,959.8	984.8	746.4	238.4	2,975.0	845.2	1,220.4	98.1		498.8	410.6
1998	4,359.6	1,089.6	790.7	298.9	3,270.0	938.1	1,308.4	96.2		497.3	526.3
1999	4,605.7	1,147.6	805.2	342.4	3,458.1	999.6	1,456.8	99.5		485.9	515.8
2000	5,027.0	1,191.6	781.6	410.0	3,835.5	1,083.7	1,637.1	129.5		532.4	582.3
2001	5,210.2	1,319.6	840.6	479.0	3,890.6	1,021.8	1,754.3	152.3		550.4	564.1
2002	5,642.7	1,509.6	1,007.0	502.5	4,133.1	960.2	2,007.2	211.7		579.0	586.7
2003	6,010.5	1,636.3	1,092.1	544.3	4,374.2	898.2	2,209.7	278.4	....	635.6	630.7
2004	6,563.6	1,728.2	1,151.1	577.0	4,835.5	918.5	2,547.8	395.2	1,077.7	685.9	683.3
2005	7,258.6	1,825.0	1,139.8	685.2	5,433.6	1,041.6	2,916.0	442.9	1,266.6	697.6	778.5
2006	8,037.8	1,962.6	1,188.6	774.0	6,075.3	1,181.2	3,355.8	466.8	1,454.3	732.1	806.2
2007	8,843.5	2,083.2	1,107.6	975.6	6,760.3	1,424.4	3,588.4	483.2	1,589.5	793.4	954.0
2008	9,372.5	2,109.4	1,240.3	869.1	7,263.1	1,617.7	3,823.2	588.0	1,726.8	861.4	960.8
2009	9,082.1	2,342.5	1,424.8	917.7	6,739.6	1,343.0	3,809.0	601.7	1,648.1	832.6	755.0
2008: Jan	8,926.2	2,075.8	1,093.7	982.0	6,850.4	1,450.7	3,612.5	487.0	1,603.6	791.7	995.6
Feb	8,965.3	2,081.2	1,090.0	991.2	6,884.1	1,468.9	3,628.8	491.6	1,618.4	794.2	992.3
Mar	9,035.4	2,082.3	1,097.6	984.7	6,953.1	1,497.6	3,670.9	496.8	1,631.6	799.5	985.2
Apr	8,976.6	2,072.7	1,096.5	976.2	6,903.9	1,512.6	3,649.5	503.0	1,640.4	804.8	937.0
May	9,001.6	2,080.0	1,105.5	974.5	6,921.6	1,518.7	3,645.6	508.6	1,648.3	808.3	948.7
June	8,992.9	2,084.9	1,117.5	967.4	6,908.0	1,531.5	3,634.3	514.5	1,659.6	813.4	928.8
July	9,021.5	2,085.1	1,122.0	963.1	6,936.4	1,544.3	3,622.3	521.6	1,663.6	823.7	946.1
Aug	9,038.2	2,072.4	1,130.1	942.3	6,965.8	1,557.7	3,623.7	526.4	1,666.7	829.5	954.9
Sept	9,195.1	2,112.7	1,149.5	963.2	7,082.4	1,581.4	3,664.1	539.8	1,674.9	834.9	1,002.0
Oct	9,541.2	2,231.5	1,217.6	1,013.9	7,309.7	1,645.6	3,822.0	578.4	1,719.2	852.6	989.5
Nov	9,406.2	2,166.8	1,252.5	914.3	7,239.4	1,636.9	3,820.4	582.6	1,723.6	858.1	923.9
Dec	9,372.5	2,109.4	1,240.3	869.1	7,263.1	1,617.7	3,823.2	588.0	1,726.8	861.4	960.8
2009: Jan	9,337.1	2,145.7	1,273.0	872.7	7,191.4	1,601.1	3,805.0	593.0	1,720.8	869.8	915.6
Feb	9,347.6	2,162.6	1,261.7	900.8	7,185.0	1,587.1	3,818.2	595.7	1,721.6	879.9	899.7
Mar	9,328.6	2,187.2	1,273.0	914.2	7,141.4	1,564.1	3,836.1	600.2	1,720.3	870.6	870.6
Apr	9,266.9	2,185.0	1,263.8	921.2	7,081.9	1,545.0	3,831.4	605.1	1,715.6	859.7	845.8
May	9,338.1	2,210.7	1,263.2	947.5	7,127.4	1,525.4	3,875.6	613.1	1,712.2	858.3	868.1
June	9,319.6	2,252.5	1,293.5	959.0	7,067.1	1,499.0	3,862.5	610.9	1,704.6	856.2	849.4
July	9,249.6	2,268.1	1,325.5	942.6	6,981.5	1,482.8	3,846.8	608.3	1,697.8	852.6	799.3
Aug	9,210.4	2,304.0	1,363.1	940.8	6,906.5	1,450.7	3,825.5	606.9	1,690.5	850.5	779.8
Sept	9,126.9	2,314.1	1,379.4	934.7	6,812.8	1,414.7	3,781.9	604.0	1,679.8	848.0	768.2
Oct	9,046.3	2,305.0	1,372.1	932.8	6,741.4	1,383.5	3,757.3	601.8	1,667.1	846.6	754.0
Nov	9,103.7	2,309.8	1,382.9	926.9	6,793.8	1,366.0	3,823.0	604.6	1,660.6	842.2	762.7
Dec	9,082.1	2,342.5	1,424.8	917.7	6,739.6	1,343.0	3,809.0	601.7	1,648.1	832.6	755.0

[1] Data are prorated averages of Wednesday values for domestically chartered commercial banks, branches and agencies of foreign banks, New York State investment companies (through September 1996), and Edge Act and agreement corporations.

[2] Includes securities held in trading accounts, held-to-maturity, and available for sale. Excludes all non-security trading assets, such as derivatives with a positive fair value or loans held in trading accounts.

[3] Excludes unearned income. Includes the allowance for loan and lease losses. Excludes Federal funds sold to, reverse repurchase agreements (RPs) with, and loans to commercial banks. Includes all loans held in trading accounts under a fair value option.

[4] Includes closed-end residential loans, not shown separately.

[5] Includes construction, land development, and other land loans, and loans secured by farmland, multifamily (5 or more) residential properties, and nonfarm nonresidential properties.

[6] Includes credit cards and other consumer loans.

[7] Includes other items, not shown separately.

Note: Data in this table are shown as of January 22, 2010.

Source: Board of Governors of the Federal Reserve System.

[Percent per annum]

Year and month	U.S. Treasury securities Bills (at auction)[1] 3-month	6-month	Constant maturities[2] 3-year	10-year	30-year	Corporate bonds (Moody's) Aaa[3]	Baa	High-grade municipal bonds (Standard & Poor's)	New-home mortgage yields[4]	Prime rate charged by banks[5]	Discount window (Federal Reserve Bank of New York)[5,6] Primary credit	Adjustment credit	Federal funds rate[7]
1929	....	....	....	....	....	4.73	5.90	4.27	....	5.50–6.00	....	5.16	....
1933	0.515	....	....	....	....	4.49	7.76	4.71	....	1.50–4.00	....	2.56	....
1939	.023	....	....	....	....	3.01	4.96	2.76	....	1.50	....	1.00	....
1940	.014	....	....	....	....	2.84	4.75	2.50	....	1.50	....	1.00	....
1941	.103	....	....	....	....	2.77	4.33	2.10	....	1.50	....	1.00	....
1942	.326	....	....	....	....	2.83	4.28	2.36	....	1.50	....	[8]1.00	....
1943	.373	....	....	....	....	2.73	3.91	2.06	....	1.50	....	[8]1.00	....
1944	.375	....	....	....	....	2.72	3.61	1.86	....	1.50	....	[8]1.00	....
1945	.375	....	....	....	....	2.62	3.29	1.67	....	1.50	....	[8]1.00	....
1946	.375	....	....	....	....	2.53	3.05	1.64	....	1.50	....	[8]1.00	....
1947	.594	....	....	....	....	2.61	3.24	2.01	....	1.50–1.75	....	1.00	....
1948	1.040	....	....	....	....	2.82	3.47	2.40	....	1.75–2.00	....	1.34	....
1949	1.102	....	....	....	....	2.66	3.42	2.21	....	2.00	....	1.50	....
1950	1.218	....	....	....	....	2.62	3.24	1.98	....	2.07	....	1.59	....
1951	1.552	....	....	....	....	2.86	3.41	2.00	....	2.56	....	1.75	....
1952	1.766	....	....	....	....	2.96	3.52	2.19	....	3.00	....	1.75	....
1953	1.931	....	2.47	2.85	....	3.20	3.74	2.72	....	3.17	....	1.99	....
1954	.953	....	1.63	2.40	....	2.90	3.51	2.37	....	3.05	....	1.60	....
1955	1.753	....	2.47	2.82	....	3.06	3.53	2.53	....	3.16	....	1.89	1.79
1956	2.658	....	3.19	3.18	....	3.36	3.88	2.93	....	3.77	....	2.77	2.73
1957	3.267	....	3.98	3.65	....	3.89	4.71	3.60	....	4.20	....	3.12	3.11
1958	1.839	....	2.84	3.32	....	3.79	4.73	3.56	....	3.83	....	2.15	1.57
1959	3.405	3.832	4.46	4.33	....	4.38	5.05	3.95	....	4.48	....	3.36	3.31
1960	2.93	3.25	3.98	4.12	....	4.41	5.19	3.73	....	4.82	....	3.53	3.21
1961	2.38	2.61	3.54	3.88	....	4.35	5.08	3.46	....	4.50	....	3.00	1.95
1962	2.78	2.91	3.47	3.95	....	4.33	5.02	3.18	....	4.50	....	3.00	2.71
1963	3.16	3.25	3.67	4.00	....	4.26	4.86	3.23	5.89	4.50	....	3.23	3.18
1964	3.56	3.69	4.03	4.19	....	4.40	4.83	3.22	5.83	4.50	....	3.55	3.50
1965	3.95	4.05	4.22	4.28	....	4.49	4.87	3.27	5.81	4.54	....	4.04	4.07
1966	4.88	5.08	5.23	4.93	....	5.13	5.67	3.82	6.25	5.63	....	4.50	5.11
1967	4.32	4.63	5.03	5.07	....	5.51	6.23	3.98	6.46	5.63	....	4.19	4.22
1968	5.34	5.47	5.68	5.64	....	6.18	6.94	4.51	6.97	6.31	....	5.17	5.66
1969	6.68	6.85	7.02	6.67	....	7.03	7.81	5.81	7.81	7.96	....	5.87	8.21
1970	6.43	6.53	7.29	7.35	....	8.04	9.11	6.51	8.45	7.91	....	5.95	7.17
1971	4.35	4.51	5.66	6.16	....	7.39	8.56	5.70	7.74	5.73	....	4.88	4.67
1972	4.07	4.47	5.72	6.21	....	7.21	8.16	5.27	7.60	5.25	....	4.50	4.44
1973	7.04	7.18	6.96	6.85	....	7.44	8.24	5.18	7.96	8.03	....	6.45	8.74
1974	7.89	7.93	7.84	7.56	....	8.57	9.50	6.09	8.92	10.81	....	7.83	10.51
1975	5.84	6.12	7.50	7.99	....	8.83	10.61	6.89	9.00	7.86	....	6.25	5.82
1976	4.99	5.27	6.77	7.61	....	8.43	9.75	6.49	9.00	6.84	....	5.50	5.05
1977	5.27	5.52	6.68	7.42	7.75	8.02	8.97	5.56	9.02	6.83	....	5.46	5.54
1978	7.22	7.58	8.29	8.41	8.49	8.73	9.49	5.90	9.56	9.06	....	7.46	7.94
1979	10.05	10.02	9.70	9.43	9.28	9.63	10.69	6.39	10.78	12.67	....	10.29	11.20
1980	11.51	11.37	11.51	11.43	11.27	11.94	13.67	8.51	12.66	15.26	....	11.77	13.35
1981	14.03	13.78	14.46	13.92	13.45	14.17	16.04	11.23	14.70	18.87	....	13.42	16.39
1982	10.69	11.08	12.93	13.01	12.76	13.79	16.11	11.57	15.14	14.85	....	11.01	12.24
1983	8.63	8.75	10.45	11.10	11.18	12.04	13.55	9.47	12.57	10.79	....	8.50	9.09
1984	9.53	9.77	11.92	12.46	12.41	12.71	14.19	10.15	12.38	12.04	....	8.80	10.23
1985	7.47	7.64	9.64	10.62	10.79	11.37	12.72	9.18	11.55	9.93	....	7.69	8.10
1986	5.98	6.03	7.06	7.67	7.78	9.02	10.39	7.38	10.17	8.33	....	6.32	6.80
1987	5.82	6.05	7.68	8.39	8.59	9.38	10.58	7.73	9.31	8.21	....	5.66	6.66
1988	6.69	6.92	8.26	8.85	8.96	9.71	10.83	7.76	9.19	9.32	....	6.20	7.57
1989	8.12	8.04	8.55	8.49	8.45	9.26	10.18	7.24	10.13	10.87	....	6.93	9.21
1990	7.51	7.47	8.26	8.55	8.61	9.32	10.36	7.25	10.05	10.01	....	6.98	8.10
1991	5.42	5.49	6.82	7.86	8.14	8.77	9.80	6.89	9.32	8.46	....	5.45	5.69
1992	3.45	3.57	5.30	7.01	7.67	8.14	8.98	6.41	8.24	6.25	....	3.25	3.52
1993	3.02	3.14	4.44	5.87	6.59	7.22	7.93	5.63	7.20	6.00	....	3.00	3.02
1994	4.29	4.66	6.27	7.09	7.37	7.96	8.62	6.19	7.49	7.15	....	3.60	4.21
1995	5.51	5.59	6.25	6.57	6.88	7.59	8.20	5.95	7.87	8.83	....	5.21	5.83
1996	5.02	5.09	5.99	6.44	6.71	7.37	8.05	5.75	7.80	8.27	....	5.02	5.30
1997	5.07	5.18	6.10	6.35	6.61	7.26	7.86	5.55	7.71	8.44	....	5.00	5.46
1998	4.81	4.85	5.14	5.26	5.58	6.53	7.22	5.12	7.07	8.35	....	4.92	5.35
1999	4.66	4.76	5.49	5.65	5.87	7.04	7.87	5.43	7.04	8.00	....	4.62	4.97
2000	5.85	5.92	6.22	6.03	5.94	7.62	8.36	5.77	7.52	9.23	....	5.73	6.24
2001	3.44	3.39	4.09	5.02	5.49	7.08	7.95	5.19	7.00	6.91	....	3.40	3.88
2002	1.62	1.69	3.10	4.61	5.43	6.49	7.80	5.05	6.43	4.67	....	1.17	1.67
2003	1.01	1.06	2.10	4.01	....	5.67	6.77	4.73	5.80	4.12	2.12	....	1.13
2004	1.38	1.57	2.78	4.27	....	5.63	6.39	4.63	5.77	4.34	2.34	....	1.35
2005	3.16	3.40	3.93	4.29	....	5.24	6.06	4.29	5.94	6.19	4.19	....	3.22
2006	4.73	4.80	4.77	4.80	4.91	5.59	6.48	4.42	6.63	7.96	5.96	....	4.97
2007	4.41	4.48	4.35	4.63	4.84	5.56	6.48	4.42	6.41	8.05	5.86	....	5.02
2008	1.48	1.71	2.24	3.66	4.28	5.63	7.45	4.80	6.05	5.09	2.39	....	1.92
2009	.16	.29	1.43	3.26	4.08	5.31	7.30	4.64	5.14	3.25	.50	....	.16

[1] High bill rate at auction, issue date within period, bank-discount basis. On or after October 28, 1998, data are stop yields from uniform-price auctions. Before that date, they are weighted average yields from multiple-price auctions.

See next page for continuation of table.

TABLE B–73. Bond yields and interest rates, 1929–2009—*Continued*

[Percent per annum]

Year and month	U.S. Treasury securities					Corporate bonds (Moody's)		High-grade municipal bonds (Standard & Poor's)	New-home mortgage yields[4]	Prime rate charged by banks[5]	Discount window (Federal Reserve Bank of New York)[5,6]		Federal funds rate[7]
	Bills (at auction)[1]		Constant maturities[2]								Primary credit	Adjustment credit	
	3-month	6-month	3-year	10-year	30-year	Aaa[3]	Baa						
											High-low	High-low	High-low	
2005: Jan	2.32	2.60	3.39	4.22	....	5.36	6.02	4.28	6.01	5.25–5.25	3.25–3.25	....	2.28
Feb	2.53	2.76	3.54	4.17	....	5.20	5.82	4.14	5.75	5.50–5.25	3.50–3.25	....	2.50
Mar	2.75	3.00	3.91	4.50	....	5.40	6.06	4.42	5.82	5.75–5.50	3.75–3.50	....	2.63
Apr	2.78	3.06	3.79	4.34	....	5.33	6.05	4.31	5.84	5.75–5.75	3.75–3.75	....	2.79
May	2.85	3.10	3.72	4.14	....	5.15	6.01	4.16	5.82	6.00–5.75	4.00–3.75	....	3.00
June	2.98	3.13	3.69	4.00	....	4.96	5.86	4.08	5.76	6.25–6.00	4.25–4.00	....	3.04
July	3.21	3.41	3.91	4.18	....	5.06	5.95	4.15	5.76	6.25–6.25	4.25–4.25	....	3.26
Aug	3.45	3.67	4.08	4.26	....	5.09	5.96	4.21	5.83	6.50–6.25	4.50–4.25	....	3.50
Sept	3.46	3.68	3.96	4.20	....	5.13	6.03	4.28	5.99	6.75–6.50	4.75–4.50	....	3.62
Oct	3.70	3.98	4.29	4.46	....	5.35	6.30	4.49	6.03	6.75–6.75	4.75–4.75	....	3.78
Nov	3.90	4.16	4.43	4.54	....	5.42	6.39	4.53	6.20	7.00–7.00	5.00–5.00	....	4.00
Dec	3.89	4.19	4.39	4.47	....	5.37	6.32	4.43	6.39	7.25–7.00	5.25–5.00	....	4.16
2006: Jan	4.20	4.29	4.35	4.42	....	5.29	6.24	4.31	6.12	7.50–7.25	5.50–5.25	....	4.29
Feb	4.41	4.51	4.64	4.57	4.54	5.35	6.27	4.41	6.40	7.50–7.50	5.50–5.50	....	4.49
Mar	4.51	4.61	4.74	4.72	4.73	5.53	6.41	4.44	6.53	7.75–7.50	5.75–5.50	....	4.59
Apr	4.59	4.71	4.89	4.99	5.06	5.84	6.68	4.60	6.64	7.75–7.75	5.75–5.75	....	4.79
May	4.72	4.81	4.97	5.11	5.20	5.95	6.75	4.61	6.69	8.00–7.75	6.00–5.75	....	4.94
June	4.79	4.95	5.09	5.11	5.15	5.89	6.78	4.64	6.79	8.25–8.00	6.25–6.00	....	4.99
July	4.96	5.09	5.07	5.09	5.13	5.85	6.76	4.64	6.81	8.25–8.25	6.25–6.25	....	5.24
Aug	4.98	4.99	4.85	4.88	5.00	5.68	6.59	4.43	6.87	8.25–8.25	6.25–6.25	....	5.25
Sept	4.82	4.90	4.69	4.72	4.85	5.51	6.43	4.30	6.72	8.25–8.25	6.25–6.25	....	5.25
Oct	4.89	4.91	4.72	4.73	4.85	5.51	6.42	4.32	6.69	8.25–8.25	6.25–6.25	....	5.25
Nov	4.95	4.95	4.64	4.60	4.69	5.33	6.20	4.17	6.55	8.25–8.25	6.25–6.25	....	5.25
Dec	4.84	4.87	4.58	4.56	4.68	5.32	6.22	4.17	6.37	8.25–8.25	6.25–6.25	....	5.24
2007: Jan	4.96	4.93	4.79	4.76	4.85	5.40	6.34	4.29	6.35	8.25–8.25	6.25–6.25	....	5.25
Feb	5.02	4.96	4.75	4.72	4.82	5.39	6.28	4.21	6.31	8.25–8.25	6.25–6.25	....	5.26
Mar	4.96	4.90	4.51	4.56	4.72	5.30	6.27	4.18	6.22	8.25–8.25	6.25–6.25	....	5.26
Apr	4.87	4.87	4.60	4.69	4.87	5.47	6.39	4.32	6.21	8.25–8.25	6.25–6.25	....	5.25
May	4.77	4.80	4.69	4.75	4.90	5.47	6.39	4.37	6.22	8.25–8.25	6.25–6.25	....	5.25
June	4.63	4.77	5.00	5.10	5.20	5.79	6.70	4.64	6.54	8.25–8.25	6.25–6.25	....	5.25
July	4.83	4.85	4.82	5.00	5.11	5.73	6.65	4.64	6.70	8.25–8.25	6.25–6.25	....	5.26
Aug	4.34	4.56	4.34	4.67	4.93	5.79	6.65	4.73	6.73	8.25–8.25	6.25–5.75	....	5.02
Sept	4.01	4.13	4.06	4.52	4.79	5.74	6.59	4.57	6.58	8.25–7.75	5.75–5.25	....	4.94
Oct	3.96	4.08	4.01	4.53	4.77	5.66	6.48	4.41	6.55	7.75–7.50	5.25–5.00	....	4.76
Nov	3.49	3.63	3.35	4.15	4.52	5.44	6.40	4.45	6.42	7.50–7.50	5.00–5.00	....	4.49
Dec	3.08	3.29	3.13	4.10	4.53	5.49	6.65	4.22	6.21	7.50–7.25	5.00–4.75	....	4.24
2008: Jan	2.86	2.84	2.51	3.74	4.33	5.33	6.54	4.00	6.02	7.25–6.00	4.75–3.50	....	3.94
Feb	2.21	2.09	2.19	3.74	4.52	5.53	6.82	4.35	5.96	6.00–6.00	3.50–3.50	....	2.98
Mar	1.38	1.53	1.80	3.51	4.39	5.51	6.89	4.67	5.92	6.00–5.25	3.50–2.50	....	2.61
Apr	1.32	1.54	2.23	3.68	4.44	5.55	6.97	4.43	5.98	5.25–5.00	2.50–2.25	....	2.28
May	1.71	1.82	2.69	3.88	4.60	5.57	6.93	4.34	6.01	5.00–5.00	2.25–2.25	....	1.98
June	1.89	2.15	3.08	4.10	4.69	5.68	7.07	4.48	6.13	5.00–5.00	2.25–2.25	....	2.00
July	1.72	1.99	2.87	4.01	4.57	5.67	7.16	4.88	6.29	5.00–5.00	2.25–2.25	....	2.01
Aug	1.79	1.96	2.70	3.89	4.50	5.64	7.15	4.90	6.33	5.00–5.00	2.25–2.25	....	2.00
Sept	1.46	1.78	2.32	3.69	4.27	5.65	7.31	5.03	6.09	5.00–5.00	2.25–2.25	....	1.81
Oct	.84	1.39	1.86	3.81	4.17	6.28	8.88	5.68	6.10	5.00–4.00	2.25–1.25	....	.97
Nov	.30	.86	1.51	3.53	4.00	6.12	9.21	5.28	6.16	4.00–4.00	1.25–1.25	....	.39
Dec	.04	.32	1.07	2.42	2.87	5.05	8.43	5.53	5.67	4.00–3.25	1.25–0.50	....	.16
2009: Jan	.12	.31	1.13	2.52	3.13	5.05	8.14	5.13	5.11	3.25–3.25	0.50–0.50	....	.15
Feb	.31	.46	1.37	2.87	3.59	5.27	8.08	5.00	5.09	3.25–3.25	0.50–0.50	....	.22
Mar	.25	.43	1.31	2.82	3.64	5.50	8.42	5.15	5.10	3.25–3.25	0.50–0.50	....	.18
Apr	.17	.37	1.32	2.93	3.76	5.39	8.39	4.88	4.96	3.25–3.25	0.50–0.50	....	.15
May	.19	.31	1.39	3.29	4.23	5.54	8.06	4.60	4.92	3.25–3.25	0.50–0.50	....	.18
June	.17	.32	1.76	3.72	4.52	5.61	7.50	4.84	5.17	3.25–3.25	0.50–0.50	....	.21
July	.19	.29	1.55	3.56	4.41	5.41	7.09	4.69	5.40	3.25–3.25	0.50–0.50	....	.16
Aug	.18	.27	1.65	3.59	4.37	5.26	6.58	4.58	5.32	3.25–3.25	0.50–0.50	....	.16
Sept	.13	.22	1.48	3.40	4.19	5.13	6.31	4.13	5.26	3.25–3.25	0.50–0.50	....	.15
Oct	.08	.17	1.46	3.39	4.19	5.15	6.29	4.20	5.14	3.25–3.25	0.50–0.50	....	.12
Nov	.06	.16	1.32	3.40	4.31	5.19	6.32	4.35	5.08	3.25–3.25	0.50–0.50	....	.12
Dec	.07	.17	1.38	3.59	4.49	5.26	6.37	4.16	5.01	3.25–3.25	0.50–0.50	....	.12

[2] Yields on the more actively traded issues adjusted to constant maturities by the Department of the Treasury. The 30-year Treasury constant maturity series was discontinued on February 18, 2002, and reintroduced on February 9, 2006.

[3] Beginning with December 7, 2001, data for corporate Aaa series are industrial bonds only.

[4] Effective rate (in the primary market) on conventional mortgages, reflecting fees and charges as well as contract rate and assuming, on the average, repayment at end of 10 years. Rates beginning with January 1973 not strictly comparable with prior rates.

[5] For monthly data, high and low for the period. Prime rate for 1929–1933 and 1947–1948 are ranges of the rate in effect during the period.

[6] Primary credit replaced adjustment credit as the Federal Reserve's principal discount window lending program effective January 9, 2003.

[7] Since July 19, 1975, the daily effective rate is an average of the rates on a given day weighted by the volume of transactions at these rates. Prior to that date, the daily effective rate was the rate considered most representative of the day's transactions, usually the one at which most transactions occurred.

[8] From October 30, 1942 to April 24, 1946, a preferential rate of 0.50 percent was in effect for advances secured by Government securities maturing in one year or less.

Sources: Department of the Treasury, Board of Governors of the Federal Reserve System, Federal Housing Finance Agency, Moody's Investors Service, and Standard & Poor's.

TABLE B-74. Credit market borrowing, 2001–2009

[Billions of dollars; quarterly data at seasonally adjusted annual rates]

Item	2001	2002	2003	2004	2005	2006	2007	2008
NONFINANCIAL SECTORS								
Domestic	1,151.9	1,408.0	1,677.7	1,991.7	2,329.2	2,398.5	2,536.7	1,870.4
By instrument	1,151.9	1,408.0	1,677.7	1,991.7	2,329.2	2,398.5	2,536.7	1,870.4
Commercial paper	−83.1	−57.9	−37.3	15.3	−7.7	22.4	11.3	7.7
Treasury securities	−5.1	257.1	398.4	362.5	307.3	183.7	237.5	1,239.0
Agency- and GSE-backed securities [1]	−0.5	.5	−2.4	−.6	−.4	−.3	−.4	.2
Municipal securities	122.8	159.4	137.6	130.5	195.0	177.4	215.6	65.4
Corporate bonds	343.4	133.4	152.2	75.5	56.7	215.6	311.2	204.6
Bank loans n.e.c.	−87.5	−108.2	−76.3	5.2	134.5	175.3	240.2	192.6
Other loans and advances	6.1	29.6	10.2	60.0	120.1	142.4	318.4	40.6
Mortgages	705.4	888.9	989.9	1,226.3	1,423.6	1,386.7	1,066.0	80.2
Home	552.0	754.7	812.3	1,014.7	1,108.6	1,059.8	695.7	−115.7
Multifamily residential	40.6	37.3	71.4	49.6	70.9	55.1	103.0	58.8
Commercial	109.1	90.1	118.5	149.5	235.0	268.5	262.7	119.1
Farm	3.8	6.9	−12.2	12.5	9.1	3.3	4.6	18.0
Consumer credit	150.6	105.2	105.5	117.0	100.3	95.3	136.9	40.2
By sector	1,151.9	1,408.0	1,677.7	1,991.7	2,329.2	2,398.5	2,536.7	1,870.4
Household sector	672.0	825.3	995.9	1,049.6	1,168.1	1,176.0	861.3	37.0
Nonfinancial business	380.0	181.0	165.7	464.7	682.5	887.9	1,252.3	551.0
Corporate	211.9	23.0	86.8	203.8	333.7	465.1	783.0	347.7
Nonfarm noncorporate	161.7	150.8	91.5	245.2	331.6	408.6	454.8	202.2
Farm	6.4	7.1	−12.6	15.8	17.3	14.2	14.6	1.1
State and local governments	105.5	144.1	120.1	115.4	171.7	151.2	185.9	43.3
Federal Government	−5.6	257.6	396.0	361.9	306.9	183.4	237.1	1,239.2
Foreign borrowing in the United States	−11.2	93.4	43.0	155.3	113.0	332.6	170.3	−129.5
Commercial paper	18.3	58.8	18.9	69.2	38.6	98.4	−69.3	−71.0
Bonds	−18.5	31.6	28.7	85.8	64.5	227.8	218.7	−62.1
Bank loans n.e.c.	−7.3	5.3	−2.5	3.8	14.5	13.8	24.1	5.1
Other loans and advances	−3.8	−2.3	−2.1	−3.6	−4.6	−7.4	−3.2	−1.5
Nonfinancial domestic and foreign borrowing	1,140.8	1,501.3	1,720.7	2,146.9	2,442.3	2,731.1	2,707.0	1,740.9
FINANCIAL SECTORS								
By instrument	874.7	876.5	1,066.7	979.8	1,118.5	1,291.0	1,791.9	888.5
Open market paper	−126.9	−99.9	−63.5	21.7	214.2	196.3	−111.4	−125.6
GSE issues [1]	304.1	219.8	250.9	75.0	−84.0	35.6	282.4	271.7
Agency- and GSE-backed mortgage pool securities [1]	338.5	326.8	330.6	47.9	167.3	295.4	626.3	497.3
Corporate bonds	310.2	388.7	487.1	669.6	743.8	798.2	693.3	−291.1
Bank loans n.e.c.	21.0	23.1	21.4	66.0	18.8	−62.3	70.9	496.1
Other loans and advances	25.5	6.8	31.2	74.1	44.4	21.2	225.8	33.3
Mortgages	2.2	11.2	8.9	25.5	14.1	6.6	4.7	6.8
By sector	874.7	876.5	1,066.7	979.8	1,118.5	1,291.0	1,791.9	888.5
Commercial banking	52.9	49.7	48.5	78.4	85.1	177.4	263.2	161.1
U.S.-chartered commercial banks	30.2	29.9	13.2	18.7	36.9	107.5	131.8	79.1
Foreign banking offices in the United States	−0.9	−.4	−.1	.1	.0	−.3	.0	−.2
Bank holding companies	23.6	20.3	35.4	59.5	48.2	70.2	131.3	82.3
Savings institutions	0.0	−23.1	35.3	91.4	22.5	−108.2	104.1	−67.1
Credit unions	1.5	2.0	2.2	2.3	3.3	4.2	13.4	8.3
Life insurance companies	0.6	2.0	2.9	3.0	.4	2.7	14.5	26.2
Government-sponsored enterprises	304.1	219.8	250.9	75.0	−84.0	35.6	282.4	271.7
Agency- and GSE-backed mortgage pools [1]	338.5	326.8	330.6	47.9	167.3	295.4	626.3	497.3
Asset-backed securities issuers	264.5	218.4	249.7	440.7	730.2	798.7	335.2	−425.2
Finance companies	10.9	66.2	111.1	134.3	33.5	34.8	34.9	−79.4
REITs [2]	3.8	27.0	32.3	94.6	55.4	15.5	10.2	−48.6
Brokers and dealers	1.4	−1.7	6.4	15.2	.1	6.4	−4.0	77.7
Funding corporations	−103.6	−10.7	−3.2	−2.9	104.7	28.3	111.6	466.4
ALL SECTORS, BY INSTRUMENT								
Total	2,015.5	2,377.8	2,787.4	3,126.8	3,560.7	4,022.0	4,498.8	2,629.4
Open market paper	−191.6	−99.1	−82.0	106.2	245.1	317.1	−169.4	−189.0
Treasury securities	−5.1	257.1	398.4	362.5	307.3	183.7	237.5	1,239.0
Agency- and GSE-backed securities [1]	642.1	547.2	579.1	122.3	82.8	330.6	908.3	769.2
Municipal securities	122.8	159.4	137.6	130.5	195.0	177.4	215.6	65.4
Corporate and foreign bonds	635.2	553.7	668.0	830.9	865.0	1,241.6	1,223.2	−148.6
Bank loans n.e.c.	−73.9	−79.8	−57.4	75.1	167.8	126.8	335.1	693.8
Other loans and advances	27.8	34.1	39.3	130.5	159.8	156.2	541.0	72.4
Mortgages	707.6	900.1	998.8	1,251.8	1,437.7	1,393.3	1,070.7	87.0
Consumer credit	150.6	105.2	105.5	117.0	100.3	95.3	136.9	40.2

[1] Government-sponsored enterprises (GSE).
[2] Real estate investment trusts (REITs).

See next page for continuation of table.

[Billions of dollars; quarterly data at seasonally adjusted annual rates]

Item	2008				2009		
	I	II	III	IV	I	II	III
NONFINANCIAL SECTORS							
Domestic	1,748.3	1,056.8	2,665.5	2,011.2	1,430.0	1,514.1	965.6
By instrument	1,748.3	1,056.8	2,665.5	2,011.2	1,430.0	1,514.1	965.6
Commercial paper	42.9	−77.3	62.8	2.2	−151.9	−145.9	−11.0
Treasury securities	411.4	310.1	2,080.2	2,154.2	1,442.8	1,896.4	1,481.2
Agency- and GSE-backed securities [1]	1.3	.3	−1.7	1.0	−3.2	−1.1	3.7
Municipal securities	95.5	61.2	98.2	6.9	120.5	117.3	158.6
Corporate bonds	181.0	354.9	92.4	190.1	579.2	395.9	262.0
Bank loans n.e.c.	256.2	85.6	368.0	60.6	−353.1	−297.3	−282.0
Other loans and advances	114.4	95.1	83.0	−130.0	−50.9	−48.5	−20.2
Mortgages	530.6	121.5	−134.2	−197.3	−64.8	−282.0	−545.2
Home	272.9	−113.3	−328.4	−293.8	−61.6	−225.5	−452.9
Multifamily residential	70.4	69.8	59.6	35.3	2.0	1.6	−5.2
Commercial	169.4	147.2	116.5	43.1	−7.4	−60.3	−89.3
Farm	17.9	17.9	18.1	18.1	2.1	2.2	2.2
Consumer credit	115.0	105.4	16.6	−76.4	−88.7	−120.8	−81.6
By sector	1,748.3	1,056.8	2,665.5	2,011.2	1,430.0	1,514.1	965.6
Household sector	431.4	31.8	−62.1	−253.3	−160.7	−214.2	−351.3
Nonfinancial business	825.6	689.9	575.7	112.8	52.9	−248.9	−283.9
Corporate	467.8	461.2	405.6	56.3	240.6	56.8	94.2
Nonfarm noncorporate	380.6	195.8	190.4	42.0	−195.1	−299.9	−368.3
Farm	−22.7	32.8	−20.3	14.5	7.5	−5.8	−9.8
State and local governments	78.6	24.8	73.3	−3.5	98.2	82.0	115.9
Federal Government	412.7	310.4	2,078.5	2,155.2	1,439.6	1,895.3	1,484.9
Foreign borrowing in the United States	325.3	103.8	−517.5	−429.8	179.7	192.0	291.4
Commercial paper	212.0	41.7	−276.4	−261.5	63.1	−23.5	200.3
Bonds	79.9	73.2	−261.8	−139.7	137.5	220.7	99.0
Bank loans n.e.c.	35.4	−9.0	21.5	−27.4	−19.4	−6.0	−8.2
Other loans and advances	−2.0	−2.1	−.8	−1.3	−1.5	.7	.3
Nonfinancial domestic and foreign borrowing	2,073.6	1,160.7	2,148.0	1,581.4	1,609.6	1,706.1	1,257.0
FINANCIAL SECTORS							
By instrument	884.5	947.9	1,167.3	554.3	−1,781.3	−2,134.4	−1,532.6
Open market paper	−231.5	−232.6	−380.6	342.3	−573.7	−565.8	−430.5
GSE issues [1]	111.7	655.8	202.4	117.0	−254.5	−680.9	−590.3
Agency- and GSE-backed mortgage pool securities [1]	533.8	666.4	503.4	285.5	304.4	555.9	481.1
Corporate bonds	83.6	−109.7	−540.4	−597.7	−431.0	−448.0	−227.7
Bank loans n.e.c.	180.8	10.2	986.6	806.7	−484.1	−627.9	−511.6
Other loans and advances	185.7	−39.6	390.0	−402.9	−348.0	−377.2	−251.5
Mortgages	20.4	−2.6	5.9	3.4	5.6	9.5	−2.1
By sector	884.5	947.9	1,167.3	554.3	−1,781.3	−2,134.4	−1,532.6
Commercial banking	228.8	299.2	259.2	−142.7	−298.7	−42.4	−152.4
U.S.-chartered commercial banks	92.0	9.2	512.3	−297.3	−307.7	−59.4	−231.2
Foreign banking offices in the United States	−0.6	−.1	.0	.0	.0	.0	.0
Bank holding companies	137.4	290.1	−253.1	154.7	9.1	17.0	78.8
Savings institutions	101.3	−76.2	−203.7	−89.9	−82.9	−336.2	−95.6
Credit unions	−15.2	27.6	32.4	−11.6	−41.2	−7.2	−.8
Life insurance companies	9.6	9.2	38.0	48.0	−9.6	−8.0	−12.0
Government-sponsored enterprises	111.7	655.8	202.4	117.0	−254.5	−680.9	−590.3
Agency- and GSE-backed mortgage pools [1]	533.8	666.4	503.4	285.5	304.4	555.9	481.1
Asset-backed securities issuers	−255.1	−454.2	−384.7	−606.6	−617.4	−556.9	−573.6
Finance companies	129.7	.8	−169.9	−278.0	−168.3	−168.9	−142.5
REITs [2]	−69.8	−24.9	−30.5	−69.2	−34.3	−46.2	−20.1
Brokers and dealers	221.2	−136.7	762.9	−536.4	−159.9	−.5	7.6
Funding corporations	−111.4	−19.0	157.8	1,838.3	−419.1	−843.0	−433.9
ALL SECTORS, BY INSTRUMENT							
Total	2,958.1	2,108.6	3,315.3	2,135.7	−171.7	−428.3	−275.6
Open market paper	23.4	−268.2	−594.2	83.0	−662.5	−735.2	−241.2
Treasury securities	411.4	310.1	2,080.2	2,154.2	1,442.8	1,896.4	1,481.2
Agency- and GSE-backed securities [1]	646.7	1,322.5	704.1	403.5	46.7	−126.1	−105.5
Municipal securities	95.5	61.2	98.2	6.9	120.5	117.3	158.6
Corporate and foreign bonds	344.5	318.3	−709.7	−547.3	285.7	168.6	133.3
Bank loans n.e.c.	472.4	86.8	1,376.1	839.9	−856.6	−931.1	−801.7
Other loans and advances	298.1	53.5	472.2	−534.2	−400.5	−424.9	−271.3
Mortgages	551.1	118.9	−128.3	−193.9	−59.2	−272.5	−547.3
Consumer credit	115.0	105.4	16.6	−76.4	−88.7	−120.8	−81.6

Source: Board of Governors of the Federal Reserve System.

[Billions of dollars]

End of year or quarter	All proper-ties	Farm proper-ties	Nonfarm properties				Nonfarm properties by type of mortgage					
							Government underwritten				Conventional [2]	
			Total	1- to 4-family houses	Multi-family proper-ties	Com-mercial proper-ties	Total [1]	1- to 4-family houses			Total	1- to 4-family houses
								Total	FHA-insured	VA-guar-anteed		
1950	72.7	6.0	66.6	45.1	10.1	11.5	22.1	18.8	8.5	10.3	44.6	26.2
1951	82.1	6.6	75.6	51.6	11.5	12.5	26.6	22.9	9.7	13.2	49.0	28.8
1952	91.3	7.2	84.1	58.4	12.3	13.4	29.3	25.4	10.8	14.6	54.8	33.1
1953	101.1	7.7	93.4	65.9	12.9	14.5	32.1	28.1	12.0	16.1	61.3	37.9
1954	113.6	8.2	105.4	75.7	13.5	16.3	36.2	32.1	12.8	19.3	69.3	43.6
1955	129.9	9.0	120.9	88.2	14.3	18.3	42.9	38.9	14.3	24.6	78.0	49.3
1956	144.5	9.8	134.6	99.0	14.9	20.7	47.8	43.9	15.5	28.4	86.8	55.1
1957	156.5	10.4	146.1	107.6	15.3	23.2	51.6	47.2	16.5	30.7	94.6	60.4
1958	171.8	11.1	160.7	117.7	16.8	26.1	55.2	50.1	19.7	30.4	105.5	67.6
1959	191.6	12.1	179.5	131.6	18.7	29.2	59.3	53.8	23.8	30.0	120.2	77.7
1960	208.3	12.8	195.4	142.7	20.3	32.4	62.3	56.4	26.7	29.7	133.1	86.3
1961	229.1	13.9	215.1	155.8	23.0	36.4	65.6	59.1	29.5	29.6	149.5	96.7
1962	252.7	15.2	237.5	170.5	25.8	41.1	69.4	62.2	32.3	29.9	168.1	108.3
1963	280.0	16.8	263.1	187.9	29.0	46.2	73.4	65.9	35.0	30.9	189.7	122.0
1964	307.4	18.9	288.4	204.8	33.6	50.0	77.2	69.2	38.3	30.9	211.3	135.6
1965	334.7	21.2	313.5	221.9	37.2	54.5	81.2	73.1	42.0	31.1	232.4	148.8
1966	357.9	23.1	334.8	234.4	40.3	60.1	84.1	76.1	44.8	31.3	250.7	158.3
1967	382.5	25.0	357.4	248.7	43.9	64.8	88.2	79.9	47.4	32.5	269.3	168.8
1968	412.1	27.3	384.8	266.1	47.3	71.4	93.4	84.4	50.6	33.8	291.4	181.6
1969	442.5	29.2	413.3	283.9	52.3	77.1	100.2	90.2	54.5	35.7	313.1	193.7
1970	474.5	30.5	444.0	298.0	60.1	85.8	109.2	97.3	59.9	37.3	334.7	200.8
1971	525.0	32.4	492.7	326.4	70.1	96.2	120.7	105.2	65.7	39.5	371.9	221.2
1972	598.2	35.4	562.9	367.0	82.8	113.1	131.1	113.0	68.2	44.7	431.7	254.1
1973	673.9	39.8	634.1	408.7	93.2	132.3	135.0	116.2	66.2	50.0	499.1	292.4
1974	734.0	44.9	689.1	441.5	100.0	147.5	140.2	121.3	65.1	56.2	548.8	320.2
1975	793.9	49.9	744.0	483.2	100.7	160.1	147.0	127.7	66.1	61.6	597.0	355.5
1976	881.1	55.4	825.7	546.4	105.9	173.4	154.0	133.5	66.5	67.0	671.6	412.9
1977	1,013.0	63.8	949.2	642.5	114.3	192.3	161.7	141.6	68.0	73.6	787.4	500.9
1978	1,165.5	72.8	1,092.8	753.7	125.2	213.9	176.4	153.4	71.4	82.0	916.4	600.3
1979	1,331.5	86.8	1,244.7	870.8	135.0	238.8	199.0	172.9	81.0	92.0	1,045.7	697.9
1980	1,467.6	97.5	1,370.1	969.7	141.1	259.3	225.1	195.2	93.6	101.6	1,145.1	774.5
1981	1,591.5	107.2	1,484.3	1,046.5	139.2	298.6	238.9	207.6	101.3	106.2	1,245.4	838.9
1982	1,676.1	111.3	1,564.8	1,091.1	141.1	332.6	248.9	217.9	108.0	109.9	1,315.9	873.3
1983	1,871.7	113.7	1,757.9	1,214.9	154.3	388.6	279.8	248.8	127.4	121.4	1,478.1	966.1
1984	2,120.6	112.4	2,008.2	1,358.9	177.4	471.9	294.8	265.9	136.7	129.1	1,713.4	1,093.0
1985	2,370.3	94.1	2,276.2	1,528.8	205.9	541.5	328.3	288.8	153.0	135.8	1,947.8	1,240.0
1986	2,657.9	84.0	2,573.9	1,732.8	239.3	601.7	370.5	328.6	185.5	143.1	2,203.4	1,404.2
1987	2,996.2	75.8	2,920.4	1,960.9	262.1	697.4	431.4	387.9	235.5	152.4	2,489.0	1,573.0
1988	3,313.1	70.8	3,242.3	2,194.7	279.0	768.6	459.7	414.2	258.8	155.4	2,782.6	1,780.5
1989	3,585.4	68.8	3,516.6	2,428.1	289.9	798.6	486.8	440.1	282.8	157.3	3,029.8	1,988.0
1990	3,788.2	67.6	3,720.6	2,613.6	288.3	818.8	517.9	470.9	310.9	160.0	3,202.7	2,142.7
1991	3,929.8	67.5	3,862.4	2,771.9	284.9	805.6	537.2	493.3	330.6	162.7	3,325.2	2,278.6
1992	4,043.4	67.9	3,975.5	2,942.0	272.0	761.5	533.3	489.8	326.0	163.8	3,442.2	2,452.2
1993	4,174.8	68.4	4,106.4	3,100.9	269.1	736.4	513.4	469.5	303.2	166.2	3,592.9	2,631.4
1994	4,339.2	69.9	4,269.3	3,278.2	269.5	721.6	559.3	514.2	336.8	177.3	3,710.0	2,764.0
1995	4,524.9	71.7	4,453.2	3,445.4	275.4	732.4	584.3	537.1	352.3	184.7	3,869.0	2,908.3
1996	4,792.5	74.4	4,718.1	3,668.4	287.6	762.1	620.3	571.2	379.2	192.0	4,097.8	3,097.3
1997	5,104.5	78.5	5,026.0	3,902.5	299.4	824.1	656.7	605.7	405.7	200.0	4,369.4	3,296.8
1998	5,589.6	83.1	5,506.5	4,259.0	333.5	914.0	674.1	623.8	417.9	205.9	4,832.4	3,635.2
1999	6,195.4	87.2	6,108.2	4,683.0	374.3	1,051.0	731.5	678.8	462.3	216.5	5,376.8	4,004.2
2000	6,754.2	84.7	6,669.4	5,107.8	403.5	1,158.2	773.1	720.0	499.9	220.1	5,896.3	4,387.8
2001	7,461.8	88.5	7,373.2	5,659.7	445.5	1,268.0	772.7	718.5	497.4	221.2	6,600.6	4,941.2
2002	8,361.9	95.4	8,266.5	6,414.4	484.5	1,367.6	759.3	704.0	486.2	217.7	7,507.2	5,710.4
2003	9,365.5	83.2	9,282.3	7,223.6	564.3	1,494.4	709.2	653.3	438.7	214.6	8,573.1	6,570.3
2004	10,627.4	95.7	10,531.8	8,248.4	617.5	1,665.9	661.5	605.4	398.1	207.3	9,870.3	7,643.0
2005	12,065.1	104.8	11,960.3	9,357.0	688.2	1,915.1	606.6	550.4	348.4	202.0	11,353.7	8,806.6
2006	13,458.4	108.0	13,350.3	10,416.8	743.6	2,189.9	600.2	543.5	336.9	206.6	12,750.2	9,873.3
2007	14,529.0	112.7	14,416.4	11,112.5	844.3	2,459.6	609.2	552.6	342.6	210.0	13,807.2	10,559.9
2008	14,616.0	130.7	14,485.3	11,005.3	909.9	2,570.2	807.2	750.7	534.0	216.7	13,678.1	10,254.6
2008: I	14,661.5	117.2	14,544.4	11,180.3	863.1	2,501.0	640.7	583.8	372.3	211.5	13,903.7	10,596.5
II	14,699.8	121.6	14,578.2	11,160.3	880.5	2,537.4	683.9	627.2	412.2	215.0	13,894.3	10,533.0
III	14,684.8	126.1	14,558.7	11,107.8	900.4	2,550.4	742.7	686.1	474.4	211.7	13,815.9	10,421.6
IV	14,616.0	130.7	14,485.3	11,005.3	909.9	2,570.2	807.2	750.7	534.0	216.7	13,678.1	10,254.6
2009: I	14,598.1	131.2	14,466.9	10,990.8	912.6	2,563.6	863.6	806.7	577.8	228.9	13,603.4	10,184.1
II	14,537.4	131.7	14,405.7	10,942.7	912.9	2,550.0	921.5	863.1	628.0	235.2	13,484.2	10,079.6
III p	14,418.7	132.3	14,286.5	10,850.0	911.6	2,524.8	940.8	881.0	697.3	183.7	13,345.7	9,969.1

[1] Includes Federal Housing Administration (FHA)–insured multi-family properties, not shown separately.
[2] Derived figures. Total includes multi-family and commercial properties with conventional mortgages, not shown separately.

Source: Board of Governors of the Federal Reserve System, based on data from various Government and private organizations.

TABLE B–76. Mortgage debt outstanding by holder, 1950–2009

[Billions of dollars]

End of year or quarter	Total	Major financial institutions				Other holders	
		Total	Savings institutions [1]	Commercial banks [2]	Life insurance companies	Federal and related agencies [3]	Individuals and others [4]
1950	72.7	51.7	21.9	13.7	16.1	2.6	18.4
1951	82.1	59.5	25.5	14.7	19.3	3.3	19.3
1952	91.3	66.9	29.8	15.9	21.3	3.9	20.4
1953	101.1	75.0	34.8	16.9	23.3	4.4	21.7
1954	113.6	85.7	41.1	18.6	26.0	4.7	23.2
1955	129.9	99.3	48.9	21.0	29.4	5.3	25.3
1956	144.5	111.2	55.5	22.7	33.0	6.2	27.1
1957	156.5	119.7	61.2	23.3	35.2	7.7	29.1
1958	171.8	131.5	68.9	25.5	37.1	8.0	32.3
1959	191.6	145.5	78.1	28.1	39.2	10.2	35.9
1960	208.3	157.5	86.9	28.8	41.8	11.5	39.3
1961	229.1	172.6	98.0	30.4	44.2	12.2	44.2
1962	252.7	192.5	111.1	34.5	46.9	12.6	47.6
1963	280.0	217.1	127.2	39.4	50.5	11.8	51.0
1964	307.4	241.0	141.9	44.0	55.2	12.2	54.1
1965	334.7	264.6	154.9	49.7	60.0	13.5	56.6
1966	357.9	280.7	161.8	54.4	64.6	17.5	59.7
1967	382.5	298.7	172.3	58.9	67.5	20.9	62.8
1968	412.1	319.7	184.3	65.5	70.0	25.1	67.3
1969	442.5	338.9	196.4	70.5	72.0	31.1	72.4
1970	474.5	355.9	208.3	73.3	74.4	38.3	80.2
1971	525.0	394.2	236.2	82.5	75.5	46.3	84.5
1972	598.2	449.9	273.6	99.3	76.9	54.5	93.8
1973	673.9	505.4	305.0	119.1	81.4	64.7	103.9
1974	734.0	542.6	324.2	132.1	86.2	82.2	109.2
1975	793.9	581.2	355.8	136.2	89.2	101.1	111.5
1976	881.1	647.5	404.6	151.3	91.6	116.7	116.9
1977	1,013.0	745.2	469.4	179.0	96.8	140.5	127.3
1978	1,165.5	848.2	528.0	214.0	106.2	170.6	146.8
1979	1,331.5	938.2	574.6	245.2	118.4	216.0	177.3
1980	1,467.6	996.8	603.1	262.7	131.1	256.8	214.0
1981	1,591.5	1,040.5	618.5	284.2	137.7	289.4	261.6
1982	1,676.1	1,021.3	578.1	301.3	142.0	355.4	299.4
1983	1,871.7	1,108.1	626.6	330.5	151.0	433.3	330.2
1984	2,120.6	1,247.8	709.7	381.4	156.7	490.6	382.3
1985	2,370.3	1,363.5	760.5	431.2	171.8	580.9	425.8
1986	2,657.9	1,476.5	778.0	504.7	193.8	733.7	447.7
1987	2,996.2	1,667.6	860.5	594.8	212.4	857.9	470.7
1988	3,313.1	1,834.3	924.5	676.9	232.9	937.8	541.1
1989	3,585.4	1,935.2	910.3	770.7	254.2	1,067.3	582.9
1990	3,788.2	1,918.8	801.6	849.3	267.9	1,258.9	610.5
1991	3,929.8	1,846.2	705.4	881.3	259.5	1,422.5	661.2
1992	4,043.4	1,770.4	627.9	900.5	242.0	1,558.1	714.9
1993	4,174.8	1,770.1	598.4	947.8	223.9	1,682.8	721.8
1994	4,339.2	1,824.7	596.2	1,012.7	215.8	1,788.0	726.6
1995	4,524.9	1,900.1	596.8	1,090.2	213.1	1,878.7	746.2
1996	4,792.5	1,981.9	628.3	1,145.4	208.2	2,006.1	804.6
1997	5,104.5	2,084.0	631.8	1,245.3	206.8	2,111.4	909.1
1998	5,589.6	2,194.6	644.0	1,337.0	213.6	2,310.9	1,084.2
1999	6,195.4	2,394.3	668.1	1,495.4	230.8	2,613.3	1,187.9
2000	6,754.2	2,619.0	723.0	1,660.1	235.9	2,834.4	1,300.8
2001	7,461.8	2,790.9	758.0	1,789.8	243.0	3,205.0	1,465.9
2002	8,361.9	3,089.3	781.0	2,058.3	250.0	3,592.2	1,680.4
2003	9,365.5	3,387.3	870.6	2,255.8	260.9	4,026.8	1,951.4
2004	10,627.4	3,926.3	1,057.4	2,595.6	273.3	4,079.1	2,622.0
2005	12,065.1	4,396.2	1,152.7	2,958.0	285.5	4,208.5	3,460.4
2006	13,458.4	4,780.8	1,074.0	3,403.1	303.8	4,525.9	4,151.6
2007	14,529.0	5,065.8	1,095.3	3,644.4	326.2	5,190.2	4,273.0
2008	14,616.0	5,044.0	860.2	3,841.4	342.4	5,759.3	3,812.7
2008: I	14,661.5	5,127.2	1,111.8	3,684.5	330.9	5,344.5	4,189.8
II	14,699.8	5,112.7	1,115.6	3,660.7	336.4	5,518.2	4,068.9
III	14,684.8	5,077.9	883.6	3,853.4	340.9	5,651.1	3,955.9
IV	14,616.0	5,044.0	860.2	3,841.4	342.4	5,759.3	3,812.7
2009: I	14,598.1	5,041.7	849.8	3,853.3	338.6	5,858.8	3,697.6
II	14,537.4	4,988.1	755.5	3,897.6	335.0	5,981.5	3,567.8
III p	14,418.7	4,857.2	728.7	3,795.5	332.9	6,112.2	3,449.4

[1] Includes savings banks and savings and loan associations. Data reported by Federal Savings and Loan Insurance Corporation–insured institutions include loans in process for 1987 and exclude loans in process beginning with 1988.

[2] Includes loans held by nondeposit trust companies but not loans held by bank trust departments.

[3] Includes Government National Mortgage Association (GNMA or Ginnie Mae), Federal Housing Administration, Veterans Administration, Farmers Home Administration (FmHA), Federal Deposit Insurance Corporation, Resolution Trust Corporation (through 1995), and in earlier years Reconstruction Finance Corporation, Homeowners Loan Corporation, Federal Farm Mortgage Corporation, and Public Housing Administration. Also includes U.S.-sponsored agencies such as Federal National Mortgage Association (FNMA or Fannie Mae), Federal Land Banks, Federal Home Loan Mortgage Corporation (FHLMC or Freddie Mac), Federal Agricultural Mortgage Corporation (Farmer Mac, beginning 1994), Federal Home Loan Banks (beginning 1997), and mortgage pass-through securities issued or guaranteed by GNMA, FHLMC, FNMA, FmHA, or Farmer Mac. Other U.S. agencies (amounts small or current separate data not readily available) included with "individuals and others."

[4] Includes private mortgage pools.

Source: Board of Governors of the Federal Reserve System, based on data from various Government and private organizations.

TABLE B–77. Consumer credit outstanding, 1959–2009

[Amount outstanding (end of month); millions of dollars, seasonally adjusted]

Year and month	Total consumer credit [1]	Revolving	Nonrevolving [2]
December:			
1959	56,010.68		56,010.68
1960	60,025.31		60,025.31
1961	62,248.53		62,248.53
1962	68,126.72		68,126.72
1963	76,581.45		76,581.45
1964	85,959.57		85,959.57
1965	95,954.72		95,954.72
1966	101,788.22		101,788.22
1967	106,842.64		106,842.64
1968	117,399.09	2,041.54	115,357.55
1969	127,156.18	3,604.84	123,551.35
1970	131,551.55	4,961.46	126,590.09
1971	146,930.18	8,245.33	138,684.84
1972	166,189.10	9,379.24	156,809.86
1973	190,086.31	11,342.22	178,744.09
1974	198,917.84	13,241.26	185,676.58
1975	204,002.00	14,495.27	189,506.73
1976	225,721.59	16,489.05	209,232.54
1977	260,562.70	37,414.82	223,147.88
1978	306,100.39	45,690.95	260,409.43
1979	348,589.11	53,596.43	294,992.67
1980	351,920.05	54,970.05	296,950.00
1981	371,301.44	60,928.00	310,373.44
1982	389,848.74	66,348.30	323,500.44
1983	437,068.86	79,027.25	358,041.61
1984	517,278.98	100,385.63	416,893.35
1985	599,711.23	124,465.80	475,245.43
1986	654,750.24	141,068.15	513,682.08
1987	686,318.77	160,853.91	525,464.86
1988 [3]	731,917.76	184,593.12	547,324.64
1989	794,612.18	211,229.83	583,382.34
1990	808,230.57	238,642.62	569,587.95
1991	798,028.97	263,768.55	534,260.42
1992	806,118.69	278,449.67	527,669.02
1993	865,650.58	309,908.02	555,742.56
1994	997,301.74	365,569.56	631,732.19
1995	1,140,744.36	443,920.09	696,824.27
1996	1,253,437.09	507,516.57	745,920.52
1997	1,324,757.33	540,005.56	784,751.77
1998	1,420,996.44	581,414.78	839,581.66
1999	1,531,105.96	610,696.47	920,409.49
2000	1,716,507.37	683,457.38	1,033,049.99
2001	1,866,189.74	715,219.04	1,150,970.71
2002	1,970,765.38	750,909.70	1,219,855.68
2003	2,076,111.26	767,737.39	1,308,373.87
2004	2,191,505.71	799,175.76	1,392,329.96
2005	2,290,975.48	829,785.83	1,461,189.65
2006	2,384,812.00	871,313.07	1,513,498.93
2007	2,519,499.68	939,625.71	1,579,873.97
2008	2,559,121.52	957,341.01	1,601,780.51
2008: Jan	2,527,135.88	945,175.89	1,581,959.99
Feb	2,536,333.46	949,645.39	1,586,688.07
Mar	2,548,117.70	955,308.35	1,592,809.34
Apr	2,559,257.25	958,195.32	1,601,061.93
May	2,563,619.01	961,352.90	1,602,266.11
June	2,574,328.52	967,194.29	1,607,134.23
July	2,581,550.22	973,600.67	1,607,949.55
Aug	2,576,113.04	975,056.42	1,601,056.63
Sept	2,578,348.57	975,160.71	1,603,187.86
Oct	2,574,966.66	970,840.41	1,604,126.25
Nov	2,564,503.55	963,952.69	1,600,550.86
Dec	2,559,121.52	957,341.01	1,601,780.51
2009: Jan	2,564,375.71	955,399.91	1,608,975.80
Feb	2,551,383.40	942,695.36	1,608,688.04
Mar	2,536,960.22	934,256.97	1,602,703.25
Apr	2,522,327.21	925,910.25	1,596,416.96
May	2,515,268.82	916,563.24	1,598,705.58
June	2,506,772.12	911,692.68	1,595,079.45
July	2,498,526.68	911,018.08	1,587,508.60
Aug	2,495,162.27	902,981.36	1,592,180.91
Sept	2,486,293.30	895,048.05	1,591,245.25
Oct	2,482,101.94	887,661.34	1,594,440.60
Nov p	2,464,608.21	873,995.62	1,590,612.59

[1] Covers most short- and intermediate-term credit extended to individuals. Credit secured by real estate is excluded.

[2] Includes automobile loans and all other loans not included in revolving credit, such as loans for mobile homes, education, boats, trailers, or vacations. These loans may be secured or unsecured. Beginning with 1977, includes student loans extended by the Federal Government and by SLM Holding Corporation.

[3] Data newly available in January 1989 result in breaks in these series between December 1988 and subsequent months.

Source: Board of Governors of the Federal Reserve System.

GOVERNMENT FINANCE

TABLE B–78. Federal receipts, outlays, surplus or deficit, and debt, fiscal years, 1943–2011

[Billions of dollars; fiscal years]

Fiscal year or period	Total Receipts	Total Outlays	Total Surplus or deficit (−)	On-budget Receipts	On-budget Outlays	On-budget Surplus or deficit (−)	Off-budget Receipts	Off-budget Outlays	Off-budget Surplus or deficit (−)	Federal debt (end of period) Gross Federal	Federal debt (end of period) Held by the public	Addendum: Gross domestic product
1943	24.0	78.6	−54.6	22.9	78.5	−55.6	1.1	0.1	1.0	142.6	127.8	180.3
1944	43.7	91.3	−47.6	42.5	91.2	−48.7	1.3	.1	1.2	204.1	184.8	209.2
1945	45.2	92.7	−47.6	43.8	92.6	−48.7	1.3	.1	1.2	260.1	235.2	221.4
1946	39.3	55.2	−15.9	38.1	55.0	−17.0	1.2	.2	1.0	271.0	241.9	222.6
1947	38.5	34.5	4.0	37.1	34.2	2.9	1.5	.3	1.2	257.1	224.3	233.2
1948	41.6	29.8	11.8	39.9	29.4	10.5	1.6	.4	1.2	252.0	216.3	256.6
1949	39.4	38.8	.6	37.7	38.4	−.7	1.7	.4	1.3	252.6	214.3	271.3
1950	39.4	42.6	−3.1	37.3	42.0	−4.7	2.1	.5	1.6	256.9	219.0	273.1
1951	51.6	45.5	6.1	48.5	44.2	4.3	3.1	1.3	1.8	255.3	214.3	320.2
1952	66.2	67.7	−1.5	62.6	66.0	−3.4	3.6	1.7	1.9	259.1	214.8	348.7
1953	69.6	76.1	−6.5	65.5	73.8	−8.3	4.1	2.3	1.8	266.0	218.4	372.5
1954	69.7	70.9	−1.2	65.1	67.9	−2.8	4.6	2.9	1.7	270.8	224.5	377.0
1955	65.5	68.4	−3.0	60.4	64.5	−4.1	5.1	4.0	1.1	274.4	226.6	395.9
1956	74.6	70.6	3.9	68.2	65.7	2.5	6.4	5.0	1.5	272.7	222.2	427.0
1957	80.0	76.6	3.4	73.2	70.6	2.6	6.8	6.0	.8	272.3	219.3	450.9
1958	79.6	82.4	−2.8	71.6	74.9	−3.3	8.0	7.5	.5	279.7	226.3	460.0
1959	79.2	92.1	−12.8	71.0	83.1	−12.1	8.3	9.0	−.7	287.5	234.7	490.2
1960	92.5	92.2	.3	81.9	81.3	.5	10.6	10.9	−.2	290.5	236.8	518.9
1961	94.4	97.7	−3.3	82.3	86.0	−3.8	12.1	11.7	.4	292.6	238.4	529.9
1962	99.7	106.8	−7.1	87.4	93.3	−5.9	12.3	13.5	−1.3	302.9	248.0	567.8
1963	106.6	111.3	−4.8	92.4	96.4	−4.0	14.2	15.0	−.8	310.3	254.0	599.2
1964	112.6	118.5	−5.9	96.2	102.8	−6.5	16.4	15.7	.6	316.1	256.8	641.5
1965	116.8	118.2	−1.4	100.1	101.7	−1.6	16.7	16.5	.2	322.3	260.8	687.5
1966	130.8	134.5	−3.7	111.7	114.8	−3.1	19.1	19.7	−.6	328.5	263.7	755.8
1967	148.8	157.5	−8.6	124.4	137.0	−12.6	24.4	20.4	4.0	340.4	266.6	810.0
1968	153.0	178.1	−25.2	128.1	155.8	−27.7	24.9	22.3	2.6	368.7	289.5	868.4
1969	186.9	183.6	3.2	157.9	158.4	−.5	29.0	25.2	3.7	365.8	278.1	948.1
1970	192.8	195.6	−2.8	159.3	168.0	−8.7	33.5	27.6	5.9	380.9	283.2	1,012.7
1971	187.1	210.2	−23.0	151.3	177.3	−26.1	35.8	32.8	3.0	408.2	303.0	1,080.0
1972	207.3	230.7	−23.4	167.4	193.5	−26.1	39.9	37.2	2.7	435.9	322.4	1,176.5
1973	230.8	245.7	−14.9	184.7	200.0	−15.2	46.1	45.7	.3	466.3	340.9	1,310.6
1974	263.2	269.4	−6.1	209.3	216.5	−7.2	53.9	52.9	1.1	483.9	343.7	1,438.5
1975	279.1	332.3	−53.2	216.6	270.8	−54.1	62.5	61.6	.9	541.9	394.7	1,560.2
1976	298.1	371.8	−73.7	231.7	301.1	−69.4	66.4	70.7	−4.3	629.0	477.4	1,738.1
Transition quarter ..	81.2	96.0	−14.7	63.2	77.3	−14.1	18.0	18.7	−.7	643.6	495.5	459.4
1977	355.6	409.2	−53.7	278.7	328.7	−49.9	76.8	80.5	−3.7	706.4	549.1	1,973.5
1978	399.6	458.7	−59.2	314.2	369.6	−55.4	85.4	89.2	−3.8	776.6	607.1	2,217.5
1979	463.3	504.0	−40.7	365.3	404.9	−39.6	98.0	99.1	−1.1	829.5	640.3	2,501.4
1980	517.1	590.9	−73.8	403.9	477.0	−73.1	113.2	113.9	−.7	909.0	711.9	2,724.2
1981	599.3	678.2	−79.0	469.1	543.0	−73.9	130.2	135.3	−5.1	994.8	789.4	3,057.0
1982	617.8	745.7	−128.0	474.3	594.9	−120.6	143.5	150.9	−7.4	1,137.3	924.6	3,223.7
1983	600.6	808.4	−207.8	453.2	660.9	−207.7	147.3	147.4	−.1	1,371.7	1,137.3	3,440.7
1984	666.4	851.8	−185.4	500.4	685.6	−185.3	166.1	166.2	−.1	1,564.6	1,307.0	3,844.4
1985	734.0	946.3	−212.3	547.9	769.4	−221.5	186.2	176.9	9.2	1,817.4	1,507.3	4,146.3
1986	769.2	990.4	−221.2	568.9	806.8	−237.9	200.2	183.5	16.7	2,120.5	1,740.6	4,403.9
1987	854.3	1,004.0	−149.7	640.9	809.2	−168.4	213.4	194.8	18.6	2,346.0	1,889.8	4,651.4
1988	909.2	1,064.4	−155.2	667.7	860.0	−192.3	241.5	204.4	37.1	2,601.1	2,051.6	5,008.5
1989	991.1	1,143.7	−152.6	727.4	932.8	−205.4	263.7	210.9	52.8	2,867.8	2,190.7	5,399.5
1990	1,032.0	1,253.0	−221.0	750.3	1,027.9	−277.6	281.7	225.1	56.6	3,206.3	2,411.6	5,734.5
1991	1,055.0	1,324.2	−269.2	761.1	1,082.5	−321.4	293.9	241.7	52.2	3,598.2	2,689.0	5,930.5
1992	1,091.2	1,381.5	−290.3	788.8	1,129.2	−340.4	302.4	252.3	50.1	4,001.8	2,999.7	6,242.0
1993	1,154.3	1,409.4	−255.1	842.4	1,142.8	−300.4	311.9	266.6	45.3	4,351.0	3,248.4	6,587.3
1994	1,258.6	1,461.8	−203.2	923.6	1,182.4	−258.8	335.0	279.4	55.7	4,643.3	3,433.1	6,976.6
1995	1,351.8	1,515.8	−164.0	1,000.7	1,227.1	−226.4	351.1	288.7	62.4	4,920.6	3,604.4	7,341.1
1996	1,453.1	1,560.5	−107.4	1,085.6	1,259.6	−174.0	367.5	300.9	66.6	5,181.5	3,734.1	7,718.3
1997	1,579.2	1,601.1	−21.9	1,187.3	1,290.5	−103.2	392.0	310.6	81.4	5,369.2	3,772.3	8,211.7
1998	1,721.7	1,652.5	69.3	1,305.9	1,335.9	−29.9	415.8	316.6	99.2	5,478.2	3,721.1	8,663.0
1999	1,827.5	1,701.8	125.6	1,383.0	1,381.1	1.9	444.5	320.8	123.7	5,605.5	3,632.4	9,208.4
2000	2,025.2	1,789.0	236.2	1,544.6	1,458.2	86.4	480.6	330.8	149.8	5,628.7	3,409.8	9,821.0
2001	1,991.1	1,862.9	128.2	1,483.6	1,516.1	−32.4	507.5	346.8	160.7	5,769.9	3,319.6	10,225.3
2002	1,853.1	2,010.9	−157.8	1,337.8	1,655.2	−317.4	515.3	355.7	159.7	6,198.4	3,540.4	10,543.9
2003	1,782.3	2,159.9	−377.6	1,258.5	1,796.9	−538.4	523.8	363.0	160.8	6,760.0	3,913.4	10,979.8
2004	1,880.1	2,292.9	−412.7	1,345.4	1,913.3	−568.0	534.7	379.5	155.2	7,354.7	4,295.5	11,685.6
2005	2,153.6	2,472.0	−318.3	1,576.1	2,069.8	−493.6	577.5	402.2	175.3	7,905.3	4,592.2	12,445.7
2006	2,406.9	2,655.1	−248.2	1,798.5	2,233.0	−434.5	608.4	422.1	186.3	8,451.4	4,829.0	13,224.9
2007	2,568.0	2,728.7	−160.7	1,932.9	2,275.1	−342.2	635.1	453.6	181.5	8,950.7	5,035.1	13,896.0
2008	2,524.0	2,982.6	−458.6	1,866.0	2,507.8	−641.9	658.0	474.8	183.3	9,986.1	5,803.1	14,439.0
2009	2,105.0	3,517.7	−1,412.7	1,451.0	3,000.7	−1,549.7	654.0	517.0	137.0	11,875.9	7,544.7	14,237.2
2010 (estimates)	2,165.1	3,720.7	−1,555.6	1,529.9	3,163.7	−1,633.8	635.2	557.0	78.2	13,786.6	9,297.7	14,623.9
2011 (estimates)	2,567.2	3,833.9	−1,266.7	1,893.1	3,255.7	−1,362.6	674.1	578.2	95.9	15,144.0	10,498.3	15,299.0

Note: Fiscal years through 1976 were on a July 1–June 30 basis; beginning with October 1976 (fiscal year 1977), the fiscal year is on an October 1–September 30 basis. The transition quarter is the three-month period from July 1, 1976 through September 30, 1976.

See *Budget of the United States Government, Fiscal Year 2011*, for additional information.

Sources: Department of Commerce (Bureau of Economic Analysis), Department of the Treasury, and Office of Management and Budget.

TABLE B–79. Federal receipts, outlays, surplus or deficit, and debt, as percent of gross domestic product, fiscal years 1937–2011

[Percent; fiscal years]

Fiscal year or period	Receipts	Outlays		Surplus or deficit (−)	Federal debt (end of period)	
		Total	National defense		Gross Federal	Held by public
1937	6.1	8.6		−2.5		
1938	7.6	7.7		−.1		
1939	7.1	10.3		−3.2	54.0	46.5
1940	6.8	9.8	1.7	−3.0	52.4	44.2
1941	7.6	12.0	5.6	−4.3	50.4	42.3
1942	10.1	24.3	17.8	−14.2	54.9	47.0
1943	13.3	43.6	37.0	−30.3	79.1	70.9
1944	20.9	43.6	37.8	−22.7	97.6	88.3
1945	20.4	41.9	37.5	−21.5	117.5	106.2
1946	17.7	24.8	19.2	−7.2	121.7	108.7
1947	16.5	14.8	5.5	1.7	110.3	96.2
1948	16.2	11.6	3.5	4.6	98.2	84.3
1949	14.5	14.3	4.8	.2	93.1	79.0
1950	14.4	15.6	5.0	−1.1	94.1	80.2
1951	16.1	14.2	7.4	1.9	79.7	66.9
1952	19.0	19.4	13.2	−.4	74.3	61.6
1953	18.7	20.4	14.2	−1.7	71.4	58.6
1954	18.5	18.8	13.1	−.3	71.8	59.5
1955	16.5	17.3	10.8	−.8	69.3	57.2
1956	17.5	16.5	10.0	.9	63.9	52.0
1957	17.7	17.0	10.1	.8	60.4	48.6
1958	17.3	17.9	10.2	−.6	60.8	49.2
1959	16.2	18.8	10.0	−2.6	58.6	47.9
1960	17.8	17.8	9.3	.1	56.0	45.6
1961	17.8	18.4	9.4	−.6	55.2	45.0
1962	17.6	18.8	9.2	−1.3	53.4	43.7
1963	17.8	18.6	8.9	−.8	51.8	42.4
1964	17.6	18.5	8.5	−.9	49.3	40.0
1965	17.0	17.2	7.4	−.2	46.9	37.9
1966	17.3	17.8	7.7	−.5	43.5	34.9
1967	18.4	19.4	8.8	−1.1	42.0	32.9
1968	17.6	20.5	9.4	−2.9	42.5	33.3
1969	19.7	19.4	8.7	.3	38.6	29.3
1970	19.0	19.3	8.1	−.3	37.6	28.0
1971	17.3	19.5	7.3	−2.1	37.8	28.1
1972	17.6	19.6	6.7	−2.0	37.1	27.4
1973	17.6	18.7	5.9	−1.1	35.6	26.0
1974	18.3	18.7	5.5	−.4	33.6	23.9
1975	17.9	21.3	5.5	−3.4	34.7	25.3
1976	17.1	21.4	5.2	−4.2	36.2	27.5
Transition quarter	17.7	20.9	4.8	−3.2	35.0	27.0
1977	18.0	20.7	4.9	−2.7	35.8	27.8
1978	18.0	20.7	4.7	−2.7	35.0	27.4
1979	18.5	20.1	4.7	−1.6	33.2	25.6
1980	19.0	21.7	4.9	−2.7	33.4	26.1
1981	19.6	22.2	5.2	−2.6	32.5	25.8
1982	19.2	23.1	5.7	−4.0	35.3	28.7
1983	17.5	23.5	6.1	−6.0	39.9	33.1
1984	17.3	22.2	5.9	−4.8	40.7	34.0
1985	17.7	22.8	6.1	−5.1	43.8	36.4
1986	17.5	22.5	6.2	−5.0	48.2	39.5
1987	18.4	21.6	6.1	−3.2	50.4	40.6
1988	18.2	21.3	5.8	−3.1	51.9	41.0
1989	18.4	21.2	5.6	−2.8	53.1	40.6
1990	18.0	21.9	5.2	−3.9	55.9	42.1
1991	17.8	22.3	4.6	−4.5	60.7	45.3
1992	17.5	22.1	4.8	−4.7	64.1	48.1
1993	17.5	21.4	4.4	−3.9	66.1	49.3
1994	18.0	21.0	4.0	−2.9	66.6	49.2
1995	18.4	20.6	3.7	−2.2	67.0	49.1
1996	18.8	20.2	3.4	−1.4	67.1	48.4
1997	19.2	19.5	3.3	−.3	65.4	45.9
1998	19.9	19.1	3.1	.8	63.2	43.0
1999	19.8	18.5	3.0	1.4	60.9	39.4
2000	20.6	18.2	3.0	2.4	57.3	34.7
2001	19.5	18.2	3.0	1.3	56.4	32.5
2002	17.6	19.1	3.3	−1.5	58.8	33.6
2003	16.2	19.7	3.7	−3.4	61.6	35.6
2004	16.1	19.6	3.9	−3.5	62.9	36.8
2005	17.3	19.9	4.0	−2.6	63.5	36.9
2006	18.2	20.1	3.9	−1.9	63.9	36.5
2007	18.5	19.6	4.0	−1.2	64.4	36.2
2008	17.5	20.7	4.3	−3.2	69.2	40.2
2009	14.8	24.7	4.6	−9.9	83.4	53.0
2010 (estimates)	14.8	25.4	4.9	−10.6	94.3	63.6
2011 (estimates)	16.8	25.1	4.9	−8.3	99.0	68.6

Note: See Note, Table B–78.

Sources: Department of the Treasury and Office of Management and Budget.

TABLE B–80. Federal receipts and outlays, by major category, and surplus or deficit, fiscal years 1943–2011

[Billions of dollars; fiscal years]

Fiscal year or period	Receipts (on-budget and off-budget)					Outlays (on-budget and off-budget)										Surplus or deficit (−) (on-budget and off-budget)
	Total	Individual income taxes	Corporation income taxes	Social insurance and retirement receipts	Other	Total	National defense		International affairs	Health	Medicare	Income security	Social security	Net interest	Other	
							Total	Department of Defense, military								
1943	24.0	6.5	9.6	3.0	4.9	78.6	66.7	....	1.3	0.1	....	1.7	0.2	1.5	7.0	−54.6
1944	43.7	19.7	14.8	3.5	5.7	91.3	79.1	....	1.4	.2	....	1.5	.2	2.2	6.6	−47.6
1945	45.2	18.4	16.0	3.5	7.3	92.7	83.0	....	1.9	.2	....	1.1	.3	3.1	3.1	−47.6
1946	39.3	16.1	11.9	3.1	8.2	55.2	42.7	....	1.9	.2	....	2.4	.4	4.1	3.6	−15.9
1947	38.5	17.9	8.6	3.4	8.5	34.5	12.8	....	5.8	.2	....	2.8	.5	4.2	8.2	4.0
1948	41.6	19.3	9.7	3.8	8.8	29.8	9.1	....	4.6	.2	....	2.5	.6	4.3	8.5	11.8
1949	39.4	15.6	11.2	3.8	8.9	38.8	13.2	....	6.1	.2	....	3.2	.7	4.5	11.1	.6
1950	39.4	15.8	10.4	4.3	8.9	42.6	13.7	....	4.7	.3	....	4.1	.8	4.8	14.2	−3.1
1951	51.6	21.6	14.1	5.7	10.2	45.5	23.6	....	3.6	.3	....	3.4	1.6	4.7	8.4	6.1
1952	66.2	27.9	21.2	6.4	10.6	67.7	46.1	....	2.7	.3	....	3.7	2.1	4.7	8.1	−1.5
1953	69.6	29.8	21.2	6.8	11.7	76.1	52.8	....	2.1	.3	....	3.8	2.7	5.2	9.1	−6.5
1954	69.7	29.5	21.1	7.2	11.9	70.9	49.3	....	1.6	.3	....	4.4	3.4	4.8	7.1	−1.2
1955	65.5	28.7	17.9	7.9	11.0	68.4	42.7	....	2.2	.3	....	5.1	4.4	4.9	8.9	−3.0
1956	74.6	32.2	20.9	9.3	12.2	70.6	42.5	....	2.4	.4	....	4.7	5.5	5.1	10.1	3.9
1957	80.0	35.6	21.2	10.0	13.2	76.6	45.4	....	3.1	.5	....	5.4	6.7	5.4	10.1	3.4
1958	79.6	34.7	20.1	11.2	13.6	82.4	46.8	....	3.4	.5	....	7.5	8.2	5.6	10.3	−2.8
1959	79.2	36.7	17.3	11.7	13.5	92.1	49.0	....	3.1	.7	....	8.2	9.7	5.8	15.5	−12.8
1960	92.5	40.7	21.5	14.7	15.6	92.2	48.1	....	3.0	.8	....	7.4	11.6	6.9	14.4	.3
1961	94.4	41.3	21.0	16.4	15.7	97.7	49.6	....	3.2	.9	....	9.7	12.5	6.7	15.2	−3.3
1962	99.7	45.6	20.5	17.0	16.5	106.8	52.3	50.1	5.6	1.2	....	9.2	14.4	6.9	17.2	−7.1
1963	106.6	47.6	21.6	19.8	17.6	111.3	53.4	51.1	5.3	1.5	....	9.3	15.8	7.7	18.3	−4.8
1964	112.6	48.7	23.5	22.0	18.5	118.5	54.8	52.6	4.9	1.8	....	9.7	16.6	8.2	22.6	−5.9
1965	116.8	48.8	25.5	22.2	20.3	118.2	50.6	48.8	5.3	1.8	....	9.5	17.5	8.6	25.0	−1.4
1966	130.8	55.4	30.1	25.5	19.8	134.5	58.1	56.6	5.6	2.5	0.1	9.7	20.7	9.4	28.5	−3.7
1967	148.8	61.5	34.0	32.6	20.7	157.5	71.4	70.1	5.6	3.4	2.7	10.3	21.7	10.3	32.1	−8.6
1968	153.0	68.7	28.7	33.9	21.7	178.1	81.9	80.4	5.3	4.4	4.6	11.8	23.9	11.1	35.1	−25.2
1969	186.9	87.2	36.7	39.0	23.9	183.6	82.5	80.8	4.6	5.2	5.7	13.1	27.3	12.7	32.6	3.2
1970	192.8	90.4	32.8	44.4	25.2	195.6	81.7	80.1	4.3	5.9	6.2	15.7	30.3	14.4	37.2	−2.8
1971	187.1	86.2	26.8	47.3	26.8	210.2	78.9	77.5	4.2	6.8	6.6	22.9	35.9	14.8	40.0	−23.0
1972	207.3	94.7	32.2	52.6	27.8	230.7	79.2	77.6	4.8	8.7	7.5	27.7	40.2	15.5	47.3	−23.4
1973	230.8	103.2	36.2	63.1	28.3	245.7	76.7	75.0	4.1	9.4	8.1	28.3	49.1	17.3	52.8	−14.9
1974	263.2	119.0	38.6	75.1	30.6	269.4	79.3	77.9	5.7	10.7	9.6	33.7	55.9	21.4	52.9	−6.1
1975	279.1	122.4	40.6	84.5	31.5	332.3	86.5	84.9	7.1	12.9	12.9	50.2	64.7	23.2	74.8	−53.2
1976	298.1	131.6	41.4	90.8	34.3	371.8	89.6	87.9	6.4	15.7	15.8	60.8	73.9	26.7	82.7	−73.7
Transition quarter ..	81.2	38.8	8.5	25.2	8.8	96.0	22.3	21.8	2.5	3.9	4.3	15.0	19.8	6.9	21.4	−14.7
1977	355.6	157.6	54.9	106.5	36.6	409.2	97.2	95.1	6.4	17.3	19.3	61.1	85.1	29.9	93.0	−53.7
1978	399.6	181.0	60.0	121.0	37.7	458.7	104.5	102.3	7.5	18.5	22.8	61.5	93.9	35.5	114.7	−59.2
1979	463.3	217.8	65.7	138.9	40.8	504.0	116.3	113.6	7.5	20.5	26.5	66.4	104.1	42.6	120.2	−40.7
1980	517.1	244.1	64.6	157.8	50.6	590.9	134.0	130.9	12.7	23.2	32.1	86.6	118.5	52.5	131.3	−73.8
1981	599.3	285.9	61.1	182.7	69.5	678.2	157.5	153.9	13.1	26.9	39.1	100.3	139.6	68.8	133.0	−79.0
1982	617.8	297.7	49.2	201.5	69.3	745.7	185.3	180.7	12.3	27.4	46.6	108.2	156.0	85.0	125.0	−128.0
1983	600.6	288.9	37.0	209.0	65.6	808.4	209.9	204.4	11.8	28.6	52.6	123.0	170.7	89.8	121.8	−207.8
1984	666.4	298.4	56.9	239.4	71.8	851.8	227.4	220.9	15.9	30.4	57.5	113.4	178.2	111.1	117.9	−185.4
1985	734.0	334.5	61.3	265.2	73.0	946.3	252.7	245.1	16.2	33.5	65.8	129.0	188.6	129.5	131.0	−212.3
1986	769.2	349.0	63.1	283.9	73.2	990.4	273.4	265.4	14.1	35.9	70.2	120.6	198.8	136.0	141.4	−221.2
1987	854.3	392.6	83.9	303.3	74.5	1,004.0	282.0	273.9	11.6	40.0	75.1	124.1	207.4	138.6	125.2	−149.7
1988	909.2	401.2	94.5	334.3	79.2	1,064.4	290.4	281.9	10.5	44.5	78.9	130.4	219.3	151.8	138.7	−155.2
1989	991.1	445.7	103.3	359.4	82.7	1,143.7	303.6	294.8	9.6	48.4	85.0	137.4	232.5	169.0	158.3	−152.6
1990	1,032.0	466.9	93.5	380.0	91.5	1,253.0	299.3	289.7	13.8	57.7	98.1	148.7	248.6	184.3	202.5	−221.0
1991	1,055.0	467.8	98.1	396.0	93.1	1,324.2	273.3	262.3	15.8	71.2	104.5	172.5	269.0	194.4	223.5	−269.2
1992	1,091.2	476.0	100.3	413.7	101.3	1,381.5	298.3	286.8	16.1	89.5	119.0	199.6	287.6	199.3	172.1	−290.3
1993	1,154.3	509.7	117.5	428.3	98.8	1,409.4	291.1	278.5	17.2	99.4	130.6	210.0	304.6	198.7	157.9	−255.1
1994	1,258.6	543.1	140.4	461.5	113.7	1,461.8	281.6	268.6	17.1	107.1	144.7	217.2	319.6	202.9	171.5	−203.2
1995	1,351.8	590.2	157.0	484.5	120.1	1,515.8	272.1	259.4	16.4	115.4	159.9	223.8	335.8	232.1	160.2	−164.0
1996	1,453.1	656.4	171.8	509.4	115.4	1,560.5	265.7	253.1	13.5	119.4	174.2	229.7	349.7	241.1	167.2	−107.4
1997	1,579.2	737.5	182.3	539.4	120.1	1,601.1	270.5	258.3	15.2	123.8	190.0	235.0	365.3	244.0	157.3	−21.9
1998	1,721.7	828.6	188.7	571.8	132.6	1,652.5	268.2	255.8	13.1	131.4	192.8	237.8	379.2	241.1	188.9	69.3
1999	1,827.5	879.5	184.7	611.8	151.5	1,701.8	274.8	261.2	15.2	141.0	190.4	242.5	390.0	229.8	218.1	125.6
2000	2,025.2	1,004.5	207.3	652.9	160.6	1,789.0	294.4	281.0	17.2	154.5	197.1	253.7	409.4	222.9	239.7	236.2
2001	1,991.1	994.3	151.1	694.0	151.8	1,862.9	304.7	290.2	16.5	172.2	217.4	269.8	433.0	206.2	243.2	128.2
2002	1,853.1	858.3	148.0	700.8	146.0	2,010.9	348.5	331.8	22.3	196.5	230.9	312.7	456.0	170.9	273.1	−157.8
2003	1,782.3	793.7	131.8	713.0	143.9	2,159.9	404.7	387.1	21.2	219.5	249.4	334.6	474.7	153.1	302.6	−377.6
2004	1,880.1	809.0	189.4	733.4	148.4	2,292.9	455.8	436.4	26.9	240.1	269.4	333.1	495.5	160.2	311.8	−412.7
2005	2,153.6	927.2	278.3	794.1	154.0	2,472.0	495.3	474.1	34.6	250.5	298.6	345.8	523.3	184.0	339.8	−318.3
2006	2,406.9	1,043.9	353.9	837.8	171.2	2,655.1	521.8	499.3	29.5	252.7	329.9	352.5	548.5	226.6	393.5	−248.2
2007	2,568.0	1,163.5	370.2	869.6	164.7	2,728.7	551.3	528.5	28.5	266.4	375.4	366.0	586.2	237.1	317.9	−160.7
2008	2,524.0	1,145.7	304.3	900.2	173.8	2,982.6	616.1	594.6	28.9	280.6	390.8	431.3	617.0	252.8	365.2	−458.6
2009	2,105.0	915.3	138.2	890.9	160.5	3,517.7	661.0	636.7	37.5	334.3	430.1	533.2	683.0	186.9	651.6	−1,412.7
2010 (estimates)	2,165.1	935.8	156.7	875.8	196.9	3,720.7	719.2	692.0	51.1	372.3	457.2	685.9	721.5	187.8	525.8	−1,555.6
2011 (estimates)	2,567.2	1,121.3	296.9	935.1	213.9	3,833.9	749.7	721.3	54.2	400.7	497.3	595.0	736.3	250.7	549.9	−1,266.7

Note: See Note, Table B–78.

Sources: Department of the Treasury and Office of Management and Budget.

Table B–81. Federal receipts, outlays, surplus or deficit, and debt, fiscal years 2006–2011

[Millions of dollars; fiscal years]

Description	Actual				Estimates	
	2006	2007	2008	2009	2010	2011
RECEIPTS, OUTLAYS, AND SURPLUS OR DEFICIT						
Total:						
Receipts	2,406,876	2,568,001	2,523,999	2,104,995	2,165,119	2,567,181
Outlays	2,655,057	2,728,702	2,982,554	3,517,681	3,720,701	3,833,861
Surplus or deficit (–)	–248,181	–160,701	–458,555	–1,412,686	–1,555,582	–1,266,680
On-budget:						
Receipts	1,798,494	1,932,912	1,865,953	1,450,986	1,529,936	1,893,113
Outlays	2,232,988	2,275,065	2,507,803	3,000,665	3,163,742	3,255,668
Surplus or deficit (–)	–434,494	–342,153	–641,850	–1,549,679	–1,633,806	–1,362,555
Off-budget:						
Receipts	608,382	635,089	658,046	654,009	635,183	674,068
Outlays	422,069	453,637	474,751	517,016	556,959	578,193
Surplus or deficit (–)	186,313	181,452	183,295	136,993	78,224	95,875
OUTSTANDING DEBT, END OF PERIOD						
Gross Federal debt	8,451,350	8,950,744	9,986,082	11,875,851	13,786,615	15,144,029
Held by Federal Government accounts	3,622,378	3,915,615	4,183,032	4,331,144	4,488,962	4,645,704
Held by the public	4,828,972	5,035,129	5,803,050	7,544,707	9,297,653	10,498,325
Federal Reserve System	768,924	779,632	491,127	769,160		
Other	4,060,048	4,255,497	5,311,923	6,775,547		
RECEIPTS BY SOURCE						
Total: On-budget and off-budget	2,406,876	2,568,001	2,523,999	2,104,995	2,165,119	2,567,181
Individual income taxes	1,043,908	1,163,472	1,145,747	915,308	935,771	1,121,296
Corporation income taxes	353,915	370,243	304,346	138,229	156,741	296,902
Social insurance and retirement receipts	837,821	869,607	900,155	890,917	875,756	935,116
On-budget	229,439	234,518	242,109	236,908	240,573	261,048
Off-budget	608,382	635,089	658,046	654,009	635,183	674,068
Excise taxes	73,961	65,069	67,334	62,483	73,204	74,288
Estate and gift taxes	27,877	26,044	28,844	23,482	17,011	25,035
Customs duties and fees	24,810	26,010	27,568	22,453	23,787	27,445
Miscellaneous receipts	44,584	47,556	50,005	52,123	82,849	87,099
Deposits of earnings by Federal Reserve System	29,945	32,043	33,598	34,318	77,083	79,341
Allowances [1]					–12,000	–9,000
All other	14,639	15,513	16,407	17,805	17,766	16,758
OUTLAYS BY FUNCTION						
Total: On-budget and off-budget	2,655,057	2,728,702	2,982,554	3,517,681	3,720,701	3,833,861
National defense	521,827	551,271	616,073	661,049	719,179	749,748
International affairs	29,499	28,482	28,857	37,529	51,138	54,192
General science, space and technology	23,584	25,525	27,731	29,449	33,032	31,554
Energy	782	–860	628	4,749	18,952	24,863
Natural resources and environment	33,028	31,732	31,825	35,574	47,039	42,537
Agriculture	25,969	17,662	18,387	22,237	26,610	25,590
Commerce and housing credit	6,187	487	27,870	291,535	–25,319	22,127
On-budget	7,262	–4,606	25,453	291,231	–31,745	17,901
Off-budget	–1,075	5,093	2,417	304	6,426	4,226
Transportation	70,244	72,905	77,616	84,289	106,458	104,189
Community and regional development	54,465	29,567	23,952	27,650	28,469	31,973
Education, training, employment, and social services	118,482	91,656	91,287	79,746	142,521	126,399
Health	252,739	266,382	280,599	334,327	372,336	400,661
Medicare	329,868	375,407	390,758	430,093	457,159	497,341
Income security	352,477	365,975	431,313	533,224	685,870	595,005
Social security	548,549	586,153	617,027	682,963	721,496	736,284
On-budget	16,058	19,307	17,830	34,071	37,629	27,664
Off-budget	532,491	566,846	599,197	648,892	683,867	708,620
Veterans benefits and services	69,811	72,818	84,653	95,429	124,655	124,539
Administration of justice	41,016	41,244	47,138	51,549	55,025	57,280
General government	18,177	17,425	20,325	22,026	29,290	27,670
Net interest	226,603	237,109	252,757	186,902	187,772	250,709
On-budget	324,325	343,112	366,475	304,856	306,176	369,789
Off-budget	–97,722	–106,003	–113,718	–117,954	–118,404	–119,080
Allowances					18,750	21,676
Undistributed offsetting receipts	–68,250	–82,238	–86,242	–92,639	–79,731	–90,476
On-budget	–56,625	–69,939	–73,097	–78,413	–64,801	–74,903
Off-budget	–11,625	–12,299	–13,145	–14,226	–14,930	–15,573

[1] Includes Allowances for Health Reform and the Jobs Bill.

Note: See Note, Table B–78.

Sources: Department of the Treasury and Office of Management and Budget.

Table B–82. Federal and State and local government current receipts and expenditures, national income and product accounts (NIPA), 1960–2009

[Billions of dollars; quarterly data at seasonally adjusted annual rates]

Year or quarter	Total government			Federal Government			State and local government			Addendum: Grants-in-aid to State and local governments
	Current receipts	Current expenditures	Net government saving (NIPA)	Current receipts	Current expenditures	Net Federal Government saving (NIPA)	Current receipts	Current expenditures	Net State and local government saving (NIPA)	
1960	134.4	123.0	11.4	93.9	86.8	7.1	44.5	40.2	4.3	4.0
1961	139.0	132.2	6.8	95.5	92.9	2.6	48.1	43.8	4.3	4.5
1962	150.6	142.9	7.7	103.6	101.2	2.4	52.0	46.8	5.2	5.0
1963	162.2	151.2	11.0	111.8	106.5	5.3	56.0	50.3	5.7	5.6
1964	166.6	159.3	7.3	111.8	110.9	.9	61.3	54.9	6.4	6.5
1965	180.3	170.6	9.8	121.0	117.7	3.2	66.5	60.0	6.5	7.2
1966	202.8	192.8	10.0	138.0	135.7	2.3	74.9	67.2	7.8	10.1
1967	217.7	220.0	–2.3	146.9	156.2	–9.3	82.5	75.5	7.0	11.7
1968	252.1	247.0	5.1	171.3	173.7	–2.4	93.5	86.0	7.5	12.7
1969	283.5	267.0	16.5	192.7	184.1	8.6	105.5	97.5	8.0	14.6
1970	286.9	295.2	–8.4	186.1	201.6	–15.5	120.1	113.0	7.1	19.3
1971	303.6	325.8	–22.2	191.9	220.6	–28.7	134.9	128.5	6.5	23.2
1972	347.0	356.3	–9.3	220.3	245.2	–24.9	158.4	142.8	15.6	31.7
1973	390.4	386.5	3.9	250.8	262.6	–11.8	174.3	158.6	15.7	34.8
1974	431.8	436.9	–5.2	280.0	294.5	–14.5	188.1	178.7	9.3	36.3
1975	442.1	510.2	–68.2	277.6	348.3	–70.6	209.6	207.1	2.5	45.1
1976	505.9	552.2	–46.3	323.0	376.7	–53.7	233.7	226.3	7.4	50.7
1977	567.3	600.3	–33.0	364.0	410.1	–46.1	259.9	246.8	13.1	56.6
1978	646.1	656.3	–10.2	424.0	452.9	–28.9	287.6	268.9	18.7	65.5
1979	728.9	729.9	–1.0	486.9	500.9	–14.0	308.4	295.4	13.0	66.3
1980	798.7	846.5	–47.8	532.8	589.5	–56.6	338.2	329.4	8.8	72.3
1981	917.7	966.9	–49.2	619.9	676.7	–56.8	370.2	362.7	7.6	72.5
1982	939.3	1,076.8	–137.5	617.4	752.6	–135.3	391.4	393.6	–2.2	69.5
1983	1,000.3	1,171.7	–171.4	643.3	819.5	–176.2	428.6	423.7	4.9	71.6
1984	1,113.5	1,261.0	–147.5	710.0	881.5	–171.5	480.2	456.2	23.9	76.7
1985	1,214.6	1,370.9	–156.3	774.4	953.0	–178.6	521.1	498.7	22.4	80.9
1986	1,290.1	1,464.0	–173.9	816.0	1,010.7	–194.6	561.6	540.9	20.7	87.6
1987	1,403.2	1,540.5	–137.4	896.5	1,045.9	–149.3	590.6	578.6	12.0	83.9
1988	1,502.4	1,623.6	–121.2	958.5	1,096.9	–138.4	635.5	618.3	17.2	91.6
1989	1,627.2	1,741.0	–113.8	1,038.0	1,172.0	–133.9	687.5	667.4	20.1	98.3
1990	1,709.3	1,879.5	–170.3	1,082.8	1,259.2	–176.4	738.0	731.8	6.2	111.4
1991	1,759.7	1,984.0	–224.2	1,101.9	1,320.3	–218.4	789.4	795.2	–5.8	131.6
1992	1,845.1	2,149.0	–303.9	1,148.0	1,450.5	–302.5	846.2	847.6	–1.4	149.1
1993	1,948.2	2,229.4	–281.2	1,224.1	1,504.3	–280.2	888.2	889.1	–.9	164.0
1994	2,091.9	2,304.0	–212.2	1,322.1	1,542.5	–220.4	944.8	936.6	8.2	175.1
1995	2,215.5	2,412.5	–197.0	1,407.8	1,614.0	–206.2	991.9	982.7	9.2	184.2
1996	2,380.4	2,505.7	–125.3	1,526.4	1,674.7	–148.2	1,045.1	1,022.1	23.0	191.1
1997	2,557.2	2,581.1	–23.8	1,656.2	1,716.3	–60.1	1,099.5	1,063.2	36.3	198.4
1998	2,729.8	2,649.3	80.5	1,777.9	1,744.3	33.6	1,164.5	1,117.6	46.9	212.6
1999	2,902.5	2,761.9	140.6	1,895.0	1,796.2	98.8	1,240.4	1,198.6	41.8	232.9
2000	3,132.4	2,906.0	226.5	2,057.1	1,871.9	185.2	1,322.6	1,281.3	41.3	247.3
2001	3,118.2	3,093.6	24.6	2,020.3	1,979.8	40.5	1,374.0	1,389.9	–15.9	276.1
2002	2,967.9	3,274.7	–306.9	1,859.3	2,112.1	–252.8	1,412.7	1,466.8	–54.1	304.2
2003	3,043.4	3,458.6	–415.2	1,885.1	2,261.5	–376.4	1,496.3	1,535.1	–38.8	338.0
2004	3,265.7	3,653.5	–387.8	2,013.9	2,393.4	–379.5	1,601.0	1,609.3	–8.4	349.2
2005	3,659.3	3,916.4	–257.1	2,290.1	2,573.1	–283.0	1,730.4	1,704.5	25.9	361.2
2006	3,995.2	4,147.9	–152.7	2,524.5	2,728.3	–203.8	1,829.7	1,778.6	51.0	359.0
2007	4,209.2	4,424.0	–214.8	2,660.8	2,897.2	–236.5	1,927.3	1,905.6	21.7	378.9
2008	4,057.6	4,740.3	–682.7	2,475.0	3,117.6	–642.6	1,974.2	2,014.4	–40.2	391.7
2009 ᵖ	....	4,993.0	....	....	3,454.5	....	....	2,015.1	....	476.6
2006: I	3,919.8	4,064.5	–144.7	2,473.8	2,681.1	–207.3	1,800.6	1,738.0	62.6	354.6
II	3,971.1	4,137.3	–166.2	2,501.8	2,731.2	–229.4	1,830.3	1,767.0	63.2	361.0
III	4,024.8	4,197.8	–173.1	2,547.4	2,762.9	–215.5	1,842.5	1,800.1	42.4	365.1
IV	4,064.9	4,192.0	–127.0	2,575.1	2,738.1	–163.0	1,845.3	1,809.4	35.9	355.5
2007: I	4,167.4	4,335.5	–168.1	2,640.1	2,841.0	–200.9	1,902.3	1,869.5	32.8	375.0
II	4,202.8	4,389.1	–186.3	2,660.1	2,881.3	–221.3	1,923.4	1,888.4	34.9	380.7
III	4,212.3	4,450.7	–238.4	2,659.9	2,918.7	–258.8	1,932.1	1,911.7	20.3	379.7
IV	4,254.2	4,520.5	–266.3	2,682.9	2,947.9	–265.0	1,951.6	1,952.9	–1.3	380.3
2008: I	4,172.0	4,625.5	–453.5	2,590.7	3,024.2	–433.5	1,963.7	1,983.8	–20.1	382.5
II	3,974.5	4,797.0	–822.5	2,372.1	3,169.0	–796.9	1,994.2	2,019.8	–25.5	391.8
III	4,087.0	4,811.7	–724.8	2,489.5	3,155.2	–665.7	1,987.5	2,046.5	–59.0	390.0
IV	3,996.8	4,726.9	–730.2	2,447.8	3,121.9	–674.1	1,954.4	2,007.5	–56.1	402.4
2009: I	3,775.0	4,780.6	–1,005.7	2,251.3	3,220.3	–969.1	1,961.4	1,998.0	–36.6	437.7
II	3,728.4	5,021.9	–1,293.5	2,237.0	3,505.9	–1,268.9	1,989.3	2,013.9	–24.6	497.9
III	3,735.0	5,077.0	–1,342.0	2,215.1	3,542.1	–1,327.0	2,003.6	2,018.6	–14.9	483.7
IV ᵖ	....	5,092.3	....	....	3,549.7	....	....	2,029.8	....	487.2

Note: Federal grants-in-aid to State and local governments are reflected in Federal current expenditures and State and local current receipts. Total government current receipts and expenditures have been adjusted to eliminate this duplication.

Source: Department of Commerce (Bureau of Economic Analysis).

TABLE B–83. Federal and State and local government current receipts and expenditures, national income and product accounts (NIPA), by major type, 1960–2009

[Billions of dollars; quarterly data at seasonally adjusted annual rates]

Year or quarter	Current receipts									Current expenditures					Net government saving
	Total	Current tax receipts				Contributions for government social insurance	Income receipts on assets	Current transfer receipts	Current surplus of government enterprises	Total 2	Consumption expenditures	Current transfer payments	Interest payments	Subsidies	
		Total 1	Personal current taxes	Taxes on production and imports	Taxes on corporate income										
1960	134.4	113.4	46.1	44.5	22.7	16.5	2.7	0.9	0.9	123.0	83.3	28.1	10.4	1.1	11.4
1961	139.0	117.1	47.3	47.0	22.8	17.1	2.9	1.1	.8	132.2	88.2	31.9	10.2	2.0	6.8
1962	150.6	126.1	51.6	50.4	24.0	19.2	3.2	1.2	.9	142.9	96.8	32.8	11.1	2.3	7.7
1963	162.2	134.4	54.6	53.4	26.2	21.7	3.4	1.3	1.4	151.2	102.7	34.3	12.0	2.2	11.0
1964	166.6	137.5	52.1	57.3	28.0	22.5	3.7	1.6	1.3	159.3	108.6	35.1	12.9	2.7	7.3
1965	180.3	149.5	57.7	60.7	30.9	23.5	4.1	1.9	1.3	170.6	115.9	38.0	13.7	3.0	9.8
1966	202.8	163.5	66.4	63.2	33.7	31.4	4.7	2.2	1.0	192.8	131.8	42.0	15.1	3.9	10.0
1967	217.7	173.8	73.0	67.9	32.7	35.0	5.5	2.5	.9	220.0	149.5	50.3	16.4	3.8	−2.3
1968	252.1	203.1	87.0	76.4	39.4	38.8	6.4	2.6	1.2	247.0	165.7	58.4	18.8	4.2	5.1
1969	283.5	228.4	104.5	83.9	39.7	44.3	7.0	2.7	1.0	267.0	178.2	64.1	20.2	4.5	16.5
1970	286.9	229.2	103.1	91.4	34.4	46.6	8.2	2.9	.0	295.2	190.1	77.3	23.1	4.8	−8.4
1971	303.6	240.3	101.7	100.5	37.7	51.5	9.0	3.1	−.2	325.8	204.7	92.2	24.5	4.7	−22.2
1972	347.0	273.8	123.6	107.9	41.9	59.6	9.5	3.6	.5	356.3	220.8	103.0	26.3	6.6	−9.3
1973	390.4	299.3	132.4	117.2	49.3	76.0	11.6	3.9	−.4	386.5	234.8	115.2	31.3	5.2	3.9
1974	431.8	328.1	151.0	124.9	51.8	85.8	14.4	4.5	−.9	436.9	261.7	135.9	35.6	3.3	−5.2
1975	442.1	334.3	147.6	135.3	50.9	89.9	16.1	5.1	−3.2	510.2	294.6	171.3	40.0	4.5	−68.2
1976	505.9	383.6	172.3	146.4	64.2	102.0	16.3	5.8	−1.8	552.2	316.6	184.3	46.3	5.1	−46.3
1977	567.3	431.0	197.5	159.7	73.0	113.9	18.4	6.8	−2.7	600.3	346.6	195.9	50.8	7.1	−33.0
1978	646.1	484.8	229.4	170.9	83.5	132.1	23.2	8.2	−2.2	656.3	376.5	210.9	60.2	8.9	−10.2
1979	728.9	537.9	268.7	180.1	88.0	153.7	30.8	9.4	−2.9	729.9	412.3	236.0	72.9	8.5	−1.0
1980	798.7	585.6	298.9	200.3	84.8	167.2	39.9	11.1	−5.1	846.5	465.9	281.7	89.1	9.8	−47.8
1981	917.7	663.5	345.2	235.6	81.1	196.9	50.2	12.7	−5.6	966.9	520.6	318.1	116.7	11.5	−49.2
1982	939.3	659.5	354.1	240.9	63.1	210.1	58.9	15.3	−4.5	1,076.8	568.1	354.7	138.9	15.0	−137.5
1983	1,000.3	694.1	352.3	263.3	77.2	227.2	65.3	16.9	−3.2	1,171.7	610.5	382.5	156.9	21.3	−171.4
1984	1,113.5	762.5	377.4	289.8	94.0	258.8	74.3	19.7	−1.9	1,261.0	657.6	395.3	187.3	21.1	−147.5
1985	1,214.6	823.9	417.3	308.1	96.5	282.8	84.0	23.4	.6	1,370.9	720.1	420.4	208.8	21.4	−156.3
1986	1,290.1	868.8	437.2	323.4	105.5	304.9	89.7	25.9	.9	1,464.0	776.1	446.6	216.3	24.9	−173.9
1987	1,403.2	965.7	489.1	347.5	127.1	324.6	85.6	27.0	.2	1,540.5	815.1	464.4	230.8	30.3	−137.4
1988	1,502.4	1,018.9	504.9	374.5	137.2	363.2	89.9	27.9	2.6	1,623.6	852.8	493.6	247.7	29.5	−121.2
1989	1,627.2	1,109.2	566.1	398.9	141.5	386.9	93.7	32.5	4.9	1,741.0	902.9	538.1	272.5	27.4	−113.8
1990	1,709.3	1,161.3	592.7	425.0	140.6	412.1	98.0	36.3	1.6	1,879.5	966.0	592.4	294.2	27.0	−170.3
1991	1,759.7	1,179.9	586.6	457.1	133.6	432.2	97.0	44.9	5.7	1,984.0	1,015.8	628.9	311.7	27.5	−224.2
1992	1,845.1	1,239.7	610.5	483.4	143.1	457.1	89.6	50.5	8.2	2,149.0	1,050.4	756.3	312.3	30.1	−303.9
1993	1,948.2	1,317.8	646.5	503.1	165.4	479.6	86.8	55.3	8.7	2,229.4	1,075.4	804.6	312.7	36.7	−281.2
1994	2,091.9	1,425.6	690.5	545.2	186.7	510.7	86.0	60.0	9.6	2,304.0	1,108.9	839.9	322.7	32.5	−212.2
1995	2,215.5	1,516.7	743.9	557.9	211.0	535.5	91.8	58.4	13.1	2,412.5	1,141.4	882.4	353.9	34.8	−197.0
1996	2,380.4	1,641.5	832.0	580.8	223.6	557.9	99.9	66.8	14.4	2,505.7	1,176.7	929.2	364.6	35.2	−125.3
1997	2,557.2	1,780.0	926.2	611.6	237.1	590.3	103.6	69.3	14.1	2,581.1	1,222.1	954.6	370.6	33.8	−23.8
1998	2,729.8	1,910.8	1,026.4	639.5	239.2	627.8	102.7	75.3	13.3	2,649.3	1,263.2	978.1	371.6	36.4	80.5
1999	2,902.5	2,035.8	1,107.5	673.6	248.8	664.6	106.4	81.7	14.1	2,761.9	1,343.9	1,014.9	357.9	45.2	140.6
2000	3,132.4	2,202.8	1,232.3	708.6	254.7	709.4	118.8	92.3	9.1	2,906.0	1,426.6	1,071.5	362.0	45.8	226.5
2001	3,118.2	2,163.7	1,234.8	727.7	193.5	736.9	114.6	98.9	4.0	3,093.6	1,524.4	1,169.0	341.5	58.7	24.6
2002	2,967.9	2,002.1	1,050.4	762.8	181.3	755.2	99.9	104.3	6.3	3,274.7	1,639.9	1,280.9	312.6	41.4	−306.9
2003	3,043.4	2,047.9	1,000.3	806.8	231.8	782.8	96.8	108.9	7.0	3,458.6	1,756.8	1,354.8	298.0	49.1	−415.2
2004	3,265.7	2,213.2	1,047.8	863.4	292.0	831.7	100.3	119.3	1.2	3,653.5	1,860.4	1,440.1	306.6	46.4	−387.8
2005	3,659.3	2,546.8	1,208.6	930.2	395.9	877.4	111.9	126.7	−3.5	3,916.4	1,977.9	1,534.9	342.7	60.9	−257.1
2006	3,995.2	2,807.4	1,352.4	986.8	454.2	926.4	129.6	136.0	−4.2	4,147.9	2,093.3	1,631.0	372.2	51.4	−152.7
2007	4,209.2	2,960.6	1,490.9	1,028.7	426.7	964.2	143.3	147.7	−6.6	4,424.0	2,214.9	1,743.3	411.0	54.8	−214.8
2008	4,057.6	2,758.0	1,432.4	1,047.3	263.3	995.6	144.2	166.7	−6.9	4,740.3	2,386.9	1,904.0	395.9	53.5	−682.7
2009 ᵖ	....	....	1,107.6	1,023.9	....	978.3	164.3	189.0	−8.1	4,993.0	2,417.8	2,136.4	379.1	59.7	....
2006: I	3,919.8	2,747.6	1,321.5	971.5	443.4	920.0	122.2	132.4	−2.4	4,064.5	2,064.8	1,590.0	354.1	55.6	−144.7
II	3,971.1	2,791.1	1,340.2	983.3	456.4	921.9	127.4	134.5	−3.8	4,137.3	2,083.1	1,627.3	375.4	51.4	−166.2
III	4,024.8	2,835.1	1,354.3	991.6	477.2	925.3	132.0	137.0	−4.7	4,197.8	2,105.8	1,651.2	391.1	49.8	−173.1
IV	4,064.9	2,855.7	1,393.5	1,000.7	439.7	938.4	136.9	139.9	−6.0	4,192.0	2,119.7	1,655.5	368.2	48.7	−127.0
2007: I	4,167.4	2,935.1	1,459.5	1,015.3	447.4	957.3	140.4	143.0	−8.4	4,335.5	2,152.2	1,730.7	403.3	49.2	−168.1
II	4,202.8	2,963.1	1,481.8	1,025.2	442.0	958.5	142.8	145.3	−6.9	4,389.1	2,197.2	1,714.4	419.1	58.3	−186.3
III	4,212.3	2,960.4	1,500.7	1,032.2	414.3	963.4	144.9	148.5	−4.9	4,450.7	2,234.3	1,744.5	415.8	56.0	−238.4
IV	4,254.2	2,983.6	1,521.9	1,042.3	403.2	977.5	145.1	153.9	−6.0	4,520.5	2,275.9	1,783.7	405.5	55.4	−266.3
2008: I	4,172.0	2,884.1	1,531.8	1,042.5	295.0	990.3	143.7	159.4	−5.6	4,625.5	2,332.5	1,825.2	414.6	53.1	−453.5
II	3,974.5	2,679.8	1,326.2	1,050.8	288.4	993.9	145.1	162.0	−6.3	4,797.0	2,381.5	1,966.7	395.9	52.9	−822.5
III	4,087.0	2,786.2	1,437.3	1,058.5	275.7	999.9	143.2	164.5	−6.9	4,811.7	2,436.4	1,898.7	423.8	52.9	−724.8
IV	3,996.8	2,681.8	1,434.3	1,037.3	194.2	998.4	144.6	181.0	−8.9	4,726.9	2,397.1	1,925.3	349.3	55.2	−730.2
2009: I	3,775.0	2,463.7	1,187.3	1,018.6	244.2	974.8	156.5	190.7	−10.7	4,780.6	2,378.6	2,009.2	337.3	55.5	−1,005.7
II	3,728.4	2,395.4	1,082.6	1,019.6	281.2	976.0	166.5	199.3	−8.8	5,021.9	2,409.0	2,175.2	382.8	54.9	−1,293.5
III	3,735.0	2,416.7	1,086.1	1,023.1	296.7	979.0	165.7	180.0	−6.3	5,077.0	2,431.0	2,174.4	403.8	67.7	−1,342.0
IV ᵖ	....	....	1,074.4	1,034.3	....	983.4	168.5	186.1	−6.6	5,092.3	2,452.4	2,186.8	392.6	60.5	....

¹ Includes taxes from the rest of the world, not shown separately.
² Includes an item for the difference between wage accruals and disbursements, not shown separately.

Source: Department of Commerce (Bureau of Economic Analysis).

TABLE B–84. Federal Government current receipts and expenditures, national income and product accounts (NIPA), 1960–2009

[Billions of dollars; quarterly data at seasonally adjusted annual rates]

Year or quarter	Total	Current tax receipts Total[1]	Personal current taxes	Taxes on production and imports	Taxes on corporate income	Contributions for government social insurance	Income receipts on assets	Current transfer receipts	Current surplus of government enterprises	Total[2]	Consumption expenditures	Current transfer payments[3]	Interest payments	Subsidies	Net Federal Government saving
1960	93.9	76.5	41.8	13.1	21.4	16.0	1.4	0.4	–0.3	86.8	49.7	27.6	8.4	1.1	7.1
1961	95.5	77.5	42.7	13.2	21.5	16.6	1.5	.5	–.5	92.9	51.6	31.4	7.9	2.0	2.6
1962	103.6	83.3	46.5	14.1	22.5	18.6	1.7	.5	–.5	101.2	57.8	32.5	8.6	2.3	2.4
1963	111.8	88.6	49.1	14.7	24.6	21.1	1.8	.6	–.3	106.5	60.8	34.2	9.3	2.2	5.3
1964	111.8	87.7	46.0	15.4	26.1	21.8	1.8	.7	–.3	110.9	62.8	35.4	10.0	2.7	.9
1965	121.0	95.6	51.1	15.4	28.9	22.7	1.9	1.1	–.3	117.7	65.7	38.5	10.6	3.0	3.2
1966	138.0	104.7	58.6	14.4	31.4	30.6	2.1	1.2	–.6	135.7	75.7	44.4	11.6	3.9	2.3
1967	146.9	109.8	64.4	15.2	30.0	34.1	2.5	1.1	–.6	156.2	87.0	52.8	12.7	3.8	–9.3
1968	171.3	129.7	76.4	16.9	36.1	37.9	2.9	1.1	–.3	173.7	95.3	59.7	14.6	4.1	–2.4
1969	192.7	146.0	91.7	17.8	36.1	43.3	2.7	1.1	–.4	184.1	98.3	65.5	15.8	4.5	8.6
1970	186.1	137.9	88.9	18.1	30.6	45.5	3.1	1.1	–1.5	201.6	98.6	80.5	17.7	4.8	–15.5
1971	191.9	138.6	85.8	19.0	33.5	50.3	3.5	1.1	–1.6	220.6	101.9	96.1	17.9	4.6	–28.7
1972	220.3	158.2	102.8	18.5	36.6	58.3	3.6	1.3	–1.1	245.2	107.6	112.7	18.8	6.6	–24.9
1973	250.8	173.0	109.6	19.8	43.3	74.5	3.8	1.3	–1.8	262.6	108.8	125.9	22.8	5.1	–11.8
1974	280.0	192.1	126.5	20.1	45.1	84.1	4.2	1.4	–1.8	294.5	117.9	146.9	26.0	3.2	–14.5
1975	277.6	186.8	120.7	22.1	43.6	88.1	4.9	1.5	–3.6	348.3	129.5	185.6	28.9	4.3	–70.6
1976	323.0	217.9	141.2	21.4	54.6	99.8	5.9	1.6	–2.2	376.7	137.1	200.9	33.8	4.9	–53.7
1977	364.0	247.2	162.2	22.7	61.6	111.1	6.7	2.0	–3.0	410.1	150.7	215.5	37.1	6.9	–46.1
1978	424.0	286.6	188.9	25.3	71.4	128.7	8.5	2.7	–2.5	452.9	163.3	235.7	45.3	8.7	–28.9
1979	486.9	325.9	224.6	25.7	74.4	149.8	10.7	3.1	–2.6	500.9	178.9	258.0	55.7	8.2	–14.0
1980	532.8	355.5	250.0	33.7	70.3	163.6	13.7	3.9	–3.9	589.5	207.4	302.9	69.7	9.4	–56.6
1981	619.9	407.7	290.6	49.9	65.7	193.0	18.3	4.1	–3.2	676.7	238.3	333.5	93.9	11.1	–56.8
1982	617.4	386.3	295.0	41.0	49.0	206.0	22.2	5.7	–2.9	752.6	263.3	363.0	111.8	14.6	–135.3
1983	643.3	393.2	286.2	44.4	61.3	223.1	23.8	6.1	–3.0	819.5	286.4	387.2	124.6	20.9	–176.2
1984	710.0	425.2	301.4	47.3	75.2	254.1	26.6	7.4	–3.4	881.5	309.9	400.8	150.3	20.7	–171.5
1985	774.4	460.2	336.0	46.1	76.3	277.9	29.1	9.7	–2.6	953.0	338.3	424.0	169.4	21.0	–178.6
1986	816.0	479.2	350.0	43.7	83.8	298.9	31.3	8.5	–1.9	1,010.7	358.0	449.9	178.2	24.6	–194.6
1987	896.5	543.6	392.5	45.9	103.2	317.4	27.5	11.0	–3.0	1,045.9	373.7	457.6	184.6	30.0	–149.3
1988	958.5	566.2	402.8	49.8	111.1	354.8	29.4	10.5	–2.3	1,096.9	381.7	486.8	199.3	29.2	–138.4
1989	1,038.0	621.2	451.5	49.7	117.2	378.0	28.0	12.7	–1.7	1,172.0	398.5	527.1	219.3	27.1	–133.9
1990	1,082.8	642.2	470.1	50.9	118.1	402.0	29.6	14.2	–5.3	1,259.2	419.0	576.2	237.5	26.6	–176.4
1991	1,101.9	635.6	461.3	61.8	109.9	420.6	29.1	18.2	–1.6	1,320.3	438.3	604.0	250.9	27.1	–218.4
1992	1,148.0	659.9	475.2	63.3	118.8	444.0	24.8	19.4	.0	1,450.5	444.1	725.4	251.3	29.7	–302.5
1993	1,224.1	713.0	505.5	66.4	138.5	465.5	25.5	21.3	–1.3	1,504.3	441.2	773.4	253.4	36.3	–280.2
1994	1,322.1	781.4	542.5	79.0	156.7	496.2	22.7	22.8	–.9	1,542.5	440.7	808.3	261.3	32.2	–220.4
1995	1,407.8	844.6	585.8	75.6	179.3	521.9	23.3	18.4	–.3	1,614.0	440.1	849.0	290.4	34.5	–206.2
1996	1,526.4	931.9	663.3	72.9	190.6	545.4	26.5	23.8	–1.2	1,674.7	446.5	896.0	297.3	34.9	–148.2
1997	1,656.2	1,030.1	744.2	77.8	203.0	579.4	25.4	21.3	–.1	1,716.3	457.5	925.4	300.0	33.4	–60.1
1998	1,777.9	1,115.8	825.2	80.7	204.2	617.4	21.2	22.6	–.8	1,744.3	454.6	954.9	298.8	35.9	33.6
1999	1,895.0	1,195.4	893.0	83.4	213.0	654.8	20.6	23.4	.8	1,796.2	473.3	995.4	282.7	44.8	98.8
2000	2,057.1	1,309.6	995.6	87.3	219.4	698.6	24.5	25.7	–1.2	1,871.9	496.0	1,047.4	283.3	45.3	185.2
2001	2,020.3	1,249.4	991.8	85.3	164.7	723.3	24.5	27.0	–4.0	1,979.8	530.2	1,140.0	258.6	51.1	40.5
2002	1,859.3	1,073.5	828.6	86.8	150.5	739.3	20.3	26.1	.2	2,112.1	590.5	1,252.1	229.1	40.5	–252.8
2003	1,885.1	1,070.2	774.2	89.3	197.8	762.8	22.8	25.6	3.7	2,261.5	660.3	1,339.4	212.9	49.0	–376.4
2004	2,013.9	1,153.8	799.2	94.3	250.3	807.6	23.2	29.0	.3	2,393.4	721.4	1,405.0	221.0	46.0	–379.5
2005	2,290.1	1,383.7	931.9	98.8	341.0	852.6	23.7	33.6	–3.5	2,573.1	765.8	1,491.3	255.4	60.5	–283.0
2006	2,524.5	1,558.3	1,049.9	99.4	395.0	904.6	26.1	38.3	–2.9	2,728.3	811.0	1,587.1	279.2	51.0	–203.8
2007	2,660.8	1,647.2	1,168.1	94.7	370.2	944.4	29.1	42.7	–2.7	2,897.2	848.8	1,688.6	312.2	47.6	–236.5
2008	2,475.0	1,421.7	1,102.5	92.0	212.3	974.5	30.3	52.3	–3.8	3,117.6	934.4	1,840.6	292.0	50.6	–642.6
2009 ᵖ	....	....	836.5	92.4	....	956.4	48.3	68.1	–4.9	3,454.5	986.8	2,137.1	272.3	58.3	....
2006: I	2,473.8	1,517.6	1,023.1	99.6	383.8	896.9	24.3	37.1	–2.1	2,681.1	810.4	1,552.4	263.1	55.2	–207.3
II	2,501.8	1,541.6	1,034.7	99.6	396.1	899.8	25.5	37.7	–2.7	2,731.2	808.5	1,588.9	282.8	51.1	–229.4
III	2,547.4	1,581.3	1,053.9	99.9	415.5	904.0	26.5	38.6	–3.0	2,762.9	813.1	1,603.7	296.7	49.4	–215.5
IV	2,575.1	1,592.8	1,088.0	98.6	384.6	917.8	28.2	39.9	–3.6	2,738.1	812.1	1,603.5	274.2	48.3	–163.0
2007: I	2,640.1	1,638.3	1,136.8	94.9	393.6	937.3	28.3	41.0	–4.8	2,841.0	821.1	1,666.2	306.4	47.4	–200.9
II	2,660.1	1,654.0	1,157.6	94.8	387.3	938.8	28.7	41.5	–2.9	2,881.3	839.9	1,672.4	321.3	47.7	–221.3
III	2,659.9	1,644.8	1,177.6	95.4	358.5	943.8	29.6	42.6	–.8	2,918.7	860.8	1,694.1	316.6	47.3	–258.8
IV	2,682.9	1,651.7	1,200.6	93.6	341.3	957.6	29.8	45.8	–2.1	2,947.9	873.4	1,721.6	304.7	48.2	–265.0
2008: I	2,590.7	1,546.0	1,195.3	92.7	243.1	970.0	29.3	47.9	–2.5	3,024.2	903.2	1,759.5	312.3	49.2	–433.5
II	2,372.1	1,322.8	984.2	93.1	231.2	973.0	31.2	48.4	–3.4	3,169.0	923.2	1,904.5	291.4	49.9	–796.9
III	2,489.5	1,435.2	1,110.1	91.8	218.5	978.5	30.6	49.0	–3.9	3,155.2	956.0	1,829.0	319.5	50.7	–665.7
IV	2,447.8	1,382.9	1,120.2	90.2	156.5	976.4	30.0	64.0	–5.4	3,121.9	955.4	1,869.5	244.6	52.4	–674.1
2009: I	2,251.3	1,191.5	900.3	85.7	192.0	953.0	40.7	72.7	–6.7	3,220.3	954.2	1,981.2	231.3	53.6	–969.1
II	2,237.0	1,157.4	829.9	91.6	223.8	954.3	50.8	79.8	–5.3	3,505.9	979.1	2,195.6	277.4	53.7	–1,268.9
III	2,215.1	1,153.2	811.0	93.5	238.1	957.1	49.5	58.7	–3.5	3,542.1	1,001.2	2,178.1	296.3	66.5	–1,327.0
IV ᵖ	....	....	804.7	98.7	....	961.3	52.1	61.2	–4.3	3,549.7	1,012.8	2,193.5	284.1	59.3	....

[1] Includes taxes from the rest of the world, not shown separately.
[2] Includes an item for the difference between wage accruals and disbursements, not shown separately.
[3] Includes Federal grants-in-aid to State and local governments. See Table B–82 for data on Federal grants-in-aid.

Source: Department of Commerce (Bureau of Economic Analysis).

TABLE B–85. State and local government current receipts and expenditures, national income and product accounts (NIPA), 1960–2009

[Billions of dollars; quarterly data at seasonally adjusted annual rates]

Year or quarter	Current receipts									Current expenditures					Net State and local government saving
	Total	Current tax receipts				Contributions for government social insurance	Income receipts on assets	Current transfer receipts [1]	Current surplus of government enterprises	Total [2]	Consumption expenditures	Government social benefit payments to persons	Interest payments	Subsidies	
		Total	Personal current taxes	Taxes on production and imports	Taxes on corporate income										
1960	44.5	37.0	4.2	31.5	1.2	0.5	1.3	4.5	1.2	40.2	33.5	4.6	2.1	0.0	4.3
1961	48.1	39.7	4.6	33.8	1.3	.5	1.4	5.2	1.3	43.8	36.6	5.0	2.2	.0	4.3
1962	52.0	42.8	5.0	36.3	1.5	.5	1.5	5.8	1.4	46.8	39.0	5.3	2.4	.0	5.2
1963	56.0	45.8	5.4	38.7	1.7	.6	1.6	6.4	1.6	50.3	41.9	5.7	2.7	.0	5.7
1964	61.3	49.8	6.1	41.8	1.8	.7	1.9	7.3	1.6	54.9	45.8	6.2	2.9	.0	6.4
1965	66.5	53.9	6.6	45.3	2.0	.8	2.2	8.0	1.7	60.0	50.2	6.7	3.1	.0	6.5
1966	74.9	58.8	7.8	48.8	2.2	.8	2.6	11.1	1.6	67.2	56.1	7.6	3.4	.0	7.8
1967	82.5	64.0	8.6	52.8	2.6	.9	3.0	13.1	1.5	75.5	62.6	9.2	3.7	.0	7.0
1968	93.5	73.4	10.6	59.5	3.3	.9	3.5	14.2	1.5	86.0	70.4	11.4	4.2	.0	7.5
1969	105.5	82.5	12.8	66.0	3.6	1.0	4.3	16.2	1.5	97.5	79.8	13.2	4.4	.0	8.0
1970	120.1	91.3	14.2	73.3	3.7	1.1	5.2	21.1	1.5	113.0	91.5	16.1	5.3	.0	7.1
1971	134.9	101.7	15.9	81.5	4.3	1.2	5.5	25.2	1.4	128.5	102.7	19.3	6.5	.0	6.5
1972	158.4	115.6	20.9	89.4	5.3	1.3	5.9	34.0	1.6	142.8	113.2	22.0	7.5	.1	15.6
1973	174.3	126.3	22.8	97.4	6.0	1.5	7.8	37.3	1.5	158.6	126.0	24.1	8.5	.1	15.7
1974	188.1	136.0	24.5	104.8	6.7	1.7	10.2	39.3	.9	178.7	143.7	25.3	9.6	.1	9.3
1975	209.6	147.4	26.9	113.2	7.3	1.8	11.2	48.7	.4	207.1	165.1	30.8	11.1	.2	2.5
1976	233.7	165.7	31.1	125.0	9.6	2.2	10.4	55.0	.4	226.3	179.5	34.1	12.5	.2	7.4
1977	259.9	183.7	35.4	136.9	11.4	2.8	11.7	61.4	.3	246.8	195.9	37.0	13.7	.2	13.1
1978	287.6	198.2	40.5	145.6	12.1	3.4	14.7	71.1	.3	268.9	213.2	40.8	14.9	.2	18.7
1979	308.4	212.0	44.0	154.4	13.6	3.9	20.1	72.7	–.3	295.4	233.3	44.3	17.2	.3	13.0
1980	338.2	230.0	48.9	166.7	14.5	3.6	26.3	79.5	–1.2	329.4	258.4	51.2	19.4	.4	8.8
1981	370.2	255.8	54.6	185.7	15.4	3.9	32.0	81.0	–2.4	362.7	282.3	57.1	22.8	.4	7.6
1982	391.4	273.2	59.1	200.0	14.0	4.0	36.7	79.1	–1.6	393.6	304.9	61.2	27.1	.5	–2.2
1983	428.6	300.9	66.1	218.9	15.9	4.1	41.4	82.4	–.2	423.7	324.1	66.9	32.3	.4	4.9
1984	480.2	337.3	76.0	242.5	18.8	4.7	47.7	89.0	1.5	456.2	347.7	71.2	37.0	.4	23.9
1985	521.1	363.7	81.4	262.1	20.2	4.9	54.8	94.5	3.2	498.7	381.8	77.3	39.4	.3	22.4
1986	561.6	389.5	87.2	279.7	22.7	6.0	58.4	105.0	2.8	540.9	418.1	84.3	38.2	.3	20.7
1987	590.6	422.1	96.6	301.6	23.9	7.2	58.2	100.0	3.1	578.6	441.4	90.7	46.2	.3	12.0
1988	635.5	452.8	102.1	324.6	26.0	8.4	60.5	109.0	4.8	618.3	471.0	98.5	48.4	.4	17.2
1989	687.5	488.0	114.6	349.1	24.2	9.0	65.7	118.1	6.7	667.4	504.5	109.3	53.2	.4	20.1
1990	738.0	519.1	122.6	374.1	22.5	10.0	68.5	133.5	6.9	731.8	547.0	127.7	56.8	.4	6.2
1991	789.4	544.3	125.3	395.3	23.6	11.6	68.0	158.2	7.3	795.2	577.5	156.5	60.8	.4	–5.8
1992	846.2	579.8	135.3	420.1	24.4	13.1	64.8	180.3	8.3	847.6	606.2	180.0	61.0	.4	–1.4
1993	888.2	604.7	141.1	436.8	26.9	14.1	61.3	198.1	9.9	889.1	634.2	195.2	59.4	.4	–.9
1994	944.8	644.2	148.0	466.3	30.0	14.5	63.3	212.3	10.5	936.6	668.2	206.7	61.4	.3	8.2
1995	991.9	672.1	158.1	482.4	31.7	13.6	68.5	224.2	13.5	982.7	701.3	217.6	63.5	.3	9.2
1996	1,045.1	709.6	168.7	507.9	33.0	12.5	73.4	234.0	15.6	1,022.1	730.2	224.3	67.3	.3	23.0
1997	1,099.5	749.9	182.0	533.8	34.1	10.8	78.2	246.4	14.2	1,063.2	764.5	227.6	70.6	.4	36.3
1998	1,164.5	794.9	201.2	558.8	34.9	10.4	81.5	265.3	12.5	1,117.6	808.6	235.8	72.8	.4	46.9
1999	1,240.4	840.4	214.5	590.2	35.8	9.8	85.8	291.1	13.3	1,198.6	870.6	252.3	75.2	.4	41.8
2000	1,322.6	893.2	236.7	621.3	35.2	10.8	94.3	313.9	10.4	1,281.3	930.6	271.4	78.8	.5	41.3
2001	1,374.0	914.3	243.0	642.4	28.9	13.7	90.0	348.0	8.0	1,389.9	994.2	305.1	83.0	7.7	–15.9
2002	1,412.7	928.7	221.8	676.0	30.9	15.9	79.6	382.3	6.1	1,466.8	1,049.4	333.0	83.5	.9	–54.1
2003	1,496.3	977.7	226.2	717.5	34.0	20.1	74.0	421.3	3.3	1,535.1	1,096.5	353.4	85.1	.1	–38.8
2004	1,601.0	1,059.4	248.6	769.1	41.7	24.1	77.1	439.4	1.0	1,609.3	1,139.1	384.3	85.6	.4	–8.4
2005	1,730.4	1,163.1	276.7	831.4	54.9	24.8	88.3	454.3	.1	1,704.5	1,212.0	404.8	87.3	.4	25.9
2006	1,829.7	1,249.0	302.5	887.4	59.2	21.8	103.5	456.7	–1.3	1,778.6	1,282.3	402.9	93.0	.4	51.0
2007	1,927.3	1,313.4	322.8	934.0	56.5	19.8	114.2	483.9	–3.9	1,905.6	1,366.1	433.7	98.7	7.1	21.7
2008	1,974.2	1,336.3	330.0	955.3	51.0	21.1	113.9	506.1	–3.2	2,014.4	1,452.4	455.0	103.9	3.0	–40.2
2009 ᵖ	....	....	271.2	931.6	....	21.9	116.0	597.5	–3.2	2,015.1	1,430.9	475.9	106.8	1.4	....
2006: I	1,800.6	1,230.0	298.4	871.9	59.6	23.1	97.9	449.9	–.3	1,738.0	1,254.5	392.2	91.0	.4	62.6
II	1,830.3	1,249.5	305.5	883.8	60.2	22.1	101.9	457.8	–1.1	1,767.0	1,274.6	399.4	92.6	.4	63.2
III	1,842.5	1,253.8	300.4	891.8	61.6	21.3	105.5	463.5	–1.6	1,800.1	1,292.7	412.6	94.5	.4	42.4
IV	1,845.3	1,262.9	305.5	902.2	55.1	20.5	108.7	455.5	–2.3	1,809.4	1,307.6	407.4	94.0	.4	35.9
2007: I	1,902.3	1,296.8	322.7	920.4	53.8	20.0	112.0	477.0	–3.6	1,869.5	1,331.2	439.5	97.0	1.9	32.8
II	1,923.4	1,309.1	324.1	930.4	54.7	19.7	114.0	484.5	–4.0	1,888.4	1,357.3	422.6	97.8	10.7	34.9
III	1,932.1	1,315.7	323.1	936.8	55.8	19.6	115.3	485.6	–4.1	1,911.7	1,373.6	430.2	99.2	8.8	20.3
IV	1,951.6	1,331.9	321.3	948.7	61.9	19.9	115.3	488.4	–3.9	1,952.9	1,402.5	442.4	100.8	7.2	–1.3
2008: I	1,963.7	1,338.1	336.4	949.8	51.9	20.3	114.4	493.9	–3.1	1,983.8	1,429.3	448.2	102.4	4.0	–20.1
II	1,994.2	1,356.9	342.0	957.7	57.2	20.8	114.0	505.4	–2.9	2,019.8	1,458.3	454.0	104.5	2.9	–25.5
III	1,987.5	1,351.0	322.1	966.7	57.1	21.4	112.7	505.5	–3.1	2,046.5	1,480.4	459.7	104.3	2.1	–59.0
IV	1,951.4	1,298.9	314.1	947.1	37.7	22.0	114.5	519.5	–3.5	2,007.5	1,441.7	458.3	104.7	2.8	–56.1
2009: I	1,961.4	1,272.2	287.0	933.0	52.2	21.8	115.8	555.7	–4.0	1,998.0	1,424.4	465.7	106.0	2.0	–36.6
II	1,989.3	1,238.1	252.7	928.0	57.4	21.7	117.7	617.4	–3.5	2,013.9	1,429.9	477.5	105.4	1.2	–24.6
III	2,003.6	1,263.5	275.2	929.7	58.6	21.9	116.2	604.9	–2.9	2,018.6	1,429.8	480.0	107.5	1.2	–14.9
IV ᵖ	....	....	269.8	935.6	....	22.1	116.4	612.1	–2.3	2,029.8	1,439.7	480.5	108.5	1.2	....

[1] Includes Federal grants-in-aid. See Table B–82 for data on Federal grants-in-aid.
[2] Includes an item for the difference between wage accruals and disbursements, not shown separately.

Source: Department of Commerce (Bureau of Economic Analysis).

TABLE B–86. State and local government revenues and expenditures, selected fiscal years, 1942–2007

[Millions of dollars]

Fiscal year [1]	General revenues by source [2]							General expenditures by function [2]				
	Total	Property taxes	Sales and gross receipts taxes	Individual income taxes	Corporation net income taxes	Revenue from Federal Government	All other [3]	Total [4]	Education	Highways	Public welfare [4]	All other [4,5]
1942	10,418	4,537	2,351	276	272	858	2,123	9,190	2,586	1,490	1,225	3,889
1944	10,908	4,604	2,289	342	451	954	2,269	8,863	2,793	1,200	1,133	3,737
1946	12,356	4,986	2,986	422	447	855	2,661	11,028	3,356	1,672	1,409	4,591
1948	17,250	6,126	4,442	543	592	1,861	3,685	17,684	5,379	3,036	2,099	7,170
1950	20,911	7,349	5,154	788	593	2,486	4,541	22,787	7,177	3,803	2,940	8,867
1952	25,181	8,652	6,357	998	846	2,566	5,763	26,098	8,318	4,650	2,788	10,342
1953	27,307	9,375	6,927	1,065	817	2,870	6,252	27,910	9,390	4,987	2,914	10,619
1954	29,012	9,967	7,276	1,127	778	2,966	6,897	30,701	10,557	5,527	3,060	11,557
1955	31,073	10,735	7,643	1,237	744	3,131	7,584	33,724	11,907	6,452	3,168	12,197
1956	34,667	11,749	8,691	1,538	890	3,335	8,465	36,711	13,220	6,953	3,139	13,399
1957	38,164	12,864	9,467	1,754	984	3,843	9,252	40,375	14,134	7,816	3,485	14,940
1958	41,219	14,047	9,829	1,759	1,018	4,865	9,699	44,851	15,919	8,567	3,818	16,547
1959	45,306	14,983	10,437	1,994	1,001	6,377	10,516	48,887	17,283	9,592	4,136	17,876
1960	50,505	16,405	11,849	2,463	1,180	6,974	11,634	51,876	18,719	9,428	4,404	19,325
1961	54,037	18,002	12,463	2,613	1,266	7,131	12,563	56,201	20,574	9,844	4,720	21,063
1962	58,252	19,054	13,494	3,037	1,308	7,871	13,489	60,206	22,216	10,357	5,084	22,549
1963	62,890	20,089	14,456	3,269	1,505	8,722	14,850	64,816	23,776	11,136	5,481	24,423
1962–63	62,269	19,833	14,446	3,267	1,505	8,663	14,556	63,977	23,729	11,150	5,420	23,678
1963–64	68,443	21,241	15,762	3,791	1,695	10,002	15,951	69,302	26,286	11,664	5,766	25,586
1964–65	74,000	22,583	17,118	4,090	1,929	11,029	17,250	74,678	28,563	12,221	6,315	27,579
1965–66	83,036	24,670	19,085	4,760	2,038	13,214	19,269	82,843	33,287	12,770	6,757	30,029
1966–67	91,197	26,047	20,530	5,825	2,227	15,370	21,198	93,350	37,919	13,932	8,218	33,281
1967–68	101,264	27,747	22,911	7,308	2,518	17,181	23,599	102,411	41,158	14,481	9,857	36,915
1968–69	114,550	30,673	26,519	8,908	3,180	19,153	26,117	116,728	47,238	15,417	12,110	41,963
1969–70	130,756	34,054	30,322	10,812	3,738	21,857	29,973	131,332	52,718	16,427	14,679	47,508
1970–71	144,927	37,852	33,233	11,900	3,424	26,146	32,372	150,674	59,413	18,095	18,226	54,940
1971–72	167,535	42,877	37,518	15,227	4,416	31,342	36,156	168,549	65,813	19,021	21,117	62,598
1972–73	190,222	45,283	42,047	17,994	5,425	39,264	40,210	181,357	69,713	18,615	23,582	69,447
1973–74	207,670	47,705	46,098	19,491	6,015	41,820	46,542	198,959	75,833	19,946	25,085	78,095
1974–75	228,171	51,491	49,815	21,454	6,642	47,034	51,735	230,722	87,858	22,528	28,156	92,180
1975–76	256,176	57,001	54,547	24,575	7,273	55,589	57,191	256,731	97,216	23,907	32,604	103,004
1976–77	285,157	62,527	60,641	29,246	9,174	62,444	61,125	274,215	102,780	23,058	35,906	112,472
1977–78	315,960	66,422	67,596	33,176	10,738	69,592	68,435	296,984	110,758	24,609	39,140	122,478
1978–79	343,236	64,944	74,247	36,932	12,128	75,164	79,822	327,517	119,448	28,440	41,898	137,731
1979–80	382,322	68,499	79,927	42,080	13,321	83,029	95,467	369,086	133,211	33,311	47,288	155,276
1980–81	423,404	74,969	85,971	46,426	14,143	90,294	111,599	407,449	145,784	34,603	54,105	172,957
1981–82	457,654	82,067	93,613	50,738	15,028	87,282	128,925	436,733	154,282	34,520	57,996	189,935
1982–83	486,753	89,105	100,247	55,129	14,258	90,007	138,008	466,516	163,876	36,655	60,906	205,080
1983–84	542,730	96,457	114,097	64,529	17,141	96,935	153,571	505,008	176,108	39,419	66,414	223,068
1984–85	598,121	103,757	126,376	70,361	19,152	106,158	172,317	553,899	192,686	44,989	71,479	244,745
1985–86	641,486	111,709	135,005	74,365	19,994	113,099	187,314	605,623	210,819	49,368	75,868	269,568
1986–87	686,860	121,203	144,091	83,935	22,425	114,857	200,350	657,134	226,619	52,355	82,650	295,510
1987–88	726,762	132,212	156,452	88,350	23,663	117,602	208,482	704,921	242,683	55,621	89,090	317,527
1988–89	786,129	142,400	166,336	97,806	25,926	125,824	227,838	762,360	263,898	58,105	97,879	342,479
1989–90	849,502	155,613	177,885	105,640	23,566	136,802	249,996	834,818	288,148	61,057	110,518	375,094
1990–91	902,207	167,999	185,570	109,341	22,242	154,099	262,955	908,108	309,302	64,937	130,402	403,467
1991–92	979,137	180,337	197,731	115,638	23,880	179,174	282,376	981,253	324,652	67,351	158,723	430,526
1992–93	1,041,643	189,744	209,649	123,235	26,417	198,663	293,935	1,030,434	342,287	68,370	170,705	449,072
1993–94	1,100,490	197,141	223,628	128,810	28,320	215,492	307,099	1,077,665	353,287	72,067	183,394	468,916
1994–95	1,169,505	203,451	237,268	137,931	31,406	228,771	330,677	1,149,863	378,273	77,109	196,703	497,779
1995–96	1,222,821	209,440	248,993	146,844	32,009	234,891	350,645	1,193,276	398,859	79,092	197,354	517,971
1996–97	1,289,237	218,877	261,418	159,042	33,820	244,847	371,233	1,249,984	418,416	82,062	203,779	545,727
1997–98	1,365,762	230,150	274,883	175,630	34,412	255,048	395,639	1,318,042	450,365	87,214	208,120	572,343
1998–99	1,434,029	239,672	290,993	189,309	33,922	270,628	409,505	1,402,369	483,259	93,018	218,957	607,134
1999–2000	1,541,322	249,178	309,290	211,661	36,059	291,950	443,186	1,506,797	521,612	101,336	237,336	646,512
2000–01	1,647,161	263,689	320,217	226,334	35,296	324,033	477,592	1,626,066	563,575	107,235	261,622	693,634
2001–02	1,684,879	279,191	324,123	202,832	28,152	360,546	490,035	1,736,866	594,694	115,295	285,464	741,413
2002–03	1,763,212	296,683	337,787	199,407	31,369	389,264	508,702	1,821,917	621,335	117,696	310,783	772,102
2003–04	1,887,397	317,941	361,027	215,215	33,716	423,112	536,386	1,908,543	655,182	117,215	340,523	795,622
2004–05	2,026,034	335,779	384,266	242,273	43,256	438,558	581,902	2,012,110	688,314	126,350	365,286	832,161
2005–06	2,189,750	358,564	417,013	268,362	53,075	452,854	639,882	2,122,967	728,922	136,495	371,997	885,552
2006–07	2,329,015	383,101	438,580	289,308	60,524	467,584	689,918	2,265,284	776,626	144,807	389,123	954,729

[1] Fiscal years not the same for all governments. See Note.

[2] Excludes revenues or expenditures of publicly owned utilities and liquor stores and of insurance-trust activities. Intergovernmental receipts and payments between State and local governments are also excluded.

[3] Includes motor vehicle license taxes, other taxes, and charges and miscellaneous revenues.

[4] Includes intergovernmental payments to the Federal Government.

[5] Includes expenditures for libraries, hospitals, health, employment security administration, veterans' services, air transportation, water transport and terminals, parking facilities, transit subsidies, police protection, fire protection, correction, protective inspection and regulation, sewerage, natural resources, parks and recreation, housing and community development, solid waste management, financial administration, judicial and legal, general public buildings, other government administration, interest on general debt, and other general expenditures, not elsewhere classified.

Note: Except for States listed, data for fiscal years listed from 1962–63 to 2006–07 are the aggregation of data for government fiscal years that ended in the 12-month period from July 1 to June 30 of those years; Texas used August and Alabama and Michigan used September as end dates. Data for 1963 and earlier years include data for government fiscal years ending during that particular calendar year.

Data prior to 1952 are not available for intervening years.

Source: Department of Commerce (Bureau of the Census).

[Billions of dollars]

End of year or month	Total Treasury securities outstanding [1]	Marketable							Nonmarketable				
		Total [2]	Treasury bills	Treasury notes	Treasury bonds	Treasury inflation-protected securities			Total	U.S. savings securities [3]	Foreign series [4]	Government account series	Other [5]
						Total	Notes	Bonds					
Fiscal year:													
1970	369.0	232.6	76.2	93.5	63.0				136.4	51.3	4.8	76.3	4.1
1971	396.3	245.5	86.7	104.8	54.0				150.8	53.0	9.3	82.8	5.8
1972	425.4	257.2	94.6	113.4	49.1				168.2	55.9	19.0	89.6	3.7
1973	456.4	263.0	100.1	117.8	45.1				193.4	59.4	28.5	101.7	3.7
1974	473.2	266.6	105.0	128.4	33.1				206.7	61.9	25.0	115.4	4.3
1975	532.1	315.6	128.6	150.3	36.8				216.5	65.5	23.2	124.2	3.6
1976	619.3	392.6	161.2	191.8	39.6				226.7	69.7	21.5	130.6	4.9
1977	697.6	443.5	156.1	241.7	45.7				254.1	75.4	21.8	140.1	16.8
1978	767.0	485.2	160.9	267.9	56.4				281.8	79.8	21.7	153.3	27.1
1979	819.0	506.7	161.4	274.2	71.1				312.3	80.4	28.1	176.4	27.4
1980	906.4	594.5	199.8	310.9	83.8				311.9	72.7	25.2	189.8	24.2
1981	996.5	683.2	223.4	363.6	96.2				313.3	68.0	20.5	201.1	23.7
1982	1,140.9	824.4	277.9	442.9	103.6				316.5	67.3	14.6	210.5	24.1
1983	1,375.8	1,024.0	340.7	557.5	125.7				351.8	70.0	11.5	234.7	35.6
1984	1,559.6	1,176.6	356.8	661.7	158.1				383.0	72.8	8.8	259.5	41.8
1985	1,821.0	1,360.2	384.2	776.4	199.5				460.8	77.0	6.6	313.9	63.3
1986	2,122.7	1,564.3	410.7	896.9	241.7				558.4	85.6	4.1	365.9	102.8
1987	2,347.8	1,676.0	378.3	1,005.1	277.6				671.8	97.0	4.4	440.7	129.8
1988	2,599.9	1,802.9	398.5	1,089.6	299.9				797.0	106.2	6.3	536.5	148.0
1989	2,836.3	1,892.8	406.6	1,133.2	338.0				943.5	114.0	6.8	663.7	159.0
1990	3,210.9	2,092.8	482.5	1,218.1	377.2				1,118.2	122.2	36.0	779.4	180.6
1991	3,662.8	2,390.7	564.6	1,387.7	423.4				1,272.1	133.5	41.6	908.4	188.5
1992	4,061.8	2,677.5	634.3	1,566.3	461.8				1,384.3	148.3	37.0	1,011.0	188.0
1993	4,408.6	2,904.9	658.4	1,734.2	497.4				1,503.7	167.0	42.5	1,114.3	179.9
1994	4,689.5	3,091.6	697.3	1,867.5	511.8				1,597.9	176.4	42.0	1,211.7	167.8
1995	4,950.6	3,260.4	742.5	1,980.3	522.6				1,690.2	181.2	41.0	1,324.3	143.8
1996	5,220.8	3,418.4	761.2	2,098.7	543.5				1,802.4	184.1	37.5	1,454.7	126.1
1997	5,407.5	3,439.6	701.9	2,122.2	576.2	24.4	24.4		1,967.9	182.7	34.9	1,608.5	141.9
1998	5,518.7	3,331.0	637.6	2,009.1	610.4	58.8	41.9	17.0	2,187.7	180.8	35.1	1,777.3	194.4
1999	5,647.2	3,233.0	653.2	1,828.8	643.7	92.4	67.6	24.8	2,414.2	180.0	31.0	2,005.2	198.1
2000	5,622.1	2,992.8	616.2	1,611.3	635.3	115.0	81.6	33.4	2,629.3	177.7	25.4	2,242.9	183.3
2001 [1]	5,807.5	2,930.7	734.9	1,433.0	613.0	134.9	95.1	39.7	2,876.7	186.5	18.3	2,492.1	179.9
2002	6,228.2	3,136.7	868.3	1,521.6	593.0	138.9	93.7	45.1	3,091.5	193.3	12.5	2,707.3	178.4
2003	6,783.2	3,460.7	918.2	1,799.5	576.9	166.1	120.0	46.1	3,322.5	201.6	11.0	2,912.2	197.7
2004	7,379.1	3,846.1	961.5	2,109.6	552.0	223.0			3,533.0	204.2	5.9	3,130.0	192.9
2005	7,932.7	4,084.9	914.3	2,328.8	520.7	307.1			3,847.8	203.6	3.1	3,380.6	260.5
2006	8,507.0	4,303.0	911.5	2,447.2	534.7	395.6			4,203.9	203.7	3.0	3,722.7	274.5
2007	9,007.7	4,448.1	958.1	2,458.0	561.1	456.9			4,559.5	197.1	3.0	4,026.8	332.6
2008	10,024.7	5,236.0	1,489.8	2,624.8	582.4	524.5			4,788.7	194.3	3.0	4,297.7	293.8
2009	11,909.8	7,009.7	1,992.5	3,773.8	679.8	551.7			4,900.1	192.5	4.9	4,454.3	248.4
2008: Jan	9,238.0	4,532.9	984.4	2,503.9	558.5	472.0			4,705.1	195.7	5.9	4,181.7	321.8
Feb	9,358.1	4,661.4	1,125.4	2,478.4	571.8	471.8			4,696.7	195.6	5.3	4,175.6	320.7
Mar	9,437.6	4,732.4	1,158.4	2,514.1	571.8	474.1			4,705.2	195.4	4.9	4,183.7	321.2
Apr	9,377.6	4,642.6	1,025.7	2,540.7	571.8	490.3			4,735.0	195.3	4.9	4,213.6	321.1
May	9,388.8	4,685.2	1,119.2	2,476.6	581.1	494.3			4,703.6	195.2	3.3	4,190.8	314.3
June	9,492.0	4,696.4	1,060.5	2,543.4	581.1	497.5			4,795.6	195.0	3.1	4,288.1	309.4
July	9,585.5	4,822.1	1,135.8	2,574.8	581.1	516.5			4,763.4	194.8	3.0	4,266.0	299.6
Aug	9,645.8	4,901.9	1,227.2	2,556.4	582.9	521.4			4,743.9	194.5	3.0	4,250.9	295.6
Sept	10,024.7	5,236.0	1,489.8	2,624.8	582.9	524.5			4,788.7	194.3	3.0	4,297.7	293.8
Oct	10,574.1	5,729.4	1,909.7	2,686.6	582.9	536.2			4,844.7	194.2	4.0	4,358.4	288.1
Nov	10,661.2	5,822.7	2,003.7	2,674.9	594.6	535.4			4,838.5	194.2	4.0	4,353.7	286.6
Dec	10,699.8	5,797.6	1,866.7	2,792.2	594.6	530.1			4,902.2	194.1	4.0	4,421.7	282.4
2009: Jan	10,632.1	5,749.9	1,798.6	2,826.0	594.6	516.7			4,882.2	193.8	5.0	4,406.0	277.3
Feb	10,877.1	6,012.4	1,985.6	2,892.0	609.4	511.5			4,864.8	194.1	5.0	4,391.4	274.3
Mar	11,126.9	6,266.1	2,033.6	3,084.5	620.5	513.1			4,860.8	194.0	6.0	4,388.7	272.2
Apr	11,238.6	6,363.4	1,994.5	3,204.5	620.5	529.9			4,875.2	194.0	7.0	4,403.9	270.3
May	11,321.6	6,454.3	2,065.4	3,211.3	632.5	531.0			4,867.3	193.9	6.5	4,399.4	267.6
June	11,545.3	6,612.1	2,006.5	3,417.7	643.7	532.3			4,933.2	193.6	6.0	4,468.6	265.0
July	11,669.3	6,782.8	2,020.5	3,547.5	654.8	548.0			4,886.5	193.3	5.5	4,431.8	256.0
Aug	11,812.9	6,939.2	2,068.5	3,638.6	667.8	552.4			4,873.6	192.8	4.5	4,425.9	250.4
Sept	11,909.8	7,009.7	1,992.5	3,773.8	679.8	551.7			4,900.1	192.5	4.9	4,454.3	248.4
Oct	11,893.1	6,947.6	1,858.5	3,818.2	691.9	567.1			4,945.5	192.2	4.4	4,501.1	247.8
Nov	12,113.0	7,174.6	1,850.5	4,039.8	704.9	567.5			4,938.5	191.8	4.4	4,497.4	244.9
Dec	12,311.4	7,272.5	1,793.5	4,181.1	717.9	568.1			5,038.9	191.3	4.4	4,597.1	246.0

[1] Data beginning with January 2001 are interest-bearing and non-interest-bearing securities; prior data are interest-bearing securities only.

[2] Data from 1986 to 2002 and 2005 to 2009 include Federal Financing Bank securities, not shown separately.

[3] Through 1996, series is U.S. savings bonds. Beginning 1997, includes U.S. retirement plan bonds, U.S. individual retirement bonds, and U.S. savings notes previously included in "other" nonmarketable securities.

[4] Nonmarketable certificates of indebtedness, notes, bonds, and bills in the Treasury foreign series of dollar-denominated and foreign-currency-denominated issues.

[5] Includes depository bonds; retirement plan bonds; Rural Electrification Administration bonds; State and local bonds; special issues held only by U.S. Government agencies and trust funds and the Federal home loan banks; for the period July 2003 through February 2004, depositary compensation securities; and beginning August 2008, Hope bonds for the HOPE For Homeowners Program.

Note: Through fiscal year 1976, the fiscal year was on a July 1–June 30 basis; beginning with October 1976 (fiscal year 1977), the fiscal year is on an October 1–September 30 basis.

Source: Department of the Treasury.

TABLE B–88. Maturity distribution and average length of marketable interest-bearing public debt securities held by private investors, 1970–2009

| End of year or month | Amount outstanding, privately held | Maturity class | | | | | Average length [1] | |
		Within 1 year	1 to 5 years	5 to 10 years	10 to 20 years	20 years and over	Years	Months
		Millions of dollars					Years	Months
Fiscal year:								
1970	157,910	76,443	57,035	8,286	7,876	8,272	3	8
1971	161,863	74,803	58,557	14,503	6,357	7,645	3	6
1972	165,978	79,509	57,157	16,033	6,358	6,922	3	3
1973	167,869	84,041	54,139	16,385	8,741	4,564	3	1
1974	164,862	87,150	50,103	14,197	9,930	3,481	2	11
1975	210,382	115,677	65,852	15,385	8,857	4,611	2	8
1976	279,782	150,296	90,578	24,169	8,087	6,652	2	7
1977	326,674	161,329	113,319	33,067	8,428	10,531	2	11
1978	356,501	163,819	132,993	33,500	11,383	14,805	3	3
1979	380,530	181,883	127,574	32,279	18,489	20,304	3	7
1980	463,717	220,084	156,244	38,809	25,901	22,679	3	9
1981	549,863	256,187	182,237	48,743	32,569	30,127	4	0
1982	682,043	314,436	221,783	75,749	33,017	37,058	3	11
1983	862,631	379,579	294,955	99,174	40,826	48,097	4	1
1984	1,017,488	437,941	332,808	130,417	49,664	66,658	4	6
1985	1,185,675	472,661	402,766	159,383	62,853	88,012	4	11
1986	1,354,275	506,903	467,348	189,995	70,664	119,365	5	3
1987	1,445,366	483,582	526,746	209,160	72,862	153,016	5	9
1988	1,555,208	524,201	552,993	232,453	74,186	171,375	5	9
1989	1,654,660	546,751	578,333	247,428	80,616	201,532	6	0
1990	1,841,903	626,297	630,144	267,573	82,713	235,176	6	1
1991	2,113,799	713,778	761,243	280,574	84,900	273,304	6	0
1992	2,363,802	808,705	866,329	295,921	84,706	308,141	5	11
1993	2,562,336	858,135	978,714	306,663	94,345	324,479	5	10
1994	2,719,861	877,932	1,128,322	289,998	88,208	335,401	5	8
1995	2,870,781	1,002,875	1,157,492	290,111	87,297	333,006	5	4
1996	3,011,185	1,058,558	1,212,258	306,643	111,360	322,366	5	3
1997	2,998,846	1,017,913	1,206,993	321,622	154,205	298,113	5	5
1998	2,856,637	940,572	1,105,175	319,331	157,347	334,212	5	10
1999	2,728,011	915,145	962,644	378,163	149,703	322,356	6	0
2000	2,469,152	858,903	791,540	355,382	167,082	296,246	6	2
2001	2,328,302	900,178	650,522	329,247	174,653	273,702	6	1
2002	2,492,821	939,986	802,032	311,176	203,816	235,811	5	6
2003	2,804,092	1,057,049	955,239	351,552	243,755	196,497	5	1
2004	3,145,244	1,127,850	1,150,979	414,728	243,036	208,652	4	11
2005	3,334,411	1,100,783	1,279,646	499,386	281,229	173,367	4	10
2006	3,496,359	1,140,553	1,295,589	589,748	290,733	179,736	4	11
2007	3,634,666	1,176,510	1,309,871	677,905	291,963	178,417	4	10
2008	4,745,256	2,042,003	1,468,455	719,347	352,430	163,022	4	1
2009	6,228,565	2,604,676	2,074,723	994,689	350,550	203,928	4	1
2008: Jan	3,805,408	1,315,046	1,295,456	710,580	319,185	165,140	4	9
Feb	3,933,939	1,454,105	1,294,886	691,672	319,156	174,120	4	8
Mar	4,127,033	1,607,155	1,323,534	702,527	319,481	174,336	4	5
Apr	4,079,776	1,509,658	1,366,837	709,124	338,330	155,827	4	6
May	4,162,323	1,618,739	1,329,756	718,171	333,602	162,056	4	6
June	4,203,441	1,580,568	1,396,177	730,327	334,145	162,224	4	6
July	4,328,809	1,668,784	1,439,791	716,694	341,086	162,453	4	5
Aug	4,386,440	1,774,790	1,390,479	706,395	351,906	162,870	4	5
Sept	4,745,256	2,042,003	1,468,455	719,347	352,430	163,022	4	1
Oct	5,238,827	2,462,352	1,496,698	764,782	352,076	162,919	3	10
Nov	5,312,125	2,540,826	1,490,667	761,948	355,148	163,536	3	10
Dec	5,307,633	2,406,537	1,607,484	776,147	354,202	163,262	3	10
2009: Jan	5,240,470	2,336,988	1,606,792	773,548	360,402	162,741	3	11
Feb	5,505,532	2,543,867	1,659,368	776,956	358,570	166,771	3	11
Mar	5,759,709	2,601,162	1,790,274	833,981	357,716	176,575	3	11
Apr	5,800,248	2,601,043	1,792,321	875,653	376,004	155,227	3	11
May	5,815,094	2,660,151	1,762,962	856,289	367,080	168,611	3	11
June	5,943,636	2,611,596	1,891,559	900,239	361,806	178,436	3	11
July	6,065,512	2,636,005	1,964,000	916,972	360,698	187,837	4	0
Aug	6,179,984	2,669,428	2,014,501	951,363	352,756	191,935	4	0
Sept	6,228,565	2,604,676	2,074,723	994,689	350,550	203,928	4	1
Oct	6,138,150	2,481,258	2,073,374	1,019,112	349,067	215,339	4	3
Nov	6,386,026	2,462,190	2,259,073	1,084,264	349,156	231,343	4	3
Dec	6,483,901	2,415,461	2,337,392	1,137,420	349,280	244,348	4	4

[1] Treasury inflation-protected securities—notes, first offered in 1997, and bonds, first offered in 1998—are included in the average length calculation from 1997 forward.

Note: Through fiscal year 1976, the fiscal year was on a July 1–June 30 basis; beginning with October 1976 (fiscal year 1977), the fiscal year is on an October 1–September 30 basis.

Data shown in this table are as of January 14, 2010.

Source: Department of the Treasury.

[Billions of dollars]

End of month	Total public debt [1]	Federal Reserve and Intragovernmental holdings [2]	Held by private investors									
						Pension funds						
			Total privately held	Depository institutions [3]	U.S. savings bonds [4]	Private [5]	State and local governments	Insurance companies	Mutual funds [6]	State and local governments	Foreign and international [7]	Other investors [8]
2000: Mar	5,773.4	2,590.6	3,182.8	237.7	185.3	150.2	196.9	120.0	222.3	306.3	1,085.0	679.1
June	5,685.9	2,698.6	2,987.3	222.2	184.6	149.0	194.9	116.5	205.4	309.3	1,060.7	544.8
Sept	5,674.2	2,737.9	2,936.3	220.5	184.3	147.9	185.5	113.7	207.8	307.9	1,038.8	529.9
Dec	5,662.2	2,781.8	2,880.4	201.5	184.8	145.0	179.1	110.2	225.7	310.0	1,015.2	509.0
2001: Mar	5,773.7	2,880.9	2,892.8	188.0	184.8	153.4	177.3	109.1	225.3	316.9	1,012.5	525.5
June	5,726.8	3,004.2	2,722.6	188.1	185.5	148.5	183.1	108.1	221.0	324.8	983.3	380.3
Sept	5,807.5	3,027.8	2,779.7	189.1	186.4	149.9	166.8	106.8	234.1	321.2	992.2	433.1
Dec	5,943.4	3,123.9	2,819.5	181.5	190.3	145.8	155.1	105.7	261.9	328.4	1,040.1	410.7
2002: Mar	6,006.0	3,156.8	2,849.2	187.6	191.9	152.7	163.3	114.0	266.1	327.6	1,057.2	388.8
June	6,126.5	3,276.7	2,849.8	204.7	192.7	152.1	153.9	122.0	253.8	333.6	1,123.1	313.8
Sept	6,228.2	3,303.5	2,924.8	209.3	193.3	154.5	156.3	130.4	256.8	338.6	1,188.6	297.0
Dec	6,405.7	3,387.2	3,018.5	222.6	194.9	153.8	158.9	139.7	281.0	354.7	1,235.6	277.4
2003: Mar	6,460.8	3,390.8	3,069.9	153.4	196.9	165.8	162.1	139.5	296.6	350.0	1,275.2	330.4
June	6,670.1	3,505.4	3,164.7	145.1	199.1	170.2	161.3	138.7	302.3	347.9	1,371.9	328.2
Sept	6,783.2	3,515.3	3,268.0	146.8	201.5	167.7	155.5	137.4	287.1	357.7	1,443.3	371.1
Dec	6,998.0	3,620.1	3,377.9	153.1	203.8	172.1	148.6	136.5	280.8	364.2	1,523.1	395.6
2004: Mar	7,131.1	3,628.3	3,502.8	162.8	204.4	169.8	143.6	141.0	280.8	374.1	1,670.0	356.3
June	7,274.3	3,742.8	3,531.5	158.6	204.6	173.3	134.9	144.1	258.7	381.2	1,735.4	340.6
Sept	7,379.1	3,772.0	3,607.0	138.5	204.1	174.0	140.8	147.4	255.0	381.7	1,794.5	371.0
Dec	7,596.1	3,905.6	3,690.6	125.0	204.4	173.7	151.0	149.7	254.1	389.1	1,849.3	394.3
2005: Mar	7,776.9	3,921.6	3,855.4	141.8	204.2	177.3	158.0	152.4	261.1	412.0	1,952.2	396.4
June	7,836.5	4,033.5	3,803.0	126.9	204.2	181.0	171.3	155.0	248.7	444.0	1,877.5	394.5
Sept	7,932.7	4,067.8	3,864.9	125.3	203.6	184.2	164.8	159.0	244.7	467.6	1,929.6	386.0
Dec	8,170.4	4,199.8	3,970.6	117.1	205.1	184.9	153.8	160.4	251.3	481.4	2,033.9	382.6
2006: Mar	8,371.2	4,257.2	4,114.0	115.3	205.9	186.7	153.0	161.3	248.7	486.1	2,082.1	475.0
June	8,420.0	4,389.2	4,030.8	117.1	205.2	192.1	150.9	161.2	244.2	499.4	1,977.8	482.8
Sept	8,507.0	4,432.8	4,074.2	113.5	203.6	201.9	155.6	160.6	235.7	502.1	2,025.3	475.8
Dec	8,680.2	4,558.1	4,122.1	114.8	202.4	207.5	157.1	159.0	250.7	516.9	2,103.1	410.6
2007: Mar	8,849.7	4,576.6	4,273.1	119.7	200.3	221.7	159.2	150.8	264.5	535.0	2,194.8	427.1
June	8,867.7	4,715.1	4,152.6	110.4	198.6	232.5	160.2	142.1	267.7	580.3	2,192.0	268.7
Sept	9,007.7	4,738.0	4,269.7	119.6	197.1	246.7	165.6	133.4	306.3	541.4	2,235.3	324.1
Dec	9,229.2	4,833.5	4,395.7	129.7	196.4	257.6	168.8	123.3	362.9	531.5	2,353.2	272.2
2008: Mar	9,437.6	4,694.7	4,742.9	125.3	195.3	270.5	169.4	129.4	484.4	521.6	2,505.8	341.2
June	9,492.0	4,685.8	4,806.2	112.7	194.9	276.7	169.1	135.5	477.2	513.4	2,587.2	339.4
Sept	10,024.7	4,692.7	5,332.0	130.0	194.2	292.5	171.6	140.6	656.1	499.3	2,799.5	448.3
Dec	10,699.8	4,806.4	5,893.4	105.0	194.2	297.2	174.6	160.5	768.8	483.1	3,075.9	634.4
2009: Mar	11,126.9	4,785.2	6,341.7	129.1	193.9	305.9	173.2	179.7	716.0	477.9	3,264.6	901.4
June	11,545.3	5,026.8	6,518.5	140.8	193.5	312.4	172.7	189.7	695.0	488.4	3,382.1	943.8
Sept	11,909.8	5,127.1	6,782.7	199.0	192.4	324.5	176.7	196.3	643.0	502.5	3,497.4	1,050.9
Dec	12,311.4	5,276.9	7,034.5	....	191.3	....	....	....	....	....	....	....

[1] Face value.
[2] Federal Reserve holdings exclude Treasury securities held under repurchase agreements.
[3] Includes commercial banks, savings institutions, and credit unions.
[4] Current accrual value.
[5] Includes Treasury securities held by the Federal Employees Retirement System Thrift Savings Plan "G Fund."
[6] Includes money market mutual funds, mutual funds, and closed-end investment companies.
[7] Includes nonmarketable foreign series, Treasury securities, and Treasury deposit funds. Excludes Treasury securities held under repurchase agreements in custody accounts at the Federal Reserve Bank of New York. Estimates reflect benchmarks to this series at differing intervals; for further detail, see *Treasury Bulletin* and http://www.treas.gov/tic/ticsec2.shtml
[8] Includes individuals, Government-sponsored enterprises, brokers and dealers, bank personal trusts and estates, corporate and noncorporate businesses, and other investors.

Note: Data shown in this table are as of January 25, 2010.

Source: Department of the Treasury.

CORPORATE PROFITS AND FINANCE

TABLE B–90. Corporate profits with inventory valuation and capital consumption adjustments, 1960–2009

[Billions of dollars; quarterly data at seasonally adjusted annual rates]

Year or quarter	Corporate profits with inventory valuation and capital consumption adjustments	Taxes on corporate income	Corporate profits after tax with inventory valuation and capital consumption adjustments		
			Total	Net dividends	Undistributed profits with inventory valuation and capital consumption adjustments
1960	53.1	22.8	30.3	13.4	16.9
1961	54.2	22.9	31.3	13.9	17.4
1962	62.3	24.1	38.3	15.0	23.2
1963	68.3	26.4	42.0	16.2	25.7
1964	75.5	28.2	47.4	18.2	29.2
1965	86.5	31.1	55.5	20.2	35.3
1966	92.5	33.9	58.7	20.7	38.0
1967	90.2	32.9	57.3	21.5	35.8
1968	97.3	39.6	57.6	23.5	34.1
1969	94.5	40.0	54.5	24.2	30.3
1970	82.5	34.8	47.7	24.3	23.4
1971	96.1	38.2	57.9	25.0	32.9
1972	111.4	42.3	69.1	26.8	42.2
1973	124.5	50.0	74.5	29.9	44.6
1974	115.1	52.8	62.3	33.2	29.1
1975	133.3	51.6	81.7	33.0	48.7
1976	161.6	65.3	96.3	39.0	57.3
1977	191.8	74.4	117.4	44.8	72.6
1978	218.4	84.9	133.6	50.8	82.8
1979	225.4	90.0	135.3	57.5	77.8
1980	201.4	87.2	114.2	64.1	50.2
1981	223.3	84.3	138.9	73.8	65.2
1982	205.7	66.5	139.2	77.7	61.5
1983	259.8	80.6	179.2	83.5	95.7
1984	318.6	97.5	221.1	90.8	130.3
1985	332.5	99.4	233.1	97.6	135.6
1986	314.1	109.7	204.5	106.2	98.3
1987	367.8	130.4	237.4	112.3	125.1
1988	426.6	141.6	285.0	129.9	155.1
1989	425.6	146.1	279.5	158.0	121.5
1990	434.4	145.4	289.0	169.1	120.0
1991	457.3	138.6	318.7	180.7	138.0
1992	496.2	148.7	347.5	188.0	159.5
1993	543.7	171.0	372.7	202.9	169.7
1994	628.2	193.1	435.1	235.7	199.4
1995	716.2	217.8	498.3	254.4	243.9
1996	801.5	231.5	570.0	297.7	272.3
1997	884.8	245.4	639.4	331.2	308.2
1998	812.4	248.4	564.1	351.5	212.6
1999	856.3	258.8	597.5	337.4	260.1
2000	819.2	265.1	554.1	377.9	176.3
2001	784.2	203.3	580.9	370.9	210.0
2002	872.2	192.3	679.9	399.3	280.6
2003	977.8	243.8	734.0	424.9	309.2
2004	1,246.9	306.1	940.8	550.3	390.5
2005	1,456.1	412.4	1,043.7	557.3	486.4
2006	1,608.3	473.3	1,135.0	704.8	430.3
2007	1,541.7	451.5	1,090.2	767.8	322.4
2008	1,360.4	292.2	1,068.2	689.9	378.3
2009 *p*				576.1	
2006: I	1,590.9	460.7	1,130.2	646.4	483.9
II	1,597.7	475.1	1,122.6	691.1	431.5
III	1,655.1	496.6	1,158.5	727.1	431.4
IV	1,589.6	460.7	1,128.8	754.5	374.3
2007: I	1,535.4	469.5	1,065.9	772.6	293.3
II	1,594.9	466.5	1,128.4	778.1	350.3
III	1,537.1	440.0	1,097.1	770.6	326.5
IV	1,499.4	430.1	1,069.3	749.9	319.4
2008: I	1,459.7	323.2	1,136.4	719.4	417.1
II	1,403.7	317.5	1,086.3	693.7	392.6
III	1,454.6	304.8	1,149.8	676.6	473.2
IV	1,123.6	223.3	900.4	669.9	230.5
2009: I	1,182.7	270.3	912.4	618.1	294.2
II	1,226.5	305.9	920.6	556.0	364.5
III	1,358.9	321.0	1,037.9	549.9	488.0
IV *p*				580.5	

Source: Department of Commerce (Bureau of Economic Analysis).

TABLE B–91. Corporate profits by industry, 1960–2009

[Billions of dollars; quarterly data at seasonally adjusted annual rates]

Year or quarter	Total	Corporate profits with inventory valuation adjustment and without capital consumption adjustment												Rest of the world
		Domestic industries												
		Total	Financial			Nonfinancial								
			Total	Federal Reserve banks	Other	Total	Manu-factur-ing [1]	Trans-porta-tion [2]	Utilities	Whole-sale trade	Retail trade	Infor-mation	Other	
SIC: [3]														
1960	51.5	48.3	8.4	0.9	7.5	39.9	23.8	7.5	....	2.5	2.8	....	3.3	3.1
1961	51.8	48.5	8.3	.8	7.6	40.2	23.4	7.9	....	2.5	3.0	....	3.4	3.3
1962	57.0	53.3	8.6	.9	7.7	44.7	26.3	8.5	....	2.8	3.4	....	3.6	3.8
1963	62.1	58.1	8.3	1.0	7.3	49.8	29.7	9.5	....	2.8	3.6	....	4.1	4.1
1964	68.6	64.1	8.8	1.1	7.6	55.4	32.6	10.2	....	3.4	4.5	....	4.7	4.5
1965	78.9	74.2	9.3	1.3	8.0	64.9	39.8	11.0	....	3.8	4.9	....	5.4	4.7
1966	84.6	80.1	10.7	1.7	9.1	69.3	42.6	12.0	....	4.0	4.9	....	5.9	4.5
1967	82.0	77.2	11.2	2.0	9.2	66.0	39.2	10.9	....	4.1	5.7	....	6.1	4.8
1968	88.8	83.2	12.8	2.5	10.3	70.4	41.9	11.0	....	4.6	6.4	....	6.6	5.6
1969	85.5	78.9	13.6	3.1	10.5	65.3	37.3	10.7	....	4.9	6.4	....	6.1	6.6
1970	74.4	67.3	15.4	3.5	11.9	52.0	27.5	8.3	....	4.4	6.0	....	5.8	7.1
1971	88.3	80.4	17.6	3.3	14.3	62.8	35.1	8.9	....	5.2	7.2	....	6.4	7.9
1972	101.6	92.1	19.2	3.3	15.8	72.9	42.2	9.5	....	6.9	7.4	....	7.0	9.5
1973	115.4	100.5	20.5	4.5	16.1	80.0	47.2	9.1	....	8.2	6.7	....	8.8	14.9
1974	109.6	92.1	20.2	5.7	14.5	71.9	41.4	7.6	....	11.5	2.3	....	9.1	17.5
1975	135.0	120.4	20.2	5.6	14.6	100.2	55.2	11.0	....	13.8	8.2	....	12.0	14.6
1976	165.6	149.1	25.0	5.9	19.1	124.1	71.4	15.3	....	12.9	10.5	....	14.0	16.5
1977	194.8	175.7	31.9	6.1	25.8	143.8	79.4	18.6	....	15.6	12.4	....	17.8	19.1
1978	222.4	199.6	39.5	7.6	31.9	160.0	90.5	21.8	....	15.6	12.3	....	19.8	22.9
1979	232.0	197.4	40.4	9.4	30.9	157.0	89.8	17.0	....	18.8	9.9	....	21.6	34.6
1980	211.4	175.9	34.0	11.8	22.2	142.0	78.3	18.4	....	17.2	6.2	....	21.8	35.5
1981	219.1	189.4	29.1	14.4	14.7	160.3	91.1	20.3	....	22.4	9.9	....	16.7	29.7
1982	191.1	158.5	26.0	15.2	10.8	132.5	67.1	23.1	....	19.6	13.5	....	9.3	32.6
1983	226.6	191.5	35.5	14.6	21.0	156.0	76.2	29.5	....	21.0	18.8	....	10.4	35.1
1984	264.6	228.1	34.4	16.4	18.0	193.7	91.8	40.1	....	29.5	21.1	....	11.1	36.6
1985	257.5	219.4	45.9	16.3	29.5	173.5	84.3	33.8	....	23.9	22.2	....	9.2	38.1
1986	253.0	213.5	56.8	15.5	41.2	156.8	57.9	35.8	....	24.1	23.5	....	15.5	39.5
1987	306.9	258.8	61.6	16.2	45.3	197.3	87.5	42.4	....	19.0	24.0	....	24.4	48.0
1988	367.7	310.8	68.8	18.1	50.7	242.0	122.5	48.9	....	20.4	21.0	....	29.3	57.0
1989	374.1	307.0	80.2	20.6	59.5	226.8	112.1	43.8	....	22.1	22.1	....	26.7	67.1
1990	398.8	322.7	92.3	21.8	70.5	230.4	114.4	44.7	....	19.6	21.6	....	30.1	76.1
1991	430.3	353.8	122.1	20.7	101.4	231.7	99.4	53.8	....	22.2	27.7	....	28.7	76.5
1992	471.6	398.5	142.7	18.3	124.4	255.8	100.8	59.2	....	25.5	29.2	....	41.1	73.1
1993	515.0	438.1	133.4	16.7	116.7	304.7	116.8	70.2	....	26.7	40.6	....	50.4	76.9
1994	586.6	508.6	129.2	18.5	110.7	379.5	150.1	85.2	....	31.8	47.2	....	65.2	78.0
1995	666.0	573.1	160.1	22.9	137.2	413.0	176.7	87.9	....	28.0	44.8	....	75.5	92.9
1996	743.8	641.8	167.5	22.5	144.9	474.4	192.0	93.7	....	40.6	53.7	....	94.5	102.0
1997	815.9	708.3	187.4	24.3	163.2	520.9	212.2	86.5	....	48.2	65.9	....	108.1	107.6
1998	738.6	635.9	159.6	25.6	134.0	476.2	173.4	81.1	....	51.7	74.7	....	95.5	102.8
1999	776.6	655.0	190.4	26.7	163.8	464.6	174.6	59.1	....	51.7	75.6	....	103.6	121.5
2000	755.7	610.0	194.4	31.2	163.2	415.7	166.5	45.8	....	55.6	71.4	....	76.4	145.6
NAICS: [3]														
1998	738.6	635.9	159.5	25.6	133.9	476.4	155.8	21.3	33.5	52.8	67.3	21.9	123.7	102.8
1999	776.6	655.0	189.3	26.7	162.6	465.7	148.8	16.5	33.7	54.8	65.7	12.5	133.6	121.5
2000	755.7	610.0	189.6	31.2	158.4	420.4	143.9	15.2	25.6	58.7	60.7	−15.5	131.8	145.6
2001	720.8	551.1	228.0	28.9	199.1	323.1	49.7	1.2	25.2	51.3	72.6	−24.4	147.4	169.7
2002	762.8	604.9	265.2	23.5	241.7	339.7	47.7	−.1	12.3	49.1	81.6	−3.8	153.0	157.9
2003	892.2	726.4	311.8	20.1	291.8	414.6	69.4	7.4	12.4	54.8	88.9	4.9	176.7	165.8
2004	1,195.1	990.1	362.3	20.0	342.3	627.8	154.1	14.4	19.4	75.6	93.4	45.6	225.2	205.0
2005	1,609.5	1,370.0	443.6	26.6	417.0	926.4	247.2	29.8	29.8	92.2	122.6	81.3	324.3	239.4
2006	1,784.7	1,527.8	448.0	33.8	414.1	1,079.9	304.5	42.1	54.4	103.7	133.2	92.4	349.6	256.8
2007	1,730.4	1,382.6	367.8	37.7	330.1	1,014.9	278.6	30.0	49.1	102.2	121.6	90.3	343.0	347.8
2008	1,424.5	1,047.3	278.9	35.7	243.2	768.4	175.5	11.4	40.1	75.1	78.2	84.7	303.4	377.2
2007: I	1,705.4	1,423.2	384.2	38.2	346.0	1,039.0	288.9	32.9	51.3	107.9	127.9	90.5	339.6	282.2
II	1,779.1	1,467.9	406.2	38.5	367.7	1,061.7	316.0	33.0	46.6	117.0	137.2	77.5	334.4	311.2
III	1,732.9	1,362.4	378.2	37.5	340.6	984.2	244.0	30.9	47.3	107.9	118.7	93.9	341.5	370.5
IV	1,704.1	1,277.0	302.5	36.5	266.0	974.5	265.7	23.4	51.2	76.0	102.4	99.4	356.4	427.1
2008: I	1,512.9	1,100.6	357.0	35.9	321.1	743.6	187.6	12.9	33.1	46.6	75.6	91.6	296.3	412.3
II	1,463.8	1,096.8	330.8	31.1	299.7	766.0	160.1	11.9	43.1	56.6	80.2	101.8	312.1	367.0
III	1,522.2	1,125.0	297.5	34.6	262.9	827.5	205.7	9.2	43.5	85.8	77.1	81.9	324.4	397.2
IV	1,199.3	866.9	130.3	41.1	89.2	736.6	148.6	11.5	40.8	111.5	79.7	63.6	280.8	332.4
2009: I	1,327.6	1,011.9	253.9	28.8	225.1	758.0	121.6	6.7	53.6	94.0	83.1	95.4	303.6	315.8
II	1,355.1	1,053.9	280.7	46.1	234.6	773.3	132.3	1.3	53.4	87.5	95.1	99.4	304.2	301.2
III	1,477.8	1,154.6	362.4	57.6	304.8	792.2	129.7	4.8	61.5	80.6	98.8	107.0	309.9	323.2

[1] See Table B–92 for industry detail.
[2] Data on Standard Industrial Classification (SIC) basis include transportation and public utilities. Those on North American Industry Classification System (NAICS) basis include transporation and warehousing. Utilities classified separately in NAICS (as shown beginning 1998).
[3] SIC-based industry data use the 1987 SIC for data beginning in 1987 and the 1972 SIC for prior data. NAICS-based data use 2002 NAICS.

Note: Industry data on SIC basis and NAICS basis are not necessarily the same and are not strictly comparable.

Source: Department of Commerce (Bureau of Economic Analysis).

Table B–92. Corporate profits of manufacturing industries, 1960–2009

[Billions of dollars; quarterly data at seasonally adjusted annual rates]

		Corporate profits with inventory valuation adjustment and without capital consumption adjustment										
		Durable goods [2]							Nondurable goods [2]			
Year or quarter	Total manufacturing	Total [1]	Fabricated metal products	Machinery	Computer and electronic products	Electrical equipment, appliances, and components	Motor vehicles, bodies and trailers, and parts	Other	Total	Food and beverage and tobacco products	Chemical products	Petroleum and coal products	Other
SIC: [3]												
1960	23.8	11.6	0.8	1.8		1.3	3.0	2.7	12.2	2.2	3.1	2.6	4.2
1961	23.4	11.3	1.0	1.9		1.3	2.5	2.9	12.1	2.4	3.3	2.3	4.2
1962	26.3	14.1	1.2	2.4		1.5	4.0	3.4	12.3	2.4	3.2	2.2	4.4
1963	29.7	16.4	1.3	2.6		1.6	4.9	4.0	13.3	2.7	3.7	2.2	4.7
1964	32.6	18.1	1.5	3.3		1.7	4.6	4.4	14.5	2.7	4.1	2.4	5.3
1965	39.8	23.3	2.1	4.0		2.7	6.2	5.2	16.5	2.9	4.6	2.9	6.1
1966	42.6	24.1	2.4	4.6		3.0	5.2	5.2	18.6	3.3	4.9	3.4	6.9
1967	39.2	21.3	2.5	4.2		3.0	4.0	4.9	18.0	3.3	4.3	4.0	6.4
1968	41.9	22.5	2.3	4.2		2.9	5.5	5.6	19.4	3.2	5.3	3.8	7.1
1969	37.3	19.2	2.0	3.8		2.3	4.8	4.9	18.1	3.1	4.6	3.4	7.0
1970	27.5	10.5	1.1	3.1		1.3	1.3	2.9	17.0	3.2	3.9	3.7	6.1
1971	35.1	16.6	1.5	3.1		2.0	5.2	4.1	18.5	3.6	4.5	3.8	6.6
1972	42.2	22.9	2.2	4.6		2.9	6.0	5.6	19.3	3.0	5.3	3.4	7.7
1973	47.2	25.2	2.7	4.9		3.2	5.9	6.2	22.1	2.5	6.2	5.4	7.9
1974	41.4	15.3	1.8	3.3		.6	.7	4.0	26.1	2.6	5.3	10.9	7.3
1975	55.2	20.6	3.3	5.1		2.6	2.3	4.7	34.5	8.6	6.4	10.1	9.5
1976	71.4	31.4	3.9	6.9		3.8	7.4	7.3	39.9	7.1	8.2	13.5	11.1
1977	79.4	38.0	4.5	8.6		5.9	9.4	8.5	41.4	6.9	7.8	13.1	13.6
1978	90.5	45.4	5.0	10.7		6.7	9.0	10.5	45.1	6.2	8.3	15.8	14.8
1979	89.8	37.2	5.3	9.5		5.6	4.7	8.5	52.6	5.8	7.2	24.8	14.7
1980	78.3	18.9	4.4	8.0		5.2	−4.3	2.7	59.5	6.1	5.7	34.7	13.1
1981	91.1	19.5	4.5	9.0		5.2	.3	−2.6	71.6	9.2	8.0	40.0	14.5
1982	67.1	5.0	2.7	3.1		1.7	.0	2.1	62.1	7.3	5.1	34.7	15.0
1983	76.2	19.5	3.1	4.0		3.5	5.3	8.4	56.7	6.3	7.4	23.9	19.1
1984	91.8	39.3	4.7	6.0		5.1	9.2	14.6	52.6	6.8	8.2	17.6	20.1
1985	84.3	29.7	4.9	5.7		2.6	7.4	10.1	54.6	8.8	6.6	18.7	20.5
1986	57.9	26.3	5.2	.8		2.7	4.6	12.1	31.7	7.5	7.5	−4.7	21.3
1987	87.5	41.3	5.5	5.6		6.1	3.8	17.7	46.2	11.2	14.6	−1.4	21.9
1988	122.5	54.8	6.6	11.3		7.8	6.3	16.7	67.7	9.7	18.8	12.9	26.4
1989	112.1	51.8	6.4	12.4		9.5	2.8	14.3	60.3	11.2	18.3	6.6	24.2
1990	114.4	44.5	6.1	12.0		8.7	−1.8	16.1	69.9	14.4	17.0	16.5	22.0
1991	99.4	35.1	5.3	5.8		10.2	−5.3	17.5	64.3	18.3	16.3	7.4	22.3
1992	100.8	41.2	6.3	7.6		10.6	−.9	17.6	59.6	18.4	16.1	−.8	25.9
1993	116.8	56.5	7.4	7.6		15.4	6.1	19.6	60.4	16.5	16.0	2.8	25.0
1994	150.1	75.8	11.2	9.3		23.2	8.0	21.7	74.3	20.4	23.6	1.5	28.9
1995	176.7	82.3	11.9	14.9		22.0	.2	26.1	94.4	27.6	28.2	7.4	31.2
1996	192.0	92.0	14.6	17.0		20.7	4.5	29.5	99.9	22.7	26.6	15.3	35.3
1997	212.2	104.8	17.1	16.9		26.0	5.2	33.3	107.4	25.2	32.4	17.6	32.3
1998	173.4	86.7	16.1	19.6		9.1	5.9	29.8	86.6	22.0	26.2	7.1	31.4
1999	174.6	77.9	16.1	12.0		5.3	7.5	28.1	96.6	28.1	24.8	4.6	39.2
2000	166.5	64.6	15.5	16.2		5.1	−1.4	28.1	101.9	26.0	15.3	29.7	30.9
NAICS: [3]												
1998	155.8	82.7	16.4	15.3	4.2	6.2	6.4	34.2	73.1	22.1	25.0	5.3	20.7
1999	148.8	71.2	16.4	11.7	−6.8	6.4	7.7	35.9	77.6	30.9	22.8	2.2	21.7
2000	143.9	60.0	15.8	7.7	4.2	5.9	−.7	27.1	83.9	26.0	13.8	27.6	16.5
2001	49.7	−26.9	9.8	2.0	−48.6	1.9	−8.9	16.8	76.6	28.2	11.6	29.7	7.1
2002	47.7	−7.7	9.1	1.4	−34.4	.0	−4.5	20.7	55.4	25.3	17.8	1.3	11.0
2003	69.4	−4.3	8.0	1.0	−14.7	2.2	−11.7	10.8	73.8	24.0	18.9	23.5	7.4
2004	154.1	40.7	12.2	7.1	−4.3	.6	−6.8	31.9	113.4	24.3	24.7	49.1	15.3
2005	247.2	95.6	18.1	14.5	9.0	−1.4	1.1	54.2	151.7	27.3	25.7	79.4	19.3
2006	304.5	118.9	18.7	19.2	17.4	11.5	−6.8	58.9	185.7	32.5	52.5	76.6	24.0
2007	278.6	96.1	21.3	19.8	11.2	−1.1	−16.4	61.3	182.6	30.2	51.9	77.8	22.7
2008	175.5	30.7	17.6	16.1	4.7	−4.1	−47.5	43.9	144.9	33.7	31.3	66.5	13.3
2007: I	288.9	105.9	19.1	20.0	17.0	3.5	−15.1	61.4	183.0	28.2	52.4	78.0	24.3
II	316.0	100.6	20.6	21.0	10.5	−2.1	−8.7	59.3	215.4	33.5	50.2	110.9	20.8
III	244.0	84.9	22.5	19.3	11.6	−4.5	−24.9	60.9	159.1	29.3	42.6	64.8	22.5
IV	265.7	92.8	23.0	19.0	5.5	−1.4	−17.0	63.7	172.9	29.8	62.4	57.5	23.2
2008: I	187.6	61.0	18.5	17.1	14.5	−3.6	−35.3	49.8	126.6	29.2	16.4	64.5	16.6
II	160.1	19.7	14.9	13.1	2.0	−2.0	−55.7	47.4	140.5	37.1	48.2	42.5	12.7
III	205.7	40.5	17.7	14.6	.1	−2.6	−45.4	56.2	165.2	37.3	39.1	79.3	9.5
IV	148.6	1.5	17.4	19.6	2.2	−8.4	−53.4	22.3	147.1	31.3	21.7	79.7	14.4
2009: I	121.6	8.0	19.3	12.8	3.2	−6.3	−54.8	33.9	113.6	34.7	29.6	29.4	19.8
II	132.3	11.9	13.7	10.4	3.9	−9.1	−38.5	31.5	120.4	33.1	39.4	15.2	32.8
III	129.7	6.7	10.9	8.1	3.1	−9.4	−16.6	10.8	122.9	35.1	37.4	15.8	34.5

[1] For Standard Industrial Classification (SIC) data, includes primary metal industries, not shown separately.
[2] Industry groups shown in column headings reflect North American Industry Classification System (NAICS) classification for data beginning 1998. For data on SIC basis, the industry groups would be industrial machinery and equipment (now machinery), electronic and other electric equipment (now electrical equipment, appliances, and components), motor vehicles and equipment (now motor vehicles, bodies and trailers, and parts), food and kindred products (now food and beverage and tobacco products), and chemicals and allied products (now chemical products).
[3] See footnote 3 and Note, Table B–91.

Source: Department of Commerce (Bureau of Economic Analysis).

TABLE B–93. Sales, profits, and stockholders' equity, all manufacturing corporations, 1968–2009

[Billions of dollars]

Year or quarter	All manufacturing corporations				Durable goods industries				Nondurable goods industries			
	Sales (net)	Profits		Stock-holders' equity²	Sales (net)	Profits		Stock-holders' equity²	Sales (net)	Profits		Stock-holders' equity²
		Before income taxes¹	After income taxes			Before income taxes¹	After income taxes			Before income taxes¹	After income taxes	
1968	631.9	55.4	32.1	265.9	335.5	30.6	16.5	135.6	296.4	24.8	15.5	130.3
1969	694.6	58.1	33.2	289.9	366.5	31.5	16.9	147.6	328.1	26.6	16.4	142.3
1970	708.8	48.1	28.6	306.8	363.1	23.0	12.9	155.1	345.7	25.2	15.7	151.7
1971	751.1	52.9	31.0	320.8	381.8	26.5	14.5	160.4	369.3	26.5	16.5	160.5
1972	849.5	63.2	36.5	343.4	435.8	33.6	18.4	171.4	413.7	29.6	18.0	172.0
1973	1,017.2	81.4	48.1	374.1	527.3	43.6	24.8	188.7	489.9	37.8	23.3	185.4
1973: IV	275.1	21.4	13.0	386.4	140.1	10.8	6.3	194.7	135.0	10.6	6.7	191.7
New series:												
1973: IV	236.6	20.6	13.2	368.0	122.7	10.1	6.2	185.8	113.9	10.5	7.0	182.1
1974	1,060.6	92.1	58.7	395.0	529.0	41.1	24.7	196.0	531.6	51.0	34.1	199.0
1975	1,065.2	79.9	49.1	423.4	521.1	35.3	21.4	208.1	544.1	44.6	27.7	215.3
1976	1,203.2	104.9	64.5	462.7	589.6	50.7	30.8	224.3	613.7	54.3	33.7	238.4
1977	1,328.1	115.1	70.4	496.7	657.3	57.9	34.8	239.9	670.8	57.2	35.5	256.8
1978	1,496.4	132.5	81.1	540.5	760.7	69.6	41.8	262.6	735.7	62.9	39.3	277.9
1979	1,741.8	154.2	98.7	600.5	865.7	72.4	45.2	292.5	876.1	81.8	53.5	308.0
1980	1,912.8	145.8	92.6	668.1	889.1	57.4	35.6	317.7	1,023.7	88.4	56.9	350.4
1981	2,144.7	158.6	101.3	743.4	979.5	67.2	41.6	350.4	1,165.2	91.3	59.6	393.0
1982	2,039.4	108.2	70.9	770.2	913.1	34.7	21.7	355.5	1,126.4	73.6	49.3	414.7
1983	2,114.3	133.1	85.8	812.8	973.5	48.7	30.0	372.4	1,140.8	84.4	55.8	440.4
1984	2,335.0	165.6	107.6	864.2	1,107.6	75.5	48.9	395.6	1,227.5	90.0	58.8	468.5
1985	2,331.4	137.0	87.6	866.2	1,142.6	61.5	38.6	420.9	1,188.8	75.6	49.1	445.3
1986	2,220.9	129.3	83.1	874.7	1,125.5	52.1	32.6	436.3	1,095.4	77.2	50.5	438.4
1987	2,378.2	173.0	115.6	900.9	1,178.0	78.0	53.0	444.3	1,200.3	95.1	62.6	456.6
1988 ³	2,596.2	215.3	153.8	957.6	1,284.7	91.6	66.9	468.7	1,311.5	123.7	86.8	488.9
1989	2,745.1	187.6	135.1	999.0	1,356.6	75.1	55.5	501.3	1,388.5	112.6	79.6	497.7
1990	2,810.7	158.1	110.1	1,043.8	1,357.2	57.3	40.7	515.0	1,453.5	100.8	69.4	528.9
1991	2,761.1	98.7	66.4	1,064.1	1,304.0	13.9	7.2	506.8	1,457.1	84.8	59.3	557.4
1992 ⁴	2,890.2	31.4	22.1	1,034.7	1,389.8	-33.7	-24.0	473.9	1,500.4	65.1	46.0	560.8
1993	3,015.1	117.9	83.2	1,039.7	1,490.2	38.9	27.4	482.7	1,524.9	79.0	55.7	557.1
1994	3,255.8	243.5	174.9	1,110.1	1,657.6	121.0	87.1	533.3	1,598.2	122.5	87.8	576.8
1995	3,528.3	274.5	198.2	1,240.6	1,807.7	130.6	94.3	613.7	1,720.6	143.9	103.9	627.0
1996	3,757.6	306.6	224.9	1,348.0	1,941.6	146.6	106.1	673.9	1,816.0	160.0	118.8	674.2
1997	3,920.0	331.4	244.5	1,462.7	2,075.8	167.0	121.4	743.4	1,844.2	164.4	123.1	719.3
1998	3,949.4	314.7	234.4	1,482.9	2,168.8	175.1	127.8	779.9	1,780.7	139.6	106.5	703.0
1999	4,148.9	355.3	257.8	1,569.3	2,314.2	198.8	140.3	869.6	1,834.6	156.5	117.5	699.7
2000	4,548.2	381.1	275.3	1,823.1	2,457.4	190.7	131.8	1,054.3	2,090.8	190.5	143.5	768.7
2000: IV	1,163.6	69.2	46.8	1,892.4	620.4	31.2	19.3	1,101.5	543.2	38.0	27.4	790.9
NAICS: ⁵												
2000: IV	1,128.8	62.1	41.7	1,833.8	623.0	26.9	15.4	1,100.0	505.8	35.2	26.3	733.8
2001	4,295.0	83.2	36.2	1,843.0	2,321.2	-69.0	-76.1	1,080.5	1,973.8	152.2	112.3	762.5
2002	4,216.4	195.5	134.7	1,804.0	2,260.6	45.9	21.6	1,024.8	1,955.8	149.6	113.1	779.2
2003	4,397.2	305.7	237.0	1,952.2	2,282.7	117.6	88.2	1,040.8	2,114.5	188.1	148.9	911.5
2004	4,934.1	447.5	348.2	2,206.3	2,537.3	200.0	156.5	1,212.9	2,396.7	247.5	191.6	993.5
2005	5,411.5	524.2	401.3	2,410.4	2,730.5	211.3	161.2	1,304.0	2,681.0	312.9	240.2	1,106.5
2006	5,782.7	604.6	470.3	2,678.6	2,910.2	249.1	192.8	1,384.0	2,872.5	355.5	277.5	1,294.6
2007	6,060.0	602.8	442.7	2,921.8	3,015.7	246.8	159.4	1,493.1	3,044.4	356.1	283.3	1,428.7
2008	6,375.6	388.1	266.3	2,994.5	2,971.0	97.9	43.4	1,494.7	3,404.6	290.2	222.9	1,499.8
2007: I	1,405.8	149.2	117.3	2,775.4	715.8	61.4	47.7	1,441.4	690.0	87.8	69.6	1,334.0
II	1,526.5	172.8	136.3	2,900.1	760.8	75.4	61.0	1,490.8	765.7	97.4	75.3	1,409.2
III	1,539.4	147.6	79.9	2,959.6	767.2	57.1	8.7	1,500.3	772.2	90.6	71.2	1,459.3
IV	1,588.3	133.2	109.2	3,052.2	771.8	52.9	42.1	1,539.9	816.5	80.4	67.1	1,512.3
2008: I	1,566.4	150.0	117.3	3,086.3	740.5	58.6	44.8	1,551.0	825.9	91.3	72.6	1,535.3
II	1,724.2	142.7	109.4	3,082.7	780.4	47.6	31.4	1,544.8	943.7	95.1	78.0	1,537.9
III	1,682.3	165.5	123.6	3,059.7	757.9	54.6	36.0	1,538.9	924.4	110.9	87.6	1,520.8
IV	1,402.8	-70.1	-84.0	2,749.2	692.2	-63.0	-68.8	1,344.0	710.5	-7.2	-15.2	1,405.3
2009: I	1,203.6	48.4	33.2	2,661.5	590.8	-6.6	-10.9	1,301.7	612.7	55.0	44.1	1,359.8
II	1,263.2	81.5	60.0	2,714.4	598.6	12.3	3.6	1,315.6	664.6	69.1	56.4	1,398.9
III	1,321.9	117.6	94.3	2,877.2	624.6	37.4	28.8	1,419.7	697.3	80.2	65.5	1,457.5

¹ In the old series, "income taxes" refers to Federal income taxes only, as State and local income taxes had already been deducted. In the new series, no income taxes have been deducted

² Annual data are average equity for the year (using four end-of-quarter figures)

³ Beginning with 1988, profits before and after income taxes reflect inclusion of minority stockholders' interest in net income before and after income taxes

⁴ Data for 1992 (most significantly 1992:I) reflect the early adoption of Financial Accounting Standards Board Statement 106 (Employer's Accounting for Post-Retirement Benefits Other Than Pensions) by a large number of companies during the fourth quarter of 1992. Data for 1993 (1993:I) also reflect adoption of Statement 106. Corporations must show the cumulative effect of a change in accounting principle in the first quarter of the year in which the change is adopted.

⁵ Data based on the North American Industry Classification System (NAICS). Other data shown are based on the Standard Industrial Classification (SIC).

Note: Data are not necessarily comparable from one period to another due to changes in accounting principles, industry classifications, sampling procedures, etc. For explanatory notes concerning compilation of the series, see *Quarterly Financial Report for Manufacturing, Mining, and Trade Corporations*, Department of Commerce, Bureau of the Census.

Source: Department of Commerce (Bureau of the Census).

TABLE B–94. Relation of profits after taxes to stockholders' equity and to sales, all manufacturing corporations, 1959–2009

Year or quarter	Ratio of profits after income taxes (annual rate) to stockholders' equity—percent [1]			Profits after income taxes per dollar of sales—cents		
	All manufacturing corporations	Durable goods industries	Nondurable goods industries	All manufacturing corporations	Durable goods industries	Nondurable goods industries
1959	10.4	10.4	10.4	4.8	4.8	4.9
1960	9.2	8.5	9.8	4.4	4.0	4.8
1961	8.9	8.1	9.6	4.3	3.9	4.7
1962	9.8	9.6	9.9	4.5	4.4	4.7
1963	10.3	10.1	10.4	4.7	4.5	4.9
1964	11.6	11.7	11.5	5.2	5.1	5.4
1965	13.0	13.8	12.2	5.6	5.7	5.5
1966	13.4	14.2	12.7	5.6	5.6	5.6
1967	11.7	11.7	11.8	5.0	4.8	5.3
1968	12.1	12.2	11.9	5.1	4.9	5.2
1969	11.5	11.4	11.5	4.8	4.6	5.0
1970	9.3	8.3	10.3	4.0	3.5	4.5
1971	9.7	9.0	10.3	4.1	3.8	4.5
1972	10.6	10.8	10.5	4.3	4.2	4.4
1973	12.8	13.1	12.6	4.7	4.7	4.8
1973: IV	13.4	12.9	14.0	4.7	4.5	5.0
New series:						
1973: IV	14.3	13.3	15.3	5.6	5.0	6.1
1974	14.9	12.6	17.1	5.5	4.7	6.4
1975	11.6	10.3	12.9	4.6	4.1	5.1
1976	13.9	13.7	14.2	5.4	5.2	5.5
1977	14.2	14.5	13.8	5.3	5.3	5.3
1978	15.0	16.0	14.2	5.4	5.5	5.3
1979	16.4	15.4	17.4	5.7	5.2	6.1
1980	13.9	11.2	16.3	4.8	4.0	5.6
1981	13.6	11.9	15.2	4.7	4.2	5.1
1982	9.2	6.1	11.9	3.5	2.4	4.4
1983	10.6	8.1	12.7	4.1	3.1	4.9
1984	12.5	12.4	12.5	4.6	4.4	4.8
1985	10.1	9.2	11.0	3.8	3.4	4.1
1986	9.5	7.5	11.5	3.7	2.9	4.6
1987	12.8	11.9	13.7	4.9	4.5	5.2
1988 [2]	16.1	14.3	17.8	5.9	5.2	6.6
1989	13.5	11.1	16.0	4.9	4.1	5.7
1990	10.6	7.9	13.1	3.9	3.0	4.8
1991	6.2	1.4	10.6	2.4	.5	4.1
1992 [3]	2.1	−5.1	8.2	.8	−1.7	3.1
1993	8.0	5.7	10.0	2.8	1.8	3.7
1994	15.8	16.3	15.2	5.4	5.3	5.5
1995	16.0	15.4	16.6	5.6	5.2	6.0
1996	16.7	15.7	17.6	6.0	5.5	6.5
1997	16.7	16.3	17.1	6.2	5.8	6.7
1998	15.8	16.4	15.2	5.9	5.9	6.0
1999	16.4	16.1	16.8	6.2	6.1	6.4
2000	15.1	12.5	18.7	6.1	5.4	6.9
2000: IV	9.9	7.0	13.9	4.0	3.1	5.1
NAICS: [4]						
2000: IV	9.1	5.6	14.3	3.7	2.5	5.2
2001	2.0	−7.0	14.7	.8	−3.3	5.7
2002	7.5	2.1	14.5	3.2	1.0	5.8
2003	12.1	8.5	16.3	5.4	3.9	7.0
2004	15.8	12.9	19.3	7.1	6.2	8.0
2005	16.7	12.4	21.7	7.4	5.9	9.0
2006	17.6	13.9	21.4	8.1	6.6	9.7
2007	15.2	10.7	19.8	7.3	5.3	9.3
2008	8.9	2.9	14.9	4.2	1.5	6.5
2007: I	16.9	13.2	20.9	8.3	6.7	10.1
II	18.8	16.4	21.4	8.9	8.0	9.8
III	10.8	2.3	19.5	5.2	1.1	9.2
IV	14.3	10.9	17.8	6.9	5.4	8.2
2008: I	15.2	11.5	18.9	7.5	6.0	8.8
II	14.2	8.1	20.3	6.3	4.0	8.3
III	16.2	9.3	23.0	7.3	4.7	9.5
IV	−12.2	−20.5	−4.3	−6.0	−9.9	−2.1
2009: I	5.0	−3.4	13.0	2.8	−1.9	7.2
II	8.8	1.1	16.1	4.7	.6	8.5
III	13.1	8.1	18.0	7.1	4.6	9.4

[1] Annual ratios based on average equity for the year (using four end-of-quarter figures). Quarterly ratios based on equity at end of quarter.
[2] See footnote 3, Table B–93.
[3] See footnote 4, Table B–93.
[4] See footnote 5, Table B–93.

Note: Based on data in millions of dollars.
See Note, Table B–93.

Source: Department of Commerce (Bureau of the Census).

TABLE B–95. Historical stock prices and yields, 1949–2003

Year	Common stock prices [1]									Common stock yields (Standard & Poor's) (percent) [5]	
	New York Stock Exchange (NYSE) indexes [2]						Dow Jones industrial average [2]	Standard & Poor's composite index (1941–43=10) [2]	Nasdaq composite index (Feb. 5, 1971=100) [2]	Dividend-price ratio [6]	Earnings-price ratio [7]
	Composite (Dec. 31, 2002= 5,000) [3]	December 31, 1965=50									
		Composite	Industrial	Transportation	Utility [4]	Finance					
1949	....	9.02	....	....	....	....	179.48	15.23	....	6.59	15.48
1950	....	10.87	....	....	....	....	216.31	18.40	....	6.57	13.99
1951	....	13.08	....	....	....	....	257.64	22.34	....	6.13	11.82
1952	....	13.81	....	....	....	....	270.76	24.50	....	5.80	9.47
1953	....	13.67	....	....	....	....	275.97	24.73	....	5.80	10.26
1954	....	16.19	....	....	....	....	333.94	29.69	....	4.95	8.57
1955	....	21.54	....	....	....	....	442.72	40.49	....	4.08	7.95
1956	....	24.40	....	....	....	....	493.01	46.62	....	4.09	7.55
1957	....	23.67	....	....	....	....	475.71	44.38	....	4.35	7.89
1958	....	24.56	....	....	....	....	491.66	46.24	....	3.97	6.23
1959	....	30.73	....	....	....	....	632.12	57.38	....	3.23	5.78
1960	....	30.01	....	....	....	....	618.04	55.85	....	3.47	5.90
1961	....	35.37	....	....	....	....	691.55	66.27	....	2.98	4.62
1962	....	33.49	....	....	....	....	639.76	62.38	....	3.37	5.82
1963	....	37.51	....	....	....	....	714.81	69.87	....	3.17	5.50
1964	....	43.76	....	....	....	....	834.05	81.37	....	3.01	5.32
1965	....	47.39	....	....	....	....	910.88	88.17	....	3.00	5.59
1966	487.92	46.15	46.18	50.26	90.81	44.45	873.60	85.26	....	3.40	6.63
1967	536.84	50.77	51.97	53.51	90.86	49.82	879.12	91.93	....	3.20	5.73
1968	585.47	55.37	58.00	50.58	88.38	65.85	906.00	98.70	....	3.07	5.67
1969	578.01	54.67	57.44	46.96	85.60	70.49	876.72	97.84	....	3.24	6.08
1970	483.39	45.72	48.03	32.14	74.47	60.00	753.19	83.22	....	3.83	6.45
1971	573.33	54.22	57.92	44.35	79.05	70.38	884.76	98.29	107.44	3.14	5.41
1972	637.52	60.29	65.73	50.17	76.95	78.35	950.71	109.20	128.52	2.84	5.50
1973	607.11	57.42	63.08	37.74	75.38	70.12	923.88	107.43	109.90	3.06	7.12
1974	463.54	43.84	48.08	31.89	59.58	49.67	759.37	82.85	76.29	4.47	11.59
1975	483.55	45.73	50.52	31.10	63.00	47.14	802.49	86.16	77.20	4.31	9.15
1976	575.85	54.46	60.44	39.57	73.94	52.94	974.92	102.01	89.90	3.77	8.90
1977	567.66	53.69	57.86	41.09	81.84	55.25	894.63	98.20	98.71	4.62	10.79
1978	567.81	53.70	58.23	43.50	78.44	56.65	820.23	96.02	117.53	5.28	12.03
1979	616.68	58.32	64.76	47.34	76.41	61.42	844.40	103.01	136.57	5.47	13.46
1980	720.15	68.10	78.70	60.61	74.69	64.25	891.41	118.78	168.61	5.26	12.66
1981	782.62	74.02	85.44	72.61	77.81	73.52	932.92	128.05	203.18	5.20	11.96
1982	728.84	68.93	78.18	60.41	79.49	71.99	884.36	119.71	188.97	5.81	11.60
1983	979.52	92.63	107.45	89.36	93.99	95.34	1,190.34	160.41	285.43	4.40	8.03
1984	977.33	92.46	108.01	85.63	92.89	89.28	1,178.48	160.46	248.88	4.64	10.02
1985	1,142.97	108.09	123.79	104.11	113.49	114.21	1,328.23	186.84	290.19	4.25	8.12
1986	1,438.02	136.00	155.85	119.87	142.72	147.20	1,792.76	236.34	366.96	3.49	6.09
1987	1,709.79	161.70	195.31	140.39	148.59	146.48	2,275.99	286.83	402.57	3.08	5.48
1988	1,585.14	149.91	180.95	134.12	143.53	127.26	2,060.82	265.79	374.43	3.64	8.01
1989	1,903.36	180.02	216.23	175.28	174.87	151.88	2,508.91	322.84	437.81	3.45	7.42
1990	1,939.47	183.46	225.78	158.62	181.20	133.26	2,678.94	334.59	409.17	3.61	6.47
1991	2,181.72	206.33	258.14	173.99	185.32	150.82	2,929.33	376.18	491.69	3.24	4.79
1992	2,421.51	229.01	284.62	201.09	198.91	179.26	3,284.29	415.74	599.26	2.99	4.22
1993	2,638.96	249.58	299.99	242.49	228.90	216.42	3,522.06	451.41	715.16	2.78	4.46
1994	2,687.02	254.12	315.25	247.29	209.06	209.73	3,793.77	460.42	751.65	2.82	5.83
1995	3,078.56	291.15	367.34	269.41	220.30	238.45	4,493.76	541.72	925.19	2.56	6.09
1996	3,787.20	358.17	453.98	327.33	249.77	303.89	5,742.89	670.50	1,164.96	2.19	5.24
1997	4,827.35	456.54	574.52	414.60	283.82	424.48	7,441.15	873.43	1,469.49	1.77	4.57
1998	5,818.26	550.26	681.57	468.69	378.12	516.35	8,625.52	1,085.50	1,794.91	1.49	3.46
1999	6,546.81	619.16	774.78	491.60	473.73	530.86	10,464.88	1,327.33	2,728.15	1.25	3.17
2000	6,805.89	643.66	810.63	413.60	477.65	553.13	10,734.90	1,427.22	3,783.67	1.15	3.63
2001	6,397.85	605.07	748.26	443.59	377.30	595.61	10,189.13	1,194.18	2,035.00	1.32	2.95
2002	5,578.89	527.62	657.37	431.10	260.85	555.27	9,226.43	993.94	1,539.73	1.61	2.92
2003 [3]	5,447.46	....	633.18	436.51	237.77	565.75	8,993.59	965.23	1,647.17	1.77	3.84

[1] Averages of daily closing prices.

[2] Includes stocks as follows: for NYSE, all stocks listed; for Dow Jones industrial average, 30 stocks; for Standard & Poor's (S&P) composite index, 500 stocks; and for Nasdaq composite index, over 5,000.

[3] The NYSE relaunched the composite index on January 9, 2003, incorporating new definitions, methodology, and base value. (The composite index based on December 31, 1965=50 was discontinued.) Subset indexes on financial, energy, and health care were released by the NYSE on January 8, 2004 (see Table B–96). NYSE indexes shown in this table for industrials, utilities, transportation, and finance were discontinued.

[4] Effective April 1993, the NYSE doubled the value of the utility index to facilitate trading of options and futures on the index. Annual indexes prior to 1993 reflect the doubling.

[5] Based on 500 stocks in the S&P composite index.

[6] Aggregate cash dividends (based on latest known annual rate) divided by aggregate market value based on Wednesday closing prices. Monthly data are averages of weekly figures; annual data are averages of monthly figures.

[7] Quarterly data are ratio of earnings (after taxes) for four quarters ending with particular quarter-to-price index for last day of that quarter. Annual data are averages of quarterly ratios.

Sources: New York Stock Exchange, Dow Jones & Co., Inc., Standard & Poor's, and Nasdaq Stock Market.

TABLE B–96. Common stock prices and yields, 2000–2009

| Year or month | Common stock prices [1] | | | | | | | Common stock yields (Standard & Poor's) (percent) [4] | |
| | New York Stock Exchange (NYSE) indexes [2,3] (December 31, 2002=5,000) | | | | Dow Jones industrial average [2] | Standard & Poor's composite index (1941–43=10) [2] | Nasdaq composite index (Feb. 5, 1971=100) [2] | Dividend-price ratio [5] | Earnings-price ratio [6] |
	Composite	Financial	Energy	Health care					
2000	6,805.89				10,734.90	1,427.22	3,783.67	1.15	3.63
2001	6,397.85				10,189.13	1,194.18	2,035.00	1.32	2.95
2002	5,578.89				9,226.43	993.94	1,539.73	1.61	2.92
2003	5,447.46	5,583.00	5,273.90	5,288.67	8,993.59	965.23	1,647.17	1.77	3.84
2004	6,612.62	6,822.18	6,952.36	5,924.80	10,317.39	1,130.65	1,986.53	1.72	4.89
2005	7,349.00	7,383.70	9,377.84	6,283.96	10,547.67	1,207.23	2,099.32	1.83	5.36
2006	8,357.99	8,654.40	11,206.94	6,685.06	11,408.67	1,310.46	2,263.41	1.87	5.78
2007	9,648.82	9,321.39	13,339.99	7,191.79	13,169.98	1,477.19	2,578.47	1.86	5.29
2008	8,036.88	6,278.38	13,258.42	6,171.19	11,252.62	1,220.04	2,161.65	2.37	3.54
2009	6,091.02	3,987.04	10,020.30	5,456.63	8,876.15	948.05	1,845.38	2.40	
2006: Jan	8,007.35	8,187.86	10,965.30	6,604.09	10,872.48	1,278.72	2,289.99	1.83	
Feb	8,044.86	8,280.82	10,741.43	6,566.87	10,971.19	1,276.65	2,273.67	1.86	
Mar	8,174.34	8,459.04	10,702.23	6,653.63	11,144.45	1,293.74	2,300.26	1.85	5.61
Apr	8,351.28	8,572.54	11,467.85	6,519.78	11,234.68	1,302.18	2,338.68	1.85	
May	8,353.45	8,608.10	11,380.52	6,488.14	11,333.88	1,290.00	2,245.28	1.90	
June	7,985.59	8,225.13	10,690.86	6,395.87	10,997.97	1,253.12	2,137.41	1.96	5.86
July	8,103.97	8,340.25	11,360.86	6,566.19	11,032.53	1,260.24	2,086.21	1.94	
Aug	8,294.89	8,574.68	11,610.65	6,763.81	11,257.35	1,287.15	2,117.77	1.92	
Sept	8,383.29	8,789.30	10,807.75	6,910.95	11,533.60	1,317.81	2,221.94	1.87	5.88
Oct	8,651.02	9,101.77	11,020.11	6,975.17	11,963.12	1,363.38	2,330.17	1.83	
Nov	8,856.30	9,251.53	11,657.36	6,845.16	12,185.15	1,388.63	2,408.70	1.80	
Dec	9,089.55	9,461.77	12,078.39	6,931.01	12,377.62	1,416.42	2,431.91	1.79	5.75
2007: Jan	9,132.04	9,575.21	11,381.56	7,083.45	12,512.89	1,424.16	2,453.19	1.81	
Feb	9,345.98	9,732.63	11,658.11	7,174.03	12,631.48	1,444.79	2,479.86	1.82	
Mar	9,120.57	9,342.66	11,503.16	6,997.30	12,268.53	1,406.95	2,401.49	1.89	5.85
Apr	9,555.98	9,658.88	12,441.16	7,332.01	12,754.80	1,463.65	2,499.57	1.84	
May	9,822.99	9,864.01	13,031.00	7,474.48	13,407.76	1,511.14	2,562.14	1.81	
June	9,896.98	9,754.29	13,639.81	7,268.42	13,480.21	1,514.49	2,595.40	1.81	5.65
July	9,985.42	9,543.66	14,318.49	7,210.07	13,677.89	1,520.70	2,655.08	1.80	
Aug	9,440.44	8,963.67	13,250.28	6,957.87	13,239.71	1,454.62	2,539.50	1.92	
Sept	9,777.59	9,060.63	14,300.99	7,138.20	13,557.69	1,497.12	2,634.47	1.88	5.15
Oct	10,159.33	9,390.30	14,976.30	7,231.60	13,901.28	1,539.66	2,780.42	1.84	
Nov	9,741.15	8,522.71	14,622.23	7,127.40	13,200.58	1,463.39	2,662.80	1.95	
Dec	9,807.36	8,447.99	14,956.77	7,306.60	13,406.99	1,479.23	2,661.55	1.93	4.51
2008: Jan	9,165.10	7,776.77	14,222.14	7,068.98	12,538.12	1,378.76	2,418.09	2.06	
Feb	9,041.52	7,577.54	13,931.92	6,674.75	12,419.57	1,354.87	2,325.83	2.10	
Mar	8,776.21	7,155.51	14,000.91	6,318.44	12,193.88	1,316.94	2,254.82	2.17	4.57
Apr	9,174.10	7,579.73	15,159.35	6,381.98	12,656.63	1,370.47	2,368.10	2.09	
May	9,429.04	7,593.63	16,365.23	6,405.40	12,812.48	1,403.22	2,483.24	2.07	
June	8,996.98	6,798.20	16,272.67	6,243.42	12,056.67	1,341.25	2,427.45	2.15	4.01
July	8,427.37	6,207.89	14,899.86	6,412.48	11,322.38	1,257.33	2,278.14	2.27	
Aug	8,362.20	6,304.58	13,772.04	6,618.92	11,530.75	1,281.47	2,389.27	2.23	
Sept	7,886.29	6,159.18	12,562.82	6,316.05	11,114.08	1,217.01	2,205.20	2.36	3.94
Oct	6,130.39	4,733.74	9,515.71	5,434.03	9,176.71	968.80	1,730.32	2.83	
Nov	5,527.63	3,779.86	9,262.07	5,088.99	8,614.55	883.04	1,542.70	3.11	
Dec	5,525.70	3,673.95	9,136.33	5,090.83	8,595.56	877.56	1,525.89	3.00	1.65
2009: Jan	5,477.14	3,337.14	9,295.97	5,256.13	8,396.20	865.58	1,537.20	3.01	
Feb	5,051.42	2,823.74	8,785.04	5,106.78	7,690.50	805.23	1,485.98	3.07	
Mar	4,739.72	2,633.65	8,266.81	4,596.81	7,235.47	757.13	1,432.23	2.92	.86
Apr	5,338.39	3,313.47	8,839.95	4,771.71	7,992.12	848.15	1,641.15	2.60	
May	5,823.10	3,819.95	9,848.66	5,051.78	8,398.37	902.41	1,726.08	2.41	
June	5,985.64	3,924.19	10,189.64	5,224.16	8,593.00	926.12	1,826.99	2.35	.82
July	6,026.55	4,000.66	9,765.09	5,410.22	8,679.75	935.82	1,873.84	2.31	
Aug	6,577.18	4,646.60	10,295.91	5,706.96	9,375.06	1,009.72	1,997.51	2.12	
Sept	6,839.88	4,844.93	10,791.73	5,838.22	9,634.97	1,044.55	2,084.75	2.06	1.19
Oct	6,986.35	4,918.07	11,342.57	5,931.28	9,857.34	1,067.66	2,122.85	2.02	
Nov	7,079.38	4,848.04	11,486.95	6,155.21	10,227.55	1,088.07	2,143.53	1.99	
Dec	7,167.51	4,734.07	11,335.23	6,430.25	10,433.44	1,110.38	2,220.60	1.95	

[1] Averages of daily closing prices.
[2] Includes stocks as follows: for NYSE, all stocks listed (in 2009, over 3,800); for Dow Jones industrial average, 30 stocks; for Standard & Poor's (S&P) composite index, 500 stocks; and for Nasdaq composite index, in 2009, over 2,700.
[3] The NYSE relaunched the composite index on January 9, 2003, incorporating new definitions, methodology, and base value. Subset indexes on financial, energy, and health care were released by the NYSE on January 8, 2004.
[4] Based on 500 stocks in the S&P composite index.
[5] Aggregate cash dividends (based on latest known annual rate) divided by aggregate market value based on Wednesday closing prices. Monthly data are averages of weekly figures, annual data are averages of monthly figures.
[6] Quarterly data are ratio of earnings (after taxes) for four quarters ending with particular quarter-to-price index for last day of that quarter. Annual data are averages of quarterly ratios.

Sources: New York Stock Exchange, Dow Jones & Co., Inc., Standard & Poor's, and Nasdaq Stock Market.

AGRICULTURE

TABLE B–97. Farm income, 1948–2009

[Billions of dollars]

Year	Income of farm operators from farming						Production expenses	Net farm income
	Gross farm income							
		Cash marketing receipts			Value of inventory changes[3]	Direct Government payments[4]		
	Total[1]	Total	Livestock and products	Crops[2]				
1948	36.5	30.2	17.1	13.1	1.7	0.3	18.8	17.7
1949	30.8	27.8	15.4	12.4	−.9	.2	18.0	12.8
1950	33.1	28.4	16.1	12.4	.8	.3	19.5	13.6
1951	38.3	32.8	19.6	13.2	1.2	.3	22.3	15.9
1952	37.7	32.5	18.2	14.3	.9	.3	22.8	14.9
1953	34.4	31.0	16.9	14.1	−.6	.2	21.5	13.0
1954	34.2	29.8	16.3	13.6	.5	.3	21.8	12.4
1955	33.4	29.5	16.0	13.5	.2	.2	22.2	11.3
1956	33.9	30.4	16.4	14.0	−.5	.6	22.7	11.2
1957	34.8	29.7	17.4	12.3	.6	1.0	23.7	11.1
1958	39.0	33.5	19.2	14.2	.8	1.1	25.8	13.2
1959	37.9	33.6	18.9	14.7	.0	.7	27.2	10.7
1960	38.6	34.0	19.0	15.0	.4	.7	27.4	11.2
1961	40.5	35.2	19.5	15.7	.3	1.5	28.6	12.0
1962	42.3	36.5	20.2	16.3	.6	1.7	30.3	12.1
1963	43.4	37.5	20.0	17.4	.6	1.7	31.6	11.8
1964	42.3	37.3	19.9	17.4	−.8	2.2	31.8	10.5
1965	46.5	39.4	21.9	17.5	1.0	2.5	33.6	12.9
1966	50.5	43.4	25.0	18.4	−.1	3.3	36.5	14.0
1967	50.5	42.8	24.4	18.4	.7	3.1	38.2	12.3
1968	51.8	44.2	25.5	18.7	.1	3.5	39.5	12.3
1969	56.4	48.2	28.6	19.6	.1	3.8	42.1	14.3
1970	58.8	50.5	29.5	21.0	.0	3.7	44.5	14.4
1971	62.1	52.7	30.5	22.3	1.4	3.1	47.1	15.0
1972	71.1	61.1	35.6	25.5	.9	4.0	51.7	19.5
1973	98.9	86.9	45.8	41.1	3.4	2.6	64.6	34.4
1974	98.2	92.4	41.3	51.1	−1.6	.5	71.0	27.3
1975	100.6	88.9	43.1	45.8	3.4	.8	75.0	25.5
1976	102.9	95.4	46.3	49.0	−1.5	.7	82.7	20.2
1977	108.8	96.2	47.6	48.6	1.1	1.8	88.9	19.9
1978	128.4	112.4	59.2	53.2	1.9	3.0	103.2	25.2
1979	150.7	131.5	69.2	62.3	5.0	1.4	123.3	27.4
1980	149.3	139.7	68.0	71.7	−6.3	1.3	133.1	16.1
1981	166.3	141.6	69.2	72.5	6.5	1.9	139.4	26.9
1982	164.1	142.6	70.3	72.3	−1.4	3.5	140.3	23.8
1983	153.9	136.8	69.6	67.2	−10.9	9.3	139.6	14.3
1984	168.0	142.8	72.9	69.9	6.0	8.4	142.0	26.0
1985	161.1	144.0	70.1	73.9	−2.3	7.7	132.6	28.5
1986	156.1	135.4	71.6	63.8	−2.2	11.8	125.0	31.1
1987	168.4	141.8	76.0	65.8	−2.3	16.7	130.4	38.0
1988	177.9	151.3	79.6	71.6	−4.1	14.5	138.3	39.6
1989	191.6	160.5	83.6	76.9	3.8	10.9	145.1	46.5
1990	197.8	169.3	89.1	80.2	3.3	9.3	151.5	46.3
1991	192.0	168.0	85.8	82.2	−.2	8.2	151.8	40.2
1992	200.6	171.5	85.8	85.7	4.2	9.2	150.4	50.2
1993	205.0	178.3	90.5	87.8	−4.2	13.4	158.3	46.7
1994	216.1	181.4	88.3	93.1	8.3	7.9	163.5	52.6
1995	210.8	188.2	87.2	101.0	−5.0	7.3	171.1	39.8
1996	235.8	199.4	92.9	106.5	7.9	7.3	176.9	58.9
1997	238.0	207.8	96.5	111.3	.6	7.5	186.7	51.3
1998	232.6	196.5	94.2	102.2	−.6	12.4	185.5	47.1
1999	234.9	187.8	92.1	95.7	−.2	21.5	187.2	47.7
2000	241.7	192.1	99.6	92.5	1.6	23.2	191.0	50.7
2001	249.9	200.0	106.7	93.4	1.1	22.4	195.0	54.9
2002	230.6	194.6	93.9	100.7	−3.5	12.4	191.4	39.1
2003	258.6	216.1	105.7	110.5	−2.7	16.5	197.7	60.9
2004	294.7	238.0	123.5	114.5	11.2	13.0	207.3	87.3
2005	298.4	241.0	124.9	116.1	−.4	24.4	219.7	78.7
2006	291.2	240.9	118.6	122.3	−3.1	15.8	232.7	58.5
2007	338.4	288.5	138.6	149.9	.6	11.9	267.5	70.9
2008	377.1	324.2	141.1	183.1	−2.4	12.2	290.0	87.1
2009 [p]	335.2	282.1	118.4	163.6	−1.0	12.5	278.1	57.0

[1] Cash marketing receipts, Government payments, value of changes in inventories, other farm-related cash income, and nonmoney income produced by farms including imputed rent of operator residences.

[2] Crop receipts include proceeds received from commodities placed under Commodity Credit Corporation loans.

[3] Physical changes in beginning and ending year inventories of crop and livestock commodities valued at weighted average market prices during the year.

[4] Includes only Government payments made directly to farmers.

Note: Data for 2009 are forecasts.

Source: Department of Agriculture (Economic Research Service).

TABLE B–98. Farm business balance sheet, 1952–2009

[Billions of dollars]

End of year	Assets										Claims			
	Total assets	Physical assets						Financial assets			Total claims	Real estate debt [5]	Non–real estate debt [6]	Propri-etors' equity
		Real estate	Non–real estate					Total [4]	Invest-ments in coopera-tives	Other [4]				
			Live-stock and poultry [1]	Ma-chinery and motor vehi-cles	Crops [2]	Pur-chased inputs [3]								
1952	133.1	85.1	14.8	15.0	7.9		10.3	3.2	7.1	133.1	6.2	7.1	119.8
1953	128.7	84.3	11.7	15.6	6.8		10.3	3.3	7.0	128.7	6.6	6.3	115.8
1954	132.6	87.8	11.2	15.7	7.5		10.4	3.5	6.9	132.6	7.1	6.7	118.8
1955	137.0	93.0	10.6	16.3	6.5		10.6	3.7	6.9	137.0	7.8	7.3	121.9
1956	145.7	100.3	11.0	16.9	6.8		10.7	4.0	6.7	145.7	8.5	7.4	129.8
1957	154.5	106.4	13.9	17.0	6.4		10.8	4.2	6.6	154.5	9.0	8.2	137.3
1958	168.7	114.6	17.7	18.1	6.9		11.4	4.5	6.9	168.7	9.7	9.4	149.6
1959	172.9	121.2	15.2	19.3	6.2		11.0	4.8	6.2	172.9	10.6	10.7	151.6
1960	174.4	123.3	15.6	19.1	6.4		10.0	4.2	5.8	174.4	11.3	11.1	151.9
1961	181.6	129.1	16.4	19.3	6.5		10.4	4.5	5.9	181.6	12.3	11.8	157.5
1962	188.9	134.6	17.3	19.9	6.5		10.5	4.6	5.9	188.9	13.5	13.2	162.2
1963	196.7	142.4	15.9	20.4	7.4		10.7	5.0	5.7	196.7	15.0	14.6	167.1
1964	204.2	150.5	14.5	21.2	7.0		11.0	5.2	5.8	204.2	16.9	15.3	172.1
1965	220.8	161.5	17.6	22.4	7.9		11.4	5.4	6.0	220.8	18.9	16.9	185.0
1966	234.0	171.2	19.0	24.1	8.1		11.6	5.7	6.0	234.0	20.7	18.5	194.8
1967	246.1	180.9	18.8	26.3	8.0		12.0	5.8	6.1	246.1	22.6	19.6	203.9
1968	257.2	189.4	20.2	27.7	7.4		12.4	6.1	6.3	257.2	24.7	19.2	213.2
1969	267.8	195.3	22.8	28.6	8.3		12.8	6.4	6.4	267.8	26.4	20.0	221.4
1970	278.8	202.4	23.7	30.4	8.7		13.7	7.2	6.5	278.8	27.2	21.3	230.3
1971	301.8	217.6	27.3	32.4	10.0		14.5	7.9	6.7	301.8	28.8	24.0	248.9
1972	339.9	243.0	33.7	34.6	12.9		15.7	8.7	6.9	339.9	31.4	26.7	281.8
1973	418.5	298.3	42.4	39.7	21.4		16.8	9.7	7.1	418.5	35.2	31.6	351.7
1974 [7]	449.2	335.6	24.6	48.5	22.5		18.1	11.2	6.9	449.2	39.6	35.1	374.5
1975	510.8	383.6	29.4	57.4	20.5		19.9	13.0	6.9	510.8	43.8	39.8	427.3
1976	590.7	456.5	29.0	63.3	20.6		21.3	14.3	6.9	590.7	48.5	45.7	496.5
1977	651.5	509.3	31.9	69.3	20.4		20.5	13.5	7.0	651.5	55.8	52.6	543.1
1978	777.7	601.8	50.1	78.8	23.8		23.2	16.1	7.1	777.7	63.4	60.4	653.9
1979	914.7	706.1	61.4	91.9	29.9		25.4	18.1	7.3	914.7	75.8	71.7	767.2
1980	1,000.4	782.8	60.6	97.5	32.8		26.7	19.3	7.4	1,000.4	85.3	77.2	838.0
1981	997.9	785.6	53.5	101.1	29.5		28.2	20.6	7.6	997.9	93.9	83.8	820.2
1982	962.5	750.0	53.0	103.9	25.9		29.7	21.9	7.8	962.5	96.8	87.2	778.5
1983	959.3	753.4	49.5	101.7	23.7		30.9	22.8	8.1	959.3	98.1	88.1	773.1
1984	897.8	661.8	49.5	125.8	26.1	2.0	32.6	24.3	8.3	897.8	101.4	87.4	709.0
1985	775.9	586.2	46.3	86.1	22.9	1.2	33.3	24.3	9.0	775.9	94.1	78.1	603.8
1986	722.0	542.4	47.8	79.0	16.3	2.1	34.4	24.4	10.0	722.0	84.1	67.2	570.7
1987	756.5	563.7	58.0	78.7	17.8	3.2	35.2	25.3	9.9	756.5	75.8	62.7	618.0
1988	788.5	582.3	62.2	81.0	23.7	3.5	35.9	25.6	10.4	788.5	70.8	62.3	655.4
1989	813.7	600.1	66.2	84.1	23.9	2.6	36.7	26.3	10.4	813.7	68.8	62.3	682.7
1990	840.6	619.1	70.9	86.3	23.2	2.8	38.3	27.5	10.9	840.6	67.6	63.5	709.5
1991	844.2	624.8	68.1	85.9	22.2	2.6	40.5	28.7	11.8	844.2	67.4	64.4	712.3
1992	867.8	640.8	71.0	84.8	24.2	3.9	43.0	29.4	13.6	867.8	67.9	63.7	736.2
1993	909.2	677.6	72.8	85.4	23.3	3.8	46.3	31.0	15.3	909.2	68.4	65.9	774.9
1994	934.7	704.1	67.9	86.8	23.3	5.0	47.6	32.1	15.5	934.7	69.9	69.0	795.8
1995	965.7	740.5	57.8	87.6	27.4	3.4	49.1	34.1	15.0	965.7	71.7	71.3	822.8
1996	1,002.9	769.5	60.3	88.0	31.7	4.4	49.0	34.9	14.1	1,002.9	74.4	74.2	854.3
1997	1,051.3	808.2	67.1	88.7	32.7	4.9	49.6	35.7	13.9	1,051.3	78.5	78.4	894.4
1998	1,083.4	840.4	63.4	89.8	29.9	5.0	54.7	40.5	14.2	1,083.4	83.1	81.5	918.7
1999	1,138.8	887.0	73.2	89.8	28.3	4.0	56.5	41.9	14.6	1,138.8	87.2	80.5	971.1
2000	1,203.2	946.4	76.8	90.1	27.9	4.9	57.1	43.0	14.1	1,203.2	84.7	79.2	1,039.3
2001	1,255.9	996.2	78.5	92.8	25.2	4.2	58.9	43.6	15.3	1,255.9	88.5	82.1	1,085.3
2002	1,259.7	998.7	75.6	96.2	23.1	5.6	60.4	44.7	15.8	1,259.7	95.4	81.8	1,082.5
2003	1,383.4	1,112.1	78.5	100.3	24.4	5.6	62.4	45.6	16.9	1,383.4	83.2	81.0	1,219.2
2004	1,588.0	1,305.2	79.4	107.8	24.4	5.7	65.5			1,588.0	95.7	86.3	1,406.0
2005	1,779.4	1,487.0	81.1	113.1	24.3	6.5	67.5			1,779.4	104.8	91.6	1,583.0
2006	1,923.6	1,625.8	80.7	114.2	22.7	6.5	73.7			1,923.6	108.0	95.5	1,720.0
2007	2,055.3	1,751.4	80.7	114.7	22.7	7.0	78.8			2,055.3	112.7	101.4	1,841.2
2008	2,005.5	1,692.7	80.6	115.8	27.6	7.2	81.6			2,005.5	130.1	108.8	1,766.6
2009 [p]	1,943.7	1,633.8	80.6	112.3	27.6	7.2	82.1			1,943.7	132.8	106.1	1,704.8

[1] Excludes commercial broilers; excludes horses and mules beginning with 1959 data; excludes turkeys beginning with 1986 data.
[2] Non–Commodity Credit Corporation (CCC) crops held on farms plus value above loan rate for crops held under CCC.
[3] Includes fertilizer, chemicals, fuels, parts, feed, seed, and other supplies.
[4] Beginning with 2004, data available only for total financial assets. Data through 2003 for other financial assets are currency and demand deposits.
[5] Includes CCC storage and drying facilities loans.
[6] Does not include CCC crop loans.
[7] Beginning with 1974 data, farms are defined as places with sales of $1,000 or more annually.

Note: Data exclude operator households. Beginning with 1959, data include Alaska and Hawaii.
Data for 2009 are forecasts.

Source: Department of Agriculture (Economic Research Service).

TABLE B–99. Farm output and productivity indexes, 1948–2008

[1996=100]

Year	Farm output				Productivity indicators	
	Total	Livestock and products	Crops	Farm-related output	Farm output per unit of total factor input	Farm output per unit of labor input
1948	44	49	42	32	47	13
1949	43	50	41	28	45	14
1950	43	52	39	30	44	14
1951	45	54	41	30	46	15
1952	46	55	42	28	47	16
1953	46	55	42	27	47	17
1954	47	58	42	26	48	17
1955	48	59	43	28	48	18
1956	49	61	42	30	49	20
1957	48	60	42	31	48	21
1958	51	62	46	35	51	24
1959	53	65	47	45	51	24
1960	55	65	49	46	54	27
1961	56	68	49	45	55	28
1962	56	69	50	44	55	28
1963	58	71	52	46	56	30
1964	57	72	50	42	57	32
1965	59	71	53	42	58	33
1966	59	73	52	40	58	36
1967	61	74	54	40	59	40
1968	62	74	56	39	60	40
1969	63	74	58	37	60	42
1970	62	77	55	33	60	43
1971	67	79	62	34	64	47
1972	68	81	62	35	64	48
1973	70	81	66	42	66	50
1974	65	78	60	41	62	47
1975	70	75	68	38	68	51
1976	71	79	68	40	67	53
1977	75	80	74	42	71	57
1978	76	80	76	45	67	59
1979	80	81	83	46	70	61
1980	77	82	75	43	67	60
1981	83	83	86	36	75	65
1982	84	83	87	72	77	71
1983	73	84	67	73	68	63
1984	83	83	84	67	79	73
1985	87	85	88	80	85	83
1986	84	86	83	76	84	79
1987	85	87	83	84	85	78
1988	81	88	73	99	81	73
1989	86	88	84	102	88	81
1990	90	90	89	96	91	91
1991	90	92	89	97	91	91
1992	96	95	97	91	98	98
1993	91	96	88	95	92	98
1994	102	101	104	92	99	95
1995	97	102	92	104	92	89
1996	100	100	100	100	100	100
1997	105	103	105	111	102	106
1998	105	104	104	122	101	111
1999	107	108	105	128	102	115
2000	107	107	107	118	107	128
2001	108	107	106	123	108	128
2002	106	109	102	117	106	124
2003	108	110	106	109	110	131
2004	113	108	116	118	117	142
2005	111	110	112	110	114	141
2006	112	113	111	118	116	152
2007	114	113	115	109	113	151
2008	113	113	113	110	120	154

Note: Farm output includes primary agricultural activities and certain secondary activities that are closely linked to agricultural production for which information on production and input use cannot be separately observed. Secondary output (alternatively, farm-related output) includes recreation activities, the imputed value of employer-provided housing, land rentals under the Conservation Reserve, and services such as custom machine work and custom livestock feeding.

See Table B–100 for farm inputs.

Source: Department of Agriculture (Economic Research Service).

TABLE B–100. Farm input use, selected inputs, 1948–2009

Year	Farm employment (thousands)[1]			Crops harvested (millions of acres)[4]	Selected indexes of input use (1996=100)											
						Capital input		Labor input			Intermediate input					
	Total	Self-employed and unpaid family workers[2]	Hired workers[3]		Total farm input	Total	Durable equipment	Total	Hired labor	Self-employed and unpaid family labor	Total	Feed and seed	Energy and lubricants[5]	Agricultural chemicals	Purchased services
1948	9,759	7,433	2,326	356	93	115	66	325	277	349	46	55	65	20	44
1949	9,633	7,392	2,241	360	97	115	78	317	257	347	52	58	72	21	43
1950	9,283	6,965	2,318	345	98	118	90	305	268	323	53	59	73	25	45
1951	8,653	6,464	2,189	344	99	120	100	293	259	311	56	61	76	25	49
1952	8,441	6,301	2,140	349	99	122	109	287	253	304	56	60	80	26	52
1953	7,904	5,817	2,087	348	99	123	114	275	246	289	56	61	81	26	50
1954	7,893	5,782	2,111	346	97	124	120	269	232	288	54	58	81	27	49
1955	7,719	5,675	2,044	340	100	124	123	263	228	281	59	65	83	28	51
1956	7,367	5,451	1,916	324	100	124	124	247	208	266	61	68	83	30	53
1957	6,966	5,046	1,920	324	100	123	123	229	199	244	63	71	82	29	54
1958	6,667	4,705	1,962	324	101	121	121	218	201	226	67	76	80	30	56
1959	6,565	4,621	1,944	324	103	121	121	217	196	227	70	77	81	34	76
1960	6,155	4,260	1,895	324	102	121	123	205	196	208	69	77	82	34	73
1961	5,994	4,135	1,859	302	101	121	121	200	195	201	69	76	84	37	72
1962	5,841	3,997	1,844	295	103	120	119	200	195	202	72	79	85	41	72
1963	5,500	3,700	1,800	298	103	120	119	192	195	190	74	82	86	45	71
1964	5,206	3,585	1,621	298	101	121	121	180	175	182	73	79	88	49	68
1965	4,964	3,465	1,499	298	101	121	123	176	165	181	73	79	89	50	70
1966	4,574	3,224	1,350	294	102	121	126	163	149	170	78	85	91	55	70
1967	4,303	3,036	1,267	306	102	122	131	154	138	161	79	86	90	62	73
1968	4,207	2,974	1,233	300	103	123	136	153	134	162	81	87	90	66	71
1969	4,050	2,843	1,207	290	105	123	139	150	135	158	83	91	92	74	69
1970	3,951	2,727	1,224	293	104	122	140	144	136	147	84	92	92	79	65
1971	3,868	2,665	1,203	305	104	121	142	142	134	145	86	94	90	86	66
1972	3,870	2,664	1,206	294	106	121	142	141	134	144	89	98	89	94	65
1973	3,947	2,702	1,245	321	107	120	145	140	136	141	91	97	90	110	70
1974	3,919	2,588	1,331	328	106	121	153	139	145	136	89	94	86	115	68
1975	3,818	2,481	1,337	336	103	123	159	137	147	131	84	91	102	79	71
1976	3,741	2,369	1,372	337	106	124	163	135	149	127	88	94	114	89	75
1977	3,660	2,347	1,313	345	106	126	169	131	145	124	89	94	120	88	74
1978	3,682	2,410	1,272	338	113	127	173	129	136	125	100	105	126	92	89
1979	3,549	2,320	1,229	348	115	128	179	131	141	125	103	109	115	100	94
1980	3,605	2,302	1,303	352	114	130	186	128	140	121	101	109	112	100	85
1981	3,497	2,241	1,256	366	110	129	187	127	140	121	95	103	108	94	81
1982	3,335	2,142	1,193	362	109	127	184	118	125	114	96	106	101	83	88
1983	3,282	1,991	1,291	306	108	125	176	117	138	106	96	106	98	77	87
1984	3,091	1,930	1,161	348	105	121	168	113	129	105	93	99	102	90	85
1985	2,760	1,753	1,007	342	102	119	159	105	117	98	91	99	91	83	87
1986	2,693	1,740	953	325	100	115	148	106	112	103	90	100	85	81	80
1987	2,681	1,717	964	302	100	112	137	108	115	105	91	99	95	78	83
1988	2,727	1,725	1,002	297	99	109	130	110	118	105	91	99	95	78	83
1989	2,637	1,709	928	318	98	107	125	106	111	103	90	95	94	84	89
1990	2,568	1,649	919	322	99	106	121	99	111	93	94	101	94	88	85
1991	2,591	1,682	909	318	99	105	118	100	110	94	96	101	94	93	89
1992	2,505	1,640	865	319	98	104	114	97	104	94	95	101	92	93	85
1993	2,367	1,510	857	308	99	103	110	93	104	88	99	103	93	95	95
1994	2,613	1,774	839	321	102	102	106	107	101	111	101	103	95	94	100
1995	2,597	1,730	867	314	105	101	103	108	105	110	105	109	100	94	105
1996	2,433	1,602	831	326	100	100	100	100	100	100	100	100	100	100	100
1997	2,432	1,557	875	333	103	100	98	99	105	96	105	105	102	103	106
1998	2,284	1,405	879	326	104	99	98	94	107	87	110	111	103	105	113
1999	2,239	1,326	913	327	105	99	98	93	112	84	114	116	105	104	117
2000	2,126	1,249	877	325	101	98	98	84	94	79	109	114	103	103	107
2001	2,084	1,211	873	321	100	98	98	84	95	78	108	111	100	100	110
2002	2,115	1,243	872	316	100	98	99	85	96	79	107	110	109	100	104
2003	2,066	1,181	885	324	98	97	100	82	94	76	105	114	91	93	101
2004	2,012	1,188	824	321	96	97	103	79	87	75	103	112	98	95	98
2005	1,988	1,208	780	321	97	98	107	79	87	74	105	113	91	96	103
2006	1,900	1,148	752	312	96	98	109	74	83	69	107	114	87	96	105
2007	1,832	1,082	750	322	101	97	109	76	90	68	114	118	100	105	115
2008	1,786	1,054	732	327	94	97	111	73	86	67	102	110	88	84	107
2009 [p]	....	....	....	319	....	....	....	....	....	....	....	....	....	....	....

[1] Persons involved in farmwork. Total farm employment is the sum of self-employed and unpaid family workers and hired workers shown here.
[2] Data from Current Population Survey (CPS) conducted by the Department of Commerce, Census Bureau, for the Department of Labor, Bureau of Labor Statistics.
[3] Data from national income and product accounts from Department of Commerce, Bureau of Economic Analysis.
[4] Acreage harvested plus acreages in fruits, tree nuts, and vegetables and minor crops. Includes double-cropping.
[5] Consists of petroleum fuels, natural gas, electricity, hydraulic fluids, and lubricants.

Source: Department of Agriculture (Economic Research Service).

TABLE B–101. Agricultural price indexes and farm real estate value, 1975–2009

[1990-92=100, except as noted]

Year or month	Prices received by farmers			Prices paid by farmers											Addendum: Average farm real estate value per acre (dollars)[3]
				All commodities, services, interest, taxes, and wage rates[1]	Production items										
	All farm products	Crops	Livestock and products		Total[2]	Feed	Livestock and poultry	Fertilizer	Agricultural chemicals	Fuels	Farm machinery	Farm services	Rent	Wage rates	
1975	73	88	62	47	55	83	39	87	72	40	38	48		44	340
1976	75	87	64	50	59	83	47	74	78	43	43	52		48	397
1977	73	83	64	53	61	82	48	72	71	46	47	57		51	474
1978	83	89	78	58	67	80	65	72	66	48	51	60		55	531
1979	94	98	90	66	76	89	88	77	67	61	56	66		60	628
1980	98	107	89	75	85	98	85	96	71	86	63	81		65	737
1981	100	111	89	82	92	110	80	104	77	98	70	89		70	819
1982	94	98	90	86	94	99	78	105	83	97	76	96		74	823
1983	98	108	88	86	92	107	76	100	87	94	81	82		76	788
1984	101	111	91	89	94	112	73	103	90	93	85	86		77	801
1985	91	98	86	86	91	95	74	98	90	93	85	85		78	713
1986	87	87	88	85	86	88	73	90	89	76	83	83		81	640
1987	89	86	91	87	87	83	85	86	87	76	85	84		85	599
1988	99	104	93	91	90	104	91	94	89	77	89	85		87	632
1989	104	109	100	96	95	110	93	99	93	83	94	91		95	668
1990	104	103	105	99	99	103	102	97	95	100	96	96	96	96	683
1991	100	101	99	100	100	98	102	103	101	104	100	98	100	100	703
1992	98	101	97	101	101	99	96	100	103	96	104	103	104	105	713
1993	101	102	100	104	104	102	104	96	109	93	107	110	100	108	736
1994	100	105	95	106	106	106	94	105	112	89	113	110	108	111	798
1995	102	112	92	109	108	103	82	121	116	89	120	115	117	114	844
1996	112	127	99	115	115	129	75	125	119	102	125	116	128	117	887
1997	107	115	98	118	119	125	94	121	121	106	128	116	136	123	926
1998	102	107	97	115	113	111	88	112	122	84	132	115	120	129	974
1999	96	97	95	115	111	100	95	105	121	94	135	114	113	135	1,030
2000	96	96	97	119	115	102	110	110	120	129	139	118	110	140	1,090
2001	102	99	106	123	120	109	111	123	121	121	144	120	117	146	1,150
2002	98	105	90	124	119	112	102	108	119	115	148	120	120	153	1,210
2003	106	110	103	128	124	114	109	124	121	140	151	125	123	157	1,270
2004	118	115	122	134	132	121	128	140	121	165	162	127	126	160	1,360
2005	114	110	119	142	140	117	138	164	123	216	173	133	129	165	1,610
2006	115	120	111	150	148	124	134	176	128	239	182	139	141	171	1,830
2007	136	142	130	161	160	149	131	216	129	264	191	146	147	177	2,010
2008	149	169	130	183	190	194	124	392	139	344	209	146	165	183	2,170
2009	131	150	112	179	183	182	115	288	147	228	223	159	178	187	2,100
2008: Jan	145	159	129	170	171	168	123	275	133	307	198	143	165	187	2,170
Feb	146	164	131	172	174	176	128	291	133	311	199	143	165	187	
Mar	146	167	129	175	178	183	125	315	134	349	199	144	165	187	
Apr	146	169	128	180	185	185	122	344	135	369	202	144	165	183	
May	152	173	134	184	192	198	127	364	136	400	207	145	165	183	
June	158	183	137	188	197	202	124	406	138	425	208	147	165	183	
July	159	182	138	192	202	216	124	441	140	429	210	148	165	179	
Aug	156	177	137	192	203	215	128	469	141	393	212	148	165	179	
Sept	154	174	133	191	201	209	125	479	143	372	214	148	165	179	
Oct	150	168	127	187	196	196	118	479	144	317	215	148	165	185	
Nov	142	158	123	183	190	191	118	443	146	247	221	147	165	185	
Dec	135	150	119	179	184	184	127	396	145	207	216	147	165	185	
2009: Jan	139	161	114	180	184	189	120	340	142	204	214	160	178	189	2,100
Feb	126	146	109	179	183	187	118	325	148	198	219	159	178	189	
Mar	126	147	109	180	184	185	119	320	151	191	220	159	178	189	
Apr	129	151	112	180	185	185	122	327	151	200	220	159	178	187	
May	130	150	113	180	185	193	118	309	151	207	220	159	178	187	
June	134	159	112	180	184	197	112	281	145	237	220	160	178	187	
July	131	150	112	179	182	190	113	271	146	230	226	159	178	184	
Aug	127	147	109	178	181	185	111	257	141	241	226	159	178	184	
Sept	126	142	108	177	180	180	109	261	142	245	227	159	178	184	
Oct	134	151	110	178	180	180	110	253	148	252	226	159	178	188	
Nov	135	153	115	179	182	182	113	254	150	265	226	158	178	188	
Dec	135	148	119	179	182	182	114	258	150	266	227	158	178	188	

[1] Includes items used for family living, not shown separately.
[2] Includes other production items, not shown separately.
[3] Average for 48 States. Annual data are: March 1 for 1975, February 1 for 1976–81, April 1 for 1982–85, February 1 for 1986–89, and January 1 for 1990–2009.

Source: Department of Agriculture (National Agricultural Statistics Service).

TABLE B-102. U.S. exports and imports of agricultural commodities, 1950-2009

[Billions of dollars]

Year	Exports							Imports					Agri-cultural trade balance
	Total [1]	Feed grains	Food grains [2]	Oilseeds and products	Cotton	Tobacco	Animals and products	Total [1]	Fruits, nuts, and vegetables [3]	Animals and products	Coffee	Cocoa beans and products	
1950	2.9	0.2	0.6	0.2	1.0	0.3	0.3	4.0	0.2	0.7	1.1	0.2	-1.1
1951	4.0	.3	1.1	.3	1.1	.3	.5	5.2	.2	1.1	1.4	.2	-1.1
1952	3.4	.3	1.1	.2	.9	.2	.3	4.5	.2	.7	1.4	.2	-1.1
1953	2.8	.3	.7	.2	.5	.3	.4	4.2	.2	.6	1.5	.2	-1.3
1954	3.1	.2	.5	.3	.8	.3	.5	4.0	.2	.5	1.5	.3	-.9
1955	3.2	.3	.6	.4	.5	.4	.6	4.0	.2	.5	1.4	.2	-.8
1956	4.2	.4	1.0	.5	.7	.3	.7	4.0	.2	.4	1.4	.2	.2
1957	4.5	.3	1.0	.5	1.0	.4	.7	4.0	.2	.5	1.4	.2	.6
1958	3.9	.5	.8	.4	.7	.4	.5	3.9	.2	.7	1.2	.2	*
1959	4.0	.6	.9	.6	.4	.3	.6	4.1	.2	.8	1.1	.2	-.1
1960	4.8	.5	1.2	.6	1.0	.4	.6	3.8	.2	.6	1.0	.2	1.0
1961	5.0	.5	1.4	.6	.9	.4	.6	3.7	.2	.7	1.0	.2	1.3
1962	5.0	.8	1.3	.7	.5	.4	.6	3.9	.2	.9	1.0	.2	1.2
1963	5.6	.8	1.5	.8	.6	.4	.7	4.0	.3	.9	1.0	.2	1.6
1964	6.3	.9	1.7	1.0	.7	.4	.8	4.1	.3	.8	1.2	.2	2.3
1965	6.2	1.1	1.4	1.2	.5	.4	.8	4.1	.3	.9	1.1	.1	2.1
1966	6.9	1.3	1.8	1.2	.4	.5	.7	4.5	.4	1.2	1.1	.1	2.4
1967	6.4	1.1	1.5	1.3	.5	.5	.7	4.5	.4	1.1	1.0	.2	1.9
1968	6.3	.9	1.4	1.3	.5	.5	.7	5.0	.5	1.3	1.2	.2	1.3
1969	6.0	.9	1.2	1.3	.3	.6	.8	5.0	.5	1.4	.9	.2	1.1
1970	7.3	1.1	1.4	1.9	.4	.5	.9	5.8	.5	1.6	1.2	.3	1.5
1971	7.7	1.0	1.3	2.2	.6	.5	1.0	5.8	.6	1.5	1.2	.2	1.9
1972	9.4	1.5	1.8	2.4	.5	.7	1.1	6.5	.7	1.8	1.3	.2	2.9
1973	17.7	3.5	4.7	4.3	.9	.7	1.6	8.4	.8	2.6	1.7	.3	9.3
1974	21.9	4.6	5.4	5.7	1.3	.8	1.8	10.2	.8	2.2	1.6	.5	11.7
1975	21.9	5.2	6.2	4.5	1.0	.9	1.7	9.3	.8	1.8	1.7	.5	12.6
1976	23.0	6.0	4.7	5.1	1.0	.9	2.4	11.0	.9	2.3	2.9	.6	12.0
1977	23.6	4.9	3.6	6.6	1.5	1.1	2.7	13.4	1.2	2.3	4.2	1.0	10.2
1978	29.4	5.9	5.5	8.2	1.7	1.4	3.0	14.8	1.5	3.1	4.0	1.4	14.6
1979	34.7	7.7	6.3	8.9	2.2	1.2	3.8	16.7	1.7	3.9	4.2	1.2	18.0
1980	41.2	9.8	7.9	9.4	2.9	1.3	3.8	17.4	1.7	3.8	4.2	.9	23.8
1981	43.3	9.4	9.6	9.6	2.3	1.5	4.2	16.9	2.0	3.5	2.9	.9	26.4
1982	36.6	6.4	7.9	9.1	2.0	1.5	3.9	15.3	2.3	3.7	2.9	.7	21.3
1983	36.1	7.3	7.4	8.7	1.8	1.5	3.8	16.5	2.3	3.8	2.8	.8	19.6
1984	37.8	8.1	7.5	8.4	2.4	1.5	4.2	19.3	3.1	4.1	3.3	1.1	18.5
1985	29.0	6.0	4.5	5.8	1.6	1.5	4.1	20.0	3.5	4.2	3.3	1.4	9.1
1986	26.2	3.1	3.8	6.5	.8	1.2	4.5	21.5	3.6	4.5	4.6	1.1	4.7
1987	28.7	3.8	3.8	6.4	1.6	1.1	5.2	20.4	3.6	4.9	2.9	1.2	8.3
1988	37.1	5.9	5.9	7.7	2.0	1.3	6.4	21.0	3.8	5.2	2.5	1.0	16.1
1989	40.0	7.7	7.1	6.4	2.2	1.3	6.4	21.9	4.1	5.1	2.4	1.0	18.2
1990	39.5	7.0	4.8	5.7	2.8	1.4	6.6	22.9	4.6	5.7	1.9	1.1	16.6
1991	39.4	5.7	4.2	6.4	2.5	1.4	7.0	22.9	4.6	5.5	1.9	1.1	16.5
1992	43.2	5.8	5.4	7.3	2.0	1.6	7.9	24.8	4.7	5.7	1.7	1.1	18.4
1993	43.0	5.0	5.7	7.3	1.6	1.3	8.0	25.1	5.0	5.9	1.5	1.0	17.9
1994	46.2	4.7	5.3	7.2	2.6	1.3	9.2	27.0	5.3	5.8	2.5	1.0	19.2
1995	56.2	8.1	6.7	8.9	3.7	1.4	10.9	30.3	5.9	6.0	3.3	1.1	25.9
1996	60.4	9.4	7.4	10.8	2.7	1.4	11.1	33.5	6.6	6.1	2.8	1.4	26.9
1997	57.1	6.0	5.3	12.1	2.7	1.5	11.3	36.1	6.9	6.5	3.9	1.5	21.0
1998	51.8	5.0	5.0	9.5	2.6	1.5	10.6	36.9	7.7	6.9	3.4	1.7	14.9
1999	48.4	5.5	4.7	8.1	1.0	1.3	10.4	37.7	8.5	7.3	2.9	1.5	10.7
2000	51.3	5.2	4.3	8.6	1.9	1.2	11.6	39.0	8.6	8.4	2.7	1.4	12.3
2001	53.7	5.2	4.2	9.2	2.2	1.3	12.4	39.4	9.0	9.2	1.7	1.5	14.3
2002	53.1	5.5	4.5	9.6	2.0	1.0	11.1	41.9	9.7	9.0	1.7	1.8	11.2
2003	59.4	5.4	5.0	11.7	3.4	1.0	12.2	47.4	10.8	8.9	2.0	2.4	12.0
2004	61.4	6.4	6.3	10.4	4.2	1.0	10.4	54.0	12.2	10.6	2.3	2.5	7.4
2005	63.2	5.4	5.7	10.2	3.9	1.0	12.2	59.3	13.4	11.5	3.0	2.8	3.9
2006	70.9	7.7	5.5	11.3	4.5	1.1	13.5	65.3	14.6	11.5	3.3	2.7	5.6
2007	90.0	10.9	9.9	15.6	4.6	1.2	17.2	71.9	16.3	12.4	3.8	2.7	18.1
2008	115.3	14.9	13.6	23.7	4.8	1.2	21.8	80.5	17.6	12.0	4.4	3.3	34.8
Jan-Nov:													
2008	107.1	14.1	13.0	21.5	4.6	1.1	20.4	73.9	16.0	10.9	4.1	2.9	33.2
2009	88.6	8.7	7.1	20.6	3.1	1.0	16.5	65.4	15.9	9.2	3.7	3.0	23.2

* Less than $50 million.

[1] Total includes items not shown separately.

[2] Rice, wheat, and wheat flour.

[3] Includes fruit, nut, and vegetable preparations. Beginning with 1989, data include bananas but exclude yeasts, starches, and other minor horticultural products.

Note: Data derived from official estimates released by the Bureau of the Census, Department of Commerce. Agricultural commodities are defined as (1) nonmarine food products and (2) other products of agriculture that have not passed through complex processes of manufacture. Export value, at U.S. port of exportation, is based on the selling price and includes inland freight, insurance, and other charges to the port. Import value, defined generally as the market value in the foreign country, excludes import duties, ocean freight, and marine insurance.

Source: Department of Agriculture (Economic Research Service).

Table B–103. U.S. international transactions, 1946–2009

[Millions of dollars; quarterly data seasonally adjusted. Credits (+), debits (−)]

Year or quarter	Goods[1]			Services				Income receipts and payments			Unilateral current transfers, net[2]	Balance on current account
	Exports	Imports	Balance on goods	Net military transactions[2]	Net travel and transportation	Other services, net	Balance on goods and services	Receipts	Payments	Balance on income		
1946	11,764	−5,067	6,697	−424	733	310	7,316	772	−212	560	−2,991	4,885
1947	16,097	−5,973	10,124	−358	946	145	10,857	1,102	−245	857	−2,722	8,992
1948	13,265	−7,557	5,708	−351	374	175	5,906	1,921	−437	1,484	−4,973	2,417
1949	12,213	−6,874	5,339	−410	230	208	5,367	1,831	−476	1,355	−5,849	873
1950	10,203	−9,081	1,122	−56	−120	242	1,188	2,068	−559	1,509	−4,537	−1,840
1951	14,243	−11,176	3,067	169	298	254	3,788	2,633	−583	2,050	−4,954	884
1952	13,449	−10,838	2,611	528	83	309	3,531	2,751	−555	2,196	−5,113	614
1953	12,412	−10,975	1,437	1,753	−238	307	3,259	2,736	−624	2,112	−6,657	−1,286
1954	12,929	−10,353	2,576	902	−269	305	3,514	2,929	−582	2,347	−5,642	219
1955	14,424	−11,527	2,897	−113	−297	299	2,786	3,406	−676	2,730	−5,086	430
1956	17,556	−12,803	4,753	−221	−361	447	4,618	3,837	−735	3,102	−4,990	2,730
1957	19,562	−13,291	6,271	−423	−189	482	6,141	4,180	−796	3,384	−4,763	4,762
1958	16,414	−12,952	3,462	−849	−633	486	2,466	3,790	−825	2,965	−4,647	784
1959	16,458	−15,310	1,148	−831	−821	573	69	4,132	−1,061	3,071	−4,422	−1,282
1960	19,650	−14,758	4,892	−1,057	−964	639	3,508	4,616	−1,238	3,379	−4,062	2,824
1961	20,108	−14,537	5,571	−1,131	−978	732	4,195	4,999	−1,245	3,755	−4,127	3,822
1962	20,781	−16,260	4,521	−912	−1,152	912	3,370	5,618	−1,324	4,294	−4,277	3,387
1963	22,272	−17,048	5,224	−742	−1,309	1,036	4,210	6,157	−1,560	4,596	−4,392	4,414
1964	25,501	−18,700	6,801	−794	−1,146	1,161	6,022	6,824	−1,783	5,041	−4,240	6,823
1965	26,461	−21,510	4,951	−487	−1,280	1,480	4,664	7,437	−2,088	5,350	−4,583	5,431
1966	29,310	−25,493	3,817	−1,043	−1,331	1,497	2,940	7,528	−2,481	5,047	−4,955	3,031
1967	30,666	−26,866	3,800	−1,187	−1,750	1,742	2,604	8,021	−2,747	5,274	−5,294	2,583
1968	33,626	−32,991	635	−596	−1,548	1,759	250	9,367	−3,378	5,990	−5,629	611
1969	36,414	−35,807	607	−718	−1,763	1,964	91	10,913	−4,869	6,044	−5,735	399
1970	42,469	−39,866	2,603	−641	−2,038	2,330	2,254	11,748	−5,515	6,233	−6,156	2,331
1971	43,319	−45,579	−2,260	653	−2,345	2,649	−1,303	12,707	−5,435	7,272	−7,402	−1,433
1972	49,381	−55,797	−6,416	1,072	−3,063	2,965	−5,443	14,765	−6,572	8,192	−8,544	−5,795
1973	71,410	−70,499	911	740	−3,158	3,406	1,900	21,808	−9,655	12,153	−6,913	7,140
1974	98,306	−103,811	−5,505	165	−3,184	4,231	−4,292	27,587	−12,084	15,503	−9,249	1,962
1975	107,088	−98,185	8,903	1,461	−2,812	4,854	12,404	25,351	−12,564	12,787	−7,075	18,116
1976	114,745	−124,228	−9,483	931	−2,558	5,027	−6,082	29,375	−13,311	16,063	−5,686	4,295
1977	120,816	−151,907	−31,091	1,731	−3,565	5,680	−27,246	32,354	−14,217	18,137	−5,226	−14,335
1978	142,075	−176,002	−33,927	857	−3,573	6,879	−29,763	42,088	−21,680	20,408	−5,788	−15,143
1979	184,439	−212,007	−27,568	−1,313	−2,935	7,251	−24,565	63,834	−32,961	30,873	−6,593	−285
1980	224,250	−249,750	−25,500	−1,822	−997	8,912	−19,407	72,606	−42,532	30,073	−8,349	2,317
1981	237,044	−265,067	−28,023	−844	144	12,552	−16,172	86,529	−53,626	32,903	−11,702	5,030
1982	211,157	−247,642	−36,485	112	−992	13,209	−24,156	91,747	−56,583	35,164	−16,544	−5,536
1983	201,799	−268,901	−67,102	−563	−4,227	14,124	−57,767	90,000	−53,614	36,386	−17,310	−38,691
1984	219,926	−332,418	−112,492	−2,547	−8,438	14,404	−109,073	108,819	−73,756	35,063	−20,335	−94,344
1985	215,915	−338,088	−122,173	−4,390	−9,798	14,483	−121,880	98,542	−72,819	25,723	−21,998	−118,155
1986	223,344	−368,425	−145,081	−5,181	−8,779	20,502	−138,538	97,064	−81,571	15,494	−24,132	−147,177
1987	250,208	−409,765	−159,557	−3,844	−8,010	19,728	−151,684	108,273	−93,891	14,293	−23,265	−160,655
1988	320,230	−447,189	−126,959	−6,320	−3,013	21,725	−114,566	136,713	−118,026	18,687	−25,274	−121,153
1989	359,916	−477,665	−117,749	−6,749	3,551	27,805	−93,142	161,287	−141,463	19,824	−26,169	−99,486
1990	387,401	−498,438	−111,037	−7,599	7,501	30,270	−80,864	171,742	−143,192	28,550	−26,654	−78,968
1991	414,083	−491,020	−76,937	−5,275	16,560	34,516	−31,136	149,214	−125,085	24,131	9,904	2,897
1992	439,631	−536,528	−96,897	−1,448	19,969	39,164	−39,212	133,766	−109,531	24,234	−36,636	−51,613
1993	456,943	−589,394	−132,451	1,383	19,714	41,040	−70,311	136,057	−110,741	25,316	−39,811	−84,805
1994	502,859	−668,690	−165,831	2,570	16,305	48,463	−98,493	166,521	−149,375	17,146	−40,265	−121,612
1995	575,204	−749,374	−174,170	4,600	21,772	51,414	−96,384	210,244	−189,353	20,891	−38,074	−113,567
1996	612,113	−803,113	−191,000	5,385	25,015	56,535	−104,065	226,129	−203,811	22,318	−43,017	−124,764
1997	678,366	−876,794	−198,428	4,968	22,152	63,035	−108,273	256,804	−244,195	12,609	−45,062	−140,726
1998	670,416	−918,637	−248,221	5,220	10,210	66,651	−166,140	261,819	−257,554	4,265	−53,187	−215,062
1999	683,965	−1,031,784	−347,819	2,593	7,085	73,051	−265,090	293,925	−280,037	13,888	−50,23	−301,630
2000	771,994	−1,226,684	−454,690	317	2,486	72,052	−379,835	350,918	−329,864	21,054	−58,645	−417,426
2001	718,711	−1,148,609	−429,898	−2,296	−3,254	69,943	−365,505	290,797	−259,075	31,722	−64,487	−398,270
2002	685,170	−1,168,002	−482,831	−7,158	−4,245	72,633	−421,601	280,942	−253,544	27,398	−64,948	−459,151
2003	715,848	−1,264,860	−549,012	−11,981	−11,475	77,433	−495,034	320,456	−275,147	45,309	−71,794	−521,519
2004	806,161	−1,477,996	−671,835	−13,518	−14,275	89,640	−609,987	413,739	−346,519	67,219	−88,362	−631,130
2005	892,337	−1,683,188	−790,851	−10,536	−13,006	99,124	−715,268	535,263	−462,905	72,358	−105,772	−748,683
2006	1,015,812	−1,863,072	−847,260	−7,119	−10,873	104,893	−760,359	682,221	−634,136	48,085	−91,273	−803,547
2007	1,138,384	−1,969,375	−830,992	−7,384	2,345	134,609	−701,422	818,931	−728,085	90,845	−115,996	−726,573
2008	1,276,994	−2,117,245	−840,252	−13,881	16,175	142,021	−695,936	764,637	−646,406	118,231	−128,363	−706,068
2008: I	315,637	−534,482	−218,846	−2,543	3,076	35,659	−182,653	202,927	−166,241	36,686	−33,330	−179,298
II	332,876	−554,372	−221,496	−3,055	4,922	36,784	−182,847	198,796	−172,521	26,274	−31,147	−187,719
III	337,912	−559,002	−221,090	−4,664	5,595	34,217	−185,942	195,319	−161,194	34,125	−32,361	−184,178
IV	290,569	−469,389	−178,820	−3,618	2,581	35,363	−144,495	167,596	−146,450	21,146	−31,527	−154,875
2009: I	249,374	−373,411	−124,036	−3,017	1,985	32,661	−92,408	135,352	−117,051	18,301	−30,343	−104,450
II	246,134	−361,621	−115,487	−1,855	3,509	32,592	−81,240	135,074	−118,404	16,670	−33,410	−97,980
III [p]	263,911	−396,050	−132,138	−2,044	3,939	32,865	−97,378	140,403	−116,694	23,709	−34,365	−108,034

[1] Adjusted from Census data for differences in valuation, coverage, and timing; excludes military.
[2] Includes transfers of goods and services under U.S. military grant programs.

See next page for continuation of table.

[Millions of dollars; quarterly data seasonally adjusted. Credits (+), debits (−)]

| Year or quarter | Capital account transactions, net | U.S.-owned assets abroad, excluding financial derivatives [increase/financial outflow (−)] | | | | Foreign-owned assets in the U.S., excluding financial derivatives [increase/financial inflow (+)] | | | Financial derivatives, net | Statistical discrepancy | |
		Total	U.S. official reserve assets [3]	Other U.S. Government assets	U.S. private assets	Total	Foreign official assets	Other foreign assets		Total (sum of the items with sign reversed)	Of which: Seasonal adjustment discrepancy
1946			−623								
1947			−3,315								
1948			−1,736								
1949			−266								
1950			1,758								
1951			−33								
1952			−415								
1953			1,256								
1954			480								
1955			182								
1956			−869								
1957			−1,165								
1958			2,292								
1959			1,035								
1960		−4,099	2,145	−1,100	−5,144	2,294	1,473	821		−1,019	
1961		−5,538	607	−910	−5,235	2,705	765	1,939		−989	
1962		−4,174	1,535	−1,085	−4,623	1,911	1,270	641		−1,124	
1963		−7,270	378	−1,662	−5,986	3,217	1,986	1,231		−360	
1964		−9,560	171	−1,680	−8,050	3,643	1,660	1,983		−907	
1965		−5,716	1,225	−1,605	−5,336	742	134	607		−457	
1966		−7,321	570	−1,543	−6,347	3,661	−672	4,333		629	
1967		−9,757	53	−2,423	−7,386	7,379	3,451	3,928		−205	
1968		−10,977	−870	−2,274	−7,833	9,928	−774	10,703		438	
1969		−11,585	−1,179	−2,200	−8,206	12,702	−1,301	14,002		−1,516	
1970		−9,337	2,481	−1,589	−10,229	7,226	7,775	−550		−219	
1971		−12,475	2,349	−1,884	−12,940	23,687	27,596	−3,909		−9,779	
1972		−14,497	−4	−1,568	−12,925	22,171	11,185	10,986		−1,879	
1973		−22,874	158	−2,644	−20,388	18,388	6,026	12,362		−2,654	
1974		−34,745	−1,467	366	−33,643	35,227	10,546	24,682		−2,444	
1975		−39,703	−849	−3,474	−35,380	16,870	7,027	9,843		4,717	
1976		−51,269	−2,558	−4,214	−44,498	37,839	17,693	20,147		9,134	
1977		−34,785	−375	−3,693	−30,717	52,770	36,816	15,954		−3,650	
1978		−61,130	732	−4,660	−57,202	66,275	33,678	32,597		9,997	
1979		−66,054	−1,133	−3,746	−61,176	40,693	−12,526	53,218		25,647	
1980		−86,967	−8,155	−5,162	−73,651	62,037	16,649	45,388		22,613	
1981		−114,147	−5,175	−5,097	−103,875	85,684	6,053	79,631		23,433	
1982	199	−127,882	−4,965	−6,131	−116,786	95,056	3,593	91,464		38,163	
1983	209	−66,373	−1,196	−5,006	−60,172	87,399	5,845	81,554		17,457	
1984	235	−40,376	−3,131	−5,489	−31,757	116,048	3,140	112,908		18,437	
1985	315	−44,752	−3,858	−2,821	−38,074	144,231	−1,119	145,349		18,362	
1986	301	−111,723	312	−2,022	−110,014	228,330	35,648	192,681		30,269	
1987	365	−79,296	9,149	1,006	−89,450	247,100	45,387	201,713		−7,514	
1988	493	−106,573	−3,912	2,967	−105,628	244,833	39,758	205,075		−17,600	
1989	336	−175,383	−25,293	1,233	−151,323	222,777	8,503	214,274		51,756	
1990	−6,579	−81,234	−2,158	2,317	−81,393	139,357	33,910	105,447		27,425	
1991	−4,479	−64,389	5,763	2,923	−73,075	108,221	17,388	90,833		−42,252	
1992	978	−74,410	3,901	−1,667	−76,644	168,349	40,477	127,872		−43,304	
1993	−1,299	−200,551	−1,379	−351	−198,823	279,758	71,753	208,005		6,898	
1994	−1,723	−178,937	5,346	−390	−183,893	303,174	39,583	263,591		−902	
1995	−927	−352,264	−9,742	−984	−341,538	435,102	109,880	325,222		31,656	
1996	−735	−413,409	6,668	−989	−419,088	547,885	126,724	421,161		−8,977	
1997	−1,027	−485,475	−1,010	68	−484,533	704,452	19,036	685,416		−77,224	
1998	−766	−353,829	−6,783	−422	−346,624	420,794	−19,903	440,697		148,863	
1999	−4,939	−504,062	8,747	2,750	−515,559	742,210	43,543	698,667		68,421	
2000	−1,010	−560,523	−290	−941	−559,292	1,038,224	42,758	995,466		−59,265	
2001	11,922	−382,616	−4,911	−486	−377,219	782,870	28,059	754,811		−13,906	
2002	−1,470	−294,646	−3,681	345	−291,310	795,161	115,945	679,216		−39,894	
2003	−3,480	−325,424	1,523	537	−327,484	858,303	278,069	580,234		−7,880	
2004	1,323	−1,000,870	2,805	1,710	−1,005,385	1,533,201	397,755	1,135,446		97,476	
2005	11,344	−546,631	14,096	5,539	−566,266	1,247,347	259,268	988,079		36,623	
2006	−3,906	−1,285,729	2,374	5,346	−1,293,449	2,065,169	487,939	1,577,230	29,710	−1,698	
2007	−1,895	−1,472,126	−122	−22,273	−1,449,731	2,129,460	480,949	1,648,511	6,222	64,912	
2008	953	−106	−4,848	−529,615	534,357	534,071	487,021	47,050	−28,905	200,055	
2008: I	−637	−251,501	−276	3,268	−254,493	426,058	208,646	217,412	−7,966	69,777	14,659
II	−682	107,343	−1,267	−41,592	150,202	2,003	178,826	−176,823	−2,355	81,410	−3,037
III	2,967	29,322	−179	−225,997	255,498	117,897	115,573	2,324	−4,075	38,067	−25,884
IV	−695	114,730	−3,126	−265,293	383,150	−11,888	−16,024	4,136	−14,509	67,236	14,264
2009: I	−710	94,734	−982	244,102	−148,387	−67,757	70,892	−138,649	8,407	69,777	10,571
II	−719	37,398	−3,632	193,750	−152,720	14,614	124,299	−109,685	11,265	35,422	−1,806
III p	−686	−294,102	−49,021	57,928	−303,009	332,407	123,584	208,823		70,416	−20,677

[3] Consists of gold, special drawing rights, foreign currencies, and the U.S. reserve position in the International Monetary Fund (IMF).

Source: Department of Commerce (Bureau of Economic Analysis).

TABLE B–104. U.S. international trade in goods by principal end-use category, 1965–2009

[Billions of dollars; quarterly data seasonally adjusted]

Year or quarter	Exports							Imports						
			Nonagricultural products							Nonpetroleum products				
	Total	Agricultural products	Total	Industrial supplies and materials	Capital goods except automotive	Automotive	Other	Total	Petroleum and products	Total	Industrial supplies and materials	Capital goods except automotive	Automotive	Other
1965	26.5	6.3	20.2	7.6	8.1	1.9	2.6	21.5	2.0	19.5	9.1	1.5	0.9	8.0
1966	29.3	6.9	22.4	8.2	8.9	2.4	2.9	25.5	2.1	23.4	10.2	2.2	1.8	9.2
1967	30.7	6.5	24.2	8.5	9.9	2.8	3.0	26.9	2.1	24.8	10.0	2.5	2.4	9.9
1968	33.6	6.3	27.3	9.6	11.1	3.5	3.2	33.0	2.4	30.6	12.0	2.8	4.0	11.8
1969	36.4	6.1	30.3	10.3	12.4	3.9	3.7	35.8	2.6	33.2	11.8	3.4	4.9	13.0
1970	42.5	7.4	35.1	12.3	14.7	3.9	4.3	39.9	2.9	36.9	12.4	4.0	5.5	15.0
1971	43.3	7.8	35.5	10.9	15.4	4.7	4.5	45.6	3.7	41.9	13.8	4.3	7.4	16.4
1972	49.4	9.5	39.9	11.9	16.9	5.5	5.6	55.8	4.7	51.1	16.3	5.9	8.7	20.2
1973	71.4	18.0	53.4	17.0	22.0	6.9	7.6	70.5	8.4	62.1	19.6	8.3	10.3	23.9
1974	98.3	22.4	75.9	26.3	30.9	8.6	10.0	103.8	26.6	77.2	27.8	9.8	12.0	27.5
1975	107.1	22.2	84.8	26.8	36.6	10.6	10.8	98.2	27.0	71.2	24.0	10.2	11.7	25.3
1976	114.7	23.4	91.4	28.4	39.1	12.1	11.7	124.2	34.6	89.7	29.8	12.3	16.2	31.4
1977	120.8	24.3	96.5	29.8	39.8	13.4	13.5	151.9	45.0	106.9	35.7	14.0	18.6	38.6
1978 [1]	142.1	29.9	112.2	34.2	47.5	15.2	15.3	176.0	42.6	133.4	40.7	19.3	25.0	48.4
1979	184.4	35.5	149.0	52.2	60.2	17.9	18.7	212.0	60.4	151.6	47.5	24.6	26.6	52.8
1980	224.3	42.0	182.2	65.1	76.3	17.4	23.4	249.8	79.5	170.2	53.0	31.6	28.3	57.4
1981	237.0	44.1	193.0	63.6	84.2	19.7	25.5	265.1	78.4	186.7	56.1	37.1	31.0	62.4
1982	211.2	37.3	173.9	57.7	76.5	17.2	22.4	247.6	62.0	185.7	48.6	38.4	34.3	64.3
1983	201.8	37.1	164.7	52.7	71.7	18.5	21.8	268.9	55.1	213.8	53.7	43.7	43.0	73.3
1984	219.9	38.4	181.5	56.8	77.0	22.4	25.3	332.4	58.1	274.4	66.1	60.4	56.5	91.4
1985	215.9	29.6	186.3	54.8	79.3	24.9	27.2	338.1	51.4	286.7	62.6	61.3	64.9	97.9
1986	223.3	27.2	196.2	59.4	82.8	25.1	28.9	368.4	34.3	334.1	69.9	72.0	78.1	114.2
1987	250.2	29.8	220.4	63.7	92.7	27.6	36.4	409.8	42.9	366.8	70.8	85.1	85.2	125.7
1988	320.2	38.8	281.4	82.6	119.1	33.4	46.3	447.2	39.6	407.6	83.1	102.2	87.9	134.4
1989 [1]	359.9	41.1	318.8	90.5	136.9	35.1	56.3	477.7	50.9	426.8	84.6	112.3	87.4	142.5
1990	387.4	40.2	347.2	97.0	153.0	36.2	61.0	498.4	62.3	436.1	83.0	116.4	88.2	148.5
1991	414.1	40.1	374.0	101.6	166.6	39.9	65.9	491.0	51.7	439.3	81.3	121.1	85.5	151.4
1992	439.6	44.1	395.6	101.7	176.4	46.9	70.6	536.5	51.6	484.9	89.1	134.8	91.5	169.6
1993	456.9	43.6	413.3	105.1	182.7	51.6	74.0	589.4	51.5	537.9	100.8	153.2	102.1	182.0
1994	502.9	47.1	455.8	112.7	205.7	57.5	79.9	668.7	51.3	617.4	113.6	185.0	118.1	200.6
1995	575.2	57.2	518.0	135.6	234.4	61.4	86.5	749.4	56.0	693.3	128.5	222.1	123.7	219.0
1996	612.1	61.5	550.6	138.7	254.0	64.4	93.6	803.1	72.7	730.4	136.1	228.4	128.7	237.1
1997	678.4	58.5	619.9	148.6	295.8	73.4	102.0	876.8	71.8	805.0	144.9	253.6	139.4	267.1
1998	670.4	53.2	617.3	139.4	299.8	72.5	105.5	918.6	50.9	867.7	151.6	269.8	148.6	297.7
1999	684.0	49.7	634.3	140.3	311.2	75.3	107.5	1,031.8	67.8	964.0	156.3	295.7	179.0	333.0
2000	772.0	52.8	719.2	163.9	357.0	80.4	117.9	1,226.7	120.3	1,106.4	181.9	347.0	195.9	381.6
2001	718.7	54.9	663.8	150.5	321.7	75.4	116.2	1,148.6	103.6	1,045.0	172.5	298.4	189.8	384.3
2002	685.2	54.5	630.7	147.6	290.4	78.9	113.7	1,168.0	103.5	1,064.5	164.6	283.9	203.7	412.2
2003	715.8	60.9	655.0	162.5	293.7	80.6	118.2	1,264.9	133.1	1,131.8	181.4	296.4	210.1	443.8
2004	806.2	62.9	743.2	192.2	327.5	89.2	134.2	1,478.0	180.5	1,297.5	232.5	344.5	228.2	492.4
2005	892.3	64.9	827.5	221.5	358.4	98.4	149.2	1,683.2	251.9	1,431.3	272.7	380.7	239.4	538.5
2006	1,015.8	72.9	942.9	263.2	404.0	107.3	168.4	1,863.1	302.4	1,560.6	300.1	420.0	256.6	584.0
2007	1,138.4	92.1	1,046.3	302.3	433.0	121.3	189.7	1,969.4	331.0	1,638.4	308.4	446.0	259.2	624.8
2008	1,277.0	118.0	1,159.0	372.0	457.7	121.5	207.9	2,117.2	453.3	1,664.0	333.1	455.2	233.8	641.9
2006: I	243.4	17.5	226.0	61.0	97.9	26.7	40.5	454.6	72.9	381.8	74.1	101.9	64.2	141.6
II	252.1	18.0	234.1	65.7	100.8	26.4	41.2	463.8	78.2	385.6	74.4	104.0	64.1	143.0
III	255.9	18.4	237.6	67.4	100.9	26.6	42.6	476.4	82.9	393.4	77.1	106.5	62.9	146.9
IV	264.4	19.0	245.3	69.1	104.4	27.6	44.3	468.3	68.4	399.9	74.5	107.5	65.4	152.4
2007: I	269.5	20.0	249.5	69.8	104.9	28.9	46.0	475.6	70.5	405.1	74.8	110.0	63.8	156.5
II	277.7	21.4	256.2	74.7	105.4	29.9	46.2	483.3	77.8	405.5	78.4	109.9	63.1	154.1
III	289.2	24.5	264.7	76.6	109.9	30.6	47.6	494.1	82.3	411.8	78.5	112.1	66.3	154.8
IV	302.0	26.2	275.8	81.2	112.9	31.8	49.8	516.4	100.4	416.0	76.7	114.1	66.0	159.3
2008: I	315.6	29.3	286.3	90.7	113.6	31.1	50.9	534.5	112.6	421.9	82.7	115.3	63.7	160.2
II	332.9	31.6	301.3	100.0	116.9	31.2	53.2	554.4	124.4	430.0	86.5	117.5	62.1	163.9
III	337.9	31.4	306.5	103.1	118.1	31.9	53.5	559.0	130.8	428.2	90.2	115.5	58.1	164.3
IV	290.6	25.7	264.8	78.2	109.0	27.3	50.3	469.4	85.4	383.9	73.7	106.9	49.9	153.5
2009: I	249.4	23.6	225.8	63.5	98.4	17.5	46.3	373.4	52.2	321.2	55.2	91.8	32.3	141.9
II	246.1	25.2	220.9	65.5	93.3	16.7	45.4	361.6	56.9	304.7	46.9	86.5	31.7	139.5
III [p]	263.9	24.8	239.2	74.4	95.5	21.6	47.6	396.1	68.9	327.2	50.0	91.1	44.5	141.6

[1] End-use commodity classifications beginning 1978 and 1989 are not strictly comparable with data for earlier periods. See *Survey of Current Business*, June 1988 and July 2001.

Note: Data are on a balance of payments basis and exclude military. In June 1990, end-use categories for goods exports were redefined to include reexports (exports of foreign goods); beginning with data for 1978, reexports are assigned to detailed end-use categories in the same manner as exports of domestic goods.

Source: Department of Commerce (Bureau of Economic Analysis).

TABLE B–105. U.S. international trade in goods by area, 2001–2009

[Millions of dollars]

Item	2001	2002	2003	2004	2005	2006	2007	2008	2009 first 3 quarters at annual rate [1]
EXPORTS									
Total, all countries	718,711	685,170	715,848	806,161	892,337	1,015,812	1,138,384	1,276,994	1,012,559
Europe	178,229	161,116	169,249	188,913	207,503	239,764	279,476	321,151	251,943
Euro area [2]	111,025	104,242	110,301	123,972	134,920	152,282	176,484	198,538	157,255
France	19,693	18,897	16,891	20,770	22,120	23,339	26,436	28,603	26,045
Germany	29,363	26,125	28,422	31,016	33,787	40,770	49,106	54,209	41,933
Italy	9,715	9,898	10,378	10,547	11,342	12,398	14,003	15,330	11,920
United Kingdom	39,701	32,627	33,233	35,336	37,842	44,526	49,395	52,868	44,793
Canada	163,259	160,915	169,929	189,982	212,192	230,983	249,949	261,872	200,239
Latin America and Other Western Hemisphere	158,969	148,337	149,049	171,800	192,257	221,626	242,312	287,806	229,384
Brazil	15,789	12,310	11,139	13,756	15,212	18,832	24,061	32,175	24,999
Mexico	101,181	97,305	97,248	110,606	120,160	133,658	135,811	151,147	124,031
Venezuela	5,600	4,021	2,827	4,761	6,413	8,994	10,193	12,604	9,453
Asia and Pacific	188,731	186,871	199,192	220,914	236,019	270,810	301,190	325,948	266,709
China	19,108	22,043	28,292	34,324	41,072	53,528	62,786	69,552	62,636
India	3,754	4,098	4,980	6,101	7,914	9,622	14,885	17,623	16,599
Japan	55,879	50,298	50,845	52,271	53,118	57,153	60,421	64,457	49,728
Korea, Republic of	21,203	21,881	23,542	25,581	27,112	31,671	33,657	33,913	26,557
Singapore	17,338	16,042	16,287	19,199	20,212	23,550	25,379	27,633	21,087
Taiwan	17,394	18,027	17,065	21,157	21,016	22,334	25,415	24,636	16,491
Middle East	18,142	18,061	18,270	21,784	29,634	34,782	42,744	52,343	40,525
Africa	11,383	9,870	10,158	12,768	14,733	17,847	22,713	27,873	23,759
Memorandum: Members of OPEC [3]	19,502	17,895	16,662	21,723	31,052	37,994	47,607	63,669	47,077
IMPORTS									
Total, all countries	1,148,609	1,168,002	1,264,860	1,477,996	1,683,188	1,863,072	1,969,375	2,117,245	1,508,109
Europe	255,988	261,340	285,282	321,505	355,431	383,816	411,205	440,802	322,091
Euro area [2]	166,509	172,762	187,948	209,767	229,233	246,867	268,798	277,728	207,759
France	30,422	28,290	29,244	31,608	33,848	37,037	41,544	44,036	33,608
Germany	59,141	62,540	68,201	77,350	84,992	89,242	94,306	97,597	68,132
Italy	23,768	24,209	25,397	28,096	30,975	32,660	35,027	36,140	26,160
United Kingdom	41,185	40,596	42,610	46,087	50,800	53,187	56,367	57,884	45,407
Canada	219,358	212,431	225,357	260,386	295,060	307,109	320,786	342,920	219,735
Latin America and Other Western Hemisphere	199,923	205,610	218,665	257,114	296,315	335,493	349,409	379,783	275,707
Brazil	14,468	15,782	17,917	21,164	24,441	26,373	25,650	30,449	19,681
Mexico	132,542	136,117	139,834	158,464	173,436	201,812	214,582	219,808	170,528
Venezuela	15,251	15,094	17,136	24,921	33,978	37,134	39,910	51,424	26,755
Asia and Pacific	411,473	432,214	462,062	542,073	608,703	684,325	718,565	729,142	577,561
China	102,404	125,316	152,671	196,973	243,886	288,139	321,688	337,963	285,835
India	9,755	11,822	13,067	15,577	18,819	21,845	24,102	25,739	21,097
Japan	126,685	121,618	118,264	130,094	138,375	148,560	146,037	139,587	90,933
Korea, Republic of	35,207	35,605	37,238	46,177	43,791	45,811	47,547	48,062	39,115
Singapore	15,080	14,821	15,162	15,407	15,131	17,712	18,423	15,891	15,624
Taiwan	33,641	32,611	32,117	34,985	35,103	38,414	38,489	36,496	27,292
Middle East	36,423	34,303	41,470	51,283	62,467	71,907	77,405	111,108	56,217
Africa	25,444	22,103	32,025	45,636	65,211	80,420	92,005	113,490	56,797
Memorandum: Members of OPEC [3]	59,755	53,247	68,346	94,109	124,942	145,367	174,340	242,575	104,260
BALANCE (excess of exports +)									
Total, all countries	−429,898	−482,831	−549,012	−671,835	−790,851	−847,260	−830,992	−840,252	−495,548
Europe	−77,759	−100,224	−116,033	−132,592	−147,928	−144,053	−131,729	−119,651	−70,149
Euro area [2]	−55,483	−68,520	−77,648	−85,795	−94,313	−94,585	−92,313	−79,190	−50,504
France	−10,729	−9,393	−12,354	−10,838	−11,727	−13,698	−15,108	−15,433	−7,564
Germany	−29,778	−36,415	−39,778	−46,334	−51,204	−48,472	−45,200	−43,387	−26,199
Italy	−14,053	−14,311	−15,020	−17,550	−19,633	−20,262	−21,024	−20,810	−14,239
United Kingdom	−1,484	−7,969	−9,377	−10,751	−12,958	−8,661	−6,971	−5,015	−615
Canada	−56,099	−51,516	−55,428	−70,403	−82,868	−76,126	−70,837	−81,049	−19,496
Latin America and Other Western Hemisphere	−40,955	−57,273	−69,615	−85,314	−104,059	−113,867	−107,097	−91,977	−46,324
Brazil	1,321	−3,472	−6,778	−7,408	−9,229	−7,541	−1,588	1,726	5,317
Mexico	−31,361	−38,812	−42,586	−47,857	−53,276	−68,153	−78,771	−68,661	−46,496
Venezuela	−9,651	−11,073	−14,309	−20,160	−27,565	−28,140	−29,717	−38,820	−17,304
Asia and Pacific	−222,742	−245,344	−262,869	−321,159	−372,684	−413,515	−417,375	−403,194	−310,852
China	−83,296	−103,274	−124,379	−162,649	−202,813	−234,612	−258,902	−268,411	−223,199
India	−6,001	−7,724	−8,088	−9,477	−10,905	−12,223	−9,217	−8,116	−4,500
Japan	−70,806	−71,320	−67,419	−77,823	−85,257	−91,407	−85,616	−75,130	−41,205
Korea, Republic of	−14,004	−13,724	−13,697	−20,596	−16,679	−14,140	−13,890	−14,149	−12,557
Singapore	2,258	1,221	1,125	3,793	5,080	5,838	6,956	11,741	5,464
Taiwan	−16,248	−14,584	−15,052	−13,829	−14,087	−16,080	−13,074	−11,860	−10,801
Middle East	−18,282	−16,242	−23,199	−29,499	−32,833	−37,126	−34,661	−58,764	−15,692
Africa	−14,062	−12,233	−21,867	−32,867	−50,479	−62,574	−69,292	−85,617	−33,036
Memorandum: Members of OPEC [3]	−40,253	−35,351	−51,684	−72,386	−93,889	−107,373	−126,733	−178,907	−57,183

[1] Preliminary; seasonally adjusted.
[2] Euro area consists of: Austria, Belgium, Cyprus (beginning in 2008), Finland, France, Germany, Greece (beginning in 2001), Ireland, Italy, Luxembourg, Malta (beginning in 2008), Netherlands, Portugal, Slovakia (beginning in 2009), Slovenia (beginning in 2007), and Spain.
[3] Organization of Petroleum Exporting Countries, consisting of Algeria, Angola (beginning in 2007), Ecuador (beginning in 2007), Indonesia (ending in 2008), Iran, Iraq, Kuwait, Libya, Nigeria, Qatar, Saudi Arabia, United Arab Emirates, and Venezuela.

Note: Data are on a balance of payments basis and exclude military. For further details, and additional data by country, see Survey of Current Business, January 2010.

Source: Department of Commerce (Bureau of Economic Analysis).

TABLE B–106. U.S. international trade in goods on balance of payments (BOP) and Census basis, and trade in services on BOP basis, 1981–2009

[Billions of dollars; monthly data seasonally adjusted]

Year or month	Goods: Exports (f.a.s. value)[1,2] Total, BOP basis[3]	Total, Census basis[3,4]	Foods, feeds, and beverages	Industrial supplies and materials	Capital goods except automotive	Automotive vehicles, parts, and engines	Consumer goods (nonfood) except automotive	Goods: Imports (customs value)[5] Total, BOP basis	Total, Census basis[4]	Foods, feeds, and beverages	Industrial supplies and materials	Capital goods except automotive	Automotive vehicles, parts, and engines	Consumer goods (nonfood) except automotive	Services (BOP basis) Exports	Services (BOP basis) Imports
1981	237.0	238.7	....	....	....	....	....	265.1	261.0	....	....	....	....	....	57.4	45.5
1982	211.2	216.4	31.3	61.7	72.7	15.7	14.3	247.6	244.0	17.1	112.0	35.4	33.3	39.7	64.1	51.7
1983	201.8	205.6	30.9	56.7	67.2	16.8	13.4	268.9	258.0	18.2	107.0	40.9	40.8	44.9	64.3	55.0
1984	219.9	224.0	31.5	61.7	72.0	20.6	13.3	332.4	[6]330.7	21.0	123.7	59.8	53.5	60.0	71.2	67.7
1985	215.9	[7]218.8	24.0	58.5	73.9	22.9	12.6	338.1	[6]336.5	21.9	113.9	65.1	66.8	68.3	73.2	72.9
1986	223.3	[7]227.2	22.3	57.3	75.8	21.7	14.2	368.4	365.4	24.4	101.3	71.8	78.2	79.4	86.7	80.1
1987	250.2	254.1	24.3	66.7	86.2	24.6	17.7	409.8	406.2	24.8	111.0	84.5	85.2	88.7	98.7	90.8
1988	320.2	322.4	32.3	85.1	109.2	29.3	23.1	447.2	441.0	24.8	118.3	101.4	87.7	95.9	110.9	98.5
1989	359.9	363.8	37.2	99.3	138.8	34.8	36.4	477.7	473.2	25.1	132.3	113.3	86.1	102.9	127.1	102.5
1990	387.4	393.6	35.1	104.4	152.7	37.4	43.3	498.4	495.3	26.6	143.2	116.4	87.3	105.7	147.8	117.7
1991	414.1	421.7	35.7	109.7	166.7	40.0	45.9	491.0	488.5	26.5	131.6	120.7	85.7	108.0	164.3	118.5
1992	439.6	448.2	40.3	109.1	175.9	47.0	51.4	536.5	532.7	27.6	138.6	134.3	91.8	122.7	177.3	119.6
1993	456.9	465.1	40.6	111.8	181.7	52.4	54.7	589.4	580.7	27.9	145.6	152.4	102.4	134.0	185.9	123.8
1994	502.9	512.6	42.0	121.4	205.0	57.8	60.0	668.7	663.3	31.0	162.0	184.4	118.3	146.3	200.4	133.1
1995	575.2	584.7	50.5	146.2	233.0	61.8	64.4	749.4	743.5	33.2	181.8	221.4	123.8	159.9	219.2	141.4
1996	612.1	625.1	55.5	147.7	253.0	65.0	70.1	803.1	795.3	35.7	204.5	228.1	128.9	172.0	239.5	152.6
1997	678.4	689.2	51.5	158.2	294.5	74.0	77.4	876.8	869.7	39.7	213.8	253.3	139.8	193.8	256.1	165.9
1998	670.4	682.1	46.4	148.3	299.4	72.4	80.3	918.6	911.9	41.2	200.1	269.5	148.7	217.0	262.8	180.7
1999	684.0	695.8	46.0	147.5	310.8	75.3	80.9	1,031.8	1,024.6	43.6	221.4	295.7	179.0	241.9	281.9	199.2
2000	772.0	781.9	47.9	172.6	356.9	80.4	89.4	1,226.7	1,218.0	46.0	299.0	347.0	195.9	281.8	298.6	223.7
2001	718.7	729.1	49.4	160.1	321.7	75.4	88.3	1,148.6	1,141.0	46.6	273.9	298.0	189.8	284.3	286.2	221.8
2002	685.2	693.1	49.6	156.8	290.4	78.9	84.4	1,168.0	1,161.4	49.7	267.7	283.3	203.7	307.8	292.3	231.1
2003	715.8	724.8	55.0	173.0	293.7	80.6	89.9	1,264.9	1,257.1	55.8	313.8	295.9	210.1	333.9	304.3	250.4
2004	806.2	814.9	56.6	203.9	327.5	89.2	103.2	1,478.0	1,469.7	62.1	412.8	343.6	228.2	372.9	353.1	291.2
2005	892.3	901.1	59.0	233.0	358.4	98.4	115.3	1,683.2	1,673.5	68.1	523.8	379.3	239.4	407.2	389.1	313.5
2006	1,015.8	1,026.0	66.0	276.0	404.0	107.3	129.1	1,863.1	1,853.9	74.9	602.0	418.3	256.6	442.6	435.9	349.0
2007	1,138.4	1,148.2	84.3	316.4	433.0	121.3	146.0	1,969.4	1,957.0	81.7	634.7	444.5	259.2	474.6	504.8	375.2
2008	1,277.0	1,287.4	108.3	388.0	457.7	121.5	161.3	2,117.2	2,103.6	89.0	779.5	453.7	233.8	481.6	549.6	405.3
2008: Jan	103.8	104.7	8.7	30.0	38.2	10.4	13.4	177.7	176.8	7.2	65.4	37.9	21.2	39.8	45.5	33.1
Feb	106.8	107.9	9.0	32.2	38.1	10.9	13.4	180.1	178.3	7.2	63.7	38.6	22.3	41.2	44.8	33.2
Mar	105.1	105.8	9.4	32.3	37.4	9.8	12.8	176.6	174.9	7.2	63.5	38.4	20.2	40.1	45.3	33.2
Apr	109.0	109.8	9.5	33.1	39.1	10.2	13.5	183.5	181.8	7.4	68.0	39.1	21.2	40.5	45.9	33.4
May	109.5	110.1	9.5	34.2	38.4	10.2	13.5	183.2	182.3	7.6	68.0	39.4	20.4	41.5	47.1	33.9
June	114.4	115.1	10.0	36.7	39.4	10.8	14.0	187.6	186.7	7.4	73.2	38.5	20.5	41.4	47.2	34.2
July	117.2	118.2	10.0	37.9	40.1	11.5	14.6	194.5	193.3	7.5	79.9	38.7	20.3	41.0	47.2	34.8
Aug	114.7	115.9	9.9	37.0	40.4	10.3	13.9	186.8	186.1	7.8	73.4	38.0	19.3	42.0	47.0	35.7
Sept	106.0	106.6	9.0	32.4	37.6	10.2	13.5	177.7	176.2	7.6	65.9	38.4	18.6	40.1	46.0	34.4
Oct	103.8	104.8	8.3	34.1	37.5	10.0	13.3	175.2	174.4	7.6	66.1	37.2	17.9	40.1	45.9	33.9
Nov	97.5	98.5	7.9	27.6	36.4	9.2	13.2	151.8	151.0	7.4	48.8	35.4	16.7	37.4	44.0	33.0
Dec	89.2	90.1	7.1	23.2	35.1	8.1	12.6	142.4	141.9	7.2	43.6	34.1	15.2	36.7	43.7	32.4
2009: Jan	82.4	83.2	7.1	22.2	33.2	5.6	11.4	130.0	129.6	6.9	38.5	31.9	11.5	36.1	41.6	30.9
Feb	84.4	85.2	7.1	22.2	33.3	6.0	12.8	121.6	121.2	6.7	34.3	30.1	10.2	34.6	40.9	30.3
Mar	82.6	83.6	7.3	22.4	31.9	6.0	12.4	121.8	121.4	6.8	34.5	29.6	10.6	35.2	40.3	30.0
Apr	80.0	80.8	7.6	21.1	30.9	5.8	11.9	119.9	119.5	6.7	33.7	28.6	10.5	35.5	41.7	30.3
May	82.1	83.1	7.9	23.2	31.0	5.4	12.1	119.3	119.0	6.8	33.1	28.9	10.2	35.5	41.4	30.0
June	84.1	85.0	8.1	24.4	31.4	5.5	12.1	122.4	122.1	6.9	37.0	28.9	11.1	33.7	42.1	30.7
July	86.8	87.8	7.8	24.8	32.2	6.8	12.4	129.5	129.3	6.8	38.3	30.1	13.4	35.4	42.6	31.3
Aug	86.8	87.6	7.9	25.7	30.9	7.3	12.3	128.8	128.4	6.7	37.5	30.1	14.7	34.8	42.9	31.2
Sept	90.3	91.1	7.5	27.1	32.5	7.5	12.8	137.7	137.3	6.7	42.9	30.9	16.3	35.4	43.1	31.4
Oct	93.5	94.8	7.7	27.6	33.7	7.9	13.7	138.6	138.2	6.9	41.1	31.9	16.9	36.6	43.5	31.6
Nov[p]	94.6	95.6	9.0	27.0	34.1	8.4	13.0	143.0	142.6	6.8	43.1	33.2	16.9	38.0	43.6	31.6

[1] Department of Defense shipments of grant-aid military supplies and equipment under the Military Assistance Program are excluded from total exports through 1985 and included beginning 1986.

[2] F.a.s. (free alongside ship) value basis at U.S. port of exportation for exports.

[3] Beginning with 1989 data, exports have been adjusted for undocumented exports to Canada and are included in the appropriate end-use categories. For prior years, only total exports include this adjustment.

[4] Total includes "other" exports or imports, not shown separately.

[5] Total arrivals of imported goods other than in-transit shipments.

[6] Total includes revisions not reflected in detail.

[7] Total exports are on a revised statistical month basis; end-use categories are on a statistical month basis.

Note: Goods on a Census basis are adjusted to a BOP basis by the Bureau of Economic Analysis, in line with concepts and definitions used to prepare international and national accounts. The adjustments are necessary to supplement coverage of Census data, to eliminate duplication of transactions recorded elsewhere in international accounts, and to value transactions according to a standard definition.

Data include international trade of the U.S. Virgin Islands, Puerto Rico, and U.S. Foreign Trade Zones.

Source: Department of Commerce (Bureau of the Census and Bureau of Economic Analysis).

TABLE B–107. International investment position of the United States at year-end, 2001–2008

[Millions of dollars]

Type of investment	2001	2002	2003	2004	2005	2006	2007	2008 [p]
NET INTERNATIONAL INVESTMENT POSITION OF THE UNITED STATES	−1,868,875	−2,037,970	−2,086,513	−2,245,417	−1,925,146	−2,184,282	−2,139,916	−3,469,246
Financial derivatives, net [1]	....	....	....	....	57,915	59,836	71,472	159,582
Net international investment position, excluding financial derivatives	−1,868,875	−2,037,970	−2,086,513	−2,245,417	−1,983,061	−2,244,118	−2,211,388	−3,628,828
U.S.-OWNED ASSETS ABROAD	6,308,681	6,649,079	7,638,086	9,340,634	11,961,552	14,428,137	18,278,842	19,888,158
Financial derivatives, gross positive fair value [1]	....	....	....	....	1,190,029	1,238,995	2,559,332	6,624,549
U.S.-owned assets abroad, excluding financial derivatives	6,308,681	6,649,079	7,638,086	9,340,634	10,771,523	13,189,142	15,719,510	13,263,609
U.S. official reserve assets	129,961	158,602	183,577	189,591	188,043	219,853	277,211	293,732
Gold [2]	72,328	90,806	108,866	113,947	134,175	165,267	218,025	227,439
Special drawing rights	10,783	12,166	12,638	13,628	8,210	8,870	9,476	9,340
Reserve position in the International Monetary Fund	17,869	21,979	22,535	19,544	8,036	5,040	4,244	7,683
Foreign currencies	28,981	33,651	39,538	42,472	37,622	40,676	45,466	49,270
U.S. Government assets, other than official reserve assets	85,654	85,309	84,772	83,062	77,523	72,189	94,471	624,100
U.S. credits and other long-term assets [3]	83,132	82,682	81,980	80,308	76,960	71,635	70,015	69,877
Repayable in dollars	82,854	82,406	81,706	80,035	76,687	71,362	69,742	69,604
Other [4]	278	276	274	273	273	273	273	273
U.S. foreign currency holdings and U.S. short-term assets [5]	2,522	2,627	2,792	2,754	563	554	24,456	554,222
U.S. private assets	6,093,066	6,405,168	7,369,737	9,067,981	10,505,957	12,897,100	15,347,828	12,345,777
Direct investment at current cost	1,693,131	1,867,043	2,054,464	2,498,494	2,651,721	2,948,172	3,451,482	3,698,784
Foreign securities	2,169,735	2,076,722	2,948,370	3,545,396	4,329,259	5,604,475	6,835,079	4,244,311
Bonds	557,062	702,742	868,948	984,978	1,011,554	1,275,515	1,587,089	1,392,903
Corporate stocks	1,612,673	1,373,980	2,079,422	2,560,418	3,317,705	4,328,960	5,247,990	2,851,408
U.S. claims on unaffiliated foreigners reported by U.S. nonbanking concerns [6]	839,303	901,946	594,004	793,556	1,018,462	1,184,073	1,239,718	991,920
U.S. claims reported by U.S. banks, not included elsewhere [7]	1,390,897	1,559,457	1,772,899	2,230,535	2,506,515	3,160,380	3,821,549	3,410,762
FOREIGN-OWNED ASSETS IN THE UNITED STATES	8,177,556	8,687,049	9,724,599	11,586,051	13,886,698	16,612,419	20,418,758	23,357,404
Financial derivatives, gross negative fair value [1]	....	....	....	....	1,132,114	1,179,159	2,487,860	6,464,967
Foreign-owned assets in the United States, excluding financial derivatives	8,177,556	8,687,049	9,724,599	11,586,051	12,754,584	15,433,260	17,930,898	16,892,437
Foreign official assets in the United States	1,109,072	1,250,977	1,562,564	2,011,899	2,306,292	2,825,628	3,403,995	3,871,362
U.S. Government securities	847,005	970,359	1,186,500	1,509,986	1,725,193	2,167,112	2,540,062	3,228,438
U.S. Treasury securities	720,149	811,995	986,301	1,251,943	1,340,598	1,558,317	1,736,687	2,325,672
Other	126,856	158,364	200,199	258,043	384,595	608,795	803,375	902,766
Other U.S. Government liabilities [8]	17,007	17,144	16,421	16,287	15,866	18,682	24,024	32,650
U.S. liabilities reported by U.S. banks, not included elsewhere [9]	134,655	155,876	201,054	270,387	296,647	297,012	406,031	252,588
Other foreign official assets	110,405	107,598	158,589	215,239	268,586	342,822	433,878	357,686
Other foreign assets	7,068,484	7,436,072	8,162,035	9,574,152	10,448,292	12,607,632	14,526,903	13,021,075
Direct investment at current cost	1,518,473	1,499,952	1,580,994	1,742,716	1,905,979	2,154,062	2,450,132	2,646,847
U.S. Treasury securities	375,059	473,503	527,223	561,610	643,793	567,861	639,715	884,965
U.S. securities other than U.S. Treasury securities	2,821,372	2,779,067	3,422,856	3,995,506	4,352,998	5,372,339	6,190,067	4,703,529
Corporate and other bonds	1,343,071	1,530,982	1,710,787	2,035,149	2,243,135	2,824,801	3,289,077	2,865,903
Corporate stocks	1,478,301	1,248,085	1,712,069	1,960,357	2,109,863	2,547,468	2,900,990	1,837,626
U.S. currency	229,200	248,061	258,652	271,953	280,400	282,627	271,952	301,139
U.S. liabilities to unaffiliated foreigners reported by U.S. nonbanking concerns [10]	798,314	897,335	450,884	600,161	658,177	799,471	1,000,430	873,227
U.S. liabilities reported by U.S. banks, not included elsewhere [11]	1,326,066	1,538,154	1,921,426	2,402,206	2,606,945	3,431,272	3,974,607	3,611,368
Memoranda:								
Direct investment abroad at market value	2,314,934	2,022,588	2,729,126	3,362,796	3,637,996	4,470,343	5,227,962	3,071,189
Direct investment in the United States at market value	2,560,294	2,021,817	2,454,877	2,717,383	2,817,970	3,293,053	3,593,291	2,556,882

[1] A break in series in 2005 reflects the introduction of U.S. Department of the Treasury data on financial derivatives.

[2] U.S. official gold stock is valued at market prices.

[3] Also includes paid-in capital subscriptions to international financial institutions and resources provided to foreigners under foreign assistance programs requiring repayment over several years. Excludes World War I debts that are not being serviced.

[4] Includes indebtedness that the borrower may contractually, or at its option, repay with its currency, with a third country's currency, or by delivery of materials or transfer of services.

[5] Beginning in 2007, includes foreign-currency-denominated assets obtained through temporary reciprocal currency arrangements between the Federal Reserve System and foreign central banks.

[6] A break in series in 2003 reflects the reclassification of assets reported by U.S. securities brokers from nonbank-reported assets to bank-reported assets, and a reduction in counterparty balances to eliminate double counting. A break in series in 2005 reflects the addition of previously unreported claims of U.S. financial intermediaries on their foreign parents associated with the issuance of asset-backed commercial paper in the United States.

[7] Also includes claims reported by U.S. securities brokers. A break in series in 2003 reflects the reclassification of assets reported by U.S. securities brokers from nonbank-reported assets to bank-reported assets.

[8] Primarily U.S. Government liabilities associated with military sales contracts and other transactions arranged with or through foreign official agencies.

[9] Also includes liabilities reported by U.S. securities brokers.

[10] A break in series in 2003 reflects the reclassification of liabilities reported by U.S. securities brokers from nonbank-reported liabilities to bank-reported liabilities and a reduction in counterparty balances to eliminate double counting.

[11] Also includes liabilities reported by U.S. securities brokers. A break in series in 2003 reflects the reclassification of liabilities reported by U.S. securities brokers from nonbank-reported liabilities to bank-reported liabilities.

Note: For details regarding these data, see *Survey of Current Business*, July 2009.

Source: Department of Commerce (Bureau of Economic Analysis).

TABLE B–108. Industrial production and consumer prices, major industrial countries, 1982–2009

Year or quarter	United States[1]	Canada	Japan	France	Germany[2]	Italy	United Kingdom
Industrial production (Index, 2002=100)[3]							
1982	54.1	53.2	74.5	73.6	69.5	73.3	72.8
1983	55.6	56.1	76.8	73.6	69.8	71.4	75.4
1984	60.5	63.1	84.0	74.9	71.9	73.8	75.5
1985	61.3	66.3	87.1	75.4	75.4	74.9	79.6
1986	61.9	65.8	86.9	76.3	76.9	77.9	81.5
1987	65.1	68.5	89.9	77.8	77.2	80.2	84.8
1988	68.4	73.1	98.5	81.0	79.9	85.3	88.9
1989	69.1	72.9	104.3	83.9	83.7	88.4	90.8
1990	69.7	70.9	108.5	89.6	88.1	88.6	90.5
1991	68.7	68.3	110.4	89.2	93.9	87.8	87.5
1992	70.6	69.2	103.7	87.5	91.8	86.8	87.8
1993	72.9	72.5	99.8	83.8	84.9	84.8	89.7
1994	76.8	77.1	100.7	87.4	87.4	89.9	94.5
1995	80.4	80.6	103.8	89.5	88.3	95.3	96.2
1996	84.0	81.6	106.0	89.2	88.4	93.6	97.5
1997	90.1	86.2	110.3	92.5	91.0	97.3	98.9
1998	95.4	89.2	102.5	95.9	94.4	98.5	99.9
1999	99.5	94.4	103.0	97.3	95.4	98.3	101.4
2000	103.7	102.6	108.4	101.0	100.8	102.4	103.2
2001	100.1	98.4	101.3	101.8	101.1	101.3	101.7
2002	100.0	100.0	100.0	100.0	100.0	100.0	100.0
2003	101.3	100.1	103.0	98.9	100.5	99.4	99.3
2004	103.8	101.7	108.0	100.2	103.6	99.0	100.4
2005	107.2	103.7	109.6	100.3	107.1	98.3	99.1
2006	109.7	102.9	114.2	101.6	113.3	101.8	99.2
2007	111.3	102.6	117.6	102.8	120.1	104.0	99.5
2008	108.8	97.2	113.6	100.4	120.1	100.5	96.4
2009 p	98.2	....	88.3	....	....	....	....
2008: I	112.0	99.0	119.8	104.1	123.6	105.6	99.6
II	110.7	98.3	118.4	102.2	122.7	104.5	98.2
III	108.1	97.6	114.5	100.9	121.3	100.0	96.2
IV	104.4	93.9	101.6	94.3	112.7	91.9	91.7
2009: I	99.1	87.7	79.1	87.7	98.2	83.2	87.1
II	96.4	84.5	85.7	87.0	97.6	80.6	86.6
III	98.0	83.8	92.0	89.6	101.2	84.1	85.8
IV p	99.7	....	96.3	....	....	....	....
Consumer prices (Index, 1982–84=100)							
1982	96.5	94.9	98.0	91.7	97.0	87.8	95.4
1983	99.6	100.4	99.9	100.3	100.3	100.7	99.8
1984	103.9	104.7	102.1	108.0	102.7	111.5	104.8
1985	107.6	108.9	104.2	114.3	104.9	121.8	111.1
1986	109.6	113.5	104.8	117.2	104.7	128.9	114.9
1987	113.6	118.4	105.0	121.1	105.0	135.0	119.7
1988	118.3	123.2	105.7	124.3	106.3	141.9	125.6
1989	124.0	129.3	108.1	128.7	109.2	150.8	135.4
1990	130.7	135.5	111.4	133.1	112.2	160.5	148.2
1991	136.2	143.1	115.0	137.3	116.7	170.6	156.9
1992	140.3	145.2	117.0	140.6	122.7	179.4	162.7
1993	144.5	147.9	118.5	143.6	128.1	187.3	165.3
1994	148.2	148.2	119.3	146.0	131.6	194.9	169.4
1995	152.4	151.4	119.2	148.6	133.9	205.2	175.1
1996	156.9	153.8	119.3	151.5	135.8	213.3	179.4
1997	160.5	156.2	121.4	153.3	138.4	217.7	185.0
1998	163.0	157.8	122.2	154.3	139.7	221.9	191.4
1999	166.6	160.5	121.8	155.2	140.5	225.6	194.3
2000	172.2	164.9	121.0	157.8	142.5	231.3	200.0
2001	177.1	169.1	120.0	160.3	145.3	237.8	203.7
2002	179.9	172.9	119.0	163.4	147.4	243.6	207.0
2003	184.0	177.7	118.7	166.9	148.9	250.1	213.0
2004	188.9	181.0	118.7	170.4	151.4	255.7	219.3
2005	195.3	185.0	118.3	173.4	153.7	260.7	225.6
2006	201.6	188.7	118.6	176.3	156.2	266.2	232.8
2007	207.342	192.7	118.7	178.9	159.7	271.1	242.7
2008	215.303	197.3	120.3	184.0	163.9	280.1	252.4
2009 p	214.537	197.9	118.7	184.1	164.5	282.3	251.1
2008: I	212.100	194.0	119.2	182.1	162.7	276.7	248.0
II	216.757	198.0	120.2	184.7	163.9	279.9	253.0
III	219.278	200.0	121.4	185.0	165.1	282.6	255.4
IV	213.075	197.1	120.5	184.1	164.1	281.4	253.2
2009: I	212.015	196.4	119.0	183.3	164.0	280.8	247.8
II	214.263	198.1	119.0	184.3	164.3	282.3	249.7
III	215.718	198.3	118.7	184.2	164.7	282.9	251.9
IV p	216.152	198.6	118.1	184.7	164.9	283.2	254.8

[1] See Note, Table B–51 for information on U.S. industrial production series.
[2] Prior to 1991 data are for West Germany only.
[3] All data exclude construction. Quarterly data are seasonally adjusted.

Note: National sources data have been rebased for industrial production and consumer prices.

Sources: As reported by each country, Department of Labor (Bureau of Labor Statistics), and Board of Governors of the Federal Reserve System.

TABLE B–109. Civilian unemployment rate, and hourly compensation, major industrial countries, 1982–2009

[Quarterly data seasonally adjusted]

Year or quarter	United States	Canada	Japan	France	Germany [1]	Italy	United Kingdom
	Civilian unemployment rate (Percent) [2]						
1982	9.7	10.7	2.4	[3]7.3	5.6	5.4	10.8
1983	9.6	11.6	2.7	7.6	6.9	5.9	11.5
1984	7.5	10.9	2.8	8.9	[3]7.1	5.9	11.8
1985	7.2	10.2	2.7	9.4	7.2	6.0	11.4
1986	7.0	9.3	2.8	9.5	6.6	[3]7.5	11.4
1987	6.2	8.4	2.9	9.6	6.3	7.9	10.5
1988	5.5	7.4	2.5	9.2	6.3	7.9	8.6
1989	5.3	7.1	2.3	8.6	5.7	7.8	7.3
1990	[3]5.6	7.7	2.1	[3]8.3	5.0	7.0	7.1
1991	6.8	9.8	2.1	8.5	[3]5.6	[3]6.9	8.9
1992	7.5	10.6	2.2	9.4	6.7	7.3	10.0
1993	6.9	10.8	2.5	10.5	8.0	[3]9.8	10.4
1994	[3]6.1	[3]9.6	2.9	11.1	8.5	10.7	9.5
1995	5.6	8.6	3.2	10.5	8.2	11.3	8.7
1996	5.4	8.8	3.4	11.1	9.0	11.3	8.1
1997	4.9	8.4	3.4	11.1	9.9	11.4	7.0
1998	4.5	7.7	4.1	10.6	9.3	11.5	6.3
1999	4.2	7.0	4.7	10.2	[3]8.5	11.0	6.0
2000	4.0	6.1	4.8	8.7	7.8	10.2	5.5
2001	4.7	6.5	5.1	7.9	7.9	9.2	5.1
2002	5.8	7.0	5.4	8.1	8.6	8.7	5.2
2003	6.0	6.9	5.3	[3]8.6	9.3	8.5	5.0
2004	5.5	6.4	4.8	9.0	10.3	8.1	4.8
2005	5.1	6.0	4.5	9.0	[3]11.2	7.8	4.9
2006	4.6	5.5	4.2	9.0	10.4	6.9	5.5
2007	4.6	5.3	3.9	8.1	8.7	6.2	5.4
2008	5.8	5.3	4.0	7.5	7.5	6.8	5.7
2009	9.3						
2008: I	5.0	5.2	3.9	7.2	7.8	6.6	5.3
II	5.3	5.3	4.1	7.4	7.6	6.9	5.4
III	6.0	5.3	4.1	7.5	7.4	6.8	5.9
IV	6.9	5.6	4.1	8.0	7.4	7.1	6.4
2009: I	8.2	6.7	4.5	8.7	7.7	7.4	7.1
II	9.3	7.5	5.3	9.3	8.0	7.6	7.8
III	9.7	7.8	5.5	9.7	8.0	7.9	7.9
IV	10.0						
	Manufacturing hourly compensation in U.S. dollars (Index, 2002=100) [4]						
1982	45.9	59.8	28.5	40.7	34.3	41.5	36.3
1983	47.3	64.0	30.7	39.3	34.1	43.3	33.7
1984	48.9	64.7	31.6	37.7	32.1	43.4	32.0
1985	51.4	64.7	32.7	39.9	32.9	44.8	34.0
1986	53.8	64.7	48.2	54.1	46.3	61.2	41.8
1987	55.6	69.3	57.8	65.0	58.4	75.9	51.8
1988	57.5	78.1	66.8	67.9	62.2	81.2	60.1
1989	59.3	85.1	65.7	66.8	61.1	85.0	59.1
1990	62.1	92.0	66.8	81.8	76.4	104.8	72.0
1991	65.8	100.2	76.6	83.5	79.1	110.1	80.3
1992	68.9	99.5	84.3	93.7	92.0	118.0	80.4
1993	70.5	94.4	98.9	91.5	92.2	96.3	69.1
1994	72.2	91.7	109.5	97.0	98.4	99.1	72.2
1995	73.4	93.4	123.1	111.1	117.4	103.7	75.8
1996	74.6	95.5	107.3	110.4	117.0	115.5	74.7
1997	76.5	96.3	99.7	99.5	103.4	109.5	81.8
1998	81.2	94.5	94.4	99.2	103.4	105.5	89.0
1999	84.8	96.4	108.6	98.2	101.4	103.3	91.9
2000	91.3	99.6	113.9	89.6	92.4	91.9	91.4
2001	94.8	98.1	102.3	89.2	92.4	92.0	90.7
2002	100.0	100.0	100.0	100.0	100.0	100.0	100.0
2003	108.0	116.6	105.7	122.5	122.4	124.2	114.1
2004	108.9	130.0	114.3	138.9	135.3	141.2	133.7
2005	112.5	145.7	113.2	144.1	137.1	145.9	140.4
2006	114.7	160.4	106.1	151.1	144.0	150.2	149.3
2007	119.6	175.4	104.5	169.4	159.9	167.5	167.5
2008	123.2	180.4	121.2	187.3	176.1	184.6	159.0

[1] Prior to 1991 data are for West Germany only.

[2] Civilian unemployment rates, approximating U.S. concepts. Quarterly data for France, Germany, and Italy should be viewed as less precise indicators of unemployment under U.S. concepts than the annual data.

[3] There are breaks in the series for Canada (1994), France (1982, 1990, and 2003), Germany (1984, 1991, 1999, and 2005), Italy (1986, 1991, and 1993), and United States (1990 and 1994). For details, see *International Comparisons of Annual Labor Force Statistics, Adjusted to U.S. Concepts, 10 Countries, 1970–2008*, October 1, 2009, Appendix B, at http://www.bls.gov/fls/flscomparelf/notes.htm#country_notes.

[4] Hourly compensation in manufacturing, U.S. dollar basis; data relate to all employed persons (employees and self-employed workers). For details on manufacturing hourly compensation, see *International Comparisons of Manufacturing Productivity and Unit Labor Cost Trends, 2008*, October 22, 2009.

Source: Department of Labor (Bureau of Labor Statistics).

[Foreign currency units per U.S. dollar, except as noted; certified noon buying rates in New York]

Period	Australia (dollar)[1]	Canada (dollar)	China, P.R. (yuan)	EMU Members (euro)[1,2]	Germany (mark)[2]	Japan (yen)	Mexico (peso)	South Korea (won)	Sweden (krona)	Switzerland (franc)	United Kingdom (pound)[1]
March 1973	1.2716	0.9967	2.2401		2.8132	261.90	0.013	398.85	4.4294	3.2171	2.4724
1988	0.7841	1.2306	3.7314		1.7570	128.17	2.273	734.52	6.1370	1.4643	1.7813
1989	.7919	1.1842	3.7673		1.8808	138.07	2.461	674.13	6.4559	1.6369	1.6382
1990	.7807	1.1668	4.7921		1.6166	145.00	2.813	710.64	5.9231	1.3901	1.7841
1991	.7787	1.1460	5.3337		1.6610	134.59	3.018	736.73	6.0521	1.4356	1.7674
1992	.7352	1.2085	5.5206		1.5618	126.78	3.095	784.66	5.8258	1.4064	1.7663
1993	.6799	1.2902	5.7795		1.6545	111.08	3.116	805.75	7.7956	1.4781	1.5016
1994	.7316	1.3664	8.6397		1.6216	102.18	3.385	806.93	7.7161	1.3667	1.5319
1995	.7407	1.3725	8.3700		1.4321	93.96	6.447	772.69	7.1406	1.1812	1.5785
1996	.7828	1.3638	8.3389		1.5049	108.78	7.600	805.00	6.7082	1.2361	1.5607
1997	.7437	1.3849	8.3193		1.7348	121.06	7.918	953.19	7.6446	1.4514	1.6376
1998	.6291	1.4836	8.3008		1.7597	130.99	9.152	1,400.40	7.9522	1.4506	1.6573
1999	.6454	1.4858	8.2783	1.0653		113.73	9.553	1,189.84	8.2740	1.5045	1.6172
2000	.5815	1.4855	8.2784	.9232		107.80	9.459	1,130.90	9.1735	1.6904	1.5156
2001	.5169	1.5487	8.2770	.8952		121.57	9.337	1,292.02	10.3425	1.6891	1.4396
2002	.5437	1.5704	8.2771	.9454		125.22	9.663	1,250.31	9.7233	1.5567	1.5025
2003	.6524	1.4008	8.2772	1.1321		115.94	10.793	1,192.08	8.0787	1.3450	1.6347
2004	.7365	1.3017	8.2768	1.2438		108.15	11.290	1,145.24	7.3480	1.2428	1.8330
2005	.7627	1.2115	8.1936	1.2449		110.11	10.894	1,023.75	7.4710	1.2459	1.8204
2006	.7535	1.1340	7.9723	1.2563		116.31	10.906	954.32	7.3718	1.2532	1.8434
2007	.8391	1.0734	7.6058	1.3711		117.76	10.928	928.97	6.7550	1.1999	2.0020
2008	.8537	1.0660	6.9477	1.4726		103.39	11.143	1,098.71	6.5846	1.0816	1.8545
2009	.7927	1.1412	6.8307	1.3935		93.68	13.498	1,274.63	7.6539	1.0860	1.5661
2008: I	.9058	1.0039	7.1590	1.5007		105.17	10.803	956.12	6.2668	1.0670	1.9790
II	.9436	1.0099	6.9578	1.5625		104.62	10.428	1,017.02	5.9862	1.0316	1.9712
III	.8879	1.0411	6.8375	1.5030		107.58	10.328	1,064.56	6.3175	1.0734	1.8924
IV	.6735	1.2115	6.8400	1.3202		96.01	13.061	1,360.86	7.7957	1.1560	1.5704
2009: I	.6644	1.2455	6.8361	1.3035		93.78	14.384	1,415.27	8.4107	1.1487	1.4344
II	.7609	1.1682	6.8293	1.3619		97.42	13.315	1,282.78	7.9239	1.1123	1.5502
III	.8332	1.0980	6.8306	1.4304		93.54	13.261	1,237.55	7.2907	1.0623	1.6410
IV	.9090	1.0557	6.8271	1.4762		89.88	13.062	1,166.70	7.0114	1.0219	1.6335

Trade-weighted value of the U.S. dollar

Period	Nominal				Real[7]		
	G-10 index (March 1973=100)[3]	Broad index (January 1997=100)[4]	Major currencies index (March 1973=100)[5]	OITP index (January 1997=100)[6]	Broad index (March 1973=100)[4]	Major currencies index (March 1973=100)[5]	OITP index (March 1973=100)[6]
1988	92.7	60.92	90.43	24.07	92.09	84.24	115.57
1989	98.6	66.90	94.29	29.61	93.83	88.58	110.11
1990	89.1	71.41	89.91	40.10	91.30	85.21	109.76
1991	89.8	74.35	88.59	46.69	89.77	83.54	108.85
1992	86.6	76.91	87.00	53.13	87.88	82.40	105.24
1993	93.2	83.78	89.90	63.37	89.23	85.65	102.61
1994	91.3	90.87	88.43	80.54	89.06	85.30	102.62
1995	84.2	92.65	83.41	92.51	86.61	81.43	102.68
1996	87.3	97.46	87.25	98.24	88.62	86.34	99.68
1997	96.4	104.43	93.93	104.64	93.34	93.63	100.73
1998	98.8	115.89	98.45	125.89	101.32	98.70	113.93
1999		116.04	96.89	129.20	100.69	98.44	112.64
2000		119.45	101.58	129.84	104.55	105.08	118.82
2001		125.93	107.67	135.91	110.56	112.54	117.35
2002		126.67	105.99	140.36	110.71	110.92	119.81
2003		119.11	92.99	143.52	104.00	97.85	121.41
2004		113.63	85.37	143.38	99.38	90.86	120.05
2005		110.71	83.71	138.89	97.75	90.67	116.38
2006		108.52	82.46	135.38	96.64	90.58	113.70
2007		103.40	77.84	130.28	92.03	86.40	108.07
2008		99.83	74.34	127.23	88.29	83.44	103.02
2009		105.87	77.75	136.68	91.84	86.55	107.53
2008: I		97.31	71.97	124.96	85.92	80.36	101.27
II		95.80	70.87	123.01	85.61	80.10	100.86
III		97.88	73.46	123.79	87.58	83.28	101.56
IV		108.35	81.19	137.18	94.06	90.03	108.39
2009: I		111.12	82.68	141.89	95.95	91.41	111.07
II		107.08	79.41	136.91	93.43	88.74	108.48
III		103.69	75.45	135.01	90.58	84.55	106.98
IV		101.61	73.58	132.91	87.41	81.51	103.59

[1] U.S. dollars per foreign currency unit.
[2] European Economic and Monetary Union (EMU) members consists of Austria, Belgium, Cyprus (beginning in 2008), Finland, France, Germany, Greece (beginning in 2001), Ireland, Italy, Luxembourg, Malta (beginning in 2008), Netherlands, Portugal, Slovakia (beginning in 2009), Slovenia (beginning in 2007), and Spain.
[3] G-10 index discontinued after December 1998.
[4] Weighted average of the foreign exchange value of the dollar against the currencies of a broad group of U.S. trading partners.
[5] Subset of the broad index. Consists of currencies of the Euro area, Australia, Canada, Japan, Sweden, Switzerland, and the United Kingdom.
[6] Subset of the broad index. Consists of other important U.S. trading partners (OITP) whose currencies are not heavily traded outside their home markets.
[7] Adjusted for changes in consumer price indexes for the United States and other countries.

Source: Board of Governors of the Federal Reserve System.

TABLE B–111. International reserves, selected years, 1972–2009

[Millions of special drawing rights (SDRs); end of period]

Area and country	1972	1982	1992	2002	2007	2008	2009 October	2009 November
World [1]	151,995	368,041	760,933	1,893,634	4,123,167	4,563,431	5,102,935	5,101,008
Advanced economies [1]	113,362	214,025	557,602	1,142,317	1,564,042	1,648,376	1,892,898	1,904,061
United States	12,112	29,918	52,995	59,160	46,820	52,396	86,925	86,149
Japan	16,916	22,001	52,937	340,088	603,794	656,178	651,148	651,393
United Kingdom	5,201	11,904	27,300	27,973	31,330	29,142	36,633	36,772
Canada	5,572	3,439	8,662	27,225	25,944	28,426	35,303	34,964
Euro area (incl. ECB) [1]	....	....	....	195,771	148,621	154,221	192,634	191,281
Austria	2,505	5,544	9,703	7,480	7,079	6,101	5,604	5,582
Belgium	3,564	4,757	10,914	9,010	6,827	6,306	10,533	10,415
Cyprus	294	490	764	2,239	3,888	416	478	483
Finland	664	1,420	3,862	6,885	4,525	4,587	5,855	5,911
France	9,224	17,850	22,522	24,268	31,855	24,630	31,246	31,436
Germany	21,908	43,909	69,489	41,516	31,896	31,846	43,177	42,103
Greece	950	916	3,606	6,083	526	350	1,068	1,092
Ireland	1,038	2,390	2,514	3,989	499	572	1,259	1,207
Italy	5,605	15,108	22,438	23,798	20,721	26,838	32,540	32,206
Luxembourg	....	....	66	114	93	220	464	463
Malta	253	999	927	1,625	2,396	239	359	356
Netherlands	4,407	10,723	17,492	7,993	7,198	8,140	12,712	12,703
Portugal	2,130	1,179	14,474	8,889	1,226	1,281	1,990	1,919
Slovak Republic	....	....	....	6,519	11,450	11,631	477	476
Slovenia	....	....	520	5,143	624	567	631	619
Spain	4,567	7,450	33,640	25,992	7,582	8,376	11,508	11,385
Australia	5,656	6,053	8,429	15,307	15,764	20,015	26,386	24,395
China, P.R.: (Hong Kong)	....	....	25,589	82,308	96,593	118,468	150,964	159,103
Denmark	787	2,111	8,090	19,924	20,663	26,347	46,378	47,382
Iceland	78	133	364	326	1,634	2,284	2,241	....
Israel	1,126	3,518	3,729	17,714	18,047	27,601	38,491	38,222
Korea	485	2,556	12,463	89,272	165,908	130,607	166,139	168,205
New Zealand	767	577	2,239	3,650	10,914	7,175	9,406	9,690
Norway	1,220	6,272	8,725	23,579	38,500	33,079	30,692	30,648
San Marino	....	....	....	135	410	459	....	....
Singapore	1,610	7,687	29,048	60,478	103,121	113,092	115,941	117,315
Sweden	1,453	3,397	16,667	12,807	17,281	16,957	28,126	27,680
Switzerland	6,961	16,930	27,100	31,693	29,432	30,426	59,638	62,100
Taiwan Province of China	957	7,866	60,333	119,381	171,532	189,864	215,097	216,099
Emerging and developing economies ..	33,295	124,025	196,245	747,475	2,555,349	2,911,295	3,206,282	3,193,432
By area:								
Africa	3,962	7,737	13,069	53,757	183,632	216,669	217,494	216,705
Developing Asia	4,882	44,490	63,596	368,403	1,354,990	1,654,342	1,902,421	1,880,812
China, P.R. (Mainland)	....	10,733	15,441	214,815	969,055	1,266,206	1,475,683	....
India	1,087	4,213	4,584	50,174	169,356	161,036	172,402	168,291
Europe	2,680	5,359	13,811	125,684	527,826	507,498	524,268	530,185
Russia	....	....	....	32,840	295,872	268,426	261,093	264,508
Middle East	8,281	60,520	40,668	80,931	206,493	209,359	228,318	230,157
Western Hemisphere	9,089	25,563	65,102	118,700	282,407	323,427	333,781	335,572
Brazil	3,853	3,566	16,457	27,593	113,585	125,239	144,701	146,226
Mexico	1,072	828	13,800	37,223	55,128	61,766	55,586	56,134
Memoranda:								
Oil-exporting countries	9,915	69,941	40,923	131,309	620,884	632,376	620,963	628,044
Non-oil developing countries	18,431	54,084	155,322	616,166	1,934,465	2,278,919	2,585,319	2,565,388

[1] Includes data for European Central Bank (ECB) beginning 1999. Detail does not add to totals shown.

Note: International reserves consists of monetary authorities' holdings of gold (at SDR 35 per ounce), SDRs, reserve positions in the International Monetary Fund, and foreign exchange.

U.S. dollars per SDR (end of period) are: 1.08570 in 1972; 1.10310 in 1982; 1.37500 in 1992; 1.35952 in 2002; 1.58025 in 2007; 1.54027 in 2008; 1.58989 in October 2009; and 1.61018 in November 2009.

Source: International Monetary Fund, *International Financial Statistics.*

TABLE B–112. Growth rates in real gross domestic product, 1991–2010

[Percent change]

Area and country	1991–2000 annual average	2001	2002	2003	2004	2005	2006	2007	2008	2009 [1]	2010 [1]
World	3.1	2.3	2.9	3.6	4.9	4.5	5.1	5.2	3.0	−.8	3.9
Advanced economies	2.8	1.4	1.7	1.9	3.2	2.6	3.0	2.7	.5	−3.2	2.1
Of which:											
United States	3.4	1.1	1.8	2.5	3.6	3.1	2.7	2.1	.4	−2.5	2.7
Japan	1.2	.2	.3	1.4	2.7	1.9	2.0	2.3	−1.2	−5.3	1.7
United Kingdom	2.5	2.5	2.1	2.8	3.0	2.2	2.9	2.6	.5	−4.8	1.3
Canada	2.9	1.8	2.9	1.9	3.1	3.0	2.9	2.5	.4	−2.6	2.6
Euro area [2]	....	1.9	.9	.8	2.2	1.7	2.9	2.7	.6	−3.9	1.0
Germany	2.1	1.2	.0	−.2	1.2	.7	3.2	2.5	1.2	−4.8	1.5
France	2.0	1.8	1.1	1.1	2.3	1.9	2.4	2.3	.3	−2.3	1.4
Italy	1.6	1.8	.5	.0	1.5	.7	2.0	1.6	−1.0	−4.8	1.0
Spain	2.9	3.6	2.7	3.1	3.3	3.6	4.0	3.6	.9	−3.6	−.6
Memorandum:											
Newly industrialized Asian economies [3]	6.1	1.2	5.6	3.1	5.9	4.7	5.6	5.7	1.7	−1.2	4.8
Emerging and developing economies	3.6	3.8	4.8	6.2	7.5	7.1	7.9	8.3	6.1	2.1	6.0
Regional groups:											
Africa	2.4	4.9	6.5	5.4	6.7	5.7	6.1	6.3	5.2	1.9	4.3
Central and eastern Europe	2.0	.2	4.4	4.8	7.3	6.0	6.6	5.5	3.1	−4.3	2.0
Commonwealth of Independent States [4]	....	6.1	5.2	7.8	8.2	6.7	8.4	8.6	5.5	−7.5	3.8
Russia	....	5.1	4.7	7.3	7.2	6.4	7.7	8.1	5.6	−9.0	3.6
Developing Asia	7.4	5.8	6.9	8.2	8.6	9.0	9.8	10.6	7.9	6.5	8.4
China	10.4	8.3	9.1	10.0	10.1	10.4	11.6	13.0	9.6	8.7	10.0
India	5.6	3.9	4.6	6.9	7.9	9.2	9.8	9.4	7.3	5.6	7.7
Middle East	4.0	2.5	3.8	6.9	5.9	5.5	5.8	6.2	5.3	2.2	4.5
Western Hemisphere	3.3	.7	.6	2.2	6.0	4.7	5.7	5.7	4.2	−2.3	3.7
Brazil	2.5	1.3	2.7	1.1	5.7	3.2	4.0	5.7	5.1	−.4	4.7
Mexico	3.5	−.2	.8	1.7	4.0	3.2	5.1	3.3	1.3	−6.8	4.0

[1] All figures are forecasts as published by the International Monetary Fund. For the United States, advance estimates by the Department of Commerce show that real GDP fell 2.4 percent in 2009.

[2] Euro area consists of: Austria, Belgium, Cyprus, Finland, France, Germany, Greece, Ireland, Italy, Luxembourg, Malta, Netherlands, Portugal, Slovak Republic, Slovenia, and Spain.

[3] Consists of Hong Kong SAR (Special Administrative Region of China), Korea, Singapore, and Taiwan Province of China.

[4] Includes Mongolia, which is not a member of the Commonwealth of Independent States but is included for reasons of geography and similarities in economic structure.

Note: For details on data shown in this table, see *World Economic Outlook* and *World Economic Outlook Update* published by the International Monetary Fund.

Sources: Department of Commerce (Bureau of Economic Analysis) and International Monetary Fund.